Lecture Notes in Computer Science

Edited by G. Goos and J. Hartmanis
Series: I.F.I.P. TC7 Optimization Conferences

40

Optimization Techniques

Modeling and Optimization in the Service of Man

Part 1

Proceedings, 7th IFIP Conference
Nice, September 8–12, 1975

Edited by Jean Cea

Springer-Verlag
Berlin · Heidelberg · New York 1976

Editor
Jean Cea
Département de Mathématiques
Faculté des Sciences
Parc Valrose
06034 Nice Cedex/France

Library of Congress Cataloging in Publication Data
IFIP Conference on Optimization Techniques, 7th, Nice, 1975.
Optimization techniques.

(Series, I. F. I. P. TC 7 optimization conferences)
(Lecture notes in computer science ; 40-41)
Sponsored by the IFIP Technical Committee on Optimization (TC 7).
1. Mathematical optimization--Congresses.
2. Mathematical models--Congresses. I. Céa, Jean, 1932- II. International Federation for Information Processing. Technical Committee on Optimization (TC 7). III. Title. IV. Series: International Federation for Information Processing. Technical Committee on Optimization (TC 7). Series, I. F. I. P. TC 7 optimization conferences. V. Series: Lecture notes in computer science ; 40-41.
QA402.5.I173 1975 001.4'24 76-9857

AMS Subject Classifications (1970): 49.02, 49A35, 49A40, 49B35, 49B40, 49D10, 49D45, 49G99, 65K05, 90C10, 90C20, 90C30, 90C50, 90C99, 90 D05, 92A15, 93.02, 93B05, 93B10, 93B20, 93B30, 93B35, 93B99, 93C20, 93E05, 93E20, 94.00
CR Subject Classifications (1974): 3.1, 3.2, 3.3, 4.9, 5.1, 5.4

ISBN 3-540-07622-0 Springer-Verlag Berlin · Heidelberg · New York
ISBN 0-387-07622-0 Springer-Verlag New York · Heidelberg · Berlin

Printed in Germany
Printing and binding: Offsetdruckerei Julius Beltz, Hemsbach/Bergstr.

PREFACE

These Proceedings are based on the papers presented at the 7th IFIP Conference on Optimization Techniques held in Nice, September 8-12, 1975. The Conference was sponsored by the IFIP Technical Committee on Optimization (TC 7) with the co-operation of:

AFCET (Association Française pour la Cybernétique Economique et Technique)

IRIA (Institut de Recherche en Informatique et en Automatique)

SMF (Société Mathématique de France)

Université de Nice, Ville de Nice and Conseil Général des Alpes-Maritimes.

The Conference was devoted to recent advances in optimization techniques and their application to modeling, identification and control of large systems. Major emphasis of the Conference was on the most recent application areas including: environmental systems, socio-economic systems, biological systems.

The Proceedings are divided into two volumes: In the first are collected the papers in which the methodological aspects are emphasized; in the second those dealing with various application areas.

The international Program Committee of the Conference consisted of:

A.V. Balakrishnan (U.S.A.), B. Fraeijs de Veubeke (Belgium), G. Nyiry (Hungary), A. Kalliauer (Austria), L.L. Lions (France), G. Marchuk (USSR), C. Olech (Poland), L.S. Pontryagin (USSR), A. Ruberti (Italy), F. Stoer (RFG), J.H. Westcott (United Kingdom), K. Yajima (Japan).

PART 1

TABLE OF CONTENTS

INVITED SPEAKERS

Convexity Properties in Structural Optimization
Fraeijs de Veubeke, B. 1

Environment and Some Problems of Optimization
Marchuk, G.I. 13

Multiregional Population Projection
Rogers, A./Ledent, J. 31

MEDICINE AND BIOLOGY

System Theoretic Control in Immunology
Barton, C.F./Mohler, R.R./Hsu, C.S. 59

Optimisation des Processus de Fermentation en Continu
Blum, J. 71

Structural Identifiability of Biological Compartmental Systems. Digital Computer Implementation of a Testing Procedure
Cobelli, C./Lepschy, A./Romanin-Jacur, G. 88

Modélisation de la Marche en Vue du Calcul des Efforts sur l'Articulation Coxo-Femorale
Bonnemay, A./Furet, J./Koukis/Sedel, L. *

Stability Analysis of Predator-Prey Models via Liapunov Method
Gatto, M./Rinaldi, S. 103

Détermination d'une Représentation des Noyaux de Volterra pour un Système Physiologique Non-Linéaire
Gautier, M./Monsion, M./Sagaspe, J.P. 110

A Combinatorial Method for Health-Care Districting
Ghiggi, C./Puliafito, P.P./Zoppoli, R. 116

Study of Waking-Sleeping Behaviour Using Automatic Analysis and Quantification
Gottesmann, Cl./Lacoste, G./ Rodrigues, L./Kirkham, P./ Rallo, J.L./Arnaud, Ch. 131

Self-Sustained Oscillations in the Jacob-Monod Mode of Gene Regulation
Grossmann, Z./Gumowski, I. 145

---

*paper not received

Optimisation in the Modelling of Digestive Tract Electrical Signals
Linkens, D.A. 155

Propagation Model of Bio-Electric Potentials through the Shells of the Brain
Nicolas, P. 170

Implementable Policies for Improving the Biomass Yield of a Fishery
Sluczanowski, P.W.R. 182

Dynamic Smoothing of E.E.G. Evoked Responses
Vidal, J./Reisenfeld, S. *

A Control and Systems Analysis of Artificial Instream Aeration
Whitehead, P.G. 207

HUMAN ENVIRONMENT (WATER POLLUTION)

Modeling Dispersion in a Submerged Sewage Field
Baron, G./Wajc, S.J./Spriet, J./Vansteenkiste, G.C. 229

The Identification and Adaptive Prediction of Urban Sewer Flows
Beck, M.B. 246

The Use of Mixed Integer Programming for the Evaluation of Some Alternate Air Pollution Abatement Policies
Escudero, L.F./Vazquez Muniz, A. 264

On the Use of Quasilinearization for the Solution of Sub-Problems in On-Line Hierarchical Control and its Application to a Water Distribution Network
Fallside, F./Perry, P.F. 273

A Computer Algorithm for Solving a Reservoir Regulation Problem under Conflicting Objectives
Fronza, G./Karlin, A./Rinaldi, S. 292

Optimal Pollution Control of a Lake
Litt, F.X./Smets, H. 315

Modélisation et Identification d'une Relation Pluie-Débit - Le modèle "SEMOIS"
Lorent, B. 331

A Mathematical Model for Analysis of Mountain Drainage Basins
Morandi Cecchi, M. 350

Modelling of a Computer Controlled Open Channel Waste Water System
Rennicke, K./Polak, E. *

Optimal Sampling System for Estimating Geographical Distributions of Natural Resource and Environmental Pollution
Taga, Y./Wakimoto, K./Ichimura, M. 363

HUMAN ENVIRONMENTS (SOCIOLOGY, URBAN SYSTEMS, PHYSICS, CHEMISTRY)

Investigation into the Use of the African Board Game, Ayo, in the Study of Human Problem-Solving
Agbalajobi, F.B./Cooper, R.L./Sonuga, J.O. 368

Numerical Modelling of a Newly Discovered Powerful Molecular Laser
Bui, T.D. *

Catastrophe Theory and Urban Processes
Casti, J./Swain, H. 388

Modelling and Simulation of the Mesoscale Mosaic Structure of the Lower Marine Trophic Levels
Dubois, D.M. 407

Optimisation et Planification des Réseaux de Télécommunications
Minoux, M. 419

World Models: A Case Study on Social Responsibility and Impact
Rechenmann, F./Rivera, E./Uvietta, P. 431

A Mathematical Model for Pressure Swing Adsorption
Sebastian, D.J.G. 440

HUMAN ENVIRONMENTS (ENERGY, WORLD MODELS)

A Four-Variable World System
Gould, F.J. 455

The Application of Gradient Algorithms to the Optimization of Controlled Versions of the World 2 Model of Forrester
De Jong, J.L./Dercksen, J.W. 470

A New Approach to Modelling in Planning of Electric Power Systems
Kalliauer, A. 496

On the Optimization of Peat Burning Plants
Kiukaanniemi, E./Uronen, P./Alander, O. 506

A Multi-Area Approach to the Economic Optimization of Electric Power System
Rakić, R./Petrović, R./Rakić, M. 518

OPERATIONAL RESEARCH

Le Problème de la Multivalence dans le Travail Continu
Bartoli, J.A./Trémolières, R. 537

Search and Montecarlo Techniques for Determining Reservoir Operating Policies
Colorni, A./Fronza, G. 557

A Model of Many Goal-Oriented Stochastic Automata with Application on a Marketing Problem
El-Fattah, Y.M. 570

The Forecast and Planning of Manpower with Implications to Higher Educational Institutions-Mathematical Models
Friedman, M. 589

Etablissement Automatique des Tableaux de Marche et Feuilles de Service dans un Réseau de Transport
Faure, R. 608

Construction Automatique des Horaires d'une Ligne d'Autobus
Heurgon, E./Présent, M./Tarim, G. 622

Regional School Districting via Mathematical Programming
De Giorgi, C./Tagliabue, G./Migliarese, P./Palermo, P.C. 637

On the Optimal Control of Natural Resource Use in the Neoclassical Economic Framework
Haurie, A./Hung, N.M. 646

Computer Elaboration of Time-Table for Single Railway Line
Jelaska, M. 657

An Interactive Implementation of Control Theory Techniques Applied to Pindyck's Model of the U.S. Economy
Johnson, O.G./Mangin, X./Rhyne, J.R. 676

Control in Economy Based on Non-Price Information
Ligeti, I./Siv́ák, J. 691

Modelling and Optimization Techniques in Accordance with the Information Requirements for Socio-Economic Development
De Man, W.H. 705

Problem Reduction and for Graphs and Dynamic Programming Revisited
Martelli, A./Montanari, U. *

Optimum Allocation of Investments in a Two-Region Economy
Nicoletti, B./Pezella, F./Raiconi, G. **

Population Planning - A Distributed Time Optimal Control Problem
Olsder, G.J./Strijbos, R.C.W. 721

On the Linear Regulator Tracking Problem and its Application to Econometrics
Terceiro, J. *

On the Optimality of a Switch-Over Policy for Controlling the Queue Size in an M/G/1 Queue with Variable Service Rate
Tijms, H. 736

Optimization of Resource Allocation in R+D Projects
Waśniowski, R. 743

Optimal Ocean Navigation
De Wit, C. 748

**This paper was received during production and has been included at the end of the volume (page 834).

The Optimization Techniques Used for Some Transportation Network Planning
Yajima, K. *

Optimization Methods in Large Scale Scheduling Problems
Zimin, I.*

ASSOCIATED SOFTWARE PROBLEMS

Design and Application of an Interactive Simulation Language
Alfonseca, M. 757

A Functional Package for Monitoring Branching Methods in Combinatorial Optimization
Barthès, J.P.A. 769

SCORPION: Système de Modélisation et d'Optimisation
Delpuech, D./Gires, A./Pere-Laperne, B./Soubies, M. 774

An Interactive System for Modeling
Galligani, I./Moltedo, L. 794

Optimal Allocation of Telephone Cable Drums to Construction Sites
Kfir, M./Resh, M./Siany, E./Rodoy, Y. *

A Network Combining Packet Switching and Time Division Circuit Switching in a Common System
De Smet, J./Sanders, R. 808

Optimum Allocation of Investments in a Two-Region Economy
Nicoletti, B./Pezella, F./Raiconi, G. 834

LIST OF AUTHORS 849

PART 2

TABLE OF CONTENTS

GAMES

Fuzzy Games
Aubin, J.P. *

On the Marginal Value of an Antagonistic Game
Hartung, J. 1

Gaming Modelling of Interrelations Among Organizational Units
Levien, R./Sokolov, V./Zimin, I. *

OPTIMAL DESIGN

Optimization of Structural Elements
Armand, J.-L. 9

The Policy Iteration Method for the Optimal Stopping of a Markov Chain with an Application
Van Hee, K.M. 22

Algorithmes pour un Problème Inverse Discret de Sturm-Liouville
Morel, P. 37

Etude de Problèmes d'Optimal Design
Murat, F./Simon, J. 54

Une Formule de Hadamard dans des Problèmes d'Optimal Design
Palmerio, B./Dervieux, A. 63

Problèmes Inverses de Valeurs Propres
Rousselet, B. 77

COMPUTATIONAL TECHNIQUES

A Decomposition Technique in Integer Linear Programming
Giulianelli, S./Lucertini, M. 86

An Integrated Theory of Problems as an Algebraic Base for Complexity Understanding and Automatic Problem Solving
Guida, G./Mandrioli, D./Paci, A./Somalvico, M. 98

Minimum Problems on Sets with Convergence and Parameter Determination in Partial Differential Equations
Kluge, R. *

---

*paper not received

Choix d'une Base dans l'Approximation d'une Fonction
Lemaire, J./Moriou, M./Pouget, J. 130

Implémentation Numérique en Filtrage Optimal Non-Linéaire: Algorithmes Parallèles et Comparaison avec d'autres Solutions
Levieux, F. 151

Méthodes de Décomposition appliquées aux Problèmes de Contrôle Impulsionnel
Maurin, S. 169

A Mixt Relaxation Algorithm Applied to Quasi-Variational Inequations
Miellou, J.C. 192

An Efficient Algorithm for Minimization that Does not Require Analytic Derivatives
Mifflin, R. *

Eclatement de Contraintes en Parallèle pour la Minimisation d'une Forme Quadratique
Pierra, G. 200

Application de la Méthode de Pénalisation aux Problèmes de Contrôle en Nombres Entiers
Saguez, C. 219

Une Nouvelle Méthode de Décomposition des Grands Systèmes ou la Partition Précède l'Affectation
Thuaire, A./Malengé, J.P. 229

On the Multivariable Control of Nuclear Reactors Using the State Feedback Approach
Tsafestas, S./Chrysochoides, N. 250

MATHEMATICAL PROGRAMMING

Un Algorithme de Minimisation de Fonctions Convexes avec ou sans Contraintes "l'Algorithme d'Echanges"
Carasso, C. 268

A Remark on Multiplier Methods for Nonlinear Programming
Cirinà, M. 283

Optimisation sans Contraintes: Construction d'une Famille d'Algorithmes à Convergence Quadratique par Linéarisation
Denel, J. 293

Optimization in Large Partly Nonlinear Systems
Drud, A. 312

A New Branch And Bound Approach for Concave Minimization Problems
Horst, R. 330

Mathematical Programming and the Computation of Optimal Taxes for Environmental Pollution Control
Jacobsen, S.E. 337

On Large Scale Linear Fractional Programs
Kovács, A./Stahl, J. 353

Some Remarks on Generalized Lagrangians
Kurcyusz, S. 362

Implicit Dynamic Equations
Luenberger, D.G. *

Subgradient Optimization, Matroid Problems and Heuristic Evaluation
Maffioli, F. 389

Theoretical and Practical Aspects of Coordination by Primal Method
Malinowski, K.B./Szymanovski, J. 397

On the Implementation of Reduced Gradient Methods
Mukai, H./Polak, E. 426

Contribution to Dubovitsky and Milyutin's Optimization Formalism
Rigby, L. 438

A Perturbation Theory Approach to Non-Linear Programming
Thurber, J./Whinston, A. 454

OPTIMAL CONTROL DETERMINISTIC

An Introduction to Bounded Rate Systems
Bruni, C./Koch, G./Germani, A. 471

Un Calcul Symbolique Non Commutatif pour les Asservissements Non Linéaires et Non Stationnaires
Fliess, M. 496

The Numerical Design of Feedback Control Systems Containing a Saturation Element by the Method of Inequalities
Gray, J.O./Al-Janabi, T.H. 510

Sur l'Approximation du Contrôle Optimal des Systèmes Gouvernés par des Equations Différentielles avec Retard par la Méthode de Différences Finies
Lasiecka, I./Hatko, A. 522

Canonical Realizations of Transfer Operators
Levan, N. 538

On Optimal Control Problems with Bounded State Variables and Control Appearing Linearly
Maurer, H. 555

On the Optimal Control of Variational Inequalities
Patrone, F. 560

Modelling and Control for Distributed Parameter Systems
Pritchard, A.J./Crouch, P.E. 566

On Bang-Bang Control Policies
Gonzalez, R./Rofman, E. 587

Optimal Control Problems in Sobolev Spaces with Weights. Numerical Approaches. Applications to Plasma Control and Time Delay Problems
Simionescu, C. 603

On Optimal Parametric Control of Parabolic System
Sokolowski, J. 623

On the Convergence of Balakrishnan's Method
Zolezzi, T. 634

OPTIMAL CONTROL STOCHASTIC

Minimum Variance Control of Discrete-Time Linear Stochastic System, Using Instantaneous Output Feedback
Blanvillain, P./Favier, G. 636

Finding a Feasible Control for Real Process under Uncertainty
Brdyś, M. 656

Infinite Dimensional Estimation Theory Applied to a Water Pollution Problem
Curtain, R.F. 685

Numerical Solution of the Operator Riccati Equation for the Filtering of Linear Stochastic Hereditary Differential Systems
Delfour, M.C. 700

On the Approximation of Time-Varying Stochastic Systems
Genesio, R./Pomé, R. 720

Stabilizing Control for Linear Systems with Bounded Parameter and Input Uncertainty
Gutman, S./Leitmann, G. 729

Application of the Optimal Control Theory with Distributed Parameters on a Searching Problem
Hellman, O. 756

About Properties of the Mean Value Functional and of the Continuous Infimal Convolution in Stochastic Convex Analysis
Hirriart-Urruty, J.B. 763

Evolution of Some Problems of Stochastic Control when the Discount Vanishes
Lasry, J.M. 790

The Effect on Optimal Consumption of Increased Uncertainty in Labor Income in the Multiperiod Case
Miller, B.L. 799

An Extension to Abstract Function Spaces of Recursive Minimum-Norm Estimation Algorithms via Innovations
Mosca, E./Zappa, G. *

Nonlinear Optimal Stochastic Control - Some Approximations when the Noise is Small
Perkins, J.D./Sargent, R.W.H. 820

Asymptotic Behavior of Posterior Distributions for Random Processes under Incorrect Models
Yamada, K. 831

LIST OF AUTHORS 847

CONVEXITY PROPERTIES IN STRUCTURAL OPTIMIZATION

B. FRAEIJS de VEUBEKE
Laboratoire de Techniques Aéronautiques et Spatiales
75, Rue du Val-Benoît, 4000 Liège, Belgique

INTRODUCTION

Optimization by a digital computer of a given structural design necessarily implies the reduction of a continuum to a finite number of degrees of freedom, be it rather large. In what follows it is understood that this discretization is achieved by a finite element method, although most of the properties to be exhibited are shared by finite difference procedures. The main variables discribing the response of the structure to its environment are either

- a finite dimensional vector of generalized displacements, noted q
- a finite dimensional vector of generalized deformations, noted e
- a finite dimensional vector of generalized stresses, noted s.

The action of the environment is limited here to the specification of sets of generalized loads, a given set being noted as a finite dimensional vector g.
The sources of such loads are multiple; they may be of gravitational, aerodynamical or thermal origin.
The optimization itself consists in the determination of finite sets of design variables for which the following hierarchy may be conveniently adopted [1,2] :

1. Transverse dimensional design variables.
   They are most easily described in terms of the discretized model of the structure. If we conceive the structure as made of a set of interconnected bars and plates, the local cross-sectional area of a bar, or thickness of a plate are design variables of this type. It is understood that the specification of such variables in a finite number of locations is accompanied by the specification of interpolation functions allowing the transverse dimensions to be known everywhere.
   It must be noted that alterations of the transverse design variables in thin-walled structures does not in principle modify either the external geometry of the structure, nor the topology of the interconnexions of its component parts.
2. Configuration variables.
   Some of them may still keep the external geometry invariant, while altering the length of bars and plates and modifying the relative angles between component parts. More generally they can also modify the external shape and the permissibility of this depends on the function the structure has to fulfill. Clearly there is more freedom in this respect for a bridge design, while there is very little for an aircraft wing, where the external shape is largely dictated by aerodynamic considerations. Configuration variables are those that do not belong to the first group but that still keep the topology of component interconnexions invariant.

3. Material properties.

While variables of the two preceding groups have continuous variations between upper and lower bounds, the choice of material properties for each component is of discrete type. For this reason the optimization of the choice of materials is largely one of direct engineering judgment, possibly a problem of direct comparison between few designs involving different options. An exception must however be made for composite materials such as fiber and matrix where fiber orientation is a continuous variable very similar to a configuration variable.

4. Topological variables.

Again differences in topology in the interconnexions cannot be mapped as a continuous change of variables. Any particular choice is mostly based on previous expérience and engineering intuition, although purely technological considerations are usually also involved.

Our conclusions about design variables is that little can be done presently in the matter of a useful mathematical formalism concerning the two last groups, except perhaps for very simple component parts. Moreover the changes in configuration variables have essentially non linear repercussions on the response of the structure, while the changes in transverse dimensions lead to simple properties of linearity or convexity. For this reason most of the efforts towards computerized optimization of structures is presently concerned, as in this paper, with the first group of variables only.

The optimality criterion itself may be very complex when aiming at a significant estimation of cost. For this reason, optimization in civil engineering where cost of materials, manufacture, manpower, delays, stock and investment are essential ingredients is totally different from optimization in aerospace as envisaged in this paper. The consideration of weight is so predominant in this last case, that it usually supersedes all other factors and leaves a very simple functional to be minimized, one that is both linear and homogeneous in the design variables of the first group. Moreover the cost of aerospace structures being high and the consequences of a bad design extremely heavy, the investments in scientific computation of the structural response and the search for optimality are more easily accepted.

We must now describe the types of constraints imposed on either the design variables themselves or on the structural response.

The transverse dimensional design variables are usually bounded from below and from above for reasons of manufacture and handling or for safegard against haphazard environmental actions that would unreasonably complicate the mathematical description of the loading cases. If c denotes the set of design variables we have thus for each component

$$0 < \underline{c}_i \leqslant c \leqslant \bar{c}_i$$

The result of a continuous approach to design variables may conflict with the use of a standardized scale of gauge thicknesses, in which case the gauge closest to the value obtained will generally be tried for the final answer.

The structural response itself receives at least the two following constraints :

1. For a specified set of external loads the elastic limit of the materials involved may not be exceeded, or a limit well below the elastic limit is set to obtain a lower bound to the safe number of loading cycles in fatigue.
2. For a specified set of external loads there may be no loss of or even bifurcation of the stability of equilibrium.

In many cases haphazard exceptional loading cases are specified for which bifurcation of the equilibrium is allowed, provided the structure continues to resist elastically with a redistributed state of stress. Loads may be envisaged under which the elastic limits are exceeded and the structure becomes permanently damaged, provided there is no catastrophic collapse leading to loss of lives.

While structures optimized under constraints of type 1 and 2 can be tested against such geometrically or materially non linear phenomena, it does not seem reasonable at present to include them in the optimization procedure itself.

The following constraints are also technically significant :

3. Some linear combination of the displacements must satisfy a given equality or inequality under a given set of loads.
   In this category we find the prescription of limitation of a global rigidity characteristic of the structure, such as the torsional rigidity of a wing under tip torque or of an automobile chassis.
   Another example is the requirement that the trailing edge of an aircraft spoiler, straight in the retracted position, should remain straight when fully opened in the air stream [3].
4. Specified values or bounds are set to the low frequency vibration spectrum of the structure.

STRUCTURAL RELATIONS

The relations between the structural response variables and the loads can conveniently be decomposed and presented in matrix form as follows [4].

There are purely kinematical relations linking generalized displacements and strains; they imply compatibility of the strains,

$$e = S^T q \tag{1}$$

and a dual relationship involves the equilibrium between loads and stresses

$$g = Ss \tag{2}$$

The global kinematical matrix S depends solely on the topology of element interconnexions and is <u>independent</u> of the values of the dimensional design variables and of material properties.

The conjugate character of displacements and loads and of stresses and strain appears clearly in the virtual work theorem

$$q^T g = q^T Ss = (S^T q)^T s = e^T s \tag{3}$$

Assuming the material properties to be linear elastic, we add the constitutive equations

$$s = Je \qquad J \text{ positive definite.} \tag{4}$$

From this we can derive the global stiffness relation between loads and displacements

$$g = K\,q \tag{5}$$

$$K = SJS^T = K^T \qquad \text{the global stiffness matrix.}$$

K is certainly non negative, it is not restrictive, even if we have to suppress some rigid body modes by adding artificial kinematical boundary conditions, to assume it also positive definite. The elements of J, hence also those of K, are linear homogeneous functions of the design parameters

$$K = \sum_i c_i \frac{\partial K}{\partial c_i} \qquad\qquad c_i > 0 \tag{6}$$

$$J = \sum_i c_i \frac{\partial J}{\partial c_i}$$

The matrices of partial derivatives depend only on material properties.

WEIGHT FUNCTIONAL and CONSTRAINTS

The weight functional is obviously a positive linear form in the design parameter

$$\omega = \sum_i p_i c_i \qquad\qquad p_i > 0 \tag{7}$$

the coefficients p_i depending on the material properties. It has the lower bound

$$\underline{\omega} = \sum_i p_i \underline{c_i} \tag{8}$$

Consider now the constraints stemming from upper bounds to the stressing of the material. In an isotropic continuum the Hüber-Hencky-Von Mises bound on the elements τ_{ij} of the local stress tensor

$$(\tau_{11}-\tau_{22})^3 + (\tau_{22}-\tau_{33})^2 + (\tau_{33}-\tau_{11})^2 + 6(\tau_{12}^2+\tau_{23}^2+\tau_{31}^2) \leq 2\sigma_e^2$$

(where σ_e is the elastic limit under uniaxial stress) is very convenient to use. It is better adapted to our purpose, when expressed in terms of the strain tensor ε_{ij}

$$(\varepsilon_{11}-\varepsilon_{22})^2 + (\varepsilon_{22}-\varepsilon_{33})^2 + (\varepsilon_{33}-\varepsilon_{11})^2 + 6(\varepsilon_{12}^2+\varepsilon_{23}^2+\varepsilon_{31}^2) \leq 2(1+\nu)^2\varepsilon_e^2$$

(ν is Poisson's ratio). For anisotropic materials the quadratic form has more complicated coefficients but remains essentially positive definite.
This explains that in any given component (finite element) of the structure the elastic

limit is nowhere exceeded if the set $e_{(e)}$ of generalized strains in this component is subjected to suitable constraints (finite in number) of the form

$$e^T_{(e)} E_e e_{(e)} \leq \alpha_e \qquad E_e \text{ positive definite matrix}$$

$$\alpha_e > 0. \tag{9}$$

As $e_{(e)}$ is a subset of e, we may write

$$e_{(e)} = B_e e \qquad B_e \text{ a Boolean matrix}$$

and, in view of equation (1), each constraint of this type is translated in a constraint on the displacement vector

$$q^T SB_e^T E_e B_e S^T q \leq \alpha_e \tag{9'}$$

Such constraints are independent of the values of the design variables but depend on the material properties.

A constraint of global rigidity type is equivalent to the requirement of a minimum value for the strain energy under the prescribed load system; hence it can be presented in the form

$$\frac{1}{2} q^T g = \frac{1}{2} g^T F g \geq \beta > 0 \tag{10}$$

where g is known and F, the global flexibility matrix

$$F = K^{-1} \rightarrow q = Fg \tag{11}$$

depends non linearly on our definition of design parameters.

If, under a given loading system g, a linear constraint

$$m^T q = \gamma$$

is imposed on the displacements, we obtain the constraint

$$m^T Fg = \gamma$$

that involves again the flexibility matrix.

The elastic stability constraints will be analyzed later.

ISOSTATICITY

The property of a structure to be isostatic is well known from simple examples of pin-jointed trusses. The concept can be extended to a continuum[5], the degree of hyperstaticity being identified with the degree of linear connectivity. The definition of isostaticity from the view point of a discretized model is that the homogeneous equation associated to (2) has only the trivial solution

$$S\,s = 0 \quad \rightarrow \quad s = 0$$

Then, provided the structure is isostatically supported, S is square and non singular and the generalized stresses can be directly determined for any loading conditions from the equilibrium equations as

$$s = S^{-1}\,g$$

We may note that this situation is seldom met in practice for more general thin-walled structures, because discretization induces artificial hyperstaticity, even if the continuum is simply connected.
An isostatic structure can be designed to be fully stressed under a single loading case. The case of constant strain elements (corresponding to first degree polynomial approximations to the displacement field) is particularly obvious in that respect. The plate thickness or bar cross-sectional area is taken to be constant within the element so that a single design parameter c_e and a single constraint (9) are to be considered. The generalized stress $s_{(e)}$ is known from statics and its relation to the generalized strain is

$$s_{(e)} = c_e \frac{\partial J_e}{\partial c_e} e_{(e)}$$

where $\partial J_e / \partial c_e$ is a positive definite matrix independant from c_e.
The weight of the element is $p_e c_e$ where p_e is some positive constant. Clearly, since c_e should be minimized, its minimum value is obtained by satisfying the constraint (9)

$$\frac{1}{c_e^2} s^T_{(e)} \left(\frac{\partial J_e}{\partial c_e}\right)^{-1} E_e \left(\frac{\partial J_e}{\partial c_e}\right)^{-1} s_{(e)} = \frac{1}{c_e^2} h_e \leq \alpha_e$$

as an equality.
If several loading cases are to be considered it is also clear that in each element the design parameter has to be choosen by the same equality constraint for the largest of the h_e values generated by the different loading cases. Hence, in general, for each case, at least one of the elements will be stressed to its limit capacity.
This concept of fully stressed design [6] has been extended to hyperstatic structures as an approximation to real minimum weight design under stress constraints alone.

HYPERSTATICITY

Isostatic structures are not efficient when, as is mostly the case, several types of loadings are to be taken into account. Cooperation of all the resisting members due to redundant coupling helps to reduce local peak stresses and is finally conducive to lighter and stiffer structures.

Hyperstatic structure possess self-stressing states, each of which is an s vector, solution of the homogeneous equation associated to (2) (g=0).

If X is a matrix, whose columns form a basis for the subspace of self-stressings, we may write

$$SX = 0 \rightarrow X^T S^T = 0 \qquad (12)$$

and, as general solution to equation (2),

$$s = S^{\#}g + Xx \qquad (13)$$

Where $S^{\#}g$ is any particular stress vector in equilibrium with the loads and x an arbitrary vector of intensities of self-stressings, usually termed <u>redundancies</u>.

Neither the particular pseudo-inverse $S^{\#}$, nor the matrix X depend on the design parameters, they depend only on the topology of interconnexions.

The determination of the redundancies rests on compatibility conditions for the strains

$$e = J^{-1} s$$

They are the existence conditions for inversion of (1), that is, in view of (12)

$$X^T e = 0 \rightarrow X^T J^{-1} S^{\#} g + X^T J^{-1} X x = 0 \qquad (14)$$

Because X is a base matrix (independent columns), this set of equations for x has a positive definite, hence invertible, matrix.

The presence of J^{-1} causes the redundancies to depend non linearly on the design parameters. The satisfaction of the stressing constraints becomes therefore difficult and iterative search techniques are needed, [7,8,9].

STRESS CONSTRAINTS AND CONVEXITY OF THE SET OF ADMISSIBLE LOADS

When several loading cases are considered, the following question arises : to which extent may the loads be linearly combined without overstressing a given design ? Consider the general linear combination

$$g = \sum_{1}^{n} \lambda_m g_{(m)} \qquad (15)$$

where the "design" loads $g_{(m)}$ are specified.

The λ_m, positive or negative, are loading factors. It is easily shown that, when all the constraints (9) are satisfied, they belong to a convex set of λ space. Observe that in g-space each form (9') of the constraints requires the q-vectors to belong to a convex, but generally unbounded set (even independent of the design variables). The intersection of all these convex sets is itself convex and bounded (again provided the kinematic degrees of freedom have been removed). The linear transformation (5) maps this convex set into a convex bounded set of g space. Hence if all the stressing constraints are satisfied for each design load, they remain satisfied for the linear combination (15) if (sufficient condition) the combination is convex

$$\lambda_m \geq 1 \qquad m = 1,2 \dots n \qquad \sum_1^n \lambda_m = 1. \tag{16}$$

Indeed each $g_{(m)}$ lies in the convex set of admissible loads and the convex combination being the smallest convex set containing the $g_{(m)}$, is also contained in the admissible set. The convex admissible set of loads depends of course through the mapping (5) on the values of the design parameters.

STABILITY OF EQUILIBRIUM AND CONVEXITY OF THE SET OF ADMISSIBLE LOADS

Under a given loading vector λg a stability matrix $\hat{S}$ (not to be confused with the kinematical matrix) can be obtained that enables the criterium of elastic stability to be placed in the form

$$u^T \hat{S} u + u^T K u \geq 0 \quad \text{for every } u \tag{17}$$

where u is a vector of perturbation of displacements. Assuming the gradients of the displacements at equilibrium in the continuum to be negligible before unity (small strains and rotations), the $\hat{S}$ matrix may be taken to be proportional to be loading factor λ, we write

$$\hat{S} = - \lambda S$$

Changing the stability criterium to

$$\lambda \mu \leq 1 \qquad \mu = \frac{u^T S u}{u^T K u} \tag{18}$$

Let $\bar{\mu}$ and $\underline{\mu}$ be respectively the maximum and minimum of the Rayleigh quotient μ.

Case 1 $\qquad \underline{\mu} < \bar{\mu} < 0$

For every u $\qquad \mu < 0$ and, as $\dfrac{1}{\bar{\mu}} < \dfrac{1}{\underline{\mu}} < 0$

the structure is unconditionally stable for positive loading factors, the negative values being limited by $\lambda \geq 1/\underline{\mu}$.

Case 2 $\quad 0 < \underline{\mu} < \bar{\mu}$

For every u $\quad \mu > 0$ and, as $\dfrac{1}{\underline{\mu}} > \dfrac{1}{\bar{\mu}} > 0$
the structure is unconditionally stable for negative loading factors, the positive values being limited by $\lambda \leq 1/\bar{\mu}$

Case 3 $\quad \underline{\mu} < 0 < \bar{\mu}$
is the general one as compression stresses prevail usually somewhere for positive as well as negative loading factors.
The loading factors are bounded in both directions

$$\frac{1}{\underline{\mu}} \leq \lambda \leq 1/\bar{\mu}$$

Consider now again the case of a linear combination (15) of several loading cases
We have $\quad \hat{S} = -\sum_{1}^{n} \lambda_m S_m$

and the stability condition

$$-\sum_{1}^{n} \lambda_m u^T S_m u + u^T K u \geq 0 \quad \text{for any perturbation } u$$

In the positive hyperoctant of λ-space we solve the eigenvalue problem for given $\lambda_m \geq 0$

$$\alpha K u = \sum_{1}^{n} \lambda_m S_m u$$

the stability condition being then $u^T Ku\ (1-\alpha) \geq 0$ or,
Since $u^T K u > 0, \quad \alpha \leq 1$.

But if $\bar{\mu}_m = \max \dfrac{u^T S_m u}{u^T K u}$

$$u^T S_m u \leq \bar{\mu}_m u^T K u \qquad \text{for any } u$$

and $\alpha u^T K u = \sum_{1}^{n} \lambda_m u^T S_m u \leq u^T K u \left(\sum_{1}^{n} \lambda_m \bar{\mu}_m \right)$

Whence the stability criterion is certainly satisfied if

$$\Sigma \lambda_m \bar{\mu}_m \leq 1 \tag{19}$$

When all the upper bounds $\bar{\mu}_m$ are positive this condition bounds the positive hyperoctant in λ-space by a hyperplane passing through the coordinates $1/\bar{\mu}_m$ on each axis. If one or several of the upper bounds are negative, the positive part of the

hyperplane is a boundary but the hyperoctant itself is unbounded.
In the hyperoctant $\lambda_1 \leq 0$, other $\lambda_m \geq 0$, it is sufficient to replace $u^T S_1 u$ by its minimum $\underline{\mu}_1 u^T K u$ and the stability conditions is seen to be satisfied by

$$\lambda_1 \underline{\mu}_1 + \sum_2^m \lambda_m \overline{\mu}_m \leq 1 \tag{20}$$

This produces the bounding hyperplane for this hyperoctant. The generalization to the other hyperoctants is obvious.
In the usual case where $\underline{\mu}_m < 0 < \overline{\mu}_m$ for all m, it is seen that the convex polyedron defined by its vertices $1/\overline{\mu}_m$ and $1/\underline{\mu}_m$ on the m axis is a domain of stability in λ-space.

The domain of stability is in fact a larger one. The characteristic surface bounding the domain in the positive hyperoctant will be shown to be convex. Suppose we know the critical perturbation shape u that, for a given set $\lambda_m \geq 0$ belonging to the characteristic surface, yields the critical eigenvalue $\alpha = 1$. Thus

$$K u = \Sigma \lambda_m S_m u \tag{21}$$

A first order perturbation gives

$$(1 + d\alpha)K(u + du) = \Sigma (\lambda_m + d\lambda_m) S_m (u + du)$$

Or, after simplifying by (21) and keeping first order terms,

$$(K - \Sigma\lambda_m S_m) du = \Sigma d \lambda_m S_m u - d\alpha Ku \tag{22}$$

The homogeneous equation, identical to the homogeneous adjoint since the matrix is symmetrical, has the non trivial solution

$$du = d\rho \, u \qquad d\rho \text{ arbitrary}$$

Hence the existence condition for a solution to the non homogeneous problem is

$$\Sigma d \lambda_m u^T S_m u - d\alpha u^T K u = 0 \tag{23}$$

For $d\alpha = 0$ we stay on the tangent plane

$$\Sigma d \lambda_m u^T Su = 0 \tag{24}$$

to the characteristic surface. Keeping first order perturbations on the loading factors, let us now examine how the critical perturbation on displacements and the eigenvalue are affected to second order

$$(1 + d\alpha + d\beta)K(u + du + dv) = \Sigma\,(\lambda_m + d\lambda_m)\,S_m\,(u + du + dv)$$

In view of (21) and (22) this already reduces to the second order terms balance

$$(K - \Sigma\,\lambda_m S_m)\,dv = \Sigma\,d\lambda_m\,S_m\,du - d\alpha\,K\,du - d\beta\,K\,u$$

The existence condition for dv, or a simple cancellation of terms obtained from (21) as

$$dv^T K u = \Sigma\lambda_m\,d\,v^T\,S_m\,u$$

yields

$$d\beta\,u^T K u = \Sigma\,d\lambda_m\,u^T S_m\,du - d\alpha\,u^T\,K\,du$$

The right-hand side can be transformed by premultiplication of (22) by u^T, hence

$$d\beta\,u^T\,K\,u = du^T\,K\,du - \Sigma\lambda_m\,du^T\,S_m\,du$$

Now as $u^T\,K\,u > 0$ and, by hypothesis

$$\max_v \frac{\Sigma\lambda_m\,v^T\,S_m v}{v^T\,Kv} = 1$$

We obtain $d\,\beta \geq 0$

This shows in particular that, when we move in the tangent plane to the characteristic surface, the eigenvalue $\alpha = 1$ receives a positive second order increase and we penetrate into the unstable region. The characteristic surface is therefore convex.

A similar conclusion is reached for the charactéristic surfaces of the other hyperoctants.

This constitutes another proof that the domain of stability is convex in λ-space.

The two preceding convexity properties provide a justification for considering a finite number of loading cases, the vertices of a convex polyedron.

REFERENCES

1. L.A. SCHMIT and R.M. MALETT.
Structural synthesis and design parameter hierarchy. Journal of the structures Division, ASCE, Vol. 89, Aug. 1963, p. 269

2. C. FLEURY and B. FRAEIJS de VEUBEKE
Structural optimization. Sixth IFIP conference on Optimization Techniques, Novosibirsk, 1974.

3. C. FLEURY
Optimization d'un spoiler d'avion avec vérification de restrictions de flexibilité. Rapport SF-33 du Laboratoire de Techniques Aéronautiques et Spatiales Université de Liège, janvier 1975.

4. B. FRAEIJS de VEUBEKE
The numerical analysis of structures . In Proceedings of 13 th International Congress of Theoretical and Applied Mechanics, Moscow 1972;
Ed. E. BECKER and E.K. MIKHAILOV.
Springer - Verlag Berlin, pp. 20-28.

5. B. FRAEIJS de VEUBEKE
Diffusion des inconnues hyperstatiques dans les structures à longerons couplés. Bulletin 24 du Service Technique de l'Aéronautique, Bruxelles, 1951.

6. R. RAZANI
Behaviour of fully stresses design of structures and its relation ship to minimum weight design.
A.I.A.A. Journal. Vol. 3, 1966, p 2262.

7. SYMPOSIUM ON STRUCTURAL OPTIMIZATION
Agard Conference Proceedings CP-36, 1969.

8. Structural Design Applications of Mathematical Programming Techniques,
Ed. L.A. Schmit and G.G. Pope, AGARD-ograph AG-149, 1970

9. Second Symposium on Structural Optimization
AGARD Conference Proceedings CP-123, 1973.

Environment and Some Problems of Optimization

G.I.Marchuk

Computing Center, Siberian Branch

USSR Academy of Sciences ,

Novosibirsk

Introduction

As a result of the rapid economic development which has taken place recently in most countries all over the world there arise more and more powerful industrial units and complexes. In view of the distribution of manpower such units are built, as a rule, in densely populated areas or nearby, therefore rational allocation of industrial units with regard for natural environment and its protection is a very important task.

The present paper describes methods of allocation of such industrial units with regard for a minimal pollution of the environment.

1. Statement of a problem

Let us assume that it is necessary to allocate new industrial units in the neighbourhood of a town or a populated area on condition that the total average pollution of the town and its alloted area (a park zone) is minimal. Let the given plant release into the air an amount of aerosol φ per unit time which is carried by air masses and diffuses under the influence of small-scale turbulence.

If u, v and w are velocity components of the air particles, the transfer of substance φ in the atmosphere is described by the equation of diffusion

$$\frac{\partial\varphi}{\partial t}+u\frac{\partial\varphi}{\partial x}+v\frac{\partial\varphi}{\partial y}+w\frac{\partial\varphi}{\partial z}-p\varphi=\frac{\partial}{\partial z}\nu\frac{\partial\varphi}{\partial z}+\mu\Delta\varphi+Q\omega(r) \qquad (1.1)$$

under the condition

$$\alpha\frac{\partial\varphi}{\partial z}+\beta\varphi=0 \quad at \quad z=0,$$

$$\frac{\partial\varphi}{\partial z}=0 \quad at \quad z=z_H, \qquad (1.2)$$

where α and β are known constants or functions (x, y).

It is supposed that at a fairly large distance from the source the aerosol, unprecipitated to the Earth's surface, has a concentration close to zero, so that

$$\varphi=0 \quad on \quad S, \qquad (1.3)$$

where S is the boundary of the region D . Let $S=\sigma\times H$ and be cylindrical where σ is projection of S onto the plane $z=0$, H domain of solution definition along the height $0\leqslant z\leqslant z_H$ where z_H is a relative upper boundary of the atmosphere. Later on S_α will denote boundaries of spatial domains D_α , σ_α those of the domains which are projections of S_α onto the plane $z=0$.

In deriving equation (1.1) we assumed that $p=\frac{1}{\tau}$ and τ is the average time of aerosol precipitation to the ground. Naturally, p is, generally, a function of coordinates and time. The turbulence coefficients ν and μ are chosen on the basis of the statistic turbulence theory and describe diffusion of the aerosol spot by small-scale turbulence.

The velocity components u , v and w in (1.1) satisfy the continuity equation

$$\frac{\partial u}{\partial x}+\frac{\partial v}{\partial y}+\frac{\partial w}{\partial z}=0 .$$

For the sake of simplicity we will assume the aerosol source of power Q to be uniformly distributed in the domain σ_ε (in the vicinity of the point M) where an industrial unit is located and aerosol is released into the atmosphere at the height $z=h$. In this way, under our assumption, the function $\omega(M)$ is of the form

$$\omega(M)=\frac{1}{\Delta\delta_\varepsilon} , \quad if \quad M\in\sigma_\varepsilon \quad and \quad z\leqslant h$$

and is zero outside the domain.

Given the source function $\omega(M)$ and its power Q, we must find a solution to problem (1.1), (1.2), (1.3), periodic in time and covering the yearly cycle T, i.e.

$$\varphi(\underline{r},0)=\varphi(\underline{r},T) . \qquad (1.4)$$

Now we will see now the functions u, v, w can be represented. Unfortunately, their detailed climatic values are not available for the most part. Therefore in order to solve the problem of aerosol diffusion we must compute vector velocity components in the planetary boundary layer by mesometeorological methods.

In this case the input data of the problem will be: pressure and temperature fields at the AT -850 mm level, relief, roughness of the underlying surface, albedo and others. Given these characteristics, it is possible to find the unknown wind velocity fields. Consideration of the velocity vector diurnal variation is of great importance. Therefore for a given type of motions on the upper surface of the boundary layer there is solved a mesometeorological problem of the fields of meteorological elements inside the layer until the solution becomes periodic. Then the data are averaged on this interval

$$u_\alpha = \frac{1}{T_m}\int_0^{T_m} u_m\, dt, \qquad v_\alpha = \frac{1}{T_m}\int_0^{T_m} v_m\, dt, \qquad w_\alpha = \frac{1}{T_m}\int_0^{T_m} w_m\, dt,$$

where u_m , v_m , w_m is a solution of the mesometeorological problem with diurnal variation, T_m is the period covering 24 hours.

After the daily means u , v and w are found, a seven-day averag ing of daily data is made taking account of the type of motion on the upper surface of the boundary layer. Let T_w be a seven-day period, then, finally, we have

$$u = \frac{1}{T_w}\int_0^{T_w} u_\alpha\, dt, \qquad v = \frac{1}{T_w}\int_0^{T_w} v_\alpha\, dt, \qquad w = \frac{1}{T_w}\int_0^{T_w} w_\alpha\, dt,$$

which are the mean vector velocity components, considering the turbulent ex- change of pulsations for a period of one hour to one week.

The average interval T_w is chosen because the period of 5 to 7 days is a more or less natural synoptic period of variability of meteorologi- cal element fields. But such averaging can also be made on the basis of climatological analysis of repeatability of the regional weather types.

2. Macroturbulent diffusion

In equation (1.1) we consider horizontal (or small-scale) turbulence diffusion. However, in solving problem (1.1) to (1.4) we have to deal with a more or less essential change of the wind direction and velocity during a year in all points of the region under consideration.

Usually such problems are solved on the basis of climatological infor- mation on the mean atmospheric wind fields and the simple macroturbulent exchange models with the use of the macrodiffusion phenomenological coefficient. However, it turns out that such a solution is a rough one and does not yield satisfactory results.

Therefore we will choose another method of solution, i.e. a direct simulation of the macroturbulent process.

For this purpose we employ the week-averaged climatological data on the wind velocity components obtained with the help of the above algorithm and solve problem (1.1) to (1.4) until it becomes periodic with respect to the annual cycle. The solution obtained is averaged over a year and, besides, the amount of precipitated aerosol is measured in any point (x, y). As a result we have the annual mean value of the aerosol concentration

$$\bar{\varphi} = \frac{1}{T} \int_0^T \varphi \, dt \,, \qquad (2.1)$$

the time-averaged and integrated-with- height aerosol concentration over a given point of the Earth's surface

$$a = \frac{1}{T} \int_0^T dt \int_0^H \varphi \, dz \,, \qquad (2.2)$$

and the mean annual value of the precipitated aerosol in the given area bounded by a cylindrical surface S_0 with projection σ_0 onto the plane $z = 0$.

$$b = \frac{1}{T} \int_0^H dz \int_0^T p\varphi \, dt \,, \qquad (2.3)$$

Since our main task is to estimate the aerosol concentration over a chosen region-in the domain D_0 -or its precipitation we introduce the integral characteristics:

$$A = \int_{\sigma_0} a \, dS \,, \qquad (2.4)$$

and

$$B = \int_{\sigma_0} b\, dS \qquad (2.5)$$

or, in an explicit form,

$$A = \frac{1}{T} \int_0^T dt \int_{D_0} \varphi\, dD , \qquad (2.6)$$

$$B = \frac{1}{T} \int dt \int_{D_0} \rho\varphi\, dD . \qquad (2.7)$$

The method of solution of the formulated problem is a rational one as it deals with a direct modelling of meteorological situations in the mean climatic sense and with calculation of these situations in the process of the substance transfer and diffusion.

Thus we solve problem of aerosol diffusion, released by the industrial units, located in the $\omega \times H$ neighbourhood of the point $\underline{r}_0(M,h)$. If we know distribution of $\bar{\varphi}$ in space, we can measure the mean aerosol concentration over the region

$$A = \int_{D_0} a\, dD \qquad (2.8)$$

and also the amount of the precipitated aerosol particles in the region D_0

$$B = \int_{D_0} b\,(x,y)\, dD . \qquad (2.9)$$

If the industrial unit is located in another point $\underline{r}_1$, then all the calculation should be repeated. It means that the solution of the problem of an optimal location (from the viewpoint of minimum B) of an industrial unit involves a large number of variants, but one can never be sure lest there might be a better variant from the viewpoint of the minimum functional B. Therefore it is necessary to look for other methods of solution, which are described in the following discussion.

3. Conjugate equations of diffusion

To solve the problem of an optimal location of an industrial unit we must introduce a conjugate problem with respect to the initial one (1.1) to (1.4).

To this end we will consider the Hilbert space of functions H with the scalar product

$$(\varphi, \psi) = \int_0^T dt \int_D \varphi\psi \, dD \tag{3.1}$$

where φ and ψ belong to F, T is the time interval, D is the do main of solution definition. Let each element of Hilbert space F satisfy boundary conditions (1.2), (1.3) and the periodicity condition $\varphi(\underline{r}, 0)=\varphi(\underline{r}, T)$.

Let us introduce the operator

$$L = \frac{\partial}{\partial t} + u\frac{\partial}{\partial x} + v\frac{\partial}{\partial y} + w\frac{\partial}{\partial z} - \rho - \frac{\partial}{\partial z}\nu\frac{\partial}{\partial z} - \mu\Delta .$$

Then in the domain $T \times D$ problem (1.1), (1.2), (1.3) can be written as

$$L\varphi = Q\omega(\underline{r}_0) . \tag{3.2}$$

In the class of real functions we introduce a conjugate operator with the help of the Lagrangian identity

$$(\varphi^*, L\varphi) = (\varphi, L^* \varphi^*) \ , \qquad (3.3)$$

where $\varphi^* \in F^*$, F^* is a new Hilbert space, and L^* is a conjugate operator. (The procedure of deriving conjugate operators and of constructing conjugate spaces F^* is presented in [1]). As a result we obtain the following operator:

$$L^* = -\frac{\partial}{\partial x} - u\frac{\partial}{\partial x} - v\frac{\partial}{\partial y} - w\frac{\partial}{\partial z} - \rho - \frac{\partial}{\partial z}\nu\frac{\partial}{\partial z} - \mu\Delta \ .$$

The Hilbert space of conjugate functions F^* consists of a sum of squared elements φ^* satisfying the following boundary conditions:

$$\begin{aligned} &\alpha\frac{\partial \varphi^*}{\partial z} + \beta\varphi^* = 0 \qquad at \ z = 0 \ , \\ &\frac{\partial \varphi^*}{\partial z} = 0 \qquad at \ z = z_H \ , \\ &\varphi^* = 0 \qquad on \ S \ . \end{aligned} \qquad (3.4)$$

Then we introduce the formal conjugate equations

$$L^* \varphi^* = \xi \ , \qquad (3.5)$$

where ξ is an unknown function of coordinates and time.

Now we write equation (3.5) in the equivalent form:

$$-\frac{\partial\varphi^*}{\partial t} - u\frac{\partial\varphi^*}{\partial x} - v\frac{\partial\varphi^*}{\partial y} - w\frac{\partial\varphi^*}{\partial z} - \rho\varphi^* = \frac{\partial}{\partial z}\nu\frac{\partial\varphi^*}{\partial z} + \mu\Delta\varphi^* + \xi \quad (3.6)$$

under conditions (3.4). We take the periodicity condition of solution within the interval T as the time data, i.e.

$$\varphi^*(\underline{r}, 0) = \varphi^*(\underline{r}, T) \quad . \quad (3.7)$$

Equation (3.6) with (3.4) can be solved as a Cauchy problem with the condition

$$\varphi^* = \varphi^*_T \quad at \quad t = T, \quad (3.8)$$

where φ^*_T is any smooth coordinate function. The solution is carried out towards the decrease of t. The analysis shows that in this case the problem is correct. Now we continue to solve the problem towards t decreasing until periodicity is reached, which will be the desired solution of problem (3.6), (3.4), (3.7).

Now we will show that the conjugate problem is very important for the air pollution estimation.

In fact, scalarly multiplying the basic equation (3.2) and the conjugate equation (3.5) by φ^* and φ respectively, and subtracting the results we have

$$(\varphi^*, L\varphi) - (\varphi, L^*\varphi^*) = (\xi, \varphi) - Q(\omega, \varphi^*) \quad . \quad (3.9)$$

Taking identity (3.3) into account we obtain

$$(\xi, \varphi) = Q\,(\omega, \varphi^*) \tag{3.10}$$

or, in the integral form,

$$\int_0^T dt \int_D \xi\varphi \, dD = \int_0^T Q\,\varphi^*(\underline{r}_0, t)\, dT \tag{3.11}$$

if Q is dependent on time and

$$\int_0^T dt \int_D \xi\varphi \, dD = Q \int_0^T \varphi^*(\underline{r}_0, t)\, dT \tag{3.12}$$

if Q is independent of time.

Here we have

$$\varphi^*(\underline{r}_0, t) = \int_{\delta_\varepsilon} dS \int_0^h dz\, \varphi^*(\underline{r}, t)$$

Comparing the left hand side of relation (3.11) and expression (3.10), we see that, if we put

$$\xi = \begin{cases} \frac{1}{T}, & \text{if} \quad r \in D_0 \\ 0 & \text{outside} \quad D_0 \end{cases} \tag{3.13}$$

then the left hand side of (3.11) will represent the overall aerosol concentration over the region σ_0, and if we choose

$$\xi = \begin{cases} \frac{p}{T}, & \text{if} \quad r \in D \\ 0 & \text{outside} \quad D, \end{cases} \tag{3.14}$$

the left hand side of equation (3.12) will represent the whole amount of aerosol precipitated in the territory σ_0 .

Thus we must have two conjugate problems: one with the right hand side as in (3.13), denoted by φ_A^* , and the other with the right hand side as in (3.14) denoted by φ_B^* . Then from relation (3.12) it follows that

$$A = Q \overline{\varphi_A^* (\underline{r}_0)} , \tag{3.15}$$

$$B = Q \overline{\varphi_B^* (\underline{r}_0)} , \tag{3.16}$$

where

$$\overline{\varphi_B^* (\underline{r}_0)} = \int_0^T \varphi_A^* (r_0 , t) \, dt ,$$

$$\overline{\varphi_A^* (\underline{r}_0)} = \int_0^T \varphi_B^* (r_0 , t) \, dt .$$

If Q is dependent on time, then, instead of (3.12), we should use (3.11).

Thus the values A and B are calculated either by solving the basic problems, as is seen from (3.10), (3.11), or the conjugate problems, in accordance with (3.15), (3.16). Here we have a duality principle in respect to the functionals of the problems.

If location of a factory is determined one can solve the basic problem (1.1), (1.2), (1.3) with the condition of a yearly periodicity by the method presented in section 2.

As a result we obtain perfect information about the climatic aerosol distribution over the whole domain D which enables us to pose a problem about the effect of aerosol pollution on the microclimate in the region S .

4. Location planning of industrial units near a populated area

Formulas (3.15), (3.16) are the basic ones for planning the industrial unit location. In fact, two conjugate problems should be solved to find the functions $\overline{\varphi_A^*(r_0)}$ and $\overline{\varphi_B^*(r_0)}$. These functions estimate suspended or continuously falling aerosols in the region if the industrial unit is located in the vicinity of the point $\underline{r}_0$. The same values could be calculated, as it was mentioned above, with the help of basic equations.

Let us give a little bit different formulation of the problem, i.e. let us assume that the location of the unit is not fixed. The coordinate $\underline{r}_0$ is regarded as moving and changeable. Then the functions $\overline{\varphi_A^*}$ and $\overline{\varphi_B^*}$, depending only on x and y, will estimate the suspended and precipitating aerosols if the aerosol source of unit power $Q = 1$ is placed at the point M with the coordinates (x and y). Here we have a solution of the conjugate problems. With the source of power Q given, we can distinguish those provinces of the region σ, which satisfy the sanitary norms of pollution for a populated area and a recreation zone.

The further choice of the proper place in the above-mentioned zone envolves economic problems and resources. This is a classical problem with constraints in linear programming. The constraints depend, in particular, on the relief, geological structure of the country, location of park zones, agricultural areas, etc.

This problem being linear, the functions $\overline{\varphi_A^*}$ and $\overline{\varphi_B^*}$ obtained can be used for planning the location of n industrial units with the aerosol release $Q_1, Q_2, \ldots, Q_n$ respectively. Then the total pollution is calculated as follows:

$$A = \sum_{i=1}^{n} Q_i \overline{\varphi_A^*(r_i)} \quad . \qquad (4.1)$$

$$B = \sum_{i=1}^{n} Q_i \, \overline{\varphi_B^*(r_i)} \qquad (4.2)$$

Here $\underline{r}_i = \underline{r}_i(M_i, h)$ and M_i are the points of the domain 6 in whose neighbourhood the industrial units are located. It is assumed that the height of aerosol release is the same for all factories. Generalization to other levels is trivial.

5. Location planning of industrial units in the neighbourhood of several populated areas

In densely populated areas the location of industrial units that release aerosols into the atmosphere appears to be even a more difficult **task** since it becomes necessary to meet the pollution sanitary norms for several populated areas, park and recreation zones and other regions. This problem can also be solved with the help of conjugate equations. In fact, let there be a number of populated areas in the domains $S_1, S_2, \dots, S_m$, respectively. For each zone S_n ($n = 1, 2, \dots, m$) we solve the problem

$$-\frac{\partial \varphi_k^*}{\partial t} - u\frac{\partial \varphi_k^*}{\partial x} - v\frac{\partial \varphi_k^*}{\partial y} - w\frac{\partial \varphi_k^*}{\partial z} - p\varphi_k^* = \frac{\partial}{\partial z}\nu\frac{\partial \varphi_k^*}{\partial z} + \mu\Delta\varphi_k^* + \xi_k \qquad (5.1)$$

under the condition

$$\alpha = \frac{\partial \varphi_k^*}{\partial z} + \beta\varphi_k^* = 0 \quad \text{at} \quad z = 0 \,,$$

$$\frac{\partial \varphi_k^*}{\partial z} = 0 \quad \text{at} \quad z = 0 \,, \qquad (5.2)$$

$$\varphi_k^* = 0 \quad \text{on} \quad S$$

periodically changing the solution with time

$$\varphi_k^* (\underline{r}, 0) = \varphi_k^* (\underline{r}, T) , \tag{5.3}$$

where

$$\xi_n = \begin{cases} \frac{1}{T} , & if \quad \underline{r} \in D_k \\ 0 & on \quad D_k \end{cases} \tag{5.4}$$

where D_n is the domain with the boundary S_n .

In solving m problems we find for each of them the domain of a possible location of an industrial unit taking account of the norms of the aerosol release over the region of interest σ_k .

Then by the intersection of all the domains of a possible location we choose, in accordance with the sanitary norms, a domain Σ if there is any. Then the location of the industrial unit in the domain Σ satisfies the sanitary norms of all regions σ_k . If such a domain does not exist, we pose a problem of a maximally admissible amount of the released aerosol over the region where an industrial unit can be built with regard for the environment control requirements.

6. General plan of ecological development and environment control

In view of the above said it is reasonable now to formulate a problem of the location of industrial units, releasing aerosols into the atmosphere, for each economic region, with regard for the environment control requirements. To this end it is necessary to make weekly climatic wind field maps taking into account the relief characteristics of the underlying surface, etc. , with the help of the methods presented in section 1. With these data available it is necessary to solve conjugate equations φ_A^* and φ_B^*

which will make it possible to find areas, in which to build future industrial units, and to estimate the permissible amounts of aerosol emission.

Ecological situation in populated areas shows, in fact, what prospective enterprises would be desirable for the development of the town and recreation zones. With these zones known beforehand, it is possible to define the functions $\varphi^*_{A_k}$ and $\varphi^*_{B_k}$. By means of these functions, one can determine prospective regions for further development of industries envolving aerosol emissions into the atmosphere, as well as the permissible amount of such emissions. Determination of these areas is, in the author's opinion, the central task in the general planning of siting industries in economic regions under consideration.

7. Minimax problem

The approaches presented above make it possible to come to the solution of the minimax problem, which can be described as follows.

1. Let D be a closed domain in space with the boundary S . There are n populated areas, recreation zones and other places requiring special protection against aerosol pollutions. Let us denote them by σ_1, $\sigma_2, \dots, \sigma_n$. We form a conjugate problem with respect to the values B_H for each domain $\sigma_k (1, 2, \dots, n)$.

For any chosen point M of a possible location of an industrial unit, releasing aerosol of power Q per unit time M with the coordinates r_0 inside D , we consider the functional

$$J(M) = \max_k B_k(M) . \qquad (7.1)$$

The minimal pollution for all regions S_k will take place when point M is chosen from the condition

$$\max_k B_k(M) = \min_{M \in S} \tag{7.2}$$

2. Let the requirements to the maximum permissible pollution norms of the given regions be considered as a constrant and let $\Sigma \in \sigma$ be the domain of a possible location of an industrial unit that satisfies these norms. As a result we have

$$\max_k B_k(M) = \min_{M \in \Sigma_0} . \tag{7.3}$$

If, with the above constraints taken into consideration, there does not exist a domain Σ , satisfying the sanitary norms of all the domains σ_n , it is necessary to reduce the aerosol release Q to the minimum which allows a solution of the minimax problem to be found. This new constraint on the aerosol emission is an obligatory technological requirement to the industrial unit being planned, i.e. it is necessary either to lower its production capacity or develop more up-to-date technological methods which will reduce aerosol emissions into the atmosphere.

3. If in the domain D there are regions which for some reasons (geological, natural resources, communications, etc.) are a priori unfit for the construction of new industrial units these regions must be left out of consideration and regarded as new constraints of the problem. Denoting the permissible (from the point of view of constraints) domain $\Sigma_0 \in \Sigma$ we arrive at a similar problem

$$\max_k B_k(M) = \min_{M \in \Sigma_0} . \tag{7.4}$$

The above minimax problems are effectively handled by a simple linear calculation. In fact, let us consider a region with the boundary S . Let there be in it several residential and recreation zones $\sigma_1, \ldots, \sigma_n$.

For each of them we formulate a conjugate problem and find the value $\varphi_B^*(M)$, which is a function of the point $M(x,y)$ of the domain S in the region S_k under consideration. By definition $\varphi_{B_k}^*(M) = B_k(M)$. Consequently we have $B_k(M)=B_k(x,y)$. Let us now form such fields for all $k=1,2,\dots,n$. As a result for each point M of the domain S we will have a set of numbers $B_1, B_2, \dots, B_k$. Choosing the maximum ones we find the functional $J(M)$ for the point M. Resetting all points M of the domain S we obtain the field of the functional $J(M)$. The point in which the functional $J(M)$ reaches its minimum is the solution of the minimax problem (7.2).

Taking into consideration the sanitary norms constraints

$$J(M) \leqslant 0 \;,$$

where C is the given constant, we find in the domain S the region $\Sigma \in 6$ where location of an industrial unit will meet the sanitary norms requirements for all the regions S_n $(n = 1, 2, \dots, n)$.

Finally, excluding from Σ those regions which do not satisfy such constraints as: geology, natural resources, communications, etc., we obtain a still more narrow region $\Sigma_0 \in \Sigma$, in which the minimax problem is solved in the form (7.4).

We have not as yet touched upon economic aspects of the problem. In a simple form this problem can be formulated as follows. In Σ there is such a variant of location, which is optimal according to the above criterion. This problem is solved by the conventional methods of mathematical programming.

All the sets of problems considered above, naturally, hold true for the case when $A_k(M) = \varphi_k^*(M)$ is taken as the basic functional.

References

1. Marchuk G.I. Methods of Numerical Analysis, Novosibirsk, "Nauka", 1973 (Russian).

2. Marchuk G.I. Numerical solution of the problems of the dynamics of the atmosphere and the ocean. L., Gidrometeoizdat, 1974, (Russian).

MULTIREGIONAL POPULATION PROJECTION

Andrei Rogers
Jacques Ledent

Population projections illuminate the impacts of current schedules of births, deaths and migration by drawing out the future consequences of the maintenance of present rates. Methods for developing population projections for single regions are well known, and the mathematics of such exercises have been documented in countless articles, and more recently, in several texts (e.g., Keyfitz, 1968; Pollard, 1973). The mathematics of population projection for multiregional systems that experience internal migration, however, are less known, and it is only recently that concepts such as the multiregional life table have given them a methodological consistency with the conventional mechanics of single-region population projection.

This paper is an exposition of the mathematics of multiregional population projection. We begin by outlining the notion of a multiregional life table. Next, we show how the stationary regional populations of such a life table serve as inputs to numerical calculations carried out with the multiregional versions of the discrete and continuous models of demographic growth [e.g., Leslie, 1945, and Sharpe and Lotka, 1911, respectively]. We then conclude with a brief consideration of some of the spatial consequences of zero population growth.

Although some mathematics is inevitable in a paper such as this, we have attempted to avoid as much of the mathematical apparatus as possible. Further details may be found in the text by Rogers (1975).

Finally, an important ingredient of effective strategies to understand and resolve complex problems of a mathematical nature is a powerful notational system. In extending the principal results of single-region population mathematics to multiregional population systems, we generalize conventional notation as set out, for example, in Keyfitz (1968); although we do not distinguish notationally between continuous and discrete functions. The regional dimension is introduced by means of two subscripts which refer to regions of birth and residence. As in the single-region theory, the argument of a variable usually refers to age, and the right superscript, also enclosed in parentheses, refers to time. The Glossary below brings together most of the variables used in this paper.

GLOSSARY

Observed Population

$_jK_i^{(t)}(x)$ = Number of individuals aged x to x+4 years at last birthday in region i at time t who were born in region j.

$F_i(x)$ = Annual rate of childbearing in region i among individuals aged x to x+4 years at last birthday.

Stationary (Life Table) Population

$_j\ell_i(x)$ = Number of individuals at exact age x in region i who were born in region j.

$q_i(x)$ = Probability of dying within the next 5 years for individuals in region i at exact age x.

$p_{ij}(x)$ = Probability of residing in region j at exact age x+5 for individuals in region i at exact age x.

$_jp_i(x)$ = Probability of residing in region i at exact age x for individuals born in region j.

$s_{ij}(x)$ = Proportion of x-to-(x+4)-year old residents of region i alive and x+5 to x+9 years in region j 5 years later.

$_jL_i(x)$ = Number of individuals aged x to x+4 years at last birthday in region i who were born in region j. (Also interpretable as the number of person-years lived in region i by j-born individuals between ages x to x+4 years.)

$_jT_i(x)$ = Total person-years lived in region i from age x to the end of life by j-born individuals.

$_je_i(x)$ = Expectation of remaining life in region i for j-born individuals at age x.

$_jR_i(0)$ = Net reproduction rate in region i of j-born individuals.

B_i = Number of births in the stationary population of region i.

Stable Population

λ = Stable 5-year growth ratio.

r = Intrinsic rate of growth.

b_j = Intrinsic birth rate in region j.

d_j = Intrinsic death rate in region j.

o_j = Intrinsic outmigration rate in region j.

i_j = Intrinsic inmigration rate in region j.

n_j = Intrinsic net migration rate in region j.

$C_j(x)$ = Proportion of the total stable population in region j that is x-to-(x+4)-years old.

$(\%)_j$ = Proportion of the total multiregional stable population that is in region j.

Y_j = Stable equivalent of region j.

Q_j = Number of births in the stable population of region j.

1. <u>The Multiregional Life Table</u>

A multiregional life table exhibits the mortality and migration history of an artificial population, called a <u>cohort</u>, as it gradually decreases in size until all of its members have died. Normally it is assumed that the age-specific mortality and migration experience to which this cohort is exposed remains constant and that the cohort is undisturbed by emigration and immigration. Consequently, changes in the cohort's membership can only occur in the form of a decrease due to deaths.

The data set out in a multiregional life table originate from a set of probabilities of outmigrating and of dying within each interval of age, $p_{ij}(x)$ and $q_i(x)$, respectively, where $\sum_{j=1}^{m} p_{ij}(x) + q_i(x) = 1$. Life tables that deal with age intervals of a year are frequently referred to as <u>complete</u> life tables, whereas those using longer intervals are called <u>abridged</u> life tables. We, however, shall ignore this somewhat spurious distinction and for convenience will, without loss of generality, deal only with 5-year age intervals throughout.

Let the <u>regional radix</u> $\ell_i(0)$ denote the number of babies born at a given instant in time in the ith region of an m-region multiregional population system. Subjecting these regional cohorts to the age-specific mortality and mobility of an observed population, we may obtain $\ell_i(x)$, the expected number of individuals who survive to exact age x in region i. However, we need to keep track of where these survivors were born. Consequently, let us introduce an additional subscript on the left-hand side of the variable to designate the region of birth, such that ${}_j\ell_i(x)$ denotes the expected number of survivors alive in region i at age x who were born in region j.

Consider the ${}_j\ell_i(x+5)$ residents of region i at age x+5 who were born in region j. They are survivors of the $\sum_{h=1}^{m} {}_j\ell_h(x)$ j-born individuals who at age x resided in any one of the m regions (h = 1, 2, ..., m). Denoting by $p_{hi}(x)$ the probability that an individual in region h at age x will survive and be in region i 5 years later, we have the relationship:

$$_j\ell_i(x+5) = {}_j\ell_1(x)p_{1i}(x) + {}_j\ell_2(x)p_{2i}(x) + \ldots = \sum_{h=1}^{m} {}_j\ell_h(x)p_{hi}(x) . \quad (1)$$

It has been estimated that the probability that a female at age 10 and residing in California in 1958 would be living in the rest of the United States 5 years later is 0.058749, and the probability that a female resident of the rest of the United States at the same age in 1958 would still be living there in 1963 is 0.985997. Thus the number of California-born life table survivors at age 15 in the rest of the United States is

$$\begin{aligned} {}_1\ell_2(15) &= {}_1\ell_1(10)p_{12}(10) + {}_1\ell_2(10)p_{22}(10) \\ &= 85{,}751\ (0.058749) + 11{,}544\ (0.985997) \\ &= 5{,}038 + 11{,}382 \\ &= 16{,}420\ , \end{aligned}$$

a quantity that appears in the second row-first column position in the lower half of the array set out in Table 1 . The regional radices for that table were both arbitrarily set to 100,000.

Let $_jL_i(x)$ denote the total person-years lived in region i, during the 5-year age interval (x, x+5) by individuals who were born in region j. Assuming a uniform distribution of outmigrations and deaths over the 5-year unit interval of age, we may define the following multiregional generalization of the single-region linear integration formula for deriving L(x):

$$_jL_i(x) = \frac{5}{2}\left[{}_j\ell_i(x) + {}_j\ell_i(x+5)\right] \quad (2)$$

TABLE 1 - STATIONARY LIFE TABLE POPULATION, REGIONAL FERTILITY RATES, AND MULTIREGIONAL NET MATERNITY FUNCTION: UNITED STATES FEMALES, 1958, TWO-REGION MODEL

Region	Age x	${}_1\ell_1(x)$	${}_2\ell_1(x)$	${}_1L_1(x)/\ell_1(0)$	${}_2L_1(x)/\ell_2(0)$	$F_1(x)$	${}_1\Phi_1(x)$	${}_2\Phi_1(x)$
	10	85,751	2,291	4.16220	0.14050	0.00032	0.00134	0.00004
	15	80,737	3,329	3.92220	0.18953	0.04959	0.19451	0.00940
	20	76,151	4,252	3.65597	0.25690	0.12323	0.45052	0.03166
	25	70,088	6,023	3.33854	0.33460	0.08945	0.29862	0.02993
California	30	63,454	7,360	3.06113	0.39018	0.05262	0.16109	0.02053
	35	58,991	8,247	2.86151	0.42907	0.02387	0.06831	0.01024
	40	55,469	8,916	2.70519	0.45559	0.00606	0.01640	0.00276
	45	52,738	9,308	2.57330	0.47038	0.00030	0.00078	0.00014
	50	50,194	9,507	2.44204	0.47586	0.00002	0.00004	0.00001
Region	Age x	${}_1\ell_2(x)$	${}_2\ell_2(x)$	${}_1L_2(x)/\ell_1(0)$	${}_2L_2(x)/\ell_2(0)$	$F_2(x)$	${}_1\Phi_2(x)$	${}_2\Phi_2(x)$
	10	11,544	94,672	0.69909	4.70382	0.00048	0.00034	0.00225
	15	16,420	93,481	0.92960	4.64493	0.04584	0.04261	0.21291
	20	20,764	92,316	1.18150	4.56260	0.12567	0.14848	0.57338
	25	26,496	90,188	1.48124	4.46573	0.09311	0.13792	0.41582
Rest of U.S.	30	32,754	88,441	1.73468	4.38419	0.05477	0.09502	0.24014
	35	36,634	86,926	1.90037	4.30997	0.02825	0.05369	0.12177
	40	39,381	85,473	2.00486	4.22927	0.00819	0.01642	0.03463
	45	40,813	83,698	2.05530	4.12971	0.00048	0.00100	0.00200
	50	41,399	81,490	2.06703	4.00307	0.00001	0.00003	0.00005

Source: Rogers (1975), p. 101.

We have estimated the number of California-born life table survivors at age 15 in the rest of the United States to be 16,420. Table 1 gives 11,544 as the corresponding total for those 5 years younger. Hence the total number of person-years lived in the rest of the United States between ages 10 and 15 by the 100,000 California-born females is

$$\begin{aligned} {}_1L_2(10) &= \frac{5}{2}\left[{}_1\ell_2(10) + {}_1\ell_2(15)\right] \\ &= \frac{5}{2}\left[11{,}544 + 16{,}420\right] \\ &= 69{,}909\ , \end{aligned}$$

or 0.69909 years per California-born female.

The remainder of the multiregional life table follows directly. First, we complete the survivorship and migration history of the multiregional cohort of babies. Next, we compute the total person-years in prospect beyond age x by region of residence, ${}_jT_i(x)$ say, for each birth cohort $\ell_j(0)$, where

${}_jT_i(x) = \sum_{y=x}^{z} {}_jL_i(y)$, z being the last age interval of life. The expectation of life beyond age x for j-born individuals then follows directly as:

$$ {}_je(x) = \frac{\sum_{i=1}^{m} {}_jT_i(x)}{\sum_{i=1}^{m} {}_j\ell_i(x)} = \frac{{}_jT(x)}{{}_j\ell(x)}\ , $$

and

$$ {}_je_i(x) = \frac{{}_jT_i(x)}{\sum_{i=1}^{m} {}_j\ell_i(x)} = \frac{{}_jT_i(x)}{{}_j\ell(x)}\ , \qquad (4) $$

Thus, we conclude that a j-born individual currently at age x can expect to live a total of ${}_je(x)$ more years, of which ${}_je_j(x)$ years will be spent in region j and ${}_je_i(x)$ years will be spent in region i, i=1, 2, ..., m, (i≠j).

Summing the various columns of person-years lived in Table 1 and adding to these totals the person-years lived by those under age 10 and over age 55, we may find the total person-years lived beyond each age, by region of residence and birth, and the corresponding expectations of remaining life at each age. From such calculations we conclude, for example, that a California-born baby girl, under the regional mobility and mortality schedules that prevailed in the United States in 1958, has an expectation of life at birth of 73.86 years of which 24.90 years, on the average, will be lived in the rest of the United States. A baby girl born in the rest of the United States, on the other hand, has a life expectancy of 73.11 years, of which only 5.75 years, on the average, will be lived in California.

Table 2 presents the regional expectations of life at birth by region of residence for the same 1958 data that generated Table 1 but disaggregates California into four regions: the San Francisco, Los Angeles, and San Diego Standard Metropolitan Statistical Areas, and the rest of California. For purposes of comparison, the corresponding expectations of life at birth for males are also included.

The data in Table 2 indicate that the migration patterns of males and females are remarkably similar, with males exhibiting slightly higher levels of geographical mobility. (The proportions of expected lifetimes to be lived in the regions of birth are higher for females born in all but the rest of California region.) The heaviest migration level out of California occurs in the San Diego region, where almost a half (45 to 47 percent) of a baby's expected lifetime is expected to be lived outside of California. This no doubt is due to the large number of births that are attributable to Navy and other military personnel stationed in that region.

TABLE 2 - REGIONAL EXPECTATIONS OF LIFE AT BIRTH BY REGION OF RESIDENCE: UNITED STATES MALES AND FEMALES, 1958, FIVE-REGION MODEL

A. Males

Region of Birth	Region of Residence 1.	2.	3.	4.	5.	Total
1. San Francisco S.M.S.A.	32.51	5.50	1.10	5.59	22.92	67.62
2. Los Angeles S.M.S.A.	4.11	36.06	1.56	3.62	22.16	67.50
3. San Diego S.M.S.A.	3.64	7.67	21.72	2.46	31.95	67.44
4. Rest of California	8.81	7.39	1.27	27.09	22.78	67.35
5. Rest of U.S.	1.34	2.69	0.58	0.87	61.26	66.74

B. Females

Region of Birth	Region of Residence 1.	2.	3.	4.	5.	Total
1. San Francisco S.M.S.A.	35.96	6.61	1.18	6.02	24.22	73.98
2. Los Angeles S.M.S.A.	4.77	40.81	1.79	3.82	22.97	74.15
3. San Diego S.M.S.A.	4.22	9.05	24.63	2.61	33.26	73.78
4. Rest of California	10.59	9.09	1.37	27.97	24.71	73.73
5. Rest of U.S.	1.42	2.99	0.55	0.83	67.35	73.14

Source: Rogers (1975), p. 72.

2. The Discrete Model of Multiregional Demographic Growth

Population projections work out the numerical consequences to an initial population of a particular set of assumptions regarding future fertility, mortality, and geographical mobility. The mechanics of such projections typically revolve around three basic steps. The first ascertains the starting age distribution and the age-specific schedules of fertility, mortality, and migration to which this population has been subject during a past period. The second adopts a set of assumptions regarding the future behavior of such schedules. And the third derives the consequences of applying these schedules to the initial population.

The discrete model of multiregional demographic growth expresses the population projection process by means of a matrix operation in which a multiregional population, set out as a vector, is multiplied by a projection matrix that survives that population forward through time [Rogers (1975), Ch. 5]. The projection calculates the region and age-specific survivors of a multiregional population of a given sex and adds to this total the new births that survive to the end of the unit time interval. This process may be described by the following system of equations:

$$K_i^{(t+1)}(0) = \sum_{x=\alpha-5}^{\beta-5} \sum_{j=1}^{m} b_{ji}(x)\, K_j^{(t)}(x) \qquad \alpha-5 \le x \le \beta-5,\ i = 1, 2, \ldots, m \tag{5}$$

$$K_i^{(t+1)}(x+5) = \sum_{j=1}^{m} s_{ji}(x)\, K_j^{(t)}(x) \qquad x=0, 5, 10, \ldots, z,\ i = 1, 2, \ldots, m \tag{6}$$

where we continue to assume a time and age interval of 5 years, and where

$b_{ji}(x)$ = the average number of (female) babies born during a 5-year unit interval and alive in region i at the end of that interval, per (female) person in region j aged x to x+4 years at the beginning of the interval;

$s_{ji}(x)$ = the probability that a (female) resident of region j aged x to x+4 years will be alive and in region i 5 years later;

$K_j^{(t)}(x)$ = the (female) population in region j aged x to x+4 years at time t;

α = the first age of childbearing;

β = the last age of childbearing;

z = the last age interval of life (e.g., 85 years and over).

As in the single-region model, survival of individuals from one moment in time to another, 5 years later, is calculated by diminishing a regional population to take into account the decrement due to mortality. In the multi-regional model, however, we also need to include the decrement due to outmigration and the increment contributed by inmigration. An analogous problem is presented by surviving children born during the 5-year interval. Some of these migrate with their parents; others are born after their parents have migrated but before the unit time interval has elapsed.

In the United States an estimated 446,634 [$=K_1^{(t)}(20)$] and 5,149,902 [$=K_2^{(t)}(20)$] women, aged 20 to 24 years at last birthday, were living in California and in the rest of the United States, respectively, at mid-year of 1958. Recalling the two-region life table population for California and the rest of the United States that appears in Table 1 and using the appropriate formula for $s_{ii}(x)$ [see Rogers (1975), p. 79] we may compute, for example,

$$s_{11}(20) = \frac{\dfrac{{}_1L_1(25)}{{}_1L_2(20)} - \dfrac{{}_2L_1(25)}{{}_2L_2(20)}}{\dfrac{{}_1L_1(20)}{{}_1L_2(20)} - \dfrac{{}_2L_1(20)}{{}_2L_2(20)}} = \frac{\dfrac{3.33854}{1.18150} - \dfrac{0.33460}{4.56260}}{\dfrac{3.65597}{1.18150} - \dfrac{0.25690}{4.56260}} = 0.90596 .$$

Analogous calculations yield the outmigration proportion $s_{21}(20) = 0.02232$.

The sum of the two products $s_{11}(20)\ K_1^{(t)}(20)$ and $s_{21}(20)\ K_2^{(t)}(20)$ gives the expected number of women aged 25 to 29 in California in 1963 [Equation (6)]:

$$K_1^{(t+1)}(25) = (0.90596)(466{,}634) + (0.02232)(5{,}149{,}902)$$
$$= 537{,}719.$$

Utilizing the appropriate formula for the fertility rates $b_{ij}(x)$ [see Rogers (1975), p. 12] we may calculate the contribution made to the first age group in the rest of the United States in 1963 by surviving female children of 20-to 24-year-old women residents of California in 1958:

$$b_{12}(20) = \tfrac{1}{2}[(0.11260)F_1(20) + (0.90596)(0.11260)F_1(25)$$
$$+ (0.09050)(4.90700)F_2(25)] \quad ,$$

into which we may substitute $F_1(20) = 0.12323$, $F_1(25) = 0.08945$, and $F_2(25) = 0.09311$ to find

$$b_{12}(20) = 0.03217.$$

Applying this rate to the estimated 446,634 females in California aged 20 to 24 years in 1958, we find their contribution to the first age group in the rest of the United States in 1963 to be 446,634 (0.03217) = 14,368 girls. Adding this total to the corresponding contribution made by 20-to 24-year-old females in the rest of the United States in 1958 we obtain the total contribution to $K_2^{(t+1)}(0)$ made by U.S. women aged 20 to 24 in 1958, and aggregating all such totals across the childbearing ages [Equation (5)], we find $K_2^{(t+1)}(0) = 9{,}638{,}313$, the resident population aged 0 to 4 at last birthday in the United States at mid-year 1963. Adding this total to the resident population at all other ages gives the rest of the United States a projected grand total of 86,612,665 females for 1963. California's projected total female population for the same year is 8,646,045. In Table 3B we find that the corresponding totals in 1958 were 80,844,419 and 7,395,438, respectively.

It is well known that a regional population which is closed to (i.e., undisturbed by) migration will, if subjected to an unchanging regime of mortality and fertility, ultimately achieve a stable constant age composition that increases at a constant stable growth ratio, λ say. In Rogers (1975) it is shown that this same property obtains region-by-region in the case of a multiregional population system the totality of which is closed to migration and subjected to an unchanging multiregional schedule of mortality, fertility, and internal migration. Knowledge of the asymptotic properties of such a population projection helps us understand the meaning of observed age-specific birth, death, and migration rates. In particular, the quantity $r = 0.2 \ln \lambda$ gives the intrinsic rate of growth that is implied by the indefinite continuation of observed schedules of mortality, fertility, and migration. Table 3 shows that this rate is 0.02064 in the 2-region projection and 0.02065 in the 5-region projection. Both rates are below the 0.02070 yielded by the single-region model. The differences are a consequence of aggregation bias.

A related but equally useful demographic measure is the <u>stable equivalent</u> Y (Keyfitz, 1969) of each region and its proportional allocation across age groups in that region, $C_i(x)$, which is the region's <u>stable age composition</u>. The former may be obtained by projecting the observed multiregional population forward until it becomes stable and dividing the resulting age-region-specific totals by the stable growth ratio λ raised to the nth power, where n is the number of iterations that were needed to achieve stability. Summing across all age groups in a region gives the regional stable equivalent Y_i, whilst dividing the number in each age group in region i by Y_i gives $C_i(x)$, region i's age composition at stability. Finally, dividing each region's stable equivalent by the sum total of all regional stable equivalents gives $(\%)_i$, the <u>stable regional share</u> of the total multiregional population in region i at stability.

Table 3 presents the above described demographic measures for our California-rest of the United States data of 1958. Also included are intrinsic rates of birth, death, and migration. Note that if the 1958 schedules of growth were to continue unchanged, California's population would ultimately stabilize at about 18 percent of the national total (doubling its 1958 share) and would increase at an annual rate of approximately 20.6 per 1000. Three-fourths of California's stable population would reside in the San Francisco and Los Angeles SMSAs and about one-third of the population would be under 15 years of age. Net migration into the state would be positive, but both the San Diego SMSA and the rest of California each would experience a slight net outmigration of about 0.4 per 1000. Both the highest birth rate and the highest proportion of the aged would be found in the San Diego SMSA, a reflection of San Diego's dual roles as military base and retirement haven.

TABLE 3 - MULTIREGIONAL PROJECTIONS TO STABILITY AND ASSOCIATED PARAMETERS: UNITED STATES FEMALES, 1958

A. FIVE-REGION PROJECTION

Projections and Stable Growth Parameters	REGION OF RESIDENCE				
	1. San Francisco S.M.S.A.	2. Los Angeles S.M.S.A.	3. San Diego S.M.S.A.	4. Rest of Cal.	5. Rest of U.S.
K(1958)	1,941,994	3,723,919	446,390	1,283,135	80,844,419
%(1958)	0.0220	0.0422	0.0051	0.0145	0.9162
K(2008)	7,561,538	14,488,817	2,334,043	4,634,969	180,567,030
%(2008)	0.0361	0.0691	0.0112	0.0221	0.8615
Y	3,620,347	6,612,727	1,023,696	2,210,093	61,171,949
%	0.0485	0.0886	0.0137	0.0296	0.8196
C(0-14)	0.3275	0.3297	0.3404	0.3520	0.3456
C(15-64)	0.5953	0.5904	0.5570	0.5717	0.5828
C(65+)	0.0773	0.0799	0.1027	0.0763	0.0716
λ	1.10878				
r	0.02065				
b	0.02593	0.02612	0.02826	0.02780	0.02744
Δ=b-r	0.00528	0.00547	0.00760	0.00714	0.00679
d	0.00652	0.00628	0.00721	0.00676	0.00665
i	0.02242	0.01832	0.03163	0.02920	0.00245
o	0.02117	0.01751	0.03202	0.02958	0.00259
n	0.00125	0.00081	-0.00039	-0.00039	-0.00014

B. TWO-REGION AND AGGREGATED MULTIREGIONAL PROJECTIONS

Projections and Stable Growth Parameters	TWO-REGION MODEL		AGGREGATIONS OF MULTIREGIONAL MODELS		SINGLE-REGION MODEL
	1. California	2. Rest of U.S.	TWO-REGION	FIVE-REGION	
K(1958)	7,395,438	80,844,419	88,239,857	88,239,857	88,239,857
K(2008)	28,704,425	180,787,223	209,491,647	209,586,397	209,416,093
Y	13,182,724	61,427,080	74,609,804	74,638,813	74,172,787
%	0.1767	0.8233	1.0000	1.0000	1.0000
C(0-14)	0.3337	0.3456	0.3435	0.3435	0.3443
C(15-64)	0.5865	0.5828	0.5835	0.5834	0.5835
C(65+)	0.0798	0.0716	0.0730	0.0732	0.0722
λ	1.10874		1.10874	1.10878	1.10905
r	0.02064		0.02064	0.02065	0.02070
b	0.02651	0.02744	0.02728	0.02727	0.02734
Δ=b-r=d	0.00587	0.00680	0.00663	0.00662	0.00664

3. The Continuous Model of Multiregional Demographic Growth

The principal contribution of the continuous model of demographic growth lies in its ability to trace through the ultimate consequences of applying a given schedule of fixed age-specific rates of fertility, mortality, and migration to a population of a single sex. It is, therefore, a natural generalization of the multiregional life table's stationary population whose total births are equal to total deaths. When births are not forced to equal deaths, but instead are assumed to occur according to rates that are forever fixed, we obtain the more interesting model of a stable multiregional population. By associating the births of a current generation with those of a preceding generation, one can develop several important constants that describe the ultimate growth and regional age distributions of such a population.

A continuous model of single-sex population growth may be defined for a multiregional population system by means of a straightforward generalization of the corresponding single-region model. Beginning with the number of female births at time t in each region, $B_i(t)$, say, we note that the number of women aged x to x+dx in region i at time t, were born since time zero and are survivors of those born x years ago anywhere in the multiregional system and now living in region i at age x, that is $\sum_{j=1}^{m} B_j(t-x)\,{}_jp_i(x)dx$, where $x \le t$. At time t, these women give birth to

$$\left[\sum_{j=1}^{m} B_j(t-x)\,{}_jp_i(x)\right] m_i(x)dx$$

children in region i per year. Here ${}_jp_i(x)$ denotes the probability that a baby girl born in region j will survive to age x in region i, and $m_i(x)dx$ is the annual rate of female childbearing among women aged x to x+dx in region i.

Integrating the above expression over all x and adding $W_i(t)$ to include births to women already alive at time zero gives the fundamental integral equation system

$$B_i(t) = W_i(t) + \int_0^t \left[\sum_{j=1}^m B_j(t-x)\,{}_jp_i(x) \right] m_i(x)dx, \qquad i = 1, 2, \ldots, m \quad (7)$$

For all t beyond the last age of childbearing, those surviving from time zero will no longer contribute to current births, i.e., $W_i(t) = 0$ for $t > \beta$, and (7) then reduces to the homogeneous equation system

$$B_i(t) = \int_0^t \sum_{j=1}^m B_j(t-x)\,{}_jp_i(x)m_i(x)dx = \int_0^t \sum_{j=1}^m B_j(t-x)\,{}_j\Phi_i(x)dx$$

$$t > \beta \qquad i = 1, 2, \ldots, m, \quad (8)$$

where ${}_j\Phi_i(x) = {}_jp_i(x)m_i(x)$ is the multiregional generalization of the net maternity function of the single-region model (Keyfitz, 1968, Ch.6). With this <u>multiregional net maternity function</u> we may associate the moments

$${}_jR_i(n) = \int_\alpha^\beta x^n\,{}_j\Phi_i(x)dx \qquad i,j = 1, 2, \ldots, m \quad (9)$$

among which ${}_jR_i(0)$ is of particular interest inasmuch as it defines the number of (girl) children expected to be born in region i to a (girl) baby now born in region j. Summing this measure over regions of residence we find the <u>region-of-birth reproduction rate</u> for region j:

$${}_jR(0) = {}_jR_1(0) + {}_jR_2(0) + \ldots = \sum_{i=1}^m {}_jR_i(0) \quad (10)$$

Alternatively, summing the same measure over regions of birth we obtain the <u>region-of-residence reproduction rate</u> for region i:

$$R_i(0) = \frac{B_1}{B_i}\,{}_1R_i(0) + \frac{B_2}{B_i}\,{}_2R_i(0) + \ldots = \sum_{j=1}^m \frac{B_j}{B_i}\,{}_jR_i(0) \ , \quad (11)$$

where the weights introduced into the summation reflect the total number of births in each region.

As in the single-region model, the solution of (7) can be found by first obtaining a solution of (8) and then choosing values for the arbitrary constants in that solution so that in addition to satisfying (8), $B_i(t)$ also satisfies (7). Following the procedure used in the single-region model (e.g., Keyfitz, 1968, Ch.5) we adopt the trial solution $B_i(t) = Q_i e^{rt}$ and rewrite (8) as

$$Q_i = \int_{\alpha}^{\beta} \sum_{j=1}^{m} Q_j e^{-rx} \, {}_jp_i(x) m_i(x) dx \ , \quad i = 1, 2, \ldots, m,$$

where the range of integration has been narrowed to take into account that $m_i(x) \neq 0$ only for $\alpha \leq x \leq \beta$. Finally, dividing both sides of the equation by Q_i gives the <u>multiregional characteristic equation system</u>

$$1 = \sum_{j=1}^{m} \frac{Q_j}{Q_i} \, {}_j\Psi_i(r) \ , \qquad i = 1, 2, \ldots, m, \tag{12}$$

where ${}_j\Psi_i(r) = \int_{\alpha}^{\beta} e^{-rx} \, {}_jp_i(x) m_i(x) dx = \int_{\alpha}^{\beta} e^{-rx} \, {}_j\Phi_i(x) dx$.

Single-region arguments may be used to show that the system of equations in (12) can have only one real root and that any complex roots which satisfy (12), must occur in complex conjugate pairs (Keyfitz, 1968, Ch.5). Furthermore, the real root r is greater than the real part of any complex root. Consequently, the birth sequence $B_i(t) = \sum_{h=1}^{\infty} Q_{hi} e^{r_h t}$ is increasingly dominated by the first term $Q_{1i} e^{r_1 t}$ as t becomes large. Thus, ultimately

$$B_i(t) \doteqdot Q_{1i} \, e^{r_1 t} = Q_i e^{rt} \quad .$$

Exponential births lead to an exponentially growing population with a stable distribution in which each age-by-region subpopulation maintains a constant proportional relationship to the total population and increases at the same <u>intrinsic rate of growth</u>, r . The influence of the initial population distribution is forgotten as time goes by, a condition known as <u>ergodicity</u>.

In the single-region model one normally evaluates $\Psi(r)$ with the numerical approximation

$$\Psi(r) = \sum_{x=\alpha}^{\beta-5} e^{-r(x+2.5)} \frac{L(x)F(x)}{\ell(0)} ,$$

in which the integral $\int_0^5 e^{-r(x+t)} p(x+t)m(x+t)dt$ is replaced by the product of $e^{-r(x+2.5)}$, $\frac{L(x)}{\ell(0)}$, and $F(x)$, the observed fertility rate. The summation is over ages x which are multiples of 5.

An analogous approach may be followed in the multiregional model. We evaluate the integral

$$\int_0^5 e^{-r(x+t)} {}_jp_i(x+t)m_i(x+t)dt$$

as the product of $e^{-r(x+2.5)}$, $\frac{{}_jL_i(x)}{\ell_j(0)}$, and $F_i(x)$.

Thus we have

$${}_j\Psi_i(r) = \sum_{x=\alpha}^{\beta-5} e^{-r(x+2.5)} \frac{{}_jL_i(x)F_i(x)}{\ell_j(0)}$$

Using the data set out in Table 1, we may compute, for example,

$${}_2\Psi_1(0) = {}_2R_1(0) = \sum_{x=10}^{50} \frac{{}_2L_1(x)}{\ell_2(0)} F_1(x) = 0.105 ,$$

which defines the number of baby girls by which a woman born in the rest of the United States will be replaced in California. Analogous computations give

$${}_1R_1(0) = 1.192 \qquad {}_1R_2(0) = 0.495 \qquad {}_2R_2(0) = 1.603 .$$

We conclude therefore, that under the 1958 schedule of growth, a girl born in the rest of the United States will be replaced, in the subsequent generation, by ${}_2R(0) = 0.105 + 1.603 = 1.708$ baby girls of whom 0.105 will be born in California. Corresponding measures for a California-born girl are 1.687 and 0.495, respectively.

But r = 0 is clearly not the solution of Equation (12). This can be readily established by substituting the values of ${}_j\Psi_i(0)$ into (12) and solving for Q_2/Q_1 and Q_1/Q_2 , respectively. Solving the first equation we obtain $Q_2/Q_1 = -1.829$; the solution to the second is $Q_1/Q_2 = -1.218$ or, equivalently, $Q_2/Q_1 = -0.821$. Since we have two different estimates of the same quantity it is clear that we have not yet found the correct value for r. By a process of iteration we ultimately converge to r = 0.02059, for which

$$ {}_1\Psi_1(r) = 0.711 \quad {}_1\Psi_2(r) = 0.282 \quad {}_2\Psi_1(r) = 0.060 \quad {}_2\Psi_2(r) = 0.941 . $$

Substituting these into Equation (12) gives $Q_2/Q_1 = 4.823$ in both cases, i.e.,

$$ 0.711 + (4.823)0.060 = 1 $$

$$ (1/4.823)0.282 + 0.941 = 1 $$

4. The Spatial Consequences of Zero Population Growth

During the past decade, several White House task forces, countless congressional committees, and scores of public interest groups have attempted to define the outlines of a desirable national population growth policy, taking as their starting point the widespread conviction that such growth is not taking place the way it should. Even though these committees and task forces span more than a decade and several administrations, their respective products have been remarkably similar in coverage, major themes, and proposals. Most begin by projecting the nation's population growth to a net increase of anywhere from 80 to 145 million Americans by the turn of the century. Almost all of these study groups then assert that without public intervention, a majority of citizens will inherit steadily growing, already overcrowded and poorly planned metropolitan areas. (See, for example, the various reports of the U.S. Commission on Population Growth and the American Future, 1972.)

The contention that America's population crisis stems from a propensity to overbreed overlooks the evident fact that any demographic imbalance in the U.S. today is less one of absolute numbers than of their maldistribution. The notion of a population distribution policy therefore has wide appeal but, unfortunately, insufficient substance. An important contributing factor to this lack of substance is our poor understanding of the dynamics of multiregional demographic growth and distribution.

Demographers agree that because of the large number of young people in America's population today, immediate zero population growth is not a practical objective. Consequently, most projected paths toward a stationary population assume an average of approximately 2.11 births per woman from now on and hold mortality fixed. On the assumption of zero or negligibly small net immigration, such a projection leads in about 70 years to a stationary population that is approximately 40 to 50 percent larger than the current population. Much has been made of the social and economic consequences of such a population and particularly important have been the analyses of its stationary age composition--an age composition that would have a higher median age and virtually constant numbers from age zero to 50. (See, for example, Coale, 1972.)

But what of the spatial distribution of such a stationary national population? What are the alternative paths in a geographic context? Will we, for example have as Alonso (1973, p. 191) puts it "a nationally stable population ... composed of many localities declining in population, many localities growing, and only some remaining stable"?

A nationally stationary population may arise out of a growth process which exhibits a zero growth rate in each short interval of time or it may develop out of a long-run average zero growth rate which occurs as a consequence of a combination of sequences of positive growth, of zero growth, and of decline. Since no obvious advantages arise from the latter case, demographers quite naturally have viewed the attainment of a stationary population as arising from a continuation of zero growth in the short-run. Thus the normal assumption involves a fixed mortality schedule and fertility set at replacement level.

An analogous situation arises in the case of a multiregional population. By augmenting the assumptions of fixed mortality and replacement level fertility with the assumption of fixed migration we may obtain a stationary multiregional population. In such a case, each region in the system will grow at a zero rate of growth. (Alternatively, we may assume that zero growth for the multiregional system is a consequence of an aggregation of zero and nonzero growth rates in its constituent regions. The dynamics of this situation are more complex and will not be considered in this paper.)

If mortality is fixed and one thousand baby girls born at each moment replace themselves, on the average, with a thousand baby girls as they move past their childbearing years, we will ultimately obtain a stationary zero growth population. But the women who survive to the childbearing ages must have enough daughters to replace not only themselves but also those women who have not survived to become mothers. Thus we specify that the net (and not the gross) reproduction rate of the female population be unity, i.e., R(0)=1. Reducing observed age-specific fertility rates proportionally to obtain a net reproduction rate of unity then is one way of achieving a stationary population. The last column in the lower half of Table 4 shows that had the U.S. female population in 1958 immediately moved to replacement levels, the 88 million female population of that year would have grown to 113 million (the stationary equivalent, Y) before attaining zero population growth.

The multiregional analog of the above calculation is straightforward. We simply reduce the observed age-specific regional fertility rates proportionally until region-of-birth net reproduction rates are all equal to unity, i.e., ${}_{j}R(0) = 1$, $j = 1, 2, \ldots, m$. The mechanics of the population projection process itself, however, remain unchanged.

Table 4 sets out some of the more interesting consequences of an immediate movement to replacement levels of fertility by the 1958 U.S. female population that has served as our numerical example throughout this paper. (Note that Table 4 is the zero growth counterpart of Table 3, which illuminated the long-run consequences of an unchanging continuance of present rates.) Several findings are of some interest and merit elaboration.

First, observe that the spatial allocations or shares of the stationary multiregional population in Table 4 do not differ significantly from those of

TABLE 4 - MULTIREGIONAL PROJECTIONS TO ZERO GROWTH AND ASSOCIATED PARAMETERS: UNITED STATES FEMALES, 1958

A. FIVE-REGION PROJECTION

jections Stable wth ameters	REGION OF RESIDENCE				
	1. San Francisco S.M.S.A.	2. Los Angeles S.M.S.A.	3. San Diego S.M.S.A.	4. Rest of Cal.	5. Rest of U.S.
(1958)	1,941,994	3,723,919	446,390	1,283,135	80,844,419
(1958)	0.0220	0.0422	0.0051	0.0145	0.9162
(2008)	4,132,157	7,869,750	1,216,643	2,398,295	95,274,261
(2008)	0.0373	0.0710	0.0110	0.0216	0.8592
Y	5,887,834	10,558,059	1,546,379	3,337,595	92,180,796
%	0.0519	0.0930	0.0136	0.0294	0.8121
(0-14)	0.1997	0.1960	0.1705	0.1979	0.2014
(15-64)	0.6296	0.6223	0.5874	0.6212	0.6309
(65+)	0.1707	0.1818	0.2422	0.1810	0.1677
λ	1.00000				
r	0.00000				
b	0.01359	0.01317	0.01178	0.01315	0.01375
Δ=b-r	0.01359	0.01317	0.01178	0.01315	0.01375
d	0.01334	0.01305	0.01599	0.01438	0.01366
i	0.01906	0.01624	0.03167	0.02775	0.00224
o	0.01931	0.01636	0.02746	0.02651	0.00233
n	-0.00025	-0.00012	0.00421	0.00124	-0.00009

B. TWO-REGION AND AGGREGATED MULTIREGIONAL PROJECTIONS

jections Stable wth ameters	TWO-REGION MODEL		AGGREGATIONS OF MULTIREGIONAL MODELS		SINGLE-REGION MODEL
	1. California	2. Rest of U.S.	TWO-REGION	FIVE-REGION	
(1958)	7,395,438	80,844,419	88,239,857	88,239,857	88,239,857
(2008)	15,442,904	95,404,038	110,846,942	110,891,106	110,653,183
Y	20,765,005	92,670,056	113,435,061	113,512,666	112,988,412
%	0.1831	0.8169	1.0000	1.0000	1.0000
(0-14)	0.1927	0.2014	0.1998	0.1997	0.2003
(15-64)	0.6249	0.6310	0.6299	0.6296	0.6308
(65+)	0.1824	0.1676	0.1703	0.1707	0.1689
λ	1.00000		1.00000	1.00000	1.00000
r	0.00000		0.00000	0.00000	0.00000
b	0.01322	0.01375	0.01365	0.01364	0.01369
Δ=b-r=d	0.01322	0.01375	0.01365	0.01364	0.01369

the stable multiregional population in Table 3. In both cases, California receives approximately 18 percent of the national population with the San Francisco, Los Angeles and San Diego SMSA's receiving 5, 9, and 1½ percent, respectively. Thus it appears that the spatial allocation effects of proportionally reduced fertility are negligible.

Although the redistributional effects of proportionally reduced fertility are negligible, the age compositional effects are not. As in the single-region model, reduced fertility produces an older population which has a much higher percentage of its members in the 65 years and over age group. However, the interaction of reduced fertility and fixed migration schedules produces an uneven regional allocation of the aged. Thus although California under zero growth would have about 18 percent of its population in the 65-year and over age group, San Diego would have more (24 percent) while San Francisco would have less (17 percent). The spatial population dynamics leading up to this result are clear. San Diego, because it is a retirement haven, receives relatively "older" inmigrants than does San Francisco. As the proportion of the aged increases nationally, San Diego will receive a heavier than average net inflow of migrants. This is why its net migration rate changes from a <u>negative</u> 0.4 per 1000 in Table 3 to a <u>positive</u> 4.2 per 1000 in Table 4. San Francisco's corresponding rates, on the other hand, exhibit a reverse shift, decreasing from a <u>positive</u> net migration rate of 1.2 per 1000 to a <u>negative</u> rate of 0.2 per 1000.

Finally, Table 4 shows that regions which exhibit higher than average birth rates prior to zero growth will have lower than average birth rates during zero growth. Once again San Diego offers an interesting case study. According to Table 3, it has the highest intrinsic birth rate of all 5 regions in the system (28 per 1000). Yet in Table 4 its intrinsic birth rate is the lowest (12 per 1000). The population dynamics producing this reversal are the same as those outlined earlier and result from the relatively older population that San Diego would have under zero growth. (Note that San Diego's intrinsic death rate is the highest both before <u>and</u> during zero growth).

In one of his contributions to the final reports produced by the Commission on Population Growth and the American Future, Peter Morrison (1972, p. 547) observed:

> "...demographic processes interact in subtle and often complex ways, and the mechanisms by which declining fertility would influence population redistribution are only partially understood."

It is hoped that this paper has identified and illuminated some of these mechanisms.

REFERENCES

Alonso, W. (1973). "Urban Zero Population Growth," Daedalus, CII, 191-206.

Coale, A.J. (1972). "Alternative Paths to a Stationary Population," in Demographic and Social Aspects of Population Growth, Ed., C.F. Westoff and R. Parke, Jr., U.S. Commission on Population Growth and the American Future (Washington, D.C.: U.S. Government Printing Office), pp.589-603.

Feeney, G. (1970). "Stable Age by Region Distributions," Demography, VI, 341-348.

Gantmacher, F.R. (1959). The Theory of Matrices, trans, K.A. Hirsch, Vol. 2 (New York: Chelsea Publishing Co.).

Keyfitz, N. (1968). Introduction to the Mathematics of Population, (Reading, Mass.: Addison-Wesley).

_________ (1969). "Age Distribution and the Stable Equivalent," Demography, VI, 261-269.

LeBras, H. (1971). "Equilibre et Croissance de Populations Soumises a des Migration," Theoretical Population Biology, II, 100-121.

Leslie, P.H. (1945). "On the Use of Matrices in Certain Population Mathematics," Biometrika, XXXIII, 183-212.

Morrison, P.A. (1972). "The Impact of Population Stabilization on Migration and Redistribution," in Population, Distribution, and Policy, Ed., S.M. Mazie, U.S. Commission on Population Growth and the American Future (Washington, D.C.: U.S. Government Printing Office), pp. 543-560.

Parlett, B. (1970). "Ergodic Properties of Population, I: The One Sex Model," Theoretical Population Biology, I, 191-207.

Pollard, J.H. (1973). Mathematical Models for the Growth of Human Populations (London: Cambridge University Press).

Rogers, A. (1966). "The Multiregional Matrix Growth Operator and the Stable Interregional Age Structure," Demography, III, 537-544.

_________ (1971). Matrix Methods in Urban and Regional Analysis, (San Francisco, Cal.: Holden-Day).

_________ (1974). "The Multiregional Net Maternity Function and Multiregional Stable Growth," Demography, XI, 473-481.

_________ (1975). Introduction to Multiregional Mathematical Demography (New York: John Wiley).

Sharpe, F.R. and A.J. Lotka (1911). "A Problem in Age-Distribution," Philosophical Magazine, Ser. 6, XXI, 435-438.

Stone, L.O. (1968). "Stable Migration Rates from the Multiregional Growth Matrix Operator," Demography, V, 439-442.

Sykes, Z.M. (1969). "On Discrete Stable Population Theory," Biometrics, XXV, 285-293.

SYSTEM THEORETIC CONTROL IN IMMUNOLOGY†

C.F. Barton, R.R. Mohler and C.S. Hsu
Department of Electrical and Computer Engineering
Oregon State University
Corvallis, Oregon 97331

ABSTRACT

A systematic overview is presented of body immune response from which a primitive mathematical model is derived as a base for more extensive research. The model provides a basic description of one basic class of cells (B-cells) with extensions for antibody switch-over and secondary response.

Introduction

The purpose of this paper is to present a kinetic model of cellular and antibody secretion changes during the immune response. The immune system can be defined as that which distinguishes between "self" and "non-self" and rejects foreign agents. This definition will be taken as a starting point for developing a mathematical model of the immune system which is comprised of:

(1) a group of cells, the lymphocytes, of which each human body possesses about 10^{12} and,

(2) a group of molecules, the antibodies, of which each human possesses about 10^{20}

When an organism is invaded by an antigen (i.e. a foreign agent which could be a virus or a bacterial product), lymphocytes and antibodies are mobilized toward a common objective - the final elimination of the antigen invader. Some subgroups of the lymphocytes will get larger (the B-cells); other subgroups of lymphocytes (the T-cells) will modify their function during the immune response by first enhancing the antibody production, and then eventually by decreasing this production rate. After elimination of the antigen the system will go back to a state of equilibrium where the immunocompetent cells will gradually cease to differentiate and produce the antibodies.

The immune response appears as a highly complex and finely controlled variable structure system [1] with each type of immunocompetent cell and response modulating the others. A systematic understanding of immunology should provide valuable clues to the solution of relevant problems in such areas as: (1) immunotherapy, where the immune response is activated and/or inactivated artificially, (2) transplant rejection, (3) viral diseases, and (4) cancer, where because of the presence of blocking factors, immunocompetent cells lose their inhibiting effect on the tumor. Further,

† Research supported in part by US-NSF Grant No. ENG74-15530.

a mathematical model of the immune response should help to extract the few most essential variables from the more complex real situation. It could therefore be valuable in correlation and interpretation of the findings of the vast number of experimental projects becoming available, and could help avoid the need for certain experiments which may be impossible to perform on human beings. Several different models are being developed - each one with the objective of interpreting a specific function of the immune system. Even the mathematical models taken together will, of course, remain an oversimplification of the real system.

Present Overview of the Immune System+

Lymphocytes are produced in the bone marrow at an approximate rate of 10^7 cells/minute. Whereupon they reach, by means of circulating antibody molecules in the blood stream, most tissues of the body. They are collected and concentrated in some parts of the immune system such as the lymph nodes, the thymus and the spleen, and in the bone marrow. When antigen enters the body, two different types of immunological reaction may occur:

(1) The synthesis and release of free antibody into the blood and other fluids (humoral immune response). The antibody reacts with antigen to form complexes which are subsequently eliminated.

(2) The production of "sensitized" lymphocytes which have antibody-like molecules on the surface. These are the effects of cell-mediated immunity.

At the rest state, the lymphocytes secrete small amounts of antibody which coats the cells and constitutes the antibody-combining sites or receptors. The antigen is formed of a large protein molecule that displays on its surface some antigenic determinant called epitopes susceptible to recognition by the cell receptors. The epitope-receptor recognition is the stimulating signal for the lymphocyte, identified then as a B-cell, to undergo proliferation and differentiation. The offspring cells form family lines called clones. Some cells, termed plasma cells, will secrete the antibody at a rate of about 10^8 molecules/cell·h. Other cells, called memory cells, return to rest and represent the "memory" of the antigen exposure. According to the clonal selection theory, all those clones generated by the stimulation of the lymphocytes are committed either to produce or to carry the memory of the same antibody which originally stimulated the lymphocyte cell. [22]

The stimulation of the lymphocytes depends on several factors:

(i) the concentration on the lymphocyte surface of recognized epitopes,

(ii) the degree of fit for epitope-combining sites,

(iii) the way epitopes are presented, either on the surface of a molecule or on the surface of a cell,

(iv) and in most humoral reactions, but not in all, on the presence of another type of lymphocyte, the T-cells.

+ For a detailed discussion the reader is referred to the excellent texts by Roitt [2] and by Abramoff and LaVia [3].

The T-cells constitute approximately 70 percent of the total lymphocyte population. They are experimentally distinguished from the B-cells, about 25 percent of the lymphocytes, rather by their function than by morphological differences. (The remaining cells not included in both counts are sometimes termed "null cells.") T-cells are processed by or in some way dependent on the thymus. They are responsible for cell-mediated immunity, and although they do not seem to secrete antibody themselves, they do play a key role in the humoral immune primary response and in the secondary response (immune response to second exposure to antigen).

Antibody and antigen react together to form an antibody-antigen complex. The chemical reaction is characterized by an intrinsic equilibrium constant or antibody affinity (k in l/mole) which refers to the energy of interaction between one site of antibody and one antigen-determinant [4]. This intrinsic affinity is not measurable experimentally since it is not possible to isolate one single site and one determinant. One rather measures a functional affinity which represents an average of all interactions of antigen combining sites in one antibody molecule with corresponding copies of specific determinants.

The final elimination of antigen follows essentially two patterns.

(1) Opsonic adherence: the antibody reacting with antigen develops an increase binding affinity for specific sites on the surface of scavenger cells such as polymorphonuclear leucocytes and macrophages. The bacteria coated with antibody become easier to be engulfed and digested.

(2) Lysis of cell by complement cascades. Complement operation requires the presence of antigen-antibody complex on the surface of bacteria and of the first complement which is a protein. The complement cascade is activated by the Ab-Ag complex whereupon several molecules of the next component in the complement sequence (at least 9 basic complements altogether) are generated. At their turn, each of these molecules generate several molecules of the next complement for an amplified cascade effect. The last molecule formed in the chain has the ability to punch "a functional hole" through the cell membrane on which they are fixed, leading to the death of the cell or lysis. Similar cascade chains and the effect of enzyme concentration to increase membrane permeability as demonstrated by lysis is discussed by Mohler [5] and Banks [6].

Kinetics of Cell Population and Antibody Production - Model I

The first mathematical analysis of the immune process was of a preliminary nature by Hege and Cole [7]. Jilek [8,9] derives a probability model of different cell types to undergo repeated contacts with specific antigens. He assumes a Poisson form of process and considers a Monte Carlo simulation. Bell [10,11,12] derives a model, which was a significant advance, for the binding of antigen to antibodies of different affinity constants. The research discussed here is most closely related to recent research conducted at the University of Rome through our joint US-Italy research program [13,14].

Basic assumptions usually made in past research include:

(a) clonal selection theory as discussed above;

(b) antigen is monovalent, but the model could be easily extended to a multivalent antigen;

(c) T-B cell cooperation is not considered;

(d) the model describes the humoral immune response, and cell-mediated immunity is not considered;

(e) existence of the numerous different types of antibodies and of different types of cells secreting them is not considered;

(f) any mutual interaction between cell receptors is neglected;

(g) system parameters are assumed to be independent of total cell population;

(h) immunological tolerance is neglected or poorly explained,

(i) switch-over phenomenon is neglected;

(j) difference between primary and secondary response is neglected.

Model I may be derived with assumption (a) to (j) as listed above. It should be noted that this model is only intended to be a base for further work and by no means a complete model of the immune system.

Consider the following classification according to state and control:

$x_1(k,t)$: population density of B-cells, which are stimulated lymphocyte cells with particular surface receptors for antigen according to the antibody affinity constant k. They may divide to produce plasma cells and/or memory cells. The latter which may further divide and enter the original pool of immunocompetent cells or stimulated lymphocytes.

$x_2(k,t)$: population density of plasma cells of given k which are non-reproducing offspring of B-cells.

$x_3(k,t)$: population density of antibody sites of given k.

$x_4(k,t)$: population density of antibody-antigen complexes.

$h(t)$: antigen concentration which triggers the response mechanism (assumed to stimulate the response according to an average specific affinity in the initial model).

This derivation assumes that antibody reacts with antigen to form the antibody-antigen complex following the law of mass action, with an antibody affinity constant k. There is a population distribution of B-cells with continuous values of the affinity constant k over a range k_1, k_2 which in Model I has an average value $\bar{k}$. A second model considers a distributed population of B-cells with respect to k.

The following parameters are used in the model:

α = birth rate constant of stimulated B-cells

p_s = probability that an antigen stimulates cell (h,k dependent)

p_d = probability that a B-cell differentiates into a plasma cell (h,k dependent)

β = rate of generation of new B-cells (from bone marrow, k dependent)

τ_1 = mean life time of B-cells

τ_2 = mean life time of plasma cells

τ_3 = mean life time of antibody cells

τ_4 = mean life time of antibody-antigen complex

τ_h = mean life time of antigen

α' = plasma cell antibody production rate

$u_1(\bar{k},h) = p_s(1 - 2p_d)$

$u_2(\bar{k},h) = p_s p_d$

$c_{\bar{k}}$ = dissociation rate of antibody-antigen complex

$\bar{k}c_{\bar{k}}$ = association rate of antibody-antigen complex

$\dot{h}_i$ = inoculation rate of antigen.

The dynamics of the population density of B-cells depends on three phenomena:

a) B-cells stimulated at a rate $\alpha p_s x_1$, disappear and differentiate into plasma cells at a rate $2\alpha p_s p_d x_1$, and into memory cells at a rate $2\alpha p_s(1-p_d)x_1$ which enter the pool of immunocompetent B-cells.

b) New B-cells are generated in the bone marrow at a rate β.

c) Immunocompetent cells have mean death rate of $\frac{x_1}{\tau_1}$.

Consequently, the sum of these three terms leads to the rate of change of immunocompetent cells:

$$\frac{dx_1}{dt} = \alpha\, p_s(1-2p_d)\, x_1 - \frac{x_1}{\tau_1} + \beta \quad , \tag{1}$$

Similarly, plasma cells, antibody sites and antibody-antigen complex for an average affinity constant $\bar{k}$ may be approximated by birth rate minus death rate equations as follows:

$$\frac{dx_2}{dt} = 2\alpha\, p_s p_d x_1 - \frac{x_2}{\tau_2} \quad , \tag{2}$$

$$\frac{dx_3}{dt} = -c_{\bar{k}}\bar{k}hx_3 - \frac{x_3}{\tau_3} + \alpha' x_2 + c_{\bar{k}}x_4 \quad , \tag{3}$$

$$\frac{dx_4}{dt} = c_{\bar{k}}\bar{k}hx_3 - (c_{\bar{k}} + \frac{1}{\tau_4})\, x_4 \quad . \tag{4}$$

The generation of a particular free antigen of given antibody affinity $\bar{k}$ may be approximated by inoculation rate - rate of catabolism - net complex association rate, or

$$\frac{dh}{dt} = \dot{h}_i - \frac{h}{\tau_h} - \bar{k}c_{\bar{k}}hx_3 + c_{\bar{k}}x_4 \tag{5}$$

Bruni, et al. [13] derive the following probability approximation:

for a given concentration of antigen with an antibody affinity constant k

$$p_d = \frac{kh}{1 + kh}$$

and

$$p_s \simeq \begin{cases} 1, \text{ for some sensitive interval, } & \gamma_1 < kh < \gamma_2 \\ 0, \text{ for other } kh. \end{cases}$$

Model I was simulated on a digital computer (OS3-system) with a program based on a RUNGE-KUTTA fourth-order method of integration. The parameters used in the simulation are listed in Table I. They all represent observed values except for the antibody-antigen complex dissociation rate c_k which was estimated; to simulate the injection of antigen in Freund's adjuvant the antigen inoculation rate was represented by the sum of two functions - a step function accounting for two-thirds of the total amount of antigen injected and an exponential function accounting for the remaining one-third.

The results of the simulation are shown in Figure 1. The kinetics of the cell and antibody molecule populations are consistent with known immunological phenomena. It is worth noting that the model is very sensitive to the dissociation rate c_k, and that experimental data for the conditions presented here were not yet available at the writing of this paper.

$$\dot{h}_i(t) = \frac{Q}{3\tau_u V} e^{-\frac{t}{\tau_u}} + \frac{2}{3}\frac{Q}{T_u V}\,\delta_{-1}(T_u - t).$$

TABLE I

α	5.780×10^{-2}	hr^{-1}
β	1.627×10^{-9}	mole/hr
τ_1	7140	hr
τ_2	71	hr
k	10^6	$mole^{-1}$
c_k	10^{-6}	hr^{-1}
α'	2×10^{-8}	hr^{-1}
τ_3	200	hr
τ_4	100	hr
τ_h	50	hr
Q	3.33×10^{-8}	mole
V	0.2	liter
T_u	1000	hr
τ_u	100	hr

Distribution Effect of k, Secondary Response and Switch-over - Model II

Model II as represented below is a refinement of Model I to take account of these three important phenomena in the immune response whereby cell clones, and antibodies are generated according to a distribution of affinities. The second response to a

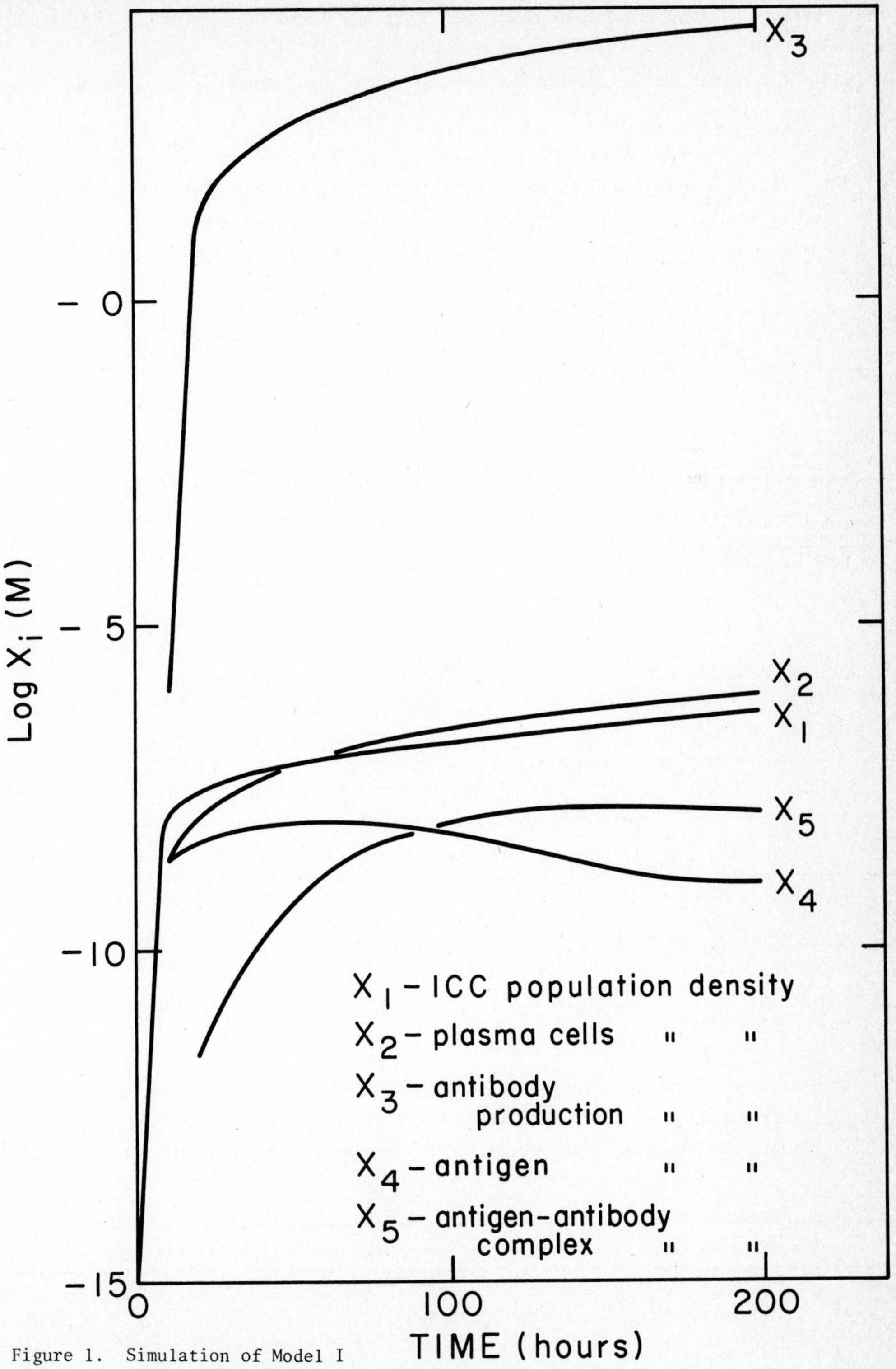

Figure 1. Simulation of Model I

given antigen is more pronounced than the first, and there is a rapid cut-off of one antibody (IgM) as another (IgG) is produced.

Similar to the immune population density (Model I) derivation above, Model II is derived as follows:

$$\frac{dx_1}{dt} = \alpha\, p_s(1 - 2p_d - 2p_m)\, x_1 - \frac{x_1}{\tau_2} + \beta\, p_c(k) \,, \qquad (6)$$

$$\frac{dx_2}{dt} = 2\alpha p_s p_d x_1 + 2\alpha_m\, p_{dm}\, x_5 - \frac{x_2}{\tau_2} \,, \qquad (7)$$

$$\frac{dx_{3M}}{dt} = -c'_k\, k'h\, x_{3M} - \frac{x_{3M}}{\tau_{3M}} + \alpha' x_2 + c'_k\, x_{4M} \,, \qquad (8)$$

$$\frac{dx_{3G}}{dt} = -c''_k\, k''h\, x_{3G} - \frac{x_{3G}}{\tau_{3G}} + \alpha'' x_2\, [t - t_s(h)] + c''_k\, x_{4G} \,, \qquad (9)$$

$$\frac{dx_{4M}}{dt} = c'_k\, k'\, h\, x_{3M} - (c'_k + \frac{1}{\tau_{4M}})\, x_{4M} \,, \qquad (10)$$

$$\frac{dx_{4G}}{dt} = c''_k\, k''\, x_{3G} - (c''_k + \frac{1}{\tau_{4G}})\, x_{4G} \,, \qquad (11)$$

$$\frac{dx_5}{dt} = 2\alpha\, p_s p_m x_1 - 2\alpha_m p_{dm} x_5 - \frac{x_5}{\tau_5} \,, \qquad (12)$$

$$\frac{dh}{dt} = \dot{h}_i - \frac{h}{\tau_h} - h \int_{k'_1}^{k'_2} k'\, c'_k\, x_{3M}(k',t)\, dk' - h \int_{k'_1}^{k'_2} k''$$

$$c''_k\, x_{3G}(k'',t)\, dk'' + \int_{k'_1}^{k'_2} c'_k\, x_{4M}(k',t)\, dk' + \int_{k''_1}^{k''_2}$$

$$c''_k\, x_{4G}(k'',t)\, dk'' \,, \qquad (13)$$

Notation used here, and not previously defined in Model I, is as follows:

p_m = probability that a B-cell differentiates into a memory cell

p_{dm} = probability that a memory cell differentiates into a plasma cell

x_{3M} = population density of antibody sites IgM,

x_{3G} = population density of antibody sites IgG,

x_{4M} = molecule density of complex antigen - IgM immunoglobulin (Ag-IgM),

x_{4G} = molecule density of complex antigen - IgG immunoglobulin (Ag-IgG),

x_5 = population density of memory cells,

c'_k = dissociation rate of Ag-IgM,
c''_k = dissociation rate of Ag-IgG,
$c'_k k'$= association rate of Ag-IgM,
$c''_k k''$= association rate of Ag-IgG,
τ_{3M} = mean lifetime of IgM,
τ_{3G} = mean lifetime of IgG,
τ_{4G} = mean lifetime of complex Ag-IgG,
τ_{4M} = mean lifetime of complex Ag-IgM,
τ_5 = mean lifetime of memory cells,
α_m = production rate of plasma cell by memory cell,
$\alpha' \neq \alpha''$ = the immunoglobulin production rates of plasma cells are different for IgM and IgG,
$t_s(h)$ = delay time associated with the switch-over mechanism,
k'_1, k'_2 = antibody affinity limits associated with IgM,
k''_1, k''_2 = antibody affinity limits associated with IgG.

1) The average affinity constant of the antibody generated during the immune response increased with respect to time as a consequence of the distributed effect of B-cells which can differentiate into antibody producing cells (plasma cells) with a large number of k (assumed continuous here) over some allowable interval k_1, k_2. Whereas in Model I, the population densities and k dependent parameters were computed for an average value of $\bar{k}$,in Model II they are determined for each particular k. Equation (1) becomes equation (6) where the production rate of B-cells β is modulated by a probability of generation $p_c(k)$.

   The amount of antigen binding with antibodies and the amount of antigen liberated by dissociation of the complexes are respectively obtained by integrating over the interval k_1, k_2 or k'_1, k'_2 and k''_1, k''_2 as explained in the next section. The model assumes that antibody is entirely generated by the plasma cells (amount of antibody generated by memory cells is neglected).

2) The secondary response is characterized by three facts observed experimentally:
   i) The interval time between antigen challenge and proliferation is smaller in the secondary response than for the primary.
   ii) The serum antibody level is higher in secondary response, there is an expanded pool of antigen-sensitive memory cells.
   iii) Higher-affinity antibodies are produced.

   Model II considers stimulated B-cells and memory cells as two distinct populations. (Note change in first term of equation (6) and the introduction of equation (12) for memory cells). It is assumed that the time interval between the antigen injection is short compared to the lifetime of a memory cell but long compared to the lifetime of a plasma cell and antibody. Also, the memory cells are not included in the population of immunocompetent cells in order to follow recent experimental findings which indicate that memory and immunocompetent cells present different affinity distributions. As stated earlier, the immunocompetent cells show at the end of the primary response a shift toward higher antibody affinity. The same phenomenon is not seen for the memory cells which present a greater heterogeneity in their affinity and therefore a larger selectivity. This provides the organism to react more adequately against a wide range of antigen doses upon secondary exposure [4]. Memory cells are stimulated and differentiate into plasma cells; this is represented by the term $2\ \alpha_m\ p_{dm} x_5$ in equation (7).

3) The B-cell switch-over phenomenon is characterized by the secretion of various antibodies after contact with antigen. The synthesis of these antibodies proceeds at different rates. Usually there is an early IgM response (generated from a μ-protein chain) which tends to fall off rapidly. And apparently, the same plasma-cells start secreting IgG (from a γ-protein chain) which builds up to its maximum over a longer time period.

The same phenomenon, this time amplified, is observed in the secondary exposure to the same antigen. The time trajectory of the IgM responses resembles that seen in the primary though the peak may be higher. By contrast the synthesis of IgG antibodies accelerates to a much higher peak, and there is a relatively slow fall-off in serum antibody levels [2]: Equation (3) of Model I has been replaced by equations (8) and (9) of Model II for the generation of IgM and IgG antibodies. IgG is produced after a time delay t_s which according to some experimental evidence depends on h. The gradual decrease in IgM production should be reflected in the model by appropriate production rates α' and α''. Until demonstrated otherwise by more precise correlation of experiment and simulation, any introduction in equation (8) for a step function to shut off the IgM production is neglected Here it is assumed $c_k' \simeq c_k''$ and $k' \simeq k''$ for a given h for the antibody-antigen complexes.

The initial conditions are:

a) At start of primary response

$$x_1 \neq 0$$

$$x_2 = x_{3M} = x_{3G} = X_{4M} = x_{4G} = x_5 = 0$$

b) At start of secondary response

$$x_1 \neq 0$$

$$x_2 \simeq x_{3M} \simeq x_{3G} \simeq x_{4M} \simeq x_{4G} \simeq 0$$

$$x_5 = \text{value at the end of primary response}$$

Discussion

At the present time Model II is simulated and biological experiments specifically designed to validate the model are performed. It seems appropriate now to review and assess the above assumptions made prior to Model II. In regards to assumption (b), Bell [15] and Bell and Delisi [16] derive simple mathematical models for specific binding of multivalent antigen to immune cell receptors when competition exists with non specific bindings of antigen to all surfaces and with binding of haptens to receptors. Effectively this competition decreases the antigen-receptor association constant. In most cases of humoral immune response the antigen is not T-cell independent and therefore assumption (c) fails. Several subpopulations of T-cells have been "identified" mainly by their distinct function in process regulation by antigenic stimulation of B-cells to be more effective, or by suppressing it. Several non-mathematical models have been proposed for the cooperation between T and B cells [17-21] - most of them assume that a stimulation signal is sent directly by the T-cells or, indirectly through the macrophages, another type of cell, to the B-cells. Several types of stimuli coming from specific T-cells or allogenic T-cells might be present in the T- and B-cells cooperation - T-B cooperation should be incorporated into the mathematical model with at least one new state variable for the T-cells. The "helper" and "suppressor" functions of T-cells may be expressed in the probability of B-cell stimulation being function of the T-cell population. The T-B interaction changes the rate of all proliferation; therefore it should be influential in the secondary response and in the switch-over phenomena for which the time-delay parameter t_s is expected to change.

Immunological tolerance and one of its counterparts graft rejection are other aspects of the immune system which could be analyzed in the T-B cell model. Experiments on thymectomized animals have shown that T-cells are involved in the rejection of grafts [2]. Assumption (g) is not always valid either since cellular proliferation and death rates depend to some extent on population density.

These assumptions are being investigated in more detail with new model refinements. Indeed, model development must proceed in an iterative manner, integrated with extensive immunological experiments such as are being conducted at the Oregon Regional Primate Research Center in conjunction with this project and that at the University of Rome.

In the long range, research of this nature is intended to bring focus to a somewhat disjointed world-wide experimental program, and eventually lead to a systematic understanding of disease control, cancer and transplant rejection.

REFERENCES

1. Raff, M.C., "T and B Lymphocytes and Immune Responses," Nature 242, 19-23, 1973.
2. Roitt, I.M., Essential Immunology, Blackwell Scientific Publication, London, 1971.

3. Abramoff, P., and LaVia, M., Biology of the Immune Response, McGraw-Hill, New York, 1970.
4. Macario, A.J., and Conway de Macario, E., "Sequential Changes and Persistence of Antibody Molecules During the Immune Response with Special Reference to the Binding Properties of the Antigen-Combining Site," Immunochemistry 12, pp 249-262, 1975.
5. Mohler, R.R., "A Basis for Variable Structure Models in Human Biology," in Variable Structure Systems with Application to Economics and Biology, Ruberti and Mohler, Eds.), pp 233-243, Springer-Verlag, 1975.
6. Banks, H.T., et al., "Nonlinear Systems in Models for Enzyme Cascades," Ibid. pp 265-277.
7. Hege, J.S., and Cole, J.L., "A Mathematical Model Relating Circulating Antibody and Antibody Forming Cells," J. Immunol. 94, pp 34-40, 1966.
8. Jikek, M., and Sterzl, J., "Modeling of the Immune Response," in Morphological and Functional Aspects of Immunity, pp 333-349, Plenum Press, New York, 1971.
9. Jilek, M., "Immune Response and its Stochastic Theory," Proc. IFAC Symposium on System Identification, The Hague, pp 209-212, 1973.
10. Bell, G.I., "Mathematical Model of Clonal Selection and Antibody Production," J. Theoret. Biol. 29, pp 191-232, 1970.
11. Ibid., Part II, J. Theoret. Biol. 33, pp 339-378, 1971.
12. Ibid., Part III, "The Cellular Basis of Immunological Paralysis," pp 379-398, 1971.
13. Bruni, C., Giovenco, M.A., Koch, G., and Strom, R., "A Dynamical Model of the Immune Response," in Variable Structure Systems with Application to Biology and Economics (Ruberti and Mohler, Eds.), Springer-Verlag, New York, 1975.
14. Bruni, C. Giovenco, M.A., Koch, G. and Strom, R., "The Immune Response as a Variable Structure System," Univ. Roma, Ist Auto. Report R. 74-25, July 1974.
15. Bell, G.I., "Model for the Binding of Multivalent Antigen to Cells," Nature 248, pp 430-431, 1974.
16. Bell, G.I. and Delisi, C.P., "Antigen Binding to Receptors on Immunocompetent Cells, 1. Simple Models and Interpretation of Experiments," Cellular Immunology 10, pp 415-431, 1974.
17. Feldmann, M., "Antigen Specific T-Cell Factors and Their Role in the Regulation of T-B Interaction," in The Immune System (E. Sercarz et al. eds.), Academic Press, 1974. pp 497-510.
18. Dutton, R.W., et al., "Is there Evidence for a Non-Antigen Specific Diffusable Chemical Mediator from the Thymus-Derived Cell in the Initiation of the Immune Response?" in Progress in Immunology, pp 355-368, Academic Press, New York, 1971.
19. Dutton, R.W., "T-Cell Factors in the Regulation of the B-Cell Response," in The Immune System (E. Sercarz et al.,eds), Academic Press, 1974, pp 485-495.
20. Gershon, R.K., "T-Cell Regulation: The Second Law of Thymodynamics," Ibid, pp 471-484.
21. Gershon, R.K., "T-Cell Control of Antibody Production," Contemporary Topics in Immunobiology, 3, pp 1-40, 1974.
22. Burnet, F.M., The Clonal Selection Theory of Acquired Immunity. Cambridge University Press, 1959.

OPTIMISATION DES PROCESSUS DE FERMENTATION EN CONTINU

J. BLUM
Laboratoire d'Analyse Numérique
C.N.R.S et PARIS VI
4, Place Jussieu
75005 - PARIS - FRANCE

Abstract.

The knowledge of a mathematical model of the kinetics of growth of single cell microorganisms and of the physical system enabling to cultivate them leads to the mathematical formulation of the problem.

Duality and gradient methods have been used to realize the minimisation of the industrial cost of the process, the production of biomasse per hour being given. Because of non linearity of the state equations and of non convexity of the cost function, Uzawa and Arrow-Hurwicz algorithms have been improved so that the convergence is obtained in 30 sec. on Univac 1110.

Ce travail entre dans le cadre de la préparation d'un Doctorat d'Etat ès Sciences Mathématiques à l'Université Paris VI. Je remercie le Professeur LIONS de m'avoir permis d'entreprendre ce travail, le Professeur KERNEVEZ de m'avoir mis en contact avec l'équipe de microbiologistes de Dijon, et le Professeur GLOWINSKI pour ses nombreux et judicieux conseils. Je remercie également toute l'équipe de la Station de Génie Microbiologique de l'INRA de Dijon, et en particulier MM. PERINGER et BLACHERE, pour leur fructueuse collaboration.

INTRODUCTION

De façon très générale, on entend par "fermentation" la production en culture de microorganismes unicellulaires à partir de matières premières appelées substrats (sucres, mélasses,...) et à l'aide d'un agent fermenteur.

On distingue trois types de telles cultures :

- la culture batch : elle se fait à l'intérieur d'un fermenteur sans adjonction ni prélèvement d'un produit , jusqu'à épuisement du substrat. Ce type de culture est utilisé pour la fabrication d'antibiotiques et de vitamines.
- la culture en continu : on injecte du substrat de façon continue et on soutire ce qui se trouve dans le fermenteur de façon à ce que le volume reste constant. Ce type de culture est récent, encore peu industrialisé, mais utilisé pour obtenir les levures fourragères servant à l'alimentation animale.
- la culture en semi-continu : c'est un procédé mixte. On laisse la fermentation se faire en batch puis,au bout d'un certain temps,on injecte du substrat avec un débit variable au cours du temps. Il se produit une expansion de volume ; quand le volume du liquide atteint celui du fermenteur, on vidange et on recommence. Ce procédé est utilisé pour la fabrication de la levure de boulangerie.

On se propose ici de réaliser une optimisation de la production de microorganismes unicellulaires en continu. La résolution de ce problème nécessite la connaissance du comportement du système biologique constitué par ces microorganismes ainsi que celle du système physique permettant de les cultiver.

La modélisation du système biologique a été étudiée en culture batch par l'équipe de la Station de Génie Microbiologique de l'I.N.R.A de Dijon [1] [2], et généralisée au cas de la culture en continu [3]. La modélisation du système physique est celle présentée par Aiba, Humphrey et Millis dans [4]. Le problème consiste alors à minimiser le coût industriel du process, dépendant des paramètres biologiques et physiques.

Deux schémas de fermentation ont été étudiés ; le premier est un schéma à un seul fermenteur standard avec recyclage, le second à deux fermenteurs couplés et avec recyclage. Les techniques employées sont présentées dans le cas le plus simple du schéma à un seul fermenteur.

I - MODELISATION.

1) Flow-sheet général.

Ce flow-sheet simplifié résume bien la réalité industrielle des fermentations en continu.

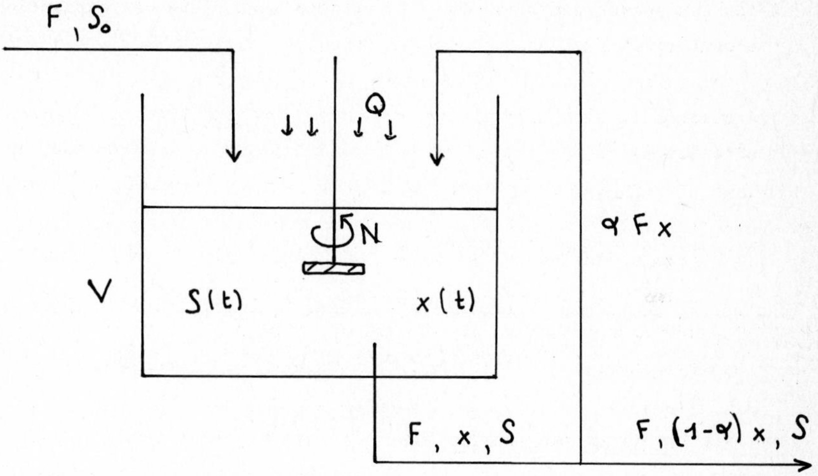

Fig. 1 Fermenteur standard avec recyclage, aération et agitation.

On injecte dans le fermenteur de volume utile V du substrat de concentration S_o avec un débit F constant au cours du temps. A chaque instant la concentration du substrat à l'intérieur du fermenteur est S(t) et celle de la biomasse produite est x(t). On soutire du fermenteur de façon continue le milieu de culture avec le même débit F de sorte que le volume reste constant. On recycle avec le coefficient de recyclage α une fraction de la biomasse soutirée et on recueille l'autre fraction ainsi que le substrat résiduel. De plus on injecte de l'air avec un débit Q constant et on agite le milieu, la vitesse de rotation de l'agitateur étant N .

• Le bilan en masse pour ce qui est de la biomasse s'écrit :

(1) $$V \frac{dx}{dt} = \mu x V - F(1-\alpha)x$$

μ étant le taux de croissance spécifique de la biomasse .

• Le bilan en masse pour ce qui est du substrat s'écrit :

(2) $$V \frac{dS}{dt} = F(S_o-S) - V_S x V$$

V_S étant la vitesse spécifique d'absorption du substrat.

• Le développement des microorganismes nécessite la consommation de l'oxygène dissous dans le milieu de culture. Cet oxygène dissous, de concentration C_L , est transféré de la phase gazeuse dans la phase liquide par l'intermédiaire de l'aération et de l'agitation de la culture. Le bilan d'oxygène s'écrit :

(3) $$\frac{dC_L}{dt} = T_R \times K_{LA} \times (100-C_L) - (V_R+V_{RE})x$$

K_{LA} étant le coefficient de transfert du système, V_R la vitesse spécifique de respiration des microorganismes, V_{RE} la vitesse spécifique de respiration endogène et T_R une constante .

• A l'équilibre on aura donc :

(4) $$\mu V = F(1-\alpha)$$

(5) $$F(S_o-S) = V_S x V$$

(6) $$T_R \times K_{LA} \times (100-C_L) = (V_R+V_{RE})x$$

• La quantité de biomasse recueillie à l'équilibre par unité de temps est

(7) $$PROD = F(1-\alpha)x$$

2) Modélisation du système biologique [1] [2] [3]

Le taux de croissance spécifique μ de la biomasse, qui caractérise le système biologique, est une combinaison linéaire de V_S et de V_R :

(8) $$\mu = P_o V_S + Q_o V_R$$

Le système biologique est donc défini par la façon dont V_S et V_R dépendent de S et de la concentration d'oxygène dissous C_L . On a :

(9) $$V_S = V_{SM} \times \frac{S}{K_S + S} \times \frac{1}{1 + \frac{BE \times C_L}{K_B + C_L}}$$

où V_{SM} est la vitesse spécifique maximale d'absorption du substrat, K_S , K_B et BE étant des constantes.

(10) $$V_R = \frac{S \times (K_2 V_1 + V_2 S)}{K_1 K_2 + K_2 (1 + \frac{K_1}{K_3}) S + WS^2} \times \frac{C_L}{K_L + C_L}$$

V_1 , V_2 , K_1 , K_2 , K_3 , K_L , W étant des constantes.

De plus, la vitesse spécifique V_{RE} de la respiration endogène est donnée par l'expression suivante :

(11) $$V_{RE} = V_{REM} \times \frac{C_L}{K_{LE} + C_L}$$

V_{REM} étant sa valeur maximale et K_{LE} une constante.

3) Modélisation du système physique [4]

Le système physique englobe la description de la géométrie du fermenteur et les divers processus de transfert de masse et d'énergie.

• La hauteur H_L du liquide dans le fermenteur cylindrique étant choisie égale au diamètre de celui-ci, le volume utile du fermenteur est donné par :

(12) $$V = \frac{\pi}{4} H_L^3$$

• L'aération du fermenteur est caractérisée par un indice NAE appelé nombre d'aération. Cet indice est lié au débit d'air injecté Q et à la vitesse de rotation de l'agitateur N par la relation :

(13) $$NAE = \alpha_1 \frac{Q}{N \times H_L^3}$$

• Soient PU la puissance absorbée par l'agitation en absence d'aération et PG celle absorbée par l'agitation en présence d'aération. PU est donnée par :

(14) $$PU = \beta_1 N^3 H_L^5$$ où β_1 est une constante.

La courbe donnant $\frac{PG}{PU}$ en fonction de NAE est une relation empirique :

(15) $$PG = PU \times h(NAE)$$

• La vitesse linéaire V_L de l'air traversant la section principale du fermenteur et ramenée à cette section vaut :

(16) $$V_L = \frac{Q}{\pi/4\ H_L^2}$$

• Le coefficient de transfert K_{LA} dépend de la géométrie du fermenteur, de la pression PR de l'air à l'intérieur du fermenteur (exprimée en mm Hg), de la puissance d'agitation PG et de la vitesse de l'air V_L par la relation :

(17) $$K_{LA} = \delta_1 \times \left[2 \times \left(1 + \frac{PR-760}{760}\right) + \frac{H_L}{10,3}\right] \times \left(\frac{PG}{V}\right)^{0,95} \times V_L^{0,67}$$

où δ_1 dépend de PR et de la température T de fermentation.

• D'une aération intense résulte une augmentation apparente du volume utile du fermenteur qui, exprimé en o/o , est appelée hold-up HOL et est donnée par la relation :

(18) $$HOL = \left[\left(\frac{PU}{V}\right)^{o,4} \times V_L^{o,5} - 2,75\right] / 0,725$$

Le volume total du fermenteur, compte-tenu d'une formation éventuelle de mousse V_o évaluée à 0,2 V, vaut alors :

(19) $$V_T = V + V \times \frac{HOL}{100} + V_o = V \times \left(1,2 + \frac{HOL}{100}\right)$$

II - FORMULATION MATHEMATIQUE DU PROBLEME

Pour optimiser le process le biologiste a la possibilité de jouer sur un certain nombre de paramètres qui, une fois fixés, déterminent totalement le système : ce sont les variables de contrôle du système.

On prendra pour vecteur de contrôle :

$$u = (F, S_o, \alpha, H_L, NAE, C_L) \quad \in R^6$$

Le vecteur d'état y est alors :

$$y = (S, x, K_{LA}, N, Q, PU, PG, V_L, HOL, V_T) \quad \in R^{10}$$

1) Equations d'état

A l'équilibre, y est déterminé à partir de u par les équations implicites (4), (5),(6) et (13) à (19). Ce système sera noté :

$$A(u,y) = 0$$

où A est non linéaire.

2) Contraintes

a) Contraintes sur le contrôle :

Les variables de contrôle sont soumises aux contraintes suivantes :

$$0 < F \leqslant F\ max$$
$$0 < S_o \leqslant S_o\ max$$
$$0 \leqslant \alpha < 1$$
$$0 < H_L \leqslant H_L\ max$$
$$0 < NAE \leqslant 12$$
$$1 < C_L < 100$$

On transformera les inégalités strictes en inégalités larges : par exemple $F > 0$ sera remplacé par $F \geqslant F_{min}$ où F_{min} est suffisamment voisin de 0 pour que la signification physique de la contrainte reste la même. On peut alors écrire : $u \in K_o$, où K_o est un convexe fermé borné de R^6.

b) Contraintes sur l'état :

Pour que le modèle du I soit valable il nous faut imposer les contraintes suivantes :

$$x \leqslant 50\ g/l$$
$$V_L \leqslant 150\ m/h$$
$$0,1\ HP/m^3 \leqslant \frac{P_G}{V} \leqslant 2,5\ HP/m^3$$
$$\frac{N \times H_L^2 \times \rho}{9 \times VIS} \geqslant 6000$$

ρ étant la densité du milieu, VIS sa viscosité, cette contrainte signifie que le nombre de Reynolds est suffisamment grand pour qu'on soit en régime turbulent.

On notera ces contraintes sous la forme : $f(u,y) \leqslant 0$ où $f \in R^5$

c) Contrainte " spéciale "

Lorsque u est fixée, pour résoudre le système des équations d'état, on utilise (4) :

$$\mu(S,C_L) = \frac{F(1-\alpha)}{\pi/4\ H_L^3}$$

Mais on doit avoir $S < S_o$ pour assurer la positivité de x et des autres vaiables d'état ; μ étant strictement croissante par rapport à S, on doit avoir :

$$F(1-\alpha) - \pi/4\ H_L^3\ \mu(S_o\ ,\ C_L) < 0$$

qu'on note $g(u) < 0$.

3) Fonction-coût :

Le coût global du process est composé par les coûts unitaires d'investissement et de fonctionnement des postes qui le composent : production (PROD), matières premières (FS_o), agitation (PG), aération (Q), épuration (FS), écoulement (F), recyclage (RE), fermenteur (V_T). Il s'écrit :

$$COUT = Q_1\ PROD + Q_2\ FS + Q_3\ FS_o + Q_4\ PG^{E_1} + Q_5\ Q^{E_2} + Q_6\ F + Q_7\ V_T + Q_8\ V_T^{E_3} + Q_9 P_G^{E_4}$$
$$+ Q_{10}\ Q^{E_5} + Q_{11}\ RE + Q_{12}\ PROD + Q_{13}$$

le coefficient de recyclage RE étant donné par :

RE = 0 si $\alpha = 0$ (pas de recyclage)

RE = 1 si $\alpha > 0$ (nécessité d'un système de recyclage)

On désire également que la production de biomasse PROD donnée par (7) soit proche d'une valeur K qui représente la production désirée de biomasse.

On prendra alors pour critère à minimiser une somme pondérée de COUT et de $(PROD-K)^2$:

$$J = COUT + C(PROD-K)^2$$

C étant la constante permettant au biologiste de donner plus ou moins d'importance à la contrainte sur la production.

COUT contient un terme non différentiable $Q_{11}RE$, qui est une fonction en escalier. J peut donc se mettre sous la forme : $J = J_o + J_1$ où J_o est différentiable et où J_1 est une fonction en escalier.

4) Formulation du problème d'optimisation :

Existe-t-il $(u_o\ ,\ y_o) \in K \times R^{10}$ tel que :

$A(u_o,y_o) = 0$, $g(u_o) < 0$, $f(u_o\ ,\ y_o) \leqslant 0$

et

$$J(u_o\ ,\ y_o) = \inf_{\substack{u \in K \\ y \in R^{10} \\ A(u,y) = 0 \\ g(u) < 0 \\ f(u,y) \leqslant 0}} J(u,y) \qquad (P)$$

III - RESOLUTION DU PROBLEME D'OPTIMISATION (P)

On démontre aisément à l'aide du théorème des fonctions implicites et par des arguments de compacité que (P) admet au moins une solution.

A étant non linéaire et J non convexe il y a tout lieu de penser qu'il existe plusieurs minima locaux. Ce sont ces minima qu'on va chercher à atteindre.

Soit $K' = \{u \in K_o : g(u) < 0\}$

g étant non convexe, K' n'est pas convexe.

Le problème de recherche des optima locaux se pose alors ainsi :

Existent-ils $(u_o , y_o) \in K' \times R^{10}$ et un voisinage V' de u_o dans R^6 tels que

$$A(u_o , y_o) = 0 \quad , \quad f(u_o , y_o) \leqslant 0$$

et

$$J(u_o , y_o) = \inf_{\substack{u \in V' \cap K' \\ y \in R^{10} \\ A(u,y) = 0 \\ f(u,y) \leqslant 0}} J(u,y) \qquad (P')$$

Principe de la méthode :

L'idée est de résoudre (P') par une méthode de type gradient, en traitant la contrainte $u \in K$ par projection, $g(u) < 0$ par continuité, $f(u,y) \leqslant 0$ à l'aide de multiplicateurs de Lagrange et $A(u,y) = 0$ par l'introduction d'un état adjoint.

1) Recherche d'un point-selle pour résoudre la contrainte $f(u,y) \leqslant 0$

Pour traiter la contrainte $f(u,y) \leqslant 0$, on introduit le lagrangien

$$\mathcal{L}(u,y,q) = J(u,y) + (q,f(u,y)) \quad , \quad q \in R^5_+$$

$\mathcal{L}$ peut se mettre sous la forme :

$$\mathcal{L} = \mathcal{L}_o + Q_{11}RE = \mathcal{L}_o + \mathcal{L}_1$$

où $\mathcal{L}_o$ est différentiable et $\mathcal{L}_1$ une fonction en escalier.

q_o est vecteur de Kuhn-Tucker [5] pour (P') si :

$$\inf_{\substack{u \in V' \cap K' \\ y \in R^{10} \\ A(u,y) = 0}} \mathcal{L}(u,y,q_o) = \inf_{\substack{u \in V' \cap K' \\ y \in R^{10} \\ A(u,y) = 0 \\ f(u,y) \leqslant 0}} J(u,y)$$

On sait que, pour que u_o et y_o soient solutions de (P') et pour que q_o soit vecteur de Kuhn-Tucker associé, il faut et il suffit que$((u_o , y_o),q_o)$ soit point-selle de $\mathcal{L}$ sur $(V' \cap K') \times R^{10} \times R^5_+$.

Du fait de la non-convexité, l'existence de point-selle n'est pas assuré, mais pour trouver u_o et y_o on emploiera malgré tout une technique de recherche de point-selle.[6] [7]

a) Algorithme (A_1) de type Uzawa

On part de $u_1 \in K'$, $q_1 \in R^5_+$.

A la n^e itération, on calcule u_n , y_n et q_n de la façon suivante :

$$(a_1)\begin{cases} u_n \in V' \cap K_n \cap K' \\ A(u_n\,,\,y_n) = 0 \\ \mathcal{L}(u_n\,,\,y_n\,,\,q_{n-1}) = \inf\limits_{\substack{u \in V' \cap K_n \cap K' \\ y \in R^{10} \\ A(u,y)=0}} \mathcal{L}(u,y,q_{n-1}) \end{cases}$$

$$q_n = \mathrm{Proj}_{R^5_+}(q_{n-1} + \rho' f(u_n\,,\,y_n)) \qquad \rho' > 0$$

Choix de K_n :

Soit k un réel positif compris entre 0 et 1 .

Soit $\mathcal{H}_n$ l'homothétie de centre u_n et de rapport k .

K_n est l'homothétique de K_0 par la transformation $\mathcal{H}_n$.

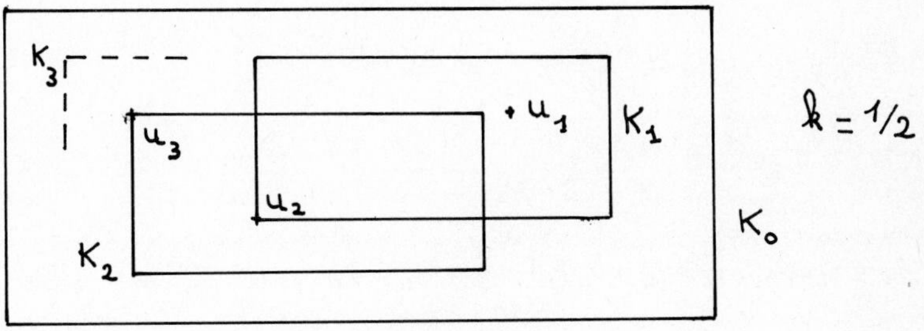

Fig. 2 : Construction de K_n (représentation dans R^2)

A chaque itération de cet algorithme, la recherche de u_n et de y_n nous amène à résoudre le problème de contrôle optimal (a_1) qu'on traitera plus bas.

Il convient également de remarquer que, si cet algorithme converge, ce sera vers un point maximin de $\mathcal{L}$ et non nécessairement vers un point-selle. Il faudra donc s'assurer que u_o et y_o sont bien solutions de (P').

b) Algorithme (A_2) de type Arrow-Hurwicz :

Du système des équations d'état $A(u,y) = 0$, on peut, comme $\frac{\partial A}{\partial y}$ est inversible, exprimer en théorie, y en fonction de u : $y = \overline{y}(u)$.

D'où $\mathcal{L}_o(u,y,q) = \mathcal{L}_o(u,\overline{y}(u),q) = \overline{\mathcal{L}}_o(u,q)$

L'algorithme (A_2) peut alors s'écrire ainsi :

- On part de $u_1 \in K'$, $q_1 \in R^5_+$.
- A la n^e itération, on calcule u_n , y_n et q_n de façon suivante :

$$\begin{cases} u_n = \mathrm{Proj}_{K_n}(u_{n-1} - \rho_n \, {}^t\frac{\partial \overline{\mathcal{L}}_o}{\partial u}(u_{n-1}\,,\,q_{n-1})) \\ A(u_n\,,\,y_n) = 0 \\ q_n = \mathrm{Proj}_{R^5_+}(q_{n-1} + \rho' f(u_n\,,\,y_n))\,, \quad \rho' > 0 \end{cases}$$

K_n est défini de la même façon que dans (A_1) et ρ_n sera précisé plus tard. Si cet algorithme converge, il faudra également s'assurer que u_o et y_o sont solutions de (P').

2) Résolution du problème de contrôle (a_1) et calcul de $\frac{\partial \bar{\mathcal{L}}_o}{\partial u}$:

L'idée, pour résoudre (a_1), est de traiter les équations d'état sous forme de contraintes [8] [9] et donc d'introduire le lagrangien :

$$M_{n-1}(u,y,p) = J(u,y) + (q_{n-1}\ , f(u,y)) + (p,A(u,y)) \quad p \in R^{10}$$

On démontre aisément le théorème suivant :

THEOREME Pour que $(u_n\ , y_n\ , p_n)$ soit point-selle de M_{n-1} sur $((V' \cap K' \cap K_n) \times R^{10}) \times R^{10}$, il faut que :

$$A(u_n\ , y_n) = 0$$

$$\frac{{}^t\partial J_o}{\partial y}(u_n,y_n) + \frac{{}^t\partial f}{\partial y}(u_n\ , y_n)\, q_{n-1} + \frac{{}^t\partial A}{\partial y}(u_n\ , y_n)\, p_n = 0$$

$$\left(\frac{{}^t\partial \bar{\mathcal{L}}_o}{\partial u}(u_n\ , q_{n-1}), u-u_n\right)_{R^6} + \mathcal{L}_1(u) - \mathcal{L}_1(u_n) \geqslant 0 \quad \forall u \in V' \cap K_n \cap K' \tag{20}$$

avec :

$$\frac{{}^t\partial \bar{\mathcal{L}}_o}{\partial u}(u_n\ , q_{n-1}) = \frac{{}^t\partial J_o}{\partial u}(u_n\ , y_n) + \frac{{}^t\partial f}{\partial u}(u_n\ , y_n)q_{n-1} + \frac{{}^t\partial A}{\partial u}(u_n\ , y_n)p_n$$

Pour résoudre le problème de contrôle (a_1) on pourra alors utiliser l'algorithme de type gradient projeté suivant:[10] [11]

- On part de $u_n^o = u_{n-1}$
- La i^e itération donnant y_n^i, p_n^i et u_n^{i+1} à partir de u_n^i s'écrit :

$$A(u_n^i\ , y_n^i) = 0$$

$$\frac{{}^t\partial J_o}{\partial y}(u_n^i\ , y_n^i) + \frac{{}^t\partial f}{\partial y}(u_n^i\ , y_n^i)\, q_{n-1} + \frac{{}^t\partial A}{\partial y}(u_n^i\ , y_n^i)p_n^i = 0$$

$$u_n^{i+1} = \mathrm{Proj}_{K_n}\left(u_n^i - \rho_n^i\left(\frac{{}^t\partial J_o}{\partial u}(u_n^i\ , y_n^i) + \frac{{}^t\partial f}{\partial u}(u_n^i\ , y_n^i)q_{n-1} + \frac{{}^t\partial A}{\partial u}(u_n^i\ , y_n^i)p_n^i\right)\right)$$

- $u_n^\infty = u_n$

Choix de ρ_n^i :

ρ_n^i sera choisi localement optimal pour le lagrangien $\mathcal{L}$, pour que l'algorithme converge vers un minimum local. Si on a par exemple une fonction $\mathcal{L}$ de ce type :

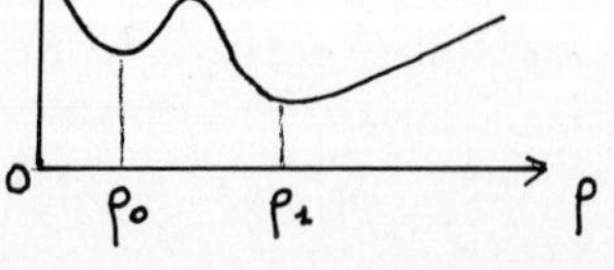

c'est ρ_o qu'on retiendra. C'est dans ce sens que la minimisation de $\mathcal{L}$ est effectuée à l'intérieur d'un voisinage V' de u_o comme cela a été défini dans l'algorithme (A_1).

ρ_n^i devra également être tel que u_n^{i+1} appartienne à K'.

• Pratiquement on déterminera d'abord $\rho^i_{n\ max}$ tel que les ρ de l'intervalle $[0,\rho^i_{n\ max}]$ soient en bijection avec les points du projeté sur K_n de la demi-droite de descente d'origine u_n^i.

Dans la recherche du ρ optimal, il n'est pas judicieux de procéder par dichotomie du fait du caractère non convexe de $\mathcal{L}$. On divisera les intervalles en dix intervalles égaux, ce qui permet de mieux suivre l'évolution de $\mathcal{L}$ en fonction de ρ.

On calculera $\mathcal{L}(\mathrm{Proj}_{K_n}(u_n^i - \frac{j}{10}\rho^i_{n\ max}\ \frac{{}^t\partial\overline{\mathcal{L}}_o}{\partial u}(u_n^i, q_{n-1})))$

et

$$g(\mathrm{Proj}_{K_n}(u_n^i - \frac{j}{10}\ \rho^i_{n\ max}\ \frac{{}^t\partial\overline{\mathcal{L}}_o}{\partial u}(u_n^i, q_{n-1})))$$

pour j allant de 1 à 10 et dès que $\mathcal{L}$ ne décroît plus ou que g devient positif (pour un certain j_o), on recommence l'opération sur l'intervalle

$$I = \left[u_n^i - \frac{j_o-2}{10}\ \rho^i_{n\ max}\ \frac{{}^t\partial\overline{\mathcal{L}}_o}{\partial u}\ ,\ u_n^i - \frac{j_o}{10}\rho_n^i\ {}_{max}\ \frac{{}^t\partial\overline{\mathcal{L}}_o}{\partial u}\right]$$

(si $j_o \neq 1$) jusqu'à ce que $\mathcal{L}$ soit minimum avec la précision qu'on souhaite. On est amené à considérer l'intervalle I ci-dessus car on peut avoir les deux configurations suivantes :

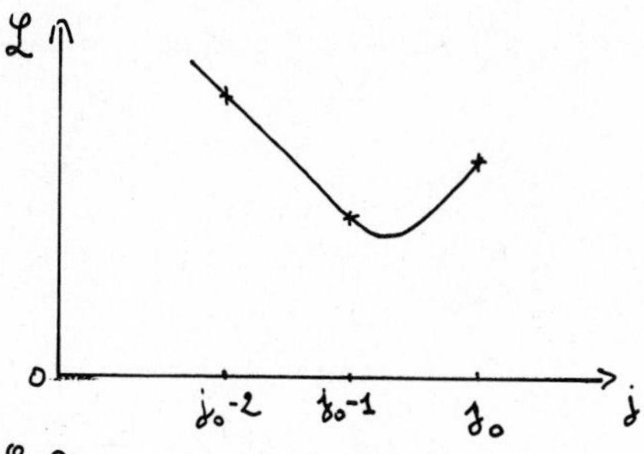

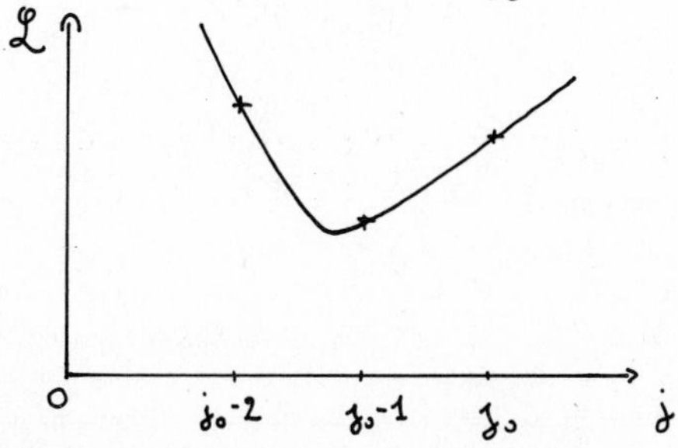

• On constate que, si on a utilisé le gradient de $\mathcal{L}_o$ dans l'algorithme, c'est $\mathcal{L}$ qu'on minimise par l'intermédiaire de ρ_n^i en accord avec (20) où $(\mathcal{L}_1(u) - \mathcal{L}_1(u_n))$ vaut soit 0 soit Q_{11}.

• ρ_n^i est donc tel que u_n^{i+1} soit le premier minimum local de $\mathcal{L}$ à partir de u_n^i sur le projeté sur K_n de la demi-droite de descente à condition que g soit resté négatif ou à défaut est tel que u_n^{i+1} annule g pour la première fois sur le projeté de cette demi-droite. C'est donc le choix de ρ_n^i qui permet de faire comme on l'a vu dans la définition de (A_1) une minimisation de $\mathcal{L}$ sur $V' \cap K_n \cap K'$, V' à cause du ρ localement optimal, K_n de la projection et K' parce qu'on oblige u_n^i à rester dans K'.

3) Formes définitives des algorithmes (A_1) et (A_2) :

a) Algorithme (A_1) :

• On part de $u_1 \in K'$, $q_1 = 0$

• On calcule u_n à partir de u_{n-1} et q_{n-1} à l'aide de l'algorithme suivant :

• $u_n^o = u_{n-1}$

• la i^e itération donnant u_n^{i+1} à partir de u_n^i s'écrit :

$$A(u_n^i , y_n^i) = 0$$

$$\frac{{}^t\partial J_o}{\partial y} (u_n^i , y_n^i) + \frac{{}^t\partial f}{\partial y} (u_n^i , y_n^i)q_{n-1} + \frac{{}^t\partial A}{\partial y} (u_n^i , y_n^i)p_n^i = 0$$

$$u_n^{i+1} = \mathrm{Proj}_{K_n} [u_n^i - \rho_n^i(\frac{{}^t\partial J_o}{\partial u} (u_n^i , y_n^i) + \frac{{}^t\partial f}{\partial u} (u_n^i , y_n^i)q_{n-1} + \frac{{}^t\partial A}{\partial u}(u_n^i,y_n^i)p_n^i)]$$

• $u_n^\infty = u_n$

• $A(u_n , y_n) = 0$

• $q_n = \mathrm{Proj}_{R_+^5} (q_{n-1} + \rho' f(u_n , y_n)) \qquad \rho' > 0$

b) Algorithme (A_2) :

On part de $u_1 \in K'$, $q_1 = 0$

• u_n , y_n et q_n se calculent à partir de u_{n-1} , y_{n-1} et q_{n-1} de la façon suivante :

$$\frac{{}^t\partial J_o}{\partial y} (u_{n-1} , y_{n-1}) + \frac{{}^t\partial f}{\partial y} (u_{n-1} , y_{n-1})q_{n-1} + \frac{{}^t\partial A}{\partial y} (u_{n-1} , y_{n-1})p_{n-1} = 0$$

$$u_n = \mathrm{Proj}_{K_n} (u_{n-1} - \rho_n(\frac{{}^t\partial J_o}{\partial u} (u_{n-1} , y_{n-1}) + \frac{{}^t\partial f}{\partial u} (u_{n-1} , y_{n-1})q_{n-1} + \frac{{}^t\partial A}{\partial u}(u_{n-1},y_{n-1})p_{n-1}))$$

$A(u_n , y_n) = 0$

$q_n = \mathrm{Proj}_{R_+^5}(q_{n-1} + \rho' f(u_n , y_n)) \qquad \rho' > 0$

ρ_n est choisi de la même façon que ρ_n^o dans (A_1) .

Remarque :

Justification du traitement spécial de la contrainte $g(u) < 0$

• Nous avons vu que cette contrainte équivaut à $S < S_o$. La contrainte $S < S_o$ aurait pu être incluse dans f et traitée par dualité, mais on constate que les algorithmes proposés nécessitent à chaque itération la résolution du système des équations d'état $A(u,y) = 0$. Or si la contrainte $S < S_o$ était traitée à l'aide de multiplicateurs de Lagrange on pourrait avoir au cours de l'algorithme $S_n > S_o$ donc $x_n < 0$ ce qui n'a plus de signification physique et empêche de résoudre le système des équations d'état.

• On aurait également pu penser traiter $g(u) < 0$ par projection sur K' au lieu de projeter sur K , mais K' n'est pas convexe et cette projection serait difficile.

• On a donc traité $g(u) < 0$ par continuité ; g étant continue, $g(u_n)$ négatif, il existe un voisinage de u_n où g est négatif et l'optimisation se fait dans ce voisinage. En fait cette contrainte ne peut devenir bloquante que dans les premières itérations car :

$$g(u) = 0 \Rightarrow x = 0 \Rightarrow PROD = 0 \Rightarrow J = COUT + CK^2$$

J est alors très grand et ne peut donc être un minimum.

IV - MISE EN OEUVRE - RESULTATS

1) Mise en oeuvre

Le choix de la valeur unitiale u_1 dans les algorithmes est important du fait de la convergence vers des minima locaux. On a effectué un maillage de K_o et étudié J, f et g aux noeuds de ce maillage. Les algorithmes ont été mis en oeuvre à partir de valeurs u_1 telles que $J(u_1)$ soit "assez petit" et que les contraintes soient vérifiées en ces points.

Rappelons que le lagrangien $\mathcal{L}$ s'écrit :

$$\mathcal{L}(u,y,q) = J(u,y) + \sum_{j=1}^{5} q_j \, f_j(u,y)$$

Pour assurer une bonne pondération dans le lagrangien entre J et les termes $q_j f_j$, on a remplacé f_j par $K_j f_j$ et choisi K_j de sorte que $q_j f_j$ ait sensiblement comme ordre de grandeur le 1/10 de la valeur de J.

La constante ρ des algorithmes (A1) et (A2) a été prise égale à 1. On a adopté pour test d'arrêt des algorithmes l'optimalité de J à 10^{-5} près et la nullité de $q_j f_j$ pour $j \in \{1,\ldots,5\}$. Les valeurs numériques adoptées sont celles de la cinétique du Saccharomyces Cerivisiae.

2) Importance du rapport d'homothetie k et comparaison de (A1) et (A2).

k \ alg.	A 1	A 2
1/2	45 itérations 37 s $J_{fin} = 3560$	200 itérations 1 mn $J_{fin} = 5085$
1	200 itérations 1 mn $J_{fin} = 4800$	81 itérations 38 s $J_{fin} = 3560$

$J_{initial} = 7017$

Fig. 3 Comparaison de (A_1) et (A_2) suivant diverses valeurs de k sur un exemple.

Les essais numériques à partir de diverses valeurs initiales u_1 montrent que l'algorithme (A1) de type Uzawa, pris avec k=1, c'est à dire avec optimisation dans tout K, converge vers un optimum médiocre après de nombreuses itérations. La raison en est que J est brutalement minimisé dans les premières itérations, que les contraintes deviennent alors fortement positives et que les multiplicateurs de Lagrange agissent alors si brutalement pour les ramener en-dessous de 0 que J atteint des valeurs très élevées, ce qui créé de très fortes oscillations de J dans les premières itérations et entraine une convergence médiocre. C'est ce qui a conduit à utiliser une restriction homothétique et on constate en général que pour k=1/2, l'algorithme (A1) converge régulièrement et vite vers de bons optima locaux.

L'algorithme (A2) utilisé avec k=1 est meilleur que (A1) avec le même k, car on ne fait qu'une descente suivant le gradient à chaque itération et l'optimisation est donc moins forte, ne créant pas de brusques oscillations. Par contre pour k plus petit l'algorithme (A2) est en général moins bon que (A1), car il converge plus lentement et même parfois vers de moins bons optima.

En définitive il semble que la meilleure méthode soit d'adopter (A1) avec k=1/2 et, si on n'a pas une bonne et rapide convergence, soit de diminuer k en utilisant toujours (A1), soit d'utiliser (A2) mais en augmentant k.

<u>REMARQUE</u> : <u>JUSTIFICATION DE L'ECRITURE DE J COMME SOMME PONDEREE DE COUT ET DE $(PROD-K)^2$</u> :

On désire que la production PROD de biomasse soit proche d'une certaine valeur K. On peut considérer cela comme une contrainte : PROD=K, ce qui revient à minimiser J=COUT et à introduire f_6=PROD-K. Mais les essais numériques sur (A1) et (A2) ne permettent pas d'obtenir une bonne convergence de u ; J tend vers une certaine valeur mais pour u_n on observe un phénomène de "zigzag" de ce type :

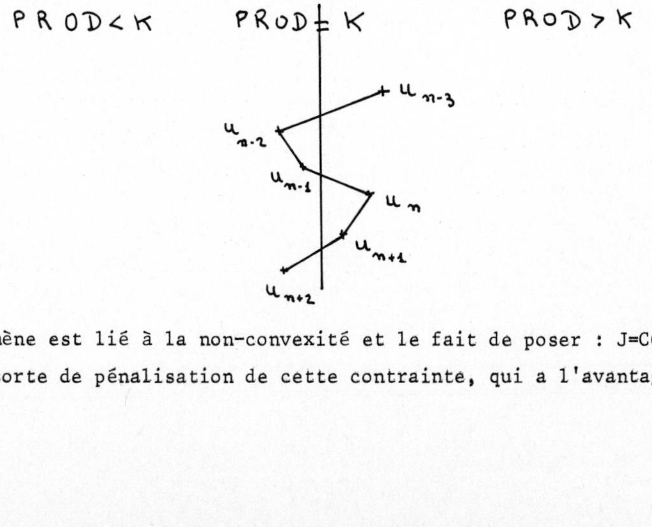

Ce phénomène est lié à la non-convexité et le fait de poser : $J=COUT + C(PROD-K)^2$ est une sorte de pénalisation de cette contrainte, qui a l'avantage de "convexifier"

J dans une certaine mesure et d'assurer une bonne convergence des algorithmes.

3°) Interprétation biologique des résultats

La recherche d'optima locaux à partir de différentes valeurs initiales de u permet de tirer un certain nombre de conclusions sur le système biologique à employer :

a) Le fait de s'imposer la production de biomasse nous impose la dimension optimale du fermenteur. En effet, en prenant une production de 20 000g/h de biomasse, tous les optima sont tels que le diamètre H_L du fermenteur est très voisin de 2m.

b) La concentration C_L d'oxygène dissous est très faible pour les u optimaux, la contrainte $C_L > 1\%$ s'avèrant en général bloquante. Cela correspond à une minimisation de K_{LA} et donc du coût du transfert de l'oxygène de la phase gazeuse dans la phase liquide.

c) Le nombre d'aération NAE, qui peut varier dans l'intervalle [0,12], est proche de 0,2 pour les optima ; en corrélation avec lui la vitesse d'aération Q est petite. Cela correspond à la minimisation du coût de l'aération. [12]

d) L'introduction d'un recyclage de la biomasse est intéressante, mais ce recyclage n'est pas indispensable quand la concentration S_o du substract injecté est grande.

CONCLUSION

L'optimisation de J nous impose la géométrie du fermenteur, nous montre l'intérêt du recyclage et nous apprend qu'il faut réduire au minimum indispensable le transfert d'oxygène de la phase gazeuse dans la phase liquide, en diminuant le plus possible l'aération. Telles sont les premières conclusions qu'on peut tirer de la mise en oeuvre de cette technique d'optimisation des processus de fermentation en continu. Une étude systématique est en cours à l'INRA de Dijon, dans l'idée de mettre en pratique ces algorithmes pour l'optimisation réelle des processus de fermentation en continu sur des installations pilotes et plus tard industrielles.

BIBLIOGRAPHIE

1. P.PERINGER,H.BLACHERE,G.CORRIEU et A.G.LANE : "Mathematical model of the kinetics of growth of Saccharomyces Cerivisiae 4th Int. Ferment. Symp.,Kyoto,Japan,1972.

2. P.PERINGER,H.BALCHERE,G.CORRIEU et A.G. LANE :"A Generalized Mathematical Model for the Growth Kinetics of Saccharomyces Cerivisiae with Experimental Determination of Parameters". Biotechnology and Bioengineering, Vol. XVI,1974.

3. J.BLUM,P.PERINGER,H.BLACHERE : "Optimal Single Cell Protein Production from Yeasts in a Continuous Fermentation Process". 1st Intersectional Congress of the International Association of Microbiological Societies. Sept.74. Tokyo.

4. S.AIBA,A.HUMPHREY,N.MILLIS : Biochemical Engineering Academic Press. 1965.

5. KUHN,TUCKER : "Non linear Programming" :Proceedings of the Second Berkeley Symposium on Mathematical Statistics and Probability" University of California Press. 1961.

6. ARROW-HURWICZ-UZAWA : Studies in Linear and Non Linear Programming : Stanford University Press. 1958.

7. R.GLOWINSKI :"Méthodes Itératives Duales pour la minimisation de fonctionnelles convexes". CIME 1971. Edizioni Cremonese. Rome 1973.

8. J.L.LIONS : Some aspects of the Optimal Control of Distributed Parameter Systems: SIAM. Philadelphia. 1972.

9. J.P. YVON : "Application des méthodes duales au contrôle optimal". Cahier de l'IRIA. 1971.

10. D.LEROY : "Méthodes numériques en contrôle optimal". Thèse 3ème cycle. Paris 1972.

11. J.CEA : Optimisation. Théorie et Algorithmes. Dunod 1971.

12. M. OKABE,S.AIBA,M.OKADA : "The modified complex Method as Applied to an Optimization of Aeration and Agitation in Fermentation". J. Ferment. Technol. Vol. 51. N°8. 1973.

STRUCTURAL IDENTIFIABILITY OF BIOLOGICAL COMPARTMENTAL SYSTEMS.

Digital Computer Implementation of a Testing Procedure

C.Cobelli, A.Lepschy, G.Romanin-Jacur

Laboratorio per Ricerche di Dinamica
dei Sistemi e di Elettronica Biomedica
del
Consiglio Nazionale delle Ricerche
Casella Postale 1075-35100 Padova (Italy)

1. Introduction

The most widely treated problem in compartmental analysis of biological systems [1,2,3] concerns the choice of the compartmental structure of the system (identification of the compartments and of their relationships: compartmentalization) and the evaluation of the system parameters via a suitable input-output experiment (identification of the transfer rate constants: estimation).

However, prior to actually performing the identification experiment, the following problem has to be considered: can the chosen experiment provide the desired information about the system? i.e., can all parameters characterizing the adopted compartmental model be estimated from the chosen experiment? (identifiability problem: [4]).

This problem is particularly important in the study of "in vivo" phenomena as the experiment is often non repeatable because of induced harm, high cost, troubles etc. (e.g., radioactive tracer experiments). The problem is to be answered, therefore, after the compartmentalization but before the estimation. In such a way the problem can be characterized as the a priori structural identifiability problem because it has to be faced only with reference to assumptions about the model structure and not about the values of its parameters (values which can be obtained only through the planned experiment); the a posteriori identifiability, on the contrary, refers to the actually estimated values of the parameters and it is connected to the statistical evaluation of the reliability of the estimates.

In this paper the structural identifiability problem is considered for multi-input multi-output compartmental systems of any structure, where each input enters one compartment only and each output is re lated to one compartment. A testing procedure for the identifiability of such systems is presented and a description of the techniques employed for a digital computer implementation of the whole procedure is given. Finally we apply the above procedures to a compartmental model of copper metabolism.

2. Some concepts on compartmental systems

It seems useful to review some general concepts about compartmental systems.

A compartment is a quantity of material which kinetically behaves in a characteristic and homogeneous way. It must be emphasized that a compartment may or may not coincide with a physiologically realizable region of space.

A compartmental system consists of interconnected compartments which exchange material either by physical transport or by chemical reaction. A compartmental system is therefore characterized by compartments and intercompartmental relations.

The differential equations describing the dynamical behaviour of a compartmental system are obtained from the mass balance equation for each compartment:

$$\dot{q}_i = \sum_{\substack{j\neq i\\ j\neq 0}} f_{ij} + m_i + u_i - \sum_{\substack{j\neq i\\ j\neq 0}} f_{ji} - f_{oi} \qquad i=1,n \qquad (1)$$

where:

q_i is the amount of material of the i-th compartment;

m_i is the net rate of production of material by metabolism (internal input);

u_i is the rate at which material enters the i-th compartment from the environment external to the system (external or perturbation input);

f_{oi} is the excretion flow from the i-th compartment to the environment;

f_{ji} is the transfer flow from the i-th to the j-th compartment;

f_{ij} is the transfer flow from the j-th to the i-th compartment.

The classical compartment theory assumes linearity and time-invariance of the system; therefore eq.(1) can be written is the form:

$$\dot{q}_i = \sum_{\substack{j\neq i\\ j\neq 0}} k_{ij}\, q_j + m_i + u_i - \sum_{\substack{j\neq i\\ j\neq 0}} k_{ji}\, q_i - k_{oi}\, q_i \qquad (2)$$

where:

k_{ij} is the (non negative) rate constant from the j-th to the i-th compartment;

k_{oi} is the (non negative) rate constant from the i-th compartment to the environment.

In <u>steady state</u> m_i is assumed to be constant, the perturbation external input u_i is equal to zero, the rate of change of q_i is zero by definition and each q_i assumes a constant steady state value q_{is}.

With reference to the (small) deviations $x_i = q_i - q_{is}$ caused by u_i, equation (2) can be rewritten in the form:

$$\dot{x}_i = \sum_{\substack{j \neq i \\ j \neq 0}} k_{ij} x_j + u_i - \sum_{\substack{j \neq i \\ j \neq 0}} k_{ji} x_i - k_{oi} x_i \qquad (3)$$

For a tracer, equation (3) also holds under the following assumptions:

i) the system is in steady state;

ii) the injected tracer has a metabolic fate identical to the fate of the non-labeled substance;

iii) the mixing of the injected tracer with the non-labeled substance within each compartment is complete and rapid in comparison with transfer rates of the substance between compartments;

iv) the amount of the injected tracer is negligible in comparison with the size of the compartment; the steady state is not altered by the injection;

v) there is no isotopic fractionation for radioactive tracer.

For an n compartmental system, the k_{ij} rate constants can be grouped into a square, n order matrix K, the main diagonal of which is null, and the k_{oi} rate constants into an n order row matrix K_o.

As far as the structural identifiability problem is concerned, we must observe that matrices K and K_o are not yet known (as no estimation has been performed), but we know which of their entries are nonzero, as this derives from compartmentalization. Namely, we know only matrices H and H_o, obtained from K, K_o through the following statement:

$$\begin{cases} h_{rs}=0 \quad \text{if} \quad k_{rs}=0 \\ h_{rs}=1 \quad \text{if} \quad k_{rs}\neq 0 \end{cases} \quad \text{with} \quad \begin{cases} r=0,n \\ s=1,n \end{cases} \qquad (4)$$

Matrix H may be viewed as the connection matrix of a directed graph with nodes corresponding to compartments and branchesto the rate constants (fig.1).

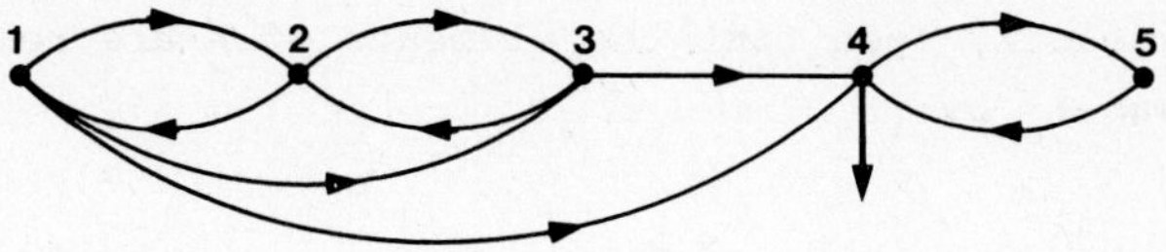

$$H = \begin{bmatrix} 0 & 1 & 0 & 0 & 0 \\ 1 & 0 & 1 & 0 & 0 \\ 1 & 1 & 0 & 0 & 0 \\ 1 & 0 & 1 & 0 & 1 \\ 0 & 0 & 0 & 1 & 0 \end{bmatrix} \qquad H_o = \begin{bmatrix} 0 & 0 & 0 & 1 & 0 \end{bmatrix}$$

Figure 1 - Directed graph of a compartmental system and corresponding H and H_o matrices.

For what follows it is useful to know whether a given compartment i can influence compartment j: with reference to the above graph, it corresponds to the existence of a path from compartment i to compartment j. As is well known, this problem may be solved by checking wether the ij entry of one of the successive powers of H is nonzero; the order of the first power of H in which such element is nonzero is equal to the number of branches of the minimum path from i to j. A system is said to be <u>strongly connected</u> when every compartment can be reached from every other compartment; in such a case matrix $R = \sum_{l=1}^{n} H^l$ has all nonzero entries. A system is said to be <u>open</u> (<u>closed</u>) when there is some exchange (no exchange) with the environment; the corresponding condition is $H_o \neq 0$ $(H_o \equiv 0)$.

The variables x_i in (3) can be clearly considered as components of the state vector x of a dynamical, linear, time invariant system:

$$\dot{x} = Ax + Bu \tag{5}$$

$$y = Cx \tag{6}$$

where $u = u_i$ is the input and y is the output formed by the measured variables.

It can be easily seen that the elements of A are related to the elements of K and K_o by:

$$a_{ij} = k_{ij} \qquad i \neq j \tag{7}$$

$$a_{ii} = -k_{oi} - \sum_{j=1}^{n} k_{ji} \tag{8}$$

Matrix A is therefore diagonally dominant and consequently its eigenvalues cannot be purely imaginary and have a non positive real part [7] ; usually however they are real and negative.

3. Statement of the problem

As previously said, in this paper we consider multi input - multi output compartmental systems of any structure where each input enters one compartment only and each output is related to one compartment.

The assumption about the structure is completely general (previous work in this field considers only strongly connected system [8,5] ; the general case is treated also in [6]); as a consequence no restrictions have to be made on matrix K (non-negativity of its entries is the only assumption).

The assumption about the inputs corresponds to the more usual case in tracer experiments. If we label the r_b inputs ($r_b \leq n$) with index j, ($j=1,r_b$), for the ($n \times r_b$) matrix B the following condition holds:

$$b_{il} = \begin{cases} 1 & \text{if input 1 enters the i-th compartment} \\ 0 & \text{otherwise} \end{cases} \tag{9}$$

The assumption about the outputs corresponds to a large class of practical cases of tracer experiments. If we label the r_c outputs ($r_c \leq n$) with index k, ($k=1,r_c$), for the ($r_c \times n$) matrix C the following condition holds:

$$c_{mi} = \begin{cases} 1 & \text{if output m is taken from compartment i} \\ 0 & \text{otherwise} \end{cases} \tag{10}$$

The most general input-output configuration where the input can fraction into several compartments and the output is related to more than one compartment (the observed output variable y_r is a linear combination of some state variables x_s) is now under study.

As far as the identifiability problem is concerned, it must be noted that if the aim of identification is to have a model of the system, by which either the response to a given input or the input causing a desired response may be computed, than any equivalent realization (A,B, C) is acceptable. In such a case, as is well known, necessary and sufficient condition for identifiability is that the system be controllable and observable; all the required information about the system is included in the transfer function matrix.

In the case of biomedical applications, however, identification has diagnostic aims, and determining the transfer function matrix of the system (i.e. one of the equivalent (A,B,C) triples) may be insufficient, while it is necessary to evaluate all the transfer rate constants k_{rs}, which are of immediate physiological significance. In the latter case controllability and observability of the system are only necessary conditions; moreover the number of mutually independent coefficients of the transfer functions is to be at least equal to the number of nonzero k_{rs} transfer rate constants. In fig.2 this situation is clearly illustrated: the system is controllable and observable, but is not structurally identifiable as only four rate constants can be uniquely estimated.

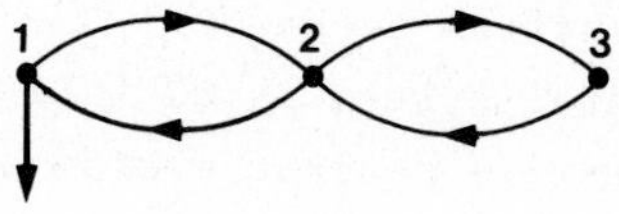

$$B = \begin{bmatrix} 1 \\ 0 \\ 0 \end{bmatrix} \qquad C = \begin{bmatrix} 0 & 0 & 1 \end{bmatrix}$$

Figure 2 - Example of a controllable, observable but non structurally identifiable compartmental system.

4. Outline of the procedure

With reference to what has been discussed in section 3, testing the structural identifiability of a compartmental system by a given input-output experiment (namely when the topological structure of input-state-output connection is completely known) consists of:
1) testing wether the necessary conditions for controllability and observability are satisfied with respect to the system structure (i.e. independently on the numerical values of nonzero k_{ij} parameters);
2) comparing (again with respect to the system structure and therefore independently on the numerical values) the number of not yet determined nonzero parameters of K and K_o matrices, and the number of mutually independent coefficients in the numerator and denominator polynomials of the $r_b \times r_c$ input-output transfer functions.

As far as topic 1 is concerned, as seen above, the problem is to be faced independently on the numerical values taken by the entries of A; therefore it seems not suitable to refer to usual controllability and observability criteria, based on the ranks of respectively controllability matrix P (constructed on the basis of the pair A,B) and observability matrix Q (constructed with A,C). On the contrary, it is useful to consider the following theorems [6] , which make use only of connection matrices H and H_o.
Theorem 1: The existence of at least one path reaching every uncontrolled compartment from a controlled one is a necessary condition for a compartmental system to be CC; the existence of at least one path from every unobserved compartment to an observed one is a necessary condition for a compartmental system to be CO.
Theorem 2.1: A compartmental system is CC in a structural sense if every uncontrolled compartment is reachable from at least a controlled one along any path.
Theorem 2.2: A compartmental system is CO in a structural sense if there is at least one path from every unobservable compartment to an observed one.

As far as topic 2 is concerned, the subject is somewhat complex and the discussion may be developed as follows.

From input and output behavior, the identification will allow one to determine, for instance, the values of numerator and denominator polynomials of the transfer functions related to every input-output pair (as controllability and observability have already been tested, the transfer function matrix uniquely corresponds to any minimal realization of the system). As seen above, the problem consists in checking wether the number of obtainable mutually independent coefficients is equal or less than the number of nonzero parameters k_{ij} of the considered compartmental model. Even if the relations between coefficients and k_{ij} are not linear, yet the given condition brings to the solvability of the problem.

Getting the analytical expressions of the numerator and denominator polynomial coefficients as functions of k_{ij} is extremely cumbersome; even if it may be used in the numerical estimation, if the system results to be identifiable, it is clearly more suitable to adopt a criterion which simply allows one to test whether the system is identifiable or not without computing the functions of k_{ij}. This is particularly useful if the systems turn out to be not identifiable and either a different experiment is to be planned, or a simpler model (identifiable through the planned experiment) is to be adopted.

For this purpose, the authors have suggested some test procedures [6], and here a new one is presented.

Consider the following expression for the transfer function matrix $\underline{G}(s)$ (cf [6] for computational details):

$$\underline{G}(s) = \frac{C.\mathrm{adj}\ (sI-A).B}{\det(sI-A)} = \frac{1}{\det(sI-A)}\Big\{CB(s^{n-1}+\alpha_1 s^{n-2}+..+\alpha_{n-1}) + \\ + CAB(s^{n-2}+\alpha_1 s^{n-3}+..+\alpha_{n-2}) +..+ CA^{n-2}B(s+\alpha_1)+CA^{n-1}B\Big\} \tag{11}$$

where $\det(sI-A) = s^n+\alpha_1 s^{n-1}+ \alpha_2 s^{n-2}+..+\alpha_n$.

$[\underline{G}(s)]_{ml}$ can be computed via (11) by taking $[CB]_{ml}, [CAB]_{ml}, \ldots, [CA^{n-1}B]_{ml}$ instead of the corresponding matrices.

In all we have $r_b r_c$ transfer functions $[\underline{G}(s)]_{ml} = N_{ml}/D$ from every input l to every output m.

Polynomial D, which is common to all transferences, is characterized by n coefficients $\alpha_1,..,\alpha_n$, and therefore it allows to write n equations in the parameters k_{ij}.

Analogously, the $r_b r_c$ numerators N_{ml} are characterized by $r_b r_c(n-1)$ coefficients; in fact the coefficient of s^{n-1} is 1 if the polynomial is of degree n-1. A knowledge of them allows one to write at most as many equations. However this number of equations must be reduced if the following situations occur:

1) N_{ml} has degree $p=n-1-v<n-1$;
2) N_{ml} has a w-th degree factor in common with D ;
3) N_{ml} has a z-th degree factor in common with one or more other numerators.

Hence it must be checked wether these situations occur and, in this case, v, w and z are to be evaluated. This purpose may be reached only by operations on the structure of the graph representing the system. In fact:

- situation 1) corresponds to the case in which in (11) all products $C A^i B$, i=0, 1...v-1 are null, which is easy to check on the graph,on the basis of the length (number of branches) of the shortest path from l to m: this length is v.
- situation 2) corresponds to the case where the subsystem controllable from l and observable from m does not coincide with the whole system as w compartments are not included (which is easily checked on the graph). In fact the reduced transfer function is a ratio of polynomials, where the denominator polynomial D' has degree n-w; if the transference is presented in standard form, with denominator polynomial D, then the numerator necessarily includes the factor D/D'.
- situation 3) corresponds to the case where the subsystem ml has a common cascade part (c.c.p.) with another subsystem m'l' which may be checked on the graph if there exist two nodes f, g such that: i) each node of c.c.p. is reachable from l and l' only through a path entering f and reaches m and m' through a path outgoing from g; ii) each node of c.c.p. can reach outer nodes only through g and can be reached from outer nodes only through f; the value of z is equal to the lowest power such that $[A^z]_{fg} \neq 0$ (see fig.3).

The number of independent equations in the k_{ij} system parameters is:

$$N = n + r_b \cdot r_c (n-1) - \sum_i v_i - \sum_j w_j - \sum_k (t_k - 1) z_k \qquad (12)$$

where, as seen above, the first addendum is related to the denominator, the second one is the maximum number of equations obtainable from the numerators, which is reduced by the terms indicated in the three sums, corresponding respectively to situations 1), 2), 3); the first sum refers to all numerators having degree less then n-1, the second one to numerators having some factors in common with the denominator and the third one to all cascade parts which are common to more ml subsystems; t_k is the number of m l subsystems having the same k-th cascade part.

N is to be compared with the total number N_k of the non zero k_{ij} to be determined. If $N<N_k$ the system is not identifiable by the chosen experiment and it is necessary either to modify the experiment or to adopt another model of simpler structure.

If $N \geq N_k$ the system is identifiable; if $N>N_k$ the system can be identified by a simpler experiment or the planned experiment allows one to identify a more complex model; however if the chosen experiment and the adopted model are used, it is possible either to utilize all equations to improve the estimates, or to delete $N-N_k$ equations to have a simpler computation (for this purpose we may eliminate either those equations which have complex analytical structure, or those which correspond to the most noisy channels, or those with highest parametric sensitivity).

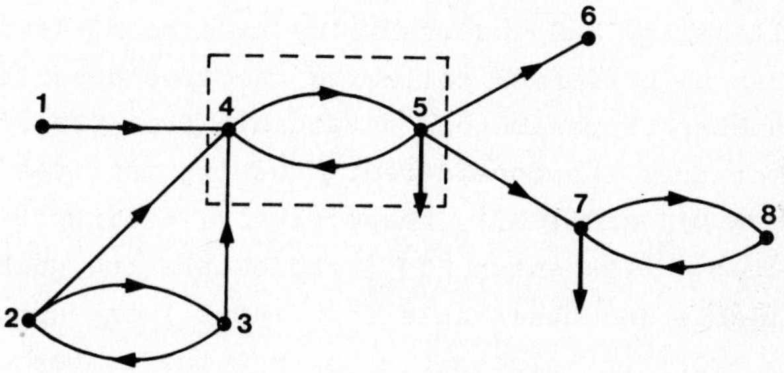

$$B = \begin{bmatrix} 1 & 0 \\ 0 & 1 \\ 0 & 0 \\ 0 & 0 \\ 0 & 0 \\ 0 & 0 \\ 0 & 0 \\ 0 & 0 \end{bmatrix} \quad ; \quad C = \begin{bmatrix} 0 & 0 & 0 & 0 & 0 & 1 & 0 & 0 \\ 0 & 0 & 0 & 0 & 0 & 0 & 0 & 1 \end{bmatrix}$$

Figure 3 - Compartments 4 and 5 form the common cascade part between the four subsystems.

5. Flow chart

As seen in section 3 and 4 controllability and observability are necessary conditions for structural identifiability.

Referring to theorems 2.1, 2.2 and to matrix $R_1 = R+I$, matrices R_1B and CR_1 can be used to test controllability and observability in a structural sense: $[R_1B]_{il} \neq 0$ denotes compartment i reachable from input l and $[CR_1]_{mi} \neq 0$ denotes compartment i observable from output m. The system is CC and CO if each row of R_1B and each column of CR_1 have at least one positive non zero entry. Note that controllability and observability always hold for strongly connected systems (see [5]).

Once controllability and observability have been tested, identifiability analysis can be performed following the line described in section 4. As the number of parameters obtainable from the denominator is always n, the numerators are considered. Putting matrices R_1B and CR_1 in boolean form, $(R_1B)_b$ and $(CR_1)_b$ respectively, their product $T=(CR_1)_b \times (R_1B)_b$ is computed. Each entry $[T]_{ml}$ represents the number of compartments controllable and observable from input l and output m. From T and A,B,C (see (12)) it is possible to know the number of parameters obtainable from the numerators, provided there are no common cascade parts. Note that for strongly connected compartmental systems each entry of T is equal to n, therefore T needs no computation (see above and section 2).

Given two subsystems ml and m'l', the possible common cascade part is a set of compartments S such that:

i) $[R_1B]_{il} > 0 \quad ; \quad [R_1B]_{il'} > 0 \quad ;$

$[CR_1]_{mi} > 0 \quad ; \quad [CR_1]_{m'i} > 0 \qquad \forall i \in S$

ii) $k_{ij} = 0 \quad \forall i \in S \quad , \forall j \notin S \quad$ except $i=f$;

$k_{ji} = 0 \quad \forall i \in S \quad , \forall j \notin S \quad$ except $j=g$.

If a common cascade part is found, a further simplification must be performed. Note that for strongly connected systems there are no common cascade parts due to their peculiar structure.
In fig.4 a general flow chart of the whole procedure is presented.

6. Example

The above presented procedure for testing identifiability was ap-

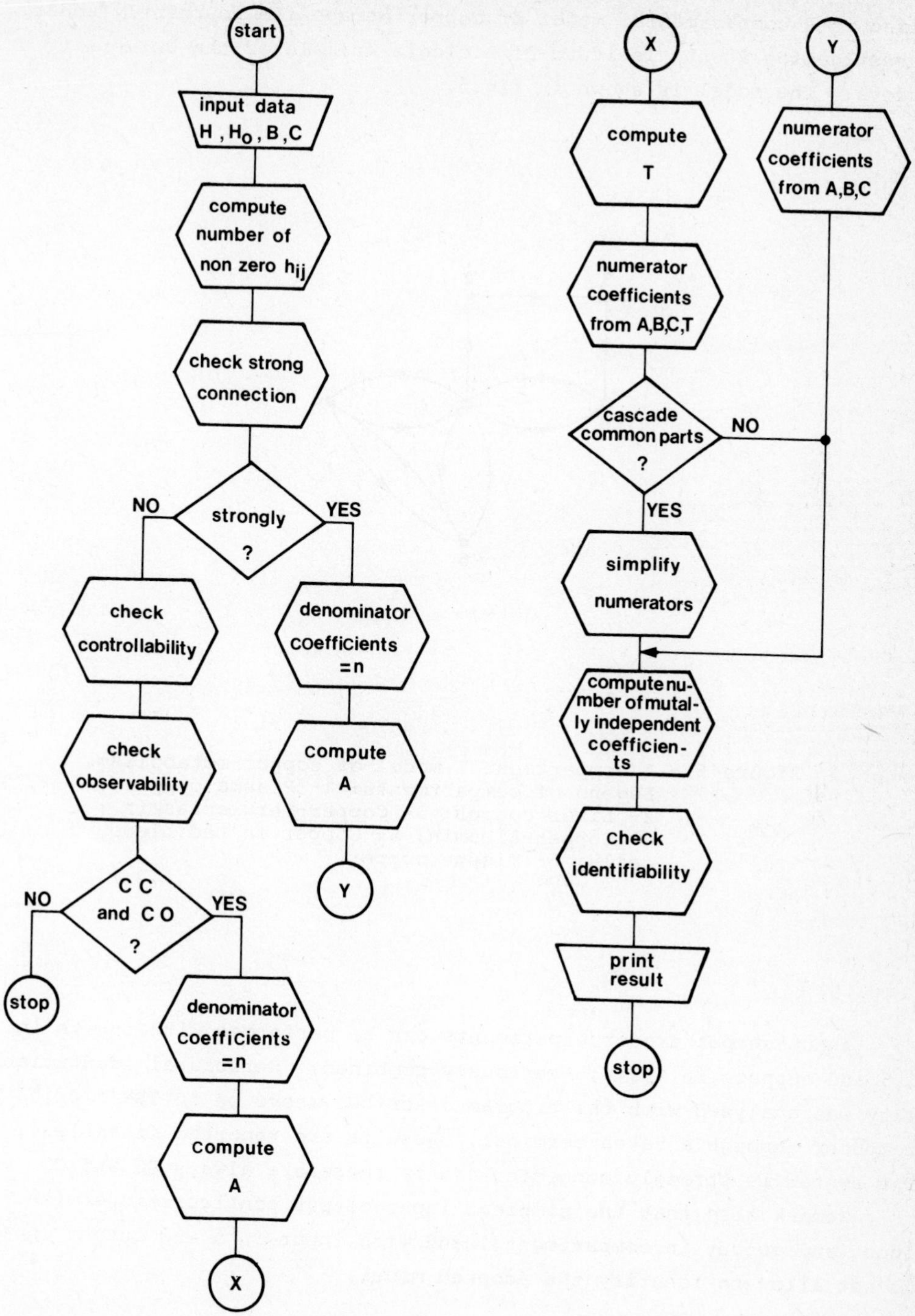

Figure 4 - The general flow chart of the procedure

plied to a compartmental model of copper metabolism, currently under investigation at the Istituto di Biologia Animale of the University of Padova. The model is shown in fig.5.

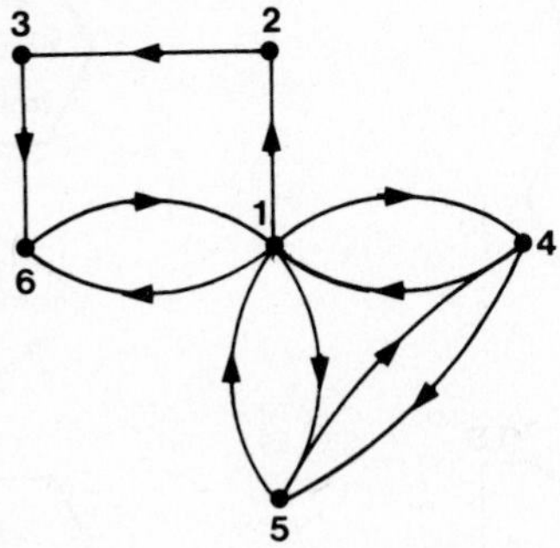

Figure 5 - A compartmental model of copper metabolism. Legend of compartments: 1- Plasma copper ; 2- Liver copper; 3- Copper-Ceruloplasmin ; 4- Copper-Albumin; 5- Copper in red blood cells; 6- Tissue copper.

Input-output tracer experiments can be performed with inputs in 1,5 and outputs in 1,3,4,5 variously combined. Structural identifiabi lity was analyzed with the program described above on an IBM 370/158 computer through a batch terminal. Results are reported in table 1. The system is strongly connected and is therefore always CC and CO.

Remark also that the simplest input-output configurations with input and output in compartment 1 and with input in 5 and output in 1 do not allow to identify the adopted model.

Table 1

Input(s) in compartments	Output(s) in compartments	Result
1	1	Not identifiable with 1 degree of freedom
1	1,3	Identifiable with 3 redundant equations
1	1,4	" " 4 " "
1	1,5	" " 4 " "
1	1,3,4	" " 8 " "
1	1,3,4,5	" " 13 " "
5	1	Not identifiable with 1 degree of freedom
5	1,3	Identifiable with 2 redundant equations
5	1,4	" " 4 " "
5	1,5	" " 4 " "
5	1,3,4	" " 7 " "
5	1,3,4,5	" " 12 " "
1,5	1	" " 4 " "
1,5	1,3	" " 11 " "
1,5	1,4	" " 14 " "
1,5	1,5	" " 14 " "
1,5	1,3,4	" " 21 " "
1,5	1,3,4,5	" " 31 " "

References

[1] Rescigno, A., and Segre, G. Drug and Tracer Kinetics. Blaisdell Publ.Co., Waltham, Mass. (1966).

[2] Atkins, G.L. Multicompartment Models for Biological Systems. Methuen and Co. Ltd., London (1969).

[3] Jacquez, J.A. Compartmental Analysis in Biology and Medicine. Elsevier Publ. Co., Amsterdam (1972).

[4] Bellman, R., and Aström, K.J. On Structural Identifiability. Math. Biosci. 7, 329-339 (1970).

[5] Cobelli, C., and Romanin-Jacur, G. Structural Identifiability of Strongly Connected Biological Compartmental Systems. Medical & Biological Engineering. In press.

[6] Cobelli, C., and Romanin-Jacur, G. Controllability, Observability and Structural Identifiability of Biological Compartmental Systems. IEEE Transactions on Biomedical Engineering. In press.

[7] Hearon, J.Z. Theorems on Linear Systems. Ann. N.Y. Acad. Sci. 108, 36-68 (1963).

[8] Hàjek, M. A Contribution to the Parameter Estimation of a Certain Class of Dynamical Systems. Kybernetika 8,165-173 (1972).

STABILITY ANALYSIS OF PREDATOR-PREY MODELS VIA LIAPUNOV METHOD

M. Gatto and S. Rinaldi

Centro per lo Studio della
Teoria dei Sistemi, C.N.R.

Milano, Italy

Abstract

As it is well known from the classical applications in the electrical and mechanical sciences, energy is a suitable Liapunov function: thus, by analogy, all energy functions proposed in ecology are potential Liapunov functions. In this paper, a generalized Lotka-Volterra model is considered and the stability properties of its non-trivial equilibrium are studied by means of an energy function, first proposed by Volterra in the context of conservative ecosystems. The advantage of this Liapunov function with respect to the one that can be induced through linearization is also illustrated.

1. Introduction

As is well-known, one of the most classical problems in mathematical ecology is the stability analysis of equilibria and, in particular, the determination of the region of attraction associated to any asymptotically stable equilibrium point. It is also known that the best way of obtaining an approximation of such regions is La Salle's extension of Liapunov method[1], [2].

Nevertheless, this approach has not been very popular among ecologists, the main reason being that Liapunov functions (i.e. functions that satisfy the conditions of Liapunov method) are in general difficult to devise.

The aim of this paper is to show how the energy function first proposed by Volterra and more recently by Kerner [3] turns out to be quite often a Liapunov function even for non-conservative ecosystems. In order to avoid complexity in notation and proofs, the only case that is dealt with in the following is the one of second order (pre -

dator-prey) systems, but the authors strongly conjecture that the results presented in this paper could be easily generalized to more complex ecological models.

2. The Volterra Function

Consider the simple Lotka-Volterra model

$$\frac{dx}{dt} = x\ (a-by) \tag{1.a}$$

$$\frac{dy}{dt} = y\ (-c + dx) \tag{1.b}$$

where x and y are prey and predator populations and (a,b,c,d) are strictly positive constants. This system has a non-trivial equilibrium (x,y) given by (x,y) = (c/d, a/b) which is simply stable in the sense of Liapunov. Moreover, any initial state in the positive quadrant gives rise to a periodic motion.

This can easily be proved by means of the energy function proposed by Volterra

$$V = (x/\bar{x} - \log(x/\bar{x})) + p(y/\bar{y} - \log(y/\bar{y})) - (1 + p) \tag{2}$$

where

$$p = b\bar{y}/d\bar{x}$$

since this function is constant along any trajectory and its contour lines are closed lines in the positive quadrant.

In other words, the Volterra function (2) is a Liapunov function because it is positive definite and its derivative dV/dt is negative semidefinite (identically zero).

In the following, the Volterra function will be used in relation with non-conservative ecosystems of the form :

$$\begin{aligned} \frac{dx}{dt} &= x(a - by + f(x,y)) \\ \frac{dy}{dt} &= y(-c + dx + g(x,y)) \end{aligned} \tag{3}$$

where f and g are continuously differentiable functions. Moreover, we assume that there exists a non-trivial equilibrium $(\bar{x},\bar{y}) > 0$ and that the positive quadrant is an invariant set for system (3) so that it can be identified from now on with the state set of the system.

3. The Volterra Function as a Liapunov Function

Consider the generalized Lotka-Volterra model (3) and the Volterra function V given by eq. (2). Then, the derivative of the Volterra function along trajectories is given by

$$\frac{dV}{dt} = \frac{\partial V}{\partial x} \cdot \frac{dx}{dt} + \frac{\partial V}{\partial y}\frac{dy}{dt} = \left(\frac{x}{\bar{x}} - 1\right)(a - by + f(x,y))$$

$$+ \frac{b\bar{y}}{d\bar{x}}\left(\frac{y}{\bar{y}} - 1\right)(-c + dx + g(x,y))$$

In order to study $\frac{dV}{dt}$ in a neighborhood of the equilibrium $(\bar{x},\bar{y})$, it is possible to expand this function in Taylor's series up to the second order terms, i.e.

$$\frac{dV}{dt} \simeq \frac{dV}{dt}\Big|_{\bar{x},\bar{y}} + \frac{d}{dx}\left(\frac{dV}{dt}\right)\Big|_{\bar{x},\bar{y}} \delta x + \frac{d}{dy}\left(\frac{dV}{dt}\right)\Big|_{\bar{x},\bar{y}} \delta y$$

$$+ \frac{1}{2}\frac{d^2}{dx^2}\left(\frac{dV}{dt}\right)\Big|_{\bar{x},\bar{y}} (\delta x)^2 + \frac{1}{2}\frac{d^2}{dy^2}\left(\frac{dV}{dt}\right)\Big|_{\bar{x},\bar{y}} (\delta y)^2$$

$$+ \frac{d^2}{dxdy}\left(\frac{dV}{dt}\right)\Big|_{\bar{x},\bar{y}} \delta x \delta y \qquad (4)$$

Since

$$\frac{dV}{dt}\Big|_{\bar{x},\bar{y}} = \frac{d}{dx}\left(\frac{dV}{dt}\right)\Big|_{\bar{x},\bar{y}} = \frac{d}{dy}\left(\frac{dV}{dt}\right)\Big|_{\bar{x},\bar{y}} = 0$$

$$\frac{d^2}{dx^2}\left(\frac{dV}{dt}\right)\Big|_{\bar{x},\bar{y}} = \frac{2\bar{f}_x}{\bar{x}}$$

$$\frac{d^2}{dy^2}\left(\frac{dV}{dt}\right)\Big|_{\bar{x},\bar{y}} = \frac{2b\bar{g}_y}{d\bar{x}}$$

$$\frac{d^2}{dxdy}\left(\frac{dV}{dt}\right)\Big|_{\bar{x},\bar{y}} = \frac{\bar{f}_y}{\bar{x}} + \frac{b\bar{g}_x}{d\bar{x}}$$

where $\bar{f}_x, \bar{f}_y, \bar{g}_x, \bar{g}_y$ are the partial derivatives of f and g evaluated at $(\bar{x},\bar{y})$, eq. (4) becomes:

$$\frac{dV}{dt} \simeq \frac{1}{2} \left[\delta x \;\; \delta y\right] \begin{bmatrix} \frac{2\bar{f}_x}{\bar{x}} & \frac{\bar{f}_y}{2\bar{x}} + \frac{b\bar{g}_x}{2d\bar{x}} \\ \frac{\bar{f}_y}{2\bar{x}} + \frac{b\bar{g}_x}{2d\bar{x}} & \frac{2b\bar{g}_y}{d\bar{x}} \end{bmatrix} \left[\delta x \;\; \delta y\right]^T \qquad (5)$$

Therefore the second order approximation of $\frac{dV}{dt}$ turns out to be a homogeneous quadratic form; by studying the negative or positive definiteness of such a form, it is possible to derive sufficient conditions for the Volterra function to be a Liapunov function. More precisely, by applying the well-known Sylvester conditions and performing easy computations, it results

$$\left.\begin{array}{l} \bar{f}_x < 0 \\ (b\bar{g}_x + d\bar{f}_y)^2 < 4bd\bar{f}_x\bar{g}_y \end{array}\right\} \Rightarrow \frac{dV}{dt} \text{ negative definite} \qquad (6)$$

$$\left.\begin{array}{l} \bar{f}_x > 0 \\ (b\bar{g}_x + d\bar{f}_y)^2 < 4bd\bar{f}_x\bar{g}_y \end{array}\right\} \Rightarrow \frac{dV}{dt} \text{ positive definite} \qquad (7)$$

Notice that these conditions are only sufficient for Liapunov methods to be applicable; thus, even if these conditions are not satisfied, it is possible that the Volterra function turns out to be a Liapunov function (see Ex. 2).

As far as the study of stability properties in the large is concerned, the Volterra function is definitely advantageous with respect to quadratic forms. This is apparent in the case of global stability; in fact, global stability can be inferred by means of Volterra function, whose contour lines in the state set are closed, while this is never possible by means of a positive definite quadratic form since the contour lines are not closed (see Ex. 1 and 2).

4. Examples

This section is devoted to clarify by means of some examples what has been previously exposed.

Example 1

The first example is a simple symmetric competition model between two species described by the following equations (see May [4]):

$$\frac{dx}{dt} = x(k_1 - x - \alpha y)$$

$$\frac{dy}{dt} = y(k_2 - y - \alpha x)$$

where k_1, k_2 and α are positive parameters.

Provided that

$$\begin{cases} \alpha k_2 > k_1 \\ \alpha k_1 > k_2 \end{cases} \quad \text{or} \quad \begin{cases} \alpha k_2 < k_1 \\ \alpha k_1 < k_2 \end{cases}$$

a non-trivial equilibrium $(\bar{x},\bar{y})$ exists and is given by

$$(\bar{x},\bar{y}) = \left(\frac{\alpha k_2 - k_1}{\alpha^2 - 1}, \frac{\alpha k_1 - k_2}{\alpha^2 - 1}\right)$$

Thus, the matrix F of the linearized system is given by

$$F = \begin{bmatrix} -\bar{x} & -\alpha\bar{x} \\ -\alpha\bar{y} & -\bar{y} \end{bmatrix}$$

and its eigenvalues have negative real parts, provided that its trace is strictly negative and its determinant is strictly positive. These conditions are obviously satisfied if $\alpha < 1$. On the other hand, also the sufficient conditions given by eq. (6) work well. In fact

$$\bar{f}_x = -1 < 0$$

and

$$(b\bar{g}_x + d\bar{f}_y)^2 = \alpha^2(1+\alpha)^2 < 4bd\bar{f}_x\bar{g}_x = 4\alpha$$

provided that $\alpha < 1$.

However, the Volterra function guarantees the global stability of the equilibrium. This can be easily understood when taking into account that there is no error in the Taylor's expansion (4), because the functions f and g are linear. Thus, $\frac{dV}{dt}$ is negative definite in the state set and global stability follows from La Salle's conditions.

Example 2

Consider the well-known modification obtained from the classical Lotka-Volterra model, when assuming, in the absence of predation, a logistic growth for the prey :

$$\frac{dx}{dt} = x(a - by - kx) \qquad\qquad k > 0$$

$$\frac{dy}{dt} = y\,(-c + dx)$$

If ad $>$ kc a non-trivial equilibrium

$$(\bar{x},\bar{y}) = \left(\frac{c}{d}, \frac{a}{b} - \frac{kc}{bd}\right)$$

exists and linearization around it yields

$$F = \begin{bmatrix} -\frac{kc}{d} & -\frac{bc}{d} \\ \frac{da-kc}{b} & 0 \end{bmatrix}$$

which has eigenvalues with negative real parts. On the other hand , it turns out that

$$\bar{f}_x = -k$$

$$4bd\bar{f}_x\bar{g}_y = (b\bar{g}_x + d\bar{f}_y)^2 = 0$$

Therefore eq. (6) is not satisfied. Nevertheless, by means of a direct computation, it results

$$\frac{dV}{dt} = - \frac{k}{b\bar{x}\bar{y}} (x - \bar{x})^2$$

i.e. $\frac{dV}{dt}$ is negative semidefinite. Since the locus $\frac{dV}{dt} = 0$ is not a trajectory of the system (easy to check), Krasowskyi conditions are met with and asymptotic stability can be inferred. Moreover, since $\frac{dV}{dt}$ is negative semidefinite in the whole state set, global stability can be straight forwardly deduced.

6. Concluding Remarks

The energy function proposed by Volterra has been used in this paper to analyze the asymptotic behaviour of non-conservative ecosystems of the predator-prey type. The main result is that the Volterra function turns out to be a well-defined Liapunov function for a large class of systems and therefore allows the discussion of the local and global stability properties of such systems. The Volterra function seems to be definitively advantageous with respect to the Liapunov functions that can be obtained through linearization particularly in the case of global stability.

Acknowledgement

The work was supported by Centro per lo studio della Teoria dei Sistemi, C.N.R., Milano, Italy and I.I.A.S.A. (International Institute for Applied Systems Analysis), Schloss Laxenburg, Austria.

REFERENCES

[1] J.P. La Salle "Some Extensions of Liapunov's Second Method" IRE Trans. on Circuit Theory, Vol. 7, pp. 520-527, 1960.

[2] R. Rosen - Dynamical System Theory in Biology Vol. 1, Wiley-Interscience, 1970.

[3] E.H. Kerner "A Statistical Mechanics of Interacting Biological Species" Bull. Math. Biophys., Volume 19, pp.121-146, 1957.

[4] R.M. May - Stability and Complexity in Model Ecosystems Princeton University Press, 1973.

DETERMINATION D'UNE REPRESENTATION DES NOYAUX DE VOLTERRA POUR UN SYSTEME PHYSIOLOGIQUE NON-LINEAIRE

M. Gautier, M. Monsion, J.P. Sagaspe
Université de Bordeaux I
Laboratoire d'Automatique
33405 Talence

I Introduction

Nous cherchons un modèle de représentation du système crânio-rachidien de l'homme à partir des enregistrements des variations de la pression intra-crânienne consécutives à des injections de liquide céphalo-rachidien artificiel dans les ventricules.

II Processus physiologique

Le système crânio-rachidien est constitué par les 3 composants : tissus nerveux, système vasculaire, liquide céphalo-rachidien, contenus dans une enceinte rigide. La pression du liquide céphalo-rachidien ou pression intra-crânienne (P.I.C.) traduit l'état d'équilibre des trois composants et l'étude dynamique de son évolution apporte des données physio-pathologiques irremplaçables dans la compréhension des situations d'hypertension intra-crânienne chez l'homme.

De façon habituelle, trois tests sont pratiqués pour induire des variations de la P.I.C. :

- Compression bilatérale des veines jugulaires.
- Respiration d'un mélange de CO_2.
- Injection incrémentale de L.C.R. artificiel à l'intérieur des ventricules.

Ces tests sont longs, délicats et parfois dangereux. Aussi avons-nous cherché à identifier globalement le système afin d'obtenir les mêmes résultats à partir de tests simples.

Le système peut être schématisé de la façon suivante :

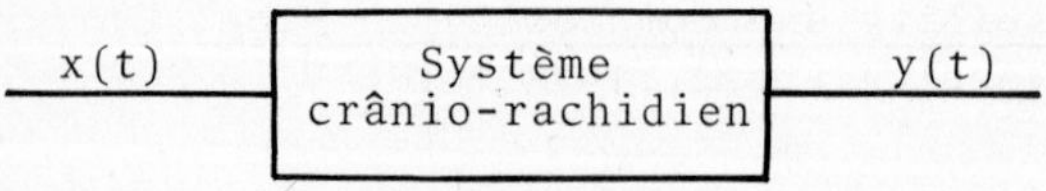

x(t), l'entrée : injection de L.C.R. artificiel
y(t), la sortie : P.I.C.

L'étude des enregistrements nous a montré que le système, déterministe, invariant, stable et continu, est non linéaire.

III Représentation de Volterra du système

Compte tenu des propriétés du processus, il est possible d'approximer la relation fonctionnelle entrée-sortie, $y(t) = k\left[x(t)\right]$, par le développement en série de Volterra.

$$y(t) = \sum_{i=1}^{N} C_i\left[h_i, x(t)\right]$$

$$\text{avec } C_i\left[h_i, x(t)\right] = C_i(t) = \underbrace{\int_0^t \ldots \int_0^t}_{i} h_i(\tau_1, \ldots, \tau_i) \prod_{j=1}^{i} x(t-\tau_j)d\tau_j$$

Ce développement peut être schématisé de la façon suivante :

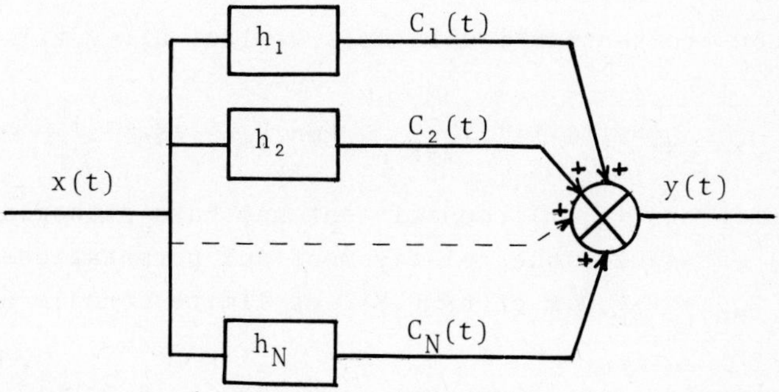

IV Détermination des fonctionnelles C_i

En utilisant la propriété d'homogénéité des C_i, $C_i\left[\lambda x(t)\right] = \lambda^i\, C_i\left[x(t)\right]$, $\lambda \in \mathbb{R}$, il est possible de calculer les N fonctionnelles $C_i(t)$ à partir de N enregistrements des réponses $y_1, y_2, \ldots, y_N$ du système à des entrées $\lambda_p\, x(t)$

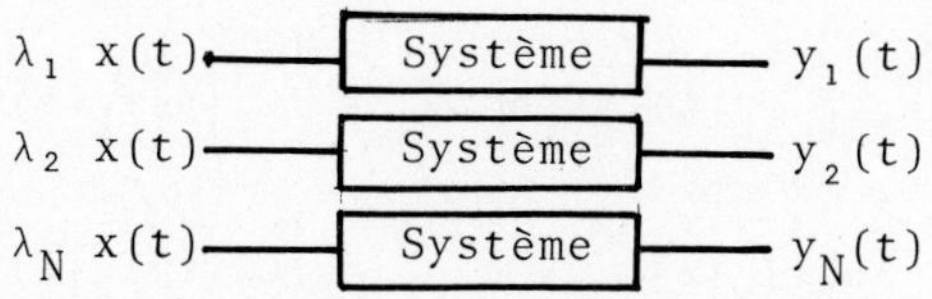

On utilise la méthode de Gardiner qui conduit à la relation :

$$\begin{vmatrix} C_1(t) \\ C_2(t) \\ \cdot \\ \cdot \\ \cdot \\ C_N(t) \end{vmatrix} = \begin{vmatrix} \lambda_1 & \lambda_1^2 \ldots & \lambda_1^N \\ \lambda_2 & \lambda_2^2 & \lambda_2^N \\ \cdot & & \cdot \\ \cdot & & \cdot \\ \cdot & & \cdot \\ \lambda_N & \ldots\ldots\ldots & \lambda_N^N \end{vmatrix}^{-1} \begin{vmatrix} y_1(t) \\ y_2(t) \\ \cdot \\ \cdot \\ \cdot \\ y_N(t) \end{vmatrix}$$

Notre problème se ramène donc à caractériser h_i, noyau d'ordre i, connaissant l'entrée x(t) et la sortie $C_i(t)$.

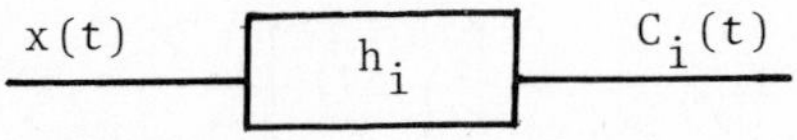

V Caractérisation d'un noyau h_i

Sans nuire à la généralité de la méthode, nous développerons les calculs pour un noyau d'ordre deux et pour des entrées échelons.

Nous construisons un modèle $\hat{h}_2(\tau_1,\tau_2)$ de $h_2(\tau_1,\tau_2)$ sous la forme :

$$\hat{h}_2(\tau_1,\tau_2) = \sum_{m=0}^{M} \sum_{n=0}^{M} B_{mn}\, g_m(\tau_1) g_n(\tau_2)$$

Les fonctions $\{g_i(\tau)\}$ constituent une base orthogonale. $h_i(\tau_1,\ldots,\tau_i)$ est symétrique relativement aux permutations des τ_i. Ceci implique que $B_{mn} = B_{nm}, \forall m$ et $n \in [0,M]$, et limite donc le nombre d'inconnues.

Nous obtenons ainsi une approximation de la sortie du noyau h_2 :

$$\hat{C}_2(t) = \sum_{m=0}^{M} \sum_{n=0}^{M} B_{mn} \int_0^t g_m(\tau)d\tau \int_0^t g_n(\tau)d\tau$$

La dernière étape consiste à déterminer les coefficients B_{mn}. Pour cela, nous décomposons $C_2(t)$ et $\hat{C}_2(t)$ sur une même base de fonctions orthonormales sur $[0,T]$ par rapport à la fonction poids w(t).

$$C_2(t) = \sum_{k=0}^{K} \gamma_k\, f_k(t) \quad \text{avec } \gamma_k = \int_0^T C_2(t) f_k(t) w(t) dt.$$

$$\hat{C}_2(t) = \sum_{k=0}^{K} \alpha_k\, f_k(t) \quad \text{avec } \alpha_k = \int_0^T \hat{C}_2(t) f_k(t) w(t) dt.$$

L'unicité de la décomposition nous permet d'assurer l'identité entre $C_2(t)$ et $\hat{C}_2(t)$ en écrivant $\alpha_k \equiv \gamma_k$, $\forall k = 0,K$. Le calcul littéral de α_k nous fournit une relation $\alpha_k = R_k(B_{mn})$. Nous obtenons ainsi un système linéaire dans lequel B_{mn} sont les inconnues et que nous pouvons résoudre, compte tenu d'un choix convenable de K, ordre de la décomposition.

VI Application

Les fonctions de base sont des fonctions de Laguerre. Nous rappelons leurs propriétés :

Définition : $\Lambda_n(t) = (-1)^n \sqrt{2}\, e^{-t}\, L_n(2t)$

avec $L_n(t) = \sum_{j=0}^{n} (-1)^j C_n^j \frac{t^j}{j!}$

Orthonormalité sur $[0,\infty]$: $\int_0^\infty \Lambda_m(t).\Lambda_n(t)dt = \delta_{mn}$

Récurrence : $(n+1)\, \Lambda_{n+1} + (2n+1-2t)\, \Lambda_n + n\Lambda_{n-1} = 0.$

Intégrale : $I_n = \int_0^t \Lambda_n(t)dt = \sqrt{2} - \Lambda_n(t) - 2 \sum_{j=0}^{n-1} \Lambda_j(t)$

Décomposition de $C_2(t)$

$$C_2(t) = \sum_{k=0}^{K} \gamma_k\, \Lambda_k(t) \quad \text{avec } \gamma_k = \int_0^\infty C_2(t)\, \Lambda_k(t)dt.$$

Décomposition de $\hat{C}_2(t)$

Expression de $\hat{C}_2(t)$:

$$\hat{C}_2(t) = \sum_{m=0}^{M} \sum_{n=0}^{M} B_{mn} \int_0^t \Lambda_m(\tau)d\tau \int_0^t \Lambda_n(\tau)d\tau.$$

$$\hat{C}_2(t) = \sum_{m=0}^{M} \sum_{n=0}^{M} B_{mn}\, I_m(t)\, I_n(t).$$

d'où la relation :

$$\hat{C}_2(t) = \sum_{k=0}^{K} \alpha_k \Lambda_k(t) \quad \text{avec } \alpha_k = \int_0^\infty \Sigma\Sigma\, B_{mn}\, I_m(t)\, I_n(t)\, \Lambda_k(t)dt.$$

$$\alpha_k = \sum_{m=0}^{M} \sum_{n=0}^{M} B_{mn}\, \beta_{mn}^k \quad \text{avec } \beta_{mn}^k = \int_0^\infty I_m(t)\, I_n(t)\, \Lambda_k(t)dt.$$

Pour k donné, nous obtenons une équation linéaire en B_{mn}

$$\sum_{m=0}^{M} \sum_{n=0}^{M} B_{mn} \beta_{mn}^{k} = \gamma_k$$

Le système obtenu en faisant varier k de 0 à K est soluble si : le nombre d'équations K+1 est supérieur ou égal au nombre d'inconnues (M+1)(M+2)/2. Le tableau ci-dessous montre que la dimension du système croît rapidement avec l'ordre i du noyau et M.

i \ M	1	2	3	4
1	2	3	4	5
2	3	6	10	15
3	4	10	20	35

Ceci constitue le seul inconvénient lors de l'implantation sur ordinateur. En effet, les coefficients β_{mn}^{k} peuvent être calculés à priori puisqu'ils ne dépendent que du choix de la base et du type d'entrée. Le calcul des $C_i(t)$ et des γ_k se réalise facilement et l'on peut dire que la méthode est globalement très rapide.

VII Conclusion

Nous proposons une méthode de détermination des noyaux de Volterra d'un système non linéaire déterministe, invariant, stable et continu. La rapidité des calculs et la simplicité des tests nécessaires en font un outil pratique et efficace dans l'aide au diagnostic relatif aux cas d'hypertension intra-crânienne.

BIBLIOGRAPHIE

1 - GAUTIER M., MONSION M., SAGASPE J.P.

Caractérisation des noyaux de Volterra d'un système non linéaire.
Electronic Letters. Vol 11 n° 15 p. 351 à 353.

2 - GARDINER A.

Identification of processus containing single-valued non-linearities.
Int. J. Control, 1973, 18, n° 5 1029 à 1039.

3 - VOLTERRA V.

Theory of functionals and of integral and integro-differential equations.
New-York, Dover.

A COMBINATORIAL METHOD FOR HEALTH-CARE DISTRICTING

C.Ghiggi P.P.Puliafito R.Zoppoli

Istituto di Elettrotecnica
Università di Genova

Viale Causa,13
16145 Genoa (Italy)

I. INTRODUCTION

The problem described in this paper arises whenever, for political or administrative reasons, a geographical region must be partitioned into an unknown number of districts so that, within each district, the total amount of service supplied by existing facilities of known location and capacity may satisfy a given demand, according to some optimality criterion.

The philosophy of the problem is quite different from that of the so-called Location Problem (see for example TOREGAS et AL. [1]), since we are neither seeking locations for new facilities nor trying to modify their capacities.

The following assumptions will define the problem more clearly.

1. The region is considered to be made up of a certain number of assigned undivisible communities of known concentrated population.
2. Each community must be univocally assigned to a district, i.e., no overlap among districts is allowed.
3. The location and capacity of every facility are assigned.
4. Each district must be connected in the geometrical sense.
5. The population of each district must lie within an assigned range.
6. The number of districts is unknown.

In the following, we shall refer to hospitals as facilities.

This work was supported by the National Council of Research of Italy (CNR).

The capacity of a facility will be simply characterized by the number of beds of the hospital. Then, the aim of the paper will be to present a partioning method for the region, such that each district can be considered as "self-sufficient" from a health care point of view, and "satisfactory" for both the planner and the citizen. Such terms will be specified later on.

It is worth noting that our problem formulation is comprehensive enough as to describe conveniently districting problemsfor other classes of facilities.

II. STATEMENT OF THE PROBLEM

Although analytical constraints may be derived from the preceding assumptions, reduction of our districting problem to a mathematical program does not seem an easy matter. Actually, as frequently happens in planning problems in which socio-economical factors are involved, it is rather unrealistic to define a single cost function that satisfactorily describes the several requirements of a health care system, which cannot always be expressed in quantitative terms.

Since a formal approach to the problem based on the multigoal decision theory is beyond the aim of this paper, we will assume,for the time being, to have achieved a "satisfactory" cost function to be minimized. Then, it will be difficult to avoid what is commonly called an "ill-structured" formulation of the problem. This cost function should include such factors as the average time (or distance) travelled by the citizen to reach the hospital he is assigned to, and the difference between the demand and the offer of bed-units within the district. Other factors might have to be minimized such as, for instance, the number of districts (in order to reduce admin istrative expenses) or the difference between a given district's population and a pre-assigned value suggested by social or administrative reasons.

To state the structure of the problem more clearly, let us consider the geographical region shown in Fig. 1. This region is subdivided into communities, a limited number of which have a hospi tal on their territory. Since the only information we need to retain from the map of Fig.1 is adjacency between communities, we will refer to the graph of Fig.2, in which nodes correspond to communities and an arc between two nodes denotes an adjacency relationship between the corresponding communities. Obviously, according to the presence of a hospital in a community, two classes of nodes (with and without a hospital) can be distinguished.

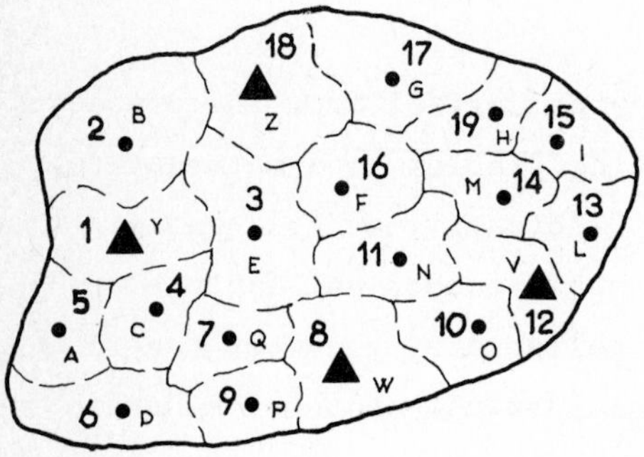

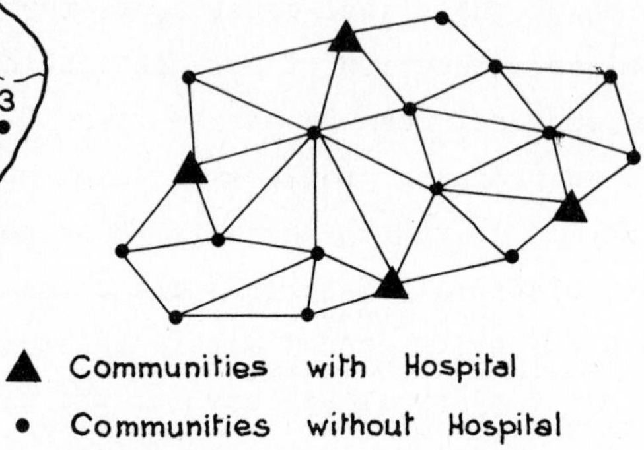

Fig.1. Geographical region

Fig.2. Graph of adjacent communities

Observe now that there is a one-to-one correspondence between the set of all trees in the graph and the set of all connected districts in the map. It follows that a tree including at least one hospital and characterized by an allowed amount of population yields a "feasible district" in the sense of the assumptions introduced in Section I. These properties will lead to a computational procedure for finding all possible districts.

Let $\mathcal{D} \triangleq \{d_1, d_2, \dots, d_n\}$ be the set of all nodes in the graph, and $\mathcal{U} \triangleq \{u_1, u_2, \dots, u_m\}$ the set of all feasible districts. Then, we define, as a "feasible solution" of the districting problem, every subset

$$s_i \triangleq \left\{u_{i_1}, u_{i_2}, \ldots, u_{i_k}\right\} \in \mathcal{U} \quad \text{such that}$$

$$u_{i_1} \cup u_{i_2} \cup \ldots \cup u_{i_k} = \mathbb{O} \tag{1}$$

$$u_{i_j} \cap u_{i_h} = \emptyset, \quad \forall\, j \neq h. \tag{2}$$

Every feasible solution s_i partitions the given region into nonoverlapping and connected districts of allowed population. Fig.3 shows an example of feasible solution. We will assume that the set of feasible solutions is not an empty set.

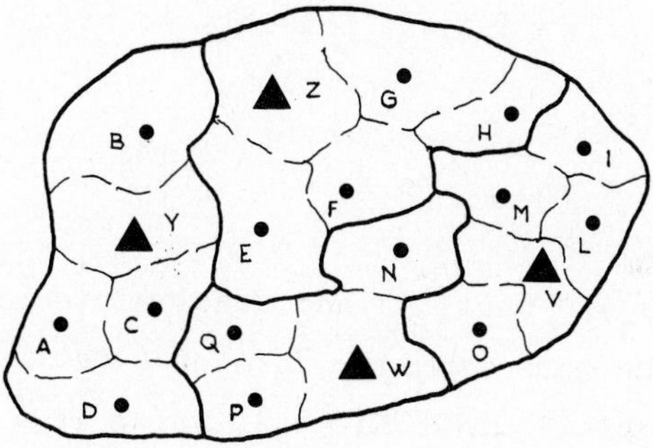

Fig.3. Example of feasible solution.

From the above definitions, an algebraic formulation of the districting problem directly follows. Let us define an n x m constraint matrix $A = [a_{ij}]$ in the following way:

- every community (i.e., every node of $\mathbb{O}$) corresponds to a row in A;
- every feasible district (i.e., every element of $\mathcal{U}$) corresponds to a column of A;
- $a_{ij} = 1$ if district j includes community i, $a_{ij} = 0$ otherwise.

Any collection of feasible districts is then represented by a zero-one vector $\underline{x} = (x_1, x_2, \ldots, x_m)$, where $x_i = 1$ if the collection includes district i, $x_i = 0$ otherwise. Then, a vector $\underline{x}$ will represent a feasible solution provided that the following constraints are verified:

$$A\underline{x} = \underline{1} \tag{3}$$

where $\underline{1}$ is an n-vector of all 1s. Constraints (3) are the algebraic version of conditions (1), (2).

Assume now that, whatever optimality criterion may have been chosen for the districting problem, it is meaningful to characterize a given feasible district i by means of a cost c_i, and this independently of the other districts selected for the feasible solution. Assume also that it is possible to "evaluate" any feasible solution by considering the total cost, which is obtained by adding the costs of all districts included in the solution.

Such "independence" and "additivity" assumptions enable us to define as "optimal solution" the feasible solution $\underline{x}^*$ that minimizes the cost function

$$z = \sum_{i=1}^{m} c_i x_i = \underline{c}' \, \underline{x} \tag{4}$$

where $\underline{c} = (c_1, c_2, \ldots, c_m)$. Cost (4) and constraints (3) give to our districting problem the more familiar form of a Set Partitioning Problem (see, for example, ARONOFSKY [2]), which is a special type in the class of integer programming problems. The solution of such a mathematical program will be discussed later on.

III. A SIMPLIFIED VERSION OF THE PROBLEM

Before we describe a method for finding all feasible districts (and thus for building the constraint matrix A) and an enumerative method for solving the Set Partitioning Problem, we must admit that the problem, as it is stated, is really usually too big for our means of solution. Then, some way must be found in order to reduce the dimensionality of the problem without wasting too much of its meaningfulness. In a typical region of Italy, the number of commu nities might easily be 400 or 500, and the number of feasible districts, for a reasonable choice of the lower and upper population bounds, will inevitably grow to several thousands of units.

One way of facing this shortcoming might consiste in discarding many feasible districts on the basis of some intuitive judgement, for instance by not allowing, for particular geographical conditions, long and narrow or starred districts. Obviously, such simplification leads to reduce the number of columns of A or, equivalently, the number of elements of the set $\mathcal{U}$. As a result of this reduction, suboptimal solution (if they exist) will in general be found.

To avoid performing such a reduction too arbitrarily, a two-level computational procedure is proposed.

1) At the first level, we reduce the set $\mathcal{U}$ to a new set $\tilde{\mathcal{U}}$ such that $\tilde{\mathcal{U}} \subset \mathcal{U}$ (then, a reduced matrix $\tilde{A}$ is obtained).

2) At the second level, we solve a simplified Set Partitioning Problem on matrix $\tilde{A}$, possibly after changing the cost vector $\underline{c}$ to a new cost vector $\underline{\tilde{c}}$, and obtain a suboptimal solution $\underline{\tilde{x}}^*$. Let $\mathcal{S}$ be the set of all feasible solutions s_i that can be derived from $\mathcal{U}$, and let $\tilde{\mathcal{S}}$ be the set that can be derived from $\tilde{\mathcal{U}}$. Clearly, $\tilde{\mathcal{S}} \subseteq \mathcal{S}$. The introduction of the new cost vector $\underline{\tilde{c}}$ would be unnecessary if one could know in advance that the optimal solution $\underline{x}^*$ still belongs to $\tilde{\mathcal{S}}$.

To be more specific, let us examine in some detail how this procedure can work in the problem we are dealing with. As we said in Section II, the global cost function should include a term, penalizing the average time (or distance) travelled by the citizen to reach the hospital he is assigned to. If by exploiting the particular structure of the cost function, we first try to minimize such a term, it is easy to show that a meaningful reduction of set $\mathcal{U}$ can be obtained, which is consistent with the intuition and simplifies the original Set Partitioning Problem by several orders of magnitude.

What we essentially want to obtain at the first level is a clustering of the communities around the most appropriate hospitals so that the average distance is minimized with the constraint that the demand of bed-units is satisfied within every cluster. A natural and straightforward way to determine such clusters consists in solving a suitable Transportation Problem (see for esample HADLEY [3]) as follows.

Let us consider the inhabitants of the region as goods to be shipped from the n communities to the l hospitals. Then, a Transportation Problem can be stated for which the cost function is given by

$$t = \sum_{i=1}^{n} \sum_{j=1}^{l} z_{ij} c_{ij}, \quad z_{ij} \geq 0 \tag{5}$$

where z_{ij} is the number of people assigned from community i to hospital j, and c_{ij} is the distance (or the travel time) between community i and hospital j. If hospital j is within community i, then $c_{ij} = 0$. Obvious constraints are the following:

$$\sum_{j=1}^{l} z_{ij} = a_i, \quad i = 1,2,\ldots,n \tag{6}$$

where a_i is the number of inhabitants of community i.

If we do not impose any other constraint, a trivial optimal solution wholly assigns every community to the nearest hospital regardless of its capacity. Recall, however, that we have assumed the number of beds for each hospital to be given. Let b_j be the number of beds of hospital j. Since bed-units and inhabitants are not homogeneous quantities, we need some comparison coefficient to meet the demand and the offer of the health-care system. Let α be such a coefficient, which specifies the number of inhabitants that can be assisted by the health services corresponding to one bed--unit. The balance between demand and offer is then expressed by the following constraints

$$\sum_{i=1}^{n} z_{ij} \leq \alpha b_j, \quad j = 1,2,\ldots,l \tag{7}$$

Clearly, since we have assumed that no new bed needs to be added, we must have

$$\sum_{i=1}^{n} a_i \leq \alpha \sum_{j=1}^{l} b_j \quad (8)$$

or, equivalently,

$$\alpha \geq \bar{\alpha} = \sum_{i=1}^{n} a_i \Big/ \sum_{j=1}^{l} b_j \quad (9)$$

The choice of α will be discussed later on. Suppose now to have solved the Transportation Problem outlined by (5), (6), (7)for a certain value of α . According to this solution, some communities will have been assigned to a unique hospital, while the remaining ones will have been shared among two or more hospitals. However, the number of the latter class of communities, which we will call "unassigned communities", is smaller than the number of hospitals, since in a Transportation Problem the number of nonnegative z_{ij} is $\leq n+l-1$. Fig.4 shows a typical solution of the Transportation Problem.

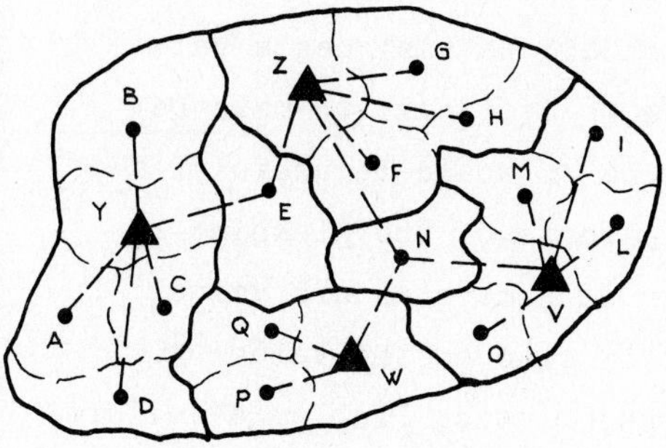

Fig.4. Solution of the Transportation Problem.

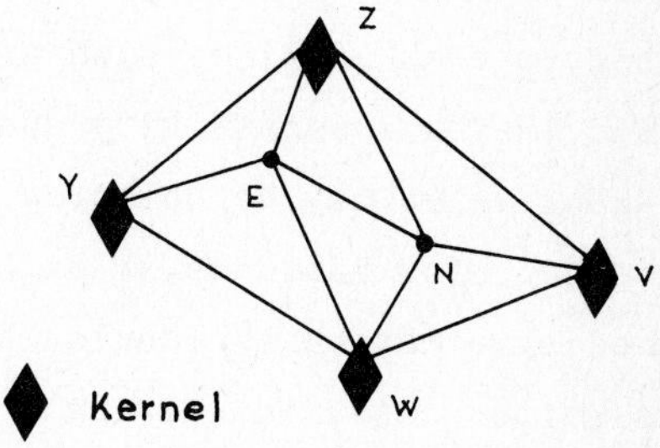

Fig.5. Reduced graph.

If the communities assigned to a hospital and the hospital itself constitute a connected subregion (and this happens most often), we define such subregion as a "kernel". It follows that the original graph of Fig.2 is reduced to a much simpler one, the nodes of which are given by kernels, unassigned communities and communities that have been assigned to a single hospital but that are not connected with the corresponding kernel (also these communities will be called "unassigned communities"). A reduced graph of this type is shown in Fig.5.

The construction of the feasible districts, as illustrated in Section II, can now be performed on this graph, yielding the reduced set of feasible districts $\tilde{\mathcal{U}}_\alpha$ (or, equivalently, the matrix $\tilde{A}_\alpha$) as required by the first computational level. The subscript α recalls that the reduced set $\tilde{\mathcal{U}}_\alpha$ and the matrix $\tilde{A}_\alpha$ depend now on the factor α .

At the second computational level, we must solve a new Set Partitioning Problem, which, however, is much simpler than the original one. Of course, the new cost vector $\tilde{\underline{c}}$ will include other terms of the global optimality criterion, but not necessarily distance or travel time.

As regards the factor α , we notice that this coefficient has, in our problem, both a mathematical and a socio-economical meaning. From a mathematical point of view, observe that the coefficient α , in the range $(\bar{\alpha}, \infty)$, should be assigned a value such that $\underline{x}^* \in \tilde{\mathcal{S}}_\alpha$. Since such a choice is difficult to make beforehand (maybe a sensitivity analysis on α would be useful), a meaningful value may be selected on the basis of the planning requirements. For instance, α might take on some standard value assigned by a national planning board, or take on the value $\bar{\alpha}$. In the latter case, in solving the Transportation Problem a uniform inhabitants / bed-units ratio would be assumed for the hospitals of the region.

In the next Section, the scheme of an algorithm to perform the two level computational procedure will be presented.

IV. ALGORITHMS FOR SOLUTION

The first step towards the solution of our reduced Set Partitioning problem consists in finding an algorithm for building the constraint matrix $\tilde{A}_\alpha$ column by column. Since the number of possible combinations with L kernels and K unassigned communities is $(2^L-1)2^K$, to enumerate all such combinations and then to select all feasible districts may clearly turn out to be prohibitive.

Therefore, the search for the feasible districts will be tried by means of the following procedure:

1) choose any kernel as a root;
2) find on the reduced graph all trees spanning from this root and having population lying between the assigned limits;
3) choose another kernel as a new root, go back to step 2), and so on for all kernels.

The process of finding all trees spanning from an assigned root is readily accomplished by means of a search technique which is similar to the "Backtrack Programming" method proposed by GOLOMB [4]. The resultant algorithm backtracks over the solution stack every time the population exceeds the upper limit or a tree is outlined that has been found before.

Once the constraint matrix $\tilde{A}_\alpha$ is found, there exist several different approaches leading to the optimal solution $\underline{\tilde{x}}^*$ (cutting planes, Balas algorithm, branch and bound, rounding off the solutions of a standard linear programming code, etc.; see also for references HU [5]). The one that seems to be the most appropriate for our problem is an implicit enumerative search technique which, by means of a previous ordering of its columns, scans matrix $\tilde{A}_\alpha$ looking for all feasible solutions.

This approach is due to PIERCE [6], who suggested a particular way of ordering the columns. Even though it may be slower than other methods, it has the great advantage of finding all feasible solutions. This might be the starting point for a multigoal optimization or, more simply, it might allow the planner to assign dif ferent costs to every feasible solution, according to different objectives, and then to choose as "the optimal solution" the one that ranks most satisfactorily with respect to all objectives.

The rows of matrix $\tilde{A}_\alpha$ are now given by the kernels and the unassigned communities, while the columns are the feasible districts; the elements of such a matrix have the same meaning as the elements of A in (3).

The columns of matrix $\tilde{A}_\alpha$ are ordered in such a way that, in reading them from the left to the right, groups of columns are found in the following order: the columns of the first group have 1 in the first row, the columns of the second group have 0,1 in the first and in the second row, respectively, and so on. The following example will clarify such a structure.

$$\tilde{A}_\alpha = \left(\begin{array}{cccc|ccc|ccc|cc} 1&1&1&1&0&0&0&0&0&0&0&0 \\ \cline{5-7} 1&0&0&0&1&1&1&0&0&0&0&0 \\ \cline{8-10} 0&0&1&0&0&0&0&1&1&1&0&0 \\ \cline{11-12} 0&1&0&0&1&0&0&1&0&0&1&1 \\ 0&0&0&0&0&1&1&0&0&1&0&1 \\ 0&1&1&0&0&0&1&0&0&0&1&0 \end{array}\right)$$

Recalling that a feasible solution is a collection of feasible districts such that each kernel, or unassigned community, belongs to one and only one district, we reckon that a feasible solution cannot have two columns covering the same kernel or unassigned community (i.e., having a 1 in the same row). Thus, for instance, two columns that appear in a feasible solution cannot belong to the same group.

The algorithm chooses one column from the first group, then one from the second, checking that they both do not cover the same row, and so on, and backtracks whenever a feasible solution may be found beginning with the current columns. FLOYD's method [7] has been used to implement the backtrack algorithm.

A realistic example about the province of Imperia, Italy, is presented with the intent of clarifying our approach. The province is made up of 67 communities and it is served by 7 non-specialistic hospitals.

Fig.6 shows the output of the Transportation Problem when an $\alpha = \bar{\alpha}$ has been chosen. Two hospitals have disappeared from the map, since their capacity was so small that, according to parameter α, they were not even big enough for their community. Thus, the two communities have been erased from the number of destinations and have been added to the number of origins (with a reduced population).

By choosing the population limits for the feasible districts P_{min} = 30.000 and P_{max} = 100.000, the algorithm has generated the sixteen feasible solutions of Fig.7.

V. CONCLUDING COMMENTS

Two essential features characterize the method proposed in the paper: 1) the reduction of the original high-dimensional problem to a smaller one by solving a suitable Transportation Problem, 2) the choice of Backtrack Programming algorithms to face the subsequent combinatorial problems. Since the simplified approach of point one is heuristic and the choice of point two may appear to be arbitrary, some comments are needed.

As regards the first point, it is worth noting that, despite the heuristic nature of the suggested simplification, the introduction of the Transportation Problem to reduce the dimensionality of the original problem is quite consistent with the intuition, since it emphasizes the role of hospitals as gravitation centers for the health-care demand. Moreover, such a reduction may be "controlled" by means of a unique parameter, i.e., the coefficient α which enables an easy sensitivity analysis significant for both a mathematical and a socio-economical interpretation.

The choice of a Backtrack Programming approach to solve the final Set Partitioning Problem is probably a questionable fact, since other combinatorial methods may perform more efficiently. For the present problem other experimental work is required. Ob

Fig.6. Output of Transportation Problem for Provincia of Imperia.

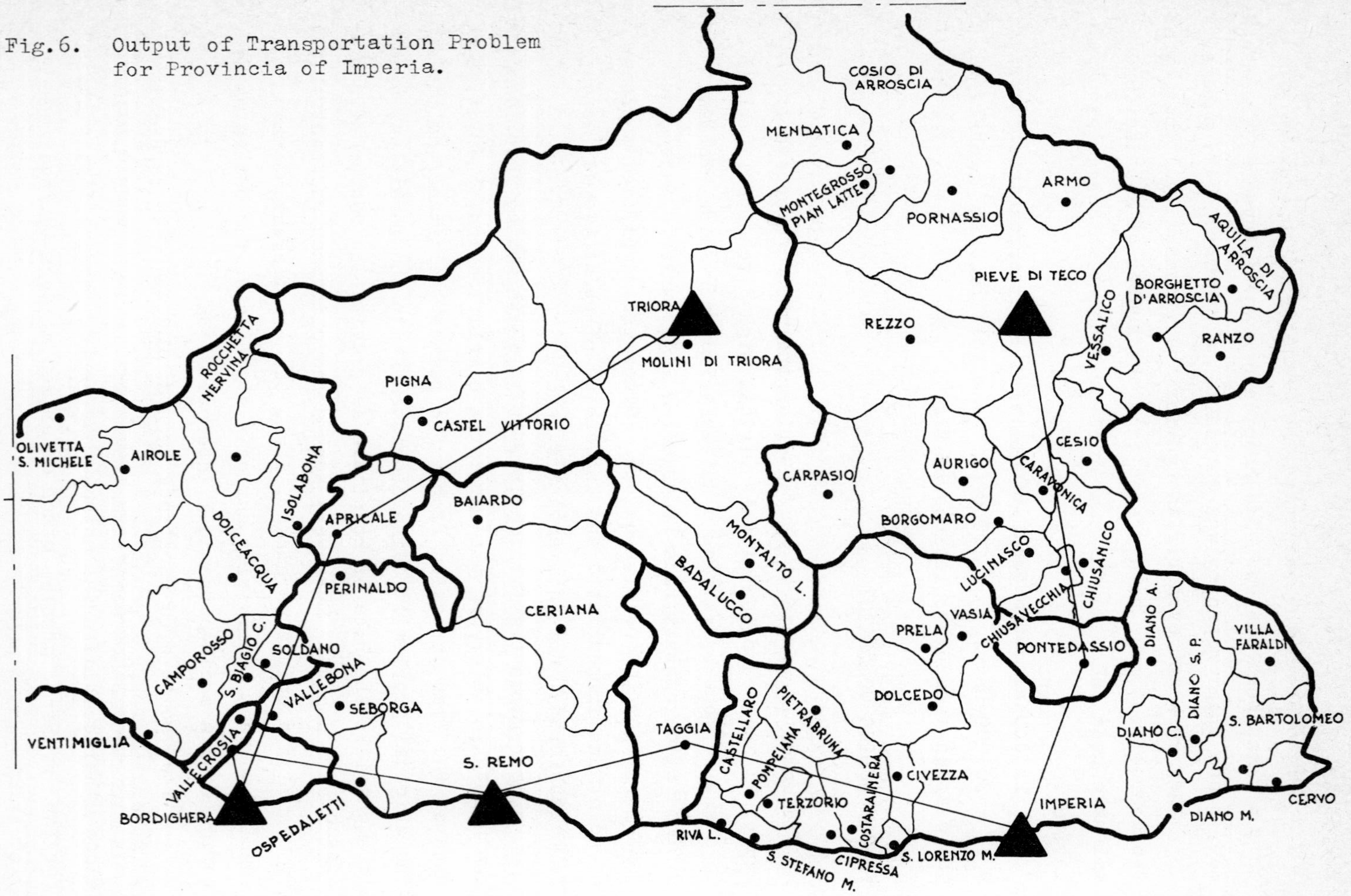

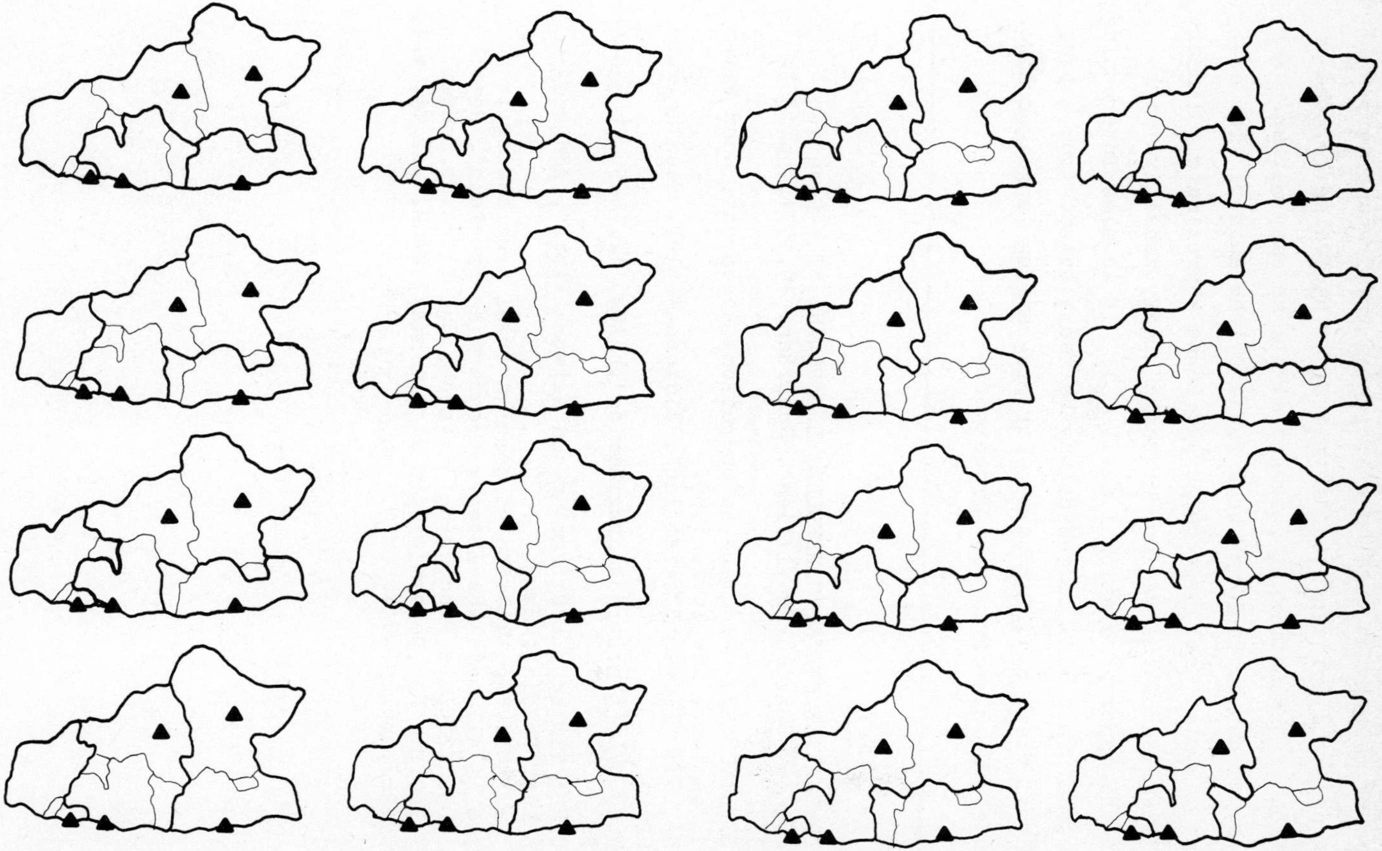

Fig. 7. Feasible districts for Provincia of Imperia.

serve, however, that, for a given solution of the Transportation Problem, the search for feasible districts, or equivalently, the determination of the matrix $\tilde{A}_\alpha$, is not at all an easy matter. For this search, no better tool has been found by the authors (for example, the computational time turns out to be approximately linear with the dimension of the region, although highly sensitive with respect to the upper population limit P_{max}). It is also interesting to observe that this kind of search may be facilitated, from a practical point of view, by using particular programming languages like, for instance, the Symmetric List Processor.

REFERENCES

[1] C.TOREGAS, R.SWAIN, C.REVELLE, L.BERGMAN: "The Location of Emergency Service Facilities", Opns.Res, 19,1971, pp.1363--1373.

[2] J.S.ARONOFSKY: "Progress in Operations Research", John Wiley and Son Inc., New York, 1969.

[3] G.HADLEY: "Linear Programming", Addison-Wesley, Reading,Mass., 1962.

[4] S.W.GOLOMB: "Backtrack Programming", JACM, 12,1965, pp.516--524.

[5] T.C.HU: "Integer Programming and Network Flows", Addison--Wesley, Reading, Mass., 1970.

[6] J.F.PIERCE: "Application of combinatorial programming to a class of all zero-one Integer Programming problems", Rept. 36.YO3, IBM Data Processing Division, Cambridge Sc.Center.

[7] R.W.FLOYD: "Non Deterministic Algorithms", JACM, vol.14, n.4, Oct.1967, pp.636-644.

STUDY OF WAKING-SLEEPING BEHAVIOUR USING AUTOMATIC ANALYSIS AND QUANTIFICATION

Cl. Gottesmann, G. Lacoste, L. Rodrigues, P. Kirkham, J.L. Rallo and Ch. Arnaud

Laboratoire de Psychophysiologie. Faculté des Sciences et des Techniques
06034 NICE Cedex

The activation of nerve and muscle cells is characterised by a low voltage activity. The study of these fluctuations of potential difference is the purpose of the electrophysiological approach widely used in clinical medecine on one hand, psychophysiological and neurophysiological research on the other.

This electrical activity has essentially two forms :

- the first is rapid, of digital type, since it is either on or off; this is what one observes in the axons, the nervous conducting paths, and single cell recordings : it is a matter of calculating a response frequency.

- the second consists of variations of potential difference with variable polarity, certain of them can last more than a second. They generally come from complex structures usually studied through several different layers of tissue. The typical example is that of the electroencephalogram recorded on the scalp or the electrocorticogram recorded directly on the cortex, the frequency of which varies from about 0.5-40 c/s. The study of this kind of activity is essential in Man for clinical medecine, in animals for fundamental and applied research.

This approach meets two major difficulties :

- the mass of information from which the critical characteristics are to be drawn.
- visual data analysis, which is slow and open to inconsistency.

This is why many research workers have set out to find automatic analysis methods, which are both rapid and accurate.

For our part, we have undertaken the automatic analysis of the different phases of waking and sleeping in the rat, fundamental behaviour on which all else is based. This approach has been complemented by automatic analysis of brain excitability and psychomotor activity. This research firstly carried out off-line, subsequently on-line, will very soon result in a system allowing the automatic analysis of the same data on animals completly free to move.

Seven phases of the waking-sleeping cycle have been selected, their physiological significance has been specified in our previous works (1, 2) : 1/ active or attentive waking, with theta activity; 2/ normal waking; 3/ slow wave sleep; 4/ deeper sleep characterised by neocortical spindles; 5/ intermediate stage which precedes and follows paradoxical sleep and is characterised by neocortical spindles and theta activity; 6/ paradoxical sleep, where dreams occur in Man; 7/ the periods of rapid eye movements during paradoxical sleep (figure 1).

In order to avoid any loss of information, we have set the unit duration of analysis at one second. It is well known that the nervous system is in permanent unstable equilibrium, even more so in a small animal with higher metabolic rate, having a very polyphasic waking-sleeping rhythm with brief activities such as spindles and the bursts of eye-movements.

Off-line approach

A/ State determination (for references, see 3, 4, 5, 6, 7).

A study of the two cerebral derivations used, has shown that signal analysis by autocorrelation or cross correlation would require computing power far beyond the means available to us and for the processing it would be difficult to reconcile signal length with the one second' "quantum" we had decided on.

Spectral analysis of the two brain derived channels has indicated that in a particular frequency band, the amount of energy in channel 1, makes it possible to distinguish between the principal sleeping and waking phases, with some overlapping. For channel 2, use is made of the ratio of energies in two frequency bands one of which is centred on the theta type activity. For the electrooculogram (channel 3) which is only taken into consideration during paradoxical sleep, the deviations from the base line are detected, then integrated. Finally, for the electromyogram (channel 4), the energy emitted in a particular frequency band is integrated; this too differs during the different behavioural phases, with overlaps. Thus each of the 3 essential derivations (1, 2, 4) is tested a certain number of times per unit of time; the energy collected is integrated over the one second base. This results in an energy value, for each derivation , which is specific to each phase of waking-sleeping behaviour with overlaps at the edges and which constitutes a partial criterion.

Each behavioural phase is also defined by a global criterion resulting from the combination of the three partial criteria. However, in certain cases one of the partial criteria is below the experimentally fixed norm, for the corresponding state. This results in a penalisation of the global criterion, which is a function of the unsatisfactory criterion's deviation from the norm. Above a certain degree of penalisation, the state is retained but qualified as "doubtful". The doubtful states are counted with their probable state and also, separately. They are thus easely deductible.

This analysis is undertaken on an IBM 1800 with 16 K words of 16 bits which processes the data at thirty-two times the speed of acquisition, which is done in analogue form on magnetic tape. The signals undergo a pre-processing by means of pass-band filters centred on zones determined by spectral analysis. Each channel is sampled at 25-50 Hz depending on the derivation. The data are then digitised,

Different rejection logics were used : for example, to eliminate heart pulses, high energy signals which are surimposed on the electromyogram; also transient states like the short periods of clonus activities during paradoxical sleep that could be taken for attentive waking.

Output :

Cards are punched with the successive states and their duration, in binary code. The doubtful states are given in decreasing order of their probability of appearance. The processing condenses 24 hours of recording into a maximum of 300 cards.

These data are then grouped by quarter of an hour, hour and total length of the recording. The values produced in a listing (figure 2A)show the percentage of time passed in each of the seven states, in waking as a whole, in sleeping as a whole, and the global percentage of doubtful states grouping together the individual percentages for each of the seven states.

Finally, an output in the form of histograms (figure 2B)indicates the evolution by quarter of an hour, of the percentage of time passed in each state and the average percentage for the whole recording.

Reliability :

The contingency studied by the C test (12) indicates the following values :

Corrector A - Corrector A : C = .89
Corrector B - Corrector B : C = .83
Corrector A - Corrector B : C = .87
Corrector A - Computer : C = .81
Corrector B - Computer ; C = .81

The perfect contingency in our experimental conditions (global contingency between 6 states) is .91. The mean percentage of correspondence, state by state (13), between the two correctors and the computer is 82%. For the different stages it is :

attentive or active waking	: 86%
normal waking	: 79,5%
slow wave sleep	: 83%
spindles	: 78,5%
intermediate state	: 81%
paradoxical sleep	: 85,5%

These results are satisfactory. In fact, since the publication of our technique KOHN et al. (14) have described a method with which they dissociate only three phases, with a 12 second period of integration and they obtain a 91% correspondence (15).

B/ Determination of brain excitability

1. Study of evoked potentials (for references, see 6, 7, 8, 9).

A central or peripheral stimulation induces in the nervous pathways and centres with which it comes into contact, an activity said to be "evoked", which gives indications about the level of excitability of the central zone studied.

The "evoked potential" is recorded in analogue form on a magnetic tape. During off-line treatment, at 16 times the acquisition speed, a synchronising signal preceding the evoked potential opens an analysis window of variable duration with a high definition (2 samples per millisecond), during which the response is registered by the computer, then stored with the responses collected in the same behavioural phase. The responses which occur during "doubtful" states are eliminated.

The mean amplitude and dispersion are automatically calculated for each sample point making up the evoked potential. Only a predetermined number of responses is retained, by hour and by state.

The output of results takes place every twelve hours in graphical analogue form. The standard deviation is also marked on the same figure ($\frac{\sigma}{2}$) -figure 3A-.

2. Analysis of induced states (for references, see 6,7,9).

Equally, a central or peripheral stimulation can also induce a change in behaviour and in the spontaneous global electrophysiological activities . A stimulus can momentarily wake the animal etc ... This possible influence is tested by the automatic comparison of the animal's state in the second which precedes and the second which follows the stimulation .

In order to avoid any interference with the state determination, the stimulus intended to induce an evoked potential always occurs at the limit of a period of state analysis .

The results of this analysis are produced as a listing showing the percentage of induced states in each phase of the cycle and the number of samples counted (figure 3B).

C/ Psychomotor activity (for references, see 7, 8, 9) .

It is important to know the rate and the distribution of psychomotor activity during the circadian period in order to characterise the behaviour of a "normal" animal and that of an experimental animal subjected to various disturbances : selective lesions of the nervous system or pharmacological influences . In order to detect movements of the preparation the electromyogram channel undergoes a second processing which allows the fluctuations in energy in successive periods of analysis to be tested . Above an experimentally determined threshold, this fluctuation is counted as a movement, which is then classified with the state during which it occurred .

This approach has, in addition, the advantage of distinguishing the drugs which create a dissociation between the behaviour and the electrocorticogram, such as morphine and atropine which tend to induce a cortical activity like slow wave sleep although the animal has a waking behaviour and moves about in its cage . This diagnostic is established where an animal present a significant increase in its movements during slow wave sleep, a phase which is usually associated with resting behaviour .

The results are given as a listing in the same way as for the states . The motor activity arising in the different states is indicated in the form of a percentage of the duration of the state .

On line approach

The off line approach, rapid and rich in information, is interesting but it nervertheless presents the following difficulties :

- it is not always possible to detect experimental problems and artefacts during the data acquisition ; the difficulties only appear after analysis.
- the determination of central excitability requires the number of stimulations to be increased, with the computer undertaking a sorting process afterwards .
- on a practical level, the analysis done outside the laboratory is very expensive, which has caused this technique to be abandoned .

The purchase of a small computer (TEXAS 980A) has allowed us to undertake the study of a program for analysis and quantification in real time . Eliminating the difficulties outlined above, it makes it possible in addition to envisage a real-time investigation of metabolic changes . At the moment, we are studying the coupling of a push-pull cannula technique, for the perfusion of a central structure by means of 2 concentric or parallel tubes, with the time basis of the computer . In this way, the output could be studied taking into account the precise state during which it was obtained, and it be easier to look for possible assimilation or elimination by the central nervous system, in terms of the different behavioural phases .

It is difficult to indicate the precise method used as this investigation is the subject of a contract . The real-time program has a better performance than the off-line one and allows the feed-back necessary for the determination of central excitability with a minimal number of stimulations .

The output data are the same as for the off-line program . Figure 4 gives an example of recording analysed in real time without the intervention of an organisational logic for the stages which would enable the rare aberrant states to be eliminated.

Real time processing of telemetry data

Ideally one wishes to work on animal which are free to move. Up to now, we have only been able to use rats equipped with recording cables, which, though light, cause the animal discomfort and favour the dislodging of the acrylic cement cap fixed to the skull.

Since a short while ago the laboratory has had at its disposal the prototype of a polygraphic microtelemetric system : 4 channels, 4 gr., 3 weeks autonomy (11). At the moment, we are in a position to demonstrate the processing in real-time of biological signals received by this method (figure 5). Although adjustments may be necessary, the results are very encouraging. A miniature telemetry technique for electrical and pharmacological stimulations will soon be added, offering a bright future for research in psychophysiology and ethology.

Conclusion :

We would like to perfect rapid and viable techniques of analysis for electrophysiological and metabolic activities in an animal living as normally as possible, a necessary condition for the advancement of knowledge of the physiological basis of behaviour.

* We wish to thank M. Rodi for his valuable assistance.

* This work was supported by D.R.M.E. (74/138), D.G.R.S.T. (75 7 0092) and C.N.R.S. grants.

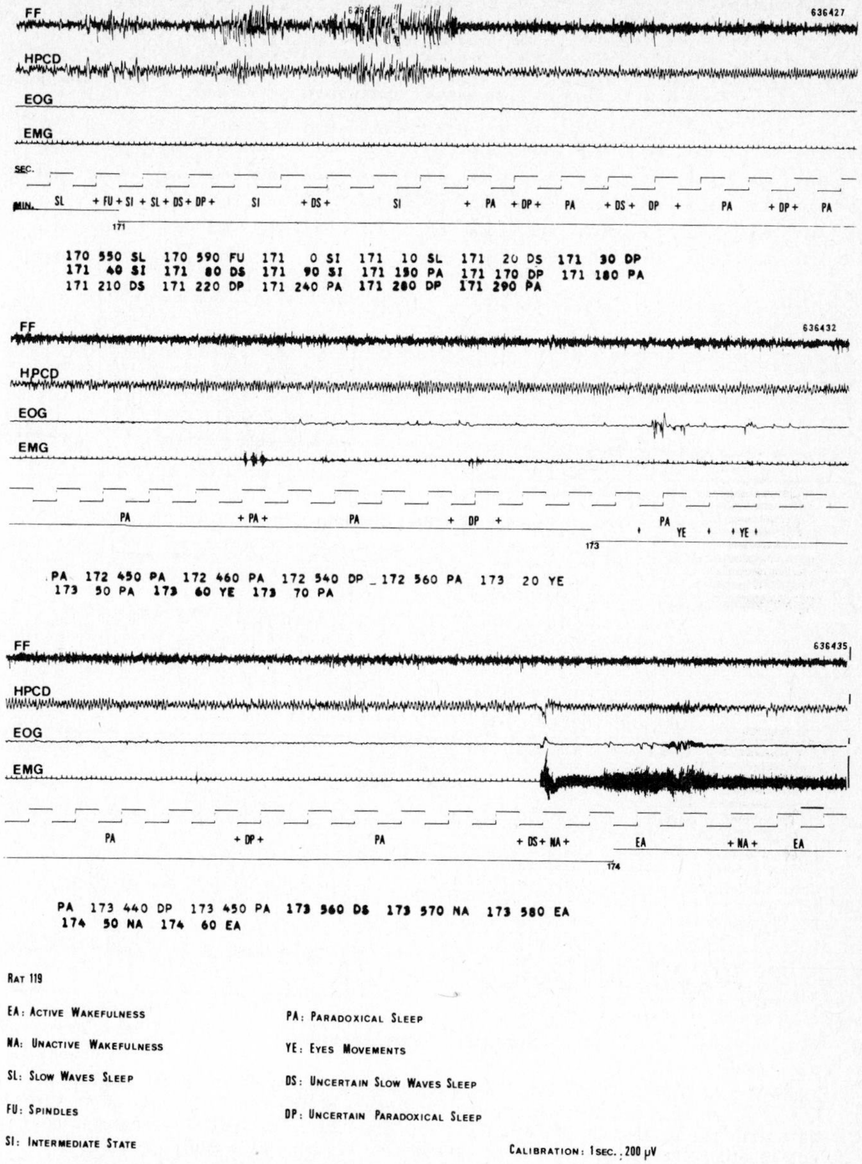

Figure 1 : DIFFERENT PHASES OF THE WAKING-SLEEPING CYCLE DETECTED BY THE OFF-LINE PROGRAM . Under each of the three parts of this recording is the corresponding listing . The first three numbers indicate the minute of recording (min.) the following three give the seconds (55.0).
On the central trace, note the intervention of the prohibitory logic (min.172, sec. 45) which indicates the appearance of paradoxical sleep despite the electromyogram which could have resulted in active waking .

Abreviations : FF : frontal cortex - HPCD : dorsal hippocampus - EOG : electrooculogram - EMG : electromyogram .

From GOTTESMANN et al., 1973 .

A *** ETATS *** RAT 214 S JOURNEE DU 21 2 72

*** POURCENTAGES PAR TRANCHES DE 0 H 15 MN 0 S ***

TRANCHE	EVEIL ACTIF		EVEIL NON ACTIF		SOMMEIL LENT		STADE DE FUSEAUX		STADE INTERMEDIAIRE		SOMMEIL PARADOXAL			EVEIL	SOMMEIL	DOUTEUX
0	17.4	0.7	1.3	0.0	44.1	5.8	9.6	0.0	19.8	0.7	7.2	0.0	0.4	18.7	80.7	7.6
1	55.5	0.0	37.6	0.0	3.8	0.2	1.3	0.0	1.5	0.0	0.0	0.0	0.0	93.1	6.6	0.2
2	68.7	0.0	31.2	0.0	0.0	0.0	0.0	0.0	0.0	0.0	0.0	0.0	0.0	99.9	0.0	0.0
3	49.1	0.0	19.2	0.0	21.5	2.3	3.3	0.1	6.1	0.3	0.5	0.0	0.1	68.3	31.4	2.8
*****	47.6	0.1	22.3	0.0	17.3	2.0	3.5	0.0	6.8	0.2	1.9	0.0	0.1	70.0	29.6	2.6

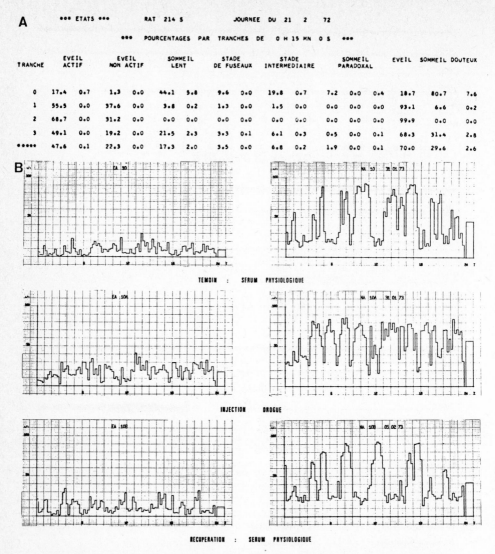

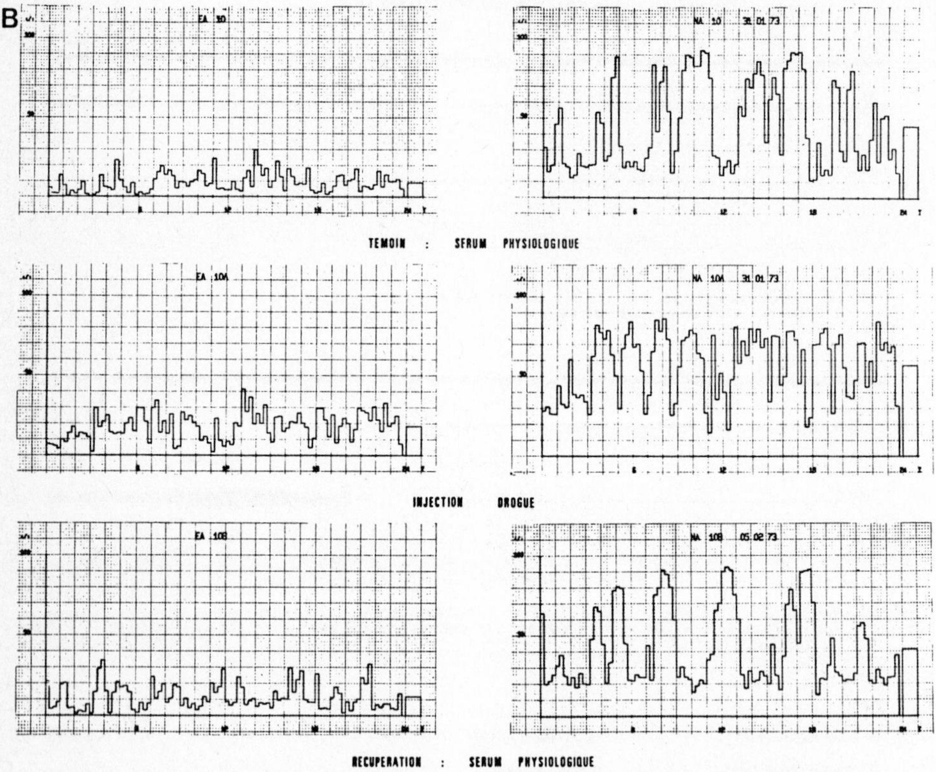

Figure 2 : A/ STATES OUTPUT LISTING . Each column, indicates for every quarter of an hour and every hour, the percentage of the total time passed in each state with the percentage of "doubtfuls" at the side . The last three columns collect together the values for waking as a whole, sleeping as a whole, and all the "doubtfuls".

B/ STATES OUTPUT ON A HISTOGRAM . An example taken from the study of a psychotropic drug . Evolution of active waking (left hand column) and normal waking (right hand column) ; during the control period (top histograms), the administering of the drug (middle), the recuperation period (bottom) . Note, on the right, the average for each state for the duration of recording.

For abreviations, see figure 1

From TASSET and GOTTESMANN (unpublished)

A

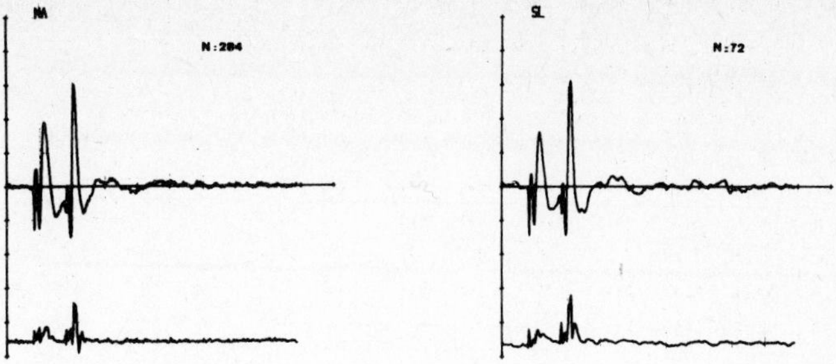

B

RAT 214 S JOURNEE DU 21 2 72

NOMBRE D'OBSERVATIONS			ETATS INDUITS EN ./.						
			EA	NA	SL	FU	SI	PA	YE
EA	592	287	64	29	5	0	1	2	0
NA	430	221	40	54	5	0	0	1	0
SL	450	226	4	3	60	12	20	0	0
FU	203	72	2	1	29	35	32	0	0
SI	337	167	1	0	29	20	50	0	0
PA	71	49	7	3	20	0	1	69	0
YE	0	0	0	0	0	0	0	0	0

Figure 3 : AUTOMATIC ANALYSIS OF CEREBRAL REACTIVITY IN THE RAT .

A/ STUDY OF EVOKED POTENTIALS .

The upper curve shows the mean amplitude of two successive potentials . The lower one represents the corresponding dispersion for the different components of the response .

B/ ANALYSIS OF INDUCED STATES .

In the left column, the numbers indicate the number of stimulations taken into account for each state for this analysis . On the right, written in percentages, are the states observed in the second following stimulation . Thus, 430 stimulations in normal waking were followed by normal waking in 54% of the cases, by active waking in 40 % of the cases, etc...

Note that this animal did not have an electrooculogram.

The second column of numbers (287, 221, etc...) shows the number of samples counted for the evoked potential analysis, the reduction being the result of logical prohibition .

For abreviations, see figure 1

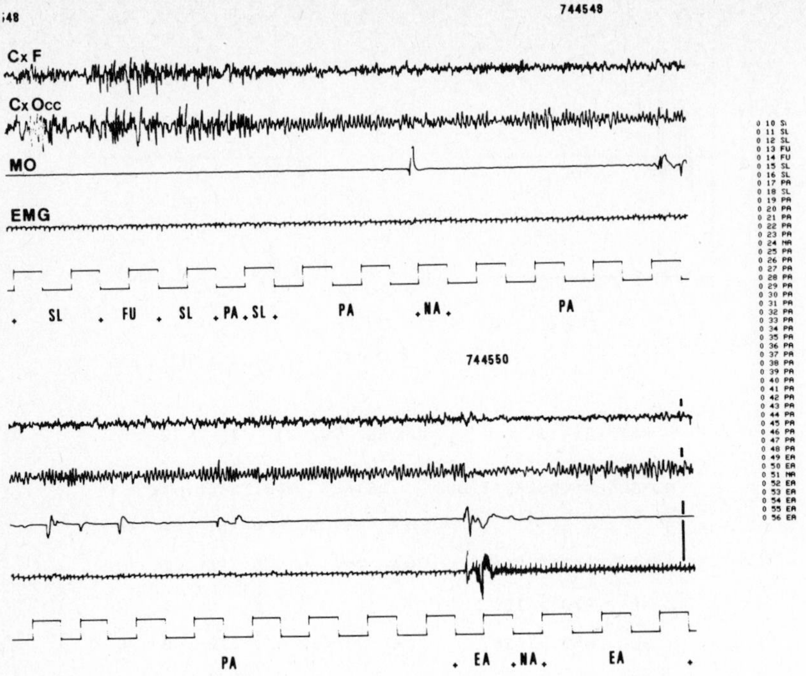

Figure 4 : DIFFERENT PHASES OF WAKING AND SLEEPING ANALYSED BY THE REAL-TIME PROGRAM .

Continuous recording with corresponding listing on the right . The analysis has been undertaken without the organisational logic which allows the elimination of the rare aberrant states . Eye movements (MO) of paradoxical sleep are not analysed . Channel 1 is filtered .

For abreviations, see figure 1

Scale : 1 sec. 100 μV

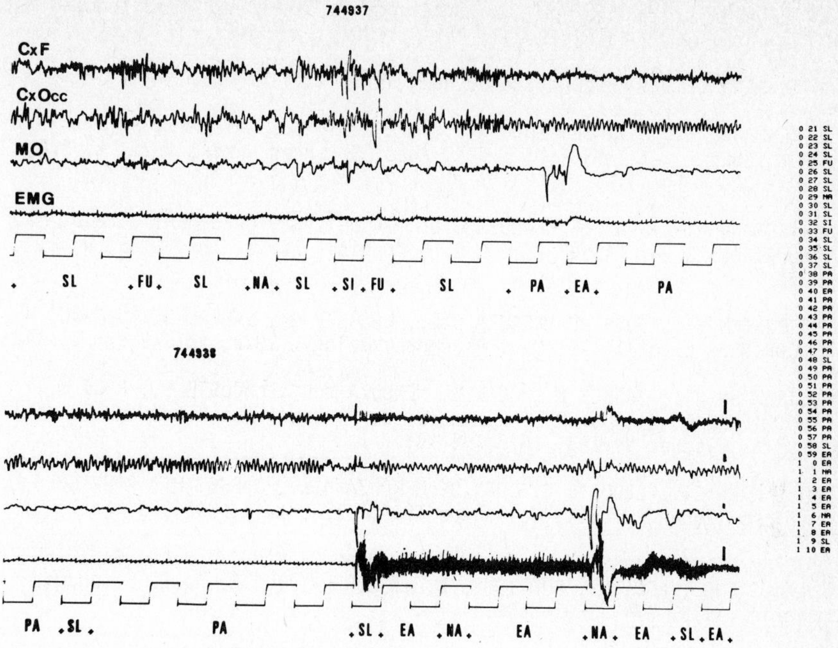

<u>Figure 5</u> : REAL-TIME ANALYSIS OF A RAT RECORDED BY TELEMETRY .

Continuous recording with corresponding listing on the right . As in figure 4, the processing was completed without the use of logical organisation of the states . Note the two short field losses in the awake rat . Eye movements (MO) of paradoxical sleep are not analysed .

<u>For abreviations</u>, see figure 1.

Scale : 1 sec. 200 µV

1. GOTTESMANN Cl. : Recherche sur la Psychophysiologie du sommeil chez le Rat. Presses du Palais-Royal, Paris, 1967, 156 pages.

2. GOTTESMANN Cl. : Année Psychologique, 1971, 71, 451-488.

3. GOTTESMANN Cl., JUAN DE MENDOZA J.L., LACOSTE G., LALLEMENT B., RODRIGUES L. et TASSET M. : C.R. Acad. Sciences Paris, 1971, t. 272, 301-302.

4. GOTTESMANN Cl., JUAN DE MENDOZA J.L., LACOSTE G., LALLEMENT B. RODI M., RODRIGUES L. et TASSET M. : C.R. Soc. Biol. Paris, 1971, 165, n° 2, 373.

5. GOTTESMANN Cl., JUAN DE MENDOZA J.L., LACOSTE G., LALLEMENT B., RODI M., RODRIGUES L. et TASSET M. : Psychophysiology, 1972, Vol. 9, n° 1, 142.

6. GOTTESMANN Cl., TASSET M., JUAN DE MENDOZA J.L., LACOSTE G., RODI M., RODRIGUES L. et ROUX R. : Symposium de Wurzburg "La Nature du Sommeil". Gustav Fischer Verlag, 1973, 98-101.

7. GOTTESMANN Cl., LACOSTE G. JUAN DE MENDOZA J.L., TASSET M., RODRIGUES L.: Informatique Médicale, Colloques IRIA, 1973, t. 1, 295-309.

8. GOTTESMANN Cl., TASSET M., RALLO J.L., JUAN DE MENDOZA J.L., GAUTHIER P. LACOSTE G., RODI M., RODRIGUES L. et ROUX R. : C.R. Acad. Sciences Paris, 1972, 274, 3601-3602.

9. GOTTESMANN Cl., TASSET M., RALLO J.L., JUAN DE MENDOZA J.L., GAUTHIER P., LACOSTE G., RODI M., RODRIGUES L. et ROUX R. : Psychophysiology, 1973.

10. GOTTESMANN Cl., LACOSTE G. et RODRIGUES L. : A.P.S.S. Edinburgh, 1975, Psychophysiology (in press).

11. GOTTESMANN Cl., RODI M. et RALLO J.L. : BIOCAPT Paris 1975 (in preparation)

12. SIEGEL S. : Non parametric statistics for behavioural sciences. The Graw Hill Co, New-York, 1956.

13. JOHNSON C. : Use of computer in sleep research. A.P.S.S. Bruges, 1971.

14. KOHN M., LITCHFIELD D., BRANCHEY M. and BREBBIA D.R.: Electroenceph. clin. Neurophysiol., 1974, 37, 518-520.

15. BRANCHEY M., BREBBIA D.R., KOHN M. and LITCHFIELD D. : Electroenceph. clin. Neurophysiol., 1974, 37, 501-506.

SELF-SUSTAINED OSCILLATIONS IN THE JACOB-MONOD MODE OF GENE REGULATION

Z. Grossman and I. Gumowski
CERN, 1211 Geneva 23, Switzerland

A plausible macroscopic model of genetic regulation by feedback repression, evolved from the original formulation of Goodwin, is considered. This model has the form of a second-order non-linear dynamic system, $\dot{x} = f_1(x,y)$, $\dot{y} = f_2(x,y)$, where $x(t) \geq 0$ describes the mRNA which codes for the protein $y(t) \geq 0$, the latter acting as a repressor. Published analytical, analog, and digital studies of this model do not report the existence of any periodic solutions. A stochastic analysis has produced some irregular undamped oscillations, but these appear to be due to the stochastic elements so introduced.

The model $\dot{x} = f_1(x,y)$, $\dot{y} = f_2(x,y)$ is known to be approximate. In particular it neglects delays of synthesis and transport of x,y from the place of production to the place of effect. Periodic solutions are found when a constant delay is introduced into y(t), or a variable one into x(t). In the latter case, analytical expressions for the amplitude and period are determined by means of a Poincaré-type expansion. In the presence of delay, sustained oscillations of x and y are found to exist in a wide parameter range.

* * *

INTRODUCTION

Under the influence of classical thermodynamics and statistical mechanics it was believed for a long time that chemical, biochemical, and biological reactions, described by a system of non-linear ordinary differential equations, have only monotonically varying transients toward or away from a state of static equilibrium. This rather entrenched belief started to evolve with the discovery of sustained oscillations in a purely chemical reaction involving an inorganic catalyst (oxydation of malonic acid by $KBrO_3$ in the presence of Ce ions) [1,2]. The presence of temporal oscillations resulted in spatial oscillations [photographs in Herschkowith-Kaufman[3]]. In due course many oscillatory phenomena were found in biochemistry [survey in Hess and Boiteux[4]]. Present interest appears to centre on glycolysis[5,6], which constitutes the next natural step in chemical (and mathematical) complexity. The present paper considers oscillations in a cellular system and, more specifically, the so-called epigenetic oscillations. Although the experimental evidence for the existence, and especially biological relevance of self-sustained epigenetic oscillations, is still a subject of debate[7-9], the study of mathematical models of such oscillations has been pursued quite intensively[10-13]. This paper falls in the scope of the latter activity.

A plausible macroscopic model of genetic regulation by feedback repression, evolved from the original formulation of Goodwin[10], is

$$\dot{x}(t) = a\left(1 + A\,y(t)\right)^{-1} - b\,x(t) \quad , \quad \dot{y}(t) = B\,x(t) - C\,y(t) \quad , \tag{1}$$

where $x(t) \geq 0$ is a mRNA which codes for the protein $y(t) \geq 0$, the latter acting as a repressor. All reaction constants in (1) are positive, and x,y represent instantaneous concentrations. This model is analoguous to the Jacob-Monod system[14,15]. The study of (1) did not disclose any self-sustained oscillations[12], except when (1) was replaced by a roughly similar stochastic process[13]. Some rather irregular undamped oscillations were then found, but these oscillations appear to be due entirely to the stochastic elements so introduced. A modification of the non-linear term to the form

$$a\,y^m\left(1 + A\,y^n\right)^{-1} \quad , \quad m,n > 0 \; , \tag{2}$$

as well as an increase of the differential order from two to three, by introducing an intermediate metabolite, also failed to produce a qualitative change in the hoped-for direction[12]. Periodic solutions were reported in a rather narrow parameter range, when m = 0, n = 2 in (2), and the number of intermediate metabolites is increased to six or more (differential order increased to eight or more) [16].

The situation is radically changed, as will be shown, when pure delay is introduced into (1) without any increase of differential order. Such a modification constitutes an improvement of the model because it permits us to take into account the finite times of transcription, synthesis, and transport (diffusion) between the place of production and effect of x and y. The biological arguments behind an unambiguous definition of these times are still a subject of study[17]. Mathematically no loss of generality occurs when x, y, and t are normalized. Keeping the same names for the normalized variables, the modified version of (1) has two reaction constants and four delays:

$$\dot{x}(t) = [1 + y(t-\tau_1)]^{-1} - b\,x(t-\tau_3)\,, \quad \dot{y}(t) = x(t-\tau_2) - c\,y(t-\tau_4)\,. \tag{3}$$

The existence of a constant steady state (static equilibrium) $x_0 = cy_0$, $y_0 = -\frac{1}{2} + \sqrt{\frac{1}{4} + 1/(bc)}$, is unaffected by the delays, but the effect on stability may become strong. For constant delays the variational and characteristic equations of (3) at (x_0, y_0) are

$$L(\tau, y) = \ddot{y}(t) + b\dot{y}(t-\tau_3) + c\dot{y}(t-\tau_4) + \beta y(t-\tau_1-\tau_2) + bc\,y(t-\tau_3-\tau_4) = 0\,, \tag{4}$$

$$s^2 + s\left(b e^{-s\tau_3} + c e^{-s\tau_4}\right) + \beta e^{-s(\tau_1+\tau_2)} + bc\,e^{-s(\tau_3+\tau_4)} = 0\,, \tag{5}$$

where $\beta = (1 + y_0)^{-2}$.

In general, (5) admits an infinity of roots s_i [eigenvalues of $L(\tau,y)$]. Let $\theta(t)$ be a sufficiently smooth function and

$$y(t) = \theta(t)\,, \quad -\tau \le t \le 0\,, \quad \tau = \max(\tau_1+\tau_2\,, \tau_3+\tau_4) \tag{6}$$

an initial condition assuring the existence of unique solutions of (3) and (4). It is known that in general the eigenvalues s_i are enumerable and can be ordered according to their moduli, i.e. so that $|s_{i+1}| \ge |s_i|$. Suppose for simplicity that all s_i are non-degenerate. The solution of (4) and (6) can then be written in the form

$$y(t) = \sum_{i=-\infty}^{\infty} C_i e^{s_i t}\,, \quad C_i = \text{complex constants} \tag{7}$$

where the C_i, $i < 0$ are so chosen that $y(t)$ is real-valued. When $\theta(t)$ is sufficiently smooth (as assumed), the sequence $\{C_i\}$ will not cause a divergence of the series in (7). A sufficient condition of stability of the steady state (x_0,y_0) is therefore $\mathrm{Re}\, s_i < 0$ for all i, whereas a sufficient condition of instability is $\mathrm{Re}\, s_i > 0$ for one i. The case $\mathrm{Re}\, s_i = 0$ for some i and $\mathrm{Re}\, s_i < 0$ for all others is a critical one (in the sense of Liapunov). The s_i depend continuously on $\tau_1, \ldots, \tau_4$. If a critical case exists in the permissible range of delays, a bifurcation of the form

$$\text{stable } (x_0,y_0) \rightarrow \text{unstable } (x_0,y_0) + \text{stable periodic solution} \tag{8}$$

becomes possible. Whether this bifurcation actually occurs depends on the form of the non-linearity in (3). The objective of this paper consists in ascertaining the conditions of such an occurence.

PERIODIC SOLUTIONS ATTRIBUTABLE TO PURE DELAY

A preliminary step in the study of periodic solutions of (3) is the determination of purely imaginary roots s_i of (5). Since (5) contains six parameters, it is expedient to examine a few special cases before drawing any general conclusions.

Consider first the case $\tau_3 = \tau_4 = 0$. The delays τ_1 and τ_2 appearing only in the combination $\tau = \tau_1 + \tau_2$, one of them may be omitted and the other replaced by τ. The requirement $s = i\omega$, ω = real, leads to the condition that the two algebraic equations

$$-\omega^2 + bc + (1+y_0)^{-2}\cos\omega\tau = 0\,, \qquad (b+c)\omega - (1+y_0)^{-2}\sin\omega\tau = 0 \tag{9}$$

resulting from (5), should admit at least one real root τ,ω. Such a root can only exist when $bcy_0^2 > 1$. This inequality is never satisfied, because (3) implies $1 = bcy_0(1+y_0) > bcy_0^2$. Constant delays τ_1 and τ_2 are therefore not a primary cause of periodic solution of (3) via the bifurcation (8), so τ_1, τ_2 can be omitted in what follows.

As a second special case consider $\tau_4 = 0$, $\tau_3 = \tau$. The algebraic equations analoguous to (9) admit a real root $\omega = \omega_0$, $\tau = \tau_0$,

$$\tau_0 = \frac{\pi}{2\omega_0}\,, \qquad \omega_0^2 = \alpha + \beta + [(\alpha+\beta)^2 + b^2c^2 - \beta^2]^{1/2}\,, \qquad \alpha = \tfrac{1}{2}(c^2 - b^2)\,, \tag{10}$$

for all b,c. An analysis of the critical case shows, however, that the bifurcation (8) does not take place, the equilibrium (x_0,y_0) becoming simply unstable when $\tau > \tau_0$. The bifurcation (8) is also absent when the non-linearity in (3) is given by (2), m = 1, 2, and n = 0, 1, 2, ½. Hence τ_3 = const is also not a primary cause of periodic solutions of (3).

The third special case $\tau_3 = 0$, $\tau_4 = \tau$ is more favourable. A real root $\omega = \omega_0$, $\tau = \tau_0$ exists for all b,c, but instead of $\tau_0 = \pi/(2\omega_0)$ in (10), one has

$$\tau_0 = \frac{1}{\omega_0}\,\mathrm{arc\,tg}\left[\frac{\omega_0}{bc}(\beta - b^2 - \omega_0^2)\right]\,, \qquad \text{modulo } \frac{\pi}{\omega_0} \tag{11}$$

For example, b = 0.5, c = 0.1 yields $\omega_0 = 0.074$, $\tau_0 = 33.4$. The bifurcation (8) occurs for a wide range of b,c, and $\tau \geq \tau_0$. Illustrative forms of the resulting periodic solutions are shown in Fig. 1 [a) in the phase plane x − y, b) in the phase plane $\dot{x} - \dot{y}$, and c) x and y as a function of t]. When $\tau/\tau_0 - 1 \ll 1$, the amplitude of these periodic solutions is a rather irregular function of the excess delay $\tau - \tau_0$.

The occurrence of the bifurcation (8) is strongly favoured by the presence of a variable delay depending on x,y. For example, when $\tau_4 = 0$, $\tau_3 = \tau$, τ_0 given by (10) and

$$\tau = \tau_0 + \bar{\delta}_0 - \bar{\delta}\,x^2(t)\,, \qquad \bar{\delta}_0, \bar{\delta} > 0\,, \tag{12}$$

periodic solutions of (3) exist for a wide range of $\bar{\delta}_0,\bar{\delta}$. Illustrative forms are shown in Fig. 2 (the same representation as in Fig. 1 is used). For the same values of b and c the oscillation periods in Fig. 2 are, however, much shorter than those in Fig. 1. When $\bar{\delta}_0, \delta \ll \tau_0$, the periodic solutions are almost sinusoïdal. The bifurcation (8) occurs also when x^2 in (12) is replaced by y^2 or $x^2 + y^2$. In fact, any smooth function g(x,y) will do, provided it assures a finite value of max τ as x,y increase. Terms of an odd degree in the expansion of g(x,y), linear ones included, have no effect on the amplitude limitation of the resulting periodic solutions. They merely cause some dissymmetry in the form of x(t), y(t). In the context of reaction dynamics the presence of a variable delay component, such as g(x,y) in (3), implies a transport time between the place of production and effect which depends on the product concentrations.

In the case of small g(x,y) the amplitude and period of periodic solution of (3) can be expressed analytically by means of a Poincaré-type expansion. Consider, for example, $\tau_1 = \tau_2 = \tau_4 = 0$, $\tau_3 = \tau$ given by (12), and let $\mu > 0$ be a small parameter. The periodic solution is sought in the form

$$\left.\begin{aligned} &\tau - \tau_0 = \mu[\delta_0 - \delta x^2(t)], \quad x(t) = x_0 + \sum_{i=0}^{\infty} x_i(\bar{t})\mu^i, \quad y(t) = y_0 + \sum_{i=0}^{\infty} y_i(\bar{t})\mu^i \\ &\bar{t} = \omega_0 t \sum_{i=0}^{\infty} h_i \mu^i, \quad \dot{y}(0) = 0, \quad L(\tau, y) = \mu N(\tau, x, y) \end{aligned}\right\} \tag{13}$$

where N(τ,x,y) is the non-linear part of (3), L(τ,y) is given by (4), h_i are undetermined constants, and $x_i(\bar{t})$, $y_i(\bar{t})$ undetermined periodic functions of period 2π. The substitution of (13) into (3), followed by a series expansion in powers of μ, leads to the usual linear recursive system

$$L(\tau_0, y_i) = f_i(y_0(\bar{t}), \dots, y_{i-1}(t)), \quad i = 1, 2, \dots, \tag{14}$$

where the functions f_i are unambiguously defined. For i = 0 one obtains

$$y_0(\bar{t}) = A_0 \cos \bar{t}, \quad h_0 = 1, \tag{15}$$

which is simply the eigenfunction of (4) corresponding to the critical eigenvalue (the so-called generating solution). The absence of secular terms in (14) yields, after some lengthy algebra,

$$A_0^2 = \frac{4}{3}\,\frac{\delta_0 + h_1\tau_0}{\delta + \varepsilon_1}, \quad h_1 = \frac{2b\delta_0 \cos\omega_0\tau_0 + \varepsilon_2}{3 - 2b\tau_0\cos\omega_0\tau_0 + \varepsilon_3}, \tag{16}$$

where ε_1, ε_2, ε_3 are some formally complicated but numerically small expressions. The equations (15) and (16) possess a qualitatively correct dependence on b,c, and τ, and for small $\bar{\delta}_0/\tau_0$, $\bar{\delta}/\tau_0$ they agree quite well with the directly computed periodic solutions of (3). For example, when b = 0.5, c = 0.1, $\delta_0 = 0.01\,\tau_0$, $\delta = \sim 1.34$, the computed amplitudes of y(t) differ from A_0 by less than 0.1%.

When other delays are introduced into (3) together with τ_3, there is generally no qualitative change, the sole effect being a weak deformation of the periodic solutions. When both τ_3 and τ_4 are non-zero, there exists a small region in parameter space where (5) simultaneously admits two critical roots. After the "composite bifurcation" the solution of (3) is still oscillatory, but apparently no longer periodic.

CONCLUSION

When pure delays are introduced into the Goodwin model of the Jacob-Monod mode of gene regulation, self-sustained stable periodic oscillations are found to exist in a wide parameter range, the parameters characterizing reaction rates, product synthesis, and transport times. Constant and concentration-dependent delays are both found to be primary causes of periodic oscillations.

Acknowledgement

The authors express their thanks to P. Rapp for his interest in the present approach and for some fruitful discussions.

Figure captions

Fig. 1: Periodic oscillations for the case of a constant delay

a) in the phase plane x-y
b) in the phase plane $\dot{x}$-$\dot{y}$
c) x and y as a function of t.

Fig. 2: Periodic oscillations for the case of a variable delay

a) in the phase plane x-y
b) in the phase plane $\dot{x}$-$\dot{y}$
c) x and y as a function of t.

Fig. 1 Periodic solution of (3), $\tau_1 = \tau_2 = \tau_3 = 0$, $\tau_4 = \tau$.

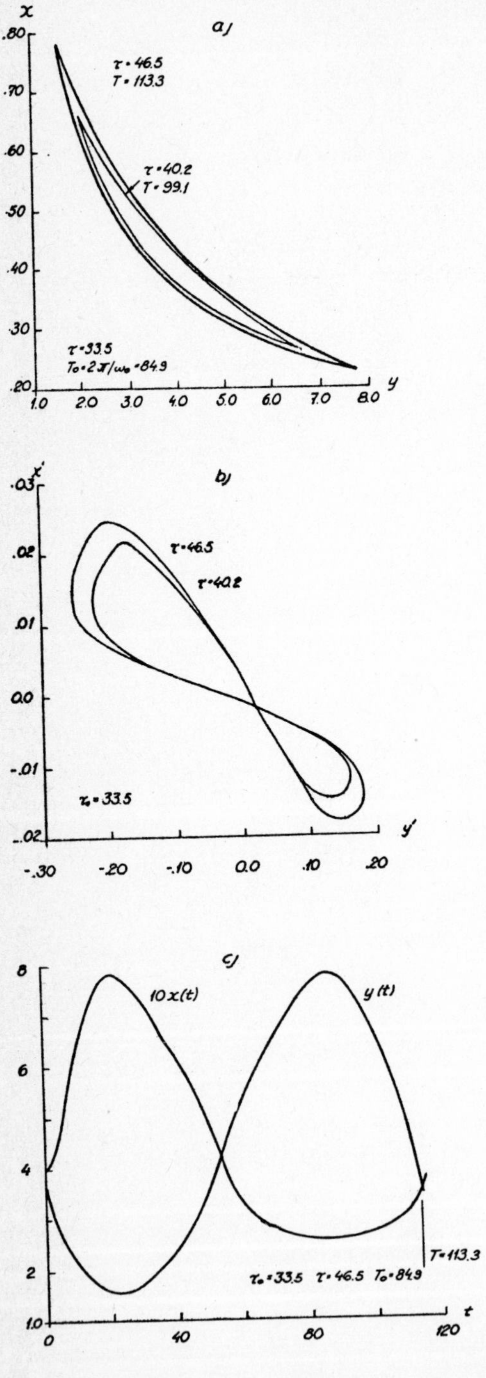

Fig. 2 Periodic solution of (3), $\tau_1 = \tau_2 = \tau_4 = 0$, $\tau_3 = \tau_0 + \bar{\delta}_0 - \bar{\delta}x^2(t)$

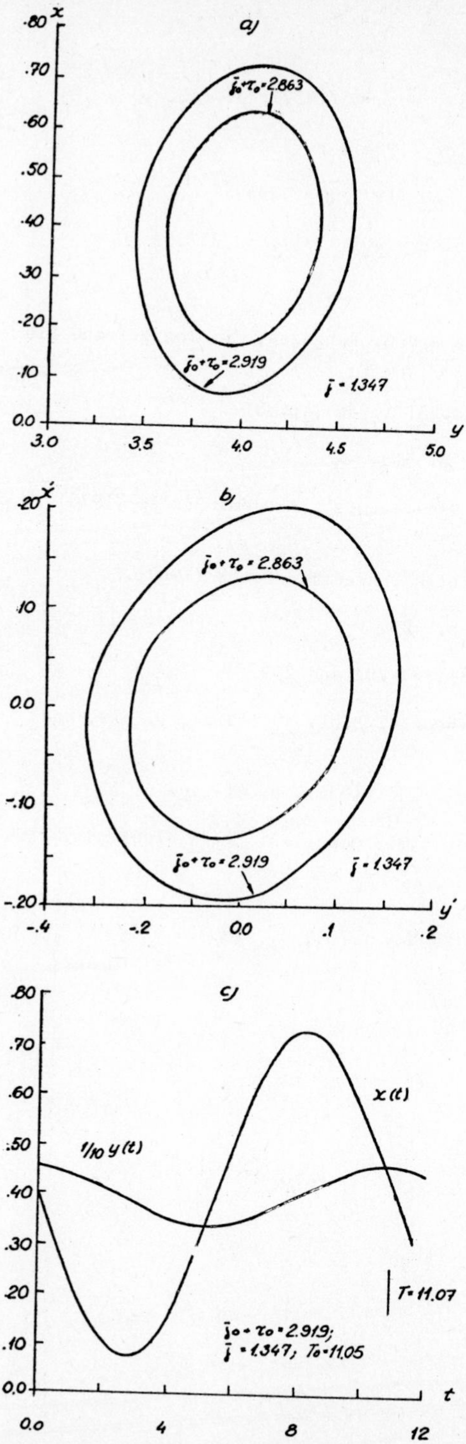

Note: The references cited are illustrative. No effort was made to assure completeness or a chronologically proper sequence.

1) B.P. Belousov, Sb. Ref. Radiat. Med. (1958), Moscow (1959), p. 145.

2) A.M. Zhabotinskii, Dokl. Akad. Nauk SSSR 157 (1964), p. 392.

3) M. Herschkowitz-Kaufman, CR Acad. Sci. C. 270 (1970), p. 1049.

4) B. Hess and A. Boiteux, Annu. Rev. Biochemistry 40 (1971), p. 237.

5) E.E. Selkov, Eur. J. Biochem. 4 (1968), p. 79.

6) J. Higgins, R. Frenkel, E. Hulme, A. Lucas and G. Rangazas, "Biological and Biochemical Oscillators", Academic Press (1973), p. 127.

7) W.A. Knorre, Biochem. Biophys. Res. Commun. 31 (1968), p. 812.

8) B.C. Goodwin, Eur. J. Biochem. 10 (1969), p. 515.

9) W.A. Knorre, "Biological and Biochemical Oscillators", Academic Press (1973), p. 425.

10) B.C. Goodwin, "Temporal organization in cells", Academic Press (1963).

11) B.C. Goodwin, Adv. Enz. Regul. 3 (1965), p, 425.

12) J.S. Griffith, J. Theoret. Biol. 20 (1968), p. 202 and 209.

13) J. Tiwari, A. Fraser and R. Beckman, J. Theoret. Biol. 39 (1973), p. 679, and 45 (1974), p. 311.

14) J. Monod and M. Cohen-Bazire, CR Acad. Sci. 236 (1953), p. 417 and p. 530.

15) J. Monod and F. Jacob, Cold Spring Harbour Symp. Quant. Biol. 26 (1961), p. 389.

16) P. Rapp, Bio. Systems 5 (1975), No 112.

17) Correspondence Ninio-Lodish, Nature 255 (29 May 1975), p. 429.

OPTIMISATION IN THE MODELLING OF DIGESTIVE TRACT ELECTRICAL SIGNALS

D. A. Linkens
Department of Control Engineering
The University of Sheffield
Sheffield, England

Abstract

Spontaneous electrical rhythms have been recorded in many parts of the digestive tract in animals and humans. The signals contain a low frequency regular oscillation which varies in frequency and waveshape between parts of the tract and between species. A mathematical model postulated for these rhythms comprises a set of mutually coupled Van der Pol oscillators. For the human small and large intestines where signals are nearly sinusoidal the method of harmonic balance is used to obtain analytical results for amplitude, phase and entrained frequency. The non-linear algebraic equations are solved using hill-climbing methods due to Rosenbrock, Powell and Fletcher-Reeves. Algorithms requiring first derivatives of the minimised functions have been found significantly faster than the Rosenbrock method.

1. INTRODUCTION

Since the 1920's it has been known that there exists spontaneous electrical activity in the digestive tract (1). Following the initial recording of signals from the surface wall of the stomach, improvements in electronic recording techniques have led to a great amount of data being obtained throughout the tract and in many species of animals (2). The outstanding feature of the electrical activity is the existence of a spontaneous low frequency oscillation often called the 'basic electrical rhythm' or pacesetter potential (3). This rhythm has been shown to be spontaneously present by the fact that small excised areas of tissue still show regular oscillations.

Although there are onsiderable differences in the electrical rhythms between species the spontaneous activity has been recorded in the stomach, small intestine, large intestine and rectum (4,5,6,7). In the stomach the rhythm is pulse-like in dogs and rectangular-like in humans. Recordings from stomachs in the resting condition with no mechanical contractions show rhythm frequencies of about 0.05Hz in humans and about 0.08Hz in dogs. In the duodenum the human recordings are nearly sinusoidal, while a typical canine recording is shown in Figure 1. The human duodenal recordings

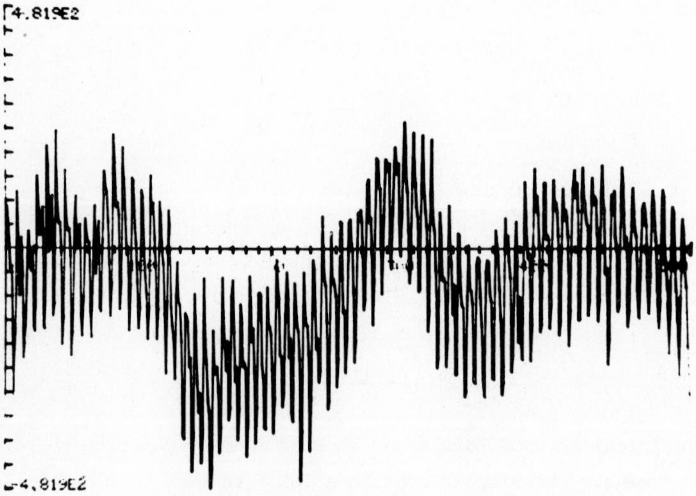

Figure 1 - Typical canine duodenal recording.

have a small amount of asymmetry which can be allowed for in the mathematical model. The duodenal frequency varies between about 0.2Hz in humans and 0.25Hz in dogs. Over the length of the duodenum there is a constant frequency known as a 'plateau' effect which has been of considerable interest in producing a mathematical model for the tract

(8). From the end of the duodenum to the ileum, the small intestine exhibits a shallow gradient of frequency with the human recording dropping to about 0.17Hz at the ileum. In the colon and rectum however there is a difference in the pattern of behaviour between humans and other species. In humans there are three patterns recorded (9). There are periods of zero activity when no regular rhythms are obtained, interspersed with two oscillations having frequencies of about 0.05Hz and 0.12Hz. These frequencies do not have a precise integer relationship and cannot therefore be viewed as a harmonic phenomenon. There is no obvious gradient of frequency along the length of the colon, but the percentage occurrence of each of the three modes does vary significantly.

Synchronised with the basic electrical rhythms are action potentials which occur whenever there are mechanical contractions in the tract. There are however long periods when no action potentials are present but the low frequency oscillations continue. The nature of the action potentials varies between species and between different parts of the tract. In the canine stomach the whole waveshape of the basic rhythm is altered giving a much larger mark-space ratio as can be seen in Figure 2. In the human duodenum, however, actional potentials comprise a burst of high-frequency pulses superimposed on top of the basic rhythm. Recordings made at the Department of Surgery,

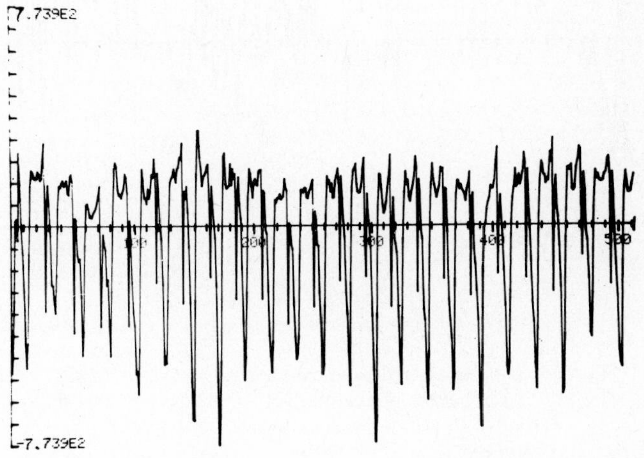

Figure 2 - Typical canine gastric recording with action potentials.

Sheffield, in the human colon have so far produced no evidence of any action potentials during mechanical contractions.

Some evidence exists that there is coordination between the stomach and duodenum

which controls the emptying of the stomach contents into the small intestine (10). A further phenomenon in the small intestine comprises a travelling wave of action potential spikes accompanied by a variation in the basic rhythm frequency (11).

Neural and hormonal modulation of the rhythms in intact organs appears to be fairly small, so that changes in frequency of greater than 10% are rare even for large drug stimulations. An exception to this is bombesin which appears to completely stop the electrical activity in the small intestine (12). Similarly, common diseases of the tract seem to have little effect upon the electrical activity except in the case of diverticular disease of the human colon which produces a higher frequency rhythm of about 0.25Hz as seen in Figure 3. Operations such as the cutting of the vagal nerve supply to the stomach produce temporary changes in the electrical patterns but considerable recovery to the normal patterns is often observed (13).

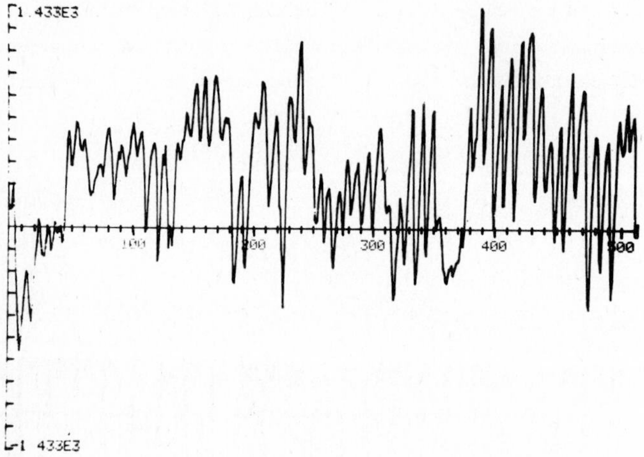

Figure 3 - Human colonic recording showing higher frequency rhythm characteristic of diverticulitis.

2. DATA RECORDING AND ANALYSIS

The electrical signals are normally recorded from stainless steel electrodes placed on either the inside or outside wall of the tract. Electrodes implanted on the outside wall are placed during an operation and the leads taken out through a drain in the abdominal wall. Six electrodes are usually implanted and removed after about two weeks. To make recordings from normal humans swallowed tubes are used which contain one or two electrodes 0.1mm. in diameter. The electrodes are surrounded by suction caps so that they can be secured to the inside wall of the gut with a negative pressure of 20cm. of mercury. A third method of recording employs surface electrodes placed over the stomach region for non-invasive measurement of gastric activity (14).

All the signals are mvolts in amplitude and are amplified before recording onto 6 channel ultraviolet paper in parallel with a 4 channel analogue FM tape recorder. Large amounts of data have been recorded from humans and dogs in this way and it has been found desirable to select visually from the ultraviolet recordings suitable 8 minute stretches of data for subsequent interactive analysis. These stretches are compressed onto another FM analogue tape by playing back the original tapes 16 times faster than real time. In this way 1000 8-minute stretches of data can be compressed onto one 1200ft. analogue tape.

The logging and analysis program used for the gastro-intestinal research forms part of a general systems analysis and identification package which has grown out of the medical application (15). There are 41 options currently available each of which can be conversationally selected by a three letter code.

The LOG option is used to continuously log the compressed data via a high speed ADC onto the 1M word disc of a GE4020 process control computer. Various display options allow for 'paging' and expansion of the data base. Amongst the analysis programs the fast Fourier transform is most commonly used for accurate measurement of the digestive rhythm frequencies. An example of this is shown in Figure 4 which is a canine duodenal transform also containing a gastric component, made evident by using a logarithmic transform. Use is also being made of a fast Walsh transform (16) and Figure 5

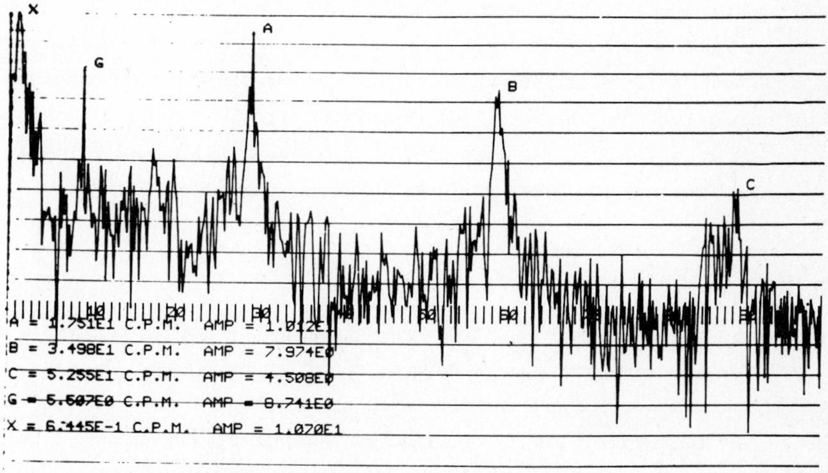

Figure 4 - Log transform of canine duodenal recording containing an additional gastric spectral peak.

is an example of this applied to a human colon with diverticular disease. The normal low frequency mode together with the higher frequency mode characteristic of diverticulitis can be clearly seen.

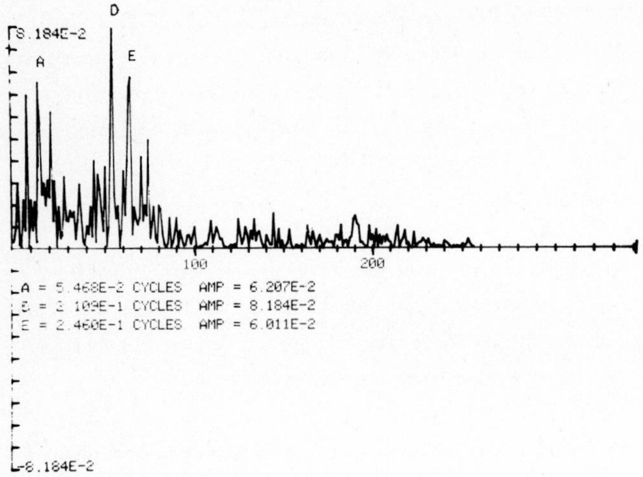

Figure 5 - Fast Walsh transform of data from a human colon with diverticulitis.

3. DIGESTIVE TRACT MODELLING

A mathematical model which reproduces all the known physiological phenomena recorded from the gastro-intestinal tract comprises a set of mutually-coupled oscillators. For the small and large intestines which have a tubular structure, a one-dimensional 'chain' of oscillators has been utilised (8), while for the stomach a two-dimensional plane is necessary (17). The simplest model for the individual oscillator units consists of a non-linear second order differential equation of the Van der Pol type

$$\ddot{x} - \varepsilon(a^2 - x^2)\dot{x} + \omega^2 x = 0$$

where frequency, waveshape and amplitude are determined by the parameters 'ω', 'ε' and 'a'. The interactive analysis techniques described briefly in the previous section are being used to set these parameters in analogue and digital simulations of the tract. Various forms of mutual coupling can be used but the normal structure employed in this work corresponds to linear resistive, capacitive and inductive coupling as shown in the equivalent circuit of Figure 6.

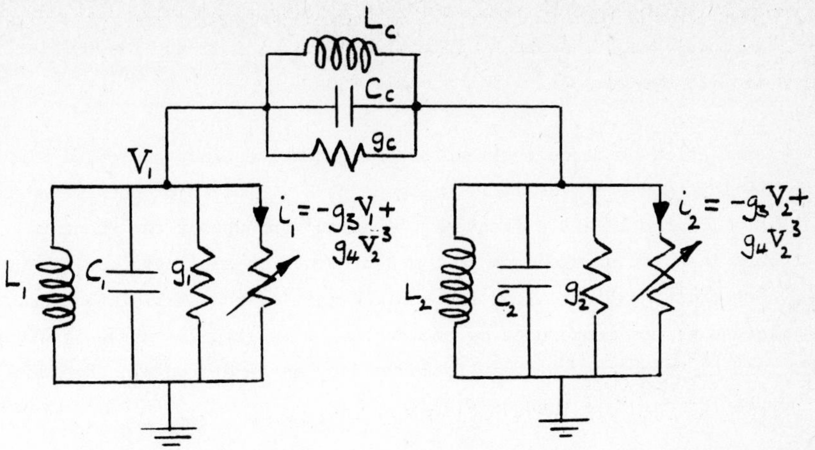

Figure 6 - Equivalent circuit of two mutually-coupled Van der Pol oscillators.

Investigation of the basic phenomena produced by this model has been done by analogue simulation of up to 8 cells. It has been found that two stable limit cycles are obtainable from mutually coupled Van der Pol oscillators for particular forms and values of coupling. This enables the human colonic data to be modelled by a ring structure of oscillators. Summation of two adjacent cells to give the model output reproduces the three modes as shown in Figure 7. The three modes in this figure were

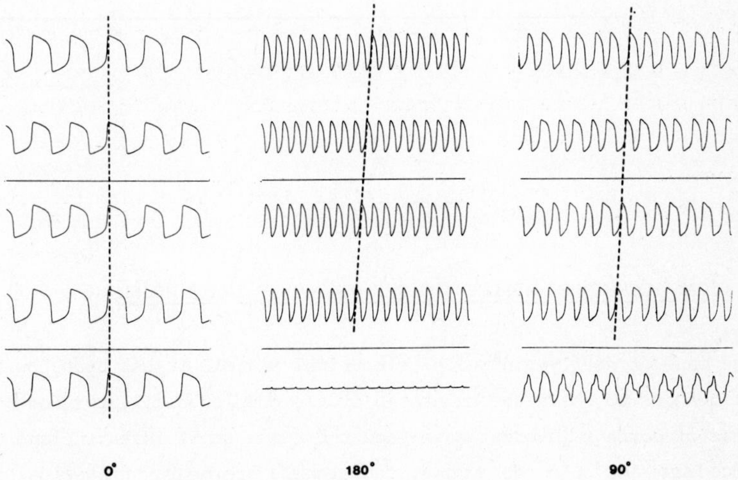

Figure 7 - A human colonic model comprising a ring of 4 Van der Pol oscillators showing three solutions.

obtained by switching on the simulation from different initial conditions. Switching between the modes can be caused by injection of sinusoidal and random disturbances or perturbations to the basic oscillator cells (18).

For simulation of large sections of the digestive tract a digital simulation comprising 100 interconnected cells is being used (8). The major phenomenon recorded from the small intestine is a frequency 'plateau' throughout the duodenum. This 'plateau' occurs in spite of the fact that measurements on small excised tissue indicate a steady frequency gradient along the whole length of the small intestine. An example of the plateau effect reproduced by the digital simulation is given in Figure 8 which also indicates a secondary plateau introduced by an 'incision' in the model matching known physiological data in dogs (19).

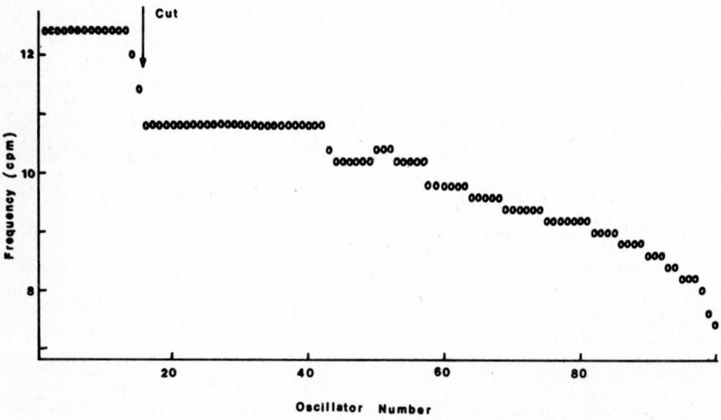

Figure 8 - 100 oscillator digital simulation showing two frequency 'plateaux' caused by an 'incision' in the model.

4. ANALYTICAL TECHNIQUES APPLIED TO THE DIGESTIVE TRACT MODEL

In the case of nearly-sinusoidal electrical signals it has been possible to use analytical methods to solve the equations of the coupled oscillator model. The particular areas of current interest have been the human small intestine and colon. In both the duodenum and colon of humans, the signals are nearly sinusoidal in nature and both areas exhibit frequency entrainment. The phenomenon of frequency entrainment of a single Van der Pol oscillator by an external forcing function has been known for many years (20). In this work the case of mutually-coupled Van der Pol oscillators is considered and the method of harmonic balance is employed to obtain approximate analytical solutions (21).

For two coupled oscillators under entrainment the harmonic balance method assumed a sinusoidal solution for each cell given by

$$x_1 = A_1 \cos(\omega_e t + \beta)$$

$$x_2 = A_2 \cos(\omega_e t + \alpha)$$

Differentiation of these solutions and ignoring second derivative terms in amplitude because of the assumption of slowly varying coefficients gives

$$\dot{x}_1 = -A_1(\omega_e + \dot{\beta})\sin(\omega_e t + \beta) + \dot{A}_1\cos(\omega_e t + \beta)$$

$$\ddot{x}_1 = -A_1(\omega_e + \dot{\beta})^2\cos(\omega_e t + \beta) - 2(\omega_e + \dot{\beta})\,\dot{A}_1\sin(\omega_e t + \beta)$$

etc.

Substitution of these expressions into the governing equations and simplification of the circular functions is followed by ignoring all the harmonic terms and retaining only the fundamental component. By equating the sine and cos terms in each equation, time is eliminated and 4 algebraic equations result. When there are 'n' interconnected oscillators, '2n' non-linear algebraic equations are obtained whose solution gives directly the values of entrained frequency, 'n' amplitudes and 'n-1' phases (the phase of the first oscillator is taken to be 0°). For the 'nth' oscillator the equations have the following typical form which here represents inductive coupling for a 'chain' model

$$(\omega_n^2 - \omega_e^2)A_n\cos\alpha_n - \lambda_n\omega_e A_{n+1}\sin\alpha_{n+1} - \lambda_{n-1}\omega_e A_{n-1}\sin\alpha_{n-1} + \varepsilon_n\omega_e A_n\sin\alpha_n -$$

$$\varepsilon_n\lambda_n A_{n+1}\cos\alpha_{n+1} - \varepsilon_n\lambda_{n-1}A_{n-1}\cos\alpha_{n-1} + \varepsilon_n A_n^2/2\left\{-A_n/2.\omega_e\sin\alpha_n + \lambda_n A_{n+1}\right.$$

$$\cos\alpha_{n+1} + \lambda_{n-1}A_{n-1}\cos\alpha_{n-1} + \lambda_n A_{n+1}/2\cos(2\alpha_n - \alpha_{n+1}) + \lambda_{n-1}A_{n-1}/2\cos$$

$$\left.(2\alpha_n - \alpha_{n-1})\right\} = 0$$

For some types of coupling between two oscillators it has been found that the algebraic equations can be solved directly when the uncoupled frequencies are equal.

Simple relationships between entrained frequency and coupling factor have been found (22) and similarly for amplitude. It has also been found that prediction of two stable limit cycles can be obtained from the harmonic balance method. Thus Figure 9 shows the good agreement between analytical and simulated results giving the minimum coupling

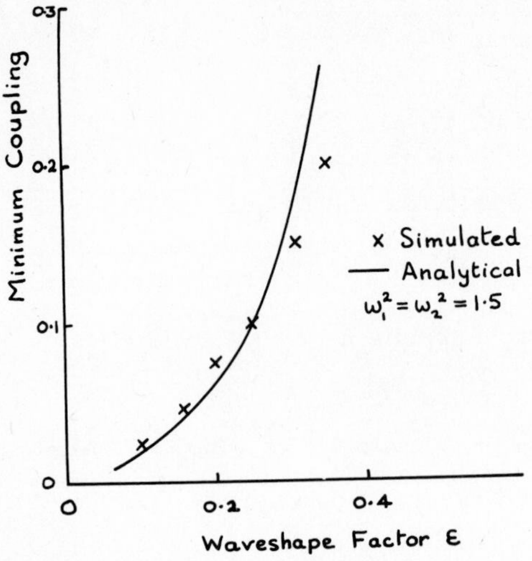

Figure 9 - The minimum coupling coefficient required to produce 2 stable limit cycles as a function of waveshape parameter.

values of waveshape factor 'ε' which produce two stable limit cycles. The analytical relationship is given by

$$\text{Minimum Coupling} = \frac{-(\omega^2 - 2\varepsilon^2) + \sqrt{[(\omega^2 - 2\varepsilon^2)^2 - 8\omega^2\varepsilon^2]}}{2\omega^2}$$

In the majority of cases the non-linear algebraic relationships cannot be solved directly and methods of hill-climbing have to be used. Provided the waveshape factor 'ε' is less than unity good correlation has been obtained between simulated and hill-climb results as can be seen in Figure 10a and b. These figures show the effect of coupling changes on entrained frequency, amplitude and phase. These results were obtained using a Rosenbrock constrained optimisation technique requiring function evaluation only (23). For realistic simulation of the human duodenum a chain of oscillators is required and Figure 11 shows the amplitudes obtained for an 18x1 chain solved with the Rosenbrock algorithm. The open-ended chain is not representative of a section of the intact organ and the large end - effects can be clearly seen in Figure 11. To make the chain represent a section of the organ, end-effect correction

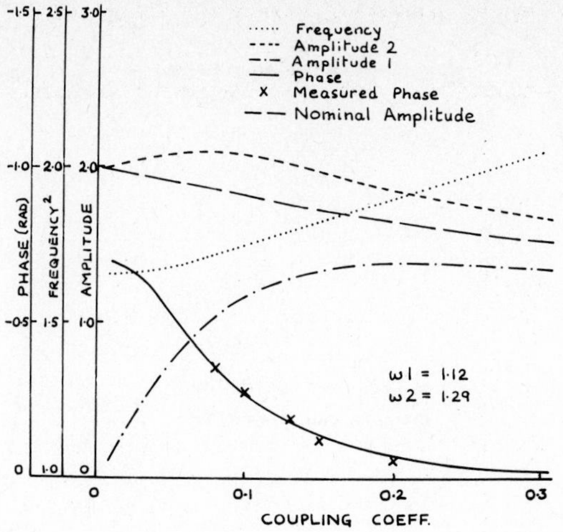

(a) in-phase mode

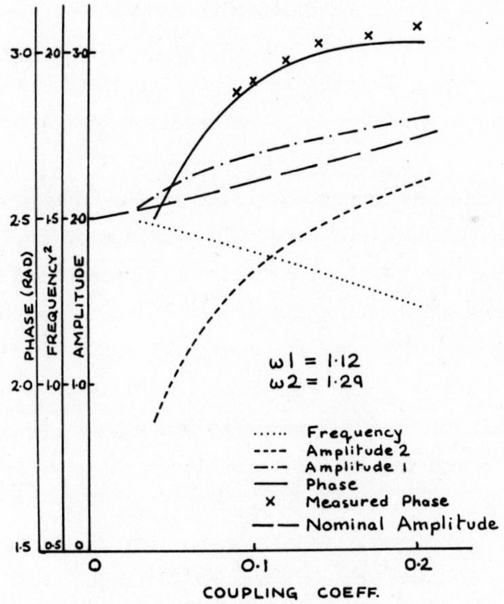

(b) anti-phase mode

Figure 10 - Variations of entrained frequency, amplitudes and phase for two coupled oscillators.

has been attempted so that the first and last oscillators have an additional input predicted from knowledge of the conditions along the chain. Figure 11 shows the result obtained by linear extrapolation of amplitude and phase from the first and last

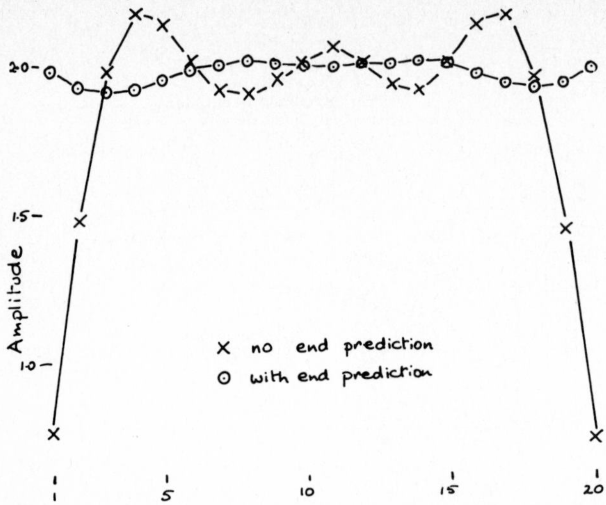

Figure 11 - Entrained amplitudes for an 18x1 chain using a Rosenbrock algorithm.

two oscillators in the chain. In this example an amplitude of 2.0 units would be expected for the whole chain since there is no gradient of uncoupled frequency.

For hill-climbing on more than 10 oscillators the Rosenbrock algorithm was found to be too slow using an ICL 1907 computer. The problem is basically unconstrained and the first partial derivatives of the functions to be minimised can be evaluated, albeit with considerable tedious algebraic manipulation. Two algorithms suited to this approach and implemented on the NAG library of the ICL 1900 series have been tried. The first is a Powell routine (24) which commences the hill-climb using steepest descent and then curves to terminate at the Newton-Raphson point. This algorithm has been found generally reliable and fairly fast. A line-printer output from this method is shown in Figure 12 which represents a tube simulation having 5 oscillators along the length and 4 around the periphery. In the graph plot the oscillators around the tube are numbered 1 to 4 and the absence of a number indicates that higher number(s) occupy the same point on the graph. For this 40 variable example 61 iterations were performed in 100 second of machine time and gave a hill-value of $2.6.10^{-2}$. The uncoupled oscillators had equal frequencies and values of amplitude and phase around the tube should have been identical. The second algorithm is a Fletcher-Reeves routine (25) which uses 'n' one-dimensional searches based on steepest descent to a local minimum. When a local minimum is located the conjugate direction is found and another one-dimensional search is commenced. This algorithm has been found to give better results both in terms of hill-values and speed. Figure 13 is the amplitude result obtained

```
ITERATION  61  FF=  0.2697001156E-01
WE=  1.360660
B=  0.494318  0.808466  0.346962 -0.360333 -0.193567  0.422500  0.764328  0.305318 -0.397767 -0.367472
 0.279440  0.636581  0.208736 -0.444437 -0.287740  0.327973  0.690317  0.253850 -0.423037
A=  0.797871  1.833107  2.454775  1.764566  0.785109  0.769528  1.701399  2.328002  1.686184  0.781842
 0.780039  1.589320  2.165885  1.625128  0.805182  0.776228  1.660002  2.257600  1.672957  0.789480

GRADIENT VALUES
WE=  0.097964
B=  0.003401 -0.024781 -0.003503 -0.003404 -0.005987  0.009909  0.018846  0.001940 -0.004097 -0.005019
 0.008083 -0.006675 -0.002401  0.000771 -0.008799 -0.010753  0.010898 -0.001963 -0.002593
A= -0.003518 -0.014593  0.026682 -0.005339 -0.006323  0.000121 -0.024292 -0.012066 -0.013591 -0.002987
 0.008211 -0.016348 -0.018432 -0.010586  0.005972  0.001006 -0.014682 -0.012780 -0.009697 -0.003091
```

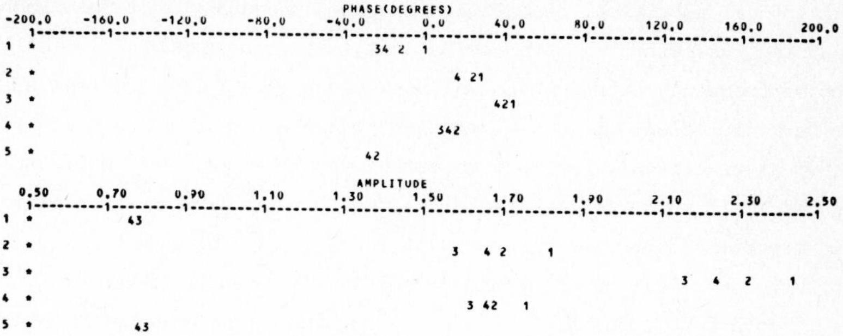

Figure 12 - Entrained amplitudes and phases for a 5 x 4 tube using a Powell algorithm.

for an 18x1 chain using the Fletcher-Reeves algorithm. 41 iterations of the 36 one-dimensional searches were obtained in 40 seconds and gave a hill-value of $2.6 \cdot 10^{-2}$. This example did not employ any form of end-correction and clearly shows the non-uniform amplitude if end-effects are not considered.

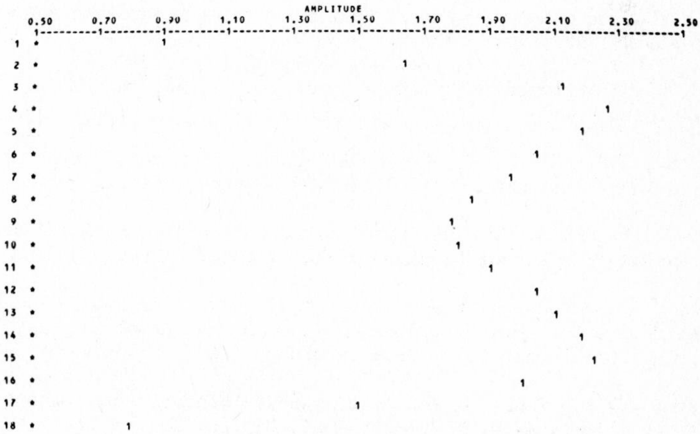

Figure 13 - Entrained amplitudes for an 18x1 chain using a Fletcher-Reeves algorithm.

5. CONCLUSIONS

A mathematical model comprising linked oscillators based on Van der Pol's equation is capable of reproducing the known phenomena recorded electrically from the surface walls of the mammalian digestive tract. For the human small and large intestines nearly-sinusoidal electrical signals are recorded and analytical solutions have been obtained using the method of harmonic balance. For the case of 'n' oscillators in a condition of frequency entrainment '2n' non-linear algebraic equations are obtained from the harmonic balance method. Solution of these equations requires hill-climbing methods and gives directly the most important variables of frequency, amplitudes and phases. For small numbers of oscillators a Rosenbrock algorithm is satisfactory and simple to programme. For large numbers of oscillators the Rosenbrock method is too slow and hence optimisation algorithms requiring first derivatives of functions have been used. Both Powell and Fletcher-Reeves routines have been satisfactory for up to 50 variables with the later algorithm being considerably faster.

6. ACKNOWLEDGEMENTS

The data on which this work is based have been obtained by a team in the University Department of Surgery, Sheffield, headed by Professor H. L. Duthie and assisted by members of the Medical Physics Department.

7. REFERENCES

1. Alvarez, W. C. and Mahoney, L. J., 'Action currents in stomach and intestine', Am. J. Physiol., 1922, 58, p.476.

2. Duthie, H. L., 'Electrical activity of gastrointestinal smooth muscle', GUT, 1974, 15, p.669.

3. Bulbring, E., 'The role of electrophysiology in the investigation of factors controlling intestinal motility', Rendic. R. Gastroenterol., 1970, 2, p.197.

4. Kwong, N. K., Brown, B. H., Whittaker, G. E. and Duthie, H. L., 'Electrical activity of the gastric antrum in man', Brit. J. Surg., 1970, 57, p.913.

5. Christensen, J., Schedl, H. P., and Clifton, J. A., 'The small intestinal basic electrical rhythm (slow wave) frequency gradient in normal man and in patients with a variety of diseases', Gastroenterology, 1966, 50, p.309.

6. Christensen, J., Caprilli, R. and Lund, G. F., 'Electric slow waves in circular muscle of cat colon', A. J. Physiol., 1969, 217, p.77.

7. Wankling, W. J., Brown, B. H., Collins, C. D. and Duthie, H. L., 'Basal electrical activity in the anal canal in man', GUT, 1968, 9, p.457.

8. Robertson-Dunn, B. and Linkens, D. A., 'A mathematical model of the slow-wave electrical activity of the human small intestine', Med. & Biol. Eng., 1974, p.750.

9. Taylor, I., Duthie, H. L., Smallwood, R., Brown, B. H. and Linkens, D. A., 'The effect of stimulation on the myoelectrical activity of the rectosigmoid in man',

GUT, 1974, 15, p.599.

10. Bedi, B. S., Code, C. F., 'Pathway of coordination of postprandial, antral and duodenal action potentials', Am. J. Physiol., 1972, 22, p.1295.

11. Szurszewski, J. H., 'A migrating electric complex of the canine small intestine', Am. J. Physiol., 1969, 217, p.1757.

12. Corazziari, E., Delle Fave, G. F., Melchiorri, P. and Torsoli, A., 'Effects of Bombesin on gallbladder and duodeno-jejunal mechanical activity in man', Proc. 4th Int. Symposium on 'Gastro intestinal Motility', Banff, Canada, Sept., 1973, p.293.

13. Sarna, S. K., Bowes, K. L. and Daniel, E. E., 'Postoperative gastric electrical control activity in man', Proc. 4th Int. Symposium on Gastrointestinal Motility, Banff, Canada, Sept. 1973, p.73.

14. Brown, B. H., Smallwood, R. H., Duthie, H. L. and Stoddard, C. J., 'Intestinal smooth muscle electrical potentials recorded from surface electrodes', Med. & Biol. Eng., 1975, p.97.

15. Linkens, D. A. and Cannell, A. E., 'Interactive graphics analysis of gastrointestinal electrical signals', IEEE Trans. Biomed. Eng., 1974, p.335.

16. Linkens, D. A. and Temel, B. Z., 'The use of Walsh transforms in the analysis of gastro-intestinal signals', Int. Symposium on Theory & Application of Walsh Functions, Hatfield, July 1975.

17. Sarna, S. K., Daniel, E. E. and Kingma, Y. J., 'Simulation of the electrical control activity of the stomach by an array of relaxation oscillators', Am. J. Dig. Dis., 1972, 17, p.299.

18. Linkens, D. A., Taylor, I. and Duthie, H. L., 'Mathematical modelling of the colorectal myoelectrical activity in humans', IEEE Trans. Bio. Med. Eng., to be published.

19. Herman-Taylor, J. and Code, C. F., 'Localisation of the duodenal pacemaker and its role in the organisation of duodenal myoelectrical activity', GUT, 1971, 12, p.40.

20. Van der Pol, B., 'Forced oscillation in a circuit with non-linear resistance (reception with reactive triode)', Phil. Mag., 1927, 3, p.65.

21. Lawden, D. F., 'Mathematics of Engineering Systems', Methuen, 1961, p.349.

22. Linkens, D. A., 'Analytical solution of large numbers of mutually coupled nearly sinusoidal oscillators', IEEE Trans. Cct. & Sys., 1974, Cas-21, p.294.

23. Rosenbrock, H. H., 'An automatic method for finding the greatest or least value of a function', Comput.J., 1960, 3, p.175.

24. Powell, M. J. D., 'A Fortran subroutine for unconstrained minimisation requiring first derivatives of the objective function', 1960 UKAEA Res.Gp. Report, AERE R6469.

25. Fletcher, R. and Reeves, C. M., 'Function minimisation by conjugate gradients', 1964, Comput.J., 7, p.149.

PROPAGATION MODEL OF BIO-ELECTRIC POTENTIALS THROUGH THE SHELLS OF THE BRAIN

Patrice NICOLAS
Institut National de la Santé et de la Recherche Médicale
Lab. Groupe de Recherches U.84
Hôpital de la Salpêtrière
75634 PARIS CEDEX 13

ABSTRACT

The discrepancy between potential distributions recorded on the scalp and on the cerebral cortex, as a result of the electric field propagation through the surrounding shells, requires development of techniques which enable us to compute one distribution as a function of the other. The method presented is based on a physical model consistent with neurophysiological patterns, and in which the sources (encephalitic charges and currents) are multipolar distributions. The general field equations, applied to a convenient closed domain, lead to a family of Helmholtz equations which govern the transmission of the potential pseudo-periodic components. Local boundary conditions having been imposed by the multipolar assumption, the solutions are deduced from an elementary source system. It is then shown that the distribution of the surface potential (on the scalp) is obtained by convolution of the cortical potential distribution and a transfer function which is a solution of the Helmholtz equation associated with an elementary source system. An approximation of the cortical distribution can be computed by discrete deconvolution. Finally, various simulation experiments on digital computer allowed us to test the model, by comparison with empirical data.

I. INTRODUCTION

The potential changes dealt with clinical and experimental neurophysiology are with few exceptions recorded from skin electrodes which are placed at a distance from the active cells; therefore, if we want to draw conclusions as to the generators of the potential, we come upon many problems due to the propagation of the field through various tissues. In spite of experimental investigation, the interpretation of brain activities recorded on the scalp is particularly problematic, because they result from numerous sources which are very heterogeneous. More precisely, by setting electrodes on the scalp, one tries to have information about the cortical sites of abnormal signals, as a consequence of pathological processes. It would be then more usefull to implant the captors in the brain; for obvious reasons, we cannot often use such an optimal procedure on man. Hence, the best thing we could try to obtain is an approximation of the cortical surface potential, proceeding from scalp records. For this purpose, we present a general model which can be used both for theoretical explanation and experimental test.

II. SETTING THE PROBLEM

The physical system under consideration can be described as follows:

The encephalon is an unknown set of electrical sources, varying both in space and time, which occupy a closed domain whose boundary is the cortical surface S.The neural generators induce two potential distributions, V_S on S and $V_{S'}$ on the scalp surface S', by propagation through several layers of media like rachidian cephalitic liquid (RCL), dura matter, skull and skin (the brain's shells). We have then to exhibit the relationship of V_S and $V_{S'}$ (fig. 1).

As a good approach, it is possible to consider each media as being linear, homogeneous and isotropic. Locally, we can also assume that the thicknesses h_i of the layers vary little in space; moreover, the radius of curvature of the various surfaces is always 'large' with respect to the distance $h = \sum h_i$ which separates S from S'. Figure 1 summarizes the local geometry of the physical system just described.

III. GENERAL EQUATIONS

The potential V is a pseudo-random function (Smith & Schadé, 1970), which is continuous everywhere and can be expressed as the resultant of a finite number of pseudo-periodic components:

$$V(x,t) = \sum_{n=1}^{N} U_n(x) \operatorname{Exp}(j\, f_n(t)). \tag{1}$$

The space functions U_n are assumed to be continuous on R^3. The phases f_n are stricly in-

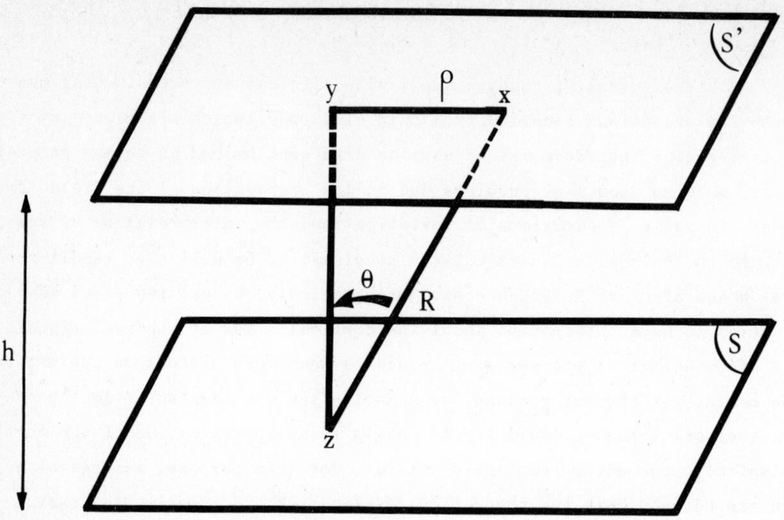

FIGURE 1.- Local geometry of the physical problem.

creasing and C^1 on every time interval; hence, their first derivatives are uniformly bounded. Moreover, within every domain which does contain no source, the propagation of the potential is governed by the following equation (Panofsky & Phillips, 1955):

$$\Delta V - \epsilon\mu\frac{\partial^2 V}{\partial t^2} - \mu\gamma\frac{\partial V}{\partial t} = 0, \tag{2}$$

where the coefficients are characteristics of the media such as:

$$\epsilon\mu \sim \frac{1}{c^2} \cdot$$

According to this latter estimate, and if we take into account the low frequency range under consideration, then we can neglect the second derivative with respect to time, and we obtain:

$$\Delta V - \mu\gamma\frac{\partial V}{\partial t} = 0. \tag{3}$$

Thus, the propagation of the bio-potential between cortex and scalp is a <u>diffusion process</u>, and more precisely a Wiener process (Dynkin, 1965).

Let k_n be now an time-dependant function such as:

(4) $$k_n^2(t) = -j\mu\gamma \frac{df_n}{dt} .$$

It follows from (1) and the equation (3) that we have then:

(5) $$\Delta U_n + k_n^2 U_n = 0,$$

for each spatial component U_n of V. This latter equation is called the Helmholtz equation of the Wiener process (Bouix, 1966). Its general solution is given by the expansion:

(6) $$U(r,\theta,\varphi) = \sum_{n=0}^{\infty} \sum_{m=0}^{n} z_n(kr)(a_{nm}\cos m\varphi + b_{nm}\sin m\varphi)P_n^m(\cos\theta),$$

where z_n and P_n^m respectively are Bessel functions and Legendre polynomials.

IV. BOUNDARY PROBLEM

The boundary conditions obviously must be compatible with physiological data, but the only thing we can assume to be known is the potential V_S, on the cortical surface S. Then, it is necessary to make one more assumption, in order to have uniqueness. For this purpose, let us consider an elementary source set; according to the structures of the neural nets, we can assume that the field which is induced by this set is locally characterized as follows:

AT ANY POINT OF THE CORTICAL SURFACE, THE ELECTRICAL IMAGE OF THE UNDERLYING GENERATORS IS IDENTICAL TO THAT OF A VIRTUAL MULTIPOLE WITH CYLINDRICAL SYMMETRY AND AXIS PERPENDICULAR TO THE SURFACE.

Such an hypothesis involves that the boundary conditions are given by a non-uniform distribution of multipolar sources. The cylindrical symmetry leads to $m = 0$, $\varphi = 0$ in the expansion (6), and we have:

(6') $$U(r,\theta) = \sum_{n=0}^{\infty} a_n z_n(kr)P_n(\cos\theta).$$

Moreover, if the elementary source sets are 2^q- poles, then we have:

(7) $$a_n = 0, \qquad n = 0,1,\ldots,q-1,$$

and:

(8) $$\sum_{n=q+1}^{\infty} a_n z_n P_n = 0\left(\frac{1}{kr}\right).$$

In other words, the main part of the expansion (6') is given by the only q-th term. Here a first optimization problem arises, which is to find the optimal q for the best approximation; it is still unresolved, because of the lack of convenient experimental data. Until now, the neurophysiologist only was interested in dipolar sheet models, or even dipoles deep within the brain (Bremer, 1949; Eccles, 1951; Bishop & Clare, 1952; Calvet et al., 1964, Geisler & Gerstein, 1961). Nevertheless, such a modelization seems to be much too simple with regard to the complexity of the neural networks, because thousands of depolarization currents spread over each cortical neuron at the same time. Therefore, a multipolar sheet hypothesis appears more realistic, at least from a theoretical point of view.

Whatever q may be, we know that $z_q P_q$ is rapidly decreasing as a function of the distance. If we take into account the background noise, the multipolar potential V approximately vanishes beyond a cylinder C, whoses bases are disks D, D' on S and S'. Let V_D be the zero-order trace of V, restricted in D. Then, for <u>one</u> multipole, we have the following boundary problem:

$$\begin{cases} \text{To find V such as: } V \in C^{o}(\bar{C}) \text{ and:} \\ \text{(i) } \Delta V + k^2 V = 0 \text{ inside C,} \\ \text{(ii) } V\big|_D = V_D \text{ on D.} \end{cases}$$

In this formulation, (i) stands for the propagation and (ii) expresses the choice of partial boundary conditions. As V must be continuous everywhere, it is easy to show that the above problem is well-posed.

Now, let x be a running point on S, and y any point on S'; according to the multipolar assumption, we have then:

$$V_{D'}(y) = V_D(x)\ z_q\left(\frac{kh}{u(\rho)}\right)\ P_q(u(\rho)), \tag{9}$$

where:

$$u(\rho) = \cos(\text{Arctg}\ \frac{\rho}{h}), \quad \text{and } \rho = |x - y|\ .$$

If $g = z_q P_q$, with an obvious change of variables we finally obtain:

$$V_{D'}(y) = V_D(x)\ g(x - y). \tag{10}$$

Hence, if we consider the real potential distribution $V_{S'}$ which is induced on S' by the whole set of cortical sources, then we have the following approximation:

$$V_{S'}(y) = \int_D V_S(x)\ g(x - y)\ dx, \tag{11}$$

where V_S is the real potential distribution on S. As g is approximately vanishing beyond the disk D which is centered on y, we can only consider its restriction g_D in D. Then we can write:

$$V_{S'} = V_S * g_D. \tag{12}$$

Stated another way, through an obvious isomorphism between D and D', we come upon a convolution. As a matter of fact, g_D depends on y through the parameter h and the function k, because the shells are not strictly uniform. Nevertheless, if we assume (as we have since the outset) that there exists a 'large enough' domain where the gradient of h and k is negligible, then g_D is unvarying by translation in such a domain. Hence, g_D will be called the transfer function of the potential, in the sense of the multipolar hypothesis. The following statement summarizes the results:

LET V_S BE A PSEUDO-PERIODIC POTENTIAL DISTRIBUTION ON THE CORTICAL SURFACE S. IF V_S OBEYS THE LOCAL MULTIPOLAR ASSUMPTION, THEN THE POTENTIAL DISTRIBUTION $V_{S'}$ WHICH IS INDUCED ON THE SCALP IS APPROXIMATED BY THE CONVOLUTION EQUATION (12).

This statement is true for pseudo-periodic potential; for any pseudo-random potential as defined in § III, we obtain analogous results by linearity.

Furthermore, there are weak eddy currents inside the shells, which do not come from the encephalitic generators. Hence, to the potential induced by these generators, one must add some background noises which are represented in the boundary problem by a convenient function F(x,t) on the right-hand side of the equation (i). We have taken it into account by choosing F as uniform random noise for further computing.

V. NUMERICAL ESTIMATES

In order to test the model with empirical data, some numerical estimates have been made, such as attenuation, vision field of the electrodes, and geometrical approximation error. For this purpose, the dipolar hypothesis has been used, because it was obviously both the most simple and the best known.

1) Attenuation

The attenuation effect is measured by the transfer function, where q = 1. Two factors are involved: frequency and distance. The first one can be considered as negligible, because the potential changes under consideration are much too slow. The shell's thickness dependance, on the contrary, have the greatest importance; for its estimate, we have computed g for five different h values. The result is a set of curves which express the attenuation of the potential as a function of the distance from a dipole, for each thickness h. More precisely, let E be an electrode (pin-point electrode) situated at the point x on the scalp, and let z be any point of the cortical surface, projected onto y on the scalp (fig. 1). The attenuation of a signal recorded by E from z is given by:

$$10 \,\mathrm{Log}_{10}(g(x - y)).$$

This function increases (in absolute value) both with the distance ρ from the dipole axis and the total thickness h of the shells. Figure 2 shows the main variations of this atte-

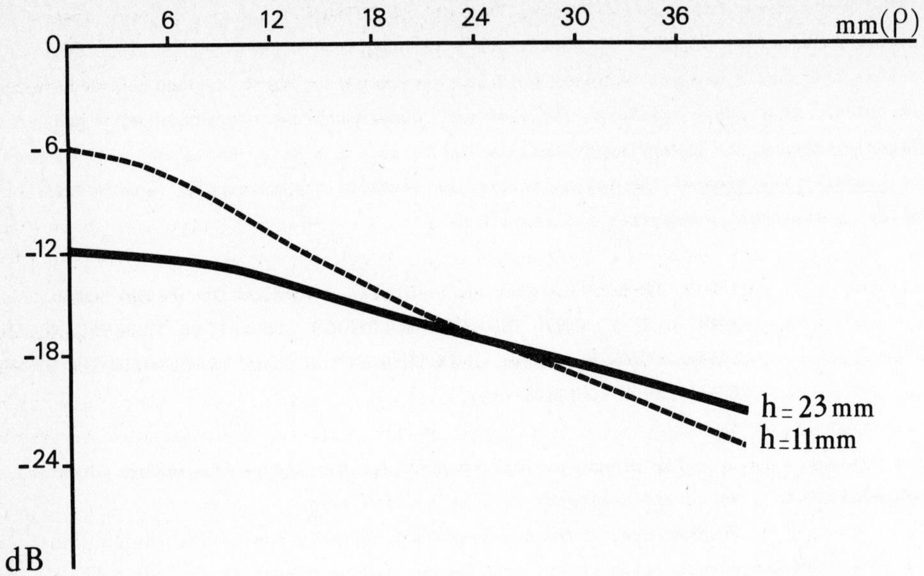

FIGURE 2.- Attenuation curves, as functions of the distance from a dipole axis (elementary source set). The dotted curve corresponds to the minimum thickness of the layers between cortex and scalp; the solid one corresponds to the maximum thickness of these layers; the middle curves (not plotted) have the same intersection as those in the figure.

nuation. All the curves are cutting each other close to -16 dB. Stated another way, the attenuation is superior to 16 dB beyond a disk of 24 mm radius which is centered over the emission point on the cortex. As this is true whatever h may be, then we can estimate that the vision field of a scalp electrode has the same radius, because the ratio signal/noise is always superior to 15 dB.

2) Geometrical error

The boundary problem is only defined in a 'rather small' cylindrical domain C, lying between scalp and cortex. The attenuation estimates allow us to stipulate the real dimensions of this cylinder; they also permit us to compute the error which is introduced by approximating locally the surfaces with their tangent planes. It follows from the preceding that the contribution of D's center (on the cortex) to the potential on the lateral boundary of C is zero. Then, let us assume that the radius of curvature of the skull is about 9.5 cm in the zone under consideration (admissible mean value in the parietal zone). Under this condition, the average error on the attenuation is less than .3 dB; the error on the radius of D is at the most .25 mm. The geometrical approximation of the model is thus admissible, at least for 'rather regular zones' of the skull.

VI. SIMULATION EXPERIMENTS

The model's behaviour has been tested on digital computer, for various cortical distributions, by the means of simulation experiments. For this purpose, the following simulated device has been used:

On the scalp, inside a circular zone of 24 mm radius, are assumed to be placed 49 electrodes, one of them central. They have a circular section of 4 mm in diameter, and occupy the nodes of a square grid having links of 6.14 mm. Any two electrodes are thus always at a minimum distance of 2.14 mm from each other. All recordings are monopolar with average reference. On the cortex, a similar montage is assumed to be set up inside a concentric circular zone of radius 48 mm. Thus, in order to take into account the preceding estimates, the simulation is restricted to a domain which is equivalent to a 'spot of vision' or visual field for scalp electrodes. In the same way, their diameter corresponds to a value in common use with real experiments. Figure 3 roughly schematizes the device such simulated.

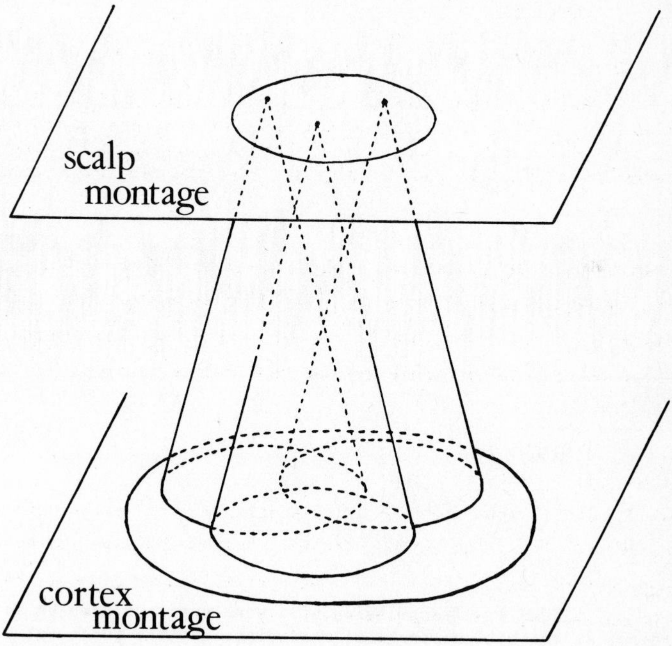

FIGURE 3.- Simulated device: each skin electrode has a fiel of vision which is a circular cortical area of 48mm in diameter.

Furthermore, we assume that the cortical area under consideration holds up three mixed pseudo-periodic activities: ALPHA waves (10 - 15 Hz), BETA waves (20 - 25

Hz) and THETA waves (3 - 7 Hz). The spatial densities of these components are respectively choosen as elliptic, exponential and parabolic distributions.

Figure 4 shows traces corresponding with two recordings from central electrodes (one of them on the cortex and the other on the scalp), during a five seconds interval for a cortical distribution having a weak stationnary gradient. These traces show almost the same types of waveshapes; nevertheless, various patterns (lettered) are rather badly reproduced, reversed or even undetected on the scalp. The average attenuation reaches - 4 dB, but the smoothing out is negligible. Such an example is a 'good case', where two superimposed electrodes receive similar signals. This is due to the regularity of the cortical distribution, whose components are spread out with minor divergences of density in the whole area which is explored.

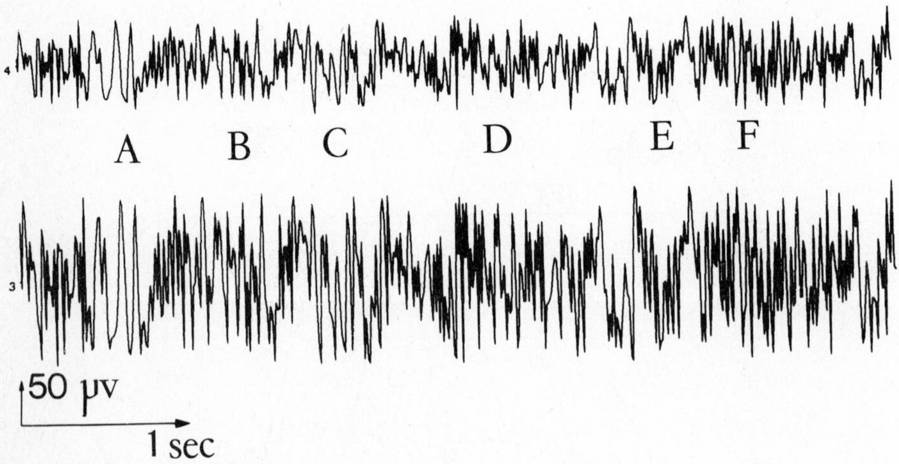

FIGURE 4.- Transmission of a weak gradient complex activity. At the top: scalp recording; at the bottom: cortical recording. Letters point out zones of discrepancy. Time constant: 10 msec.

On the contrary, the traces of figure 5 show the effect of a strong gradient cortical distribution. In this simulated experiment, an ample BETA rhytm is localized in a 5 sq. cm cortical area which is centered on the electrodes axis; a weak ALPHA wave is spread out the whole 'spot' which is seen by the skin electrode. Under this condition, there is a total discrepancy between the two recordings: the ALPHA waveshape is detected on the scalp, whereas the only BETA rhytm does exist inside the underlying cortical zone.

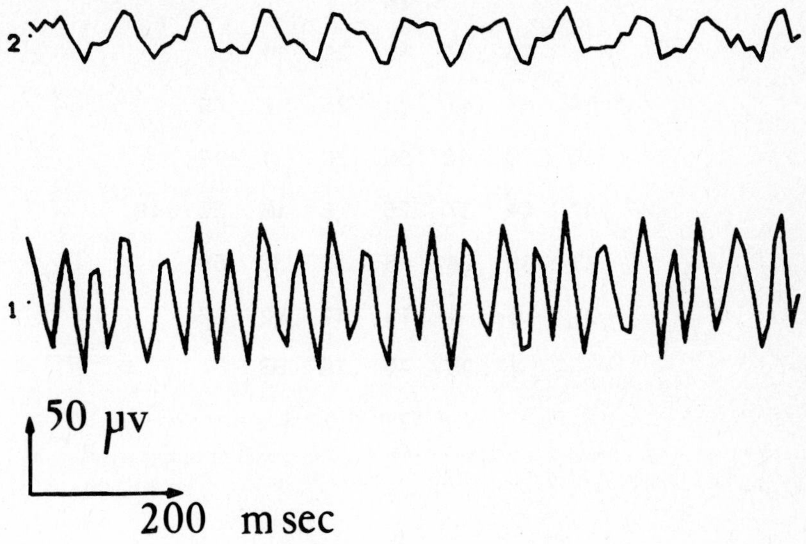

FIGURE 5.- Transmission of a complex activity having a strong space gradient. At the top: the scalp recording; at the bottom: the cortical recording. There is a total discrepancy between the levels.

In figure 6 we give the distributions of surface potential, for fixed time, inside the two homologous 'spots' on cortex and scalp. Here we see that the maximum BETA and THETA activity completely disappears from the scalp. Moreover, the extension of negative potentials is larger on the scalp, and it tends to the middle of the disk, whereas the amplitudes are stronger in the upper left quadrant. This latter effect is due to large amplitude potentials beyond the boundary of the disk which is shown in figure 6. In the main, however, the gradient is weaker on the scalp, and there is a spatial smoothing of the distributions.

Remark

The above simulated traces do not aim at being realistic; more precisely, they are not intended to simulate real traces, and their only purpose is helping us to see in what way various shapened activities can be transmitted from cortex to scalp, in the sense of the model.

				25				
		48	37	31	21	11		
	54	47	41	33	25	8	-5	
	50	50	42	36	20	-1	-17	
42	47	44	37	25	6	-16	-36	-49
	37	35	24	5	-17	-39	-59	
	21	16	4	-19	-42	-62	-82	
		-4	-25	-46	-70	-92		
				-71				

				16				
		11	21	19	11	-1		
	28	23	39	47	46	13	-11	
	25	41	58	68	71	30	-16	
23	34	58	64	48	47	9	-32	-44
	63	68	57	36	1	-47	-93	
	37	45	13	-26	-53	-69	-76	
		14	-25	-55	-69	-78		
				-69				

FIGURE 6.- Potential distributions inside homologous 'spots' of48 mm in diameter. At the top: the scalp distribution; at the bottom: the cortical distribution. The potential values are expressed in microvolts. The circle and the rhomb respectively mark the THETA and BETA maximum activities on the cortex level; they are not detected on the scalp.

VII. CONCLUSION

The results of the simulation essentially arise from the well-known properties of convolution. Indeed, the integration tends to smooth over the strong gradient images, while better spread components remain detectable, even if they are absent from the sub-jacent cortical area. A small amplitude activity can be transmitted if it occupies a sufficiently large cortical zone, while other, although of far greater amplitude, are not seen on the scalp. These results are tallied with the empirical observations. Moreover, it is easy to see that any multipolar assumption would provide results of the same type, within numerical deviations. This tolerance reinforces the generality of the model, but limits the span of the classical hypotheses made on the cortical sources patterns.

The convolution defines $V_{S'}$ as a function of V_S and g. In practice, for clinical applications, the question is rather how to compute V_S on the cortex, using the values of $V_{S'}$ which are picked up on the scalp. In other words, we have to reverse the convolution, and the main problem is to find an optimal method for the best approximation, which takes into account both the small number of captors and the noise level. However, given an appropriate definition of experimental conditions, it seems possible to compute the electrocorticogram as a function of the surface EEG, in the sense of the model, with a sufficient accuracy.

REFERENCES

BISHOP G.H. & CLARE M.H.: Sites of origin of electric potential in striate cortex. J. Neurophysiol., 1958, 10 : 201-220.

BOUIX M.: Les discontinuités du rayonnement électromagnétique. Dunod, Paris, 1966, 241 pp.

BREMER F.: Considérations sur l'origine et la nature des "ondes" cérébrales. EEG clin. Neurophysiol., 1949, 1: 177-193.

CALVET J., CALVET M.C. & SCHERRER J.: Etude stratigraphique de l'activité EEG spontanée. EEG clin. Neurophysiol., 1964, 17: 109-125.

DYNKIN E.B.: Markov Processes. Springer-Verlag, Berlin, 1965, t.1, 357 pp.

ECCLES J.C.: Interpretation of action potentials evoked in the cerebral cortex. EEG clin. Neurophysiol., 1951, 19: 217-229.

GEISLER C.D. & GERSTEIN G.L.: The surface EEG in relation to its sources. EEG clin. Neurophysiol., 1961, 13: 927-934.

PANOFSKY W.A. & PHILLIPS M.: Classical electricity and magnetism. Addison-Wesley, Reading, Mass., 1955, 400 pp.

SMITH J. & SCHADE J.P.: Computer Programming for parameter Analysis of the Electroencephalogram. In Computers and Brain. Progress in Brain Research, vol.33, Amsterdam, 1970.

IMPLEMENTABLE POLICIES FOR IMPROVING THE BIOMASS YIELD OF A FISHERY

Philip W. R. Sluczanowski
Dept. of Computing and Control
Imperial College
London SW7,
United Kingdom

Chapter 1. Introduction

The Beverton-Holt Model of a fishery was first presented in [1] and is still the main tool in planning policies where the age structure of the fish is considered important (see [2] - [4]), even though Leslie Matrix techniques have been applied. The model assumes that no stock-recruitment relationship exists and that fishing mortality depends on the net choice and the applied fishing intensity. This paper deals with choosing mesh sizes and planning fishing strategies to improve yields.

[2], [3], [5] have given various analyses of the optimal way to harvest a single year class under various restriction. Chapter 2 solves the general problem formulated in [2] subject to an implementable class of controls and presents a simple numerical way of computing the optimal solution. A method for choosing optimal mesh sizes for maximum sustainable yields is then presented, based on a technique given in [6].

[4], [7], [8] considered the effect of all the year classes being fished together, since no net is completely selective. Chapter 3 defines periodicity in fisheries control policies and analyses the structure of periodic solutions, allowing one to obtain better long term yields than the maximum sustainable yield. [2], [3], [4], [7], [8], [9] have discussed the concept of "pulse fishing", whereby one fishes with maximum possible intensity at certain times. "Bang-bang" solutions to the periodic problem of this type are then discussed.

Assuming that one has chosen a long-term policy, necessary conditions on the age structure are presented in Chapter 4 that insure that future average yields over periods of fixed duration are at least as good as the long term average yield. This allows one to formulate strategies for recovering overexploited fisheries in a control theoretic framework. A numerical example provides some interesting insights.

CHAPTER 2

THE SINGLE YEAR-CLASS MODEL

The Beverton-Holt Model of a fishery deals with a stock of a given species contained within certain geographical limits that does not interact with other fish of the same species. Whereas most of the fishery economics literature deals with aggregated numbers of fish, or their total weight, the Beverton-Holt Model also considers their age structure. Each year-class is regarded as having dynamics such as mortality and weight growth independent of the others.

At the beginning of each successive year i a number of fish, called the recruitment R_i, enter the fishery. These are considered to be independent of previous populations, an assumption that is not as rash as it initially sounds when one investigates the available stock-recruitment models. Considering that a single female cod can produce millions of eggs, that of the order of 99.998% of the eggs fail to survive, and that survivorship depends largely on local environmental conditions, it is not surprising that recruitments can vary by factors of more than a hundred and are considered random, uncorrelated with previous populations.

Suppose that at time t = 0, a number of fish R arrive at the fishery. At any future time t the number of fish in this year-class N(t) suffers natural mortality M and fishing mortality $F_M(t)$, both proportional to N(t). An upper limit T on the fishes' lives is also decided upon, above which no fish can survive:

$$\frac{dN(t)}{dt} = -[M + F_M(t)]\,N(t), \quad 0 \le t < T, \quad M > 0, \quad F_M(t) \ge 0 \tag{2.1}$$

$$N(0) = R > 0$$

$$N(t) = 0 \quad , \quad t \ge T$$

Associated with the year-class is a weight function w(t) which describes the average weight of a fish of age t. We require w(t) to have continuous first derivative, increasing and bounded for $t \in [0,T]$, and $\frac{\dot{w}}{w}(t)$ decreasing, a standard property of natural growth curves. (The von Bertallanfy curve $w(t) = w_\infty\ [1 - e^{-r(t-t_0)}]^3$ is often a good fit).

We assume too that the fishing mortality $F_M(t)$ is linearly dependent on fishing intensity, a function of the number of vessels used, their tonnage, and the time spent fishing. (see [1], [3], [8]).

We shall henceforth use F(t) instead of $F_M(t)$ in (2.1) and call it fishing intensity. It is piecewise continuous and physically bounded as follows:

$$0 \le F(t) \le \bar{F} \tag{2.2}$$

Given a constant fixed cost per unit fishing effort c, a fixed unit price for fish, and having decided on a discount rate r, Clark et al. [2] showed that the present value of the stock PV is given by the following expression:

$$PV = \int_0^\infty e^{-rT} F(t) \{N(t)w(t) - c\} \, dt \quad r \geq 0, \quad c \geq 0 \tag{2.3)'}$$

We are concerned with finding strategies $F(t)$, $t \in [0,T]$ which maximize this quantity.

If $F(t) = 0$, $t \in [0,T]$, then the natural biomass curve $B(t) = N(t)w(t)$ has shape as in Fig. 1. We assume that c is such that either $c > B(0)$ in which case we define $t^* = 0$, or else $\exists t^* \in [0,T]$ such that $B(t^*) = c$ and $\dot{B}(t^*) > 0$. Otherwise the value of the stock never exceeds the cost of extracting it. Either $B(T) > c$ in which case we define $t^{**} = T$ or else $\exists\, t^{**} \in [t^*,T]$ where $B(t^{**}) = 0$ and $B(t^{**}) < 0$. We also define the value curve $V(t)$ for any $F(t)$:

$$V(t) = e^{-rt} \{N(t)\, w(t) - c\} \tag{2.4}$$

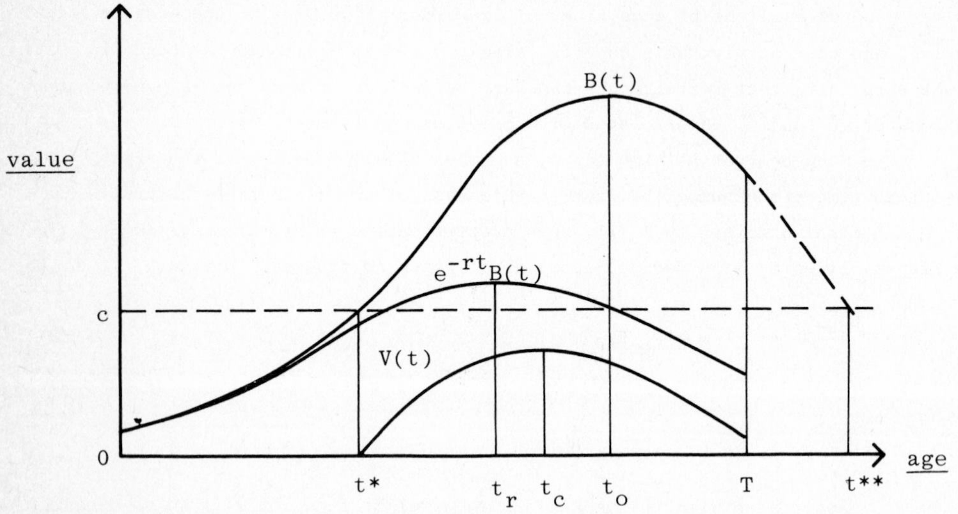

Fig. 1. Dynamics of Single year Class.

These curves are plotted in Fig. 1, together with $e^{-rt}B(t)$, and defining the ages at which they achieve their respective maxima t_o, t_c, and t_r, it is easily seen that these can be computed from the following relationships:

$$t_o \in (t^*, \infty) \qquad \text{where } \frac{\dot{w}}{w}(t_o) = M \tag{2.5a}$$

$$t_c \in (t^*, \infty) \qquad \text{where } B(t_c)\left\{r+M - \frac{\dot{w}}{w}(t_c)\right\} = cr \tag{2.5b}$$

$$t_r \in [0, \infty) \qquad \text{where } \frac{\dot{w}}{w}(t_r) = M+r \tag{2.5c}$$

Because $\frac{\dot{w}}{w}(t)$ is decreasing and since $r, M, c \geq 0$, it can also be seen from (2.5a) - (2.5c) that:

$$t_r \le t_c \le t_o \tag{2.6}$$

Note: It is possible that $T < t_r$. (2.6)

Implementable Optimal Solutions of the One-dimensional Problem:

If $\bar{F}$ is very large, the situation corresponds to our being able to harvest all the fish in one fell swoop. If we wish to maximize the biomass yield, it is obvious that we should do so at the point this curve reaches its peak, i.e. at t_o. Clark et al. [2] and Hannesson [3] used on investment technique first described by Fisher to show that the point of "instant fishing" for a given c and r is t_c or that the optimal policy for $\bar{F}$ large enough was one with controls not piecewise constant, and therefore not easily implementable. Thus bounds on the point of harvest are given by (2.6) for any cost c, given r.

In practice, however, $\bar{F}$ is relatively small (e.g. $\bar{F} < 1.5$ for $M \approx .15$). This means that we shall require more time within which to harvest the year-class. It will be shown that the optimal implementable policy for any $\bar{F}$ will be of the form:

$$\begin{aligned} F(t) &= 0 & 0 \le t < t_1 \\ &= \bar{F} & t_1 < t < t_2 \\ &= 0 & t_2 < t \le T \end{aligned} \tag{2.7}$$

where $t_1 \le t_c < t_2$. That is, there is only one period of fishing (t_1, t_2) and it must include t_c. A simple numerical method for determining t_1 and t_2 will then be outlined.

Definition: $\begin{matrix} t_1 \\ t_2 \end{matrix} \in [0,T]$ is called a $\begin{matrix} \text{switching-on} \\ \text{switching-off} \end{matrix}$ time if

$$\begin{matrix} F(t_1 - \delta) = 0 \\ F(t_2 - \delta) = F \end{matrix} \quad \text{and} \quad \begin{matrix} F(t_1 + \delta) = \bar{F} \\ F(t_1 + \delta) = 0 \end{matrix} \quad \forall\, \delta \in (0,\varepsilon),\ \text{some } \varepsilon > 0. \tag{2.8}$$

Using standard optimization techniques (see [10]) we form the Hamiltonian of the system described by (2.1) and (2.3):

$$\begin{aligned} H(t) &= -F(t)e^{-rt}\,\{N(t)w(t) - c\} - \lambda(t)\,\{M+F(t)\}\,N(t),\ t\in [0,T] \\ &= -F(t)\,\{V(t) + \lambda(t)N(t)\} \quad -\lambda(t)MN(t) \end{aligned} \tag{2.9}$$

where $V(t)$ is as in (2.4) and $\lambda(t)$, the adjoint variable, is defined by:

$$- \dot{\lambda}(t) = \frac{\partial H}{\partial N}$$

$$= - \{M+F(t)\} \lambda(t) - F(t)\ w\ (t) e^{-rt} \tag{2.10a}$$

and satisfies the transversality condition $\lambda(T) = 0$ (2.10b)

Using a strong variation of the Maximum Principle we know that, except for singular subarcs, the optimal $F(t)$ will minimize $H(t)$ $\forall t \epsilon [0,T]$ subject to (2.2). Along a singular subarc over I, a finite subset of $[0,T]$, we have:

$$V(t) + \lambda(t)\ N(t) = 0 \quad \forall t \epsilon I$$

i.e.

$$\dot{V}(t) + \dot{\lambda}(t)N(t) + \lambda(t)\dot{N}(t) = 0 \quad \forall t \epsilon I$$

or

$$\{\frac{\dot{w}}{w}(t) - M - r\}\ N(t)\ w\ (t) + \ rc=0 \quad \forall t \epsilon I$$

This is the singular arc that Clark et al [2] and Hannesson [3] proposed as the optimal policy for $c,r \neq 0$, and $\bar{F}$ large enough such that the path can be followed. Further differentiation yields the corresponding control:

$$F(t) = \frac{\ddot{w}(t) - (M+r)\ \dot{w}(t)}{\dot{w}(t) - (M+r)\ w(t)} - M$$ which can be satisfied only for $t \epsilon I c [t_c, t_o]$.

However, as they pointed out, such a policy is not feasible practically, and we shall therefore search for extremal solutions that yield piecewise constant controls (and exclude sequences of these that may tend weakly to the singular solution). Henceforth we shall regard this as our class of admissible controls. For $\bar{F}$ not large enough to follow singular arcs, our solutions are the same as those from the class of piecewise continuous controls. [Numerical examples show the differences between the singular solutions and those proposed below are < 1%]. Our implementable solution must therefore minimize $H(t)$, which yields:

$$F(t) = \bar{F} \qquad V(t)+\lambda(t)N(t) > 0$$
$$= 0 \qquad\qquad " \qquad < 0 \tag{2.11}$$

and since the switching curve is continuous we have that at the switching times t_i:

$$V(t_i) + \lambda(t_i)N(t_i) = 0 \tag{2.12}$$

<u>Lemma 1</u>: If t_1 is a switching-on time, then $\dot{V}\ (t_1 -) > 0$.
Similarly $\dot{V}\ (t_2 +) < 0$ for t_2 switching-off time. (2.13)

<u>Proof</u>: We first show that:

$$F(t) = 0 \quad \forall t \epsilon [a,b] \Rightarrow \lambda(t)N(t) = \text{constant on } [a,b].$$

$$F(t) = 0 \Rightarrow \dot{N}(t) = -MN(t),\ \dot{\lambda}(t) = M\lambda(t)$$

$$\frac{d}{dt}[\lambda(t)N(t)] = \dot{N}(t)\lambda(t) + N(t)\dot{\lambda}(t) = 0$$

$$\Rightarrow \quad \lambda(t)N(t) = \text{constant}$$

(2.8), (2.11), $\Rightarrow \{V(t) + \lambda(t)N(t)\}_{t_1-\delta} < 0$ some $\delta > 0$

(2.12) $\Rightarrow \{V(t) + \lambda(t)N(t)\}_{t_1} = 0$

Therefore: $$\frac{V(t_1-\delta) - V(t_1) + \lambda(t_1-\delta)\ N(t_1-\delta) - \lambda(t_1)N(t_1)}{\delta} > 0$$

$$(2.14) \Rightarrow \lim_{\delta \to 0+} \frac{V(t_1-\delta) - V(t_1)}{\delta} > 0$$

i.e. $\dot{V}(t_1-) > 0$ since derivative obviously exists where $F(t)$ is constant. Similarly $\dot{V}(t_2+) < 0$.

Theorem 1. If t_1 is an optimal switching-on time and t_2 is an optimal switching-off time, then:

i) There is at most one fishing period.

ii) $t_1 \in [0,t_c]$

iii) $t_2 \in [t_c,T]$

Proof. i) Suppose that there is more than one switching-on time in $[0,T]$. Then let t_2^a correspond to the switching-off time of a period followed by a switching-on time $t_1^b < T$.

Then by Lemma 1:

$$\dot{V}(t_2^a+) < 0 \Rightarrow e^{-rt_2^a+} \{(\frac{\dot{w}}{w}(t_2^a+) - M - r)\, B(t_2^a+) + rc\} < 0$$

If $t_2^a < t_o$, then $t \in [t_2^a, t_o]$ imply $B(t)$ increasing, $\frac{\dot{w}}{w}(t)$ decreasing; while $V(t)$ is decreasing $\forall\ t \geq t_o$ (by (2.6)). Together these imply that $\dot{V}(t) < 0$ $\forall\ t \in (t_2^a, T)$, which implies $\dot{V}(t_1^b-) < 0$, contradicting Lemma 1.

So there is at most one switching-on time $t_1 \in [0,T]$.

ii) A switching-on time t_1 must exist; then from the shape of $V(t)$ in Fig. 1., (2.5b) and (2.13), it is obvious that $t_1 \leq t_c$.

iii) Let t_2 be the subsequent switching-off time and suppose that

$$t_2 < \min\ \{t_c, T\}$$

Together with Lemma 1 this implies that $\exists\ \delta t > 0$ such that $\dot{V}(t+\delta t) < 0$ so putting $t_3 = t_2 + \delta t$ we get $e^{-rt_3}\ \{(\frac{\dot{w}}{w}(t_3) - M - r)\ w(t_3)\ N(t_2)\ e^{-M(t_3-t_2)} + rc\} < 0$

$$\Rightarrow N(t_2) > \frac{rc}{w(t_3) e^{-M(t_3-t_2)}\ \{M+r - \frac{\dot{w}}{w}(t_3)\}} \triangleq k$$

But from (2.5b) and the shape of natural $V(t)$ we have that $e^{-rt_3}\ \{(\frac{\dot{w}}{w}(t_3) - M - r)\ w(t_3)\ \bar{N} e^{-M(t_3-t_2)} + rc\} > 0$ where $\bar{N} = Re^{-Mt_2} \Rightarrow \bar{N} < k < N(t_2)$

But $N(t_2) = Re^{-Mt_1 - (M+\bar{F})(t_2-t_1)} = \bar{N}e^{-\bar{F}(t_2-t_1)} < \bar{N}$ contradiction.

Therefore $\underline{t_2 \geq \min\ \{t_c, T\}}$

This theorem implies that the optimal fishing period must include time t_c. Being the maximum of the natural "value curve" it can be thought of as the time of "most efficient fishing", i.e. the time at which one gets most for one's effort.

Note: It is readily seen that $t_1 \geq t^*$ and $t_2 \leq t^{**}$, for otherwise one is unnecessarily adding negative parts to the objective function.

The shape of the biomass curve under fishing is next discussed.

a) If $\{N(T)w(T) - c\} \geq 0$, such as when $c=0$, then by (2.11) $F(T) = \bar{F}$, i.e. $t_2 = T$ and $\lambda(t_2) = 0$.

b) If $\{N(T)w(T) - c\} > 0$, then $F(T) = 0$ and $t_2 < T$.

(2.10) => $\lambda(t_2) = 0$, and (2.12) gives $N(t_2)\, w\, (t_2) = c$.

These imply that

$$t_2 = \min\, \{T, \tau\} \quad \text{where } N(\tau)w(\tau) = c \tag{2.15}$$

Since $\lambda(t_2) = 0$ (2.10a) gives

$$\lambda(t_1) = \bar{F} \int_{t_2}^{t_1} e^{-rs}\, w(s)\, e^{(M+\bar{F})(t_1 - s)}\, ds$$ and substituting into (2.12)

we get:

$$e^{-rt_1} \{N(t_1)w(t_1) - c\} = \bar{F} \int_{t_1}^{t_2} e^{-rs}\, N(s)\, w\,(s)\, ds \tag{2.16}$$

where the left hand side is the natural value curve, independent of $\bar{F}$ for given c. As $\bar{F} \to 0+$, right hand side $\to 0$; so by choosing $\bar{F}$ small enough one can make t_1 as close to t^* as one wishes. Also as $\bar{F} \to 0+$, $N(t_2) \to N(\min\, \{T, t^{**}\})$

i.e. $\bar{F} \to 0$ => the optimum fishing period $(t_1, t_2) \to (t^*, \min\, \{T, t^{**}\})$. Fig. 2 illustrates the varying trajectories for different $\bar{F}$'s using data for plaice from [1]. with r = .1 and c = .05.

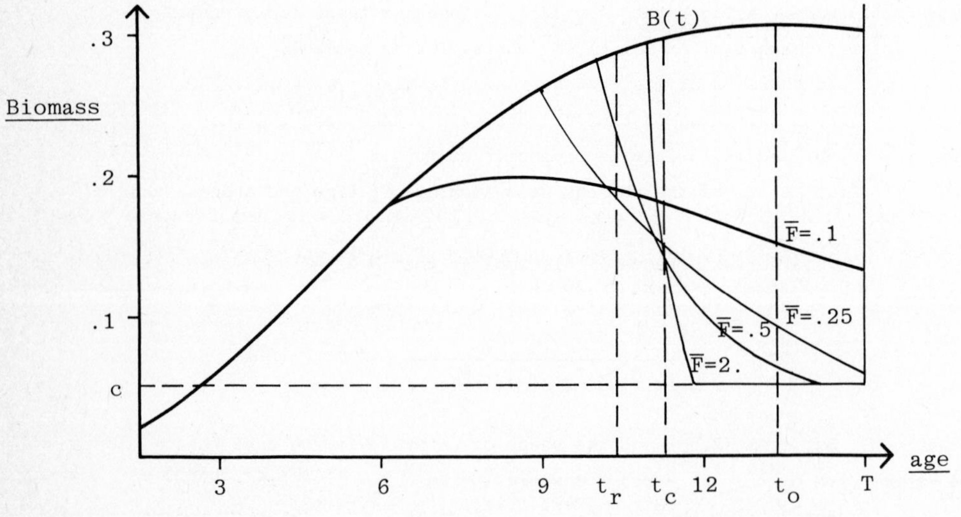

Fig.2. Optimal Implementable Trajectories.

From (2.16) can also be derived the following expression:

$$e^{-rt_1} \{B(t_1) - c\} = \bar{F} \int_{t_1}^{t_2} e^{-rs} \{B(s) - c\}\, ds + \bar{F}\, c \int_{t_1}^{t_2} e^{-rs}\, ds$$

i.e. The instantaneous value of the fishery at starting time

= expected revenue + discounted cost.

This is a generalization of the result Goh [5] proved for c,r = 0.

Implementing Numerical Algorithms to solve the 1-D Problem

The problem is to find $(t_1,t_2) \subset [t^*,T]$ which maximizes

$$J = \bar{F} \int_{t_1}^{t_2} e^{-rs} \{N(s)w(s) - c\} \, ds$$

Now given t_1, (2.15) allows us to calculate a corresponding t_2 which will be optimal if t_1 is. So the problem reduces to a one-dimensional minimization problem, with a convenient starting interval for the search, $[t^*, t_c]$.

$$\min_{t_1 \in [t^*, t_c]} V(t_1) = -\bar{F} \int_{t_1}^{t_2(t_1)} e^{-rs} \{ N(s)w(s) - c \} \, ds \tag{2.17}$$

where $t_2(t_1) = T$ if $N(t_1)e^{-(M+\bar{F})(T-t_1)} w(T) > c$

$= \underset{\tau \in [t_1, T]}{\text{solution of}}\ N(t_1)e^{-(M+\bar{F})(\tau-t_1)} w(\tau) = 0$ otherwise.

A Numerical Example and some Observations

The above algorithm was used to compute the optimal fishing periods for various costs, discount rates, and $\bar{F}$'s. The parameters used are those for North Sea Plaice as above, although the below observations apply also to other data used (North Sea Cod). It must be remembered that we assume that we are exploiting each year-class optimally, i.e. that we do not expend any fishing effort on the year-class after t_2, a condition not easy to implement.

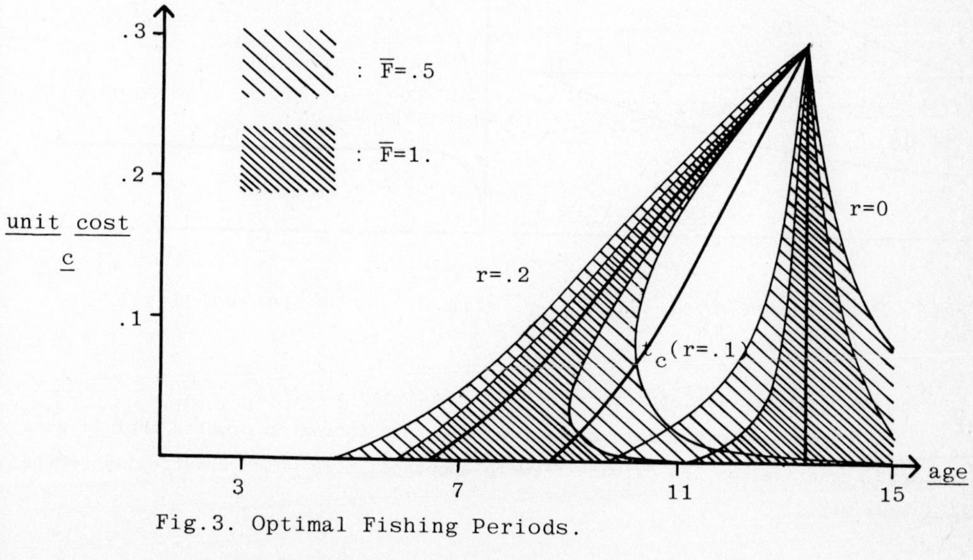

Fig.3. Optimal Fishing Periods.

i) Fig. 3 shows the optimal fishing periods for different costs and discount rates. It is interesting to note that as costs increase to max $\{B(t)\}$, the period becomes a pulse at t_o. This is because at high costs $t\epsilon[0,T]$ the profit margin is low and $[t^*,t^{**}]$ gets smaller while $t_c\epsilon[t^*,t^{**}]$. Thus high costs eliminate the advantage of considering discount rates.

ii) It is instructive to consider the situation from the viewpoint of a private company, interested in maximizing its profits from a single year stock. If r represents the rate of interest in other forms of investment, then the profit from the stock at time T is:

$$P = \int_0^T F(t)\, e^{r(T-t)} \{N(t)w(t) - c\}\, dt \tag{2.18}$$

which has the same optimal solution (t_1,t_2) as (2.3)

$$P_{opt} = e^{rT}\, \bar{F} \int_{t_1}^{t_2} V(t)\, dt \tag{2.19}$$

The profits that can be gained using differing interest rates, and the corresponding drop in the actual mass of fish-meat extracted are illustrated in Fig.4.

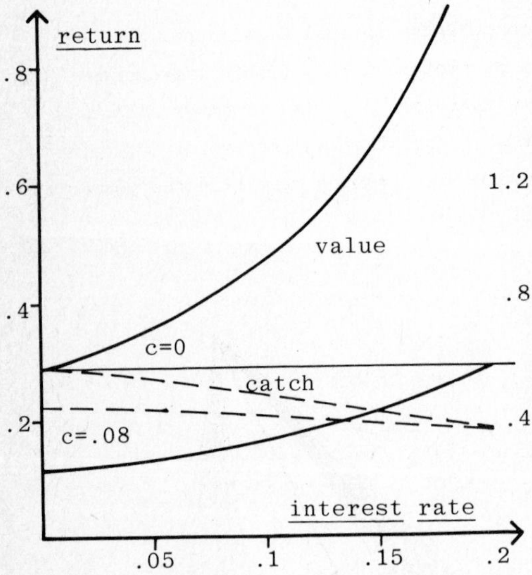

Fig.4. Profits due to interest.

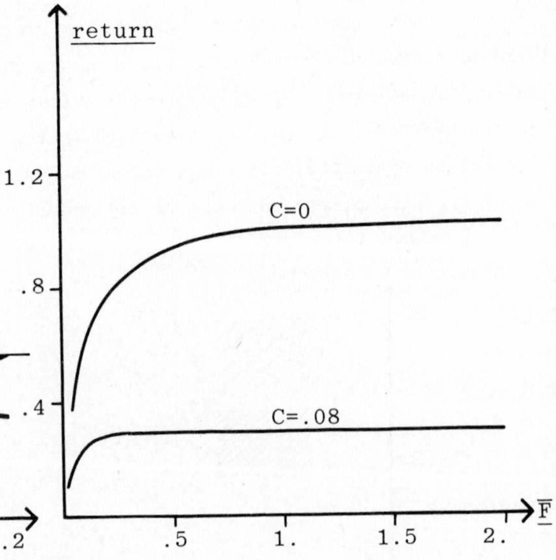

Fig.5. Yields for varying $\bar{F}$'s.

Two features are apparent:

1) A high interest rate makes possible such increased profits that it acts as a large incentive for the private firm to adopt policies which drastically reduce the biomass yield.

2) High fishing costs tend to nullify this effect somewhat, a fact that should be considered when planning taxation.

iii) Fig. 5 illustrates how much improvement in profits is possible by increasing fishing capacity. It shows that for $\bar{F} > .4$, very little extra revenue is gained, implying that a rather conservative policy of using low intensity effort for a long time is not only more stable, but also almost as profitable. Increasing costs accentuate this trend.

Application to choice of mesh size

In practice the fishing effort $F(t)$ does not affect the fishing mortality $F_M(t)$ of all the age groups equivalently. Depending on the mesh size of the net, the same fishing effort has more effect on old fish than on young ones. This can be represented by means of a selectivity curve $s(t)$, a monotonic increasing function of the age of the fish t.

i.e. $\quad F_M(t) = s(t)\, F(t) \quad 0 \le s(t) \le 1, \; t \in [0,T]$

So $s(t)$ represents the probability of a t-year old fish being affected by the net.

A class of nets can be parameterized by a parameter such as the mean cut-off age. Denote $s_p(t)$ the curve corresponding to parameter $p \in \bar{P}$, a closed subset of R^1. (2.20)

Knife-edge Selection and Sustainable Yields

Since the number of fish of any year-class after T years is too low to significantly affect results, the precise choice of T is not very important (see [1]). We can therefore choose T to be integral which implies that at any time there are T distinct year classes in the fishery.

Beverton and Holt [1] observed that if one fishes constantly with $F(t) = F_s$ the catch in one year due to all the T year classes, is equal to the total yield of one year class over T years (2.21).

A useful simplification that we shall consider first is to regard a net as exploiting all fish above a cut-off age t_K equally, and not affecting younger fish.

$$s_{t_K}(t) = 0 \quad 0 \le t \le t_K$$
$$= 1 \quad t_K < t \le T \qquad (2.22)$$

Assuming that $c = 0$ and that one can select a knife-edge mesh with parameter t_K as in (2.22), choosing $t_K = t_1$ for the given $\bar{F}, r$ will obviously give the maximum possible sustained yield since, as Goh [5] and Clarke et al [2] pointed out, one is then best exploiting each year-class individually.

If $c \neq 0$, then one can use a technique very similar to that described by Turvey [6] to compute the optimal choice of t_K and $\bar{F}$ for a long term yield. The method is described here both for completeness and because it presents a simply computable explicit solution to a well defined problem, as opposed to Turvey's theoretical formulation.

Using the observation (2.21), the problem is to choose $\bar{F}$, t_K so as to find the maximum sustainable yield Y_s.

$$Y_s = \max_{(t_K \in [0,t_o],\ \bar{F})} \int_0^T \bar{F}e^{-rt} \{s_{t_K}(t)\ N(t)w(t) - c\}\ dt$$

$$= \max_{\bar{F}} \{\max_{t_K} \bar{F}\int_{t_K}^{T} e^{-rt} N(t)w(t)\ dt - c\bar{F} \int_0^T e^{-rt}\ dt\} \tag{2.23}$$

since S_{t_K} is knife-edge. The solution of the eumetric curve

$$E(\bar{F}) = \max_{t_1} \int_{t_1}^{T} \bar{F}\ e^{-rt} N(t)w(t)\ dt \tag{2.24}$$

was derived above and one can plot this function and the corresponding optimal cut-off ages $t_K(\bar{F}) = t_1(\bar{F})$ for varying $\bar{F}$'s as in Fig. 6.

$E(\bar{F}) \to N(t_r)w(t_r)$, and $t_K(\bar{F}) \to t_r$ as $\bar{F} \to \infty$.

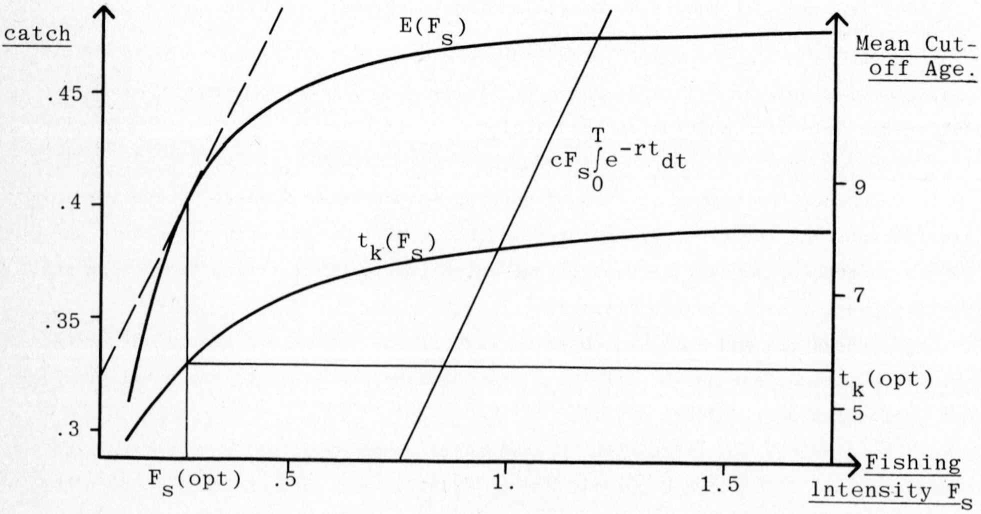

Fig.6. Max. Sust. Yield Policy ($c \neq 0$).

The second term in (2.23) is linear in $\bar{F}$ and can easily be drawn for a given c. Solving (2.23) now requires choosing $\bar{F}$opt such that the distance between the two curves is greatest. The solution to this is of the Golden Rule type, where t the slope of the eumetric curve is $c\int_0^T e^{-rt}dt$. t_{Kopt} is the corresponding best cut-off point.

Extensions for Different Nets

The above method can easily be extended to more general descriptions of nets. All that is different is that the eumetric curve is derived from minimizing with respect to a parameter p instead of t_K. Nets are never actually knife-edge, although most treatments to date have searched for the optimal mean cut-off age t_M by identifying it with the optimal cut-off age t_K.

By considering the solutions of the knife-edge problems, it is obvious that its yields must be greater than those from any other selectivity curve. The curves due to different $\bar{F}$'s for a mean cut-off class of meshes with selectivity curve slope equal to .5 is shown in Fig. 6. They are very similar to those for knife-edge selection (<.1%) and show that when considering sustainable yields the approximation mentioned above is fairly accurate.

This technique can be easily used for any class of meshes parameterized by a parameter p. The use of computers to numerically integrate functions makes it feasible to parameterize as accurately as possible sets of selectivity curves, giving more accurate choices of mesh. However, the general crudeness of the model probably gives such exercises little significance.

Optimum Solution of Conglomerate Problem for large $\bar{F}$ and c

It can be seen from Fig. 3 that for large values of $\bar{F}$ and c, the optimal harvesting of a single year-class may require fishing for less than one year. In this case it is possible by a suitable choice of net to obtain a periodic solution which makes full use of the available $\bar{F}$, rather than using $\bar{F}$opt as calculated above.

Given $\bar{F}$, r and c we can compute the optimal fishing period for a single year class $(t_1, t_2) < 1$. Suppose that we fish each year class when its age corresponds to this period.

Then provided the following conditions hold:

$$\begin{aligned} s_p\,t) &= 0 \qquad t < t_2 - 1 \\ s_p(t) &= 1 \qquad t > t_1 \end{aligned} \tag{2.25}$$

each year class is optimally exploited, without interfering significantly in the dynamics of the other year classes.

Since fishing is traditionally periodic in a sense, (2.25) could provide a convenient method for establishing mesh sizes.

CHAPTER 3

THE CONGLOMERATE YEAR-CLASS PROBLEM

In considering strategies for maximizing the long-term yield of a fishery, it is worth considering what forms of control are likely not only to be effective, but also implementable. Limiting the size of the harvested fish or the extent of catches is not easily enforced. Planning $\bar{F}$ by means of controlling the building and power of fleets, and changing mesh sizes, are long-term measures, difficult to implement legislatively because of the "momentum" of the present fishing capital. In what follows we shall assume that we are dealing with a fixed sub-optimal net, and a given $\bar{F}$. The implementable measures we shall consider are:

a) closing certain areas

b) declaring closed times

c) controlling the extent of fishing.

These can be summarized as follows

Find $F(t)$, $t \geq 0$, $0 \leq F(t) \leq \bar{F}$

We shall assume $c = 0$ for simplicity, but the analysis that follows is easily adapted to include it. Similarly discount rates are not considered; these could in fact be regarded as being included in a modified weight function $e^{-rt} w(t)$ since such stringent conditions on the shape of $w(t)$ are no longer needed. The T-dimensional model can now be described:

Let each component $N_i(t)$ of $N \epsilon R^T$ be the number of fish in the age group $[i-1,i)$. Then

$$\frac{dN(t)}{dt} = -\{M + F(t)S(t)\} N(t) \text{ for almost all } t \geq 0 \qquad (3.1)$$

$$N(0) = N_0 \geq 0$$

where M = unit matrix x natural mortality

$F(t) \varepsilon R$, $0 \leq F(t) \leq \bar{F}$, $t \geq 0$ represents fishing intensity

$$S(t) = \begin{bmatrix} s_p(\tau) & & & \\ & s_p(\tau+1) & & 0 \\ & & \ddots & \\ 0 & & & s_p(\tau+T-1) \end{bmatrix}$$

where τ is the fractional part of t and $s_p(t)$ is the selectivity curve as described above for some parameter p.

The objective function is now:

$$\max J = \int_0^\infty F(t)\, W^T(t)\, S(t)\, N(t)\, dt \qquad (3.2)$$

where $W(t) = (w(\tau), w(\tau+1), \ldots, w(\tau+T-1))^T$, τ is the fractional part of t and w(t) is the weight function.

Note that the definition of N(t), S(t), W(t) implies that at times t = 1,2,3 there are discontinuous boundary conditions similar to those used by Walters [7]. Specifically for $j \varepsilon I^+ = \{0,1,2,3,\ldots\}$

$$\begin{array}{lll} N_1(j) = R_j & W_1(j) = w(o) & S_1(j) = S_p(0) \\ N_2(j) = N_1(j-) & W_2(j) = W_1(j-) & S_2(j) = S_1(j-) \\ N_3(j) = N_2(j-) & W_3(j) = W_2(j-) & S_3(j) = S_2(j-) \\ \vdots \quad \vdots & \vdots \quad \vdots & \vdots \\ N_T(j) = N_{T-1}(j-) & W_T(j) = W_{T-1}(j-) & S_T(j) = S_{T-1}(j-) \end{array} \quad (3.3)$$

These relationships are illustrated in Fig. 7.

The system is a T-dimensional Bilinear system as discussed in [11].

We shall also assume that recruitments are equal, stationary, and independent.

$R_j = R \quad j \in I^+.$

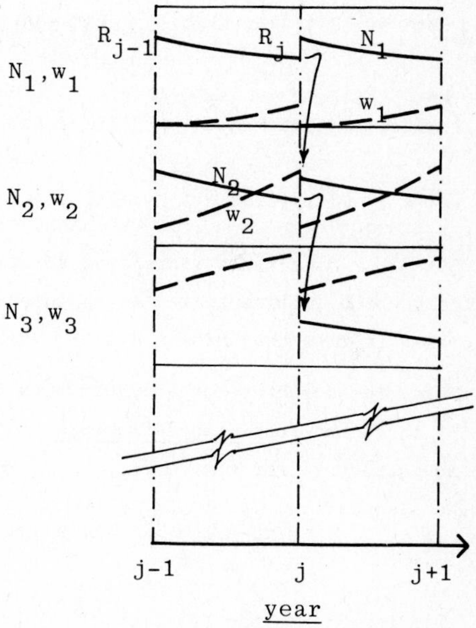

Fig.7. Boundary Conditions.

Periodic Solutions and their Structure

Since the system must be optimized over infinite time, it is reasonable both theoretically and practically to search for periodic solutions.

Definition. The system described by (3.1) and (3.3) is said to be periodic with period P if $F(t) = F(t+P)\ \forall t \geq 0$ and $\bar{t} > 0$ such that $N(\bar{t}) = N(\bar{t}+P) = N(\bar{t}+2P) = \ldots$ (3.4)

The following theorem follows immediately:

Theorem. For any control, if the system described by (3.1) and (3.3) is periodic, then the period time P is an integer.

Proof. Suppose P, the period time is not an integer and let $\bar{t}$ be as in (3.4).

Then $N_1(\bar{t}) = N_1(\bar{t}+P)$ (3.5)

Now choose $t^* = \min\{\ulcorner\bar{t}\urcorner, \ulcorner\bar{t}+P\urcorner\}$

$t^*+\Delta t = \max\{\ulcorner\bar{t}\urcorner, \ulcorner\bar{t}+P\urcorner\}$ where $\ulcorner x\urcorner$ is the fractional part of $x \varepsilon R$.

Since $N_1(i) = R\ \forall i \varepsilon I^+$, and $F(t)$ is periodic

$$(3.5) \Rightarrow Re^{-Mt^* - \int_0^{t^*} F(t+\Delta t)s(t)dt} = Re^{-M(t^*+\Delta t) - \int_0^{t^*+\Delta t} F(t)s(t)dt}$$

i.e. $$\int_0^{t^*} F(t+\Delta t)s(t)dt = M\Delta t + \int_0^{\Delta t} F(t)s(t)dt + \int_{\Delta t}^{t^*+\Delta t} F(t)s(t)dt$$

or $$M\Delta t + \int_0^{\Delta t} F(t)s(t)dt + \int_0^{t^*} F(t+\Delta t)\,\{s(t+\Delta t) - s(t)\}\,dt = 0$$

But $M\Delta t > 0$, $s(t)$ is increasing so all right hand terms ≥ 0. So we get a contradiction, which implies that P is an integer.

Note. Theorem 2 implies that $N(t) = N(t+P)\ \ \forall t \geq 0$.

Next, the structure of a system with integral period P is considered. We define $N^s(0)$ to be the stable age structure at the beginning of the period, with $N^s(t)$ the age structure for $t \in [0,P)$.

We also define:

$$f_i(t_1,t_2) = e^{-M(t_2-t_1) - \int_{t_1}^{t_2} F(t)\ s(i+t)dt} \quad \text{for } (t_1,t_2) \subset [0,P]$$

This represents the fraction of fish left at time t_2 if we start fishing at t_1 and i indicates the age of the fish when we start fishing. Similarly define

$$g_i(t_1,t_2) = \int_{t_1}^{t_2} F(t)w(t)e^{-M(t-t_1) - \int_{t_1}^{t} F(t)s(i+t)dt}dt$$ the total catch from the same year-class over the same time with unit starting conditions.

Periodicity implies that $N^s(0-) = N^s(P-)$

This allows us to construct $N^s(0)$ and define $\alpha_i \varepsilon R$, i=1,2, ... as follows:

$$
\begin{aligned}
N^s_1(O) &= R \\
N^s_2(O) &= N^s_1(P-) = Rf_o(P-1,P) = R\,\alpha_1 \\
N^s_3(O) &= N^s_2(P-) = Rf_o(P-2,P) = R\,\alpha_2 \\
&\vdots \\
N^s_p(O) &= N^s_{p-1}(P-) = Rf_o(1,P) = R\,\alpha_{P-1} \qquad (3.6)\\
N^s_{p+1}(O) &= N^s_p(P-) = N^s_1(O)\ f_o(O,P) \\
N^s_{p+2}(O) &= N^s_{p+1}(P-) = N^s_2(O)\ f_1(O,P) \\
&\vdots \\
N^s_T(O) &= N^s_{T-1}(P-) = N^s_{T-p}(O)\ f_{T-p-1}(O,P) = R\alpha_{T-1}
\end{aligned}
$$

Fig. 8 clarifies what αi, βi represent. Note that constructing $N^s(O)$ from $F^s(t)$, $t\varepsilon[O,P]$ computationally merely requires "wrapping around" the $N^s_i(P-)$ for each i to $N^s_{i+1}(O)$ as illustrated.

It is also apparent that after T years of applying a periodic control to a system with constant recruitment, a stable age structure $N^s(O)$ will be constructed by (3.6)

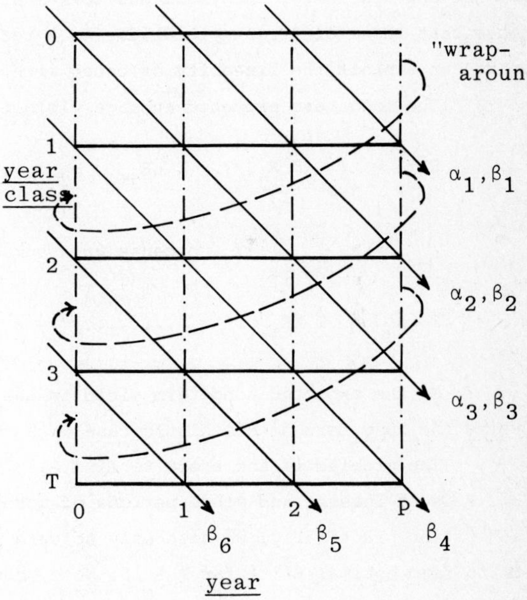

Fig.8. Periodic Structure.

Fig. 8. αi is the fraction of fish left after being fished "along the appropriate "arrow", βi the corresponding catch (T=S,P=3).

We define β_i in a similar way:

If $f_j(t_1,t_2) = \alpha_i$, then $\beta_i = g_j(t_1,t_2)$ $\quad i = 1,2,\ldots T-1$

$$\begin{aligned} \text{and}\quad \beta_T &= g_{T-P}\ (0,P) \\ \beta_{T+1} &= g_{T-P+1}\ (0,P-1) \\ &\vdots \\ \beta_{T+P-1} &= g_{T-1}\ (0,1) \end{aligned} \tag{3.7}$$

Associated with this control and period P is the cost functional derived from (3.2).

$$\text{average yield} = \frac{1}{P} \int_0^P F^s(t)W^T(t)S(t)\ N^s(t)\ dt \tag{3.8}$$

Applying a periodic policy for a long while implies that any recruitment R_j is subject to one of P fishing policies, depending on where within the cycle [0,P] it appears. [e.g. The yield due to R=1 at t=2 in Fig. 8. is $\gamma_3 = \beta_1 + \alpha_1\beta_4$.] Suppose that these different yields due to a recruitment R=1 are $(\gamma_1, \gamma_2, \ldots, \gamma_p)$; then we can exploit the linearity of catch with recruitment as follows.

The long term expected average yield is given by:

$$E[Y] = \sum_{j=0}^{\infty} (E[R_j]\ \gamma_1 + E\ [R_{j+1}]\ \gamma_2 + \ldots + E\ [R_{j+p}]\ \gamma_p)$$

$$= R \sum_{j=0}^{\infty} \sum_{i=1}^{p} \gamma_i \quad \text{because we assumed } R_i\text{'s independent and}$$

$$E\ [R_j] = E\ [R_{j+1}] = \ldots\ldots = R$$

So the expected long term yield is the same as that obtained by considering the long term deterministic case with constant recruitment R.

The problem is therefore to find P, $F^s(t)$ for $t \in [0,P]$ so as to maximize (3.8). P is an integer and since periods of more than fifteen years are beyond consideration practically, we need only solve a finite number of optimizations of (3.8) to find optimal $F^s(t)$ for $P \leq 15$. Note, however, that we do not claim to solve the long-term problem, only the periodic one.

Numerical Solutions of the Periodic Problem

The periodic formulation of the problem can be transformed into a standard P-dimensional problem as discussed in [11]. It can be solved using numerical algorithms for constrained control such as those in [11], [12], [13].

The Switching-Time-Variation Method (STVM) by Mohler [11] was used to find controls that satisfied the Strong Maximum Principle and could reasonably be assumed to be global solutions. However, the implementation of the algorithm is difficult and computationally time consuming (especially evaluating the switching curve). Several other simply implementable techniques were also used to get suboptimal solutions. The three procedures are described below.

i) Following Hannesson [3] and to a certain extent Pope [4] we assume that we fish for one of every P years. A one-dimensional minimization is then carried out on the degree of fishing intensity during that year. However, above a certain low P, the required intensity rapidly exceeds physical bounds. Hannesson [3] achieved better results because he was also selecting the cut-off age of the mesh t_k. The results, however, were inferior to ii) below.

ii) In this method the full fishing capacity $\bar{F}$ was implemented and it was assumed that the single stretch of fishing during [O,P] would end at P. The starting time $t_1 \varepsilon [O,P]$ was then chosen to maximize the yield. The results of this crude method were surprisingly good. A two-dimensional search on both the starting and finishing times $[t_1, t_2] \subset [O,P]$ improved the yield marginally (<1%).

iii) The Switching-Time-Variation Method was used with much difficulty. Forming the Hamiltonian, one must define an adjoint variable as in the single-dimensional case and deduce boundary conditions at integral times similar to (3.3) (see [10]). A version of the Strong Maximum Principle indicates that the optimal strategy must be "bang-bang".

If the selectivity curve was very steep, then the best policy within a period usually consisted of about P/2 gradually lengthening pulses, the total duration of which was roughly the solution of ii) above. Shallow selectivity curves tended to reduce the number of pulses within each period. Again their total duration was that of ii).

Notes

1) Two one-year periods are a local solution of the two-year single period problem and similarly for longer periods. This is an example of a Hamiltonian with several local minima in function space.

2) Yields of up to 9.34% increase on the maximum sustainable yield were possible with current data on the North Sea 3N-O cod stock with $\bar{F}$=2., a reasonable figure. It was generally indicated that improvements in yield due to periodic policies are chiefly attained due to using the full available intensity for a certain length of time.

3) The yields are relatively insensitive to the actual distribution of this length of time, the optimal yield using iii) never exceeding that of ii) by more than 1% in the examples used. This indicates that simple optimizations such as ii), possibly extended to two dimensions, would yield results as good practically as those by the sophisticated but

much more difficult techniques.

4) It is important to realize that if one is pulsing with large fishing intensity, the solution is more sensitive to small variations in the total length of fishing time, so this must be strictly determined and implemented.

5) When $c \neq 0$ or $r \neq 0$ larger improvements than the above are envisaged, partly due to policies like those discussed earlier (chapter 2), and also due to profitability arguments. (e.g. If the total biomass is less than the cost of extracting it, one wouldn't consider fishing. See also [2]).

Table 1 compares the yields obtained by methods i), ii), iii) to the maximum sustainable yield. The data used is that for the ICNAF 3N-O North Sea Cod Fishery. In this case the solution by iii) is the same as the two-dimensional version of ii), i.e. there is only one period of fishing.

The figures refer to percentage improvements on the maximum sustainable yield obtained by F^s (optimal) = .285.

Period	1	3	6	10
i) $\bar{F}$ opt ≤ 2	.285	.883	2.	2.
Increase	0	.59	4.67	decreasing
ii) t_1 (opt)	.86	2.57	4.94	8.22
Increase	1.00	1.54	4.77	9.23
iii) $[t_1,t_2]$(opt)	[.86,1.00]	[3.36,2.07]	[4.36,5.35]	[7.86,9.67]
Increase	1.00	1.62	5.05	9.25

Table 1. Percentage Improvements in Max. Sust. Yield.

CHAPTER 4

NECESSARY CONDITIONS FOR CONTINUED SUSTAINABLE YIELDS

Suppose that we have established a periodic control with period P. Then using (3.6), (3.7) we can construct the corresponding α_i, i=1,T.
β_i, i=1,2,...T+P-1.

Next we define:

$$\bar{b} \in R^p = (\beta_1, \beta_2, \ldots\ldots \beta_p)^T \qquad (4.1)$$
$$b \in R^T = (\beta_{p+1}, \beta_{p+2}, \ldots \beta_{p+T-1}, 0)^T$$
$$a \in R^T = (\alpha_1, \alpha_2, \ldots \alpha_p, 0, \ldots 0)^T$$

$$A \in R^{T\times T} = \left[\begin{array}{ccc} 0 & & 0 \\ \hline \alpha_{p+1} & & \\ & \alpha_{p+2} \quad 0 & \\ 0 & \ddots & 0 \\ & & \alpha_T \end{array}\right] \begin{array}{l} P \\ \\ T-p \\ \\ \\ \end{array}$$

Then just before the beginning of the period of control, we have the age structure N(O-). At the end of the period the new age structure will be N(P-) and they are related as follows:

$$N(P-) = AN(O-) + Ra \qquad (4.2)$$

and the corresponding catch

$$C = b^T N(O-) + (R,R, \ldots R)\, \bar{b} \qquad (4.3)$$

$$= b^T N(O-) + R\beta \qquad \text{where } \beta = \sum_{i=1}^{p} b_i$$

But the stable age structure N^s is invariant under (4.2)

i.e. $\quad N^s(p-) = N^s(O-) = AN^s(O-) + Ra \qquad (4.4)$

or $\quad N^s(O-) = (I-A)^{-1}\, Ra$, a unique solution

(Note $(I-A)^{-1} = I + A + A^2 + \ldots$ converges in a finite number of steps).

$$C_s = R\,\{b^T (I-A)^{-1} a + \beta\} \qquad (4.5)$$

(4.4) and (4.5) are useful expressions for the stable age structure and catch.

We seek conditions on N(O-) that ascertain that the expected yield with variable recruitments R_j ($E[R_j] = R$, $co[R_i, R_j] = 0$, $i \neq j$) from time t = 0 is at least as much as if we had the stable age structure $N^S(0-)$. Thus we can judge whether the fishery is in good shape with respect to its age structure or not. It also provides a convenient target set in planning strategies for the "recovery" of a fishery, understood to mean the above.

Suppose that the age structure just before we start applying the periodic control is $N(0-)$. Note that the two right hand terms in expression (4.3), refer respectively to the catch from the known age structure and future expected recruitments. Then in the first period of control the expected catch:

$EC_1 = b^T N(0-) + E_1$ where E_1 is the expected yield due to new recruitments.

To satisfy the above conditions we require:

$$EC_1 \geq EC_s$$

i.e. $$b^T N(0-) + E_1 \geq b^T N^S(0-) + E_1$$

or $$b^T N(0-) \geq b^T (I-A)^{-1} Ra$$ because recruitments are independent

Similarly we require that in the second period after $t = 0$

$$EC_2 = b^T AN(0-) + E_2 \geq b^T AN_s(0-) + E_2$$

or $$b^T AN(0-) \geq b^T A(I-A)^{-1} Ra$$

The year-classes in $N(0-)$ will only affect the yields over the next $(T-1)$ years or n_p = (integer above $\{(T-1)/p\}$) periods. (Note: $A^{n_p} = 0$).

Proceeding as above we obtain the conditions

$$b^T A^a N(0-) \geq b^T A^i \ (I-A)^{-1} Ra \qquad i=0,1,2,\ldots,(n_p-1) \tag{4.6}$$

As i increases $b^T A^i$ has fewer non-zero elements, so the conditions applies to fewer elements of $N(0-)$, namely, the younger age groups. (3.14) defines a closed non-empty set ($N^S(0-)$ belongs to it) within which we are assured of further yields at least as good as "sustainable" yields with our chosen control policy.

Note that we assume that the <u>average</u> yield over <u>each period</u> of P years is above a certain minimu. The smaller P is, the larger the number of constraint equations on $N(0-)$. This corresponds to controlling the variance of future yields more strictly. For instance, assuring a certain average yield over ten years is easier than assuring the same average yield over each of two five year periods. So we need also to decide how regular we require future yields to be.

A computable constraint equation of the form (4.6) allows us for the first time to formulate strategies for the recovery of a fishery in a control theoretic framework. We first decide on the long term policy we wish to apply (i.e. P and $F(t)$, $t \in [0,P]$). Suppose we decide that Y years is the time within which we wish the fishery to recover if possible. Then, knowing the current age structure N_c, we can construct the constraint set (4.6) and solve the system described by (3.1) and (3.2) with:

$$N(0) = N_c \qquad (4.7)$$

$$\text{and} \quad b_i^T N(Y-) = a_i \qquad i = 0,1,2,\dots(n_{p-1})$$

A Numerical Example

Below are the constraint equations corresponding to being able to preserve a four-yearly average using the maximum-sustainable-yield long term policy for the North Sea ICNAF 3N-O cod stock.

$$F_{max.sust.yield} = .285, \quad T = 12$$

If $N(0-) \in R^{12}$ is the age structure we require:

$$\begin{bmatrix} .70 & 1.04 & 1.61 & 2.16 & 2.76 & 3.41 & 4.16 & 4.98 & 5.01 & 4.47 & 2.99 & 0 \\ .53 & .53 & .60 & .72 & .72 & .64 & .43 & 0 & 0 & 0 & 0 & 0 \\ .14 & .10 & .06 & 0 & 0 & 0 & 0 & 0 & 0 & 0 & 0 & 0 \end{bmatrix} N(0-) \geq \begin{bmatrix} 3.83 \\ 1.39 \\ .198 \end{bmatrix} \qquad (4.8)$$

The following are examples of age structures that satisfy the condition (4.8).

i) The stable age structure $N^s(0-)$ obviously satisfies (4.8) with equality: (.819,.624,.413,.254,.156,.0967,.0595,.0366,.0221,0137,.0087,.0053)

ii) $N^N(0)$, the age structure for constant recruitments R=1 and no fishing, provides upper bounds on the components for constant recruitments. (.819,.670,.549,.449,.368,.301,.247,.202,.165,.135,.111,.091).

iii) In fact, a little less than the first five terms of ii) satisfy (4.8) (.819, .670, .549, .449, .214, 0, 0, 0, 0, 0, 0, 0)
This implies that if the recruitments over the last five years were all R = 1 and we do not interfere with them, the fishery can be said to have recovered, even if there are very few fish of any other age group there.

iv) (5.44, 0, 0, 0, 0, 0, 0, 0, 0, 0, 0, 0).
This shows that one recruitment of 5.44/.819 = 6.72 and no fishing in the subsequent year will also recover the fishery.

v) (2.73, 1.83, 0, 0, 0, 0, 0, 0, 0, 0, 0, 0).
Similar to iv), but requires two recruitments of 3.34 each and two years of no fishing.

These arguments ignore stock-recruitment aspects which could well be affected in such a consideration. However, we have a simple method of determining how to recover a fishery as we learn what the current age structure is. (e.g. We do not fish until the current age structure satisfies 4.8).

The terminal time constraint also allows us to describe an elementary feedback policy in the sense that if we know the current age structure, we can maximize the expected yield over the next t years and still make sure that the expected age structure N(t-) is such that the fishery age-structure is still viable.

CHAPTER 5
COMMENTS

Perhaps the most striking observation throughout this study is that increases in fishing intensity above the level of maximum sustainable yield suffer greatly from diminishing returns, and in fact the best increases over these were less than 10%. Increasing costs reduce the level of intensity even further, provided meshes are correctly selected.

Although the Maximum Principle implies that optimal policies will be "bang-bang", these interact much more strongly with the fishery if they are slightly misused. It may be wiser to sacrifice the slight increase in yield possible by such methods for greater long term stability by using more conservative, low intensity, sustainable yield policies. However, higher costs should yield more benefits from pulse fishing, and the analysis of Chapter 3 could be carried out for a more realistic cost function.

Perhaps the next important improvement to the economic model described in Chapter 2 should be a removal of the assumptions of constant price of fish and constant cost per unit fishing effort. These two variables are closely linked to the discount rate and costs are certainly not linear in fishing effort. A more realistic financial description would probably be solvable by methods such as those described above, but with greater significance.

CHAPTER 6

REFERENCES

1 Beverton, R.J.H. and Holt, S.J., On the Dynamics of Exploited Fish Populations, Fish.Invest. Ser. II, vol. 19, H.M.S.O., London, 1957.

2 Clark, C.G. Edwards and Friedlander, M., J. Fish. Res. Board Can., vol. 30, pp 1629-1640, (1973).

3 Hannesson, R., Economics of Fisheries: Some Problems of Efficiency, Lund Economic Studies, vol. 9, Studentlitteratur , Lund, (1974).

4 Pope, J.G., In The Mathematical Theory of the Dynamics of Biological Populations, edit. M-S. Bartlett and R.W. Hiorns, Academic Press, London and N.Y., pp 23-34, (1973).

5 Goh, B.S., Proc. 6th Hawaii International Conf. System Science, Jan. 8-12, (1972).

6 Turvey, R., Amer. Econ. Rev., Vol. 54, pp 64-77, (1964).

7 Walters, C.J., Trans. Am. Fish. Soc., 98(3): 505-512, (1969).

8 Report of the ICFS/ICNAF Working Group on Cod Stocks in the North Atlantic, Cooperative Research Reports, No. 33, Edit. D.J. Garrod, International Council for the Exploitation of the Sea, Charlottenlund, (1973).

9 Clark, C.W., Mathematical Economics, (in press)

10 Byson, A.E. and Ho, Y., Applied Optimal Control, Ginn & Co., Waltham, Toronto, London (1969).

11 Mohler, R.R., Bilinear Control Processes, Academic Press, London and N.Y., (1973).

12 Jacobson, D.H. and Mayne, D.Q., Differential Dynamic Programming, Elsevier Press, N.Y., (1970).

13 Mayne, D.Q. and Polak, E., J. Optimiz. Theory Applic., vol. 16, no. 3/4, pp. 277-302, (1975).

A CONTROL AND SYSTEMS ANALYSIS OF ARTIFICIAL INSTREAM AERATION

P.G. Whitehead*
Control and Systems Group
Department of Engineering
University of Cambridge
England

ABSTRACT

The identification and estimation of discrete-time models of BOD-DO (Biochemical Oxygen Demand-Dissolved Oxygen) in river systems is considered using a multivariable extension of the instrumental variable approximate maximum likelihood techniques of time series analysis. The dynamic water quality models relate water quality at specific points on the river and are used in a design study to evaluate the performance of artificial aerators in the River Cam. Operating schemes are developed which utilise closed loop state variable feedback control and feedforward control to maintain adequate levels of dissolved oxygen in the river.

1. Introduction

In 1972 a programme of research was initiated in the Control Group at Cambridge in collaboration with the Great Ouse River Division of the Anglian Water Authority and the Department of the Environment. The research has been directed towards obtaining robust, low order models of water quality states in river systems; models that are dynamic and describe the day to day variation in water quality and are stochastic and account for the inevitable uncertainties associated with the system. At the same time the models are designed to be of practical utility and one such design application is described in this paper for the control of oxygen regimes in river systems.

The steadily deteriorating condition of the River Cam in South East England in recent years has led to frequent summer fish mortalities, a condition that may be alleviated in the long term by improved effluent treatment. In the short term, however, artificial instream aeration is considered a viable alternative providing an inexpensive means of improving oxygen regimes in the river. As shown in Figure 1, the effluent from Cambridge Sewage Works produces an oxygen sag, the minimum of which occurs approximately four kilometres downstream. The objective of the aerator system is to raise the level of the dissolved oxygen in the river in order to prevent the dangerously low levels of oxygen at the minimum. The performance of the aerators depends largely on the day to day variations of water quality and environmental conditions and it is necessary therefore to identify and estimate a dynamic water quality model for this stretch of the River Cam prior to the design of a control strategy.

---

*Paul Whitehead is a member of Wolfson College

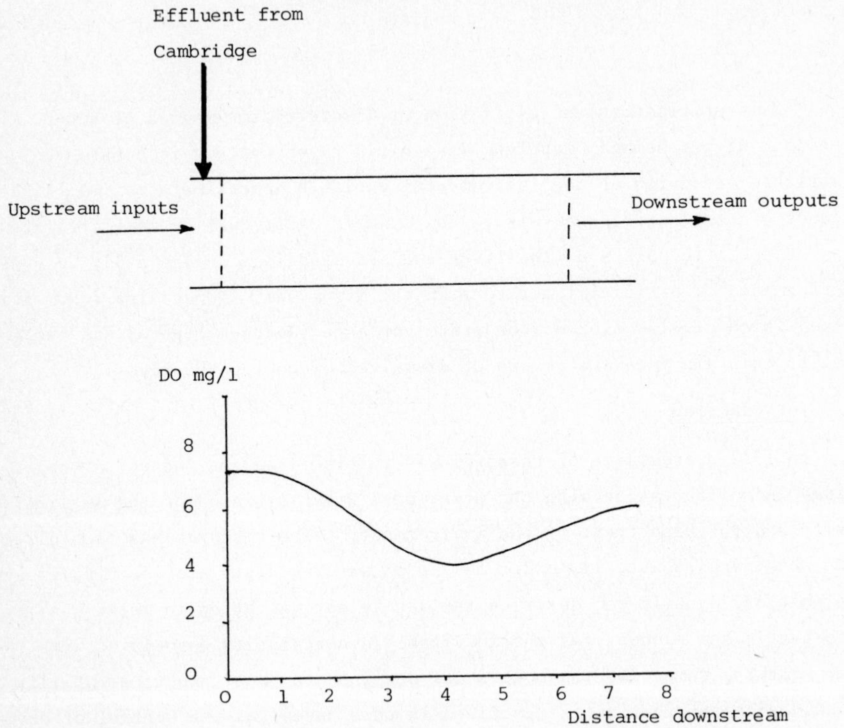

Figure 1 River reach downstream of Cambridge and the Dissolved Oxygen profile.

2. Identification and Estimation of BOD-DO Models

During the early stages of the river system modelling exercises both for the River Cam (see Beck and Young 1974) and for another river, the Bedford Ouse (see Whitehead and Young 1974), the extended Kalman filter (EKF) has proved to be a flexible tool with which to identify suitable dynamic water quality model structures. An initial model is formulated based on some heuristic feeling or physico-chemical understanding of the system, and the EKF is then used to test the efficacy of these models and, where necessary, to supplement the basic model with additional terms to account for disturbances (Beck and Young 1975).

For example by considering bias terms on the system equations as random variables, it was possible to obtain recursive estimates of their variation over the sample period. These estimates showed most variation during periods of prolonged sunlight and, as a result, it was concluded that the discrepancies between the model response and the observed data was most probably due to photosynthetic effects.

Further investigation revealed that in the case of the River Cam, the release of oxygen by photosynthetic activity on algae populations and the BOD load exerted by the mass deaths of algae were both suitably accounted for in terms of a pseudo-empirical relationship dependent upon temperature and sunlight conditions. In order to estimate the effects of photosynthetic activity in the Ouse, chlorophyll A data was recorded in addition to temperature and sunlight and an alternative empirical oxygen production equation was developed which incorporated the algal effects directly. A complete statistical analysis of the BOD-DO model using a continuous discrete version of the EKF is described by Beck and Young (1974).

The identification of the model structure represents an important phase in the analysis and the flexibility of the EKF is an enormous advantage during this initial stage. However, the flexibility can lead to inefficiency, both computation and statistical, when used to *estimate* the parameters that characterise the identified model structure.

An approach to multivariable system parameter estimation which is both more systematic than the EKF and appears to provide a considerable improvement in statistical efficiency involves a multivariable extension of the Instrumental Variable - Approximate Maximum Likelihood (IVAML) method of time-series analysis, previously applied to single input, single output model estimation (Young 1974, Young et al, 1971). The approach is restricted to discrete time, vector matrix equations and requires that most of the state vector is available for measurement.

Consider the following discrete-time, state-space representation of a multivariable (multi-input, multi-output), linear dynamic system,

$$\underline{x}_k = A\underline{x}_{k-1} + B\underline{u}_{k-1} \qquad (1)$$

where $\underline{x}_k = [x_{1k}\ x_{2k}\ \dots\ x_{nk}]^T$ is an n dimensional vector of state variables that characterise the system at the kth instant of time, $\underline{u}_k = [u_{1k}\ u_{2k}\ \dots\ u_{mk}]^T$ is an m dimensional vector of deterministic input variables, also sampled at the kth time instant, while A and B are, respectively, n×n and n×m matrices with elements a_{ij} (i,j = 1,2,...,n) and b_{ij} (i = 1,2,...,n; j = 1,2,...,m).

Suppose now that each element x_{ik} of the state vector $\underline{x}_k$ is available for measurement but is contaminated by a zero mean lumped noise disturbance ξ_{ik} which is assumed to include the effects of all stochastic inputs and other disturbances as well as measurement hoise. The vector of observations $\underline{y}_k = [y_{1k}\ y_{2k}\ \dots\ y_{nk}]^T$ at the kth instant is then defined by

$$\underline{y}_k = \underline{x}_k + \underline{\xi}_k \tag{2}$$

Here $\underline{\xi}_k = [\xi_{1k}\ \xi_{2k}\ \dots\ \xi_{nk}]^T$ is the n dimensional vector of the lumped noise disturbances which is assumed to have the following statistical properties

$$E\{\underline{\xi}_k\} = 0 \quad ; \quad E\{\underline{\xi}_k\underline{\xi}_k^T\} = Q \quad ; \quad E\{\underline{\xi}_k\underline{u}_j^T\} = 0 \text{ , for all } k,j \tag{3}$$

In other words, the noise disturbances are assumed to be zero mean random variables which may, in general, be both serially correlated in time and correlated with each other at the same instant of time, but which are completely uncorrelated with the deterministic input variables that compose the input vector $\underline{u}_k$.

Substituting from equation (2) into (1) we obtain the following relationship between the measured variables

$$\underline{y}_k = A\underline{y}_{k-1} + B\underline{u}_{k-1} + \underline{\eta}_k \tag{4}$$

where $\underline{\eta}_k$ represents the combined effects of the system stochastic disturbances and is defined as

$$\underline{\eta}_k = \underline{\xi}_k - A\underline{\xi}_{k-1} \tag{5}$$

In practice a discrete time model such as (1) could be obtained either by direct analysis of the physical system in discrete time terms, by transformation of an equivalent continuous-time state-space model using standard methods of transformation (Dorf, 1965), or by a combination of both.

The water quality model developed for the River Cam and the Bedford Ouse is in the form of equation (1) with the multivariable model describing the relationships between Biochemical Oxygen Demand (BOD) and Dissolved Oxygen (DO) at the output of a single reach in a non-tidal river system. This model takes the form of two coupled first order equations and can be written as

$$\text{BOD:} \quad x_{1k} = k_1 \frac{Vm}{Q_{k-1}} x_{1,k-1} + k_2u_{1,k-1} + k_3S_{k-1} \tag{6}$$

$$\text{DO:} \quad x_{2k} = k_4x_{1,k-1} + k_5 \frac{Vm}{Q_{k-1}} x_{2,k-1} + k_6u_{2,k-1} + k_7S_{k-1} + k_8C_{s,k-1} \tag{7}$$

where x_1 is the BOD at the output of the reach, which can be considered as an aggregate or macro measure of the oxygen absorbing potential of substances in the stream (such as decaying organic material from effluent discharges), and is defined as the oxygen absorbed in mg ℓ^{-1} over a five day period by a sample of river water in the absence of light at a constant temperature of 20°C;

x_2 is the DO at the output of the reach (mg ℓ^{-1});

Q is the volumetric flow rate in the stream (m^3 day $^{-1}$);

V_m is the mean volumetric hold-up in the reach (m^3);

u_1 is the input BOD from the previous upstream reach in the river system (mg ℓ^{-1});

u_2 is the input DO from the previous upstream reach (mg ℓ^{-1});

S is the term dependent upon sunlight hours and chlorophyl A level to account for photosynthetic effects such as algal growth and decay;

C_s is the saturation concentration of DO (mg ℓ^{-1});

and

$k_1, k_2, \ldots, k_8$ are coefficients or parameters which will be either constant or slowly time-variable depending on the period of observation.

Equations (6) and (7) may be easily written in the vector matrix form of equation (1) by defining the matrices (A;B) and the vectors ($\underline{x}_k$;$\underline{u}_k$) in the following manner:

$$A = \begin{bmatrix} k_1 \frac{V_m}{Q_{k-1}} & 0 \\ k_4 & k_5 \frac{V_m}{Q_{k-1}} \end{bmatrix} \quad ; \quad B = \begin{bmatrix} k_2 & 0 & k_3 & 0 \\ 0 & k_6 & k_7 & k_8 \end{bmatrix} \tag{8}$$

$$\underline{x}_k^T = \begin{bmatrix} x_{1k} & x_{2k} \end{bmatrix} \quad ; \quad \underline{u}_k^T = \begin{bmatrix} u_{1k} & u_{2k} & S_k & C_{s,k} \end{bmatrix}$$

Sampled values for both states can be obtained from a planned experiment: DO is easily measurable by an instream probe; BOD, on the other hand, is somewhat more difficult to estimate since a sample of river water must be kept in controlled conditions for 5 days, as indicated in its definition (indeed the measurement is sometimes termed "5 day BOD"). The resulting measurement equations can be written in the vector form (2) with the elements y_{1k} and y_{2k} of the vector $\underline{y}_k$ denoting the BOD and DO observations, respectively, and with ξ_{1k} and ξ_{2k} denoting the effects of stochastic disturbances and unavoidable measurement noise.

The basic estimation problem posed by equations (1) and (2) is to use the noisy observations of the state variables given in (2) to obtain consistent estimates of the $n^2 + nm$ parameters that characterise the A and B matrices in (1). In order to solve this problem we first note that the ith elemental row of the composite equation (3) can be written as

$$y_{ik} = \underline{z}_k^T \underline{a}_i + \eta_{ik} \tag{9}$$

where
$$\underline{z}_k^T = [y_{1,k-1}\ y_{2,k-1} \ldots y_{n,k-1}, \ldots, u_{m,k-1}]$$
$$\underline{a}_i = [a_{i1}, a_{i2} \ldots a_{in}, b_{i1}, \ldots, b_{im}]^T$$
and
$$\eta_{ik} = \xi_{ik} - a_{i1}\xi_{1,k-1} - , \ldots, - a_{in}\xi_{n,k-1}$$

Thus one simple approach to the problem of estimating the unknown parameters is to decompose the overall estimation problem into n separate sub-problems, each defined in terms of an estimation model such as (9) which is linear in an $n + m$ subset of the $n^2 + nm$ unknown parameters.

In order to obtain a consistent estimate of the parameter vector $\underline{a}_i$ a least squares regression algorithm is modified using the instrumental variable approach described by Young (1970). A recursive algorithm is obtained in which the estimate $\hat{\underline{a}}_{ik}$ after k samples is obtained as the linear sum of the previous estimate $\hat{\underline{a}}_{i,k-1}$ plus a corrective term based on new information y_{ik}, $\underline{z}_k$ and $\hat{\underline{x}}_k$, where $\hat{\underline{x}}_k$ is a vector of instrumental variables (see Young and Whitehead 1974). The recursive estimation algorithm is of the following form.

$$\hat{\underline{a}}_{ik} = \hat{a}_{i,k-1} - \underline{K}_k\{\underline{z}_k^T\hat{\underline{a}}_{i,k-1} - y_{ik}\} \qquad \text{I(1)}$$

where $\underline{K}_k$ is a gain vector defined by

$$\underline{K}_k = \hat{P}_{k-1}\hat{\underline{x}}_k\,[1+\underline{z}_k^T\hat{P}_{k-1}\hat{\underline{x}}_k]^{-1}$$

and the matrix $\hat{P}_k$ is obtained by a second recursive algorithm

$$\hat{P}_k = \hat{P}_{k-1} - \hat{P}_{k-1}\hat{\underline{x}}_k\,[1+\underline{z}_k^T P_{k-1}\hat{\underline{x}}_k]^{-1}\,\underline{z}_k^T\hat{P}_{k-1} \qquad \text{I(2)}$$

The problems of choosing suitable instrumental variable $\hat{\underline{x}}_k$ are discussed in detail by Young and Whitehead (1974) together with a discussion of the modelling problems associated with the noise vector $\underline{\eta}_{ik}$.

The estimation algorithms have been applied to field data obtained from both the Bedford Ouse and the River Cam and a deterministic forecast of BOD and DO is given in Figure 2 for the reach of the Cam where the system model was estimated as

$$\underline{x}_k = \begin{bmatrix} 0.36\dfrac{V_m}{Q_{k-1}} & 0 \\ -0.25 & -0.26\dfrac{V_m}{Q_{k-1}} \end{bmatrix} \underline{x}_{k-1} + \begin{bmatrix} 0.27 \\ 0.33 \end{bmatrix} \begin{bmatrix} L_{k-1} \\ C_{k-1} \end{bmatrix} + \begin{bmatrix} 0.43 \\ 0.84 \end{bmatrix} S_{k-1} + \begin{bmatrix} 0 \\ 0.1 \end{bmatrix} C_{s_{k-1}}$$

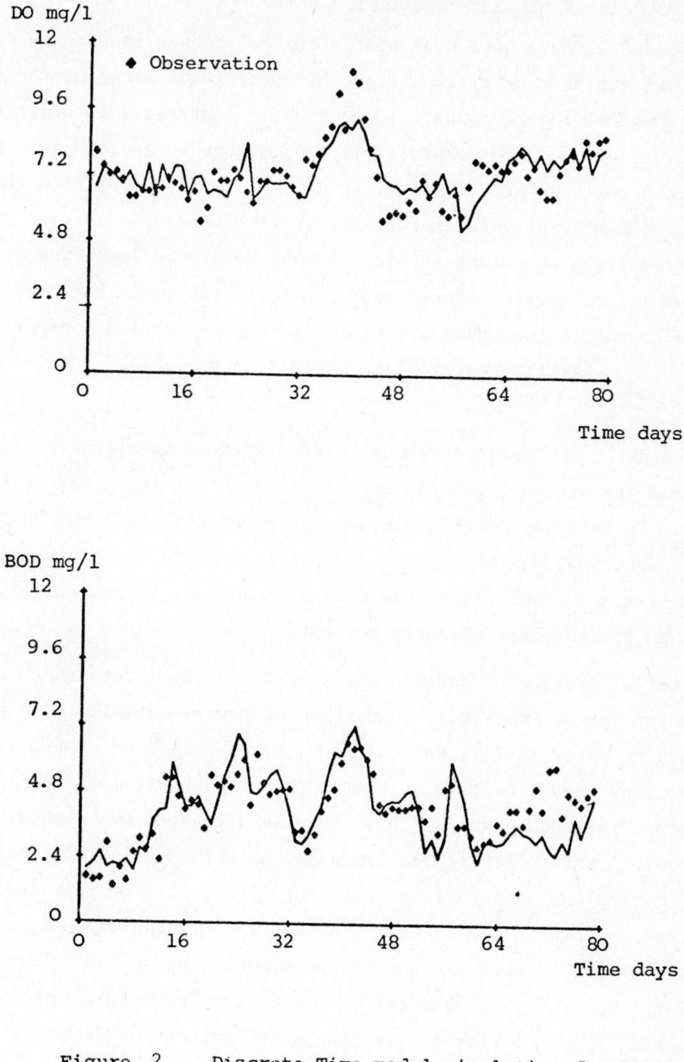

Figure 2 Discrete Time model simulation for BOD-DO on River Cam.

This simple discrete time model adequately describes the dynamic behaviour of BOD and DO over the 80 day summer period in 1972 and may be used in an aerator design study.

3. Techniques for Water Quality Control

Dynamic models have been used widely in the process industries for the design and evaluation of engineering systems from the operational management viewpoint. Often complex chemical reactions have to be closely controlled in order to meet product specifications and, for example, it is possible by continuously monitoring a quality state downstream of a reactor, to detect any deviation from the specified desired level and take whatever remedial action is required to correct the situation. The idea of monitoring, detecting an error from a reference level and then taking remedial action is, of course, closed loop control; the loop is closed either by the operational managers, who take a decision to change certain appropriate variables in the system or by automatic controllers which directly adjust the input control variables.

The design of automatic feedback control systems is aided considerably by a dynamic model of the system which can be used in place of the plant in an "off-line" design study. In this way experimentation on the plant, which may be both expensive and dangerous, can be avoided. Bearing in mind the experience of the Process Industries, it seems clear that feed back control is potentially an extremely useful technique in the water resource context.

One control problem of particular interest is the maintenance of dissolved oxygen levels in rivers immediately downstream of sewage outfalls. A recently formed Cam working party (1974), for instance, has the task of controlling dissolved oxygen in the River Cam downstream of Cambridge sewage works in order to prevent fish mortalities. Young and Beck (1974) have investigated two methods of maintaining the DO level in this reach of the Cam using either a variable effluent quality from the treatment plant or a variable effluent discharge rate into the river. For both control systems it was assumed that BOD information was not available and that only the dissolved oxygen was continuously monitored at the downstream point. Such schemes are, however, high capital cost solutions requiring long term justification and, for full flexibility, the Water Authority may often have to look for lower cost, albeit temporary, alternatives.

On low-cost alternative approach to the maintenance of dissolved oxygen levels in a river system is by artificial aeration using mechanical aerators. This has obvious practical advantages since it does not rely on purpose built treatment plants and avoids the high capital cost of building such plants. However, artificial aerators should always be viewed as a temporary solution since they cannot cope with a continually worsening effluent from an overloaded sewage works; indeed this may well tend to mask a slowly deteriorating situation.

Artificial aeration of polluted rivers has been investigated both experimentally and theoretically by Whipple et al (1970) and it has been used for some time in practical situations as a method of alleviating pollution problems. The principle is simply to increase the air-water interfacial area, either by the additional turbulence introduced by mechanical aerators or by the entrained bubbles generated by a diffuser, and thereby to increase the rate of transfer of oxygen from the air to the water.

If instream aeration is proposed as a short term solution to a particular river water quality problem then it is clearly desirable to have some form of control system to operate the aerators so as to maintain the desired level of DO. And it is for the design of such a control scheme that a dynamic model of BOD-DO can be of particular relevance.

4. An instream aeration control study on the Bedford-Ouse

Conventional controllers for aerator equipment utilise an upstream probe to monitor continuously dissolved oxygen. The aerator equipment is switched on immediately a low level of upstream DO is detected. This may not be satisfactory if high levels of BOD are present since it is the DO level downstream of the aerator that will tend to be depressed (i.e. fish mortalities occur at the minimum point of the dissolved oxygen sag which mught often occur downstream of the aerator). On the other hand a dissolved oxygen probe located close to the average minimum DO position would feedback information on the critical DO level and aerator operation would be on the basis of this measurement. The influence of upstream water quality is still important, however, since it gives prior warning of high BOD loads: the upstream DO probe measures this input disturbance and provides "feedforward" information to the controller.

A feedforward-feedback control strategy is shown on the left of the block diagram in Figure 3 where the gains k_1, k_2 and k_3 represent controller parameters; k_1 influences the direct DO feedback, k_2 is the gain on the integrated error between the dissolved oxygen and the reference level y_r and k_3 is the gain on the feed-forward signal. The summation of these three effects is related to the oxygen input required at the aerators to maintain a constant level of dissolved oxygen at the downstream point. The controller gains affect the transient response of the system and therefore can be designed to meet certain specifications.

For instance, we would require a reasonably fast response to maintain good control but the effect of having large control gains consistent with such performance could be to produce an oscillatory response or large disturbances which would put the model states outside the range over which they have been estimated. Such non - linear or oscillatory conditions are clearly not satisfactory.

There are several techniques for the design of "satisfactory" control systems (see Box and Jenkins, 1974 or Astrom, 1970) but one purely deterministic

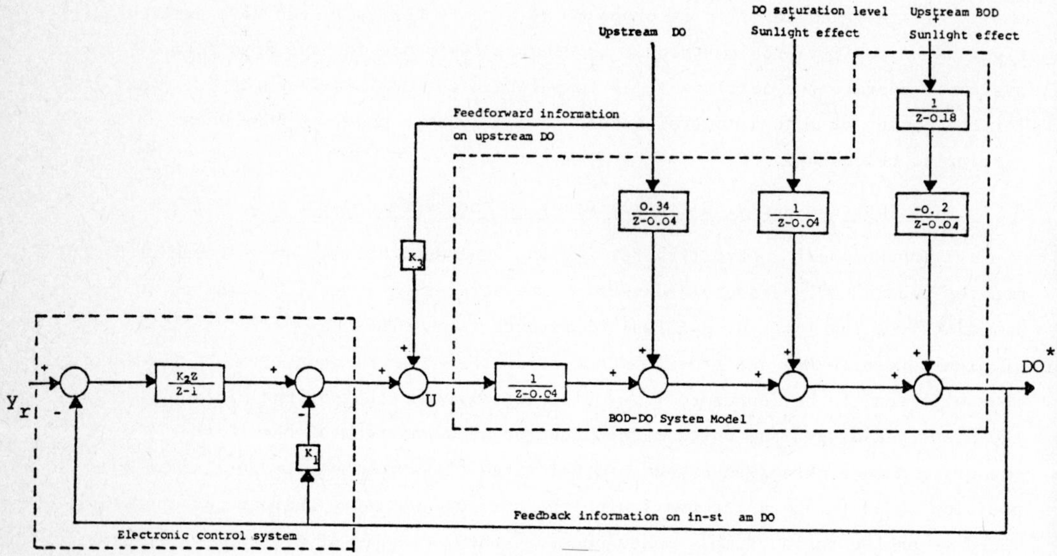

Figure 3 Block diagram of Ouse model and control scheme.

DO^* controlled downstream DO level
U DO input at aerators
y_r DO reference level

technique developed by Young and Willems (1972) is servomechanism "pole assignment". Here the control system gains are chosen to ensure that the dynamic modes of behaviour of the closed loop system are of a suitable frequency and damping; and at the same time, that the steady state or equilibrium characteristics are consistent with the specified "acceptable" levels of DO.

In discrete time terms, the servomechanism pole assignment technique has been described by Young and Beck (1974) and we shall consider it briefly for completeness.

Consider the discrete-time system described by the state equations

$$\begin{aligned} \underline{x}_{k+1} &= F\underline{x}_k + G\underline{u}_k \\ \underline{y}_k &= C\underline{x}_k \end{aligned} \tag{10}$$

where $\underline{x}_k$ represents the system states at time k (i.e. downstream BOD and DO)

$\underline{u}_k$ represents the control input vector at time k

$\underline{y}_k$ represents the state observations at time k

F, G and C are matrices of coefficients.

In order to introduce an "integral of error" term between the desired reference level $[\underline{y}r]_{k+1}$ and the controlled state $\underline{y}_{k+1}$ an additional equation is adjointed to the system equations (see Young and Beck 1974)

$$\underline{w}_{k+1} = \underline{w}_k + T\left([\underline{y}r]_{k+1} - C\underline{x}_{k+1}\right) \tag{11}$$

We see that provided the system is stable so that a steady state exists then $\underline{w}_{k+1} = \underline{w}_k$ and as desired $\underline{y}_k = C\underline{x}_k = \underline{y}_r$.

On substituting from the system equations (10), we see that equation (11) becomes

$$\underline{w}_{k+1} = \underline{w}_k + T\left([\underline{y}r]_{k+1} - CF\underline{x}_k - CG\underline{U}_k\right) \tag{12}$$

The overall system equation is then obtained by combining the two equations (10) and (12) above as follows

$$\begin{bmatrix} \underline{x} \\ \underline{w} \end{bmatrix}_{k+1} = \begin{bmatrix} F & 0 \\ -TFC & I \end{bmatrix} \begin{bmatrix} \underline{x} \\ \underline{w} \end{bmatrix}_k + \begin{bmatrix} G \\ -TCG \end{bmatrix} u_k + \begin{bmatrix} 0 \\ TI \end{bmatrix} [\underline{y}_r]_{k+1} \tag{13}$$

The state variable feedback control law is now defined as

$u = -(k_1 x_{1k} + k_2 x_{2k} \ldots k_n x_{nk})$ or in vector form

$$u = -k^T \underline{x}_k \tag{14}$$

where $k_1, k_2 \ldots k_n$ are controller gains used to assign the poles of the closed loop system to arbitrary (within physical reason) positions inside the unit circle in the complex plane, and to provide reasonable closed loop control dynamics.

In the above context, the control problem of aerating the river reduces to a single variable problem on the DO state since the BOD state cannot be controlled by re-aeration and, for the purposes of control can be considered simply as an additional distrubance term.

Under this assumption the linear state variable feedback law equation (14) u_k reduces therefore to

$$u_k = -(k_1 x + k_2 w) \qquad (15)$$

with state variable feedback on the DO state, x, together with the integral error, w.

Evaluating equation (13) for the Bedford Ouse reach (see Whitehead and Young, 1974) for the summer condition of mean $v/_Q = 2.0$ gives

$$\begin{bmatrix} x_{k+1} \\ w_{k+1} \end{bmatrix} = \begin{bmatrix} 0.04 & 0 \\ -0.04 & 1 \end{bmatrix} \begin{bmatrix} x_k \\ w_k \end{bmatrix} + \begin{bmatrix} k^T \\ -k^T \end{bmatrix} \begin{bmatrix} x_k \\ w_k \end{bmatrix} + \begin{bmatrix} 0 \\ 1 \end{bmatrix} [y_r]_{k+1}$$

which can be written concisely

$$\begin{bmatrix} Z-0.04+k_1 & k_2 \\ 0.04-k_1 & Z-1-k_2 \end{bmatrix} \begin{bmatrix} x_k \\ w_k \end{bmatrix} = \begin{bmatrix} 0 \\ 1 \end{bmatrix} [y_r]_{k+1} \qquad (16)$$

where Z is the z transform or forward shift operator, i.e. $Zx_k = x_{k+1}$.

The closed loop characteristic equation can then be obtained in the usual manner (see Takahashi 1970) as the

$$\det \begin{bmatrix} Z - 0.04 + k_1 & k_2 \\ 0.04-k_1 & Z-1-k_2 \end{bmatrix} = 0$$

$$\text{i.e. } Z^2 + Z(k_1 - k_2 - 1.04) + (0.04-k_1) = 0 \qquad (17)$$

The desired closed loop pole positions in the Z plane can be obtained in various ways but here they were set at -0.06 ± 0.13 in order to yield for a damping ratio of 0.7 and a natural frequency of 2 rad/day. These pole positions give a characteristic equation of the form

$$Z^2 + 0.12 + 0.017 \qquad (18)$$

and, equating the coefficients of (17) and (18), produces the following laws, which will theoretically ensure the desired closed loop pole positions.

$$0.12 = k_1 - k_2 - 1.04$$

and

$$0.017 = 0.04 - k_1$$

giving

$$k_1 = 0.023$$

$$k_2 = 1.14$$

At this stage we have defined the closed loop characteristics but we still require to minimise the input DO disturbance.

A possible deterministic method of minimising this unwanted disturbance is to insert into the system a feedforward branch whose input is the unwanted disturbance. The method is only applicable to those systems in which a disturbance can be physically detected but in the river system the upstream input DO may be measured continuously or discretely via an instream probe. The principle of invariance (D'Azzo and Houpis 1966) is used to determine the gain k_3 on the feed-forward branch where k_3 is chosen to minimise the input DO effect. From Figure 3 we see that the DO disturbance is given by

$$D = \frac{0.34}{(Z-0.04)}$$

and, the total effect of the feedforward compensator F_c is

$$F_c = \frac{k_3}{(Z-0.04)} \tag{19}$$

The effect of the observed disturbance will be cancelled if we set the compensation to

$$F_c = \frac{-0.34}{(Z\ 0.04)}$$

i.e. $k_3 = -0.34$ (20)

Such deterministic feedforward control is particularly sensitive to errors in the model parameters and should, therefore, be used with caution in a practical situation; indeed the design should always be checked by extensive stochastic simulation prior to any attempt at implementation.

In the latter connection, it will be noted that following the lead of Young and Beck (1974) purely deterministic control system design has been considered here despite the fact that stochastic models are available. This was considered advisable in the first instance since it is simple and because it provides a reference against which to judge stochastic designs that may be conceived at a later stage. Too often in the current control theory orientated world of control, "optimal" and complex solutions are considered first and, in consequence, simpler possibilities receive less than adequate attention.

Figure 4 shows the simulated response of the control system designed above to a step change in the reference level from six to seven mg/l on day 15; immediately the error between the downstream DO and the reference level is observed the control signal increases and the instream DO moves up to the new desired level

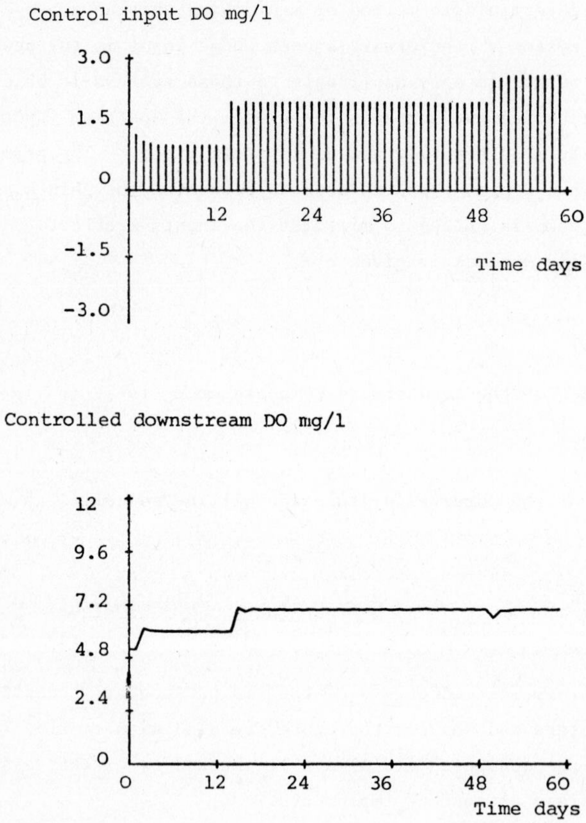

<u>Figure 4</u> Downstream DO and input control signal

with a response speed defined by the control system design. On day 50 the response of the system to a step change of 3mg/l in the BOD is shown; here the DO decreases initially but the controller acts to minimise the discrepancy from the desired level and the DO slowly recovers again in a manner defined by the control system design.

Figure 4 illustrates the control action with no additional distrubances, such as algal or sunlight effects. Figure 5, on the other hand, shows the simulated response of the hypothetical reaeration control system acting on the reach over a "typical" summer period based primarily on the 1973 data but assuming an additional BOD load of 5mg/l in the river. With the DO desired reference level at 6 mg/l, it is clear that the reaerator control signal varies continuously over the period in order to minimise the effects of all the disturbances and the instream DO level oscillates only slightly around the reference level, indicating the efficacy of the control system design at least from the simulation viewpoint.

5. An application of instream aeration in the River Cam

The possibility of maintaining automatic control over water quality in a river system is of immediate interest to the Great Ouse River Division of the Anglian Water Authority following the report of the GORD working party on dissolved oxygen in the Cam (1975). The steadily deteriorating situation in the river downstream of Baits-Bite appears to be due to the combined effects of unsatisfactory sewage effluents caused by overloading at Cambridge sewage works, pumping station overflows, and finally, the marked diurnal variations in DO that appear in the reach during prolonged periods of dry, sunny weather and are probably due to the presence of large algae populations that become established in the nutrient rich environment downstream of the sewage outfall (Beck and Young 1975). The influents tend to depress the overall DO level and this, combined with the large diurnal variations, provide a DO level at night which is sometimes insufficient to support fish life. Fish mortalities and pollution have occurred in the reach from Baits-Bite to Bottisham - the reach of the Cam studied by Beck in 1972.

The planned expansion of the sewage works will not be operational until 1978 and the recommendation of the working party was, therefore, to alleviate the short term problem by installing artificial aerators in the Cam downstream of Baits-Bite. Since the transient violations of water quality are of importance in this problem the dynamic model may be used to assess the effect of the aerators and develop a possible control strategy.

The discrete dynamic BOD-DO model for the Cam described in section 2 was based on the mid-day DO levels. In the present study, therefore, it was necessary to re-estimate the model using the 7 am DO values which represented approximately the daily minimum of the diurnal cycle. The model obtained from this analysis was as follows for mean $Vm/Q_{k-1} = 0.9$ days

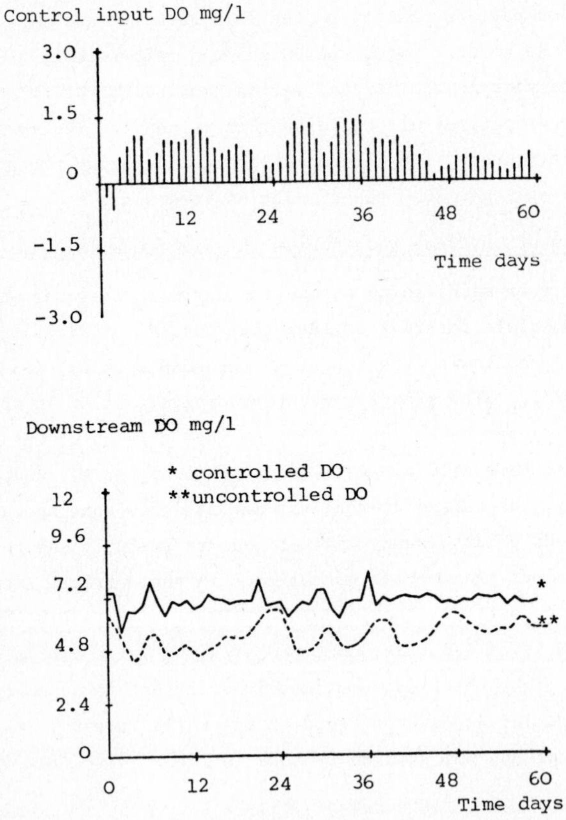

Figure 5 Downstream DO level and Control signal using 1973 summer data on the River Ouse.

$$x_k = \begin{bmatrix} 0.32 & 0 \\ -0.41 & 0.02 \end{bmatrix} x_{k-1} + \begin{bmatrix} 0.41 & 0 \\ 0 & 0.05 \end{bmatrix} \begin{bmatrix} L_{k-1} \\ C_{k-1} \end{bmatrix}$$

$$+ \begin{bmatrix} 0.14 \\ 0.21 \end{bmatrix} S_{k-1} + \begin{bmatrix} 0 \\ 0.73 \end{bmatrix} C_{s_{k-1}} \qquad (21)$$

On the basis of the above model a feedback-feedforward control scheme similar to that for the Ouse was developed, in which the controller gains were found to be

$k_1 = 0.003$
$k_2 = -1.03$
$k_3 = -0.05$

An additional facility is included in the Cam controller so that the control only operates when the dissolved oxygen level falls below the reference level of 6 mg/l. This is an obvious practical requirement since it is unnecessary to operate the aerators when high DO levels exist.

The controller was applied initially to the Cam Model using the 1972 summer data. Figure 6 shows the sustained high levels of DO throughout the summer and the control signal or aerator input remains zero for much of the time and only 1 mg/l of dissolved oxygen was required after day 46. In order to test the control scheme under more difficult conditions, an additional effluent loading of 5 mg/l of BOD was input into the reach model and a typical simulation run with control under these conditions is shown in Figure 7. The controlled response is reasonably constant at 6 mg/l but, as with the Ouse example, the discrete control law cannot counteract all the disturbances and some minor oscillation about the reference is obtained. The control signal shows an input of oxygen over the entire period and this increases to a maximum of about 3 mg/l after day 45 at the end of the sunny period. The control input during the sunny period is reduced since there is a net input of DO from the photosynthetic and respiratory effects.

The analysis indicates that, during poor quality conditions, up to 3 mg/l of additional downstream dissolved oxygen will be required. On the basis of WRPL tests on the proposed aerator equipment three aerators would be required to provide the additional DO and so help to prevent the possibility of a fish kill. It is clear, however, that at certain times less reaeration is required and one or two aerators would suffice to maintain satisfactory instream DO. It is necessary, therefore, to consider how the control system can be modified to allow for the efficient and flexible operation of the three aerators.

The aerator efficiency R is related to the power rating P by the following relationship

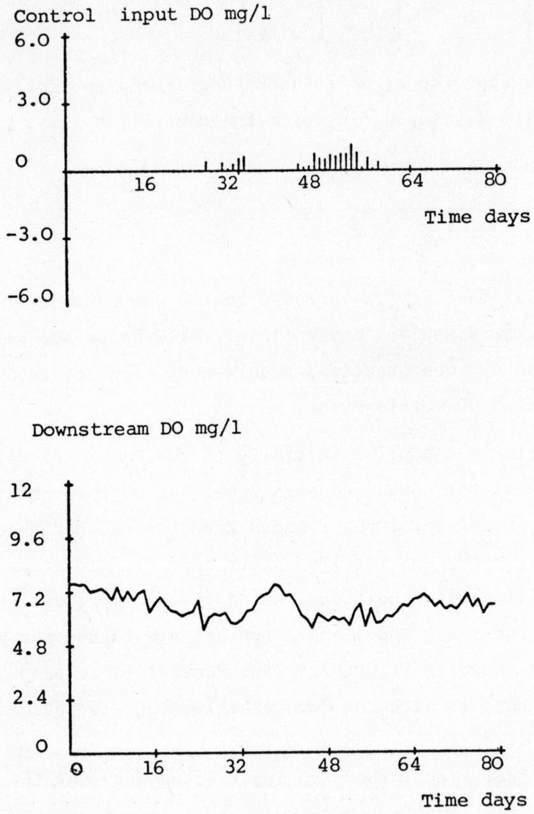

Figure 6 Downstream DO level and associated control input for the Cam over Summer 1972.

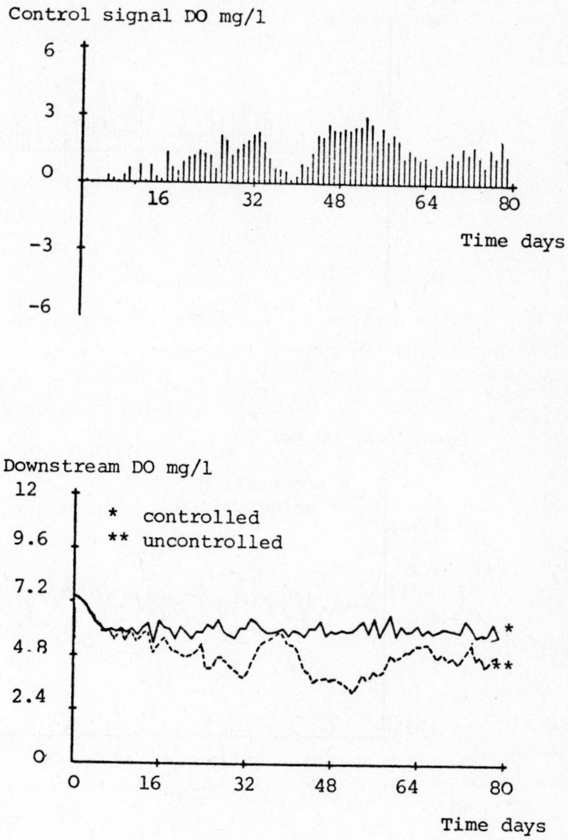

Figure 7 Controlled downstream DO for River Cam given additional effluent loading.

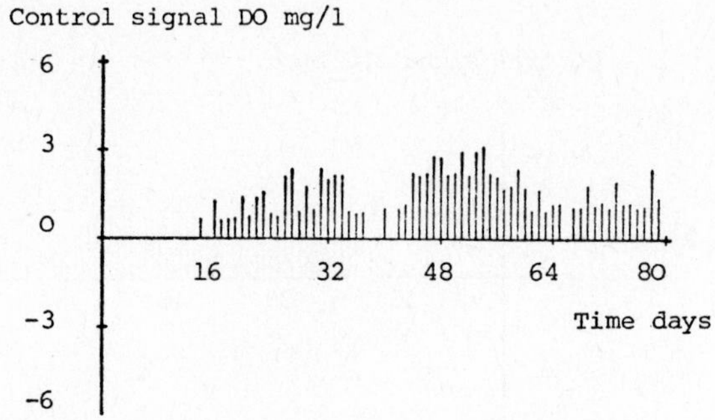

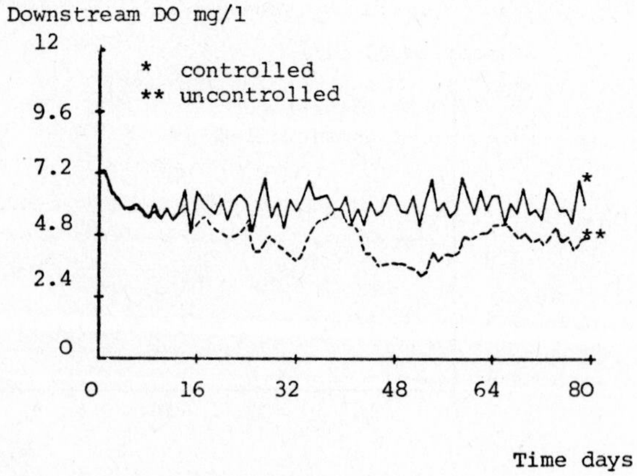

Figure 8 Control using three aerators.

$$R = \frac{k(C_s - C)}{P} \qquad (22)$$

where $C_s - C$ is the saturation oxygen deficit and k is a coefficient of aeration. At the low flow conditions in the Cam k/P is calculated from the manufacturers' literature and the WPRL trials as 0.18. The siting of the aerators on the river is likely to influence their performance since if the aerated water stream from an upstream aerator passes into the intake of a second aerator, the efficiency of the second aerator will be low. The aerators should, therefore, be separated by a suitable distance to ensure adequate mixing. Even so, the saturation deficit will be successively smaller at the second and third aerator and this effect can be assessed using equation (22): at each aerator the new saturation deficit is determined and the oxygen level increases in a stepwise fashion down the river each time with a successively smaller step.

The theoretical control signal shown in Figure 7 does not contain this kind of stepwise operation and a modified control signal including the aerator efficiency factor is determined such that, at each step, the best use of the available aerators is achieved. In effect, a three level control signal is used consistent with the three levels available for the aeration equipment. This modified control scheme is shown in Figure 8 and a clear stepwise input is obtained. Of course, the step size does vary slightly according to the saturation deficit which itself varies with temperature: but nevertheless the three level control action still maintains an adequate DO level in the river despite the obvious quantisation error introduced by the use of only three discrete levels of control.

6. Conclusions

This preliminary study has shown that the application of aerators in the Cam appears to be a satisfactory solution to the problem of maintaining safe DO levels in the river. The Great Ouse River Division have now purchased three aerators for use in the River Cam and it is proposed that the control system be evaluated on-line.

The application of relatively simple feedforward-feedback controllers to the problems of water quality control immediately downstream of major sewage discharges is considered a highly practical approach and one that will become increasingly attractive as sewage plants become more flexible.

In addition, the application of the recursive algorithms to the estimation of model parameters provides models which are statistically efficient and which may be estimated from field data, data that is often corrupted by high levels of measurement noise.

References

Beck, M.B., and Young, P.C.,(1975), Identification and Parameter Estimation of DO-BOD models using the Extended Kalman Filter, CUED/F - CONTROL/TR93 (1975). University of Cambridge. Engineering Department.

Beck, M.B., and Young, P.C., (1975), A Dynamic Model for BOD-DO Relationships in a Non-Tidal River, Water Research, to be published 1975.

Box, G. and Jenkins, G.M., (1970), Time Series Analysis Forecasting and Control, Holden Day.

D'Azzo, J.J., and Houpis, C.H., Feedback Control Analysis and Synthesis, McGraw Hill, 1966.

Dorf, R.C., Time Domain Analysis and Design of Control Systems, Addison-Wesley, 1965.

Report of the Working Party on Dissolved Oxygen, Artificial Aeration of the River Cam, Anglian Water Authority, 1974.

Takahashi, Y. Rabins, M.J., Auslander, D.M., Control and Dynamic Systems, Addison-Esley, 1970.

Young, P.C., (1970) Automatica, Vol.7, No.2 p 271.

Young, P.C., Shellswell, S.H., Neethling, C.G., (1971), Tech. Report., Dept. of Engineering, University of Cambridge, CUED/B - CONTROL/TR16.

Young, P.C., and Beck, M.B., (1974). The Modelling and Control of Water Quality in a River System, Automatica Vol.10 No.5 pp 455-468.

Young, P.C., and Whitehead, P.G., (1974). 77 Recursive Approach to Time-Series Analysis for Multivariable Systems, Proc. IFIP Working Conference on Modelling and Simulation of Water Resource Systems, Ghent, Belgium (July/August), North Holland, Amsterdam.

Whipple, W.N., Coughlan, F.P., and Yu, S.L., Instream Aeration for Polluted Rivers, ASCE, JSED, October 1970.

Whitehead, P.G., and Young, P.C., (1974), A Dynamic Stochastic Model for Water Quality in part of the Bedford Ouse River System, Proc. IFIP Working Conf. on Modelling and Simulation of Water Resources Systems. Ghent. Belgium (July/August) North-Holland. Amsterdam.

MODELING DISPERSION IN A SUBMERGED SEWAGE FIELD

J. SPRIET
G.C. VANSTEENKISTE
University of Ghent and Brussels
BELGIUM

G. BARON
S.J. WAJC
University of Brussels
BELGIUM

Several large urban communities located on a sea shore utilise - or consider utilizing - a deceptively simple system of disposal of their sewage water : after a rough preliminary treatment (sedimentation), the liquid is pumped to a linear diffusor anchored on the sea-floor, at several km from the shore under a submergence of some 50 m. The diffusor itself is a sparger pipe, 2 to 4 m in diameter, and pierced with equidistant side holes of 5 to 10 cm diameter. When the sea current is naught, the buoyant jets formed at the side holes unite near the diffusor into a linear vertical buoyant plume whose behaviour was studied in great detail for the case of laminar flow [1, 2, 3] and for that of turbulent flow [4, 5, 6]. It has been shown, for instance, that the maximum density difference between sea water and the plume decreases asymptotically (when the distance to the diffusor, y, increases) like $y^{-3/5} F_o^{4/5}$ for laminar flow, and like $y^{-1} F_o^{2/3}$ for turbulent flow. As the submergence is finite, these plumes are eventually deflected into horizontal buoyant plumes, either at the sea surface or at the level of a thermocline (see infra) if the flux of density difference per unit length of diffusor, F_o, is small enough.

The structure of these horizontal buoyant plumes has not yet been thoroughly investigated, and therefore prevailing design methods of marine sewage disposal systems [6] take only the dispersion in vertical plumes into account. It has occured to us that a detailed study of the dispersion properties horizontal buoyant plumes might be rated higher than an academic exercise by people willing to swim along the French Riviera. This paper then gives our main results for the case of linear laminar horizontal buoyant plumes ; the turbulent case and the axisymetric cases will be published elsewhere.

1. Asymptotic form of the conservation equations

When the Boussinesq hypothesis pertaining to natural convection in a quasi-incompressible fluid applies, the momentum and energy equations assume the following form for bi-dimensional flow [Ox is horizontal, Oy is vertical upwards] :

$$\frac{\partial(\Delta\psi,\psi)}{\partial(x,y)} = -\frac{\partial\Theta}{\partial x} + \frac{1}{Gr^{1/2}} \Delta^2 \psi \qquad (1.1)$$

$$\frac{\partial(\Theta,\psi)}{\partial(x,y)} = \frac{1}{Pr.Gr^{1/2}} \Delta\Theta \qquad (1.2)$$

The plumes studied here are in fact Prandtl boundary layers along the Ox axis. To find their asymptotic solution for $Gr \to \infty$ in the vicinity of $y = o$ (inner solution), one has to stretch y and ψ as follows :

$$Y = y.Gr^{2/10} \qquad \text{and} \qquad \Psi = \psi.Gr^{3/10} \qquad (1.3)$$

The fundamental term in the inner solution satisfies then :

$$\frac{\partial\Psi}{\partial Y}\frac{\partial^3\Psi}{\partial x\,\partial Y^2} - \frac{\partial\Psi}{\partial x}\frac{\partial^3\Psi}{\partial Y^3} = -\frac{\partial\Theta}{\partial x} + \frac{\partial^4\Psi}{\partial Y^4} \qquad (1.4)$$

$$\frac{\partial\Psi}{\partial Y}\frac{\partial\Theta}{\partial x} - \frac{\partial\Psi}{\partial x}\frac{\partial\Theta}{\partial Y} = \frac{1}{Pr}\frac{\partial^2\Theta}{\partial Y^2} \qquad (1.5)$$

The inner solution will be valid to order $O(Gr^{-2/10})$

2. Superficial horizontal buoyant plumes

When the plume is formed at the sea-surface, the solution of (1.4) (1.5) must satisfy the following boundary conditions :

$Y = o$: $\Psi = o$ (the surface is a stream-line) (2.1)

$\frac{\partial^2\Psi}{\partial Y^2} = o$ (no shear stress at the surface) (2.2)

$\frac{\partial\Theta}{\partial Y} = o$ (no heat flux to the atmosphere) (2.3)

$Y = \infty$ $\frac{\partial\Psi}{\partial Y} = o$ (no velocity in the x direction far from the surface) (2.4)

$\Theta = o$ (no effect on specific mass far from the surface) (2.5)

This problem admits the following similarity solution :

$$\Psi = \sqrt{x}\,.\,f(\eta) \quad , \qquad \Theta = \frac{1}{\sqrt{x}}\,.\,g(\eta) \qquad (2.6)$$

where the similarity variable is

$$\eta = \frac{Y}{\sqrt{x}} \tag{2.7}$$

The functions f and g satisfy the system :

$$f''' = -\frac{1}{2} f f'' - \frac{1}{2} \eta g \tag{2.8}$$

$$g' = -\frac{Pr}{2} fg \tag{2.9}$$

and the boundary conditions :

$$\eta = o \quad : \quad f = f'' = o \tag{2.10}$$

$$\eta = \infty \quad : \quad f' = o \tag{2.11}$$

Moreover, to completely determine the solution, the enthalphy flux is normalized :

$$\int_{-\infty}^{\infty} u \, \Theta \, dY = \int_{-\infty}^{\infty} f' g \, d\eta = 1 \tag{2.12}$$

This problem was solved with an optimization scheme (5.). For numerical integration a 4th order Runge-Kutta-Gill method was used. Figures 1 and 2 give the interesting functions $f'(\eta)$ and $g(\eta)/\sqrt{Pr}$ for $0.01 \leqslant Pr \leqslant 300$. It is possible to check that the numerical solution is correct for large values of Prandtl (the asymptotic solution is easily found) ; for instance :

$$\lim_{Pr \to \infty} g(\eta) = g(o) \exp\left(-\frac{Pr.f'(o)}{4} \eta^2\right) \tag{2.13}$$

and

$$\lim_{Pr \to \infty} \frac{g(o)\sqrt{f'(o)}}{\sqrt{Pr}} = \frac{1}{2\sqrt{\pi}} \tag{2.14}$$

Figures 3 and 4 give the streamlines and the isotherms for Pr = 1 and Pr = 10. Far from the (virtual) source, near y = o, the streamlines become parallel to Ox and equidistant : the potential energy given by the source to the fluid is completely transformed into kinetic energy and the shear stress along the surface is naught. The larger Pr, the closer the isotherms are to y = o (as indicated by 2.13). Near x = o, the similarity solution, as most boundary layer-type solutions, supports "the curse of the leading edge"...

It is worth remarking that the dilution along the surface is by no means negligible : $\Theta(o)$ varies like $x^{-1/2} F_o^{5/6}$, while the superficial velocity is independant of x (and proportional to $F_o^{1/3}$).

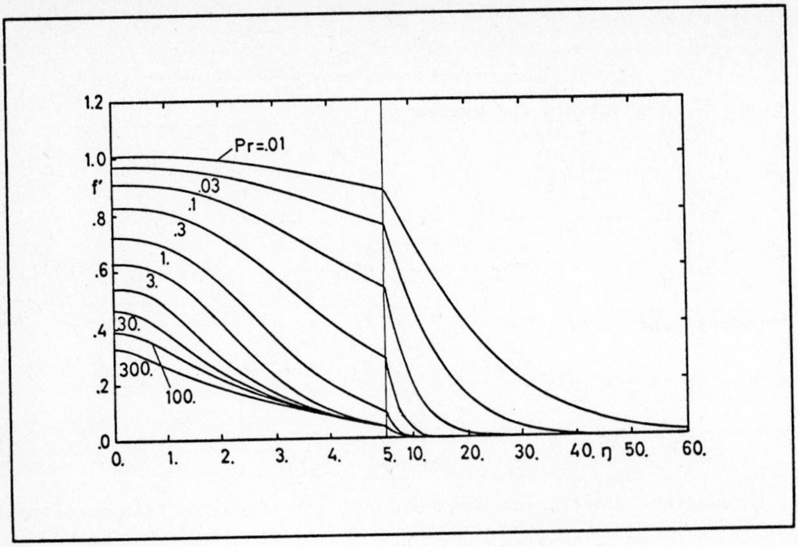

Fig. 1 : Dimensionless velocity profile (superficial plume)

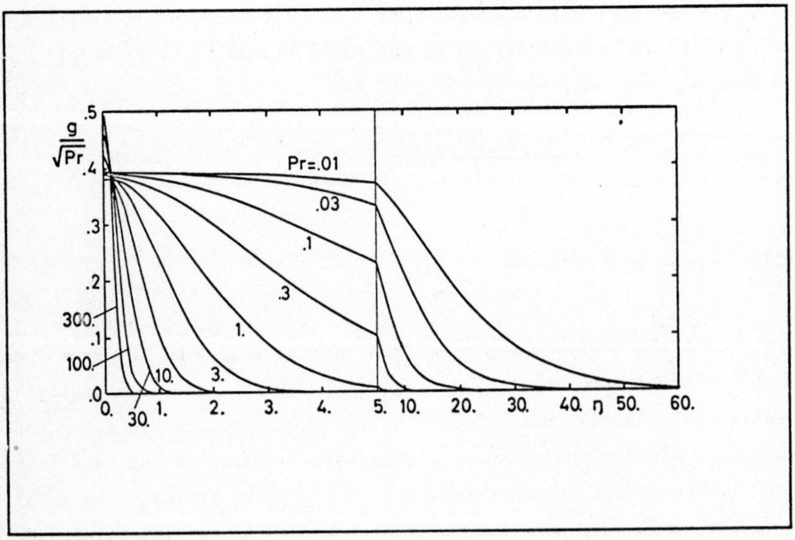

Fig. 2 : Dimensionless density-difference profile (superficial plume)

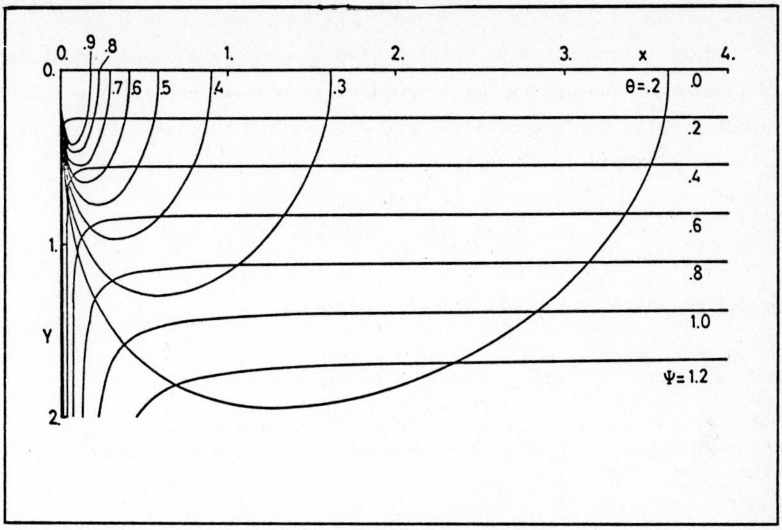

Fig. 3 : Flow pattern in a superficial plume (Pr = 1)

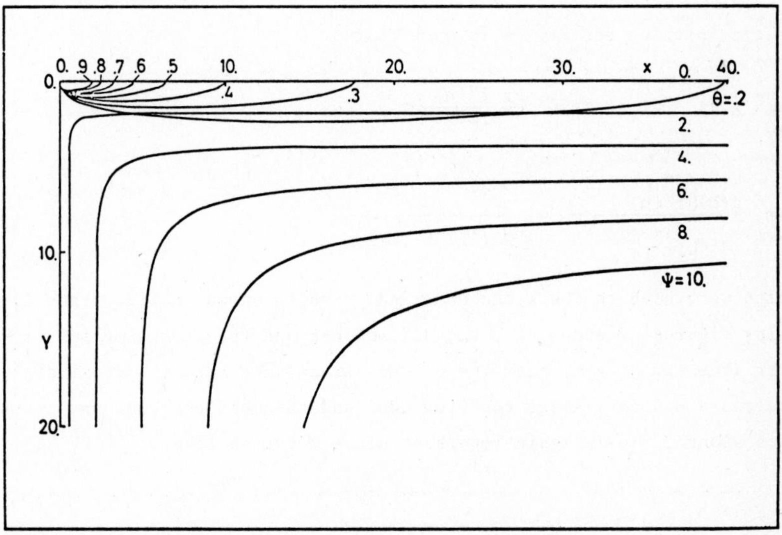

Fig. 4 : Flow pattern in a superficial plume (Pr = 10)

3. Horizontal buoyant plumes on the sea floor

If instead of urban sewage water one would pump some dense industrial effluent to the distributor, the boundary layer would now spread on the sea-floor. The velocity field and density difference field are again given by (1.4), (1.5), (2.1), (2.3), (2.4), (2.5) and (instead of (2.2)) :

$$Y = o \quad : \quad \frac{\partial \Psi}{\partial Y} = o \quad \text{(the velocity is zero on the sea floor)} \tag{3.1}$$

The similarity solution (2.6), (2.7) still applies :

$$\Psi = \sqrt{x}\, .\, f(\eta) \qquad \text{and} \qquad \Theta = \frac{1}{\sqrt{x}}\, g\,(\eta)$$

where f and g are given by (2.8), (2.9) but under the boundary conditions :

$$\eta = o \quad : \quad f = o, \quad f' = o \tag{3.2}$$

$$\eta = \infty \quad : \quad f' = o \tag{3.3}$$

and with the conservation equation for the enthalpy flux :

$$\int_{-\infty}^{\infty} f' \; g \; d\eta = 1 \tag{3.4}$$

The asymptotic solution for $Pr \to \infty$ is such that :

$$\lim_{Pr\to\infty} \; g(\eta) = g(o) \; \exp \; (- \frac{Pr \; f''(o)}{12} \; \eta^3) \tag{3.5}$$

and

$$\lim_{Pr\to\infty} \; \frac{g(o)[\, f''(o)\,]^{1/3}}{[\, Pr\,]^{2/3}} = \frac{3}{2.(12)^{2/3}.\Gamma(\frac{2}{3})} \tag{3.6}$$

These results were used to check the numerical results shown on fig. 5 and 6. Again, the following figures, 7 and 8 give the streamlines and the isotherms for Pr = 1 and Pr = 10. Far from the origin, near Y = o, the streamlines become approximately parabolic : the solid boundary slows the flow down and thickens the boundary layer. The dilution along Y = o is again important since Θ varies like $x^{-1/2}\; F_o^{5/6}$.

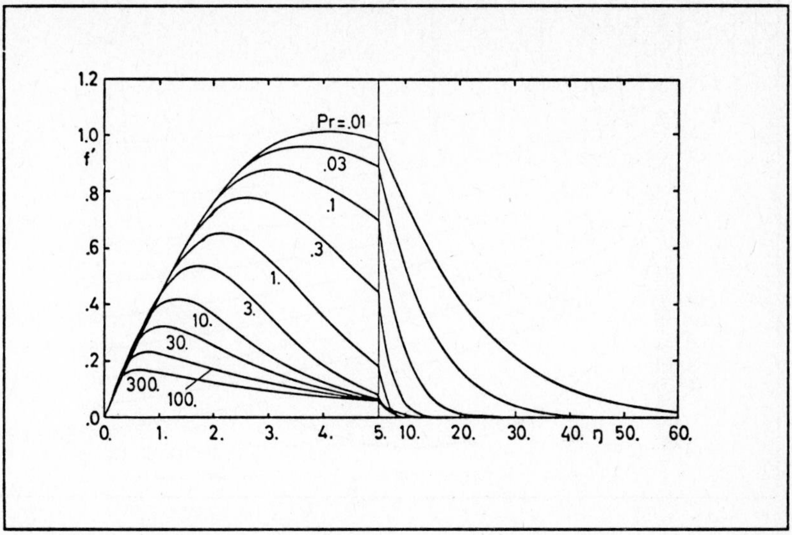

Fig. 5 : Dimensionless velocity profile (floor plume)

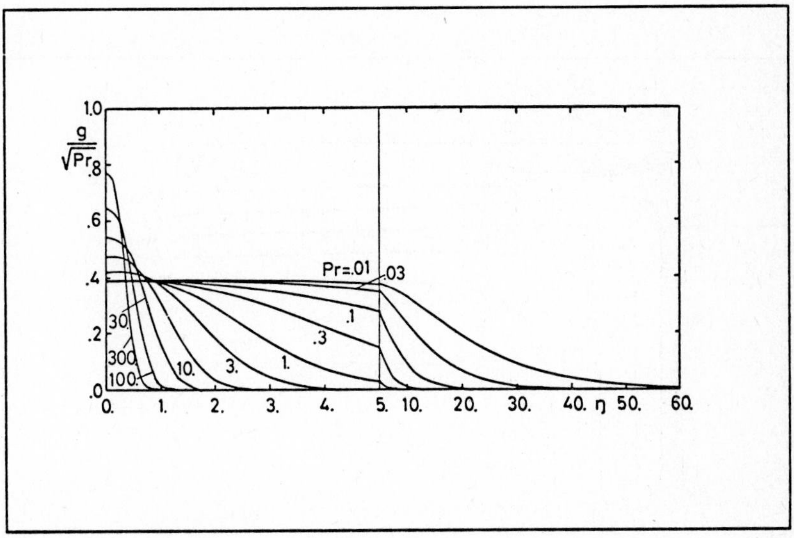

Fig. 6 : Dimensionless density-difference profile (floor plume)

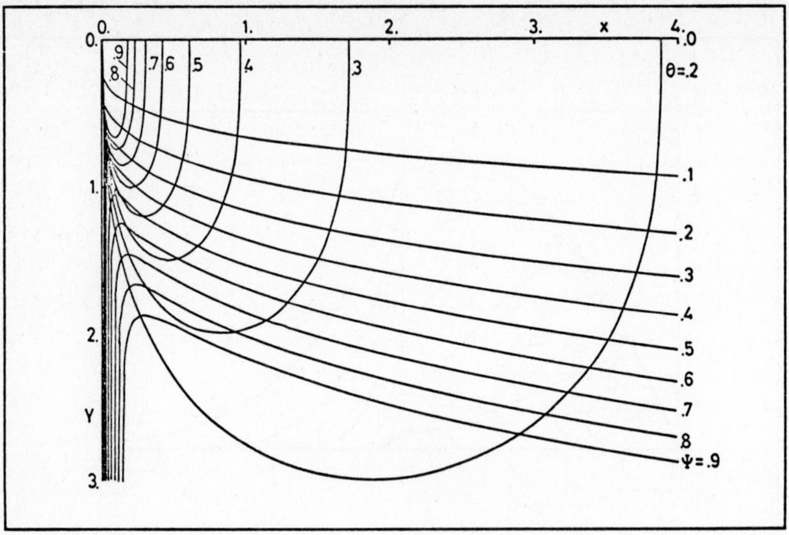

Fig. 7 : Flow pattern in a floor plume (Pr = 1)

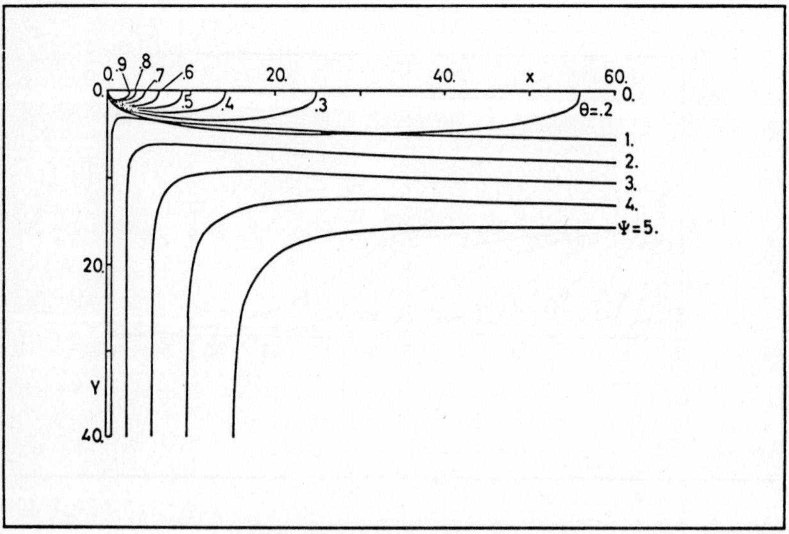

Fig. 8 : Flow pattern in a floor plume (Pr = 10)

4. Horizontal buoyant plume submerged at the level of a thermocline

When the sea density increases with depth, one says that the sea is stably stratified. A vertical density profile then typically displays two or more plateaus, some 10 to 100 m deep, separated by transition zones of only 1 m depth, the thermoclines. If a vertical plume reaching a thermocline has lost enough buoyancy underway it will be deflected horizontally and feed a so-called submerged sewage field. To model this field, suppose that a known flow of liquid of density equal to the mean density between those of the adjacent plateaus is injected at the level of the (infinitely thin) thermocline. The resulting plume will be symmetric with respect to 0x and the equations describing this free shear boundary layer are again (1.4), (1.5) with the boundary conditions :

$Y = o \qquad \Psi = o$ (0x is a streamline) (4.1)

$\frac{\partial^2 \Psi}{\partial Y^2} = o$ (the horizontal velocity profile is symmetric with respect to 0x) (4.2)

$\Theta = o$ (by symmetry) (4.3)

$Y = \infty \qquad \frac{\partial \Psi}{\partial Y} = o$ (far from the plume, the velocity is purely vertical) (4.4)

$\Theta = 1$ (density is given) (4.5)

Let us adapt Schlichting's [7] solution for the linear isothermal jet and look for a Blasius-Howarth [8] expansion of the form :

$$\Psi = x^{1/3} \sum_{i=o}^{\infty} x^{4i/3} f_i(\eta) \tag{4.6}$$

$$\Theta = \sum_{i=o}^{\infty} x^{4i/3} g_i(\eta) \tag{4.7}$$

where the similarity variable is :

$$\eta = \frac{Y}{x^{2/3}} \tag{4.8}$$

The fundamental terms of these expansions are

$$f_o = 6\,\alpha \tanh \alpha\,\eta \tag{4.9}$$

$$g_o = \frac{\int_o^{\eta} \frac{d\eta}{\cosh^{2\,Pr} \alpha\eta}}{\int_o^{\infty} \frac{d\eta}{\cosh^{2\,Pr} \alpha\eta}} \tag{4.10}$$

where α is related to the momentum flux by :

$$M = 2\,\rho \int_o^{\infty} u^2 \, dY = 48\,\rho\,\alpha^3 \tag{4.11}$$

and the enthalpy flux in the x direction is naught (by antisymmetry). This first term gives an impression of the first part of the development of the plume (figs 9, 10)

For the practical case of disposal of urban sewage in sea-water, the density difference is essentially due to the concentration difference in sodium chloride. The interesting pollutants might be present in minute concentrations and would then diffuse through this plume, but without disturbing its density or its velocity-field, If the concentration of such a pollutant is c, a solution of the following form exists

$$c = x^{-1/3} \sum_{i=o}^{\infty} x^{4i/3}\, h_i(\eta) \tag{4.12}$$

satisfying

$$\frac{\partial c}{\partial x}\frac{\partial \Psi}{\partial Y} - \frac{\partial c}{\partial Y}\frac{\partial \Psi}{\partial x} = \frac{1}{Sc}\frac{\partial^2 c}{\partial Y^2} \tag{4.13}$$

$$Y = o \; : \; \frac{\partial c}{\partial Y} = o \quad \text{(by symmetry)} \tag{4.14}$$

$$Y = \infty \; : \; c = o \quad \text{(the dilution far from the plume is complete)} \tag{4.15}$$

It is easy to show that the fundamental term in (4.12) is :

$$h_o = \frac{h_o(o)}{\cosh^{2\,Sc} \alpha\eta} \tag{4.16}$$

Once again, the dispersion in this horizontal plume, less important than in a vertical one, is however not negligible : $c(Y = o)$ varies like $x^{-1/3}\, P_o$. Figs. 11 and 12 show, for $Sc = 100$, the sharp pollutant tongue at the level of the thermocline.

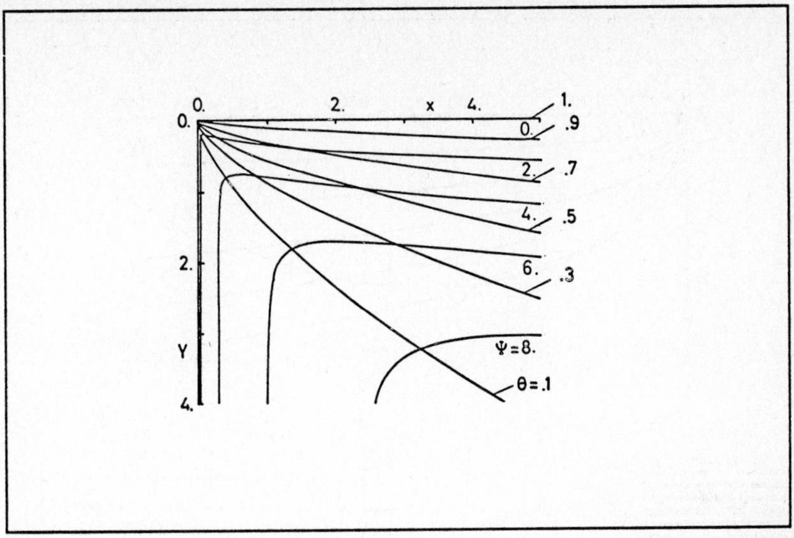

Fig. 9 : Flow pattern in a submerged plume (Pr = 1)

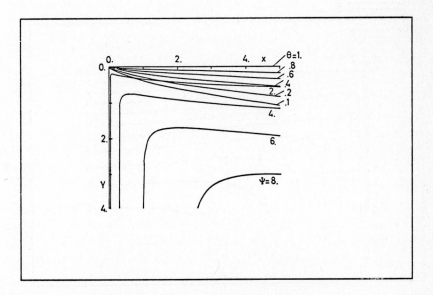

Fig. 10 : Flow pattern in a submerged plume (Pr = 10)

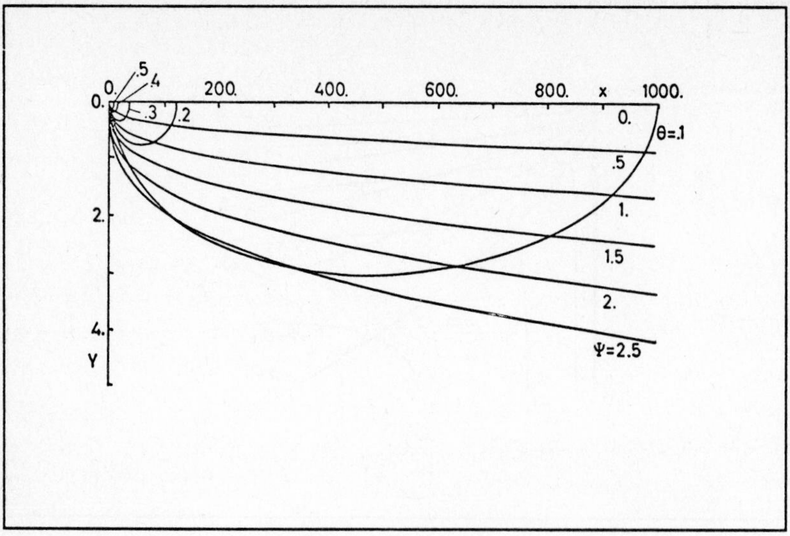

Fig. 11 : Pollutant dispersion in a submerged plume (Sc = 100)

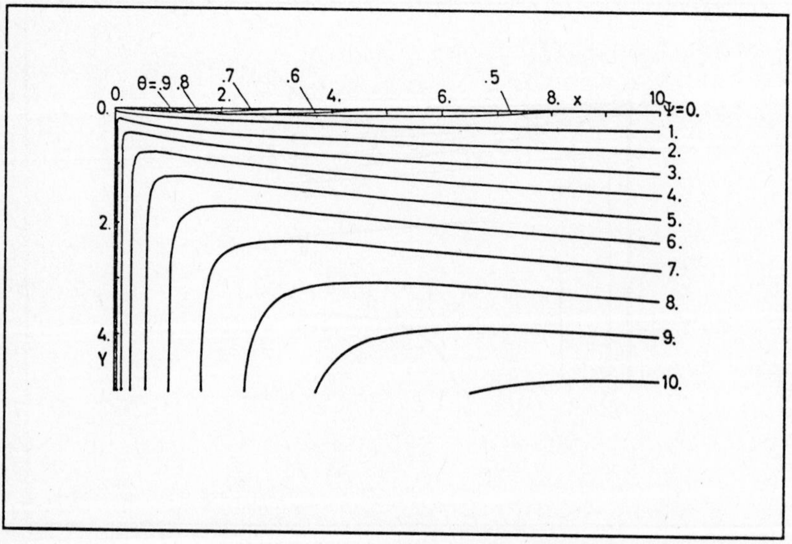

Fig. 12 : Pollutant dispersion in a submerged plume (Sc = 100)

5. Optimization technique

Boundary value problems can be solved using an optimization scheme. The expression :

$$f = \alpha_1 \left(\int_{-\infty}^{+\infty} f'g \, d\eta - 1 \right)^2 + \alpha_2 f'^2(\infty)$$

for instance is a suitable objective function for the solution of (2.8), (2.9), (2.10), (2.11), (2.12). For the case of analog integration in a hybrid configuration, machine noise disturbs the correct evaluation of the criterium function. If the partial derivatives cannot be determined analytically, the numerical evaluation of the derivatives is jeopardized by noise. A good and fast direct search technique is preferable . The method chosen here is a modified rotating coordinate technique. The algorithm has been provided of an efficient line search for determining the minimum point in a given direction.

line search

The line search is a combination of direct search and curve fitting in such a way that under fairly general conditions convergence to the minimum is guaranteed [9].

Let $\underline{x}_k$ be the present point, $\underline{d}_k$ the direction of search and α_k a given step. Following function evaluations are done

$$f(\underline{x}_k + \alpha_k \underline{d}_k), \; f(\underline{x}_k + 2\alpha_k \underline{d}_k), \; f(\underline{x}_k + 4\alpha_k \underline{d}_k) \ldots\ldots$$

till three points $\underline{x}_1 = \underline{x}_k + \alpha_1 \underline{d}_k$,

$\underline{x}_2 = \underline{x}_k + \alpha_2 \underline{d}_k$,

$\underline{x}_3 = \underline{x}_k + \alpha_3 \underline{d}_k$ are obtained

which satisfy the condition

$$f(\underline{x}_1) > f(\underline{x}_2) < f(\underline{x}_3)$$

If the function $f(\underline{x})$ is strictly unimodal in the given direction the coordinate α_m of the minimum point $\underline{x}_1 + \alpha_m \underline{d}_k$ will be in the interval (α_1, α_3). Then a curve fitting procedure is started which does not require derivatives.

A quadratic

$$q(\alpha) = \sum_{i=1}^{3} f(\underline{x}_i) \frac{\prod_{j\neq i} (\alpha - \alpha_j)}{\prod_{j\neq i} (\alpha_i - \alpha_j)}$$

is passed through the three points and the coordinate of the extremum

$$\alpha_e = \frac{1}{2} \frac{(\alpha_2^2 - \alpha_3^2) f(\underline{x}_1) + (\alpha_3^2 - \alpha_1^2) f(\underline{x}_2) + (\alpha_1^2 - \alpha_2^2) f(\underline{x}_3)}{(\alpha_2 - \alpha_3) f(\underline{x}_1) + (\alpha_3 - \alpha_1) f(\underline{x}_2) + (\alpha_1 - \alpha_2) f(\underline{x}_3)}$$

is warranted to be a minimum and contained in the interval (α_1, α_3) ; $f(\underline{x}_k + \alpha_e \underline{d}_k)$ is evaluated. If $\alpha_e < \alpha_2$ a new point $\underline{x}_1 = \underline{x}_k + \alpha_e \underline{d}_k$ is introduced reducing (α_1, α_3) to (α_e, α_3).
If $\alpha_e > \alpha_2$, $\underline{x}_3 = \underline{x}_k + \alpha_m \underline{d}_k$ is calculated and (α_1, α_3) reduces to (α_1, α_e). A new quadratic fit is performed on the reduced interval.
If $\alpha_1 = \alpha_2$, the interval $(\alpha_2, \alpha_i) - \alpha_i$ is the coordinate of $\underline{x}_i$ being the argument of $f_i = \max(f(\underline{x}_1), f(\underline{x}_2))$-is divided to obtain a new point $\underline{x}_n$ in such a way that the new interval is smaller than the preceding one. It can be proved by the Global Convergence Theorem [9] that this algorithm converges to the solution if the objective function is continuous and unimodal in α. The order of convergence is known to be about 1.3 [9]. In practice the search procedure has to be terminated before it has converged. For these problems α_m is determined to within a fixed percentage of its true value. A constant c, $o < c < 1$ is selected (c = 0.01) and α is found so as to satisfy $|\alpha - \bar{\alpha}| \leq c|\bar{\alpha}|$ where $\bar{\alpha}$ is the lower bound α_1 on the true minimizing value of the parameter if α_1 is different from zero or equal to the termination value for the complete algorithm if α equals zero.

optimization algorithm [10]

In a simple coordinate descent method the coordinate directions ($\underline{e}_1$, $\underline{e}_2$, $\underline{e}_3$... $\underline{e}_n$) are cyclically used to provide the directions for individual line searches. If the objective functions has continuous partial derivatives this method is globally convergent [9], and the convergence rate is affected by rotation of the coordinates. However if the first partial derivatives are not continuous objective functions and coordinate directions can be found so that the algorithm will not find the minimum. By rotating the coordinate system after n line searches an attempt is made to solve this problem. If at the same time one axis is oriented towards the direction of the valley, locally estimated in a way analoguous to the method used in the parallel tangent algorithm it has been found by some trial objective functions that the convergence rate is improved. An efficient method for obtaining a new orthonormal set is that of Powell [11], which requires $O(n^2)$ multiplications instead of $O(n^3)$.

The final algorithm is the following :

Given $\underline{x}_o$ and the current set of orthogonal directions $D = (\underline{d}_o, \underline{d}_1, \dots d_{n-1})$ a set of β_j's are computed using n line searches :

$$\beta_j = \min_\beta f(\underline{x}_j + \beta \underline{d}_j) \qquad \text{with} \quad \underline{x}_{j+1} = \underline{x}_j + \beta_j \underline{d}_j$$

$$\text{for} \quad j = 0, 1, 2 \dots, n-1$$

The orders of the directions d_j is changed yielding $D' = (\underline{d}'_o, \underline{d}'_1, \dots \underline{d}'_{n-1})$ so that the first k directions have β-values different from zero $(\beta_o, \beta_1, \beta_2, \dots, \beta_k, o, o, \dots o)$. Then a new set of directions is computed.

1 Set $\quad j = k$

$\tau = (\beta_k)^2$

$\underline{\sigma} = \beta_k \underline{d}'_k$

2 if $j = o$ terminate the process, otherwise compute

$$d_j^n = \frac{(\tau \underline{d}'_{j-1} - \beta_{j-1} \underline{\sigma})}{[\tau(\tau + \beta_{j-1}^2)]^{1/2}}$$

3 Set $\quad j = j - 1$

$\tau = \tau + (\beta_j)^2$

$\underline{\sigma} = \underline{\sigma} + \beta_j \underline{d}'_j \quad ; \quad$ go to 2

4 The remaining vectors are obtained as follows

$$\underline{d}_o^n = \frac{\underline{\sigma}}{\sqrt{\tau}} \qquad \underline{\sigma} = \sum_{j=o}^{k} \beta_j \underline{d}'_j \qquad \tau = \sum_{j=o}^{k} (\beta_j)^2$$

$$\underline{d}_k^n = \underline{d}'_k \qquad \text{for } j = k+1, k+2, \dots, n-1$$

We now have a new set $D^n = (\underline{d}_o^n, \underline{d}_1^n, \dots, \underline{d}_{n-1}^n)$ to repeat the procedure.

To minimize the number of objective function evaluations a suitable step for the line search is necessary. If the step is too small ; the initial value has to be doubled too many times. If the step is too large, too many curve fittings have to be performed. Therefore the step is adjusted during the optimization. For every coordinate relaxation (n line searches) $a = \frac{1}{n} \sum_{j=o}^{n-1} \beta_j$ is computed. The series $\{a_k\}$ converges at least linearly for the quadratic case [9]. The convergence rate is dependent of the special objective function under study but experimentally it has been found that if a fraction of a (say a/8) is used as step for the next coordinate search an improvement in overall computation time is observed for the different objective functions encountered in the problem.

6. Conclusion

The classical methods of boundary layer theory allow us to accurately model linear laminar horizontal buoyant plumes. Using the modern developments of the theory (matched asymptotic expansions) we could even produce still better solutions of the non-linear problems considered. However, for any reasonable design, the unit flux F_o is likely to be so large that the flow would be turbulent rather than laminar. The results of our forthcoming study of turbulent horizontal plumes are more qualitative, but the general approach to modeling closely resembles the one used here.

Notations

u	horizontal velocity component
x	horizontal distance
y	vertical distance
F_o	density difference flux per unit length of diffusor
Gr	GRASHOF-number
P_o	mass flux of pollutant per unit length of diffusor
Pr	PRANDTL-number
α	thermal expansion coefficient
ψ	streamfunction
Θ	reduced density difference
ρ	specific mass
Γ	GAMMA-function

References

[1] Tetsu Fujü, Itsuki Morioka and Haruo Uehara, *Buoyant Plume Above a Horizontal Line Heat Source*, Int. J. Heat and Mass Transfer, 16, 755-768, 1973.

[2] Gebhart B., Pera L. and Schorr A.W., *Steady laminar natural convection plumes above a horizontal line heat source*, Int. J. Heat and Mass Transfer, 13, 161-171, 1970.

[3] Spalding D.B. and Cruddace R.G., *Theory of the steady laminar buoyant flow above a line heat source in a fluid of large Prandtl number and temperature-dependent viscosity*, Int. J. Heat and Mass Transfer, 3, 55-59, 1961.

[4] Tennekes H. and Lumley J.L., *A First Course in Turbulence*, M I T Press, Cambridge, U.S.A., 135-144, 1972.

[5] Turner J.S., *Buoyant Plumes and Thermals*, in : Annual Reviews of Fluid Mechanics Annual Reviews Inc. - Palo Alto, Cal., U.S.A., 1, 29, 1969.

[6] Koh, R.C.J. and Brooks N.H., *Fluid Mechanics of Waste Water Disposal in the Ocean*, in : Annual Reviews of Fluid Mechanics - Annual Reviews Inc. - Palo Alto, Cal., U.S.A., 7, 187, 1975.

[7] Rosenhead, L., ed., *Laminar Boundary Layers*, Oxford, Clarendon Press, 254, 1963.

[8] Rosenhead, L., ed., *Laminar Boundary Layers*, Oxford, Clarendon Press, 260, 1963.

[9] Luenberger, D., *Introduction to linear and nonlinear programming*, Addison & Wesley, 1973.

[10] Jacoby, S., Kowalik, J., Pizzo, J., *Iterative methods for nonlinear optimization problems*, Prentice-Hall, 1972.

[11] Powell, M., *On the calculation of orthogonal vectors*, Computer Journal, 11, 302, 1968.

THE IDENTIFICATION AND ADAPTIVE PREDICTION OF URBAN SEWER FLOWS

M.B. Beck
University Engineering Department,
Control Engineering Group,
Mill Lane,
Cambridge,
CB2 1RX.

1. Introduction

Unlike most process industries a wastewater treatment plant receives a raw input material whose variations with time are large and imprecisely defined. Some of these disturbances, which result from rainfall-runoff into the urban sewer network, are quite disruptive for the operation of the treatment plant and may also cause a subsequent overloading of the receiving river's self-purification capacity. The effluent from a sewer network, i.e. the influent to a wastewater treatment plant, is as it were, the fulcrum about which the control of the sewer network and the treatment plant is balanced. Therefore, an advance knowledge of the dynamic variations of the influent flow would play an important role in the more efficient operation of the treatment plant and the minimisation of storm-water overflows from the sewers.

Most previous models for urban rainfall-runoff/sewer effluent flow relationships tend to be of the large, deterministic, internally descriptive type. For certain control objectives it may, in practice, be sufficient to use a much simpler black box conception of the system. In this paper results are presented for the identification of a stochastic input/output, time-series model using the method of maximum likelihood: the data are taken from the Käppala treatment plant and meteorological stations in the district surrounding Stockholm. The identification phase of the analysis is an introductory stage in the examination of the potential applicability of an on-line, adaptive predictor for the influent flow to the treatment plant. The prediction problem is separated into two steps: in the first step the parameters of the black box model are estimated recursively with a least squares technique; the second step makes a prediction of the plant influent flow on the basis of the newly updated model and parameter estimates.

The predictor is adaptive in the sense that it automatically adjusts the model parameters to any unknown changes in the process dynamics. It is practical in the sense that it assumes very little on-line instrumentation of the system: in general, the innovation of an automatic control for water quality is severely hampered by a lack of the relevant, reliable, and robust measuring equipment. From a comparison of the prediction with the observed Käppala data it turns out that a good advance knowledge of the influent flow variations can be obtained in the absence of any measurements of the rainfall incident on the urban land surface.

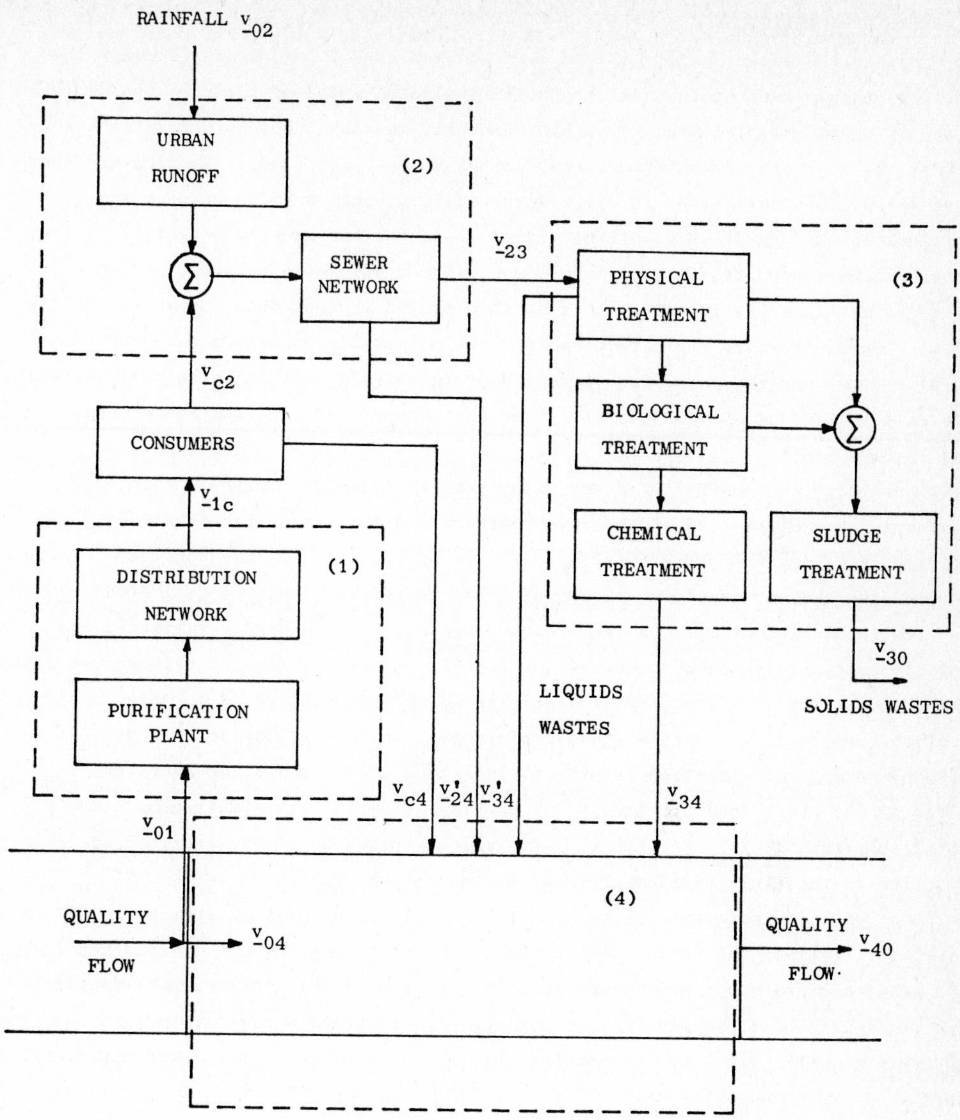

SUBSYSTEMS:

(1) POTABLE WATER ABSTRACTION, PURIFICATION, AND SUPPLY NETWORK
(2) URBAN LAND RUNOFF AND THE SEWER NETWORK
(3) WASTEWATER TREATMENT PLANT
(4) A STRETCH OF RIVER

Figure 1 The water quality system.

2. PROBLEM FORMULATION

Consider the water quality system defined by figure 1. Consider further the competing demands made on the quality "resources" of a reach of river by the assimilation of waste material from one urban community and the supply of potable water to a second, adjacent, downstream urban community. A proper understanding and control of the dynamic variations in river water quality would seem to be of vital importance to the organisation of the river's resource and amenity potential. Yet, although we have seen this stated many times before, automatic control, a common feature of most process industries, is notable by its absence from the water quality system. Much effort is still required to obtain suitable dynamic models for subsequent control system synthesis; a review of this field, with particular reference to the application of system identification and parameter estimation techniques, is given in BECK (1975)[4].

A knowledge and control of river water quality dynamics implies a knowledge of the dynamic characteristics of the sewer network and the wastewater treatment plant. In particular, figure 1 shows that the periodic oscillations of the consumer effluent, $\underline{v}_{c2}$, and the sudden, impulsive nature of urban runoff from any rainfall event, $\underline{v}_{02}$, makes the input raw material to the treatment plant, $\underline{v}_{23}$, a highly variable, and generally imprecisely known, quantity. Control objectives for the network and plant become, then, very much a matter of acquiring advance knowledge of the flow component, y, of the vector $\underline{v}_{23}$. Such a knowledge permits, in theory, the prior organisation of the network/plant operation for the minimisation of the polluting overflows $\underline{v}'_{24}$ and $\underline{v}'_{34}$ to the river, and ultimately, it provides a basis for establishing a truly controllable input to the treatment plant, which implies a greater flexibility in the regulation of the final treated effluent to the stream, $\underline{v}_{34}$.

Thus, given measurements of the rainfall u_i, say, at several spatial locations i ($i=1,2, \ldots, m$) on the urban land surface, we wish to determine a dynamic model which relates u_i to y, the effluent from the sewer network; this is the identification problem. Most previous investigations of this problem have divided it into two sub-problems: (i) given u_i, determine the inlet discharge to the sewer network from runoff (e.g. CHEN and SHUBINSKI (1971)[7], PAPADAKIS and PREUL (1973)[19]); (ii) given all flows entering the network, determine the output flow-rate y (e.g. HARRIS (1970)[13]). One striking feature of the currently available models is their purely deterministic and highly complex structure. Clearly these large, internally descriptive models reflect the complexity of the laws which describe the underlying physical phenomena governing the system's behaviour. Yet a theoretically complete analysis produces an unwieldy and possibly intractable model, with a multitude of parameters to be evaluated, and it is admitted that "to a varying degree most of these methods rely upon empirical relationships and experience" (PAPADAKIS and PREUL (1973)[19]). It seems, therefore, that a stochastic model derived from time-series analysis, herein the maximum likelihood method (ÅSTRÖM and BOHLIN (1965)[2]), might yield equally usable results. Such an input/output, black box model for the relationships between u_i and y assumes little or no a priori knowledge of the physical laws of the system and takes a relatively macroscopic view of the cause/effect relationships involved. A similar approach to sewage flow modelling, after BOX and JENKINS (1970)[6], has been adopted by GOEL and LaGREGA (1972)[11]. For adaptive prediction of the effluent sewer flow the identification part of the analysis is required primarily for the determination of a suitable order and structure for the predictor model. The prediction problem can be stated as follows: at time t, given the noisy observations y(t), y(t-1), ..., of the present and past values of the influent to the plant and a model for the dynamic variations of y, we wish to make a k-step ahead prediction of y(t+k). In addition, the predictor should be simple, adaptable to changes in the process dynamics, and require little on-line instrumentation.

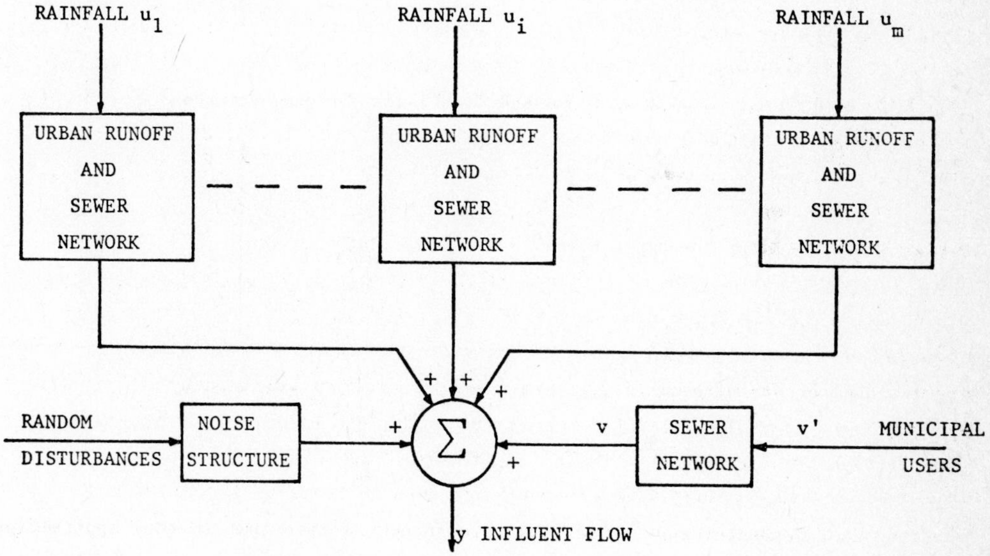

Figure 2 A schematic representation of the system for the identification of input/output flow models

3. IDENTIFICATION and ADAPTIVE PREDICTION

The class of models to be examined is one of parametric, linear, time-invariant models of a canonical form. They are black box models in the sense that they assume no knowledge of physical relationships between the system's inputs and output other than that the inputs should produce observable responses in the output.

3.1. Maximum Likelihood Identification.

In the general case, given the set of input/output data samples ($u_i(t)$, $i = 1, 2, \ldots, m$; $y(t)$; $t = 1, 2, \ldots, N$), where $u_i(t)$, $i = 1, 2, \ldots, m$ are the m input signals, $y(t)$ is the output signal and t is the time of the tth sampling instant, the identification problem is to find an estimate of the parameters of the system model (ÅSTRÖM and BOHLIN (1965)[2], GUSTAVSSON (1969)[12]),

$$A(q^{-1})y(t) = \sum_{i=1}^{m} B_i(q^{-1})u_i(t) + \lambda C(q^{-1})e(t) \qquad (1)$$

in which e(t) is a sequence of independent, normal (0,1) random variables and q denotes the shift operator

$$q\{y(t)\} = y(t+1) \quad \text{etc.} \qquad (2)$$

$A(q^{-1})$, $B_i(q^{-1})$, $i = 1, 2, \ldots, m$, and $C(q^{-1})$ are the polynomials

$$\left.\begin{aligned} A(q^{-1}) &= 1 + a_1 q^{-1} + \ldots + a_n q^{-n} \\ B_i(q^{-1}) &= b_{i0} + b_{i1} q^{-1} + \ldots + b_{in} q^{-n} \qquad i = 1,2,\ldots,m \\ C(q^{-1}) &= 1 + c_1 q^{-1} + \ldots + c_n q^{-n} \end{aligned}\right\} \qquad (3)$$

The residual errors of eqn. (1), $\{\varepsilon(t), t = 1, 2, \ldots, N\}$, defined by

$$C(q^{-1})\varepsilon(t) = A(q^{-1})y(t) - \sum_{i=1}^{m} B_i(q^{-1})u_i(t) \qquad (4)$$

are thus an independent and normal $(0,\lambda)$ sequence. Notice that in this application the inputs of the system correspond to the rainfall u_i measured at the locations $i = 1, 2, \ldots, m$ and the output y is the influent flow to the treatment plant (see figure 2).

3.2. Adaptive Prediction

For the derivation of an adaptive predictor (WITTENMARK (1974)[22]) let us consider once again the discrete-time process, eqn.(1), which we rewrite as,

$$A(q^{-1})y(t) = \sum_{j=1}^{m'} B_j(q^{-1})v_j(t) + \lambda C(q^{-1})\, e(t) \qquad (5)$$

Here $v_j(t)$, $j = 1,2,\ldots, m'$, are auxiliary variables which aid in the characterisation of the time-series y (see eg. WITTENMARK (1974)[22], HOLST (1974)[14]); more specifically, for reasons which become apparent later, v_j may be thought of either as a suitable deterministic, synthetic signal, e.g. a periodic function, or as measurements of the process input variable u_i (eqn.(1)). Now denote the k-step ahead prediction of the output signal y based on the sampled observations y(t),y(t-1), ..., and the signals $v_j(t+k)$, $v_j(t+k-1)$, ..., (j=1,2,..., m'), by $\hat{y}(t+k|t)$. Introducing the loss function

$$V_k(t) = E\{\varepsilon(t+k)^2\} \tag{6}$$

where E{...} is the expectation operation and $\varepsilon(t+k)$ is the prediction error,

$$\varepsilon(t+k) = y(t+k) - \hat{y}(t+k|t) \tag{7}$$

the predictor which minimises eqn.(6) is derived in ÅSTRÖM (1970)[1] for the case where the process, eqn. (5), has <u>known</u> A, B_j, C polynomials. According to Åström, using the identity,

$$C(q^{-1}) = A(q^{-1})\,F(q^{-1}) + q^{-k}\,G(q^{-1}) \tag{8}$$

where

$$\left.\begin{aligned} F(q^{-1}) &= 1 + f_1 q^{-1} + \ldots + f_{k-1} q^{-k+1} \\ G(q^{-1}) &= g_o + g_1 q^{-1} + \ldots + g_{n-1} q^{-n+1} \end{aligned}\right\} \tag{9}$$

The k-step ahead predictor for eqn. (5) is given by

$$\hat{y}(t+k|t) = \frac{G(q^{-1})y(t)}{C(q^{-1})} + \frac{F(q^{-1})}{C(q^{-1})} \sum_{j=1}^{m'} B_j(q^{-1})\, v_j(t+k) \tag{10}$$

Alternatively, if the polynomials A, B_j, C are unknown, they can be estimated off-line by the method outlined in section 3.1 above and then substituted into eqns. (8) and (10) to obtain the predictor.

However, for an on-line predictor of an unknown process we should prefer to identify the process and make predictions "simultaneously". In other words, we have a learning (or adaptive, self-tuning) procedure in which the parameters of the <u>predictor</u>, eqn. (10), are <u>recursively</u> estimated at each time t, rather than estimating a priori the parameters of the <u>process</u>, eqn. (5). WITTENMARK (1974)[22] solves this problem by transforming it into the already solved problem of an adaptive regulator (WITTENMARK (1973)[21]).

In the current application a slightly modified version of Wittenmark's algorithms are employed (HOLST (1974)[14]). The derivation is briefly as follows. Rearranging eqn. (10), and introducing $\varepsilon(t)$ from eqn. (7), we have at time t,

$$y(t) = G(q^{-1})y(t-k) - (C(q^{-1}) - 1)\hat{y}(t|t-k) + F(q^{-1}) \sum_{j=1}^{m'} B_j(q^{-1})\, v_j(t) + \varepsilon(t) \tag{11}$$

Eqn. (11) is now re-written as,

$$y(t) = A^*(q^{-1})y(t-k) - B^*(q^{-1})\hat{y}(t|t-k) + \sum_{j=1}^{m'} \Gamma_j^*(q^{-1})v_j(t) + \varepsilon(t) \tag{12}$$

such that we have the identities,

$$\left.\begin{aligned} A^*(q^{-1}) &\equiv G(q^{-1}) \quad ; \quad B^*(q^{-1}) \equiv C(q^{-1}) - 1 \\ \Gamma_j^*(q^{-1}) &\equiv F(q^{-1})\, B_j(q^{-1}) \quad j=1,2,\ldots,m' \end{aligned}\right\} \tag{13}$$

with the polynomial definitions,

$$\left.\begin{aligned} A^*(q^{-1}) &= \alpha_o + \alpha_1 q^{-1} + \ldots. + \alpha_{n-1} q^{-n+1} \\ B^*(q^{-1}) &= \beta_1 q^{-1} + \ldots. + \beta_n q^{-n} \\ \Gamma_j^*(q^{-1}) &= \gamma_{jo} + \gamma_{j1} q^{-1} + \ldots + \gamma_{j,n+k-1}\, q^{-n-k+1} \qquad j=1,2,\ldots,m' \end{aligned}\right\} \tag{14}$$

Eqn. (12) forms the basis of the adaptive predictor algorithms, whereby (HOLST (1974)[14]):

Step 1 : Estimation

At time t, upon receipt of a new observation y(t), the parameters, $\alpha_o,\ldots,\alpha_{n-1}$, $\beta_1,\ldots,\gamma_{1o},\ldots,\gamma_{1,n+k-1},\ldots,\gamma_{m'o}, \ldots, \gamma_{m',n+k-1}$ are estimated in the prediction model,

$$y(t) = A^*(q^{-1})\, y(t-k) - B^*(q^{-1})\hat{y}(t|t-k) + \sum_{j=1}^{m'}\Gamma_j^*\, (q^{-1})v_j(t) + \varepsilon(t) \tag{15a}$$

by the method of least squares;

Step 2 : Prediction

Using the estimates $\hat{A}^*(q^{-1})$, $\hat{B}^*(q^{-1})$, and $\hat{\Gamma}_j^*(q^{-1})$ obtained in eqn. (15a), make a k-step ahead prediction,

$$\hat{y}(t+k|t) = \hat{A}^*(q^{-1})y(t) - \hat{B}^*(q^{-1})\, \hat{y}\, (t+k|t) + \sum_{j=1}^{m'} \hat{\Gamma}_j^*(q^{-1})\, v_j(t+k) \tag{15b}$$

Since a least squares estimation is readily implemented in recursive form, the

the predictor is well suited to real-time applications with each step of the procedure being repeated at each sampled instant of time. Thus, if the following vectors are defined as

$$\underline{z}^T(t) = \Big[y(t-k),\ldots,y(t-k-n+1),\ -\hat{y}(t-1|t-k-1),\ldots,-\hat{y}(t-n|t-k-n),\ v_1(t),\ldots,$$
$$v_1(t-k-n+1),\ \ldots,\ v_{m'}(t),\ \ldots,\ v_{m'}(t-k-n+1)\Big]$$

$$\underline{a}(t) = \Big[\alpha_o,\ldots,\alpha_{n-1},\beta_1,\ldots,\beta_n,\gamma_{1o},\ldots,\gamma_{1,n+k-1},\ldots,\gamma_{m'o},\ldots,\gamma_{m',n+k-1}\Big]^T$$

eqn. (15a) becomes $y(t) = \underline{z}^T(t)\,\underline{a} + \varepsilon(t)$ (16)

and the well known recursive least squares algorithms for the estimates $\hat{\underline{a}}$ of $\underline{a}$ are given by (e.g. YOUNG (1969)[23], YOUNG (1974)[24]),

$$\hat{\underline{a}}(t) = \hat{\underline{a}}(t-1) - P(t-1)\underline{z}(t)\Big(1 + \underline{z}^T(t)\,P(t-1)\underline{z}(t)\Big)^{-1}\Big[\underline{z}^T(t)\,\hat{\underline{a}}\,(t-1) - y(t)\Big] \quad \text{(a)}$$
$$P(t) = P(t-1) - P(t-1)\underline{z}(t)\Big(1+\underline{z}^T(t)\,P(t-1)\underline{z}(t)\Big)^{-1}\underline{z}^T(t)\,P(t-1) \quad \text{(b)} \qquad (17)$$

in which $P(t) \triangleq \left[\sum_{j=1}^{t} \underline{z}(j)\underline{z}^T(j)\right]^{-1}$ (18)

Remarks

(i) Estimation bias: If $C(q^{-1}) = 1$ in eqn. (5) it can be shown that $\varepsilon(t) = \lambda e(t)$ and, providing that $e(t)$ is not correlated in time and is independent of $y(t)$, $v_j(t)$ $(j=1,2,\ldots,m')$, the estimates $\hat{\underline{a}}$ are unbiased. In practice however, where it is more probable that $C(q^{-1}) \neq 1$, the predictor still appears to behave nicely; notice that if the estimates $\hat{\underline{a}}$ converge to $\underline{a}$, it implies that certain covariances and cross-covariances equal zero (HOLST (1974)[14], WITTENMARK (1974)[22]).

(ii) Time-varying parameters: In view of the nature of this particular application (see section 4.2) it is useful to allow for the estimation of time-varying parameters. One method of achieving this is with exponential weighting of past data (e.g. YOUNG (1969)[23], EYKHOFF (1974)[8]); introducing a weighting factor μ, where $0 \ll \mu < 1$, the recursive least squares algorithms of eqn. (17) are modified to give (EYKHOFF (1974)[8]),

$$\hat{\underline{a}}(t) = \hat{\underline{a}}(t-1) - P(t-1)\underline{z}(t)\Big(\mu + \underline{z}^T(t)\,P(t-1)\underline{z}(t)\Big)^{-1}\Big[\underline{z}^T(t)\hat{\underline{a}}(t-1) - y(t)\Big] \quad \text{(a)}$$
$$P(t) = \frac{1}{\mu}\Big\{P(t-1) - P(t-1)\underline{z}(t)\Big(\mu + \underline{z}^T(t)\,P(t-1)\underline{z}(t)\Big)^{-1}\underline{z}^T(t)\,P(t-1)\Big\} \quad \text{(b)} \qquad (19)$$

where now $P(t) \triangleq \left[\sum_{j=1}^{t} \mu^{t-j}\underline{z}(j)\underline{z}^T(j)\right]^{-1}$

(iii) Auxiliary variables: When measurements of any process inputs, e.g. rainfall in this instance, are to be used as auxiliary variables, note that the measurements $v_j(t+k)$, $v_j(t+k-1),\ldots,$ are required at time t for prediction according to eqn. (15b).

Clearly, additional information of this kind is only of real benefit providing $\gamma_{jo} = \gamma_{j1} = \ldots = \gamma_{jk} = 0$, i.e. there exists a pure time delay τ in the input/output process dynamics where $\tau \geq k$. Other forms of auxiliary variables are typically (here) average weekly and daily periodic dry-weather flow profiles.

A full analysis of the adaptive predictor of eqn. (15) will appear in a forthcoming report (HOLST (1975)[15]).

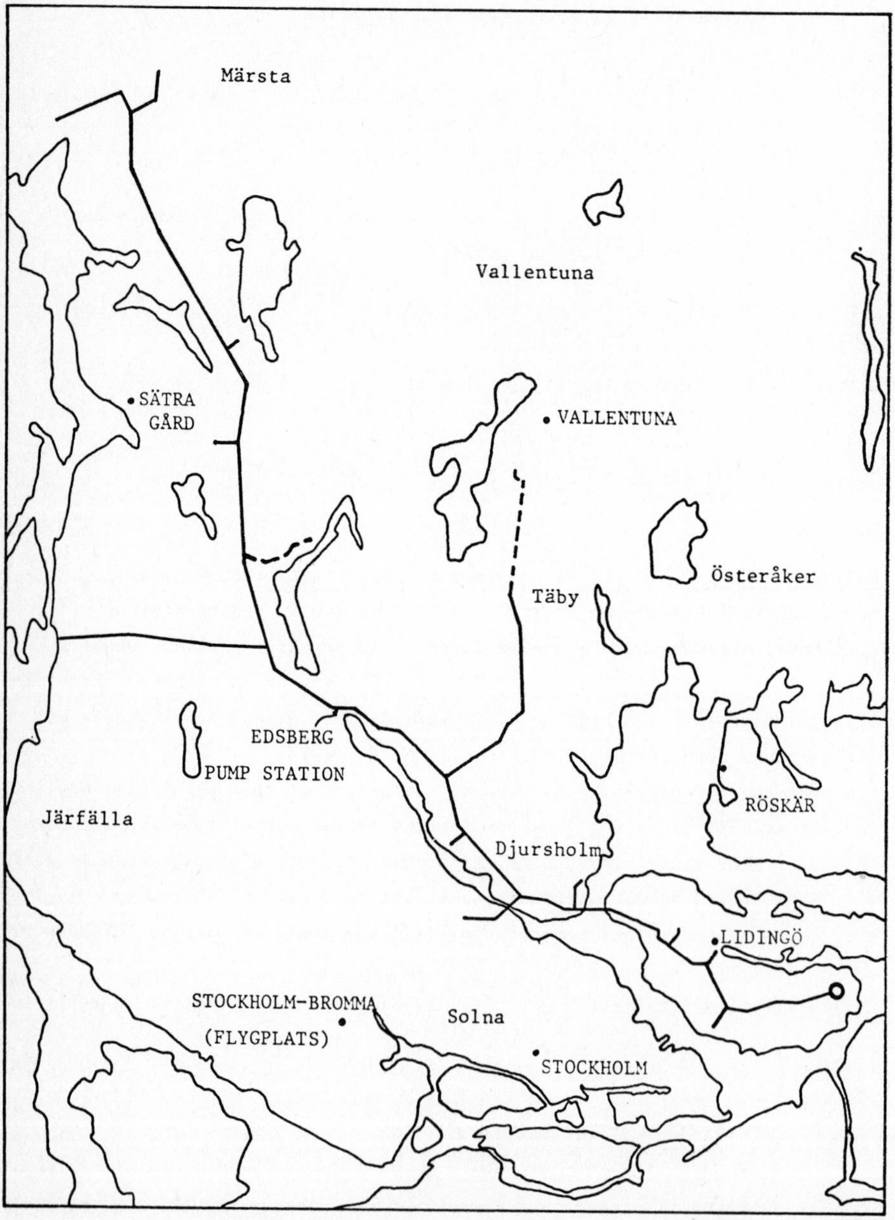

Figure 3 The Käppala sewer tunnel system

• = Meteorological station
o = Käppala treatment plant

4. A CASE STUDY - THE KÄPPALA PLANT, STOCKHOLM.

Figure 3 shows the sewer tunnel system which collects waste water from an area of some 1191 km^2 covering part of the City of Stockholm and it's surrounding districts and serving a population of 290,000. The observed influent flow-rate to the Käppala plant is analysed for the period between October 1st (08.00 hrs) and October 31st (07.00 hrs), a total of 720 hourly samples. For the same interval data are available (from the Swedish Institute of Meteorology and Hydrology, Stockholm) for the rainfall measured at four stations, Röskär, Stockholm-Bromma, Stockholm, and Lidingö (see figure 3). Because of several imperfections in the data, notably the presence of large pumping disturbances in the flow-rate measurements and the low frequency of the sampling in the rainfall measurements, e.g. once, twice, per day, it is particularly difficult to obtain suitably identified input/output model for the urban runoff/sewer effluent dynamics.

4.1. Identification.

The problems of the data and of maximum likelihood identification are discussed in greater detail elsewhere (BECK (1974)[3]). Briefly, it is necessary to low-pass filter the data before any useful analysis can be attempted. A rainfall-runoff flow (RRF) model, which incorporates a deterministic component describing the dry-weather weekly flow periodicity and a stochastic model for rainfall-runoff flows, is identified:

$$y_r(t) = -a_1 y_r(t-1) + b_3\, u(t-3) + b_7(t-7) + \lambda(e(t) + c_1 e(t-1)) \qquad (20)$$

where

$$y_r(t) = y(t) - \bar{y}_w\,(t) \qquad (21)$$

$y_r(t)$ may be considered as the excess flow resulting from runoff sources ($m^3\, s^{-1}$), $y(t)$ is the (low pass filtered) observation of the treatment plant influent ($m^3 s^{-1}$), and $\bar{y}_w(t)$ is a mean weekly dry-weather flow pattern ($m^3\, s^{-1}$) computed a priori from the (low-pass filtered) data on $y(t)$; the input $u(t)$ is a signal representing a single (low-pass filtered), spatially-averaged rainfall time-series (mm). The estimates of the parameters are given by,

$$a_1 = -0.739 \pm 0.028 \;,\; b_3 = 0.063 \pm 0.032 \;;\; b_7 = 0.086 \pm 0.031 \;;$$
$$c_1 = 0.984 \pm 0.001 \;;\; \lambda = 0.027 \pm 0.001.$$

Figure 4 shows the data, deterministic output response, and model error for the deterministic component of eqn. (20) substituted in eqn. (21) to obtain $y(t)$. The effects of the pumping disturbances are visible as regularly placed (approx. once daily) spikes in the observed output and model error sequences; there are also recognisable daily and weekly fluctuations in $y(t)$ with additional peak responses from the

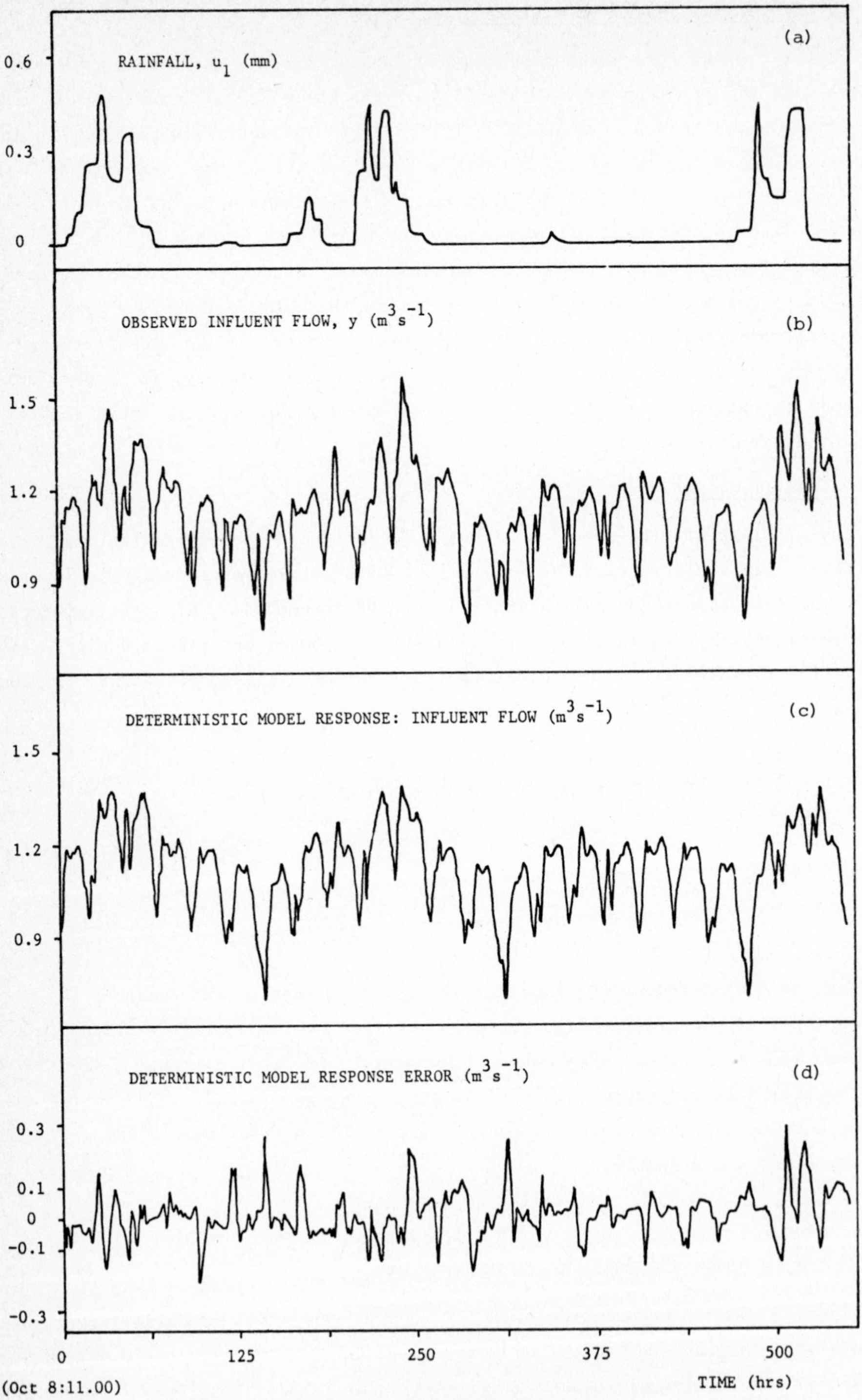

Figure 4 Comparison between the deterministic response of an RRF model (superimposed upon a mean weekly profile) and the observed influent flow

rainfall-runoff. The residuals $\varepsilon(t)$ of the stochastic model, eqn. (20), have a standard deviation (λ) of $\pm$ 0.027 ($m^3 s^{-1}$), a large part of which is contributed by the pumping disturbances. Notice that these residuals are also the one-step ahead prediction errors of the model, eqn. (20), c.f. section 4.2. In short, there are considerable difficulties in the estimation of the $B(q^{-1})$ and $C(q^{-1})$ polynomials and the model is only as good as the quality of the data, which, as we have indicated, leaves much to be desired.

4.2. Adaptive prediction.

In an initial study of the feasibility of an on-line adaptive predictor it would have been advantageous to identify the process, eqn. (1) by maximum likelihood methods, compute the optimal (minimum variance) predictor through eqns. (8) and (10), and then compare the adaptive predictor, eqn. (15), for the unknown process with the optimal predictor for the known process. The preceding remarks do not really support the use of such a procedure, although, at the very least, it is possible to conclude that a suitable predictor would have low-order $A^*(q^{-1})$ and $B^*(q^{-1})$ polynomials.

We consider the case where we have only (low-pass filtered) measurements of the influent flow-rate to the treatment plant, $y(t)$.

One-step ahead prediction

It is found that an appropriate structure for the one-step ahead predictor ($k=1$) is defined by,

$$\hat{y}(t+1|t) = \alpha_o y(t) - \beta_1 \hat{y}(t|t-1) + \gamma_{1o} v_1(t+1) + \gamma_{11} v_1(t) + \gamma_{2o} v_2(t+1) + \gamma_{21} v_2(t) \qquad (22)$$

where $v_1(t) = \bar{y}_w(t)$ and $v_2(t) = \bar{y}_d(t)$ are respectively synthetic, deterministic, weekly and daily dry-weather flow profiles computed a priori from the data. Given the a priori estimates $\underline{\hat{a}}(0)$,

$$\hat{\alpha}_o(0) = 1.20 \qquad \hat{\gamma}_{1o}(0) = 0.47 \qquad \hat{\gamma}_{2o}(0) = 0.37$$

$$\hat{\beta}_1(0) = 0.42 \qquad \hat{\gamma}_{11}(0) = -0.27 \qquad \hat{\gamma}_{21}(0) = -0.30$$

and a priori diagonal matrix $P(0) = (0.1)\ I$, where I is the identity matrix, for the algorithms of eqn. (10) (exponential weighting factor $\mu = 0.995$), the results of figures 5 and 6 are obtained for the adaptive predictor of eqn (22). Despite the inevitable errors from the pumping disturbances, the one-step ahead prediction is, perhaps surprisingly, remarkably close to the observed data; in particular, the runoff from rainfall is well described, even though the predictor is operating in the absence of any information on these events. Notice that the recursive parameter estimates are relatively insensitive to the intermittent effects of runoff, which are

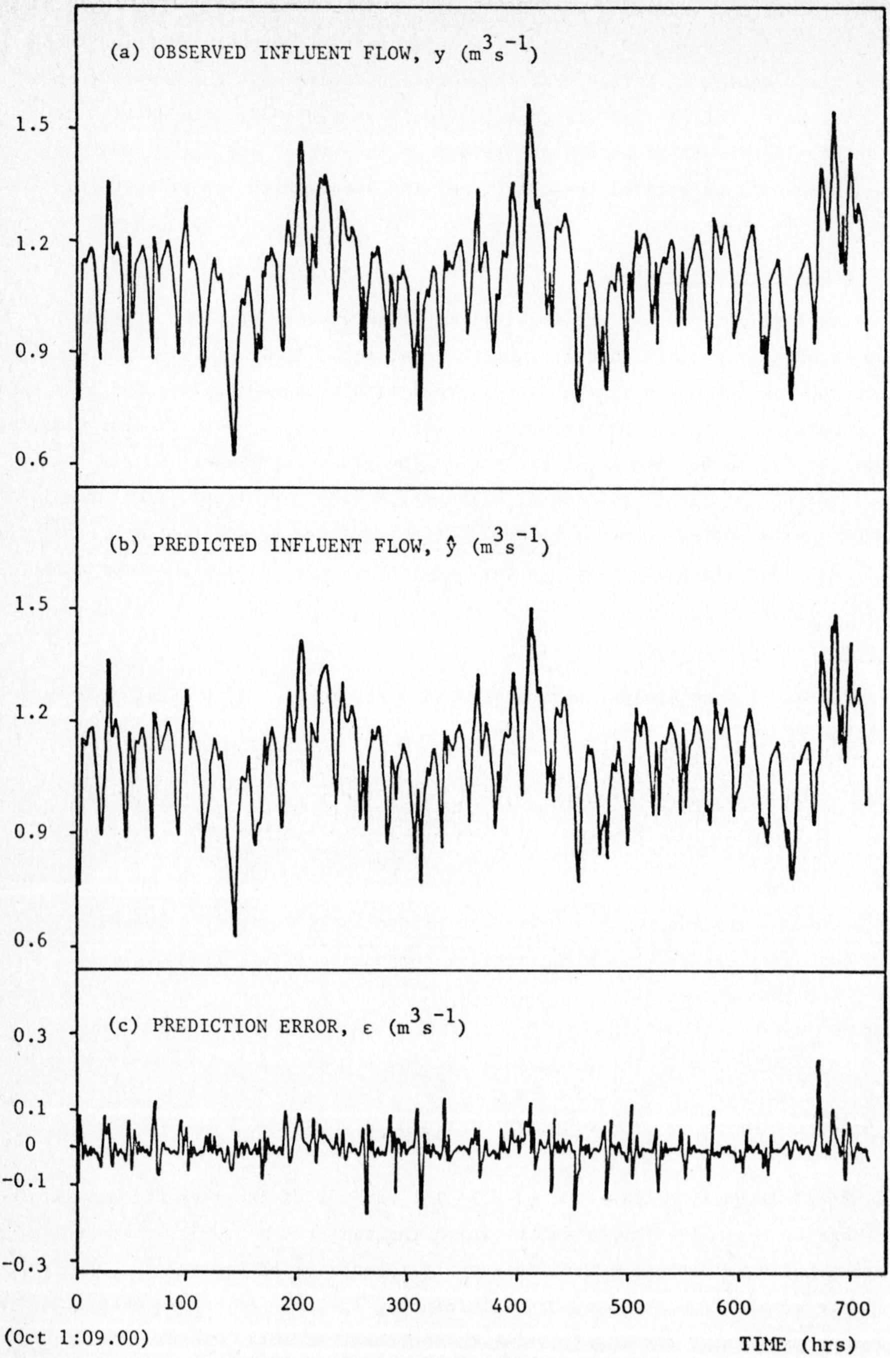

Figure 5 The results of the one-step ahead adaptive predictor

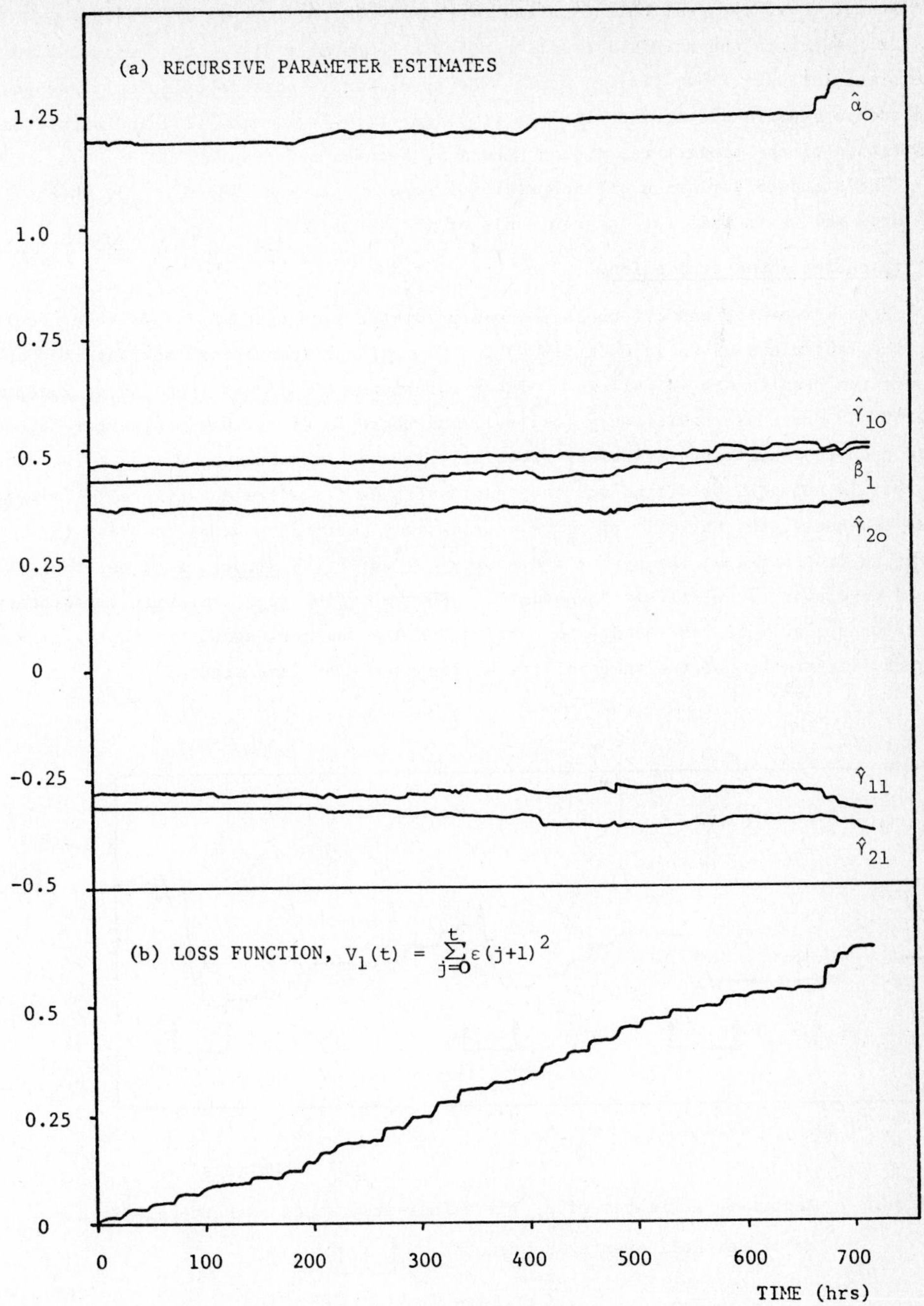

Figure 6 The results of the one-step ahead adaptive predictor

tantamount to an apparent change in the process dynamics. It is argued that a spatially-distributed rainfall event produces a temporally distributed response in the plant influent flow, $y(t)$. Hence the predictor is capable of quickly recognising such a dynamic disturbance through $y(t)$ and $\hat{y}(t|t-1)$ in eqn. (22) and significant adaptation of the parameters, e.g. α_o and β_1 , becomes redundant.

The standard deviation of the predictor errors ε is $\pm$ 0.029 ($m^3 s^{-1}$), which compares well with that for the residuals of the RRF model.

Multiple-step ahead prediction.

Both a two-step and a four-step ahead predictor have been analysed; some results for the latter are given in BECK (1974)[3]. The salient features of the four-step ahead prediction results are as follows. The prediction $\hat{y}(t+4|t)$ is found to be independent of the previous prediction $\hat{y}(t+3|t-1)$ and there is altogether a stronger dependence upon the auxiliary variables, especially the weekly component $v_1(t)$. The runoff process is not well predicted and the resultant peak flows are substantially attenuated. Simultaneously, the estimate of α_o is considerably adapted in order to track the changing properties of the system's dynamics, of which the structure of the four-step ahead predictor is relatively "ignorant". However after such temporary disturbances $\hat{\alpha}_o$ returns slowly to its steady-state value for dry-weather conditions thus giving a good illustration of the adaptability of the predictor (see figure 7).

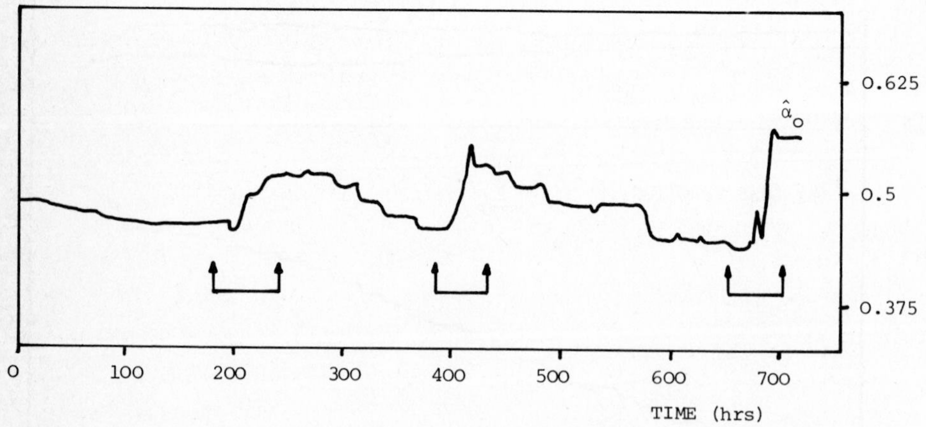

Figure 7 Recursive estimates of α_o for a four-step ahead adaptive predictor

Major rainfall events are denoted

5. SOME COMMENTS ON ADAPTIVE PREDICTION AND CONTROL APPLICATIONS.

Time-varying parameters: Exponential weighting of past data (EWP) is one method of allowing for the recursive estimation of time-varying parameters. But it is a method which does not allow any prior selection between those parameters which may be expected to be time-varying and those which are not. For instance, we might expect the $\Gamma^*_j(q^{-1})$ polynomials for the auxiliary variables to be constant, while the $A^*(q^{-1})$ and $B^*(q^{-1})$ polynomials could be expected to vary much more. Furthermore, the EWP method is only appropriate for the case of slowly-varying parameters, yet the rainfall-runoff is a relatively fast, almost impulsive, disturbance of the system. It seems likely, therefore, that a more sophisticated, but easily programmed, technique of time-variable parameter estimation could improve the operation of an adaptive predictor. For example, if the parameters $\underline{a}(t)$ are assumed to vary in a simple random-walk manner, a modified version of the least squares algorithms, eqn. (17), are given by (YOUNG (1969)[23], YOUNG (1974)[24]),

$$\left.\begin{aligned}
\hat{\underline{a}}(t) &= \hat{\underline{a}}(t-1) - [P(t-1) + D]\, \underline{z}(t)\left(1+\underline{z}^T(t)\,[P(t-1) + D]\,\underline{z}(t)\right)^{-1}\cdot \\
&\qquad \cdot\left[\underline{z}^T(t)\,\hat{\underline{a}}(t-1) - y(t)\right] && \text{(a)} \\
P(t) &= P(t-1) - [P(t-1) + D]\,\underline{z}(t)\left(1+\underline{z}^T(t)\,[P(t-1) + D]\,\underline{z}(t)\right)^{-1}\cdot \\
&\qquad \cdot\, \underline{z}^T(t)\,[P(t-1) + D] && \text{(b)}
\end{aligned}\right\} \quad (24)$$

where D is a positive, definite, (usually) diagonal matrix which reflects the expected rates of change in the parameters $\underline{a}$ (c.f. eqn. (19)).

Auxiliary variables and additional measurements: For higher values of k the use of rainfall measurements would be of benefit to the predictor. Note that from eqn. (20) there is good reason to believe that the Käppala sewer system has a pure time delay $\tau \simeq 3$ (hrs). In a practical situation, therefore, an on-line predictor could cope with a delay of up to 3 hours in the receipt of rainfall measurements, although the time to the peak runoff response $\tau_p (> \tau)$ is perhaps a more critical measure for determining the benefits of using these data. It is, after all, the peak flows which cause the greatest upset to the operational control of the network and treatment plant.

Sewer network flow control: Sewer flow control is exercised largely by the installation of storage tanks in the network, although a small amount of storage is available in the sewers themselves (see e.g. PEW et al (1973)[20]). This large-scale control problem seems to be amenable to the hierarchical approach (e.g. LABADIE et al (1975)[16]). (Similar approaches have been applied to the analogous problem of potable water supply network control, FALLSIDE and PERRY (1975)[9], FALLSIDE et al (1975)[10]).

Wastewater treatment plant control: Currently there are many more problems than solutions in wastewater treatment plant control (e.g. OLSSON et al (1973)[18]). However, the prediction and control of the influent flow has wide-ranging implications not only for the treatment plant but also for the whole water quality system (YOUNG and BECK (1974)[25], BECK (1975)[4]: the essential point is that flow control alleviates gross overloading of the water quality system and, at the same time, it regulates the dynamic behaviour of many of the unit processes of wastewater treatment. A first study of flow equalisation, i.e. the modulation of diurnal variations, shows that significant benefits might accrue, for example, in the operation of sedimentation processes (LaGREGA and KEENAN (1974)[17]). Of course, flow prediction is only a part of the problem of characterising the plant input raw material; in addition, it is necessary to describe the quality of the sewage flow. Recently, BERTHOUEX et al (1975)[5] have used similar time-series analysis techniques (BOX and JENKINS (1970)[6]) for the modelling of plant input biochemical oxygen demand variations.

6. CONCLUSIONS

The major limitation in this study of the adaptive prediction of urban sewer flows has been the poor quality of the data. In any future study it can be expected that, while pumping disturbances may not be eliminated completely, better data would be available for analysis. With a view to on-line implementation of the predictor it would,therefore, be important to site the flow-measuring equipment at a carefully chosen location.

One-step ahead forecasts of the plant influent flow are obtained from an adaptive predictor which closely approaches the satisfaction of the practical constraints on the system: namely, as little automated instrumentation as possible should be assumed. The salient feature of the black box model for the predictor is its simplicity and compactness when compared with other, largely deterministic, models based on the physical laws of the system behaviour. For it should be remembered that the currently existing technology of wastewater treatment favours the simple rather than the sophisticated.

ACKNOWLEDGEMENTS

This work was carried out while the author was visiting the division of Automatic Control at the Lund Institute of Technology, Sweden. It is with gratitude that he acknowledges the assistance and advice provided by Professor Karl-Johan Åström and his Department. The author is deeply indebted to Jan Holst who gave much time to the discussion of adaptive predictors. Further thanks are due to Björn Wittenmark, Ivar Gustavsson, and especially to Gustaf Olsson for his continual encouragement and useful comments. Finally, the author is grateful to Kjell-Ivar Dahlqvist of the Käppala treatment plant for the receipt of the data.

REFERENCES

1. ÅSTRÖM K.J., "Introduction to stochastic control theory", Academic Press, New York, 1970.
2. ÅSTRÖM K.J., and BOHLIN T., "Numerical identification of linear dynamic systems from normal operating records", Proc. IFAC symp. Theory of self-adaptive control systems, Teddington, England, 1965.
3. BECK M.B., "The identification and prediction of urban sewer flows - a preliminary study", Report 7432(C), Lund Inst. Techn., Div. Aut. Contr., 1974.

4. BECK, M.B., "Dynamic modelling and control applications in water quality maintenance", Report CUED/F - Contr/TR92, Control Group, Univ. Eng. Dept., Cambridge, 1975.
5. BERTHOEUX P.M., HUNTER W.G., PALLESEN L.C., and SHIH C-Y., "Modelling sewage treatment plant influent data", Proc. A.S.C.E., J. Env. Eng. Div., Vol.101, No. EE1, pp 127-138, Feb. 1975.
6. BOX G.E.P., and JENKINS G.M., "Time-series analysis, forecasting and control", Holden-Day, San Francisco, (1970).
7. CHEN C.W. and SCHUBINSKI R.P., "Computer simulation of urban storm water runoff", Proc. A.S.C.E., J. Hydr. Div., Vol.97, No.HY2, pp 289-301, Feb. 1971.
8. EYKHOFF P., "System identification-parameter and state examination", John Wiley and Sons, London, 1974.
9. FALLSIDE F., and PERRY P.F., "Hierarchical optimisation of a water supply network", Proc. IEE, Vol. 122, No.2., pp 202-208, Feb. 1975.
10. FALLSIDE F., PERRY P.F., and RICE P.D., "On-line prediction of consumption for water supply network control", Reprints 6th IFAC Congress, Boston, Massachusetts, Aug. 1975.
11. GOEL A.L., and LaGREGA M.D., "Stochastic models for forecasting sewage flows", Paper presented at 41st Natl. Meeting, Operations Res. Soc. Amer., New Orleans, 1972.
12. GUSTAVSSON I.,"Parametric identification of multiple input, single output linear dynamic systems", Report 6907, Lund Inst. Techn., Div. Aut. Contr., 1969.
13. HARRIS G.S., "Real time routing of flood hydrographs in storm sewers", Proc. A.S.C.E., J. Hydr. Div., Vol.96, No.HY6, pp 1247-1260, June, 1970.
14. HOLST J., "The use of self-tuning predictors for forecasting the loading of a power system" (in Swedish), Report 7433C,Lund Inst. Techn., Div. Aut. Contr., 1974.
15. LABADIE J.W., GRIGG N.S., and BRADFORD B.H., "Automatic control of large-scale combined sewer systems", Proc. A.S.C.E., J. Env. Eng. Div., Vol.101, No. EE1, pp. 27-39, Feb. 1975.
17. LaGREGA M.D., and KEENAN J.D., "Effects of equalising wastewater flows", J.W.P.C.F., Vol.46, No.1, p.p. 123-132, Jan. 1974.
18. OLSSON, G., DAHLQVIST K-I., EKLUND K., and ULMGREN L., "Control problems in wastewater treatment", Report, Axel Johnson Inst. for industr. Res., Nynäshamn, Sweden, 1973.
19. PAPADAKIS C.N., and PREUL H.C., "Testing of methods for determination of urban runoff", Proc. A.S.C.E., J. Hydr. Div., Vol.99 No. HY9, pp. 1319-1335, Sept.1973.
20. PEW K.A., CALLERY R.L., BRANDSETTER A., and ANDERSON J.J., "Data acquisition and combined sewer controls in Cleveland", J.W.P.C.F., Vol.45, No.11, pp.2276-2289, Nov.1973.
21. WITTENMARK B., "A self-tuning regulator", Report 7311, Lund. Inst. Techn.,Div. Aut. Contr., 1973.
22. WITTENMARK B., "A self-tuning predictor", I.E.E.E., Trans. Aut. Contr., Vol.AC-19 No.6, pp. 848-851, Dec. 1974.
23. YOUNG P.C., "Applying parameter estimation to dynamic systems - Part I", Control Engng., Vol.16, No.10, pp. 119-125, Oct.1969.
24. YOUNG P.C., "A recursive approach to time-series analysis", Bull Inst. Maths. Appl. (IMA), Vol.10, Nos.5/6, pp. 209-224, May/June, 1974.
25. YOUNG P.C., and BECK M.B., "The modelling and control of water quality in a river system", Automatica, Vol.10, No.5, pp. 455-468, Sept. 1974.

THE USE OF MIXED INTEGER PROGRAMMING FOR THE EVALUATION OF SOME ALTERNATE AIR POLLUTION ABATEMENT POLICIES

L.F. Escudero and A. Vazquez Muñiz
Universidad Autónoma de Madrid - IBM Scientific Center
Po. de la Castellana, 4. Madrid (Spain)

INTRODUCTION

As a part of the preliminary work performed in the Nervion River Valley Bilbao Air Pollution Study, the following method has been developed for the evaluation and selection of emission control policies and standards.

Escudero and Jimenez, 1975 describes a methodology used to estimate the probability distribution of pollutant concentrations in each receptor grid square of a studied area for a seasonal time period, given the predicted pollutant emissions due to the point and area sources with significant influence on the pollutant concentration. This probability distribution is estimated over the total range of different meteorological conditions that affect the concentration significantly.

The probability distribution, which is estimated on the basis of a stochastic diffusion model, gives the probability for each meteorological condition and set of contributing emissions that the concentration in each grid square will exceed the maximum limit of concentration.

A polluted grid square is considered to be one in which this probability is greater than the maximum probability allowed, called the relative limit. A contributing areas is the set of point sources and area sources which affect the concentration in the receptor grid square. A polluted area is defined as the set of contributing areas and polluted grid squares which have at least one grid square or emitter source in common.

GENERAL OBJECTIVE AND CONDITIONS FOR THE MASC-AP MODEL

The objective of this model is to evaluate the alternatives for reducing the emission at the point and area sources so that the problem area will no longer be polluted area.

The reduction alternatives may be programmed for a single seasonal period or for a set of these periods adapting the reduction alternative for each emitter source to fixed and constant abatement levels for the entire period programmed (Escudero, 1973). This paper treats a single seasonal period, and in contrast to other types of models (Gorr and Kortanek, 1970; Kortanek and Gorr, 1971; Teller, 1968), the probabilistic limits of the real concentration are used, as it is one of the principal characteristics of the reduction model.

The probabilistic limits of the concentration include the new average theoretical concentrations in the polluted grid square when the emissions are reduced (Escudero and Jimenez, 1975). These concentrations correspond to a given set of probabilities that the real concentration exceed the absolute limit, so that once the new theoretical concentration has been estimated it is assumed that it is the upper limit of the interval which corresponds to it in the limit concentrations relative to the given set of probabilities. In this way an estimate is made of the probability of excess real concentration for each theoretical concentration, and therefore for each emission reduction alternative.

The emission reduction alternatives are estimated such that the emission reduction to be imposed on each influence source be both the minimum possible and be in proportion to its influence on the polluted area.

THE ELEMENTS OF THE EMISSIONS REDUCTION MODEL

The elements needed for using this mixed integer programming model for each problem area are the following:

The receptor grid square $r \forall r \in R$ which makes up the polluted area where the concentration is to be reduced.

The influence emitter grid square $e \forall e \in E$ within the problem area.

The meteorological condition $m \forall m \in M$ in grid square r which, given the set of emissions, causes the real concentration C_{rm} to exceed the absolute limit AL in the seasonal period under consideration.

The type of probability $p \forall p \in P$ which corresponds to the probability PAL_{rmp} of the limit concentration UC_{rmp}.

The predicted pollutant emission AQA_e (μg/s) for the seasonal period under consideration coming from the area sources located in emitter grid square e. Idem (μg/s) for point sources (AQP_e).

The theoretical unit influence KA_{rem} of the area emissions from emitter grid square e upon grid square r under meteorological condition m, according to the stochastic diffusion model. Idem for the point source emissions (KP_{rem}).

The average theoretical pollutant concentration TC_{rm} (μg/m^3) which, in the stochastic diffusion model, is found in grid square r, under meteorological condition m, given the actual set of emissions AQA_e and AQP_e. The pollutant concentration TC_{rm} is represented by:

$$TC_{rm} = a_{rm} + \sum_{e=1}^{E} (KA_{rem} AQA_e + KP_{rem} AQP_e) \qquad \forall m \in M,\ e \in R \tag{1}$$

where a_{rm} is an independant term considering the background concentration and others.

The frequency MP_m of meteorological condition m during the seasonal period under consideration. Only those meteorological conditions are taken into account whose probability MP_m is significant.

The meximum allowable probability (relative limit) RL that the real concentration C_r in any grid square exceed the absolute limit AL.

The theoretical concentration UC_{rmp} in grid square r under meteorological condition m corresponding to probability PAL_{rmp}.

The given set of probabilities PAL_{rmp} that the real concentration in each situation rm exceed the absolute limit AL. Using the stochastic diffusion model, the theoretical concentration is obtained for each possible set of emissions. It is assumed that the probability that the real concentration exceed the limit AL is the probability estimated by the UC_{rmp} value inmediately above the corresponding theoretical concentration.

The probability that for the predicted set of emissions AQA_e and $AQAP_e$ the real concentration in grid square r under meteorological condition m exceed the maximun limit AL, taking into consideration the probability of the meteorological condition, so that $PC_{rm} = MP_m \; PAL_{rm}$.

The probability PAL_{rm} that, for the predicted set of emissions, the real concentration exceeds the absolute limit will be equal to PAL_{rmP}. Therefore, $UC_{rmP} = TC_{rm}$.

The influence WA_e of the area sources in emitter grid square e during the seasonal period considered upon the pollutant concentration in all the grid squares which make up the polluted area under all the meteorological conditions considered (Escudero and Jimenez, 1975). Idem for the point sources (WP_e). The influences WA_e and WP_e are represented by:

$$WA_e = \sum_{r=1}^{R} \sum_{m=1}^{M} KA_{rem} \; AQA_e \; PC_{rm} \tag{2a}$$

$$WP_e = \sum_{r=1}^{R} \sum_{m=1}^{M} KP_{rem} \; AQP_e \; PC_{rm} \tag{2b}$$

The maximum percent MRA_e of the reduction allowed of the predicted emission AQA_e in emitter grid square e, based upon socioeconomic considerations. Idem for the point sources $AQP_e (MRP_e)$.

The variables used in the model are: The pollutant emission XQA_e to be reduced in the area source of emitter grid square e during the entire seasonal period being considered. Idem for the point sources (XQP_e). The new average theoretical concentration XC_{rm} in situation rm corresponding to the new emission from each emitter grid square. The binary variable Y_{rmp} whose value is 1 if the theoretical concentration UC_{rmp} is the upper limit of the concentration XC_{rm}. If not its value is 0.

THE FORMULATION OF THE MASC-AP MODEL

Using the elements described above, the model for the reduction of emissions that will eliminate the polluted area is the following:

Minimize in a weighted form the emission reduction:

$$\text{Min. } QR = \sum_{e=1}^{E} \left(\frac{1}{WA_e} XQA_e + \frac{1}{WP_e} XQP_e \right) \tag{3}$$

such that, with the conditions being the same, priority is given to the emission in the grid square that pollutes most.

Minimization of the Equation (3) is subject to the following conditions:

1) The estimation of the new theoretical average concentration XC_{rm} corresponding, according to the stochastic diffusion model, to the new set of emissions.

$$XC_{rm} = TC_{rm} - \sum_{e=1}^{E} (KA_{rem} \; XQA_e + KP_{rem} \; XQP_e) \qquad \forall m \in M,\ r \in R \tag{4}$$

2) The necessity that only variable Y_{rmp} take on the value 1 if UC_{rmp} is the limit inmediately above the new average theoretical concentration XC_{rm} $\forall m \in M$, $r \in R$.

$$XC_{rm} \le \sum_{p=1}^{P} UC_{rmp} \; Y_{rmp} \qquad \forall m \in M,\ r \in R \tag{5}$$

$$1 = \sum_{p=1}^{P} Y_{rmp} \qquad \forall m \in M,\ r \in R \tag{6}$$

3) The equation (8) is the principal condition of the model requiring the probability

$$\sum_{m=1}^{M} MP_m \; PAL_{rmp} \; Y_{rmp} \tag{7}$$

that the real concentration C_r exceed the absolute limit AL not be greater than the relative limit RL in any of the polluted grid square.

$$\sum_{m=1}^{M} \sum_{p=1}^{P} MP_m \; PAL_{rmp} \; Y_{rmp} \le RL \qquad \forall r \in R \tag{8}$$

In this regard it is important to note that Equation (6) demands that each case have only one Equation (7) different from zero.

4) The variables for the amount of emission reduction are represented by:

$$XQA_e \le MRA_e \; AQA_e \tag{9a}$$

$$XQP_e \le MRP_e \; AQP_e \tag{9b}$$

The principal results of the reduction model are:

a) The reduction values, expressed in percentages, for the point and area sources of each grid square for the time period considered.

b) The values of the corresponding new emissions.

c) The new probabilistic distribution of concentration for each receptor grid square which makes up the polluted area.

d) The probability that the new concentration exceed the limit established.

THE BRANCH AND BOUND POSSIBILITIES IN THE MASC-AP MODEL

The model for the reduction of the pollutant emissions needs the use of mixed integer programming techniques, since the Y variables are binary being able to take on only the values 0 and 1. Among the many algorithms existing for its solution (Geoffrion and Marsten, 1972) the MASC-AP reduction model is based on the IBM MPSX/MIP system using the following possibilities.

SOS conditions

A Special Order Set is a set (Beale and Tomlin, 1969) of binary variables of which one and only one has the value 1. In the emissions reduction model the SOS conditions are included in Equation (6) so that if one variable has the value 1 the others must be null. Accompanying each SOS row there must be another condition or some weighting that is responsible for the important attributed to it. For the SOS condition the corresponding weighting is the probability PC_{rm} that the concentration C_r exceed the maximum limit AL.

Accompanying each SOS row there is another weighting row that represents the importance attributed to each SOS variable, in this case to each Y_{rmp} variable. For the SOS row (Equation 6) the corresponding weighting row is the Equation (5).

The SOS rows possibility is used in the branch and bound phase, once the continuous optimum solution is obtained, when at a certain node the branching integer variable (in this case, SOS row) is selected. To branch the SOS row, the value of its weighting row (Equation 5) is analyzed, so that (Escudero, 1975b) if it were the case, for example that

$$1 = Y_1 + Y_2 + Y_3 + Y_4 + Y_5 \qquad \text{(SOS row)} \qquad (10)$$

$$W = 750Y_1 + 500Y_2 + 250Y_3 + 100Y_4 + 50Y_5 \qquad \text{(weighting row)} \qquad (11)$$

and the SOS row did not have any binary variable with a value of 1, the value of W is noted, and if this is, for example, 300, then, since the only other alternatives would be 750, 500, 250, 100 and 50, either $W > 300$ (in which case W is 750 or 500) or $W < 300$ (in which case W is 250 or 100 or 50). To establish this dichotomy it is necessary that in the first case $Y_3 = Y_4 = Y_5 = 0$ and in the second case that $Y_1 = Y_2 = 0$, so that in the corresponding branch 3 and 2 SOS variables respectively have been fixed, when in the normal procedure (Benichou et al., 1971) only one of the variables would have been acted upon.

Quasi-integer variables

In the optimization models with integer variables, it is necessary, in the optimum, that these variables take on integer values (0 or 1 in this case), but often in the branching formation the candidate nodes have some variables with integer values and others with quasi-integer values (for example, 0.001; 0.995) which means having many successor nodes in order to make them integers (primarily if the number of integer variables is high and their coefficients in the objective function are not very different).

The need in our case for binary variables only is motivated by the requirement in Equation (8) that the probability that the concentration exceed the absolute limit not be greater than the relative limit. Thus, even though the binary variables had only quasi-integer values, the objective would also be achieved, since the quasi-integrality of the binary variables will really bring about the probability of exceeding the absolute limit, even though it were not the relative limit, but were a value very close to it. Given the probabilistic form of the model this would not ruin the plan adopted for the reduction of the emissions.

Pseudo-cost of the integer variables

There exist in the literature many controversies over the strategy to be used in the branch and bound phase, mainly in regard to the choice of the next branching node and the choice of the branching variable. Although in the choice of the branching node the criterium may be used of the best functional value (Roy et al., 1970) or a mixed criterium, the best functional value until the first integer solution and then the best estimated value (Benichou et al., 1971), the MASC-AP model uses the criterium of the best estimated value. In regard to the branching variable, although the penalties criterium may be adopted (Roy et al., 1970), the MASC-AP model uses the criterium of the pseudo-costs (Benichou et al., 1971) since it has been observed experimentally that it better incorporates the influence of each variable upon the objective function.

Therefore, using the SOS rows as the "branching variables" (Escudero, 1975b), the elements of this strategy are the following:

$\bar{W}_c$. The real value of the weighting row W_c of the "branching SOS row" in the optimum solution of the subproblem (or node) k.

$f_c^{(r)}$. The sum of SOS variables ($\sum_{j\le r} Y_j$) that make up the SOS row c, being fixed to zero in the first branch of the dichotomy r. In the case of Equations (10) and (11), r=2 then $f_c^{(2)} = Y_1 + Y_2$. Therefore, for the second branch of the dichotomy r we have $1 - f_c^{(2)} = Y_3 + Y_4 + Y_5$.

F^k. The optimum functional value in subproblem k.

F^{n+1}. The optimum functional value in the subproblem (n+1).

F^{n+2}. The optimum functional value in the subproblem (n+2). The subproblems (n+1) and (n+2) have been generated by means of branching on the SOS row with the dichotomy r.

The pseudo-costs lower and upper of the SOS row in the dichotomy r (if they have not been obtained previously) are estimated as follows:

$$PCL_c^{(r)} = \frac{|F^k - F^{n+1}|}{f_c^{(r)}} \tag{12}$$

$$PCU_c^{(r)} = \frac{|F^k - F^{n+2}|}{1 - f_c^{(r)}} \tag{13}$$

So that, if for each dichotomy r (in our case r=1, 2, 3 and 4) of each SOS row i we have obtained the value $\delta_i^{(r)}$:

$$\delta_i^{(r)} = \min \{PCL_i^{(r)} f_i^{(r)}, PCU_i^{(r)} (1-f_i^{(r)})\} \quad (14)$$

the estimations of each node are obtained in the following way. Using the pseudo-costs of the I SOS rows in which one SOS variable has not taken the value 1 in the node (k), the calculation is made on the basis of the formula:

$$E^k = F^k + \sum_{i=1}^{I} \delta_i^{(r)} \quad (15)$$

where r is the corresponding dichotomy of each of the I SOS rows considered. Equation (15) represents the funcional value E^k of the best integer solution which is estimated may be obtained with the nodes generated from the node k.

The pseudo-costs (Equations 12 and 13) represent the deteriorization of the optimum value (F^k) of the function for every unit of change in the corresponding SOS row. These values depend on the node in which they have been obtained. However, on the basis of the preliminary experiments which have been carried out, it may be assumed that although they do not remain constant, they have generally the same order of magnitude.

THE MASC-AP MODEL STRATEGY

The strategy of the MASC-AP model, since it has a large percentage of binary variables and can thus be considered "quasi-pure", is the following.

The selection of the branching variable and the branching node.

The SOS row in Equation (6) to bifurcate will be that which has not yet reached an integer or quasi-integer value, whose associated value PC_{rm} is greater, since this is the most difficult SOS condition to fulfill, and therefore the condition which causes a greater deteriorization in the objective function. Once the first integer solution is obtained, the SOS row is chosen whose value $\delta_i^{(r)}$ (Equation 14) is the one which offers a greater deteriorization in the objective function.

These deteriorizations are classified in dynamic order such that the "list" of the different deteriorizations is composed by the actualized pseudo-costs. When the SOS row to bifurcate has been selected, the criterium for creating the two successor nodes is based on Equation (5).

Except in the node (0), before selecting the branching SOS row it is necessary to select the branching node from among all the candidate nodes. The criterium adopted by the MASC-AP model is to choose the node with the best estimated value so that, since the pseudo-costs are not calculated for the SOS rows which are not yet branching SOS rows, the estimated value in the first branches, and practically until some integer solution is reached, differs very little from the functional value.

Dropped nodes and selection of the candidate nodes

Before obtaining the optimum continuous solution, the MASC-AP model obtains a feasible integer solution such that in the branch and bound phase those nodes are dropped whose functional value is worse than that of the previously obtained integer solution.

Once the integer solution has been obtained, the branch and bound phase drops the nodes whose functional value is greater say by 10% than that of the integer solution. Also, this phase "postpones" nodes whose functional value even if it is greater than the value of the integer solution does not have a difference greater than the previous value (e.g. 10%), so that once the optimality of the best integer solution has been proved it is observed whether among the postponed succesor nodes there is some integer solution which differs from the optimum solution by no more than 10%. In this way, different alternatives for the reduction of emissions are produced.

Now, given that the alternatives for the emission are estimated, since the effects of each emitter source on the pollution of the problem area are estimated for only the polluted area, a node is not admitted as candidate node if its functional value is not better, say, as a minimum by 10%, than the value of the best integer solution. In this way much of the CPU time is saved, and at the same time little of the accuracy of the quasi-optimum integer solution is lost.

CONCLUSION

The model presented in this paper must be considered to be an effective tool for establishing bases for corrective alternatives for an abatement problem of air pollution. It should also be considered a very useful instrument for qualifying, within the development policies for a given area, the standards that are more and more indispensible for protecting our air environment.

It should be noted that the basic statistical parameter considered in the formulation of the model is the maximum probability allowed that the concentration in a given grid square exceed the maximum limit allowed, in contrast to models which use averages as their standards of quality. This methods avoids the danger of large concentrations being masked with smaller concentrations. This probability depends conjointly on the probabilistic matrix of the typology by which the different meteorological factors have been stratified and the probability that for a theoretical concentration estimated on the basis of a predicted set of emissions the real concentration might exceed the maximum limit permited.

It is of interest to point out that in order to estimate the concentration in each grid square, stochastic diffusion models have been used for each meteorological stratum, depending on the emissions, so that the tabular form of the model is in function with the emitter grid squares.

The criterium which minimize the model is the weighted reduction of the emission levels for each contributing grid square in accord with the effect it has on the pollutant concentration in the sum of the grid squares which make up the polluted area.

REFERENCES

Beale, E.M.L. and J.A. Tomlin (1969) Special facilities in a general mathematical programming system for non-convex problem using ordered sets of variables. 5th Inter. Conf. on O.R., North-Holland, 447-454.

Benichou, M. et al. (1971) Experiments in mixed-integer linear programming. Mathematical Programming, 1, 1:76-94.

Escudero L.F. (1973) Formulación matemática de un modelo probabilístico de estimación y reducción de contaminantes atmosféricos. Centro de Investigación UAM-IBM, PCI-10.73, 71-78.

Escudero, L.F. (1975a) The Air Pollution Abatement MASC-AP Model. Mathematical Models for Environment Problems, University of Southampton, England.

Escudero, L.F. (1975b) Programación lineal contínua, entera y mixta, vol. I, chap. 10.7, ed. Deusto, Bilbao, Spain.

Escudero, L.F. and J. Jimenez (1975) Estimación de zonas contaminadas. I Congreso Iberoamericano del Medio Ambiente, Madrid.

Fahlander, K., S-A. Gustafson, and L.E. Olsson (1974) Computing optimal air pollution abatement strategies-some numerical experiments on field data. Proceedings of the Fifth Meeting of the Expert Panel on Air pollution Modeling, Nato Committee on the Challenges to Modern Society, 27.

Geoffrion, A.M. and R.E. Marsten (1972) Integer programming algorithms: a framework and state-of-art-survey. Man. Sci., 18, 9:465-491.

Gorr, W.I. and K.O. Kortanek (1970) Numerical aspect of Pollution abatement problem: Constrained generalized moment techniques. Inst. of Physical Planning, Carnegie-Mellon University, 12.

Gorr, W.I., S-A. Gustafson and K.O. Kortanek (1972) Optimal control strategies for air quality standards and regulatory policies. Environment and Planning, 4:183-192.

Gustafson, S-A. and K.O. Kortanek (1972) Analytical properties of some multiple-source urban diffusion models. Enviroment and planning 4:31-34.

Gustafson, S-A. and K.O. Kortanek (1973) Mathematical Models for air pollution control: determination of optimum abatement policies. Models for Environment pollution control (ed. R.A. Deininger), Ann Arbor Science Publ., 251-265.

Gustafson, S-A. and K.O. Kortanek (1975) On the calculation of Optimal long-term air pollution abatement strategies for multiple-source areas. Mathematical Models for Environment Problems, University of Southampton, England.

IBM (1975) MPSX/MIP/370, SH19-1094/1095/1099, N.Y.

Khon, R.E. (1970) Linear Programming Model for air pollution control: a pilot study of the St. Louis Airshed. Journ. Air Poll. Contr. Assoc., 20:78-82.

Kortanek, K.O. and W.I. Gorr (1971) Cost benefit measures for regional air pollution abatement models, I. of P.P., 5.

Roy, B. et al. (1970) From SEP procedure to the mixed ophelie program. Integer and non-linear programming (ed. J. Abadie), North-Holland, 419-436.

Teller, A. (1968) The use of linear programming to estimate the cost of some alternate air pollution abatement policies. Proc. IBM 320-1953, N.Y., 345-354.

ON THE USE OF QUASILINEARIZATION FOR THE SOLUTION OF SUB-PROBLEMS IN ON-LINE HIERARCHICAL CONTROL AND ITS APPLICATION TO A WATER DISTRIBUTION NETWORK

F. Fallside* and P.F. Perry**

Summary

Due to the difficulties of handling non-linearities in many large systems to which on-line optimal control is being applied, many applications have had to be restricted to the linear model-quadratic cost case. In particular, if the calculations are performed in a decentralized manner, the sub-system problems must yield a rapid solution and in the simple linear-quadratic case analytic solutions to these sub-problems may be obtained. The method of quasilinearization for the resolution of boundary-value problems arising in the solution of non-linear differential equations has been widely developed. This paper examines the use of quasilinearization algorithms for the solution of sub-problems arising in a problem decomposition using Lagrangian duality. The good convergence properties of the algorithms make them particularly useful for the solution of the sub-system problems. The actual improvement in operating costs obtained by handling more general sub-system non-linearities is compared with the increased computational burden for an actual on-line water control scheme.

* Reader in Electrical Engineering, Cambridge University.

** Research student in Electrical Engineering, Cambridge University.

1. Introduction

The determination of optimal controls for on-line implementation is, in general, a most difficult task. Only in restricted cases, such as linearized process models and quadratic cost expansions, can analytic solutions to the control problems be obtained, and consequently determination of optimal controls and the associated optimal trajectories must often be obtained iteratively on a computer. Since many practical systems are non-linear it is desirable to have a control algorithm capable of handling such non-linearities. The dynamic programming method[1-3] is capable of handling a very general type of problem, but has enormous high speed memory and computational requirements. State increment dynamic programming[4] reduces high speed memory requirements but still requires much computing time, while the successive approximation method[4] requires an equal number of state and control variables, although the time requirements are somewhat reduced. Thus a considerable amount of computing power has to be sacrificed if more general systems are to be handled using dynamic programming methods.

For the solution of very large problems formulated in a decentralized manner clearly none of the above methods are appropriate, since any hierarchical control algorithm involves the repetitive solution of many sub-system problems. The quasilinearization method,[5] developed by Bellman and Kalaba, is a useful method of obtaining an approximate solution to the non-linear sub-system boundary-value problem. It basically solves a sequence of linearized problems which hopefully converge on the true solution of the non-linear problem. Although convergence is in no sense guaranteed, in cases where it does work it provides a computationally efficient method of solving the non-linear sub-system problems.

If this method is to be of use in solving many non-linear sub-system problems in a hierarchical structure, clearly it must converge very rapidly. In this paper the quasilinearization algorithm is used for the solution of non-linear sub-system problems arising from the spatial decomposition technique used in Lagrange duality theory.[7] A modified[6] algorithm, which uses a scaling factor in the sub-system variations and has a descent property in the error indices, is assessed for its usefulness in speeding up sub-system convergence. The method is applied to a water supply control scheme, which includes sub-problems of a fairly general form, involving the minimization of a functional subject to differential, non-differential, inequality and terminal constraints. A comparison is made between pump energy requirements as predicted by linear and non-linear models at the sub-systems, and the increased computational burden of handling the non-linear case.

2. Statement of problem

The subject of this paper is the optimal control of a large dynamical system whose hierarchical structure allows it to be described as a set of N interconnected dynamical sub-problems[7] in the following way:

$$\min_{\underline{x}_i,\underline{u}_i,\underline{m}_i,\underline{y}_i} \sum_{i=1}^{N} \{F_i(\underline{x}_i(t_f)) + \int_{t_o}^{t_f} f_i(\underline{x}_i,\underline{u}_i,\underline{y}_i,\underline{m}_i,t)\,dt\}$$

subject to

$$\begin{aligned}
\dot{\underline{x}}_i &= \underline{g}_i(\underline{x}_i,\underline{u}_i,\underline{y}_i,\underline{m}_i,t)\\
\underline{x}_i(t_o) &= \underline{x}_{io}\\
\underline{h}_i(\underline{x}_i,\underline{u}_i,\underline{y}_i,\underline{m}_i,t) &\leq \underline{0} \qquad\qquad i = 1,2,\ldots,N\\
\underline{H}_i(\underline{x}_i(t_f)) &\leq \underline{0}\\
\underline{q}_i(\underline{x}_i,\underline{u}_i,\underline{y}_i,\underline{m}_i,t) &= \underline{0}\\
\underline{Q}_i(\underline{x}_i,\underline{u}_i,\underline{y}_i,\underline{m}_i,t_f) &= \underline{0}
\end{aligned} \tag{1}$$

$$\begin{aligned}
\sum_{i=1}^{N} \underline{G}_i(\underline{x}_i,\underline{u}_i,\underline{y}_i,\underline{m}_i,t) &= \underline{0}\\
\sum_{i=1}^{N} \underline{R}_i(\underline{x}_i,\underline{u}_i,\underline{y}_i,\underline{m}_i,t) &\leq \underline{0}
\end{aligned} \tag{2}$$

where $\underline{x}_i$ are the states, $\underline{u}_i$ the controls, $\underline{y}_i$ the dependent variables, $\underline{m}_i$ the coordinating variables, F_i the terminal cost, f_i the instantaneous cost, all for the ith sub-problem. Using the additive separability of the Lagrangian,[7] the following N sub-problems may be defined

$$\min_{\underline{x}_i,\underline{u}_i,\underline{m}_i} \{F_i(\underline{x}_i(t_f)) + \int_{t_o}^{t_f} f_i^*\,dt\}$$

subject to constraints (1) and (2), where

$$f_i^* = f_i + \langle\underline{\beta},\underline{G}_i\rangle + \langle\underline{\gamma},\underline{R}_i\rangle \tag{3}$$

where $\underline{\beta}$ and $\underline{\gamma}$ are appropriate N-vector multipliers, giving the well-known Goal Coordination Algorithm which maximizes the dual function at one level and repetitively solves a set of N sub-problems at a lower level until overall convergence is reached. A similar decomposition in discrete time may also be obtained. This paper is primarily concerned with the derivation of efficient solution methods for general sub-problems of this form within this hierarchical structure. In particular, if true model non-linearities are used, is the increased computational burden associated with obtaining solutions by a modified quasilinearization method worthwhile in terms of the increased cost savings over the results for the linear case?

Ignoring the subscripts, clearly each sub-system problem is of the form

$$\min_{\underline{x},\underline{u},\underline{m},\underline{y}} J = F(\underline{x}(t_f)) + \int_{t_o}^{t_f} f(\underline{x},\underline{u},\underline{y},\underline{m},t)\, dt$$

where

$$\begin{aligned} \dot{\underline{x}} &= \underline{g}(\underline{x},\underline{u},\underline{y},\underline{m},t) \\ \underline{x}(t_o) &= \underline{x}_o \\ \underline{h}(\underline{x},\underline{u},\underline{y},\underline{m},t) &\leqslant \underline{0} \\ \underline{h}_f(\underline{x},\underline{u},\underline{y},\underline{m},t_f) &\leqslant \underline{0} \\ \underline{q}(\underline{x},\underline{u},\underline{y},\underline{m},t) &= \underline{0} \\ \underline{Q}(\underline{x},\underline{u},\underline{y},\underline{m},t_f) &= \underline{0} \end{aligned} \tag{4}$$

Defining the multipliers $\underline{\lambda}(t)$ to handle the differential constraints, $\underline{\rho}(t)$ to handle the equality constraints, and a constant $\underline{\mu}$ to handle the terminal time constraints, this problem may be written

$$\min_{\underline{x},\underline{u},\underline{y},\underline{m},\underline{\lambda},\underline{\rho},\underline{\mu}} J = \int_{t_o}^{t_f} (\underline{\lambda}^T\dot{\underline{x}}+H)\, dt + G \tag{5}$$

where the Hamiltonian is defined

$$H \triangleq f - \underline{\lambda}^T\underline{g} + \underline{\rho}^T\underline{q} \tag{6}$$

and

$$G \triangleq F(\underline{x}(t_f)) + \underline{\mu}^T\underline{Q} \tag{7}$$

If standard optimal control theory is applied, the following conditions of optimality are obtained:

$$\begin{aligned} &\dot{\underline{x}} - \underline{g} = \underline{0} \qquad \underline{x}(t_o) = \underline{x}_o \\ &\underline{q} = \underline{0} \\ &\underline{Q}(t_f) = \underline{0} \\ &\dot{\underline{\lambda}} - \underline{H}_x = \underline{0} \\ &\underline{H}_u = \underline{0} = \underline{H}_y = \underline{H}_m \\ &(\underline{\lambda}+\underline{G}_x)_{t_f} = \underline{0} \end{aligned} \tag{8}$$

subject to the inequality constraints at each interval. The object is to find controls and states satisfying these equations to a specified degree of accuracy. Defining a norm function

$$N(\underline{\xi}) = \underline{\xi}^T \underline{\xi} = \|\underline{\xi}\|^2 \tag{9}$$

we may specify the optimal control problem in terms of the minimization of the cumulative errors

$$J = J_1 + J_2 \tag{10}$$

where

$$J_1 = \int_{t_o}^{t_f} \{N(\underline{\dot{x}}-\underline{g}) + N(\underline{q})\}dt + N(\underline{Q}(t_f)) \tag{11}$$

$$J_2 = \int_{t_o}^{t_f} \{N(\underline{\dot{\lambda}}-\underline{H}_x) + N(\underline{H}_x) + N(\underline{H}_y) + N(\underline{H}_m)\}dt + N(\underline{\lambda}+\underline{G}_x)_{t_f} \tag{12}$$

and stop the iterations when J is smaller than some pre-specified accuracy. The normal quasilinearization algorithm corresponds to updating the current $\underline{x},\underline{u},\underline{y},\underline{m},\underline{\lambda},\underline{\rho},\underline{\mu}$ by increments derived from the solution of the first order expansions of the optimality conditions (8). A new expansion point is then obtained which reduces J, and the procedure repeated until convergence is achieved.

The inequality constraints may in general be handled by penalty methods with very little modification of the quasilinearization method. In this present work, however, attention is restricted to what is the most important case in engineering problems, simple upper and lower physical bounds on the variables. In this case, a gradient projection method due to Rosen[8] may be used. This basically checks the variables at each iteration to see if the limits are violated. If a variable exceeds the limit, it is set equal to that limit, and the next step in the minimization proceeds along the projection of the gradient along that limit.

The object of this paper, then, is to obtain solutions to very general subsystem problems and to coordinate their solutions into a coordination algorithm for the hierarchical control of the system.

3. Quasilinearization algorithm

The standard method of solving the problem outlined in the previous section is to consider the linearized set of optimality conditions defined by

$$(\dot{\underline{x}}-\underline{g})^k + \delta(\dot{\underline{x}}-\underline{g}) = \underline{0}$$
$$\delta\underline{x}_o = \underline{0}$$
$$\underline{q}^k + \delta\underline{q} = \underline{0}$$
$$\underline{Q}^k + \delta\underline{Q}(t_f) = \underline{0}$$
$$(\dot{\underline{\lambda}}-\underline{H}_x)^k + \delta(\dot{\underline{\lambda}}-\underline{H}_x) = \underline{0} \tag{13}$$
$$\underline{H}_u^k + \delta\underline{H}_u = \underline{0}$$
$$\underline{H}_y^k + \delta\underline{H}_y = \underline{0}$$
$$\underline{H}_m^k + \delta\underline{H}_m = \underline{0}$$
$$\delta(\underline{\lambda}+\underline{G}_x)_{t_f} + (\underline{\lambda}+\underline{G}_x)_f^k = \underline{0}$$

where the linearization is performed about some nominal operating point at the kth iteration, denoted by the superscript k. These may be expanded to yield the following set of differential equations:

$$\begin{aligned}
&\Delta\dot{\underline{x}} - \underline{g}_x^T\Delta\underline{x} - \underline{g}_u^T\Delta\underline{u} - \underline{g}_y^T\Delta\underline{y} - \underline{g}_m^T\Delta\underline{m} + (\dot{\underline{x}}-\underline{g})^k = \underline{0} \\
&\Delta\dot{\underline{\lambda}} - \underline{H}_{xx}^T\Delta\underline{x} - \underline{H}_{xu}^T\Delta\underline{u} - \underline{H}_{xy}^T\Delta\underline{y} - \underline{H}_{xm}^T\Delta\underline{m} - \underline{H}_{x\rho}^T\Delta\underline{\rho} + (\dot{\underline{\lambda}}-\underline{H}_x)^k - \underline{H}_{x\lambda}^T\Delta\underline{\lambda} = 0
\end{aligned} \tag{14}$$

subject to the algebraic constraints

$$\begin{aligned}
&\underline{q}_x^T\Delta\underline{x} + \underline{q}_u^T\Delta\underline{u} + \underline{q}_y^T\Delta\underline{y} + \underline{q}_m^T\Delta\underline{m} + \underline{q}^k = \underline{0} \\
&\underline{H}_{ux}^T\Delta\underline{x} + \underline{H}_{uu}^T\Delta\underline{u} + \underline{H}_{uy}^T\Delta\underline{y} + \underline{H}_{um}^T\Delta\underline{m} + \underline{H}_{u\lambda}^T\Delta\underline{\lambda} + \underline{H}_{u\rho}^T\Delta\underline{\rho} + \underline{H}_u^k = \underline{0} \\
&\underline{H}_{yx}^T\Delta\underline{x} + \underline{H}_{yu}^T\Delta\underline{u} + \underline{H}_{yy}^T\Delta\underline{y} + \underline{H}_{ym}^T\Delta\underline{m} + \underline{H}_{y\lambda}^T\Delta\underline{\lambda} + \underline{H}_{y\rho}^T\Delta\underline{\rho} + \underline{H}_y^k = \underline{0} \\
&\underline{H}_{mx}^T\Delta\underline{x} + \underline{H}_{mu}^T\Delta\underline{u} + \underline{H}_{my}^T\Delta\underline{y} + \underline{H}_{mm}^T\Delta\underline{m} + \underline{H}_{m\lambda}^T\Delta\underline{\lambda} + \underline{H}_{m\rho}^T\Delta\underline{\rho} + \underline{H}_m^k = \underline{0}
\end{aligned} \tag{15}$$

and the initial and terminal conditions

$$\begin{aligned}
&(\Delta\underline{x})_{t_o} = \underline{0} \\
&(\underline{Q}_x^T\Delta\underline{x})_{t_f} + (\underline{Q}_u^T\Delta\underline{u})_{t_f} + (\underline{Q}_y^T\Delta\underline{y})_{t_f} + (\underline{Q}_m^T\Delta\underline{m})_{t_f} + \underline{Q}(t_f) = \underline{0} \\
&(\Delta\underline{\lambda})_{t_f} + \{\underline{G}_{xx}^T\Delta\underline{x} + \underline{G}_{xu}^T\Delta\underline{u} + \underline{G}_{xy}^T\Delta\underline{y} + \underline{G}_{xm}^T\Delta\underline{m} + \underline{G}_{x\mu}^T\Delta\underline{\mu}\}_{t_f} + (\underline{\lambda}+\underline{G}_x)_{t_f} = \underline{0}
\end{aligned} \tag{16}$$

The solutions $\Delta\underline{x},\Delta\underline{\lambda},\Delta\underline{u},\Delta\underline{m},\Delta\underline{y},\Delta\underline{\mu},\Delta\underline{\rho}$ may then be added to the current estimate of the solution to yield an estimate at the kth iteration of

$$\begin{aligned}
\underline{x}^{k+1} &= \underline{x}^{k} + \Delta\underline{x} \\
\underline{\lambda}^{k+1} &= \underline{\lambda}^{k} + \Delta\underline{\lambda} \\
\underline{u}^{k+1} &= \underline{u}^{k} + \Delta\underline{u} \\
\underline{m}^{k+1} &= \underline{m}^{k} + \Delta\underline{m} \\
\underline{y}^{k+1} &= \underline{y}^{k} + \Delta\underline{y} \\
\underline{\mu}^{k+1} &= \underline{\mu}^{k} + \Delta\underline{\mu} \\
\underline{\rho}^{k+1} &= \underline{\rho}^{k} + \Delta\underline{\rho}
\end{aligned} \tag{17}$$

This leads to a change in the performance index of

$$\delta J_1 + \delta J_2 \tag{18}$$

where

$$\delta J_1 = 2\int_{t_o}^{t_f} \{(\dot{\underline{x}}-\underline{g})^T\delta(\dot{\underline{x}}-\underline{g}) + \underline{q}^T\delta\underline{q}\}dt + 2\underline{Q}^T(t_f)\delta\underline{Q}(t_f) \tag{19}$$

$$= -2J_1 \tag{20}$$

$$\delta J_2 = 2\int_{t_o}^{t_f} \{(\dot{\underline{\lambda}}-\underline{H}_x)^T\delta(\dot{\underline{\lambda}}-\underline{H}_x) + \underline{H}_u^T\delta\underline{H}_u + \underline{H}_y^T\delta\underline{H}_y + \underline{H}_m^T\delta\underline{H}_m\}dt + 2(\underline{\lambda}+\underline{G}_x)_{t_f}^T\,\delta(\underline{\lambda}+\underline{G}_x)_{t_f} \tag{21}$$

$$= -2J_2 \tag{22}$$

substituting in for the incremental changes of equation (13) and using the definitions of J_1 and J_2. Thus

$$\delta J = -2J \tag{23}$$

showing a reduction in the value of J at each iteration.

The modified[6] quasilinearization method uses the following linearized version of the optimality conditions for $0 \leq \alpha \leq 1$

$$\begin{aligned}
(\dot{\underline{x}}-\underline{g})^k &+ \alpha\delta(\dot{\underline{x}}-\underline{g}) &= \underline{0} \\
&\alpha\delta\underline{x}_o &= \underline{0} \\
\underline{q}^k &+ \alpha\delta\underline{q} &= \underline{0} \\
\underline{Q}^k &+ \alpha\delta\underline{Q}(t_f) &= \underline{0} \\
(\dot{\underline{\lambda}}-\underline{H}_x)^k &+ \alpha\delta(\dot{\underline{\lambda}}-\underline{H}_x) &= \underline{0} \\
\underline{H}_u^k &+ \alpha\delta\underline{H}_u &= \underline{0} \\
\underline{H}_y^k &+ \alpha\delta\underline{H}_y &= \underline{0} \\
\underline{H}_m^k &+ \alpha\delta\underline{H}_m &= \underline{0} \\
(\underline{\lambda}+\underline{G}_x)_f^k &+ \alpha\delta(\underline{\lambda}+\underline{G}_x)_f^k &= \underline{0}
\end{aligned} \tag{24}$$

which, if expanded, leads to a reduction in the performance index

$$\delta J = -2\alpha J \tag{25}$$

and hence, by suitable choice of α at each iteration, the performance index may be rapidly extremized. This optimum choice of α may be obtained by a one-dimensional search on $J(\alpha)$ at each iteration.

4. Soltuon of two-point boundary value problem

The previous section has formulated the quasilinearization approach for a general control problem. Here, the solution algorithm for the linearized two-point boundary-value problem is described.

Consider the problem of solving the differential equations (14) subject to the algebraic constraints (15) and the initial and terminal conditions (16). Clearly it is possible to solved equations (15) for $\Delta\underline{u},\Delta\underline{y},\Delta\underline{m},\Delta\underline{\rho}$ all as functions of $\Delta\underline{x}$ and $\Delta\underline{\lambda}$, since then there are 4 equations in 4 unknowns. Substituting these values into equations (14) and defining

$$\underline{z}^{k+1} = \begin{bmatrix} \underline{x}^{k+1} \\ \underline{\lambda}^{k+1} \end{bmatrix} = \begin{bmatrix} \underline{x}^{k} + \Delta\underline{x} \\ \underline{\lambda}^{k} + \Delta\underline{\lambda} \end{bmatrix} \tag{26}$$

the problem may be restated as the solution of the linearized equation

$$\frac{d}{dt}\,\underline{z}^{k+1} = \underline{F}(\underline{z}^{k}) + \underline{J}(\underline{z}^{k})(\underline{z}^{k+1}-\underline{z}^{k}) \tag{27}$$

subject to the boundary conditions

$$\begin{aligned} z_i(t_o) &= z_{io} \qquad i = 1,2,\ldots,n \\ z_i(t_f) &= z_{if} \qquad i = n+1,\ldots,2n \end{aligned} \tag{28}$$

where z_i is the ith component of the $2n\times 1$ vector $\underline{z}$, and $\underline{J}$ is the system Jacobian with ij^{th} element

$$J_{ij} = \frac{\partial F_i}{\partial z_j} \tag{29}$$

It is convenient at this stage to write the boundary conditions as

$$\begin{aligned} z_1(t_o)a_{k_1} + z_2(t_o)a_{k_2} + \ldots\ z_{2n}(t_o)a_{k_{2n}} &= b_k \\ z_1(t_f)a_{\ell_1} + z_2(t_f)a_{\ell_2} + \ldots\ z_{2n}(t_f)a_{\ell_{2n}} &= b_\ell \end{aligned} \tag{30}$$

where there are k initial conditions and ℓ final conditions on $z_i(t)$.

Writing equation (27) as

$$\frac{d}{dt}\underline{z}^{k+1} = \underline{J}(\underline{z}^k)\underline{z}^{k+1} + \underline{F}(\underline{z}^k) - \underline{J}(\underline{z}^k)\underline{z}^k \tag{31}$$

it is clear that the general solution consists of two parts

$$\underline{z}^{k+1}(t) = \underline{\Phi}^{k+1}(t,t_o)\underline{z}^{k+1}(t_o) + \underline{P}(t) \tag{32}$$

The first part or transient response is determined by solving

$$\frac{d}{dt}\underline{\Phi}^{k+1}(t,t_o) = \underline{J}(\underline{z}^k)\underline{\Phi}^{k+1}(t,t_o) \tag{33}$$

subject to

$$\underline{\Phi}^{k+1}(t_o,t_o) = \underline{I} \tag{34}$$

where $\underline{I}$ is the $2n\times 2n$ identity matrix. The particular integral satisfies

$$\frac{d}{dt}\underline{P}^{k+1}(t) = \underline{J}(\underline{z}^k)\underline{P}^{k+1}(t) + \underline{F}(\underline{z}^k) - \underline{F}(\underline{z}^k)\underline{z}^k \tag{35}$$

and the general solution is

$$\underline{z}^{k+1}(t) = \underline{\Phi}^{k+1}(t,t_o)\underline{C}^{k+1} + \underline{P}^{k+1}(t)$$

where $\underline{C}^{k+1}$ is the $2n\times 1$ vector of constants of integration determined by the equations (30) which may be rewritten in the form

$$\begin{aligned} &<\underline{C}^{k+1},\underline{a}_i> = b_i & i = 1,2,\ldots n \\ &<\underline{\Phi}^{k+1}(t_f,t_o)\underline{C}^{k+1}+\underline{P}^{k+1}(t_f),\underline{a}_j> = b_j & j = n+1,\ldots 2n \end{aligned} \tag{36}$$

where

$$\underline{a}_i = [a_{i_1}, a_{i_2}, \ldots, a_{i_{2n}}]^T \tag{37}$$

The iterations continue until

$$\|\underline{C}^{k+1}-\underline{C}^{k}\| \leqslant \varepsilon \tag{38}$$

where ε is an arbitrarily small quantity. The basic steps of the solution algorithm are shown on the flowchart of Fig.1.

The following section provides an illustration of the practical use of this technique for solving non-linear sub-system problems in a hierarchical structure arising from the spatial problem decomposition using Lagrangian duality.

5. Solution of a non-linear water supply problem

Consider the problem of obtaining the minimum pumping cost control for a water supply system[9] described by the following differential equations:

$$\frac{dx_1}{dt} = 0.075\times u_1 - 4.66\times 10^{-4}\times S_1(x_1-x_2) - 2.367\times 10^{-3} \tag{39}$$

$$\frac{dx_2}{dt} = 9.527\times 10^{-4}\times S_1(x_1-x_2) + 0.1533\times u_2 - 2.485\times 10^{-3}\times S_2(x_2-x_5) - 3.629\times 10^{-3} \tag{40}$$

$$\frac{dx_3}{dt} = 0.1\times u_3 - 0.0239 \tag{41}$$

$$\frac{dx_4}{dt} = 0.25\times u_4 - 3.726\times 10^{-3}\times S_3(x_4-239)^{0.54} - 2.95\times 10^{-3} \tag{42}$$

$$\frac{dx_5}{dt} = 0.05\times u_5 + 8.1\times 10^{-4}\times S_2(x_2-x_5) - 8.97\times 10^{-3} \tag{43}$$

$$\frac{dx_6}{dt} = 0.1712\times u_6 + 1.25\times 10^{-3}\times S_4(375-x_6) + 9.922\times 10^{-4}\times S_5(540-x_6) - 1.35\times 10^{-3} \tag{44}$$

subject to $\underline{x}(0) = \underline{x}_o$, where

$$J = \int_0^{24} \{\tfrac{1}{2}\|\underline{x}-\underline{x}^d\|^2_{\underline{Q}} + \underline{Q}_L\underline{x} + \tfrac{1}{2}\|\underline{u}-\underline{u}^d\|^2_{\underline{R}} + \underline{R}_L\underline{u}\}dt \tag{45}$$

is a second-order expansion of operating costs. In this problem $\underline{x}$ is the vector of states or reservoir levels on the system, $\underline{u}$ is the vector of pump controls, and $\underline{x}^d, \underline{u}^d$ are their desired values respectively. All vectors are of dimension 6 , and $\underline{Q}, \underline{Q}_L, \underline{R}, \underline{R}_L$ are the appropriate 6×6 weighting matrices.

This regulator control problem arises from an actual control scheme developed on a computer-controlled water supply network, described in detail in reference 9.

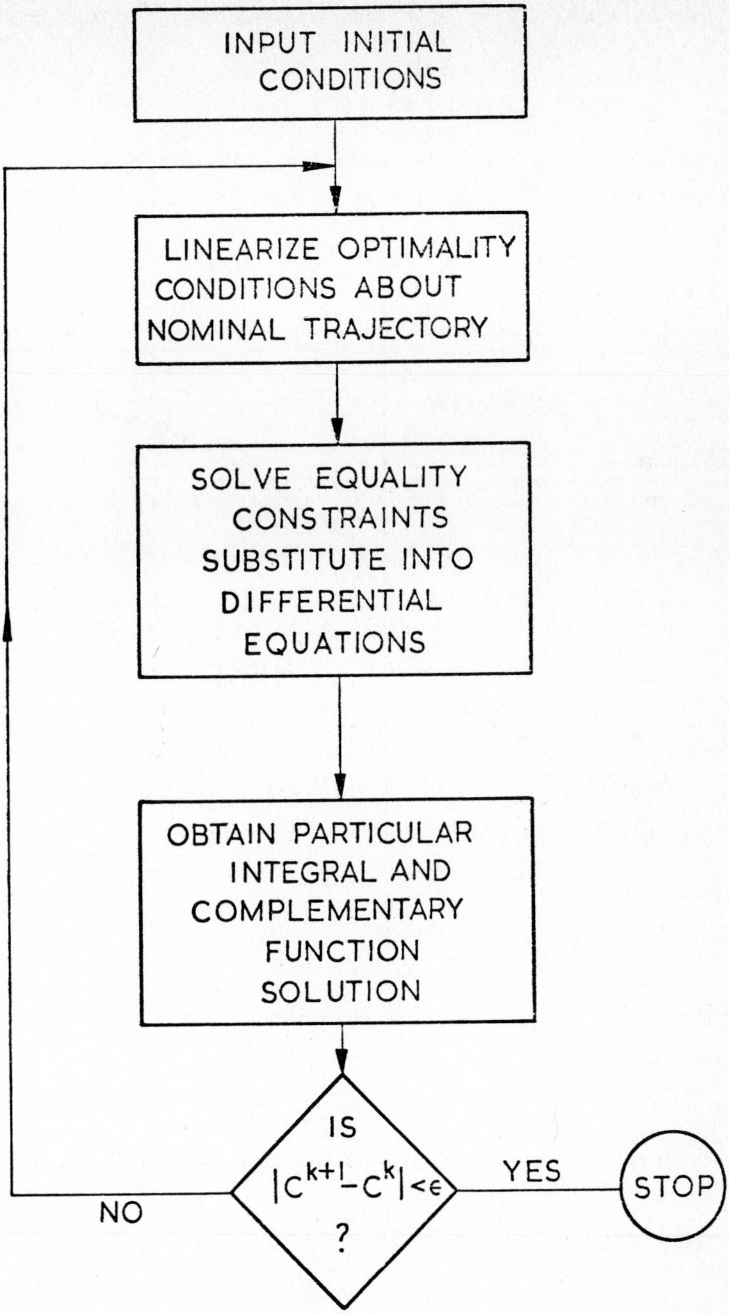

FIG.1 QUASILINEARISATION ALGORITHM FOR SOLVING SUB-SYSTEM PROBLEMS

The non-linearities $S_1 \ldots S_6$ appearing in this formulation are of the general form

$$S_i(\zeta) = \mathrm{Sgn}(\zeta)|\zeta|^{0.54} \qquad i = 1,2,\ldots 5 \tag{46}$$

which is in fact the steady state flow along a pipe of unit resistance, the head drop along the pipe being ζ . A graph of this is shown in Fig.2.

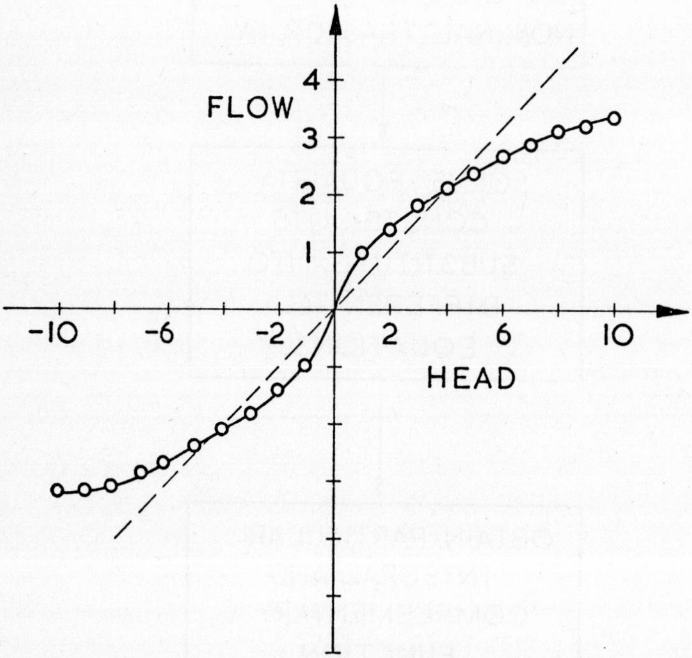

FIG.2 STEADY-STATE HEAD-FLOW RELATIONSHIP FOR A PIPE

This problem may be decomposed by introducing the coupling variables

$$\begin{aligned} \xi_{11} &= x_2 \\ \xi_{21} &= x_1 \\ \xi_{22} &= x_5 \\ \xi_{51} &= x_2 \end{aligned} \tag{47}$$

where ξ_{ij} is the jth coupling variable in the ith sub-system. In this way the following 6 sub-problems are defined:

Sub-problem 1:

$$\underset{x_1,u_1,\xi_{11}}{\text{Min}} \int_0^{24} \{\frac{1}{2} u_1^2 + \frac{1}{2}(x_1-765)^2 + \beta_{11}(\xi_{11}-x_2)\}dt + F_1(x_1(t_f))$$

S.t. $\dot{x}_1 = 0.075\times u_1 - 4.66\times 10^{-4}\times S_1(x_1-\xi_{11}) - 2.367\times 10^{-3}$
$x_1(0) = 765$
$u_1(t) \leq 1$

Sub-problem 2:

$$\underset{x_2,u_2,\xi_{21},\xi_{22}}{\text{Min}} \int_0^{24} \{\frac{1}{2}(x_2-535)^2 + \frac{1}{2} u_2^2 + \beta_{21}(\xi_{21}-x_1) + \beta_{22}(\xi_{22}-x_5)\}dt + F_2(x_2(t_f))$$

S.t. $\dot{x}_2 = 9.527\times 10^{-4}\times S_1(\xi_{21}-x_2) + 0.1533\times u_2 - 2.48\times 10^{-3}\times S_2(x_2-\xi_{22}) - 3.629\times 10^{-3}$
$x_2(0) = 535$
$u_2(t) \leq 1$

Sub-problem 3:

$$\underset{x_3,u_3}{\text{Min}} \int_0^{24} \{\frac{1}{2}(x_3-489)^2 + \frac{1}{2} u_3^2\}dt + F_3(x_3(t_f))$$

S.t. $\dot{x}_3 = 0.1\times u_3 - 0.0239$
$x_3(0) = 489$
$u_3(t) \leq 1$

Sub-problem 4:

$$\underset{x_4,u_4}{\text{Min}} \int_0^{24} \{\frac{1}{2}(x_4-307)^2 + \frac{1}{2} u_4^2\}dt + F_4(t_f))$$

S.t. $\dot{x}_4 = 0.25\times u_4 - 3.726\times 10^{-3}\times S_3(x_4-239) - 2.95\times 10^{-3}$
$x_4(0) = 307$
$u_4(t) \leq 1$

Sub-problem 5:

$$\underset{x_5,u_5,\xi_{51}}{\text{Min}} \int_0^{24} \{\frac{1}{2}(x_5-393)^2 + \frac{1}{2} u_5^2 + \beta_{51}(\xi_{51}-x_2)\}dt + F_5(x_5(t_f))$$

S.t. $\dot{x}_5 = 0.05\times u_5 + 8.1\times 10^{-4}\times S_2(\xi_{51}-x_5) - 8.97\times 10^{-3}$
$x_5(0) = 393$
$u_5(t) \leq 1$

Sub-problem 6:

$$\min_{x_6,u_6} \int_0^{24} \{\tfrac{1}{2}(x_6-245)^2 + \tfrac{1}{2}u_6^2\}dt + F_6(x_6(t_f))$$

S.t. $\dot{x}_6 = 0.1712\times u_6 + 1.25\times10^{-3}\times S_4(375-x_6) + 9.922\times10^{-4}\times S_5(540-x_6) - 1.35\times10^{-3}$

$x_6(0) = 245$

$u_6(t) \lessgtr 1$

Using a goal coordination algorithm, each of these sub-problems is solved for a given value of the coupling multiplier $\underline{\beta}$. The solution $\underline{x}_i^*$, $\underline{u}_i^*$ and $\underline{\xi}_i^*$ of the sub-system problems are then used to update the multiplier according to

$$\underline{\beta}^{k+1} = \underline{\beta}^k + \alpha\underline{d}^k \tag{48}$$

where

$$\underline{d}^k = \nabla_{\underline{\beta}}\psi(\underline{\beta}) \tag{49}$$

for a linear search or

$$\underline{d}^k = [\nabla_{\underline{\beta}}\psi(\underline{\beta})]^k + \frac{\|\nabla_{\underline{\beta}}\psi(\underline{\beta})\|_k^2}{\|\nabla_{\underline{\beta}}\psi(\underline{\beta})\|_{k-1}^2}\,\underline{d}^{k-1} \tag{50}$$

for a conjugate gradient minimization of the dual function $\psi(\underline{\beta})$. In this case, the gradient is simply the error in the coordinating relations, and when this tends to zero, the solution has been obtained. In this case the dual function is

$$\psi(\underline{\beta}) = \min_{\underline{x}_i,\underline{u}_i,\underline{\xi}_i} \{\sum_{i=1}^{6} [F_i + \int_{t_o}^{t_f} (f_i + \langle\underline{\beta},\underline{G}_i\rangle)dt]\} \tag{51}$$

and from this

$$\nabla_{\underline{\beta}}\psi(\underline{\beta}) = \sum_{i=1}^{6} \underline{G}_i \tag{52}$$

for the minimizing values of $\underline{x}_i,\underline{u}_i,\underline{\xi}_i$.

Minimizing the Hamiltonian H_i for each sub-system, as in Section 2, leads to the optimality conditions

$$\begin{aligned}\dot{\underline{x}}_i &= \frac{\partial H_i}{\partial \underline{\lambda}_i}\\ \dot{\underline{\lambda}}_i &= -\frac{\partial H_i}{\partial \underline{x}_i}\end{aligned} \tag{53}$$

$$\frac{\partial H_i}{\partial \underline{u}_i} = \underline{0}$$

$$\frac{\partial H_i}{\partial \underline{\xi}_i} = \underline{0} \qquad (54)$$

The values of $\underline{u}_i$ and $\underline{\xi}_i$ in terms of $\underline{x}_i$ and $\underline{\lambda}_i$ may be solved for from equations (54) and the problem reduces to the solution of the two-point boundary-value problem defined by equations (53), subject to the initial conditions

$$\underline{x}_i(0) = \underline{x}_{io} \qquad \underline{\lambda}_i(t_f) = \underline{\lambda}_{if}$$

For all of the sub-problems, 24 integration steps are used, and the integration of the differential equations performed using a 4th order Runge-Kutta procedure.

6. Results

The above problem has been solved on an IBM 370/165 computer, and a typical system response to a step disturbance for the first sub-problem is shown in Fig.3. The described quasilinearization algorithm has been used to obtain sub-system solutions. The convergence requirements for each sub-system are summarized in Table 1, together with the initial values of the multipliers. The global problem converges in about 30 iterations using a simple linear search.

The optimum controls are calculated to minimize the control effort and the deviations of the state from desired levels when a step demand is placed on the system. As shown in Fig.3, a step demand for water is met by reducing the pump flow control as much as possible and meeting the difference by reducing the reservoir level. For example, the final control for sub-system 1 is

$$u_1^*(24) = 0.075 \times u_1(24) = 2.367 \times 10^{-3} \text{ mgd} \qquad (55)$$

and this is the minimum allowable pumped quantity of water.

In general, this zone will be subjected to a time varying deterministic disturbance which is obtained by forecasting the water demand from past data. Fig.3 merely shows the response to the steady state or average of this demand.

An important practical consideration in the proposed on-line implementation of a scheme designed to handle non-linear models is whether the increased computational burden is justifiable in terms of cost savings.

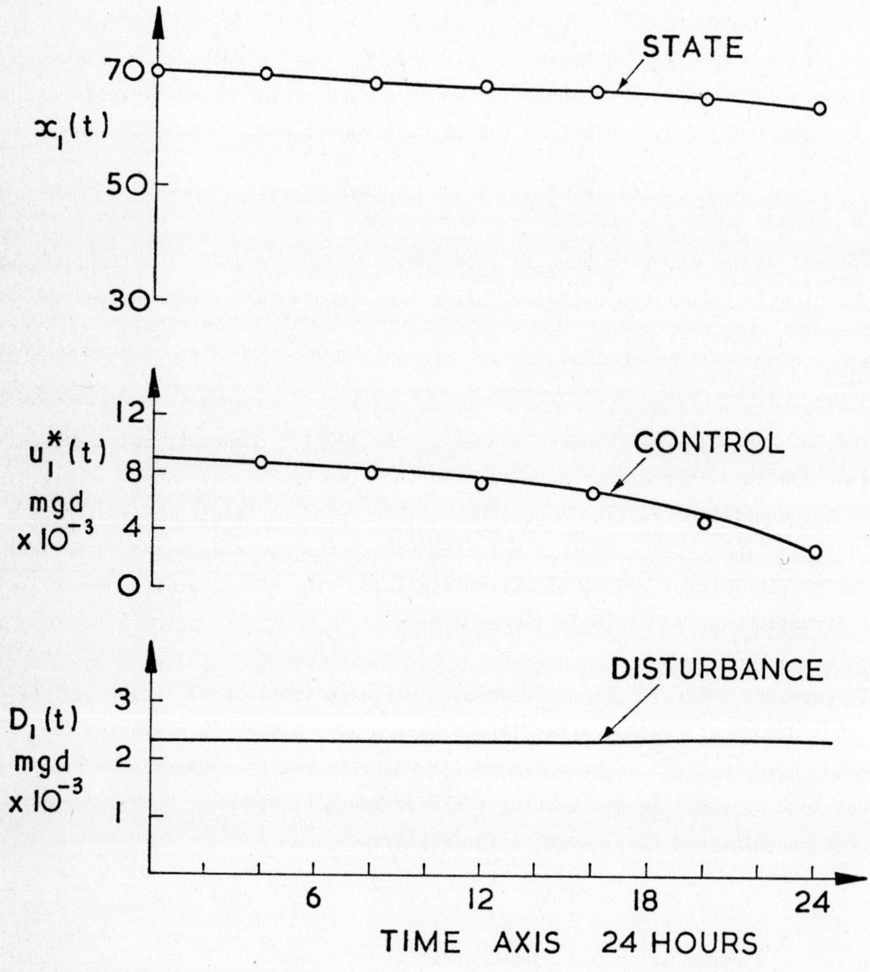

FIG.3 OPTIMAL CONTROL AND STATE FOR SUB-PROBLEM 1

Table 1

Sub-problem i	No. of iterations* for convergence	Initial multipliers $\lambda_i(t)$ $0 \leq t \leq 24$	$\lambda_i(24)$
1	3	0.4	0.4
2	2	0.15	0.15
3	2	2.39	2.39
4	12	0.047	0.047
5	3	3.58	3.58
6	20	0.0457	0.0457

*iterations are terminated when

$$\| C^{k+1} - C^k \| \leq 10^{-6}$$

To examine this, consider the solution to the first sub-system problem, using firstly a linear model and secondly a non-linear model. In the first case, the model is linearized about an operating point and the quadratic costs calculated. The results are tabulated in Table 2. Then, for a full non-linear model, solved by quasilinearization, the trajectories are obtained and quadratic costs calculated, the results being shown in Table 3.

Table 2

t	$\Delta x_1 = 765 - x_1$	$(\Delta x_1)^2$	$\lambda_1(t)$	$\lambda_1^2(t)$
4	9.766×10^{-3}	95.374×10^{-6}	1.489	2.21855
8	21.729×10^{-3}	472.149×10^{-6}	1.429	2.04209
12	36.621×10^{-3}	134.109×10^{-5}	1.312	1.746283
16	53.711×10^{-3}	288.487×10^{-5}	1.146	1.31265
20	75.928×10^{-3}	576.506×10^{-5}	0.886	0.78503
24	104.98×10^{-3}	110.208×10^{-4}	0.513	0.26273

$$\sum_t (\Delta x_1)^2 = 21579.352\times10^{-6}$$

$$\sum_t \lambda_1^2 = 8.3677339$$

Table 3

t	$\Delta x_1 = 765 - x_1$	$(\Delta x_1)^2$	$\lambda_1(t)$	$\lambda_1^2(t)$
4	9.521×10^{-3}	90.649×10^{-6}	1.491	2.22243
8	21.729×10^{-3}	472.149×10^{-6}	1.430	2.04622
12	36.377×10^{-3}	132.328×10^{-5}	1.323	1.75080
16	53.467×10^{-3}	285.872×10^{-5}	1.140	1.29969
20	75.195×10^{-3}	565.43×10^{-5}	0.880	0.776108
24	104.492×10^{-3}	109.185×10^{-4}	0.512	0.26245

$$\sum_t (\Delta x_1)^2 = 21317.67\times10^{-6}$$

$$\sum_t (\lambda_1)^2 = 8.357703$$

The quadratic costs in the first case are

$$\begin{aligned} J_1 &= \sum_t (\Delta x_1)^2 + \sum_t (u_1)^2 \\ &= \sum_t (\Delta x_1)^2 + (0.075)^2 \sum_t (\lambda_1)^2 \\ &= 686.546\times 10^{-4} \end{aligned}$$

and in the second case

$$J_2 = 683.297\times 10^{-4}$$

which is a percentage reduction of about 0.5% . The computational burden in terms of time requirements for handling the non-linearity is increased by a factor of 3 . Clearly the increase depends on the number of iterations required in total to solve all the sub-system problems, and these can be reduced to a minimum using modifications of the quasilinearization algorithm. Experience has shown that the number of iterations to convergence can be halved using the modified algorithm and optimizing with respect to the choice of initial multipliers over the time interval.[6] Thus, for a 50% increase in computer time requirements, pumping costs can be reduced by ½% .

This additional saving of ½% in costs may be well worthwhile if the dynamics of the system under consideration are slow enough to allow the computer to calculate the optimal controls within one sampling interval, as is the case with the water supply problem. If, however, the additional time requirements of the quasilinearization algorithm mean that a more powerful computer must be installed to control the system, then the savings will have to be compared with the additional computer costs to determine if it is worthwhile increasing the computer capacity to save the additional ½% operating costs.

Conclusions

The method of quasilinearization has been used to solve non-linear sub-system problems arising from a problem decomposition using Lagrangian duality. The method has been applied to a practical water supply problem, and results indicate that it is worthwhile handling non-linear models for on-line implementation in this application.

Acknowledgements

The authors are grateful to R.H. Burch and K.C. Marlow, of East Worcestershire Waterworks Company, for financial support, and to A.R. Farmer and M.S. Jennions of Kent Automation Systems, for technical cooperation. They are also grateful to M. Singh and J. Galy of Laboratoire d'Automatique et d'Analyse des Systemes du C.N.R.S., for a computer program on which these calculations are based, and to

P.D. Rice, of this department, for data processing. Thanks are also due to the Science Research Council and Peterhouse, Cambridge, for financial support.

References

1. R. Bellman: "Dynamic Programming", Princeton University Press, Princeton, New Jersey, 1957 (book)

2. R. Bellman and S. Dreyfus: "Applied Dynamic Programming", Princeton University Press, Princeton, New Jersey, 1962 (book).

3. R.A. Howard: "Dynamic Programming and Markov Processes", John Wiley and Sons Inc., New York, 1960 (book)

4. R.E. Larson: "State Increment Dynamic Programming", John Wiley and Sons Inc., New York, 1960 (book)

5. R. Bellman and R.E. Kalaba: "Quasilinearization and Nonlinear Boundary-Value Problems", American Elsevier Publishing Company, Inc., New York, 1965 (book)

6. A. Miele, A. Mangiavacchi and A.K. Aggarwal: "Modified Quasilinearization Algorithm for Optimal Control Problems with Nondifferential Constraints", Journal of Optimization Theory and Applications, Vol.14, No.5, 1974

7. F. Fallside and P.F. Perry: "Decentralized Optimum Control Methods for Water Distribution System's Optimization", Cambridge University Engineering Dept., TR 31 (elec) 1974

8. J.B. Rosen: "The Gradient Projection Method for Nonlinear Programming - Pts 1 & 2", Journal Soc.Ind.Appl.Math., 1960, 8, pp.181-217

9. F. Fallside and P.F. Perry: "Hierarchical Optimization of a Water-Supply Network", Proc.IEE, Vol.122, No.2, Feb. 1975, pp.202-208

A COMPUTER ALGORITHM FOR SOLVING A RESERVOIR REGULATION PROBLEM UNDER CONFLICTING OBJECTIVES

G. Fronza (°), A. Karlin (°), S. Rinaldi (°)

(°) Istituto di Elettrotecnica ed Elettronica
Centro Teoria dei Sistemi - Politecnico di Milano

1. INTRODUCTION

In recent years, many problems concerning the design and operation of water resources systems have been solved through mathematical programming techniques (mostly linear [1] , dynamic [2], [3], non linear [4] , [5] and chance constraints [6] programming) or efficient search-simulation schemes [7] . The validity of these approaches lies on the crucial assumption that there exists a single decision maker with a single objective function, where all the economic goals to be pursued can be summarized.

With the aim of a closer connection to real situations, different viewpoints have been considered. Specifically, the two following cases have mainly been taken into account.

a) One decision-maker without complete knowledge of the economic framework and then bound to consider a set of alternative targets. This approach leads to the use of multiobjective mathematical programming techniques (see, for instance, [8] - [10]).

b) Many decision centers, each pursuing an individual objective and hierarchically subjected to a supervisor. This approach leads to the use of multilevel systems analysis techniques (see, for instance [11] - [13]).

In many cases, however, the real situation is conspicuously different even from the ones considered in a), b). In particular, it is often characterized by the existence of many decision makers, each pursuing an individual objective in conflict with the others. Such a situation has not yet been extensively analyzed in the literature. Among the few examples, the approach has been followed in [14] , [15] , [16] for different kinds of problems: in both cases the solution has been found by means of game theory techniques.

The "conflictual" decision-making structure is also considered in the present paper, where the authors discuss the operation problem of a short-term regulated lake. Specifically, the operating rule is assumed to result from a tradeoff between the consociated users of the reservoir outflows and the "recreational user", the population living along the sides. The analysis is carried out in Section 3 by following the classical game theory approach [17] , under some additional hypotheses about the economy of the system (Section 2). More in detail, the basic viewpoint of neglecting the losses due to contract failures, provided that their amount is not "too large", is adopted (see also [18], [19]). Furthermore the operating rule to be determined is bound to belong to a given class, so that the problem is turned into a finite dimensional game.

In Section 3, it is shown how the formulation of the lake regulation problem as a game leads to a very simple solution in the non-cooperative situation. Moreover, as pointed out in the final example (Section 4), such a solution can be determined by means of an efficient search algorithm, to be easily run on a computer. The example is drawn from the analysis of the Lake Maggiore regulation system, presently carried out by the authors. The lake, which lies partly in Switzerland and partly in Italy, where all downstream users are situated, is managed with a short-term policy somehow similar to the one considered here and changed practically twice during the year. The operating rule parameters, here considered as the decision variables of the game players are presently fixed by a law resulting from a past tradeoff. However, in front of an increasing demand of downstream water it is worthwhile questioning whether these values can be "reasonably" changed.

2. PROBLEM FORMULATION

Consider a lake which supplies water for a certain number of consociated downstream users and contemporarily provides a recreational benefit to the population living along its sides.
Let the following assumptions about the regulation and the economy of the system be true.

a) Operating rule and decision variables

The reservoir is continuously regulated, i.e. at every instant of time a decision must be taken about the flow-rate to be released at that instant. This assumption simplifies the derivation of the results, which, anyway, can be extended to the case of short-term (e.g. daily) regulation (see the example below).

Consider the lake continuity equation

$$\frac{ds(t)}{dt} = a(t) - r(t) \qquad (s(t_1)=s_1) \tag{2.1}$$

where

$s(t)$ = storage at time t;
$a(t)$ = inflow flow-rate at time t;
$r(t)$ = release flow-rate at time t;
t_1 = initial regulation time;
s_1 = given initial storage.

Moreover assume that the decision on the release is taken in accordance with an operating rule of the following kind (fig. 1) :

$$r(t) = \begin{cases} g(s(t)) & 0 \leq s(t) < x_1 \ , \quad s(t) > x_2 \qquad (2.2.a) \\ g(x_1) & x_1 \leq s(t) \leq x_2 \qquad (2.2.b) \end{cases}$$

where

$g(s(t))$ = maximum admissible release flow-rate when the storage is $s(t)$;

x_1, x_2 = bounds of the regulation range = decision variables of the regulation problem.

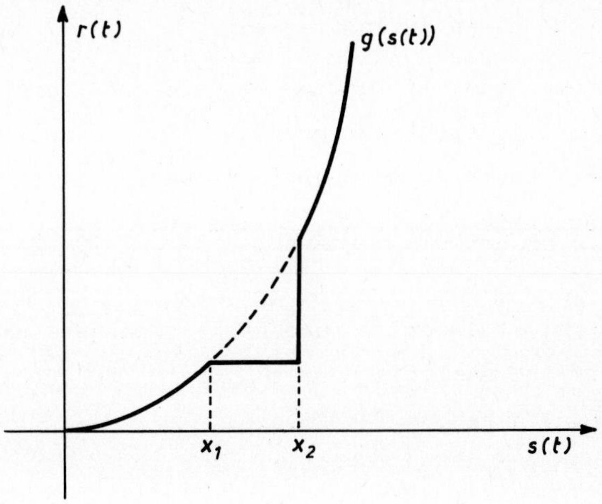

Fig.1 Operating rule

In other terms, for given x_1 and x_2, the release is chosen only on the basis of the present storage: other possible information, such as inflows forecast, is not considered. The operating rule (2.1) is the same for the different periods of the year. However, the procedure here developed for determing (x_1,x_2) under the one-season hypothesis can be used as a subroutine for the multiple season case (see the example of the last section again).

Furthermore, the results obtained under (2.2) do also hold when replacing (2.2.b) by any non-decreasing function of the storage. This, together with the consideration that x_1 and x_2 are not fixed a priori but are the decision variables of the problem make the assumption of (2.2) less restrictive.

Let T = 1 year and NT denote a given time horizon. If the inflows are introduced into (2.1) as a given segment $\hat{a}_{[t_1,t_1+NT)}$ (taken from historical record, for instance) then, in view of (2.1), (2.2), both the storage and the release at time t only depend on (x_1,x_2). In the following $\hat{s}(\cdot,x_1,x_2)$ and $\hat{r}(\cdot,x_1,x_2)$

will denote the storage and release segments corresponding to $\hat{a}_{[t_1,t_1+NT)}$. They must be regarded to as obtained by means of a "system simulation", i.e. by solving (2.1), (2.2) in correspondence with (x_1,x_2) and the given inflow segment.

On the other hand, if the inflows are considered as a T-periodic stochastic process, then, for every (x_1,x_2), both storages and releases must be dealt with as stochastic processes $s(.;x_1,x_2)$ and $r(.;\ x_1,x_2)$ respectively, ($\hat{s}(.;\ x_1,x_2)$ and $\hat{r}(.,\ x_1,x_2)$ being (incomplete) realizations).

Furthermore, it is quite reasonable to assume and it may be proved by means of the analysis carried out in [20], that both processes asymptotically tend to become T-periodic.

b) The economy of the system

In periods of normal conditions, i.e. when water is neither scarce nor in excess a constant flow-rate $g(x_1)$ is released downstream (Eq. 2.2.b). Hence $g(x_1)$ has the economic meaning of a target outflow (contract).

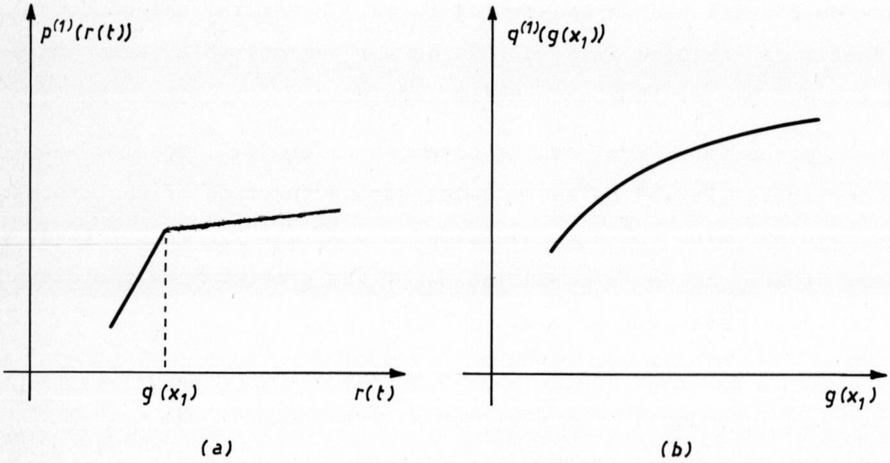

Fig. 2 The downstream users' benefit (a) and target benefit (b) curves

A typical behaviour [21] of the downstream users' benefit curve $p^{(1)}(r(t))$ is shown in Fig. 2.a, where it is clear that the extra-return due to the flow-rate, supplied in excess of the target, is practically negligible. On the other hand, outflows less than the contract correspond to rapidly decreasing benefits or even economic losses. The target benefit line $q^{(1)}(g(x_1))$ is drawn in Fig. 2.b. Instead of making direct use of $p^{(1)}(.)$, here the criterion suggested in [18], [19] is adopted, i.e. it is assumed that losses due to contract failures may be negligible provided that "their amount is not too large". More in detail, only the yearly target profit $T.q^{(1)}(g(x_1)) = P^{(1)}(x_1)$ will be taken into account, together with a constraint on yearly failures. Specifically, define the downstream users' deficit at time t

$$h^{(1)}(t) = \begin{cases} 0 & s(t) \geq x_1 \\ g(x_1) - r(t) & s(t) < x_1 \end{cases} \qquad (2.3)$$

and subsequently the k-th year deficit volume

$$f^{(1)}(k) = \int_{t_1+(k-1)T}^{t_1+kT} h^{(1)}(t)\, dt \quad . \qquad (2.4)$$

If the inflows are represented by a given segment $\hat{a}_{[t_1, t_1+NT)}$ then, for any (x_1, x_2), it is possible to determine the corresponding yearly failures sequence $\{\hat{f}^{(1)}(k;\, x_1, x_2)\}_{k=1}^{N}$ by simulation :

$$\hat{f}^{(1)}(k;\, x_1, x_2) = \int_{t_1+(k-1)T}^{t_1+kT} \hat{h}^{(1)}(t,\, x_1, x_2) dt \qquad k=1,2,\ldots,N \quad (2.5)$$

where

$$\hat{h}^{(1)}(t;\, x_1, x_2) = \begin{cases} 0 & \hat{s}(t; x_1, x_2) \geq x_1 \\ g(x_1) - \hat{r}(t; x_1, x_2) & \hat{s}(t;\, x_1, x_2) < x_1 \end{cases} \qquad (2.6).$$

On the other hand, if the inflows are represented by a stocha-

stic T-periodic process, for a fixed (x_1,x_2) also the yearly failures must be regarded to as a discrete stochastic process $\{f^{(1)}(k;x_1,x_2)\}_k$. Apparently, in view of (2.3), (2.4) and the properties of $s(\cdot;x_1,x_2)$, $r(\cdot;x_1,x_2)$, the process $\{f^{(1)}(k;x_1,x_2)\}_k$ must be considered as asymptotically becoming a stationary one $\{f_\infty^{(1)}(k;x_1,x_2)\}_k$.
This allows to define the following deficit index :

$$w^{(1)}(x_1,x_2) = E\, f_\infty^{(1)}\,(k;x_1,x_2).$$

In practical terms (see the example below), the effect of the initial storage can be considered as negligible after a very short interval and hence $\{f^{(1)}(k;\ x_1,x_2)\}_k$ can be approximately regarded to as a stationary process. Therefore, for N large enough, $w^{(1)}(x_1,x_2)$ can be determined via simulation :

$$w^{(1)}(x_1,x_2) \cong \frac{1}{N} \sum_{k=1}^{N} \hat{f}^{(1)}\,(k;x_1,x_2). \qquad (2.7)$$

It is then possible to specify when yearly failures may be considered as tolerable by setting the constraints

$$w^{(1)}(x_1,x_2) \leq W^{(1)}$$

where $W^{(1)}$ denotes a given volume.
Of course, instead of the index (2.7), different percentiles of the distribution of $f^{(1)}(k;x_1,x_2)$ might be used in order to define the constraint on failures.

As for the recreational user, it is here assumed that his benefits only depend upon the storage, in accordance with the curve $p^{(2)}(\cdot)$ drawn in Fig. 3.
The storage exceeding a given s* corresponds to a flood situation on the lake and causes rapidly decreasing benefits and economic losses. By following the same viewpoint adopted for the other user, a "yearly target profit" is defined and considered as the user's performance index, while setting a constraint on lake floods.

Specifically (see (Fig. 3) let :

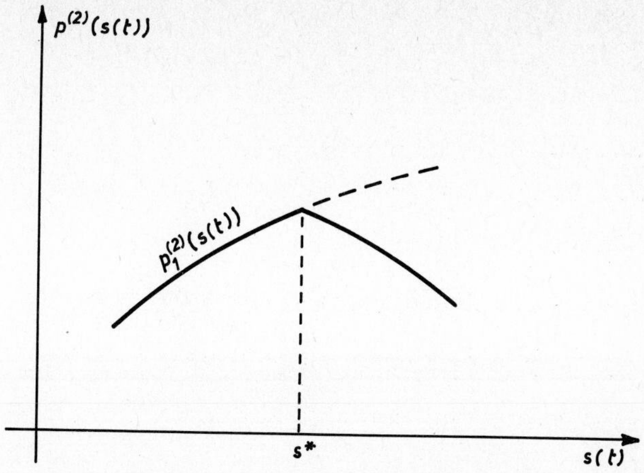

Fig. 3 The recreational users' benefit curve.

$$q^{(2)}(k) = \int_{t_1+(k-1)T}^{t_1+kT} p_1^{(2)}(s(t))\, dt$$

represent the target profit for the k-th year.

Again, if the inflows are introduced into the continuity equation as the segment $\hat{a}_{[t_1,t_1+NT)}$, for any (x_1,x_2) it is possible to determine the corresponding yearly target profit sequence $\{\hat{q}^{(2)}(k;x_1,x_2)\}_{k=1}^{N}$ by simulation :

$$\hat{q}^{(2)}(k, x_1,x_2) = \int_{t_1+(k-1)T}^{t_1+kT} p_1^{(2)}(\hat{s}(t;x_1,x_2))dt \qquad (2.8)$$

If a (.) is regarded to as a T-periodic process, then the yearly target profits must be considered as a process $\{q^{(2)}(k;\ x_1,x_2)\}_k$, which tends to become a stationary one $\{q_\infty^{(2)}\ (k;x_1,x_2)\}_k$. Hence it is possible to define a "yearly target profit" as

$$p^{(2)}(x_1,x_2) = Eq_{\infty}^{(1)}(k;\ x_1,x_2)\ .$$

Approximately it turns out to be

$$p^{(2)}(x_1,x_2) \cong \frac{1}{N}\sum_{k=1}^{N} \hat{q}^{(2)}(k;\ x_1,x_2) \qquad (2.9)$$

for N large enough.

Similarly it is possible to define a "reservoir flood" at time t

$$h^{(2)}(t) = \begin{cases} 0 & s(t) \leq s^* \\ s(t) - s^* & s(t) > s^* \end{cases}$$

a k-th year flood index

$$f^{(2)}(k) = \frac{1}{T}\int_{t_1+(k-1)T}^{t_1+kT} h^{(2)}(t)\,dt$$

a stationary process $\left\{f_{\infty}^{(2)}(k;x_1,x_2)\right\}_k$ and a yearly flood index

$$w^{(2)}(x_1,x_2) = E\ f_{\infty}^{(2)}(k;\ x_1,x_2).$$

Moreover, simulation in correspondence with (x_1,x_2) and $\hat{a}_{[t_1,\ t_1+NT)}$ allows to determine

$$\hat{h}^{(2)}(t;\ x_1,x_2) = \begin{cases} 0 & , \quad \hat{s}(t;x_1,x_2) \leq s^* \\ \hat{s}(t;x_1,x_2) - s^* & , \quad \hat{s}(t;x_1,x_2) > s^* \end{cases} \qquad (2.10)$$

and

$$\hat{f}^{(2)}(h;\ x_1,x_2) = \int_{t_1+(k-1)T}^{t_1+kT} \hat{h}^{(2)}(t;x_1,x_2)\,dt\ . \qquad (2.11)$$

It turns out to be

$$w^{(2)}(x_1,x_2) \cong \frac{1}{N}\sum_{k=1}^{N} f(k;\ x_1,x_2) \qquad (2.12)$$

so that it is finally possible to specify when reservoir floods may

be considered as tolerable by setting the bound

$$w^{(2)}(x_1,x_2) \leq W^{(2)}$$

where $W^{(2)}$ is an assigned volume.

c) <u>The decision making structure of the system</u>

In presence of a single decision maker, the regulation problem could be expressed by the following mathematical program:

$$\max_{x_1,x_2} \; p^{(1)}(x_1) + p^{(2)}(x_1,x_2) \tag{2.13}$$

$$x_2 \geq x_1 \geq 0 \tag{2.14}$$

$$w^{(m)}(x_1,x_2) \leq W^{(m)} \qquad m = 1,2 \quad . \tag{2.15}$$

This is the decision making structure usually assumed in the literature. In many real situation however there does not exist any supervisor or "water seller", but the management results from a direct tradeoff between the users. In this case a more satisfactory formulation of the lake regulation problem is given by the following two person non-zero sum game :

$$\max_{x_1} p^{(1)}(x_1) \tag{2.16}$$

$$x_2 \geq x_1 \geq 0 \tag{2.17}$$

$$w^{(1)}(x_1,x_2) < W^{(1)} \tag{2.18}$$

for the downstream user

$$\max_{x_2} p^{(2)}(x_1,x_2) \tag{2.19}$$

$$x_2 \geq x_1 \tag{2.20}$$

$$w^{(2)}(x_1,x_2) \leq W^{(2)} \tag{2.21}$$

for the recreational user. In fact, as in the case described in the example, the decision process evolution may assumed to be roughly the following :

I) the downstream users decide to build the dam in order to make a satisfactory "guaranteed water" $g(x_1)$ available to them;

II) the population living along the lake sides care that the extra-storages, due to the dam construction, do not become excessive by requiring a proper regulation range (x_1, x_2) and specifically a proper x_2, the parameter which mostly influences the floods on the lake.

In the next section the characteristics of the game (2.16)-(2.21) will be discussed and an algorithm for determining the solution will be given.

3. PROBLEM SOLUTION

First the characteristics of the feasible regions of the optimization problems (2.16)-(2.18) and (2.19)-(2.21), respectively, are examined. Such an analysis enables to draw some conclusions about the existence and the uniqueness of the solution of the game (2.16)-(2.21), and allows to choose an efficient solution algorithm. In fact, it must be recalled that $w^{(1)}(\cdot,\cdot)$ and $w^{(2)}(\cdot,\cdot)$ are defined via simulation, so that, a priori, the solution of the game must be found by using (2.1), (2.2), (2.5)-(2.7), (2.10)-(2.12) a certain number of times, each time corresponding to a different pair (x_1,x_2).

Let $\mathcal{D} = \{(x_1,x_2): x_2 \geq x_1 \geq 0\}$ and let $\mathcal{R}^{(1)}, \mathcal{R}^{(2)}$ be the subregions of $\mathcal{D}$ where (2.18) and (2.21) are respectively satisfied. The following property leads to obtain useful informations about the shape of $\mathcal{R}^{(m)}$, m=1,2.

Proposition

The functions $w^{(1)}(\cdot,x_2)$ and $w^{(2)}(x_1,\cdot)$ are non-decreasing, the functions $w^{(1)}(x_1,\cdot)$ and $w^{(2)}(\cdot,x_2)$ are non-increasing.
To justify the statement, recall [19] that $\hat{s}(t;\cdot,x_2)$ is non-increasing while $\hat{s}(t;x_1,\cdot)$ is non decreasing. Hence the conclusions about the flood index follow by applying (2.10)-(2.12). In particular, with respect to (2.10), note that the non-flood interval $\{t: \hat{s}(t;\cdot,x_2) \leq s^*\}$ is non-increasing while the non-flood interval $\{t: \hat{s}(t;x_1,\cdot) \leq s^*\}$ is non-decreasing.
Moreover, in view of (2.2), it turns out that $\hat{r}(t;x_1,\cdot)$ is a non-increasing function while $\hat{r}(t;\cdot, x_2)$ is a non-decreasing one. This directly yields the conclusions about the deficit index, if (2.5)-(2.7) are taken into account. Apparently the boundary of $\mathcal{R}^{(m)}$ consists of the vertical axis, the bisector $x_2 = x_1$, as well as of the curve implicitly defined by

$$w^{(m)}(x_1,x_2) = W^{(m)} \qquad (3.1.m)$$

Let $x_2 = x_2^{(m)}(x_1)$ represent the explicit form of (3.1m).

Since

$$\frac{dx_2^{(m)}(x_1)}{dx_1} = -\frac{\dfrac{\partial w^{(m)}(x_1,x_2)}{\partial x_1}}{\dfrac{\partial w^{(m)}(x_1,x_2)}{\partial x_2}} \qquad (3.2)$$

in view of the Proposition it turns out that $x_2^{(m)}(.)$ is a non-decreasing function. Moreover, by remarking that $w^{(1)}(0,x_2)=0$ while $w^{(2)}(x_1,x_1) = \text{const} = \min_{x_2} w^{(2)}(x_1,x_2)$, it is possible to guess the behaviour of the curves $w^{(2)}(x_1,x_2) = \text{const.}$ and, in particular, of the contours of $\mathcal{R}^{(1)}$ and $\mathcal{R}^{(2)}$.

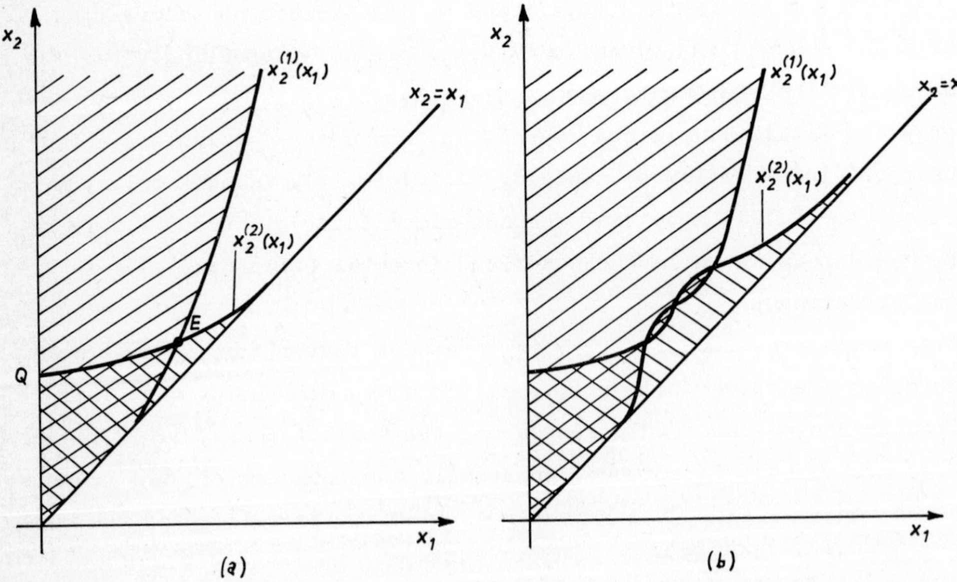

Fig. 4 The single (a), the multiple (b) intersection case

Property (3.2) is not enough to ensure the uniqueness of the intersection between the two curves, since situations of the kind described in Fig. 4.b might occur. However, apart from problems characterized by peculiar values of the data s^*, $\hat{a}_{[t_1,t_1+NT]}$, $g(.)$, $W^{(1)}$, $W^{(2)}$, the most common case is the one described in Fig. 4a. From now onwards the existence of a unique intersection E will be assumed: the analysis however could also be carried out in the multiple intersection case.

First note that in view of (2.8), (2.9) and the above mentioned property of the storage, $P^{(1)}(., x_2)$ is a non-increasing function, while $P^{(2)}(x_1,.)$ is a non-decreasing one. Moreover consider $Q(0, x_2^{(2)}(0))$ and let M and l_M respectively denote any point of the curve segment $\widehat{QE}$ and the tangent to $\widehat{QE}$ in M. Then it is possible to specify which is the Pareto optimal **line** for the game (2.16)-(2.21), i.e. the set

$$\mathcal{B} = \left\{(\hat{x}_1,\hat{x}_2) : \nexists (x_1,x_2) \in \mathcal{R}^{(1)} \cap \mathcal{R}^{(2)} : P^{(1)}(x_1) \geq P^{(1)}(\hat{x}_1), P^{(2)}(x_1,x_2) \geq P^{(2)}(\hat{x}_1,\hat{x}_2)\right\} .$$

Specifically, the shape of $\mathcal{R}^{(1)} \cap \mathcal{R}^{(2)}$ as shown in Fig. 4.a allows to conclude that, in the present case,

$$\mathcal{B} = \{E\} \cup \mathcal{B}^*$$

where

$$\mathcal{B}^* = \left\{(\hat{x}_1,\hat{x}_2) : (\hat{x}_1,\hat{x}_2) \in \widehat{QE} \; , \; \left.\frac{\partial P^{(2)}(x_1,x_2)}{\partial l_M}\right|_{\substack{x_1=\hat{x}_1 \\ x_2=\hat{x}_2}} < 0\right\} \qquad (3.3)$$

A basic characteristic of the game (2.13)-(2.18) is that $E(\hat{x}_{1E},\hat{x}_{2E})$ is the unique equilibrium strategy of the game, i.e. if the first user plays $\hat{x}_{1E}$, the second one must play $\hat{x}_{2E}$ otherwise either he violates his constraint or he does not maximize his payoff. Viceversa, if the second user plays $\hat{x}_{2E}$, the first is must select $\hat{x}_{1E}$ for the same reason. Hence E, being both a Pareto optimal and an equilibrium strategy, may be assumed as the solution of the game (2.16)-(2.21) in the non-cooperative case. Of course since the contour of $\mathcal{R}^{(1)} \cap \mathcal{R}^{(2)}$ is not explicitly given, the intersection E must be found via simulation, in accordance with some efficient search scheme (see the example below).

The cooperative case, which is much more complicated if $\mathcal{B}^*$ is nonempty, is briefly discussed in the following.
More in detail, the solution can be looked for

i) by solving the mathematical program (2.13)-(2.15);

ii) by assuming a "right" bargain rule, i.e. a division of the extra-profit due to cooperation.

For instance if $(\tilde{x}_1^{(o)}, \tilde{x}_2^{(o)})$ is a solution supplied by step i), then a bargain rule may be the following [17] :

$$P^{(1)} = P^{(1)}(\tilde{x}_{1E}) + \frac{\Delta_1 - \Delta_2}{2}$$

to the first user

$$P^{(2)} = P^{(2)}(\tilde{x}_{1E}, \tilde{x}_{2E}) + \frac{\Delta_1 - \Delta_2}{2}$$

where

$$\Delta_1 = P^{(1)}(\tilde{x}_1^{(o)}) - P^{(1)}(\tilde{x}_{1E})$$

$$\Delta_2 = P^{(2)}(\tilde{x}_{1E}, \tilde{x}_{2E}) - P^{(1)}(\tilde{x}_1^{(o)}, \tilde{x}_2^{(o)}).$$

Note that, while the determination of the non cooperative solution does not imply the knowledge of the explicit form of $P^{(1)}(\cdot)$ and $P^{(2)}(\cdot,\cdot)$. On the contrary such knowledge is fundamental when analysing the cooperative case, which hence requires a much greater amount of data.

4. EXAMPLE

This section summarizes the results of an analysis performed on data taken from the lake Maggiore system (Northern Italy).

a) Data

The maximum admissible release curve g(s(t)) has been plotted in Fig. 5.

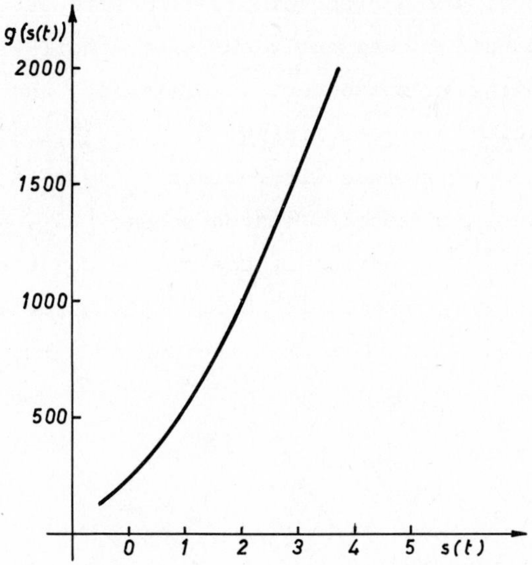

Fig.5 The maximum admissible release curve for the example

The historical record 1943-1967 has been used as the hydrological input for the simulation. For the sake of convenience, the constraints on failures and on floods have been respectively expressed in terms of percents of deficitary and flood days over the time horizon instead of using volumes:

$$\bar{w}^{(1)}(x_1,x_2) \leq \bar{W}^{(1)}$$

$$\bar{w}^{(2)}(x_1,x_2) \leq \bar{W}^{(2)} \quad .$$

The behaviour of the corresponding feasible regions is obviously quite similar to the one of $\mathcal{R}_1$ and $\mathcal{R}_2$.

b) Solution Algorithm

A situation of the kind described in Fig. 4a, i.e. the existence of a unique equilibrium point has been a priori assumed and verified a posteriori. The point E has been found through the angular bisection-bisection search algorithm, whose k-th step is illustrated in Fig. 6. More in detail, the (k-1)-th step provides a sector S_k and a search analysis along the bisector b_k is carried out at the k-th step, in order to determine the bisector position with respect to the unknown equilibrium and subsequently to select the (k+1)-th sector by properly discarding an emisector. Specifically, the search along b_k consist of a simulation for determining $\bar{w}^{(1)}(x_1^{(j)}, x_2^{(j)})$ and $\bar{w}^{(2)}(x_{1k}^{(j)}, x_{2k}^{(j)})$ in correspondence with points $A_k^{(j)}=(x_{1k}^{(j)}, x_{2k}^{(j)})$ chosen in accordance with a bisection search scheme [22]. When the search leads to a point $A_{jk}^{(j)}$ where only one of the constraints (2.18), (2.21) is satisfied, then it is possible to determine the bisector position. The algorithm stops when the sector width becomes smaller than a fixed value.

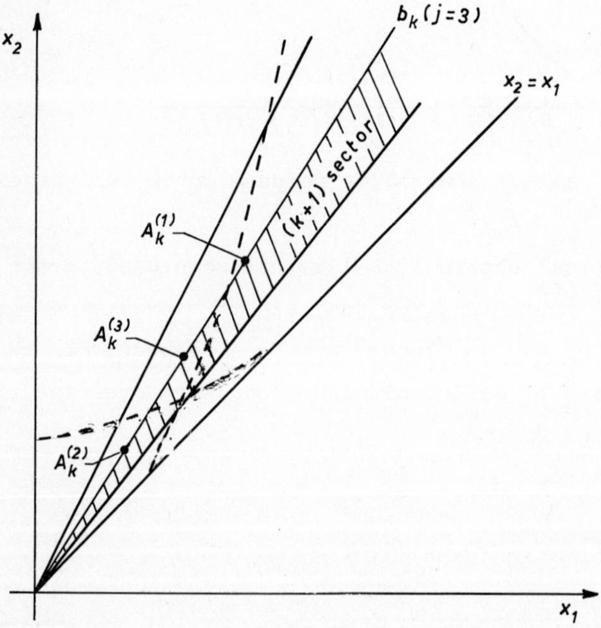

Fig. 6 The k-th step of the solution algorithm

c) Results

The solution has been found under different data s*, $\bar{W}^{(1)}$, $\bar{W}^{(2)}$. More in detail, the behaviour of ($\hat{x}_{1E}$, $\hat{x}_{2E}$) versus $\bar{W}^{(1)}$, for fixed s*, $\bar{W}^{(2)}$, is shown in Fig. 7. On the other hand, Fig. 8 exhibits the effect of the flood level s* on the solutions of the game.

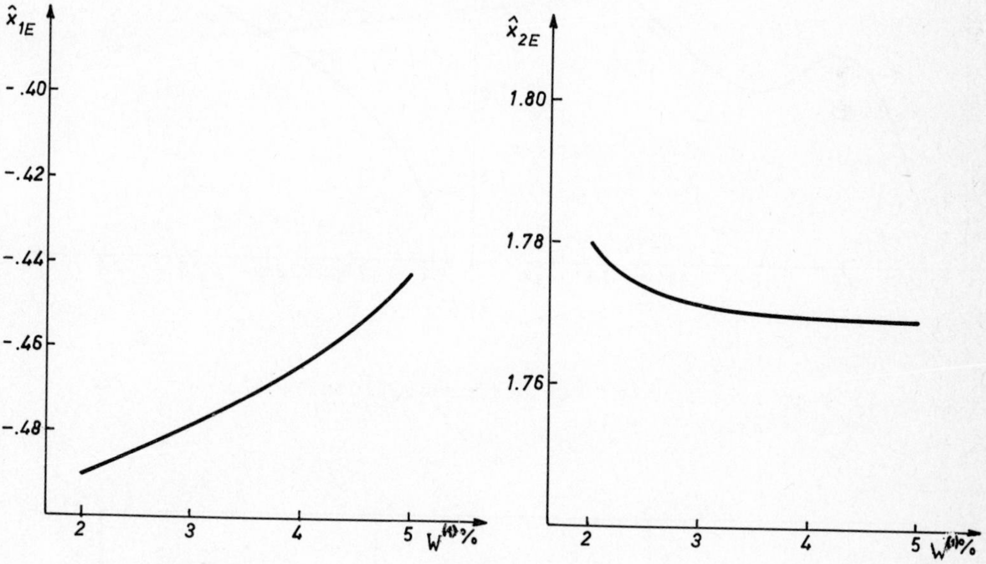

Fig. 7 Problem solution (m) for different failure constraints (s*=2.5 m, $W^{(2)}$= 1%).

Finally, the case when the operating policy parameters are changed twice during the year, in correspondence with a "summer" and a "winter" season respectively, has been considered. Apart from the double dimension of the game, there is no substantial difference with the one-season case and the above mentioned algorithm can be used as a subroutine when looking for the two-season equilibrium point. The results in two cases corresponding to s* = 2.5 m are reported in Table 1, where the index s and w denote the summer and the winter season respectively (the upper pair is the summer solution, the lower pair is the winter one).

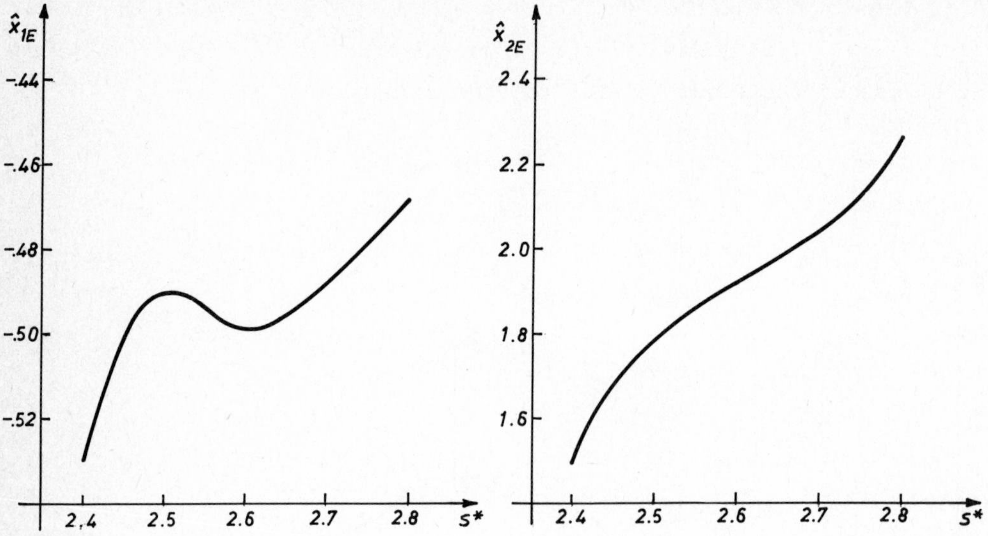

Fig. 8 Problem solution (m) for different flood levels $s^*(W^{(1)}=2\%,\ W^{(2)}=1\%)$

Data	Summer Solution	Winter Solution
$W_s^{(1)} = W_w^{(1)} = 2\%$ $W_s^{(2)} = W_w^{(2)} = 1\%$	- 0.225, 1.578	- 0.626 , 2.141
$W_s^{(1)} = W_w^{(1)} = 4\%$ $W_s^{(2)} = W_w^{(2)} = 2\%$	- 0.144, 1.964	- 0.610 , 2.348

Table 1 Solution (m) of the two seasonal problem s* = 2.5 m

5. CONCLUDING REMARKS

A short-term regulation problem of a lake has been discussed in this paper and formulated as a non-cooperative game. The solution does not require an explicit knowledge of the players' performance indexes. The estimation of such benefits, specially the ones concerning recreation on the lake, is a major drawback for solving the problem in the cooperative case. A certain amount of criticism may involve the economy of the system as assumed in the paper. An alternative and a priori more rigorous way would apparently be the one of introducing dificits and floods into the objective function instead of using target benefits and considering losses in the constraints set.
When following this view point, however, it would be quite difficult to determine structural properties of the problem able to suggest on efficient search-simulation scheme.

REFERENCES

[1] Thomas A., Fiering M., "The Nature of the Storage Yield Function", in "Operations Research in Water Quality Management" Harvard University Water Program, Cambridge, U.S.A., 1963.

[2] Buras N., "Scientific Allocation of Water Resources", American Elsevier, New York, 1972

[3] Hall W., Butcher W., Esogbue A., "Optimization of the Operation of a Multiple Purpose Reservoir by Dynamic Programming", Water Resources Research, June 1968.

[4] MaassA. et al., "Design of Water Resource Systems", Harvard University Press, Cambridge, U.S.A., 1962.

[5] Young G., Pisano M., "Non Linear Programming Applied to Regional Water Resource Planning", Water Resources Research, Vol.6, no.1, Feb. 1970

[6] Revelle C., Joeres E., Kirby W., "The Linear Decision Rule in Reservoir Management and Design 1: Development of the Stochastic Model", Water Resources Research, Vol. 5, no. 4, Aug. 1969.

[7] Hufschmidt M., Fiering M., "Simulation Techniques for Design of Water Resource Systems", Harvard University Press, Cambridge, Massachussets, 1966.

[8] Cohon J., Marks D., "Multiobjective Screening Models and Water Resource Investment", Water Resources Research, Vol. 9, no. 4, Aug. 1973.

[9] Cohon J., Marks D., "A Review and Evaluation of Multiobjective Programming Techniques", Water Resources Research, Vol. 11, no.2, April. 1975.

[10] Haimes Y., Hall W., "Multiobjectives in Water Resources System Analysis: The Surrogate Worth Trade Off Method", Water R sources Research, Vol. 10, no. 4, 1974.

[11] Haimes Y., "Decomposition and Multilevel Approach in the Modelling

and Management of Water Resources Systems", in "Decomposition of Large Scale Problems", Himmelblau D. Editor, North Holland Publ. Co., 1973.

[12] Haimes Y., "Multilevel Dynamic Programming Structure for Regional Water Resource Management", in "Decomposition of Large Scale Problems" Himmelblau D. Editor, North Holland Publ. Co., 1973.

[13] Hall W., Dracup J., "Water Resources Systems Engeneering", Mc Graw-Hill Inc., 1970.

[14] Hipel J., Ragade R., Unny T., "Metagame Analysis of Water Resources Conflicts", Proc. of the A.S.C.E., vol. 100, no. HY 10, Oct. 1974.

[15] Rogers P., "A Game Theory Approach to the Problems of International River Basins", Water Resources Research, Vol. E, no. 4, Aug. 1969.

[16] Fronza G., Karlin A., Rinaldi S., "Multipurpose Reservoir Operation under Conflicting Objectives" Int. Rep. 75-1, Istituto di Elettrotecnica ed Elettronica, Politecnico di Milano, Milano, Italy.

[17] Luce D., Raiffa H., "Games and Decisions", John Wiley and Sons Inc. New York, 1967.

[18] Yeh W., Askew A., Hall W., "Optimal Planning and Operation of a Multiple Purpose Reservoir", Proc. of the 7th Mathematical Programming Synposium, The Hague, Sept. 1970.

[19] Fronza G. et al., "Optimal Reservoir Operating Policies via Search Methods" in Proc. of IFAC/UNESCO Workshop on "Systems Analysis and Modelling Approaches in Environment Systems", Zakopane (Poland), Sept. 17-22, 1973.

[20] Rozanov Y., "Some System Approaches to Water Resources Problems II. Statistical Equilibrium of Processes in Dam Storage", Res. Rep. RR-75-4, IIASA, Feb. 1975.

[21] Bryant G., "Stochastic Theory of Queues Applied to Design of Im-

pounding Reservoirs", doctorial dissertation, Harvard University, 1961.

[22] Wilde D., Beightler C. "Foundations of Optimization", Prentice Hall Inc. 1967.

OPTIMAL POLLUTION CONTROL OF A LAKE (+)

F.X. LITT (*) and H. SMETS (**)

ABSTRACT

This paper considers a lake in which a pollutant is dumped at a rate whose maximum value is constant. We assume that the quantity of pollutant eliminated by natural processes is proportional to the total amount of pollutant contained into the lake. With this process we associate a cost which is the sum of two terms : the first one represents the cost of cleaning up a fraction of the pollutant and the second term is a measure of the damage done to the environment.

We then determine the optimal dumping policy, i.e., the policy which minimizes that cost integrated over a fixed period of time by solving an optimal control problem

---

(+) Research supported by OECD under the Transfontier Pollution Programme.

(*) Chargé de cours associé, Université de Liège, Belgium.
(**)Environment Directorate, OECD, Paris, chargé de cours, Université de Liège, Belgium.

1. Introduction

We are concerned with the time history of the pollution of a lake by a pollutant dumped at a time rate where maximum value is constant.

Two cases are examined : either the pollutant is non-degradable (purely cumulative system), or the pollutant is disappearing exponentially with time (phenomenon of sedimentation, renewal of lake's water or radio-active decay).

The goal is to compute the cleaning policy such that the discounted sum of the costs (cleaning plus damage to the environment) extended over a fixed period of time is minimal. That goal is achieved by solving an optimal control problem. This is done in the four distinct situations obtained by combining constant or linear marginal cost of cleaning up with constant or linear marginal cost of damage to the environment.

We shall find that while in conventional environmental economics (static case), the optimal strategy consists in setting a cleaning up standard, the optimal strategy in this case amounts to a fixed standard in a few instances and to selecting time varying clean up standards in most cases.

2. Statement of the problem

The sources of pollution are emitting the pollutant at a constant time rate q_o. At time τ the fraction $q(\tau)$ is dumped into the lake and the fraction $q_o - q(\tau)$ is cleaned up. This gives rise to the cleaning cost :

$$cq_o\left[\frac{q_o - q(\tau)}{q_o}\right]^p, \qquad c > 0, \quad p \geqslant 1 \tag{1}$$

and $q(\tau)$ is constrained according to :

$$0 \leqslant q(\tau) \leqslant q_o \tag{2}$$

On the other hand, if $Q(\tau)$ is the total amount of pollutant contained into the lake at time τ, the cost due to the damage done to the environment will be :

$$bQ_M\left[\frac{Q(\tau)}{Q_M}\right]^n, \qquad b > 0, \quad n \geqslant 1 \tag{3}$$

where the quantity Q_M will be defined later.

The total cost extended over a fixe period of time $[o, T]$ will then be :

$$\int_o^T \left\{ cq_o\left[\frac{q_o - q(\tau)}{q_o}\right]^p + bQ_M\left[\frac{Q(\tau)}{Q_M}\right]^n \right\} e^{-at}dt \qquad (4)$$

where $a > 0$ is the discount factor.

If we assume that the quantity of pollutant disappearing by a natural process (e.g. sedimentation, renewal of lake's water or radio-active decay) is proportional to the total amount of pollutant $Q(\tau)$ contained into the lake, $Q(\tau)$ and $q(\tau)$ are related by the following ordinary differential equation :

$$\frac{dQ(\tau)}{d\tau} = -fQ(\tau) + q(\tau) \qquad (5)$$

where $f \geqslant 0$ and $f = 0$ for the purely cumulative system.

We call social horizon, the inverse $1/a$ of the discount factor. Through the relation :

$$\frac{1}{a} = \int_o^\infty e^{-at}d\tau \qquad (6)$$

the social horizon can be interpreted as a discounted sum of intervals of time : the largest the discount factor, the smallest is the social horizon.

Next, we define the quantity Q_M of (3) : it is the amount of pollutant contained into the lake at the social horizon for the purely cumulative system when no clean up is performed and when the initial amount $Q(o)$ is zero :

$$Q_M = \int_o^{1/a} q_o d\tau = \frac{q_o}{a} \qquad (7)$$

We are looking for a policy $q(\tau)$, $\tau \varepsilon [o,T]$, which minimizes (4) under the constraints (2) and (5).

Defining the non dimensionnal variables :

$$t = a\tau, \qquad u = \frac{q_o - q}{q_o}, \qquad x = \frac{Q}{Q_M} \qquad (8)$$

and the parameters :

$$t_f = aT, \qquad k = \frac{b}{ac}, \qquad \ell = \frac{f}{a} \tag{9}$$

we obtain the following optimal control problem :

Find the optimal control $u^*(t)$, $t\varepsilon[o,t_f]$ *and the corresponding optimal trajectory* $x^*(t)$, $t\varepsilon[o,t_f]$ *which minimizes*

$$\int_o^{t_f} [kx^n(t) + u^p(t)]e^{-t}dt \tag{10}$$

with $k > 0$, $n \geqslant 1$, $p \geqslant 1$, *under the constraints :*

$$\dot{x}(t) = -\ell x(t) + 1 - u(t), \quad 0 \leqslant u(t) \leqslant 1, \; t\varepsilon[0,t_f] \tag{11}$$

with $\ell \geqslant 0$, *starting with initial condition* $x(0) = x^o \geqslant 0$. *We ask further that the optimal control* $u^*(t)$, $t\varepsilon[o,t_f]$ *belongs to the class of piecewise continuous functions.*

Recall that $u(t) = 1$ corresponds to no pollution and $u(t) = 0$ to maximum pollution; also, $\ell = 0$ for a purely cumulative system.

We shall study the 4 cases corresponding to p and n equal to 1 or 2, for finite and infinite terminal time.

3. Technique of analysis

To solve the problem, we use the maximum principle of Pontryagin [1]. Hence, consider the hamiltonian

$$H(t,\lambda,x,u) = \lambda_o(kx^n + u^p)e^{-t} + \lambda(-\ell x + 1 - u) \tag{12}$$

where $\lambda_o = -1$ if $t_f \neq \infty$ and $\lambda_o \leqslant 0$ if $t_f = \infty$ [2].

The optimal control $u^*(t)$ must satisfy the condition

$$H(t,\lambda(t),x(t),u^*(t)) \geqslant H(t,\lambda(t),x(t),u) \quad \forall u\varepsilon[0,1] \tag{13}$$

whenever $\lambda(t)$ satisfy the ordinary differential equation :

$$\dot{\lambda}(t) = -\frac{\delta H}{\delta x} = -\lambda_o nkx^{n-1}(t)e^{-t} + \ell\lambda(t) \tag{14}$$

Furthermore, since $x(t_f)$ is free, $\lambda(t_f)$ must satisfy the transversality condition :

$$\lambda(t_f) = 0 \tag{15}$$

The problem is thus reduced to the solution of the two points boundary value problem given by relation (11), (13), (14) and (15), when t_f is finite. Indeed, condition (15) does not hold when t_f is infinite [2]. In this last case, we must integrate the system for arbitrary initial condition $\lambda(0)$ in order to compute the cost and find which $\lambda(0)$ minimizes it : the problem is reduced to parameter optimization.

4. Results

The solution of the two points boundary value problem (t_f finite), as well as the solution of the parameter optimization (t_f infinite) are straightforward, so that the details will not be given here. More details can be found in [3]-[5].

In the sequel, MCD will stand for marginal cost of damage and MCC for marginal cost of cleaning up.

4.1. Constant MCD ($n = 1$) and constant MCC ($p = 1$)

For a finite t_f we get :

$$u^*(t) = 0, \quad x^*(t) = e^{-\ell t}(x^o - \frac{1}{\ell}) + \frac{1}{\ell}$$

if $k \leqslant \ell + 1$ or $k > \ell + 1$ and $t_f \leqslant \frac{1}{\ell+1} \ln \frac{k}{k-1-\ell}$,

and

$$u^*(t) = \begin{cases} 1 & t \varepsilon [0, t_1[\\ 0 & t \varepsilon [t_1, t_f] \end{cases}$$

$$u^*(t) = \begin{cases} e^{-\ell t} x^o & t \varepsilon [o, t_1) \\ e^{-\ell(t-t_1)}(e^{-\ell t_1} x^o - \frac{1}{\ell}) + \frac{1}{\ell} & t \varepsilon [t_1, t_f] \end{cases}$$

where $t_1 = \frac{1}{\ell+1} (t_f - \ln \frac{k}{k-1-\ell})$

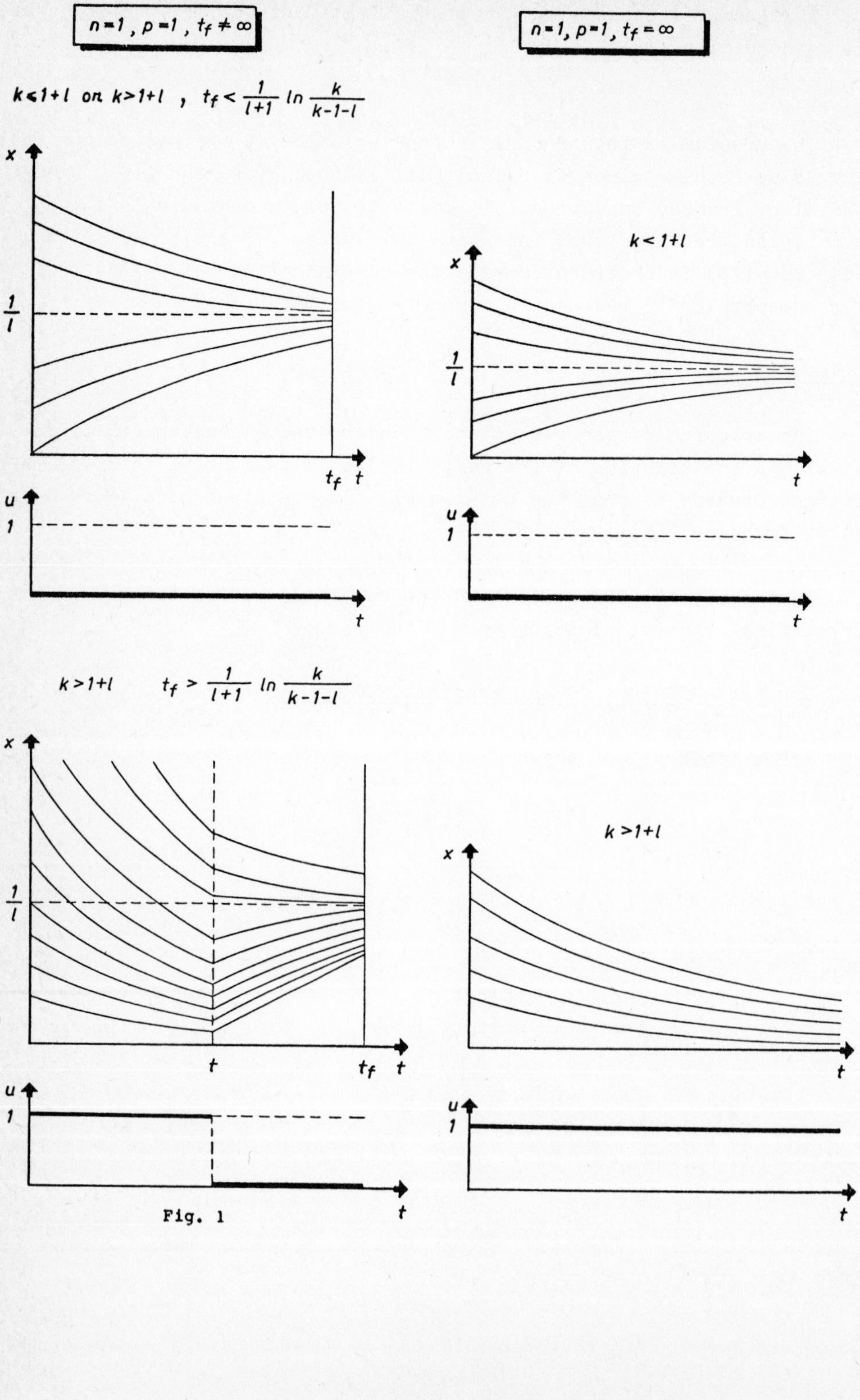

n=1 , p=1 , t_f ≠ ∞
n=1, p=1, t_f = ∞
k<1+l on k>1+l , t_f < 1/(l+1) ln k/(k-1-l)
k < 1+l
k >1+l   t_f > 1/(l+1) ln k/(k-1-l)
k >1+l
x
u
1/l
1
t
t_f

Fig. 1

if $k > \ell + 1$ and $t_f > \frac{1}{\ell+1} \ell n \frac{k}{k-1-\ell}$

For $t_f = \infty$, we get :

$u^*(t) = 0$ if $k < \ell + 1$, and $u^*(t) = 1$ if $k > \ell + 1$.
When $k = \ell + 1$, any control is optimal; indeed in that case it is possible to integrate the cost by parts and then realize that it depends only upon x^o.

We see that the optimal policy does not depend upon the initial level of pollution x^o but depends upon the parameters k, ℓ and t_f. For $k > 1 + \ell$ and t_f sufficiently large but finite, there is a switch from $u = 1$ to $u = 0$; that switch disappears when t_f becomes infinite. For all other cases the optimal policy is constant.

The situation is described on fig. 1.

4.2. Constant MCD ($n = 1$) and linear MCC ($p = 2$)

For a finite t_f we get :

$$u^*(t) = \frac{k}{2(\ell+1)} \left[1 - e^{-(\ell+1)(t_f-t)}\right]$$

if $k \leqslant 2(\ell+1) / \left[1 - e^{-(\ell+1)t_f}\right]$

$$u^*(t) = \begin{cases} 1 & t \varepsilon [0, t_1) \\ \frac{k}{2(\ell+1)} \left[1 - e^{-(\ell+1)(t_f-t)}\right] & t \varepsilon [t_1, t_f] \end{cases}$$

where $t_1 = t_f + \frac{1}{\ell+1} \; n \frac{k-2(\ell+1)}{k}$

if $k > 2(\ell+1) / \left[1 - e^{-(\ell+1)t_f}\right]$

For $t_f = \infty$, we get :

$$u^*(t) = \frac{k}{2(\ell+1)} = u_\infty \qquad \text{if } k \leqslant 2(\ell + 1)$$

$$u^*(t) = 1 \qquad \text{if } k > 2(\ell + 1)$$

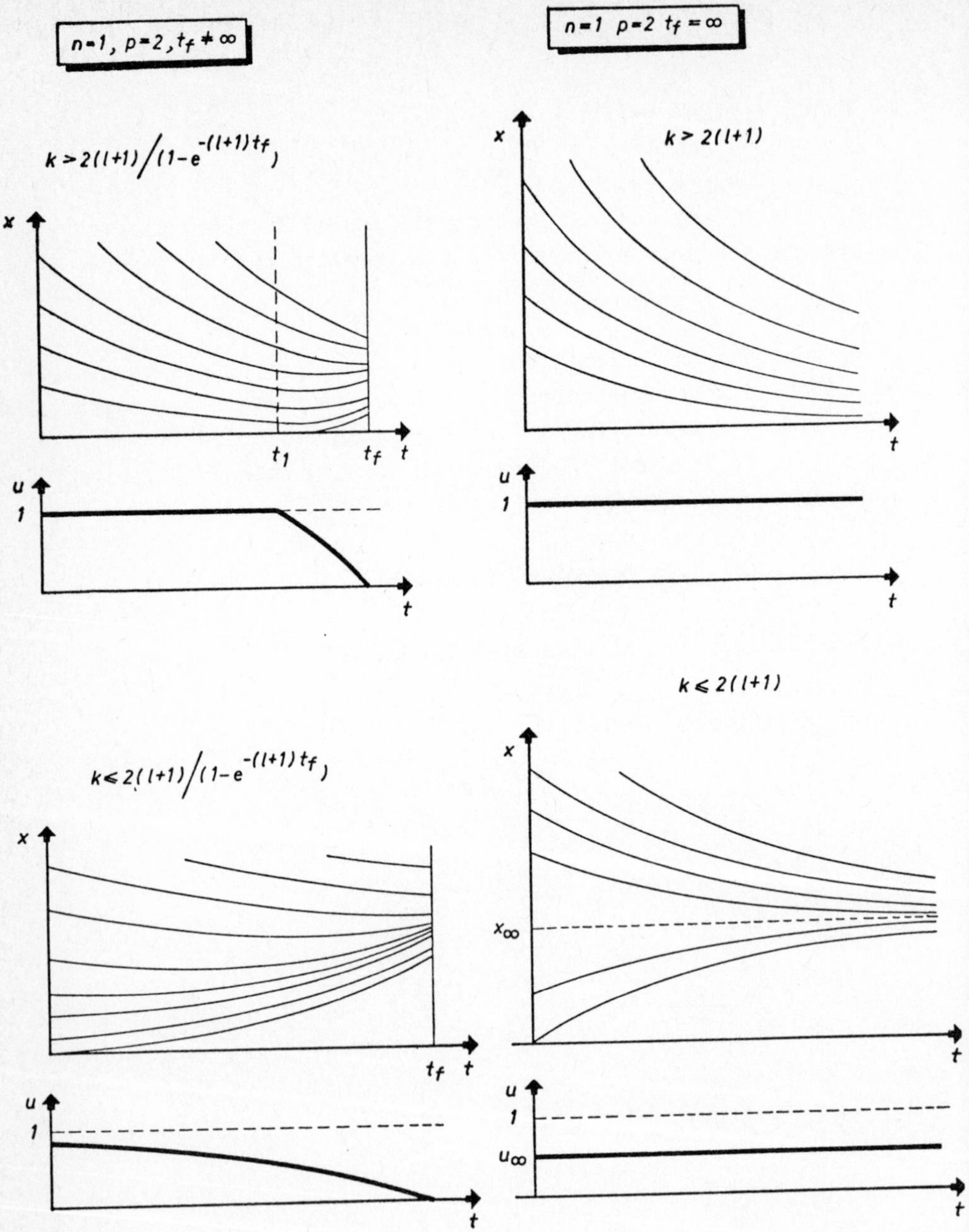
n=1, p=2, t_f ≠ ∞
n=1 p=2 t_f = ∞
k > 2(l+1)/(1-e^-(l+1)t_f)
k > 2(l+1)
x
t_1
t_f
t
u
1
k ≤ 2(l+1)
k ≤ 2(l+1)/(1-e^-(l+1)t_f)
x_∞
u_∞

Fig. 2

Again, the optimal policy does not depend upon the initial level of pollution x^o, but depends upon the parameters k, ℓ and t_f. The optimal policy is constant for an infinite t_f but is partly or totally of exponential type when t_f is finite.

The situation is described on fig. 2.

4.3. Linear MCD (n = 2) and constant MCC (p = 1)

For a finite t_f, there is in the plane (t,x) a locus AB (see fig. 3 and 4) along which the optimal control will switch from u = 1 to u = 0. The equation of that locus is :

$$x = \frac{\ell[(\ell+1)(2\ell+1)-2k]-2k[(\ell+1)e^{-(2\ell+1)(t_f-t)}-(2\ell+1)e^{-(\ell+1)(t_f-t)}]}{2k\ell(\ell+1)[1-e^{-(t_f-t)}]}$$

That locus has a vertical asymptote given by $t = t_f$ and an horizontal one given by $x = \tilde{x}$ with

$$\tilde{x} = \frac{(\ell+1)(2\ell+1)-2k}{2k(\ell+1)}$$

For $t_f \to \infty$, the limit of the locus is its horizontal asymptote.

There is further, under certain conditions, a singular arc given by :

$$u_s = 1 - \frac{\ell(\ell+1)}{2k}, \qquad x_s = \frac{\ell+1}{2k}$$

(i) $x_s \geqslant 1/\ell \Rightarrow$ no singular arc.

For a finite t_f, if we define $\hat{x}$ as the intersection of the locus AB and the x axis, we get :

$$u^*(t) = 0 \qquad \text{if } x^o \leqslant \hat{x}, \text{ and}$$

$$u^*(t) = \begin{cases} 1 & t \in [0,t_1) \quad \text{if } x^o > \hat{x} \\ 0 & t \in [t_1,t_f] \end{cases}$$

where $(t_1, x(t_1))$ is a point of the locus AB.

The results are the same for $t_f = \infty$ provided we replace $\hat{x}$ by $\tilde{x}$ and

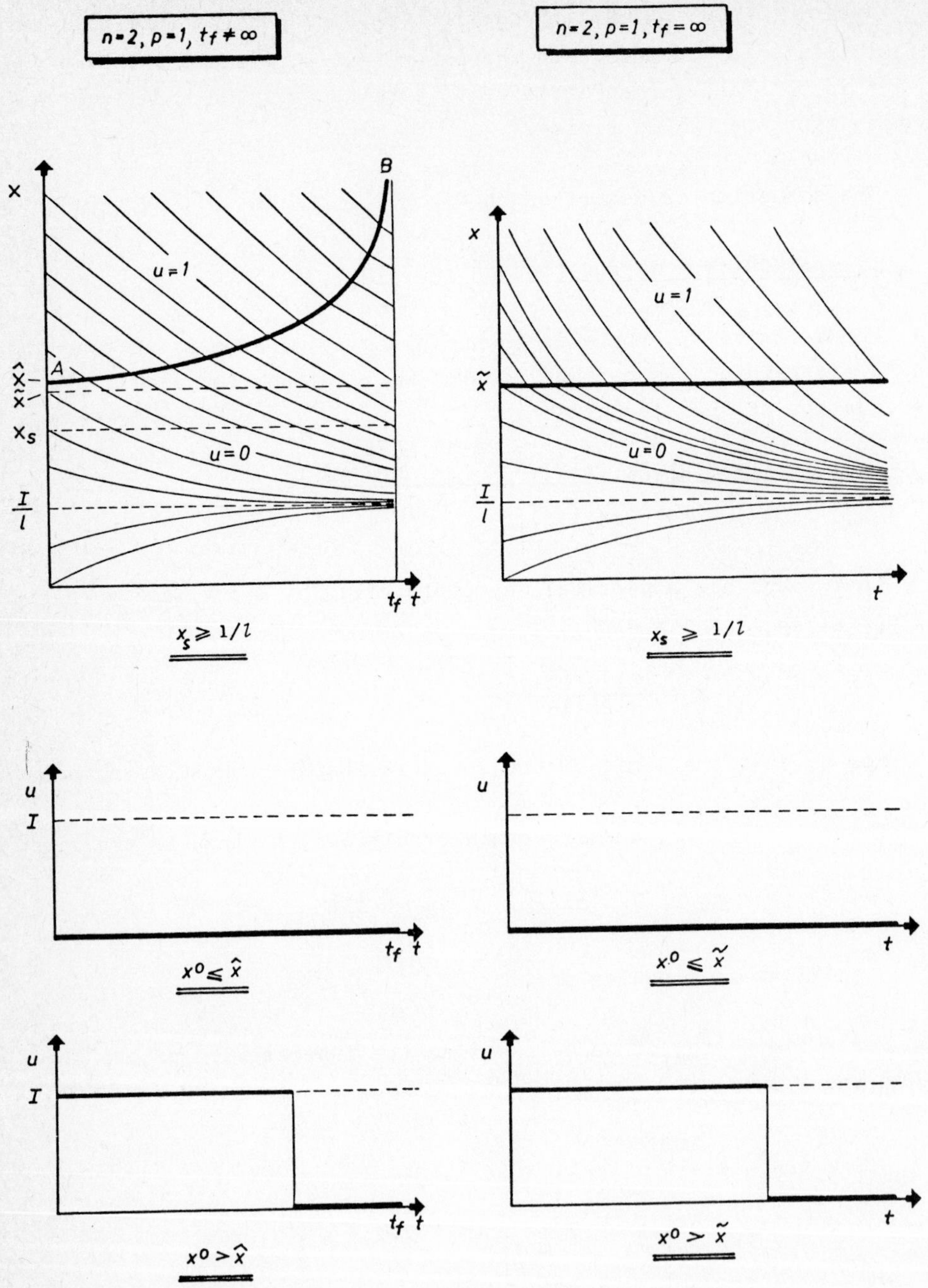
n=2, p=1, $t_f \neq \infty$
n=2, p=1, $t_f = \infty$
x
B
u=1
A
$\hat{x}$
$\tilde{x}$
x_s
u=0
I/l
t_f t
t
$x_s \geq 1/l$
$x_s \geq 1/l$
u
I
$x^0 \leq \hat{x}$
$x^0 \leq \tilde{x}$
$x^0 > \hat{x}$
$x^0 > \tilde{x}$

Fig. 3

the curve AB by its horizontal asymptote $x = \tilde{x}$.

(ii) $x_s < 1/\ell \Rightarrow$ there is a singular arc.

For a finite t_f, we get :

$$u^*(t) = \begin{cases} 0 & t \varepsilon [0,t_1) \\ u_s & t \varepsilon [t_1,t_2) \\ 0 & t \varepsilon [t_2,t_f] \end{cases} \qquad \text{if } x^o \leqslant x_s$$

where $t_1 = -\frac{1}{\ell} \ln \frac{\ell x_s - 1}{\ell x^o - 1}$ and t_2 is at the intersection of the locus AB and the horizontal x_s.

$$u^*(t) = \begin{cases} 1 & t \varepsilon [0,t_1) \\ u_s & t \varepsilon [t_1,t_2) \\ 0 & t \varepsilon [t_2,t_f] \end{cases} \qquad \text{if } x_s < x^o < x_s e^{\ell t_2}$$

$$u^*(t) = \begin{cases} 1 & t \varepsilon [0,t_1) \\ 0 & t \varepsilon [t_1,t_f] \end{cases} \qquad \text{if } x_s e^{\ell t_2} \leqslant x^o$$

where $(t_1, x(t_1))$ is a point on the locus AB.

For $t_f = \infty$, we get :

$$u^*(t) = \begin{cases} 0 & t \varepsilon [0,t_1) \\ u_s & t \geqslant t_1 \end{cases} \qquad \text{if } x^o \leqslant x_s$$

where $t_1 = -\frac{1}{\ell} \ln \frac{\ell x_s - 1}{\ell x^o - 1}$

$$u^*(t) = \begin{cases} 1 & t \varepsilon [0,t_1) \\ u_s & t \geqslant t_1 \end{cases} \qquad \text{if } x_s < x^o$$

where $t_1 = -\frac{1}{\ell} \ln \frac{x_s}{x_o}$.

We see that in this case, the optimal control depends upon both the initial level of pollution and the parameters of the problem.

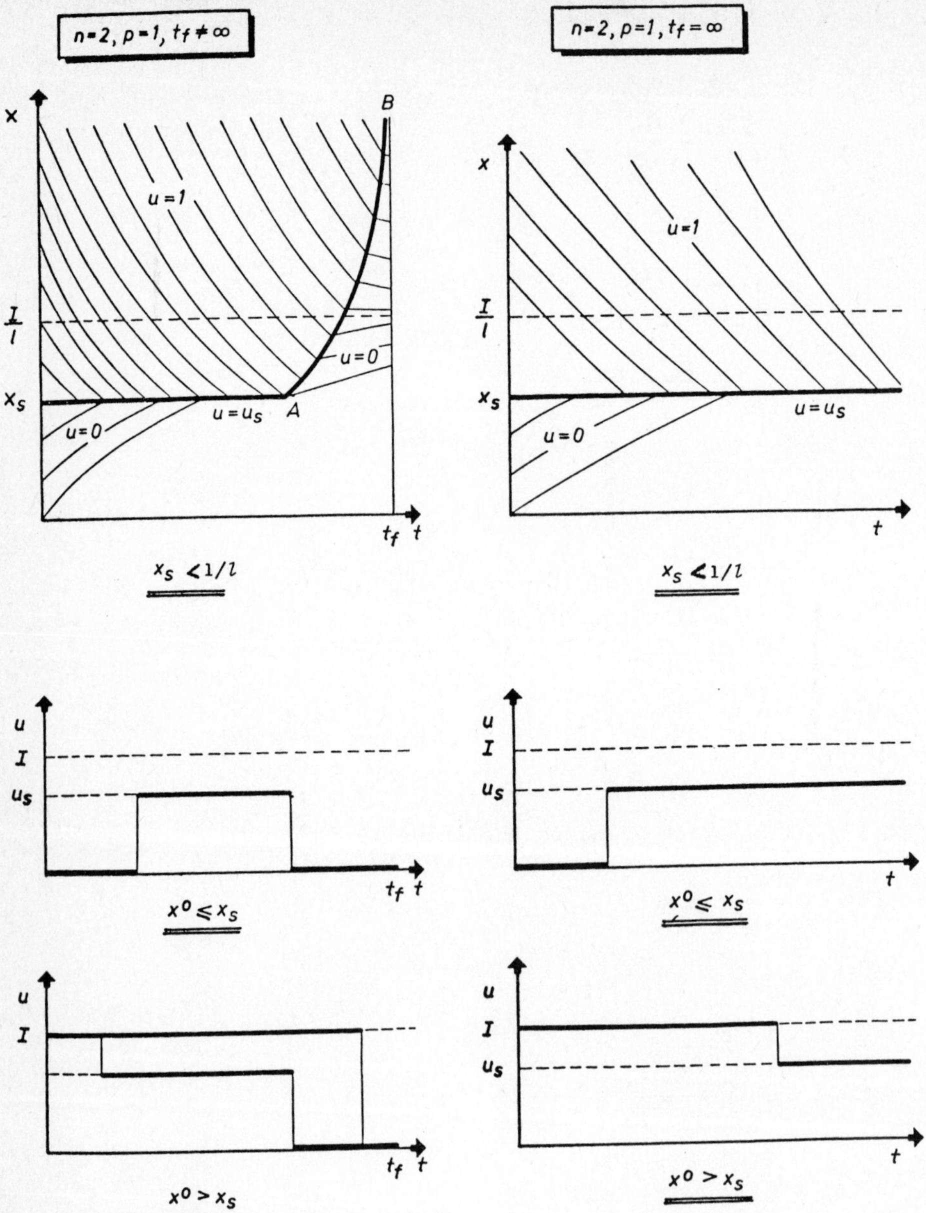

n=2, p=1, $t_f \neq \infty$
n=2, p=1, $t_f = \infty$
x
B
u=1
I/l
u=0
x_s
u=0
$u=u_s$
A
t_f
t
x
u=1
I/l
x_s
$u=u_s$
u=0
t
$x_s < 1/l$
$x_s < 1/l$
u
I
u_s
t_f
t
u
I
u_s
t
$x^0 \leq x_s$
$x^0 \leq x_s$
u
I
t_f
t
u
I
u_s
t
$x^0 > x_s$
$x^0 > x_s$

Fig. 4

4.4. Linear MCD (n = 2) and linear MCC (p = 2)

For a finite t_f, there is in the plane (t,x) a locus AB (see fig. 5) along which the optimal control will change from the boundary value $u(t) = 1$ to values in the interior of the interval $[0,1]$. The equation of that locus is :

$$x = \frac{k(s_1-s_2)-\ell(\ell+1)[s_2 e^{s_1(t_f-t)} - s_1 e^{s_2(t_f-t)}]}{kh[e^{s_1(t_f-t)} - e^{s_2(t_f-t)}]} + \frac{\ell+1}{k}$$

where $h = \ell(\ell+1) + k$, $\quad s_1 = \frac{1+\sqrt{4h+1}}{2}$, $\quad s_2 = \frac{1-\sqrt{4h+1}}{2}$.

That locus has a vertical asymptote given by $t = t_f$ and an horizontal one given by $x = \bar{x}$ with :

$$\bar{x} = \frac{\ell+1}{kh}(h - \ell s_2)$$

For $t_f \to \infty$, the limit of the locus is its horizontal asymptote.

For a finite t_f, if we define $\bar{\bar{x}}$ as the intersection of the locus AB and the x axis, we get :

$$u^*(t) = \frac{k}{h} + \frac{ka_1}{\ell+s_2} e^{s_1 t} + \frac{ka_2}{\ell+s_1} e^{s_2 t} \qquad \text{if } x^o \leqslant \bar{\bar{x}}$$

where
$$a_1 = \frac{h-[hx^o-(\ell+1)](\ell+s_2)e^{s_2 t_f}}{h[(\ell+s_1)e^{s_1 t_f}-(\ell+s_2)e^{s_2 t_f}]}$$

$$a_2 = \frac{h-[hx^o-(\ell+1)](\ell+s_1)e^{s_1 t_f}}{h[(\ell+s_1)e^{s_1 t_f}-(\ell+s_2)e^{s_2 t_f}]}$$

$$u^*(t) = \begin{cases} 1 & t\varepsilon[0,t_1) \\ \frac{\ell+1}{h} + a_1 e^{s_1(t-t_1)} + a_2 e^{s_2(t-t_1)} & t\varepsilon[t_1,t_f] \end{cases} \qquad \text{if } x^o > \bar{\bar{x}}$$

where $a_1 = \frac{\ell+1+s_1(\ell+s_2)x(t_1)}{s_1(s_1-s_2)}$, $\quad a_2 = \frac{\ell+1+s_2(\ell+s_1)x(t_1)}{s_2(s_1-s_2)}$

and $(t_1, x(t_1))$ is a point of the locus AB.

For $t_f = \infty$, we get :

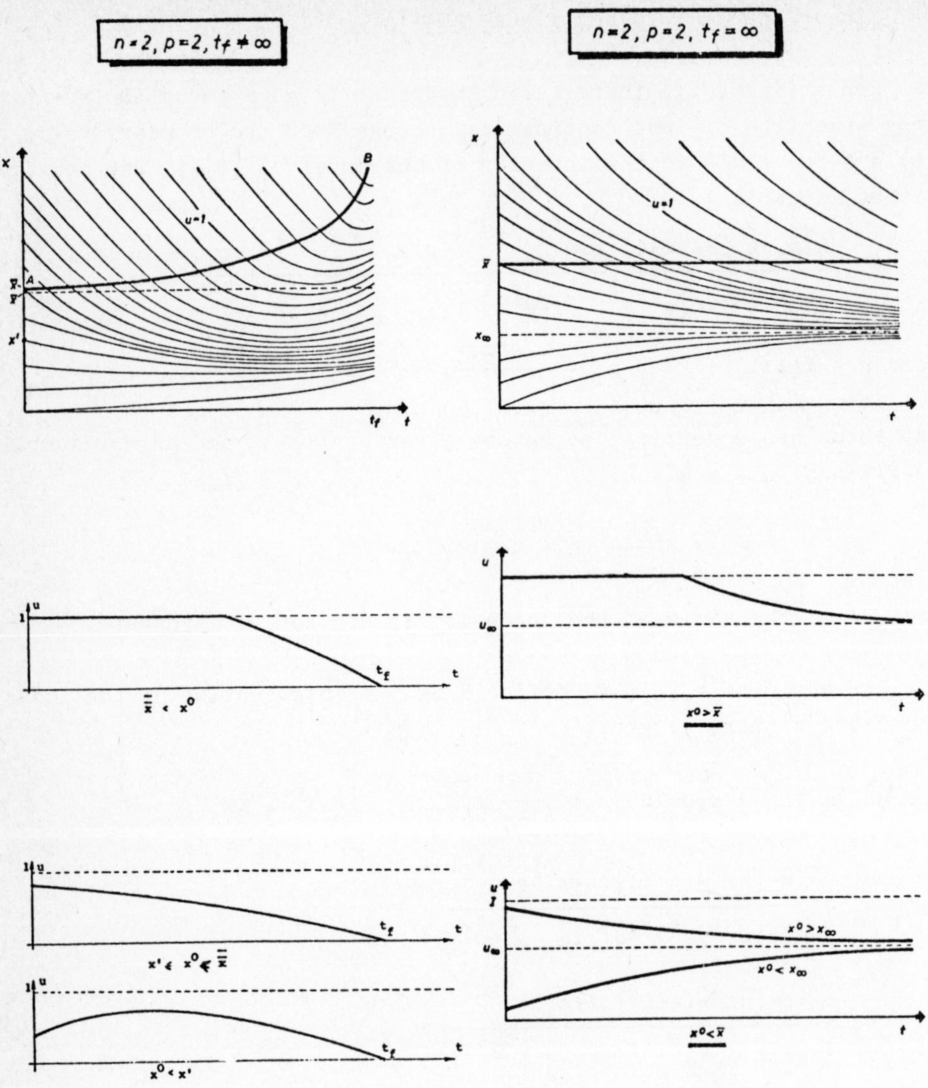

Fig. 5

$$u^*(t) = \frac{k}{h}\left[1 + \frac{hx^o-(\ell+1)}{\ell+s_1} e^{s_2 t}\right] \qquad \text{if } x^o \leqslant \bar{x}$$

$$u^*(t) = \begin{cases} 1 & t\varepsilon[0,t_1) \\ \frac{k}{h} + \frac{k[\ell+1+s_2(\ell+s_1)\bar{x}}{s_2(s_1-s_2)(\ell+s_1)} e^{s_2(t-t_1)} & t \geqslant t_1 \end{cases}$$

if $x^o > \bar{x}$, and t_1 is defined by : $t_1 = -\frac{1}{\ell}\ell n\frac{\bar{x}}{x^o}$

All the above results have been written for $\ell > 0$, but the results for the limit case $\ell = 0$ (purely cumulative system) can be everywhere obtained by taking the limit of the above results when $\ell \to 0$. For more details, the interested reader is refered to [3].

5. Conclusions

When the MCD is constant (n = 1), the optimal policy does not depend upon the initial level of pollution but depends only upon the parameters of the problem in the following way : for a given initial level of pollution, a large value of the ratio b/c (cost of damage/cost of cleaning up) leads to a more severe policy (more cleaning up) while large values of either the discount factor (a) or the disappearing coefficient (f) lead to a less severe policy.

Moreover, in that case (n = 1), the optimal policy for an infinite t_f is always constant. This last fact can be checked a priori. Indeed, by performing an integration by parts on the cost of damage, it is easy to see that the total cost takes on the form :

$$J = \frac{k}{\ell+1}\,[x(0)+1] + \int_o^\infty [u^p(t)-\frac{k}{\ell+1}u(t)]e^{-t}dt$$

Hence we shall find the optimal control by solving :

$$\min_{0\leqslant u\leqslant 1} [u^p - \frac{k}{\ell+1}\, u]$$

So the case MCD constant leads, like for the static case, to setting a cleaning up standard.

When the MCD is linear (n = 2), the optimal policy is influenced by both the initial level of pollution and the parameters of the problem. In this case the optimal strategy varies with time but monotonically.

This study gives quantitative results : if the parameters of the problem can be known, then we just have to apply some formula to find what the optimal strategy should be. An important factor is the discount coefficient a. It is probably the most uncertain parameter in the problem because it is not a physical parameter. Rather it has to be chosen according to what value we give to the future. The formulae we gave allow us to measure the impact of that parameter on the optimal strategy.

An other parameter we have to decide upon a priori, is the terminal time t_f. We can see from the results that given the same initial level of pollution, the optimal policy for finite t_f is in all cases at least as polluting and in most cases more polluting than the optimal policy for infinite t_f.

Finally we can say that the results do not contain any revolutionary idea : rather they are in accordance with common sense.

References

[1] PONTRYAGIN L.S., et al., "The mathematical Theory of Optimal Processes", *Interscience*, New York, 1967.

[2] HALKIN H., "Necessary conditions for optimal control problems with infinite horizons", *Econometrica*, vol. 42, No. 2, 1974.

[3] LITT F.X., "Politique optimale de dépollution dans un système accumulatif", *RART 74/01*, Université de Liège, juillet 1974.

[4] LITT F.X., "Politique optimale de dépollution dans un système non strictement cumulatif", *RART 74/03*, Université de Liège, septembre 1974.

[5] LITT F.X., "Politique optimale de dépollution dans un système non strictement cumulatif : suite. Conclusions de l'étude", *RART 74/05*, Université de Liège, novembre 1974.

MODELISATION ET IDENTIFICATION
D'UNE RELATION PLUIE-DEBIT

Le modèle " SEMOIS "

Bernard LORENT
Centre Interuniversitaire
des Sciences de l'Environnement
Fondation Universitaire Luxembourgeoise
rue des Déportés, 140
6700 - ARLON (Belgique)

RESUME : Cet article présente un modèle performant de prévision et de simulation du débit d'une rivière à l'exutoire de son bassin versant. Ce modèle est construit à partir de la connaissance du débit à l'exutoire, des précipitations en plusieurs stations ainsi que d'une estimation de l'évapotranspiration potentielle. Un premier sous-modèle non-linéaire, permet le calcul d'une pluie nette, d'une fonction de stockage superficiel et d'un terme d'infiltration. Ensuite, un second sous-modèle simple simule le débit de base de la rivière. Enfin, un modèle utilisant une équation aux différences, décrit le processus pluie nette-débit de ruissellement. A la fin de cet article, les résultats pratiquement obtenus sont présentés et discutés.

I. INTRODUCTION.

I.1. Nous présentons dans ce texte, quelques résultats importants d'une étude en cours, dont l'objectif principal est la réalisation d'un modèle de prévision et de simulation des débits de la Semois à l'exutoire de son bassin versant belge (Membre). Pour atteindre cet objectif, nous utilisons actuellement des mesures journalières collectées de 1967 à 1973. Ces données sont : le débit de la rivière à Membre, une estimation de l'évapotranspiration potentielle du bassin versant [1] et des relevés pluviométriques en quelques dix stations. Ces données nous ont été aimablement fournies par les soins de la section d'Hydrologie de l'Institut Royal Météorologique (I.R.M.) et du Service d'Etude Hydrologique (SETHY) du Ministère des Travaux Publics.

Précisons enfin que la Semois est un affluent ardennais de la Meuse et que son bassin versant limité à Membre a une superficie de 1229 km^2. Le lecteur désireux d'avoir une description détaillée des caractéristiques hydrométéorologiques de ce bassin lira avec intérêt la référence [2].

I.2. S'il nous fallait concevoir un modèle de relation pluie-débit à partir de l'observation des phénomènes physiques qui interviennent dans ce processus, notre tâche deviendrait rapidement impossible. En effet, en tout lieu, il conviendrait de

préciser les caractères physiques de sol, de pente, de couverture végétale ... et ensuite de décrire l'interaction entre ces différents éléments et les conditions météorologiques pour tenter d'estimer localement l'infiltration, le stockage superficiel, l'écoulement de surface ... Et après avoir mis en équation tous les phénomènes complexes localement déterminants, il faudrait encore préciser comment toute cette eau parvient à l'exutoire ... .

Fort heureusement, une alternative s'offre à nous. En effet, la dynamique de la relation pluie-débit est directement fonction des caractères physiques du bassin. Nous allons dès lors considérer le bassin comme une boite noire dont nous étudierons uniquement les caractéristiques entrées-sorties.

La relation pluie-évaporation-débit est toutefois non-linéaire et ses caractéristiques varient suivant la saison. Aussi, reviendrons-nous à certaines considérations hydrologiques importantes afin de dégager une structure de modèle simple et proche de la réalité physique. Nous sommes bien sûr conscients de ce que nous ferons de considérables simplifications dans la description des phénomènes mais nous le ferons, convaincus de ce que cette méthode conduit à des modèles de prévision et de simulation efficaces.

I.3. Le modèle présenté est conçu en temps discret. La période d'échantillonnage sera désignée par T et nous ne considérerons donc les différentes grandeurs qu'aux instants : (k-1).T , k.T , (k+1).T ...
X(k) représentera ainsi la grandeur X au temps k.T

Toutefois, en raison du type de mesures utilisées, les grandeurs X(k) représenteront le plus souvent non pas des valeurs instantanées mais des moyennes sur l'intervalle de temps k compris entre (k-1/2).T et (k+1/2).T, c'est-à-dire que :

$$X(k) = \frac{1}{T} \int_{(k-1/2).T}^{(k+1/2).T} x(t).dt$$

II. DESCRIPTION GLOBALE DU MODELE [3] , [4] , [5] .

II.1. Appelons Q(k) le débit de la rivière à l'instant k. Nous considérons, de manière classique, que ce débit est composé de deux termes, l'un le débit de ruissellement R(k) et l'autre le débit de base B(k).

Le débit de ruissellement R(k) sera la fraction du débit que nous supposerons être due directement aux pluies du fait du ruissellement superficiel.

Par contre, le débit de base B(k) est un terme que nous supposerons provenir de la vidange des nappes et qui dépend des pluies moyennant un terme d'infiltration en profondeur.

Nous écrirons donc :

$$Q(k) = B(k) + R(k) \quad (1)$$

Lorsque le terme R(k) devient négligeable, nous dirons que nous sommes en période d'étiage. Par contre, lorsque le terme R(k) est important, nous dirons que nous sommes en période de crue.

II.2. Le volume total d'eau PB(k) précipitée en un point durant l'intervalle de temps k peut se décomposer comme suit :

$$PB(k) = PN(k) + E1(k) + SI(k) \quad (2)$$

où : PN(k) est la pluie nette, c'est-à-dire la fraction de la pluie PB(k) qui est supposée atteindre l'exutoire du bassin par ruissellement superficiel et qui influencera rapidement le débit de la rivière. La pluie nette PN(k) engendrera le débit de ruissellement R(k).

E1(k) est la fraction du volume d'eau PB(k) qui sera évaporée durant l'intervalle de temps k.

SI(k) est la fraction de la pluie PB(k) qui est supposée rester sur place à la fin de l'intervalle de temps k, soit sur la végétation par interception, soit dans des dépressions superficielles ou dans les quelques premiers centimètres du sol. Une partie de ce volume SI(k) s'infiltrera ensuite en profondeur tandis qu'une autre s'évaporera plus tard, soit directement, soit à travers les mécanismes de transpiration des plantes.

Le coefficient de ruissellement au temps k est défini comme suit :

$$r(k) = \frac{PN(k)}{PB(k)} \quad (3)$$

II.3. A la surface du sol, nous écrirons l'équation de continuité :

$$S(k) = S(k-1) + SI(k) - I(k) - E2(k) \quad (4)$$

où : S(k), que nous appellerons le " stockage superficiel ", représente le volume d'eau accumulé à la surface du sol à la fin de l'intervalle de temps k, cette accumulation se faisant, soit dans la végétation, soit dans les dépressions superficielles ou encore dans les quelques premiers centimètres du sol.

I(k) est le volume d'eau qui s'infiltre en profondeur vers les nappes durant l'intervalle de temps k.

E2(k) est le volume d'eau qui s'évapore à partir du stockage superficiel, soit directement, soit par transpiration.

II.4. Le terme d'infiltration I(k) alimente les nappes qui fournissent le débit de base B(k). Nous considèrerons donc B(k) comme une fonction de I(k).

II.5. Le processus pluie-débit est finalement décrit par le schéma de la figure 1.

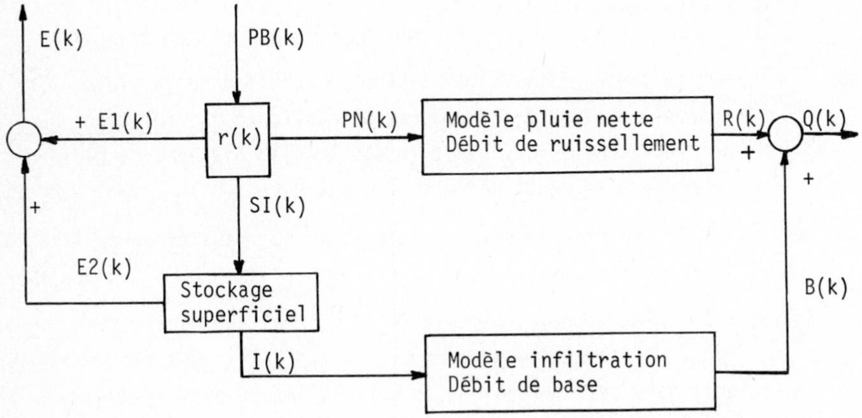

Fig. 1

On observera que l'évaporation totale résulte de l'addition des termes E1(k) et E2(k).

Remarque : Idéalement, un terme correspondant à la remontée capillaire des eaux de nappes vers la surface devrait être introduit : ceci peut être effectué par exemple en admettant que I(k) peut prendre des valeurs négatives.

III. LE MODELE DE CALCUL DE LA PLUIE NETTE [6], [7].

III.1. S'il est relativement aisé de schématiser les phénomènes par les équations de bilan (2) et (4), il est beaucoup plus difficile, sinon parfois impossible, de quantifier rigoureusement les lois physiques qui régissent ces relations. Localement, le problème est déjà bien ardu, et il devient encore plus complexe à l'échelle d'un bassin en raison de la diversité des caractéristiques dans l'espace. Aussi, afin de surmonter cette difficulté, proposons-nous un modèle non-linéaire

basé sur les quelques importantes observations hydrologiques suivantes :

- Le coefficient de ruissellement augmente avec la saturation du sol en eau : un sol et une végétation sèche pourront absorber beaucoup d'eau et par contre, une végétation détrempée et un sol saturé d'eau provoqueront un ruissellement important. Dès lors, nous lierons le coefficient de ruissellement au stockage superficiel en sorte que pour un stockage faible, le coefficient de ruissellement soit proche de zéro et que pour un stockage élevé, le coefficient de ruissellement soit proche de l'unité.
- Pour un état donné de l'humidité du sol et de la végétation au début d'une averse, le coefficient de ruissellement augmente avec l'intensité de l'averse : ceci signifie que, dans notre modèle, le stockage superficiel S(k-1) au début de l'intervalle de temps k ne déterminera pas un coefficient de ruissellement unique mais un ensemble de coefficients de ruissellement qui seront fonction du volume d'eau PB(k) précipitée durant l'intervalle de temps k.
- L'infiltration est importante lorsque le sol est saturé en eau et elle devient nulle quand le sol est sec ou faiblement humide : notre modèle devra également en tenir compte.

III.2. Ces observations nous conduisent ainsi au modèle décrit ci-dessous :

III.2.1. Considérons les deux relations déjà proposées :

$$PB(k) = PN(k) + E1(k) + SI(k) \qquad (2)$$

$$S(k) = S(k-1) + SI(k) - I(k) - E2(k) \qquad (4)$$

Ces deux relations peuvent être considérées en des endroits précis, ou bien à l'échelle d'un bassin ou d'un sous-bassin.

Supposons que le stockage superficiel S(k) ait une valeur maximale que nous appellerons Smax. Cette valeur maximale de S(k) correspond à un sol tout à fait saturé en eau et à une végétation totalement détrempée. Introduisons maintenant la notion de déficit de stockage en désignant ce déficit par la différence entre Smax et S(k). On écrira :

$$D(k) = Smax - S(k) \qquad (5)$$

Le rapport S(k)/Smax devient dans notre modèle un indice de saturation en eau du bassin tandis que le rapport D(k)/Smax correspond à un indice de capacité d'absorption de l'eau de pluie.

III.2.2. Appelons ETP(k) l'évapotranspiration potentielle durant l'intervalle de temps k et supposons, pour plus de simplicité, que l'évaporation se fait à un taux potentiel d'abord à partir de l'eau précipitée durant l'intervalle de temps considéré. Nous distinguerons deux situations :

a) $PB(k) \leqslant ETP(k)$

c'est-à-dire que l'évapotranspiration potentielle excède le volume d'eau précipitée. Dans ce cas, nous considérons que toute l'eau précipitée est directement évaporée et qu'il n'y a ni ruissellement, ni eau stockée sur place à l'issue de l'intervalle de temps considéré. Dès lors : $E1(k) = PB(k)$, $PN(k) = 0$, $SI(k) = 0$

b) $PB(k) > ETP(k)$

Dans ce cas-ci, il y aura possibilité de ruissellement et de stockage.

Comme nous supposons, comme précisé plus haut, que l'évaporation se fait au taux potentiel d'abord à partir de l'eau précipitée, nous avons d'abord : $E1(k) = ETP(k)$

Désignons par PE(k) le volume d'eau qui reste disponible pour le ruissellement et le stockage superficiel : $PE(k) = PB(k) - ETP(k)$

Il nous faut déterminer maintenant une loi de répartition entre les termes SI(k) et PN(k).

En raison des phénomènes physiques évoqués plus haut, nous proposons une loi de répartition du type :

$$SI(k) = D(k-1) \, . \, (1-e^{-PE(k)/b}) \tag{6}$$

avec la condition : $b \geqslant D(k-1)$ qui est imposée du fait que SI(k) doit toujours être inférieur à PE(k). Dès lors :

$$PN(k) = PE(k) - SI(k) \tag{7}$$

$$\text{ou} \quad PN(k) = PB(k) - ETP(k) - D(k-1) \cdot (1-e^{-(PB(k) - ETP(k))/b}) \tag{7bis}$$

Les relations SI = f(D,PE) et PN = f(D,PE) se trouvent clairement illustrées par les graphiques des figures 2 et 3 pour différentes valeurs de D(k-1).

III.2.3. Nous avons ainsi déterminé les relations qui commandent l'équation de bilan (2).

Pour l'équation de bilan (4), considérons à nouveau les deux situations :

a) $PB(k) \leqslant ETP(k)$

Nous avons alors également $E1(k) \leqslant ETP(k)$. Nous considérons qu'il peut alors y avoir évaporation à partir du stockage superficiel, et qu'elle se fera en sorte que l'évapotranspiration totale atteigne le taux potentiel à condition que le stockage superficiel soit suffisant. Dès lors, si : $S(k-1) \geqslant ETP(k) - E1(k)$ on prendra : $E2(k) = ETP(k) - E1(k)$

Par contre, si : $S(k-1) < ETP(k) - E1(k)$ alors : $E2(k) = S(k-1)$

b) $PB(k) > ETP(k)$

Dans ce cas, nous considèrerons que toute l'évaporation s'est opérée à partir de PB(k) et nous aurons donc : $E2(k) = 0$

Finalement, en ce qui concerne le terme d'infiltration en profondeur I(k), il est plausible, à défaut de mieux, de supposer qu'il est proportionnel à un taux de saturation en eau de la surface du lieu considéré et d'écrire :

$$I(k) = I_{max} \cdot \frac{S(k-1) + SI(k) - E2(k)}{Smax} \qquad (8)$$

et, en posant $A = Imax/Smax$, on a finalement :

$$S(k) = (1-A) \cdot (S(k-1) + SI(k) - E2(k)) \qquad (9)$$

On observera qu'ainsi S(k) n'excèdera jamais la valeur de (1-A).Smax Il y aura donc toujours une fraction de PB(k) qui sera absorbée pour compenser l'infiltration.

Le schéma de la figure 4 résume le fonctionnement du modèle.

III.3. Actuellement, les valeurs des paramètres que nous avons retenues pour le calcul de la pluie nette journalière moyenne dans le bassin de la Semois sont :

Smax = 85 mm de hauteur d'eau
Imax = 1 mm/jour
b = D(k-1)/0.875

Ces valeurs sont choisies par minimisation de l'erreur quadratique moyenne du modèle global tout en tenant compte d'une conservation des volumes d'eau entre la pluie nette et le débit de ruissellement.

La figure 5 illustre clairement l'efficacité de la méthode appliquée au bassin de la Semois. On observera de haut en bas, les courbes : de l'évapotranspiration potentielle (ETP) - de la pluie brute moyenne (PB) - du stockage superficiel (S) - de la pluie nette (PN) - du débit à Membre (Q). Les unités utilisées sont le 0.1 mm/jour ou le 0.1 mm. Le débit a donc été ramené à sa lame d'eau équivalente. Les performances de ce modèle sont quant à elles explicitées au paragraphe VI de cet article.

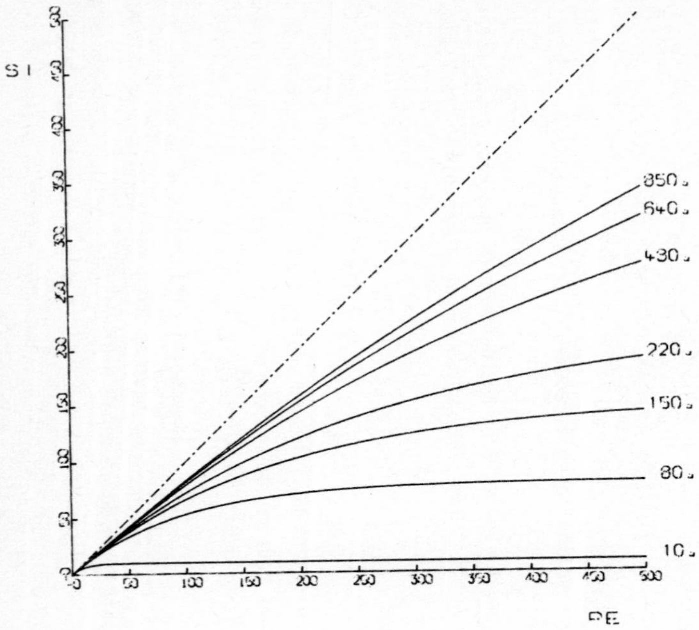

Fig. 2 - Graphique du terme du stockage SI en fonction de PE pour différentes valeurs du déficit de stockage D

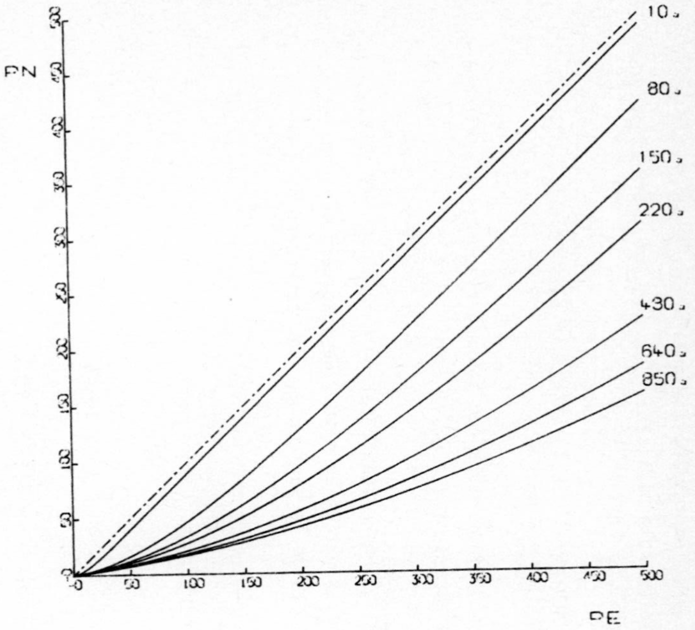

Fig. 3 - Graphique de la pluie nette (PN) en fonction de PE pour différentes valeurs du déficit de stockage D

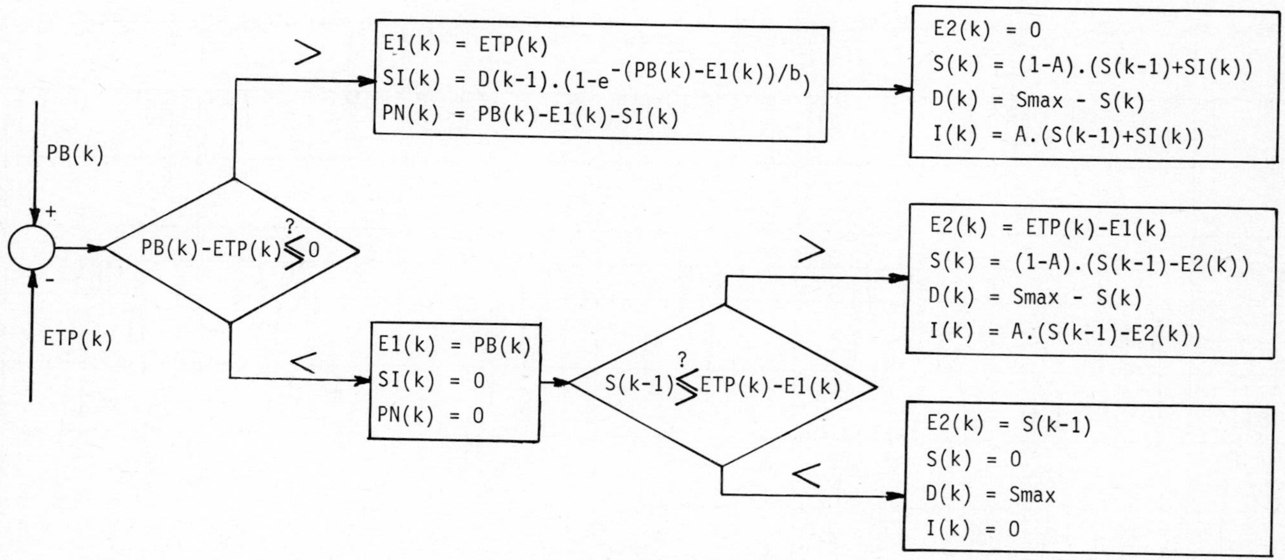

Pour la Semois : Smax = 85 mm
Imax = 1 mm/jour
b = D(k-1)/0.875

A = Imax/Smax

Fig. 4 - Modèle de calcul de la pluie nette.

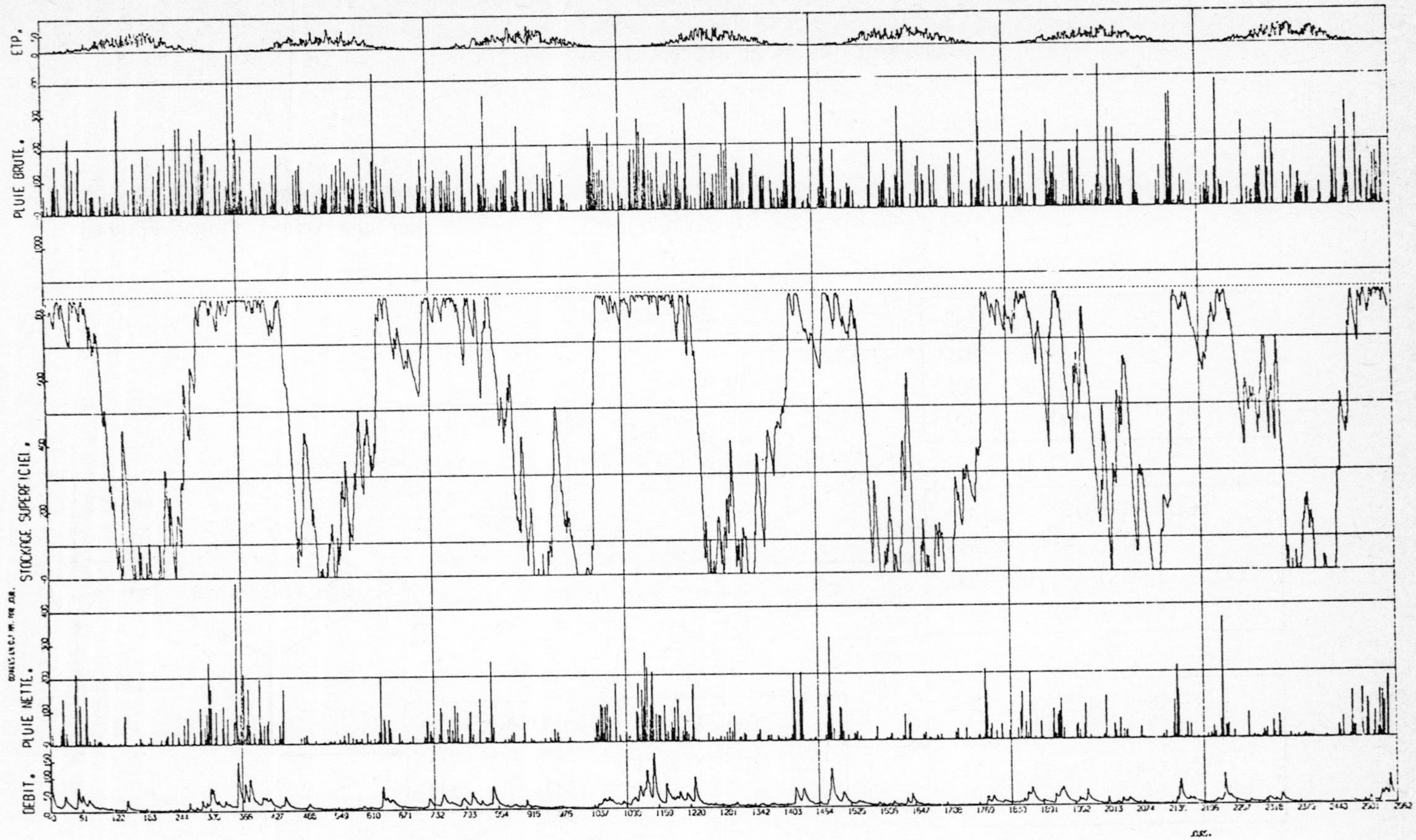

Fig. 5 - BASSIN DE LA SEMOIS - EXUTOIRE : MEMBRE.

IV. MODELISATION DU DEBIT DE BASE.

IV.1. Lorsque le cours d'eau n'est plus alimenté que par les nappes, la décroissance du débit est décrite par ce que l'on appelle " la courbe de tarissement de la rivière " qui est une caractéristique importante de celle-ci.

Classiquement, la courbe de tarissement sera approximée par l'une des deux relations :

$$Q(t) \cong Q_0 \, . \, e^{-(t-t_0)/TH} \quad (10)$$

$$Q(t) \cong \frac{Q_0}{(1 + a.(t-t_0))^2} \quad (11)$$

où : Q_0 est la valeur du débit à l'instant t_0 du début du tarissement.

[3] , [4] , [5].

IV.2. L'étude des périodes d'étiage de la Semois nous a permis de constater qu'effectivement la courbe de tarissement peut être bien approximée par une exponentielle décroissance à condition de faire intervenir un terme constant caractéristique de l'année considérée. On aura ainsi à la place de (10), la relation :

$$Q(t) - B_0 \cong (Q_0 - B_0) \, . \, e^{-(t-t_0)/TH} \quad (12)$$

où B_0 varie lentement d'une période à l'autre.

Il nous a paru dès lors logique de modéliser le débit de base B(t) en considérant qu'il était composé de deux termes. Ainsi,

$$B(k) = BR(k) + BL(k) \quad (13)$$

Le terme BR(k) est un terme qui évolue relativement vite et qui peut être attribué à des nappes, qui, situées près de la surface du sol, subiraient rapidement les effets de recharge et de décharge. Par contre, BL(k) est un terme qui peut se modifier lentement d'année en année et qui serait du à des nappes beaucoup plus stables.

Remarque : Dans le cas de la Semois, le terme rapide du débit de base décroit avec une constance de temps TH d'environ 15 jours. Celle-ci est bien différente de la constante de temps des décrues qui est de l'ordre de 4 ou 5 jours.

IV.3. Pour réaliser une bonne simulation du débit d'une rivière, il importe d'avoir une estimation plausible du débit de base tout au long de l'année. C'est à nouveau un problème délicat, d'abord en raison de l'impossibilité qu'il y a de distinguer a priori le débit de base et le débit de ruissellement lorsque ces deux termes coexistent et ensuite, du fait que la dynamique de l'écoulement souterrain est encore très mal connue. En conséquence, nous opterons pour un modèle très rudimentaire mais que nous estimons efficace.

IV.4. Nous modéliserons les termes BR(k) et BL(k) suivant le même schéma.

Considérons tout d'abord BR(k).

En période de tarissement, nous savons que BR(k) décroit quasiment comme une exponentielle. Dès lors, l'estimée $\widetilde{BR}(k)$ répondra à la relation :

$$\widetilde{BR}(k) = \alpha . \widetilde{BR}(k-1) \tag{14}$$

avec

$$\alpha = e^{-1/TH} \tag{15}$$

où TH est la constante de temps de la décroissance exponentielle.

Pour décrire la dynamique de BR(k) en période de recharge des nappes, nous utiliserons le volume d'eau $\mathcal{V}R(k)$ stockée par l'ensemble des nappes à réponse rapide :

$$\mathcal{V}R(k) = \sum_{j=k_o+1}^{k} \left[IR(j) - \widetilde{BR}(j) \right] + \mathcal{V}R(k_o) \tag{16}$$

Dans cette expression, IR(j) représente le terme d'alimentation de ces nappes par infiltration. Nous supposerons que :

$$\widetilde{BR}(k) = n . \mathcal{V}R(k) \tag{17}$$

En conséquence :

$$\widetilde{BR}(k) = \alpha . \widetilde{BR}(k-1) + (1-\alpha) . IR(k) \tag{18}$$

avec :
$$\alpha = \frac{1}{1+n} \tag{19}$$

Lorsque IR(k) s'annule, nous retrouvons ainsi la relation (14).

En utilisant l'opérateur de retard Z^{-1}, on écrira :

$$\widetilde{BR}(k) = \frac{1-\alpha}{1-\alpha . Z^{-1}} . IR(k) \qquad (20)$$

En procédant de la même manière pour BL(k), nous aurons :

$$\widetilde{BL}(k) = \frac{1-\beta}{1-\beta Z^{-1}} . IL(k) \qquad (21)$$

où cette fois, β correspondra à une constante de temps beaucoup plus grande.

Il reste à préciser les termes IR(k) et IL(k).

Nous allons simplement supposer que ce sont des fractions du terme d'infiltration I(k) évoqué dans le paragraphe III moyennant l'utilisation d'un terme de retard correspondant au temps que l'eau met à gagner la nappe. Dès lors :

$$IR(k) = p . I(k-dr) \qquad (22)$$

$$IL(k) = q . I(k-dl) \qquad (23)$$

Les différents paramètres α, p, dr, β, q, dl de ce modèle sont optimalisés en utilisant des relevés de débit en période sèche et en minimisant l'erreur quadratique moyenne entre le débit de base calculé et observé. Nous avons ainsi retenu les valeurs :

p = 0.30	q = 0.69
dr = 5 jours	dl = 30 jours
$\alpha \rightarrow$ 15 jours	$\beta \rightarrow$ 244 jours

On Observera que la somme de p et q est voisine de l'unité. Le bilan infiltration - débit de base est ainsi respecté.

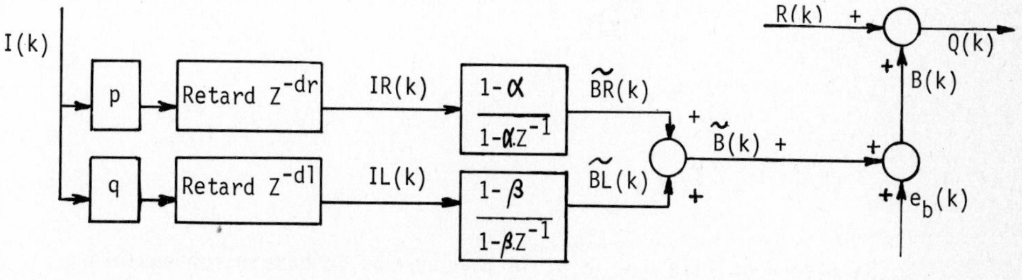

Fig. 6 - Modèle du débit de base

V. LE MODELE PLUIE NETTE - DEBIT DE RUISSELLEMENT.

V.1. L'expérience a montré que des modèles linéaires entre la pluie nette et le débit de ruissellement donnaient de très bons résultats. Ainsi s'explique le succès de la méthode de l'hydrogramme unitaire. [3], [4], [5]

Nous modéliserons le débit de ruissellement R(k) par l'expression :

$$\tilde{R}(k) = \sum_{i=1}^{N} \left[\sum_{j=0}^{M} H(i,j) \, . \, PN(i,k-j) \right] \qquad (24)$$

où : PN(i,k) est la pluie nette de la station i pour l'intervalle de temps k

H(i,k) est la valeur au temps k de l'hydrogramme instantané du sous-bassin correspondant à la station i

L'expression (24) a toutefois l'inconvénient de contenir un très grand nombre de termes : dans le cas de la Semois, un hydrogramme ne s'annule qu'après 25 ou 30 jours. Il est dès lors plus intéressant d'utiliser l'équation aux différences équivalente :

$$\tilde{R}(k) = \sum_{i=1}^{N} \left[\sum_{j=1}^{S} a_j^i . R(i,k-j) + \sum_{j=0}^{T} b_j^i . PN(i,k-j) \right] \qquad (25)$$

ou l'approximation :

$$\tilde{R}(k) = \sum_{j=1}^{S} a_j . R(k-j) + \sum_{i=1}^{N} \left[\sum_{j=0}^{T} b_j^i . PN(i,k-j) \right] \qquad (26)$$

En utilisant l'opérateur de retard Z^{-1}, on écrira plus facilement :

$$\tilde{R}(k) = A'(Z^{-1}) \, . \, R(k-1) + \sum_{i=1}^{N} B^i(Z^{-1}) \, . \, PN(i,k) \qquad (27)$$

où $A'(Z^{-1}) = a_1 + a_2 Z^{-1} + a_3 Z^{-2} + \ldots$

$B^i(Z^{-1}) = b_o{}^i + b_1^i Z^{-1} + b_2^i Z^{-2} + \ldots$

Si l'on n'utilise que la pluie moyenne sur le bassin, on emploiera le modèle plus simple :

$$\tilde{R}(k) = A'(Z^{-1}) \,.\, R(k-1) + B(Z^{-1}) \,.\, \overline{PN}(k) \qquad (28)$$

Si $\xi(k)$ est l'erreur du modèle :

$$\xi(k) = R(k) - \tilde{R}(k) \qquad (29)$$

et en posant : $A(Z^{-1}) = 1 - A'(Z^{-1}) \,.\, Z^{-1}$ (30)

le modèle s'écrira :

$$A(Z^{-1}) \,.\, R(k) = B(Z^{-1}) \,.\, \overline{PN}(k) + \xi(k) \qquad (31)$$

Le rapport $\dfrac{B(Z^{-1})}{A(Z^{-1})}$ est la fonction de transfert du système et, par division longue, on peut retrouver la réponse impulsionnelle du système PN-R laquelle est encore appelée hydrogramme instantané dans le contexte hydrologique présent.

La figure 6 montre l'hydrogramme instantané caractéristique de la Semois : ce graphique représente le débit de ruissellement qui serait engendré par une pluie nette de valeur unité qui surviendrait au temps zéro.

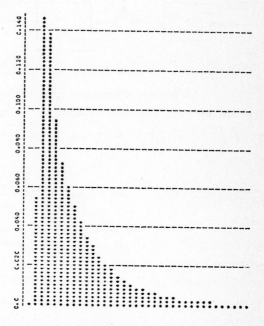

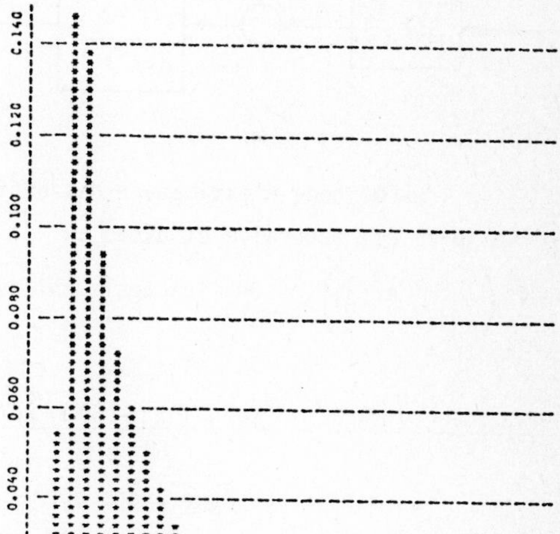

Fig. 6

V.2. Pour identifier les paramètres du modèle décrit par la relation (28), nous devons d'abord connaître R(k). Pour ce faire, nous pourrons utiliser l'estimée de R(k) obtenue par la relation :

$$\hat{R}(k) = Q(k) - \tilde{B}(k) \qquad (32)$$

où $Q(k)$ est le débit total mesuré et $\tilde{B}(k)$ le débit de base estimé par le sous-modèle du débit de base.

L'erreur $\xi(k)$ a actuellement été modélisé par l'expression :

$$\xi(k) = C(Z^{-1}) \cdot e(k) + c \tag{33}$$

où $C(Z^{-1}) = 1 + c_1 . Z^{-1} + c_2 . Z^{-2} + \ldots$

$e(k)$ est supposé être un bruit blanc discret non corrélé avec l'entrée PN du modèle.

Le modèle est ainsi décrit par le schéma :

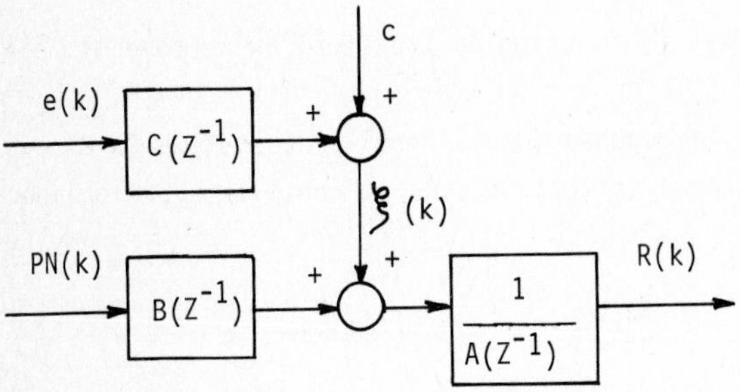

La méthode d'estimation des différents paramètres est explicitée dans [8]. Celle-ci est récursive et basée sur la minimisation de l'erreur quadratique moyenne $\left(\frac{1}{K}\sum_{j=1}^{K} e^2(j)\right)$. On lira également avec intérêt [10].

VI. APPLICATIONS ET RESULTATS SIGNIFICATIFS.

VI.1. Le modèle que nous avons décrit peut tout d'abord servir à la prédiction. Connaissant les pluies et les débits jusqu'aujourd'hui, quel sera le débit le plus probable demain ? Nous avons accordé un intérêt tout particulier à cette question et ci-dessous, le lecteur trouvera quelques résultats significatifs.

L'identification du modèle de prédiction à un jour s'est opérée avec un volume de données correspondant à sept années dont avaient été exclues les périodes de neige. Il y avait ainsi 2066 jours de données disponibles.

Bien que, ni les débits, ni la pluie ne soient des processus gaussiens, nous nous contenterons cependant de les caractériser par le contenu du tableau ci-dessous :

	DEBIT	PLUIE
Moyenne (0.1 mm/jour)	11.7	27.9
Variance	159.4	2740
Ecart-type	12.6	52.3

Le tableau suivant reprend les performances de plusieurs modèles élémentaires de prévision à 1 jour en regard de celles du modèle global présenté dans cet article. les différents modèles sont comparés au moyen de la variance de l'erreur de prédiction (σ_e^2), de l'écart-type de cette erreur (σ_e) et du coefficient ρ_g définit par :

$$\rho_g = \sqrt{1 - \frac{\sigma_e^2}{\sigma_Q^2}} \tag{34}$$

où σ_Q^2 est la variance du débit.

Prédicteurs du débit Q(k)	σ_e^2	σ_e	ρ_g
$\hat{Q}(k/k-1) = a.Q(k-1)+c$	11.88	3.45	0.962
$\hat{Q}(k/k-1) = a_1.Q(k-1)+a_2.Q(k-2)+a_3.Q(k-3)$ $+C_1.e(k-1)+C_2.e(k-2)+C_3.e(k-3)+c$	10.51	3.24	0.966
$\hat{Q}(k/k-1) = a_1\ Q(k-1)+a_2\ Q(k-2)$ $+\sum_{i=1}^{4} b_i.PB(k-i)$ $+\sum_{i=1}^{3} C_i.e(k-i) + c$	7.03	2.65	0.978
$\hat{Q}(k/k-1) = \tilde{B}(k/k-1)$ $+a_1.\hat{R}(k-1)+a_2.\hat{R}(k-2)$ $+ \sum_{i=1}^{4} b_i.PN(k-i)$ $+ \sum_{i=1}^{3} C_i.e(k-i)+c$	3.63	1.91	0.989

On observera l'efficacité du modèle présenté ici.

La référence [10] décrit clairement comment concevoir des prédicteurs à plus long terme.

VI.2. Ce modèle global peut également être utilisé pour de la simulation et par exemple pour :

- Préciser le débit possible dans les jours qui viennent à partir des différentes conditions météorologiques probables. Il suffira simplement pour les temps k futurs de remplacer dans les modèles les termes e(k) par 0 et Q(k) par les valeurs calculées et d'introduire pour les entrées pluie et évapotranspiration potentielle les valeurs probables (fig. 7).
- Simuler le débit à partir des relevés de pluies lorsque l'on est en présence de mesures manquantes du débit. A nouveau on remplacera dans le modèle les termes e(k) par 0 et le débit Q(k) par les valeurs calculées

Un article en préparation développera en détail ces applications possibles.

Fig. 7

Simulation (trait discontinu) du débit de la Semois en supposant connues les pluies jusqu'à la veille et les débits 5 jours auparavant.

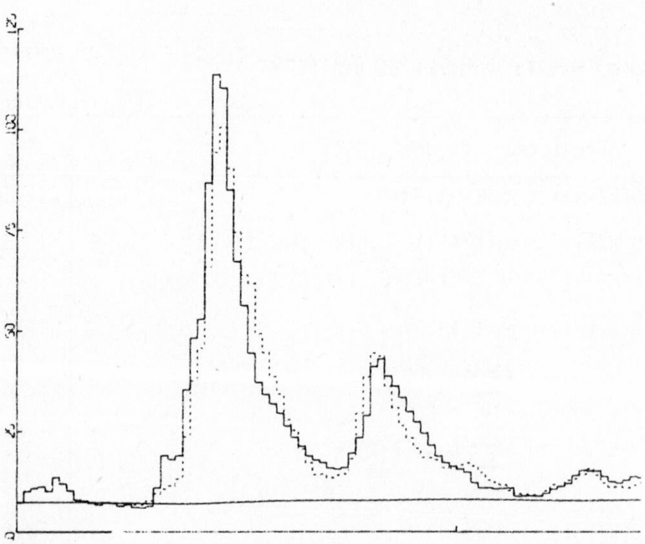

CONCLUSION : Nous avons présenté dans cet article la structure d'un modèle efficace de relation pluie-débit. Il pourra certes être amélioré et un des problèmes délicats à étudier sera celui de la fonte des neiges, sujet qui n'a pas été abordé ici.

Il importe en tout cas de rappeler que les modèles dynamiques en hydrologie constituent un outil précieux, pour tout qui, à partir d'une meilleure connaissance des phénomènes, souhaite mettre en oeuvre une politique cohérente de gestion des ressources en eau d'un bassin. Et à ce titre, des modèles capables de quantifier l'incidence des pluies sur les débits et de prévoir en conséquence l'évolution possible de ceux-ci, s'avèrent être très utiles.

REFERENCES :

[1] BULTOT, F. et DUPRIEZ, G.L. - *Estimation des valeurs journalières de l'évapotranspiration potentielle d'un bassin hydrologique.* Jl of Hydrology, vol. 21, Amsterdam (1974).

[2] BULTOT, F. et DUPRIEZ, G.L. - *Etude hydrométéorologique des précipitations sur les bassins hydrographiques belges. I. Bassin de la Semois.* Institut Royal Météorologique de Belgique, Publications, série A, n° 64.

[3] LARRAS, J. - *Prévision et prédétermination des étiages et des crues.* Eyrolles, Paris (1972).

[4] ROCHE, M. - *Hydrologie de surface.* Gauthier-Villars, Paris (1963).

[5] REMENERIAS - *L'hydrologie de l'ingénieur.* Eyrolles, Paris (1972).

[6] BULTOT, F., DUPRIEZ, G.L. et BODEUX, A. - *Interception de la pluie par la végétation forestière. Estimation de l'interception journalière à l'aide d'un modèle mathématique.* Jl of Hydrology, 17, (1972), 193-223.

[7] de MARSILY, G. - *La relation pluie-débit dans le bassin versant de l'Hallue.* Ecole Nationale des Mines de Paris, Centre d'Informatique Géologique (77 - Fontainebleau, 35 rue Saint-Honoré) (1971).

[8] KASHYAP, R.L. et RAO, A.R. - *Real time recursive prediction of river flows.* Automatica 9 (1973), 175-183.

[9] CORLIER, F. - *Modèle mathématique des débits journaliers de la Sambre.* Faculté des Sciences Agronomiques de Gembloux, Belgique (1974).

[10] JENKINS, G.M. et BOX, G.E.P. - *Time series analysis forecasting and control.* Holden Day (1970).

A MATHEMATICAL MODEL FOR ANALYSIS OF MOUNTAIN DRAINAGE BASINS

Maria Morandi Cecchi
I.E.I. of CNR Via S. Maria 46 Pisa

1. Introduction

To develop a mathematical model for analysis of mountain drainage basins is necessary to recall all concept of morphometry. This is done to be able to introduce, a quantization of geological concepts and to prepare a file of geological data able to give a complete description of the morphology and litology of the territory.

The method of the morphometical analysis are applied to the two foundamental aspects of the territory: the river branches and the river sides.

The topic of this paper is related to the hydrographyc basins considered as hollow regions of the lithosphere where the meteoric waters inflow and in different ways outflow to the final collector that discharge them into the sea or into a lake.

The study is mostly important when applied to the mountain basins that are of relative small area but play a fundamental role into the dynamics of the flow.

Infact every thing may happen in the environment of the mouth of a hydrological system of a certain amount of waters (such as rivers, torrents, etc.) and the behaviour of such sections is strictly tied to the general systematization of the totality of the related mountain basins, infact are exactly the mountain basins that may generate regular or unregular flows.

It is clear that the litology (the composition of the rocks) and the tectonics (the lay of the rocks) are very important factors to be taken into account in the study of the mountain drainage basins. The geological control of the mountain basins is therefore necessary to give a good interpretation of the data. The method proposed is the following: to use the morphometry to evaluate automatically a monodimensional model for the river branches in its drainage area. Such formulation is based on statistics because only with an analysis of the recurrences of the phenomena observed and with an analysis of the data, it is possible to obtain feasible frequency laws. This method was proposed in [1] and is convenient to build a data file of the branches of the rivers and of the sides of the rivers.

2. The method proposed

The key of the method is the hierarchisation of hydrographic basins having determined the mesh of the watersheds as preference road for the waters (rain of snow melting) to flow out.

The hierarchy defined is very simple, the first order is defined with those branches that do not receive any other branch, channels of the second order are defined those that are generated by the junction of two branches of the first order.

The third order is defined as the function of two branches of the second order, and so on. It is obvious that such ordering is a function of the topographic chard used. Infact the ordering is defined on the chards and the scale of such chards is 1:25.000 or 1:100.000 very important in this study are the anormalous inflows that appear when a branch of a certain order does not flows into the branch of the following order but instead flows into some branch of an other higher order.

Such anomalous cases are of fundamental importance to undestand the degree of systematization of a drainage basin.

Therefore the number of anomalous cases is evaluated for every order and the frequency is evaluated two. A parameter that is also evaluated is the ratio of the frequency over the hierarchical order.

If higher is the number of anomalous cases less settled is the basin itself. A great number of anomalous cases may be the cause of a messy and unforeseeable flow.

On the contrary a hierarchisation completely normal; i.e. without anomalous branches, would give a perfectly regular flow.

To illustrate more deeply the ideas presented here see specific geological literature as in [2][3][4][5][6][7][8][9][10][11][12][13][14][15].

3. The monodimensional model of river branches.

The water system mesh is analysized using the hierarchisation automatically by the computer, the watersheds mesh gives the boundary of the drainage area associated to every branch of river under consideration, the considered model is related to the surface waters and to the gathered waters neglecting instead the dispersion for infiltration into the soil and for evaporation. For an hydrographic basin is intended that area where each element of it collects and drains a certain amount of water that comes from the inner part of the basin itself.

An example is given of the torrent Branega in Liguria where either the monodimensional and the tree-dimensional model is applied.

In fig. 1 the hierarchisation of the basin is shown and in fig. 2 all the drainage basin of every branch of the river is shown.

The length of every branch is been evaluated, an average was obtained for every order and also the ratio between the average length of an order and of the following order is obtained.

Summing the lenghts average of the preceeding order one obtain the average of the basin and from it also the ratio length are evaluated. All the value of the area of every channel are evaluated, the averages are calculated and summed to the drainage area of the preceeding orders that inflow into branches of that order.

Informations are also taken into account about the kind of development i.e. the problem of the erosion of the rocks in a certain drainage area. A classification is made of different kind of soil and different classes of soils are specified. The first class collects all kinds of soil were a free development is allowed.

In the second class are included all soils for which a partially obliged development is allowed but for which the erosion is impossible. In the third class are the soils for which the development is partially obliged but the erosion is possible.

In the fourth class the development is completely obliged.

The quantisation obtained permit the comparison of the behaviour of different types of drainage basins.

All the quantities evaluated have been recorded into a data file to optimize the allocation and the use of territory resources.

4. A three-dimensional model of the sides of drainage basins of rivers branches.

Such model gives the knowledge of the surfaces of drainage basins sides, and it is based on a triangular mesh. This mesh is made automatically using as a starting point a given axis in the direction Sud-North, every drainage area is subdivided into 16 triangle, all of these triangles have one vertex in the theoretical center of the drainage area.

Automatically the surface and the planimetric area of the sides are evaluated and also the angles of the sides are evaluated. With the phisiographic aspects that are introduced in the way exposed, it is important to consider also the permeability of the soil and the information is given for the drainage basin of every branch.

A coefficient was introduced to measure the degree of permeability.

All these informations are obtained and elaborated and give a complete morphometric knowledge of the territory and this knowledge consitues the geological data file to be used if a control of the flow of water has to be made.

The control is intended mostly in consideration of problems of erosion and sedimentation.

5. An optimization algorithm for forecast of erosion.

A forecast of the behaviour of erosion and sedimentation is based on an algorithm of search of the preference path for erosion and of a measure of the possible erosion of every path.

One is looking for the path of maximum erosion such path will be chosen on the base of having maximum difference in height between initial and final node, minimum total lenght, the total lenght beeing obtained summing all the lenghts of each path from every sping point to the final point, the final point beeing either the mouth of the river or the point where the river goes into a lake etc. and if the river runs across a territory where in a certain measure erosion is possible.

Let consider the graph that it is possible to obtain by the computer using the informations in the data file,fig. 3 in the case of Branega, in an interval $[o,t]$ of the real line, a differential equation of the form:

$$\dot{y}(x,t) = f(y(x,t),\ e(x,t)) \qquad (1)$$

it is considered where $y(x,t)$ is a function of state $e(x,t)$ is a control function, f is a mapping.

Equation (1) describes a dynamics systems which where supplied with an initial state $y(x,o)$ and a control input function e produces a function y.

$$y(x,o) = k(x) \qquad (2)$$

$$\mathcal{E} = \int_0^t u(y,e)\, dt$$

and a finite number of terminal constraints

$$\mathcal{G}_i(y(t)) = c_i \qquad i = 1,2,...r \tag{3}$$

y(x,t) is a function that describes the sedimentation e (x,t) is the erosion function of a particular path considered. The function u and $\mathcal{G}_i$ are assumed to possess continuous partial derivatives with respect to their arguments. The optimal control is then that of finding the pair of function (y,e) maximising $\mathcal{E}$ while satisfying the equilibrium condition between sedimentation and erosion and the initial and terminal conditions (2) and (3). The procedure applied is completely classical. In the special case of torrent Branega in Liguria the optimization method was applied and the numerical results indicate a path as the preference path for the maximum of possible erosion and the numerical answer give a numerical measure of a parameter of erosion that coincide reasonably with observations on the territory considered.

The method has also been applied to a more extended region: the region of Cornia in Toscana; in the following figures are indicated the drainage areas and the hierarchisation applied and corrisponding to the data file. The evaluations have been made in a modular way and connected to the collector part of the region. In this part the hierarchy has reached the order 9.

In fig. 4, 5, 6, 7 one may see the regions considered.

REFERENCES

[1] CECCHI MORANDI M., DEL GROSSO A., LIMONCELLI B., "Un'applicazione dell'Informatica alla Geologia: un modello monodimensionale per lo studio dei reticoli fluviali ed uno tridimensionale per lo studio dei versanti." (to appear)

[2] MONKHOUSE, "Dizionario di Geografia", Zanichelli, Bologna (1974). (Versione italiana di "Dictionary of Geography", second edtion, Edward Arnold Publishers, Ltd. 1970).

[3] TRICART J. e CAILLEAUX A., "Traité de Géomorphologie, SEDES, Paris, Vol.1 (1965).

[4] PANIZZA M., "Elementi di Geomorfologia", Pitagora Ed., Bologna (1973).

[5] MORTON R.E., "Erasional development of streams and their drainage basins; hydrophysical approach to quantitative morphology". Geol. Soc. of America Bulletin, Vol. 56, New York (1945).

[6] SCHUMM S.A., "Evolution of drainage systems and slopes in Badlands at Perth Amboy, New Jersey". Geol. Soc. of America Bulletin, Vol. 67, New York (1956).

[7] STRAHLER A.N., "Quantitative analysis of watershed geomorphology". Amer. Geophys. Union Trans., Vol. 38, Washington (1957).

[8] DEL GROSSO A., LIMONCELLI B., "Proposta di un criterio di raccolta di dati delle analisi geomorfiche dei reticoli fluviali finalizzata ad elaborazione automatica". Atti del III Convegno Nazionale di Studi sui Problemi della Geologia Applicata, Firenze (1973).

[9] SHREVE R.L., "Statistical law of stream numbers". Journ. Geology, Vol. 74 Chicago (1966).

[10] AVENA G.C., GIULIANO G., "Considerazioni teorico-pratiche sulla applicazione dell'analisi geomorfica quantitativa ai reticoli fluviali". L'universo, a. 47, Vol. 2, Firenze (1967).

[11] AVENA G.C., GIULIANO G., LUPIA PALMIERI E., "Sulla valutazione quantitativa della gerarchizzazione ed evoluzione dei reticoli fluviali". Boll. Soc. Geol. It., Vol. 86, Roma (1967).

[12] LAMBE T.W., WHITMAN R.V., "Soil mechanics". John Wiley and Sons, New York (1969).

[13] BOULES J.E., "Foundation analysis and design". Mc Grow Hill. New York (1968).

[14] CASTANY G., "Traité pratique des eaux souteraines". Dounod, Paris.

[15] MELTON M.A., "Geometric properties of nature drainage systems and their representation in an E4 phase space". Journ. of Geology, Vol. 66, Chicago (1958).

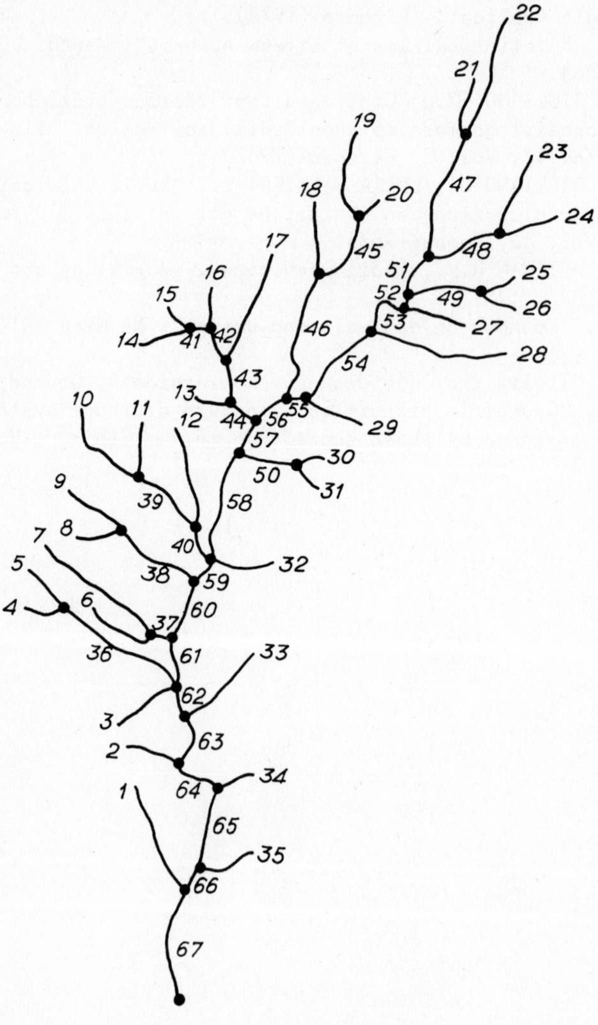
1
2
3
4
5
6
7
8
9
10
11
12
13
14
15
16
17
18
19
20
21
22
23
24
25
26
27
28
29
30
31
32
33
34
35
36
37
38
39
40
41
42
43
44
45
46
47
48
49
50
51
52
53
54
55
56
57
58
59
60
61
62
63
64
65
66
67

Fig. 1

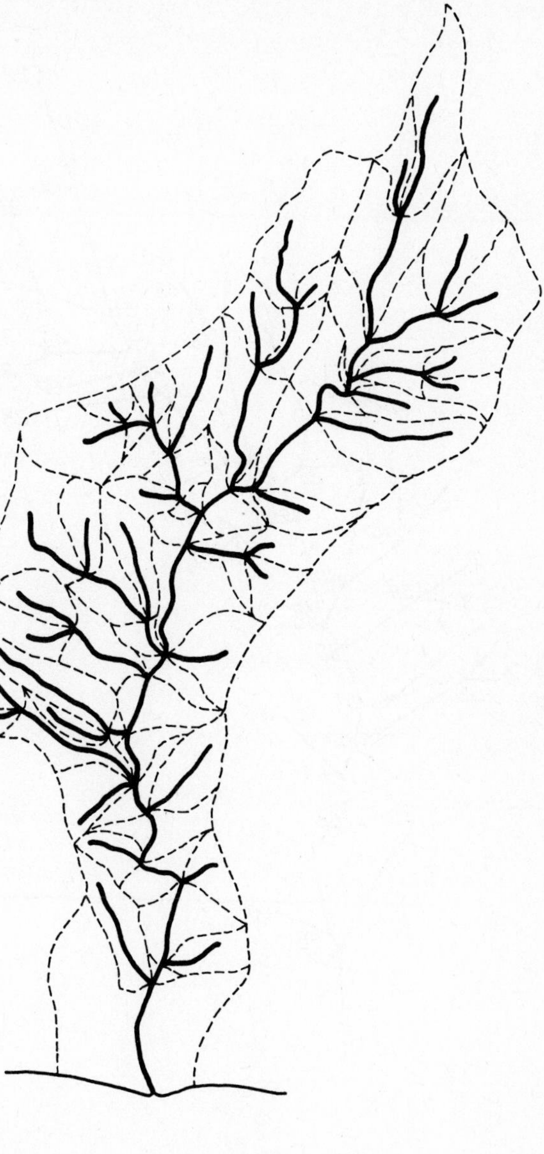

Fig. 2

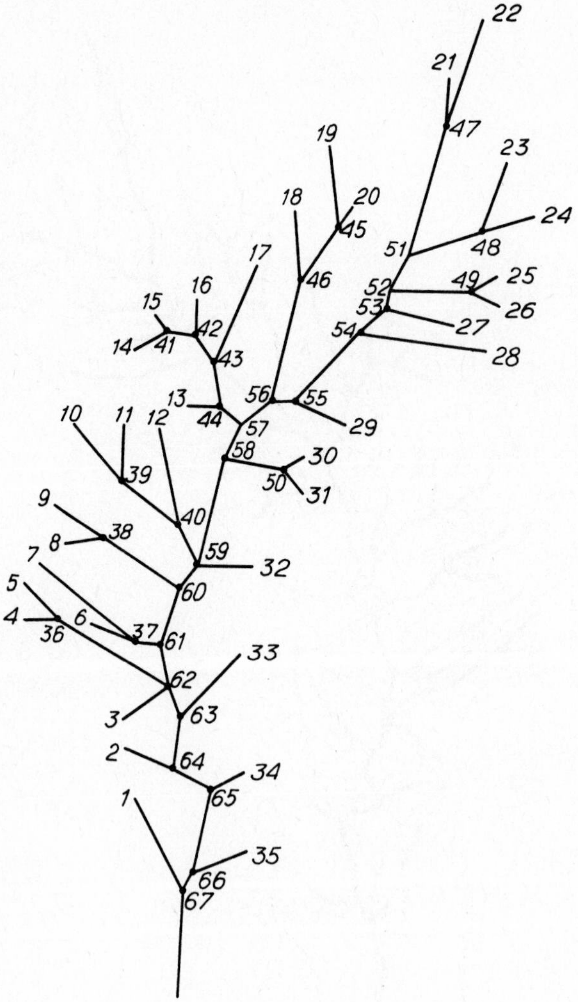
1
2
3
4
5
6
7
8
9
10
11
12
13
14
15
16
17
18
19
20
21
22
23
24
25
26
27
28
29
30
31
32
33
34
35
36
37
38
39
40
41
42
43
44
45
46
47
48
49
50
51
52
53
54
55
56
57
58
59
60
61
62
63
64
65
66
67

Fig. 3

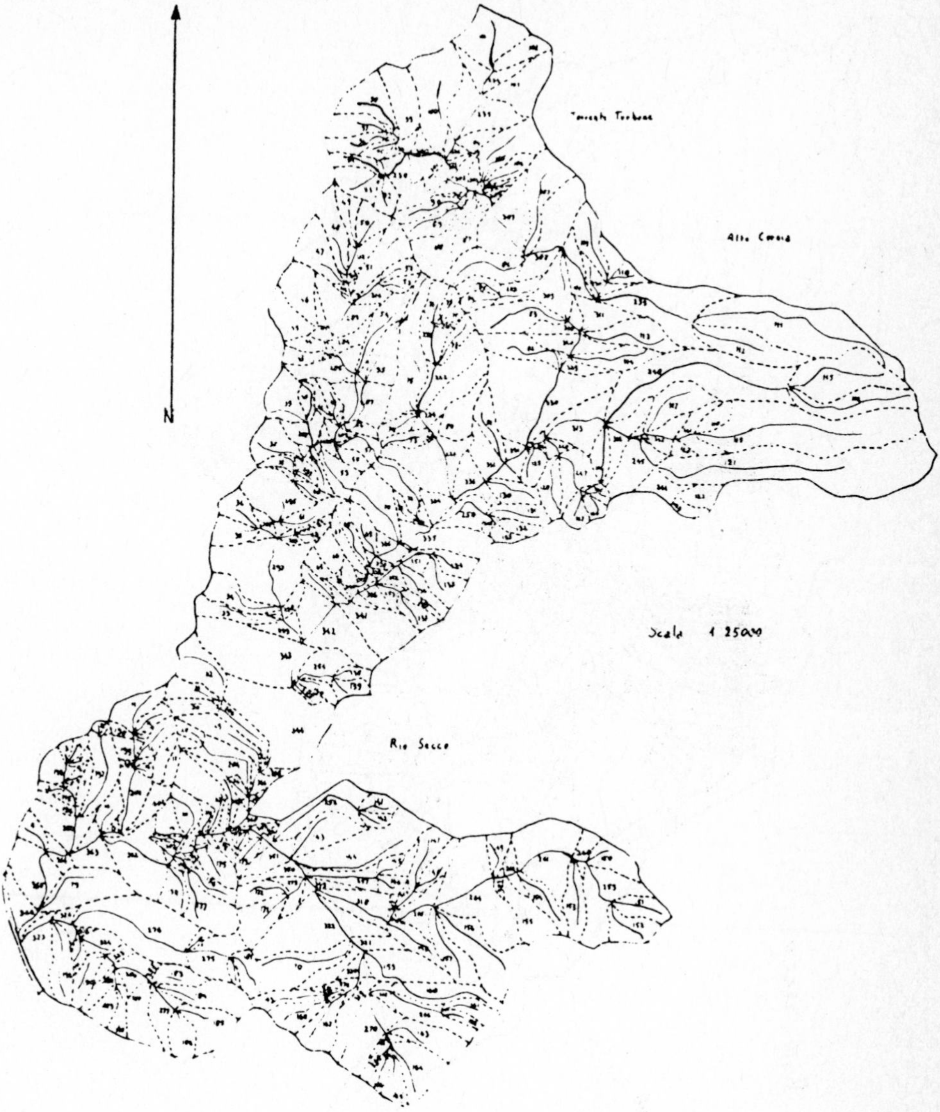

FIG 4

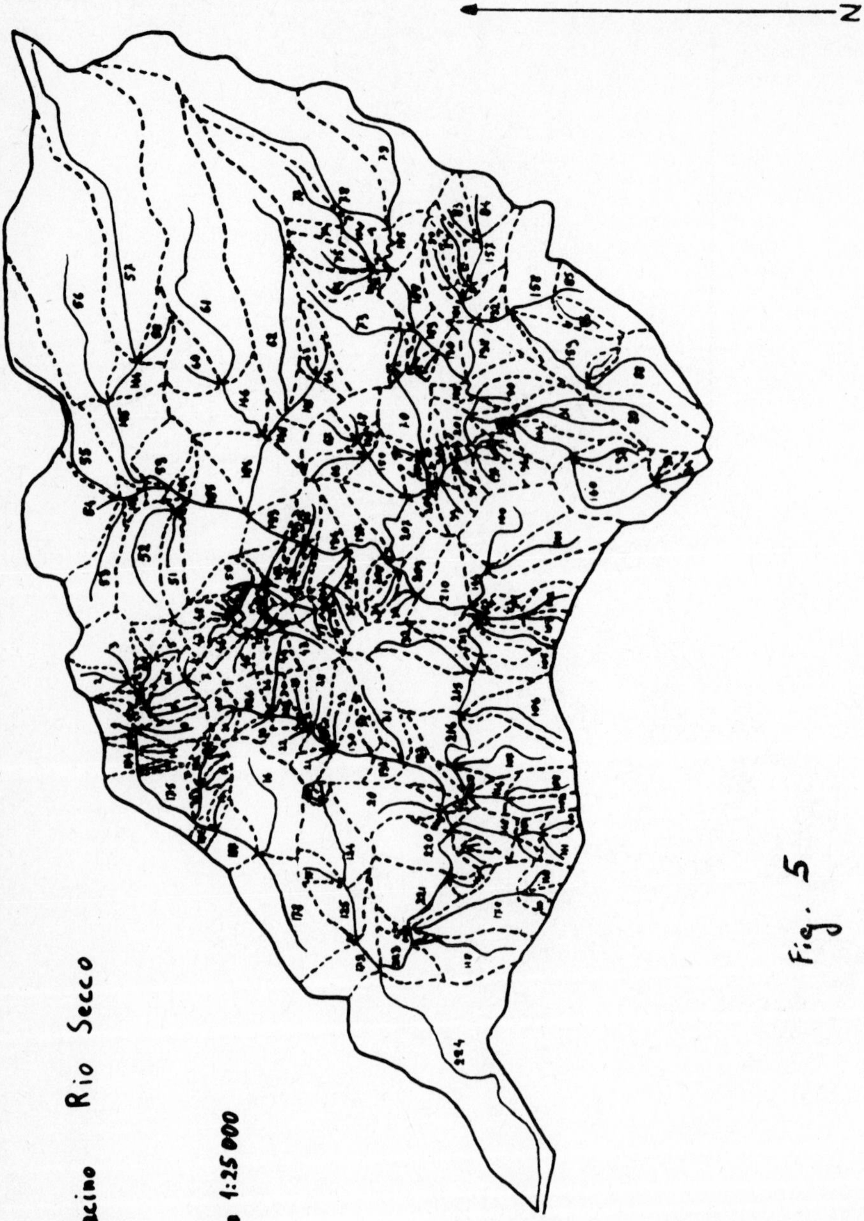

Fig. 5

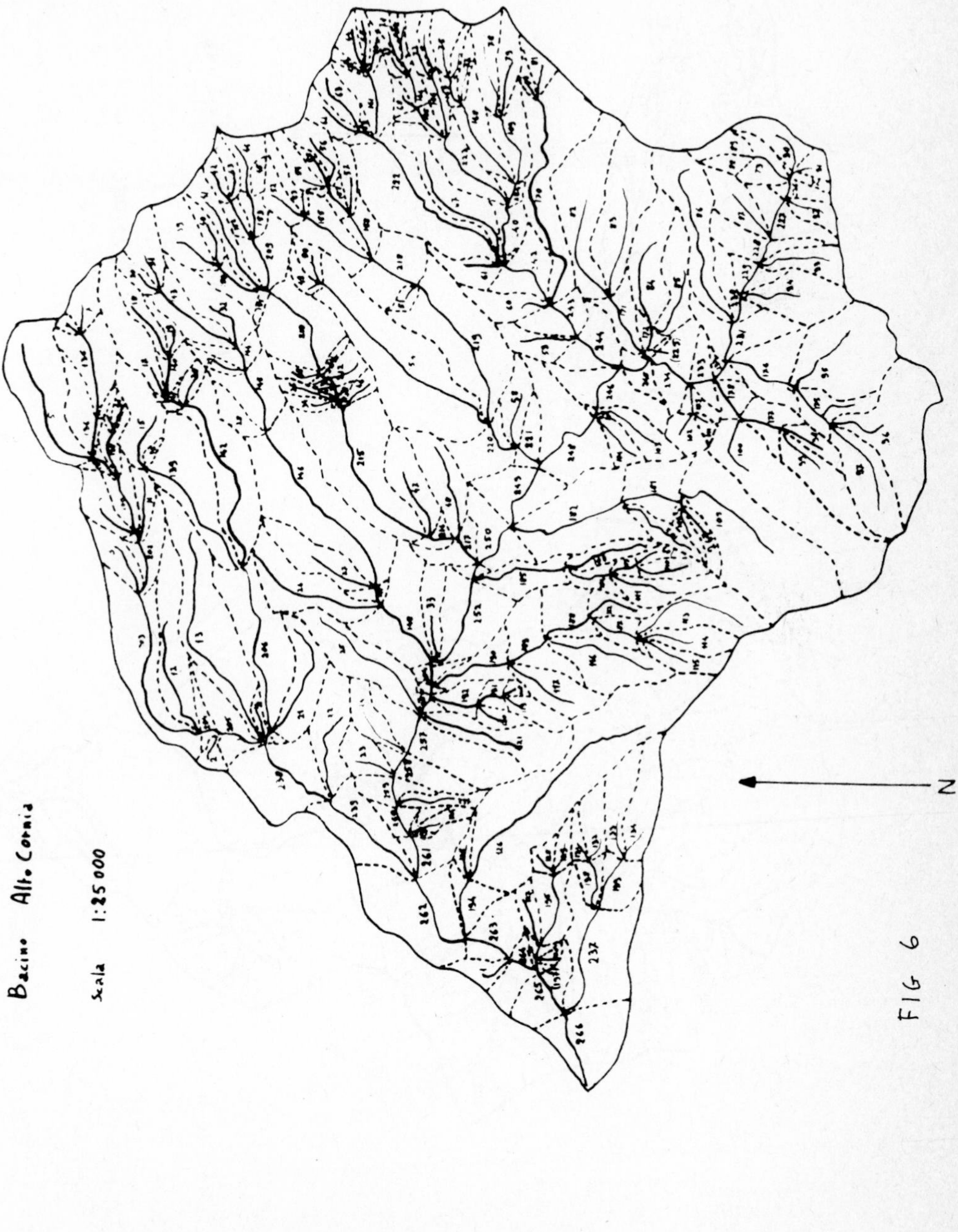

Bacino Alto Cornia

Scala 1:25 000

FIG 6

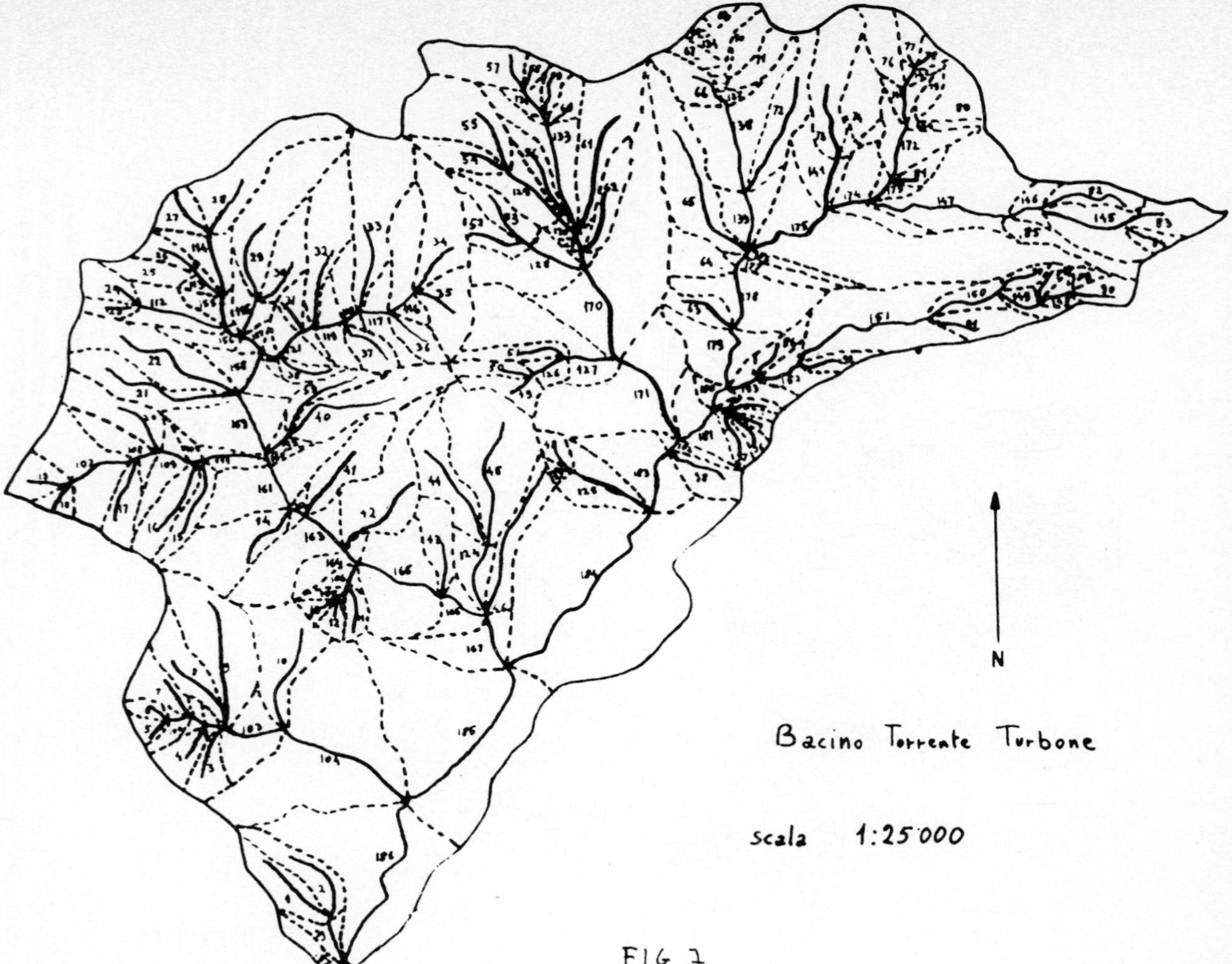

N

Bacino Torrente Turbone

scala 1:25000

FIG 7

Optimal sampling system for estimating geographical distributions of natural resource and environmental pollution

Yasushi Taga — Shizuoka Univ.
Kazumasa Wakimoto — Okayama Univ.
Minoru Ichimura — Okayama coll.of Sci.

1. Introduction

Suppose some kind of natural resource or chemical substance be distributed geographically according to an unknown density function $f(\underline{x})$ in a certain region D.

Suppose $f(\underline{x})$ be approximated fairly well in D by $exp\{P_k(\underline{x})\}$ where $P_k(\underline{x})$ is a polynominal of degree k, and let $z_1, \cdots, z_m$ be observed values of the density $f(\underline{x})$ at m points $\underline{x}_1, \cdots, \underline{x}_m$ to be selected randomly in the region D. Then the coefficients of $P_k(\underline{x})$ may be estimated by the least squares method such that the sum of squares of differences between u_i's and $P_k(\underline{x}_i)$'s is to be minimized where $u_i = log z_i$, $1 \leqq i \leqq m$.

Thus we can get the estimated density function $\hat{f}(\underline{x})$ of $f(\underline{x})$ in D, and then the whole region D may be divided into subregions $D_1, \cdots, D_l$ by the method for optimum stratification in sampling theory.

Then n_i points are randomly selected in each D_i $(1 \leqq i \leqq l)$ so that the integral $I = \int_D f(\underline{x}) d\underline{x}$ is to be estimated precisely.

2. Estimation of $f(\underline{x})$

In the approximate expression $\exp\{P_k(\underline{x})\}$ of the density function $f(\underline{x})$, we may take the degree k of polynominal $P_k(\underline{x})$ for some suitable even number. For simplification we shall state our method in the case where $k=2$ and the dimension of $\underline{x}$ is also two, i.e. $x=(\xi,\eta)$.

Let $P_2(\underline{x})$ be quadratic function of $\underline{x}$ expressed as

$$P_2(\underline{x})=a\xi^2+b\xi\eta+c\eta^2+d\xi+e\eta+g, \tag{2.1}$$

and m random points $\underline{x}_1=(\xi_1,\eta_1),\cdots, \underline{x}_m=(\xi_m,\eta_m)$ be mutually independently and identically distributed according to the uniform distribution in the region D. Then the values of density $f(\underline{x})$ at each point $\underline{x}_i$ are measured, and denoted by z_i for $i=1,2,\cdots,m$. Here we assume that measurements of density could be done without errors, i.e. $z_i=f(\underline{x}_i)$ for $i=1,2,\cdots,m$.

Now we consider that $u_i=\log z_i$ may be approximated fairly well by $P_2(\underline{x}_i)=a\xi_i^2+b\xi_i\eta_i+c\eta_i^2+d\xi_i+e\eta_i+g$ for $i=1,2,\cdots,m$, and so that coefficients $a,b,\cdots,g$ could be estimated by the least squares method, namely by minimizing the sum S of squares of differences between u_i and $P_2(\underline{x}_i)$. Let us denote estimates of $a,b,\cdots,g$ by $\hat{a},\hat{b},\cdots,\hat{g}$ which can be obtained by solving the following equations:

$$\frac{\partial S}{\partial a}=0,\ \frac{\partial S}{\partial b}=0,\ \frac{\partial S}{\partial c}=0,\ \frac{\partial S}{\partial d}=0,\ \frac{\partial S}{\partial e}=0 \text{ and } \frac{\partial S}{\partial g}=0, \tag{2.2}$$

where $S=\sum_{i=1}^{m}[u_i-P_2(\underline{x}_i)]^2$.

This system of equations reduces to the following one:

$$\hat{g}=\bar{u}-(\hat{a}\overline{\xi^2}+\hat{b}\overline{\xi\eta}+\hat{c}\overline{\eta^2}+\hat{d}\bar{\xi}+\hat{e}\bar{\eta}),$$

$$\begin{aligned}
&\hat{a}S_{20\cdot20}+\hat{b}S_{20\cdot11}+\hat{c}S_{20\cdot02}+\hat{d}S_{20\cdot10}+\hat{e}S_{20\cdot01}=S_{\cdot20}\\
&\hat{a}S_{11\cdot20}+\hat{b}S_{11\cdot11}+\hat{c}S_{11\cdot02}+\hat{d}S_{11\cdot10}+\hat{e}S_{11\cdot01}=S_{\cdot11}\\
&\hat{a}S_{02\cdot20}+\hat{b}S_{02\cdot11}+\hat{c}S_{02\cdot02}+\hat{d}S_{02\cdot10}+\hat{e}S_{02\cdot01}=S_{\cdot02}\\
&\hat{a}S_{10\cdot20}+\hat{b}S_{10\cdot11}+\hat{c}S_{10\cdot02}+\hat{d}S_{10\cdot10}+\hat{e}S_{10\cdot01}=S_{\cdot10}\\
&\hat{a}S_{01\cdot20}+\hat{b}S_{01\cdot11}+\hat{c}S_{01\cdot02}+\hat{d}S_{01\cdot10}+\hat{e}S_{01\cdot01}=S_{\cdot01}
\end{aligned} \tag{2.3}$$

where $S_{\cdot\alpha\beta} = \frac{1}{m}\sum_{i=1}^{m}(u_i-\bar{u})(\xi_i^{\alpha}\eta_i^{\beta}-\overline{\xi^{\alpha}\eta^{\beta}})$

$$S_{\alpha\beta\cdot\gamma\delta} = \frac{1}{m}\sum_{i=1}^{m}(\xi_i^{\alpha}\eta_i^{\beta}-\overline{\xi^{\alpha}\eta^{\beta}})(\xi_i^{\gamma}\eta_i^{\delta}-\overline{\xi^{\gamma}\eta^{\delta}})$$

$$\bar{u} = \frac{1}{m}\sum_{i=1}^{m}u_i, \quad \overline{\xi^{\alpha}\eta^{\beta}} = \frac{1}{m}\sum_{i=1}^{m}\xi_i^{\alpha}\eta_i^{\beta},$$

and $\alpha, \beta, \gamma, \delta = 0, 1, 2$.

Solving the system of equations (2.3) we can obtain the estimated function $\hat{f}(\underline{x})$ of density function $f(\underline{x})$ in D. The precision of approximation may be given by the correlation coefficient $r_m = Cov(\hat{f},f)/S_{\hat{f}}S_f$,

where $S_f^2 = \frac{1}{m}\sum_{i=1}^{m}[f(\underline{x}_i)]^2 - [\frac{1}{m}\sum_{i=1}^{m}f(\underline{x}_i)]^2$,

$$S_{\hat{f}}^2 = \frac{1}{m}\sum_{i=1}^{m}[\hat{f}(\underline{x}_i)]^2 - [\frac{1}{m}\sum_{i=1}^{m}\hat{f}(\underline{x}_i)]^2,$$

and $Cov(\hat{f},f) = \frac{1}{m}\sum_{i=1}^{m}\hat{f}(\underline{x}_i)f(\underline{x}_i) - [\frac{1}{m}\sum_{i=1}^{m}\hat{f}(\underline{x}_i)][\frac{1}{m}\sum_{i=1}^{m}f(\underline{x}_i)]$.

The above method may apply to the density function $f(\underline{x})$ with a polynomial $P_k(\underline{x})$ of any degree k, but $f(\underline{x})$ with $P_4(\underline{x})$ of degree four is well applicable to various situations by our experiances.

3. Estimation of I and Optimum Subdivision of D

The total amount or integral $I=\int_D f(\underline{x})d\underline{x}$ may be estimated by

$$(3.1) \qquad T = \frac{A}{n}\sum_{j=1}^{n}f(\underline{x}_j)$$

where A denotes the area D and $\underline{x}_1,\cdots,\underline{x}_n$ are independently and identically distributed according to the uniform distribution $U(D)$ in the region D.

It is easily shown that T is an unbiased estimator of I, i.e.

$$(3.2) \qquad E\{T\} = I,$$

and the variance of T is given by

(3.3) $$V(T) = (A/n)\int_D [f(\underline{x})-\mu]^2 d\underline{x},$$

where $\mu=I/A$ is the mean density in D.

Now let us suppose D is divided into l subregions $D_1,\cdots,D_l$, and n_i points $\underline{x}_{i1},\cdots,\underline{x}_{in_i}$ are taken randomly in each D_i $(1\leqq i\leqq l)$. Then an unbiased estimator of I is given by

(3.4) $$T_l = \sum_{i=1}^{l}(A_i/n_i)\sum_{j=1}^{n_i} f(\underline{x}_{ij}),$$

and the variance of T_l is given by

(3.5) $$V(T_l|\mathcal{D}) = \sum_{i=1}^{l}(A_i/n_i)\int_{D_i}[f(\underline{x})-\mu_i]^2 d\underline{x},$$

where A_i denotes the area of D_i, $\mu_i=I_i/A_i$ the mean density in D_i, and $\mathcal{D}=\{D_1,\cdots,D_l\}$ a subdivision of D.

Let us call a subdivision $\mathcal{D}^*$ optimum if $V(T_l|\mathcal{D}^*)\leqq V(T_l|\mathcal{D})$ for any subdivision $\mathcal{D}$ under the condition that l, $n=\sum_{i=1}^{l} n_i$ and allocation $(n_1,\cdots,n_l)$ are preassigned.

In case of proportional allocation $(n_i=nA_i/A)$, an optimum subdivision $\mathcal{D}^*=\{D_i^*\}$ is given such that

(3.6) $$D_i^* = \{\underline{x}\ ;\ t_{i-1}^*<f(\underline{x})\leqq t_i^*\},$$

where t_i^*'s are $(l-1)$ increasing real numbers satisfying the relations

(3.7) $$t_i^* = \frac{1}{2}(\mu_i^*+\mu_{i+1}^*),\quad \mu_i^*=I_i^*/A_i^* \text{ for } 1\leqq i\leqq l-1$$ (see [1],[2]).

The optimum division points $t_1^*,\cdots,t_{l-1}^*$ may be obtained making use of a simple recursive alogrithm if the density function $f(\underline{x})$ is given.

However $f(\underline{x})$ is unknown to us in advance, so we have to use the estimated density function $\hat{f}(\underline{x})$ based on the first observation $z_1,\cdots z_m$ as stated in section 2. Then we obtain approximately optimum division points $\hat{t}_1^*, \cdots, \hat{t}_{l-1}^*$ using $\hat{f}(\underline{x})$, *i.e.* the empiric distribution function of the sample $z_1, \cdots, z_m$.

By our experiences $V(T_l|D^*)$ is smaller than one twentieth of $V(T)$ when $l=5$. If $a \leqq f(\underline{x}) \leqq b$ for any $\underline{x}$ in D, and if l is sufficiently large, we can get the approximate value $\widetilde{V}(T_l|D^*)$ of $V(T_l|D^*)$ as

$$(3.8) \qquad \widetilde{V}(T_l|D^*) = \frac{A^2(b-a)^2}{12l^2n} .$$

References

[1] Taga,Y (1967): On optimum stratification for the objective variable based on concomitant variables using prior information; *Ann. Inst. Statist. Math.* 19, 101-129.

[2] Isii,K. and Taga,Y. (1969): On optimal stratifications for multivariate distributions; *Skand. Aktuartidskr.*, 52, 24-38.

"INVESTIGATION INTO THE USE OF THE AFRICAN BOARD GAME, AYO, IN THE STUDY OF HUMAN PROBLEM-SOLVING"

AGBALAJOBI, F.B.
(University of Lagos, Nigeria; currently at University College London)

COOPER, R.L.
(Royal Free Hospital London)

SONUGA, J.O.
(University of Lagos, Nigeria; currently at Imperial College London)

ABSTRACT

An investigation conducted into the use of a computer presentation and simulation of a game, AYO, reveals its usefulness in the study of human problem-solving since opponents whose level of sophistication can be varied systematically can be provided; subject's performance under various psychological conditions can be analytically examined and simulated. Pilot studies consisting of three experiments involving subjects whose familiarity with game playing and interaction with computers varied enormously, are reported.

INTRODUCTION

The use of games in the study of cognitive processes has been proposed by many workers (2,3,4,6,7). However, research work has in the past concentrated on such games as chess, checkers, GO etc. - games widely played in European and Asiatic cultures. Most of these games lend themselves to mathematical and algorithmic formulation, with the result that both the creation of hypotheses for testing and the simulation of the games by computer programs are relatively simple. Most of the games used so far also have a highly developed literature built up around them and competence at the highest level often involves many years of study and application. In this paper, the authors seek to introduce a game from a completely different environment. The game, AYO, is widely played among the peoples of West Africa and is a game of the Kalah family, which is largely unknown to Eurasian cultures. Despite the large population who play this game, detailed information on such sophistications as opening theory, various styles of play or how to play endgames have been lacking although the game is at least as complicated as some Western games for which these have been developed - Checkers or Backgammon for example. AYO is here considered as a tool for research into cognitive characteristics of the problem approach among the large population familiar with the game as well as a tool for studying the acquisition of the skill in players drawn from a different population which is largely unfamiliar with the task.

The use of AYO is hereby discussed with respect to three different areas of psychological testing: cognitive research; one-off testing of a subject for clinical assessment; and the serial assessment of one subject's performance as external variables (such as therapeutic conditions) are manipulated. Two basic approaches adopted by clinical psychologists, as discussed by Jones and Weinman (5) are: the classical rigorous psychometric approach and a more intuitive clinical approach, dealing with each subject in isolation. The latter approach is adopted in this paper where the emphasis is more on the analysis of a subject's method of working and the characteristics of his performance. Data collection is therefore geared towards obtaining such parameters that measure problem-solving skills and give the characteristics of the performance of subjects who play AYO. The argument in support of the use of games in cognitive research as against the use of puzzles is contained in Elithorn and Telford (4). Furthermore, the idea of computer control of item presentation as an effective contribution towards the work of a clinical psychologist is taken up and pursued. The characteristics of AYO have a simplicity which makes it particularly amenable to computer control of the strength of the opponent which the subject is pitted against, so that the subject can always be set against a program which is about his own standard.

Armed with these concepts a computerized version of the game, AYO, was developed and implemented on a PDP 8/E computer. A basic program was written to present the game, together with various subroutines for selecting which move the computer would play. The subroutines have parameters of strength which can be changed at the start of every game to set the task difficulty of the subject. The program was felt to have three different functions:

(i) providing opponents whose sophistication could be varied systematically;

(ii) becoming analytical tools to examine the subject's performance by comparison of the move the programs would have made with that which the subject makes; and

(iii) simulating the subject's performance.

Other programs for analysis were developed on ICL 1904S of Queen Mary College (University of London), utilizing its large storage facility.

A brief description of the board and the rules of the game, AYO, were given in a paper in Lagos, Nigeria by Sonuga (8). However, a detailed and differently connotated description will be given here. Following this, the role of AYO in psychological testing will be discussed and then the experimental method and some small experiments will be described. Finally, analysis techniques and the analyses of our experiments will be set out.

THE GAME AYO

AYO is played between two players on a wooden board called "OPON" which is almost rectangular in shape, and from which two rows of six hemispherical holes have been dug. The pieces are spherical seeds of a tree found in various parts of West Africa; but any convenient stones (for example, the stones used in GO game) can be used instead. The size of each piece is such as to allow each hole of the board to hold at least twenty seeds before overflowing. There are forty-eight pieces in a game of AYO and unlike some of the other board games, there is no difference between the pieces. For simplification, the convention adopted in this paper is to denote

(a) the holes on the side of the player P to move by P_1, P_2, ...P_6, in the left to right order and those of the opponent by Q_1, Q_2, ..., Q_6 (see figure 1);

(b) the number of seeds in hole P_1 say by (P_1) and

(c) the capture made by player P by C(P).

OPPONENT Q

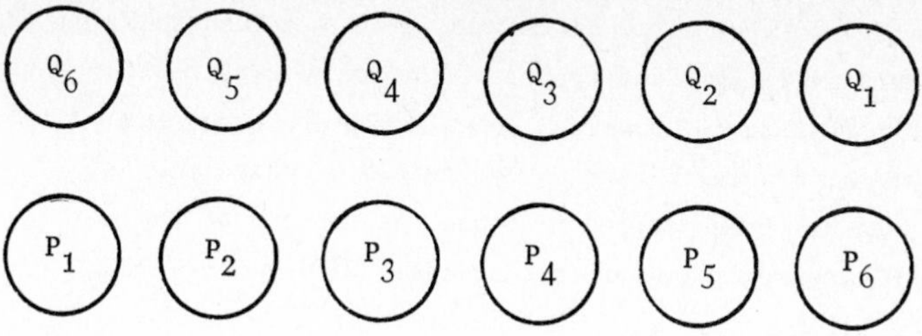

Subject P

Figure 1. Notation

Play is commenced with four seeds in each hole of the players. The first one to move is decided in one of several ways. Like most board games, there is an apparent initial "advantage" to the first player.

A player makes a move by selecting one of his holes, P_i say. He then picks all the seeds from P_i and starts to drop one seed in each hole starting with the hole immediately to the right of P_i (i.e., P_{i+1} if $1 \leq i < 6$ or Q_1 if $i = 6$) and proceeding counter-clockwise. If there are more than eleven seeds picked, then the hole P_i is always skipped during that move, so that at the end of the move, P_i is empty. The move ends when all the seeds picked up have been dropped. The player must, if possible, make a move which leaves the opponent with a move. If the last seed is dropped into one of the player's holes, the move ends and the opponent plays.

However, if the last seed is dropped into one of the opponent's holes, Q_m say ($1 \leq m \leq 6$) then the content of Q_m is examined leading to the following consequences:

(a) if (Q_m) is different from 2 or 3 after the last seed has been dropped into Q_m, then the move ends and the opponent, Q, plays next;

(b) if (Q_m) is 2 or 3 then

(i) all the seeds in Q_m are removed; and

(ii) working consecutively backwards in a clockwise direction, the contents of preceeding holes Q_k (where $1 \leq k \leq m$) are examined and removed if (Q_k) is 2 or 3; stopping when either the content of the preceeding hole is different from 2 or 3 or all the holes are exhausted and the opponent plays next;

(c) if a capture leaves all the opponent's holes empty, i.e., $(Q_n) = 0$ for all n satisfying $1 - n - 6$ then such a capture is illegal and the player makes no capture if he makes that move. Figure 2 shows a capture occurring in opponent's holes Q_5 and Q_6 but not in Q_2 where the last seed has been dropped into Q_5. At the end of the move, P captures five more seeds, i.e. $C(P) = 5$

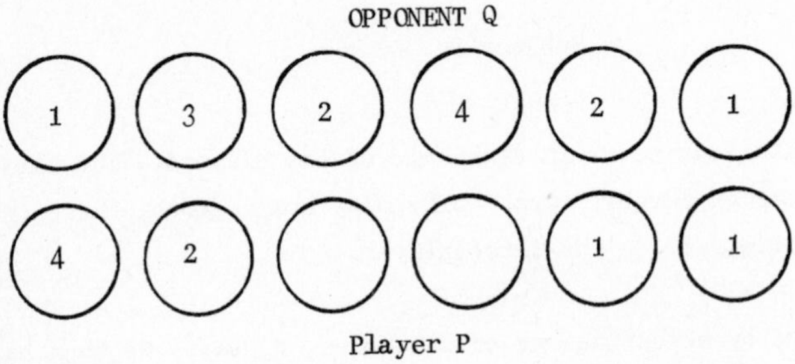

Figure 2: P makes a capture on dropping the last seed into Q_5.

In normal play, the game ends when one of the players has captured more than 24 seeds or he is left with no moves.

COMPUTER BASED TOOL FOR PSYCHOLOGICAL TESTING

i) Psychological Testing

We wish to distinguish three different uses of psychological testing: research into cognitive functioning; one-off testing of a subject to assess whether there is any impairment to his intellectual abilities; and the serial assessment of a subject to assess whether his performance deteriorates or improves as external conditions (for instance therapy) are varied.

In cognitive research, we require tasks that expose to as great an extent possible the underlying thought processes behind the subject's performance. It is also of value for a task to be varied in such a way as to place emphasis on different aspects of performance, for instance, varying the memory component or changing the sense modality (as in presenting memory span visually or aurally.)

For one-off assessment, either a standard battery of tests is given and the subject's performance is compared to normative data or preset sequence of items arranged in order of difficulty is presented and testing ends when the subject begins to fail most of the items, a cut-off point between failed items and passed items indicating the level of performance. Thus a task should be capable of having its difficulty varied and before it can be used for this form of assessment a normative study should be run.

For serial assessment, there are completely different requirements, not a single series of items, but a large pool of items at each level of difficulty is needed. Serial assessment will then consist of one or more test sessions to set the subject's level of performance and then at subsequent sessions, items of about this level will be presented and fluctuations in the standard of performance noted.

ii) The Use of the Computer

For all three of these areas, computer control of item presentation is of great value. A fuller discussion of this point is given in Jones and Weinman (5), some benefits from computer presentation being: a tighter control of experimental conditions; the collection of more detailed information regarding test performance; the ability of the computer (given a suitable task) to generate countless items at any one level of difficulty; the ability to easily vary the difficulty as a function of previous performance; the immediate capture of data in a form amenable to further analysis; and the possible increase in subject motivation caused by interaction with the computer (1,5).

For research purposes, the tight control over conditions and ease of manipulating variables given by the computer makes it an essential aid. For routine assessment, a standard battery of tests can be automated, restandardised for the new set of conditions and then new subjects can be run by relatively untrained staff, thus freeing the clinician for more important work. If the subject's level of performance at a particular task is required, it is much easier for the computer to run a process controlled assessment, than for the clinician who would need after each item to score that item, calculate the level of difficulty to be given for the next item, find or generate an item of that difficulty and then present it to the subject. This may be relatively simple for tasks such as memory span, where length of series constitutes an easy measure of difficulty to manipulate and a simple list of numbers forms an easily accessible pool of items, but for more complex tasks this method of presentation is unworkable without the use of computer controlled presentation. In the case of serial testing, computer presentation again is valuable in the large-scale item generation necessary, as well as freeing the clinician from what would be a time-consuming job.

iii) The Use of Games

So far, these ideas of using computer presentation for the test items which are versions of standard psychological tests and which are essentially problems for which a solution possibly needs to be found have been developed - memorising a sequence of digits and then repeating them correctly or finding a path through a maze (5). We seek to extend some of these ideas to the use of automated games as a tool for psychological testing. The performance of a subject in playing an intellectual game is clearly no less an indicator of psychological functioning than performance on the puzzles which form the basis of many psychometric tests (4). The problem in using unautomated games is that it is even more difficult for the tester to provide a standardised opponent than it is for him to perform a process controlled assessment as described above. The variation introduced into the results by the unstandardised procedure by which the tester selects his moves will obscure any conclusions which can be drawn from them. If, however, the computer is used to simulate an opponent with a fixed strategy, then not only do we have a standard test situation for examining many subjects, but by varying the quality of the strategy provided we may also provide opponents of varying difficulty and so can home in on the subject's level of performance in much the same way as has been suggested for standard psychological tests. It should be pointed out here that it is unlikely that the construction of just one really strong opponent (the aim of workers in the field of artificial intelligence) will be of much value.

There are some desirable features which a game should have to be of use in the test situation. For a start, the game must be well-defined, in the sense of being formally describable and the simpler the description the better, since the game will then be easier to program and so make the creation of many opponents possible. The game should not however be easy, but should allow for considerable variation of expertise, which variation should be easily describable as a hierarchy of strength of performance. It is also desirable that there be many different strategies available to the player, so that the strategy adopted by the subject may be a reflection of his personality. If there are also a number of tactics to master it will prove illuminating to observe how a novice subject learns to use them. The degree of outward manifestation of thought processes behind a subject's performance is also an important parameter in the selection of a game. While protocols may be used to make performance more explicit, information derived from the performance itself is more reliable. Finally, if the form of presentation may be changed to place greater emphasis on one aspect of performance or another, then the game will be even more useful.

iv) The Selection of Ayo

With these criteria in mind, we were satisfied that Ayo was a useful game to try. It is simple to implement, the small number of available moves at each position meaning that programs which simply perform a complete search to a fixed depth of look-ahead can provide an effective opponent since the depth can be set much larger than that for many board games without running into time trouble. A large range of look-ahead also means that look-ahead is an effective index of strength on its own.

The game is not easy, but there are many identifiable strategies and tactics which can be built into opponents and which can be searched for in the subject's performance. The explicit data available from a game is not much, but the simple perceptual structure of the board makes it particularly amenable to eye-movement analysis.

Finally, we can vary the presentation in a number of ways. The standard presentation gives the board as a set of rectangles representing the holes with figures in them representing the number of seeds. Transition from one position to the next upon input of a move is instantaneous. Two ways of changing this presentation to examine different factors are making the transition period slower, giving more visual information to the subject regarding the move being played, and changing the presentation of the number of seeds to dots placed in the rectangle. For the first point, the example of examining the improvement in play of a novice, comparing subjects who get the instantaneous transition and subjects who get more information would be interesting. Changing the representation of the number of seeds in the holes, is of use in situations in which there are large numbers of seeds in some holes. As the game is played between humans, there is a rule governing this situation, which says that a player may count the seeds in his own holes by picking them up, but not those of his opponent, so that a memory component is introduced into the game. This may be simulated on the computer in a number of ways. For a start, if the computer builds up a large number of seeds in one hole, the number displayed may be set to upper limit, for instance, 10. Alternatively, the number of seeds may be displayed as dots, either spaced regularly, or, more usefully, irregularly, the difficulty of counting thus growing with the number in the hole in a way which exactly mirrors the real life situation. A further reason for using dot display, is the universality of counting which makes it applicable in non-European situations and in areas where the use of conventional numerals may impose some constraints on its acceptability.

Finally, a particular reason for using Ayo is that the familiarity with the game may be more easily controlled than with European games. The average non-African subject will have little familiarity not only with Ayo but with any game like it, and so it is possible to study the growth of ability from absolute beginnings to mastery, without having the cross-over effect from other games inherent in the use of European games.

THE PRESENTATION OF THE GAME

i) The Equipment

The experiments described were all run on a PDP 8/E computer with 12K of core (of which only 4K was needed by the computer), attached to which was a point-plot display on which the game was presented and an ASR33 teletype for recording responses. A real-time clock was used to record response times and this was set to record in tenths of a second, this figure being adequate to distinguish decision times and also being the shortest time easily recordable on our 12-bit machine. Responses and times were captured on paper tape for later analysis.

ii) The Test

The subject is seated at a teletype, with the display at eye-level immediately behind the keyboard. The variable parameters for that particular test are preset at both the console and the clock interface as follows: depth of look ahead and the controlling parameters for the strategy are "toggled" in, while the appropriate switches are manipulated for required timing. The testing program is then started.

The subject is confronted with the position of the board represented as twelve rectangular boxes (Figure 3), in two rows, the upper six rows representing the simulated opponent's (or the computer program's) holes and the lower row representing the subjects'. In each box, a number is displayed representing the number of seeds in that hole. Above the boxes are two numbers - the left one represents the last move made by the computer while the other represents the score, or the number of seeds captured, of the simulated opponent. Similar numbers are displayed below the boxes for the subject's side. Initially, these numbers are set to zero and each box contains 4.

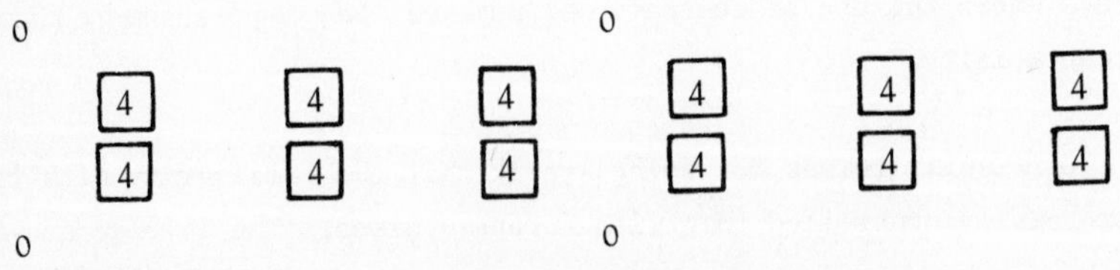

Figure 3: Test Presentation on the computer

The clock is started; the subject is then invited to type in one of the numbers 1 to 6, representing his move (1 represents that he desires to play from the leftmost hole, while 6 represents the rightmost hole). The display changes instantaneously to the position following that move unless the hole selected has no seed in it (or the key pressed is not within the range) in which case the response is ignored. The valid response is recorded both on the teletype and in core. If the subject is not satisfied with the move, he has the option of typing "R" (which is also recorded for subsequent analysis) to retract the move whereupon the display instantaneously reverts to its previous position and the subject may make a different choice. If, however, the subject is satisfied with the result of this move, he types "N" and the computer selects a move (sometimes removing the display for a short time) and changes the board instantaneously to represent the position after its move. In this case, the computer's move, the time taken for the subject to make the move, and (if the score has changed) the scores of the subject and the opponent, are recorded. Illegal moves which leave the computer with no move are not, as yet, trapped and result in the end of the game as the computer program desperately searches forever for a move. A legal end of the game occurs when the board is reduced to three seeds when no more captures are expected.

iii) The Simulated Opponent

Of the great range of possible strategies which may be programmed, the simplest only so far have been programmed. The first program, AYOR, selects its move randomly and is expected to simulate a "blind" player with no goals. It will be shown later that such a program is easily beaten by the merest novice. The second range of programs, AYOLn, use a complete search of the next n halfmoves from the position making a maximin estimation of the values of the available moves based solely on the number of seeds captured as an index of value and selecting the move with the highest value. The depth of look-ahead, n, is a variable parameter of the program and is used as the main component in a measure of the opponent sophistication. The strategy employed to choose between moves of equal values forms the other component of program difficulty. One variation, AYOLnD, of AYOLn, selects the leftmost hole of the equally-valued holes (that is preferring Q_1 to Q_2 etc), thus employing an essentially attacking strategy. Analyses of a few games revealed that AYOLnD provided a more powerful opponent than did AYOLnA and so the strength of programs are in the order AYOR, AYOLIA, AYOL1D, AYOLnA, AYOLnD, etc.

iv) The Experiments

The experiments reported here were all in the nature of pilot studies, to familiarise ourselves with the test situation and to try to find some of the important variables of performance and obtain some measures of performance. All of the subjects were of graduate level, although their familiarity with the game Ayo, game playing in general, and interaction with computers, varied enormously.

Experiment I was an initial attempt to examine the effect of opponent strength upon performance. Three opponents were selected, AYOR, AYOL2A and AYOL2D and three subjects, JJ, SN and JOL (all of whom were relatively inexperienced at the game) were tested on all three opponents in one test session. The order of presentation was balanced for the three subjects in such a way that each opponent appeared as the first opponent of one subject, the second opponent of another subject and the third opponent of the remaining subject. We would predict that the final score of the game would be related to opponent strength but, given an objective measure of move quality, we would also be interested to see if this were related to opponent strength.

Experiment II turned to the effect of different quality of subjects all playing the same opponent. Opponent AYOL2D was chosen and eight subjects, four rated as inexperienced subjects (the three subjects from Experiment I and the subject JH from Experiment III) and four rated as relatively experienced Ayo players (RC, BO, AS and FA). We would predict that the scores of the games would be related to subject quality, but would also be interested to test our objective measure of move quality and also to see the effect on other variables such as average time of move.

Experiment III was a pilot run for an examination of the effect of learning on one subject's performance. Novice subject JH was tested on two opponents each day for 14 days; the first day the subject played against AYOR and AYOL1A (the two easiest programs) and on subsequent days the difficulty of the opponents was adjusted in a subjective manner, so that the subject was required to play a better opponent if she performed well, an easier one if she performed badly. We were interested in examining improvements in her performance over time, as well as making the technique more rational. We would expect that if our measures of competence were valid that they would improve over time, and that other parameters such as time would also vary.

RESULTS AND ANALYSIS

The subject's performance can be examined from the following angles: (i) what strategies are the subjects employing; (ii) how far ahead is the subject able to plan; (iii) what errors in carrying out his plan is the subject making. In the analysis, use is made of the responses, times and captures to extract underlying plans from the game. For instance, examples of a long response time followed by a series of short times culminating in a capture may be said to show a plan being formulated and then being executed over the moves. Similarly, if a computer simulation of a particular strategy gives the same moves as the subject makes, there is reason to believe that the subject is carrying out this strategy. Analysis of this kind is complicated by two factors: two different strategies may give the same response; and errors in the subject's application may indicate that the subject is attempting to carry out a different strategy than the one he is following. Averaging over many moves should bring out whether there is any plan consistent with most moves and at the same time spotlight deviations from this general strategy.

The output of a sample is given as appendix A and consists of the moves selected by the subject, as well as those tried and rejected (S), the moves selected by the computer (C), the subject's response time (T) and the scores (SS and CS). In the analysis of a particular game, the immediately availables - the scores and average response times - were examined before the data was subjected to more detailed analysis to obtain the distribution of holes selected, the distribution of response times and the captures made by the subject. Finally, we attempted to match the subject's responses with those that would have been made by some simulated opponents, from which we derived an objective measure of move quality, by considering the best of the simulated opponents.

In examining the distribution of holes selected, the percentage of moves made from each of the six holes were calculated and the distribution was tested by a one-way X^2 to see if it deviated from the uniform distribution.

Analysis of the response times concentrated on the long times, the distribution of the number of moves between each long time giving an indication of existence of planning. Sample traces of response time are given as figures 4 and 5. These show three main phases of the game - a short opening where the subject has no firm indication of the nature of the game and has medium-length response times; a middle game characterized by long planning times; and end game in which a few medium length planning times are tempered by many very short times.

Next, the performance relating to each capture was considered. The sequence of times leading up to each capture were examined to see if long-term planning preceded this capture. Another indication of planning was felt to be the case where the hole selected for the capture, had not been selected for sometime before. This was felt to show that the move was being prepared for some time in advance.

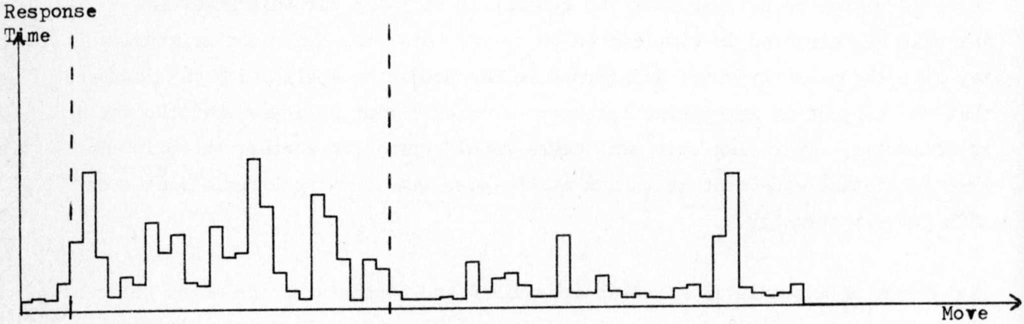

Figure 4: Response Times of Subject RC versus AYOL2D

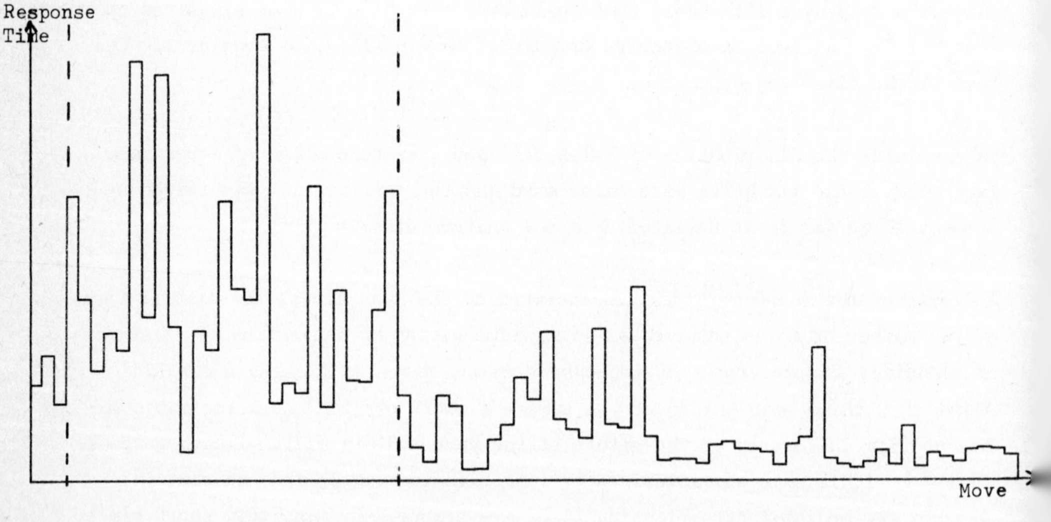

Figure 5: Response Times of Subject SN versus AYOL2D

The final analysis was at first just an attempt to discover if any underlying strategies of performance exist. The technique was to input each of the positions that the subject encountered in his game to a program which simulated a given strategy. The program then output for each position its evaluation of each of the moves, together with the number of moves it considered better, equal and worse than the move the subject chose. These numbers were then summed over the whole game giving totals B (better moves) E (equal) and W (worse moves) and the index $\frac{W}{B + W}$ was felt to be an index of the subjects agreement with the strategy. Contributions to the total B indicate where the strategy and subject part company and these situations can either be due to the subject not using the strategy at that point or to an error in carrying out his plan. The only strategies so far used are the simplistic AYOLn strategies - in which complete search of look-ahead n, for values of n ranging from 1 to 8, was tried. At this point, it was felt that AYOL8 was our best objective estimate of a good move-simulated opponent, AYOL8D being able to defeat our best subject (a very experienced Ayo player). So, it was felt that the value $\frac{W}{B + W}$ obtained from look-ahead 8 should be used as an index of game "quality". In averaging this value over several games, W and B were calculated for all the games considered as a whole and $\frac{W}{B + W}$ recalculated; rather than averaging $\frac{W}{B + W}$ separately. Testing the difference between the quality of two games or the set of games could then be achieved by use of X^2 test between pairs (B,W) of the games.

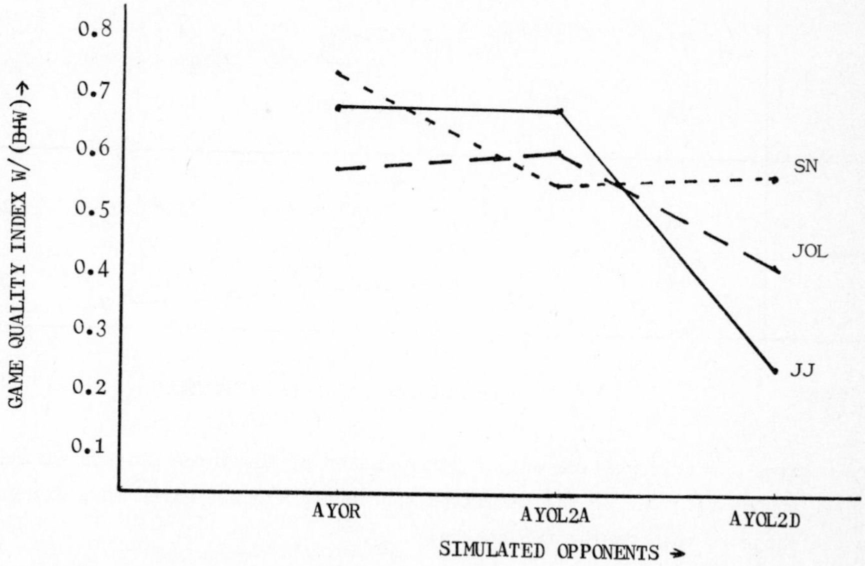

FIGURE 6: PERFORMANCE OF 3 SUBJECTS AGAINST 3 OPPONENTS

Experiment I

Table I sets out the results of the analysis of the three games of each subject. In the first three columns, the subjects simulated opponent, the subject and the sequence in which the subject played this opponent are given. Then the score of the game (subject score first), average response time and quality score for the game are given. As expected all subjects defeated AYOR, the random opponent, thus showing the existence of sufficient prior knowledge for a naive subject to perform better than random. All three subjects lost narrowly to AYOL2A and while one subject managed a draw with AYOL2D, the other two lost heavily. From the combined computor scores of the three subjects an index of strength of the three opponents' strength, AYOR = 34, AYOL2A = 69, AYOL2D = 74 giving the order of strength described above, (this order is confirmed by data gathered more informally).

Simulated Opponent	Subject	Seq	Score	Av. Time	$\frac{W}{B + W}$
R	JJ	1	27-10	39.8	.681
	JOL	3	33-11	25.5	.572
	SN	2	32-13	22.2	.744
AYOL2A	JJ	2	20-22	24.5	.675
	JOL	1	21-23	21.7	.603
	SN	3	19-24	13.0	.545
AYOL2D	JJ	3	3-38	17.8	.282
	JOL	2	7-34	15.6	.407
	SN	1	22-22	20.2	.569

Table I: STRENGTH OF SIMULATED OPPONENTS

Figure 6 gives a representation of the performances of the three players against the three opponents. One of the simulated opponents, AYOL2D, gives more discrimation among the subjects than do the two others.

Turning to more objective measures, the average response time appears to drop with opponent, but this is more likely to be due to games against poorer opponents tending to be of shorter duration and so to be lacking the short times characteristic of the final part of the game. The results with move "quality" are more complex. There are no differences between subjects, but there appears to be a significant deterioration of performance as the opponent gets stronger. This effect is however confused by other apparent effects - a fatigue effect (the third game being worse than the first two) and a morale effect, as games following defeats seem to be played somewhat worse than games following wins and draws. The small number of games makes it impossible to untangle these features.

Experiment II

In Experiment I, opponent AYOL2D gave more discrimination between the subjects than the other programs and so it was selected for use in the analysis of subjects of varying competences. The eight subjects fall into roughly two groups - four experienced and competent Ayo players and four relatively naive subjects. Table II gives the results of the eight subjects. It can immediately be seen that the more experienced subjects do much better than do the naive subjects against the common opponent and take less time over their moves. The objective measure also distinguishes the two groups, the worst of the experienced subjects being better than the best of the naive subjects.

Subject	Score	No. Moves	Av. time	$\frac{W}{B+W}$
JJ	3-38	22	17.8	.292
JOL	7-34	45	15.6	.407
SN	22-22	78	20.2	.569
JH	25-15	39	18.8	.739
BO	25-20	100	9.2	.840
RC	25-21	61	8.0	.822
AS	37-8	42	14.6	.794
FA	32-14	51	5.6	.797

Table II: Two groups of subjects vs. a common opponent, AYOL2D.

Day No.	Opponent	No. Moves	Score	Av. Time	$\frac{W}{B + W}$
1	R	54	41-4	26.8	.807
	1A	44	35-10	18.5	.865
2	1D	37	27-12	18.2	.760
	2A	140	10-32	16.7	.753
3	2A	84	20-22		.805
	1D	32	24-18		.702
4	2A	156	35-7	11.8	
	-				
5	2D	71	23-21		.756
	3A	43	14-18	27.2	.813
6	3A	40	8-32	12.8	.745
	2D	97	25-18	11.4	.803
7	3A	43	24-20	27.7	.868
	2D	39	15-25	18.8	.739

Table III: Serial Results of the first 7 test days of subject, JH.

Experiment III

It is to be expected that if other conditions are kept constant, putting a subject through a series of runs on the game should produce some performance affected by learning. Improvement over time and a pattern of approach to problem-solving should be exhibited. Table III gives the analysis obtained from the data of the first seven days of the experiment. Improvement in time is noted as Figure shows. However, the index, $\frac{B}{B + W}$ for measuring move quality within a game does not show any particular trend.

Problem-solving Approach (Planning)

In examining the characteristics of the performance of the subjects, a general picture of the whole game is considered as against individual variables like time, score and total number of moves. The first indication that a subject is not playing randomly is shown in an uneven distribution of hole-selection. Table IV gives the

Subject	1	2	3	4	5	6	1+2+6
JJ	22.7	18.2	13.6	9.1	13.6	22.7	63.3
JOL	26.7	15.6	11.1	11.1	13.3	22.2	64.5
SN	17.9	14.1	19.2	16.7	16.7	15.4	47.4
JH	12.8	25.6	23.1	12.8	7.7	17.9	56.3
BO	17.0	25.0	13.0	18.0	17.0	10.0	56.0
RC	11.5	21.3	21.3	21.3	11.5	13.1	44.9
AS	14.3	16.7	14.3	23.8	21.4	9.5	40.5
FA	17.6	11.8	21.6	23.5	11.8	13.7	43.1

Table IV: Percentages of Selection of each hole

percentages of each subject playing from each hole. An immediate difference is noticed between the values for experienced and inexperienced players.

Three of the four experienced players make less than 45% of their moves from holes 1, 2, and 6 whereas three of the four inexperienced players make more than 55% of their moves from these end holes. The game of the only inexperienced player SN deviating from this trend is discussed at length later. This shows that the inexperienced players, as expected, tend to concentrate their attention on the sides of the board where pieces seem to them to be more vulnerable. The experienced players, who have come to realise that this is not the case, do not make this type of inadequate judgement.

In real life situations, attacking players tend to play from the rightmost holes (i.e. 5 and 6) so as to get pieces in the opponent side for subsequent capture. From the games analysed and reported, none of the subjects exhibit this trait. On the other hand the defending players make most of their moves from the leftmost holes (1 and 2). The results show that subjects JJ,JOL and JH in Group 1 and BO in Group 2 fall into this category.

Group 1 subjects make more of planned captures than group 2 subjects, as shown in the table below where each major capture is preceeded by a high response time a few moves before the capture. It is expected that if the subject is clear in his mind that the plan is sound, the response times leading to the final execution of the plan should be lower than the time spent in planning.

Subjects	Major Capture	Move No.	Time for Move	Preceeding times Prior to Capture
JJ	3	16	67	34, 55, 92, 406
JOL	3	19	215	81, 94,111, 176
SN	8	26	403	155, 620
JH	6	37	49	114, 24, 60, 26, 108
BO	10	27	267	39, 71,142
RC	8	16	179	50, 57,103
AS	12	16	468	128,148,217
FA	14	12	64	180

TABLE V : PROBABLE INDICATION OF SUBJECT PLANNING.

The Special Subject, SN

SN's results are worthy of separate analysis and comments. We hesitate to hypothesise that the personality of the player shows immediately in one single game. However, SN's approach to problem-solving and new challenges (e.g. performance at a new game ADVICE) has shown that she calculates her moves quite methodically and is known not to possess extreme tendencies. Her average time of 20.18 and total moves of 78 in Table II point in this direction. In Table IV, her hole selection is fairly uniform and the fact that her game, of all, ends in a draw is a further indication. Figure 6 (Graph) gives a clear picture of the characteristics of her game as being immediately (or spontaneously) methodical.

SUMMARY

Having created an automated version of the game, Ayo, whose strength can be varied at will, and run a few subjects through the test situation, we feel able to suggest that the test generates sufficient information to be of use in the psychological laboratory. However, a more useful stage can be achieved when the simulated opponent can be made flexible enough to modify its strategy to match the competence of the subject. The requirements at this stage will be larger storage facility, faster processor and more efficient searching algorithm.

Indication not only of problem solving competence and planning ability, but also of performance style and personality, which are the features of any demanding game can be quantified by the use of a standardised test procedure. By varying the presentation of the test, different facets of performance can be investigated. The game can also take its place alongside Chess, Checkers and GO in the field of cognition research, particularly as the board has a simplicity, which makes it an ideal task for analysis by eye-movement methods. In short, with sufficient refinement, the automatic, test presentation of Ayo should prove extremely useful in many areas.

ACKNOWLEDGEMENTS

The authors are indebted to Dr Alick Elithorn and the staff of the Department of Psychological Medicine, at the Royal Free Hospital, London, for their advice and support during our investigations. Thanks are also due to all our subjects, espcially to Mrs Jacque Hagan, Miss Sue Nash, Mrs Bola Odunlami and Mr James Ladapo, for their patience and to all those who helped us in various capacities during the investigation.

Appendix A. Sample Output from a Game

S	C	T	SS	CS
6	1	274		
4	1	78		
6	1	202		
5	1	288		
1	4	187	0	4
1	6	480	0	6
3	3	383	0	12
2	4	83	0	15
3	1	488		
4	3	121		
5	2	169		
6	6	406	0	23
5	1	92		
6	3	55		
1	5	34	0	28
6	4	67	3	34
1	2	120		
2	6	43	3	38
1	3	69		
2	4	35		
3	5	57		
2	6	183		

REFERENCES

1) Andreewsky, E. (1975). "Man-Machine Interaction in Normal Subjects and in Disorder of the Central Nervous System". Comput. Biol. Med., 5, 89-95

2) Chase, W.G. and Simon, H.A. (1973). "Perception in Chess". Cognitive Psychology 4, 55-81

3) Groot, A.D. de (1965). "Thought and Choice in Chess". The Hague: Mouton

4) Elithorn, A. and Telford, A. (1973). "Design Considerations in Relation to Computer Based Problems". In "Artificial and Human Thinking" - Elithorn and Jones (eds), Elsevier

5) Jones, D. and Weinman, J. (1973). "Computer Based Psychological Testing". In "Artificial and Human Thinking" - Elithorn and Jones (eds), Elsevier

6) Newell, A. and Simon, M.A. (1972). "Human Problem Solving". Prentice Hall

7) Reitman, W. (1973). "Problem-solving, Comprehension and Memory". In "Process Models in Psychology" - Dalenoort, G.J. (ed), Rotterdam University Press

8) Sonuga, J. "Playing the AYO Game with the Computer". Lecture to Nigerian Computer Society, Lagos in 1970

CATASTROPHE THEORY AND URBAN PROCESSES

John Casti and Harry Swain

Research Scholars at the
International Institute for
Applied Systems Analysis

Schloss Laxenburg
A-2361 Laxenburg, Austria

Abstract

Phenomena exhibiting discontinuous change, divergent processes, and hysteresis can be modelled with catastrophe theory, a recent development in differential topology. Exposition of the theory is illustrated by qualitative interpretations of the appearance of functions in central place systems, and of price cycles for urban housing.

Introduction

A mathematical theory of "catastrophes" has recently been developed by the French mathematician Réné Thom [6,7] in an attempt to rationally account for the phenomenon of discontinuous change in behaviors (outputs) resulting from continuous change in parameters (inputs) in a given system. The power and scope of Thom's ideas have been exploited by others, notably Zeeman [10,11], to give a mathematical account of various observed discontinuous phenomena in physics, economics, biology, [4] and psychology. We particularly note the work of Amson [1] on equilibrium models of cities, which is most closely associated with the work presented here. With the notable exception of Amson's work, little use has been made of the powerful tools of catastrophe theory in the study of urban problems. Perhaps this is not surprising since the theory is only now becoming generally known in mathematical circles. However, despite the formidable mathematical appearance of the basic theorems of the theory, the application of catastrophe theory to a given situation is often quite simple, requiring only a modest understanding of simple geometric notions. In this regard, catastrophe theory is much like linear programming in the sense that it is not necessary to understand the mechanism in order to make it work--a fairly typical requirement of the working scientist when faced with a new mathematical tool.

Thus, our objective in this article is twofold: first, to supply a brief introduction to the basic philosophy of catastrophe theory in a form which we hope will be congenial to workers in the urban field, and second, to illustrate the applications of the theory to some classical problems in urban economic geography. Specifically, we consider an example for central place theory in which the simplest type of nontrivial catastrophe provides a satisfactory global picture of the observed developmental patterns of functions provided to the population. A second example illustrates application of one of the more complex elementary catastrophes to the issue of equilibrium residential property prices in urban land markets. Although these examples are provided primarily as qualitative illustrations of the theory, it is hoped that they may be of interest in their own right as providing an alternative and possibly more comprehensive account of the dynamics of these problems than those obtained by other methods.

Catastrophe Theory

In this section, we present a brief discussion of the basic assumptions and results of catastrophe theory in a form useful for applications. For details and proofs, we refer to [8,9].

Let $f: R^k \times R^n \to R$ be a smooth (infinitely differentiable) function representing a dynamical system Σ in the sense that R^k is the space of input variables (controls, parameters) while R^n represents the space of output variables (responses, behaviors). We assume that $k \leq 5$, while n is unrestricted. The fundamental assumption is that Σ attempts to locally minimize f. We hasten to point out that in applications of catastrophe theory, it is not necessary to know the function f. In fact, in most cases f will be a very complicated function whose structure could never be determined. All we assume is that there *exists* such a function which Σ seeks to locally minimize.

Given any such function f, if we fix the point $c \epsilon R^k$, we obtain a local potential function $f_c : R^n \to R$ and we may postulate a differential equation

$$\dot{x} = - \text{grad}_x f \quad ,$$

where $x \epsilon R^n$, $\text{grad}_x f = \text{grad } f_c = \left(\frac{\partial f}{\partial x_1}, \ldots, \frac{\partial f}{\partial x_n}\right)$.

Thus, the phase trajectory of Σ will flow toward a minimum of f_c; call it x_c. The stable equilibria are given by the minima of f_c, and, since there are usually several minima, x_c will be a multivalued function of c; that is, $x_c : R^k \to R^n$ is *not* one-to-one. The objective of catastrophe theory is to analyze this multivaluedness by means of the theory of singularities of smooth mappings.

We first state the fundamental result of catastrophe theory in relatively precise mathematical language. We then interpret each of the conclusions of the main theorem in everyday language to show their reasonableness and applicability for real-world problems.

For completeness, and to round out the mathematical theory, we consider not only the minima but also the maxima and other stationary values of f_c. Define the manifold $M_f \subset R^{k+n}$ as

$$M_f = \{(x,c) : \text{grad}_x f_c = 0\} \quad ,$$

and let $\chi_f : M_f \to R^k$ be the map induced by the projection of $R^{k+n} \to R^k$. χ_f is called the catastrophe map of f. Further, let J be the space of C^∞-functions of R^{k+n} with the usual Whitney C^∞-topology. Then the basic theorem of catastrophe theory (due to Thom) is the following.

<u>*Theorem:*</u> *There exists an open dense set $J_o \subset J$, called generic functions, such that if $f \varepsilon J_o$*

(i) M_f *is a k-manifold;*

(ii) *any singularity of* χ_f *is equivalent to one of a finite number of elementary catastrophes;*

(iii) χ_f *is stable under small perturbations of f.*

<u>Remarks</u>:

1. Here *equivalence* is understood in the following sense: maps $\chi : M \to N$ and $\bar{\chi} : \bar{M} \to \bar{N}$ are equivalent if there exist diffeomorphisms h, g such that the diagram

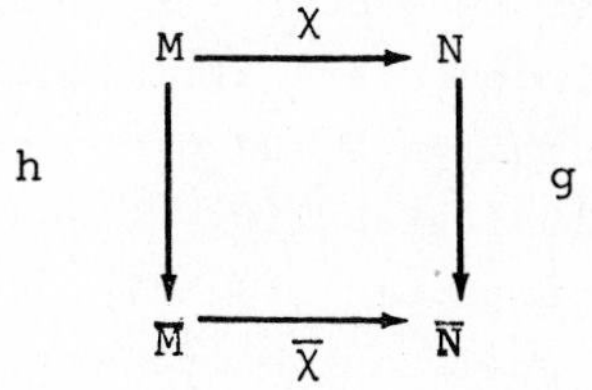

is commutative. If the maps χ, $\bar{\chi}$ have singularities at $x \varepsilon M$, $\bar{x} \varepsilon \bar{M}$, respectively, then the singularities are equivalent if the above definition holds locally with $hx = \bar{x}$.

2. *Stable* means that χ_f is equivalent to χ_g for all g in a neighborhood of f in J (in the Whitney topology).

3. The number of elementary catastrophes depends only upon k and is given in the following table:

k	1	2	3	4	5	6
number of elementary catastrophes	1	2	5	7	11	∞

A finite classification for $k > 6$ may be obtained under topological, rather than diffeomorphic, equivalence but the smooth classification is more important for applications.

4. Roughly speaking, J_o being open and dense in J simply means that if the potential function $f \varepsilon J$ were to be selected at random, then $f \varepsilon J_o$ with probability one. Thus, a given system function f is almost always in J_o, and furthermore, if it is not, an arbitrarily small perturbation will make it so.

5. The importance of M_f being a k-manifold is that M_f is the place where controlling influence is exerted: from the standpoint of the decision maker, M_f is the manifold which he may manipulate. Thus, the dimension of the behavior or output space does not enter into

the classification at all. Since n, the dimension of the behavior space, may be very large, this conclusion enables us to focus attention upon a much smaller set in investigating where and when catastrophic changes in behavior will occur. To summarize, M_f is where the action is.

6. Conclusion *(ii)* shows that, mathematically speaking, only a very small number of distinctly different catastrophes can occur. Intuitively, catastrophes are equivalent if they differ only by a change of coordinate system. Since the coordinate system chosen to describe a phenomenon is not an intrinsic feature of the system, we may restrict our attention to the analysis of only a small handfu of mathematical catastrophes, safe in the knowledge that more comple: forms cannot possibly occur. In addition, as indicated below, the elementary catastrophes are all described by simple polynomials which make their analysis and properties particularly simple.
7. The last conclusion, stability, means that should the potential f describing Σ be perturbed slightly, the new potential will also exhibit the same qualitative catastrophic behavior as f. Since no physical system is know precisely, this fact enables us to feel confident about various predictions based upon use of any $f \varepsilon J_o$.

Discontinuity, Divergence, and the Cusp Catastrophe

Our critical assumption is that Σ, the system under study, seeks to minimize the function f: that is, Σ is dissipative. Thus, the system behaves in a manner quite different from the Hamiltonian systems of classical physics. In this section we shall mention two striking features displayed by catastrophe theory which are not present in Hamiltonian systems but which are observed in many physical phenomena.

The first basic feature is *discontinuity*. If β is the image in R^k of the set of singularities of χ_f, then β is called the bifurcation set and consists of surfaces bounding regions of qualitatively different behavior similar to surfaces of phase transition. Slowly crossing such a boundary may result in a sudden change in the behavior of Σ, giving rise to the term "catastrophe". Since the dimension of the output space does not enter in the classification theorem, all information about where such catastrophic changes in output will occur is carried in the bifurcation set β which, by a corollary of conclusion *(i)* of the Theorem, is a subset of the input space R^k. Hence, even though Σ may have an output space of inconceivably high dimension, the "action" is on a manifold of low dimension which may be analyzed by ordinary geometric and analytical tools.

The second basic feature exhibited by catastrophe theory is the phenomenon of *divergence*. In systems of classical physics a small change in the initial conditions results in only a small change in the future trajectory of the process, one of the classical concepts of stability. However, in catastrophe theory the notion of stability is relative to perturbations of the system itself (the function f), rather than just to perturbations of the initial conditions, and so the Hamiltonian result may not apply. For example, adjacent tissues in a homogeneous embryo will differentiate.

Let us now illustrate the above ideas by considering the *cusp* catastrophe. It will turn out that a minor modification of this catastrophe is also the appropriate catastrophe for one of the main examples of this paper, the problem of central place discontinuities.

Let k = 2, n = 1, and let the control and behavior space have coordinates a, b, and x, respectively.

Let $f : R^2 \times R^1 \to R$ be given by

$$f(a,b,x) = \frac{x^4}{x} + \frac{ax^2}{2} + bx \quad .$$

The manifold M_f is given by the set of points $(a,b,x) \subset R^3$ where

$$\mathrm{grad}_x f(a,b,x) = 0 \quad ,$$

that is,

$$\frac{\partial f}{\partial x} = x^3 + ax + b = 0 \quad . \tag{1}$$

The map $\chi_f : M_f \to R^2$ has singularities when two stationary values of f coalesce, that is,

$$\frac{\partial^2 f}{\partial x^2} = 3x^2 + a = 0 \quad . \tag{2}$$

Thus, Equations (1) and (2) describe the singularity set S of χ. It is not hard to see that S consists of two fold-curves given parametrically by

$$(a,b,x) = (-3\lambda^2, 2\lambda^3, \lambda) \quad , \qquad \lambda \neq 0 \quad ,$$

and one cusp singularity at the origin. The bifurcation set β is given by

$$(a,b) = (-3\lambda^2, 2\lambda^3)$$

which is the cusp $4a^3 + 27b^2 = 0$. Since M_f and S are smooth at the origin, the cusp occurs in β and not in S. Figure 1 graphically depicts the situation.

It is clear from the figure that if the control point (a,b) is fixed outside the cusp, the function f has a unique minimum, while if (a,b) is inside the cusp, f has two minima separated by one maximum. Thus, over the inside of the cusp, M_f is triple-sheeted.

The phenomenon of smooth changes in (a,b) resulting in discontinuous behavior in x is easily seen from Figure 1 by fixing the control parameter a at some negative value, then varying b. On entering the inside of the cusp nothing unusual is observed in x; but upon further change in b, resulting in an exit from the cusp, the system will make a catastrophic jump from the lower sheet of M_f to the upper, or vice versa, depending upon whether b is increasing or decreasing. The cause of the jump is bifurcation of the differential equation $\dot{x} = -\mathrm{grad}_x f$, since the basic assumption is that Σ always moves so as to minimize f. As a result, no position on the middle sheet of maxima can be maintained and Σ must move from one sheet of minima to the other.

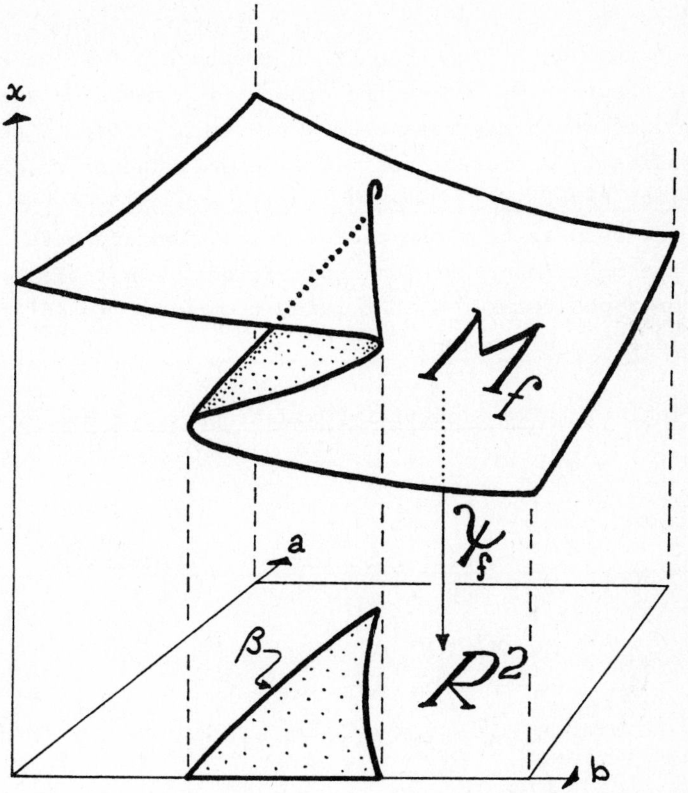

Figure 1. The Cusp Catastrophe

A *hysteresis* effect is observed when moving b in the opposite direction from that which caused the original jump: the jump phenomenon will occur only when leaving the interior of the cusp from the opposite side to the point of entry.

To see the previously mentioned divergence effect, consider two control points (a,b) with $a > 0$, $b \gtrless 0$. Maintaining the b values fixed with decreasing a, the point with positive b follows a trajectory on the lower sheet of M_f, while the other point moves on the upper sheet. Thus, two points which may have been arbitrarily close to begin with end up at radically different positions depending upon which side of the cusp point they pass.

While the cusp is only one of several elementary catastrophes, it is perhaps the most important for applications. In Table I, we list several other types for $k \leq 4$, but refer the reader to [6] for geometrical details and applications.

Table I. The Elementary Catastrophes for $k \leq 4$.

Name	potential function f	control space dimension	behavior space dimension
fold	$x^3 + ux$	1	1
cusp	$x^4 + ux^2 + vx$	2	1
swallowtail	$x^5 + ux^3 + vx^2 + wx$	3	1
butterfly	$x^6 + ux^4 + vx^3 + wx^2 + tx$	4	1
hyperbolic umbilic	$x^3 + y^3 + uxy + vx + wy$	3	2
elliptic umbilic	$x^3 - xy^2 + u(x^2 + y^2) + vx + wy$	3	2
parabolic umbilic	$x^2y + y^4 + ux^2 + vy^2 + wx + ty$	4	2

Central Place Catastrophes

To illustrate the cusp catastrophe in an urban context, consider the supply of goods and services to an urban-centered market area under all the normal postulates of classical (geometric, static, deterministic) central place theory. Then there exist spatial monopoly profits, π, in the distribution of that vast majority of goods whose threshold lies between the size of the existing market and that of the market that would be required to induce a competing supplier to locate there. The argument is similar for the number of *establishments* handling that good, the number of *functions* in a given central place, and the *order* of that central place (cf. Dacey [3] for definition of terms).

But not let there be emigration from that market area, or some other process producing a slow leakage of aggregate local purchasing power. Then $\pi \to 0$, the *minimum threshold*, at which point the good ceases to be distributed.

The threshold for (re-) appearance of the good (establishment, function) is, however, higher than $\pi = 0$ since an entrepreneur would choose that combination of good and market area offering maximal spatial monopoly profits (the *upper threshold*). Thus we have the characteristic discontinuity and hysteresis effects of catastrophe theory.

The cusp catastrophe provides a reasonable global picture for these central place phenomena. Let the independent or control variables be x, the population of a market area, and y, the disposable income per capita. The behavior or output variable can then be interpreted as the order of the central place, or number of functions or goods provided there; all three may be generally referred to as the *functional level*, m, of the central place or market area. (The implicit potential function for this system is, in contradistinction to the prior discussion, maximized by the action of the central place process. Thus we operate with -f and apply the preceding theory.) The relevant picture is given in Figure 2. Each point on the manifold M represents a functional level corresponding to given levels of aggregate local purchasing power. But though x and y determine the functional level, the fact that M is triple-sheeted within a region near the relevant thresholds means that m can take on two distinct stable equilibrium values; values, moreover, which depend on the trajectory (history or direction of change) in x and y. Thus in Figure 2 it may be readily seen that, for a fixed level of disposable income per capita, smooth increases in population will have but small effects on the functional level of the central place until the locus of that trajectory crosses the right-hand cusp border into region II (see a). At this point the

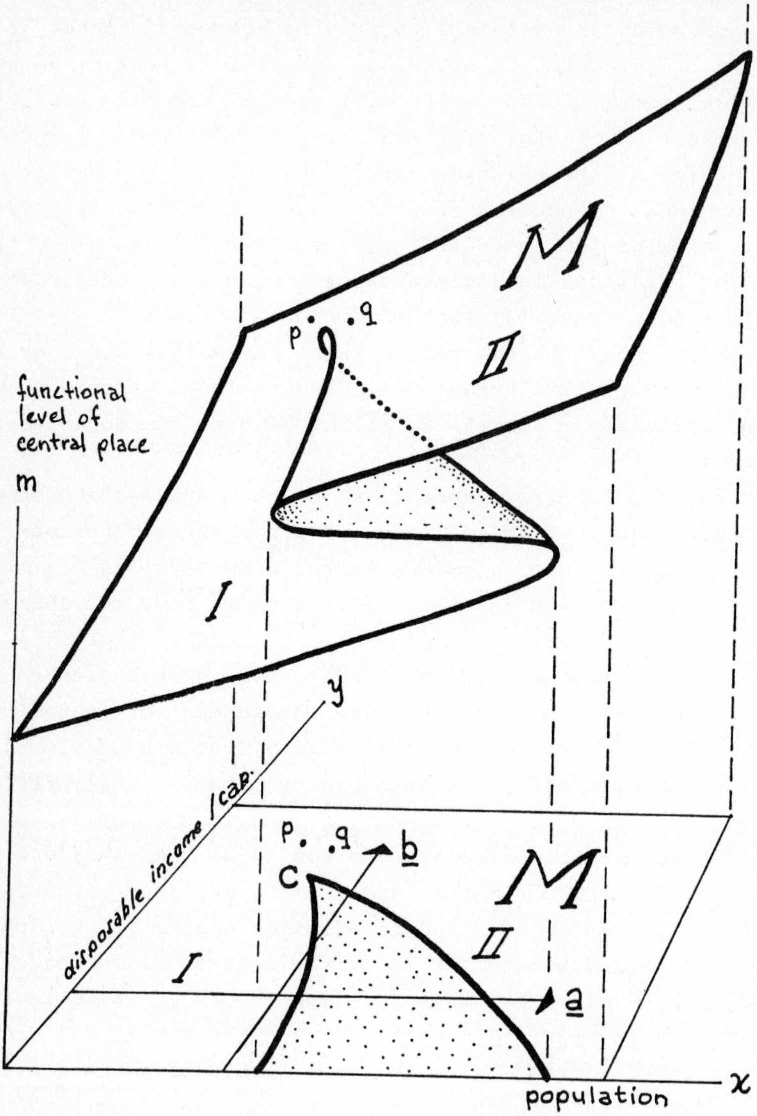

Figure 2. A Manifold for Central Place Catastrophes

functional level jumps dramatically from the lower sheet of M to the upper (the middle sheet shown in Figure 2 corresponds to relative minima and is of no interest here). The vector b shows the same qualitative result, and clearly various combinations of a and b will do the same provided such combinations pass through the x, y projection of the multi-sheeted part of M.

The hysteresis effect can be demonstrated by examining m for, say, fixed income and changing population. Let population increase along a as before; thus the cusp region is entered from I and no discontinuous output; the point then leaves I and enters region II with a positive jump in functional level. But then let population smoothly decrease (-a): the cusp is entered from II at the same point as before, and the point exits into I as before. The only difference is that this time the catastrophic jump downwards in functional level takes place when entering I and not II. Only an exit from the cusp region across a different boundary than the entry branch gives rise to catastrophic change. Thus the cusp catastrophe illustrates the theoretical prediction, and observed fact, that the threshold for (re-) appearance of a function is higher than for its disappearance. Note that this qualitatively nice behavior is obtained even with the highly restrictive and unrealisitic postulates of classical central place theory. More realistic models incorporating entrepreneurial inertia (lagged feedback plus conservative behavior in the face of uncertainty), non-zero entry costs, and substantial indivisibilities would only serve to accentuate the hysteresis effect.

The third basic feature, divergence, can be appreciated by examining the change in functional level from nearby initial points p and q as disposable income falls for a fixed population. The trajectory in M from p passes to the left of the cusp point C, and consequently m drops smoothly to levels on the lower sheet of M. On the other hand, the point q, which began with a population close to p, has a trajectory which takes it to the right of C; m is thus maintained, for a while at least, at "artificially" or "anomalously" high levels. The critical factor is that slow change of the same sort in real regional systems with similar initial conditions may lead to fundamentally different futures, depending on the location and orientation of cusp points. Moreover, one would expect these m-anomalies to be most glaring at low levels of population and income.

Property Prices and the Butterfly Catastrophe

The cusp catastrophe is probably useful in many other urban settings. Casual observation suggest that many of the lifestyle definition processes or our proliferating subcultures--processes noted for teenage gangs long before becoming part of the conventional wisdom about the post-industrial middle classes [2]--may exhibit the characterisitic non-Hamiltonian divergence of catastrophe theory, and may under special conditions display discontinuities and even hysteresis [5]. We discuss a more prosaic example, the purchase price of urban dwellings, not so much to exploit the cusp further but to use it as a vehicle to introduce a generalization which is perhaps the second-most-important elementary catastrophe for applied work, the so-called *butterfly* catastrophe.

Let r represent the real rate of change of housing prices in a particular urban market. In the first approximation, we assume that there are two types of buyers who are interested in this sort of property, and that the combined level of their activities in the property market dictates r. Call there buyers *consumers* and *speculators*. The former are interested in a wide range of attributes of the housing bundle and their demand is strongly price-elastic, especially in volatile or cyclical markets. Speculators, on the other hand, are overwhelmingly concerned with short-term (and often highly leveraged) capital gains. Since the two groups have fundamentally different objectives, time horizons, and price elasticities, they may reasonably be thought of as disjoint sets of investors. If D_c represents the demand for property by consumers and D_s the demand by speculators, then the global behavior of property prices may in this simple case be as depicted in Figure 3.

Increasing either D_c or D_s tends to increase r, but the key to catastrophic rises and falls lies with the speculators; changes in D_c for constant D_s cause only smooth changes in r. All of the features observed in the previous example--divergence, discontinuity, and hysteresis--are also present here. Moreover, in empirical applications there is frequently a relation between the location of the cusp point and the time constants of the system, with loci avoiding the multi-sheeted parts of M tending to be slower. In this example, suppose the process starts at O' in the D_c-D_s space. There are then two possiblities for passage through the cusp region and back to O', the paths OPQRO and OPQSO. The first corresponds to a spurt of speculative demand causing, after a short lag, a jump in prices from P to Q, followed by a profit-taking sell-off by speculators with only moderate increase in consumer demand, triggering a collapse of prices at R. This sort of process is

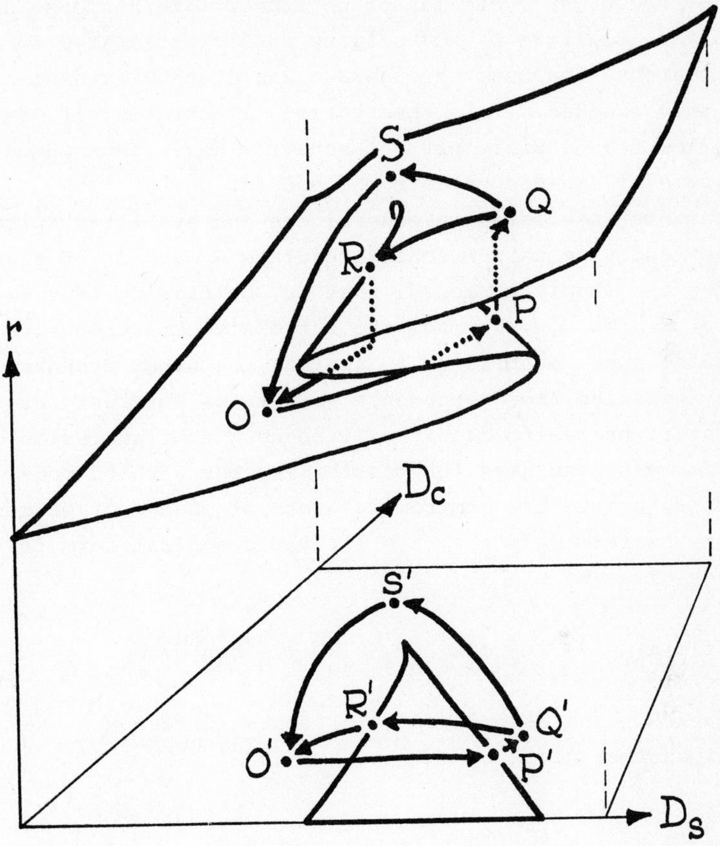

Figure 3. Catastrophe Manifold for Urban Proberty Prices

characteristic of the high-frequency components of r and is quite typical in speculative markets. The demand by consumers for market intervention is related to both the magnitude of r and the amplitude of these relatively short-term "boom-and-bust" cycles. Slowing the frequency of the OPQRO cycle may be an appropriate response under such conditions, if it allows D_c to build up sufficiently at Q to drive the return path around the cusp through S. Rapid and distressing falls in price are thus avoided. This observation illustrates, if crudely, the fast time-slow time ("silly putty") behavior divergence which is characteristic of dynamic catastrophe models.

Governments interested in orderliness and stability in housing markets--low and viscous r--usually regulate D_c and D_s by tightening or loosening the supply of money, that is, by raising or lowering interest rates. We now show how the butterfly catastrophe, a generalization of the cusp, enables us to upgrade the urban property price example by including time dependence as well as interest rate changes in the catastrophe manifold. It will be seen that inclusion of these important factors generates the possibility for a third mode of stable behavior of r, a type of "compromise" rate of change of prices.

For the butterfly (k = 4, n = 1), the canonical form for the potential is given by

$$f(c,x) = \frac{x^6}{6} + \frac{1}{4} c_1 x^4 + \frac{1}{3} c_2 x^3 + \frac{1}{2} c_3 x^2 + c_4 x \quad ,$$

where $c \varepsilon R^4$, $x \varepsilon R$. The associated catastrophe surface M is the four-dimensional surface given by

$$\frac{\partial f}{\partial x} = x^5 + c_1 x^3 + c_2 x^2 + c_3 x + c_4 = 0 \quad .$$

The surface $M \subset R^5$ and the bifucation set $\beta \subset R^4$. We draw two-dimensional sections of β to show how it generalizes the cusp. When the *butterfly factor* $c_1 > 0$, the x^4 term swamps the x^6 term and we obtain the cusp. The effect of the *bias factor* c_2 is merely to bias the position of the cusp. When the butterfly factor $c_1 < 0$, then the x^4 term conflicts with the x^6 term and causes the cusp to bifurcate into three cusps enclosing a pocket. This pocket represents the emergence of a compromise behavior midway between the two extremes represented by the upper and lower surfaces of the cusp.

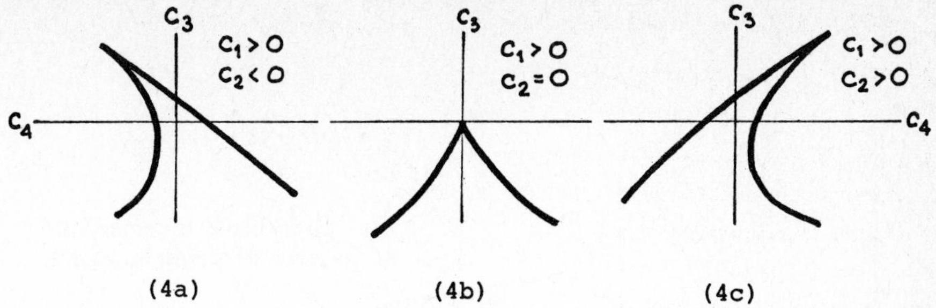

To employ the butterfly catastrophe in the urban property price setting, we let the bias factor represent the interest rate i, while the butterfly factor is the negative of time, -t. Thus normalizing the nominal interest rate at i = 0, we have the picture of Figure 5.

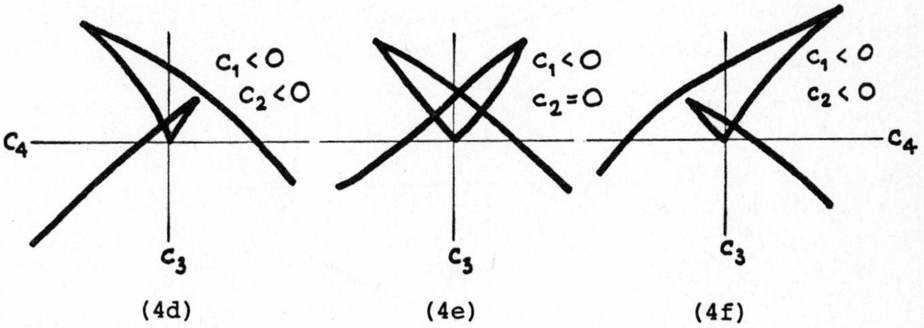

Figure 4. <u>Two-Dimensional Sections of the Butterfly Catastrophe</u>

Figure 5 shows that an increase of speculative demand coupled with a sufficiently high consumer demand will lead to a control space trajectory intersecting the interior pocket of intermediate r, rather than resulting in a dramatic jump to the upper or lower surfaces of M^2. As the previous diagrams showed, manipulation of the interest rate i influences both the size and position of this pocket of intermediate behavior, thereby in theory preventing catastrophic jumps or drops in property price rates--but at a price in secular inflation.

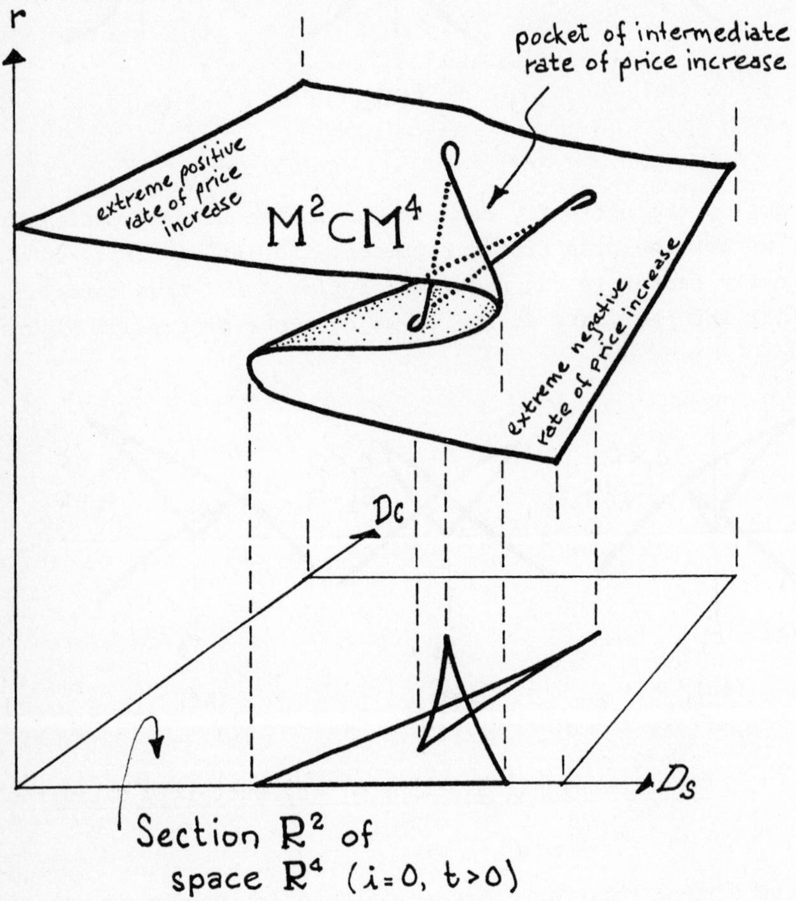

Figure 5. The Butterfly Catastrophe

Conclusions

In this note we have presented some speculation on roles for catastrophe theory in urban studies. While the simple examples provided indicate that the mathematical theory may have something relevant to say about urban processes, it is clear that much work remains before these notions can be made into operational tools for predictive and prescriptive action. In particular, to make these ideas useful in actual decision-making contexts, the qualitative analysis given here must be made quantitative. This means the isolation cf the particular surface, or family of equivalent surfaces, pertinent to the process under study. To accomplish this task, it will be necessary to use experimental data to isolate the appropriate range of parameters which appear in the canonical potential functions. We hope to examine this circle of ideas in future work.

Literature Cited

[1] AMSON, J. "Equilibrium Models of Cities: 1 - An Axiomatic Theory," *Environment and Planning*, 4 (1972), 429-44.

[2] BELL, D. *The Coming of Post-Industrial Society: A Venture in Social Forecasting*, London: Heinemann, 1974.

[3] DACEY, M.F. "The Geometry of Central Place Theory," *Geografiska Annaler* 47B:2 (1965), 111-24.

[4] JONES, D.D. "The Application of Catastrophe Theory to Biological Systems," paper presented at Systems Ecological Conference, Logan, Utah, 20-23 February 1975.

[5] KAHN, H. and A.J. WIENER, *The Year 2000*, New York: MacMillan, 1967.

[6] THOM, R. "Topological Models in Biology," *Topology*, 8 (1969), 313-35.

[7] THOM, R. *Stabilité Structurelle et Morphogenèse*, Reading, Massachusetts: Addison-Wesley, 1972.

[8] WASSERMAN, G. *Stability of Unfoldings, Springer Lecture Notes in Math*, vol. 393, New York: Springer-Verlag, 1974.

[9] WOODSTOCK, A.E.R. and T. POSTON, *A Geometrical Study of the Elementary Catastrophes, Springer Lecture Notes in Math*, vol. 373, New York: Springer-Verlag, 1974.

[10] ZEEMAN, E.C. "Differential Equations for the Heartbeat and Nerve Impulse," in C. WADDINGTON, ed., *Towards a Theoretical Biology*, 4, Edinburgh University Press, 1972.

[11] ZEEMAN, E.C. "Applications of Catastrophe Theory," Mathematics Institute, University of Warwick, March, 1973.

MODELLING AND SIMULATION OF THE MESOSCALE MOSAIC STRUCTURE OF THE LOWER MARINE TROPHIC LEVELS

Daniel M. DUBOIS
University of Liège
Dept. of Applied Statistics
Institute of Mathematics
Avenue des Tilleuls, 15
B-4000 LIEGE (Belgium)

ABSTRACT

Marine ecology deals with biological and chemical processes in interaction with their aquatic environment. The possibility of using more of the products of the sea as human food has created at present a keen interest in the study of marine plankton. It is of importance to understand the production of phytoplankton and the predator-prey relationships between phyto- and zooplankton, the path by which the organic matter produced finally reaches the fish.

In the sea, plankton populations are almost entirely at the mercy of water movement. In spite of this diffusive process, these populations display a spatio-temporal structure.

The spectral analysis of the spatial organization of phytoplankton populations exhibits two main classes of behaviour depending on the range of spatial scale. Below 5 km, the phytoplankton behaves as a passive scalar

i) from zero to 100 m, the spatial variability of phytoplankton is controlled by turbulence and its spectrum is similar to the spectrum of homogeneous and spatially isotropic turbulence according to Kolmogorov's theory,

ii) from 100 m to 5 km, the coherence between chlorophyll and temperature are high. Beyond 5 km and until 100 km, the phytoplankton dynamics in promoting patchiness, i.e. mesoscale spatial heterogeneity, dominates over that of the physical diffusive processes in eroding it.

A model is proposed to explain the mechanism of this mosaïc structure. The partial differential equations take into account advection, shear and eddy diffusivity and non-linear ecological interactions. The properties of the solutions of these equations are studied by simulation of simplified sub-models dealing with asymptotic behaviour of the ecological system. The horizontal structure is generated by local spatial instabilities. The most important characteristic is the disposition of the ecosystem to amplify microscopic excitations (fluctuations) to a macroscopic level leading to the emergence of new space and time patterns.

I. INTRODUCTION

The possibility of using more of the products of the sea as human food has created at present a keen interest in the study of marine plankton. The plankton is considered a potential source of human food. It is of importance to understand the production of phytoplankton and the relationship between phytoplankton and zooplankton, the path by which the organic matter produced finally reaches the fish.

Rather different views of the problems connected with marine plankton have been referred from time to time. Without in any way attempting to review the study of plankton as a whole we may here consider one particular problem very important for budget evaluations of primary and secondary production, the so-called patchiness effect. In the sea, plankton populations such as phytoplankton and herbivorous zooplankton are in a prey-predator relationship. Plankton populations are almost entirely at the mercy of water movement. In spite of the diffusive process, plankton populations display spatially heterogeneous patterns. This paper deals with physical and mathematical modeling of interaction of fluid flow with such biological and chemical processes.

As plankton can be considered as small organisms of identical size embedded in a turbulent flow [Pielou (1969)], their number is sufficientIy large so that only statistical properties can be possibly studied. The characteristic time of ecological response is of the order of

$$\omega^{-1} = (k_1\ k_3)^{-1/2}$$

where k_1 and k_3 are respectively the rates of natality-mortality of phytoplankton and herbivorous zooplankton. From experimental values, ond finds that the characteristic time is of the order of a few days.

Hence, if we average the evolution equations over a time which is short compared to the characteristic time of ecological response but still cover several tidal periods we smooth out the effects of oscillation and fluctuations of the sea without affecting significantly the process under study.

Let $\underline{U}$ be the horizontal component of the average velocity (residual currents), U_z its vertical component and C_i the average concentration of species i at position $\underline{r}$ and time t, respectively. The general equation of the distributions of species i can be written

$$\partial C_i/\partial t + \underline{U} \cdot \nabla C_i + U_z \, \partial C_i/\partial z = \langle f_i \rangle + \nabla.(\tilde{K} \nabla C_i) + \partial(\tilde{k} \, \partial C_i/\partial z) \quad (1)$$

where ∇ is the horizontal differential vector operator, i.e. $\nabla \equiv \underline{1}_x \partial/\partial x + \underline{1}_y \partial/\partial y$, $\langle f_i \rangle$ the time-averaged chemical and biological interactions, and $\tilde{K}$ and $\tilde{k}$ the turbulent diffusivity.

It may be noted that in marine systems, the horizontal and vertical spatio-temporal physical, chemical and biological properties are characterized by completely different scales. In considering the case of the Southern North Sea, it is generally sufficient to consider the average concentrations over the depth. A depth-averaged interactions model may be governed by equations derived from the three-dimensional ones (eq. 1) by depth integration.

The depth-averaged motion is described in terms of the mean velocity $\underline{u}$

$$\underline{u} = H^{-1} \int_{-h}^{\zeta} \underline{U} \, dz \quad (2)$$

where H is the total depth, i.e. : $H = h + \zeta$ where h is the depth and ζ the surface elevation.

One defines the mean vertical concentration

$$N_i = H^{-1} \int_{-h}^{\zeta} C_i dz \quad (3)$$

The local deviations around the means are given by

$$\underline{U} = \underline{u} + \underline{w} \quad (4)$$

$$C_i = N_i + c_i \quad (5)$$

the depth-averaged $\underline{w}$ and c_i being zero.

The depth-averaged equation is then written

$$\partial N_i/\partial t + \underline{u}.\nabla N_i = \langle F_i \rangle + \nabla.(K \nabla N_i) \qquad (6)$$

where K is a new dispersion coefficient. Indeed, for hydrodynamic models concerned with the circulation over extended regions of the sea, the combined effect of the turbulent and shear dispersions can be simply taken into account by adjusting the diffusion term in modifying the values of the dispersion coefficient.

It is rather remarkable to point out that the depth-averaged model (eq. 6) is quite similar to the precedent one (eq. 1) by just dropping the derivatives with respect to z in eq.1 (in appendix the demonstration is made). Moreover, in eq. 1 the divergence of the velocity vector is zero, i.e. $\nabla.\underline{U} + \partial U_z/\partial z = 0$ meanwhile for the depth-averaged velocity vector, one has $\nabla.(\underline{u}\,H) = 0$. Due to the fact that the depth H is a function of the considered region, $\nabla.\underline{u} \equiv - H^{-1}\underline{u}.\nabla H \neq 0$ which is not zero.

2. THE THREE SPATIAL SCALES OF PATCHINESS

a. The turbulent patchiness

At very small spatial scale (from zero to 100 m) the turbulent diffusivity is the main source of dispersion. In this case, plankton population behavesas a passive scalar and the spectrum of its spatial variability (controlled by turbulence) is similar to the spectrum of turbulence. The turbulent diffusivity depends on the horizontal scale of the phenomenon, i.e.

$$K \sim \ell^{4/3} \qquad (7)$$

Experimentally this conclusion was pointed out by Platt et al.(1975).

b. The shear effect patchiness

At small spatial scale (from 100 m to 5 km) the shear effect will be the main source of dispersion. But now, contrary to the preceding case the shear effect diffusivity does not depend on the horizontal scale and may be taken as a constant (Ronday 1974), i.e.

$$K \sim \text{constant} \qquad (8)$$

Here also plankton population behavesas a passive scalar but its spatial variability is not controlled by the shear effect coefficient, because it remains constant in the full spatial scale. In this case the spatial variability depends on the temperature fluctuations spectrum (see below the temperature dependance of ecological parameters in the model). This conclusion is also in agreement with Platt et al. (1975) experimental data : from 100 m to 5 km, they found high coherences between chlorophyll (i.e. phytoplankton concentration indicator) and temperature.

c. The eddy diffusivity patchiness

Beyond 5 km and until 100 km, eddy diffusivity is predominant. The diffusivity K may be expressed by (Joseph and Sendner, 1958)

$$K \sim P\ell \qquad (9)$$

where P is the diffusion velocity and ℓ the characteristic length of the horizontal variations. As plankton dynamics in promoting spatial heterogeneity dominates over that of the physical diffusive processes in eroding it, an optimal value of the diffusivity K is calculated in taking into account the fact that (i) an optimal numerical value of the diffusion velocity P is of the same order as the residual currents

$$P \sim \|\underline{u}\| \qquad (10)$$

and (ii) the characteristic length ℓ of the horizontal variations of plankton concentration is of the same order as the Dubois' (1975) critical spatial wavelength

$$\ell \sim 2\pi\ (2K/\omega)^{1/2} \qquad (11)$$

where ω^{-1} is the characteristic time of the ecological response. So, ecological interactions and dispersion are competitive and a "natural selection" by resonance of fluctuations due to advective currents (residual circulation) leads to space-time patterns.

The mechanism of this mesoscale patchiness is based on the fact that the spatio-temporal structures are generated by local spatial instabilities characterized by a critical wavelength λ_c meanwhile the whole ecosystem exhibits a global spatial stability which prevents it from destruction. In general, the same type of pattern appears quasi-periodically with a period $T = 2\pi/\omega$. The most important characteristic is the disposition of the ecosystem to amplify microscopic excitations (fluctuations) to a macroscopic level leading to the emergence of new space and time patterns. Moreover, the ecosystem behaves like a filter ; perturbations with a wavelength smaller than λ_c are smoothed out by the diffusive processes meanwhile perturbations of greater wavelength are amplified by the non-linear interactions. The primitive master equations (model II) showed that the physical mechanism of patchiness is characterized by a continuous generation of ecological waves.

One can refer to them as dissipative structures (Glansdorff, P. and Prigogine , 1971). These structures (ecological waves)are far from equilibrium and their maintenance requires a steady supply of energy. The production of entropy which corresponds to a degradation of the energy is compensated continually by an exterior input of energy under the form of light and nutrients (coefficient k_1). The earliest example of dissipative structure dealt with the chemical basis of morphogenesis (Turing, 1952).

A regular spatial distribution of structures can also be generated by a process of random structures initiation. Indeed, the process of structuration is initiated by these random fluctuations which are afterwards amplified by the activatory field, i.e. the prey population which behaves like an activator. With a time lag, a growing zone of inhibition is established by the predator population which behaves like an inhibitor. This spreading inhibitory field prevents new structures formation during a time corresponding to its refractory period. Activatory and inhibitory fields are transmitted by diffusion transport and the meeting of two active waves leads to their annihilation. A statistical mechanics of these expanding fields can be made to obtain more information on the mean number of structures by using methods as described by Glass et al, 1973 .

Finally, in view of pointing out some global information about this statistics of ecological waves, the concept of diversity can be used. Margalef, 1967, has introduced the Shannon-Weaver entropy H of the information content of a collection of species as an index of diversity. This formula is identical to the definition of entropy in statistical mechanics. Moreover entropy constitutes a criterion of stability for closed systems of particles around an equilibrium state, i.e. the Boltzmann H-theorem which states that at equilibrium entropy is maximum. When the system is slightly perturbed from its equilibrium state, entropy decreases of a quantity $\Delta H > 0$. In these conditions, entropy is a criterion of stability in the sence of Lyapunov (Zubov, 1964). But these conclusions are only available for closed systems and we know that ecological systems are open systems far from equilibrium maintained at a steady state through an input of energy flow (Morowitz, 1968). This steady state is no more characterized by a maximum of entropy. Nevertheless, a Lyapunov function D_0 can be deduced (Dubois, 1973) from the index of diversity in calculating the second variation of entropy around a reference state. For small fluctuations around the reference state, this function D_o looks like a weighted variance. We suggested to call such a function an index of fluctuations. Diversity, stability and structuration through fluctuations are narrowly related. Recently a model was presented which relates disturbance to pattern : "hypotheses concerning the relation between pattern and diversity translate immediately into relationships between disturbance and diversity"(Levin and Paine, 1974). We arrive at the same conclusion from the concept of index of fluctuations in a quite general framework.

3. MASTER EQUATIONS FOR PHYTO-ZOOPLANKTON PATCHINESS

Explicit expression of the interaction term $\langle F_i \rangle$ is given in the case of pray-predator plankton populations.

For the phytoplankton, one can write

$$\langle F_1 \rangle = k_1 N_1 - k_2' \left[1 - \exp \left(-\delta (N_1 - N_1') \right) \right] N_2 \qquad (12)$$

where N_1 and N_2 are respectively phyto-and zooplankton biomasses expressed in their organic carbon content per unit volume (mg C m^{-3}), k_1 the rate of growth of phytoplankton. The coefficient of N_2 is a modification (Parsons et al, 1967) of an expression due to Ivlev (1945) and represents the rate of ingestion per unit concentration of grazer at phytoplankton concentration, k_2' is the maximum rate of ingestion attainable by the zooplankters, δ is a constant defining the rate of change of ingestion with food concentration, and N_1' is the concentration of phytoplankton at which feed-food concentration, and N_1' is the concentration of phytoplankton at which feeding begins. The growth of phytoplankton is related to temperature, sunlight intensity and nutrient concentration. Averaging over the depth H and over time, k_1 can be written (O'Connor et al, 1973)

$$k_1 = K_1 T ef(K_e H)^{-1} \left(\exp(-\alpha_1) - \exp(-\alpha_o) \right) N/(K_N + N) \qquad (13)$$

where K_1 is the slope of the maximum growth rate versus temperature, T the temperature, e the base of the natural log, K_e the extinction coefficient, H the depth, f the fraction of daylight, N the nutrient concentration, K_N the half saturation constant for the nutrient N, $\alpha_1 = \alpha_o \exp(-K_e H)$ with $\alpha_o = I_{av}/I_s$ where I_{av} is the mean daily incident solar radiation and I_s the optimal light intensity. It may be noted that the extinction coefficient is an important component in the growth rate expression which is related to a number of physical and biological variables : turbidity due to the inorganic composition of the water and the self-shading of the growing phytoplankton. This last effect can be taken into account using the correlation developed by Riley (1963), i.e. $K_e = K'_e + 0.008N_1 + 0.054N_1^{2/3}$, where K'_e is the extinction coefficient without the phytoplankton-related extinction and N_1 is the phytoplankton chlorophyll *a* content (in mg m^{-3}).

For the herbivorous zooplankton, the interaction function $\langle F_2 \rangle$ is written

$$\langle F_2 \rangle = - k_3 N_2 + \beta k'_2 \left[1-\exp\left(-\delta(N_1-N'_1)\right)\right] N_2 \tag{14}$$

where k_3 is the rate of decay of zooplankton as a function of temperature and predation of the higher trophic levels, and β is the ratio of phytoplankton carbon ingested to zooplankton carbon produced (utilization coefficient). In first approximation k_3 can be expressed as a linear function of temperature, i.e. $k_3 = K'_3 T + k''_3$.

Substituting eqs. (10) and (12) in eq.(16) for $i = 1,2$, the master equations for phyto-zooplankton horizontal structuration are written

$$\partial N_1/\partial t + \underline{u}.\nabla N_1 = K_1 T ef(K_e H)^{-1}\left(\exp(-\alpha_1)-\exp(-\alpha_o)\right) N/(K_N+N)$$

$$- k'_2\left[1-\exp\left(-\delta(N_1-N'_1)\right)\right] N_2 + \nabla.(K \nabla N_1) \tag{15}$$

$$\partial N_2/\partial t + \underline{u}.\nabla N_2 = - (k'_3 T + k''_3) N_2$$

$$+ \beta k'_2\left[1-\exp\left(-\delta(N_1-N'_1)\right)\right] N_2 + \nabla.(K \nabla N_2) \tag{16}$$

These general master equations are quite original. Their properties can be pointed out in considering asymptotic solutions. For this, several simplified models can be deduced (from eqs. (15) and (16)) which exhibit most aspects of the spatial structuration mechanism of phyto- and zooplankton populations.

(i) *Model I :*

When the behaviour of phyto-and zooplankton populations are only considered on a short period of time, parameters like T, f and I_{av} do not change drastically. To take into account the variation of the extinction coefficient and nutrient concentration with the concentration of phytoplankton, a logistic law can be used to approximate the growth rate k_1 , i.e.

$$k_1 = k'_1(1-N_1/N''_1) \tag{17}$$

where N''_1 is the maximum concentration of phytoplankton which can be found in the sea. Obviously, N_1'' is large as compared to the mean concentration of phytoplankton.

With these assumptions, eqs. (15) and (16) are written

$$\partial N_1/\partial t + \underline{u}.\nabla N_1 = k_1'(1-N_1/N_1'')N_1 - k_2'\left[1-\exp\left(-\delta(N_1-N_1')\right)\right]N_2 + \nabla.(K\nabla N_1) \qquad (18)$$

$$\partial N_2/\partial t + \underline{u}.\nabla N_2 = -k_3N_2 + \beta k_2'\left[1-\exp\left(-\delta(N_1-N_1')\right)\right]N_2 + \nabla.(K\nabla N_2) \qquad (19)$$

(ii) Model II :

When the physical mechanism of patchiness is assumed working in the linear region of the grazing, the term $\exp\left(-\delta(N_1-N_1')\right)$ can be developed in series. Knowing that $N_1' < k_3/\beta k_2' \delta << N_1''$, eqs. (18) and (19) become

$$\partial N_1/\partial t + \underline{u}.\nabla N_1 = k_1N_1 - k_2N_1N_2 + \nabla.(K\nabla N_1) \qquad (20)$$

$$\partial N_2/\partial t + \underline{u}.\nabla N_2 = -k_3N_2 + \beta k_2 N_1N_2 + \nabla.(K\nabla N_2) \qquad (21)$$

where $k_2 = k_2'\delta$.

These equations exhibit a non-zero stationary solution uniformly distributed in space (with $\underline{u} = 0$)

$$N_{10} = k_3/\beta k_2 \qquad (22)$$

$$N_{20} = k_1/k_2 \qquad (23)$$

and we see that $N_1' < N_{10} << N_1''$. For small fluctuations of populations around (N_{10}, N_{20}), analytical solutions of eqs. (20) and (21) are given in the one-dimensional case (Dubois, 1975). The stationary spatial structuration is characterized by a wavelength given by

$$\lambda_c = 2\pi(2K/\omega)^{1/2} \qquad (24)$$

where $\omega = (k_1 k_3)^{1/2}$ is the frequency of the ecological response.

Eqs. (20) and (21) were simulated on computer in one and two spatial dimensions (Dubois, 1975). The basic mechanism of a spatial structuration of prey-predator was well exhibited. Three fundamental "laws" for the space and time behaviour of this structuration were deduced :

a) the creation of a prey-predator wave,
b) the propagation of this wave with constant intensity and velocity,
c) the annihilation of two meeting waves.

A remarkable property is that this wave looks like an all-or-none response (active wave), the prey behaving like an activator and the predator like an inhibitor (with a refractory period during which the generation of a new wave cannot occur). In two dimensions, the wave exhibits a ring structure the radius of which increases with time.

Taking into account the transport by advection due to the residual circulation, eqs. (20) and (21) were integrated on computer to simulate the spatial structuration of a patch of prey-predator plankton populations in the Southern Bight of the North Sea (Dubois and Adam, 1975). During its drift in the Southern Bight, the horizontal structuration of the patch is given by a growing circular disc which loses its centre (ring structure) and breaks into segments. Due to advection, the highest densities lie in a series of areas surrounding the empty region. In other words, the initial patch transforms into a series of patches surrounding an empty region (initial patch). The same succession of events was observed experimentally in following patches during a few weeks (Wyatt, 1973).

(iii) Model III :

When the grazing is saturated, $\exp\left(-\delta(N_1-N_1')\right)$ drops in eqs.(18) and (19). One obtains

$$\partial N_1/\partial t + \underline{u}.\nabla N_1 = k_1'N_1(1-N_1/N_1'') - k_2'N_2 + \nabla.(K\nabla N_1) \qquad (25)$$

$$\partial N_2/\partial t + \underline{u}.\nabla N_2 = (-k_3 + \beta k_2')N_2 + \nabla.(K\nabla N_2) \qquad (26)$$

Eq.(26) shows that the zooplankton is no more feedbacking with the phytoplankton and its behaviour is essentially due to a balance between its decay rate and grazing, i.e. $(-k_3+\beta k_2')$. The temperature and predation on zooplankton can become command parameters for the survival of plankton populations. When k_3 is greater than $\beta k_2'$, the zooplankton population decreases and as a consequence the quantity of phytoplankton reaches its saturation point, N_1''. One can then assist to the phenomenon of "red tide" for patches where these dramatic conditions hold. When k_3 is smaller than $\beta k_2'$, the zooplankton population increases and eq. (25) shows that the phytoplankton population will decrease leading to a non-saturated grazing. In this case, zooplankton controls phytoplankton behaviour. The spatial pattern of the growth of zooplankton is characterized by a critical length L_c deduced from a study of the stability of eq. (26) (The same type of equation was considered by Kierstead et al (1953), but for phytoplankton), i.e.

$$L_c = \pi\left(K/(-k_3 + \beta k_2')\right)^{1/2} \qquad (27)$$

ACKNOWLEDGEMENTS

This paper was prepared at the Fisheries and Marine Service, Marine Ecology Laboratory, Bedford Institute of Oceanography, Dartmouth, N.S. (Canada). The author is grateful to the "Fonds National de la Recherche Scientifique" for the financial support of his stay in Canada. The author should like to thank Dr. F. Ronday for interesting discussions.

REFERENCES

Dubois D.M. (1973). Aspect mathématique de l'invariant en cybernétique: applications en écologie et en biologie. Cybernética (Namur). 16, 161.

Dubois D.M. (1975). Hydrodynamic aspects in environmental and ecological enhancement. Proceedings of the Second World Congress on Water Resources, New Delhi, India (in press). Also : the influence of the quality of water on ecological systems. IFIP Working Conference on Modeling and Simulation of Water Resources Systems, Ghent, Publ. by North Holland, Amsterdam, ed. by G.C. Vansteenkiste, pp. 535-543.

Dubois D.M. (1975). A model of patchiness for prey-predator plankton populations. Ecological Modeling 1 : 67-80.

Dubois D.M. (1975)."Random fluctuations and spatio-temporal structuration of biological populations:simulation of the horizontal distribution of plankton in the North Sea" (in French). Ph. D. thesis, University of Liège, 1974-75, (Belgium).

Dubois D.M. and Y. Adam (1975). Spatial structuration of diffusive prey-predator biological populations : simulation of the horizontal distribution of plankton in the North Sea. Proc. of the 2nd IFIP Working Conference on Biosystems Simulation in Water Resources and Waste Problems, Ghent, 3/5 sept. 1975, Publ. by North Holland, Amsterdam, ed. by G.C. Vansteenkiste, 13 p. (in press).

Glansdorff P. and I. Prigogine (1971). Thermodynamics of structure, stability and fluctuations, Wiley, Interscience, New York.

Glass L. (1973). Stochastic generation of regular distributions. Science, 180, 1061-1063. Also : Armstrong R.A., Jackson J.J. and Glass L. (1974). Dynamics of expanding inhibitory fields. Science, 183, 444-446.

Ivlev V.S. (1945). The biological productivity of waters. Usp. Sovrem. Biol., 19, (1), 88-120.

Joseph J. and H. Sendner (1958). Über die horizontale Diffusion in Meere. Dtsch. Hydrogr. Z., 11, 49-77.

Kierstead H. and L.B. Slobodkin (1953). The size of water masses containing plankton blooms. J. of Marine Research, XII, 1, p. 141.

Levin S.A. and R.T. Paine (1974). Disturbance, patch formation, and community structure. Proc. Nat. Acad. Sci. USA, 74(7), 2744-2747.

Margalef R. (1967). Some concepts relative to the organization of plankton. Oceanogr. Mar. Biol. Ann. Rev., 5, 257-289.

Morowitz H. (1968). Energy flow in biology, Academic Press.

O'Connor D.J., D.M. DiToro, J.L. Mancini (1973). Mathematical model of phytoplankton population dynamics in the Sacramento San Joaquin Bay Delta. Working paper. Modeling of Marine Systems. Ofir, Portugal, 4th to 8th June.

Parsons T.R., R.J. LeBrasseur and J.D. Fulton (1967). Some observations on the dependence of zooplankton grazing on cell size and concentration of phytoplankton blooms. J. Oceanogr. Soc. Japan, 23 (1), 10-17.

Pielou E.C. (1969). An introduction to mathematical ecology. Wiley, New-York.

Platt T. and K.L. Denman (1975). Spectral analysis in ecology. Ann. Rev. of Ecol. and Syst., 6.

Ronday F.C. (1974). Influence du cisaillement des courants sur l'anisotropie des coefficients de diffusion - dispersion. Bull. Soc. Roy. Sci. Liège, n° 11-12, pp. 609-624.

Ronday F.C. (1975). Modèles de circulation hydrodynamique en Mer du Nord. Ph. D. Dissertation, Liège Univ. , 180 p. (in press).

Riley G.A. (1963). On the theory of food chain relations in the sea. In "The Sea" 2 Ed. by M.N. Hill, N.Y., Interscience Publ., 438-63.

Turing A.M. (1952). The chemical basis of morphogenesis. Proc. Roy. Soc. Lond. B 237: 37-72.

Wyatt T. (1973). The biology of Oikopleura dioica and Fritillaria borealis in the Southern Bight, Marine Biology, 22, 137.

Zubov V.I. (1964). Methods of A.M. Lyapunov and their application. Noordhoff-Groningen. The Netherlands.

OPTIMISATION ET PLANIFICATION
DES RESEAUX DE TELECOMMUNICATIONS

M. MINOUX

Centre National d'Etudes
des Télécommunications
30-40 R. du Général Leclerc,
92131 ISSY (FRANCE)

ABSTRACT: The problem of minimum cost extension of an existing communication network, over a given time period $[0,T]$, is stated and formulated. A two phase solution method is then described, in which: a) an optimal long-range configuration is sought, assuming static routing all over the period $[0,T]$; b) the optimal dynamic routing problem is solved by relaxing the fixed routing assumption, and taking into account the results obtained in phase a).

I- INTRODUCTION

Le problème central en matière de planification de réseaux de Télécommunications peut se résumer de la façon suivante: déterminer une politique optimale d'investissements (au sens du moindre coût actualisé) sur une période donnée $[0,T]$, permettant de répondre à une demande en trafic centre à centre croissante au cours du temps.

La connaissance des règles d'acheminement du trafic permet, pour une valeur moyenne souhaitée de la qualité de service, de convertir la demande en trafic en une demande en circuits de transmission (cf. [1], [4]). Cette demande $d_{ij}(t)$, définie pour chaque couple (i,j) de centres (elle peut être nulle pour certains couples) et pour chaque instant $t=0,1,..T$

représente le nombre total de circuits de transmission devant être en service à l'instant t entre i et j .

Satisfaire la demande $d_{ij}(t)$ suppose:

a) l'installation de matériels de commutation et de modulation en quantité suffisante dans les centres extrémités i et j ,

b) l'installation de matériels de transmission de capacités suffisantes sur un ou plusieurs itinéraires (routages) reliant physiquement i et j . (câbles coaxiaux, faisceaux hertziens, guides d'ondes .... avec leurs supports: tranchées, tours hertziennes, etc...)

c) l'installation de materiel de transfert de circuits en chacun des centres intermédiaires de ces itinéraires (routages).

On voit immédiatement que, pourvu qu'il n'y ait pas création de nouveaux centres, le problème se décompose en deux problèmes indépendants:

(P1): détermination d'une politique optimale d'investissements en matériels de commutation et de modulation dans chaque centre.

(P2): détermination d'une politique optimale d'investissements en matériels de transmission et de transfert sur l'ensemble des artères et des centres.

En effet, les investissements de commutation et de modulation restent toujours les mêmes, quelle que soit la structure du réseau de transmission. (NB: pour les réseaux téléphoniques, une restriction doit être faite lorsqu'on envisage l'introduction de nouvelles techniques de transmission et de commutation non compatibles avec les anciennes. C'est le cas p. ex. de la transmission numérique et de la commutation temporelle).

La suite de cet article sera consacrée a la résolution de (P2). Il s'agit essentiellement d'apporter une réponse aux trois questions suivantes:

(Q1): où investir? (détermination de la structure optimale du graphe des extensions).

(Q2): quoi investir? (parmi tous les matériels de transmission utilisables, quels sont ceux qui, sur chaque artère, permettent de répondre à la demande de la façon la plus économique?).

(Q3): quand investir? (détermination des dates optimales des nouveaux investissements -infrastructures et extensions sur chaque artère du réseau).

Les problèmes de taille réelle (une centaine de centres, plusieurs centaines d'artères) ne pouvant être résolus de façon exacte (il s'agit de programmes en nombres entiers comportant des dizaines de milliers de variables entières) la méthode de résolution adoptée se décompose en deux phases:

PHASE 1: (planification à long terme)
Réponse à (Q1) et à (Q2). En supposant que le routage des circuits est fixe dans le temps, le problème dynamique est ramené à un problème statique de multiflot à coût minimal, avec fonctions de coût concaves (cf. références [7], [12], [14]).

PHASE 2: (planification à court et moyen termes)
Réponse à la question (Q3). On résout le problème dynamique (datation des investissements) compte tenu des résultats obtenus dans la PHASE 1 (cf. [8])

Nous commencerons par préciser les données de base indispensables à la résolution du problème (P2).

II- LES DONNEES DE BASE DU PROBLEME

1) Le réseau étudié est représenté par un graphe non-orienté $G=[X,U]$ où:
- $X= 1,2,\ldots N$ est l'ensemble des noeuds correspondant aux centres de commutation, de modulation et de transit.
- $U \subset X^2$ est l'ensemble des arêtes (i,j) correspondant aux artères de transmission, soit existantes, soit susceptibles d'être crées.

2) L'intervalle de temps $[0,T]$ (période d'étude) est découpé en T intervalles de durée égale à l'unité (généralement: une année).

3) A chaque instant t, le graphe G est parcouru par $K=\frac{N(N-1)}{2}$ flots indépendants, notés $\varphi_{ij}(t)$, pour $i=1,\ldots N$ $j=1,\ldots N$ et $i<j$. Chaque flot $\varphi_{ij}(t)$ a pour extrémités i et j, et sa valeur est une donnée imposée: $d_{ij}(t)$. On supposera en outre que les $d_{ij}(t)$ sont des nombres entiers vérifiant: $d_{ij}(0) \leq d_{ij}(1) \leq \ldots \leq d_{ij}(T)$, ($\forall i=1,\ldots N$ $j=1,\ldots N$ et $i<j$).

4) Par ailleurs, on donne la liste des différents systèmes de transmission susceptibles d'être installés sur les artères du réseau, avec leurs capacités et leurs coûts. Pour chaque système $s=1,2,\ldots S$, ces coûts dépendent de la longueur l de l'artère considérée, et se décomposent en:

- un coût d'infrastructure (élevé) I(s).

- un coût d'extension E(s) (correspondant à l'équipement d'un canal de transmission supplémentaire)

On note $\nu(s)$ le nombre d'extensions possibles du système s (nombre total de canaux de transmission) et Q(s) la capacité (en nombre de circuits) d'une extension (d'un canal). La capacité totale du système s est donc: $\nu(s).Q(s)$.

REMARQUE: pour différents systèmes utilisant la même technique (technique Hertzienne p.ex.) le coût d'infrastructure I(s), qui est le plus important, ne croît que lentement avec la capacité maximale du système ($\nu(s).Q(s)$); il en résulte que le coût moyen d'un circuit décroit avec la capacité totale installée. Ce phénomène est connu sous le nom d'économie d'échelle (cf. § III ci-dessous). La décroissance du coût moyen suit la loi, dite "des volumes économiques" (cf. [2], [9]):

$$\frac{I(s)+\nu(s).E(s)}{\nu(s).Q(s)} = B\left[\nu(s).Q(s)\right]^{-b}$$

où b est un paramètre généralement voisin de 0.5 .

Cette loi, effectivement valable pour la plupart des matériels de transmission connus, ne doit pas être extrapolée hâtivement dans le domaine des fortes capacités, où les systèmes de transmission correspondants ne sont pas bien connus.

5) Les coûts de transfert en un noeud quelconque $i \in X$, peuvent être considérés comme des fonctions linéaires du nombre de circuits transférés. Soit f le coût de transfert d'un circuit. Pour en tenir compte, il suffit de les intégrer aux coûts d'extension. Ainsi pour un système s, on prendra les nouveaux coûts d'extension: $E'(s)=E(s)+f.Q(s)$.

6) L'état initial du réseau (à l'année t=0) est connu par la donnée, pour chaque artère $u=(i,j) \in U$, de: la capacité résiduelle disponible (c.a.d. installée mais non encore utilisée) à l'année 0 ; le numéro du dernier système installé sur l'artère u.

7) On notera τ le taux d'actualisation.

III- PROGRAMMATION A LONG TERME

On étudie l'évolution du réseau sur la période $[0,T]$. Les routages des flots antérieurs à l'année 0 (origine de l'étude), ainsi que l'organisation du réseau existant, ne sont pas remis en question. Autrement dit, on s'intéresse simplement au routage des accroissements de demande

$d_{ij}(t)-d_{ij}(0)$ $(t=1,\ldots T)$. Les capacités résiduelles des systèmes existants, mais non encore saturés à l'année 0, sont évidemment utilisées.

1) Les hypothèses

L'hypothèse fondamentale du modèle à long terme est:

(H1): Les routages sont déterminés une fois pour toutes à l'année 0, et invariants dans le temps.

(H1) n'est pas très restrictive en pratique: on constate, en effet, que les routages s'écartent en moyenne assez peu des plus courts chemins géographiques.

Le problème dynamique se ramène ainsi à un problème statique: $\forall i,j$ $(i<j)$, trouver pour tous les flots $\varphi_{ij}(t)$ un routage conduisant à un coût actualisé d'extension minimum.

En plus de l'hypothèse (H1), nous supposerons une certaine homogèneité dans la croissance des fonctions $d_{ij}(t)$:

(H2): Les vitesses de croissance $v_{ij}(t)=d_{ij}(t+1)-d_{ij}(t)$ sont toutes de la forme:

$$v_{ij}(t)=v_{ij}(0).g(t)$$

où $g(t)$ est une fonction (positive) du temps, définie $\forall t=1,\ldots T$.

(Autrement dit, les vitesses de croissance des différents flots peuvent être différentes, mais la loi de variation de ces vitesses est supposée la même pour tous les flots).

Pour rechercher, avec les hypothèses (H1) et (H2), un ensemble de routages optimal, il faut avant tout savoir calculer le coût actualisé total de développement du réseau pour un ensemble de routages donné. Soit un routage défini, pour chaque couple (i,j), par la donnée d'une chaîne L_{ij} reliant i et j dans G. Alors, la vitesse de croissance de l'artère $u \in U$ est, à chaque instant $t=1,\ldots T$:

$y_u.g(t)$ où: $y_u = \sum v_{ij}(0)$ (somme sur tous les i,j t.q. $u \in L_{ij}$)

est la vitesse de croissance initiale de l'artère u (en nombre de circuits supplémentaires par an).

(N.B.: ce qui précède se généralise immédiatement au cas où plusieurs chaînes L^1_{ij} , L^2_{ij} ,.... sont utilisées pour le routage des circuits entre i et j)

La charge de l'artère u (nombre de circuits supplémentaires par rapport à l'année 0) est alors définie à chaque instant par:

$$Y_u(t) = y_u.\sum_{j=0}^{t-1} g(j)$$

Ainsi, l'évolution des besoins futurs sur l'artère u, est caractérisée par la donnée d'un seul paramètre y_u.

Le problème se décompose donc, artère par artère: étant donnée la vitesse de croissance initiale y_u, il s'agit de déterminer une politique d'investissements de coût actualisé minimum sur la période $[0,T]$. On peut alors envisager plusieurs hypothèses sur la fonction g(t).

2) Vitesse de croissance constante (réseau stationnaire).

Dans ce cas on a: $g(t)=1 \quad \forall t$.

Une politique optimale a long terme est alors nécessairement stationnaire, c.a.d. consiste en la répétition indéfinie du même système $s^*(y_u)$. Pour trouver $s^*(y_u)$, il suffit de comparer entre eux les différents systèmes sur une période de même durée.

Pour un système s quelconque, on montre que le coût actualisé de développement sur $[0,t_\circ]$ est:

$$C(s,y_u) = \left[\frac{I(s)}{1-\rho^{\nu(s)}} + \frac{E(s)}{1-\rho}\right]\left[1 - \frac{1}{(1+\tau)^{t_\circ}}\right]$$

avec: $\rho = (1+\tau)^{-\frac{\Omega(s)}{y_u}}$

Quand $t_\circ \to +\infty$, $C(s,y_u)$ tend vers le "coût à l'infini":

$$C_\infty(s,y_u) = \frac{I(s)}{1-\rho^{\nu(s)}} + \frac{E(s)}{1-\rho}$$

Pour y_u donné, le meilleur système est celui qui vérifie:

$$C^*(y_u) = C_\infty(s^*,y_u) = \underset{s=1,..S}{\text{Min.}} \left\{ C_\infty(s,y_u) \right\}$$

et le coût actualisé de développement optimal sur la période $[0,T]$ est:

$$\Phi_u(y_u) = C^*(y_u) \cdot \left[1 - \frac{1}{(1+\tau)^T}\right]$$

Ainsi (à une homothétie près) la courbe $\Phi_u(y_u)$ est l'enveloppe inférieure de la famille de courbes $C_\infty(s,y_u)$, s=1,...S.

Chaque courbe $C_\infty(s,y_u)$ a pour ordonnée à l'origine: $I(s) + E(s)$, (qui représente le coût de premier investissement), et admet comme asymptote la droite de pente: $\frac{1}{\tau}\left[\frac{I(s)}{\nu(s).\Omega(s)} + \frac{E(s)}{\Omega(s)}\right]$ passant par l'origine.

En fait, dans l'intervalle de validité de chaque système (ensemble des y tels que: $C_\infty(s,y) = C^*(y)$), chaque courbe peut être assimilée à une droite, et par suite la courbe $\Phi_u(y_u)$ peut être considérée comme l'enveloppe inférieure d'une famille finie de droites.

Si la famille des systèmes s=1,...S satisfait la loi "des volumes économiques" (cf. § II-4), alors on peut montrer que, pour une vitesse de croissance initiale y, le meilleur système à employer est celui pour lequel la durée de remplissage: $x = \frac{\nu(s).Q(s)}{y}$ vérifie:

$$(1 + \tau)^x = 1 + \frac{x.\tau}{1 - b} \quad \text{(x ne dépend donc que de } \tau \text{ et de b).}$$

3) Vitesse de croissance variable.

Nous envisagerons le cas simple où g(t) est de la forme:

$$g(t) = (1 + \alpha)^t$$

($\alpha > 0$ correspond à un réseau en expansion; $\alpha < 0$ correspond à une hypothèse de saturation de la demande).

Notons $\gamma(y)$ le coût d'installation d'un circuit supplémentaire lorsque la vitesse de croissance de l'artère est y. On peut établir et vérifier expérimentalement (cf. [9]) que $\gamma(y)$ suit la loi des "volumes économiques":

$$\gamma(y) = K_1 . y^{-b} \qquad \text{.... (1)}$$

Ceci permet de calculer simplement le coût actualisé de développement de l'artère u sur la période [0,T]. En effet:

$$\Phi_u(y_u) = \sum_{t=0}^{T-1} \frac{y.\gamma(y)}{(1+\tau)^t} = y_u . \gamma(y_u) . \frac{1 - \rho^T}{1 - \rho}$$

avec: $\rho = \frac{(1+\alpha)^{1-b}}{1 + \tau}$, et par suite:

$$\Phi_u(y_u) = K_1 . (y_u)^{1-b} . \frac{1 - \rho^T}{1 - \rho}$$

Pour les grandes valeurs de y, $\gamma(y)$ ne tend pas vers 0, mais vers le coût moyen K_2 du système de plus grosse capacité. On a alors:

$$\Phi_u(y_u) = K_1 . (y_u)^{1-b} . \frac{1 - \rho^T}{1 - \rho} + K_2 . y_u . \sum_{t=0}^{T-1} \left(\frac{1 + \alpha}{1 + \tau}\right)^t$$

Dans les deux cas, la fonction Φ_u est une fonction concave de y_u.

REMARQUE:

Dans les calculs précédents, il est facile de tenir compte des capacités résiduelles disponibles sur l'artère u à l'année 0. Supposons que le système existant se sature à l'année $t_1 > 0$, et soit $H(y_u)$ le coût actualisé d'extension jusqu'à l'année t_1. En régime de croissance linéaire, par exemple, on aurait:

$$\Phi_u(y_u) = H(y_u) + \frac{1}{(1+\tau)^{t_1}} C^*(y_u) . \left[1 - \frac{1}{(1+\tau)^{T-t_1}} \right]$$

4) Résolution du problème à long terme.

Quelles que soient les hypothèses de croissance retenues, le problème à long terme se ramène à un problème de multiflot de valeur fixée et de coût minimum. Pour chaque artère $u \in U$ du réseau, le coût actualisé de développement sur la période $[0,T]$ est une fonction $\Phi_u(y_u)$ du paramètre y_u (vitesse de croissance initiale de l'artère).

Dans tous les cas, les fonctions $\Phi_u(y_u)$ sont:

- monotones non décroissantes (l'installation de toute capacité supplémentaire est coûteuse);
- concaves (le coût marginal d'un circuit supplémentaire décroît avec la capacité installée).

Avec ces propriétés, il est facile de démontrer qu'un routage optimal est nécessairement un <u>uniroutage</u> (chaque flot φ_{ij} s'écoule sur un seul itinéraire). De nombreux travaux ont été consacrés à ce sujet: Dans [12], B. YAGED a proposé une méthode itérative (linéarisations successives) dans laquelle on recherche à chaque étape un routage optimal au sens des coûts marginaux (dérivées des fonctions Φ_u) relatifs à la solution courante. Dans [14], ZADEH montre que le critère du coût marginal est peu approprié dans le cas où les fonctions Φ_u présentent une concavité ou un cout fixe importants, et suggère un certain nombre de critères permettant d'améliorer localement une solution.

Dans [6] et [7], on trouvera un algorithme exact (de type "Branch and Bound") pour le cas particulier des fonctions de coût linéaires avec coût fixe (il ne s'applique malheureusement qu'aux réseaux de faibles dimensions: $N \simeq 12$).
On y trouvera également un certain nombre de méthodes heuristiques (recherche arborescente "profondeur d'abord") pour le cas général des fonctions de coût non linéaires quelconques; ces méthodes semblent bien adaptées au problème, et conduisent le plus souvent à de très bonnes solutions approchées. Elles ont en outre l'avantage de pouvoir s'appliquer à des problèmes de grandes dimension (N = 100 à 200 noeuds).

IV- PROGRAMMATION A COURT ET A MOYEN TERME.

La résolution du problème à long terme a permis de déterminer:

- la structure du graphe optimal des extensions $G^* = [X,U^*]$ par la liste de ses artères $U^* \subset U$.

- pour chaque artère u $\in U^*$, une séquence d'investissements Σ_u (optimale avec la contrainte du routage fixe dans le temps)

Chaque séquence Σ_u est définie par:
P(u) = le nombre d'investissements prévus sur l'artère u $\in U^*$
et, pour p = 1,....P(u) ,
J(u,p) = le coût total des p premiers investissements,
K(u,p) = la capacité totale installée après le $p^{\text{ième}}$ investissement.

Dans le modèle a moyen terme, ces résultats sont considérés comme des données de base, c'est à dire que l'on ne remettra en cause sur chaque artère u $\in U^*$, ni la nature ni l'ordre des investissements de la séquence Σ_u , mais uniquement les dates de leur réalisation.

1) Définition d'un échéancier d'investissements sur $[0,T]$.

Toute solution du problème (P2) sur la période $[0,T]$ peut être décrite par un échéancier d'investissements $\mathcal{E}$ c'est à dire par la donnée d'un tableau F(u,t) défini $\forall$ u $\in U^*$ et $\forall$ t = 0,1,.... T-1 . Par définition F(u,t) est le numéro du dernier investissement de la séquence Σ_u réalisé à l'année t. Ainsi, les investissements réalisés à l'année t sont tous ceux dont le numéro est compris entre F(u,t-1) + 1 et F(u,t) . (Par convention F(u,-1) = 0).

Suivant ces notations, le coût actualisé de l'échéancier $\mathcal{E}$ est:

$$\sum_{u \in U^*} \sum_{t=0}^{T-1} \frac{J(u,F(u,t)) - J(u,F(u,t-1))}{(1 + \tau)^t}$$

Le programme à long terme fournit un échéancier $\mathcal{E}^\circ = \{F^\circ(u,t)\}$ qui a la particularité d'être optimal lorsque le routage est fixe dans le temps. En abandonnant maintenant l'hypothèse du routage fixe, et en utilisant d'autre part la possibilité de diversifier les routages, certains investissements vont pouvoir être soit retardés,soit supprimés pour conduire à des solutions de coût actualisé inférieur.

2) Réseaux admissibles et échéanciers minimaux.

Pour t donné, ($0 \leq t \leq T$), associons à chaque arète u $\in U^*$ de G^* la capacité $Y_u(t)$ (en nombre de circuits).
On dit que le réseau $R(t) = [G^*, Y(t)]$ est admissible à l'instant t si les capacités $Y_u(t)$ (u $\in U^*$) permettent d'écouler simultanément tous les flots $\varphi_{ij}(t)$. Autrement dit, s'il existe sur G^* un multiflot

$\{\varphi_{ij}(t)\}$ compatible avec les capacités $Y_u(t)$ (cf. [11]).
Evidemment, pour tout échéancier $\mathcal{E} = \{F(u,t)\}$ les réseaux $R(t)=[G^*,Y(t)]$ avec: $Y_u(t) = K(u,F(u,t-1))$ sont admissibles ($\forall t=1,..T$).

On dit qu'un échéancier $\mathcal{E} = \{F(u,t)\}$ est <u>minimal</u> à l'instant t si le réseau cesse d'être admissible à l'instant t lorsqu'on supprime un quelconque des investissements qui le composent. On démontre (cf. [5] [8] que tout échéancier de coût actualisé minimum sur la période $[0,T]$ est nécessairement <u>minimal</u> à chaque instant $t=0,1,....T$.

3) <u>La méthode</u>.

Son principe est le suivant: partant de la solution $\mathcal{E}^0$ (déduite du programme à long terme), on engendre une séquence $\mathcal{E}^1, \mathcal{E}^2, ... \mathcal{E}^r$ de solutions de coûts actualisés décroissants, jusqu'à obtention d'un échéancier minimal $\mathcal{E}^*$.
Pour cela, on examine successivement toutes les années $t=0,1,....T-1$, et,à chaque année, on cherche à reporter le maximum d'investissements sur l'année suivante.

a) $t=0$; $\mathcal{E}^0 = \{F^0(u,t)\}$ solution optimale du problème statique.

b) Soit $\mathcal{E}^r = \{F^r(u,t)\}$ la solution courante.
$\forall u \in U^*$, déterminer le nombre maximum $q(u)$ d'investissements prévus à l'année t et pouvant être retardés.
Si $q(u) = 0$ $\forall u \in U^*$, alors $\mathcal{E}^r$ est minimal; aller en e).
Sinon:

c) Parmi toutes les possibilités envisagées en b) on détermine la décision la plus économique - retarder q_0 investissements sur l'artère u_0 - suivant un critère $\mathcal{C}$ (à définir).

d) La nouvelle solution est alors:

$$F^{r+1}(u,t) = F^r(u,t) \qquad \forall u \neq u_0$$
$$F^{r+1}(u_0,t) = F^r(u_0,t) - q_0$$

Faire: $r \longleftarrow r+1$. Retourner en b).

e) Faire: $t \longleftarrow t+1$, et retourner en b).

Nous avons montré dans [5] et [8] sur des exemples réels, que cette méthode permet d'améliorer notablement le coût actualisé des solutions obtenues dans le modèle à long terme (avec l'hypothèse des routages invariants dans le temps).
Il existe un grand nombre de possibilités pour le choix du critère $\mathcal{C}$

à l'étape c): on pourra par exemple, chercher à différer en priorité l'investissement le plus coûteux; ou encore, l'investissement de coût moyen maximum (rapport entre la valeur de l'investissement et le flot total qu'il permet d'écouler dans la solution courante). Ainsi, si $Y_u(t)$ est le nombre de circuits sur l'artère u à l'instant t, on cherchera u_o et q_o maximisant:

$$\frac{J(u,F(u,t)) - J(u,F(u,t)-q)}{Y_u(t) - K(u,F(u,t)-q)}$$

$\forall u \in U^*$ et $1 \leq q \leq q(u)$.

4) Résolution du problème de l'admissibilité.

La procédure précédente suppose que l'on puisse vérifier rapidement l'admissibilité du réseau dans un grand nombre de configurations différentes.

Le problème de la recherche d'un multiflot compatible sur un graphe G^* non orienté muni de capacités est classique et peut être résolu par la programmation linéaire. Cependant, cette technique de résolution présente deux inconvénients: elle est coûteuse en temps de calcul et en encombrement mémoire; elle fournit des solutions fractionnaires.

Dans [8], nous proposons une méthode d'approximations successives (présentant quelques analogies avec la Phase 1 de la méthode "SIMPLEX" en programmation linéaire) qui maintient à chaque itération le caractère entier de la solution, et qui permet de traiter des réseaux de grandes dimensions (N = 200 noeuds ou plus). Le temps de calcul est de l'ordre de N^4, mais peut être considérablement réduit lorsqu'on dispose d'une bonne solution de départ (Ainsi, la procédure donnée en IV-3 peut être rendue très efficace en utilisant à chaque fois comme solution de départ la dernière solution trouvée). L'expérience montre, par ailleurs, que les résultats fournis s'écartent très peu de l'optimum "en continu" (les différences sont toujours inférieures à 1% en valeur relative), ce qui permet d'affirmer que les solutions obtenues sont très proches de l'optimum en nombres entiers.

REMARQUES:

Lorsque les routages sont variables dans le temps, il en résulte, chaque année, des coûts de gestion supplémentaires (mutation des circuits). Ces coûts peuvent être facilement pris en compte lors de la recherche des routages admissibles (par pénalisation des changements de routage).

La méthode s'étend également sans difficulté au cas où l'on impose des contraintes de sécurité (cf. [8], chap. VI).

V- CONCLUSION

Nous avons montré dans [5] que le choix d'une politique d'extension d'un réseau de Télécommunications ne doit pas seulement être guidé par des impératifs à court terme, mais tenir compte également de l'évolution prévisible,à long terme, de la demande et des matériels, afin d'améliorer la rentabilité des investissements effectués.
L'approche que nous avons adoptée - planification à long terme, puis utilisation des résultats obtenus pour la planification à moyen terme - se trouve ainsi justifiée.
Terminons en signalant que les méthodes exposées dans cet article commencent à rentrer en exploitation pour la préparation des plans d'investissements en transmission 1976 et 1977 sur le réseau interurbain français.

REFERENCES:

[1] AYMAR (J.P.) "VOICI: un programme permettant d'évaluer les besoins futurs dans un réseau interurbain". Echo des Recherches (C.N.E.T.) Octobre 1970.

[2] ELLIS (L.W.) "La loi des volumes économiques appliquée aux Télécommunications". Rev. Telecom. N°50,1 (1975).

[3] HARTMAN (J.K.) LASDON (L.S.) "A generalized Upper Bounding algorithm for multicommodity network flow problems". Networks,1 (1972).

[4] MAURY (J.P.) "Planification des réseaux de Télécommunications". Annales des Télécom. 25, N°5-6 (1970).

[5] MINOUX (M.) "Multiflots dynamiques de coût actualisé minimal". Annales des Télécom. 30, N°1-2 (1975).

[6] MINOUX (M.) "Recherche de la configuration optimale d'un réseau de Télécommunications". (à paraître).

[7] MINOUX (M.) "Recherche de la configuration optimale d'un réseau de Télécommunications avec fonctions de coût concaves". Annales des Télécom. 29, N°1-2 (1974).

[8] MINOUX (M.) "Planification à court et moyen terme d'un réseau de Télécommunications". Annales des Télécom. 29, N°11-12 (1974).

[9] MOULON (M.) "Comparaison économique des systèmes à large bande: la méthode du coût équivalent". Revue F.I.T.C.E. Mai-Juin 1972.

[10] SCOTT (A.J.) "The optimal network problem: some computationnal procedures". Transp. Res. 3,(1969) pp. 201-210.

[11] TOMLIN (J.A.) "Minimum cost multicommodity network flows". Ops. Res. 14, N°1 (1966).

[12] YAGED (B.) "Minimum cost routing for static network models". Networks 1, N°2 (1971).

[13] YAGED (B.) "Minimum cost routing for dynamic network models". Networks 3, N°3 (1973).

[14] ZADEH (N.) "On building minimum cost communication networks". Networks 3, N°4 (1973).

[15] ZADEH (N.) "On building minimum cost communication networks over time". Networks 4, N°1 (1974).

WORLD MODELS

A CASE STUDY ON SOCIAL RESPONSABILITY AND IMPACT

F. RECHENMANN
E. RIVERA
P. UVIETTA
ENSIMAG BP. 53
38041 GRENOBLE-CEDEX

Only recently have socio-economic world models been developed. This can be explained by two reasons : the world approach is recent although the problem on the international level has been approached quite some time ago; on the other hand, such an approach requires the bringing together of manifold disciplines, which makes the implementation of such projects difficult.

World models, as all Human Science models, have a social aim and function : explanation and/or decision. Some of these models have been privileged by the Club of Rome publications in the "general public". In this case, the social impact is of a different nature, more especially as for the Club of Rome they are the source of proposed choices of Society (1), (2).

The analysis of the methodology used for the construction of these two models will allow us to point out the biases induced by the model-makers themselves, as well as the authors of the publications.

From this analysis, we will show the issueing impact on society.

It will therefore neither be a matter of suggestion an internal criterium of the models themselves nor of setting methodological standarts.

1 - The Methodology Analysis

The first aim of the analysis will be to determine the nature of the methodological biases which show that the model makers are responsible before society.

1 - 1. Publication of information on the model :

One of the main characteristics of large models is their complexity, not so much of the equations themselves but rather of the global understanding of the system and model.

In this case, the close analysis of the model will not guarantee the pointing out of all the hypotheses made as they are not systematically explained. The set of hypotheses made and the knowledge of the models global structure are fundamental elements for the understanding, on account too of the complexity.

The analysis on a world wide level is an additional element of complexity. As not very developed, elements for comparison are few. Moreover, such an approach refering to various fields of study, does not make the global understanding easy for the specialists of each field taken separately. For these reasons, it is absolutely necessary to easily know the fundamental hypotheses as well as the global structure when reading the documentation supplied by the model-makers.

1 - 1.1. Explanation of the hypotheses : If alone the widely read works are analyzed, the first report (1) allows one to establish an already lengthy list of the hypotheses laid down.

As examples we will quote :

- the five fundamental variables are characterized by an exponential growth
- a certain number of regulation factors exist
- no social upheaval will occur

On the other hand, the second report (2), gives less information in this respect. It is only possible to reconstitute the general approach rather than the hypotheses themselves. Strictly speaking, the only hypotheses expressed are the following :

- regional partitioning in order to render an account of the specificities (organic growth)
- the gap between regions can be reduced with financial help from the most developed regions
- the present and future problems set by raw materials are of the same nature as those set by oil at the present time
- the food problems are the same in the different under-developed regions

1 - 1.2. Global structure of the model : Therefore, already on this point, wether the general public or other model makers are concerned, it is difficult to have an opinion of the model. More determinant, is the availability of the global structure of the model. Working from this, the well informed reader can find out the causal links between variables and furthemore can, from this, reconstitute a certain number of non-expressed hypotheses. After an attentive analysis, it is possible to know, in a concentrated form, the variables kept as elements of the model and system dynamic, their causal relations and of the way in which they set.

On this point too, it cannot but be noticed that the second report gives little information. Only a small part of the global structure is made available to the reader. It is thus impossible to know what the model contains and consequently to make any critical analysis.

One of the MESAROVIC team's contributions was not so much the world regionalisation -the reason for this will begiven later- as the use of a modular construction : demographic, economic, energy models... The methodological advantage is obvious, and bears in particular, on the solving of the problem how to cut up the system into blocks. This, of course, is not mentionned in (2) as already the structure diagrams are, according to the authors, too complicated to be shown in their entirety, Cf.(2), p.63. Neither is this mentioned in the various technical reports published at the time of the Club of Rome meetings in Salzbourg end 73 (4), or in Vienna in April-May 74 (5). There is no doubt that this problem, if solved, should have formed the subject of a publication, because a solution to this problem should allow progress in modeling.

Moreover, the reading of the technical reports show that the effort to respect the regional disparities has perhaps not been carried very far : for the economic model it appears that 3 distinct models have been elaborated : developed countries, under-developed countries, socialist countries. The contribution towards the first report is certain, but it is not understandable why the distinct regions have been established. In the paragraph 2.2. the consequences of this problem are shown.

On the other hand, D. MEADOWS's team has, also for the general public, expounded the global structure of its model (2)(pp.212-13). With this element alone, it is possible for everyone to see the relative importance given to each of the five key-variables. Furthermore, a specialist, for example an economist, will easily be able to analyze the way in which to consider the problems relating to the "Industrial Capital" variable.

1 - 1.3. Documentation and possibility of critical analysis : from the methodological point of view, it is necessary for the model-maker to supply the information needed for the understanding of this model and for that which he wishes to show. This is essential with respect to the general public, especially if the model is widely distributed, but ever more so in respect to other model makers. It is clear that progress in modeling is possible, particularly world modeling if elements of comparison are available.

With this as aim, D. MEADOWS's team produced a very detailed technical report (3), unfortunately with some delay, as a number of criticisms had already been made before its publication. It has been possible for the first report to be widely discussed more particularly among the economists who gave themselves up to the criticisms of the hypotheses kept.

In 73, a team from the University of Sussex published a critical counter-report (6), which in detail analyses the whole model. Due to the scare information available, the second one hat not been widely discussed. At most, only the results obtained or the scenarios kept are a source of discussion. A rare example is Pr. W. BECKERMAN's article (7).

1 - 2. Reliability of the results

Another methodological bias should be pointed out : the reliability of the results obtained. The statistical data available, as proved by O. MORGENSTERN (8), are generally not reliable. Thereby, the results obtained reflect these errors. When, moreover, the causal relations are not established with certainty, as is the case for the construction of world models, to comment on the figures obtained and therefore to give them a high credibility in order to draw the conclusions necessary to help the decision making, appears dangerous if not illusory. It is desireable to stop at the analysis of the behaviour mode as D. MEADOWS and his team partly did : (1) pp.229-230. This concretely reveals the methodological differences between the two teams.

J.W. FORRESTER, D. MEADOWS have adopted a methodology which can be described as follows : the model is elaborated and then used in order to solve the behaviour mode problems and not for forecasting. Above all the correctness of the model structure is important while the accuracy of the data ranks after.

Solely the reading of the technical reports (5) allows to show that the actual methodology of MESAROVIC's team appears similar to an econometric approach. This is particularly clear in the World Economic Model : it is a Cobb-Douglas type model. These methodologies differ : both are a research in the understanding, but the second, is more a research in the correctness of the results with regard to the statistical series. The first approach, owing to the fact that the knowledge of the problems on a world scale is not yet very wide, is,doubtless, prudent.

1 - 3. Sensitivity tests and scenarios

A last point, concerning the tests realized on the two models, will be analysed. It appears that the first report presents sensitivity tests on the model as application of policies. This shows a misunderstanding which arose between model and system, as O. RADEMAKER pointed out (9)(p.13) : "Sensitivity analyses serve to find out how great is the influence of the choice of certain coefficient values, functional relations, and initial values, and not of finding the effect of particular real-world measures".

MESAROVIC's team has supplied a contribution in so far as scenarios have been really built and used.

The analysis of the methodological biases that we have pointed out will now allow us to show their impact on society.

2 - Models, Ideology and Society

2 - 1. Refusal of the ideology

The field of analysis of Social Sciences, to which the world models belong, in cludes ideology, i.e. pseudo-explanatory type of approaches.

The limits of ideology are fuzzy particularly in fields of study such as economy. A large number of discussions between economists on the equilibrium models may in fact be brought down to an ideological discussion.

If refusing to admit that the analyses in Social Sciences, including and above all on the basis of models, partly involve ideology, an inevitable bias crops up : results of the model are given as accurate as they have been mathematically "proved".

Were the controversies on the equilibrium models in the 60's not partly provoked by the discussion on more or less explicit hypotheses, and more fundamentally by the real but not expressed aims of the model makers themselves?

The ideology springs from the fact that a model is built for a specific aim, be it one of demonstration or are of decision making. On this sense, a model can therefore be neither neutral nor "objective".

Thus, for the model maker there is a responsibility factor, more particularly so when the results obtained are supposed to help political choices. In this case, the social impact takes a 'world-wide' dimension, not because the two models analyse the world system, but because they are widely read. This world dimension was much more perceptible at the time of the first report's publication : almost simultaneously growth problems were tackled in various claims among others :

- UNESCO meeting in Paris
- U.N. Conference on Environment, held in Stockolm
- CNUCED in Santiago

One must admit that the second report neither had the same impact, nor provoked a comparable awareness of the problems tackled, but it possesses as large a social impact by means of its conclusions.

2 - 2. Global approach and consideration of the specificities

The wish for a global approach led to a theoretical contradiction in the realization of the two models : denial of the ideology, but analysis biased by ideology. The approach by which the object analyzed is a system, is doubtless necessary for a better understanding. Here, the problem set is to know what appropriate degree of aggregation is to be kept, and what phenomena belong to this level of analysis.

This global approach has clearly led to covey a same ideology, inspite of divergent methodologies. Whether the approach was deliberate or not on the part of the modelmakers is not the problem.

The stress has been placed on the identity of the nature of the problems for all the countries, be it a question of food, pollution, energy, etc... But, as a matter of fact, the heart of the problem is concealed. Can one admit that the food problems in the Sahel and in South-East Asia are identical? That the provisionning in energy sets the same problems to Europe as it does to the under developed countries?

That pollution in Africa and in North America are the same? The answer is obviously negative, and goes for each crisis factor dealt with in both reports. To set the problem of pollution cannot have the same signification for a western country as for an under developed country. For the former it is a matter of questioning growth which the latter would wish to have. In this respect, the effort to regionalise the world, i.e. to take into consideration the differences, reveals itself as illusory : the regions kept are not as homogenous as the authors would make us believe. As we are not making an internal criticism of the model, let us accept the partitioning suggested. But, why problems of a given region are transposed to others (food problems for ex), if the analysis proved the necessity to explain the differences between regions?

Apparently, the second report has taken into account the existence of under development. Many authors had reproached D. MEADOWS's team with not having done this. 6 of the 10 regions are indeed under developed countries. But, the progression is only apparent. Growth remains expressed in global terms, which is to know it superficially : to ask the question whether the under developed countries will one day realise their economic take-off and follow the growth of the western countries, is once again to analyse growth in terms of stages of growth, as is done by Rostow.
C. FURTADO (10) had already showed this up in connection with the first report. The criticisms of the second report remain identical. Basically, the problem is set in the same terms; it is, for example, said p.73 (2) that...."the gap between the world various regions continually increases".

Many tested scenarios show that the authors are looking for solutions in order to diminish the gaps. But, here again it shows a refusal to ask oneself if the developed countries have not reached such a economic growth thanks to the dominating relations which they have imposed.

If the existance of such a bias is accepted, the solutions proposed in the two reports, such as aid towards development by the means of capital, will probably have a large social impact on the economic development and with regards to public opinion. The readers of the two reports will find in them a confirmation, given as strictly accurate, of what they already know, by means of media, on help towards development which has been practised in the form of financial help since the end of WW.II. From this time onwards the general public is strongly influenced given the fact that by definition, it does not have all the information necessary at its disposal in order to have a truly personal opinion and to recognize such biases.

2 - 3. Analysis of growth and crisis

For some time too, the reader of the second report has been made aware of a second point dealing with an aspect of growth : this concerns the problem of the present crisis(es). The diversity of the vocabulary reveals the complexity of the problem : partial crises are spoken such as, for example, the "food crisis", the "energy crisis"

or the crisis at a global level : the world crisis
the crisis of the capitalist system, etc...

The explanations suggested are at least as numerous as the terms employed. Finally, in fact, the uncertainty as to determine when exactly the crisis began is just as great.. As yet, it has not been possible to make a coherent socio-historical analysis, partly as the crisis is at present continuing.

It is therefore very significant to notice the slide performed on the crisis factors between the two reports. According to D. MEADOWS's team, population, pollution and depletion of natural resources are the factors which in the future will stop growth. On the second report, the blockage has already occured with the development of oil supply and food problems.

It is clear that the explanations proposed are not of the same nature and diverge. The reader will certainly be more satisfied with the second report as problems which concern his every day life (especially energy) are dealt with. But the question of the validity of the theses presented must be put. The most striking example is that of the 1972 famine. The USSR, which had not foreseen a sufficient increase in the cultivated surfaces of wheat, is alone held responsible for this famine according to the authors ((2), pp.39-40). There could have been an error of forecasting by the USSR, but this does not give an explanation of the reason why other regions are, for the past few years, experiencing famine owing to exceptional drought. Moreover in many countries this famine problem is not recent. In the same way, the analysis of the petrol crisis seems biased : the problem is set as that of the transfer of economic power. Inevitably such an analysis leads to the proposing of solutions by means of cooperation. This in plain language means to take care of the producing and consuming countries interests in order to avoid all conflict, through prices or force. In this connection, one can wonder if the analysis is complete. The reader may have been surprised at the fact that, as in the first report, the phenomenon of Multinational Corporations is generally ignored. Owing to the fact that in the analysis things happen as if these oil firms do not exist, the reader does not have at his disposal the information necessary when reading the solutions suggested : MESAROVIC's team demonstrates that nuclear energy will have to act only as a transition before the exploitation of solar energy. The model makers have not taken into consideration the fact that for some time already the oil firms have been investing in the energy sources, particularly nuclear energy, and that this strategy is not applied for a short period of time.

The existence of biases such as those described above lays down a certain number of methodological precautions to the model maker if the wishes to avoid the risk of being considered as a propagator of an ideology and therefore as a technocrat.

2 - 4. Technocratism

The denial of the ideology and the expressed wish of scientificity may appear as a definitive form of technocratism, in so far as the aim decided on is help for the making of decisions. The research made and the results obtained are meant to be indisputable as it is a matter of scientific work.

The methodology adopted by D. MEADOWS's team should be a partial guarantee against this bias. The main aim is firstly to have a better understanding of the system. But, this then presupposes two points : not to fall into the trap of confusing model/system, and above all not to have as only aim help towards decision making.

An approach of econometric inspiration, as the one adopted for the second report, leads to a more or less stated aim of forecasting. This leads to the proposing of a large amount of numerical outputs to the reader. This approach is hazardous as the accusation of technocratism can be even more easily made. It is obvious that the credibility of the conclusions is always greater when numerical outputs are joined to them as they are therefore accurate and therefore as a guarantee for their accuracy.

CONCLUSION

Ideology appears to be difficult to avoid : in so far as the knowledge of the systems analyzed remains incertain. However, the social impact of the models being a reality, it is desirable to adopt a methodology which allows one to avoid a certain number of biases presented here. In the opposite case it is the appraisement of the very model-makers' contributions which incurs the risk of being altered. The presence of non explicit hypotheses or other elements of information leads to the following problem : was this voluntary on the part of the model-maker? It is clear that the effort to explain the hypotheses made is an element of more complete knowledge on the model for the model makes himself.

J.W. FORRESTER's "Systems Dynamics" is an appreciable contribution towards accessibility and on the methodological level. However, if non computer science specialists are to have access to such works, it is essential to go further in the methodological effort, which is conceived as an aid towards the construction and comprehension of the model built. This therefore parallely implies the suggestions of more adapted and accessible languages which simultaneously give a methodology adapted to the problems to be dealt with (11).

BIBLIOGRAPHY

1) MEADOWS D. et al : "Halte à la croissance?", Paris, Fayard 1972.

2) MESAROVIC M., PESTEL E. : "Stratégie pour demain", Paris, Seuil 1974.

3) MEADOWS D. et al : "Dynamics of growth in a finite world", Cambridge, Wright-Allen Press 1974.

4) MESAROVIC M., PESTEL E. : "Critical choices for mankind : Limits to independence", Report for Salzburg, Dec. 1973.

5) MESAROVIC M., PESTEL E., dir :
- Construction of regionalized world economic model
- Energy models : ressources, demand, supply
- Population model

Vienne, may 1974.

6) COLE H.D.S., et al : "Models of Doom. A Critique of the Limits to Growth", New-York, Universe Books 1973.

7) BECKERMAN W. : "Réquisitoire contre le Club de Rome", Expansion, mars 1975, pp.106-111.

8) MORGENSTERN O. : "Précision et incertitude des données économiques", Paris, Dunod 1972.

9) RADEMAKER O. : "Project Group Global Dynamics",Progress Report n°1, Eindhoven 1972.

10) FURTADO C. : "Le mythe du développement et le futur du Tiers-Monde", Revue Tiers-Monde, janv - mars 1974.

11) RECHENMANN F. : "Structuration et introduction de la notion d'espace dans les langages de simulation continue". Toulouse, Journées AFCET : "L'approche dynamique des systèmes socio-économiques", 19-20 juin 1975.

A MATHEMATICAL MODEL FOR PRESSURE SWING ADSORPTION

D.J.G. Sebastian
BOC Limited, UK

1. Introduction

Pressure Swing Adsorption (PSA) as a physical method of separation of gas mixtures has rapidly gained importance. The incentive for a mathematical model comes from the fact that accuracy of prediction is essential for optimal plant design.

The PSA principle of gas separation is based on two fundamental facts:

1) Some substances adsorb some gases in preference to other gases.
2) The amount adsorbed for any given gas increases as the pressure of the gas increases.

As an illustration, consider the following two-step adsorption cycle to purify helium diving gas. Helium diving gas is principally a mixture of oxygen and helium. When the diving chambers are depressurised, the contaminated gas will consist mainly of carbon dioxide, oxygen and helium. Traditionally this waste gas has been thrown away. The PSA cycle described below is a method of purifying this gas and recovering expensive helium.

The adsorbent chosen has a strong preference for adsorbing all gases except helium.

Step 1. Purification

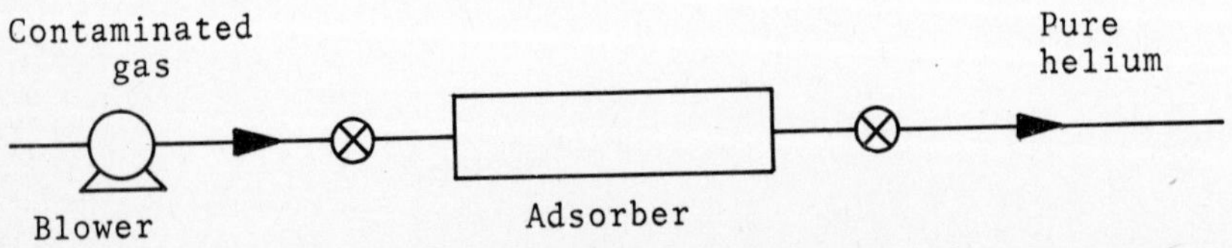

During the high pressure purification step oxygen and the contaminants are preferentially adsorbed and the output from the bed is pure helium. The bed will gradually become saturated, and when it is no longer able to purify the input gas, it is changed over to regeneration.

Step 2. Regeneration

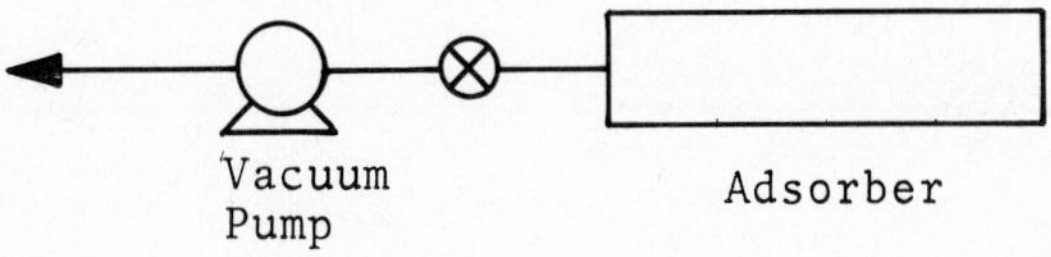

As the bed is evacuated its capacity to hold gases decreases, thus losing oxygen and the contaminants. At the end of the evacuation the bed is ready for purification again.

The term pressure swing comes from the fact that a swing in the pressure between the steps is essential for the process to function. In actual practice the cycles are, in general, more complex than the one described, but the principles of operation remain the same.

This paper describes a model which has been developed for simulating the evacuation step.

2. Equations Forming the Model

a) Partial Differential Equations for the Bed.

The equations themselves are based on standard chemical engineering principles and their derivation is not given here. The variables of the model are set out below:

Independent Variables

- x - distance along the bed
- θ - time

Dependent Variables

- u - flow rate
- v - gas phase composition
- w - pressure

i) Overall Mass Balance Equation

$$\frac{\partial u}{\partial x} + \left[\frac{a\varepsilon}{RT} + a\xi(v,w) \right] \frac{\partial v}{\partial \theta} + a\eta(v,w) \frac{\partial w}{\partial \theta} = 0 \qquad 2.1$$

ii) Single Component Mass Balance Equation

$$\frac{\partial vw}{\partial x} + \left[\frac{a\varepsilon}{RT} + a\gamma(v,w) \right] \frac{\partial vw}{\partial \theta} + a\delta(v,w) \frac{\partial w}{\partial \theta} = 0 \qquad 2.2$$

iii) Momentum Balance Equation

$$w \frac{\partial w}{\partial x} + \alpha u + \beta u^2 = 0 \qquad 2.3$$

In the above equations α, β, a, ε, R and T are constants.

b) The Initial and Boundary Conditions

$$\begin{aligned} u(x,0) &= 0 \\ v(x,0) &= y_0 \qquad\qquad 0 \le x \le 1 \\ w(x,0) &= p_0 \end{aligned} \qquad 2.4$$

Two of the boundary conditions are at x = 1 and are straightforward.

$$\begin{aligned} u(1,\theta) &= 0 \qquad\qquad \theta > 0 \\ v(1,\theta) &= y_0 \end{aligned} \qquad 2.5$$

The vacuum pump, pipework and fittings are incorporated into the model through the third boundary condition. This is specified at x = 0 in the form of the nonlinear algebraic equation

$$\phi(u(0,\theta),w(0,\theta)) = 0 \qquad \theta > 0 \qquad 2.6$$

This form of the boundary condition gives rise to two difficulties

i) Unlike the case, for example, of the linear diffusion equation, the boundary value problem cannot be solved explicitly. It is necessary to start with a first approximation for the solution and by successive iteration force it to satisfy boundary condition 2.6.

ii) The non-linearity of the boundary condition leads to multiplicity of solution.

As the fitting of the boundary condition is iterative, occasionally an unwanted solution is obtained. When this occurs it is usually in the form of switching from one solution to the other.

However, certain monotonicity conditions shown in the next section may be imposed on the solution to prevent switching to the unwanted solution.

c) Monotonicity Conditions

These conditions are derived from physical consideration

i) For $x_1 > x_2$ and $\theta > 0$,

$$w(x_2,\theta) < w(x_1,\theta)$$
$$u(x_2,\theta) < u(x_1,\theta)$$

ii) For $\theta_1 > \theta_2$,

$$w(1,\theta_1) < w(1,\theta_2)$$

In addition, for $\theta > 0$, $0 \leq x < 1$

$$u(x,\theta) < 0$$

While the desired solution satisfies all the above conditions, the unwanted solution will violate at least one of them beginning with i). Thus the algorithm is given a test for detecting when there is a chance of switching to the unwanted solution.

The extreme importance of these conditions will become clearer when the technique of solution is described. Their use has been entirely successful in eliminating the unwanted solution and is thus sufficient to ensure uniqueness of solution.

d) The Type of Equations

The three partial differential equations are first order quasi-linear. They are hyperbolic-parabolic in the sense that there are only two distinct characteristics, and the third characteristic coincides with one of the first two. All the three characteristics are real and are given by

$$\frac{dx}{d\theta} = \frac{u}{(\gamma' - \xi' v)}$$

$$d\theta = 0$$

and $$d\theta = 0$$

where
$$\gamma' = \left[\frac{a\varepsilon}{RT} + \gamma(v,w)\right] w$$

$$\xi' = \frac{a\varepsilon}{RT} + \xi(v,w)$$

This is useful in studying the propagation of discontinuities in the boundary conditions and numerical stability.

3. The Method of Solution

a) General Approach

The partial differential equations are replaced by finite difference equations which are consistent with them. The iterative procedure for fitting the boundary conditions is carried out with a one-variable minimization method starting with a first approximation. At $x = 1$ boundary conditions fix the values of $u(1,\theta)$ and $v(1,\theta)$. Let $w^*(1,\theta)$ be the approximation for $w(1,\theta)$ which is as yet unknown. Using $u(1,\theta)$, $v(1,\theta)$ and $w^*(1,\theta)$ the finite difference equations can be solved to give $u^*(0,\theta)$ and $w^*(0,\theta)$ as approximations for $u(0,\theta)$ and $w(0,\theta)$ respectively. When $w^*(1,\theta)$ is the correct value

$$\phi(u^*(0,\theta), w^*(0,\theta) = 0$$

This value is determined by minimizing $\phi^2(u^*(0,\theta), w^*(0,\theta))$ with respect to $w^*(1,\theta)$. The minimization method employed is successive quadratic fitting.

b) The Finite Difference Scheme

The differential equations are retained in the first order, and the numerical scheme is explicit. A judicious choice of finite differences results in a simple scheme of solution. Some attractive looking schemes were intractable for stability analysis and were abandoned.

The final numerical scheme used is as follows.

$$u_{i,j} = u_{i,j+1} + ar\{(\frac{\varepsilon}{RT} + \xi)(v_{i,j+1} - v_{i-1,j+1}) + \eta(w_{i,j+1} - w_{i-1,j+1})\} \quad . \quad 3.1$$

$$w_{i,j} = w_{i,j+1} - \delta x(\alpha u_{i,j} + \beta u_{i,j}^2)/w_{i-1,j+1} \quad 3.2$$

$$v_{i,j} = \frac{\{-u_{i,j} v_{i,j+1} + v_{i-1,j}(\frac{a\varepsilon}{RT} + a\gamma)(w_{i,j+1} + w_{i,j} - w_{i-1,j}) - a\delta(w_{i,j} - w_{i-1,j})\}}{u_{i,j+1} - 2u_{i,j} + a(\frac{\varepsilon}{RT} + \gamma)w_{i,j+1}} \quad 3.3$$

where ξ, η, γ and δ are calculated at the grid point $i-1,j$ and $r = \frac{\delta x}{\delta}$.

The notation used for the grids is

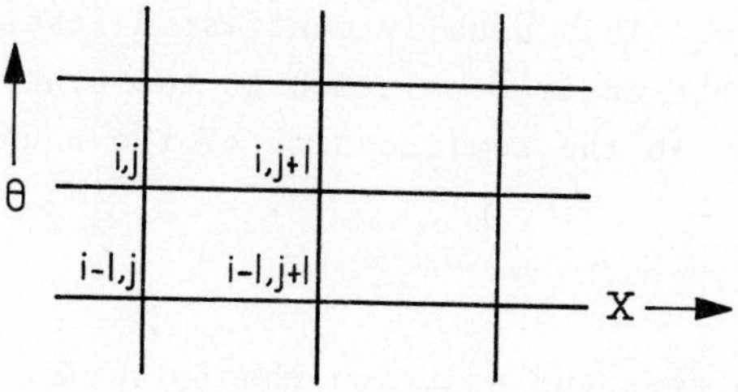

c) Consistency and Stability

It is easily verified that the finite difference equations are consistent with partial differential equations and the truncation errors are of the first order.

To study stability the error propagation equations are linearized. The eigen values characterizing the propagation of errors at time step i are bounded by

$$\lambda_{i\,max} = \max_{j} \left| \frac{ar(\frac{\varepsilon}{RT} + \gamma)(w_{ij} - 2w_{i-1,j})}{u_{i,j+1} - u_{i,j} + ar(\frac{\varepsilon}{RT} + \gamma)w_{i,j+1}} \right| \qquad 3.4$$

As one would expect with nonlinear equations, λ itself depends on the solution. It is therefore not possible to calculate $\lambda_{i\,max}$ 'a priori'. Any bound one can put on $\lambda_{i\,max}$ is also unrealistic.

However, stability analysis is invaluable in evaluating a method. Some numerical schemes were shown to be intrinsically unstable. Some other schemes were detected to be prone to instability, which was often revealed by a hand calculation.

Furthermore, the stability test enables the algorithm to detect it when stability is lost.

d) Multiplicity of Solution

What has been discussed so far is concerned with the conventional ideas of consistency, stability, characteristics and so on. One of the most unusual and interesting features of this problem is the fact that the solution is not unique. This usually manifested itself in the form of sudden switching from the desired solution to the other. The cause of this can be pinned down to the nonlinearity of the boundary condition,

$$\phi(u(0,\theta), w(0,\theta)) = 0 \qquad 2.6$$

In order to eliminate the unwanted solution the following points must be noted:

i) The algorithm must be able to detect the unwanted solution. As mentioned earlier when the solution is not the desired one at least one of the monotonicity conditions will be violated and this can be built into the algorithm.

ii) The algorithm must suppress the tendency to move towards the unwanted solution. This is achieved by applying a penalty function during the minimization.

Consider what happens at time θ_i. Let $w^{(n)}(1,\theta_i)$ represent the n th approximation to $w(1,\theta_i)$. There exists $\overline{w}(1,\theta_i)$, such that whenever $w^{(n)}(1,\theta_i) > \overline{w}(1,\theta_i)$ the monotonicity conditions are violated and vice versa. The value of $\overline{w}(1,\theta_i)$ is itself unknown and so it is not possible to put an explicit constraint on $w^{(n)}(1,\theta_i)$. The only alternative is to apply a penalty function whenever a monotonicity condition is violated, which is done as follows:

If $\quad u^{(n)}(x_{ij},\theta_i) < u^{(n)}(x_{ij+1},\theta_i) \qquad$ for $1 \le j \le n-1$

then no penalty is added.

$$p(w^{(n)}(1,\theta_i)) = \begin{cases} 10^4(1+(w^{(n)}(1,\theta_i)-w(1,\theta_{i-1}))^2), & \text{if } w^{(n)}(1,\theta_i)>w(1,\theta_{i-1}) \\ 10^4 \dfrac{1}{1+(w^{(n)}(1,\theta_i)-w(1,\theta_{i-1}))^2}, & \text{if } w^{(n)}(1,\theta_i)\le w(1,\theta_{i-1}) \end{cases}$$

The following graphs represent schematically the functions involved.

a) $\quad \phi^2(u^*(0,\theta_i),\ w^*(0,\theta_i))$

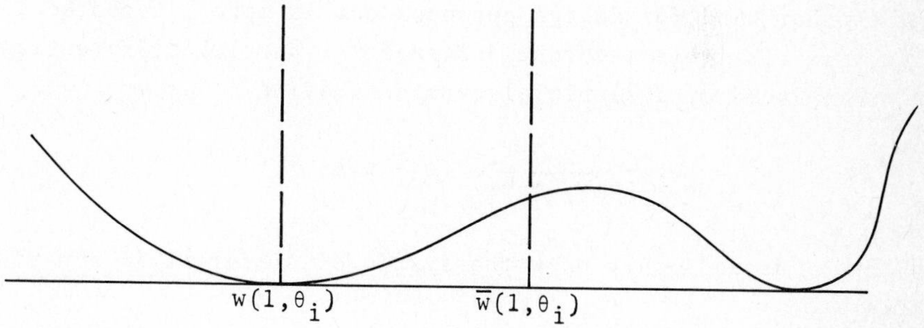

b) $\quad p(w^{(n)}(1,\theta_i))$

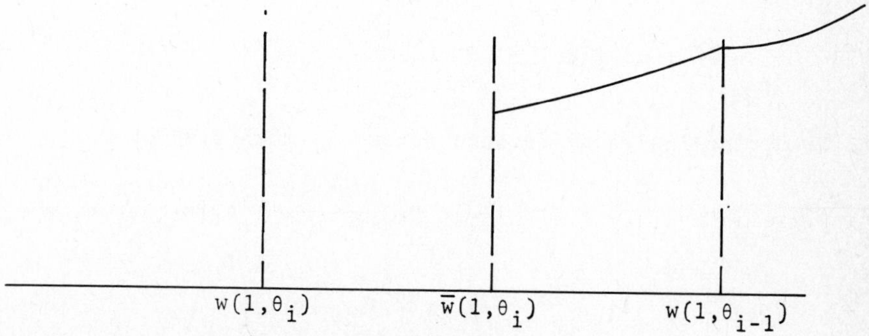

c) $\phi^2(u^*(0,\theta_i),\ w^*(0,\theta_i) + p(w^{(n)}(1,\theta_i))$

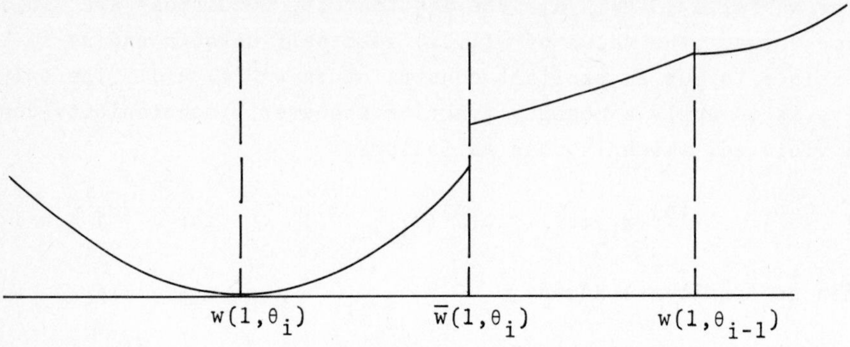

There is a discontinuity in the function to be minimized at $\overline{w}(1,\theta_i)$ but this cannot be helped as $\overline{w}(1,\theta_i)$ is unknown. In any case, this gave rise to no difficulty with the minimization method.

4. Simplification of the Model for Design Use

For process evaluation one would like to calculate u, v and w. On the other hand for design purposes one is more interested in u and w while v is of little interest. Therefore, partial differential equation 2.2 is replaced by a simple algebraic equation

$$v = v_1 + \frac{(v_2 - v_1)}{(w_2 - w_1)}(w - w_1) \qquad 4.1$$

Now that v depends only on w the system of differential equations reduces to

$$\frac{\partial u}{\partial x} + \zeta(w)\frac{\partial w}{\partial \theta} = 0 \qquad 4.2$$

$$w\frac{\partial w}{\partial x} + \alpha u + \beta u^2 = 0 \qquad 4.3$$

The resulting finite difference scheme is much simpler.

$$u_{i,j} = u_{i,j+1} + ar\{(\frac{\varepsilon}{RT} + \xi)\frac{(v_2-v_1)}{(w_2-w_1)} + \eta\}(w_{i,j+1}-w_{i-1,j+1}) \qquad 4.4$$

$$w_{i,j} = w_{i,j+1} - \delta x(\alpha u_{ij} + \beta u_{ij}^{\ 2})/w_{i-1,j} \qquad 4.5$$

The eigen values characterizing the propagation of the errors are bounded at time step i by

$$\lambda_{i\ max} = \max_{j} \left| \frac{w_{i,j} - w_{i,j+1}}{w_{i-1,j}} \right| \qquad 4.6$$

The rest of the procedure is exactly the same as in section 3.

5. Programming Details

The first approximation for $w(1,\theta_i)$ is obtained by

$$w^{(1)}(1,\theta_i) = 1.8\ w(1,\theta_{i-1}) - 0.8\ w(1,\theta_{i-2}) \qquad 4.7$$

The stopping criterion for the minimization procedure is

$$\phi^2(u^{(n)}(0,\theta),\ w^{(n)}(0,\theta)) \leq \varepsilon'$$

The value of ε' is set by the program depending on the plant size and is of the order of 10^{-7}. In general the one-variable minimization is rapid and the solution is found in about eight function evaluations. During the first time step, occasionally the number of function evaluations was as much as 20, which is because equation 4.7 cannot be used to obtain a first approximation. The use of the penalty function has little effect on the performance, as it is not transgressed often.

6. Results

The results obtained are presented in a graphical form. The full model is used in studying how the composition varies along the length of the bed at a given time. The simplified model on the other hand is used for predicting how the pressure at the end of the bed and the vacuum pump suction pressure vary with time.

Graph 1 was obtained using the full model, while graphs 2, 3 and 4 were obtained using the simplified model. The simplified model was, in particular, very useful in plant design. This model has been tested in 3 stages:

i) Simulating an existing plant - Graph 2.

ii) Predicting the behaviour of a pilot plant and comparing it with observations - Graph 3.

iii) Designing a full scale plant and then testing the design against actual performance - Graph 4.

In each case the correspondence was exceptionally good and the technique has proved reliable and accurate in every instance.

7. References

1 Ames, W.F. (1969) Numerical Methods for Partial Differential Equations, London, Thomas Nelson and Sons.

2 Armond, J.W. and Smith, K.C. (1973) Adsorption as a Technique for Gas Separation, Cryotech 73 Proceedings.

3 Smith, G.D. (1971) Numerical Solution of Partial Differential Equations, London, Oxford University Press.

4 Smith, M.G. (1967) Theory of Partial Differential Equations, London, Van Nostrand

5 Webber, D.A. (1972) Adsorptive Removal of Carbon Dioxide from Air at Intermediate Low Temperatures, The Chemical Engineer.

Acknowledgements:

I would like to thank BOC Ltd for allowing me to present this paper and, in particular, Mr. K.C. Smith for his personal interest.

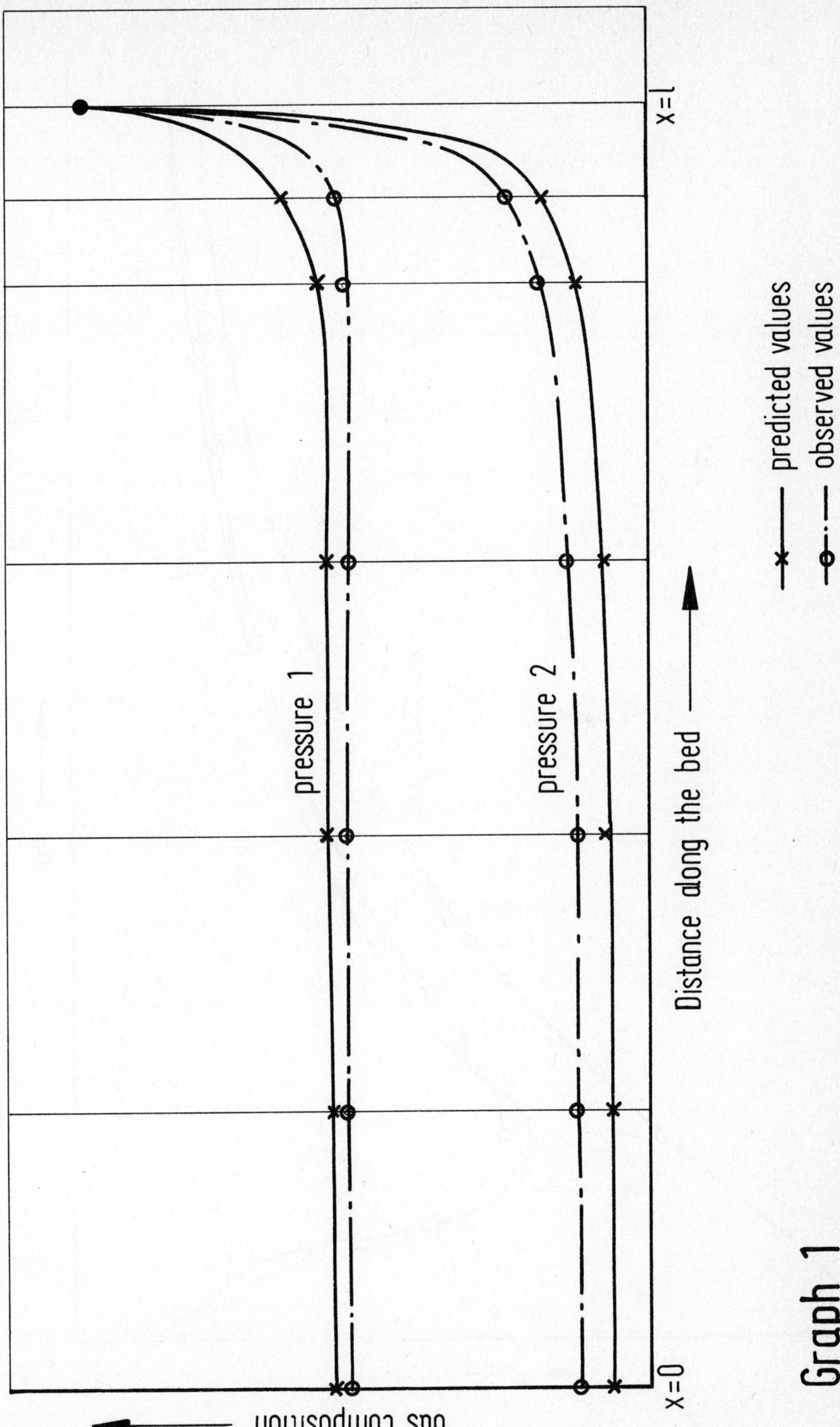
Gas composition
x=0
x=l
pressure 1
pressure 2
Distance along the bed
predicted values
observed values

Graph 1

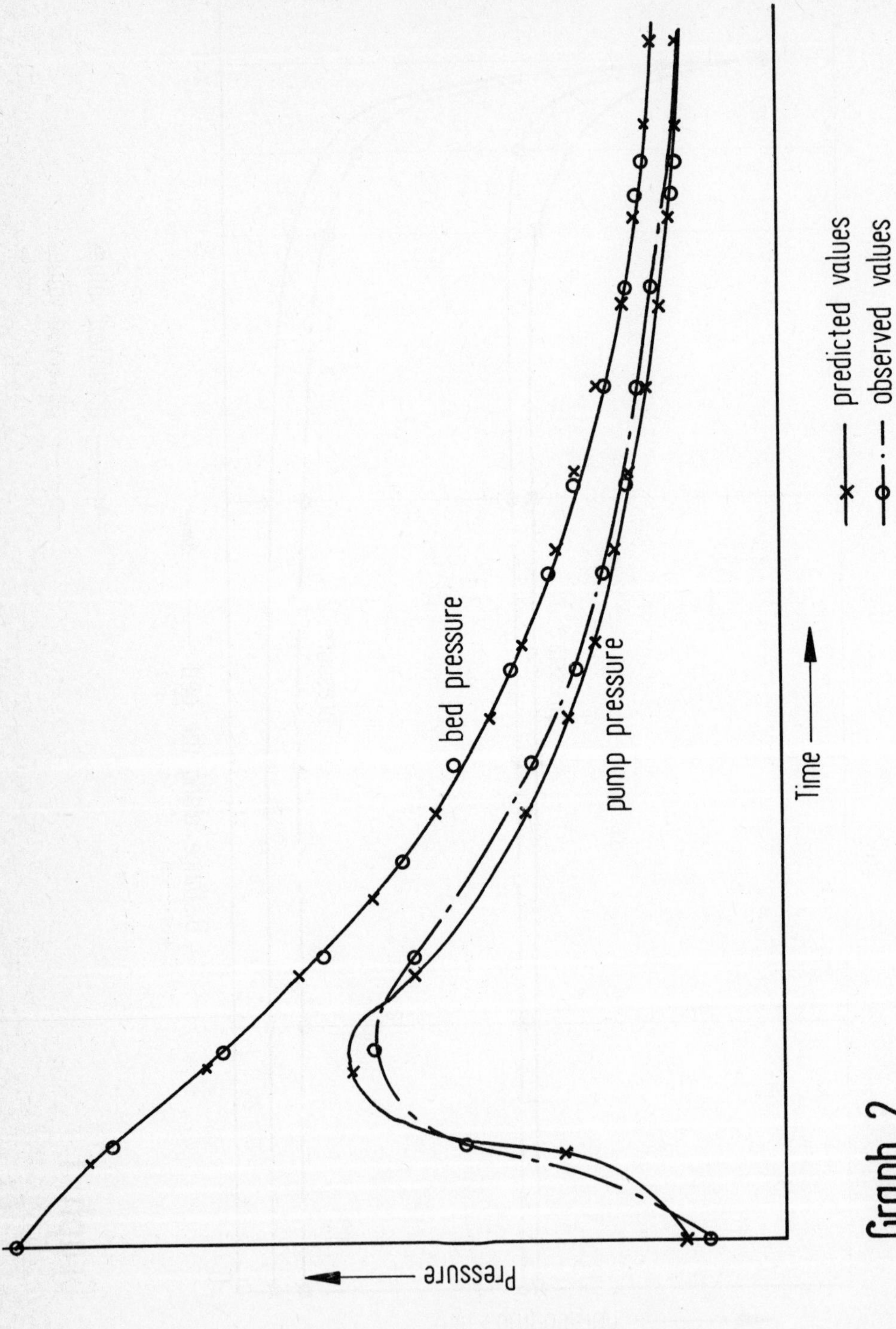

bed pressure
pump pressure
Pressure
Time
predicted values
observed values

Graph 2

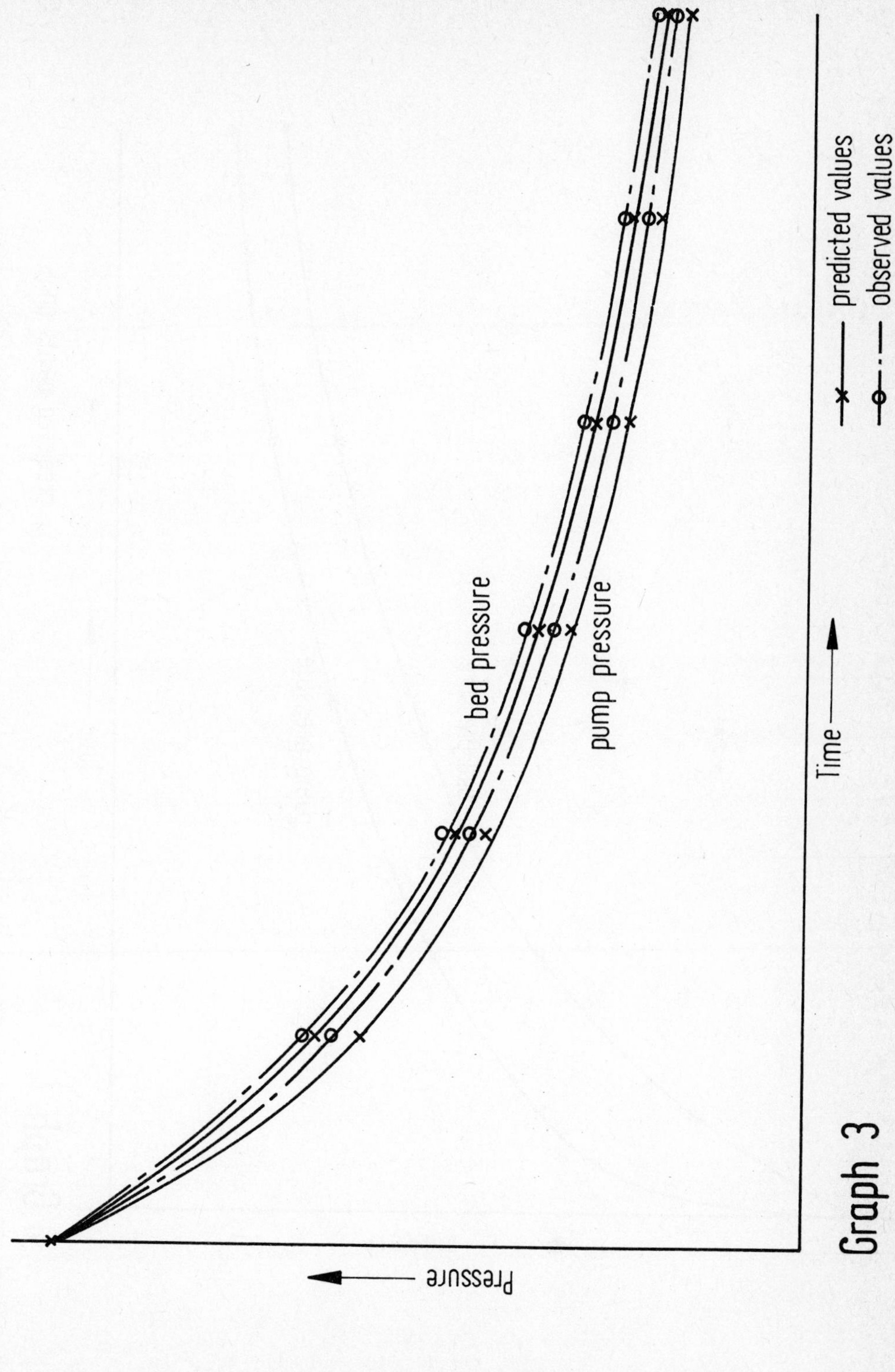
bed pressure
pump pressure
Pressure
Time
predicted values
observed values

Graph 3

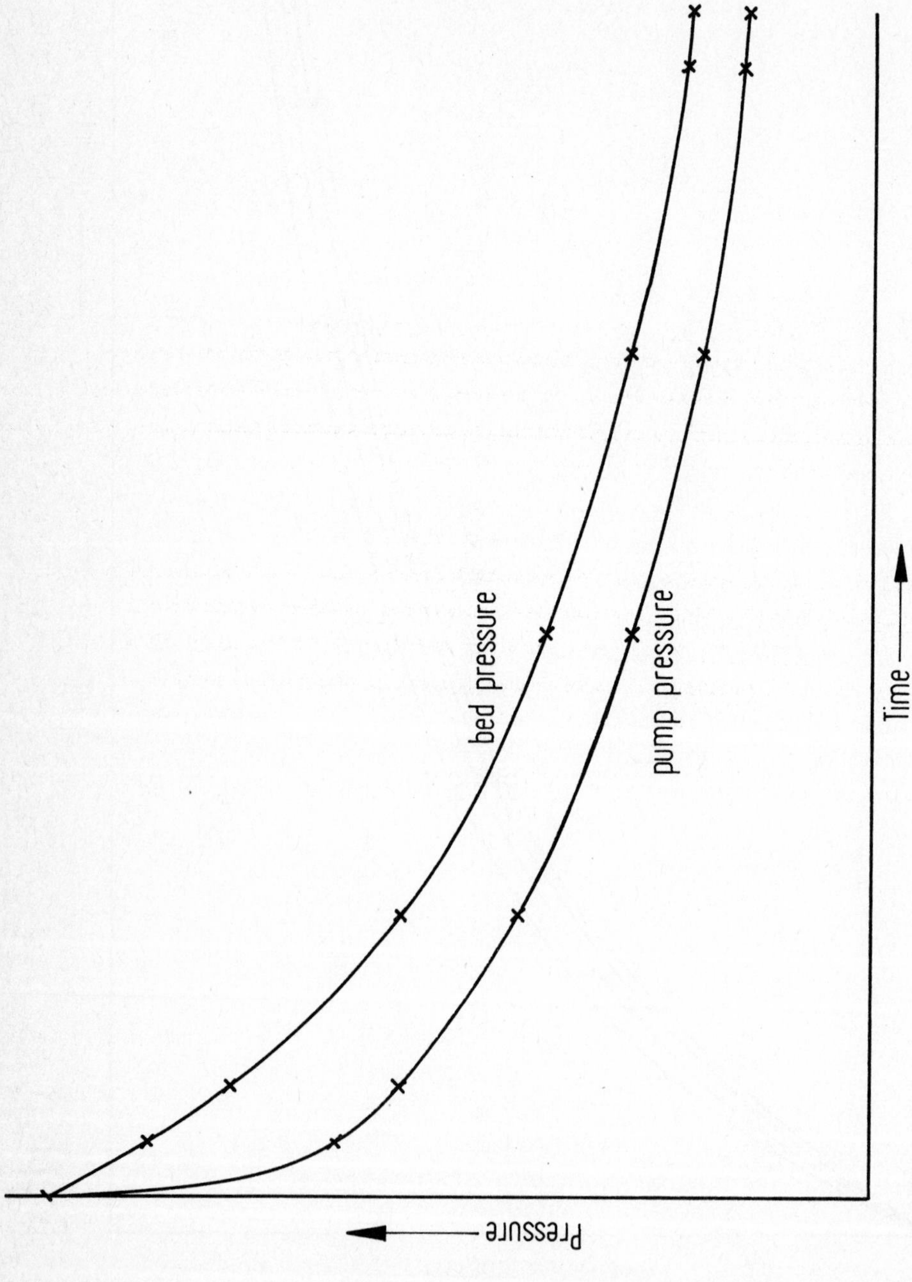

predicted points only

Graph 4

A FOUR-VARIABLE WORLD SYSTEM *

Floyd J. Gould
University of Chicago
Chicago, Illinois 60637/USA

ABSTRACT

This is a model to study aspects of the short and long-range growth and balance between four world quantities: food, energy, fertilizer, and population. The model may be used as a tool to study implications of various policies for coordinated world planning. The model operates as follows: The world is subdivided into a number of regions. Consider time period t. In each region two factors, investments and population, are used to determine supplies of fertilizer, energy, arable acreage, and workforce availability. The regional investment stream is an exogenous input to the system. In each region, demand functions are specified for foods, fertilizer, energy for agriculture, energy for other uses, acreage, and labor. These demands are functions of all prices, population, and income in period t - 1. A spatial equilibrium model links all regions and determines equilibrium imports, exports, and prices for each region. This gives, for each region, the income in period t, and specific consumption of fertilizer, energy for agriculture, acreage, and workforce. Based on this consumption, and taking account of weather, regional agricultural outputs are determined. This provides an exogenous food supply for the spatial equilibrium model in year t + 1. The supplies in t + 1 of fertilizer, energy, acreage and labor are determined, as functions of population and the investment stream, and the procedure is repeated.

* Since the writing of this material preliminary reports have been released on the MOIRA model of H. Linnemann and Associates. Because of this timing of circumstances it should be explicitly stated that this document was written prior to any knowledge of the Linnemann efforts and hence the latter must be excepted from any comments herein which refer to other works in global modeling.

A FOUR-VARIABLE SYSTEM*

I. Introduction

The purpose of this paper is to sketch a framework for investigating some aspects of the short and long-range growth and balance between four world quantities: food, energy, fertilizer, and population. The model may be used as a tool to study the implications of various policies for coordinated world planning.

We shall describe the overall flow of the system with its important links and couplings. At the outset it should be emphasized that many of the details are only briefly indicated and remain to be filled in by individuals with expertise in the areas treated.

The model operates as follows. The world is subdivided into a number of regions. Consider time period t. In each region two factors, investments and population, are used to determine supplies of fertilizer, energy, arable acreage, and workforce availability. The regional investment stream is an exogenous input to the system. The population growth is an endogenous model which remains to be filled in. In each region, demand functions are specified for foods, fertilizer, energy for agriculture, energy for other uses, acreage, and labor. These demands are functions of all prices, population, and income in period $t - 1$. A spatial equilibrium model links all regions and determines equilibrium imports, exports, and prices for each region. This gives, for each region, the income in period t, and specific consumption of fertilizer, energy for agriculture, acreage, and workforce. Based on this consumption, and taking account of weather, regional agricultural outputs are determined. This provides an exogenous food supply for the spatial equilibrium model in year $t + 1$. The supplies in $t + 1$ of fertilizer, energy, acreage and labor are determined, as functions of population and the investment stream, and the procedure is repeated (see Figures 1, 2, and 3).

Previous efforts in global modeling are reported and critiqued in [1], [2], [3], [4], and [5]. The approach described herein differs from these previous works in several respects. By way of brief comparison:

i. Speaking generally, previous studies tend to describe the world with unrealistic minimally structured functions and restrictive logic. This logic is usually in the form of difference equation/simulation models which are built at a modest level of methodology, though this is claimed to have been appropriate, given the level of

* I am grateful to G. B. Dantzig, J. Duloy, H. R. Hesse, D. G. Johnson, M. L. Kastens, A. Laffer, S. P. Magee, and J. P. Gould for helpful discussions of a previous draft of this material and on related topics.

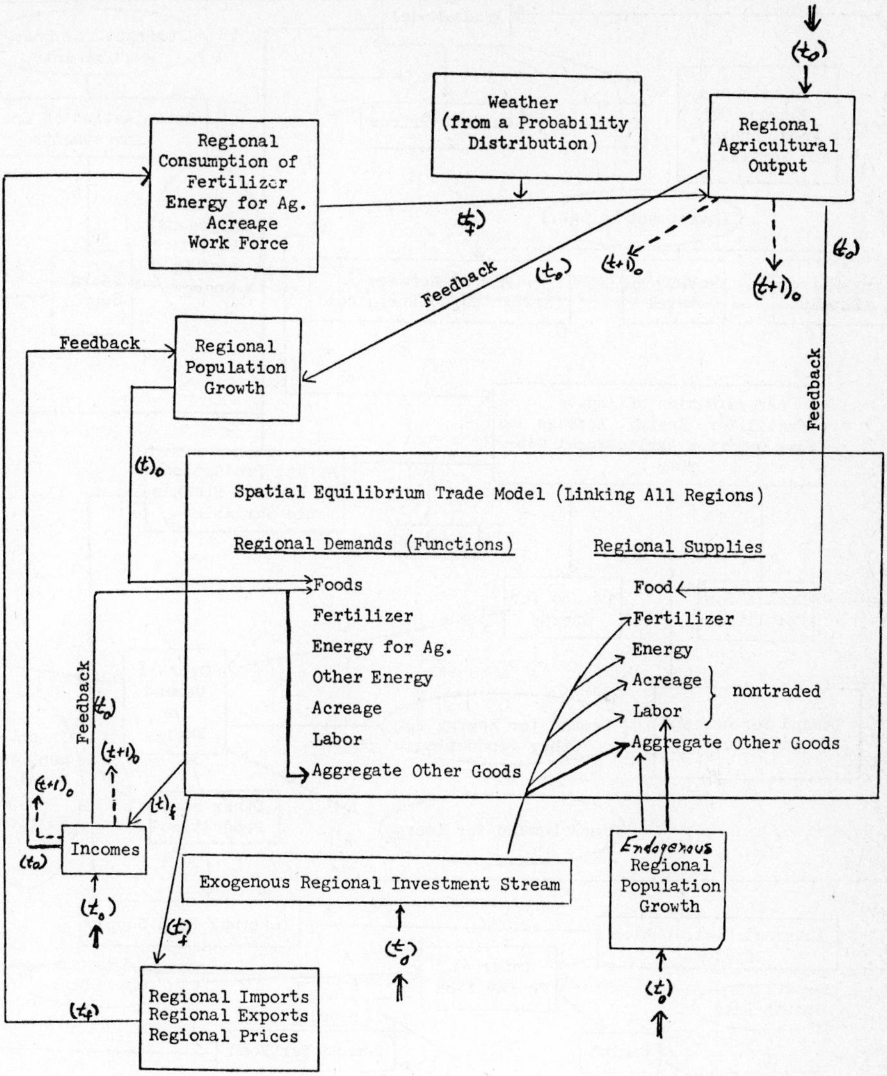

FIGURE 1: OVERALL SYSTEM

0 subscript = beginning of period
f subscript = end of period
⇒ initiating conditions

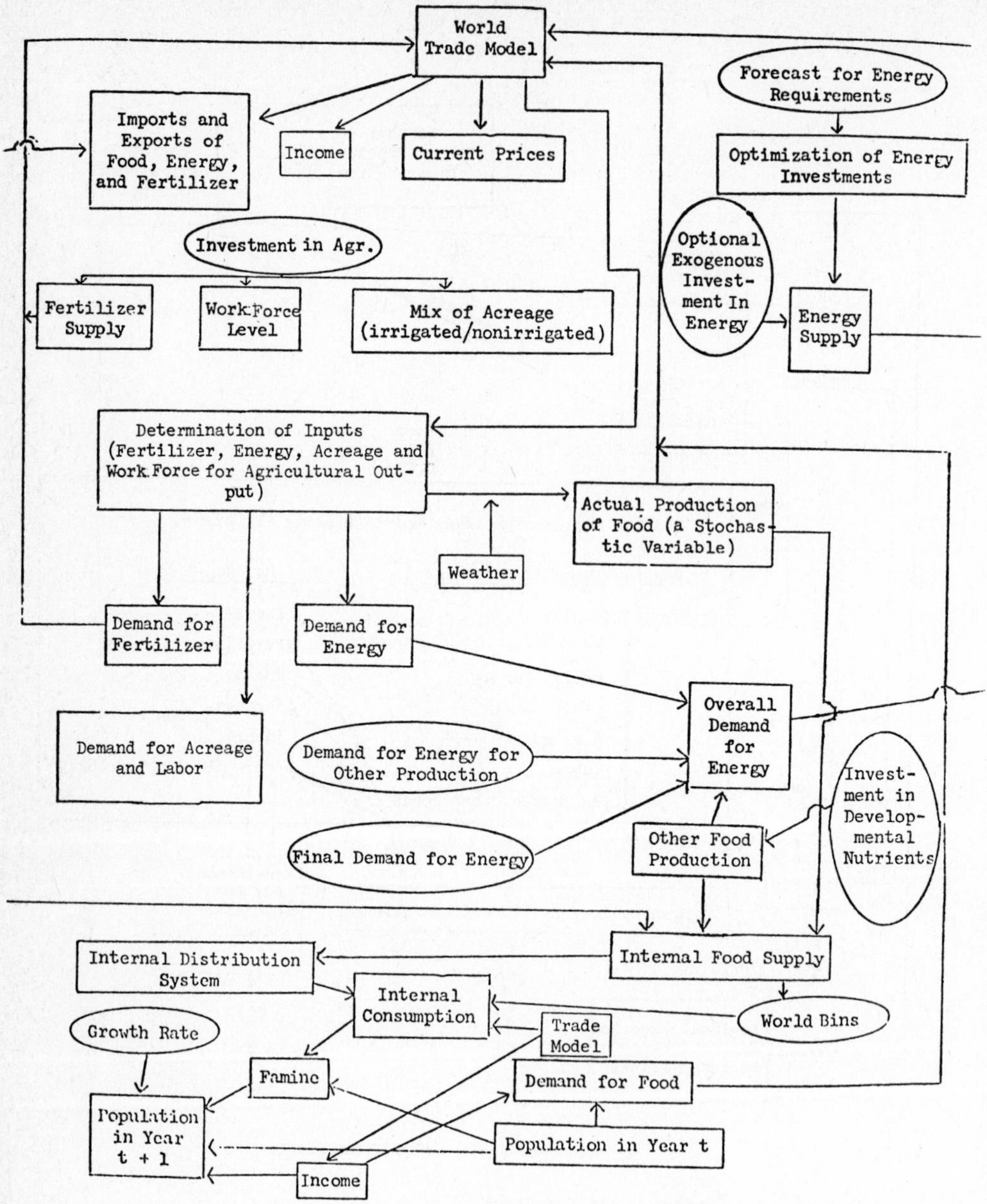

FIGURE 2: PROTOTYPE REGIONAL MODEL, DETAILED

(ellipse) = Exogenous Inputs

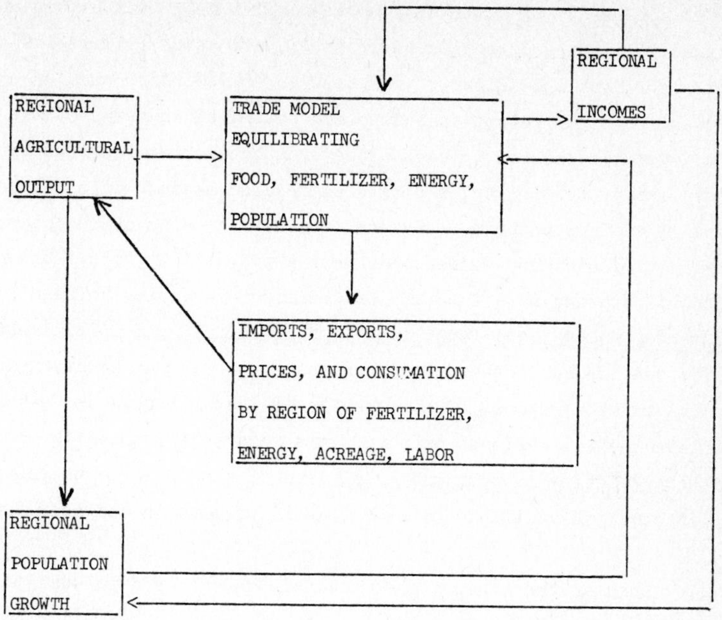

FIGURE 3: DYNAMIC LOOPS

available information and the levels of approximation inherent in the technical structure of the model. The approach herein is along more basic methodological lines, justified by the belief that, ceteris paribus, a stronger technical base will produce more interesting results. Moreover, the accomplishments of mathematical programming and operations research in large-scale cost-effectiveness studies are now abundantly evident in defense, transportation, and other areas of planning in both government and industry. This would seem to provide further support for the prospects of such an approach.

ii. Speaking more specifically, previous models for estimation of grain output tend to be log linear extrapolations over time. This provides estimates which are at best only grossly sensitive in an aggregate sense to changes in inputs and climatological probabilities, and entirely insensitive to potential new trends that can develop via the motivations of humans, organizations, and government. At worst, such estimates can be very misleading, and indeed are thought to be misleading by some prominent workers in the field. By contrast, the regional models in the present discussion are designed to produce agricultural output functions as climate-induced probability distributions. More specifically, for several commodities, such as corn, wheat, rice, and soybeans, regional output functions are estimated in terms of the following input variables: acreage planted in each of several categories (such as irrigated or non-irrigated), labor, fertilizer, a single aggregated measure of all other energy inputs, and, finally, weather patterns. Several weather patterns are defined, and based on the probabilities of these various patterns a probability distribution for regional output can be obtained as a function of the input variables. The mix of inputs for labor, acreage, energy, and fertilizer is derived from the spatial equilibrium trade model. The weather can either be exogenously input or can be drawn from a probability distribution for the region. The selection of factor inputs and weather then leads to a simulated actual regional output. This food supply model is more structured than anything existing in previous models and it should serve to provide the most specific information available on global grain outputs in the near future.

iii. None of the known global analysis models tend to deal in any depth with international trade. Much of the discussion of the food situation confuses need with market demand. During all of the years of the so-called food "surpluses" in North America there was much undernourishment and starvation in the world and even in the U.S. The disappearance of the grain reserves in 1972-1973 was caused not only by a coincidence of crop failures but by a spurt in demand brought about by heightened affluence in Europe and Japan and a policy decision in the USSR. The world food market is outstandingly a price market--concessional sales notwithstanding. Even trade restrictions and subsidies tend to work to a large extent through the price mechanism. Consequently price determination is seen as a key component of the present work. The spatial equilibrium model determines, for each region, exports and imports of foods, energy, and fertilizer along with the appropriate market clearing prices. Though a number of International Trade Models are currently being developed [6], [7], none are linked in a dynamic way to the other systems modeled in this project (food, energy, fertilizer, and population).

It is contemplated that the system we have outlined can serve several functions Certainly it can provide a useful tool for the study and analysis of alternatives. It can offer assistance in decision making at many levels. Another objective could be to provide a tool for studying the implications of various policies for coordinated world planning. Related to this is another important function, more pedagogic in nature: the model may be used as a powerful learning tool. The possibility for making alternative exogenous inputs is consistent with the idea of a parallel "gaming version" of the model. This would be a man-machine interactive mode of operation along the following lines. Experts in such areas as public policy, financial investment, agronomy, energy, international trade, and nutrition would assemble with executives and policy analysts for periods of several days during which the model would be executed, interactively, and a future of events would unfold in accord with a variety of exogenously input constraints and decisions. Such an environment of mock decision making, guided by expert advice, with continous updating of information, has proved in other contexts to be an effective way of expanding horizons and maturing judgment. In terms of the massive dynamics of the problems herein confronted a device for "hands-on" experience, even in a mock scenario, can help to bring the situation home.

One of the most recent and distinguished efforts on world modeling is the work of Mesarovic and Pestel reported in [5]. Their results seem not only to generally support the type of earlier results reported by Meadows et al., but even to outline potentials for more dire consequences for several regions of the world. The Mesarovic-Pestel group has disaggregated the world into about ten regions, and regional submodels have been constructed with numerous interacting components. Though there is a repeated emphasis in the Mesarovic-Pestel discussion on the need for coordinated world planning, satisfaction of overall objectives, etc., there is little if anything along the lines of optimization or suboptimization in their model. The quantity of detail in their logical structure is enormous, but at least qualitatively the functional specifications seem not unlike the systems of proportionalities of the earlier Meadows effect. It is our contention that optimization results can be useful at a minimum in guiding the search for acceptable policies and that the state of the art has reached the point that optimization options can be built-in and successfully handled. Moreover, it is felt that more complex mathematical representations will better approximate the non-linear interactions in world dynamics, and, again, the state of the art is able to handle the added complexity.

We wish not to detract from the fact that other projects on world models have made important and initiative steps in shedding light on policy issues in areas where global activities and interactions are influential. Our basic assumption is merely that by making systematic use of more information, more data, more structure, and more methodology, we at least allow for the possibility of improved, more sensitive forecasting, and this in turn will produce more feasible, perhaps more convincing, world plans for further study and consideration.

The spirit of this effort can be illustrated by reference to the work of Forrester, Meadows, and associates [1], [2], [3] who have produced well-publicized scenarios of doom in perhaps as little as a hundred years based on projections of current technologies and trends. By comparison, the economists' view, at least, as expressed by T. W. Schultz, tends to be generally calm and unsympathetic, for, as Schultz argues, regaring food [8]:

"There are two wholly inconsistent views of the future availability of food. The natural earth view is one of space, depletion of energy and a virtually fixed land area suitable for growing good crops that make it impossible to feed the increasing world population. The social-economic view is based on the ability and intelligence of man to lessen his dependency on cropland and on traditional agriculture, and thereby to reduce the real costs of producing food even in spite of the current population growth. Is is possible to resolve this extraordinary inconsistency? I shall try, but it will not be easy because of the strong prevailing commitment to the natural earth view. I find it ironic that economics, which has long been labelled the dismal science, must bear the cross of showing that the bleak earth outlook for food is not compatible with economic behavior."

The framework herein described should assist in reconciling these two positions, the "limited-earth" view and the more optimistic "social-economic" view. The proponents of the latter position argue that as new needs and conditions are perceived, modifications of behavior, investments in research and technology, etc., will ward off disaster. The limited-earth/exponential growth theorist basically claims that economic adjustments are not instantaneous, lead times are required, and unwittingly we may not allow for enough time.

From one point of view it might be said that the general model to be discussed is an effort toward allowing for "enough time." We seek to recognize explicitly the investment process in various new technologies, both in food and in energy, and to tune accurately enough to changing interactions so that there is sufficient lead time to modify policy and redirect resources without paying catastrophic costs. The remaining sections of this paper describe in more detail the overall framework.

II. Overall Logic of the System

This discussion is a nontechnical summary. It should be mentioned that optional capabilities can be developed for suboptimizing (or otherwise computing) more of the components which are presently described as purely exogenous. It may be helpful to refer back to Figures 1 and 3 during the following discussion.

1. Investment

In each region an investment stream is input for agriculture and energy. In agriculture this includes fertilizer technology, acreage development, irrigation, and work force training. Moreover, there is allowance for investment in selected developmental nutrients. In energy, the investment stream includes development of new technologies. All investments are exogenous.

2. Agricultural Production and Food Supply

For each region a production methodology has been developed for agriculture.

Input levels are derived from the trade model. Given any choice of factor inputs (acreage of various types planted, work force, fertilizer, and other energy inputs) a probability distribution of output can be determined as a function of regional weather patterns. Other possible stochastic shocks may be included (attacks of insects, fungus, etc.). In each region, a simulated actual (as opposed to expected) food production can be obtained by using a Monte Carlo technique with the probability distribution obtained from weather and any other stochastic factors. However, agricultural production cannot be equated with food supply, since much of the labor, capital, energy technology, and material that goes into the food supply system is expended after the crop leaves the farm. Such factors as internal storage facilities and the logistics of land transport are considered in an internal distribution component. There is also provision in the model for a subsystem of other nutrient production to augment agricultural output. These "other foods" supply functions remain to be developed.

3. Supply of Energy and Fertilizer

Supply functions are to be developed for fertilizer and for a variety of energy technologies. These will be dependent on the input investment stream. For fertilizer and energy, for each technology, time dependent cost functions will be estimated and the derived marginal cost curves will represent the supply functions. In the short run supplies are fairly inelastic with respect to price.

4. Demands for Food, Energy, Fertilizer, Acreage, and Labor

Regional demands for food as a function of all prices, population, and income must be estimated. Demands for fertilizer, acreage, workforce and energy for agriculture are derived from solving the agricultural output optimization model with alternative prices. Demands for energy for all other products (including energy production) and for final usage are exogenous.

III. The Agricultural Production System

A. The Inputs

Weather. Along with technology weather is a major determinant of regional and global output. The influence of weather is mainly stochastic, and with a given technology and specified inputs the probability of various levels of yield of a given crop can be related to the probabilities of various weather conditions at specified critical periods of the crop cycle. Examples of methods for describing and analyzing these stochastic relations are found in references [9], [10], [11]. In general, it is important that the analysis be disaggregated with respect to region, crop, and time (intraseasonal variations must be recognized).

Though the influence of weather on yields is qualitatively obvious, the implication of the quantitative importance of this factor on U.S. grain yields may be less appreciated, at least to the extent suggested by the following excerpt from a U.S. Department of Agriculture study performed in 1973 [12]:

> The conclusions [of this study] indicate very strongly that the production of grain in the United States has been favored by extremely good weather in recent years. Any national policy that does not take into consideration the fact that less favorable weather is far more likely than recent nearly optimum conditions, is likely to place us in most unfortunate circumstances. . . . The weather in recent years has been extremely favorable for high grain yields. ... the recent string of consistent high yields, especially for corn, is a weather phenomenon. It is without any basis to suppose that technology has removed the susceptibility of yields to weather fluctuations.

Technology. This is input in the forms of acreage, labor, fertilizer, and energy. Acreage will be classified as irrigated or not, and also according to the variety of seed in the sense of high or low yield. All inputs other than labor and fertilizer (i. e., machines, fuel, pesticides, herbicides, etc.) will be measured in units of energy and aggregated into a single energy input. The feasibility of aggregating in terms of energy has been demonstrated in [13] and [14].

B. Definition of Terms in the Agricultural Production Model

1. Region: A subset of the world assumed self-ruling and independent in terms of policy, trade, and production.

2. Zone: A subset of a region which is homogeneous with regard to weather.

3. Acreage Type: In each zone there are three possible types of acreage: irrigated with a high yield variety; nonirrigated with a high yield variety; and nonirrigated with a low yield variety.

4. Crops and Planting: In each zone on each acreage type there are four possible crops, some of which may be planted more than once a year on the same acreage: wheat, corn, soybeans, and rice.

5. Weather Pattern: Three key time periods are specified for each growing season (each such period being an interval of a specified number of days at a specified time of the year). For each time period weather is characterized as being in one of the conditions good, normal, or poor. A weather pattern is one of the 27 possible triples of such conditions.

6. Total output of crop i in planting j on acreage of type k in zone z, given weather pattern w, is given by

$$Q^T_{ijkzw}(L^T_{ijkz}, F^T_{ijkz}, E^T_{ijkz}, A^T_{ijkz})$$

where

L^T_{ijkz} = total labor input on ijkz

F^T_{ijkz} = total fertilizer input on ijkz

E^T_{ijkz} = total energy input other than fertilizer on ijkz

A^T_{ijkz} = total acreage devoted to ijkz

Assuming Q^T is homogeneous of degree 1 we write

$$Q_{ijkzw}(L_{ijkz}, F_{ijkz}, E_{ijkz})$$

for output per acre as a function of inputs per acre.

7. Expected output of crop i in planting j in region R

$$ERO_{ij} = \sum_z \sum_w P_{wz} \sum_k A^T_{ijkz} \cdot Q_{ijkzw}(L_{ijkz}, F_{ijkz}, E_{ijkz})$$

where

P_{wz} = probability of weather pattern w in zone z .

C. <u>A Maximization Model for Determining Factor Demands</u>

$$\max \sum_{i,j} [\pi_i ERO_{ij} - \sum_{k,z} (\pi_{A_i} A^T_{ijkz} + \pi_F F^T_{ijkz}) - \sum_z (\pi_{E_{ik}} E^T_{ijkz} + \pi_{L_{ik}} L^T_{ijkz})] ,$$

where

π_i = current regional price of food type i

π_{A_i} = regional rental price of acreage of type i

π_F = current regional price of fertilizer

$\pi_{E_{ik}}$ = current regional price of energy input to acreage of type k for crop i

$\pi_{L_{ik}}$ = current regional price of labor employed for production of crop i on acreage of type k .

As prices are varied, and the model re-solved, approximations are obtained for the demand functions for fertilizer, energy, acreage, and labor. Each of these is a function of $(\pi_i, \pi_{A_i}, \pi_F, \pi_{E_{ik}}, \pi_{L_{ik}})$.

D. Methodology for the Agricultural Production System

Econometric methods must be used to estimate the production function Q_{ijkzw} given in (6) above. Initially a log linear form independent of Region might be investigated.

The problem in C must be analyzed after the complication of the Q function is discovered. It may be desirable to add constraints to the problem, in which case potential algorithms include piecewise linearization, decomposition, and generalized Lagrangian techniques developed and previously reported in published literature [15], [16], [17], [18], [19], [20], [21].

IV. The Energy and Fertilizer Components

Regional cost curves must be obtained for producing given amounts of energy with various technologies. Let the cost of producing x_{it} kilocalories of energy in period t with technology i, given past investments $k_{i1}, k_{i2}, \ldots, k_{i,t-1}$, be given by functions

$$C_{it} = H_{it}(k_{i1}, k_{i2}, \ldots, k_{i,t-1}, x_{it}) \quad .$$

Given these relations, for each technology (in each region) the marginal cost relations and supply functions can be derived.

There is also an opportunity to optimize investment and operating expenditures over the various energy technologies so as to satisfy estimated or forecast requirements at minimum cost over a given time horizon. For example

$$x_{it} = O_{it}(k_{i1}, k_{i2}, \ldots, k_{i,t-1}, C_{it})$$

gives output as a function of expenditures. One can then formulate the nonlinear program

$$\min \sum_{t=1}^{T} \sum_{i=1}^{K} k_{it} + C_{it}, \quad \text{s.t.}$$

$$O_{it}(k_{i1}, k_{i2}, \ldots, k_{i,t-1}, C_{it}) \geq R_t, \quad t = 1, \ldots, T$$

which will allocate funds to technologies so as to satisfy estimated requirements $R_1, \ldots, R_T$ at minimum overall cost. It may be of interest to disaggregate this problem over certain subsets of technologies.

Methods similar to the above will be used for the fertilizer sector.

References, in Order of Appearance

1. The Limits to Growth, Donella H. Meadows, Dennis L. Meadows, Jørgen Randers, and William W. Behrens, III. Second Edition, November 1974, Universe Books.

2. Dynamics of Growth in a Finite World, Dennis L. Meadows, William W. Behrens III, Donella H. Meadows, Roger F. Naill, Jørgen Randers, and Erich K. O. Zahn. 1974, Wright-Allen Press.

3. Toward Global Equilibrium: Collected Papers, Dennis L. Meadows, and Donella H. Meadows. 1973, Wright-Allen Press.

4. Models of Doom, H. S. D. Cole, Christopher Freeman, Marie Jahoda, and K. L. R. Pavitt. 1973, Universe Books.

5. Mankind at the Turning Point, Mihajlo Mesarovic and Eduard Pestel. The Second Report to the Club of Rome. Dutton and Co., Reader's Digest Press, 1974.

6. "A Multilateral, Multi-Commodity Model of International Trade Flows," J. Stuart McMenamin, Jean-Paul Pinard, R. Robert Russell, Richard Boyce, and John W. Hooper. CIA Trade Flow Model, IPA Report, October 1974.

7. "Prices, Incomes, and Foreign Trade," Stephen P. Magee. A Paper Prepared for the Conference on Research in International Trade and Finance, International Finance Section, Princeton University, March 30-31, 1973.

8. "The Food Alternatives Before Us: An Economic Perspective," Theodore W. Schultz. Agricultural Economics Paper No. 74:6, Department of Economics, University of Chicago, revised July 1974.

9. Discussion Paper: "Climatic Probabilities and the Estimation of Food Crop Production in Developing Countries," C.D. Throsby. Macquarie University, Sydney, Australia. Food and Agricultural Organisation of the United Nations, Rome, January 1974.

10. "Calculation of Confidence Limits of Monthly Rainfall," H. L. Manning. J. Agric. Sc., Vol. 47, No. 2 (April 1956), pp. 154-156.

11. "Confidence Limits for Seasonal Rainfall: Their Value in Kenya Agriculture," T. Woodhead. Exptal. Agric., Vol. 6, No. 2 (April 1970), pp. 81-86.

12. "The Influence of Weather and Climate on United States Grain Yields: Bumper Crops or Droughts." A Report to the Administratior, National Oceanic and Atmospheric Administration from the Associate Administrator for Environmental Monitoring and Prediction, December 14, 1973.

13. "Energy Use in the U.S. Food System," John S. Steinhart and Carol E. Steinhart. Science, Vol. 184, No. 4134 (April 19, 1974), pp. 307-316.

14. "Food Production and the Energy Crisis," David Pimentel, L. E. Hurd, A. C. Bellotti, M. J. Forster, I.N. Oka, O. D. Sholes, and R. J. Whitman. Science, Vol. 182 (November 2, 1973), pp. 443-449.

15. "Extensions of Lagrange Multipliers in Nonlinear Programming," F. Gould. SIAM Journal of Applied Mathematics, Vol. 17, No. 6 (November 1969), pp. 1280-1297.

16. "A Class of Inside-Out Algorithms for General Programs," F. Gould. Management Science, Vol. 16, No. 5 (January 1970), pp. 350-356.

17. "Nonlinear Tolerance Programming," F. Gould. Numerical Methods for Nonlinear Optimization, Chapter 24. Academic Press, 1972. Edited by F. A. Lootsma.

18. "A General Saddle Point Result for Constrained Optimization," F. Gould, Kenneth J. Arrow and Stephen M. Howe. Mathematical Programming, Vol. 5, No. 2 (October 1973), pp. 225-234.

19. "Nonlinear Pricing: Applications to Concave Programming," F. Gould. Operations Research, Vol. 19, No. 4 (July-August 1971), pp. 1026-1035.

20. "An Existence Theorem for Penalty Function Theory," F. Gould and John P. Evans. SIAM Journal on Control, Vol. 12, No. 3 (August 1974), pp. 509-516.

21. "Exact Penalty Functions in Nonlinear Programming," F. Gould, John P. Evans and Jon W. Tolle. Mathematical Programming, Vol. 4, No. 1 (February 1973), pp. 72-97.

22. "A Unified Approach to Complementarity in Optimization," F. Gould and Jon W. Tolle. Discrete Mathematics, Vol. 7, Nos. 3-4 (February 1974), pp. 225-271.

23. "A Simplicial Algorithm for the Nonlinear Complementarity Problem," F. Gould and Marshall L. Fisher. Mathematical Programming, Vol. 6, No. 3 (June 1974), pp. 281-300.

24. "A Simplicial Approximation Algorithm for Solving Systems of Nonlinear Equations," F. Gould, Marhsll L. Fisher and Jon W. Tolle. To appear in the Proceedings of the Conference on Mathematical Programming and Its Applications, National Institute of Higher Mathematics, City University, Rome, Italy, April 1974.

25. "A New Simplicial Approximation Algorithm with Restarts: Relations Between Convergence and Labeling," F. Gould, Marshall L. Fisher and Jon W. Tolle. To appear in the Proceedings of the Conference on Computing Fixed Points with Applications, Department of Mathematical Sciences, Clemson University, Clemson, South Carolina, June 1974.

THE APPLICATION OF GRADIENT ALGORITHMS TO THE OPTIMIZATION OF CONTROLLED VERSIONS OF THE WORLD 2 MODEL OF FORRESTER

J.L. de Jong
Department of Mathematics
Eindhoven University of Technology

and

J.W.Dercksen
Netherlands Organization for the Advancement of Pure Research (Z.W.O.)
Department of Physics
Eindhoven University of Technology
P.O.Box 513, Eindhoven, The Netherlands

1. *INTRODUCTION*

In early 1972, shortly after the results in Forrester's book "World Dynamics" (Forrester (1971)) had arosed the interest of many people in the study of world models, a project group, named "Global Dynamics" was started in the Netherlands (cf.Rademaker (1972)) which set itself as one of its goals to study the effects of the incorporation of controls into the world models considered by the M.I.T. groups of Forrester and Meadows under sponsorship of the Club of Rome (cf. Meadows (1972)).

One way to get a better understanding of a controlled system is to determine the optimal controls given suitably chosen optimization criteria and to study the sensitivity of these optimal controls to changes in model and criterion parameters. An essential tool in such a study is an efficient algorithm (or better: computer program) for the numerical solution of optimal control problems of the particular type at hand. In case of the "Global Dynamics" project, in which several Dutch universities and companies cooperated, several groups set out to test different classes of known numerical optimal control algorithms in order to select the one best suited to generate the many optimal solutions required for the project. Two of these groups already reported their results (cf. Olsder & Strijbos (1973), Dekker & Kerckhoffs (1974)).

At Eindhoven University of Technology a special experimental program was set up to compare the performance of different known gradient type algorithms. These were applied to the common test problem of the project which consisted of a simplified version of the controlled world model of Forrester (with 4 instead of 5 state variables and with linear approximations of the sectionally linear table functions in Forrester's model). The results of this experimental program as well as the results of the application of the better algorithms to the complete controlled World 2 model are presented in this paper.

The outline of the paper is as follows: In Chapter 2 a precise statement is given of the complete controlled World 2 model and of the test problem, the simplified controlled World 2 model. In Chapter 3 an outline is given of the different gradient algorithms considered in the experimental program together with a discussion of the two different techniques tried out to take into account the bounds on the values of the control variables. Also in this chapter some remarks are made on the scaling of the variables. In Chapter 4 the numerical results for the different applications of the algorithms are presented and discussed. A short summary of the conclusions, an acknowledgement, a list of references, 5 tables and 4 figures conclude the paper.

2. *THE CONTROLLED WORLD 2 MODEL*

2.1 *The World 2 model of Forrester*

The World 2 model which Forrester developed for the Club of Rome and which formed the basis of the results in his book "World Dynamics" (Forrester (1971)) consists of a set of 5 interacting nonlinear difference equations which describe the evolution of 5 "level" or state variables:

P : Population

CI : Capital Investment

CIAF : Capital Investment in Agriculture Fraction

POL : Pollution

NR : Natural Resources

Differential equations in a notation more common to control engineers and equivalent to the difference equations of Forrester were given in Cuypers (1973)

$$\begin{aligned}
\dot{P} &= 0.04.P.F_3(MSL).F_{16}(CR).F_{17}(FR).F_{18}(POLR) \\
&\quad -0.028.P.F_{11}(MSL).F_{12}(POLR).F_{13}(FR).F_{14}(CR) \\
\dot{CI} &= -0.025.CI + 0.05.P.F_{26}(MSL) \\
\dot{CIAF} &= -(CIAF - F_{36}(FR).F_{43}[F_{38}(MSL)/F_{40}(FR)])/15 \\
\dot{POL} &= -\ POL/F_{34}(POLR) + P.F_{32}(CIR) \\
\dot{NR} &= -\ P.F_{42}(MSL)
\end{aligned} \tag{2.1}$$

The functions $F_k(\cdot)$ in these equations are *coupling functions* given by Forrester as sectionally linear functions of their arguments. (The index k corresponds to the number of the section in Chapter 3 of Forrester (1971) in which the corresponding coupling function is presented). The arguments of these functions are, respectively, the normalized variables:

$CR = P/PS$ (PS = Population Standard = $3.5775.10^9$)

$CIR = CI/P$

$POLR = POL/POLS$ (POLS = Pollution Standard = $3.6.10^9$)

$NRFR = NR/NRI$ (NRI = Natural Resources Initial = 9.10^{11})

and the auxiliary variables MSL (= Material Standard of Living) and FR (= Food Ratio) defined as

$$MSL = (CI/P)((1-CIAF)/(1-CIAFN)).F_6(NRFR) \tag{2.2}$$

and

$$FR = F_{20}(CR).F_{21}(CIRA).F_{28}(POLR) \tag{2.3}$$

where

$$CIRA = (CI/P)(CIAF/CIAFN) \qquad (CIAFN = CIAF\ Normal = 0.3)$$

Initial conditions for the differential equations (2.1) were specified by Forrester for the year 1900. Integration of the differential equations up to the year 1970 yields the following initial conditions for the year 1970 (cf. Cuypers (1973)).

$$\begin{aligned} P(1970) &= 3.67830938.10^9 & POL(1970) &= 2.88957159.10^9 \\ CI(1970) &= 3.83097633.10^9 & NR(1970) &= 7.7680742.10^{11} \\ CIAF(1970) &= 0.28031694 \end{aligned} \tag{2.4}$$

2.2 *The complete controlled World 2 model*

The most natural way to introduce regulating or control variables into this model (cf. Burns & Malone (1974)) is to assume that the magnitude of some of the coefficients in the differential equations (2.1) can be manipulated within certain bounds. The basis of the introduction of control variables into the World 2 model in case of the "Global Dynamics" project was the assumption that fractions U_P, U_{CI}, U_{POL} and U_{NR} of the total amount of goods and services not designated for agriculture, which amount was defined as

$$\begin{aligned} ISO &= CI.(1-CIAF).F_6(NRFR).U_r \\ &= P.MSL.(1-CIAFN).U_r \end{aligned} \tag{2.5}$$

(where ISO stands for Industrial and Service Output and where U_r is an efficiency factor (= the reciprocal of the capital coefficient with the standard value $U_r = 1/3$), can be allocated for respectively i) birthcontrol, ii) reinvestment, iii) pollution control and iv) protection of the natural resources. In addition, it was assumed that for the items i), iii) and iv) a law of diminishing returns would apply. Thus, the following *control multipliers* were postulated.

$$\begin{aligned} G_1(U_P) &= \exp\ (-\gamma_1.U_P.MSL) \\ G_3(U_{POL}) &= \exp\ (-\gamma_3.U_{POL}.(MSL/F_{32}(CIR))) \\ G_4(U_{NR}) &= \exp\ (-\gamma_4.U_{NR}) \end{aligned} \tag{2.6}$$

where γ_1, γ_3 and γ_4 are constants with the standard values

$$\gamma_1 = 25 \qquad \gamma_3 = 10 \qquad \gamma_4 = 3.5 \tag{2.7}$$

The assumed possibility to control the fraction of the ISO for reinvestment was realized by replacing the second differential equation of (2.1) by

$$\begin{aligned}\dot{CI} &= -0.025.CI + ISO.U_{CI} \\ &= -0.025.CI + P.MSL.(1-CIAFN).U_r.U_{CI}\end{aligned} \quad (2.8)$$

Given the standard values CIAFN = 0.3 and U_r = 1/3, the state equations of the controlled World 2 model become

$$\begin{aligned}\dot{P} &= 0.04.P.F_3(MSL).F_{16}(CR).F_{17}(FR).F_{18}(POLR).\exp(-\gamma_1 U_P.MSL) \\ &\quad - 0.028\ P.F_{11}(MSL).F_{12}(POLR).F_{13}(FR).F_{14}(CR) \\ \dot{CI} &= -0.025.CI + (0.7/3).P.MSL.U_{CI} \\ \dot{CIAF} &= -(CIAF - F_{36}(FR).F_{43}[F_{38}(MSL)/F_{40}(FR)])/15 \\ \dot{POL} &= -POL/F_{34}(POLR) + P.F_{32}(CIR).\exp(-\gamma_3 U_{POL}(MSL/F_{32}(CIR))) \\ \dot{NR} &= -P.F_{42}(MSL).\exp(-\gamma_4 U_{NR})\end{aligned} \quad (2.9)$$

As part of the numerical investigations of the "Global Dynamics" project polynomial approximations were determined of the coupling functions $F_k(\cdot)$ which could replace the sectionally linear functions of Forrester in the ranges of interest for the optimization. The coefficients of these polynomials are given in *Table 2.1*.

Given the meaning of the control variables the following control constraints are self evident

$$U_P \geq 0 \qquad U_{CI} \geq 0 \qquad U_{POL} \geq 0 \qquad U_{NR} \geq 0 \quad (2.10)$$

and

$$U_P + U_{CI} + U_{POL} + U_{NR} \leq 1 \quad (2.11)$$

In addition, in order to prevent the optimization procedures to generate unrealistic values, the only control variable appearing linearly in the differential equation was given a simple upper and lower limit

$$0.198 \leq U_{CI} \leq 0.242 \quad (2.12)$$

To measure the quality of different controls a performance criterion should be defined. In case of the "Global Dynamics" project several criteria were considered of which the following, Bolza-type criterion became the standard one

$$J[u] = \int_{1970}^{2100} QL(\tau)P(\tau)d\tau + \lambda_P.P(2100) + \lambda_{POL}.POL(2100) + \lambda_{NR}.NR(2100) \quad (2.13)$$

In this expression the symbol QL (= Quality of Life) stands for almost the same performance measure as introduced by Forrester

$$QL = F_{38}(CMSL).F_{39}(CR).F_{40}(FR).F_{41}(POLR), \quad (2.14)$$

the difference being that the argument of the coupling function $F_{38}(\cdot)$ is not MSL but CMSL (= Consumption Material Standard of Living) which was defined by

$$CMSL = MSL.(1-U_P-U_{CI}-U_{POL}-U_{NR})/0.7828 \tag{2.15}$$

The constants λ_P, λ_{POL} and λ_{NR} in (2.13) were given the standard values

$$\lambda_P = 10 \quad \lambda_{POL} = -0.5P(1970)/POLS \quad \lambda_{NR} = 100P(1970)/NR(1970) \tag{2.16}$$

The optimal control problem thus derived, which will be called the *complete controlled World 2 model* to distinguish it from the simplified controlled World 2 model to be discussed in the next section, can now be summarized as follows:

"Given the state equations (2.9) with the initial conditions (2.4), find the control variables U_P, U_{CI}, U_{POL} and U_{NR} as functions of the time which satisfy the control constraints (2.10), (2.11) and (2.12) and which maximize (or minimize the negative of) the performance criterion (2.13)".

2.3 The simplified controlled World 2 model

The presence in the state equations (2.9) of the coupling functions, the values of which are to be determined by interpolation or polynomial approximation,considerably increase the computer time required for integration. For that reason, it was decided in an early phase of the numerical optimization experiments to make use of a simpler model which should have roughly the same characteristics as the original model but would be much easier to integrate. This object was realized by first linearizing all coupling functions around the standard uncontrolled trajectory and thereafter simplifying the complex of linear coupling functions in such a way, that in the uncontrolled case the results of Forrester were reasonably reproduced. Following this approach it was found that the state variable CIAF, which stayed fairly constant under standard conditions, could be replaced by a constant. Thus, the number of state equations was reduced from 5 to 4. Similarly, a number of coupling functions could be omitted as their values under standard conditions hardly differed from 1.0. This led to the following simple state equations

$$\begin{aligned}
\dot{P} &= 0.04.P.f_1(POL).f_2(CMSL).\exp(-25U_P.MSL)-0.028.P.f_3(POL).f_4(CMSL)\\
\dot{CI} &= -0.025\ CI + P.MSL.U_{CI}\\
\dot{POL} &= -POL/f_7(POL) + P.f_6(CI/P).\exp(-10U_{POL})\\
\dot{NR} &= -P.MSL.\exp(-3.5U_{NR})
\end{aligned} \tag{2.17}$$

where

$$\begin{aligned}
f_1(POL) &= 1.015 - 0.015\ POL & f_4(CMSL) &= 2.6 - 1.6\ CMSL\\
f_2(CMSL) &= 1.15 - 0.15\ CMSL & f_6(CI/P) &= -1.0 + 2(CI/P)\\
f_3(POL) &= 0.95 + 0.05\ POL & f_7(POL) &= 0.8333 + 0.1667.POL
\end{aligned} \tag{2.18}$$

and

$$MSL = (CI/P)(NR/NR(1970)) \quad (2.19)$$

and

$$CMSL = MSL.(0.7 - U_P - U_{CI} - U_{POL} - U_{NR})/0.7 \quad (2.20)$$

The corresponding initial conditions became

$$P(1970) = 1.0 \quad CI(1970) = 1.0 \quad POL(1970) = 1.0 \quad NR(1970) = 800/3.6 \quad (2.21)$$

and the control constraints

$$U_P \geq 0 \qquad U_{POL} \geq 0 \qquad U_{NR} \geq 0 \quad (2.22)$$

$$0.04027 \leq U_{CI} \leq 0.05527 \quad (2.23)$$

and

$$U_P + U_{CI} + U_{POL} + U_{NR} \leq 0.7 \quad (2.24)$$

As performance criterion was chosen

$$J[u] = \int_{1970}^{2100} QL(\tau)P(\tau)d\tau + 5.P(2100) - 0.05.POL(2100) + 0.4NR(2100) \quad (2.25)$$

where QL was defined as

$$QL = (0.8+0.2CMSL)(1.5-0.5P)(1.02-0.02P) \quad (2.26)$$

Thus, in summary, the following optimal control problem, to be called *the simplified controlled World 2 model* resulted

"Given the state equations (2.17) and the initial conditions (2.21), find the control variables U_P, U_{CI}, U_{POL} and U_{NR} as functions of time which satisfy the control constraints (2.22) - (2.24) and which maximize (or minimize the negative of) the performance criterion (2.25)".

It should be noted that although the standard (uncontrolled) behavior of this simplified model compared quite well with the results of Forrester, the optimal behavior turned out to be quite different from the optimal behavior of the complete controlled World 2 model. One of the main reasons for this was the coupling function f_4(MSL), which for values of MSL larger than 1.625 have unrealistic negative values. This turned out to have a large influence on the optimal behavior. After the discovery of the imperfection the use of the model was continued for reason of its good properties as a test problem.

3. *OUTLINE OF THE ALGORITHMS TESTED*

3.1 *Gradient algorithms for solving optimal control problems*

Both optimal control problems specified in the preceding sections were of the following basic form:

"Given the state equations

$$x = f(x,u) \qquad x:[t_b,t_f] \to R^n,\ u:[t_b,t_f] \to R^m \quad (3.1)$$

and the initial conditions

$$x(t_b) = x_b \tag{3.2}$$

find the control vector $u(t), t\varepsilon[t_b,t_f]$ which satisfies the constraints

$$u_{i,min} \leq u_i(t) \leq u_{i,max} \qquad t\varepsilon[t_b,t_f] \ , \ i=1,\ldots,m \tag{3.3}$$

and which generates the least value of the performance criterion

$$J[u] = k(x(t_f)) + \int_{t_b}^{t_f} \ell(x(\tau),u(\tau))d\tau \ \text{"} \tag{3.4}$$

From a computational point of view this type of optimal control problem is rather simple: The initial and final times are fixed and there are no terminal constraints. Except for the presence of the constraints on the values of the control variables, a problem which will be dealt with below in a special section, this control problem formulation is well suited for the gradient type of algorithms, as will be seen.

Gradient methods for solving optimal control problems are iterative methods in which the control vector function is modified in each iteration so as to improve the performance criterion. Most of the algorithms contain the following basic steps

(o) assume $u^{(o)}(t), t\varepsilon[t_b,t_f]$, given and set i: = 0;

(i) evaluate the performance criterion $J[u^{(i)}]$ corresponding to $u^{(i)}$ (by integrating the state equations (3.1) forward) and the gradient $\nabla_u J^{(i)}(t), t\varepsilon[t_b,t_f]$ as to be discussed below (i.e. by integrating the costate equations (3.7) backward);

(ii) test: if $u^{(i)}$ optimal, stop; otherwise:

(iii) determine a new search direction $d^{(i)}(t), t\varepsilon[t_b,t_f]$;

(iv) set $u(t): = u^{(i)}(t)+\alpha d^{(i)}(t)$ and determine the scalar value $\alpha^{(i)}$ of α for which the performance criterion considered as a function of α reaches its minimum value (or in some algorithms: reaches a lower value which satisfies certain specifications)

(v) set $u^{(i+1)}(t): = u^{(i)}(t)+\alpha^{(i)}d^{(i)}(t)$, set i: = i+1 and return to step (i).

The step in this algorithm by which the different algorithms are distinguished is step (iii). Over the years a great number of search directions have been proposed, most of which, however, have in common that they make use of the gradient (with respect to the control) of the performance criterion (considered as a functional of the control only). This gradient is, as is well known (cf. Bryson & Ho (1969)), at each time instant equal to

$$\nabla_u J^{(i)}(t) = H_u^{(i)T}(t) = (\ell_u^{\ T}+f_u^{\ T}\lambda)^{(i)}(t) \tag{3.5}$$

where H_u is the partial derivative with respect to the control of the *Hamiltonian*, which is defined as:

$$H(x,u,\lambda) = \ell(x,u)+\lambda^T f(x,u) \tag{3.6}$$

and where $\lambda(t), t\varepsilon[t_b,t_f]$ is the *costate* or *adjoint vector* which is the solution of the costate or adjoint equation

$$\dot{\lambda} = -f_x^T\lambda - \ell_x^T \tag{3.7}$$

with the "initial" condition

$$\lambda(t_f) = k_x^T(x(t_f)) \tag{3.8}$$

The gradient $\nabla_u J^{(i)}(t)$ corresponding to a particular $u^{(i)}$ can be computed by one backward integration of the costate equations (corresponding to that $u^{(i)}$).

3.2 Methods tested

Most gradient methods in use for solving optimal control problems may be considered the infinite dimensional equivalents of the better known gradient methods for solving unconstrained finite dimensional minimization problems. The methods actually tested in the numerical experiments to be described were the infinite dimensional equivalents of the following finite dimensional methods (cf. Murray (1972), Jacoby, Kowalik & Pizzo (1972)):

a) SD(= Steepest Descent) method
b) PARTAN (= Parallel Tangents) method
c) CGI (= Conjugate Gradient I) method (of Fletcher-Reeves)
d-e) CGII (= Conjugate Gradient II) method (of Hestenes-Stiefel)
f) DFP (= Davidon-Fletcher-Powell) method

Given the definitions of the infinite dimensional inner product and the corresponding norm (in $\mathcal{L}_2^m[t_b,t_f]$)

$$<g^{(i)},h^{(i)}> = \int_{t_b}^{t_f} g^{(i)^T}(\tau)h^{(i)}(\tau)d\tau \qquad ||v|| = <v,v>^{\frac{1}{2}} \tag{3.9}$$

the search directions of the infinite dimensional counterparts of the methods a) - e) are, respectively, given by

a') SD-method (cf. Kelley (1962) Bryson & Denham (1962)):

$$d^{(i)}(t) := -\nabla_u J^{(i)}(t) \tag{3.10}$$

b') PARTAN-method (cf. Wong, Dressler & Luenberger (1971)):

$$d^{(2i)}(t) := -\nabla_u J^{(2i)}(t) \qquad i = 0,1,2,... \tag{3.11}$$

$$d^{(2i+1)}(t) := ||\nabla_u J^{(2i)}|| \frac{(u^{(2i+1)}(t)-u^{2(i-1)}(t))}{||u^{(2i+1)}-u^{2(i-1)}||} \quad i = 1,2,... \qquad := 0 \quad i = 0 \tag{3.12}$$

c') CGI-method (cf. Lasdon, Mitter & Waren (1967)):

$$d^{(i)}(t) = -\nabla_u J^{(i)}(t)+\beta^{(i)} d^{(i-1)}(t) \tag{3.13}$$

where

$$\beta^{(i)} = \frac{<\nabla_u J^{(i)},\nabla_u J^{(i)}>}{<\nabla_u J^{(i-1)},\nabla_u J^{(i-1)}>} \tag{3.14}$$

d') CGIIA-method (cf. Pagurek & Woodside (1968))

$$d^{(i)}(t) := -\nabla_u J^{(i)}(t)+\beta^{(i)} d^{(i-1)}(t) \tag{3.15}$$

with

$$\beta^{(i)} := \frac{<\nabla_u J^{(i)},v^{(i)}>}{<d^{(i-1)},v^{(i)}>} \tag{3.16}$$

where $v^{(i)}(t)$ (which is the infinite dimensional equivalent of the matrix-vector product $G^{(i)} d^{(i-1)}$ where $G^{(i)}$ is the local Hessian), can be determined from

$$v^{(i)}(t) := f_u^T w^{(i)}(t)+H_{ux} z^{(i)}(t)+H_{uu} d^{(i-1)}(t) \tag{3.17}$$

where $z^{(i)}(t)$ is the solution of

$$\dot{z}^{(i)} = f_x z^{(i)}(t)+f_u d^{(i-1)}(t) \qquad z^{(i)}(t_b) = 0 \tag{3.18}$$

and $w^{(i)}(t)$ is the solution of

$$\dot{w}^{(i)} = -f_x^T w^{(i)}-H_{xx} z^{(i)}-H_{xu} d^{(i-1)} \qquad w^{(i)}(t_f) = k_{xx} z^{(i)}(t_f) \tag{3.19}$$

e') CGIIB-method (cf. Sinnott & Luenberger (1967)):
As CGII-A-method with the replacement of H_{ux}, H_{uu} in (3.17) and H_{xx} and H_{xu} in (3.19) by respectively ℓ_{ux}, ℓ_{uu}, ℓ_{xx} and ℓ_{xu}

f') DFP-method (cf. Tripathi & Narendra (1968)):

$$d^{(i)}(t) = -\nabla_u J^{(i)}(t) - \sum_{k=0}^{i-1} \frac{<s^{(k)},\nabla_u J^{(i)}>}{<s^{(k)},y^{(k)}>} s^{(k)}(t) + \sum_{k=0}^{i-1} \frac{<a^{(k)},\nabla_u J^{(i)}>}{<a^{(k)},y^{(k)}>} a^{(k)}(t) \tag{3.20}$$

where

$$a^{(k)}(t) := y^{(k)}(t) + \sum_{j=0}^{k-1} \frac{<s^{(j)},y^{(k)}>}{<s^{(j)},y^{(j)}>} s^{(j)}(t) - \sum_{j=0}^{k-1} \frac{<a^{(j)},y^{(k)}>}{<a^{(j)},y^{(i)}>} a^{(j)}(t) \tag{3.21}$$

with

$$s^{(j)}(t) := u^{(j+1)}(t)-u^{(j)}(t) \quad , \qquad y^{(j)}(t) := \nabla_u J^{(j+1)}(t)-\nabla_u J^{(j)}(t) \tag{3.22}$$

In the process of executing this DFP-algorithm, it is required that in each iteration two new vector functions, $s^{(i)}(t)$ and $a^{(i)}(t)$, are stored. This implies that the required computer memory increases with the number of iterations. To cure this, it is customary to restart the algorithm periodically after a fixed number of iterations.

It may be noticed that in both methods, the CGIIA method and the CGIIB method, one extra forward integration (of (3.18)) and one extra backward integration (of (3.19)) are required to evaluate $\beta^{(i)}$. The CGIIB method has as advantage over the CGIIA method that no second order partial derivatives of the state equations are required which implies less programming effort and less computing time for integration.

3.3 *Techniques for bounded controls*

a) Clipping-off-technique

The first technique which was used for taking care of bounds on the values of the control components is known as the clipping-off-technique (cf. Quintana & Davison (1974)) and amounts to setting the control components back at their bounds as soon as these are violated in the search for a line minimum. This implies the following modification in step (iv) of the standard algorithm: Evaluate

$$u_{j,unclipped}(t) := \bar{u}_j^{(i)}(t) + \alpha d^{(i)}(t) \tag{3.23}$$

and set

$$\begin{aligned} \bar{u}_j(t) &:= u_{j,max} && \text{if} \quad u_{j,uncl}(t) \geq u_{j,max} \\ &:= u_{j,uncl}(t) && \text{if} \quad u_{j,min} < u_{j,uncl}(t) < u_{j,max} \\ &:= u_{j,min} && \text{if} \quad u_{j,uncl}(t) \leq u_{j,min} \end{aligned} \tag{3.24}$$

In case of no bounds on the values of the control components, the gradient tends to zero when the minimum is approached. Most gradient algorithms make implicitly use of this fact. When the minimum is attained at the boundary of the feasible region, the corresponding gradient (component) does not become small. This may spoil the search direction calculations. For instance, without modification, the values of the inner products in $\beta^{(i)}$ in (3.14) would almost completely be determined by the large gradient components corresponding to the control components at their bounds, and $\beta^{(i)}$ erroneously would get the value of approximately 1.0 in all iterations. In order to cure that situation the algorithms a') - f') were modified with the aid of *clipped functions* which are defined as

$$\begin{aligned} \bar{q}_j^{(i)}(t) &:= 0 && \text{if} \quad \bar{u}_j^{(i)}(t) \textit{ and } \bar{u}_j^{(i-1)}(t) \text{ at boundary} \\ &:= q_j^{(i)}(t) && \text{otherwise} \end{aligned} \tag{3.25}$$

With this definition the modified search directions may be written as:

a') method of steepest descent

no change

b') PARTAN-method

$$d^{(2i)}(t) := -\nabla_u J^{(2i)}(t) \qquad i = 0,1,2,\ldots$$

$$d^{(2i+1)}(t) := ||\nabla_u J^{(2i)}(t)|| \frac{(\bar{u}^{(2i+1)}(t)-\bar{u}^{2(i-1)}(t))}{||(\bar{u}^{(2i+1)}(t)-\bar{u}^{2(i-1)}(t)||} \qquad i = 1,2,\ldots \tag{3.26}$$

$$= 0 \qquad i = 0$$

c') CGI-method

$$d^{(i)}(t) := -\nabla_u J^{(i)}(t) + \frac{\langle \overline{\nabla_u J}^{(i)}, \overline{\nabla_u J}^{(i)} \rangle}{\langle \overline{\nabla_u J}^{(i-1)}, \overline{\nabla_u J}^{(i-1)} \rangle} d^{(i-1)}(t) \tag{3.27}$$

d'-e') CGII-methods

$$d^{(i)}(t) := -\nabla_u J^{(i)}(t) + \frac{\langle \overline{\nabla_u J}^{(i)}, \tilde{v}^{(i)} \rangle}{\langle s^{(i-1)}, \tilde{v}^{(i)} \rangle} s^{(i-1)}(t) \tag{3.28}$$

where

$$\tilde{v}^{(i)}(t) := f_u^T \tilde{w}^{(i)}(t) + H_{ux}^{(\ell)} \tilde{z}^{(i)}(t) + H_{uu}^{(\ell)} s^{(i-1)}(t) \tag{3.29}$$

with $\tilde{z}^{(i)}(t)$ satisfying

$$\dot{\tilde{z}}^{(i)} = f_x \tilde{z}^{(i)} + f_u s^{(i-1)} \qquad \tilde{z}^{(i)}(t_b) = 0 \tag{3.30}$$

and $\tilde{w}^{(i)}(t)$ satisfying

$$\dot{\tilde{w}}^{(i)} = -f_x^T \tilde{w}^{(i)} - H_{xx}^{(\ell)} \tilde{z}^{(i)} - H_{xu}^{(\ell)} s^{(i-1)} \qquad \tilde{w}^{(i)}(t_f) = k_{xx} \tilde{z}^{(i)}(t_f) \tag{3.31}$$

f') DFP-method

$$d^{(i)}(t) := -\nabla_u J^{(i)}(t) - \sum_{k=0}^{i-1} \frac{\langle s^{(k)}, \overline{\nabla_u J}^{(i)} \rangle}{\langle s^{(k)}, \bar{y}^{(k)} \rangle} s^{(k)}(t) + \sum_{k=0}^{i-1} \frac{\bar{a}^{(k)}, \overline{\nabla_u J}^{(i)}}{\bar{a}^{(k)}, \bar{y}^{(k)}} \bar{a}^{(k)}(t) \tag{3.32}$$

with

$$a^{(k)}(t) := y^{(k)}(t) + \sum_{j=0}^{k-1} \frac{\langle s^{(j)}, \bar{y}^{(k)} \rangle}{\langle s^{(j)}, \bar{y}^{(j)} \rangle} s^{(j)}(t) - \sum_{j=0}^{k-1} \frac{\langle \bar{a}^{(j)}, \bar{y}^{(k)} \rangle}{\langle \bar{a}^{(j)}, \bar{y}^{(j)} \rangle} \bar{a}^{(j)}(t) \tag{3.33}$$

It may be remarked that, in line with the replacement of $d^{(i-1)}(t)$ by $s^{(i-1)}(t)$ in the formulae (3.28)-(3.31) of the CGII-methods, the replacement of $d^{(i-1)}(t)$ by $(\alpha^{(i-1)})^{-1} s^{(i-1)}(t)$ in the CGI-method would have been logical (and conform the essence of one of the suggestions of Quintana and Davison (1974)). However, numerical experiments with this alternative showed that the convergence behavior was worse with replacement of $d^{(i-1)}(t)$ than without. The numerical evidence of this will be presented in the next chapter.

b) Transformation technique

The second well-known technique (cf. Jacoby, Kowalik & Pizzo (1972)) for taking care of bounded controls in gradient algorithm is the transformation technique. This technique consists of replacing the original control variables by new variables by means of a transformation which guarantees that the bounds on the original variables are automatically satisfied while the new variables are unconstrained. In particular, in case of a lower bound only, e.g. $u_j(t) \geq 0$, a common transformation is

$$u_j(t) = k_j v_j^2(t) \tag{3.34}$$

and similarly, in case of a lower and an upper bound, e.g. $a \leq u_j(t) \leq b$, a common transformation is

$$u_j(t) = \tfrac{1}{2}(a+b)-\tfrac{1}{2}(b-a)\cos(\pi k_j v_j(t)) \tag{3.35}$$

in which expressions the k_j's are arbitrary scale factors. The transformations in these cases have the property that whenever a control component approaches its bound in the original system, the corresponding gradient component with respect to the new variables tends to zero.

Against the advantage of having unconstrained instead of constrained variables,the transformation technique was found to have three smaller disadvantages for application in connection with control problems:

i) whenever a control component is at its boundary on a particular time interval at some instant during the iteration process, then there is no way when using gradient methods to leave that boundary. This property eliminates in particular a number of otherwise useful startsolutions

ii) the transformation "distorts" the object function (3.4) very severely in the neighborhood of the bounds which impairs the rate of convergence whenever the optimum happens to be near or partly on the boundary.

iii) the transformation implies an extra programming effort, which, especially in case of the CGII methods, is considerable.

One aspect of the minimization procedure which became clear when using the transformation technique was the importance of good scaling for the convergence behavior. This will be discussed in more detail in the next section.

3.4 Scaling

The convergence behavior of gradient algorithms depends, as is well known, very much on the scaling of the variables relative to the function to be minimized. This phenomenon may be explained with the observation that in gradient algorithms steps are taken which are more or less proportional to the gradient. Whenever a certain gradient vector component is large relative to the other components, which means that the object function is very sensitive to changes in the corresponding variable, then a step proportional to the gradient implies a large change in that particular variable, while the opposite would be desirable. The idea behind scaling is therefore to try to make all gradient components of the same order of magnitude, or equivalently, to make the object function equally sensitive to changes in all the variables.

In the simplified controlled World 2 model the original control variables turned out to be reasonably well scaled and no effort was put in to obtain a better scaling. As soon as the transformed variables v(t) (3.34)-(3.35) were introduced instead of the original control variables u(t), the need for scaling became more apparent: The gradient components relative to the new variables become

$$(\nabla_v J(t))_j = (\nabla_u J(t))_j \cdot 2k_j v_j \qquad j = 1,3,4 \qquad (3.36)$$

and

$$(\nabla_v J(t))_2 = (\nabla_u J(t))_2 \cdot \tfrac{1}{2}(b-a)\pi k_2 \sin(\pi k_2 v_2(t)) \qquad j = 2 \qquad (3.37)$$

Given the situation that the original gradient vector components $(\nabla_u J(t))_j$ are of roughly the same size, the new gradient vector will also be of the same size if

$$k_2/k_j \simeq \frac{2v_j}{\tfrac{1}{2}(b-a)\Pi} \qquad (3.38)$$

for the simplified controlled World 2 model, where $v_j \simeq 0.1$ and $(b-a) = 0.015$ a reasonable scaling was obtained with the scale factor values

$$k_1 = k_3 = k_4 = 1 \qquad k_2 = 10 \qquad (3.39)$$

In the complete controlled World 2 model the gradient components were no longer of the same order of magnitude. In particular, the gradient component corresponding to the population control variable U_P turned out to become much larger than the other components. A closer look at the control multipliers (2.6) explained this: With MSL $\simeq$ 12 and $F_{32}(CI/P) \simeq 8$ in the neighborhood of the optimal solution, these control multipliers became

$$\begin{aligned} G_1(U_P) &= \exp(-\gamma_1 U_P MSL) \simeq \exp(-300\, U_P) \\ G_2(U_{CI}) &= U_{CI} \\ G_3(U_{POL}) &= \exp(-\gamma_3 U_{POL}(MSL/F_{32})) \simeq \exp(-15\, U_{POL}) \\ G_4(U_{NR}) &= \exp(-\gamma_4 U_{NR}) = \exp(-3.5\, U_{NR}) \end{aligned} \qquad (3.40)$$

An obvious way to scale the control variables in this particular case was to reformulate the optimal control problem with as new control variables

$$\tilde{u}_1 = 25\, U_P MSL \qquad \tilde{u}_3 = 10\, U_{POL} MSL/F_{32}(CI/P)$$

$$\tilde{u}_2 = -\ln(U_{CI}) \qquad \tilde{u}_4 = 3.5\, U_{NR} \tag{3.41}$$

This approach, which will be called the *reformulation technique*, used in conjunction with the clipping-off technique to take into account the translated bounds on the $\tilde{u}$-variables, turned out to improve the convergence of the application of the gradient algorithms considerably. Numerical evidence of this will be discussed in the next chapter.

4. *NUMERICAL RESULTS*

4.1 *Optimization results*

The optimal control histories and the corresponding optimal state space trajectories are given in Fig.4.1 for the simplified model and in Fig.4.2 for the complete model.The optimal state space trajectories can be compared with the trajectories in case of no control (i.e. Forrester's standard results) which are presented by dotted curves in the same figures. A discussion of these results falls outside the scope of this paper: for this the reader is referred to Rademaker (1972). One remark should be made, however, and that is, that a comparison of the optimal control and state space trajectories for the two different models shows that at most only the tendencies in the behaviors roughly compare. The actual results are quite different. In fact, the optimal criterion values of the simplified model satisfies

$$J[u^*] > 178.911 \tag{4.1}$$

whereas for the complete model

$$J[u^*] > 500.042 \tag{4.2}$$

For the larger part this difference between the results for the two models can be attributed to the difference in coupling functions. In the case of the complete model much larger values of the CMSL (2.17), and through the CMSL much larger values of the QL(2.16), are generated than in the case of the simplified model. This underlines the fact that the models are indeed quite different.

4.2 *Comparison of the application of different methods to the simplified controlled World 2 problem*

In order to compare their relative efficiency all methods to be applied on the simplified model were programmed as special subroutines within one general computer program for solving optimal control problems. Two versions of this general program were used, one of which made use of the clipping-off technique for taking into account the bounds on the values of the control variables, the other one making use of the transformation technique. The aim of this approach was to obtain a comparison of the methods which should be independent of the particular way of programming of the algorithm. The drawback of such an approach was of course the fact that none of the methods was programmed in an optimally efficient way.

In the general program the *integration* of the differential equations was carried out by a standard fourth order Runge-Kutta routine. After some experimentation a stepsize of 2 years was found to be the best compromise between accuracy and required computer time. For the *line search* use was made of a quadratic search routine in which first three points on the line are determined which include the line minimum. For the initial stepsize in this search routine, which influences of course the number of function calls, two strategies were tried out, the first one consisting of using in every new line search the same small initial stepsize (α_{start} = 0.001 in the clipping-off-version and α_{start} = 0.01 in the transformation-version of the general program), the second one consisting of using an initial stepsize which was equal to half the optimal stepsize $\alpha^{(i-1)}$ in the preceding iteration. The result of this experiment is given in Table 4.6 which will be discussed in more detail below. As *convergence criterion* for terminating the iterative process use was made of the criterion that in two successive steps the performance criterion should not change in absolute value more than ε_{conv} = 0.0001. Whenever this criterion is satisfied one extra line minimization is performed with as search direction the negative of the local gradient. Only in the case that the convergence criterion is satisfied again the iterative process is terminated, otherwise the process is continued.

The results of the application of the different methods to the *simplified controlled World 2 model* are given in the Tables 4.3 to 4.6, in which the number of iterations, the number of function (= performance criterion) evaluations, the value of the performance criterion, the total computer time (on a Burroughs B 6700 multiprocessing system), the average number of calls per interation and the average amount of computer time per call are listed. The computer times given should not be taken as hard figures but only as an indication for the relative performance. The computer used being a multiprocessing machine, the actual process time may differ from case to case up to 30% depending on what other programs are processed simultaneously.

The numbers in the individual tables apply to iteration processes with the following initial controls:

In case of Table 4.3 and 4.5

$$u_1^{(o)}(t) \equiv 0 \qquad u_2^{(o)}(t) \equiv 0.04777 \qquad u_3(t) \equiv 0.05 \qquad u_4(t) \equiv 0 \tag{4.3}$$

and in case of Table 4.4 and 4.6

$$v_1^{(o)}(t) \equiv 0.1 \qquad v_2^{(o)}(t) \equiv 0.05 \qquad v_3^{(o)}(t) \equiv 0.1 \qquad v_4^{(o)}(t) \equiv 0.1 \tag{4.4}$$

which, with the actual transformations used

$$\begin{array}{ll} u_1(t) = v_1^2(t) & u_2(t) = 0.04777-0.0075\cos(\pi.10.v_2(t)) \\ u_3(t) = v_3^2(t) & u_4(t) = v_4^2(t) \end{array} \tag{4.5}$$

are equivalent to initial controls in terms of u equal to

$$u_1^{(o)}(t) \equiv 0.01 \qquad u_2^{(o)}(t) \equiv 0.04777 \qquad u_3(t) \equiv 0.01 \qquad u_4(t) \equiv 0.01 \qquad (4.6)$$

Table 4.3 shows the results of the tests with the different methods in combination with the use of the clipping-off technique. As known in the literature (cf. Pierson & Rajtora (1970)) it is advantageous to periodically restart the iteration process. To determine the best number after which to restart as well as to get more data on the same method all methods were tried with periodic restarts after respectively 6, 12 and 18 iterations (In the PARTAN method application periodic restarts were made after respectively 6, 12 and 18 PARTAN directions of search, i.e. after respectively 13, 25 and 37 line searches following (3.26)). From the results listed in the table it is immediately clear that the most efficient method in terms of number of iterations, number of function evaluations as well as computer time is the CGI method. The second best method in terms of number of iterations is the CGIIA method. Unfortunately, however, this method also requires the most computer time per iteration, which makes it into the most time consuming method. The third best method in number of iterations and at the same time the second best in terms of computer time is the DFP method, which makes this method a good second choice. Of interest in Table 4.3 is furthermore the relative poor performance of the CGIIB method in comparison with the CGIIA method mentioned above and the similarly poor performance of the PARTAN method in comparison even with the SD method. It should be remarked in this context that the number of iterations of the PARTAN method in the present case is defined as the number of search directions, a definition which is different from the one used by Wong, Dressler and Luenberger (1971). In addition to the results for the different methods of Section 3.2, Table 4.3 also lists the results for an experimental method, in which the search direction is calculated in the same way as in the CGI method (following (3.13)) but with a fixed value of $\beta^{(i)} = 1.0$. The results show clearly that such a simple-minded method is much inferior to the hardly more complicated CGI method and also inferior to the other methods of Section 3.2.

Table 4.4 shows results similar to Table 4.3 for the case that the transformation technique is used instead of the clipping-off technique. Again the CGI method is the most efficient method in terms of the amount of computer time. On the average the CGIIA method requires less iterations, however, with the highest amount of computer time per call, the method is at the same time one of the most time consuming methods. The second best method in terms of computer time is in this case the PARTAN method with the DFP-method being third. Again, the poorer performance of the CGIIB method relative to the CGIIA method in terms of number of iterations and number of function evaluations is evident.

In order to make a comparison possible of the application of the transformation technique versus the application of the clipping-off technique, Table 4.4 also lists the results for the CGI method with the clipping-off technique applied to a case with initial controls (4.6) equivalent to the initial controls (4.5) used to generate the other results in the table. Comparison shows that the clipping-off technique requires less iterations, less function evaluations and less computer time. Also the clipping-off technique leads in general to higher values of the performance criterion than the transformation technique. From detailed results on the convergence behavior not given here,it appeared that the initial convergence using the transformation technique was faster than using the clipping-off technique, whilst the final convergence on the other hand was much slower. Reasons for this phenomenon may be on one hand the simplification of the optimization problem in case of the clipping-off technique caused by the elimination of all control variable components on their bounds and on the other hand the distortion of the equi-cost surfaces by the transformation from the u-variables to the v-variables.

Table 4.5 shows the results of some more experiments to determine the best reset or restart value for the two most efficient methods, the CGI method and the DFP method,both with the clipping-off technique. In addition results are presented for a modification of the CGI method (cf..Section 3.3), in which the previous search direction $d^{(i-1)}(t)$ in (3.27) is replaced by $s^{(i-1)}(t)/\alpha^{(i-1)}$. It follows that the best reset value for both versions of the CGI method is 18, whereas for the DFP method a reset value of 30 or higher is best. Both these reset values are higher than commonly suggested in the literature (cf. Pierson & Rajtora (1970, Keller & Sengupta (1973)). It also follows that the CGI method with $d^{(i-1)}(t)$ is superior to the same method with $s^{i-1)}(t)/\alpha^{i-1)}$ replacing $d^{(i-1)}(t)$. This result is of interest since it contradicts the suggestion of Quintana and Davison (1974). It may be remarked in this context that in the CGIIA method as well as in the CGIIB method the use of $s^{(i-1)}(t)$ instead of $d^{(i-1)}(t)$ as prescribed by the algorithm (3.28)-(3.31) turned out to be almost imperative: In a number of, though not all, tests with the CGIIA and CGIIB methods with $d^{(i-1)}(t)$ instead of $s^{(i-1)}(t)$, the iterative process did not converge at all.

Table 4.6 lists the results of some extra experiments with a different stepsize strategy in the line search procedure. In particular, for three cases listed in Table 4.4 and repeated here, i.e. the CGI method and the DFP method with the transformation technique and the CGI method with the clipping-off technique the results are presented which were generated while using as initial stepsize in the line search procedure $\alpha_{start} := 0.5\alpha^{(i-1)}$ instead of a constant fixed value. The table shows that while on the average the number of iterations does not differ too much, the total number of function evaluations as well as the average number of function evaluations per iteration are considerably less. The result clearly indicates the superiority of the strategy to let the initial stepsize α_{start} depend on the preceding optimal stepsize $\alpha^{(i-1)}$.Unfortunately however there is one important proviso and that is that in no iteration such large steps are generated that computer overflow results. In fact, in a great number of trials this happened, for which reason the strategy was not used for the comparison runs presented in the preceding tables.

4.3 *Some numerical experiments with the complete controlled World 2 model*

After the numerical experiments described in the preceding section had indicated the superiority of the CGI algorithm for solving optimal control problems of the type of the controlled World 2 model, only a limited number of comparison runs (with the same initial controls and the same overall conditions) were tried out with the complete World 2 model. (The computer time for one function (= performance criterion) evaluation was roughly 2.5 times as long as in case of the simplified model). One set of comparison runs which was tried was concerned with four runs with respectively the SD method, the PARTAN method, the CGI method and the DFP method, all four in combination with the transformation technique, restarting the process after every 6 iterations. The convergence histories of these runs are presented (up to the 40th iteration) in *Figure 4.7*. From this figure it follows that the CGI method is again the fastest converging method followed by the PARTAN method, the SD method and the DFP method, which order is reasonably well in agreement with the results presented in Table 4.4. The dotted line segments in the figure show the convergence behavior of the PARTAN method for the case that the iteration definition of Wong, Dressler and Luenberger (1971) is followed. (One iteration is then defined to consist of one search along the negative gradient followed by one search along the PARTAN direction). It is of interest to note the little difference between the convergence histories of the CGI method and the thus defined PARTAN method (in which per iteration roughly twice as much work has to be done).

A second set of comparison runs which was tried was concerned with four runs with the CGI method, with restarts after every 6 iterations, in combination with four different strategies for taking care of the bounds on the values of the control variables:the use of the clipping-off technique, the use of the transformation technique, the use of a mixture of these techniques (first 15 iterations with the clipping-off technique, thereafter the transformation technique) and finally the use of the clipping-off technique after a reformulation or rescaling of the control variables as discussed in Section 3.4. The convergence histories of these runs are presented in *Figure 4.8*. It follows that the best convergence behavior is obtained through the use of rescaling or reformulation in combination with the clipping-off technique. The second best strategy is to alternate between the clipping-off technique and the transformation technique.The pure strategies, i.e. using the transformation technique of the clipping-off technique for all interations produced a less good convergence behavior.

5. *CONCLUSIONS*

Numerical experiments have been carried out with six different gradient methods for the determination of the optimal control of a simplified version of the controlled World 2 model of Forrester. The main conclusion of these experiments was that the most efficient method in terms of computer time and generally also in terms of number of iterations and number of function evaluations was the CGI method (i.e. the infinite dimensional equivalent to the Conjugate Gradient method of Fletcher and Reeves, first suggested by Lasdon, Mitter & Waren (1967)) in combination with a clipping-off technique (as described by Pagurek and Woodside (1968)) to take care of bounds on the values of the control variable components and periodically restarted every 18 iterations. A good second choice proved to be the DFP method (i.e. the infinite dimensional equivalent of the Davidon-Fletcher-Powell method following the algorithm of Tripathi-Narendra (1968)) in combination with the clipping-off technique, which in general turned out to be a more efficient method to take care of bounded controls than the transformation of variables technique.

The results of numerical experiments with the determination of the optimal control of the complete controlled World 2 model of Forrester showed in general good agreement with the results obtained for the simplified model. Again the CGI method in combination with the clipping-off technique turned out to be the most efficient method when the problem first had been rescaled by means of a reformulation of the control variables. Scaling proved in this case to be one of the most important factors for convergence.

6. *ACKNOWLEDGEMENTS*

The authors should like to acknowledge the contributions of the former students J.G. van der Velden, E.J. Mendieta, J.H. Kessels, P.F.G. Vereijken and H. Paulissen to the research reported here. They are very much indebted to Mr. R. Kool of the Department of Mathematics for his numerous improvements and suggestions while actually transforming written-out algorithms into working computer programs.

7. REFERENCES

BRYSON, Jr, A.E. and HO, Y.C. (1969): Applied Optimal Control, Blaisdell Publ. Cy, Waltham, Mass.

BRYSON, Jr. A.E. and DENHAM, W.F. (1962): A Steepest Ascent Method for Solving Optimum Programming Problems. Trans ASME, J.Appl.Mech. 29, pp. 247-259.

BURNS, J.R. and MALONE, D.W. (1974): Optimization Techniques Applied to the Forrester Model of the World, IEEE Trans.Syst.Man.Cybern., SMC-4, pp. 164-172.

CUYPERS, J.G.M. (1973): Two simplified versions of Forrester's model. Automatica, 9, pp. 399-401.

DEKKER, L. and KERCKHOFFS, E.H.J. (1974): Hybrid simulation of a World model, AICA J. 16, nr.4 pp. 10-14.

FORRESTER, J.W. (1971): World Dynamics, Wright-Allen Press Inc., Cambridge, Mass.

JACOBY, S.L.S., KOWALIK, J.S. and PIZZO, J.T. (1972): Iterative methods for nonlinear optimization problems, Prentice Hall, Inc., Englewood Cliffs, N.J.

KELLER, Jr., E.A. and SENGUPTA, J.K. (1973): Relative efficiency of computing optimal growth by conjugate gradient and Davidon methods, Int.J. Systems Sci, 4, pp. 97-120.

KELLEY, J.H. (1962): Methods of Gradients, Ch. 6 of Optimization Techniques. G. Leitmann (Ed.), Academic Press New York, pp. 206-252.

LASDON, L.S., MITTER, S.K. and WAREN, A.D. (1967) The Conjugate Gradient Method for Optimal Control Problems,IEEE Trans. Aut. Contr., AC-12, pp. 132-138.

MEADOWS, D.H. et al. (1972): The Limits to Growth, Universe Books, New York.

MURRAY, W. (ed) (1972): Numerical methods for unconstrained minimization problems, Academic Press, London.

OLSDER, G.J. and STRIJBOS, R.C.W. (1973). World Dynamics, a dynamic optimization study, Annals of Systems Research, 3, pp. 21-37.

PAGUREK, B. and WOODSIDE, C.M. (1968): The conjugate gradient method for optimal control problems with bounded control variables. Automatica, 4, pp. 337-349.

PIERSON, B.L. and RAJTORA, S.G. (1970): Computational Experience with the Davidon Method Applied to Optimal Control Problems, IEEE Trans Syst.Sci and Cybern., SSC-6, pp. 240-242.

QUINTANA, V.H. and DAVISON, E.J. (1974). Clipping-off gradient algorithms to compute optimal controls with constrained magnitude, Int.J. Control, 20, pp. 245-255.

RADEMAKER, O. (1972): Project Group Global Dynamics, Progress Reports nrs. 1,2 (1972), 3,4 (1974). Available from author, Address: T.H.E., P.O.Box 513, Eindhoven, The Netherlands.

SINNOTT, J.F. and LUENBERGER, D.G. (1967): Solution of Optimal Control Problems by the Method of Conjugate Gradients. JACC 1967 Preprints, pp. 566-574.

TRIPATHI, S.S. and NARENDRA, K.S. (1968): Conjugate direction methods for nonlinear optimization problems, Proc. 1968 NEC (Chicago, Ill.), pp. 125-129.

WONG, P.J., DRESSLER, R.M. and LUENBERGER, D.G. (1971): A combined Parallel-Tangents/ Penalty-Function Approach to Solving Trajectory Optimization Problems, AIAAJ 9, pp. 2443-2448.

F_3(MSL) (BRMM)	F_{12}(POLR) (DRPM)	F_{17}(FR) (BRFM)	F_{28}(POLR) (FRM)	F_{36}(FR) (CFIFR)	F_{40}(FR) (QLF)
1.16452528	9.27142853 -1	1.07788100 -1	1.03523809	1.0009320	-2.56917756 -2
-1.80875430 -1	1.37142858 -2	1.07280700	-1.21587300 -2	-8.7828670 -1	1.13038139
2.07672036 -2	2.07142857 -3	-1.96197200 -1	-5.33333337 -4	6.2762180 -2	-1.11816125 -1
-7.27686482 -4	F_{13}(FR) (DRFM)	1.19048700 -2	7.77777778 -6	1.78613100 -1	F_{41}(POLR) (QLP)
F_6(NRFR) (NREM)	4.36114600	F_{18}(POLR) (BRPM)	F_{32}(CIR) (POLCM)	-6.50349800 -2	1.04928571
7.00241120 -2	-6.46689100	1.02925871	-7.17151600 -2	6.66666680 -3	-1.86865081 -2
-4.20335073 -1	4.24544000	-9.48015873 -3	4.79241100 -1	F_{38}(MSL) (QLM)	-3.54761899 -4
3.79442180	-1.37198100	-5.63095238 -4	1.05333300	2.17053700 -1	6.38888884 -6
-2.49366758	2.19004600 -1	7.77777778 -6	-2.80868200 -1	9.36667000 -1	F_{42}(MSL) (NRMM)
F_{11}(MSL) (DRMM)	-1.38490000 -2	F_{20}(CR) (FCM)	2.90083700 -2	-1.0012200 -1	-5.66460900 -3
2.97868000	F_{14}(CR) (DRCM)	1.57662780	-1.35139100 -3	3.3387600 -3	1.13683700
-3.04801000	9.00000000 -1	-6.60394837 -1	2.36467500 -5	F_{39}(CR) (QLC)	-1.38493300 -1
1.53463000	5.00000000 -2	8.98694540 -2	F_{34}(POLR) (POLAT)	1.99832182	1.06418400 -2
-3.99813000 -1	5.00000000 -2	F_{21}(CIRA) (FPCI)	5.92857148 -1	-1.66214850	-2.62043700 -4
5.79524000 -2	F_{16}(CR) (BRCM)	5.09934300 -1	1.6480159 -1	8.99824969 -1	F_{43}(F_{38}/F_{40})(CIQR)
-4.69843000 -3	1.04801587	5.43464300 -1	2.80952381 -3	-2.86928923 -1	5.55944000 -1
1.98890000 -4	2.81084673 -2	-5.57696700 -2	-2.77777777 -6	3.73391612 -2	7.69541600 -1
-3.41888000 -6	-7.63888896 -2	1.83614000 -3			-8.60140000 -2
	1.01851852 -2				-2.64180300 -3

Table 2.1. Coefficients of the nonnegative powers of the polynomial approximations of the coupling functions of Forrester.

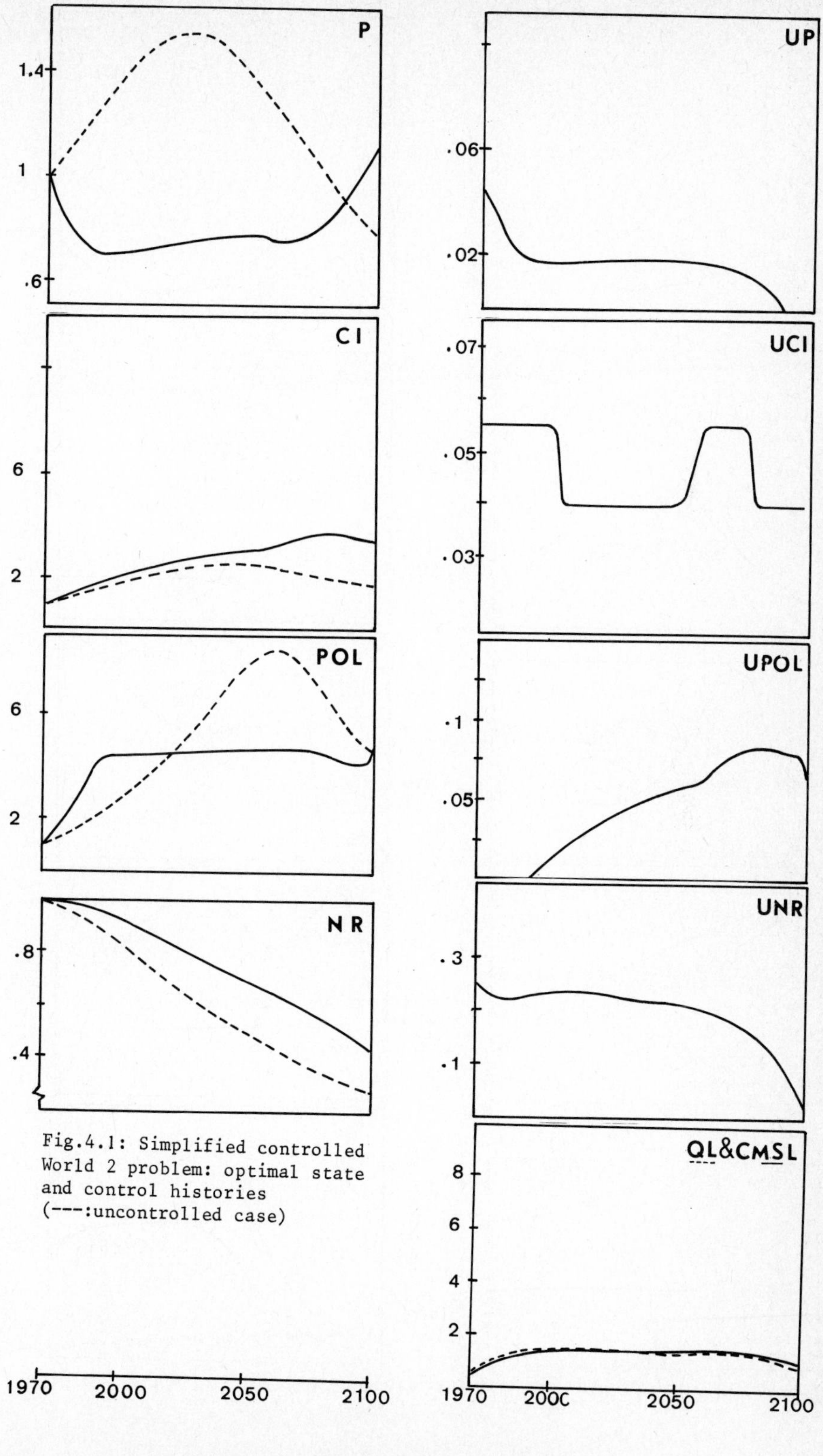

Fig.4.1: Simplified controlled World 2 problem: optimal state and control histories (---:uncontrolled case)

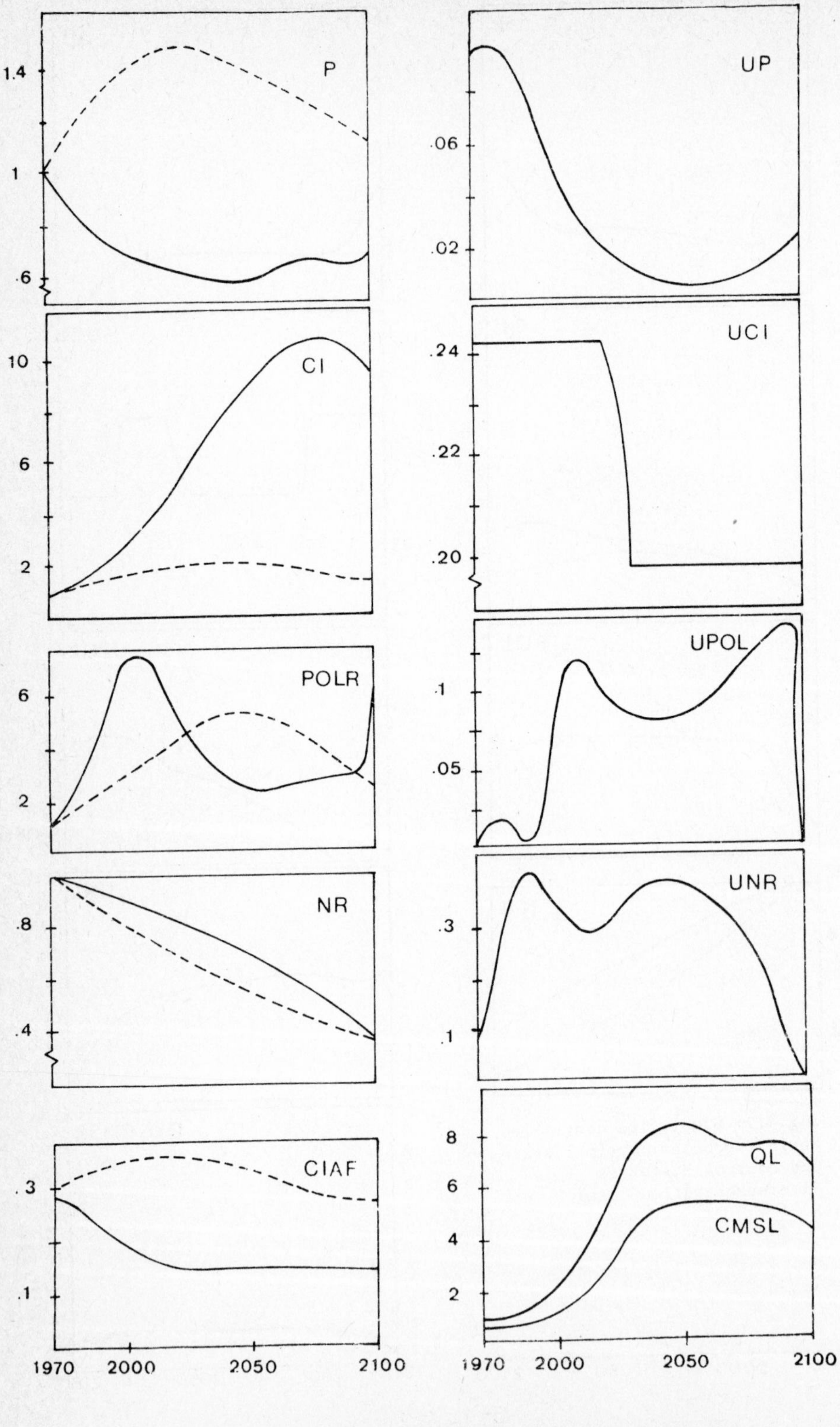

Fig.4.2: Complete controlled World 2 problem: optimal state and control histories (----- uncontrolled case)

METHOD	RESET	ITER-S	CALLS	CRITERION	TIME	C/I	T/C
SD	1	62	324	178.910560	618	5.2	1.9
PARTAN	6	82	431	.910651	804	5.3	1.9
	12	89	434	.910814	838	4.9	1.9
	18	> 100	496	.909531	862	5.0	1.7
CGI	6	42	226	.910866	376	5.4	1.7
	12	38	204	.910802	338	5.4	1.7
	18	33	188	.910624	263	5.7	1.4
CGIIA	6	50	260	.910909	1493	5.2	5.7
	12	44	233	.911205	1262	5.3	5.4
	18	48	244	.910993	1358	5.1	5.6
CGIIB	6	61	308	.910996	1464	5.1	4.8
	12	56	271	.910523	1128	4.9	4.1
	18	64	300	.910754	1182	4.7	3.9
DFP	6	51	317	.910923	459	6.2	1.4
	12	51	339	.910856	668	6.6	2.0
	18	48	312	.910846	627	6.5	2.0
$\beta^{(i)}=1.0$	6	56	268	.910480	480	4.8	1.8
	12	77	310	.910704	704	4.0	2.3
	18	92	360	.910848	848	4.0	2.4

Table 4.3: Simplified controlled World 2 model: Numerical results of the application of different methods in combination with the clipping-off technique. (">": convergence conditions not yet satisfied).

METHOD	RESET	ITER-S	CALLS	CRITERION	TIME	C/I	T/C
SD	1	92	523	178.910867	901	5.7	1.7
PARTAN	6	81	486	.907703	787	6.0	1.6
	12	72	444	.909202	671	6.2	1.5
	18	71	435	.909373	717	6.1	1.6
CGI	6	38	228	.908535	350	6.0	1.5
	12	69	413	.910531	686	6.0	1.7
	18	64	340	.910400	624	5.3	1.8
CGIIA	6	46	294	.907522	1539	6.4	5.2
	12	> 46	300	.910353	2000	6.5	6.7
	18	49	315	.910747	1783	6.4	5.6
CGIIB	6	62	373	.908684	1393	6.0	3.7
	12	57	333	.906983	1882	5.8	5.7
	18	> 65	343	.905315	1989	5.3	5.8
DFP	6	59	319	.910806	611	5.4	1.9
	12	> 94	459	.908187	907	4.9	2.0
	18	> 89	413	.904944	905	4.6	2.2
CGI	6	40	214	.910855	430	5.3	2.0
(clip)	12	37	196	.910946	394	5.3	2.0
	18	35	191	.911046	371	5.5	1.9

Table 4.4: Simplified controlled World 2 model: Numerical results of the application of different methods in combination with the transformation technique. (">": convergence conditions not yet satisfied).

METHOD	RESET	ITER-S	CALLS	CRITERION	TIME	C/I	T/C
CGI	3	64	316	178.910590	556	4.9	1.8
	6	42	226	.910866	376	5.4	1.7
	12	38	204	.910802	338	5.4	1.7
	18	33	188	.910624	263	5.7	1.4
	24	37	207	.910701	268	5.6	1.3
	30	40	223	.910836	357	5.6	1.6
	100	45	237	.910747	480	5.3	2.0
DFP	3	64	372	.910694	706	5.8	1.9
	6	51	317	.910923	459	6.2	1.4
	12	51	339	.910856	668	6.6	2.0
	18	48	312	.910846	627	6.5	2.0
	24	49	323	.910921	476	6.6	1.5
	30	45	295	.910964	594	6.6	2.0
	100	45	302	.910965	637	6.7	2.1
CGI	3	61	304	.910519	604	5.0	2.0
(modif.)	6	62	293	.910976	550	4.7	1.9
	12	51	253	.910996	400	5.0	1.6
	18	50	252	.910926	476	5.0	1.9
	24	51	341	.910782	444	4.7	1.8
	30	57	368	.910942	515	4.7	1.9
	100	98	371	.910984	814	3.8	2.2

Table 4.5: Simplified controlled World 2 model: Comparison of different reset values for three methods in combination with the clipping-off technique.

	METHOD	RESET	ITER-S	CALLS	CRITERION	TIME	C/I	T/C
A	CGI	6	43	185	178.909905	364	4.3	2.0
	(trsf)	12	47	203	.910616	512	4.3	2.5
		18	59	251	.911060	516	4.2	2.1
	DFP	6	52	279	.908612	670	4.7	2.5
	(trsf)	12	90	438	.909496	997	5.4	2.4
		18	> 74	352	.903749	905	4.9	2.3
	CGI	6	44	201	.911001	373	4.6	1.9
	(clipp.-	12	40	181	910982	409	4.5	2.3
	off)	18	36	167	911382	365	4.6	2.2
B	CGI	6	38	228	.908535	350	6.0	1.5
	(trsf)	12	69	413	.910531	686	6.0	1.7
		18	64	340	.910400	624	5.3	1.8
	DFP	6	59	319	.910806	611	5.4	1.9
	(trsf)	12	> 94	459	.908187	907	4.9	2.0
		18	> 89	413	.904944	905	4.6	2.2
	CGI	6	40	214	.910855	430	5.3	2.0
		12	37	196	.910946	394	5.3	2.0
		18	35	191	.911046	371	5.3	1.9

Table 4.6: Simplified controlled World 2 model: Comparison of different initial stepsize strategies in linesearch:
(A): $\alpha_{Start} = 0.5\alpha^{(i-1)}$; (B): α_{start} = fixed.
(">" : convergence conditions not yet satisfied.)

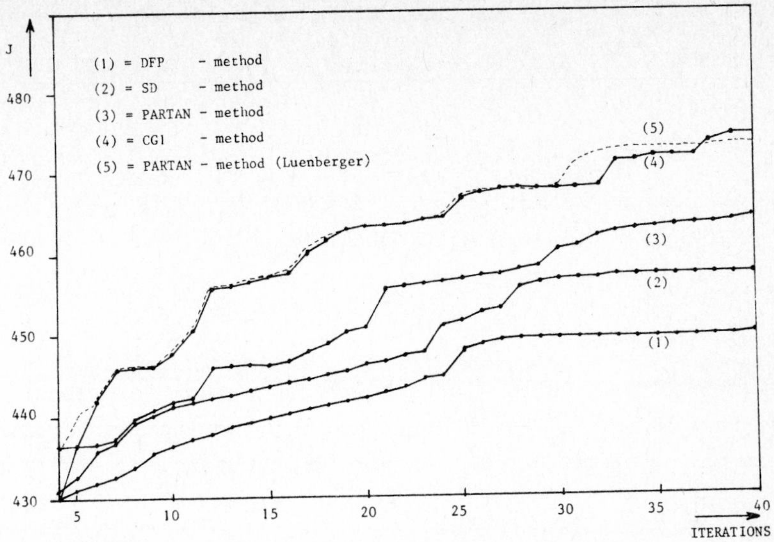

Fig.4.7 Complete controlled World 2 model: Convergence histories of 4 gradient methods in combination with the transformation technique with ($k_1=k_2=k_3=k_4=1.0$)

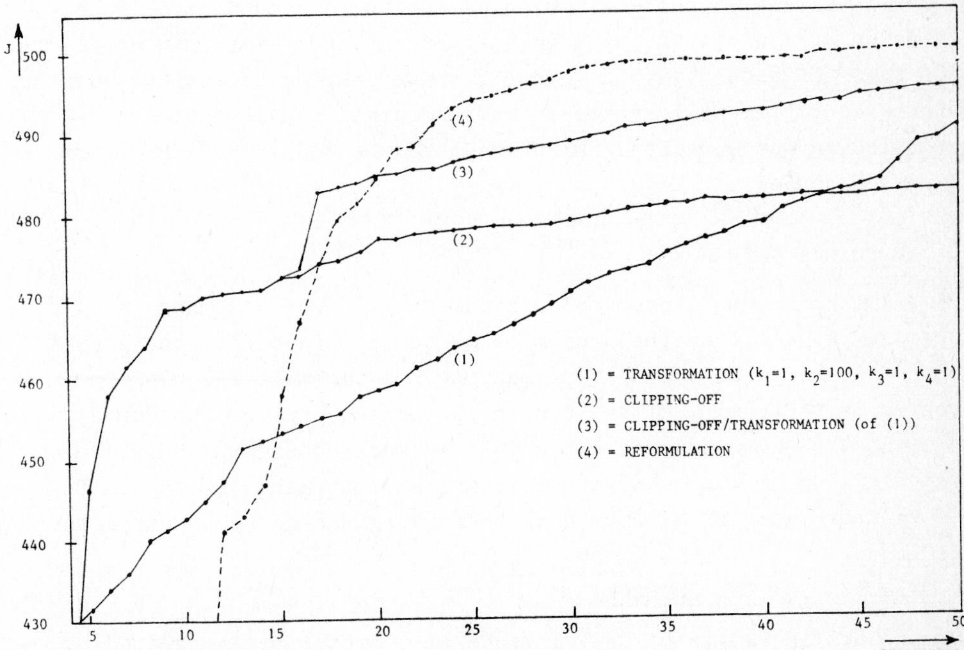

Fig.4.8 Complete controlled World 2 model: Convergence histories of the CGI-method in combination with different techniques for taking into account bounds on the values of the control variables.

A NEW APPROACH TO MODELLING IN PLANNING OF ELECTRIC POWER SYSTEMS

A. Kalliauer

Österreichische
Elektrizitätswirtschafts-
Aktiengesellschaft

1o1o Wien, AUSTRIA

ABSTRACT

The Paper shows the structure of a planning concept for electricity supply systems which, although developed for the Austrian system, is applicable on a general basis to other, more extensive, environmental systems.

1. INTRODUCTION

A system to be studied can be characterised by its elements and their relationships. The operation of such a system consists in using its elements to meet a (public) demand. A growth in demand entails an extension of the system and this in turn involves aims that conflict with those of other systems (other systems serving to meet the demand or other environmental systems). This requires consideration of global variables and constraints, which leads to the consideration of more extensive systems.

2. THE PLANNING PROBLEM

The elements of the system under study (e.g. power stations) are successively added to the system so as to keep pace with the growing requirements of the system (meeting the demand). The planning problem is the timing of the system extensions. Due to the mutual influences between several extensions we must consider a relatively long planning period. The aim of planning is to make the system fulfil certain tasks at minimum cost, observing the given constraints.

3. TREATMENT OF THE PROBLEM

Let the configuration of the elements of a system be denoted by "state". As the state changes with time, it can be expressed as a function of time:

$$z(t)\ ,\ t \in [t_o, t_e]\ ,$$

where $z(t)$ is a vector whose component $z_i(t)$ indicates the number of realisations (e.g. power stations placed in operation) of the ith element at time t ; if z_i denotes a particular project, either $z_i(t)=0$ or $z_i(t)=1$; if it is a standard unit (a power station type that can be realised any number of times), then $z_i(t)=k$ with k being a non-negative integer.

e.g. $z(t)$ for some t :

0 1 0 1	0 2 3 0 4 1
projects	standard units

We are trying to find $z^*(t)$ with $\mathcal{K}(z^*) = \min\limits_{z \in \mathcal{D}} (\mathcal{K}(z))$.

Let $\Delta z(t) := \lim\limits_{\varepsilon \to +0} (z(t) - z(t-\varepsilon))$.

$$\mathcal{K}(z) = \mathcal{K}^{op}(z) + \mathcal{K}^{inv}(\Delta z)$$

The dependence of $\mathcal{K}$ on $\Delta z(t)$ is primarily given by the investment costs of unit additions, or more exactly, the total costs which arise from the decision to extend the system.
The dependence of $\mathcal{K}$ on $z(t)$ is expressed by the operating costs. If $z(t)$ cannot meet the demand subject to the constraints this is expressed by $\mathcal{K}(z) = \infty$.

For a finite number of points t_{ij} : $\Delta z(t_{ij}) > 0$.
Hence we can write:

$$\mathcal{K}^{inv}(\Delta z) = \sum_i \sum_j K_i^{inv}(\Delta z(t_{ij}), t_{ij}) .$$

Let $y_z(t) = (y_1(t), \ldots, y_i(t), \ldots, y_n(t))$ denote the vector of output of components ("operation variables").
We have to include in our consideration the optimal operating costs:

$$\mathcal{K}^{op*}(z) = \mathcal{K}^{op}(z, y_z^*) = \min_{y_z \in Y} \mathcal{K}^{op}(z, y_z) .$$

For the purpose of studying the operation of the system we subdivide the study period into intervals Δt whose length is based on the longest operating cycle in the system (e.g. one year in the Austrian hydro system). With respect to system operation, these time intervals can be regarded as being independent and we can study the relationships within each interval T_j separately.

$$T_j = [t_0 + (j-1) * \Delta t, t_0 + j * \Delta t]$$

then:

$$\mathcal{K}^{op*}(z) = \sum_j \mathcal{K}^{op*}_{T_j}(z) = \sum_j \left(\min_{y_z \in Y_j} \mathcal{K}^{op}_{T_j}(z, y_z) \right)$$

with $Y_j \subset Y$.

As in most of the other methods of treating this problem (see e.g. (1),(3),(4)), we make this problem a discrete one with respect to these intervals and we apply a discrete Dynamic Programming algorithm. This means that we allow changes in state only at the times $t_o, t_o + \Delta t$, $t_o + 2 * \Delta t, \dots$ and calculate the operating costs for each interval $[t_o + (j-1)\cdot\Delta t, t_o + j\cdot\Delta t]$ separately.

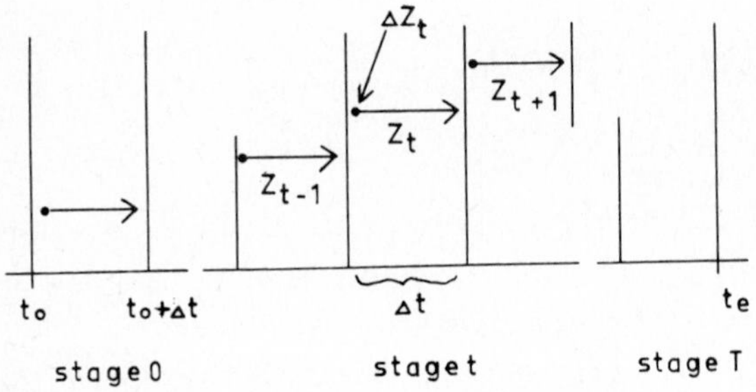

Let $z_t \in D_t$ and $z_t = z_o + \sum_{\tau=1}^{t} \Delta z_\tau$

The problem can be written:

$$\min_{\Delta z_\tau, \tau=1,\dots,T} \left(\sum_{\tau=0}^{T} K^{op*}_\tau(z_\tau) + \sum_{\tau=1}^{T} K^{inv}_\tau(\Delta z_\tau) \right).$$

Now define:

$$K_t(z_t) := \min_{\Delta z_\tau, \tau=1,\dots t} \left(\sum_{\tau=0}^{t} K^{op*}_\tau(z_\tau) + \sum_{\tau=1}^{t} K^{inv}_\tau(\Delta z_\tau) \right)$$

then:

$$K_t(z_t) = \min_{\Delta z_t} \left(K^{inv}_t(\Delta z_t) + K_{t-1}(z_{t-1}) \right) + K^{op*}_t(z_t)$$

Since hydro power accounts for a large proportion of the Austrian system, the operation model is very complex. To deal both with the questions of long-term planning and with questions of detail, two programs have been developed:

(a) an extension planning program with special routines for defining the states, with a simplified nonoptimising operation simulation model checked with the help of program (b).

(b) an operation scheduling program which can solve large-scale Nonlinear Programming problems and is used to solve questions of detail (especially for the hydro system), and to assist in planning by means of model (a).

4. STRUCTURE OF THE EXTENSION PLANNING MODEL (Fig. 1)

Let $z_t = (z_{1t}, \dots z_{it}, \dots z_{nt})$ denote a state at t with $1 \le t \le T$.

We now must generate all the $z_t \in D_t$:

This is done by using a GENER model, which "sieves out" feasible states, i.e. those which satisfy the given constraints associated with stage t .

Other models are now applied to the sets of states so generated, yielding results which we associate with each state. Thus e.g.: The SECUR model determines a security level of a state; or the SIMUL model determines the operating cost over a year calculated on the basis of a suitable but non-optimising operation strategy.

Running the problem with different security levels, we study only the respective associated values and temporarily delete some states if these do not meet the requirements. (We superimpose a mask $\bar{D}_t \subset D_t$ on the sets of states). In the case of running the problem with different parameters, some of the models need be run only once. In each case, however, the DP algorithm must be run.

This is done in the STEP model:
It serves to associate in each DP step from stage $t-1$ to stage t the total cost value $K_t(z_t)$ with each z_t . These values are the optimal costs in relation to state z_t if state $z_t \in \bar{D}_t$ has been reached by an optimal path through the stages 1 to t . The optimal extension alternative results from the optimal path to z^*_T of the last stage with

$$K_T(z^*_T) = \min_{z_T \in \bar{D}_T} K_T(z_T) .$$

5. OPERATION SCHEDULING OPTIMISATION MODEL

As stated earlier, large-scale systems must be studied. The relationships between their elements can usually be subdivided, in a multistage manner, into "global" and "local" ones, that is to say, we can subdivide the total system into subsystems (as e.g. overall generating system and hydro power stations on a certain river), which in turn contain local relationships. These can again be subdivided into global and local ones. Thus we obtain a multi-level structured system model.

Now consider the operation scheduling model to treat questions of detail.

The dimension of the operation model results from the great number of intervals of which the optimisation period consists, and from the fact that we express the period (year) by some characteristic daily load curves. We can derive the following NLP problem:

The thermal subsystem provides a cost basis for evaluating the hydro system. This results in the following objective function:

$$max \sum_{t \in T_y} v_t (PH_t)$$

where v_t is a nonlinear evaluation function for the hydro capacity PH_t and $PH_t = \sum_{i \in \mathcal{U}} PH_{it}$, where PH_{it} denotes the capacity of power plant $i \in \mathcal{U}$ at time interval t.

Let Q_{it} be the flow rate at power station i at time interval t. Then we can write $PH_{it} = f_i(Q_{it})$.

For Q_{it}, we have to consider lower and upper bounds

$$Q_{i_{min}} \leq Q_{it} \leq Q_{i_{max}} \qquad \forall i \in \mathcal{U}, \forall t \in T_y .$$

Let us define a storage - unit - incidence matrix as shown in Fig. 2.

Let V_{kt} be the volume of storage node k at the beginning of the time interval t, then $V_{kt} = V_{k0} + \sum_{\tau=1}^{t-1} \Delta V_{k\tau}$ with $\Delta V_{kt} = \sum_{i \in \mathcal{U}} (-ic_{ki}) * Q_{it}$.

The V_{kt} are constrained by $V_{k_{min}} \leq V_{kt} \leq V_{k_{max}}$.

This results in a NLP problem in the variables Q_{it} with the linear constraints resulting from those of the V_{kt}.

Let us now consider these constraints: If we are faced with a structured problem, this is expressed by the ic -matrix, which might e.g. take the following form:

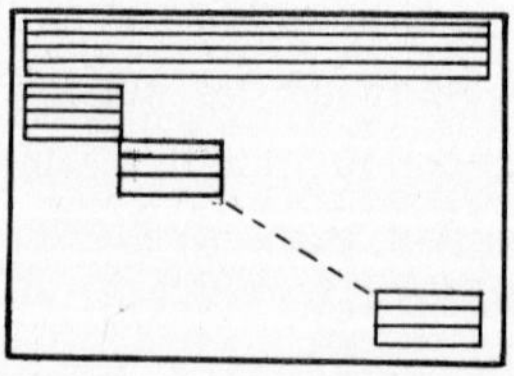

That means that we can subdivide the nodes $k \in K$ into
(1) coupling storage nodes $k \in K_c$ and
(2) storage nodes in subsystem S_i : $k \in K_{S_i}$.

Since in hydro power systems individual storages are scheduled on different cycles (daily, weekly and yearly cycles), we can also define "subsystems" with respect to time, because the constraints for the V_{kt} do not extend beyond the operation period of the power stations.

That is: $K = \underset{\text{yearly}}{K_y} + \underset{\text{weekly}}{K_w} + \underset{\text{daily cycle}}{K_d}$.

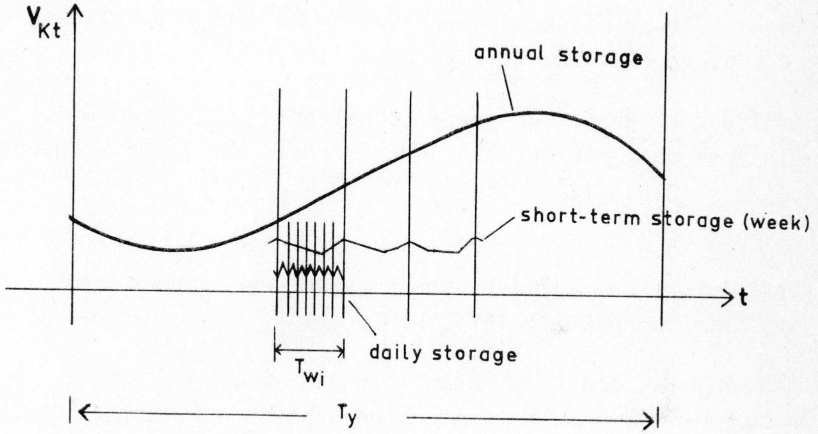

Let: $K_{dc} := K_d \cap K_c$, $K_{dS_i} := K_d \cap K_{S_i}$.

Thus we obtain a multi-level structure with coupling constraints as shown in Fig. 3.

6. APPLICATION OF A MULTI-LEVEL ALGORITHM

The above NLP problem has been handled by a method taking advantage of the structure of the constraint matrix. The projection p of the gradient g is used as a feasible direction. Instead of calculating the projection vector by the projection matrix $P = I - Q(Q^TQ)^{-1}Q^T$ and $p = Pg$ where $Q = (q_1, \ldots q_m)$ is the matrix of active constraints (as e.g. in Rosen's Gradient Projection Method), we use orthogonal vectors $\tilde{q}_1, \ldots, \tilde{q}_m$, which form a basis for the linear space $L(q_1, \ldots, q_m)$.

The projection vector p can be expressed as follows:

$$p = g - \sum_{i=1}^{m} \tilde{\lambda}_i \cdot \tilde{q}_i \quad , \quad \tilde{\lambda}_i = (g, \tilde{q}_i) / |\tilde{q}_i|^2 \quad ,$$

where (a,b) denotes the inner product of vectors a, b.

The advantage of the given structure is that constraints from parallel subsystems (i.e. from subsystems whose variable vectors have disjoint index sets) are a priori orthogonal.

REFERENCES:

(1) Dale, K.M.:
Dynamic Programming Approach to the Selection and Timing of Generation-Plant Additions. Proc. IEE, Vol 113 (1966), No 5.

(2) Feßl,K., A. Kalliauer und G. Schiller:
Die Anwendung von Optimierungsverfahren zur Kraftwerksausbauplanung. ÖZE, 27.Jg. (1974), H. 1o.

(3) Neumann, G.:
Optimierung des Ausbaues von Energieversorgungssystemen. VGB Kraftwerktechnik 53, 1973, H. 7.

(4) Oatman,E.N., and L.J. Hamant:
A Dynamic Approach to Generation Expansion Planning. Power Apparatus and Systems, 1973, No 6.

(5) Rosen,J.B.:
The Gradient Projection Method for Nonlinear Programming. Part I. Linear Constraints. SIAM 8, 196o.

Fig. 1: Structure of the Program

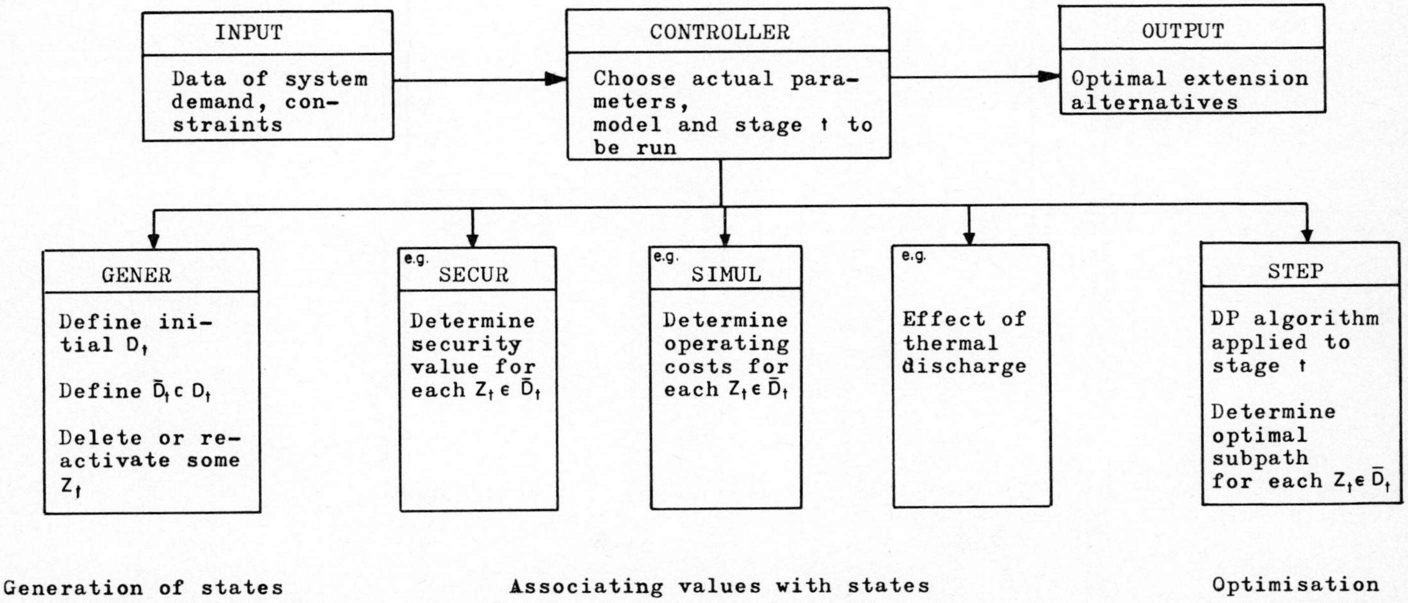

Fig. 2: Example of storage system with its incidence matrix

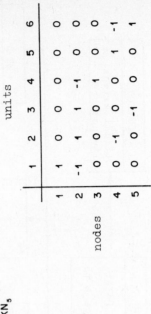

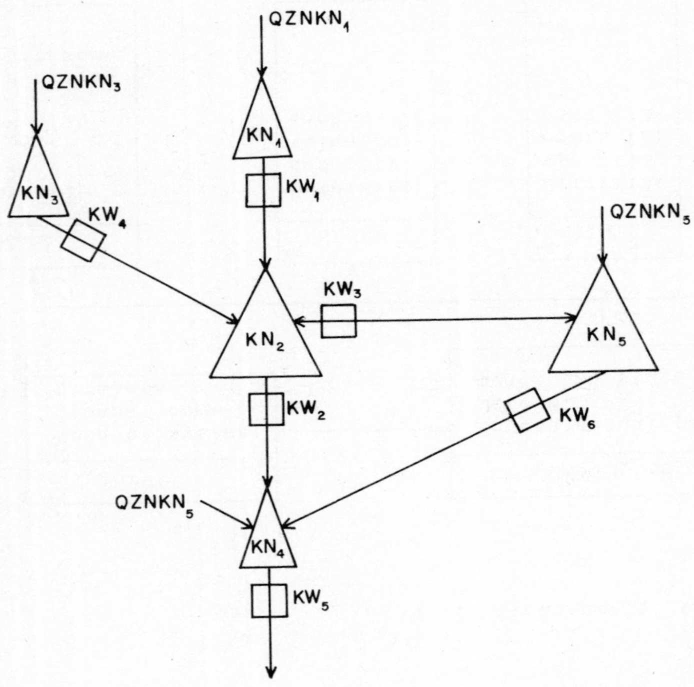

nodes \ units	1	2	3	4	5	6
1	1	0	0	0	0	0
2	-1	1	1	-1	0	0
3	0	0	0	1	0	0
4	0	-1	0	0	1	-1
5	0	0	-1	0	0	1

Fig. 3: Example of multilevel constraint matrix and adjoint subsystem tree

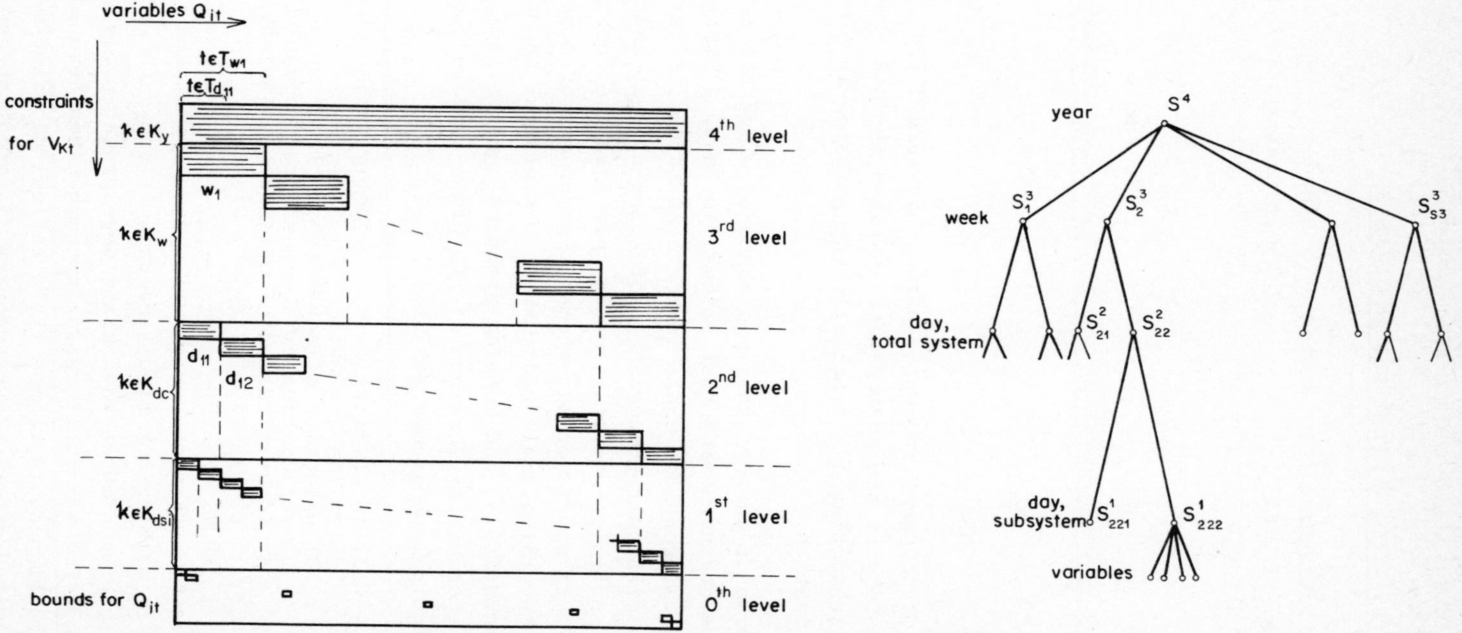

ON THE OPTIMIZATION OF PEAT BURNING PLANTS

E. Kiukaanniemi, P. Uronen
Univ. of Oulu
90100 Oulu 10, Finland

O. Alander
Kymin Osakeyhtiö-Kymmene Aktiebolag
18100 Heinola 10, Finland

1. PREFACE

Recent development in energy prices has turned the attention of man to energy sources: new sources are searched for and conventional means of energy production are critically investigated in order to optimize their utilization.

One source of energy, the importance of which has been realized with the advance of increasing fuel prices, is peat, a renewing resource of nature typical for some areas in northern Europe. Because of the comparatively difficult processing properties of peat and the quite short history of efficient development on this area the technology of peat burning plants now needs a systematic programme of development, especially concerning small and middle-sized plants. The present work is aimed at identifying and mapping practical possibilities for optimizing the total economic performance of the plant type in question. The following principal programme was used:

1. identification of the optimization objectives for existing plants
2. selection of subjects of closer study
3. realization of the most recommendable studies
4. identification of optimization objectives to be considered for future plants

The present work necessarily will have a practical character due to the specific problem but simultaneously it shows the need for modelling and optimization studies when plant development procedures in generally are planned. The straightforward approach taken here partly reflects also a situation quite common for practical decision making: available data is limited and also non-numerical information has to be used.

1. OPTIMIZATION OBJECTIVES FROM A COST SUDY AND OPERATING EXPERIENCES

In order to select optimally the subjects of studies aimed at improving the profitability of a plant, the cost structure of the plant has to be investigated. Combined with operating experience a cost study can give useful information, both for users of present plants and for designers of future plants.

Prior to attacking more specific details and overall weighting of optimization objectives will be a recommendable type of preliminary study, especially for a plant which is in the phase of development and has not yet reached its 'best', final construction. In small and middle-sized peat burning plants this situation clearly will be valid. Thus when developing this type of plant we first have to define individual subjects of development work or a set of studies and then among them to pick up in order of priority those subjects, which will satisfy adequately the following general requirements:

R1: realizable with existing resources
R2: economically profitable
R3: recommendable from the plant user's point of view (1)

A cost study combined with operating experience will show if a proposed study satisfies requirements R2 and R3. Resources for carrying out studies and development work are very different for the designer and user of a plant. Thus especially in the case of plant user the value of obtainable development may be strongly limited. The requirement R1 can be naturally satisfied optimally by a well-organized co-operation between plant users, designers and financiers of development work.

1.1. COST STUDY AND OPERATING EXPERIENCE

In any producing plant the following types of cost can be separated:

1. capital costs
2. costs of energy needed in plant operation
3. maintenance costs
4. fuel costs (2)
5. salaries

There are additionally some minor costs as taxes, insurances etc., which are not discussed here. In the test plant the above grouping of costs resulted in the distribution of procentual annual costs given in Table 1. The column 'chances of cost reduction' summarizes shortly recommendable subjects of study. The information about possibilities to reduce different costs actually forms a qualitative model for plant development, which in practice proceeds through individual decisions concerning subjects such as shown in Table 1.

TABLE 1. RELATIVE COSTS AND SOME CENTRAL TOPICS OF DEVELOPMENT
(relative costs from the test plant in-74)

cost type	percentage	chances of cost reduction, c_j, j=1,...,11
1. capital costs	28.	1. lighter building and silo constructions could be considered in future plants
2. energy costs	8.	2. dryer feed i.e. less energy would be consumed in blowing water vapor in flue gases /1/ 3. improvements of the design of flue gas ways in cyclon and boiler 4. improvements of the design of feeder systems according to minimum energy consumption
3. maintenance	7.	5. eliminating part of the moisture in feed, especially the peaks (may solidify ashes on the cyclon walls) 6. improvements of the design in: -silos (channeling) -feeder equipment (wear-out failures) (random failures) 7. scheduling maintenance actions/2/according to minimum down-time and thus minimum use of alternative fuel
4. fuel costs	38.	8. efficiency improvements in heat production lines, as an example improved waste heat recovery by pre-drying peat with flue gases 9. minimizing the use of alternative fuel (used during down-times due to larger failures and repairs, especially the down-times due to the cyclon should be avoided)
5. salaries	18.	10. less supervision would be needed if obtainable improvements were carried out in: -silos (channeling avoided) -feeder eq. (wear-out, random failures) -cyclon (extraction of ashes in fluidized phase) -ash handling (no manual operations) 11. decreased need of supervision might reduce costs paid as salaries. Thus also an effective system for the very supervising work should be considered; depending on the size of the plant it could consist of: -a centralized control room -TV-facilities and automation of a suitable degree. Computer supervising system might be economic enough in larger plants.
	100.	

The potential available for cost reductions in a peat burning plant can be studied by beginning with a similar table as above and analyzing it with an accuracy suitable for the purpose. A similar table with about the same elements in the rightmost column could be evidently formed also for other present small and middle-sized peat burning plants with different constructions.

1.2. SELECTION OF SUBJECTS OF CLOSER STUDY

The utilization of the information in Table 1. demands selection of a few central subjects of closer study, because a simultaneous investigation of all subjects would need very large resources. In order to evaluate the quantitative weights of each chance c_j the requirements (1) should be tested. Then for each c_j, $j=1,\ldots,11$ here, a weight w_j of the form (3) can be estimated.

$$w_j = \sum_{i=1}^{3} k_i R_{ij}, \text{ where} \qquad (3)$$

i = current number of requirements (1)
k_i = coefficient of the mutual weighting of requirements (1)
R_{ij} = parameter expressing the degree according to which a given subject of study c_j will satisfy requirements (1)

In practice we can expect that some additional subjects of study can be defined which will affect on several types of costs, for example pre-drying would do so. Thus the sum of type (4) would give the summed weight w_{mix} for each of such 'mixed' subjects of study, which also may lead, when succeeded, to cost reducing improvements.

$$w_{mix} = \sum_{j=1}^{j_{max}} w_j, \text{ where} \qquad (4)$$

j = current number of c_j's in Table 1
j_{max} = total number of c_j's, the available chances of cost reduction.

In this preliminary study we have not explicitly carried out the evaluation of Eqs. (3) and (4) but have represented the equations here to show that a quantitative discussion of c_j's in Table 1. would be possible if needed. In practice the selection of subjects of closer study was carried out very much according to the principle involved in above equations: those subjects were selected, which apparently are central in Table 1., satisfy requirements (1) and the cost effects of which concern several types of costs:

1. failure behaviour of the plant
2. pre-drying of the peat

Additional support for the selection could obviously be obtained by applying Eqs. (3) and (4) to the selected tasks.

The identification of parameters needed in weighting Eqs. (3) and (4) clearly will be quite laborious but gives useful information for decision making.

2. FAILURE BEHAVIOUR OF THE PLANT

The central type of failure in a peat burning plant appears to be deterministic i.e. the time of occurrence of a failure can be approximately predicted. Quite pure wear-out failures will occur in the feeder system (screw conveyors, feed blowers and flue gas blowers). Failures in the cyclon can be regarded as indirect wear-out failures (caused by frequent extraction of ashes); these failures clearly show a need for extracting ashes in fluidized phase. An additional deterministic type of failure has shown to be the shanneling of peat in silos. Also this failure shows a need for improvements in the design of silos or buffer store by demanding quite regular attention of the supervising personnel. This task of supervising in turn will cause indirectly a part of the costs paid as salaries.

2.1. PRESENT VALUES OF PERIODIC FAILURES

Assuming that mean time between failures for a component remains approximately constant or no improvements in the failing component are made, we can estimate the average annual cost due to a given failure and regard it as an annual payment or annuity. For an annuity we can obtain the corresponding present value H_j when the total time of annually paid costs is known /4/, as Eq. (5):

$$H_j = a_j x \frac{(1+i)^n-1}{i(1+i)^n} \text{, where} \quad (5)$$

H_j = present value of a periodically paid cost due to component j

a_j = an estimate of the average annual cost due to component j

i = present rate of interest

n = total time of periodic costs.

A suitable estimate for the total time of periodically paid costs could be the expected useful life of the total plant equipment, taken usually as 10-20 years for heat producing equipments.

The total sum of the present values for the periodic failure costs in a plant actually represents the available economic potential for component improvements. Therefore it can be used as one evaluable measure when performances of peat burning plants with different constructions are compared. For the test plant this sum will be about half of the corresponding present value for expectable costs of maintenance to be paid in ten years time. This shows that a considerable potential for component improvements exists.

3. PRE-DRYING OF THE PEAT

In the test plant the temperature of gases leaving the preheater of burning air varies, 140-190°C, depending on the air excess and the moisture content of the peat. Because of the low sulphur content of peat, about 0.2 w-%, the temperature of flue gases could be lowered without a significant risk of corrosion in the flue gas channels. Thus a more efficient recovery of the heat content of flue gases would be physically 'allowed'. This heat content would be efficiently utilized when used in pre-drying the peat, which improvement according to Table 1., for example, would be very desirable. The main effects of pre-drying are schemed below.

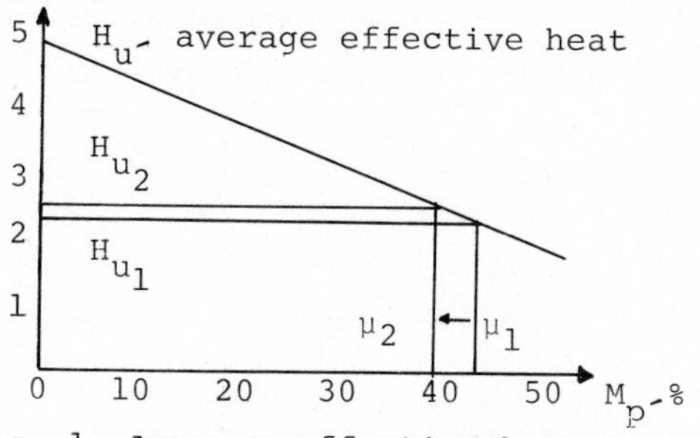

Fig. 1. Average effective heat H_u vs moisture content of the peat M_p /1/

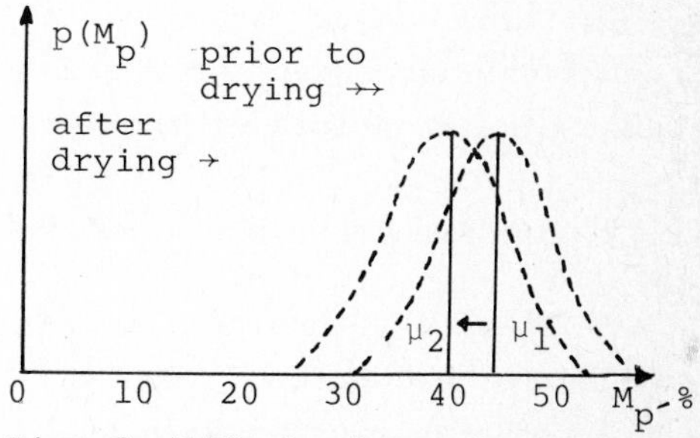

Fig. 2. Effect of pre-drying on the probability distribution of M_p, the moisture content of the peat

The use of flue gases in pre-drying would naturally cause additional costs due to recirculation equipment and energy. Therefore these negative cost effects of the pre-drying should be weighted against the following positive effects:

1. improved utilization of the waste heat of flue gases; for example a drying result of 10% would mean a 5% reduction in fuel costs
2. direct costs of maintenance obviously decreased (cyclon repairs)
3. decreased need of supervision because of an imrpoved continuity of the combustion
4. better possibilities of extracting the ashes from the cyclon in fluidized phase continuously and automatically, because a temperature higher than in present cyclons could be maintained
5. possibly small reductions in the size of the boiler
6. the plant as a whole less sensitive for variations in fuel moisture and thus reductions in the need of supervision expectable.

Some preliminary experimental results of pre-drying have already been obtained at Kymin Osakeyhtiö, Heinola, and they are favourable for the continuation of the study.

5. A COST MODEL FOR SEEKING OPTIMAL PLANT COMPOSITIONS

Plants using different fuels need different equipments for fuel storing, handling and combustion. This fact results in that also the corresponding distributions for the annual relative costs (2) will be different, which as such would be an interesting subject of study for different pairs of fuels because of the continuous development in fuel prices.

In this discussion, however, the differences in the cost structures of two plants using different fuels are interpreted as a potential for seeking optimal plant compositions for future two-fuel plants. Preliminary studies show that for plants of small capacity the two-fuel composition can be more profitable than the corresponding one-fuel alternatives, dependent on the annual demand characteristics and the ratio of unit prices of the two fuels.

5.1. COST STRUCTURE FOR A TWO-FUEL PLANT

Facilities for using alternative fuel in a heating plant may be needed for a couple of reasons:

- expectable changes in fuel prices
- uncertain availability and quality of the base fuel
- possible technical difficulties in maintaining continuous heat production using only the base fuel

The practical reasons will show a need for modelling the cost structure of a two-fuel plant, in order to compare it with the limiting one-fuel alternatives. Especially for peat-oil plants the above reasons seem to be relevant, because the technology of peat combustion units in plants of low capacity still allows development.

In a two-fuel plant part of the demand will be satisfied by the base fuel and the rest by the alternative fuel, called here aid fuel. The effective share of the designed aid fuel capacity will be decisive for the total economy of the two-fuel plant. Therefore we have selected it as the free variable in the following model of annual costs for a two-fuel plant. In the following discussion the total costs of a two-fuel plant are formed as a sum of the main cost types. The effect of plant capacity will be implicitly taken into account through the relative magnitudes of the cost types involved in the cost function.

The presented cost model is primarily constructed for peat-oil plants and therefore the following discussion will concentrate on the features characteristic for this specific type of two-fuel plants.

1. <u>Fuel costs</u>. The annual demand curve for a given heating plant usually shows that the plant must be flexibly adaptable to both short and long term variations of the demand, the minimum capacity needed being in practice about half of the maximal demand of capacity. A cycle of the annual long term variation is shown schematically in Fig. 4. assuming a smoothed (effective) representation for a typical annual demand curve.

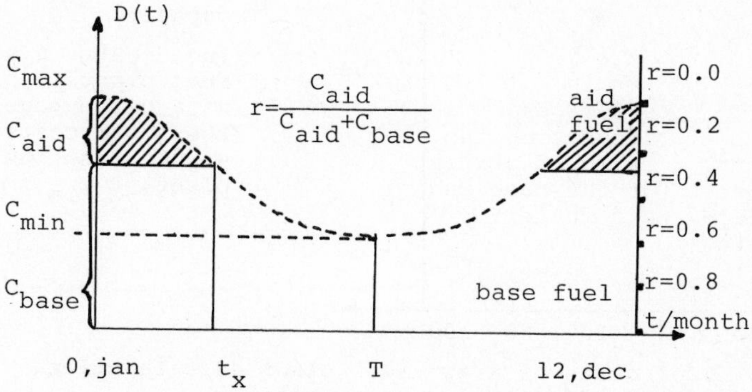

Fig. 4. Sharing of the heat production capacity between the base and aid fuels

Using the notations of the above figure we obtain for the fuel costs of a two-fuel plant:

$$\frac{1}{2}C_{fuel}(r) = \frac{w_{aid}}{w_{base}} \int_{o}^{t_x} \{D(t)-C_{base}\}dt + \int_{o}^{t_x} C_{base}dt \qquad (6)$$

$$+\int_{t_x}^{T} D(t)dt, \text{ where}$$

w_{base} = coefficient for the unit price of the base fuel

w_{aid} = coefficient for the unit price of the aid fuel

$t_x(r)$ = an aid variable to be estimated using the demand curve D(t)

T = time corresponding to the minimum demand C_{min}

Depending on the shape of the demand curve and ratio of prices of the two fuels the total fuel costs (6) as a function of the increasing r will be an increasing function (7) as shown in Fig. 5.

In real plants the shape of the long term demand curve can vary considerably depending on the type of load in the network. The two extremes are a constant demand and a demand which occurs seasonally. Between these two extremes is the present case of demand which is usual in small district heating plants.

$$\frac{d\{C_{fuel}(r)\}}{dr} \geq 0 \forall r \varepsilon [0.,1.0] \tag{7}$$

As can be seen in Fig. 5., the cost effect of using more expensive aid fuel is smallest for lower values of the r.

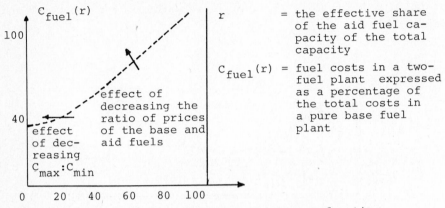

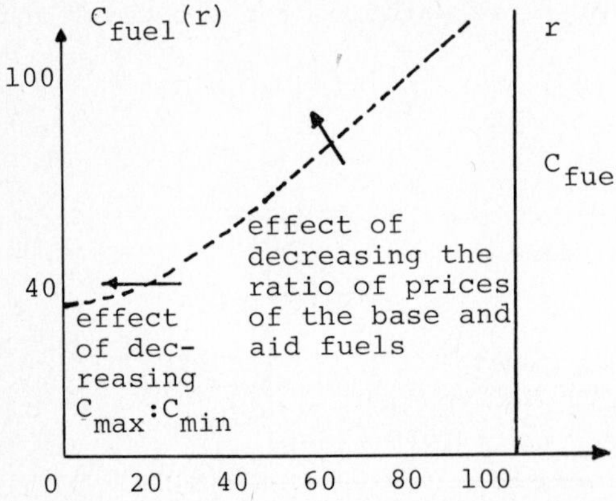

r = the effective share of the aid fuel capacity of the total capacity

$C_{fuel}(r)$ = fuel costs in a two-fuel plant expressed as a percentage of the total costs in a pure base fuel plant

Fig. 5. Fuel costs of a two-fuel plant as a function of the effective capacity ratio r.

A similar principal study concerning the rest of the main costs as a function of the r will be of interest especially for low values of the r.

2. Capital costs. The construction of the heating plant will be actually selected among three choices: one-fuel plant for the base fuel, a two-fuel plant for the base and aid fuels and a one-fuel plant for the aid fuel. Thus the capital costs will be in practice fixed by the selection of the plant composition.

In a heating plant there usually are at least two heat production units, preferably one separate units for the base load and for the more variable peak load. In a peat-oil plant one of the units, recommendably the unit for the peak demand, could be replaced by a cheaper oil unit. This change in plant composition would clearly offer means for reducing the initial plant investment so also the capital costs. Therefore the principal form of the capital cost curve as a function of the r will be of decreasing type. Small discontinuities at both ends can be expected due to changes in plant composition.

3. Maintenance costs. The decreasing function will be evident also for the costs of maintenance, because the oil units clearly need less maintenance than the present peat combustion units. Thus when replacing

a peat unit by an oil unit, considerable savings in maintenance costs can be expected.

4. Energy costs. Mainly because of the feeder system for the fuel and the system for blowing combustion air and flue gases a peat unit consumes more energy than a corresponding oil unit. Thus replacement of a peat unit by an oil unit will reduce cost of energy used in the plant. A decreasing function of energy costs as a function or the r will result.

5. Salaries. Salaries of the supervising personnel is cost factor which reflects the ease of operating the plant. A peat unit needs, at least using present plant constructions, much more attention of the supervising personnel than an oil unit. Thus replacement of a peat unit by an oil unit clearly reduces the need of supervision and correspondingly also costs paid as salaries. Therefore also here a decreasing function of costs will result when the r is increased.

The above principal discussion shows that, except for the fuel costs, all costs will show different types of decreasing tendencies as one or more peat units in a heating plant are replaced by oil units. Approximating the sum of capital, energy, maintenance and salary costs with a linear dependence as a function of the r, we obtain the following function for the total annual costs in a two-fuel plant:

$$J(r) = k_1(c_o - k\cdot r) + 2k_2\left[\left\{\frac{w_{aid}}{w_{base}}\int_o^{t_x}\{D(t)-C_{base}\}dt + \int_o^{t_x} C_{base}\,dt + \int_{t_x}^{T} D(t)\,dt\right\}\right] \qquad (8)$$

where

$k_{2,1}$ = coefficients for the relative shares of fuel costs and non-fuel costs respectively in a one-fuel plant using only base fuel

c_o = relative share of non-fuel costs in a one-fuel plant using only base fuel

k = decay factor for non-fuel costs, other notations same as in Eq. (6).

The total costs $J(r)$ must be solved numerically in order to study if a minimum for the total costs can be found for an $r \in (0.,1.0)$. If an optimum can not be found, one of the limiting one-fuel plants will be optimal as to the total costs.

The continuous representation of non-fuel costs in Eq. (8) is not strictly correct, because the possible combinations of available peat and oil units will form a discrete set of alternatives. The linear function adopted thus represents the first approximation for a set of discrete points.

The relative shares of different cost types will be also a function of plant capacity. The fuel costs will be dominant in plants of large capacity and in small and middle-sized plants the share of other costs, capital, maintenance, energy costs and salaries, will be more significant. This effect is clearly of importance in selecting the most profitable plant compositions especially for plants of small capacity. The cost function of type (8) can be used to verify numerically cost effects represented schematically in Fig. 6.

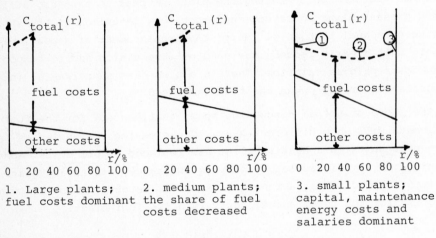

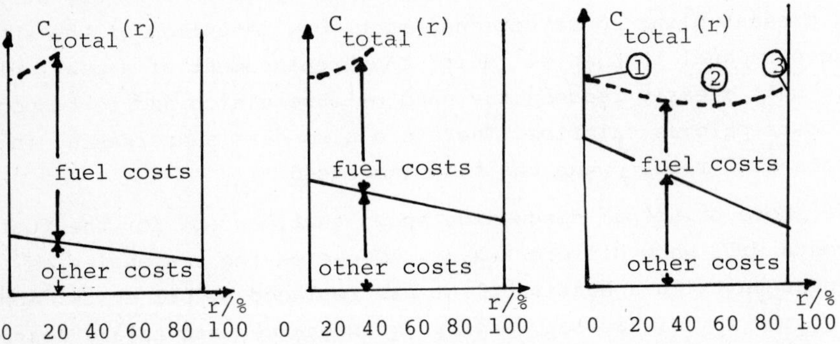

1. Large plants; fuel costs dominant

2. medium plants; the share of fuel costs decreased

3. small plants; capital, maintenance energy costs and salaries dominant

Fig. 6. Effect of plant capacity on relative costs in a two-fuel plant

The estimation of the total cost curve as a function of the r for a given plant capacity requires estimation of the economic parameters and the demand curve involved in Eq. (8). The estimation of the parameters will presuppose knowledge of the actual plant construction alternatives and availability of real cost information, which sometimes is difficult to achieve. However, the cost model of Eq. (8) will offer a possibility to study the following important topics:

1. the existence of the optimum for total costs in small heating plants i.e. the locations of the points ①, ② and ③ in Fig. 6. can be tested numerically and, consequently, the corresponding most profitable plant composition can be established
2. numerical simulation of the cost effects caused by changes in different economic parameters, for example fuel prices, can be carried out for two-fuel plants.

The applicability of the model is clearly limited to two-fuel plants where unit prices of the two fuels differ considerably from each other and different heat production units are used for the base fuel and the aid fuel. In peat-oil plant the situation will be this provided that different boilers are used for peat and oil.

6. SUMMARY

A systematic approach for seeking and selecting optimization objectives for small and middle-sized peat burning plants has been proposed. The main possibilities available for plant optimization have been stated and discussed referring to the example plant. Partly qualitative and partly quantitative grounds for employing a new component, the pre-dryer of the peat, have been found and considered to be adequate for laboratory scale studies. Preliminary results appear to be favourable.

A model for seeking optimal plant compositions for a two-fuel plant has been introduced. The model allows numerical studies of the expectable profitability of different plant compositions for future peat-oil plants, thus accomplishing the previous discussion on plant optimization.

Future studies concerning peat burning plants will concentrate on studying mechanisms of enlargements for heating plants subject to given demand characteristics.

LITERATURE CITED AND SUGGESTED READINGS:

1. Enqvist, E., On the Combustion of Peat, Work of Diploma, TKK 1972, pp. 8-19.
2. Jardine, A.K.S., Operational Research in Maintenance, Manchester Univ. Press, 1970, pp. 20-43.
3. Hirvonen, E., Cost Calculations, Second Ed., Turku 1974, pp. 126-9.
4. Peters, M.S., Timmerhaus, K.D., Plant Design and Economics for Chemical Engineers, McGraw-Hill, Sec. Ed., 1968, pp. 242-3, 265-6.
5. Wells, G.L., Process Engineering with Economic Objective, Intertext 1973.

ACKNOWLEDGEMENTS:

This work was supported in part by the Ministry of Commerce and Industry and the Building Department of the Ministry of Defence.

Experiments needed were carried out by Kymin Osakeyhtiö-Kymmene Aktiebolag, Heinola, Finland.

A MULTI-AREA APPROACH TO THE ECONOMIC OPTIMIZATION OF ELECTRIC POWER SYSTEM

Radmila Rakić Radivoj Petrović Milan Rakić

Mihailo Pupin Institute,
Belgrade, Yugoslavia

A B S T R A C T

In this paper, the problem of short-term economic dispatch of active power in a combined hydro-thermal electric power system is considered. The problem studied is a 24 hours optimization, with operational cost as associated criterion. It is assumed that consumer´s demand, defined as a number of time functions, as well as technical constraints concerning power production units, and transmission line capabilities are satisfied within the period of optimization. The deterministic time discrete mathematical model of the above stated problem consists of a set of nonlinear algebraic equations and a set of nonequalities. The power system is decomposed into a number of interconnected power areas. Consequently, a number of local less dimensional area optimization subproblems are defined. Each of them is a typical nonlinear programming problem. Coordination among subproblem solutions is performed by a higher level decision making effort. It is done by specially derrived coordination algorithm.

It is shown that the proposed multi-area approach is computationally effective and fast. This property has a particular importance since in practice the system under control is influenced by frequent structural disturbances (failures of production units and/or transmission lines) causing power generation rescheduling. Using the presented algorithm a short term dynamic optimization problem of 220 kV network of Serbia has been solved. The results of this solution are also discussed in the paper.

INTRODUCTION

Considerable activity in the field of electric power systems control in recent years has been devoted to the development and application of various optimization methods to achieve optimum system economy. In studies of economic operation of a combined hydro-thermal electric power system, attention has to be paid to the number of imporant factors such as: operating efficiency of available sources, customer requirements and supply security, water inflows, transmission losses, etc.

The need to solve the problem has rapidly grown with increased use of computers in control of electric power systems, which allow significant savings in system´s operational costs by use of optimization theory in scheduling systems operation. There have been numerous papers discussing the problem of hydro-thermal system optimization and the application of various optimization methods[/1,2,3/].

The problem,considered here, appears to be quite common. It is a problem of short-term economic dispatch of active power in a combined hydro-thermal electric power system. The optimization problem is formulated as minimization of the system´s operational cost within a 24 hour period. The main system´s characteristics are:

(a) Consumer demand is known and given by a number of time functions representing power demands in all passive nodes of a network.

(b) The set of thermal power plants belonging to the system is given. Economic efficiency of each power plant is described by generation cost curve.

(c) The hydro power generation schedules are arranged as piece-wise constant during discrete time intervals. The total amounts of water available for hydro power generation during 24 hours are given in advance for each hydro power plant.

(d) Transmission losses are taken into account in the usual simplified quadratic form.

(e) A number of constraints are imposed on both control and state variables: (i) output of each power plant is limited between technical minimum, and technical maximum, (ii) the transmission lines power capacities are limited, (iii) flows through each turbine are limited.

A common way to overcome the computational difficulties, that arise in optimization due to a high problem dimensionality, is to decompose the problem on subproblems and to coordinate the process of obtaining their solutions. Decomposition procedure presented in this paper is not a standard one. It is characterized by adoption of decomposition technique already developed /5/, and some kind of its modification. The modification consists of linearization of the integral criterion functional with respect to hydro power generation, and successive hydro power scheduling by use of minimization of a linearized functional. Solution of the problem of optimal power generation scheduling is obtained iteratively. Optimal scheduling of thermal power generation and hydro generation scheduling are the two subroutines that are successively applied until the optimal solution of hydro and thermal power generation schedule has been reached.

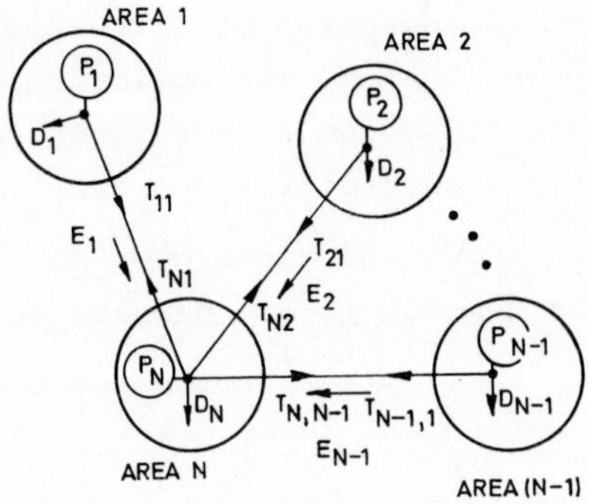

Fig. 1. Schematic representation of an electric power system composed of N interconnected areas

FORMAL PROBLEM STATEMENT

It is assumed that the system under consideration consists of a number of active and passive nodes connected by high voltage lines. It is also assumed that the system is decomposed in N areas, Fig. 1., with sufficiently independent power production and consumption. Each area i=1,..., N, has numbers h_i and s_i of hydro and steam power plants, respectively. The hydro and steam power generation H_{ij}^t, S_{ij}^t, $\forall i$ and $j=1,\dots,h_i$ (or s_i) of each production plant are discrete functions of time t, t=1,..., 24. They form column vectors of hydro and thermal power production H_i^t, S_i^t, $\forall i,t$.

Each area is characterized by a given demand D_i^t, $\forall i,t$, so that the total system demand at time t equals $D^t = \sum_{i=1}^{N} D_i^t$. Each area exchanges power with other areas. Power exchange of an area i, E_i, $\forall i$, is an algebraic sum of powers through transmission lines connecting i-th areas with others

$$E_i^t = \sum_{r=1}^{r_i} T_{ir}, \quad \forall i, \tag{1}$$

T_{ir} being a power of r-th power line connecting i-th area with other areas. With line losses neglected, the area power exchange satisfy the following relation

$$\sum_{i=1}^{N} E_i^t = 0. \tag{2}$$

Due to the technical characteristics of the interconnection transmission lines, the powers of the interconnection transmission lines are subject to the constraints of the type

$$|T_{ir}^t| \le |T_{ir}\max|, \quad \forall i,t, \text{ and } r=1,\dots,r_i. \tag{3}$$

It is supposed that hydro power plant is a constant head one. Power production of the j-th power station belonging to the i-th area, at time t, is described by a linear relation

$$H_{ij}^t = k_{ij} q_{ij}^t, \quad \forall i,t \text{ and } j=1,\dots,h_i, \tag{4}$$

where q_{ij}^t is the flow of water through the turbines of the j-th hydro power station in i-th area at time t and k_{ij} constant coeficients $\forall i$ and $j=1,\dots,h_i$. The flow of water is subject to the following constraints

$$0 \le q_{ij}^t \le q_{ij\,\max}, \quad \forall i,t, \text{ and } j=1,\dots,h_i, \tag{5}$$

which are a consequence of the power plant characteristics and

$$\sum_{t=1}^{24} q_{ij}^t \leq kQ_{ij}, \quad \forall i, \text{ and } j=1,\dots,h_i, \tag{6}$$

which are imposed by weekly operation planing. In (5) and (6) $q_{ij\,max}$ is maximum allowed flow of water through the turbines of the j-th plant in the i-th area and Q_{ij} is a volume of water available for hydro power production of the same plant during the whole interval of 24 hours.

Relations (4) can be represented in a simplified matrix notation by introducing a column vector of area water flows through turbines $(q_i^t)' = (q_{i1}^t,\dots,q_{ih_i}^t)$, $\forall i,t$, $((\cdot)'$ denoting a transpose operation) and a diagonal area matrix of constant coeficients $k_i = \text{diag}\,(k_{i1},\dots,k_{ih_i})$. The column vector of area hydro power production is according to (4)

$$H_i^t = k_i q_i^t, \quad \forall i,t. \tag{7}$$

It is convenient to introduce a column vector of area thermal power generation $(S_i^t)' = (S_{i1}^t, S_{i2}^t,\dots,S_{is_i}^t)$, $\forall i,t$. Thermal power production is normally subject to the constraints of the type

$$S_{i\,min} \leq S_i^t \leq S_{i\,max}, \quad \forall i,t, \tag{8}$$

where $S_{i\,min}$ and $S_{i\,max}$ are corresponding column vectors representing technical minimum and maximum outputs of thermal power stations belonging to i-th area. It is also convenient to write the state of the energy production and interchange for each area and time as a triplet $P_i^t = (S_i^t, H_i^t, T_i^t)$, where T_i^t represents a vector of power flows in the transmission lines connecting i-th area with other areas.

According to H. Happ/5,6/, the transmission losses in the whole system can be written, in terms of area hydro and thermal generation powers and transmission line powers, in the usual quadratic form

$$L^t = \sum_{i=1}^{N} L_i^t = \sum_{i=1}^{N} (P_i^t)' B_i P_i^t \tag{9}$$

where B_i are matrices of known B-coefficients for each area $i=1,\dots,N$.

Balance equations for the first N-1 areas are the following

$$D_i^t = \sum_{j=1}^{h_i} H_{ij}^t + \sum_{j=1}^{s_i} S_{ij}^t - L_i^t - E_i^t, \quad i=1,\dots,N-1, \ \forall t, \tag{10}$$

and for the N-th area, due to the relation (1)

$$D_N^t = \sum_{j=1}^{h_N} H_{Nj}^t + \sum_{j=1}^{s_N} S_{Nj}^t - L_N^t + \sum_{i=1}^{N-1} E_i^t, \quad \forall t. \qquad (11)$$

The associated performance criterion functional, representing system operational costs written in discrete form, is

$$F = \sum_{t=1}^{24} \sum_{i=1}^{N} \sum_{j=1}^{s_i} F_{ij}(S_{ij}^t). \qquad (12)$$

In order to simplify notation, it is convenient to introduce column vector functions for area production costs, defined by the cost functions of thermal power plants belonging to the area

$$(F_i(S_i^t))' = (F_{i1}(S_{i1}^t), \ldots, F_{is_i}(S_{is_i}^t)), \quad \forall i,t. \qquad (13)$$

The dynamic optimization problem is stated as follows. Find S_{ij}^t, and H_{ij}^t, $\forall i,j,t$, that minimize functional F defined by (12), taking into account the conditions (10) and (11) which have to be satisfied for any $t=1,\ldots,24$, and the constraints (3), (5), (6) and (8), which are imposed on values of state and control variables.

A METHOD TO SOLVE A PROBLEM

Stated problem belongs to the class of nonlinear dynamic optimization problems. Problems of this class are intensively treated in literature[/2,3/]. In a number of papers[/5,6,10/] decomposition technique has been applied in determination of optimal control of strictly thermal power systems. However, this technique is useful in treating combined hydro--thermal power systems[/9/].

The method presented in this paper represents imbeding of a previously developed method of a multi-area approach to a hydro-thermal power system optimization with hydro power generation schedule given in advance[/10/]. It should be noted that a multi-area approach in its original versions[/5,6/] was not used for dynamic optimization of hydro-thermal power systems.

Method developed to handle complete process of optimal power generation scheduling, control and rescheduling, consists of three subroutines:

(1) Subroutine for Initial Hydro Power Generation Scheduling.

(2) Subroutine for Optimal Thermal Power Generation Scheduling by use of Multi-Area Approach.

(3) Subroutine for Hydro Power Generation Rescheduling.

These subroutines are incorporated in algorithm for a multi-area dynamic optimization of a combined hydro-thermal power system as shown in Fig.2.

Each subroutine is briefly described in the following part of the paper.

Initial Scheduling of Hydro Power Generation (ISHPG)

Initial schedules for hydro power generation are usually determined by area dispatchers, and their determination is a matter of skill and experience. If initial schedules are not given, they can be determined by use of the following simple algorithm.

An initial hydro power production schedule of the j-th hydro power station, located in the i-th area, $\forall i$ and $j=1,\ldots,h_i$, is

$$H_{ij}^t = \begin{cases} \xi_{ij}(D_i^t - W_i), & \text{if } 0 \leq \xi_{ij}(D_i^t - W_i) \leq H_{ij\,max}, \\ H_{ij\,max}, & \text{if } \xi_{ij}(D_i^t - W_i) \geq H_{ij\,max}, \\ 0 & \text{if } \xi_{ij}(D_i^t - W_i) < 0, \end{cases} \quad \forall i,t \text{ and } j=1,\ldots,24, \tag{14}$$

where:

$$\xi_{ij} = \frac{k_{ij}Q_{ij}}{\sum_{j=1}^{h_i} k_{ij}Q_{ij}}, \quad \forall i \text{ and } j=1,\ldots,h_i, \text{ are constants,}$$

- W_i is adjusted by the algorithm so that, taking into account relations between powers of hydro power stations, H_{ij}^t, and flow of water through turbines, q_{ij}^t (relation (4)), hydro power generation H_{ij}^t, obtained by (14), satisfy constraints (5), and (6) imposed on water flow q_{ij}^t.

The subroutine constructed on the basis of (14) provides initial schedules of hydro power generation such that every thermal power plant operates on a constant level, during the interval of optimization, unless the constraints (5) and (6) are violated.

The flow chart of the subroutine for initial area hydro power production scheduling, constructed according to equations (14), (4), (5) and (6) is illustrated on the Fig. 3.

Initial hydro power production schedules obtained by use of the described subroutine are not necessarily close to the optimal schedules of hydro power generation. Since the schedules made by area dispatchers are often rather good, the subroutine should be applied only if

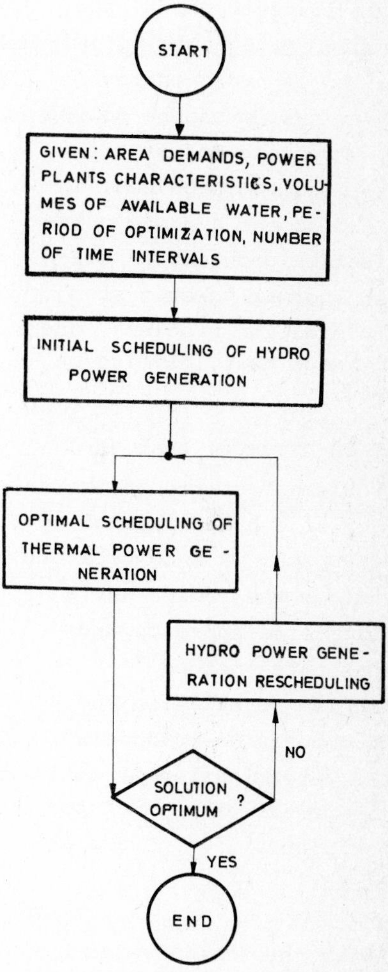

Fig. 2. Flow chart of algorithm for multi-area dynamic optimization of a combined hydro-thermal power system

initial schedules do not exist.

Optimal Schedule for Thermal Power Generation (OSTPG)

Given consumers demand and hydro power stations generation for every hour, the problem of dynamic optimization of hydro-thermal power system can be solved as a sequence of static otpimization problems. Instead of one dynamic optimization problem, 24 static thermal power system otpimization problems, one for each hour, have to be solved.

It is assumed, that the problem of static optimization of a hydro-thermal power system is a complex one. That is the reason why a multi-area approach and Diakoptics method[4,7] in problem formulation and decomposition method in the determination of optimal powers of thermal power plants[6,9,10] are applied.

After the schedules of hydro power plants are determined, the determinati-

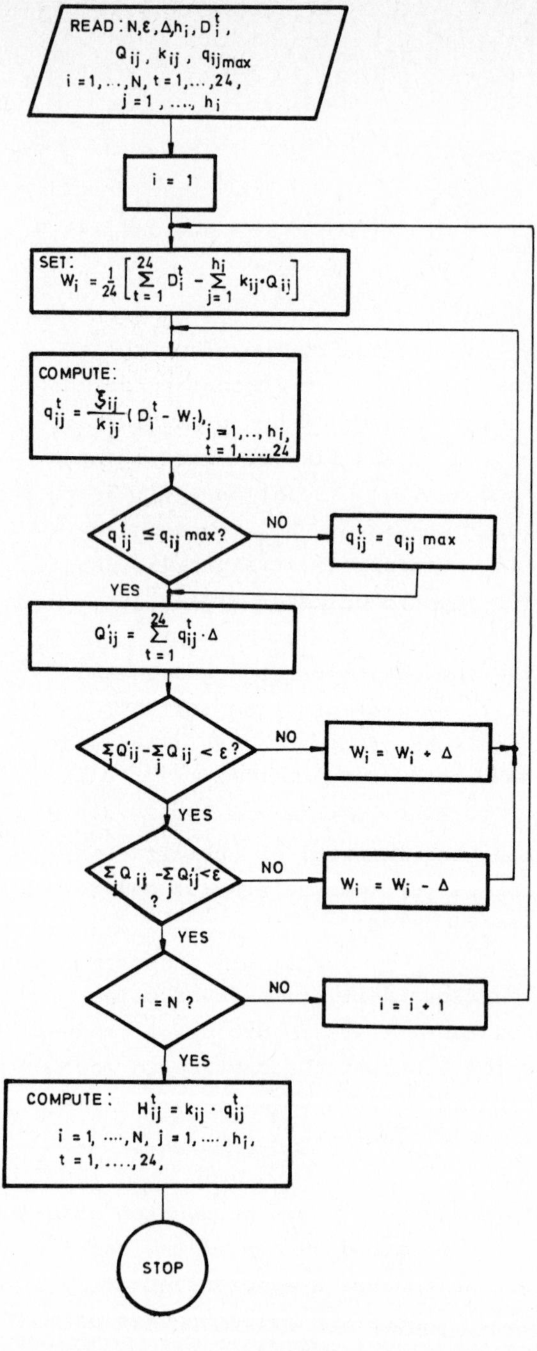

Fig. 3. Initial hydro power generation scheduling

on of the corresponding thermal power schedules becomes a nonlinear programming problem. If a Lagrangian functional is formed from criterion function (12), relations (10) and (11), and constraints (3) and (8), optimal values of variables representing powers of thermal power stations and powers of transmission lines have to satisfy the following sets of equations representating necessary conditions for optimality:

(a) The set of area vector equations

$$\frac{dF_i(S_i^t)}{dS_i^t} - \lambda_i^t\left(1 - \frac{\partial L_i^t}{\partial S_i^t}\right) + \mu_i^t(S_{imax} + S_{imin} - 2S_i^t) = 0, \quad \forall i,t, \tag{15}$$

(b) The set of inter-area equations

$$\lambda_i^t + \sum_{m=1}^{N-1} \lambda_m^t \frac{\partial L_m^t}{\partial E_i^t} = \lambda_N^t - \lambda_N^t \frac{\partial L_N^t}{\partial E_i^t} + 2\sum_{r=1}^{r_i} \nu_{ir}^t T_{ir}^t \frac{\partial T_{ir}^t}{\partial E_i^t}, \quad \forall t \text{ and } i=1,\dots,N-1, \tag{16}$$

(c) The set of equations (10) and (11) representing area balance between production and consumption of electric power.

(d) The set of constraints obtained from Kuhn-Tucker conditions

$$\begin{aligned} &(S_{ijmax} - S_{ij}^t)(S_{ij}^t - S_{ijmin}) \geq 0, \\ &\mu_{ij}(S_{ijmax} - S_{ij}^t)(S_{ij}^t - S_{ijmin}) = 0, \\ &(T_{irmax}^2 - (T_{ir}^t)^2) \geq 0, \\ &\nu_{ir}^t(T_{irmax}^2 - (T_{ir}^t)^2) = 0, \end{aligned} \tag{17}$$

$$\forall i,t \text{ and } j=1,\dots,s_i, \quad r=1,\dots,r_i.$$

In equations (15) to (17) λ_i^t, μ_{ij}^t, ν_{ir}^t, $\forall i,t$ and $j=1,\dots,s_i$, $r=1,\dots,r_i$, are Lagrange multipliers, and μ_i^t and ν_i^t are row vector multipliers, $\mu_i^t = (\mu_{i1}^t,\dots,\mu_{is_i}^t)$, $\nu_i^t = (\nu_{i1}^t,\dots,\nu_{ir_i}^t)$.

The optimal schedules of thermal power generation for given hydro power schedules are determined iteratively. One of areas (say area N) is chosen to be a reference area, and initial values of the corresponding reference multipliers λ_N^t, $\forall t$, are sellected.

Given λ_N^t, initial values for thermal power generation are arbitrarily chosen $\forall t$ and values of multipliers for other areas are obtained from the system of N-1 equations (16). It can be represented in explicit form by use of multipliers ratio vector[6,11]

$$\begin{bmatrix} \lambda_1^t \\ \cdot \\ \cdot \\ \cdot \\ \lambda_{N-1}^t \end{bmatrix} = \begin{bmatrix} \text{multipli-} \\ \text{ers ratio} \\ \text{vector} \end{bmatrix} \cdot \lambda_N^t + R(T_1^t,\dots,T_{N-1}^t), \tag{18}$$

where R is a column vector which is zero vector when all T_i^t satisfy conditions (17).

Given λ_i^t, consumer demand D_i^t, and initial hydro generation schedule of every hydro power plant H_{ij}^t, $\forall i,t$ and $j=1,\dots,h_i$, optimal values of S_i^t are obtained by solving Equations (15) and (17). If area balance Equations (10) and (11) are not satisfied, new values of λ_N^t, $\forall t$ are determined using a single area iterative algorithm[1].

New value of λ_N^t at iteration k is calculated according to

$$(\lambda_N^t)^k = (\lambda_N^t)^{k-1} + (P_T^d - P_T^{k-1})\frac{(\lambda_N^t)^{k-1} - (\lambda_N^t)^{k-2}}{P_T^{k-1} - P_T^{k-2}}, \tag{19}$$

where superscript k indicates the iteration being started,

k-1 = iteration just completed

k-2 = preceeding iteration

$P_T^k = \sum_{i=1}^{N} \sum_{j=1}^{s_i} (S_{ij}^t)^k$ = total thermal power generation at iteration k

$P_T^d = \sum_{i=1}^{N} [D_i^t - \sum_{j=1}^{h_i} H_{ij}^t]$ = total desired thermal power generation.

Multipliers ratio matrix is computed for new values of S_i^t, and new values of multipliers of other areas are obtained by use of (18). The optimal schedules of thermal power generation are obtained when constraints (10) and (11) are satisfied $\forall i$ and $\forall t$. The flow chart for thermal power generation scheduling is presented on the Fig. 4.

Hydro Power Generation Rescheduling (HPGR)

In order to obtain optimal hydro and thermal power generation schedule, the nonlinear dynamic optimization problem is linearized in a neighbourhood of initial solution of hydro power generation schedule, obtained by ISHPG subroutine, and optimal solution of thermal power generation schedule, obtained by OSTPG subroutine.

If all but j-th thermal power station in the i-th area are assumed to generate power at constant level, small variations of its power can be compensated by variations of the production of hydro power stations in the same area so that Equations (10) and (11) are always satisfied. If the powers of interconnection lines are constant, for a given demand, sufficiently small variation of thermal power can be compensated by variations of outputs of hydro power stations belonging to the same area according to

$$dS_{ij}^{t} = \frac{1}{\left(1 - \dfrac{\partial L_i^t}{\partial S_{ij}^t}\right)} \sum_{r=1}^{h_i} \left(1 - \frac{\partial L_i^t}{\partial H_{ir}^t}\right) dH_{ir}^{t}, \tag{20}$$

$\forall i,t$ and $j=1,\ldots,s_i$.

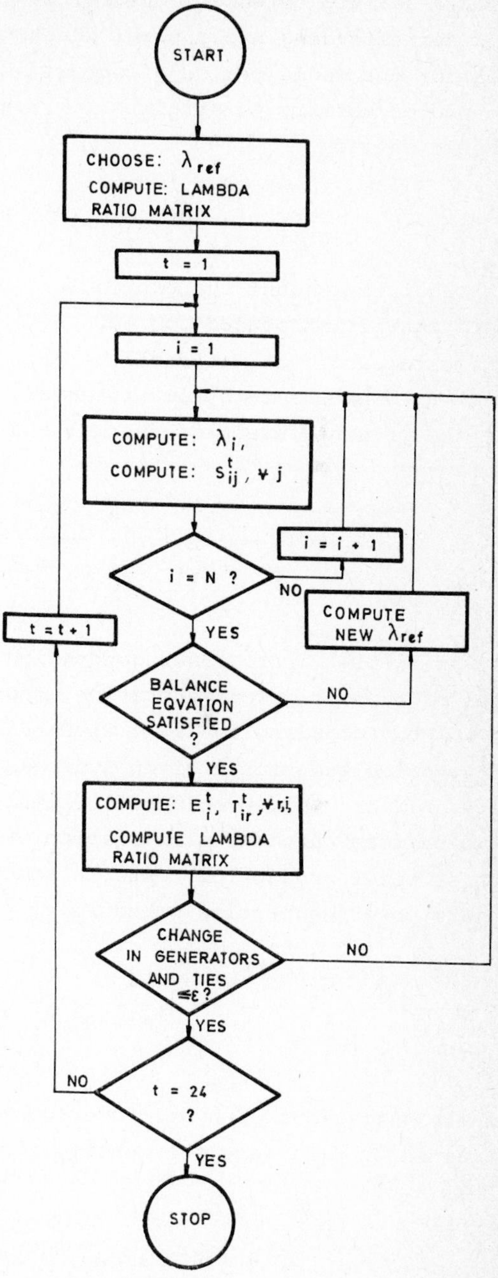

Fig. 4. The flow chart of optimal scheduling for thermal power generation

Since the flow of water through turbines of each hydro power station should satisfy integral constraints (6), flow of water variations and the corresponding hydro power generation variations have to be considered for the whole period of optimization. Since current flow of water schedules satisfy constraints (6), variations of hydro power generation should satisfy

$$\sum_{t=1}^{24} dH_{ij}^{t} = 0, \ \forall i \text{ and } j=1,\dots,h_i. \qquad (21)$$

Taking into account the expression (20), an "incremental worth of water" can be introduced for each hydro power station at every hour. Incremental worth of water of the j-th hydro power station, belonging to i-th area,at the t-th time interval, $\forall i,t$ and $j=1,\dots,h_i$, calculated at the present levels of thermal and hydro power generation is

$$C_{ij}^{t} = \left(1 - \frac{\partial L_i^t}{\partial H_{ij}^t}\right) \sum_{j=1}^{s_i} \frac{F_i(S_{ij}^t)}{dS_{ij}^t} \Big/ \left(1 - \frac{\partial L_i^t}{\partial S_{ij}^t}\right) \Bigg|_{S_{ij}^t, H_{ij}^t}, \ \forall i,t \qquad (22)$$

Given initial hydro power generation schedule and corresponding schedules of thermal power generation, incremental worth of water, C_{ij}^t, is determined according to (22). Given values of incremental worth of water, C_{ij}^t, calculated for a given hydro and thermal power generation schedules, H_{ij}^t and S_{ij}^t, problem of optimal hydro power generation rescheduling can be formulated as minimization of a linear form representing variation of power production costs in some neighbourhood of current values of hydro power generation schedule

$$\min dF = \min_{\{dH_{ij}^t\}} \left\{ \sum_{t=1}^{24} \sum_{i=1}^{N} \sum_{j=1}^{h_i} C_{ij}^t \cdot dH_{ij}^t \right\}, \qquad (23)$$

where variations of hydro power generation have to satisfy constraints defined by (21) and the constraints corresponding to those defined by (5)

$$0 \le H_{ij}^t + dH_{ij}^t \le H_{ij\max}, \quad \forall i,t \text{ and } j=1,\dots,h_i \qquad (24)$$

For a small finite variations of dH_{ij}^t in the neighbourhood of current hydro generation schedule

$$dH_{ij}^t \varepsilon [H_{ij}^t - \delta, \quad H_{ij}^t + \delta], \quad \forall i,t, \text{ and } j=1,\ldots,h_i, \tag{25}$$

the problem of hydro generation schedule improvement is a linear programming problem vith the criterion function defined by (23) and constraints given by (21), (24) and (25).

The constraints (21), (24) and (25) are such that instead of one, N smaller linear programming subproblems, one for each area, have to be solved.The i-th subproblem, $\forall i$, has the following form

$$\min Z_i = \min\{ \sum_{t=1}^{24} \sum_{j=1}^{h_i} C_{ij}^t \cdot dH_{ij}^t \}, \tag{26}$$

under constraints

$$\sum_{t=1}^{24} dH_{ij}^t = 0$$

$$0 \leq H_{ij}^t + dH_{ij}^t \leq H_{ijmax}$$

and

$$dH_{ij}^t \varepsilon [H_{ij}^t - \delta, H_{ij}^t + \delta].$$

The problem of hydro power generation rescheduling defined by (21), (23) and (24) is solved if N linear programming subproblems defined by (26) were solved independently since

$$\min dF = \sum_{i=1}^{N} \min Z_i. \tag{27}$$

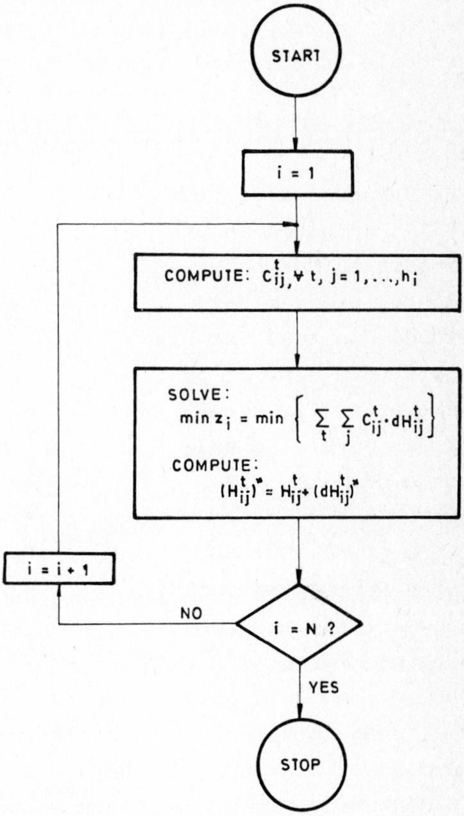

Fig. 5. The flow chart of hydro power generation rescheduling subroutine

After the defined linear programming problem is solved,a new hydro power generation schedule is obtained

$$(H_{ij}^{t})^{*} = H_{ij}^{t} + (dH_{ij}^{t})^{*}, \ \forall i,t \text{ and } j=1,\ldots,h_i. \quad (28)$$

The flow chart of HPGR subroutine as presented on the Fig. 5.

A new hydro generation schedule is used as input to OSTPG subroutine, which is previously described. OSTPG and HPGR subroutines are applied successively until an optimal solution of hydro-thermal power generation schedule is obtained for the whole area.

Example

On the basis of algorithm which is explained in previous part of the paper, a computer program was developed and test example of short term dynamic optimization of 220 kV network for Serbia is solved on a computer IBM 370/135.

A 220 kV Serbian network is schematically represented on the Fig. 6. The 220 kV system includes 2 thermal power stations, 3 hydro power stations and 8 consumers with considerable consumption connected to the network. The whole system is decomposed into 2 areas, as it is shown on the Fig. 6. The corresponding area demands, and B-coeficient matrices, for each area, as well as coefficient matrix of an interconnection subsystem, are calculated.

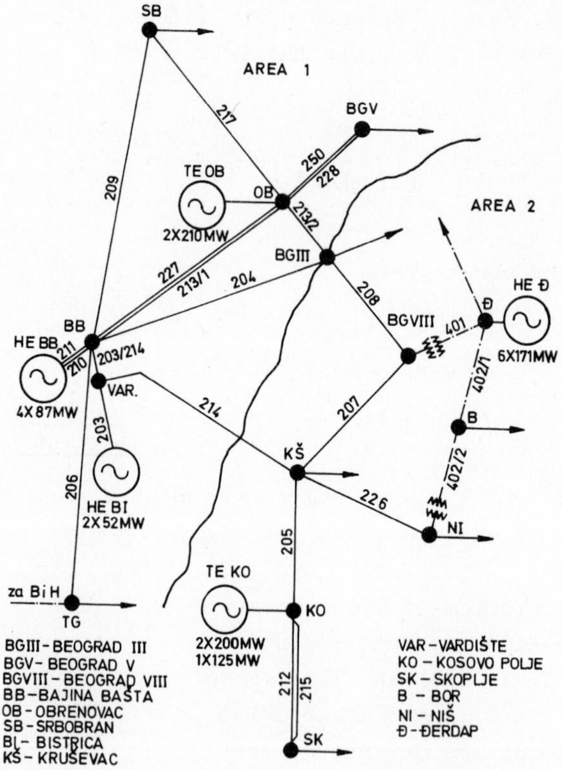

Fig. 6. A schematic representation of a 220 kV Serbian network

For a given area demands D_1^t and D_2^t, Fig. 7. (a), and total volumes of water available for hydro generation for every hydro power plant, accor-

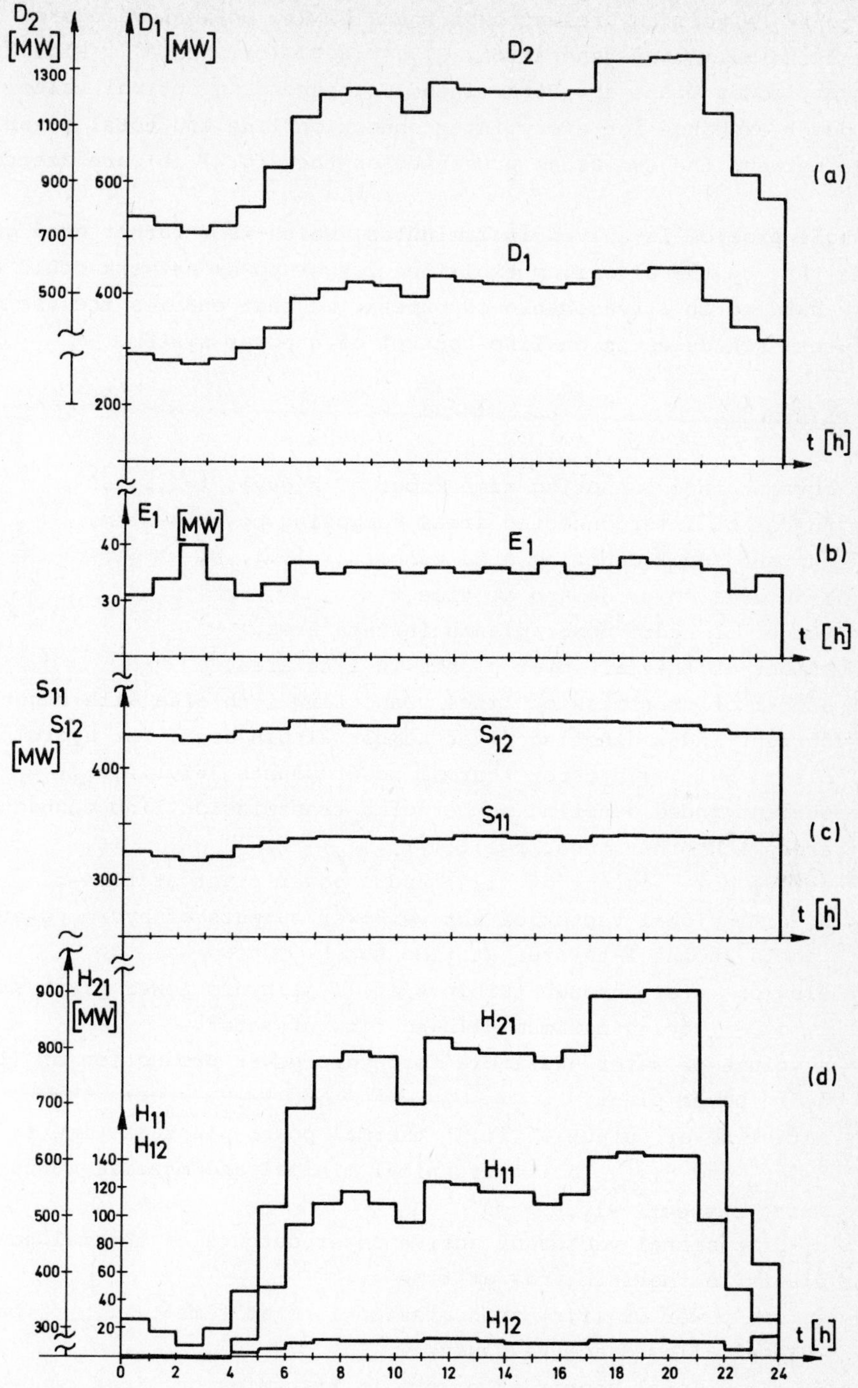

Fig. 7. Diagram of consumer demand and optimal values of power generation

ding to the algorithm presented on the Fig. 2., optimal values of hydro and thermal power generation, S_{ij}^t, Fig. 7 (c), and H_{ij}^t, Fig. 7 (d), for every power plant are determined. Corresponding optimal values of area power exchange for every interconnection line and total power exchange between the two areas presented on the Fig. 7 (b) are determined.

The whole problem is solved in 2 minutes, which is a rather good guarantee that by the algorithm explained larger power network could be easily handled in a reasonable computer time that enables the use of short-term schedules in on-line control of a power system.

List of symbols

t = current index denoting time (hour of a day), $t=1,\dots,24$,

N = number of interconnected areas composing power system,

i = current index denoting area number, $i=1,\dots,N$,

D_i^t = i-th area power demand at time t,

h_i = number of hydro power plants in i-th area,

s_i = number of thermal power plants in i-th area,

r_i = number of transmission lines connecting i-th area with other ones,

j = current index denoting plant number within area; for hydro power plants $j=1,\dots,h_i$, for thermal power plants $j=1,\dots,s_i$,

r = current index denoting number of a transmission line connecting area with other ones, $r=1,\dots,r_i$,

H_{ij}^t = active power output of (i,j) hydro power plant at time t,

H_i^t = h_i-dimensional vector of active power outputs of hydro power plants in the i-th area at time t,

q_{ij}^t = flow of water through turbines of (i,j) hydro power plant at time t, q_{ijmax} being maximum allowed flow of water,

Q_{ij} = a volume of water available for hydro power production of (i,j) hydro power plant,

S_{ij}^t = active power output of (i,j) thermal power plant at time t; S_{ijmin} and S_{ijmax} being technical minimal and maximal output powers, respectively,

S_i^t = s_i-dimensional vector of active power outputs of thermal power plants in the i-th area at time t,

T_{ir}^t = active power of (i,r) transmission line at time t, T_{irmax} being maximal allowed active power,

T_i^t = r_i-dimensional vector of powers in transmission lines connecting i-th area with all others at time t,

P_i^t = $(s_i+h_i+r_i)$-dimensional vector of power production and interchange in the i-th area at time t, $P_i^t = (S_i^t, H_i^t, T_i^t)$,

E_i^t = active power exchange of i-th area at time t,

L_i^t = transmission losses in the i-th area at time t,

L^t = transmission losses in the whole system at time t,

B_i = $(h_i+s_i+r_i) \times (h_i+s_i+r_i)$ - dimensional matrix of B-coefficients of area i,

$F_{ij}(S_{ij}^t)$ = operational cost of (i,j) thermal power plant at time t, if active oputput power is S_{ij}^t,

$F_i(S_i^t)$ = s_i-dimensional column vector function of area production costs,

λ_i^t, μ_{ij}^t, ν_{ir}^t = Lagrange multipliers,

μ_i^t = s_i-dimensional row vector multiplier,

ν_i^t = r_i-dimensional row vector multiplier,

k = current index denoting the number of iteration,

C_{ij}^t = worth of water of (i,j) hydro power plant at time t.

REFERENCES

/1/ Kirchmayer K.L.: "Economic Operation of Power Systems", John Wiley, New York, N.Y., (1958).

/2/ Bernholtz B., Graham Z.J.: "Hydrothermal Economic Scheduling", Part I, II, III, IV, Transactions of AIEE, Part III, Vol. 79, 80, (1960).

/3/ Kirchmayer L.K., Reengly R.J.: "Optimal Control of Thermal-Hydro Systems Operation", Proceedings of the II IFAC Congress, Basel, (1963).

/4/ Kron G.: "Diakoptics - The Piecewise Solution of Large-Scale Systems MacDonald, London, (June 1957 - February 1959).

/5/ Happ H.H.: "Diakoptics - Introduction and Basic Concepts", University of Wisconsin, Conf. Publication on Modern Techniques for the Analysis of Large-Scale Engineering Systems, (Nov. 1965).

/6/ Happ H.H.: "The Inter-Area Matrix: A Tie Flow Model for Power Pools" IEEE Winter Power Meeting, January, 1970., paper No. 40.

/7/ Gavilović M., Petrović R., Rakić M.: "Long-Term Scheduling and Short - Term Economic Operation of Combined Hydro-Thermal Control Plants", Proceedings of the International Seminar on Automatic Control in Production and Distribution of Electric Power, Bruxelles, (1966), pp. 464-469.

/8/ Petrović R., Rakić M.: "Short-Term Economic Operation of Combined Hydro-Thermal Control Plants", Automatika, No. 1, (1967), pp. 21-26.

/9/ Rakić R.: "Decomposition Applied to Determination of Optimal Active Power Production Dispatch with Application in 220 kV Network of SR Serbia", M.Sc. thesis, Dept. of Electrical Engineerging, University of Belgrade, (1973), (in Serbian).

/10/ Rakić R.: "Decomposition Applied to Determination of Optimal Active Power Production Dispatch in 220 kV Network of the Socialist Republic of Serbia", XI Electrical Engineer´s Conference, CIGRÉ, Ohrid, (1972), paper No. 41.06, pp. 65-79 (in Serbian).

/11/ J.F. Aldrich, H.H. Happ, J.F. Leuer: "Multi-Area Dispatch", PICA, (1971), pp. 39-47.

LE PROBLEME DE LA MULTIVALENCE DANS LE TRAVAIL CONTINU

Jacques-André Bartoli - Raymond Trémolières

I.A.E. - Université de Droit, d'Economie et
des Sciences d'Aix-Marseille
29, Av. R. Schuman - 13617 AIX-EN-PROVENCE - FRANCE

PRESENTATION

L'étude généralise un précédent travail consacré à l'automatisation des plannings de roulements de quarts. Alors que la première étude concernait le travail posté en monovalence, nous abordons ici le problème de la multivalence, situation plus générale dans laquelle un ou plusieurs opérateurs peuvent travailler en alternance sur plusieurs postes. Cette hypothèse permet d'étudier le cas où l'on affecte un nombre fractionnaire d'ouvriers sur un même poste. De tels problèmes se posent assez souvent dans le travail continu où l'on cherche à déterminer, compte-tenu d'un certain taux d'absentéisme, le nombre minimum d'ouvriers nécessaire pour assurer un travail donné. La constitution des plannings en roulements de quarts étant chose plus que fastidieuse, sinon impossible à échelle humaine, nous donnons ici les moyens d'obtenir des plannings cycliques en multivalence de façon automatique.

1. INTRODUCTION

Cet article fait suite à une première étude (cf. (1)) consacrée à la génération automatique de cycles de roulements de quarts en monovalence. Pour familiariser le lecteur avec le problème, nous donnons ci-après un planning de roulements de quarts à la Raffinerie de Reichstett.

Cette étude a été réalisée pour la Compagnie Rhénane de Raffinage de Reichstett (Alsace)

Semaine	1	2	3	4	5
Opérateurs	L M M J V . .	L M M J V . .	L M M J V . .	L M M J V . .	L M M J V . .
1 ———	N N N N N N N	- - S S S S S	S S - M M M M	M M M - - - -	J J J J - - -
2 ———	J J J J - - -	N N N N N N N	- - S S S S S	S S - M M M M	M M M - - - -
3 ———	M M M - - - -	J J J J - - -	N N N N N N N	- - S S S S S	S S - M M M M
4 ———	S S - M M M M	M M M - - - -	J J J J - - -	N N N N N N N	- - S S S S S
5 ———	- - S S S S S	S S - M M M M	M M M - - - -	J J J J - - -	N N N N N N N

<u>TABLEAU 1</u> : Roulements de quarts standard de 40 h. (Reichstett), cycle de 5 semaines

Chaque ligne de ce tableau définit le planning de travail d'un ouvrier. Les colonnes correspondent aux jours de la semaine. Le planning se répète identiquement à lui-même de 5 semaines en 5 semaines. On remarquera (et nous prendrons ceci comme hypothèse) que les ouvriers ont tous, à un décalage près dans le temps, les mêmes plannings.

Dans le tableau ainsi que dans le texte, les symboles N, S, M, J définissent les "quarts" de travail dont la durée est généralement de 8 h.

N = nuit, généralement de 21 h à 5 h
S = soir, généralement de 13 h à 21 h
M = matin, généralement de 5 h à 13 h
J = "journée normale", généralement de 8 heures.

Les symboles "-" ou "." marqueront une journée de repos.

Nous appellerons "tour" une suite ininterrompue d'un même quart, et "cycle" le planning d'un opérateur, qui se répète identique à lui-même.

Ainsi, dans le tableau 1, l'ouvrier 1 commence par un tour de 7 nuits et son cycle est de 5 semaines.

Dans ce tableau, on peut vérifier que chaque "jour" ou, plus exactement que dans chaque colonne, il y a toujours un N, un S, et un M. Autrement dit, 24 h sur 24 h, il y a toujours un opérateur présent. Le planning ainsi défini assure donc la présence constante d'un ouvrier et d'un seul sur un certain poste de travail .

Disons tout de suite que les journées normales, notées J, ont pour raison essentielle d'assurer que les opérateurs travaillent en "moyenne" un certain nombre d'heures par semaine, qui, dans le cas présenté plus haut, est de 40 heures. Pendant les quarts de J, les opérateurs sont généralement affectés à d'autres tâches (maintenance, technique, ...) que celles requises par le poste où ils sont affectés. Lorsqu'il n'y a pas de "réserves" d'ouvriers, les ouvriers en J sont souvent les premiers appelés pour remplacer les absents .

Dans le planning précédent, les 5 ouvriers sont attachés exclusivement à un seul et même poste de travail réclamant une présence permanentede 24h sur 24 h. Nous parlons alors de *monovalence*. Dans ce cas, il est bien évident que le nombre d'ouvriers affectés à un même poste est forcément un nombre entier. Cette hypothèse formait le cadre de travail de l'étude présentée dans (1) .

Dans l'étude présente, nous rejetons cette hypothèse et considérons le cas général où à un poste de travail peut être affecté un nombre fractionnaire d'ouvriers. Pour éclairer les choses, nous donnons ci-après un planning cyclique sur 9 semaines.

Dans ce planning, les opérateurs 1, 2, 3, 4 sont affectés exclusivement à un même poste - disons le poste 1 -, et les opérateurs 6, 7, 8, 9 sont affectés exclusivement à un deuxième poste - le poste 2 - . L'opérateur 5 a un rôle particulier et est communément appelé "briseur de quarts". On remarquera, en effet, qu'il passe alternativement d'un poste sur un autre et que ceci permet d'assurer qu'il y ait chaque "jour" un N, un M, et un S sur chacun des 2 postes, autrement dit, chacun des 2 postes est bien sous contrôle continu.

Nous parlerons de *multibriseurs* et de *multivalence* [1] dans le cas général où il n'y a pas forcément qu'un seul ouvrier capable de passer d'un poste sur un autre. Pour que cette hypothèse soit recevable, il est bien évident qu'il faut trouver au moins un ouvrier capable de "tenir" 2 ou plus de 2 postes différents. Ceci est en fait

---

(1) terme souvent confondu avec celui de polyvalence, qui signifie en fait tout autre chose.

Semaine	1	2	3	4	5
Opérateurs	L M M J V . .	L M M J V . .	L M M J V . .	L M M J V . .	L M M J V . .
1	N N N N N - -	J J J J J - -	- M M M M M M	M - S S S S S	S S - N N N N
2	S S S S - N N	N N N N N - -	J J J J J - -	- M M M M M M	M - S S S S S
3	M M M - S S S	S S S S - N N	N N N N N - -	J J J J J - -	- M M M M M M
4	- - - M M M M	M M M - S S S	S S S S - N N	N N N N N - -	J J J J J - -
5=bivalent	N N N - - - -	- - - M M M M	M M M - S S S	S S S S - N N	N N N N N - -
6	S S - N N N N	N N N - - - -	- - - M M M M	M M M - S S S	S S S S - N N
7	M - S S S S S	S S - N N N N	N N N - - - -	- - - M M M M	M M M - S S S
8	- M M M M M M	M - S S S S S	S S - N N N N	N N N - - - -	- - - M M M M
9	J J J J J - -	- M M M M M M	M - S S S S S	S S - N N N N	N N N - - - -

Semaine	6	7	8	9
Opérateurs	L M M J V . .	L M M J V . .	L M M J V . .	L M M J V . .
1	N N N - - - -	- - - M M M M	M M M - S S S	S S S S - N N
2	S S - N N N N	N N N - - - -	- - - M M M M	M M M - S S S
3	M - S S S S S	S S - N N N N	N N N - - - -	- - - M M M M
4	- M M M M M M	M - S S S S S	S S - N N N N	N N N - - - -
5= bivalent	J J J J J - -	- M M M M M M	M - S S S S S	S S - N N N N
6	N N N N N - -	J J J J J - -	- M M M M M M	M - S S S S S
7	S S S S - N N	N N N N N - -	J J J J J - -	- M M M M M M
8	M M M - S S S	S S S S - N N	N N N N N - -	J J J J J - -
9	- - - M M M M	M M M - S S S	S S S S - N N	N N N N N - -

<u>TABLEAU 2</u> - Roulements de quarts en multivalence sur 2 postes, un ouvrier bivalent (pratiqué dans une usine de chimie de la région marseillaise).

possible plus fréquemment qu'on ne pense, soit que les postes ne demandent pas de qualifications particulières, soit que les qualifications soient très proches.

Avant d'entamer l'étude, disons qu'il est très fréquent de trouver dans l'industrie et dans les services des plannings dans lesquels 2 postes sont assurés en liaison avec un ou plusieurs briseurs de quarts. Le cas le plus fréquent est celui où l'on rencontre des plannings du type du Tableau 2.

Notre étude a pour but de donner les moyens de construire automatiquement des plannings de roulements de quarts dans lesquels puissent figurer des "multibriseurs".

On aura ainsi la possibilité d'assurer par exemple :

2 postes avec 9, 10, 11, 12 ... ouvriers
3 postes avec 12, 13, 14, 15, ... ouvriers
....

Pour ne pas reprendre les diverses considérations présentées dans (1) sur les journées normales, les passages de consigne, les week-ends, etc..., nous restreindrons notre étude à la définition des cycles "bruts" c'est-à-dire ceux où l'on se désintéresse du positionnement des journées normales.

2. DEFINITION DU PROBLEME

Pour faciliter le problème, nous le présenterons dans une version légèrement simplifiée.

Etant donné

- un nombre P d'ouvriers,
- un nombre R de postes à assurer de façon continue par les P ouvriers,
- un nombre minimum de jours de repos devant succéder à chacun des tours (N, S, M),
- des bornes inférieures a et supérieures b pour la longueur (i.e. le nombre de quarts) de chacun des tours (N, S ou M),

il s'agit de trouver un moyen d'engendrer tous les plannings cycliques vérifiant ces hypothèses et tels que chaque ouvrier ait, à un décalage près dans le temps, exactement le même cycle que les autres ouvriers.

Nous supposerons, d'autre part, que les tours d'un cycle doivent se succéder dans un ordre déterminé qui peut être le suivant : un tour de nuits, puis un tour de soirs, puis un tour de matins, puis de nouveau un de nuits, etc...

3. RESULTATS GENERAUX

Nous donnons un premier résultat dont la démonstration est triviale en considérant que chaque "jour" il y a un nombre constant de N, de S et de M.

Lemme 1 : Considérons le planning commun à P ouvriers et concernant R postes. Si un ouvrier termine un tour (de N par exemple) à une date t (le dernier quart du tour se trouve à t), il y a alors nécessairement un autre ouvrier qui commence un tour de N à la date t + 1.

Ce lemme nous sera utile pour définir un algorithme permettant d'engendrer le cycle.

Nous aurons aussi besoin du résultat suivant.

Lemme 2 : Avec P ouvriers assurant R postes, le nombre total n de N (ou de S, ou de M) dans le cycle est :

$$n = \frac{LR}{P}$$

ou L est la longueur d'un cycle. Le nombre n doit être un multiple entier de 7.

La longueur L des cycles vérifie alors

$$L = n \frac{P}{R}$$

et L doit être entier et multiple de 7.

Démonstration :

Chaque "jour" on doit trouver R nuits d'où au total LR nuits dans le planning commun au P ouvriers. Comme les ouvriers ont tous des mêmes cycles, on doit donc trouver LR/P nuits (ou soirs, ou matins) dans un cycle. D'autre part, du fait de "l'égalité" des cycles, chaque ouvrier doit faire un même nombre de nuits (ou de soirs,...) pour chaque jour de la semaine. On a donc n = LR/P et n doit être un multiple de 7. On en déduit immédiatement les propriétés de L.

4. THEOREME CONCERNANT LES PLANNINGS EN DECALAGES REGULIERS

Dans (1) nous avons donné une méthode générale permettant d'obtenir tous les cycles possibles en monovalence. Nous avons vu, d'autre part, que la connaissance des débuts de cycles dans un planning cyclique permettait d'améliorer sensiblement la rapidité de définition des cycles. Dans ce qui suit, nous nous baserons à nouveau sur l'hypothèse que l'on recherche des cycles tels qu'ils puissent être rangés en décalage régulier dans un planning.

Précisons de quoi il s'agit :

Un planning cyclique (c'est-à-dire se reproduisant identiquement à lui-même) est dit en décalage régulier si les cycles de chacun des P opérateurs débutent à des dates régulièrement espacées. Comme il s'agit de problèmes cycliques, le mot "débuter" n'a, en fait, guère de signification. Nous l'utiliserons cependant dans le sens suivant : par convention, le cycle du premier opérateur (en haut du planning) débutera un lundi et il commencera avec le plus petit tour de nuits. (En toute généralité, ce cycle pourra effectivement débuter un autre jour de la semaine, il suffit pour cela de le décaler de 1, 2, ... 7 jours). Deux opérateurs seront dits en décalage de d, si le planning du premier s'identifie, après un décalage de d jours (modulo la longueur du cycle) avec le planning du second opérateur. Nous dirons qu'un planning cyclique pour P ouvriers est en décalage régulier s'il est possible de réordonner les lignes du planning de façon que les cycles apparaissent, en descendant, avec un décalage constant et dans le même sens.

Avant de donner un théorème fondamental sur la non redondance des plannings cycliques, nous allons démontrer quelques résultats préliminaires.

Lemme 3 : Soit un planning (P, R) définissant le planning de P ouvriers assurant R postes. Si dans ce planning les cycles de chacun des opérateurs i = 1,..., P débutent à des dates t_i régulièrement espacées de d :

$$t_i = 1 + (i - 1) d, \; i = 1, \ldots, P$$

alors le planning (P, R) considéré de la date t = 1 à la date t = Pd se reproduit identiquement à lui-même.

Démonstration :

En supposant que l'ouvrier 1 (haut du planning) fasse un N à la date t = 1 (ce que l'on peut toujours supposer nous allons tout d'abord démontrer qu'il fait nécessairement un N à la date t = Pd + 1. Comme chaque jour il y a R "N" à assurer, nous allons supposer que ces R "N" sont effectués à la date t = Pd + 1 par des ouvriers $i_1, i_2, \ldots i_R$, avec $i_j \neq 1, \forall_j = 1, \ldots R$. Du fait de l'égalité des cycles, il faut alors introduire R "N" à la date t = 1 + (P - 1) d pour les opérateurs $i_j - 1$, j = 1, ..., R. Par ailleurs l'ouvrier P fait déjà une "N" à la date t = 1 + (P - 1) d et puisque $i_j - 1 \neq P, \forall_j = 1, \ldots, R$ on trouverait donc R + 1 "N" en t = 1 + (P - 1) d. Comme ceci est impossible, c'est que l'ouvrier 1 reprend bien une "N" en t = Pd + 1. De proche en proche on démontre alors trivialement le résultat.

Pour faciliter les choses, nous allons nous intéresser aux plannings (P, R) dont la longueur L est un multiple de Pd[1] (d multiple de 7). Dans l'intervalle de temps défini par L on peut définir en général de nombreux plannings en décalage régulier de d avec Pd diviseur de L.

---

(1) Si P est divisible par R il y a en fait de nombreux plannings possibles de longueur L inférieure à un multiple de Pd, mais ces plannings se retrouvent dans ceux dont la longueur est un multiple de Pd.

Nous allons voir que certains de ces plannings peuvent être redondants par rapport à d'autres. Pour préciser le vocabulaire, soient 2 plannings de longueur L en décalages réguliers de d_1 et d_2 respectivement. Nous dirons que les plannings (d_2) sont redondants par rapport aux plannings (d_1) si toute configuration que l'on peut obtenir en imposant que les débuts de cycles soient en décalage de d_2 peut être obtenue en imposant que les débuts de cycles soient en décalage de d_1.

THEOREME : Soient deux familles de plannings en décalages réguliers, l'une en décalage de d_1 pour P opérateurs, l'autre en décalage de d_2 pour P opérateurs. Supposons que Pd_1 et Pd_2 soient des diviseurs d'un même nombre L. Une condition nécessaire est suffisante pour que les plannings engendrés par d_2, $(d_2 < d_1)$ soient *redondants* par rapport aux plannings engendrés par d_1 est que

(1) Pd_1 divise $(d_1, Pd_2)^*$

et

(2) Pd_2 divise $(Pd_1, d_2)^*$

où l'on note $(a, b)^*$ le p.p.c.m de a et b.

Démonstration :

soient n_1 et n_2 tels que

$$n_1 \, Pd_1 = n_2 \, Pd_2 = L$$

et supposons $d_2 < d_1$

D'après le lemme 3 on a les considérations suivantes :

Dans un planning d_1 on a des nuits aux dates (que l'on peut considérer comme des lundis) :

$$s_{ih}^{(1)} = 1 + (i - 1)\, d_1 + hPd_1 \,,$$

$i = 1, \ldots, P$ et $h = 0, \ldots, n_1 - 1$.

Dans un planning d_2 on a des nuits aux dates

$$s_{jk}^{(2)} = 1 + (j - 1)\, d_2 + kPd_2$$

$$j = 1, \ldots, P \text{ et } k = 0, \ldots, n_2 - 1$$

Nous allons établir le théorème par une suite de résultats.

Résultat 1 : Nous allons voir tout d'abord que les deux suites $(s_{ih}^{(1)})$ et $(s_{jk}^{(2)})$ ainsi définies ont nécessairement au moins 2 éléments en commun (si $p > 1$). Comme $s_{10}^{(1)} = s_{10}^{(2)}$ il reste à trouver un deuxième élément.

Il est clair que les deux équations suivantes, en i, h, j, k :

$$(i - 1) + hP = n_1 \qquad i \in (1, P),\ h \in (0, n_1)$$

$$(j - 1) + kP = n_2 \qquad j \in (1, P) \quad k \in (0, n_2).$$

ont au moins une solution et que cette solution ne peut être $(i = 1,\ j = 1,\ h = 0,\ k = 0)$ puisque $d_2 < d_1$, donc $n_2 > n_1$). D'autre part cette solution vérifie

$$h < n_1 \quad \text{et} \quad k < n_2 \qquad (p > 1)$$

D'où l'existence de i, h, j, k tels que

$$s_{ih}^{(1)} = 1 + n_1 d_1 = s_{jk}^{(2)} = 1 + n_2 d_2 = \frac{L}{P} < L \quad (P > 1)$$

Ce qui établit le résultat.

Résultat 2 : Considérons maintenant l'ensemble des éléments communs aux deux suites finies $(s_{ih}^{(1)})$ et $(s_{jk}^{(2)})$.

Soit $\Omega = (t_r,\ r = 1, 2, \ldots)$

cet ensemble, et notons (i_r, h_r) (j_r, k_r) les éléments correspondants à t_r. D'après le résultat 1 cet ensemble contient au moins 2 éléments.

Nous allons examiner deux propriétés possibles de Ω :

Propriété 1 :

si $\exists$ (t_r, t_s), $r \neq s$ tels que l'on ait ($i_r = i_s$ et $j_r \neq j_s$) alors les décalages d_1 et d_1 ne peuvent engendrer les mêmes plannings : en effet, dans ce cas, un au moins des opérateurs d'un planning d_1 (ou d_2) a au moins 2 "N" à faire tandis que dans les plannings d_2 (ou d_1) ces 2 "N" sont répartis entre 2 opérateurs différents.

Propriété 2 :

si $\forall$ (t_r, t_s), $r \neq s$ on a

($i_r = i_s$ et $j_r = j_s$) (cas a)

ou bien

($i_r \neq i_s$ et $j_r \neq j_s$) (cas b)

alors la famille des plannings engendrés par d_2 est une sous famille de celle des plannings en décalage de d_1.

Pour établir cette propriété, nous allons voir qu'il est impossible d'avoir le cas (a) uniquement. Supposons en effet

($i_r = i_s$ et $j_r = j_s$), $\forall$ (t_r, t_s) , $r \neq s$.

On a alors : $t_r - t_s$ = multiple de Pd_1

= multiple de Pd_2

avec $t_r - t_s < L$. Or, d'après le Lemme 3, les plannings de longueur L ainsi définis ne peuvent être que des répétitions des sous-plannings définis avec les mêmes d_1 et d_2 sur une longueur $L^* = (Pd_1, Pd_2)^*$.

Autrement dit on aurait Pd_1 et Pd_2 divise $t_r - t_s < L^*$, ce qui est impossible.

Raisonnons alors sur le cas (b) qui est alors certain si l'on n'a pas les conditions de la propriété 1.

Soient : $t_1, t_2, \ldots t_p$

les dates où l'on retrouve les débuts de cycles dans les 2 plannings (d_1) et (d_2). Examinons tout d'abord l'exemple suivant portant sur $P = 5$, $d_1 = 2$, $d_2 = 1$.

1 3 5 7 9	← dates (numéro de semaine par exemple)
1 2 3 4 5	← débuts de cycles de chacun des opérateurs

1 3 5 7 9	← dates (numéro de semaine par exemple)
1234512345	← débuts de cycles de chacun des opérateurs

On a :

r	1	2	3	4	5
t_r	1	3	5	7	9
t_r	1	2	3	4	5
j_r	1	3	5	2	4

On est bien dans le cas (b). Définissons alors :

$$j'_r = i_r, \; r = 1, 2, \ldots$$

On a : $j'_1 = 1$, $j'_2 = 2$, $j'_3 = 3$, $j'_4 = 4$, $j'_5 = 5$.

En renumérotant les opérateurs de d_2 on arrive ainsi à voir que les plannings d_2 peuvent être obtenus avec les plannings d_1. Pour que ce ne soit pas possible, il faudrait que pour 2 j_r : j_{r_1} et j_{r_2} avec $j_{r_1} = j_{r_2}$ on ait $i_{r_1} \neq i_{r_2}$. Or ceci contredit le cas (b).

Il nous reste à montrer que la condition

$$(0)\ \exists\,(t_r, t_s) : \begin{cases} (i_r = i_s \text{ et } j_r \neq j_s) & \text{(cas 0 - 1)} \\ (i_r \neq i_s \text{ et } j_r = j_s) & \text{(cas 0 - 2)} \end{cases}$$

est équivalente à la suivante :

$$(1)\ \begin{array}{ll} Pd_1 \text{ ne divise pas } (d_1, Pd_2)^* & \text{(cas 1-1)} \\ \text{ou} & \\ Pd_2 \text{ ne divise pas } (Pd_1, d_2)^* & \text{(cas 1-2)} \end{array}$$

Plaçons nous dans le cas (0-1)

Posons $D = t_s - t_r$. On a alors

$$\begin{aligned} D &= \text{divisible par } Pd_1 \\ &= \text{non divisible par } Pd_2 \\ &= \text{multiple de } d_2 \end{aligned}$$

autrement dit, Pd_2 ne divise pas un multiple de $(Pd_1, d_2)^*$ donc ne divise pas $(Pd_1, d_2)^*$.

La réciproque est immédiate en partant d'un multiple D de Pd_1 vérifiant les propriétés précédentes.

L'examen du cas 0-2 se fait parallèlement.

Le théorème précédent nous donne ainsi un moyen de se fixer des décalages réguliers non redondants avec d'autre.

5. ALGORITHME DE GENERATION DE PLANNINGS EN MULTIVALENCE

Nous admettrons dans ce qui suit que les plannings communs aux P ouvriers assurant R postes sont constitués de cycles en décalages réguliers.

Nous savons que chaque ouvrier doit assurer n "N" dans son cycle, n "S" et n "M".

Dans un planning cyclique de longueur L on doit trouver R "N" (ou "S" ou "M) chaque jour.

Occupons nous d'abord de remplir le planning en assurant un "N" chaque jour. Du fait du Lemme 3, nous supposons L = Pd. Pour assurer un "N" chaque jour, il faut alors porter d "N" dans le cycle commun aux P opérateurs. Comme les tours de N ne peuvent excéder certaines longueurs, nous effectuons un découpage de d en d_1, d_2, ... $d_1 + d_2 + \ldots = d$ et d_i est la longueur d'un "ième" tour de nuits. En tenant compte des débuts de cycles on opère alors comme dans (1) pour le positionnement de ces d "N". On opère de même pour assurer un "S" et un "M" chaque jour. Si R = 1 on a obtenu ainsi un planning.
Si R = 2 il nous faut positionner une seconde batterie de d "N", de d "S" et de d "M". (Nous parlons alors de nuit-bis, de soir-bis, ...) et ceci en tenant toujours compte des débuts de cycles et des diverses contraintes, en particulier de celles concernant les jours de repos entre les tours. On continue jusqu'à ce que chaque jour on ait R "N", R "S" et R "M" dans le planning.

Nous donnons ci-après deux exemples obtenus par ordinateur :

<u>Exemple 1</u> : tours de 3 et 4 quarts, 9 ouvriers, cycle de 9 semaines - N,A = nuits ; S,B = soirs ; M,C = matins

```
***********************************************************************
L M M J V S . L M M J V S . L M M J V S . L M M J V S . L M M J V S .
N N N . . . S S S . . M M M . . A A A . . B B B B . C C C . . N N N N
. C C C C . . N N N . . . S S S . . M M M . . A A A . . B B B B . C C
A A . . B B B . C C C C . . N N N . . . S S S . . M M M . . A A A . .
M M M M . A A A A . . B B B . C C C C . . N N N . . . S S S . . M M M
. . S S S S . M M M M . A A A A . . B B B . C C C C . . N N N . . . S
C . . N N N N . . S S S S . M M M M . A A A A . . B B B . C C C C . .
B B B B . C C C . . N N N N . . S S S S . M M M M . A A A A . . B B B
. . A A A . . B B B B . C C C . . N N N N . . S S S S . M M M M . A A
S S . . M M M . . A A A . . B B B B . C C C . . N N N N . . S S S S .
***********************************************************************
L M M J V S . L M M J V S . L M M J V S . L M M J V S .
. . S S S S . M M M M . A A A A . . B B B . C C C C . .
C . . N N N N . . S S S S . M M M M . A A A A . . B B B
B B B B . C C C . . N N N N . . S S S S . M M M M . A A
. . A A A . . B B B B . C C C . . N N N N . . S S S S .
S S . . M M M . . A A A . . B B B B . C C C . . N N N N
N N N . . . S S S . . M M M . . A A A . . B B B B . C C
. C C C C . . N N N . . . S S S . . M M M . . A A A . .
A A . . B B B . C C C C . . N N N . . . S S S . . M M M
M M M M . A A A A . . B B B . C C C C . . N N N . . . S
```

Exemple 2 : tours de 5 quarts, 9 ouvriers, cycle de 45 semaines :

L	M	M	J	V	S	.	L	M	M	J	V	S	.	L	M	M	J	V	S	.	L	M	M	J	V	S	.	L	M	M	J	V	S	.
N	N	N	N	N	.	.	S	S	S	S	S	.	.	M	M	M	M	M	.	.	A	A	A	A	A	.	.	B	B	B	B	B	.	.
S	S	.	.	M	M	M	M	M	.	.	A	A	A	A	A	.	.	B	B	B	B	B	.	.	.	.	.	C	C	C	C	C	.	.
.	A	A	A	A	A	.	.	B	B	B	B	B	.	.	.	.	.	C	C	C	C	C	.	.	N	N	N	N	N	.	.	S	S	S
B	B	B	.	.	.	.	.	C	C	C	C	C	.	.	N	N	N	N	N	.	.	S	S	S	S	S	.	.	M	M	M	M	M	.
C	C	C	.	.	N	N	N	N	N	.	.	S	S	S	S	S	.	.	M	M	M	M	M	.	.	A	A	A	A	A	.	.	B	B
.	.	S	S	S	S	S	.	.	M	M	M	M	M	.	.	A	A	A	A	A	.	.	B	B	B	B	B	.	.	.	.	.	C	C
M	M	M	M	.	.	A	A	A	A	A	.	.	B	B	B	B	B	.	.	.	.	.	C	C	C	C	C	.	.	N	N	N	N	N
A	.	.	B	B	B	B	B	.	.	.	.	.	C	C	C	C	C	.	.	N	N	N	N	N	.	.	S	S	S	S	S	.	.	M
.	.	.	C	C	C	C	C	.	.	N	N	N	N	N	.	.	S	S	S	S	S	.	.	M	M	M	M	M	.	.	A	A	A	A

L	M	M	J	V	S	.	L	M	M	J	V	S	.	L	M	M	J	V	S	.	L	M	M	J	V	S	.	L	M	M	J	V	S	.
.	.	.	C	C	C	C	C	.	.	N	N	N	N	N	.	.	S	S	S	S	S	.	.	M	M	M	M	M	.	.	A	A	A	A
N	N	N	N	N	.	.	S	S	S	S	S	.	.	M	M	M	M	M	.	.	A	A	A	A	A	.	.	B	B	B	B	B	.	.
S	S	.	.	M	M	M	M	M	.	.	A	A	A	A	A	.	.	B	B	B	B	B	.	.	.	.	.	C	C	C	C	C	.	.
.	A	A	A	A	A	.	.	B	B	B	B	B	.	.	.	.	.	C	C	C	C	C	.	.	N	N	N	N	N	.	.	S	S	S
B	B	B	.	.	.	.	.	C	C	C	C	C	.	.	N	N	N	N	N	.	.	S	S	S	S	S	.	.	M	M	M	M	M	.
C	C	C	.	.	N	N	N	N	N	.	.	S	S	S	S	S	.	.	M	M	M	M	M	.	.	A	A	A	A	A	.	.	B	B
.	.	S	S	S	S	S	.	.	M	M	M	M	M	.	.	A	A	A	A	A	.	.	B	B	B	B	B	.	.	.	.	.	C	C
M	M	M	M	.	.	A	A	A	A	A	.	.	B	B	B	B	B	.	.	.	.	.	C	C	C	C	C	.	.	N	N	N	N	N
A	.	.	B	B	B	B	B	.	.	.	.	.	C	C	C	C	C	.	.	N	N	N	N	N	.	.	S	S	S	S	S	.	.	M

L	M	M	J	V	S	.	L	M	M	J	V	S	.	L	M	M	J	V	S	.	L	M	M	J	V	S	.	L	M	M	J	V	S	.
A	.	.	B	B	B	B	B	.	.	.	.	.	C	C	C	C	C	.	.	N	N	N	N	N	.	.	S	S	S	S	S	.	.	M
.	.	.	C	C	C	C	C	.	.	N	N	N	N	N	.	.	S	S	S	S	S	.	.	M	M	M	M	M	.	.	A	A	A	A
N	N	N	N	N	.	.	S	S	S	S	S	.	.	M	M	M	M	M	.	.	A	A	A	A	A	.	.	B	B	B	B	B	.	.
S	S	.	.	M	M	M	M	M	.	.	A	A	A	A	A	.	.	B	B	B	B	B	.	.	.	.	.	C	C	C	C	C	.	.
.	A	A	A	A	A	.	.	B	B	B	B	B	.	.	.	.	.	C	C	C	C	C	.	.	N	N	N	N	N	.	.	S	S	S
B	B	B	.	.	.	.	.	C	C	C	C	C	.	.	N	N	N	N	N	.	.	S	S	S	S	S	.	.	M	M	M	M	M	.
C	C	C	.	.	N	N	N	N	N	.	.	S	S	S	S	S	.	.	M	M	M	M	M	.	.	A	A	A	A	A	.	.	B	B
.	.	S	S	S	S	S	.	.	M	M	M	M	M	.	.	A	A	A	A	A	.	.	B	B	B	B	B	.	.	.	.	.	C	C
M	M	M	M	.	.	A	A	A	A	A	.	.	B	B	B	B	B	.	.	.	.	.	C	C	C	C	C	.	.	N	N	N	N	N

L	M	M	J	V	S	.	L	M	M	J	V	S	.	L	M	M	J	V	S	.	L	M	M	J	V	S	.	L	M	M	J	V	S	.
M	M	M	M	.	.	A	A	A	A	A	.	.	B	B	B	B	B	.	.	.	.	.	C	C	C	C	C	.	.	N	N	N	N	N
A	.	.	B	B	B	B	B	.	.	.	.	.	C	C	C	C	C	.	.	N	N	N	N	N	.	.	S	S	S	S	S	.	.	M
.	.	.	C	C	C	C	C	.	.	N	N	N	N	N	.	.	S	S	S	S	S	.	.	M	M	M	M	M	.	.	A	A	A	A
N	N	N	N	N	.	.	S	S	S	S	S	.	.	M	M	M	M	M	.	.	A	A	A	A	A	.	.	B	B	B	B	B	.	.
S	S	.	.	M	M	M	M	M	.	.	A	A	A	A	A	.	.	B	B	B	B	B	.	.	.	.	.	C	C	C	C	C	.	.
.	A	A	A	A	A	.	.	B	B	B	B	B	.	.	.	.	.	C	C	C	C	C	.	.	N	N	N	N	N	.	.	S	S	S
B	B	B	.	.	.	.	.	C	C	C	C	C	.	.	N	N	N	N	N	.	.	S	S	S	S	S	.	.	M	M	M	M	M	.
C	C	C	.	.	N	N	N	N	N	.	.	S	S	S	S	S	.	.	M	M	M	M	M	.	.	A	A	A	A	A	.	.	B	B
.	.	S	S	S	S	S	.	.	M	M	M	M	M	.	.	A	A	A	A	A	.	.	B	B	B	B	B	.	.	.	.	.	C	C

L	M	M	J	V	S	.	L	M	M	J	V	S	.	L	M	M	J	V	S	.	L	M	M	J	V	S	.	L	M	M	J	V	S	.
.	.	S	S	S	S	S	.	.	M	M	M	M	M	.	.	A	A	A	A	A	.	.	B	B	B	B	B	.	.	.	.	.	C	C
M	M	M	M	.	.	A	A	A	A	A	.	.	B	B	B	B	B	.	.	.	.	.	C	C	C	C	C	.	.	N	N	N	N	N
A	.	.	B	B	B	B	B	.	.	.	.	.	C	C	C	C	C	.	.	N	N	N	N	N	.	.	S	S	S	S	S	.	.	M
.	.	.	C	C	C	C	C	.	.	N	N	N	N	N	.	.	S	S	S	S	S	.	.	M	M	M	M	M	.	.	A	A	A	A
N	N	N	N	N	.	.	S	S	S	S	S	.	.	M	M	M	M	M	.	.	A	A	A	A	A	.	.	B	B	B	B	B	.	.
S	S	.	.	M	M	M	M	M	.	.	A	A	A	A	A	.	.	B	B	B	B	B	.	.	.	.	.	C	C	C	C	C	.	.
.	A	A	A	A	A	.	.	B	B	B	B	B	.	.	.	.	.	C	C	C	C	C	.	.	N	N	N	N	N	.	.	S	S	S
B	B	B	.	.	.	.	.	C	C	C	C	C	.	.	N	N	N	N	N	.	.	S	S	S	S	S	.	.	M	M	M	M	M	.
C	C	C	.	.	N	N	N	N	N	.	.	S	S	S	S	S	.	.	M	M	M	M	M	.	.	A	A	A	A	A	.	.	B	B

<u>Exemple 2</u> (suite)

L	M	M	J	V	S	.	L	M	M	J	V	S	.	L	M	M	J	V	S	.	L	M	M	J	V	S	.	L	M	M	J	V	S	.
C	C	C	.	.	N	N	N	N	N	.	.	S	S	S	S	S	.	.	M	M	M	M	M	.	.	A	A	A	A	A	.	.	B	B
.	.	S	S	S	S	S	.	.	M	M	M	M	M	.	.	A	A	A	A	A	.	.	B	B	B	B	B	.	.	.	.	.	C	C
M	M	M	M	.	.	A	A	A	A	A	.	.	B	B	B	B	B	.	.	.	.	.	C	C	C	C	C	.	.	N	N	N	N	N
A	.	.	B	B	B	B	B	.	.	.	.	.	C	C	C	C	C	.	.	N	N	N	N	N	.	.	S	S	S	S	S	.	.	M
.	.	.	C	C	C	C	C	.	.	N	N	N	N	N	.	.	S	S	S	S	S	.	.	M	M	M	M	M	.	.	A	A	A	A
N	N	N	N	N	.	.	S	S	S	S	S	.	.	M	M	M	M	M	.	.	A	A	A	A	A	.	.	B	B	B	B	B	.	.
S	S	.	.	M	M	M	M	M	.	.	A	A	A	A	A	.	.	B	B	B	B	B	.	.	.	.	.	C	C	C	C	C	.	.
.	A	A	A	A	A	.	.	B	B	B	B	B	.	.	.	.	.	C	C	C	C	C	.	.	N	N	N	N	N	.	.	S	S	S
B	B	B	.	.	.	.	.	C	C	C	C	C	.	.	N	N	N	N	N	.	.	S	S	S	S	S	.	.	M	M	M	M	M	.

L	M	M	J	V	S	.	L	M	M	J	V	S	.	L	M	M	J	V	S	.	L	M	M	J	V	S	.	L	M	M	J	V	S	.
B	B	B	.	.	.	.	.	C	C	C	C	C	.	.	N	N	N	N	N	.	.	S	S	S	S	S	.	.	M	M	M	M	M	.
C	C	C	.	.	N	N	N	N	N	.	.	S	S	S	S	S	.	.	M	M	M	M	M	.	.	A	A	A	A	A	.	.	B	B
.	.	S	S	S	S	S	.	.	M	M	M	M	M	.	.	A	A	A	A	A	.	.	B	B	B	B	B	.	.	.	.	.	C	C
M	M	M	M	.	.	A	A	A	A	A	.	.	B	B	B	B	B	.	.	.	.	.	C	C	C	C	C	.	.	N	N	N	N	N
A	.	.	B	B	B	B	B	.	.	.	.	.	C	C	C	C	C	.	.	N	N	N	N	N	.	.	S	S	S	S	S	.	.	M
.	.	.	C	C	C	C	C	.	.	N	N	N	N	N	.	.	S	S	S	S	S	.	.	M	M	M	M	M	.	.	A	A	A	A
N	N	N	N	N	.	.	S	S	S	S	S	.	.	M	M	M	M	M	.	.	A	A	A	A	A	.	.	B	B	B	B	B	.	.
S	S	.	.	M	M	M	M	M	.	.	A	A	A	A	A	.	.	B	B	B	B	B	.	.	.	.	.	C	C	C	C	C	.	.
.	A	A	A	A	A	.	.	B	B	B	B	B	.	.	.	.	.	C	C	C	C	C	.	.	N	N	N	N	N	.	.	S	S	S

L	M	M	J	V	S	.	L	M	M	J	V	S	.	L	M	M	J	V	S	.	L	M	M	J	V	S	.	L	M	M	J	V	S	.
.	A	A	A	A	A	.	.	B	B	B	B	B	.	.	.	.	.	C	C	C	C	C	.	.	N	N	N	N	N	.	.	S	S	S
B	B	B	.	.	.	.	.	C	C	C	C	C	.	.	N	N	N	N	N	.	.	S	S	S	S	S	.	.	M	M	M	M	M	.
C	C	C	.	.	N	N	N	N	N	.	.	S	S	S	S	S	.	.	M	M	M	M	M	.	.	A	A	A	A	A	.	.	B	B
.	.	S	S	S	S	S	.	.	M	M	M	M	M	.	.	A	A	A	A	A	.	.	B	B	B	B	B	.	.	.	.	.	C	C
M	M	M	M	.	.	A	A	A	A	A	.	.	B	B	B	B	B	.	.	.	.	.	C	C	C	C	C	.	.	N	N	N	N	N
A	.	.	B	B	B	B	B	.	.	.	.	.	C	C	C	C	C	.	.	N	N	N	N	N	.	.	S	S	S	S	S	.	.	M
.	.	.	C	C	C	C	C	.	.	N	N	N	N	N	.	.	S	S	S	S	S	.	.	M	M	M	M	M	.	.	A	A	A	A
N	N	N	N	N	.	.	S	S	S	S	S	.	.	M	M	M	M	M	.	.	A	A	A	A	A	.	.	B	B	B	B	B	.	.
S	S	.	.	M	M	M	M	M	.	.	A	A	A	A	A	.	.	B	B	B	B	B	.	.	.	.	.	C	C	C	C	C	.	.

L	M	M	J	V	S	.	L	M	M	J	V	S	.	L	M	M	J	V	S	.	L	M	M	J	V	S	.	L	M	M	J	V	S	.
S	S	.	.	M	M	M	M	M	.	.	A	A	A	A	A	.	.	B	B	B	B	B	.	.	.	.	.	C	C	C	C	C	.	.
.	A	A	A	A	A	.	.	B	B	B	B	B	.	.	.	.	.	C	C	C	C	C	.	.	N	N	N	N	N	.	.	S	S	S
B	B	B	.	.	.	.	.	C	C	C	C	C	.	.	N	N	N	N	N	.	.	S	S	S	S	S	.	.	M	M	M	M	M	.
C	C	C	.	.	N	N	N	N	N	.	.	S	S	S	S	S	.	.	M	M	M	M	M	.	.	A	A	A	A	A	.	.	B	B
.	.	S	S	S	S	S	.	.	M	M	M	M	M	.	.	A	A	A	A	A	.	.	B	B	B	B	B	.	.	.	.	.	C	C
M	M	M	M	.	.	A	A	A	A	A	.	.	B	B	B	B	B	.	.	.	.	.	C	C	C	C	C	.	.	N	N	N	N	N
A	.	.	B	B	B	B	B	.	.	.	.	.	C	C	C	C	C	.	.	N	N	N	N	N	.	.	S	S	S	S	S	.	.	M
.	.	.	C	C	C	C	C	.	.	N	N	N	N	N	.	.	S	S	S	S	S	.	.	M	M	M	M	M	.	.	A	A	A	A
N	N	N	N	N	.	.	S	S	S	S	S	.	.	M	M	M	M	M	.	.	A	A	A	A	A	.	.	B	B	B	B	B	.	.

6. LA RECHERCHE DES BRISEURS DE QUARTS

Le planning étant ainsi obtenu, il reste à répartir les ouvriers suivant les postes. Soient $P_1, P_2, \ldots, P_R$ les R postes.

Une manière d'opérer est de construire une arborescence dont on comprendra facilement le principe à partir de l'exemple suivant où il s'agit de répartir les ouvriers entre 2 postes :

Pour l'ouvrier 1 on a 3 choix suivant qu'on l'affecte

- exclusivement au poste 1
- exclusivement au poste 2
- aux 2 postes en tant que briseur de quart

On a les mêmes choix pour les ouvriers restants.

On est donc en présence d'une arborescence traduisant 3^P possibilités a priori. (Dans le cas où il y a plus de 2 postes, le nombre de possibilités est bien plus considérable). En se référant au planning on peut éliminer certaines sous-arborescences issues de certains arcs.

Par exemple, une sous-arborescence pour laquelle la racine est extrémité d'un chemin pour lequel on trouverait par exemple deux ouvriers sur un même poste effectuant le même jour un même quart, est à supprimer.

Les chemins qui restent et qui vont de la racine aux noeuds terminaux fournissent des solutions possibles.

Nous donnons ci-après un exemple de planning obtenu par ordinateur avec un briseur unique (1 = poste 1, 2 = poste 2, BQ = briseur de quart).

Exemple 3

```
   L M M J V S . L M M J V S . L M M J V S . L M M J V S . L M M J V S .
1  N N N N N . . S S S S S . . M M M M M . . A A A A A . . . B B B B B .
1  S S . . M M M M M . . A A A A A . . . B B B B B . . . . C C C C C . .
2  . A A A A A . . . B B B B B . . . . C C C C C . . N N N N N . . S S S
2  B B B B . . . . C C C C C . . N N N N N . . S S S S S . . M M M M M .
1  C C C . . N N N N N . . S S S S S . . M M M M M . . A A A A A . . . B
1  . . S S S S S . . M M M M M . . A A A A A . . . B B B B B . . . . C C
2  M M M M . . A A A A A . . . B B B B B . . . . C C C C C . . N N N N N
2  A . . . B B B B B . . . . C C C C C . . N N N N N . . S S S S S . . M
BQ . . . C C C C C . . N N N N N . . S S S S S . . M M M M M . . A A A A

   L M M J V S . L M M J V S . L M M J V S . L M M J V S . L M M J V S .
1  . . . C C C C C . . N N N N N . . S S S S S . . M M M M M . . A A A A
1  N N N N N . . S S S S S . . M M M M M . . A A A A A . . . B B B B B .
2  S S . . M M M M M . . A A A A A . . . B B B B B . . . . C C C C C . .
2  . A A A A A . . . B B B B B . . . . C C C C C . . N N N N N . . S S S
1  B B B B . . . . C C C C C . . N N N N N . . S S S S S . . M M M M M .
1  C C C . . N N N N N . . S S S S S . . M M M M M . . A A A A A . . . B
2  . . S S S S S . . M M M M M . . A A A A A . . . B B B B B . . . . C C
2  M M M M . . A A A A A . . . B B B B B . . . . C C C C C . . N N N N N
BQ A . . . B B B B B . . . . C C C C C . . N N N N N . . S S S S S . . M

   L M M J V S . L M M J V S . L M M J V S . L M M J V S . L M M J V S .
1  A . . . B B B B B . . . . C C C C C . . N N N N N . . S S S S S . . M
1  . . . C C C C C . . N N N N N . . S S S S S . . M M M M M . . A A A A
2  N N N N N . . S S S S S . . M M M M M . . A A A A A . . . B B B B B .
2  S S . . M M M M M . . A A A A A . . . B B B B B . . . . C C C C C . .
1  . A A A A A . . . B B B B B . . . . C C C C C . . N N N N N . . S S S
1  B B B B . . . . C C C C C . . N N N N N . . S S S S S . . M M M M M .
2  C C C . . N N N N N . . S S S S S . . M M M M M . . A A A A A . . . B
2  . . S S S S S . . M M M M M . . A A A A A . . . B B B B B . . . . C C
BQ M M M M . . A A A A A . . . B B B B B . . . . C C C C C . . N N N N N

   L M M J V S . L M M J V S . L M M J V S . L M M J V S . L M M J V S .
1  M M M M . . A A A A A . . . B B B B B . . . . C C C C C . . N N N N N
1  A . . . B B B B B . . . . C C C C C . . N N N N N . . S S S S S . . M
2  . . . C C C C C . . N N N N N . . S S S S S . . M M M M M . . A A A A
2  N N N N N . . S S S S S . . M M M M M . . A A A A A . . . B B B B B .
1  S S . . M M M M M . . A A A A A . . . B B B B B . . . . C C C C C . .
1  . A A A A A . . . B B B B B . . . . C C C C C . . N N N N N . . S S S
2  B B B B . . . . C C C C C . . N N N N N . . S S S S S . . M M M M M .
2  C C C . . N N N N N . . S S S S S . . M M M M M . . A A A A A . . . B
BQ . . S S S S S . . M M M M M . . A A A A A . . . B B B B B . . . . C C

   L M M J V S . L M M J V S . L M M J V S . L M M J V S . L M M J V S .
1  . . S S S S S . . M M M M M . . A A A A A . . . B B B B B . . . . C C
1  M M M M . . A A A A A . . . B B B B B . . . . C C C C C . . N N N N N
2  A . . . B B B B B . . . . C C C C C . . N N N N N . . S S S S S . . M
2  . . . C C C C C . . N N N N N . . S S S S S . . M M M M M . . A A A A
1  N N N N N . . S S S S S . . M M M M M . . A A A A A . . . B B B B B .
1  S S . . M M M M M . . A A A A A . . . B B B B B . . . . C C C C C . .
2  . A A A A A . . . B B B B B . . . . C C C C C . . N N N N N . . S S S
2  B B B B . . . . C C C C C . . N N N N N . . S S S S S . . M M M M M .
BQ C C C . . N N N N N . . S S S S S . . M M M M M . . A A A A A . . . B
```

Exemple 3 (suite)

	L M M J V S . L M M J V S . L M M J V S . L M M J V S . L M M J V S .
1	C C C . . N N N N N . . S S S S S . . M M M M M . . A A A A A . . . B
1	. . S S S S S . . M M M M M . . A A A A A . . . B B B B B . . . . C C
2	M M M M . . A A A A A . . . B B B B B . . . . C C C C C . . N N N N N
2	A . . . B B B B B . . . . C C C C C . . N N N N N . . S S S S S . . M
1	. . . C C C C C . . N N N N N . . S S S S S . . M M M M M . . A A A A
1	N N N N N . . S S S S S . . M M M M M . . A A A A A . . . B B B B B .
2	S S . . M M M M M . . A A A A A . . . B B B B B . . . . C C C C C . .
2	. A A A A A . . . B B B B B . . . . C C C C C . . N N N N N . . S S S
BQ	B B B B . . . . C C C C C . . N N N N N . . S S S S S . . M M M M M .

	L M M J V S . L M M J V S . L M M J V S . L M M J V S . L M M J V S .
1	B B B B . . . . C C C C C . . N N N N N . . S S S S S . . M M M M M .
1	C C C . . N N N N N . . S S S S S . . M M M M M . . A A A A A . . . B
2	. . S S S S S . . M M M M M . . A A A A A . . . B B B B B . . . . C C
2	M M M M . . A A A A A . . . B B B B B . . . . C C C C C . . N N N N N
1	A . . . B B B B B . . . . C C C C C . . N N N N N . . S S S S S . . M
1	. . . C C C C C . . N N N N N . . S S S S S . . M M M M M . . A A A A
2	N N N N N . . S S S S S . . M M M M M . . A A A A A . . . B B B B B .
2	S S . . M M M M M . . A A A A A . . . B B B B B . . . . C C C C C . .
BQ	. A A A A A . . . B B B B B . . . . C C C C C . . N N N N N . . S S S

	L M M J V S . L M M J V S . L M M J V S . L M M J V S . L M M J V S .
1	. A A A A A . . . B B B B B . . . . C C C C C . . N N N N N . . S S S
1	B B B B . . . . C C C C C . . N N N N N . . S S S S S . . M M M M M .
2	C C C . . N N N N N . . S S S S S . . M M M M M . . A A A A A . . . B
2	. . S S S S S . . M M M M M . . A A A A A . . . B B B B B . . . . C C
1	M M M M . . A A A A A . . . B B B B B . . . . C C C C C . . N N N N N
1	A . . . B B B B B . . . . C C C C C . . N N N N N . . S S S S S . . M
2	. . . C C C C C . . N N N N N . . S S S S S . . M M M M M . . A A A A
2	N N N N N . . S S S S S . . M M M M M . . A A A A A . . . B B B B B .
BQ	S S . . M M M M M . . A A A A A . . . B B B B B . . . . C C C C C . .

	L M M J V S . L M M J V S . L M M J V S . L M M J V S . L M M J V S .
1	S S . . M M M M M . . A A A A A . . . B B B B B . . . . C C C C C . .
1	. A A A A A . . . B B B B B . . . . C C C C C . . N N N N N . . S S S
2	B B B B . . . . C C C C C . . N N N N N . . S S S S S . . M M M M M .
2	C C C . . N N N N N . . S S S S S . . M M M M M . . A A A A A . . . B
1	. . S S S S S . . M M M M M . . A A A A A . . . B B B B B . . . . C C
1	M M M M . . A A A A A . . . B B B B B . . . . C C C C C . . N N N N N
2	A . . . B B B B B . . . . C C C C C . . N N N N N . . S S S S S . . M
2	. . . C C C C C . . N N N N N . . S S S S S . . M M M M M . . A A A A
BQ	N N N N N . . S S S S S . . M M M M M . . A A A A A . . . B B B B B .

7. REMARQUES

On remarquera que la méthodologie présentée ici s'applique à des problèmes beaucoup plus généraux que celui où la même charge de travail doit être assurée 24 h sur 24 h.

Par exemple, si l'on ne positionne, au moyen de l'algorithme, que des N, des S, des M, et, par exemple, des M "bis", on aura dans le planning, chaque jour un N, un S et deux M ; autrement dit, 2 ouvriers le matin au lieu de 1 le reste du temps sur un poste.

On peut, bien sûr, supprimer aussi dans les plannings obtenus un ou plusieurs quarts certains jours (par exemple le dimanche). La méthode permet ainsi d'engendrer tous les plannings cycliques en continu ou en semi-continu dans lesquels les ouvriers ont, à un décalage près dans le temps, les mêmes plannings de travail.

Référence

1 - R. TREMOLIERES : Le problème des roulements de quarts pour les entreprises à feu continu.
(à paraître dans RAIRO, Janvier 1976).

SEARCH AND MONTECARLO TECHNIQUES FOR DETERMINING RESERVOIR OPERATING POLICIES.

A. Colorni (°), G. Fronza (°)

(°) Istituto di Elettrotecnica ed Elettronica
Centro Teoria dei Sistemi - Politecnico di Milano

1. INTRODUCTION

The problem of determining the optimal design and operation of a reservoir has been considered under many different viewpoints. Standard engineering procedures such as mass curves techniques [1] or classical hydrologic methods of analysis (see [2] - [5] for instance), have gradually been replaced by the use of mathematical programs, mainly separable [6] and dynamic [7], [8] ones, both in the deterministic and in the stochastic environment. In control theory terminology, these approaches correspond to open loop optimization schemes. It is an apparent drawback in presence of a stochastic input into the system such as the inflow. Of course, more reliable solutions can be obtained by introducing control laws (operating rules), that is when applying to feedback schemes. In this case, the problem of determining the optimal regulation, i.e. the optimal operating rule, is usually turned into a finite dimensional one by assuming a specific class of rules. In the most common case, the release in any period is made to depend upon the total available water in the period (initial storage plus inflow). Because of the constraints on the reservoir storage, the choice of the rule class cannot a priori be quite comfortable, for instance it is not possible to apply to linear functions. As a matter of fact, the great majority of existing applications considers Z-shaped rules, such as the normal ones. This prevents the optimization problem from being formulated as a mathematical program of a standard type. Three main different approaches have been proposed in the literature.

a) Pure simulation, based on the superimposition of a grid in the decision variables space [9].

b) A procedure consisting of the two following steps [10].

b1) Solution of the open loop control problem via dynamic programming in the deterministic environment supplied by a long synthetic record (see [11] - [14] for instance and the next section).

b2) Least squares optimization for choosing the operating rule that yields a sequence of releases best fitting the optimal open loop sequence.

c) Bypass of the question (see the formulations in the stochastic environment in [15], [16]) by setting the constraints that the "tails" of the Z-shaped rule are never effective, i.e. in no period the reservoir remains either empty or full.

In this case, the release turns out to be a linear function of the total available water. It must remarked, however, that on a monthly or a yearly basis, the constraint that the reservoir must never stay full is not justified by economic reasons and, in design problems, yields unnecesserarily large dam sizes.

In this paper, the simulation approach is followed, while taking a structural property of the optimization problem into account. Such a property enables to apply an efficient search-simulation scheme for determining the solution and hence to obtain a considerable decreas of the computational effort with respect to the "brute force" approach.

2. PROBLEM STATEMENT

Consider the problem of designing and operating a reservoir on a yearly basis, while assuming the following characteristics.

a) The reservoir is regulated by means of the normal operating rule $f(\cdot, x_1, x_2)$ shown in Fig. 1, where

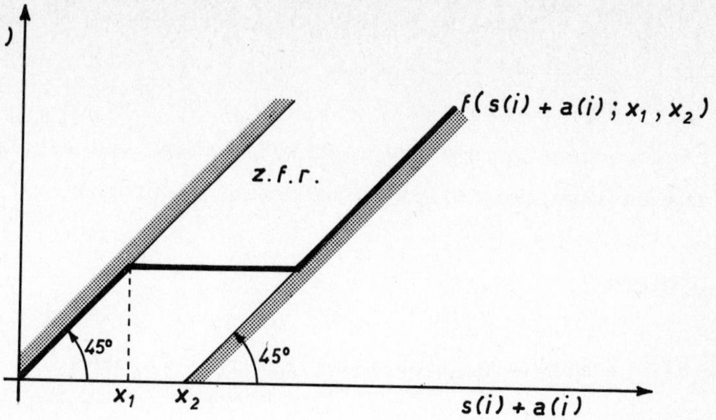

Fig. 1 Normal operating rule (z.f.r. = zone of feasible releases)

s(i) = storage at the beginning of the i-th year, i=0,1,...,n-1;
a(i) = total inflow during the i-th year;
r(i) = total release during the i-th year;
x_1 = lower bound of the regulation range (decision variable)
x_2 = reservoir capacity (decision variable).

b) The release in any year is required to be not less than x_1, the guaranteed minimum (contract). This means the downstream users are assumed to plan their activities only on the basis of the contract, so that the profit due to the reservoir operation turns out to depend only on x_1, the extra water possibly supplied having no economic value. Let $g(x_1)$ represent such profit (Fig. 2a) and c(.) the total cost function of the reservoir (Fig. 2b).

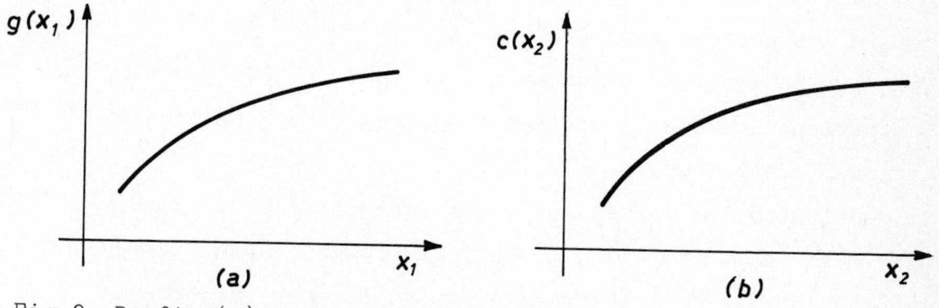

Fig.2 Profit (a) and cost (b) functions

Therefore, if the initial storage is assumed to be a given s_o and the continuity equation

$s(i+1) = s(i) + a(i) - r(i)$

is taken into account, then the reservoir design and regulation problem is turned into the follosing mathematical program

$(x = |x_1\ x_2|')$:

$$\max_x g(x_1) - c(x_2) \tag{2.1}$$

$$s(i+1) = s(i) + a(i) - f\ (s(i) + a(i);\ x_1,x_2) \quad (s(o)=s_o)\ i = 0,1,\ldots,n-1 \tag{2.2}$$

$$s(i) + a(i) \geq x_1 \tag{2.3}$$

$$x_1, x_2 \geq 0 \quad . \tag{2.4}$$

This should be regarded to as a program in the stochastic environment (see [16]), in view of the nature of a(.). In particular, if $x^{(o)}(n)$ denotes the optimal solution of (2.1)-(2.4), that is in correspondence with a planning horizon of n years, the sequence $\{x^{(o)}(n)\}_{n=1}$ should be considered as a stochastic process.

(i) Such a process is a priori non-stationary because of the arbitrary choice of s_o. However it is reasonable to assume that, for n large, the process tends to become a stationary one.

(ii) The distribution of such "asymptotic" stationary process has small variance, i.e. the long run solution is not much affected by the introduction of a particular realizazion of the inflow process into (2.1) - (2.4).
This may be verified a posteriori by solving (2.1) - (2.4) in correspondence with different synthetic long records of inflows (see below).
In conclusion, it is reasonable to replace n in (2.1)-(2.4) by N = kn (e.g. n $\simeq$ 20 , k = 50) and to introduce a given record $\{\hat{a}(i)\}_{i=o}^{N-1}$ into (2.2)-(2.3), so that the program is formulated in the deterministic environment :

$$\max_{x} \; g(x_1) - c(x_2) \tag{2.5}$$

$$s(i+1)=s(i)+\hat{a}(i)-f(s(i)+\hat{a}(i);x_1,x_2)(s(0)=s_o), \quad i=0,1,\ldots,N-1 \tag{2.6}$$

$$s(i)+\hat{a}(i) \geq x_1 \qquad i=0,1,\ldots,N-1 \tag{2.7}$$

$$x_1, x_2 \geq 0 \tag{2.8}$$

The sequence $\left\{\hat{a}(i)\right\}_{i=0}^{N-1}$ is usually obtained by the much shorter historical datum through synthetic hydrology methods.

Specifically, the following procedure is adopted

I) The historical data $\left\{\hat{a}(i)\right\}_{i=-m}^{-1}$ are considered as a (partial) realization of an ergodic process. Of course, the distribution of the random variables of the process turns out to be skewed since the inflow is a non-negative variable (usually a lognormal or a Pearsom type III distribution can be assumed). Then the data are normalized or quasi-normalized [13]

$$\hat{b}(i) = h\,(\hat{a}(i))$$

via a proper transformation h(.)

and subsequently standardized

$$\hat{c}(i) = \frac{\hat{a}(i) - \mu_b}{\sigma_b}$$

where μ_b and σ_b represent the mean and variance of the normalized process respectively.

II) If $\left\{c(i)\right\}_i$ is the process that admits $\left\{\hat{c}(i)\right\}_{i=-m}^{-1}$ as a realization, then a model of $\left\{c\;(i)\right\}_i$ is built.

Usually such a model is selected among the ARMA (p,q) stationary models [17]

$$c(i+1)= \phi_1 c(i)+\phi_2 c(i-1)+\ldots+\phi_p c(i-p+1)- \varepsilon(i)-\theta_1 \varepsilon(i-1)-\ldots- \theta_q \varepsilon(i-q) \tag{2.9}$$

where

$\left\{\varepsilon(i)\right\}_i$ = purely random stationary gaussian process with zero mean and variance σ_ε ;

and

$\left\{\phi_j\right\}_{j=1}^{p}$, $\left\{\theta_k\right\}_{k=1}^{q}$ and σ_ε = model parameters to be estimated on the basis of the data $\left\{\hat{c}(i)\right\}_{i=-m}^{-1}$.

In most cases q = 0 or 1, while p = 0 or 1, or 2.

III) A realization $\left\{\hat{c}(i)\right\}_{i=0}^{N-1}$ is obtained by generating a realization of $\left\{\varepsilon(i)\right\}_i$ by means of a Montecarlo technique (see [18] for example) and subsequently introducing it into (2.9).

IV) A realization $\left\{\hat{a}(i)\right\}_{i=0}^{N-1}$ (synthetic record) is supplied by anti-standardizing and subsequently anti-normalizing the sequence $\left\{\hat{c}(i)\right\}_{i=0}^{N-1}$.

3. PROBLEM SOLUTION

Turning to program (2.5)- (2.8) and letting $s(\cdot, x_1, x_2)$ denote the result of a "system simulation", i.e. the solution of (2.6), it is possible to choose an efficient algorithm by means of the following property (the proof is given in the Appendix).

Proposition

The function $s(i;\cdot,x_2)$ is non-increasing, the fucntion $s(i;x_1,\cdot)$ is non-decreasing.

Furthermore let

$$p(i;x_1,x_2) = s(i; x_1,x_2) + a(i) - x_1 \tag{3.1}$$

Program (2.5) - (2.8) is then turned into the following :

$$\max_x \; g(x_1)-c(x_2) \tag{3.2}$$

$$p^*(x_1,x_2) \geq 0 \tag{3.3}$$

$$x_1,x_2 \geq 0 \tag{3.4}$$

where

$$p^*(x_1,x_2) = \min_{0 \leq i \leq N-1} p(i;x_1,x_2) .$$

In view of the proposition and (3.1), the functions $p^*(\cdot,x_2)$ and $p^*(x_1,\cdot)$ turn out to be non-increasing and non-decreasing respectively. Hence, the optimal solution of (3.2)-(3.4) apparently lies on the curve implicitly defined by

$$p^*(x_1,x_2) = 0 . \tag{3.5}$$

Let $x_2(x_1)$ denote the explicit form of (3.5). Since

$$\frac{dx_2(x_1)}{dx_1} = - \frac{\dfrac{\partial p^*(x_1,x_2)}{\partial x_1}}{\dfrac{\partial p^*(x_1,x_2)}{\partial x_2}}$$

the function $x_2(\cdot)$ is a non-decreasing one. No convexity property, however, can be established in correspondence with any inflow datum $\hat{a}(\cdot)$, so that optimality situations of different kinds might occur (Fig. 3). Recall that the feasible region F, which has been defi-

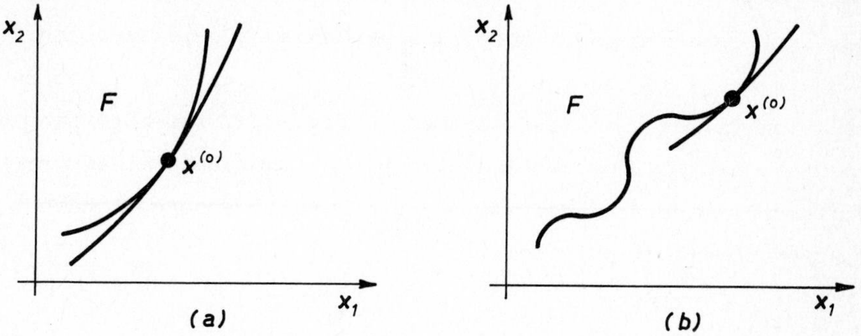

Fig. 3 Different optimality condition (F = feasible region)

ned via simulation is not explicitly known. Then assume the case is the one described in Fig. 3a and consider the solution algorithm, whose k-th step is the following.

i) The data at the beginning of the step is an interval $\mathcal{J}_k=(x_{11}^{(k)},x_{12}^{(k)})$

such that $x_{11}^{(k)} \leq x_{1}^{(o)} \leq x_{12}^{(k)}$, as well as the pairs $(x_{21}^{(k)}, x_{22}^{(k)})$, $(z_1^{(k)}, z_2^{(k)})$ where $x_{2j}^{(k)} = x_2(x_{1j}^{(k)})$, $z_j^{(k)} = g(x_{1j}^{(k)}) - c(x_{2j}^{(k)})$, $j = 1,2$.

In $\mathfrak{J}_k$ select a couple $(\tilde{x}_{11}^{(k)}, \tilde{x}_{12}^{(k)})$ in accordance with a Fibonacci search scheme [19].

ii) Determine $\tilde{x}_{2j} = x_2(\tilde{x}_{1j}^{(k)})$, $j = 1,2$, that is values of x_2 such that $p^*(\tilde{x}_{11}^{(k)}, \tilde{x}_{21}^{(k)}) = 0$ and $p^*(\tilde{x}_{12}^{(k)}, \tilde{x}_{22}^{(k)}) = 0$ respectively. These zeroes can be evaluated by means of simulation of (2.6), in accordance with a bisection search scheme, since $p^*(x_1, \cdot)$ is a monotonic function.

iii) Compute $\tilde{z}_j^{(k)} = g(\tilde{x}_{1j}^{(k)}) - c(\tilde{x}_{2j}^{(k)})$, $j = 1,2$ and select $\mathfrak{J}_{k+1}$, on the basis of $z_j^{(k)}$ and $\tilde{z}_j^{(k)}$ $j = 1,2$ and through the criterion usually followed in the Fibonacci search.

The algorithm stops when $k = \bar{k}$ such that $\mathfrak{J}_{\bar{k}}$ is smaller than a preassigned interval. The use of search methods allows to obtain the solution with remarkable precision, a characteristic of some interest when dealing with problems where couspicuous profits and costs are involved.

To obtain the same degree of precision by means of grid sampling techniques would imply a much greater amount of computation. Of course if the situation is not the one described in Fig. 3.a, the algorithm may yield a local optimum instead of a global one. Some attempts with different starting intervals $\mathfrak{J}_o$ are usually enough to have a screening of the local solutions.

5. AN EXAMPLE

The algorithm has been used in the case of a reservoir, whose yearly inflow may be described by an AR(1) lognormally distributed stationary process characterized by :

mean = 75.10^6 m^3/sec

st.dev.= 29.10^6 m^3/sec

corr.coeff.= 0.105.

The value of N has been set equal to 500. Profit and cost functions of the respective forms.

$$g(x_1) = 10^9 \, (1-e^{-10^{-7}\lambda_1})$$

$$c(x_2) = 10^9 \, (1- e^{-25.10^{-9}\lambda_2})$$

has been used for different values of the parameters λ_1 and λ_2. The results are summarized in Table 1,

λ_1 \ λ_2	0.2	0.6	1.0	1.4	1.8
0.6	35 34	30 28	24 22	18 17	13 12
	72	49	34	23	15
1.0	31 29	22 20	18 16	15 13	13 11
	82	63	50	41	33
1.4	25 23	18 16	15 13	13 11	11 9
	86	70	60	52	45
1.8	21 19	15 13	12 10	11 9	10 8
	88	75	66	59	53

Table 1 Optimal solutions for different λ_1, λ_2.

where in each box $x_1^{(o)}$ (10^6 m^3), $x_2^{(o)}$(10^6 m^3) and $g(x_1^{(o)})-c(x_2^{(o)})$ (10^7 £) are reported from top to bottom. The computer time required to solve all cases described in Table 1 has been 2.22 min, on a UNIVAC 1108 computer.

5. CONCLUDING REMARKS

The problem of determining the optimal design and contract release of a reservoir has been described in the paper and a solution algorithm, based on the alternative use of well-known search procedure has been proposed.

A general remark concerns the use of policies, such as the normal operating rule, that make the decision on the release in any period also depend on the inflow in the period. Hence the choice of the outflow volume should be based on an information, not available at the beginning of the period, when the decision is actually taken.

A more reasonable viewpoint would be the one of using operating rules based on the storage as well as on inflow forecast, supplied by the stochastic model of the inflow process. This approach, anyway, has not yet been widely investigated in water resources literature.

REFERENCES

[1] W. Rippl, "The Capacity of Storage Reservoir for Water Supply", Proceedings of the I.C.E., Vol. 71, 1883.

[2] H. Hurst, "Methods of Using Long Term Storage in Reservoirs", Proceedings of the I.C.E., paper 6059, 1956.

[3] W. Feller, "The Asymptotic Distribution of the Range of Sums of Indipendent Random Variables", Annual of Mathematical Statistics, Vol. 22, 1951.

[4] A. Anis, H. Lloyd, "On the Range of Partial Sums of a Finite

Number of Independent Normal Variates", Biometrika, Vol. 42, 1955.

[5] P. Moran: "The Theory of Storage", Methuen, London, 1959.

[6] R. Dorfman, "Mathematical Models: the Multistructure Approach" in A. Maass et al.: "Design of Water-Resource Systems", Harvard University Press, Cambridge (USA), 1962.

[7] Hall W., Butcher W., Esogbue A., "Optimization of the Operation of a Multiple Purpose Reservoir by Dynamic Programming", Water Resources Research, June 1968.

[8] Buras N., "Scientific Allocation of Water Resources", American Elsevier, New York, 1972.

[9] Hufschmidt, M., and M. Fiering, "Simulation Techniques for Design of Water-Resource Systems", Harvard University Press, 212 pp., Cambridge, Massachusetts, 1966.

[10] G. Young, "Finding Reservoir Operating Rules", Proceedings of the A.S.C.E., Vol. 93, n. HY6, 1967.

[11] Thomas A., Fiering M., "The Nature of the Storage Yield Function", in "Operations Research in Water Quality Management" Harvard University Water Program, Cambridge, U.S.A., 1963.

[12] N. Matalas, J. Wallis, "Statistical Properties of Multivariate Fractional Noise Processes", Water Resources Research, v.7, n. 6, December 1971.

[13] P.E. O'Connell, "Stochastic Modelling of Long-term Persistence in Steamflow Sequences" Imperial College - London, Hydrology Section, Internal Report 1973-2.

[14] R. Clarke, "Mathematical Models in Hydrology", Irrigation and Drainage Paper 19 - F.A.O. - Roma 1973.

[15] C. Revelle, E. Joeres, W. Kirby, "The Linear Decision Rule in Reservoir Management and Design Development of the Stochastic Model", Water Resources Research, Vol. 5, n. 4, 1969.

[16] Eisel L.M., "Chance Constrained Reservoir Model", Water Resources Research, v. 8, n. 2, April 1972.

[17] G. Box, G. Jenkins, "Time Series Analysis: Forecasting and Control", San Francisco, Holden-day Inc.

[18] J. Hammersley, D. Handscomb, "Monte Carlo Methods", Metheun, London, 1965.

[19] Wilde D., Beightler C. "Foundations of Optimization", Prentice Hall Inc. 1967.

APPENDIX

Proof of the Proposition

Only the property of $s(i;\cdot,x_2)$ is proved, since quite similar arguments hold for $s(i;x_1,\cdot)$.
The proof is based on induction. Consider x_1', x_1'' with $x_1' \geq x_1''$: since, in view of the continuity equation,

$$s(1;\, x_1',x_2)-s(1;x_1'',x_2) = f(s_o+\hat{a}(0);x_1'',x_2) -f(s_o+\hat{a}(0);\, x_1',\, x_2)$$

it turns out that

$$s(1;x_1',x_2)\leq s(1;\, x_1'',\, x_2).$$

Moreover assume that $s(i;x_1',\, x_2) \leq s(i;\, x_1'',\, x_2)$. Then

$$s(i+1);\, x_1',x_2) - s(i+1;x_1'',\, x_2) = s' - s'' + f'' - f'$$

where, for simplicity of notation,

$$s' = s(i;\, x_1',\, x_2)$$
$$s'' = s(i;\, x_1'',\, x_2)$$
$$f' = f(s' + \hat{a}(i);\, x_1',\, x_2)$$
$$f'' = f(s'' + \hat{a}(i);\, x_1'',\, x_2)$$

i) If $s' + \hat{a}(i) \leq x_1'$, then $s(i+1;\, x_1',\, x_2) = 0$, so that

$$s(i+1;\, x_1',\, x_2) \leq s(i+1;\, x_1'',\, x_2).$$

ii) If $s''+a(i) \geq x_1'' + x_2$ then $s(i+1;\, x_1'',\, x_2) = x_2 \geq s(i+1;\, x_1',\, x_2)$.

iii) Finally if

$$x_1' \leq s'+ \hat{a}(i) \leq s'' + \hat{a}(i) \leq x_1'' + x_2$$ it turns out that

$f' = x_1'$, $f'' = x_1''$ and hence

$$s(i+1;\, x_1' ,\, x_2) - s(i+1;\, x_1'',\, x_2) = (s'-s'') + (x_1''- x_1')\leq 0$$

A MODEL OF MANY GOAL-ORIENTED STOCHASTIC AUTOMATA WITH APPLICATION ON A MARKETING PROBLEM

by

Y.M. EL-FATTAH

University of Liège

Liège, Belgium

ABSTRACT

Here presented is a model of many goal-oriented stochastic automata. The goal of each automaton is the extremum of the absolute mean value of a certain utility function. That function depends explicitly on the automaton strategy and the environment response. Without need of any a priori knowledge each automaton adapts its structure in the process of achieving its own goal. By suitably setting the environment characteristics the automata model can be useful for the analysis of some operations research problems. As example that model is used for the study of the price formation process in a free competitive market. The results demonstrated the convergence of the automata updating scheme as well as the influence of a number of interesting physical parameters (like the buyers tactics, the sellers psychology, etc...) on the equilibrium condition.

1. INTRODUCTION

Tsetlin [1] has proposed different norms of behavior of a finite automaton working in a random environment. In that work the environment is assumed to either penalize or reward each action of the automaton according to certain unknown probabilities. The bahavior of an automaton is called expedient if the average penalty is less than the value corresponding to choosing all actions with equal probabilities. The behavior is called optimal or ε- optimal according to whether the average penalty is equal or arbitrarily close, respectively, to the minimum value. Krylov and Tsetlin [2] introduced the concept of games between automata and studied in particular Two-Automaton Zero-Sum games.

Stochastic automata with variable structure have been introduced by Varshavskii and Vorntsova [3] to represent learning automata attempt-ting a certain norm of behavior in an unknown random environment. Since the date of that work a respectable number of works has appeared, studying different aspects of learning automata and applying it in simulating very simple norms of behavior (like that introduced by Tsetlin) and also simple automata games (such as Two-Automaton Zero-Sum games). For a survey on the subject we refer to Narendra and Thathacher [4].

The contribution of this paper is to direct the attention of using learning automata to simulate an important class of problems of collective behavior whose deterministic version has been the subject of recent investigation mainly by Malishevskii and Tenisberg, see [5] - [7]. In that class of problems there exists a type of relation in the collective where the behavior of the participants possesses a definite mutual opposition. Such situation can arise for example in economic systems : the case of price regulation in a competitive market [8]; or in management systems : the problems of resource allocation [9].

In the model introduced in this paper a collectice of interacting stochastic automata is considered. Each automaton has a behavioral tactic directed towards the realization of its own goal, taken to be the extremun of a certain utility function. That function depends explicitly on the automaton strategy and the environment response. The automata interactions arise from the dependence of the environment response on the whole set of strategies used by the collective of automata. That dependence is generally stochastic and unknown to all the automata. Furthermore, any automaton does not know neither the utility functions, nor even the number of the other automata. The only available knowledge to each automaton is the realization of its utility function following the use of a certain strategy.

The use of automata game to model the process of market price regulation (or optimization), described in Karlin [8], from the viewpoint of collective behaviour was demonstrated by Tenisberg [5]. In his work, Tenisberg [5] made two assumptions. The first assumption is connected with the substitution of the probability characteristics of the buyers' demand by deterministic characteristics (mean value). This is equivalent to the assumption that the transactions are sufficiently numerous. The second assumption is that already in a time small compared to the characteristic time of the system a fairly large number of interactions between the sellers and the buyers occur. These assumptions permit the model to be described approximately by deterministic differential equations. Later Malishevskii and Tenisberg [6] formulated theorems about the existence and uniqueness of the equilibrium situation in the game (in the sense of Nash) and the attainability of this situation in the process of the automata game.

Krylatykh [10] modified the deterministic model of Tenisberg [5] by taking into consideration the psychological attitudes of sellers and buyers with respect to the market situation. This has the effect of including nonlinear utility function instead of a linear one in the Tenisberg model [5]. This corresponds to the cases when the automata are not able to perceive the created situations adequately; simulating the individual psychological peculiarities of the buyers and sellers, who in reality are not necessarily always objective (corresponding to a linear utility function).

Applying the present stochastic automata model the assumptions of Tenisberg [5] are not needed; in particular the stochastic nature of the buyers demand will be respected. In addition the stochastic model reveals the effect of a number of interesting factors - like the sellers psychology - on the modes of collective behaviour which has no analog in deterministic modelling as shown in section 5.

2. AUTOMATA MODEL

As model of collective behavior we consider the following game of N stochastic automata $A^1, A^2, \ldots, A^N$. The automata operate on a discrete time scale $t = 0,1,2,\ldots$ The input $s^i(t)$ to each i-th automaton can acquire one of the values $s_1, s_2, \ldots, s_m$. The output $f^i(t)$ of the automaton A^i will be assumed to take one of the k_i values $f_1^{\,i}, \ldots, f_{k_i}^{\,i}$ which will be called its strategies. We will say that the automaton A^i uses the j-th strategy if $f^i(t) = f_j^{\,i}$.

A play f(t) carried out at time t will be the name given to a set $f(t) = (f^1(t), \ldots, f^N(t))$ of the strategies used by the automata $A^1, \ldots, A^N$ at time t. The outcome s(t) of a play f(t) is a set $s(t) = (s^1(t), \ldots, s^N(t))$ of the refree or environment responses at time t. The model is depicted schematically in Fig.1. The environment is completely characterized by the probability P(f(t),s(t)) of the outcome s(t) for every play f(t). As only stationary environments will be considered, the aforementioned probability can simply be written as P(f,s). The game of N automata A^i is considered to be a game with independent outcomes, i.e.

$$P(f,s) = \prod_{i=1}^{N} P^i(f,s^i) \tag{2.1}$$

Let us introduce the indicator functions $\Phi^i(f)$ defined by

$$\Phi^i(f) = M_s^i\{ F^i [\theta^i(f^i,s^i)]\}$$
$$= \sum_s F^i[\theta^i(f^i,s^i)]P^i(f,s^i) \quad (i=1,\ldots,N) \tag{2.2}$$

where M_s^i denotes the mean value with respect to s^i, F^i is an utility function of the incentive (or utility) θ^i. The incentive θ^i depends explicitely on the automaton strategy f^i and the environment response s^i.

The objective of each i-th automaton is to choose its strategy f^i in order to minimize the absolute value of its own indicator function (2.2), i.e. to minimize

$$Q^i(f) = |\Phi^i(f)| \tag{2.3}$$

In classical N-person games, each player possesses an adequate a priori knowledge of the game, i.e. the criteria and the sets of pure strategies for all the players. It is defined that the i-th player uses the mixed strategy $p^i = (p_1^i,\ldots,p_{ki}^i)$ if the uses his pure strategy f_j^i with probability $p_j^i (j=1,\ldots,k_i)$, $\sum_{j=1}^{k_i} p_j^i=1)$. Nash's basic theorem states that any finite N-person game has at least one equilibrium situation in mixed strategies $(p^1,\ldots,p^N)$, that is

$$\overset{-i}{Q}(p^{1*},\ldots,p^{i*},\ldots,p^{N*}) \le \overset{-i}{Q}(p^{1*},\ldots,p^{i},\ldots,p^{N*}) \tag{2.4}$$

for all p^i, $i=1,\ldots,N$, where

$$\overset{-i}{Q}(p^1,\ldots,p^N) = \sum_{j_1 j_2 \cdots j_N} p_{j_1}^1 \, p_{j_2}^2 \cdots p_{j_N}^N \, Q^i(f_{j_1}^1,f_{j_2}^2,\ldots,f_{j_N}^N) \tag{2.5}$$

also denoted by $\overset{-i}{Q}(p)$, is the mathematical expectation of the gain of the i-th player when the set of mixed strategies $p=(p^1,\ldots,p^N)$ is used.

Unlike N-person, players automata in automata games do not possess any a priori information about the game. They know neither about the criteria (2.3) nor even the number of game partners. They must choose their strategies (or which is the same their probability vectors p^i) in the course of the game by using the only available information : the realizations of their incentive functions $\Theta^i(f^i,s^i)$. In studying automata games we thus come to know the behavior of the players in the game process.

The indicator functions $\Phi^i(f), i=1,\ldots,N$ given by (2.2) are assumed to satisfy the conditions of individual and group contramonotonicity [6], i.e. for any subset I of the set of indexes $\{i\}=\{1,..,N\}$ the function.

$$\Phi^I = \sum_{i\varepsilon I} \Phi^i(f)$$

decreases in the set of own variables f^i, $i\varepsilon I$ and does not decrease in the set of foreign variables $f^j, j\varepsilon \bar{I}$ ($\bar{I}$ is the complement of I).

If each automaton A^i knows its own indicator function Φ^i, and its strategy f^i can take any value in the continuous interval $[f_1{}^i, f_{ki}{}^i]$ then the optimal tactic can be given by the simple differential relation [5] - [7]

$$\overset{\circ}{f}{}^i(t) = \bar{\Phi}^i(f(t)) \tag{2.6}$$

where

$$\bar{\Phi}^i(f) = \begin{cases} 0 & \text{if } f^i=f_1{}^i, \Phi^i < 0 \text{ or } f^i=f_{ki}{}^i, \Phi^i > 0 \\ \Phi^i(f) & \text{in all other cases.} \end{cases} \tag{2.7}$$

This means that the trajectories of the system (2.6) converge to the Nash point f^* if exists.

Let us emphasize that in the present model of collective behavior the goal of each automaton is not fully determinate, i.e. known only up to certain parameters for which there is no a priori information. Specifically automaton A^i does not know its own indicator function $\Phi^i(f)$; all what is known to it is the incentive function $\Theta^i(f^i,s^i)$, see eqn. (2.2).

Let us arrange the set of strategies of the i-th automaton such that $f_{j}^{i} > f_{k}^{i}$ for all $j > k$. For any strategy $f_j^i (1 < j < k_i)$ we call f_{j+1}^{i} the next supremal strategy and f_{j-1}^{i} the next infimal strategy. The strategies f_1^i and $f_{k_i}^{i}$ are the infimal and supremal absorbing strategies, respectively of the i-th automaton.

Inspired by the behavioral conception represented by eqn.(2.6) we propose the following model of learning automata.

Let us introduce the functions,

$$u^i = \begin{cases} +1 & \text{if } \theta^i > 0 \\ 0 & \text{if } \theta^i = 0 \\ -1 & \text{if } \theta^i < 0 \end{cases} \tag{2.8}$$

and

$$\bar{\theta}^i(f^i, s^i) = \begin{cases} 0 & \text{if} \quad f^i = f_1^i, \theta^i < 0, \text{ or } f^i = f_{k_i}^i, \theta^i > 0 \\ \theta^i(f^i, s^i) & \text{in all other cases} \end{cases} \tag{2.9}$$

The idea underlying the functioning of a learning automaton in the present model can be loosely stated as follows. At any time step provided that an automaton is not at either of the absorbing states and the automaton action has elicited an environment response for which the incentive function θ^i is greater than zero than at the next time step the probability of the next supremal action is increased; on the other hand if the incentive function is less than zero then the probability of the next infimal action is increased. Otherwise, that is if the automaton is at either of the absorbing states or the incentive function is zero, the automaton remains in the status quo. That idea can be analytically represented by the following updating scheme for the automata strategis. Provided that $f^i(t) = f_j^i$ then

$$p^i_{j+u^i}(t+1) = p^i_{j+u^i}(t) + \gamma(t+1) u^i F^i(\bar{\theta}^i(f^i(t), s^i(t)))$$

$$p^i_m(t+1) = p^i_m(t) - \frac{\gamma(t+1)}{N+1} u^i F^i(\bar{\theta}^i(f^i(t), s^i(t))), \tag{2.10}$$

$$m = 1, \ldots, k_i, m \neq j + u^i$$

where $\gamma(t)$ satisfies the classical conditions of stochastic approximation schemes

$$\gamma(t) > 0 \quad , \quad \sum_{t=1}^{\infty} \gamma(t) = \infty \quad , \quad \sum_{t=1}^{\infty} \gamma^2(t) < \infty \tag{2.11}$$

A function block diagram for each i-th automaton may be represented as shown in Fig. 2.

3. ENVIRONMENT MODEL

As said before the environment is completely characterized by the probability $P(f,s)$ of the outcome $s(t)$ for every play $f(t)$. That probability also fully specifies the interaction between the automata.

In the following we present two different models of the environment, named the "pairwise comparison" and the "proportional utility".

3.1. Pairwise comparison.

Let the environment be constituted of υ elements $j=1,..,\upsilon$. The j-th element finds out the strategies f^i and f^k of two randomly chosen (with equal probabilities) automaton, the i-th and the k-th($i,k=1,..,N$). The j-th element then responds in a probabilistic manner to only one of the chosen pair of automata; say with probability $p^j(f^i,f^k)$ to the i-th and with probability $p^j(f^k,f^i)=1-p^j(f^i,f^k)$ to the k-th.

We shall assume $p^j(f^i,f^k)=\psi(\delta^j(f^i,f^k)) = 1/2 + \mu(\delta^j(f^i,f^k))$ where $\delta^j(f^i,f^k)$ is a certain utility index for the j-th element, and $\mu(x)$ is a monotonically increasing odd function $\mu(+\infty)=\mu(-\infty) = 1/2$.

The total probability of a response from the j-th element of the environment to the i-th automaton can be written thus

$$p^{jni}(f) = \frac{2}{N(N-1)} \sum_{\substack{\ell=1 \\ \ell\neq i}}^{N} \psi(\delta^j(f^i,f^\ell)) \tag{3.1}$$

Notice that

$$0 \le p^{j,i} \le 1 \quad , \quad \sum_{i=1}^{N} p^{j,i} = 1 \tag{3.2}$$

The response of the j-th element of the environment to the i-th automaton is considered to be in the form

$$s^{j,i} = \omega^j(f^i) \tag{3.3}$$

where $\omega^j(.)$ is a piecewise continuous function.

Indeed eqs.(3.2) and (3.3) permit to write the conditional probability of the environment response s^i for a play f of the automata as follows,

$$p^i(s^i \leq \sum_{j=1}^{\ell} s^{j,i}/f) = \sum_{j=1}^{\ell} p^{j,i}(f) \quad , \quad (\ell=1,..,\upsilon) \qquad (3.4)$$

3.2. Proportional utility.

In this model each element of the environment responds to the automata with probabilities proportionable to the utilities of their strategies. The probability of a response from an element increases as the utility of an automaton strategy increases and becomes maximum for maximum utility. Hence the probability that the j-th element responds to the i-th automaton can be expressed thus,

$$p^{j,i}(f) = \phi(\delta^j(f^i))/\sum_{j=1}^{N} \phi(\delta^j(f^i)), j=1,..,\upsilon; \quad i=1,..,N \quad (3.5)$$

where $\phi(.)$ is some positive non-decreasing function, and $\delta^j(f^i)$ is the utility of the i-th automaton strategy f^i for the j-th element.

Eqs.(3.3) and (3.4) again complete the environment model description after replacing the probabilities $p^{j,i}(f)$ in eqn.(3.4) by the expression of eqn.(3.5).

4. APPLICATION - Price Formation in a Competitive Market.

Consider N sellers in a market trading in one specific commodity. Each i-th seller (i=1,..,N) is assumed to be supplied by a constant q^i units of that commodity per time increment (the interval between any two successive time steps). The strategy of any i-th seller f^i represents the price he specifies for his commodity. Let the i-th seller receives a demand π^i in monetary units for buying his commoditu at the specified price f^i. The financial incentive for the i-th seller is simply the difference between the demand and supply in monetary units, i.e.

$$\theta^i = \pi^i - q^i f^i \quad , \quad (i=1,..,N) \qquad (4.7)$$

The utility of that incentive may be interpreted differently by the sellers; each according to his psychological type. That interpretation is embodied in the utility function $F^i(.)$ of an i-th seller which may be considered in the following form,

$$F^i(\theta^i) = a^i(\exp(b^i\theta^i)-1) + d^i\theta^i \quad , \quad (i=1,..,N) \qquad (4.8)$$

The constants a^i, b^i, and d^i simulate the psychological type of the i-th seller as follows,

$$\begin{array}{lll} \text{Cautious type} & : a^i,b^i < 0 \quad , & d^i = 0 \\ \text{Objective type} & : a^i,b^i = 0 \quad , & d^i > 0 \\ \text{Hazardous type} & : a^i,b^i > 0 \quad , & d^i = 0 \end{array} \qquad (4.9)$$

The nonlinearity of the utility function F^i for a cautious or hazardous seller indicates the lack of objectivity of such psychological types. Thus a hazardous type overestimates the importance of a good deal ($\delta^j > 0$) and underestimates the importance of the deal in the opposite situation ($\delta^j < 0$). A cautious type overestimates the importance of bad deals and underestimates the good ones.

The objective of each seller is to find a price strategy maximizes its utility function, or what amounts to the same ensures the least harmful situation (according to a certain psychology) created by the mismatch between commodity supply and demand in monetary units. Hence, each seller attempts to minimize the function (2.3) where the indicator function Φ^i is given by eqs. (2.2),(4.7), and (4.8).

The automata scheme (2.10) is used to simulate the behavior of the sellers.

In the case of pairwise comparison tactic of the buyers [5] the environment is simulated as in sec. 3.1. In this case the utility of the j-th buyer making his purshase from the i-th seller is given by

$$\delta^j(f^i,f^k) = f^k - f^i \qquad (4.10)$$

The ψ function in eqn. (3.1) may be taken thus,

$$\psi(x) = \begin{cases} 1 & x > \Delta \\ (x+\Delta)/2 \quad , & -\Delta < x < \Delta \quad , \\ 0 & x < -\Delta \end{cases} \qquad (4.11)$$

Here $(-\Delta,\Delta)$ represents the "active zone of the function". The function ω^j in eqn. (3.3) may be considered as

$$\omega^j(f^i) = \begin{cases} \beta^j & , \beta^j \geq f^i \\ 0 & , \beta^j < f^i \end{cases} \qquad (4.12)$$

This means that the purshasing transaction between the j-th buyer and the i-th seller will be completed only when the buyer's available amount of money β^j equals or exceeds the price f^i of a unit of the commodity.

In the case of reference prices tactic of the buyers [5] the environment is simulated as in section 3.2. In this case the utility of the j-th buyer making his purchase from the i-th seller is given by

$$\delta^j(f^i) = h^j - f^i \qquad (4.13)$$

where h^j is the reference price of the j-th buyer. The function $\phi(.)$ is taken to be the same as $\psi(.)$ defined by (4.11).

5. SIMULATION RESULTS.

In all the simulation experiments the following market parameters are considered,

Number of sellers $N=3$, Sellers' psychology :
Number of buyers $\upsilon=12$ Cautious $a^i=-1$, $b^i=-0.005$
Objective $d^i=0.02$
Hazardous $a^i=1$, $b^i=0.005$

Commodity supply $q^1=2$, $q^2=2$, $q^3=3$
Available money to each buyer $\beta^j=150$
Buyers' utility $\alpha=0.05$, see eqs. (4.10),(4.13)
The sequence $\gamma(t)$, see eqn. (2.10), were taken as

$$\gamma(t) = \frac{\gamma_o}{t} \quad , \quad \gamma_o=\text{const.}, \ t=1,2,.. \qquad (5.1)$$

The sellers sets of prices are first taken as :

c^i_k k \ i	1	2	3
1	100	100	140
2	140	130	170
3	-	170	200

The initial price probabilities for the different sellers are assumed

$p_k^i[o]$ k \ i	1	2	3
1	0.5	0.2	0.5
2	0.5	0.5	0.3
3	-	0.3	0.2

5.1. "Pairwise price comparison" tactic.

Let the number of buyers $\upsilon=12$, and consider different psychological classes of sellers.

5.1.1. Objective sellers.

The width of the active zone, see eqn. (4.11) was taken first as $\Delta=200$. The effect of the constant γ_0, see eqn. (5.1), on the convergence of the sellers price probabilities was examined. It is concluded that a very small value of γ_0 (i.e. $0 < \gamma_0 << 1$) leads to a very sluggish convergence. On the other hand a value of γ_0 as big as 1 leads to a rather vigorous and oscillatory convergence. An optimum value for γ_0 seems to exist somehow in between, see Fig. 3.

Taking $\gamma_0 = 0.1$, a satisfactory convergence has been attained at $n = 100$. At that time step, the average of price probabilities (corresponding to 10 trials) are

Table 1

$E\{p_k^i[100]\}$ k \ i	1	2	3
1	0.0528	0.0010	0.6708
2	0.9472	0.4972	0.3292
3	-	0.5018	0

which, presumably, is close to the equilibrium point.

The influence of the width Δ of the active zone was also tested with objective types of sellers and $\gamma_0 = 0.1$. With $\Delta = 2$ (which means that ψ was equal to 0 or 1 when the prices were different) we obtained the following mean probability matrix (the mean of 10 trials) :

Table 2

$E\{p_k^i[100]\}$	k \ i	1	2	3
	1	0.0355	0	0.5961
	2	0.9645	0.3397	0.4039
	3	-	0.6603	0

and with Δ = 2000 we obtained :

Table 3

$E\{p_k^i[100]\}$	k \ i	1	2	3
	1	0.1154	0.0010	0.6827
	2	0.8846	0.5133	0.3173
		-	0.4857	0

The last two tables demonstrate the tendency to increase the prices as Δ gets smaller, which can be demonstrated as follows .

According to eqn. (4.11) of the function ψ , it is clear that if as a result of pairwise comparison

$$\max\{|\delta^j(f^i,f^k) \ , \ |\delta^j(f^k,f^i)|\} \geq \Delta \qquad (5.2)$$

then the j-th buyer making that comparison will be definitely captured by one of them; specifically by the i-th if $\delta^j(c^i,c^k) \geq \Delta$ and by the k-th if $\delta^j(c^k,c^i) \geq \Delta$. An uncertain decision by the j-th buyer only happen when the prices are fairly close so that $\max\{|\delta^j(c^i,c^k)|,|\delta^j(c^k,c^i)|\} < \Delta$. In this case we shall say that "active competition" exists between the i-th and k-th sellers; we shall call the interval $(-\Delta,\Delta)$ the "active zone" of the function $\psi(x)$.

As $\Delta \to 0$, the competition by the prices tends to be uneffective; as the demand will be basically determined by the money flux into the market, and the commodity supply available to each seller. In such condition, it seems natural that each seller attempts to specify the highest possible price for his commodity. If the commodity supplies to the different sellers vary only slightly, the limit prices tend to be almost the same. This is verified by the simulation results.

Also, as in the deterministic case (cf. Tenisberg [5]), the effect of a small Δ, is more or less an equalization of prices in the market. This can be demonstrated by changing the set of prices of the second seller to include the price 140 instead of 130, as well as changing the number of buyers to have no abundant demands. Thus, take $\upsilon = 7$ and

c_k^i k \ i	1	2	3
1	100	100	140
2	140	140	170
3	-	170	200

With objective sellers and $\Delta = 2$ we obtained :

$E\{p_k^i[100]\}$ k \ i	1	2	3
1	0.1674	0.0607	0.8670
2	0.8326	0.7464	0.1330
3	-	0.1929	0

This demonstrates that the sellers have all increased the probability of the price 140 which indicates the tendency of equalization of prices, compare with Table 5.

5.1.2. Hazardous sellers.

We put $\gamma_0 = 0.1$ and $\Delta = 200$. The mean probability matrix at $n = 100$ became

$E\{p_k^i[100]\}$ k \ i	1	2	3
1	0.0457	0	0.3265
2	0.9543	0.1639	0.6735
3	-	0.8361	0

which, presumeably, is fairly close to the equilibrium point.

5.1.3. Cautious sellers.

We put $\gamma_0 = 0.1$ and $\Delta = 200$. The mean probability matrix at $n = 100$ became :

$E\{p_k^i[100]\}$ k \ i	1	2	3
1	0.3715	0.0009	0.9332
2	0.6285	0.7919	0.0668
3	-	0.2072	0

which, according to the simulation trials, should be close to the equilibrium point.

Compared to the objective case, the last two tables demonstrate that the hazardous sellers tend to increase the probability of higher prices, while the cautious sellers tempt to increase the probability of lower prices. This result has no analog in deterministic modelling; where the sellers psychology does not affect the equilibrium prices, cf. Krylatykh [10]. In stochastic modelling, however, the expectation of the utility being zero does not imply that the expectation of the utility is zero due to the nonlinear from of the utility function in the case of hazardous or cautious types. In any case; the previous result agrees more with intuition and favors stochastic modelling for more realistic simulation. Let us now reduce the number of buyers. Take $\upsilon = 7$. This means less money flow into the market. All the other market parameters remain the same as before.

Considering objective sellers, the following mean price probabilities have been reached at $n = 100$, for different widths of the active zone :

Table 4

$\Delta = 200$:

$E\{p_k^i[100]\}$ k \ i	1	2	3
1	0.3921	0.0287	0.8877
2	0.6079	0.7539	0.1123
3	-	0.2174	0

Table 5

$\Delta = 2$:

$E\{p_k^i[100]\}$ k \ i	1	2	3
1	0.2177	0	0.8586
2	0.7823	0.5279	0.1414
3	-	0.4721	0

Table 6

$\Delta = 2000$:

$E\{p_k^i[100]\}$ k \ i	1	2	3
1	0.4874	0.0329	0.8803
2	0.5126	0.7453	0.1197
3	-	0.2218	0

Comparing in respective order tables 4,5,6 with Tables 1,2,3 (where $\upsilon = 12$) it is clear that the probability of lower prices in the case of $\upsilon = 7$ have been significantly increased for all values of Δ. This agrees with the intuition that as the money flow into the market decreases, the probability of lower prices increases. This conclusion holds for all sellers psychological types.

5.2. "Reference-Price" tactics.

Let the reference price for all buyers be the same :

$$h^j = 130 \quad , \quad j=1,..,12$$

and consider the other market parameters unchanged. For $\Delta = 200$, and $\gamma_0 = 0.1$ the following simulation results have been obtained.

5.2.1. Objective sellers.

With objective type of sellers we obtained :

$E\{p_k^i[100]\}$ k \ i	1	2	3
1	0.0689	0.0010	0.6722
2	0.9311	0.5097	0.3278
3	-	0.4893	0

For this case we have also computed the absolute mean values of the utility function versus time in order to demonstrate the learning capability of the sellers automata. A plot of the optimality criterion for the second seller $\bar{Q}^2$ is shown in Fig. 4 (each point is the mean of 100 trials).

5.2.2. Hazardous seller's.

With hazardous type of sellers we obtained :

$E\{p_k^i[100]\}$ k \ i	1	2	3
1	0.0760	0	0.3292
2	0.9240	0.1903	0.6708
3	-	0.8097	0

5.2.3. Cautious sellers.

With cautious type of sellers we obtained :

$E\{p_k^i[100]\}$ k \ i	1	2	3
1	0.3828	0.0006	0.9338
2	0.6172	0.7947	0.0662
3	-	0.2047	0

Comparing these results with the results of sec. 5.1 we see that they differ slightly.

Changing the reference prices h^j did not bring significant changes to the equilibrium probabilities.

5. CONCLUSIONS.

A model of many goal-oriented stochastic automata is introduced for the study of a certain class of problems of operations research. That class is characterized by the existence of a definite mutual opposition in the behavior of the participants in the collective. In the model the goals of the participants are assumed to be known only up to certain indeterminate parameters for which there is no a priori information available. Such class of problems cannot be solved by the theory of N-person games. By means of that automata model a numerical solution to the behavioral dynamics and the equilibrium conditions of the participants in the collective can be obtained.

Besides the automata model can demonstrate the effect of certain interesting factors like participants psychology, stimulation laws, behavioral tactics, etc... on the mode of collective behavior. As example, the model is used for the simulation of the price formation process in a free market. The result obtained demonstrate the applicability of the present automata model.

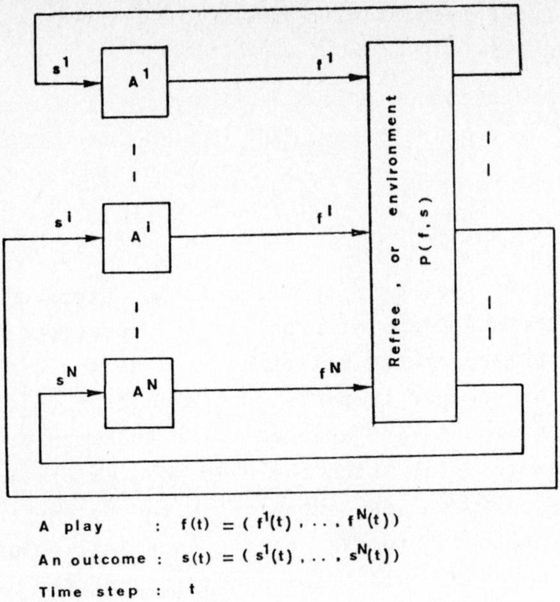

Fig. 1. N-automaton game.

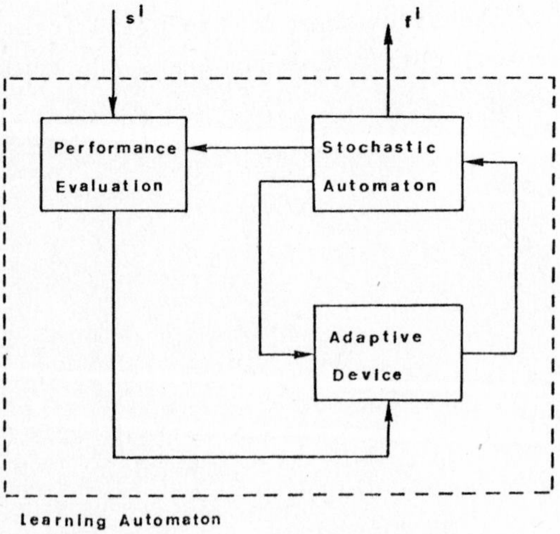

Fig. 2. Learning automaton.

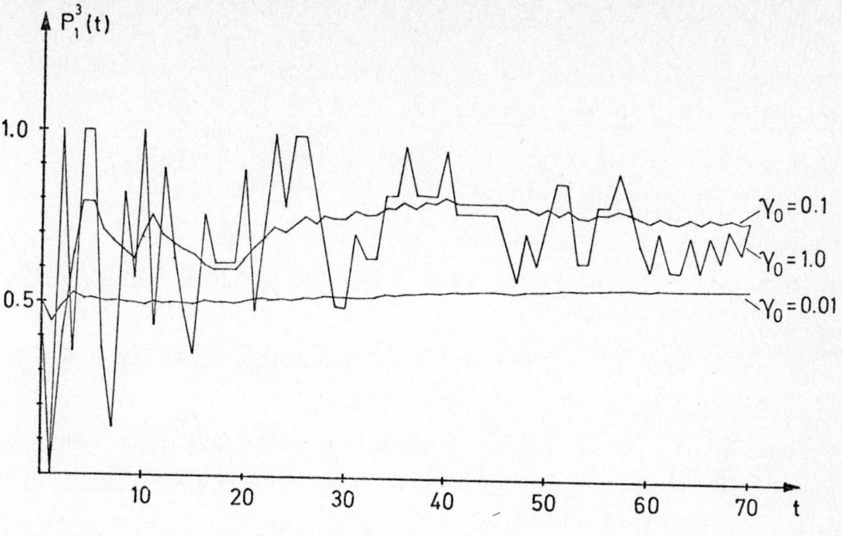

Fig. 3. Third seller first price probability versus time.

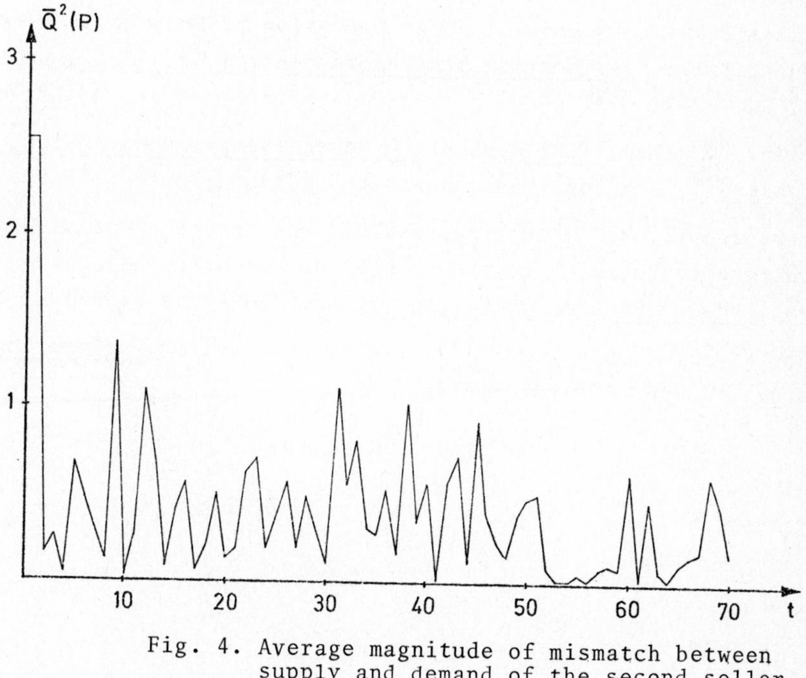

Fig. 4. Average magnitude of mismatch between supply and demand of the second seller commodity.

REFERENCES

1 L. Tsetlin, "On the Behavior of Finite Automata in Random Media", Automation and Remote Control, 22, p. 1210-1219 (1961).

2 V. Yu.Krylov, and M.L.Tsetlin., "Game between Automata", Automation and Remote Control, 24, pp. 889-899 (1962).

3 V.I.Varshavskii, and I.P.Vorontsova., "On the Behavior of Stochastic Automata with Variable Structure , Automation and Remote Control, 24, pp. 327-333 (1963).

4 K.S.Narendra, and M.L.A.Thathachar., "Learning Automata - A Survey", IEEE Trans., SMC-4, pp. 323-334 (1974).

5 Yu.D.Tenisberg., "Some Models of Collective Behavior in Dynamic Processes of Market Price Formation", Automation and Remote Control, n° 7, pp. 1140-1148 (1969).

6 A.V.Malishevskii, and Yu.D.Tenisberg., "One Class of Games Connected with Models of Collective Behavior," Automation and Remote Control, n° 11, pp. 1828-1837 (1969).

7 A.V.Malisheskii., "Models of Joint Operation of Many Goal-Oriented Elements,I,II, " Automation and Remote Control, n° 11,12, pp.1828-1845, 2020-2028 (1971).

8 S.Karlin., "Mathematical Methods in Games Theory, Programming, and Economics, I, Reading, Massachussetts, Addison-Wesley (1959).

9 V.I.Varshavskii, M.V.Meleshina, and V.T.Perekrest., "Use of Model of Collective Behavior in the Problem of Resources Allocation", Automation and Remote Control, n° 7, pp. 1107-1114 (1968).

10 L.P.Krylatykh., "On a Model of Collective Behavior",Engineering Cybernetics, pp. 803-808 (1972).

* * * *
* * *
* *
*

THE FORECAST AND PLANNING OF MANPOWER WITH IMPLICATIONS TO HIGHER EDUCATIONAL INSTITUTIONS-MATHEMATICAL MODELS

Moshe Friedman

Arizona State University
Tempe, Arizona 85281/USA

ABSTRACT: The article investigates the possibilities of planning a national higher educational system, namely the ways and the means wherein a desired output of the system is to be obtained from a given input. This examination generates guidelines whereupon a detailed mathematical model can be erected to effectuate the planning objectives. However, since the actual construction of the model involves a bulk of mathematical machinery and notations too burdensome to be comprised in the manuscript, the model itself is not developed here. Rather, a detailed exemplification of the planning operations is illustrated on a lilliputian system which serves as a demonstrative vehicle.

1. INTRODUCTION

This article considers the managerial aspects of a national higher educational system.

It is customary to think, on one hand, that its "raison d'etre" is to enable any knowledge pursuer the accomplishment of his wishes, thereby preserving a free educational process. On the other hand, the phenomenon of surplus and shortage in graduates of either this or that profession in the economy is widely recognized; a phenomenon that raises the question: Isn't it possible to regulate the process that transforms candidates to graduates so that these gaps will be diminished?

The latter viewpoint regards the higher educational system as an input/output system absorbing students as inputs and producing professionals as outputs.

The movement of students in the system is partly affected by factors that do not depend on the students themselves or their capabilities but on matters that may be controlled externally. These are composed of factors that directly influence the students, as: scholarships, help in securing accommodation and employment etc., and means affecting the absorption capacity of the various departments, like: numbers of teachers, classrooms, laboratories, etc.

Maneuvers in the allocation of these resources may yield distinct outputs to a same given input by routing the flow in the system with their aid. If there exists a desired output for the economy, it is possible to direct the flow towards it. The location of these means-and their appropriate utilization-which will enable the regulation of the movement in such a way that a desired output will be obtained from a given input, amounts to manpower planning in the higher educational institutions.

A survey of the possibilities to accomplish this goal with the aid of a mathematical model demonstrated on a simulative lilliputian educational system is the core of the present manuscript. The general approach supporting this review and employed to solve the manpower planning problem is the mathematical programming approach.

A voluminous literature exists on the subject of planning educational systems via mathematical models; see the detailed surveys of Correa [2], McNamara [3], Charnes et al. [1] and the series of papers published at the University of California at Berkeley [4], to mention only a few. The principal contribution of the present work is in developing a mathematical model of a higher educational system as an input-output system for professional manpower, and in utilizing this model for operating the possible planning means to regulate the students' flow in the system. This model constitutes an extension, a unification and an improvement compared to existing models in the literature which do not consider all the characteristics of this complicated manpower planning problem.

2. A LILLIPUTIAN PROBLEM.

We proceed to introduce a lilliputian problem that illuminates the ideas of the model. The presentation will be made without using explicit mathematical machinery. The lilliputian problem is computerized in the APL language and is available for free usage.

2.1 A Lilliputian System.

Consider a higher educational system consisting of two institutions. The first institution comprises two departments, an engineering department and an economics department. The engineering department confers one degree towards which one studies two studying units, whereas the economics department confers one degree towards which one studies one studying unit. The second institution contains one department, of engineering, which confers two consecutive degrees for each one of them one studies one studying unit.

The system includes, then, three departments and five studying units that, for the sake of convenience, will be enumerated from 1 to 3 and from 1 to 5, respectively, by their order of appearance. Thus, studying units 1, 2 are in department 1; studying unit 3 is in department 2; and studying units 4, 5 are in department 3.

A planning policy is operated on the system during 2 periods and keeps its impact for 3 periods, i.e., one period beyond the planning period itself. In real life, both a studying unit and a period may be interpreted as a year.

The description of the input-output activities of the system consists of two main elements, namely, the flow of students, and the changes in the inventory levels of the teaching facilities as a consequence of budgets allocations. A transformation which translates the quantities of teaching facilities to absorption capacity of students links the two parts. Hence, the process under study is: allocations of budgets which affect the quantities of teaching facilities. Those are translated to absorption capacity of students that with the numbers of enrolled students and the flow rates yield the output of the system.

2.2 The Flow of Students in the Lilliputian System.

Table 22.1 summarizes the flow of students to, within, and from the higher educational system. The table consists of three parts - from top to bottom - each giving a snapshot of the numbers of students in one period. Every part contains five rows that represent the studying units. The lines between the rows group the studying units in the appropriate departments. For instance, studying units 4, 5 are in department 3 (see column (1)). Column (2) shows the numbers of students in the system at the beginning of each period before absorbing the new students. For example, in the beginning of the second period, the number of students in the third studying unit before absorbing the new students is 2.55. Evidently, for period 1 this column discloses the numbers of students that are inherited from the pre-planning period, and serves as a known initial condition. Column (3) gives the numbers of the newly enrolled, qualified students. These numbers are known via statistical forecasts. Column (4) comprises the numbers of students that can be

Table 22.1

The Flow of Students in the Lilliputian System

Period t=1

(1) i	(2) $n^1 = k^0$	(3) e^1	(4) g^1	(5) k^1	(6) m^1	(7) n^2	(8) ℓ^1	(9) d^1	(10) $\ell^1 - d^1$	(11) α_1^1	(12) α_2^1	(13) α^1	(14) $\alpha^1 \lvert \ell^1 - d^1 \rvert$
1	2	10	3	1	3	0.96	0	0	0	0	0	0	0
2	6	0	7	0	6	3.16	4.2	3	1.2	3	1	1	1.2
3	3	7	7.5	4.5	7.5	2.55	3.6	2	1.6	4	2	2	3.2
4	1	8	3.6	2.6	3.6	1.01	2.06	3	-0.94	3	2	3	2.82
5	4	11	6	2	6	3.76	2.6	4	-1.4	2	3	2	2.8
													10.02

Period t=2

(1) i	(2) n^2	(3) e^2	(4) g^2	(5) k^2	(6) m^2	(7) n^3	(8) ℓ^2	(9) d^2	(10) $\ell^2 - d^2$	(11) α_1^2	(12) α_2^2	(13) α^2	(14) $\alpha^2 \lvert \ell^2 - d^2 \rvert$
1	0.96	8	6	5.04	6	0.50	0	0	0	0	0	0	0
2	3.16	1	14	1	4.16	4.88	3.7	5	-1.3	4	1	4	5.2
3	2.55	9	11.1	8.55	11.1	4.63	7.48	6	1.48	5	1	1	1.48
4	1.01	5	8	5	6.01	0.50	2.76	4	-1.24	2	1	2	2.48
5	3.76	8	8	4.24	8	3.73	5.36	4	1.36	3	4	4	5.44
													14.60

Period t=3

(1) i	(2) n^3	(3) e^3	(4) g^3	(5) k^3	(6) m^3	(7) n^4	(8) ℓ^3	(9) d^3	(10) $\ell^3 - d^3$	(11) α_1^3	(12) α_2^3	(13) α^3	(14) $\alpha^3 \lvert \ell^3 - d^3 \rvert$
1	0.50	12	6.8	6.3	6.8		0	0	0	0	0	0	0
2	4.88	3	25.2	3	7.88		7.18	7	0.18	2	3	3	0.54
3	4.63	14	12.3	7.67	12.3		10.80	11	-0.20	4	5	4	0.80
4	0.50	15	9	8.5	9		4.25	5	-0.75	5	1	5	3.75
5	3.73	6	9	5.27	9		6.13	8	-1.87	6	2	6	11.22
													16.31
													40.93

absorbed by the system according to the quantities of its teaching facilities and according to the intensity of their utilization. This column, namely the "absorption capacity" of the system, is controllable by the planning policy as will be explicated in the sequel.

Column (5) contains the numbers of the new actually absorbed students in every period. They depend on the system's absorption capacity, on the number of students found in the studying units at the beginning of the period, and on the number of enrolled students. The number of vacancies in each studying unit is the difference between the corresponding numbers in Columns (4), (2), whereas the numbers of the qualified, newly enrolled students is shown in Column (3). Hence, the entry in Column (5) is the smaller of these two values. For instance, the absorption capacity of studying unit 4 in period 1 is 3.6. Since there is already 1 student in the studying unit inherited from the past (Column (2)), it is possible to absorb in it at most 2.6 students out of 8 enrolled (Column (5)). On the other hand, the absorption capacity of the same studying unit in period t=2 is 8 students (Column (4)), and the number of students from previous periods in it is 1.01 (Column (2)). Thus, the number of absorbable students is 6.99. However, there are only 5 newly enrolled students (Column (3)). Consequently, these 5 are accepted (Column (5)). Obviously, this 5 is an upper bound and it is possible to accept only part of the enrolled students. In the first example there is a surplus of enrolled students, and 5.4 of them will be left out. In the second example there is a deficiency in qualified, enrolled students and 1.99 studying places are left vacant after the absorption of the new students. Column (6) introduces the total numbers of students in the system in each period; i.e., the sum of Columns (2) and (5).

Column (7) includes the numbers of students to be in the system at the beginning of the next period before the absorption of the newly enrolled students and, actually, it is identical, by definition, to Column (2) of the next part. The entries of this column are obtained by transitions of students from all the previous time periods. Column (7) in period t=2 was figured out, for instance, from transitions of students from Columns (5) of periods t=1 and t=2 in addition to transitions from Column (2) of period t=1. Column (7) in the bottom was obtained from transitions of students from Columns (5) of all parts of Table 22.1 in addition to transitions from Column (2) of the top. For example, the number 4.88 in studying unit 2 of Column (7) in period t=2 is computed in the following manner:

$$0.4\times1+0.1\times4.5+0.7\times5.04+0.1\times5 = 4.88.$$

The transition rates (the decimal fractions) of students in the system are obtained through statistical estimates which are based upon the movement of students in it in periods preceding the planning horizon and which are not found in Table 22.1. Tracing the calculation it is apparent that, from Column (2) of period t=1 no student was transferred, 0.4 of the students of studying unit 1 of Column (5) of period t=1 and 0.1 of the students of studying unit 3 of this column moved to studying unit 2 in period t=3, 0.7 of the students of studying unit 1 and 0.1 of the students of studying unit 4 of Column (5) of period t=2 moved also to studying unit 2 in period t=3. It is conspicuous that the possible transitions are the most diversified ones; progressing in studies, tarrying in one studying unit more than one period, altering studying orbits, dropping out, etc.

Column (8) gives the numbers of graduates at the end of every period, i.e., the system's output. It is also obtained, similar to Column (7), through graduating rates of students from all previous Columns (5) of the Table, including the section in which the particular Column (8) is located, in addition to graduating rates of students from Column (2) of the top section. These are based upon graduating rates in periods preceding the planning time and are not found in the Table.

The entry 3.6, for instance, in studying unit 3 of Column (8) of period t=1 was obtained as follows:

$$0.6\times 3+0.4\times 4.5 = 3.6 \quad .$$

Namely, 0.6 of the students of studying unit 3 of Column (2) of period t=1 and 0.4 of the students of studying unit 3 of Column (5) of the same period graduated at the end of period t=1 in studying unit 3. The first component of Column (8) is identically 0 since studying unit 1 does not confer any degrees.

Column (9) includes the desired numbers of graduates that ought to be produced by the system. It is estimated according to the predicted demand of the economy for academic manpower. Column (10) gives the differences between the actual output and the desired one. A negative sign stands for a deficiency in graduates of the profession whereas a positive sign stands for a surplus.

Columns (11), (12) introduce the penalties incurred for a deficiency, surplus of one graduate, respectively. These penalties represent the losses of the economy that are implied by dissatisfying its demand to academic manpower. Note that they vary with the studying unit, with surplus and shortage, and with the period as well. For instance, the penalty for surplus of one graduate in studying unit 3 in period t=1 is 2, whereas the same penalty in period t=2 is 1. In period t=1, the penalty for shortage in the graduates of studying unit 3 is 4.

Column (13) gives the relevant penalties of the current case according to the signs of the numbers in Column (10).

Column (14) contains the total penalty for either shortage or surplus in each studying unit, i.e., the products of the corresponding numbers in Columns (10) and (13). Its sum is the total penalty incurred for either surplus or shortage in graduates against the desired numbers in every period. The sum of these penalties, for all the periods, is found in Column (14) at the bottom of Table 22.1.

The total incurred penalty is 40.93. This sum is implied by Column (4) of Table 22.1, which stems from certain allocations of the budgets. Distinct allocations will yield different entries in Column (4) and thereby, a different penalty amount.

The objective of the planning model is to detect that allocation of the budgets that will minimize the total penalty in the period during which the system is subject to the planning policy.

2.3 <u>The Growth of the Absorption Capacity of the Lilliputian System as a Result of the Allocations of the Development Budgets</u>.

We shall commence with the exemplification of the impact of the development budgets on the growth of the inventory levels of the teaching facilities of the system. The effect of this budget is a fundamental one and is complemented by that of the current budget.

Table 23.1 summarizes the information about the growth of the inventory levels of the teaching facilities of the system. The table is partitioned into 3 parts, each of them devoted to one period. Every part consists of 6 rows which correspond to the teaching facilities. The lines between the rows group them in the appropriate departments. For instance, facilities 4, 5 and 6 serve in deparment 3, which in Table 22.1 contains studying units 4 and 5 (see Column (1)).

Column (2) shows the initial inventory levels of the teaching facilities in each time period. These inventory levels stem from previous periods and hence in t=1, this column gives the quantities inherited from the preplanning time. The initial inventory level of teaching facility 4 in the beginning of period t=2 is, for example, 3.

Column (3) comprises the numbers of money units that were allotted for investments in teaching facilities in every time period. For instance, in period t=1, out of a total sum of 41 money units the planner has allotted 7 units to teaching facility 5. This allocation is the controlled factor that, via a sequence of stages, establishes the total incurred penalty, namely 40.93 of Table 22.1. The goal of the optimization problem is to find the allocation that will yield the minimal penalty.

Columns (4), (5) and (6) introduce the incremented quantities that are added to the inventory levels of the teaching facilities in every period as a consequence of an investment of 1 money unit in periods t=1, t=2, t=3, respectively. Therefore, an investment of 1 money unit in teaching facility 2 in period t=1 will increase the inventory level in 0.2 units of it in period t=2 (row 2 in Column (4) of the middle part of Table 23.1). Obviously, materializations of investments from later time periods are identically zero.

Columns (7), (8), (9) give the increments to the inventory levels of the teaching facilities in the appropriate period as resulted from the development budget's money units allotted to them in periods t=1, t=2, t=3, respectively. The number 1.4 in row 5 of Column (7) of period t=2 is the increment to the inventory level of teaching facility 5 in the beginning of period t=2 as a consequence of an

Table 23.1

The Growth of the Inventory Levels of Teaching Facilities of the Lilliputian System as a Result of the Allocation of the Development Budgets

Period t=1

(1) j	(2) $\underline{c}^0$	(3) $\underline{y}^1$	(4) $\underline{h}^{11}$	(5) $\underline{h}^{12}$	(6) $\underline{h}^{13}$	(7) $\underline{\Delta c}^{11}$	(8) $\underline{\Delta c}^{12}$	(9) $\underline{\Delta c}^{13}$	(10) $\underline{c}^1$	(11) $\underline{f}^1$	(12) $\underline{x}^1$
1	1	5	0	0	0	0	0	0	1	0.5	2
2	1	5	0.2	0	0	1	0	0	2	0.4	5
3	4	10	0.1	0	0	1	0	0	5	0.5	10
4	3	10	0	0	0	0	0	0	3	0.2	15
5	2	7	0.3	0	0	2.1	0	0	4.1	0.4	10.25
6	1	4	0.2	0	0	0.8	0	0	1.8	0.3	6
		41									48.25

Period t=2

(1) j	(2) $\underline{c}^1$	(3) $\underline{y}^2$	(4) $\underline{h}^{21}$	(5) $\underline{h}^{22}$	(6) $\underline{h}^{23}$	(7) $\underline{\Delta c}^{21}$	(8) $\underline{\Delta c}^{22}$	(9) Δc^{23}	(10) $\underline{c}^2$	(11) $\underline{f}^2$	(12) $\underline{x}^2$
1	1	8	0.2	0	0	1	0	0	2	0.5	4
2	2	3	0.1	0.2	0	0.5	0.6	0	3.1	0.4	7.75
3	5	4	0.2	0.1	0	2	0.4	0	7.4	0.5	14.8
4	3	5	0.1	0	0	1	0	0	4	0.2	20
5	4.1	3	0.2	0.3	0	1.4	0.9	0	6.4	0.4	16
6	1.8	10	0.1	0.2	0	0.4	2	0	4.2	0.3	14
		33									76.55

Period t=3

(1) j	(2) $\underline{c}^2$	(3) $\underline{y}^3$	(4) $\underline{h}^{31}$	(5) $\underline{h}^{32}$	(6) $\underline{h}^{33}$	(7) $\underline{\Delta c}^{31}$	(8) $\underline{\Delta c}^{32}$	(9) $\underline{\Delta c}^{33}$	(10) $\underline{c}^3$	(11) $\underline{f}^3$	(12) $\underline{x}^3$
1	2	0	0	0.2	0	0	1.6	0	3.6	0.5	7.2
2	3.1	0	0	0.1	0.2	0	0.3	0	3.4	0.4	8.5
3	7.4	0	0	0.2	0.1	0	0.8	0	8.2	0.5	16.4
4	4	0	0	0.1	0	0	0.5	0	4.5	0.2	22.4
5	6.4	0	0	0.2	0.3	0	0.6	0	7	0.4	17.5
6	4.2	0	0	0.1	0.2	0	1	0	5.2	0.3	17.3
		0									89.30
		74									214.10

investment of 7 money units in period t=1 (row 5 of column (3) of the top part of Table 23.1). These 7 money units multiplied by 0.2 (row 5 of Column (4) in the middle part) will bring about a growth of 1.4.

Column (10), which is the sum of Columns (2), (7), (8) and (9), discloses the current inventory levels of teaching facilities in each period. Column (10) of every part is, in fact, Column (2) of the next one.

Column (11) presents the quantities of teaching facilities that are maintained during the relevant period by 1 money unit. Consequently, Column (12), which is Column (10) divided by Column (11), gives the necessary amounts of money units needed to keep up the current inventory levels of the teaching facilities.

It is left now to translate the inventory levels of the teaching facilities of Table 23.1 to absorption capacity of students (Column (4) of Table 22.1).

We shall demonstrate how the entry in row 1 of Column (4) of period t=1 of Table 22.1 was calculated. Department 1 uses teaching facilities 1 and 2. It was decided that on the account of one unit of teaching facility 1, 3 students can be absorbed, and each unit of teaching facility 2 can absorb 2 students. These figures establish the extent of the intensity of the utilization of the teaching facilities and cannot be found in the Tables. It follows that according to the inventory level of teaching facility 1 owned by department 1 in period t=1 (row 1 of Column (10) in the top of Table 23.1) it can absorb 3 students whereas according to the inventory level of teaching facility 2 owned by it in this period (row 2 in the same column), it can absorb 4 students. The final absorption capacity is the smallest over all the teaching facilities; i.e., the smaller of the numbers 3 and 4, namely 3. Teaching facility 1 is then the bottleneck in period t=1 to students' absorption by department 1. In the same manner the transformation maps the inventory levels of teaching facilities to absorption capacity of students for all the studying units.

We have obtained that a certain allocation of 74 money units of the development budget during the planning period that caused a certain allocation of 214.10 money units of the current budget - which is not yet taken as controllable - incurred a total penalty of 40.93 money units for deviations of graduates' numbers from the demand of the economy. Our task is to find the allocation that will minimize the penalty.

2.4 The Impact of the Current Budget on the Inventory Levels of Teaching Facilities of the Lilliputian System.

The values of Table 22.1 were calculated based on the assumption that the required sums of the current budget needed to maintain the growing inventory levels of the teaching facilities are automatically allotted. We shall now drop this supposition and incorporate the current budget into the control means.

Table 24.1 summarizes the modifications that occur in the quantities of the facilities due to the controlled allocations of the current budgets. The missing columns are identical to those of Table 23.1.

The pattern of Table 24.1 is essentially the same as that of Table 23.1. The meanings of its first five columns, from the left, are identical to the corresponding ones of Table 23.1 according to their title number. The entries themselves in the first four columns from the left are equal to those of Table 23.1. The distinction lies in the fifth column (with title number (12)), namely the current budget column. It shows the amounts of money units that were allotted for maintaining the inventory levels of the teaching facilities. These allow only the maintenance of the inventory levels that are given in the column with title number (13). The values of the last column are obtained as products of the corresponding numbers in its two preceding columns. For instance, the allocation of 14 money units to a current maintenance of teaching facility 5 in period t=2, instead of 16 as before, yielded a decrease in its active inventory level from 6.4 to 5.6 units.

The inventory levels of teaching facilities of Column (13) are translated to absorption capacity of students in the same manner that was outlined above.

Due to the lessening in these inventory levels, some modifications will occur in Columns (2), (5) and (8) of Table 22.1. The reason is that the students' absorption

Table 24.1

The Impact of the Current Budget on the Inventory Levels of Teaching Facilities of the Lilliputian System.

Period t=1

(1) j	(2) $\underline{c}^0$	(10) $\underline{c}^1$	(11) $\underline{f}^1$	(12) $\underline{x}^1$	(13) $\underline{c}_1^1$
1	1	1	0.5	2	1
2	1	2	0.4	5	2
3	4	5	0.5	10	5
4	3	3	0.2	15	3
5	2	4.1	0.4	10.25	4.1
6	1	1.8	0.3	6	1.8
				48.25	

Period t=2

(1) j	(2) $\underline{c}^1$	(10) $\underline{c}^2$	(11) $\underline{f}^2$	(12) $\underline{x}^2$	(13) $\underline{c}_1^2$
1	1	2	0.5	4	2
2	2	3.1	0.4	6	2.4
3	5	7.4	0.5	12	6
4	3	4	0.2	20	4
5	4.1	6.4	0.4	14	5.6
6	1.8	4.2	0.3	13	3.9
				69	

Period t=3

(1) j	(2) $\underline{c}^2$	(10) $\underline{c}^3$	(11) $\underline{f}^3$	(12) $\underline{x}^3$	(13) $\underline{c}_1^3$
1	2	3.6	0.5	7	3.5
2	3.1	3.4	0.4	6	2.4
3	7.4	8.2	0.5	13	6.5
4	4	4.5	0.2	21	4.2
5	6.4	7	0.4	15	6
6	4.2	5.2	0.3	14	4.2
				76	
				193.25	

capacity of the studying units is changed and consequently the numbers of actually absorbed students and the numbers of graduates have changed as well. These modifications are summarized in Table 24.2 and obviously will affect also the total incurred penalty which is now 55.28.

We have obtained that the same allocation of the 74 money units of the development budget during the planning period and a certain allocation of a trimmed current budget of 193.25 money units instead of 214.10, caused an increase from 40.93 to 55.28 in the total penalty. The purpose of the optimization procedure in this case is to point out the allocation of the development and current budgets that will minimize the total penalty.

2.5 Feedbacks in the Lilliputian System.

The illustration of the feedback phenomena will be done only for period t=1. The data is taken from Tables 22.1, 23.1 and is based on the assumption that the current budget is not subject to control.

In addition to the teaching facilities of Column (10) of Table 23.1, a certain portion of the students themselves, Columns (2) and (5) of Table 22.1, serve in academic positions as teaching assistants, thus being considered as part of the teaching facilities contributing to the absorption capacity of the studying units. This phenomenon will be named "the internal feedback". The "external feedback" will be termed after graduates that join the academic staff. These phenomena may phenomena may constitute a considerable share of the absorption capacity and cannot be ignored in delineating the input-output activities of the system. Since now Columns (4) and (5) of Table 22.1 mutually establish each other, the only way to determine them is rather by a solution of a system of equations and not by the direct method that was applied above. The formulation of the set of equations is quite cumbersome and is beyond the scope of this article.

Table 24.2

The Modifications in Table 22.1 Due to Cuts in the Current Budgets of the Lilliputian System.

Period t=1

(1) i	(2) $\underline{n}^1=\underline{k}^0$	(5) $\underline{k}^1$	(8) $\underline{\ell}^1$
1	2	1	0
2	6	0	4.2
3	3	4.5	3.6
4	1	2.6	2.06
5	4	2	2.6

Period t=2

(1) i	(2) $\underline{n}^2$	(5) $\underline{k}^2$	(8) $\underline{\ell}^2$
1	0.96	3.84	0
2	3.16	1	3.7
3	2.55	6.45	6.22
4	1.01	5	2.76
5	3.76	4.24	5.356

Period t=3

(1) i	(2) $\underline{n}^3$	(5) $\underline{k}^3$	(8) $\underline{\ell}^3$
1	0.384	4.416	0
2	4.038	3	6.338
3	3.674	6.076	7.927
4	0.384	8.016	4.008
5	3.732	4.668	5.773

Table 25.1

The Flow of Students in the Lilliputian System With Feedbacks

Period t=1

(1) i	(2) $\underline{n}^1\equiv\underline{k}^0$	(3) $\underline{k}^1$	(4) $Q^{20}\underline{k}^0$	(5) $Q^{21}\underline{k}^1$	(6) $\underline{n}^2$	(7) $P^{10}\underline{k}^1$	(8) $P^{11}\underline{k}^1$	(9) $\underline{\ell}^1$
1	2	2	0.50	0.66	1.16	0	0	0
2	6	0	2.40	0.76	0.76	2.94	0	2.94
3	3	7	1.10	2.30	2.30	1.44	1.96	3.40
4	1	2.6	0.20	0.96	0.96	0.45	1.40	1.85
5	4	5	2.70	2.26	2.26	4.80	0.75	5.55

Table 25.1 presents the modifications in Table 22.1 which happen due to the feedbacks. Columns (1) and (2) are identical to those of Table 22.1. Column (3) contains the numbers of absorbed students (the column which corresponds to Column (5) of Table 22.1) that will be obtained after the solution of the system of equations. Columns (4), (5) show the numbers of students to be in the system at the beginning of period t=2 out of Columns (2), (3), respectively, while Column (6) is their sum; i.e., the corresponding column to Column (7) of Table 22.1. The decomposition of Column (6) as the sum of Columns (4) and (5) is now necessary since the internal feedback rates, namely students' rates serving in teaching positions, for period t=2 are derived from the components of the numbers of students in the system sorted by their absorption period, Columns (4) and (5) of Table 25.1, in addition to the currently absorbed students.

Columns (7), (8) give the numbers of graduates in the end of period t=1 which are implied by Columns (2), (3), respectively, after discarding the external feedback, namely graduates that join the academic staff.

Column (9) introduces the numbers of graduates of the system which are directed to the economy to satisfy its demand for academic manpower; i.e., the corresponding column to Column (8) of Table 22.1. Trivially, it is the sum of Columns (7) and (8). The external feedback rates in our case show, for instance, that only 0.8, 0.7 of the graduates in the end of period t=1 that come from the absorbed students of Columns (2) and (3), respectively, are directed to meet the economy's needs for academic manpower. The rest returned and joined the system as part of the teaching facilities. The rates 0.7 and 0.8 are not found in Table 25.1 and are estimated by statistical methods based upon past observations.

The total incurred penalty in this period for surplus and shortage in academic manpower is 11.08. Again, the optimization procedure must reveal the allocation of budgets that will minimize this penalty.

In case we assume that the current budget is also controllable, the feedback's rates are not constants but depend on its allocation. This extension highly complicates the problem and will not be demonstrated here.

2.6 A Summary of the Budgetary Activities of the Lilliputian System

Table 26.1 summarizes the budgetary activities of the Lilliputian System during the three periods, see Column (1). Column (2) exhibits the total amounts of the development budgets in each period. Columns (3), (4) give the total amounts of the current budget needed to keep up the growing inventory levels of teaching facilities, the penalties incurred for either surplus or shortage in graduates, respectively.

Table 26.1

Summary of the Budgetary Activities of the Lilliputian System

(1) t	(2) $\bar{y}^t$	(3) $\bar{x}^t$	(4) u^t	(5) $\bar{x}^t$	(6) u^t	(7) u^t
1	41	48.25	10.02	48.25	10.02	11.08
2	33	76.55	14.60	69	13.34	12.43
3	0	89.30	16.31	76	31.92	
	74	214.10	40.93	193.25	55.28	

Columns (5), (6) follow the same pattern as Columns (3), (4), respectively, except that the current budget is subject to control. Column (7) shows the penalties in case there are feedbacks and the current budget is provided to maintain the full growing inventory levels of teaching facilities.

When the current budget is not controllable, the optimization's task is to find the allocation of the development budget that will yield the minimal value of the penalty. In case there is a possibility to cut the current budget as a control means, the optimization procedure ought to detect the allocation of the development as well as the current budgets for the sake of obtaining the minimal penalty. Similar cases exist when the feedback phenomena of the system are considered. A detailed technical formulation of the mathematical model and the optimization procedure - which may be either linear or not, depending on the assumptions concerning the functions of the model - is rather involved. It is strongly hoped that the lilliputian system has succeeded in conveying the principal ideas, and has acutely pinpointed the vertices on which intelligent, controlled operations may be implemented thereby enabling the planning of a national higher educational system.

2.7 Overview

The starting point of the planning model is the controlled allocations of the budgets. This allocation establishes the inventory levels of the teaching facilities. These are translated to absorption capacity of students. The absorption capacity, the numbers of students that are in the system from previous years, and the flow from outside determine the numbers of actually absorbed students. The flow rates of students in the system will yield the numbers of graduates. A comparison between the graduates' numbers and the economy's demand appropriately weighted gives the total penalty incurred for shortage or surplus in academic manpower. The goal of the optimization procedure of the planning model is to single out the allocation of budgets that will minimize the total penalty.

3. REFERENCES

1. Charnes, A. and Cooper, W. W. and Niehaus, R. J. "Studies in Manpower Planning", Office of Civilian Manpower Management, Department of the Navy, Washington, D. C., July 1972.
2. Correa, H. "A Survey of Mathematical Models in Educational Planning", OECD Report, Paris, 1967.
3. McNamara, J. F., "Mathematical Programming Models in Educational Planning", Review of Research, University of Oregon, 1971.
4. Research Projects in University Administration, Ford Grant #68-267, University of California at Berkeley, 1968-1973.

ETABLISSEMENT AUTOMATIQUE DES TABLEAUX DE MARCHE ET FEUILLES DE SERVICE DANS UN RESEAU DE TRANSPORT

Robert FAURE
Professeur associé au Conservatoire national des Arts et Métiers
Conseiller scientifique à la Régie autonome des transports parisiens
53 ter quai des Grands-Augustins Paris (6e) France

J'aborde devant vous une question concrète fort complexe ; le résumé qui est entre vos mains ne donne d'ailleurs qu'une idée assez faible de cette complexité.

Il s'agit, en fait, d'un problème essentiellement pratique, autour duquel tournent, depuis que l'ordinateur existe, et dans la plupart des pays, les informaticiens des entreprises de transport public, sans que jamais, avant 1973/74, on n'ait pu annoncer des résultats effectivement opérationnels.

Plusieurs équipes de la RATP ont travaillé durant cinq ou six ans avant de fournir ces premiers et importants résultats, mais il reste encore beaucoup à faire et elles continuent d'oeuvrer pour compléter et perfectionner leurs acquis.

I - LE PROBLEME GENERAL

Permettez-moi d'aborder rapidement le problème.

Dans toute entreprise de transport urbain, lorsqu'on se propose de répondre de la manière la plus rationnelle à la demande de la clientèle, compte tenu des moyens en personnel et matériel disponibles, surgissent de nombreux problèmes que la recherche opérationnelle et le calcul automatique peuvent aider à résoudre.

Les méthodes de collecte des éléments statistiques nécessaires sur l'environnement (demande de transport, en fonction de la date et de l'heure, conditions de circulation pour les véhicules utilisant des sites banalisés, etc.) ne seront pas décrites ici, ni leur utilisation en vue de définir la configuration (ou la restructuration) d'un réseau, puis la mise en service (détermination du nombre des véhicules, des fréquences, de l'effectif du personnel, etc.).

Mais une fois ces décisions prises, grâce à des méthodes appropriées, la direction de l'exploitation se trouve devant une série de problèmes (figure 1), qui doivent être résolus successivement, dans l'ordre précisé ci-dessous.

CHAINE D'EXPLOITATION D UNE LIGNE D'AUTOBUS

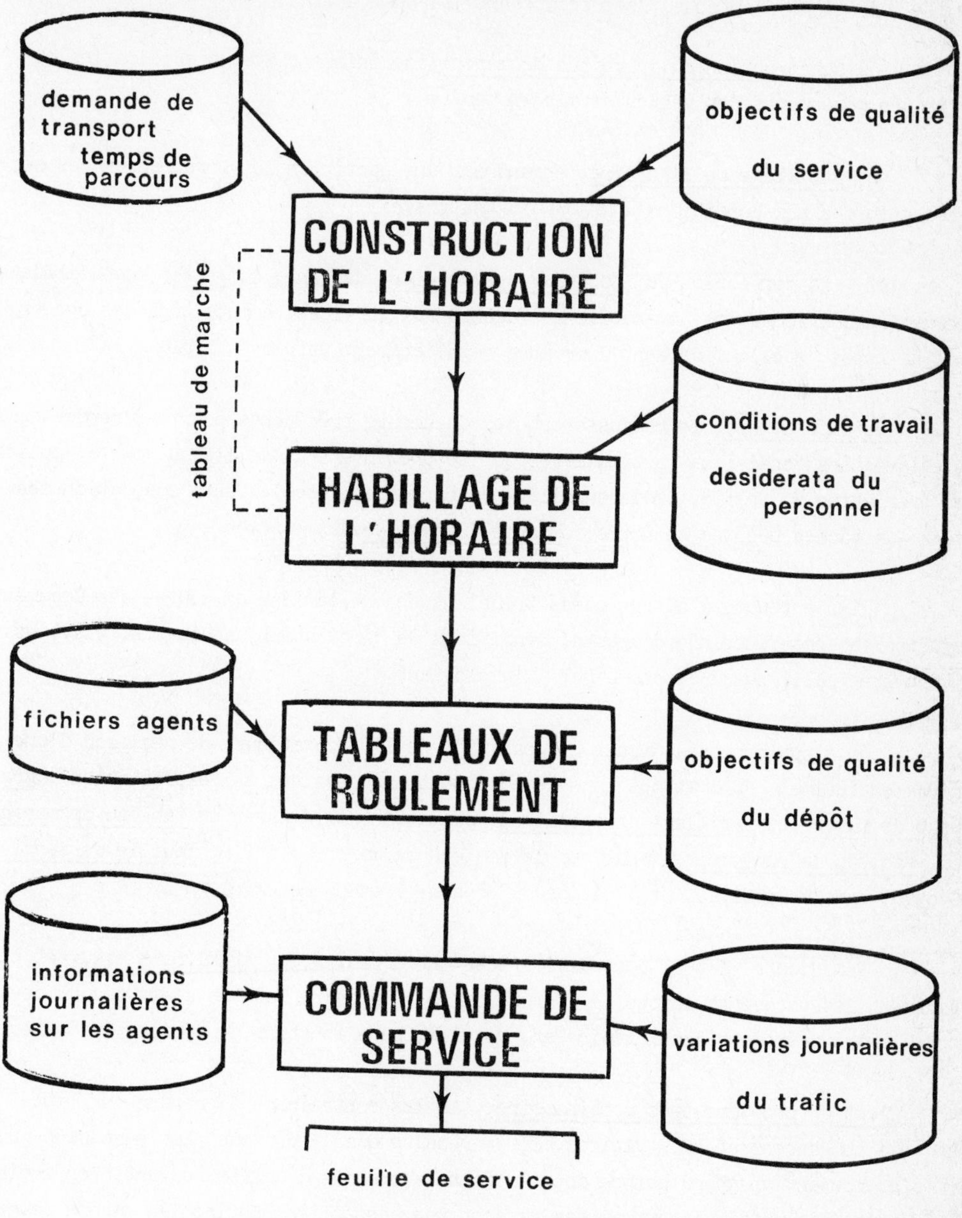

Figure 1

1 - Prévisionnellement (c'est-à-dire de un à trois mois à l'avance)

1.1 - L'établissement du tableau de marche de l'unité d'exploitation (par exemple, une ligne d'autobus), se décomposant lui-même en :

a) Construction du graphique de marche, définissant avec précision les horaires des mouvements des véhicules mis en oeuvre ;

b) Habillage de l'horaire, engendrant une partition des horaires en des services conformes aux conditions statutaires de travail.

1.2 - La confection du tableau de roulement destiné, comme son nom l'indique, à permettre l'affectation nominative des agents aux services, compte tenu des congés, jours de repos, etc. qui doivent leur être régulièrement attribués.

2 - Quotidiennement, le réajustement des documents précédents pour les rendre compatibles avec les conditions particulières qui se présentent la veille du jour d'application (variation du trafic, indisponibilité du personnel, etc.). Cette adaptation des moyens aux tâches réelles se nomme commande du service.

Bien entendu, d'autres aléas troublent encore la mise en oeuvre des documents réajustés (absence inopinée d'agents, conditions de circulation, accidents, etc.) et doivent être palliés sur-le-champ par l'exploitant.

On s'est proposé, depuis l'apparition de l'informatique, de réaliser d'une manière entièrement automatique tous les documents nécessaires à l'exploitation : graphique de marche et habillage des horaires, permettant de dresser le tableau de marche ; puis, tableau de roulement, fondé sur le tableau de marche ; enfin, feuille de service, prévoyant dans le détail l'utilisation du personnel et du matériel.

Sans doute a-t-on poursuivi l'idée que l'ordinateur établirait mieux et plus rapidement les documents jusque là confectionnés à la main. Mais on s'est trouvé devant un problème extrêmement combinatoire et, de plus, sans fonction économique évidente.

- C'est un problème très combinatoire, car les contraintes à prendre en compte sont très nombreuses et très variées. Il en résulte d'ailleurs que plusieurs sous-problèmes comportent un grand nombre de solutions, alors que d'autres peuvent n'en avoir pas du tout, si certaines contraintes ne sont pas assouplies. Enfin, les divers sous-problèmes en lesquels se décompose le problème général ne sont pas indépendants et rétroagissent même les uns sur les autres.

- C'est un problème sans fonction économique directe. Les objectifs vagues exposés plus haut n'ont pu être précisés dans le détail : en remplaçant les millions de coups de crayon par une procédure automatique, bien plus qu'une économie sur l'établissement des documents, c'est la recherche d'une plus grande maniabilité, d'une rapidité accrue et d'une nouvelle souplesse qui semble prévaloir.

De plus, à la RATP du moins, les moyens étant définis à l'avance, ce ne sont pas des économies de personnel ou de matériel qu'on espère en automatisant la réalisation des documents nécessaires à l'exploitation. Tout au plus pourrait-on envisager de diminuer le "temps supplémentaire" accordé aux agents pour certaines tâches de service (dont l'amplitude dépasse douze heures, par exemple).

En fait, on s'est aperçu assez rapidement, qu'il importait d'obtenir de "bons tableaux" de service, ce qui imposait de se renseigner sur les aspirations des agents et d'établir une "fonction économique" à partir des desiderata du personnel. De bonnes âmes étaient bien venues prôner le contraire : de tels problèmes, murmuraient-elles, se résolvent aisément; puisqu'il n'y a pas de fonction économique, n'importe quel recouvrement exact convient ; bref, nous étions bien bêtes de ne pas emprunter "le chemin de ronde" de la première simulation venue. Bien que les responsables des équipes ne soient pas aujourd'hui convaincus du rôle essentiel qu'elle a joué dans les progrès qu'ils ont accomplis, je maintiens que la laborieuse détermination de la fonction économique actuellement utilisée a donné un contenu, j'oserais même dire sa véritable signification, au problème, et, par là-même, a contribué à le transformer en un problème bien posé.

De la même façon, bien qu'aujourd'hui les auteurs des programmes prétendent avoir rapidement assimilé la structure du problème, il me suffira, pour les rappeler à plus de réalisme, d'évoquer les longs mois qui ont été nécessaires pour qu'ils y soient véritablement plongés et à même de distinguer l'essentiel de l'accessoire, les règles générales des cas particuliers et de me faire l'écho des incertitudes qu'ils manifestent parfois sur la pérennité des méthodes, pour le cas où interviendraient des modifications drastiques des conditions de travail.

Pour revenir à l'optimisation proprement dite, l'auditeur se rendra compte tout à l'heure qu'il a été nécessaire d'essayer de nombreux algorithmes, plus ou moins classiques, puis de modifier les plus adaptés d'entre eux pour venir à bout de chacun des sous-problèmes. Il verra aussi que l'aspect informatique n'est pas du tout négligeable. D'abord parce qu'il existe, comme on l'a déjà dit, des liens considérables entre les divers sous-problèmes (et même des retours en arrière) ; ensuite, parce qu'il est indispensable d'écrire d'excellents programmes lorsque ceux-ci doivent servir d'une manière répétitive, comme c'est le cas ici.

Rappelons enfin que, dans cet exposé, nous nous limiterons à la confection des documents d'exploitation pour des lignes d'autobus (chaque ligne étant traitée à part) et n'aborderons pas les problèmes analogues, mais plus lourds encore, concernant des lignes de métropolitain ou des réseaux entiers.

II - DETERMINATION DES INTERVALLES THEORIQUES OPTIMAUX

Tout commence, dans la chaîne de sous-problèmes que nous allons envisager, par la détermination des intervalles théoriques optimaux, c'est-à-dire le calcul de la fréquence optimale à partir des éléments statistiques sur la demande de transport et l'environnement, compte tenu des :

- désutilités ressenties par les clients ;
- charges d'exploitation.

a) Il y a sept ou huit ans, des stagiaires de l'Ecole des Mines de Paris s'étaient attaqués au problème, avec l'aide de cadres de la RATP [9].

De lointains aboutissements de cette recherche sont les modèles AUTOMEDON et ALKIMEDON [10], dont les usages sont plutôt réservés au long terme (choix de types d'autobus) ; de tels modèles prennent en compte les charges d'exploitation des lignes et les coûts d'attente des voyageurs.

A_i, B_i, et C_i étant des coûts unitaires constants pour toute période i et I_i, l'intervalle à cette même période, on minimise la fonction :

$$F = \sum_{i=1}^{p} \underbrace{A_i \, I_i}_{\text{coût d'attente}} + \underbrace{B_i + \frac{C_i}{I_i}}_{\text{coût d'exploitation}} ,$$

sous les contraintes suivantes : 1) tout voyageur doit accéder au premier véhicule qui se présente ; 2) le nombre d'autobus à chaque période est borné par le nombre d'autobus utilisés à la pointe.

b) En mai 1972, F.J. Salzborn [11] a proposé un modèle s'inspirant des résultats de G.F. Newell [8] et les concrétisant pour une ligne réelle. Il revient à minimiser, sous certaines contraintes, une intégrale représentant le temps total d'attente.

C'est de ces idées que sont partis des stagiaires de l'Ecole Polytechnique travaillant à la RATP pour établir un modèle dans lequel interviennent :

- le coût marginal, fonction du temps, $P_B(t)$, d'un autobus de capacité B ;
- le nombre de voyageurs empruntant le tronçon le plus chargé de la ligne qui montent dans un autobus parti à l'instant t , par unité de temps, soit c (t) ;
- le nombre total de voyageurs montant dans un autobus parti à l'instant t, par unité de temps, soit c (t) ;
- la valeur P_A du temps d'attente pour le client ;
- le taux de départ d (t) des autobus au temps t.

Pendant la révolution de pointe $[\tau-\lambda, \tau]$, le problème consiste à répartir une pénurie de voitures et donc à appliquer une politique du même type que celle proposée par Salzborn:

$$d(t) = \frac{c(t)}{B},$$

qui revient à faire partir les autobus dès qu'ils sont pleins.

Aux heures creuses, on est conduit à minimiser le coût pour la collectivité. Par exemple, pour l'avant-pointe, on a :

$$\int_0^{\tau-\lambda} \left[P_A \frac{a(t)}{d(t)} + P_B(t)\, d(t) \right] dt ,$$

sous la contrainte du nombre maximal d'autobus :

$$\int_{t-\lambda}^{t} d(t)\, dt \leqslant n = \int_{\tau-\lambda}^{\tau} \frac{c(t)}{B}\, dt .$$

Une méthode du <u>calcul des variations</u> a été employée et l'on a pu introduire un temps d'attente subjectif, qui tient compte de l'irrégularité des voitures.

c) En réalité ce qui précède ne peut guère s'appliquer qu'à des <u>dessertes homogènes</u> ce qui, malheureusement, n'est pas toujours le cas. Sur beaucoup de lignes existent des antennes, des navettes, etc., ce qui empêche d'isoler facilement les fonctions de demande intervenant dans le calcul. En outre, une difficulté apparaît dans le fait que seule une des pointes se révèle contraignante, l'autre étant saisie "en aval".

C'est pourquoi nous avons été obligés d'envisager la simplification, au moins pour les lignes non simples (et même peut-être pour toutes, car nous ne sommes pas certains de régler ainsi le véritable problème qui consiste en quelque sorte à répartir une pénurie !), du modèle dont il vient d'être question.

Dans le travail en cours, les deux points font leur réapparition et l'on "comble l'intervalle" ; nous pensons que, dans ces conditions, la <u>programmation dynamique</u> sera utilement mise en oeuvre.

III - CONSTRUCTION DU GRAPHIQUE DE MARCHE

Je me permettrai de passer assez rapidement sur ce point, car la communication suivante [5], présentée à cette même session par Mme Présent, vous permettra d'obtenir tous les détails.

Rappelons qu'il s'agit, lors de cette phase, de confectionner le graphique de marche, c'est-à-dire d'établir l'horaire des voitures.

Là encore, on part de données autant que possible fournies, d'après des enquêtes (1), par le réseau routier de la RATP (ce sont, essentiellement, les temps de parcours) ; la liaison avec la demande de transport étant encore à l'étude, comme on l'a vu au paragraphe 2, les temps de battement souhaitables et minimaux sont toujours déterminés manuellement.

Mme Présent va donc décrire comment, pour réaliser la construction proprement dite de l'horaire, après la définition des tours, qui est triviale, les opérations ont été divisées en deux phases :

1. raccordement des tours à horaire fixe ;
2. harmonisation des temps de battement, introduisant une variation de l'horaire, à raccordements donnés (2).

Là encore, le choix d'une méthode a été précédé de plusieurs tentatives de résolution. Si, pour la seconde phase, il a toujours semblé bon d'utiliser un programme linéaire, pour la première on est passé d'une méthode heuristique, s'appuyant sur des règles de priorité simples, à un algorithme de calcul d'un flot maximal à coût minimal.

D'ailleurs, c'est seulement lorsque, de la première phase, résultent certains temps de battement inférieurs aux temps minimaux, qu'on est contraint d'aborder la seconde.

---

(1) Tout un ensemble d'appareils enregistreurs automatiques devraient prochainement entrer en service, qui accumuleront les données statistiques de toute nature sur les mouvements des véhicules et des voyageurs.

(2) Pour le vocabulaire employé ici, prière de se reporter à la communication [5], § I Définitions et figure 2.

On a aussi changé de fonction économique pour le programme linéaire de cette seconde phase. Naguère était retenue une fonction quadratique des écarts entre temps de battement solutions et temps de battement souhaitables, qu'on s'empressait de linéariser.

Aujourd'hui, on a recours à la minimisation d'une somme pondérée des valeurs absolues des variations de l'horaire, par rapport à l'horaire initial, car les résultats de la première phase fournissent des temps de battement proches des temps de battement souhaités.

Mais déjà on prévoit qu'une meilleure connaissance des faits statistiques amènera une refonte de la phase 1. Du reste, peut-être la dernière phase, coûteuse en temps de calcul, disparaîtra-t-elle si l'on sait, par un programme conversationnel, permettre à l'inspecteur de ligne de mieux préparer les données, à partir d'une console reliée à un ordinateur (partie décentralisée du système).

Enfin, la liaison de ce sous-problème avec le suivant, l'habillage des horaires, est évidemment très étroite ; il semble qu'on faciliterait la résolution du second en instituant encore un système conversationnel, cette fois à la disposition du bureau central des horaires, pour aider à améliorer l'interface (partie centralisée).

IV - HABILLAGE DE L'HORAIRE

Ce n'est pas non plus la première fois qu'il est question de l'habillage des horaires dans un congrès. Melle Heurgon, une des meilleures spécialistes de la question, a fait plusieurs communications et articles à ce sujet [6], [7] ; en outre, en avril 1975, un séminaire consacré entièrement aux méthodes d'habillage (très variables selon la diversité des conditions de travail) s'est tenu à Chicago et l'on a pu y constater que beaucoup de systèmes avaient été imaginés, mais que très peu étaient devenus opérationnels, [1*] à [7*].

Pour nous, construire l'habillage d'une ligne, c'est rendre l'horaire exécutable au moyen de services réglementaires, en tenant compte des préférences du personnel. Pour d'autres, ces préférences ne jouent pas de rôle. De toute manière, les problèmes varient d'une entreprise à l'autre, du fait de la disparité des conditions de travail. On pourrait constater qu'ils varient même d'une ligne à l'autre d'un même réseau, l'âge moyen et les aspirations des machinistes étant différents.

A la RATP, le problème de l'habillage a été transformé en un problème de recouvrement exact d'un ensemble par N éléments (N, le nombre d'équipes, étant fixé).

Il existe, d'autre part, certaines contraintes supplémentaires, assurant de ne pas dépasser, pour chaque tableau de marche, un décalage maximal connu.

Pour rendre possible la résolution du problème, il convient d'engendrer à l'avance des services statutaires, en nombre suffisant pour assurer de bonnes chances de trouver des solutions, entre lesquelles la fonction économique fera un choix.

Evidemment, plus on "tronque" le générateur de services, moins il y a de solutions (voire pas du tout). Moins on le tronque, plus le problème devient combinatoire et long à résoudre.

Pour donner une idée de la difficulté de la question, rappelons simplement qu'un grand constructeur d'ordinateurs, consulté il y a quelque dix ans sur la possibilité de résoudre le problème au moyen d'un ordinateur avait répondu par la négative, au bout de plusieurs années d'étude ! La RATP peut donc se flatter d'être parvenue à un ensemble de programmes opérationnels consistant essentiellement, après l'intervention du générateur de services :

1) à utiliser un programme linéaire continu, qui suffit d'ailleurs à résoudre le problème de recouvrement exact dans un tiers des cas ;

2) lorsque le précédent programme donne des résultats partiellement non entiers, à utiliser ces résultats (partie entière, indicateurs marginaux, etc.) pour entreprendre dans de bonnes conditions la seconde phase du calcul.

Cette seconde phase consiste actuellement en un programme de recherche arborescente, qui donne satisfaction, tant au point de vue du temps de calcul, qu'au point de vue de la qualité des résultats obtenus.

Mais l'un des chercheurs de l'équipe de Melle Heurgon a pu établir [3] qu'une méthode de troncatures bien maniée pourrait permettre de parvenir au bout du problème en des temps comparables à ceux exigés par le programme ci-dessus.

Je voudrais me permettre de faire quatre observations principales sur l'état de développement actuel de la question de l'habillage à la RATP. Elles concernent :

a) le délai écoulé : il y a maintenant six ans que le problème a commencé à être abordé sérieusement ; il n'y a que deux ans que la solution a commencé à devenir opérationnelle ;

b) <u>les méthodes essayées</u> : on a dû d'abord se rendre compte qu'une énumération implicite sans solution partielle imposée était impraticable. Il a donc fallu étudier les propriétés fines des tableaux optimaux d'un programme linéaire pour essayer d'obtenir, à partir d'un calcul en nombres réels, une solution partielle utilisable pour démarrer la phase de recherche arborescente. Enfin, ce n'est que beaucoup plus tard qu'on s'est aperçu que la méthode de Gonrory I, pour les programmes en entiers, convenait aux problèmes de recouvrement, à condition de savoir choisir, à chaque étape, les contraintes les plus efficaces dans le groupe cyclique engendré par les congruences tirées du tableau optimal ;

c) <u>la fonction économique</u> : on a passé des mois et des mois à en discuter, à l'établir, puis à l'améliorer à maintes reprises. Il a été nécessaire de s'apercevoir que la minimisation du temps compensateur accordé aux agents effectuant un travail excédant les normes ne pouvait permettre de "séparer" les solutions. Quand il est devenu évident qu'il importait de réaliser les habillages conformes aux desiderata du personnel, il a fallu se renseigner sur les aspirations des agents, en fonction d'une certaine typologie des services, etc. ;

d) <u>l'absence éventuelle de solution</u> en calcul automatique, alors que le bureau des horaires, en introduisant certaines "souplesses" sur les contraintes ou les données, pourrait en construire une, manuellement. Comment parvenir, par programme, à obtenir les mêmes souplesses en calcul automatique ? Plusieurs chercheurs de l'équipe concernée estiment que cette prétention est parfaitement irréalisable. Quant à moi, je pense demander de vérifier tout de même si une formulation de certaines contraintes utilisant le concept de <u>relation floue</u> (au sens de Zadeh) ne serait pas susceptible d'ouvrir cette voie.

V - ETABLISSEMENT DU TABLEAU DE ROULEMENT

Voici l'une des phases <u>presque purement informatique</u> de l'ensemble de nos problèmes enchaînés. Rappelons qu'au terme des deux phases précédentes, par la fusion du graphique de marche et de l'habillage, on obtient le <u>tableau de marche</u>.

A partir des nombres de services requis par les différents habillages d'une même semaine, on élabore <u>le tableau de roulement</u> : il consiste à intercaler sur une semaine-type, qui se répète ensuite par glissement dans toute la période de validité du tableau, les jours de repos et les périodes de travail, de manière à équilibrer au mieux les services des agents les uns par rapport aux autres et chacun pris individuellement.

Enfin, la numérotation des services est effectuée. Elle revient, à partir des résultats de l'habillage, d'une part, à construire des suites de services réalisables la même semaine par un même agent (avec un repos suffisant entre deux journées consécutives), d'autre part à établir des séquences de semaines respectant les contraintes imposées par le roulement et répartissant au mieux les services pénibles.

Dans cette même conférence, MM. J.A. Bartoli et R. Trémolières aborderont le problème général du roulement des quarts, dans lequel apparaissent certaines propriétés arithmétiques qui facilitent l'établissement des tableaux de roulement [1] .

Il faut bien comprendre que, pour l'instant, on n'a pas, à la RATP, d'algorithme issu de la recherche opérationnelle pour confectionner le tableau de roulement et, pourtant, il est évident qu'il est nécessaire de veiller à la qualité de ce document, afin d'éviter de favoriser (impersonnellement) certains agents, au détriment des autres. En fait, les spécialistes de l'équipe qui s'est occupée de cette phase, arguent qu'il existerait peu de solutions acceptables, ce qui facilite les choix, à partir d'une méthode heuristique.

VI - CONFECTION DE LA FEUILLE DE SERVICE

La partie prévisionnelle des opérations s'arrête au tableau de roulement. Il reste à faire servir à l'exploitation quotidienne l'ensemble des travaux précédents.

La veille du jour d'exploitation, les conditions ont changé (variations du trafic, personnel indisponible, etc.). Or, il s'agit de définir ici les listes nominatives d'affectation "définitives" des agents aux services, en mettant en présence des listes mises à jour selon les indisponibilités et des horaires aménagés pour tenir compte des variations du trafic.

On y parvient grâce à la méthode hongroise, après avoir défini des poids d'incompatibilité entre machinistes et services. On obtient alors la feuille de service.

Le jour même de l'exploitation se présentent des situations encore nouvelles (absences, accidents, etc.) ; il faut donc remanier de nouveau la feuille de service. Le téléphone et le crayon sont, jusqu'à présent, les instruments de l'exploitant. Mais on envisage également, à ce stade, des programmes conversationnels, à l'échelon de l'inspecteur de ligne, pour y aider (le terminal utilisé étant le même que celui dont il a été question à la fin du § 3).

Telles sont les remarques qu'on a pu faire, sous l'angle de la recherche opérationnelle, entre 1968 et 1975, à propos de l'établissement automatique des tableaux de marche et feuilles de service de la RATP.

VII - CONCLUSIONS

On a l'habitude de décrire l'analyste opérationnel comme un personnage féru de mathématiques, capable de trouver d'élégantes optimisations, dans les situations les plus diverses de l'entreprise.

Cette image ne correspond pas du tout au labeur des équipes qui ont travaillé sur les problèmes cités plus haut. Elles se sont trouvées au sein de problèmes pratiques, que l'exploitant avait peine à formuler, et dans lesquels l'informatique joue un rôle au moins aussi important que la recherche opérationnelle.

Il a fallu une alliance étroite du client, des programmeurs et des chercheurs des groupes de recherche opérationnelle pour parvenir à comprendre, dégrossir, puis enfin résoudre les questions.

On a, bien sûr, rencontré des problèmes "passionnants", qui ont donné lieu à des recherches de niveau élevé, à des thèses de docteur-ingénieur à l'Université [3], ou des mémoires d'ingénieurs de grandes écoles [2], mais, plus souvent, il a fallu faire face à la rédaction de programmes "classiques", dont on a seulement retenu qu'ils devaient être écrits très soigneusement, en raison de leur caractère répétitif.

Il a été nécessaire, en tout cas, de convenir que le système est encore loin d'être opérationnel lorsque, à force d'essais et de tâtonnements, les méthodes et algorithmes ont été définis. L'informatique reprend ses droits, car un algorithme moins performant vaut peut-être mieux qu'une mauvaise chaîne de programmes d'ordinateur !

En un mot, dans la pratique, pour le chercheur opérationnel aux prises avec le problème réel, la découverte de la méthode d'optimisation n'est qu'un moment des longs travaux qui sont nécessaires pour l'appliquer. C'est pourquoi seuls les efforts coordonnés de plusieurs équipes peuvent venir à bout d'un ensemble complexe de sous-problèmes, dépendant les uns des autres et réagissant entre eux.

Peut-être n'est-il pas inintéressant de revenir sur cet aspect des choses, après quelques années de travaux consacrés à un problème de longue haleine ?

Tous mes remerciements vont aux membres des équipes, grandes ou petites, et nombreuses, qui, chacune, ont affronté des difficultés en résolvant tel ou tel problème de la chaîne décrite. J'ai bien conscience de leur avoir peu apporté, hormis quelques remarques de caractère pratique ou quelques données théoriques, alors que leurs travaux de grande valeur m'ont permis de réfléchir à ce grand exemple; qu'ils me pardonnent si certaines de mes conclusions leur semblent hasardeuses.

BIBLIOGRAPHIE

1. BARTOLI, J.A., et TREMOLIERES, R., Le problème de la multivalence dans le travail continu, 7e conférence IFIP sur les techniques d'optimisation. Nice, 8-13 septembre 1975
2. BOUTILLON, Catherine, Construction automatique des horaires des lignes d'autobus, Mémoire d'ingénieur de l'IIE, juin 1944
3. DELORME, Jacques, Contribution à l'étude du problème de recouvrement : méthodes de troncatures, Paris VI, thèse de docteur-ingénieur, 26 juin 1974
4. DELORME, Jacques, et HEURGON, Edith, Problèmes de partitionnement : exploration arborescente de méthode de troncatures ? RAIRO (verte), V, n° 2, juin 1975

4 bis. HERVILLARD, R., et HEURGON, E., Habillage automatique des horaires d'une ligne d'autobus. Revue de l'UITP, janvier 1975

5. HEURGON, E., PRESENT, M., TARIM, G., Construction automatique des horaires d'une ligne d'autobus, 7e conférence IFIP sur les techniques d'optimisation. Nice 8-13 septembre 1975
6. HEURGON, E., Un problème de recouvrement : l'habillage des horaires d'une ligne d'autobus. RAIRO (verte), 6e année, V, n° 1, 1972
7. HEURGON, E., Développement actuel des méthodes de construction automatique des tableaux de service, à paraître dans RAIRO (verte)

7 bis. d° Preprints : Workshop on automated techniques for scheduling of vehicle operators for urban public transportation services, ORSA Transportation Science Section, Chicago, April 27-29 1975

7 ter. HEURGON E., CAMUT Y, Elaboration automatique des tableaux de marche d'une ligne d'autobus. Affectation par ordinateur du personnel d'exploitation des dépôts du réseau routier, in Approches Rationnelles dans la gestion du personnel, Monographies de l'AFCET, Dunod 1972

8. NEWELL, G.F., Dispatching policies for a transportation route, Transportation Science,?, n° 5, p 91-105 ? 1971
9. PHAETON (modèle publié par le centre de gestion scientifique de l'Ecole nationale supérieure des Mines de Paris), 1969.
10. RATP, Optimisation des caractéristiques d'exploitation des lignes urbaines du réseau routier, décembre 1970
11. SALZBORN, J.F., Optimimum bus scheduling, Transportation Science, 6, n° 2, p. 137-148, mai 1972

BIBLIOGRAPHIE SUPPLEMENTAIRE

(Quelques-unes des principales communications présentées au symposium de Chicago, avril 1975)

1*. Constraints for scheduling operators for urban public transit systems, by Gunter P. Sharp, Atlanta, USA

2*. Approximation techniques for automated manpower scheduling, by Lawrence Bodin, A. Kydes, D. Rosenfield

3*. Preparing duty rosters for bus routes by computer, by Edith Heurgon, RATP, France

4*. An automated technique for scheduling motormen and conductors for the New York City subways, by Richard T. Jenkins, New York, USA

5*. A General computer method for bus crew scheduling, by Barbara Manington et Anthony Wren, Leeds, England

6*. Overview of the RUCUS package driver run cutting program (RUNS), by Eugène Wilhelm, the Mitre Corporation, USA

7*. Automated formation of staff schedules and duty rosters, by Helmut Kregeloh, HHA, Hambourg, West Germany

CONSTRUCTION AUTOMATIQUE DES HORAIRES D'UNE LIGNE D'AUTOBUS

Edith Heurgon; Manoëlle Présent; Güzin Tarim
RATP, Service de la Recherche Opérationnelle et du Calcul Economique

Mettre au point des méthodes rationnelles d'exploitation est un souci constant, dans une entreprise de transport. Dans cette perspective, M. Robert Faure a présenté à ce congrès la chaîne de programmes, mise au point à la RATP, pour construire par ordinateur les tableaux de marche, de service et de roulement du réseau d'autobus. Les avantages que l'on peut attendre de cette automatisation sont :

- suppression de tâches répétitives et fastidieuses d'où économie de personnel et possibilité, pour certains agents, de se consacrer à un travail plus intéressant et plus rentable ;
- meilleure adaptation de l'offre à la demande de transport ;
- normalisation des méthodes, objectif difficile à atteindre actuellement, car il s'agit d'opérations manuelles exigeant une grande expérience ;
- possibilité d'effectuer rapidement des simulations et des prévisions afin de répondre en toute connaissance de cause aux demandes du personnel.

Cet exposé se limite au seul problème de la construction automatique de l'horaire d'une ligne d'autobus.

Afin de bénéficier de l'expérience acquise par les spécialistes des dépôts et de ne pas leur retirer la responsabilité d'un travail intéressant, l'automatisation est étudiée en vue d'apporter une aide à la décision, probablement sous la forme d'un système interactif.

A partir d'un niveau de dépenses préalablement défini, l'objectif recherché est de construire un horaire assurant une bonne qualité de service, réaliste du point de vue des temps de parcours et, si possible, régulable en cas de perturbation du trafic. Divers critères secondaires doivent également être pris en compte : les contraintes imposées par l'habillage des horaires, maillon suivant de la chaîne, ou celles relatives à l'entretien des voitures, etc. (figure 1).

I - DEFINITIONS

Pour une ligne donnée, exploitée entre deux terminus A et B, on appelle : (figure 2)

- dépôt : l'établissement où les voitures sont remisées et entretenues,
- tour : le trajet d'une voiture qui part de A vers B pour revenir en A,
- temps de trajet : la durée du tour y compris temps de battement en B,

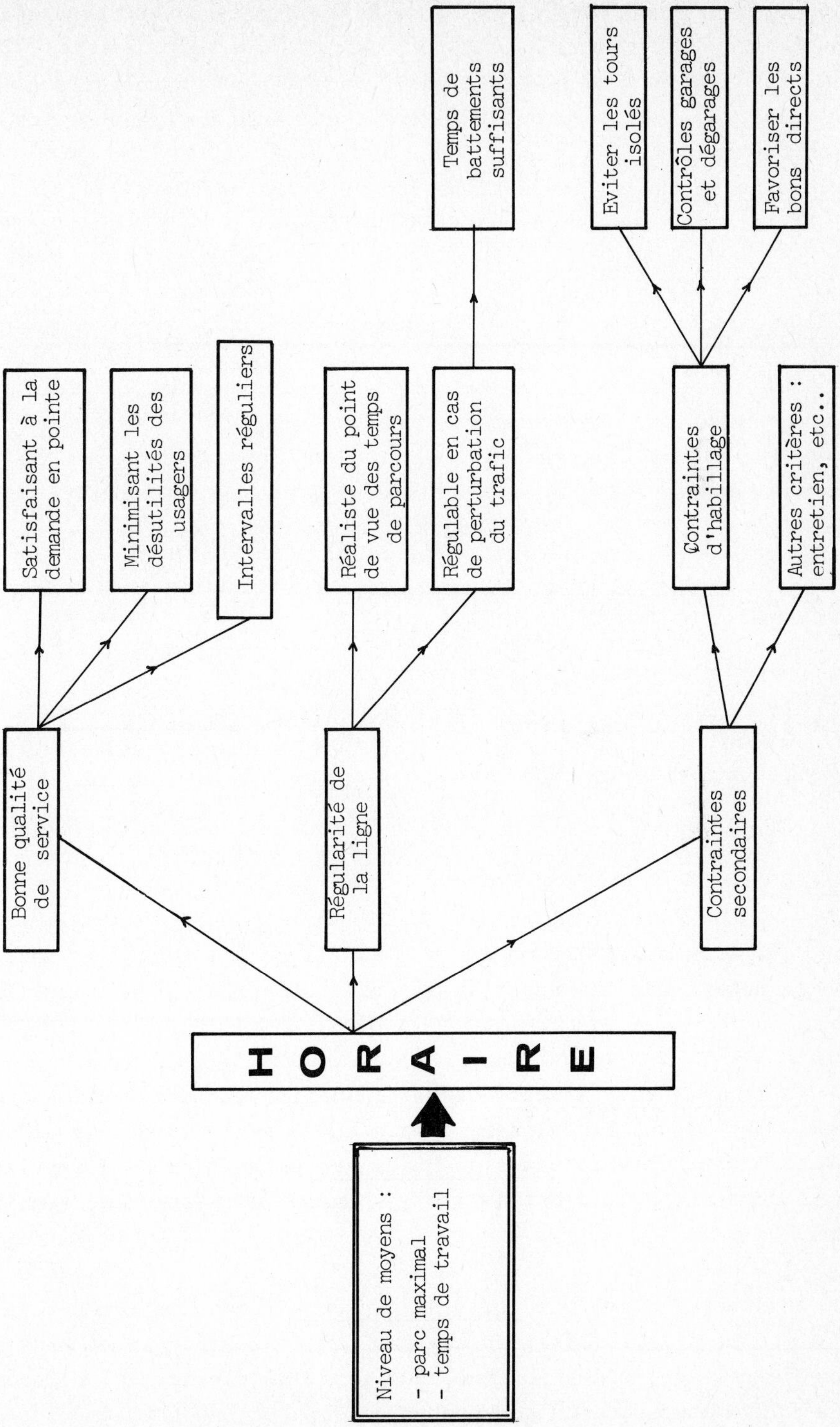
Niveau de moyens :
- parc maximal
- temps de travail
HORAIRE
Bonne qualité de service
Satisfaisant à la demande en pointe
Minimisant les désutilités des usagers
Intervalles réguliers
Régularité de la ligne
Réaliste du point de vue des temps de parcours
Régulable en cas de perturbation du trafic
Temps de battements suffisants
Contraintes secondaires
Contraintes d'habillage
Eviter les tours isolés
Contrôles garages et dégarages
Favoriser les bons directs
Autres critères : entretien, etc..

Figure 1

- temps de battement : temps de stationnement accordé à une voiture au terminus entre deux tours,
- temps de révolution : temps passé entre deux départs successifs d'une même voiture, au même terminus (la somme du temps de trajet et du temps de battement),
- raccordement des tours : deux tours sont dits raccordés s'ils sont effectués consécutivement par une même voiture.

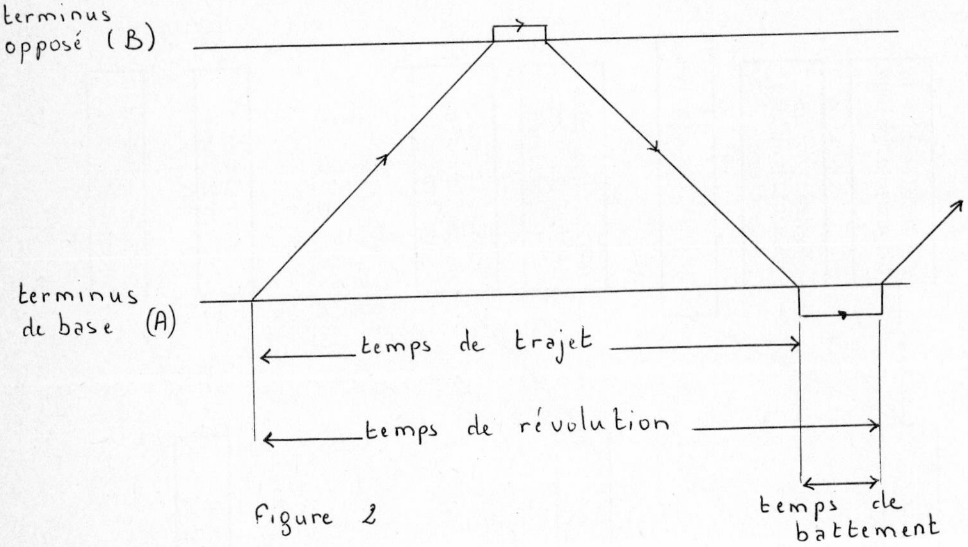

figure 2

II - DONNEES

Pour construire les horaires d'une ligne d'autobus, il faut connaître la demande de transport et les conditions de circulation (figure 3).

La demande de transport permet de définir le service à assurer, c'est-à-dire les tâches à réaliser, tandis que les conditions de circulation, données sous forme de temps de parcours, permettent de déterminer la capacité de transport, c'est-à-dire les moyens permettant de réaliser les tâches.

La détermination des temps de parcours (temps de roulage des voitures et temps d'immobilisation aux arrêts), aux différentes heures de la journée, est une opération très délicate. Elle exige la collecte, manuelle ou automatique, d'un bon nombre de données, un traitement statistique approprié et un lissage assurant la continuité des résultats.

Doivent être précisés également les temps de battement que l'on souhaite accorder aux terminus, selon l'heure de la journée. Une juste appréciation de ces temps - dits temps de battement souhaitables -, fonction de l'irrégularité de la ligne, semble être un facteur essentiel à la construction d'un bon horaire. Trop faibles, ils contribuent à étendre les retards d'un tour sur le suivant ; trop forts, ils réduisent inutilement la capacité de transport offerte. On définit, en outre, des temps de battement minimaux, en dessous desquels il n'est pas admis de descendre.

Un arbitrage judicieux doit aussi être fait entre temps de parcours et temps de battement, ceux-ci étant principalement déterminés en fonction de la variabilité de ceux-là.

Un modèle de simulation d'une ligne d'autobus est en cours d'élaboration à la RATP. Il permettra, en particulier, de tester différentes stratégies dans la construction des horaires et d'ajuster les valeurs des nombreux paramètres mis en jeu.

III - POSITION DU PROBLEME

A partir des données précédentes, deux opérations doivent être réalisées pour établir l'horaire d'une ligne d'autobus.

1/ Définir le niveau de service à offrir, sous la forme de fréquences de passages des autobus, et déterminer le parc des véhicules à utiliser (compte tenu, éventuellement, d'un parc maximal et d'un nombre d'heures de travail donnés). Les critères retenus visent tant à satisfaire à la demande (de pointe principalement) qu'à minimiser les désutilités des usagers (attente, inconfort, etc.).

2/ Construire l'horaire proprement dit, c'est-à-dire ajuster au mieux le service à offrir aux moyens mis en oeuvre. Pour cela, définir et agencer les tours de manière à assurer des intervalles réguliers d'une part, d'autre part à présenter des temps de battement, les plus proches possibles des souhaitables et toujours supérieurs aux minimaux. Doivent ainsi être précisées, pour chaque voiture, les heures de sortie du dépôt, de passage aux différents terminus, de rentrée au dépôt.

D'un point de vue théorique, il s'agit donc de définir simultanément les heures de départ des tours (d'après les fréquences calculées en 1/) et leurs raccordements, de manière à établir des suites de tours exécutables par un même autobus. Certes, ce problème peut se formuler comme un programme linéaire à variables mixtes. Mais le temps de résolution qu'il exigerait et le caractère répétitif de l'opération à réaliser (plus de 3 000 horaires doivent être établis chaque année à la RATP ont

CONSTRUCTION DE L'HORAIRE

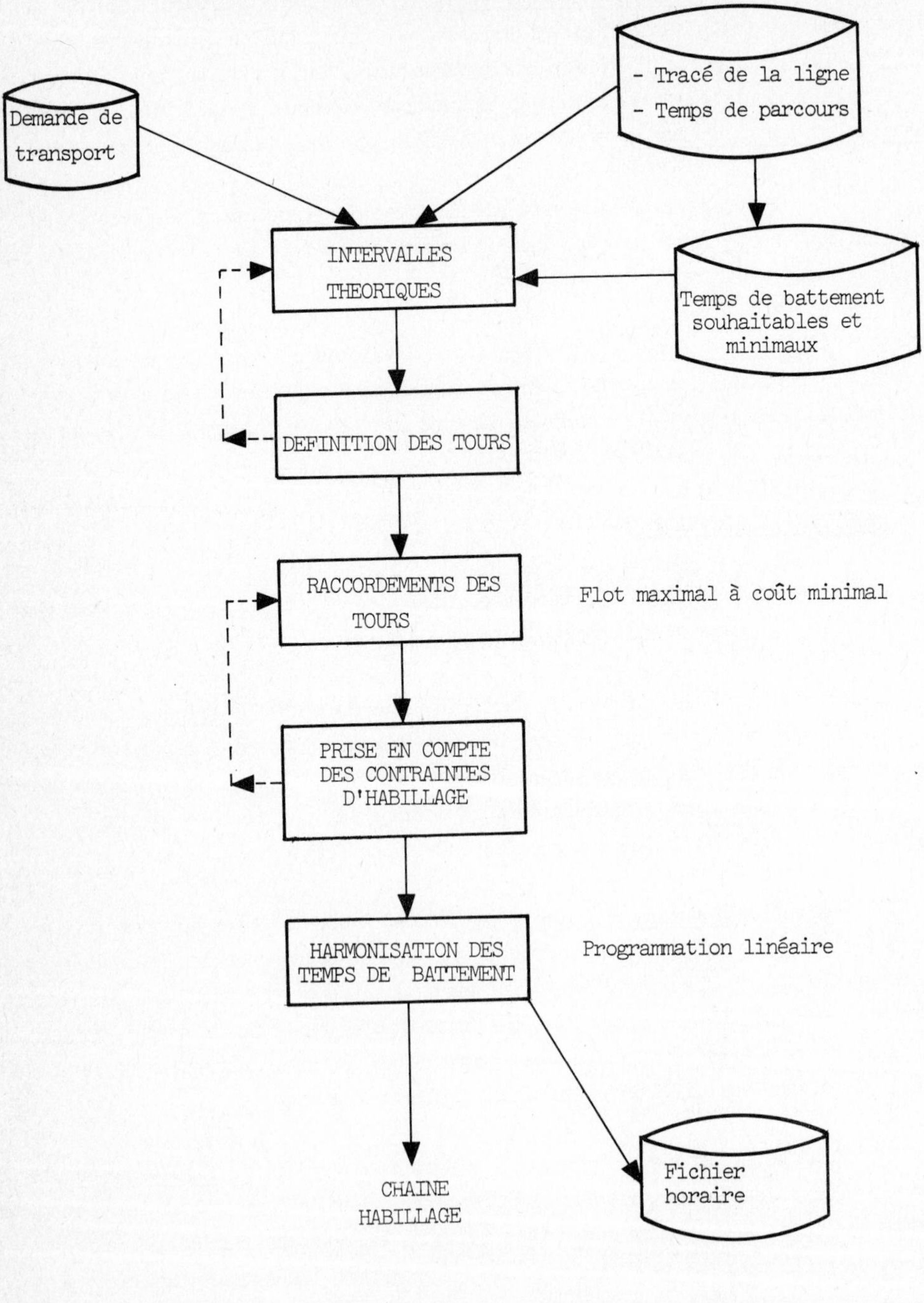

Figure 3

conduit à le décomposer en trois phases principales. On en réduit ainsi le caractère fortement combinatoire.

PHASE 1 - Définition des tours : à partir des fréquences théoriques, des temps de trajet et des heures imposées de début et de fin de service, fixer les heures de départ et d'arrivée des tours.

PHASE 2 - Raccordement des tours à horaire fixe, de manière à assurer des temps de battement les plus proches possibles des souhaitables et, selon les cas, soit en minimisant le nombre de voitures, soit en utilisant un parc donné.

PHASE 3 - Harmonisation des temps de battement en maintenant les raccordements fixes : Supposer les heures de départ fixes, lors de la phase 2, restreint la généralité du problème. Si, donc, la solution ne paraît pas satisfaisante - par exemple, si certains temps de battement sont inférieurs aux minimaux - une phase complémentaire est nécessaire. Elle consiste, sans trop altérer les intervalles initiaux et en maintenant les raccordements fixes, à introduire de légères variations sur les heures de départ des tours, afin d'assurer des temps de battement toujours supérieurs aux minimaux et à les répartir au mieux tout au long de la journée.

L'organigramme de la chaîne complète est présenté à la figure 3.

IV - DIFFERENTES ETAPES DE LA MODELISATION

IV.1 - Premières recherches

a) La première opération est supposée accomplie. Cette situation est d'ailleurs celle dans laquelle se placent les inspecteurs de ligne chargés de la construction manuelle de l'horaire. Sont donc donnés, d'une part, les intervalles à assurer aux différentes heures de la journée, d'autre part, le nombre de voitures disponibles au dépôt.

b) La phase 1 de définition des tours est triviale.

c) La phase 2 de raccordement des tours à horaire fixe est réalisée par une procédure heuristique locale, très rapide, du genre "premier arrivé, premier parti". Compte tenu du nombre limité de voitures, certains temps de battement trop petits, voire même négatifs, peuvent en résulter.

ETAPES DE LA MODELISATION

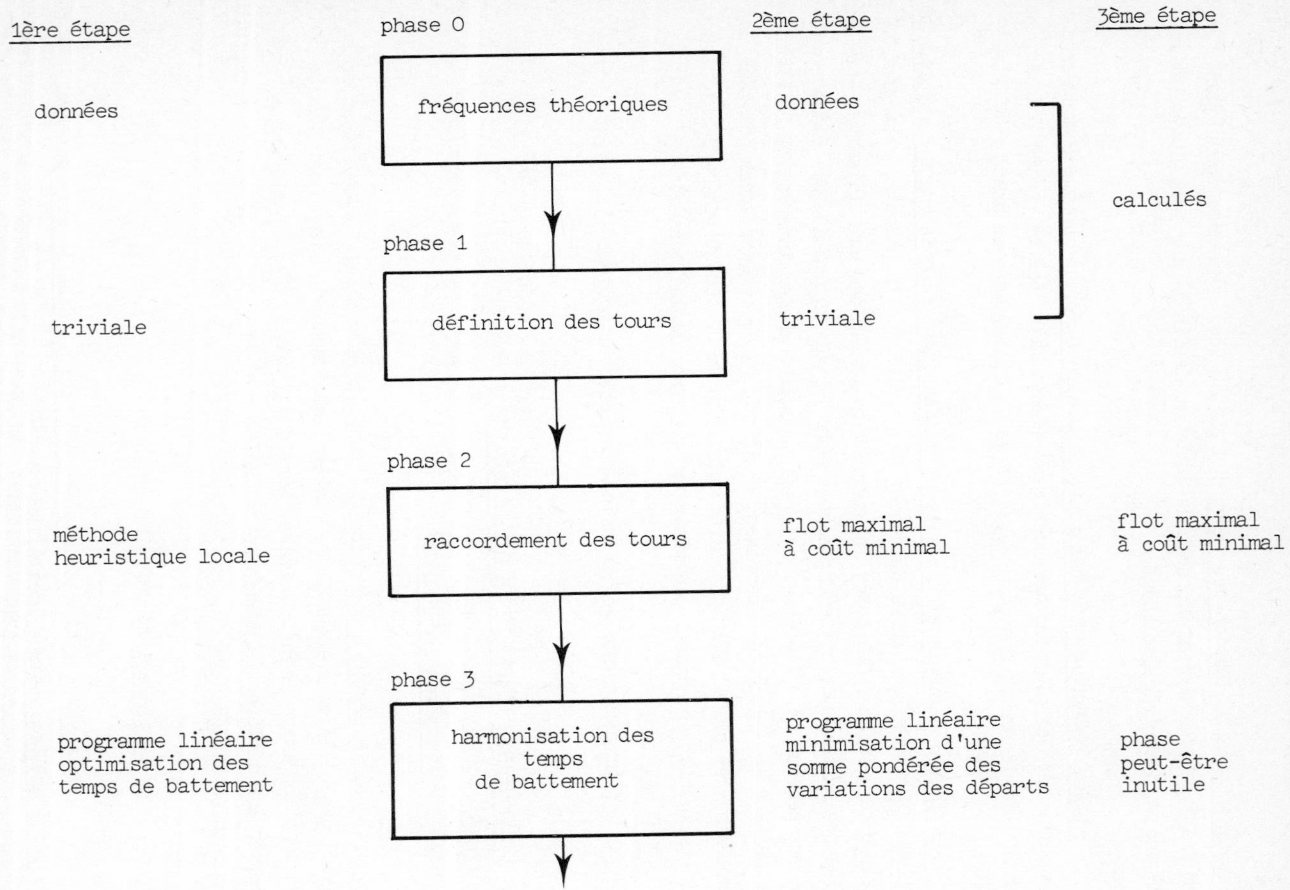

d) La phase 3 d'harmonisation des temps de battement est donc la plus importante. Elle doit permettre de trouver une solution réalisable satisfaisante, qui assure une bonne répartition des temps de battement, tous supérieurs aux minimaux, sans trop détériorer les intervalles de départ.

Ce problème se formule comme un programme linéaire.

Supposons les départs numérotés chronologiquement du début à la fin de la journée. Pour chacun d'eux, soient :

. t_{B_i}, le temps de battement, accordé dans la phase précédente, à la voiture qui doit effectuer le $i^{\text{ème}}$ départ (s'il ne correspond pas à une sortie de dépôt) ;

. t_{Bmin_i} et t_{BS_i}, respectivement les temps de battement minimal et souhaitable avant le ième départ.

Définissons alors les variables X_i comme étant la variation (positive ou négative) qu'il convient d'apporter à la $i^{\text{ème}}$ heure de départ. Soit j le numéro du départ précédent effectué par la même voiture.

Contraintes du programme linéaire

(1)	$X_j - X_i$	$\leqslant t_{B_i} - t_{Bmin_i}$	$\forall$ i qui n'est pas une sortie	
(2)	$\lvert X_i \rvert$	$\leqslant K_i$	$\forall i$	K_i donné
(3)	$\lvert X_i - X_{i-1} \rvert$	$\leqslant \lambda_i$	$\forall i$	λ_i donné

Les contraintes (1) imposent à tout temps de battement d'avoir une valeur au moins égale au minimum. Les inégalités (2) limitent en valeur absolue les variations apportées aux heures de départ. Enfin, les contraintes (3) empêchent de trop perturber les intervalles initiaux.

Fonction économique

Diverses fonctions économiques ont été successivement étudiées. Il convient de concilier les deux objectifs suivants : assurer des temps de battement proches des souhaitables, ne pas trop altérer les intervalles. En termes de programmation mathématique, la première exigence conduit à minimiser l'écart des temps de battement réels et des temps de battement souhaitables, la seconde, par exemple, à minimiser les écarts des intervalles transformés et des intervalles initiaux. Dans le premier temps, c'est l'objectif n° 1 qui a été retenu. Cependant, la minimisation d'écarts, appréciés d'ailleurs différemment selon l'heure de la journée, n'est pas une fonction linéaire. Le mieux serait, semble-t-il, de considérer une somme pondérée des carrés de ces écarts. Cependant, pour éviter la résolution d'un programme quadratique, nous avons admis, en première approximation, de minimiser une somme pondérée des valeurs absolues de ces écarts, les poids étant plus forts aux heures de pointe qu'aux heures creuses.

Linéarisation du problème

On peut linéariser la fonction économique de ce problème en introduisant un jeu de variables supplémentaires. Soit θ_{Bi} le temps de battement résultant du programme linéaire. Notons alors :

$$Y_i = \theta_{Bi} - t_{BSi} = X_i - X_j + t_{Bi} - t_{BSi}$$

Décomposons maintenant Y_i de la manière suivante :

$$Y_i = Y'_i - Y''_i \quad \text{avec :} \quad Y'_i = \text{Max}\,(0, -Y_i) \quad \text{et} \quad Y''_i = \text{Max}\,(0, +Y_i)$$

Comme, pour un départ i, l'une au moins des variables Y'_i ou Y''_i est nulle, le programme linéaire admet la formulation suivante (I notant l'ensemble des départs) :

$$\text{Min} \sum_{i \in I} \alpha_i\, Y'_i + \beta_i\, Y''_i \qquad (\alpha_i\,,\ \beta_i \geqslant 0)$$

sous les contraintes :

(1) $X_i - X_j - Y'_i + Y''_i = t_{BSi} - t_{Bi}$ $\quad \forall\, i \in I$

(2) $- \lambda_i \quad X_i - X_{i-1} \leqslant \lambda_i$ $\quad \forall\, i \in I$

(3) $0 \leqslant Y''_i \leqslant t_{BSi} - t_{Bmin_i}$ $\quad \forall\, i \in I$

$0 \leqslant Y'_i$

(4) $- K_i \leqslant X_i \leqslant K_i$ $\quad \forall\, i \in I$

Si d désigne le nombre de départs à assurer sur la ligne, ce programme linéaire comporte 3d variables et moins de 2d contraintes (en effet, pour les départs qui correspondent à des sorties, le premier type de contraintes n'existe pas). Ce programme est actuellement résolu à l'aide du code L.P. 6000, disponible sur l'ordinateur HB 6050 de la RATP.

e) Critique des résultats

Les résultats de la phase 2 sont très insuffisants et ne peuvent pas être corrigés par la phase 3, qui ne remet pas en cause les raccordements. D'une part, comme la procédure de raccordement locale ne permet pas de contrôler avec précision les garages et les dégarages des voitures, on obtient un grand nombre de tours isolés, qui rendent l'habillage de l'horaire extrêmement difficile ; d'autre part, il est fréquent que le programme linéaire, résolu à la phase 3, n'admette aucune solution réalisable. En revanche, lorsqu'il en trouve une, cette phase remplit parfaitement son rôle d'harmonisation des temps de battement.

IV.2 - Forme actuelle du modèle

On a donc cherché, pour résoudre la phase 2, une méthode plus efficace.

a) Phase 2 : Méthode mathématique

Définition du graphe : La procédure retenue fait appel à la théorie des graphes. Soit $G = (X, U)$ le graphe orienté sans circuit, où X désigne l'ensemble des tours et U celui des raccordements possibles (un raccordement entre deux tours i et j est dit possible, si le temps de battement qui en résulte est compris dans l'intervalle (T_o, T_1) préalablement défini). A chaque arc u de U, on associe un coût C_u, proportionnel à l'écart (à une puissance quelconque) entre les temps de battement réels et les temps de battement souhaitables. On pénalise, en outre, fortement les arcs correspondant à un temps de battement inférieur au minimal.

Formulation du problème

Appelons séquence une suite de tours raccordés, donc réalisables, par un même autobus. Supposons, dans un premier temps, pour les commodités de l'exposé, qu'une voiture ne puisse exécuter, pendant la période considérée, qu'une seule séquence. Cherchons alors une solution :

- qui minimise le nombre total de voitures,
- ou qui utilise un parc donné.

Réaliser les raccordements avec un nombre minimal d'autobus revient à décomposer le graphe G en un nombre minimal de chemins disjoints

Considérons le réseau de transport construit à partir du graphe biparti G' = (S, T, U'), correspondant à G, où S = T = X et U' désigne l'ensemble des raccordements possibles. Chaque arc est doté d'un coût C_u et d'une capacité 1.

Décomposer le graphe G en un nombre minimal de chemins disjoints revient à chercher dans le réseau de transport ainsi défini un flot maximal.

Si l'on veut, en outre, obtenir des temps de battement optimaux, le problème consiste à trouver un flot maximal de coût minimal.

Si le nombre des voitures est donné, il s'agit de déterminer un flot de valeur donnée et de coût minimal.

Choix d'un algorithme

Plusieurs algorithmes permettent de trouver, dans un réseau de transport, un flot maximal de coût minimal. Citons, par exemple : l'algorithme "out of Kilter", la méthode hongroise, l'algorithme présenté par Horps et Roy dans [11]. Nous avons choisi ce dernier, qui fait appel à la notion de graphe d'écart, pour les raisons suivantes :

- Le graphe est très épars ; pour chaque tour, il y a, au maximum, cinq ou six raccordements possibles. De ce fait, la méthode hongroise, qui travaille sur la matrice associée au graphe, est à rejeter.

- L'algorithme Horps-Roy, qui procède par itération sur la valeur du flot, fournit des solutions pen optimales du problème. En outre, il s'adapte très simplement au cas où le nombre de voitures est connu.

Décomposition du problème

En fait, dans une journée, et compte tenu des phénomènes de pointe qui caractérisent toute ligne de transport urbain, un même autobus peut exécuter successivement plusieurs séquences. Il n'y a donc pas correspondance immédiate entre le parc de voitures disponibles et le nombre des séquences.

Pour pallier cet inconvénient d'une part, pour interdire à une même voiture de réaliser plus de deux séquences d'autre part, enfin pour réduire les temps de calcul par l'algorithme de Roy, on a procédé à un découpage de la journée en deux, séparant ainsi pointe du matin et pointe du soir. A cet égard, c'est le nombre des séquences, pour chaque sous-problème, qu'il convient soit de minimiser, soit de maintenir fixe. On peut ainsi aisément contrôler les dégarages et garages des autobus.

b) Phase 3 : changement de fonction économique

Dès lors, les raccordements, établis à la phase 2, présentent des temps de battement aussi proches que possible des souhaitables. Si aucun d'eux n'est inférieur au minimum, la phase 3 devient inutile. Dans le cas contraire, l'objectif est bien d'assurer la réalisabilité du problème, en opérant les plus légères variations sur les heures de départ des tours.

La fonction économique du programme linéaire consiste alors à minimiser une somme pondérée (selon les heures de la journée) des valeurs absolues de ces variations.

$$\text{Min} \sum_i \alpha_i \, |x_i|$$

c) Analyse des résultats

Quatre lignes urbaines de la RATP ont été choisies pour faire des essais. Les résultats obtenus ont été jugés très satisfaisants par les exploitants du réseau routier, tant en ce qui concerne l'homogénéité des temps de révolution que la régularité des intervalles. Toutefois, comme les données ont été construites par simple lissage de l'horaire établi à la main, il n'est guère étonnant que les résultats n'en diffèrent pas essentiellement. Il est probable que, lorsque la collecte d'un nombre suffisant de données permettra la définition rigoureuse des temps de parcours et de battement, la procédure informatique se justifiera de manière plus nette. Des difficultés surgiront, peut-être, en revanche, si l'on ne vérifie pas a priori la compatibilité des intervalles théoriques et des temps de parcours (ce qui est fait, implicitement, dans l'horaire manuel). La phase 1 risque alors de devenir insuffisante.

Le tableau suivant présente les temps d'exécution sur l'ordinateur HB 6050 de la RATP.

	Ligne 75	Ligne 61	Ligne 22	Ligne 84
Phases 1 et 2	10.8 secondes	14.4 secondes	12.9 secondes	15.5 secondes
Nombre de tours	86	95	106	127
Nombre de battements $<$ min à l'issue de la phase 2	8	8	1	0
Programme linéaire temps	33.1 s	31 s	29.5 s	-
Nombre d'itérations	64	38	1	-

A l'exception du code linéaire LP 6000, utilisé à la phase 3, tous les programmes ont été écrits en FORTRAN.

On peut observer sur ce tableau que les temps d'ordinateur requis par la phase 3 sont largement supérieurs à ceux qu'exigent les phases 1 et 2 réunies. Comme cette phase 3 n'est utile que si les raccordements issus de la phase 2 présentent des temps de battement inférieurs aux minimaux, il paraît avantageux de tenter, par une élaboration plus poussée de la phase 1, de garantir cette réalisabilité dans la plupart des cas.

IV.3 - Développements futurs

C'est donc maintenant non seulement la phase 1, mais aussi la phase préliminaire de calcul des fréquences théoriques, qui doivent être considérées selon une optique nouvelle. Il faut bien admettre, en effet, qu'un préalable indispensable à l'établissement par ordinateur d'horaires satisfaisants est la détermination sur des bases objectives du service que l'on veut offrir compte tenu des moyens disponibles.

Dans cette perspective et en vue d'éliminer la phase 3, des études sont en cours qu'il est un peu prématuré de décrire ici.

Cette première partie sera réalisée à l'aide de programmes conversationnels ; pourront être ainsi remis en cause non seulement le parc, mais aussi le nombre de tours et divers autres éléments laissés à l'appréciation de l'utilisateur.

b) Contraintes d'habillage

Le maillon suivant de la chaîne, l'habillage des horaires, est déjà automatisé à la RATP. On a constaté que si certaines contraintes pouvaient être introduites au niveau de la construction de l'horaire, l'habillage en serait nettement facilité et son coût réduit. Il s'agit donc véritablement, à ce niveau-là, de traiter l'interaction entre ces deux applications. Un module sera donc intercalé entre les phases 2 et 3 et pourra fonctionner également de manière conversationnelle.

En conclusion, c'est bien à une recherche en cours que s'est attaché cet exposé. Dans le cadre de ce congrès sur la modélisation et l'optimisation au service de l'homme, il nous a paru intéressant d'insister d'une part sur les différentes étapes de la modélisation et de la résolution de ce problème, d'autre part sur l'utilisation des programmes qui en résultent sur le mode conversationnel, permettant ainsi aux spécialistes du réseau d'autobus de disposer d'un véritable instrument d'aide à la décision.

BIBLIOGRAPHIE

1. BJELKAKER, S., SCHEELE, S., "Optimization methods for bus systems in urban areas". A literature review, LINKOPING University, Department of Mathematics, Report : May 1973.

2. BOUTILLON, C., "Construction automatique des horaires des lignes d'autobus". Mémoire de diplôme d'ingénieur I.I.E., Juin 1974.

3. CHAMORRO, Alfredo, "Optimisation d'une flotte aérienne par la méthode ATEM". R.I.R.O., Vol. 3, p. 67-86 (1968).

4. DELORME, Jacques, et HEURGON, Edith, "Problèmes de partitionnement : exploration arborescente ou méthode de troncatures ?". Revue R.A.I.R.O. 9e année Vol. 2, Juin 1975.

5. FORCINA, J.L., "Une approche simple de certains problèmes de location, de distribution et de transport". Revue R.A.I.R.O., vol. 2, p. 39-59, Mai 1974.

6. HEURGON, Edith, "Un problème de recouvrement : l'habillage des horaires d'une ligne d'autobus", revue R.A.I.R.O. 6e année, V. 1, 1972.

7. LEVIN, A., "Scheduling and fleet routing models for transportation systems". Transportation Science, Vol. 5, No. 3, p. 232-255, août 1971.

8. MARTIN-LÖF, Anders, "A branch-and-bound algorithm for determining the minimal fleet size of a transportation system". Transportation Science, Vol. 4, No 2, p.159-163, Mai 1970.

9. MOSQUERA, F., "Optimisation d'une flotte aérienne : une méthode de regret pour le cas à horaire variable" (non publié).

10. NEWELL, G.F., "Dispatching policies for a transportation route". Transportation Science. No 5, p. 91-105, 1971.

11. ROY, B., "Algèbre moderne et théorie des graphes". Dunod, Paris, Tome II, p. 492, 1970.

12. SAHA, J.L., "An algorithm for bus scheduling problems". Operational Research Quarterly, Vol. 21, No. 4, p. 463-474.

13. SALZBORN, F.J., "Optimum bus scheduling". Transportation Science, Vol. 6, No. 2, p. 137-148, Mai 1972.

14. TARIM, Güzin, "Construction automatique des horaires d'une ligne d'autobus". Thèse à l'Université de Paris VI, 19 juin 1975.

REGIONAL SCHOOL DISTRICTING VIA MATHEMATICAL PROGRAMMING

C. De Giorgi, G. Tagliabue
TECHINT - COMPAGNIA TECNICA INTERNAZIONALE - Milano

P. Migliarese, P.C. Palermo
ISTITUTO DI ELETTRONICA, POLITECNICO di Milano

INTRODUCTION

This paper outlines a regional districting model, which concerns the spatial organisation of the Italian High Educational System, according to a national program implemented since november '74.
The main objects of the program, aiming to perform the regional balance and the efficiency of the educational structures, were:

- to determine the location and the sizes of polyvalent school units (in the following, district centres), supplying all the kinds of High Education and satisfying the regional demand;
- to partition the Regions into school districts in order to share the student population upon district centres according to the main goals of the program.

The structure of this problem corresponds to a well known family of mathematical models (location - allocation models): given a number n of areas, each with a known demand of services or goods, and a number m of alternative sites where the supply centres may be built to satisfy these demands, determine the location and the size of the centres and which demand areas are to be served by a given centre, in order to optimize a given objective function. Obviously, the real problem cannot be solved by mathematical programming model, i.e. by a pure quantitative approch, but such a model may be useful developped within a suitable methodological framework, connecting empiric-qualitative analyses and evaluations with automatic computations.
In this sense a multistage and iterative procedure has been proposed in

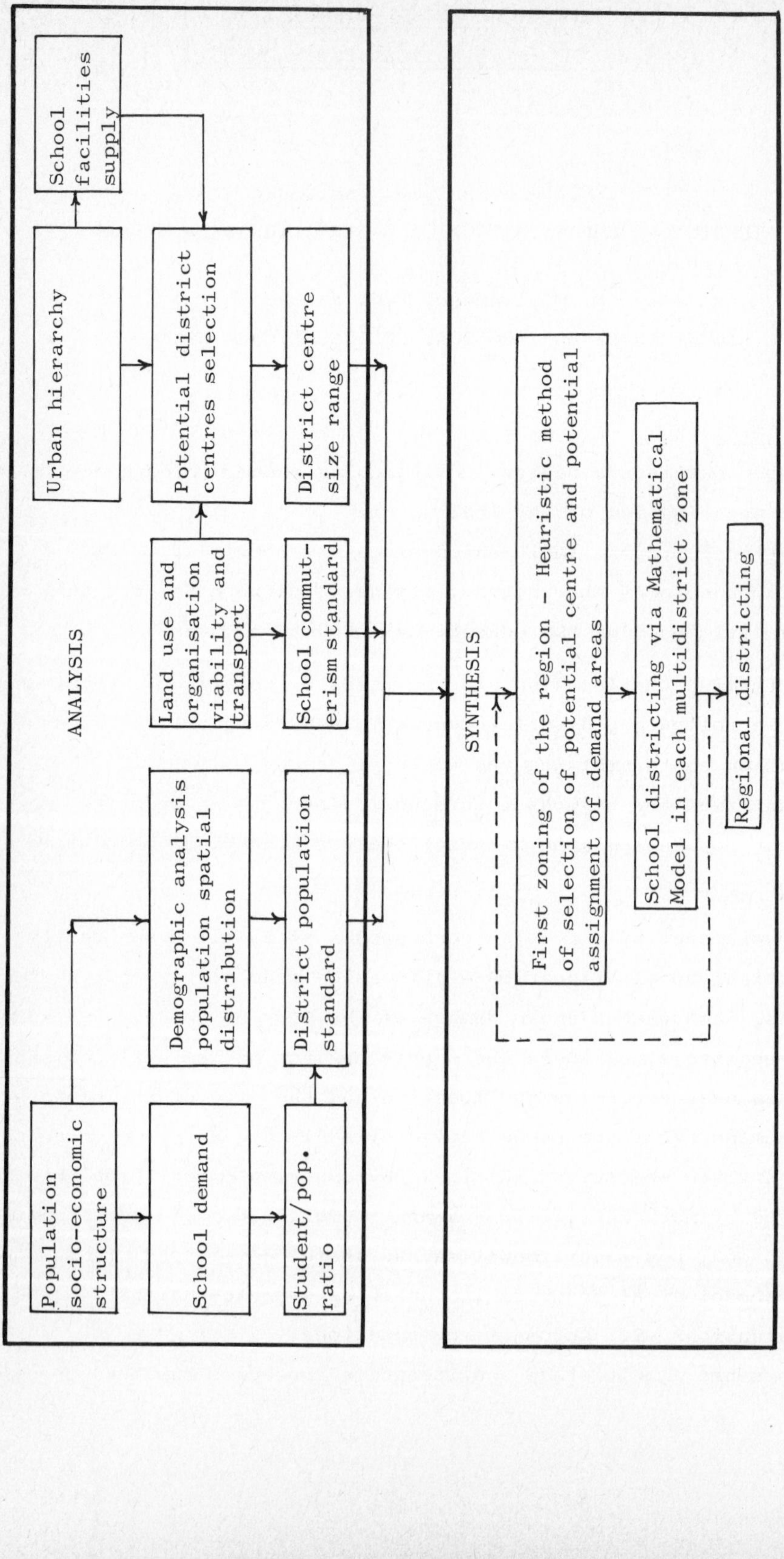
ANALYSIS
Population socio-economic structure
School demand
Student/pop. ratio
Demographic analysis population spatial distribution
District population standard
Land use and organisation viability and transport
School commut-erism standard
Urban hierarchy
School facilities supply
Potential district centres selection
District centre size range
SYNTHESIS
First zoning of the region - Heuristic method of selection of potential centre and potential assignment of demand areas
School districting via Mathematical Model in each multidistrict zone
Regional districting

Fig. 1

previous works /1/; an essential logical scheme is reported in Fig. 1. Here we will remark only that:

- parameters and constraints of the model are determined in the analysis phase;
- the first level zoning takes into account socio-political and "strategic" factors (often qualitative) and assures the feasibility of the model from a computational point of view in the meantime;
- the main task of the model is to assure the economic efficiency of the plan, given dominant political and social options;
- the iteration of the procedure, as in a simulation process, define a pay-off rate between socio-political goals and economic costs;
- the output of the study isn't "the plan", rather a balance sheet of qualitative-quantitative evaluations of some relevant alternatives.

In this framework a capacited plant location model with capacity indivisibility and side constraints has been developped.
In the following the structure of the model and the algorithm are presented, while experiments and computational results are described in other works /1/,/2/.

MODEL FORMULATION

With reference to a given zone the following entities are defined:

a) - a set $J = \{j / j = 1, \dots, m\}$ where j represents a potential district centre
 - a vector $q_j = \{q_{jk} / k = 1, \dots, k_j\}$ where q_{jk} represents the k-th capacity level of centre j (k = 1 corresponds to a closed centre)
 - a vector $f_j = \{f_{jk} / k = 1, \dots, k_j\}$, where f_{jk} represents the production cost for centre j of k-th level
 - a location variable vector $y_j = \{y_{jk} / k = 1, \dots, k_j\}$, $y_{jk} = \begin{cases} 0 \\ 1 \end{cases}$ 1), where if $y_{jk} = 1$ centre j is opened of k-th level

$$\sum_{k=1}^{k_j} y_{jk} = 1 \, , \forall j \in J \qquad 2)$$

b) - a matrix $\{h_{js}\}$ $[m \times m]$, $h_{js} = \begin{cases} 0 \\ 1 \end{cases}$, representing the compatibility among potenzial district centres, i.e. if $h_{js} =$ s j and s are mutually exclusive

$$\sum_{s=1}^{m} h_{js} (1 - y_{s1}) \leqslant 1 , \forall j \in J \qquad 3)$$

c) - two parameters NMIN and NMAX representing lower and upper bounds for the zone district number

$$NMIN \leqslant \sum_{j} (1 - y_{j1}) \leqslant NMAX \qquad 4)$$

d) - a set $I = \{i/i = 1,\dots, n\}$, where i represents elementary areas, with demand r_i.

The problem is feasible if the following data relation is verified:

$$\sum_{i=1}^{n} r_i \leqslant \sum_{j=1}^{m} q_{jk_j}$$

e) - an allocation variable matrix $\{x_{ij}\}$ $[n \times m]$, where x_{ij} $0 \leqslant x_{ij} \leqslant r_i$ 5), represents the ratio of demand r_i allocated to centre j. Obviously the allocation must not exceed the centre capacity, i.e.

$$\sum_{i=1}^{n} x_{ij} \leqslant \sum_{k=1}^{k_j} q_{jk} \; y_{jk} \; , \forall j \in J \qquad 6)$$

The demand of each centre must be satisfied:

$$\sum_{j=1}^{m} x_{ij} = r_i \quad \forall i \in I \qquad 7)$$

f) - a transportation cost matrix $\{c_{ij}\}$ $[n \times m]$

$c_{ij} = \infty$ if i cannot be allocated to j

g) - the objective function

$$F(x,y) = (1-\beta) \sum_{j=1}^{m} \sum_{k=1}^{k_j} f_{jk} \; y_{jk} + \sum_{i=1}^{n} \sum_{j=1}^{m} c_{ij} \; x_{ij}$$

i.e. the weighted sum between amortized production and transportation cost.

Our problem correspondes to:

$\min_{x,y}$ F (x,y) subject to constraints 1,..., 7

Parameter β in the objective function permits to experiment different pay-off rates between public and private costs of school service.

THE ALGORITHM

A two level tree-search algorithm has been developped. First of all a tree (main tree) is scanned, where each node represents a solution of the location problem:

determine $y_{jk} = \begin{cases} 1 \\ 0 \end{cases}$, $\forall j \in J$, $k = \begin{cases} 1 \\ k_j \end{cases}$

In the initial node $y_{jk_j} = 1, \forall i \in J$; the centres are progressively "closed" ($y_{j1} = 1$, j given) according to some preference ordering.

Let J_0^P be, at a given node P, the set of "opened" centres

$(y_{jk_j} = 1,\; j \in J_0^P)$

The node P is feasible if:

- the constraints 2,3,4 (side constraints) are satisfied and

- $\sum_{i \in I} r_i \leqslant \sum_{j \in J_0^P} q_{jk_j}$ 8)

In this case the transportation subroutine is applied in order to determine a feasible solution of the model. Otherwise the node P is fathomized and a backtrack process occurs. A secondary tree is generated in corrispondence with each feasible node of the main tree, where the capacity levels of the "opened" centres are tried to be reduced. The node PS, corresponding to node P of the main tree, represents a solution of the location problem:

$$\text{determine} \quad y_{jk} = \begin{cases} 1 \\ 0 \end{cases}, \qquad j \in J_0^P, \quad k = 2, \ldots, k_j$$

The node PS may be fathomized if:

- a feasibility check analogous to 8) is not satisfied or
- an usual bounding condition occurs.

Otherwise the transportation subroutine is applied.

The lower bound, at the node PS of the secondary tree deriving from node P of the main tree, is the sum of two components:

- a <u>transportation cost</u> defined as

$$\min_{x_{ij}} \sum_{i} \sum_{j \in J_0^P} c_{ij} \; x_{ij} \qquad \text{with constraints}$$

$$\sum_{i} x_{ij} \leqslant q_{jk_j} \qquad \forall j \in J_0^P$$

$$\sum_{i \;\; J_0^P} x_{ij} = r_i \qquad \forall i \in I$$

$$x_{ij} \geqslant 0 \qquad \forall i \in I, j \in J_0^P$$

- a <u>fixed cost</u> defined as

$$\sum_{j \;\; J^{PS}} f_{jk(j)} + CF, \text{ where}$$

$J^{PS} = \left\{ j \;\; J_0^P / y_{jk(j)} = 1 \right\}$ i.e. the set of opened centres whose capacity level $k(j)$ is fixed on the secondary tree.

$$CF = \min_{z_{jk}} \sum_{k=1}^{k_j} \sum_{j \left\{ J_0^P - J^{PS} \right\}} f_{jk} \; z_{jk} \qquad \text{with constraints}$$

$$z_{jk} = \begin{cases} 0 \\ 1 \end{cases}$$

and $\sum_{i=1}^{n} r_i - \sum_{j \in J^{PS}} q_{jk(j)} \sum_{k=1}^{k_j -} \sum_{j \in \{J_0^P - J^{PS}\}} q_{jk} \; z_{jk}$

The fixed cost is the sum of two terms. The former is the cost of the capacity levels of the nodes backward and that of the node PS, namely of the nodes whose capacities are already fixed. The letter, here denoted as CF, is the minimum cost referring to capacity levels of the nodes foreward that satisfy the demand.

CF is computed via Parametric Dynamic Programming because it must be evaluated several times corresponding to different levels of residual demand.

DETAILED ALGORITHM

Define:

$$R = \sum_{i=1}^{n} r_i$$

$$y = \{y_1, y_2 \dots y_m\}$$

$$q(y) = \sum_{j=1}^{m} q_j^T \; y_j$$

h_i, H_i fathomization indexes

INIZIALIZATION

1) $\bar{z} = \infty$; $h_j = -1$, $y_{jk_j} = 1 \; \forall j$
2) if $q(y) \geqslant R$ go to 3) else ERROR go to 9)
3) if y satisfies side constraints go to 4) else go to 8)
4) $z = F(x,y)$ (x generated via transportation subroutine)
5) if $z < \bar{z}$ go to 6) else go to 7)
6) $\bar{z} = z$
7) CALL TREE 2
8) CALL TREE 1

9) STOP

TREE 1

1) $j = m;\ y_{j1} = 1 \ \forall j$
2) if $h_j < 0$ go to 3) else go to 11)
3) $h_j = 0$
4) if y satisfies side constraints go to 5) else go to 10)
5) if $q(y) \geq R$ go to 6) else go to 9)
6) $z = F(x,y)$
7) if $z < \bar{z}$ go to 8) else go to 9)
8) $\bar{z} = z$
9) CALL TREE 2
10) if $j \neq m$ go to 1) (branch) else go to 11) (backtrack)
11) $h_j = -1;\ y_{jk_j} = 1;\ j = j-1;\ y_{j1} = 1$
12) if $j = 0$ go to 13) else go to 2)
13) RETURN

TREE 2

1) $H_j = -1 \ \forall j \mid y_{jk_j} = 1$
2) $j = m^*$, where m^* is the number of opened centres
3) if $H_j < 0$ go to 4) else go to 13) (backtrack)
4) $H_j = k_j - \bar{k} - 1$, where $\bar{k} = \min_k \ q_{jk} \mid q_{jk} \geq R - \sum_{s \neq j} q_s^T y_s$
5) if $H_j > 0$ go to 6) else go to 13) (backtrack)
6) $F_{jk}^* = \min_k LB_{jk}$, $\bar{k} \leq k \leq k_j$, where LB_{jk} is a lower bound on $F(x,y)$ at node $(\{y - y_j\}, y_{jk})$
7) if $F_{jk}^* \leq \bar{z}$ go to 8) else go to 13) (backtrack)
8) $LB_{jk}^* = \infty;\ H_j = H_j - 1$
9) $z = F(x,y)$
10) if $z < \bar{z}$ go to 11) else go to 12)

11) $\bar{z} = z$

12) if $j \neq m^*$ go to 2) (branch) else go to 5)

13) $H_j = -1$; $j - 1$

14) if $j > 0$ go to 15) else go to 17)

15) if $H_j = 0$ go to 13) else go to 16)

16) if $H_j < 0$ go to 4) else go to 6)

17 RETURN

This algorithm has been coded in FORTRAN V and tested on UNIVAC 1108, as in reference /1/.

REFERENCES

/1/ P. Maggiolini, P.C. Palermo, G. Tagliabue, P.P. Vecchi "Regional Planning of Educational Systems: Methodology and Mathematical Models" AIRO Symposium, Milan, 1975 (in italian)

/2/ C. De Giorgi, P.C. Palermo, G. Tagliabue, M. Valdata "School Districting Model" AIRO Symposium, Milan 1975 (in italian)

/3/ C. Revelle, D. Marks, J.C. Liebman "An Analysis of Private and Public Sector Location Models" Manag. Sci. Vol. 16, N. 11, 692-707 (1970)

/4/ G. Sà "Branch - and - Bound and Approximate Solution to the Capacited Plant-Location Problem" O.R., Vol. 17 1005-1015 (1969)

/5/ R.J. O'Brien "Model for Planning the Location and Size of Urban School" Socio. Econ. Plan. Sci., Vol. 2, 141-153 (1969)

ON THE OPTIMAL CONTROL OF NATURAL RESOURCE USE IN THE NEOCLASSICAL ECONOMIC FRAMEWORK*

A. Haurie and N. M. Hung

Ecole des Hautes Etudes Commerciales, Montréal.

Abstract:

One considers a class of neoclassical economic growth models where one commodity is a natural resource. Turnpike properties are proved for the finite horizon dynamic optimization problem and conditions are given for the existence of optimal programmes in the infinite horizon case. Some simple examples illustrate these findings.

Acknowledgements:

We would like to thank W.A. Brock who suggested the approach used for the existence problem. Of course all remaining errors are ours.

1.- Introduction.

This paper is an attempt to deal rigorously with some fundamental mathematical problems arising from the consideration of natural resources in the neoclassical framework of optimal economic growth. The theory of optimal economic growth initiated by Ramsey 1928 and developed by many others has benefited considerably from an optimal control formulation, see for example Shell 1967. Incidentally it posed two interesting problems which seem to be typical of these economic models.

The first one concerns the precise formulation of the *Turnpike Property*, see Cass 1966, the second one is the definition and the characterization of *the optimality when the time interval considered is infinite* and the formulation of *existence conditions* for such an optimal solution, see Koopmans 1965. It appeared that the two problems are linked together through the important role played in both problems by an *optimal steady state* suitably defined.

In the case of optimal exploitation of a natural resource, the *Turnpike Property* is well illustrated by the very simple model of optimal fish harvest studied by Cliff and Vincent 1973. Those authors showed that, for their particular model, any optimal trajectory on a sufficiently large interval would contain a singular arc where the fish population is maintained at its *level of maximal yield*, this singular arc being independent of the initial and terminal conditions. When, in a given economy, more than one commodity,some of them being natural resources, enter into production, a similar property is expected to prevail. In section 2.2 it is shown that this is

* This research was supported by Canada Council (Grant S74-1122) and by the Ministère de l'Education du Québec DGES, FCAC.

true: the Turnpike Property exhibited is expressed as a bound for the measure of the time spent away from the *Von Neumann Set* of the economy, a set which always contain the optimal steady state (s). When the cost of extraction does not depend on the importance of the stock of natural resource, an optimal steady state corresponds necessarily to the level of maximal yield for the natural resource.

When an *exhaustible* natural resource is *essential* in the production process, the concept of optimal steady states loses much of its significance since it corresponds to the degenerate situation with no production and no consumption. However another kind of property will be proved in section 2.3 which establishes a link between optimal programmes when a resource is exhaustible and the optimal steady state of a similar economy but where the natural resource is unexhaustible. Of course, that kind of Turnpike property is now dependent on the initial stock of the exhaustible resource.

In section 2.4 the existence of an optimal programme on the infinite horizon is proved. As noted by Solow 1975 one can have doubts that Time discount is defensible on the time scale appropriate for those models. The zero discount case is not a simple one since the use of the sufficient conditions of Arrow and Kurz 1970 is in general not possible and the sufficient conditions given by Rockafellar 1973 are not easily implemented. However, if there exists a unique optimal steady state the existence of an optimal programme is assured for the class of models under study. It is interesting to observe that the optimality concept introduced is stronger than those considered by Brock 1968 for a discrete time model and more recently by Halkin 1974 for an extension of the maximum principle.

Finally it should be noted that the method used to derive these results is quite general. Although the proofs make sometimes use of the peculiarities of the model defined in section 2.1, the same approach could be repeated for another model with more commodities. In fact these results could be obtained for a general class of convex control systems as shown by Rockafellar 1973, Haurie 1976, Haurie and Brock 1976.

2. Turnpike and Existence Theorems for a Dynamic Economy with Natural Resource.

In this section a model of an economy with a natural resource is introduced. We suppose that there exists a single consumption good which can reproduce itself in conjunction with the use of a commodity extracted from the environment: the natural resource. By not considering Time discount, this planning problem can be represented as being one of optimal control of an autonomous system. Our aim is to obtain a Turnpike property for optimal programmes and conditions for existence of an optimal programme when the planning horizon becomes infinite, under a minimal set of assumptions. The approach used is an adaptation to that particular model of the more abstract developments found in Haurie 1976 or Haurie and Brock 1976.

2.1 The system under study.

It is given by the following equations:

$$\dot{W} = U(C) \tag{2.1}$$

$$\dot{K} = I - \mu K, \quad \mu > 0 \text{ given} \tag{2.2}$$

$$\dot{R} = G(R) - E \tag{2.3}$$

$$I + C \leq F_1(K_1, E) \tag{2.4}$$

$$E \leq F_2(K_2, R) \tag{2.5}$$

$$K_1 + K_2 \leq K \tag{2.6}$$

$$0 \leq R,\ 0 \leq C,\ 0 \leq I,\ 0 \leq E,\ 0 \leq K_1,\ 0 \leq K_2 \tag{2.7}$$

Where the *state variables* are: the accumulated utility for the system W, the stock of the reproducible composite commodity K and the stock of the natural resource R. The *control variables* are : the consumption flow C, the investment I, the flow E of natural resource into production, the part K_1 of the stock K devoted to production of the composite commodity and the part K_2 devoted to the activity of extraction of the natural resource. U(.) is a *concave functional* defining the instantaneous utility of consumption, $F_1(.)$ and $F_2(.)$ are *concave and differentiable functionals* describing respectively the production and extraction opportunities. μ is the depreciation rate and G(.) is a *concave, differentiable* functional describing the regeneration process of the natural resource, as given for example by the Verhulst-Pearl équation.

Various models recently proposed for the investigation of the optimal use of natural resources can be cast in the form of the system (2.1) - (2.7). This is particularly the case for those developed by Dasgupta and Heal 1975, Hung 1975, Plourde 1970.

The following terminology will be used:

Definition 2.1:

a) A *programme* $\tilde{\pi}_T$ emanating from (K^o, R^o) is a map $\tilde{\pi}_T : [0, T] \to R^8$ ($[0,\infty) \to R^8$ when $T = \infty$) such that:

(i) $\tilde{\pi}_T(t) \triangleq (\tilde{W}(t), \tilde{K}(t), \tilde{R}(t), \tilde{C}(t), \tilde{I}(t), \tilde{E}(t), \tilde{K}_1(t), \tilde{K}_2(t))_T$

(ii) Almost everywhere on $[0, T]$ Eqs. (2.1) - (2.3) are satisfied.

(iii) Everywhere on $[0, T)$ the constraints (2.4) - (2.7) are verified.

(iv) $\tilde{W}_T(0) = 0$, $\tilde{K}_T(0) = K^o$, $\tilde{R}_T(0) = R^o$

b) To a given programme $\tilde{\pi}_T$ will be associated:

(i) The *trajectory*: $\tilde{y}_T : [0, T] \to R^3$, $\tilde{y}_T(t) = (\tilde{W}(t), \tilde{K}(t), \tilde{R}(t))_T$

(ii) The *state path*: $\tilde{x}_T : [0, T] \to R^2$, $\tilde{x}_T(t) = (\tilde{K}(t), \tilde{R}(t))_T$

c) A programme $\tilde{\pi}^*_T$ emanating from (K^o, R^o) is optimal if for any other programme $\tilde{\pi}_T$ emanating from (K^o, R^o) the following holds:

if $T < \infty$, $\tilde{W}^*_T(T) \geq \tilde{W}_T(T)$

$$\text{if } T = \infty,\ \forall\, \varepsilon > 0,\ \exists\, \tau,\ \forall\, t > \tau \quad \tilde{W}^*_\infty(t) > \tilde{W}_\infty(t) - \varepsilon \quad \blacksquare \tag{2.8}$$

This system satisfies the classical assumptions of optimal control theory as given by Lee and Markus 1967 and for $T < \infty$ fixed, the existence of an optimal programme is assured.

2.2 Statement and Proof of the Turnpike Property.

Consider the following optimization problem:

$$\left.\begin{array}{l} \bar{U} = \text{Max } U(C) \\ \text{under the constraints (2.4)-(2.7) and} \\ \dot{K} = I - \mu K \geq 0 \\ \dot{R} = G(R) - E \geq 0 \end{array}\right\} \tag{2.9}$$

This is a concave programming problem, thus if there exists a solution where none of the constraints (2.7) are active then there exists* a vector of Lagrange multipliers:

$$\bar{\sigma} \triangleq (\bar{p}, \bar{q}, \bar{\lambda}, \bar{\nu}, \bar{\theta}) \geq 0$$

such that for all vectors:

$$Z \triangleq (K, R, C, I, E, K_1, K_2) \in R^7,\ Z \geq 0$$

* See Mangasarian 1969.

the following holds:

$$\bar{U} \geq U\,(C) + \bar{p}\,(I - \mu K) + \bar{q}\,(G(R) - E) + \bar{\lambda}\,(F_1(K_1,E) - I - C) + \bar{\nu}\,(F_2(K_2,R) - E) + \bar{\theta}\,(K - K_1 - K_2) \triangleq L\,(Z, \sigma) \qquad (2.10)$$

and for at least one $\bar{Z}$ satisfying the constraints:

$$\bar{U} = U\,(\bar{C}) \qquad (2.11)$$

Let F denote the subset of all vectors $Z \geq 0$ for which the equality holds in (2.10), this is the *Von Neumann Set* of the economy. For a given Z we are interested in the distance:

$$d\,(Z,F) \triangleq \text{Inf}\,\{\|Z - Z'\|: Z' \in F\}.$$

Lemma 2.1 :

Let X be a given compact subset of R^7 then the following holds:

$$\forall\, \varepsilon > 0\ \exists\, \delta > 0 \text{ s.t. } Z \in X \text{ and } d\,(Z,F) > \varepsilon \Rightarrow \bar{U} - \delta > L\,(Z,\bar{\sigma}) \qquad (2.12)$$

Proof: Similar to the one given by Atsumi 1965, McKenzie 1968 or Haurie 1976 ∎

Now the Turnpike Property can be established:

Theorem 2.1: Let us assume that:

a) There exists a compact subset $X \subset R^7$ such that, for any $T > 0$, any programme $\tilde{\pi}_T \triangleq (\tilde{W}\,,\,\tilde{Z}\,)_T$ is such that:

$$\forall\, t \in [0,\, T] \quad \tilde{Z}_T(t) \in X$$

b) There exists a programme $\tilde{\pi}^+_\infty$ emanating from (K^0,R^0) such that:

$$\exists\, \bar{T} > 0\,,\ \forall\, t \geq \bar{T} \quad U\,[\tilde{C}^+_\infty(t)] = \bar{U} \qquad (2.13)$$

Then for $T > \bar{T}$, any optimal programme will necessarily verify:

$$m_T(\varepsilon) < \frac{1}{\delta}\,[\bar{U}\,\bar{T} + \bar{p}\,(\tilde{K}^*_T(T) - K^0) + \bar{q}\,(\tilde{R}^*_T(T) - R^0)] \qquad (2.14)$$

where $m_T(\varepsilon)$ is the Lebesgue measure of the subset of $[0,T]$ defined by:

$$\mathbb{E}_T(\varepsilon) \triangleq \{t \in [0,\, T]: d\,(\tilde{Z}^*_T(t),\, F) > \varepsilon\,\} \qquad (2.15)$$

Proof: Since $\tilde{\pi}^*_T$ is optimal, and since $U\,(\tilde{C}^+_\infty(t)) = \bar{U}$ for $t \geq \bar{T}$ one has:

$$\tilde{W}^*_T(T) \geq \tilde{W}^+_\infty(T) \geq \bar{U}\,(T - \bar{T}) \qquad (2.16)$$

Now, for an optimal programme the constraints (2.4)-(2.6) will always be active and thus, using (2.10)-(2.12) and integrating between 0 and T one obtains:

$$\tilde{W}^*_T(T) < \bar{U}\,T - \bar{p}\,(K^*_T(T) - K^0) - \bar{q}\,(\tilde{R}^*_T(T) - R^0) - \delta m_T(\varepsilon) \qquad (2.17)$$

where $m_T(\varepsilon)$ has been defined as the measure of the set (2.15). Now (2.16) and (2.17) lead to:

$$m_T(\varepsilon) < \frac{1}{\delta} [\bar{U}\,\bar{T} + \bar{p}\,(\tilde{K}^*_T(T) - K^o) + \bar{q}\,(\tilde{R}^*_T(T) - R^o)]$$

that is (2.14).■

2.3 Interpretation of the Turnpike Property.

2.3.1 The role of the compact set X is essential in the proof of Theorem 2.1. Such a set will be naturally defined if there exists $K_{max} > K^o$ and $R_{max} > R^o$ such that under (2.2)-(2.7) one necessarily has the following implication

$$K > K_{max} \text{ and } R > R_{max} \Rightarrow \dot{K} < 0 \text{ and } \dot{R} < 0$$

2.3.2 The upper bound given in (2.15) means that, for large values of T, an optimal programme $\tilde{\pi}^*_T$ spends most of the period in the vicinity of the set F. When F reduces to a single element $\bar{Z}$, the free disposal assumptions (2.4) and (2.5) imply that $\bar{Z}$ corresponds to *the optimal steady state* of the economy.

2.3.3 Let us write the Pontryagin necessary conditions* for an optimal trajectory $\tilde{y}^*_T$ of the system (2.1)-(2.7). Defining the Lagrangian L (Z,σ) as in (2.10) the following holds when none of the constraints (2.7) are active:

$$\frac{\partial L}{\partial C} = U'(C) - \lambda = 0 \qquad \frac{\partial L}{\partial I} = p - \lambda = 0$$

$$\frac{\partial L}{\partial E} = -q + \lambda\frac{\partial F_1}{\partial E} - \nu = 0 \qquad \frac{\partial L}{\partial K_1} = \lambda\frac{\partial F_1}{\partial K_1} - \theta = \frac{\partial L}{\partial K_2} = \nu\frac{\partial F_2}{\partial K_2} - \theta = 0$$

$$\frac{\partial L}{\partial K} = \theta - \mu\, p = -\dot{p} \qquad \frac{\partial L}{\partial R} = q\, G'(R) + \nu\frac{\partial F_2}{\partial R} = -\dot{q}$$

while the constraints (2.2)-(2.6) are satisfied. Those conditions lend themselves to the standard interpretation in terms of marginal utility and marginal productivity. If there exists a unique solution to these equations when $\dot{p} = \dot{q} = \dot{K} = \dot{R} = 0$, F reduces to a single element $\bar{Z}$ toward which the economy is driven.

2.3.4 The two limiting cases of an unexhaustible resource ($G(R) \equiv \infty$, $\partial F_2/\partial R \equiv 0$) and of a non replenishable resource ($G(R) \equiv 0$) deserve a particular attention.

In the first case the state equation (2.3) is no longer a constraint and (2.14) is replaced by:

$$m_T(\varepsilon) < \frac{1}{\delta} [\bar{U}\,\bar{T} + \bar{p}\,(\tilde{K}^*(T) - K^o)] \tag{2.18}$$

Now consider the second case. If the resource does not replenish itself, a steady state requires $E \equiv 0$ and it becomes clear that F cannot reduce to a single element (any value for R is compatible with $E = 0$); furthermore the Turnpike property loses its significance since the optimal steady states correspond to a degenerate situation where the natural resource is not used in the economy.

---

* for simplicity one will assume that U (.) is differentiable.

However a different kind of "Turnpike" could be exhibited. First, we notice that the only difference between unexhaustible and non replenishable resources is that any positive rate of extraction can be maintained in the first case while no positive rate of extraction can be maintained in the second case. Nevertheless, if the initial stock is large enough, and if $\partial F_2/\partial R \equiv 0$, it may be possible to reach at time $\bar{T}$ the steady state $\bar{Z}$ corresponding to the unexhaustible case and then to maintain the extraction at level $\bar{E}$ until exhaustion of the resource at time $\hat{T}$. For all $T > \hat{T}$ an optimal programme $\tilde{\pi}^*_T$ will certainly verify.

$$\tilde{W}^*(T) \geq (\hat{T} - \bar{T})\, \bar{U} \tag{2.19}$$

Assuming that $\bar{Z}$ is unique and defining $m'_T(\varepsilon)$ as the measure of the set:

$$\Xi'_T(\varepsilon) \overset{\Delta}{=} \{t \in [0, T]: d\,(\tilde{Z}^*_T(t), \bar{Z}) > \varepsilon\}$$

a repetition of the arguments of Theorem 2.1 gives:

$$m'_T(\varepsilon) < \frac{1}{\delta}\,[\bar{U}\,(T - \hat{T} + \bar{T}) + \bar{p}\,(\tilde{K}^*(T) - K^0)] \tag{2.20}$$

For T fixed, when R^0 increases $\hat{T}$ tends to be close to T and thus (2.20) does not differ strongly from (2.18). The relation (2.19) says that when the initial stock of a non replenishable resource is large, an optimal programme will first drive the economy toward the steady state $\bar{Z}$ as if the resource was in infinite supply and only at the end of the period will the scarcity of the resource be taken seriously into account.

To illustrate that behaviour consider the following particular system:

$$\dot{W} = C \quad , \quad \dot{K} = I - \mu K \quad , \quad \dot{R} = -E$$

$$I + C \leq A\, K_1^{\alpha}\, E^{1-\alpha} \quad , \quad A > 0 \text{ given} \quad , \quad \alpha \in [0, 1] \text{ given}$$

$$E \leq B\sqrt{K_2} \quad , \quad B > 0 \text{ given} \quad ,$$

$$K_1 + K_2 \leq K$$

$$0 \leq E, \quad 0 \leq K, \quad 0 \leq R, \quad 0 \leq I, \quad 0 \leq C, \quad 0 \leq K_1, \quad 0 \leq K_2$$

The gradient of the Langrangian $L(Z,\sigma)$ is given by:

$$\left.\begin{aligned}
&\frac{\partial L}{\partial C} = 1 - \lambda \qquad \frac{\partial L}{\partial I} = p - \lambda \qquad \frac{\partial L}{\partial E} = -q - \nu + \lambda A\,(1-\alpha)\left(\frac{K_1}{E}\right)^{\alpha} \\
&\frac{\partial L}{\partial K_1} = \lambda A\,\alpha\left(\frac{K_1}{E}\right)^{\alpha-1} - \theta \qquad \frac{\partial L}{\partial K_2} = \frac{\nu B}{2\sqrt{K_2}} - \theta \\
&\frac{\partial L}{\partial K} = \theta - p\mu = -\dot{p} \qquad \frac{\partial L}{\partial R} = 0 = -\dot{q}
\end{aligned}\right\} \tag{2.21}$$

If appears that an optimal trajectory will be composed of regular arcs where $C \equiv 0$ or $I \equiv 0$ and of a singular arc characterized by the condition: $p \equiv 1$.

Along such an arc the necessary conditions imply:

$$\theta = \mu, \quad \frac{K_1}{E} = \left(\frac{\alpha A}{\mu}\right)^{\frac{1}{1-\alpha}} \quad , \quad E = \frac{\nu B}{2\mu} \quad , \quad q + \nu = A\,(1-\alpha)\left(\frac{K_1}{E}\right)^{\alpha}$$

Since q and K_1/E are constants ν is also a constant and thus E is a constant too. It appears that the singular arc is uniquely defined as a steady state and it would be easy to check that it corresponds to the optimal steady state when the resource is unexhaustible.

2.4 Existence of an optimal programme on the infinite horizon.

Theorem 2.2 : Under the assumptions of Theorem 2.1 and if F reduces to the single element $\bar{Z}$ then there exists an optimal programme $\tilde{\pi}^*_\infty$ emanating from (K^0, R^0).

Proof: Define: $L'(x,\bar{\sigma}) \triangleq \text{Sup}\{L(Z,\bar{\sigma}): (C, I, E, K_1, K_2) \geq 0$, with (2.4)-(2.6)$\}$.

$$L_0(x) \triangleq L'(x,\bar{\sigma}) - \bar{U} \leq 0 \tag{2.22}$$

$L_0(x)$ is non positive by (2.10). Since there exists a programme $\tilde{\pi}^+_\infty$ for which

$$U[\tilde{C}^+_\infty(t)] \equiv \bar{U} \ \forall t \geq \bar{T}$$

One has certainly:

$$\theta^* = \text{Sup}\{\int_0^\infty L_0(\tilde{x}_\infty(t))\,dt: \ \tilde{K}(0) = K^0, \ \tilde{R}(0) = R^0\} > -\infty$$

where the sup is over all state paths $\tilde{x}_\infty$ with given initial values K^0, R^0.
Now there exists a sequence $\{\tilde{x}^n_\infty\}_{n\in N}$ of state paths such that:

$$\lim_{n\to\infty} \int_0^\infty L_0(\tilde{x}^n_\infty(t))\,dt = \theta^*$$

By (2.21) and using the dominated convergence theorem one has also:

$$\int_0^\infty \lim_{n\to\infty} L_0(\tilde{x}^n_\infty(t))\,dt = \theta^* \tag{2.23}$$

Varaiya 1967 has shown that for a system having the compactness and convexity properties assumed here the set of state paths $\tilde{x}_\infty$ emanating from (K^0, R^0) is compact in the topology of uniform convergence on finite intervals. Thus the sequence $\{\tilde{x}^n_\infty\}_{n\in N}$ has at least one cluster point $\tilde{x}^*_\infty$ for which, by (2.23) and by the continuity of $L'(.,\bar{\sigma})$, one has:

$$\theta^* = \int_0^\infty L_0(\tilde{x}^*_\infty(t))\,dt \tag{2.24}$$

To the state path $\tilde{x}^*_\infty$ corresponds a programme $\tilde{\pi}^*_\infty$. We have to verify that $\tilde{\pi}^*_\infty$ is optimal. Consider any other programme and form:

$$E(T) \triangleq \int_0^T [U(\tilde{C}^*_\infty(t)) - U(\tilde{C}_\infty(t))]\,dt \tag{2.25}$$

By (2.10) and (2.22) the following holds:

$$\begin{aligned} E(T) \geq &\int_0^T [L_0(\tilde{x}^*_\infty(t)) - L_0(\tilde{x}_\infty(t))]\,dt \\ &- \bar{p}\,[\tilde{K}^*_\infty(T) - \tilde{K}_\infty(T)] \\ &- \bar{q}\,[\tilde{R}^*_\infty(T) - \tilde{R}_\infty(T)] \end{aligned} \tag{2.26}$$

Assume that *one does not have:*

$$\lim_{t \to \infty} \tilde{K}(t) = \bar{K} \qquad \text{and} \qquad \lim_{t \to \infty} \tilde{R}(T) = \bar{R}$$

Thus one necessarily has $m_\infty(\varepsilon) = \infty$ and from (2.12):

$$\int_0^\infty L_0 (\tilde{x}_\infty(t))\, dt = -\infty \tag{2.27}$$

Now it is clear, by (2.23) and (2.27) that the following convergence property holds for the state path $\tilde{x}^*_\infty$

$$\lim_{t \to \infty} \tilde{K}^*_\infty (t) = \bar{K} \qquad \text{and} \qquad \lim_{t \to \infty} \tilde{R}^*_\infty(T) = \bar{R}$$

If $\tilde{x}_\infty$ converges toward $(\bar{K}, \bar{R})$, then for any $\varepsilon > 0$, if T is chosen large enough one has:

$$E(T) > \int_0^T [L_0 (\tilde{x}^*_\infty(t)) - L_0 (\tilde{x}_\infty(t))]\, dt - \varepsilon$$

and therefore

$$\int_0^\infty [U (\tilde{C}^*_\infty(t)) - U (\tilde{C}_\infty(t))]\, dt \geq 0 \tag{2.28}$$

If $\tilde{x}_\infty$ is not converging toward $(\bar{K}, \bar{R})$, the terms $\bar{p}\, \tilde{K}_\infty(T)$ and $\bar{q}\, \tilde{R}_\infty(T)$ stay bounded while, by (2.27):

$$\lim_{T \to \infty} \int_0^T [L_0 (\tilde{x}_\infty(t)) - L_0 (\tilde{x}_\infty(t))]\, dt = \infty$$

Therefore (2.28) holds in this case too and $\tilde{\pi}^*_\infty$ is an optimal programme. ■

2.5 Interpretation of the existence theorem.

2.5.1 The unicity of the optimal steady state $\bar{Z}$ is essential for the proof of Theorem 2.2. Thus the existence Theorem does not apply to the case of a non replenishable resource. Dasgupta and Heal 1975 using the approach suggested by Arrow and Kurz 1970 showed the existence of optimal programmes for a particular system with non replenishable resource and it does not seem to be possible to get more general results.

2.5.2 The method used to etablish the existence theorem is reminiscent of the approach of Pitchford 1974 to study optimal population growth. Mimicking his approach we would consider the problem:

$$\text{Max} \int_0^T [U (\tilde{C}(t)) - \bar{U}]\, dt \quad \text{with} \quad \tilde{K}(T) = \bar{K},\ \tilde{R}(T) = \bar{R}$$

and under the constraints (2.2)-(2.7) with T free. It is clear that a solution of this problem would define an optimal programme on the infinite horizon. From a theoritical point of view, the main weakness of this approach is that for most cases a solution does not exist with a finite value of T. Thus contrarily to what is claimed by Pitchford, the existence theorem of Lee and Markus does not hold in that case since it requires an upper bound for the admissible values for T.

2.5.3 As an illustration consider the following particular system:

$$\dot{W} = C\ ,\ \dot{K} = I - \mu K$$

$$\dot{R} = GR\ (R_{max} - R) - E\ ,\ G > 0\ ,\ R_{max} > 0 \text{ given}$$

$$I + C \leq AK_1^{\alpha}\ E^{1-\alpha}\ ,\ A > 0 \text{ given}\ ,\ \alpha \in [0,\ 1] \text{ given}$$

$$E \leq B\ \sqrt{K_2}\ ,\ B > 0 \text{ given}\ ,\ K_1 + K_2 \leq K$$

$$0 \leq K\ ,\ 0 \leq R\ ,\ 0 \leq I\ ,\ 0 \leq C\ ,\ 0 \leq E\ ,\ 0 \leq K_1\ ,\ 0 \leq K_2$$

The gradient of the Lagrangian as computed in (2.21) still holds excepted for the last component $\partial L/\partial R$ which becomes:

$$\frac{\partial L}{\partial R} = G\ (R_{max} - 2R)\ q = -\ \dot{q}$$

A singular arc is still characterized by $p \equiv 1$ and thus one has:

$$\theta = \mu\ ,\ \frac{K_1}{E} = \left(\frac{\alpha A}{\mu}\right)^{\frac{1}{1-\alpha}}\ ,\ E = \frac{\nu B}{2\mu}$$

$$q + \nu = A\ (1 - \alpha)\ \left(\frac{K_1}{E}\right)^{\alpha}$$

If $R = \frac{1}{2} R_{max}$ one has $\dot{q} = 0$ and the singular arc corresponds to the optimal steady state.

If $R \neq \frac{1}{2} R_{max}$ then $\frac{K_1}{E}$ remains a constant and:

$$\dot{E} = -\ \frac{B}{2\mu}\dot{q} = \frac{GB}{2\mu}\ (R_{max} - 2R)\ q \quad \begin{cases} > 0 \text{ if } R < \frac{R_{max}}{2} \\ = 0 \text{ if } R = \frac{R_{max}}{2} \\ < 0 \text{ if } R > \frac{R_{max}}{2} \end{cases}$$

It appears that the singular arc leads asymptotically to the optimal steady state.

3.- Conclusion.

The results of section 2 are obtained under the general assumptions of optimal control theory and concave programming. Therefore they hold even when the functions U (.) and F_1 (.) are not differentiable. Moreover no assumption of homogeneity is required for the production function and even the Inada conditions are replaced by the weaker assumption of the existence of the compact set X.

From the economic viewpoint, the Turnpike Property is of great help in guiding the planner for the set-up of optimal economic policies. The planner's task is simplified once he has characterized the optimal steady state in the neighbourhood of which an optimal programme should stay for the most part of the planning period. Plourde 1970 obtained a qualitative result of the same kind for a one commodity model, the commodity being a replenishable resource.

When capital is introduced into the model, the characterization of optimal policies is possible by using the policy switching technique of Pitchford 1972. Such an analysis is done by Hung 1975. However the existence of optimal programmes on an infinite planning horizon was not correctly asserted in these earlier works. In this paper this gap is hopefully filled.

References

ARROW, K.J. and KURZ, M. 1970, *Public Investment, The Rate of Return and Optimal Fiscal Policy,* J. Hopkins Press.

ATSUMI, H. 1965, Neoclassical Growth and the Efficient Programm of Capital Accumulation, *Review of Economic Studies* 32: 127 - 136.

BROCK, W.A. 1970, On Existence of Weakly Maximal Programmes in a Multisector Economy, *Review of Economic Studies* 37: 275 - 280.

CASS, D. 1966, Optimum Growth in an aggregative model of capital accumulation: A Turnpike Theorem. *Econometrica* 34: 833 - 850.

CLIFF, E.H. and VINCENT T.L. 1973, An optimal Policy for a Fish Harvest, *Journal of Optimization Theory and Applications* 12: 485 - 496.

DASGUPTA, P. and HEAL G. 1975, The Optimal Depletion of Exhaustible Resources, *Review of Economic Studies* Symposium: 3 - 28.

HALKIN, H. 1974, Necessary Conditions for Optimal Control Problems with Infinite Horizon, *Econometrica* 42: 267 - 273.

HAURIE, A. 1976, Optimal Control on an Infinite Time Horizon: The Turnpike Approach, *Journal of Mathematical Economics*, to appear.

HAURIE, A. and BROCK, W.A. 1976, On Existence of Optimal Trajectories over an Infinite Time Horizon, miméo, to appear.

HUNG, N.M. 1975, *Essay on the Optimal Dynamic Exploitation of the Natural Resources and the Social Discount,* Ph.D. Thesis Univ. of Toronto.

KOOPMANS, T.C. 1965, On the Concept of Optimal Economic Growth in *The Economic Approach to Development Planning*, North Holland.

LEE, E.B. and MARKUS, L. 1967, *Foundations of Optimal Control Theory*, J. Wiley.

MANGASARIAN, O.L. 1969, *Nonlinear Programming*, McGraw-Hill.

MC KENZIE, L.W. 1968, Accumulation Programmes of Maximum Utility and the Von Neumman Facet, in J.N. Wolfe edit. *Value Capital and Growth*, Aldine.

PITCHFORD, J. 1972, Population and Optimal Growth, *Econometrica*, 40: 103 - 106.

PLOURDE, C.G. 1970, A Simple Model of Replenishable Natural Resource Exploitation, *American Economic Review*, 60: 518 - 523.

RAMSEY, F.P. 1928, A Mathematical Theory of Saving, *Economic Journal*, 38: 543 - 559.

ROCKAFELLAR, T. 1973, Saddle Points of Hamiltonian Systems in Convex Problems of Lagrange, *Journal of Optimization Theory and Applications*, 12: 367 - 390.

SHELL, K. edit. 1967, *Essays in the Theory of Optimal Economic Growth*, M.I.T. Press.

SOLOW, R.M. 1975, Intergenerational Equity and Exhaustible Resources, *Review of Economic Studies*, Symposium: 29 - 46.

VARAIYA, P. 1967, On the Trajectories of a Differential System, in *Mathematical Theory of Control*, Balakrishnan, Newstadt edit, Academic Press.

COMPUTER ELABORATION OF TIME-TABLE FOR SINGLE RAILWAY LINE

Miroslav JELASKA
Institute for Transportation,
Railway Enterprise Ljubljana
61000 Ljubljana, Yugoslavia

ABSTRACT

This paper presents an introduction of computer techniques for the elaboration of railway time-tables. A single track line section is treated.

A short survey on data-processing organization is given including the automatic preparation of output data: the drawing of train diagram and the printing of train data.

Particularly, the method for solving the time-table problem is formally described and the appropriate criterion function is presented.

INTRODUCTION

The most considerable part of researches having for subject the introduction of data-processing techniques for the elaboration of a railway time-table have for their starting point the final product - the train diagram. This problem being obviously very large is however, due to its complexity, generally dealt with only partially. The most considerable contributions in this field are listed in references herewith under items (1),(2),(3),(4) and (5). Our way of taking into consideration this problem is quite similar. Aiming to master as large part of the problem as possible, we have started with the purpose of mastering the implements for line sections. This is only a part of the field that can be considered. Obviously there remains open the question what completion of the entire data-processing and programming package would be optimal, or where the desired automatization level occurs. Whether it would be worth trouble to embrace the largest possible area at any rate or it would be necessary to take into account the proportion between the cost of product and its efficiency. This paper has for its subject the task which is to automatize the last phase of operation - elaboration of train diagram and train schedule on line section. Should we adopt in the course of time a kind of two-phase processing, fig.1 represents the following: our actual level of results is represented by shaded areas, while within the elaboration of time-table for a part of railway network the first phase would represent the rough processing determining the tasks for line sections, while the detailed elaboration of time-tables for line sections would be embraced by the second phase.

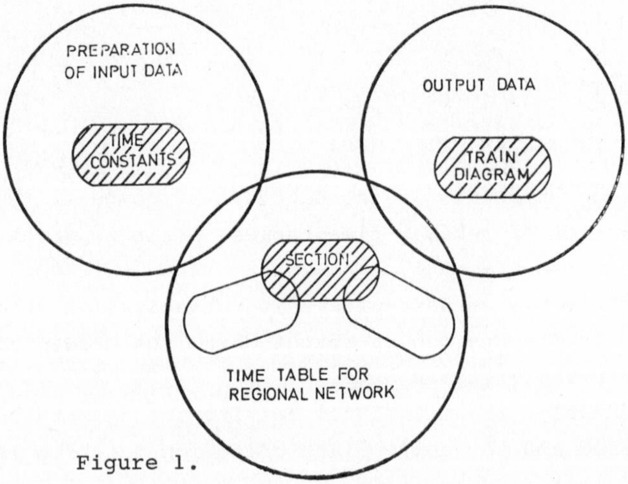

Figure 1.

The choice of adequate methods is not quite simple, since each Railway accentuates in the first place its own specific problems, and there is a lack of uniformity of attitudes in that field. There are some opinions that the universal solution would not be efficient. Even if we treat only single line section there are numerous possible solutions yet not easy to be estimated. Then we apply additional conditions and rules thus entering the field of heuristics and with this renouncing the optimum (except in the case it is occasionally found). Due to the existence of numerous solutions we apply the Monte Carlo technique of random testing. The next characteristic is the look-ahead method for solving conflicting situations. These would be the three basic characteristics of method applied.

The input data are quite heterogenous and their preparation is hard to be automatized. A part of data was collected from appropriate services, some were prepared by means of a programming package in use with Yugoslav Railways, the paper listed in references herewith under item (6) gives a good survey of the latter.

The output data represent the train diagram and the data on trains necessary for the time-table booklet officialy in use (e.g. the post of engine-driver is provided with the booklet ...). Both are represented on fig.6 and 7. With the exception of intermediate controls and corrections the way to the final product is automatized.The drawing embraces marks for minutes,numbers of trains and lines which represent the train trajectory. The fig.7 represents the output schedule for one train, fig.6 reproduces the drawing with an OFF-line plotter.

The fig.2 gives the rough flow chart of elaboration. It can be seen that it consists of two parts. The first part is the preparation. The time when to effect the preparation has not been determined, it can be effected much in advance or just before the execution. The second part is the execution in a limited sense to be effected when there is necessity of a new final product. The first correction has for its purpose to reprocess those data which have been modified and to choose the trains for line section. Thus an incomplete work file is prepared, it represents only a basis for elaboration of time-table, since during the optimization the file is completed in such a way that we can obtain from it the necessary informations for drawing train diagram and printing.

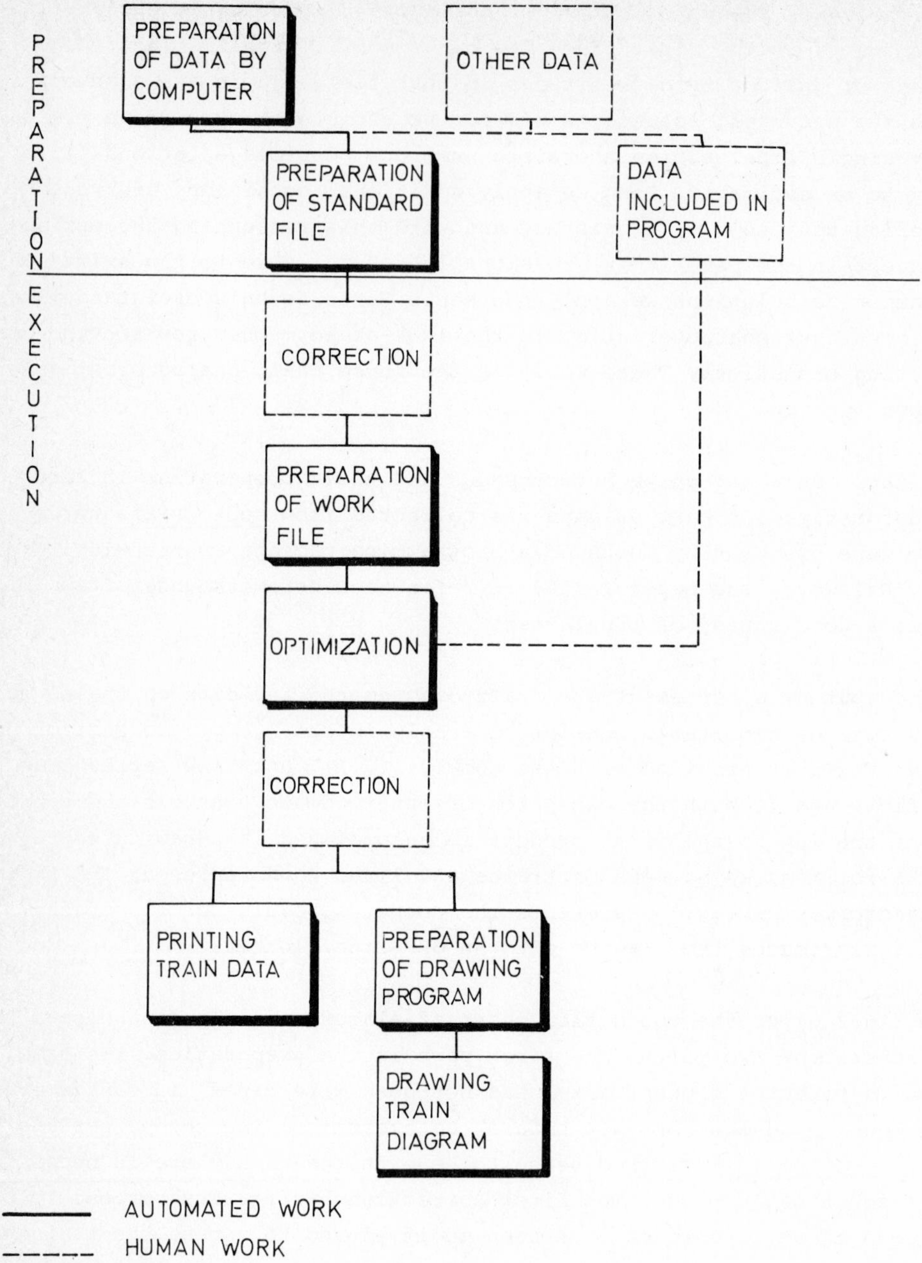
PREPARATION
EXECUTION
PREPARATION OF DATA BY COMPUTER
OTHER DATA
PREPARATION OF STANDARD FILE
DATA INCLUDED IN PROGRAM
CORRECTION
PREPARATION OF WORK FILE
OPTIMIZATION
CORRECTION
PRINTING TRAIN DATA
PREPARATION OF DRAWING PROGRAM
DRAWING TRAIN DIAGRAM
AUTOMATED WORK
HUMAN WORK

DATA AND NOTATION

To facilitate the understanding of the applied method we shall list hereunder the necessary notations and partially present the data which are being used. The input data have been classified in accordance to the mode of preparation to those prepared by means of computer and the ones provided by adequate services. As for the execution itself there is a more useful classification of data, namely data used in the optimization process and data used for preparation,printing or drawing. The first lot is more important and will be formally enumerated while other data are not so essential (e.g. for printing of train itinerary, for data needed for each single category of train such as: percentages of braked weight, maximum speeds etc., for estimation and printing of necessary elements on line sections where local passenger trains have to wait in stopping-places, a series of elements for previously effected simulations, various sizes for printing and drawing etc.).

Notation:

c	category of train
d	solution of conflicting situation
e	estimation of energy consumption for traction
f	criterion function
g	physical weight
i	station or section between two neighbour stations
j	direction
k	level in the tree of conflicting situations
l	locomotive type
n,m,ν	train
p	distance statistical data
q	conflict of two trains
r	weighted value of train
t	time
u	mode of running between two stations
w	sample of solution of conflict tree
x	binary switch
y	stop switch
α	coeff. of prices
γ	decision coeff. for "obvious" conflicting situations
δ	unit step function

ε interval for choice of time segments

λ number of tracks in station

Θ time statistical data

$\Delta\tau^{int}$ time intervals needed for trains in traffic

$\Delta\tau^{r}$ running time

$\Delta\tau^{s}$ minimum waiting time

τ^{l} time limit for locomotive delay

τ^{t} time limit for train delay

τ^{o} time after the train is available at initial station

CRITERION FUNCTION AND TRAIN WEIGHTING

The criterion function reflects a relation between incomes and expenses, i.e. we shall make efforts in obtaining the best possible results for a line section. The criterion function is constructed in such a way as to facilitate the comparison of two trains as well as of two different time-tables. It seems to us that it is essential to introduce train weighting in the criterion function. The mode of train weighting will be given priority treatment. Although it is difficult to estimate incomes and expenses, (these can be determined from various analysis), the main problem consists in how to determine or take into account the train priority class which has no quantitative indicator. The strict appliance of priority treatment for the higher priority train must be sometimes given up especialy on particularly busy section where it is difficult to operate the desired volume of traffic. Therefore we take simultaneously all trains into treatment and try to keep a certain proportion between the running time and waiting time by means of train weighting. From statistical data it is possible to determine a relationship among the following quantities:

actual running time	Θ_1
actual traveling time	Θ_2
actual distance	p
category of train	c

The value r_c is determined for each group of trains of the same category which were in operation during the period of time for which we have the available data:

$$r_c = p/(\theta_2 - \theta_1) \quad (1)$$

The value of r_c obtained for some categories of trains can be found in fig.3.

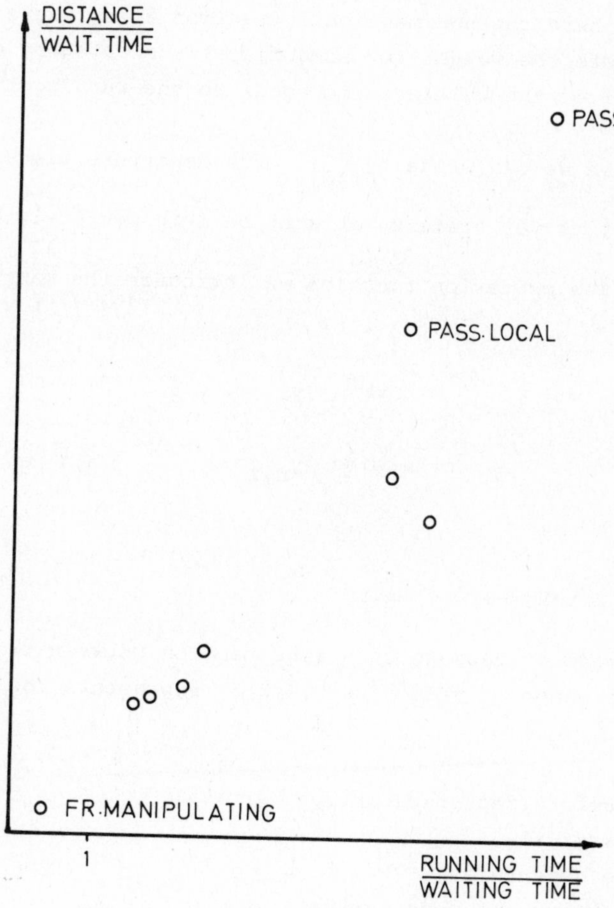

Figure 3.

The value r_c can be explained as the average number of km lost due to unit waiting time. This gives the possibility of valuating the waiting time of a train by means of the lost gross transport operation, and can be included into the criterion function. If we want, notwithstanding the statistical data, to obtain better relative results with trains of category c we can increase the value r_c over the one obtained from p, Θ_2 and Θ_1. It is essential to try to estimate how a unit of waiting time reduces the income since this does not represents a productive transport operation. We can apply here the undimensional fraction r_c/r_o where r_o is constant and represents the weight for some fictitious category of train having $\Theta_2=2\cdot\Theta_1$, i.e. the waiting time equal to the running time.

According to the notation we can write t_{n,i,j_n} for departure time and $t_{n,i,1-j_n}$ for arrival time for train n, at station i respectively. For some other elements in the criterion function we introduce the matrix for stopping $\left[y_{n,i}\right]$:

$$t_{n,i,j_n}=t_{n,i,1-j_n} \quad \Rightarrow \quad y_{n,i}=0 \qquad \text{otherwise} \quad y_{n,i}=1 \tag{2}$$

and the function:

$$u=2\cdot y_{n,i+2j_n-1} + 1\cdot y_{n,i} \tag{3}$$

which illustrates the mode of passage on a line section between two neighbour stations. The range of values $u\in\{0,1,2,3\}$ represents the following:

u=0 no waiting either before departure or upon arrival,
u=1 waiting only upon arrival,
u=2 waiting only before departure,
u=4 waiting before departure and upon arrival.

Coefficients α^a , $a\in\{1,2,...,6\}$ represent:

α^1 income per gross ton km,
α^2 expense per gross ton minute,
α^3 expense per minute of locomotive delay,
α^4 expense per minute of train delay,
α^5 expense per kwh for traction energy,

α^6 expense per stopping.

In order of appearance the expressions in the criterion function have the following meaning: 1.) estimate of income per train from gross effected transport work, 2.) estimate of expense or lost income for gross weight-time where the running time is not weighted while the waiting time is weighted with r_c/r_o , 3.)estimate of expense due to locomotive delay, 4.) estimate of expense due to train delay, 5.) estimate of expense due to the energy consumption for traction, 6.) estimate of additional expense for those stoppings that have been subsequently introduced.

The criterion function is:

$$f = \sum_n f_n \tag{4}$$

where

$$\begin{aligned} f_n = {} & \alpha^1_{c_n} \cdot P \cdot g_n - \\ & -\alpha^2_{c_n} \cdot g_n \Big(\frac{r_n}{r_o} \sum_i (t_{n,i,j_n} - t_{n,i,1-j_n}) + \sum_{i'} (t_{n,i_a,1-j_n} - t_{n,i,j_n}) \Big) - \\ & -\alpha^3_{l_n} \, (t_{n,I \cdot j_n + 1 - j_n, 1-j_n} - \tau^l_n) \cdot \delta(t - \tau^l_n) - \\ & -\alpha^4 \, (t_{n,I \cdot j_n + 1 - j_n, 1-j_n} - \tau^t_n) \cdot \delta(t - \tau^t_n) - \\ & -\alpha^5 \sum_{i'} e_{c_n, 1+u_{n,i'}, i'} - \\ & -\alpha^6 \sum_{i,\Delta\tau^s = 0} y_{n,i} \end{aligned}$$

$\delta(t)$ represents unit step function, $i \in \{1,2,\ldots,I\}$ stations and $i' \in \{1,2,\ldots,I-1\}$ sections between two neighbour stations.

DESCRIPTION OF PROCEDURE

We take into consideration the 24-hour time-table embracing the N_o set of trains. The solution would represent the determination of matrix elements $t_{n,i,j}$ along with fulfillment of condition (13). The procedure can be simplified in such a way as to treat each train n N_o only in the look-ahead method (and in the computer central memory). Consequently the time-table cycle of 24 hours will not be closed and it is therefore necessary to point out two facts:

-the first train to be treated, that is, the reference time t_o before the beginning of the procedure, must be chosen in such a way to facilitate the conclusion of the time-table cycle and to choose within a set of trains of sufficiently high priority class,

-upon the end of the procedure there remain some unsettled conflicts (in our case studie there remained two to five conflicts), which are solved within the correction work, provided we give priority to trains from the beginning of the cycle and thus assure there are no further influences to the already settled trains.

The notation for stations i=1, i=2, ..., i=I rises in the direction j=1 of increasing number of kilometers. The section between two neighbour stations i and i+1 is marked i´=i. If j_n determined the direction of train n , it can be seen that at the departure of train n from the station i the section i´ has been passed:

$$i'=i+j_n-1 \tag{5}$$

and that the following station i_a is:

$$i_a=i+2\cdot j_n-1 \tag{6}$$

We then subsequently treat one part after another of the time table represented by sub set $N\subset N_o$ of trains:

$$t_o-\varepsilon_1\le t_{n,i_o,j_n}<t_o+\varepsilon_2 \quad \Rightarrow \quad n\in N \tag{7}$$

$$i_o=1\cdot j_n+I\cdot(1-j_n)$$

Where $\varepsilon_1,\varepsilon_2>0$ are according to experiences determined sufficiently large time intervals.

Each time a new train is inserted into the set N we set its "ideal" trajectory. This trajectory represents the determination of elements $t_{n,i,j}$ in such a way as if there were no other trains on the line section In this case the train n departs from its initial station i_o at a moment τ_n^o when available. The waitings are determined only in those stations where the minimum allowed waiting time is greater than zero:

$$\Delta\tau^{s}_{n,i}>0 \quad \Rightarrow \quad y_{n,i}=1 \tag{8}$$

$$\text{otherwise} \quad y_{n,i}=0$$

and

$$t_{n,i_a,1-j_n}=t_{n,i,j_n}+\Delta\tau^{r}_{c_n,i',1}+u_{n,i} \tag{9}$$

where $i_a=i+2\cdot j_n-1$ and $i'=i+j_n-1$.

We can see that the train with the ideal trajectory would have the smallest traveling time and as a rule will have the biggest f_n (though the value of the expression for the consumed traction energy does not decrease). When condition (13) is fulfilled new waitings and deformations of train trajectory are introduced.

For each $t_{n,i,j}$, $(n\in N)$ occurring after t' the following relation must be valid:

$$t'<t_{n,i,j} \tag{10}$$

Therefore if a segment of the time-table, treated through the set N embraces also midnight, a simple linear transformation is required. Obviously this must be taken into account when forming the final data for the set N_o of trains.

To ascertain the existence of a conflict for train n on section i between two neighbour stations we must check whether condition (13) has been fulfilled.

$$t_{\nu,i_a,j_\nu}\geq t_{n,i_a,j_n}>t_{\nu,i_a,1-j_\nu} \quad \Rightarrow \quad x_{st}(\nu)=1 \tag{11}$$

$$\text{otherwise} \quad x_{st}(\nu)=0$$

According to fig.4:

$$(t_1<t_I<t_2)\vee(t_{II}<t_4 \;\&\; t_5<t_{III})\vee(t_7<t_{IV}<t_8)\vee$$

$$\vee(t_{11}<t_I<t_{12})\vee(t_3<t_{II} \;\&\; t_{III}<t_6)\vee(t_9<t_{IV}<t_{10}) \quad \Rightarrow \quad x_r=1 \tag{12}$$

$$\text{otherwise} \quad x_r=0$$

we have:

$$(\lambda_i > \sum_{\substack{\nu\in N\\ \nu\neq n}} x_{st}(\nu)) \;\&\; x_r=0 \tag{13}$$

If condition (13) has been fulfilled we set $x_c=0$, otherwise $x_c=1$. The times t_b , $b\in\{I,II,III,IV\}$, representing the running of the second train ν through section $i+j_n-1$ between two neighbour stations:

$$\begin{aligned} t_I &= t_{\nu,i,1-j_n} \\ t_{II} &= t_{\nu,i,j_n} \\ t_{III} &= t_{\nu,i+2j_n-1,1-j_n} \\ t_{IV} &= t_{\nu,i+2j_n-1,j_n} \end{aligned} \tag{14}$$

The time limits t_z , $z\in\{1,2,...,12\}$ are given in fig.4 and are obtained by means of time intervals needed for trains in traffic:

$$t_z = t^{dep/arr} \pm \Delta\tau^{int}_{i,j_n} \tag{15}$$

where $t^{dep/arr}\in\{t_{n,i,j_n}, t_{n,i,1-j_n}\}$ and $int\in\{1,2,...,5\}$ for five different intervals.

Therefore:

$$x_c=1 \quad\Rightarrow\quad m=\nu \tag{16}$$

m is the second train in conflict, or the "conflicting" train to the train n on the section $i+j_n-1$.

In order to find what are the consequences of solving that conflict we form the binary conflict tree (see fig.5) so that for the chosen number of levels K in the tree we look for $Q=2^K-1$ nodes and form the tree by means of the sequence $q\in\{1,2,...,Q\}$. One node of the tree corresponds to each single conflict. For each conflict $q<2^{K-1}$ we look for the next two conflicts where the first and second trains are:

conflict	q	2q	2q+1
first train	n	n	m
second train	m	m_{2q}	m_{2q+1}

The trains m_{2q} and m_{2q+1} are the "new-conflicting" ones.

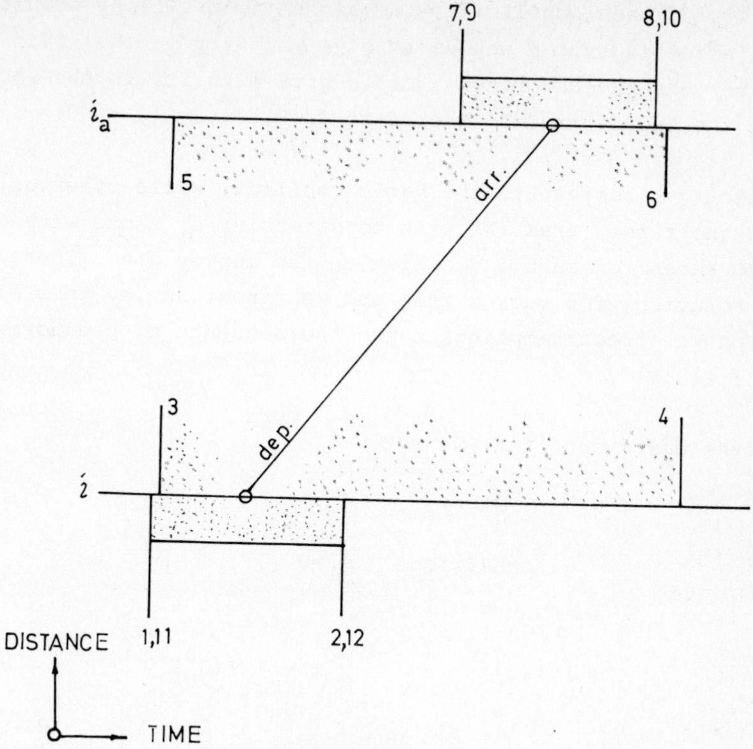
7,9
8,10
i_a
5
6
arr.
3
4
dep.
i
1,11
2,12
DISTANCE
TIME

Figure 4.

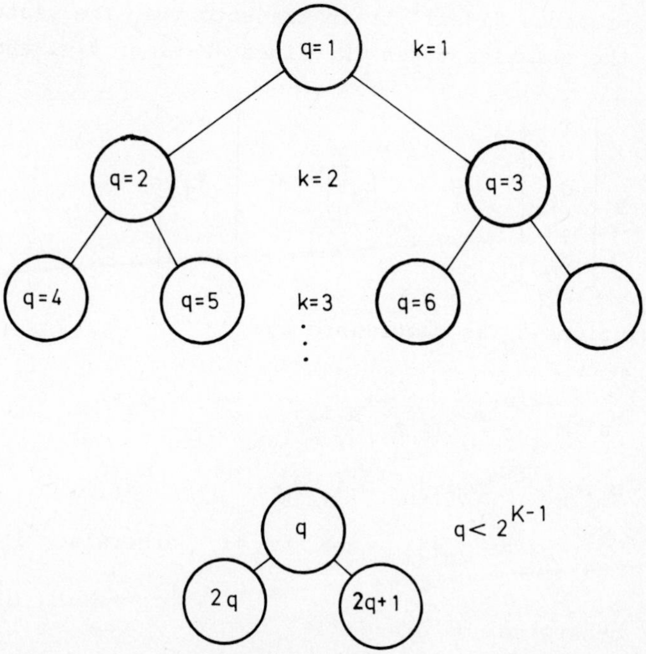
q= 1
k=1
q=2
k=2
q=3
q=4
q=5
k=3
q=6
q
q< 2^{K-1}
2q
2q+1

The solution of each conflict in the sense of fulfilling condition (13) can be effected in such a way as to give priority to the train n, for which we set the indicator d=1 , or to give priority to the second train m and set the indicator d=0. Therefore $d \in \{0,1\}$.

The conflict q=1 represents the basic conflict, while other $q \in \{2,3,\dots,Q\}$ represent the survey area. We wish to determine d_1 along with estimating the consequences of such a decision on the survey area. There are 2^Q possible solutions for such a tree and we cannot survey them all. For that reason we effect samplings using the sequence of pseudorandom numbers $\{\rho_v\}$, $\rho \in \{0,1\}$.

For q=1 (the basic conflict) we set:

$$f^1 > f^0 \quad \Rightarrow \quad d_1 = 1 \qquad \text{otherwise} \quad d_1 = 0 \tag{17}$$

where

$$f^1 = \sum_w f(d_w^1) \qquad\qquad f^0 = \sum_w f(d_w^0) \tag{18}$$

and $w \in \{1,2,\dots,W\}$ is the index which illustrates one sampling. Upon each sampling the solution is evaluated and then cancelled in such a way as to set again the previous "ideal" train trajectories. The vector d_w which determines the solution takes 2W values (W-times $d_1=1$ and W-times $d_1=0$) :

$$\left[d_w^1\right] = \begin{bmatrix} 1 \\ d_2 \\ d_3 \\ \vdots \\ d_Q \end{bmatrix} \qquad\qquad \left[d_w^1\right] = \begin{bmatrix} 0 \\ d_2 \\ d_3 \\ \vdots \\ d_Q \end{bmatrix} \tag{19}$$

For "obvious" solutions d_q is determined by:

$$\gamma_{c_n,c_m} < \Delta t = t_{m,i_\gamma,j_m} - t_{n,i,j_n} \quad \Rightarrow \quad d_q = 1$$

$$\gamma_{c_m,c_n} < \Delta t = t_{n,i,j_n} - t_{m,i_\gamma,j_m} \quad \Rightarrow \quad d_q = 0 \tag{20}$$

$$(\text{for } j_n \neq j_m \quad \Rightarrow \quad i_\gamma = i_a \quad \text{otherwise} \quad i_\gamma = i)$$

$$\text{otherwise} \qquad d_q = \rho_v$$

We thus obtain that the number of possible solutions is reduced 2^{Q_d} times if among Q conflicts there are Q_d conflicts with "obvious" solutions. $[\gamma]$ is a CxC square matrix that contains those times which according to experience guarantee that it is not worth while to check another inferior alternative.

After d_1 has been determined, again all trajectories are set in the way they have been previous to sampling, except the conflict q=1 which has been solved since that moment and is not modified any more. The solution is in accordance with the chosen d_1 , of course.

The choice of the following conflict is done by chosing from the set N the train n having the departure time from station i nearest to the reference time t_o and at the same time that it is possible to obtain for (n,i) the conflicting train m:

$$(t_{min}=t_{n,i,j_n}-t_o) \ \& \ (x_c=1) \qquad \begin{matrix} n,m\in N \\ n\neq m \end{matrix} \qquad (21)$$

Along with the solution of conflicts t_{min} increases and we must take care that:

$$t_{min}<t_{critical} \qquad (22)$$

If t_{min} exceeds $t_{critical}$ there remains the risk that we have not included on time some train from N_o in the set N. If this train had been in N it would have been included in one of the conflicts q. To avoid this, $t_{critical}$ has to be chosen in such a way as to complete the set N early enough. Then a new reference time is set:

$$t_o=t_o'+t_{critical} \qquad (23)$$

The trains that passed the entire line section are excluded from the set N since they will not be in further use.

We continue with this procedure until all trains have passed the line section. It is understood that, since within the last time segment there are no treatment of trains which have been solved already in the first one, some unsolved conflicts remain.

DESCRIPTION OF RESULTS

As shown in fig.2 the elaboration is concluded with the drawing of a time-table diagram for single-track line section and the printing of train data. Figure 6 shows a part of the train diagram for single-track section Ljubljana Jesenice which is a part of one of the main lines connecting the middle and south-east Europe. The drawing is effected in three phases. Phase 1 consists of drawing those lines which represent the train trajectories. There exists the possibility of drawing with various thickness of pen as well as with continous or broken line. The second phase consists of drawing the minute marks. The location for the inscription of minute mark is determined from $t_{n,i,j}$,(according to existing regulations the inscription is done only for minute digit for departure and arrival if the train is provided with waiting time, while the hour and ten-minute digit can be read from the time axis), and the small shift is subjected to the cosinus of the angle made by train line and time axis.Since the plotter drawing requires quite a lot of time, we used it only in the case when a certain alternative has been already corrected and approved. The survey diagram which is used for checking the results, conclusion of time-table cycle etc., is produced on printer in a simplified version. After the correction the programming statements for drawing are generated and set on the magnetic tape. The complete file with the statements and appertaining data consists of approx. 240,000 char. or approx. 3,000 char. per train. The comparatively large number of necessary characters is due to the fact that the plotter was not provided with enough powerful software support and it was necessary to write the elementary statements, this being one reason more why we decided in favour of automatic generating of program statements on the main computer (IBM 360/30 with 128 K).

The printing of train data for the time-table booklet is in our case effected almost simultaneously with the drawing of diagram. With the standard non-EDP procedure this would follow only upon the execution of the diagram. The reason for it was obviously in the fact that the graphic version is more easily surveyed by the constructor. Thus, the clasical preparation of the time-table booklet was reduced merely to the transformation and transcription of data. The direct printing will dispense the diagram constructor from that time consuming operation. We proceed to give explanations for the reading of adequate train data from fig.7.

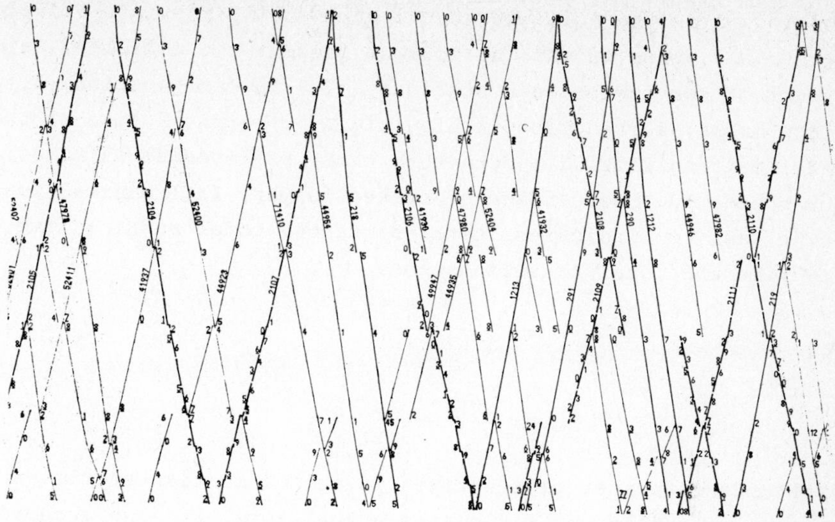

Figure 6.

TAUERN EKSPRES

EKSPRESNI VLAK ŠT. 218
SPLIT ZAGREB LJUBLJANA JESENICE MUNCHEN OOSTENDE

''SZ''   1 IN 2 RAZRED

Q 362= 700 T

1	2	3	4	5	6	7	8	9	10	11
	LJUBLJANA ISK:35									
1.0	LJUBLJANA ŠTSKA		1.5			11 52.5		75	70	
5.4	VIŽMARJE		3.5			54.0		100		1.0
6.1	MEDVODE		3.5			57.5				
7.5	ŠKOFJA LOKA		4.5			12 01.0				
8.8	KRANJ		6.5	12 12.0	3.0	05.5				
10.4	PODNART		9.0			15.0		75		6.0
12.0	LESCE-BLED		10.0			24.0				8.5
5.0	ŽIROVNICA		4.0			34.0		100		
5.1	SLOVENSKI JAVORNIK		4.0			38.0		75		
	USK:35					42.0				
2.8	JESENICE	SP	3.0	12 45.0						
64.1	VOZNI ČAS: 0 49.5			POSTANKI: 0 03.0			POTOVANJE: 0 52.5			

Figure 7.

EKSPRESNI VLAK ŠT. = Express train No.
1 IN 2 RAZRED = 1st and 2nd class
VOZNI ČAS = Running time
POSTANKI = Waiting time
POTOVANJE = Traveling time

The heading gives the following data: number of train, its itinerary, locomotive and gross weight.The columns present the following data: 1.) lenght of section between stations , 2.) name of station, 3.)passing-loop marks, 4.) section running time, 5.) arrival time at the station, 6.) waiting time, 7.) departure time, 8.) special waitings, 9.) maximum speed, 10.) percentage of braked weight, 11.) minimal running time. The last row indicates: total distance, total running time, total waiting time and total traveling time.

CONCLUSION

Notwithstanding further prospectives in automatization of time-table elaboration on the larger field, the actual level is also acceptable. It is an aid in making some alternative time-tables and allows the influence of the constructor in the choice of data and corrections. The particular purpose of the task will be more evident if the EDP would be extended to the time-table for regional railway network.

The proposed method does not assure the achievement of an optimum as far as the criterion function is concerned, but it facilitates the quite prompt searching of a good solution. The possibility is open for a more detailed analysis of parameters K,W and γ, their influence on the speed and quality, as well as analysis of the proposed method for weighting of trains.

REFERENCES

1.) E.Brettmann: Aplication of a Digital Computer to Compilation of a Clock Face Time-Table for a Single Track Line: Monthly Bulletin of the International Railway Congress Association, Cybernetics and Electronics on the Railway: Vol.5,(1968),No.10, pp 373-394.

2.) И.Т.Козлов, Г.Н.Тихонов: Составление однопутных непакетных графиков движения поездов на ЭВМ: Вестник Всесоюзн. научно-исслед. ин-та. ж.-д. транспорта: 1971,№.7, с. 17-21.

3.) N.Inada, Y.Iida: Train Traffic Planing System Through Computers: Japanese Railway Engineering: Vol.10.(1969),No.4, pp 24-27.

4.) A.L.Cherniavsky: A Program for Time-Table Compilation ba a Look-ahead Method: Artificial Inteligence: 1972,No.3, pp 61-67.

5.) I.Amit, D.Goldfarb: The Time-Table Problem for Railway: Developments in OR: Gordon and Breach,New York, Vol.2,(1971), pp 379-387.

6.) M.Vušković, B.Lušičić: Methodology and Programming Package for Railway Traction Simulation: Traffic Control and Transportation Systems: North-Holland, Amsterdam,1974, pp 453-466.

AN INTERACTIVE IMPLEMENTATION OF CONTROL THEORY TECHNIQUES APPLIED TO PINDYCK'S MODEL OF THE U.S. ECONOMY

O. G. Johnson, X. Mangin, J. R. Rhyne
Computer Science Department
University of Houston
Houston, TX 77004/USA

I. INTRODUCTION

Pindyck and others introduced the use of control theory in econometric models in the 1960's, [14], [15]. These models, although the most advanced of all econometric techniques, involve considerable trial and error in the selection of nominal trajectories and weighting factors.

Thus, only with an interactive implementation can these techniques be efficient as tools for evaluating alternative scenerios.

This paper reports the design and implementation of a general state regulator control model which utilizes interactive techniques. This model is then applied to Pindyck's model of the U.S. Economy. The interactive functions have been selected to minimize both original computation time as well as re-computations due to parameter and data changes.

II. THE STATE REGULATOR MODEL AND ALGORITHMS FOR ITS SOLUTION

The state regulator model is called, variously, the linear regulator model (or problem), the linear quadratic tracking model or the linear tracking model with quadratic cost criterion. The model appears in the literature in both continuous and discrete form. In econometric models, the discrete form of the problem is implied since most data consist of monthly or quarterly time series.

The linear quadratic tracking problem is that of minimizing

$$J=1/2 \sum_{i=0}^{N} (x_i-\hat{x}_i)'Q(x_i-\hat{x}_i)+1/2 \sum_{i=0}^{N-1} (u_i-\hat{u}_i)'R(u_i-\hat{u}_i). \qquad (1)$$

Each x_i is an n vector which represents the value of n state variables and each u_i represents r control variables at time i.

Q is an n×n matrix which is either positive semi-definite or positive definite. Often in tracking models Q is diagonal and positive semi-definite. The matrix R is r×r and positive definite. The vectors

$\hat{x}_i$ i=0,...,N and $\hat{u}_i$ i=0,...,N-1 are the desired or nominal states and controls.

The solution sequences u_i^* i=0,...,N-1 and x_i^* i=0,...,N must satisfy the equations

$$x_0=\xi \tag{2}$$

$$x_{i+1}-x_i=Ax_i+Bu_i+Cz_i \quad i=0,\dots,N-1 \tag{3}$$

The matrices A, B, C, have dimension n×n, n×r and n×k respectively. The vectors z_i are known exogeneous variables of dimension k.

The standard indirect solution to this problem is to form the Hamiltonian of the system or, alternatively, the Lagrangian

$$L\equiv J+\sum_{i=0}^{N-1} p'_{i+1}(-x_{i+1}+x_i+Ax_i+Bu_i+Cz_i) \tag{4}$$

and observe that, if a solution, x_i^*,u_i^*,p_i^* exists which extremizes the Lagrangian then, necessarily

$$p_{i+1}^*-p_i^*=-Q(x_i^*-\hat{x}_i)-A'p_{i+1}^* \quad i=1,\dots,N-1 \tag{5}$$

$$u_i^*=-R^{-1}B'p_{i+1}^*+\hat{u}_i \quad i=0,\dots,N-1 \tag{6}$$

$$p_N^*=Q(x_N^*-\hat{x}_N) \tag{7}$$

In addition, x_i^* and u_i^* satisfy equations (2) and (3).

One then makes the assumption (and later proves) that

$$P_i^*=K_ix_i^*+g_i \quad i=1,\dots,N \tag{8}$$

It can then be shown that the n×n matrices K_i i=1,...,N satisfy the initial condition

$$K_N=Q$$

and the Riccati difference equations

$$K_i=Q+(I+A)'(K_{i+1}-K_{i+1}B(R+B'K_{i+1}B)^{-1}B'K_{i+1})(I+A) \tag{10}$$

$$i=N-1,N-2,\dots,1$$

The vectors g_i i=1,...,N satisfy

$$g_N=-Q\hat{x}_N \tag{11}$$

and

$$g_i=-(I+A)'(K_{i+1}-K_{i+1}B(R+B'K_{i+1})B^{-1}B'K_{i+1})BR^{-1}B'g_{i+1} \tag{12}$$

$$+(I+A)'g_{i+1}+(I+A)'(K_{i+1}-K_{i+1}B(R+B'K_{i+1}B)^{-1}B'K_{i+1})(B\hat{u}_i$$

$$+Cz_i)-Q\hat{x}_i \quad i=N-1,N-2,\dots,1$$

From the knowledge of K_i and g_i i=1,...,N

u_i^* $i=0,\ldots,N-1$ can be computed from the equation

$$u_i^* = -(R+B'K_{i+1}B)^{-1}B'K_{i+1}[(I+A)x_i^* - BR^{-1}B'g_{i+1} + B\hat{u}_i + Cz_i] - R^{-1}B'g_{i+1} + \hat{u}_i \tag{13}$$

The solution state sequence x_i^* $i=0,\ldots,N$ can then be computed from the original difference equation. Details of the derivation of this algorithm are available in [13] and [14]. These derivations are the discrete analogues of the derivations in [1].

The modified Lagrange direct algorithm is to differentiate the Lagrangian with respect to each of the variables x_i, p_i and u_{i-1} $i=1,\ldots,N$. The resulting linear system is that given in Figure 1. The matrix in

$$\left[\begin{array}{cccc|cccc|cccc}
Q & & & & & & & & I & D' & & \\
 & Q & & & & & & & & I & D' & \\
 & & \ddots & & & & & & & & \ddots & \\
 & & & Q & & & & & & & & I \\
\hline
 & & & & R & & & & -B' & & & \\
 & & & & & R & & & & -B' & & \\
 & & & & & & \ddots & & & & \ddots & \\
 & & & & & & & R & & & & -B' \\
\hline
I & & & & -B & & & & & & & \\
D & I & & & & -B & & & & & & \\
 & \ddots & \ddots & & & & \ddots & & & & & \\
 & & D & I & & & & -B & & & &
\end{array}\right]
\begin{bmatrix} x_1 \\ x_2 \\ \vdots \\ x_N \\ u_0 \\ u_1 \\ \vdots \\ u_{N-1} \\ P_1 \\ P_2 \\ \vdots \\ P_N \end{bmatrix}
=
\begin{bmatrix} Q\hat{x}_1 \\ Q\hat{x}_2 \\ \vdots \\ Q\hat{x}_N \\ R\hat{u}_1 \\ R\hat{u}_2 \\ \vdots \\ R\hat{u}_{N-1} \\ -D\xi+Cz_0 \\ Cz_1 \\ \vdots \\ Cz_{N-1} \end{bmatrix}$$

$D \equiv -(I+A)$

The Lagrangian Matrix
Figure 1

Figure 1, although sparse, is quite large, $(2n+r)N \times (2n+r)N$. Examination of Figure 1 reveals that band structure can be obtained by eliminating some of the variables. The rows of the Lagrangian in Figure 1 are partitioned into three sections. The first section corresponds to the necessary conditions (5) and (7); the second section to condition (6) and the third section corresponds to equations (2) and (3). Conditions (5) and

(7) can be used to explicitly solve x_i in terms of p_i and p_{i+1}. Condition (6) can be used to solve u_i in terms of p_i. (If Q is semidefinite, a slight perturbation will make it positive definite).

$$x_i=Q^{-1}(p_{i+1}-p_i+A'p_{i+1})+\hat{x}_i\equiv x_i(p_i,p_{i+1}) \quad i+1,\ldots,N-1 \tag{14}$$

$$x_N=Q^{-1}p_N+\hat{x}_N\equiv x_N(p_N) \tag{15}$$

$$u_i=-R^{-1}B'p_{i+1}+\hat{u}_i\equiv u_i(p_{i+1}) \quad i=0,\ldots,N-1 \tag{16}$$

By the Courant extremum principle [9], each of these necessary relationships can be inserted into the Lagrangian without altering the solution in any way. Thus inserting (3), (14), (15) and (16) in (4) the Lagrangian becomes

$$\begin{aligned} L=&-1/2 \sum_{i=1}^{N-1} [x_i(p_i,p_{i+1})-\hat{x}_i]'Q[x_i(p_i,p_{i+1})-\hat{x}_i] \\ &-1/2 \sum_{i=0}^{N-1} [u_i(p_{i+1})-\hat{u}_i]'R[u_i(p_{i+1})-\hat{u}_i] \\ &-(x_N(p_N)-\hat{x}_N)'Q(x_N(p_N)-\hat{x}_N) \\ &-(\xi-\hat{x}_0)'Q(\xi-\hat{x}_0) \end{aligned} \tag{17}$$

From equation (17) the following can be deduced:

1. Since $x_i(p_i,p_{i+1})$ $i=1,\ldots,N-1$, $u_i(p_{i+1})$ $i=0,\ldots,N-1$ and $x_N(p_N)$ are all linear functions of the vector $P=(p_i,\ldots p_N)'$, L is a negative definite form in p.
2. Since p_j only occurs in L in terms with p_{j-1} and p_{j+1}, L is block tridiagonal, and thus band structured.

Hence, if L, thus modified, is differentiated with respect to each of p_i $k=1,\ldots,N$, the resulting matrix is that which is displayed in Figure 2.

Solution of this system of linear equations is faster computationally than the Ricatti algorithm. Also recomputations due to changes in $\hat{x}$, $\hat{u}$, C, or Z are minimal. See [13] for details. The above remarks are summerized in Figure 3.

III. THE INTERACTIVE PROCESS

Figure 4 is a general schematic of the interactive system in which the model is embedded. In the following X=x, U=u, Z=z, XH=$\hat{x}$, UH=$\hat{u}$

The available functions are:

$$
\begin{bmatrix}
M_0 & M_1 & & \\
M_1' & M_2 & M_1 & \\
 & M_1' & M_2 & M_1 \\
 & & \ddots & \\
 & & M_1' & M_2
\end{bmatrix}
\begin{bmatrix}
P_1 \\ P_2 \\ P_3 \\ \vdots \\ P_N
\end{bmatrix}
=
\begin{bmatrix}
\hat{x}_1-\xi-A\xi-B\hat{u}_0-Cz_0 \\
\hat{x}_2-\hat{x}_1-A\hat{x}_1-B\hat{u}_1-Cz_1 \\
\hat{x}_3-\hat{x}_2-A\hat{x}_2-B\hat{u}_2-Cz_2 \\
\vdots \\
\hat{x}_N-\hat{x}_{N-1}-A\hat{x}_{N-1}-B\hat{u}_{N-1}-Cz_{N-1}
\end{bmatrix}
$$

$M_0=-Q^{-1}-BR^{-1}B'$

$M_1=Q^{-1}+Q^{-1}A$

$M_2=-M_1-M_1'-BR^{-1}B'-AQ^{-1}A'$

The Modified Langrangian Matrix
Figure 2

CREATE: Retrieve a set of data from a file or input it directly. Initialize local variables.

COMPUTE: Perform the Cholesky decomposition of M (i.e., compute M^{-1} essentially) and the values of variables X and U.

DISPLAY: Display the values of any variable (of the set of data or results).

UPDATE: Update any variable or any element of a variable of the set of data.

SAVE: Save a set of results in a file for future comparative plotting.

RESET: Erase the set of previously saved results.

PLOT: Display a comparative plot of an optimized state control variable and the corresponding nominal trajectory or display a comparative plot of the various sets of results already computed and saved.

INIT: Initialize the file in which different sets of data are to be saved.

PUT: Save the present set of data on file with given name.

GET: Retrieve the set of data with given name from file.

DELETE: Delete the set of data under a given name in file.

MENU: List the available functions.

STOP: Terminate the program.

The word "FUNCTION?" is typed whenever the system requests a new function. A succession of line feeds or carriage returns will always lead to a request for a "FUNCTION?".

PROBLEM I

GIVEN: $\hat{x}_t$, $\hat{u}_t$ and z_t for t=0 to N -1 and $\hat{x}_N$

COMPUTE: x_t for t= 1 to N

u_t for t=0 to N - 1

such that

$$x_{t+1}=x_t+Ax_t + Bu_t + Cz_t \quad t=0,\ldots,N-1$$

and minimizing

$$\text{Cost}= \sum_{t=0}^{N} (x_t-\hat{x}_t)'Q(x_t-\hat{x}_t)+ \sum_{t=0}^{N-1} (u_t-\hat{u}_t)'R(u_t-\hat{u}_t)$$

x : State variables

$\hat{x}$: Nominal state trajectories

u : Control variables

$\hat{u}$: Nominal control trajectories

z : Exogeneous variables

A :

B : Transformations

C :

PROBLEM II

GIVEN : M matrix tri-diagonal block symetric

P vector

COMPUTE: Y such that

M Y = P

M : Tri-diagonal block symetrix matrix of figure 2

M : is only function of A,B,Q,R

P : Right hand side of figure 2

Figure 3

INTERACTIVE PROCESS

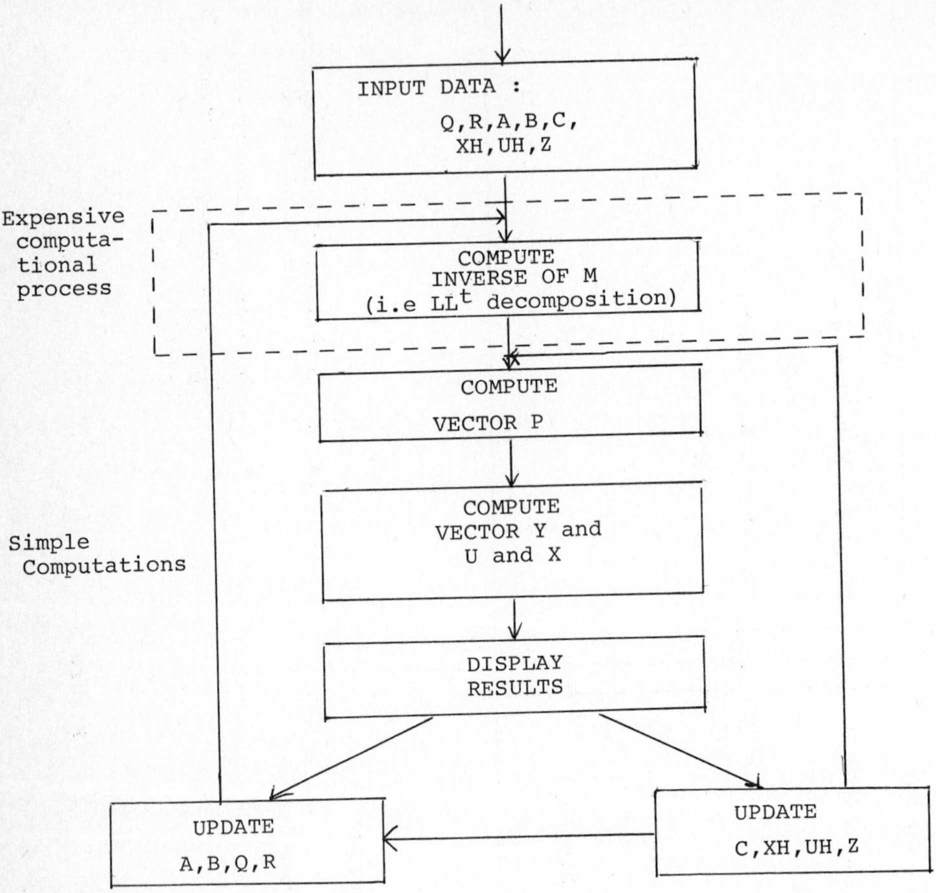

Figure 4

Three files are associated with the program. A file for the creation of data (Fortran File I/0 Unit 7), a file to save and retrieve sets of data, corresponding to different problems (File I/0 Unit 8), and a file to save and retrieve sets of results, corresponding to different problems (File I/0 Unit 9).

The following section details the use of the different functions.

1) CREATE

Type "CREATE".

Create allows the creation of a completely new set of data (for a new problem). At this time and only at this time, the dimensions n, r, k, and N can be modified.

The system responds: "IS THE DATA TO BE FETCHED FROM FILE?"

a) If the user answers "YES" the data will be retrieved from the file associated with I/0 Unit 7. The file, for keeping previous sets of results, will be initiated and an "END OF DATA TRANSFER" will be printed before the next "FUNCTION?" to indicate that the transfer was successful.

b) If the user answers "NO" the data must be entered through the terminal console. The system responds: "GIVE THE NUMBER OF STATE VARIABLES, CONTROL VARIABLES, EXOGENEOUS VARIABLES, AND TIME PERIOD RESPECTIVELY LESS THAN (maximum range for the dimensions in format 4I4)". The scalars n, r, k and N are to be entered in format 4I4. Then for each variable A, B, C, Q, R, Z, UH, XH, the following procedure will be repeated. (Remember UH=$\hat{u}$, XH=$\hat{x}$).

α) "IS MATRIX (VECTOR) variable name (first dim., second dim.) TO BE INPUT NON-ZERO ELEMENTS ONLY (IF SO TYPE (ELE)) OR IS THE ENTIRE ARRAY TO BE INPUT (IF SO TYPE ALL)".

* If the answer is ALL the user will get: "GIVE FORMAT OF INPUT (Type NO for default format)".
* If the response is NO, the input will be read in under Format control 5E12.4.
* Otherwise the format will be read and afterwards the variables(s) will be read in the format. (Only the part of the format between the two external parenthesis is entered). The system will now return to α), if there are still variables to read; otherwise it will proceed to β).
* If the answer is ELE the system will respond: "GIVE THE FORMAT OF INPUT OR TYPE 'NO' FOR DEFAULT I2, 1X, I2, 1X, E12.4 A NEGATIVE SUBSCRIPT WILL TERMINATE".
  - If the answer is NO each non-zero element of the variable must be given in the form:

```
ddbddb±ddd.dddd±dd      (d stands for digit)
↑  ↑
row| number
   |
   column number
```

A negative row number terminates input and the system returns to α) if there is still a variable to read; otherwise the system proceeds to β).

β) For each variable XNAM, UNAM, ZNAM the system prints "GIVE THE NAME OF THE ROWS OF variable name (Format 10(A6,1X))". Then the user enters the names of the different state variables, if variable name = X; control variables, if variable name = U; exogeneous variables, if variable name = Z in the form <u>ccccccbccccccb--------bcccccc</u>, where b is ignored.

The file for saving sets of results will be initiated and upon completion of β) a "FUNCTION?" will appear.

2) <u>COMPUTE</u>

From a set of data in memory (A, B, C, Q, R, Z, UH, XH) the system computes the optimal state variables and control variables X and U. If A, B, Q, and R are unchanged between two COMPUTER functions, only the part depending on the other variables is recomputed (right hand side of the linear system.) When "FUNCTION?" is printed, the computation is completed.

3) <u>DISPLAY</u>

This function displays any variable in the model. First appears: "COMPARATIVE DISPLAY OF X, XH OR U, UH?"; there are 4 possible answers:

α) "X" will give the names of the different state variables with their associated number. The response is a two digit number corresponding to the variable chosen. (If the number is not valid, [i.e., too big or zero or negative], the program returns to the state: "COMPARATIVE DISPLAY OF X, XH, OR U, UH?"); otherwise, the state variable corresponding to the number is printed; first the optimal result; then the nominal state trajectory. One may then enter a new number corresponding to another state variable.

β) "U" - The process is the same a in α) but for the control variables.

γ) "NO" - Go to the display of one variable.

δ) Any other response will cause the program to print "FUNCTION?"

* Display one variable.

The system displays "PRINT THE NAME OF THE VARIABLE TO BE DISPLAYED X, U, XH, UH, Z, A, B, C, Q, R, OR OUT IF DISPLAY IS TO BE TERMINATED".

α) If X, U, XH, UH, or Z is entered, the different names associated with the variables X or U or XH or UH or Z will be printed with their associated numbers. The response is the 2 digit number corresponding to the variable to be printed. If the number is not valid (too big or zero or negative) the program comes back to the step: Display one variable; otherwise, the corresponding variable is printed and the next variable number is given.

α) If A, B, C, Q, or R is entered, the entire matrix is printed row by row and the program comes back to the step: Display one variable.

β) If "OUT" is entered (or any other response) the program prints "FUNCTION?" and waits for the next function.

4) UPDATE

This function allows the updating of any variable of the model. The program prints: "GIVE THE VARIABLE OR THE MATRIX TO BE UPDATED XH, UH, Z, A, B, C, Q, OR ANY OTHER RESPONSE CAUSES "FUNCTION?" to appear". After the name of the variable to be updated has been entered, the program prints: "DISPLAY OF variable name (# of rows, # of columns)?". If the answer is "YES" the variable will be first displayed and the following will be printed: "ANSWER: NO CORRECTION (NO); CORRECTION OF ALL THE ELEMENTS (ALL); CORRECTION ELEMENT BY ELEMENT (ELE)".

α) If the answer is "ALL", the system will print: "GIVE THE FORMAT OF INPUT OR TYPE "NO" FOR DEFAULT FORMAT OF 5E12.4. The user enters the entire new variable. The program returns to "GIVE THE VARIABLE OR THE MATRIX TO BE UPDATED..."

β) If the answer is "ELE", it will print: "GIVE THE FORMAT OF INPUT OR TYPE FOR DEFAULT FORMAT OF I2, 1X, I2, 1X, E12.4 A NEGATIVE SUBSCRIPT WILL TERMINATE". The user enters "NO" or the part of the format (between the two extreme parentheses) in which the input is to be read. This format must read, by line, 2 integers and a real number. The first integer is the row number; the second is the column number, and the third is the value updated. A subscript out of range will cause the system to branch to "DISPLAY OF____ ____ ____?"

γ) If the answer is "NO" the system branches to: "GIVE THE VARIABLE OR THE MATRIX TO BE UPDATED XH, UH, _ _ _"

5) SAVE

This function saves on the file corresponding to I/0 Unit 9, up to 5 sets of results catalogued under a given number (from

1 to 5). The following is printed: "NUMBER BY WHICH THE RESULT IS TO BE REFERENCED (1-5)". The user gives a digit by which the set of results, in memory (X and U), is to be referenced in this file. If the digit is not in the range 1 to 5, "INVALID REFERENCE NUMBER number" is printed and the program asks for the next function. If the number is in the range 1 to 5, * and a set of results have been catalogued under this number, the following is printed: "LAST SET OF RESULTS number TO BE DESTROYED?". If user responds "YES" the new set of results is written over the last one. If the response is "NO" the system branches to the step: "NUMBER ON WHICH THE RESULTS IS TO - - - - -" and there is no set of results catalogued under this number. The set of results is transferred to file. At the end of transfer, "END OF DATA TRANSFER" is printed.

6) RESET

All the sets of results catalogued in the file corresponding to I/0 Unit 9 are decatalogued.

7) PLOT

This function allows the plotting of data and computed results. For instance, one can displya a given state variable, compare the optimized solution variable with the nominal trajectory, or display sets of results in file unit 9 simultaneously. The first time PLOT is referenced "NUMBER OF LINE ON THE TTY (EX:15)" is printed. The response is a two digit number, giving the number of lines on which the plot must extend (a page of the device). At every reference, "LAST RESULT (L) OR ALL SAVED RESULTS (G)" is printed. If the user responds with L, the set of result in memory will be plotted, with the nominal trajectory in comparison. If the answer is G, all the sets of results in the file unit 9 will be plotted on the same plotting. After the response "L" or "G", "GIVE THE VARIABLE TO BE PLOTTED, X OR U" will be printed. If a response other than X or U is typed then "FUNCTION?" will appear, ready to receive the next function. If the response is X or U, the corresponding names of the variables will appear, with their reference numbers. In order to choose a variable, one types the two digits number corresponding to the variable. If the number is invalid, the system returns to the message "GIVE THE VARIABLE TO BE PLOTTED, X OR U" else the plotting will occur and the system will wait for the next two digit variable designator.

8) INIT

This function initializes the file corresponding to I/0 unit 8. This function must be given when a new file is to be used or to reset an existing file. This file corresponds to a file containing different sets of data catalogued under given name. A "FUNCTION?" is typed at the completing of the process.

9) PUT

This function puts a set of data A, B, C, Q, R, Z, UH, XH (the one in memory) in the file I/0 Unit 8 and references it under a given name (6 characters). * If there are already 9 sets of data in the file, a message "ALREADY 9 SETS OF DATA, FILE FULL, A DELETION MUST BE MADE FIRST" appears and "FUNCTION?" is typed. * Otherwise, "GIVE THE NAME BY WHICH THE SET OF DATA IS TO BE CATALOGUED" appears and the user must answer by a name of 6 characters. Then at the end of transfer: "TRANSER COMPLETED" and "FUNCTION?" appears.

10) GET

This function retrieves a set of data under a given name from file Unit 8. First a list of the names under which sets of data have been referenced appears: "WHICH OF THE FOLLOWING DATA DO YOU WANT *** name 1 *** name 2 . . . *** name N". The response is one of the names listed. If the user does not give a proper name, "FUNCTION?" will appear and no set of data will have been retrieved. Otherwise, the proper set of data is retrieved and "TRANSFER COMPLETED" and "FUNCTION?" appears.

11) DELETE

This function decatalogues a set of data and packs the rest of the file. The system responds "GIVE THE SET OF DATA TO BE DELETED" *** name 1 *** name 2 . . . *** name N. The user gives the name of the set of data which is to be deleted. * If the name is incorrect "FUNCTION?" will appear asking for the next function. No deletion occurs. * If the name is correct, it is deleted from the dictionary, the file is packed and a "DELETION COMPLETED" and "FUNCTION?" appears.

12) MENU

This function lists the available functions with a short description of each one.

13) STOP

"RUN STOPPED BY USER. PROCESSING TERMINATED" is printed and the program stops.

IV. CONVERSION TO FULL SCALE GRAPHICS TERMINAL

As implemented now, the system is interactive with limited graphics capabilities. In the next few months the central programming effort will be directed toward software development for interfacing an IMLAC graphics minicomputer as a terminal to the central processor, a UNIVAC 1108.

The IMLAC PDS-1D Graphics system consists of two processors which share 8192 words (16 bits) of memory. One of the processors drives the deflection amplifiers of the CRT and is responsible for creating a display. The other processor can perform arithmetic, logical and branching operations, transfer data to and from peripheral devices, and can start and stop the display processor. This processor constructs display programs, refreshes the display by starting and stopping the display processor and communicates with the external devices.

Because of the dual processor construction of the IMLAC PDS-1D, it can function as a stand alone display system. In this mode of operation, there is an assembler which assembles programs for both processors, a test editor, and a debugging program. The IMLAC PDS-1D was used used in this fashion in conjunction with a course in interactive computer graphics which was taught during the summer of 1974.

The IMLAC PDS-1D is most useful when it is connected to a large scale digital computer, as its computational abilities are quite limited. The University of Houston Computing Center has a UNIVAC 1108 system and the IMLAC PDS-1D is being linked to the 1108. There were three methods by which the data transfer link could be established: (1) A direct channel connection, (2) connection via a synchronous serial data communications channel, or (3) connection via an asynchronous serial data communications channel. Alternative (2) was chosen because alternative (1) would have involved desinging and building a special interface at a very great cost, and alternative (3) would have resulted in a data transfer rate of approximately 15 words per second. The synchronous serial data communication channel offers a transfer rate of 1250 words per second in both directions simultaneously at a cost of under $400 for the necessary cable and interface circuitry. The hardware for this connection was designed and built by an M.S. student in Computer Science and is currently being tested.

Preliminary drive programs have been written for the 1108 and for the IMLAC PDS-1D. There are a number of unsatisfactory aspects of the 1108 program in its present form; it requires that a program using the IMLAC PDS-1D as a peripheral be locked into memory and it contributes a substantial amount of overhead in the communications processing routines of the operating system.

A new version of the EXEC-8 operating system will make it possible to swap a program that uses the IMLAC PDS-1D in and out of memory exactly as is done with other interactive programs. This revision of the operating system implements input and output queues for communications devices on a high speed (4 msec) drum. If the program using the IMLAC PDS-1D is swapped out, any incoming messages from the IMLAC PDS-1D are queued on the drum until the program is swapped back in again.

A series of local revisions to the communications routines of EXEC-8 will substantially reduce the overhead of communication with the IMLAC PDS-1D. These revisions will implement a "buddy system" method of allocating communications buffers that will allow variable length messages to be received without frequent interrupts to check on the status of the input. This overhead will be further reduced when a communication "front end" processor is made a part of the 1108 system.

Univac is contributing a complete graphics processing package for the 1108 which was developed in Japan for the use with Adage graphics systems. After the communications link is established and stablized between the 1108 and the IMLAC PDS-1D, work will begin on converting this program to handle the IMLAC PDS-1D.

In the meantime, a special purpose program has been developed and is being debugged to allow the IMLAC PDS-1D and the 1108 to be used in this research project.

REFERENCES

[1] M. Athans and P. Falb, Optimal Control--An Introduction To The Theory And It's Applications, McGraw-Hill, New York, 1966.

[2] James R. Bunch, "Equilibration of Symmetric Matrices in the Max-norm," Journal of the ACM, vol. 18, no. 4, October 1971, pp. 566-572.

[3] James R. Bunch, "Analysis of the Diagonal Pivoting Method, "SIAM J. Numerical Analysis, vol. 8, no. 4, December 1971, pp. 656-680.

[4] James R. Bunch, and B. N. Parlett, "Direct Methods for Solving Symmetric Indefinite Systems of Linear Equations, SIAM J. Numerical Analysis, vol. 8, no. 4, December 1971, pp. 639-655.

[5] W. E. Bosarge, Jr., and O. G. Johnson, "Direct Method Approximation To The State Regulator Control Problem Using A Ritz-Trefftz Suboptimal Control," IEEE Transactions on Automatic Control, December 1970, pp. 627-631.

[6] W. E. Bosarge, Jr., and O. G. Johnson, "Error Bounds of High Order Accuracy for the State Regulator Problem via Piecewise Polynomial Approximations," SIAM J. Control, vol. 9, no. 1, February 1971, pp. 15-28.

[7] W. E. Bosarge, Jr., and O. G. Johnson, "Numerical Properties of the Ritz-Treffrz Algorithm for Optimal Control," Communications of the ACM, vol. 14, no. 6, June 1971, pp. 402-406.

[8] W. E. Bosarge, Jr., and O. G. Johnson, R. S. McKnight, and W. P. Timlake, "The Ritz-Galerkin Procedure For Nonlinear Control Problems," SIAM J. Numerical Analysis, vol. 10, no. 1, March 1973, pp. 94-111.

[9] R. Courant and D. Hilbert, Methods of Mathematical Physics, vol. 1, Interscience, New York, 1953.

[10] E. H. Cuthill and R. S. Barga, "A Method of Normalized Block Iteration," Journal of the ACM, vol. 6, pp. 236-244.

[11] International Mathematical and Statistical Libraries Newsletter, no. 5, October, 1973.

[12] O. G. Johnson, "Convergence, Error Bounds, Sensitivity, and Numerical Comparisons of Certain Absolutely Continuous Raleigh-Ritz Methods For Sturm-Liouville Eigenvalue Problem," Technical Report No. 23, Computer Center, University of California, Berkeley, 1968.

[13] O. G. Johnson, B. C. McInnis, J. W. Nowakowski, "An Assessment of Discrete Linear Quadratic Tracking Problem Algorithms," IEEE Auto. Cont. (Submitted.)

[14] R. S. Pindyck, "An Application of the Linear Quadratic Tracking Problem To Economic Stabilization Policy," IEEE Transactions On Automatic Control, vol. AC-17, no. 3, June 1972, pp. 387-400.

[15] R. S. Pindyck, Optimal Planning for Economic Stabilization, North-Holland Publishing Company, Amsterdam, 1973.

CONTROL IN ECONOMY BASED ON NON-PRICE INFORMATION

I.LIGETI - J.SIVÁK
Institute of Economic Planning
1370.Budapest, Pf.610.
HUNGARY

In his Anti-Equilibrium J.Kornai analyzed the various components of the functioning of economic systems /Kornai, 1971/. Apart from the two extreme control mechanisms - control by prices and control by instructions - he discusses also the so called autonomous control mechanism. One of the simplest cases of autonomous control is the control based on stock signals. In an article J.Kornai and B.Martos discussed the case of control based on stock signals in a simple model of a Leontief-type economy /Kornai-Martos, 1973/.

The present paper aimes to throw light on some new components of autonomous functioning relying on a simple model. Analogy between economic processes and physical phenomena plays an important part here.

The first part of the paper describes the model. Then we proceed to analyze the conditions of the functioning of the economic system. This is followed by the generalization of the model after removing some of the simplifying assumptions.[1/]

N o t a t i o n s

a/ Variables /all variables are functions of time/

- ij - indexes of economic units $(i,j = 1,2,\dots n)$
- x - vector of the production,
- X - diagonal matrix of vector x, where $x_{ii} = x_i$
- u - vector of the producer's stock
- V - matrix of the user's stock
  - V_{ij} - stock at the j-th sector of the product of the i-th sector
- Y - matrix of the user's purchase

1/ We are indebted to István Dancs for his valuable and efficient guidance in our research of autonomous control. The same is due to Csaba Csernátony for his assistance in preparing the final version of the present paper.

Y_{ij} - the j-th sector's purchase from the product of the i-th sector

w - vector of the consumer's stock

z - vector of the consumer's purchase

b/ Constant values

$g = g(t) \geqq 0$ - the given vector of consumption

$F = F(t) \geqq 0$ - the given matrix of the input coefficients

u^*, V^*, w^* - normal stock concerning the corresponding variables

$C > 0$ - diagonal matrix of control parameters /c_i, are control parameters of the i-th sector/

x^o, u^o, ...- initial values of the variables at point $t = 0$.

Small letters indicate vectors of n components, capital letters indicate matrices. The components of the vectors and elements of the matrices are marked with superscript. The e_j denotes the j-th unit vector, by e we denote the summarizing vector. The unit matrix is denoted by E.

1. The Model of a Leontief-type Economy

The economy is divided into two spheres: the sphere of r e a l processes and the sphere of c o n t r o l . Material processes /production, transport, consumption, etc./ take place in the real sphere. In the sphere of control the information necessary for the control is collected and it is also here that the decisions are made.

According to Kornai's definition the a u t o n o m o u s c o n t r o l m e c h a n i s m satisfies the following conditions:

- the economy has only one level /independent economic units exist only and there is no central co-ordinating unit/,
- decision-making is completely decentralized,
- decision-making and the control of the functioning of economic units take place through non-price-type parameters /e.g. signalling based on production, stocks/.

A simple case of autonomous control is control based on stock signals. The individual economic units make their own decisions by comparing their own stock level with some pre-fixed normative stock level. Thus, if the stocks exceed the given normative level, the producer diminishes the output and vica versa. It means that the economic unit has such primary activities which are autonomously controlled by the system according to a primary adjustment rule. In essense this type of control is similar to the functioning of the sympathetic nervous system /Kornai, 1971/.

The assumptions of the model

1. The variables of the model are continuously differentiable with regard to time $t \geqq 0$. The values of the variables for $t = 0$ are given as constants: x^0 etc.

2. All the variables are practically observable magnitudes and of deterministic character.

3. One single consumer is considered.

4. The real sphere of the economy is of closed Leontief-type.

5. The input-coefficient matrix $F(t)$ is nonnegative, continuously differentiable and its spectral radius is less than 1 for $t \geqq 0$.

6. Starting stocks u^0, V^0, w^0 are positive magnitudes.

On the basis of assumptions 1-6 and according to the two spheres the model takes the following from: [1/]

Balance equations:

$$\begin{aligned} \dot{u} &= x - Ye - z \\ \dot{V} &= Y - FX \\ \dot{w} &= z - g \end{aligned}$$

/I/

Rules of behaviour

$$\begin{aligned} \dot{x} &= \dot{Y}e + \dot{z} + C^2(u^* - u) \\ \dot{Y} &= F\dot{X} + \dot{F}X + C^2(V^* - V) \\ \dot{z} &= \dot{g} + C^2(w^* - w) \end{aligned}$$

1/ A discrete version of the model has also been elaborated/Dancs I.-Hunyadi L. 1972.,1973/. However, here we rely on the continuous form of the model only.

Taking into consideration that $\ddot{u} = \dot{x} - \dot{Y}e - \mathring{z}$ and inserting this into the equation $\dot{x} = \dot{Y}e + \dot{z} + C^2\,(u^* - u)$ we get:

$$\ddot{u} = C^2\,(u^* - u)$$

By using similar substitutions the original model can be transformed into the following from:

B a l a n c e   e q u a t i o n s

$$\dot{u} = x - Ye - z$$
$$\dot{V} = Y - FX$$
$$\dot{w} = z - g$$

/II/

R u l e s   o f   b e h a v i o u r 1/

$$\ddot{u} = C^2(u^* - u)$$
$$\ddot{V} = C^2(V^* - V)$$
$$\ddot{w} = C^2(w^* - w)$$

This new system of equations is called the transformation of the original model. It is easy to prove, that this system is equivalent to the original one given in the article of Kornai-Martos.

2. The solution of the model

The solution of this model - which is naturally the same as that of the original model - takes the following form:

$$u = u^* + \cos Ct\,(u^o - u^*) + C^{-1}\sin Ct\,(x^o - Ye^o - z^o)$$
$$V = V^* + \cos Ct\,(V^o - V^*) + C^{-1}\sin Ct\,(Y^o - F^o X^o)$$
$$w = w^* + \cos Ct\,(w^o - w^*) + C^{-1}\sin Ct\,(z^o - g^o)$$
$$Y = FX - C\sin Ct\,(V^o - V^*) + \cos Ct\,(Y^o - F^oX^o)$$
$$z = g - C\sin Ct\,(w^o - w^*) + \cos Ct\,(z^o - g^o)$$
$$x = (E - F)^{-1}\left[g - C\sin Ct\,(u^o - u^* + V^oe - V^*e + w^o - w^*) + \right.$$
$$\left. + \cos Ct\,(x^o - F^oX^o_e - g^o)\right]$$

1/ The "rules of behaviour" describe the behaviour of the economic units. In the control-theory the rules of this type are often called response functions.

For the analysis of the properties of this solution let us regard the j-th co-ordinate of u:

$$u_j = u_j^* + \cos c_j t \ (u_j^o - u_j^*) + \frac{1}{c_j} \sin t \ (x_j^o - \sum_l Y_{jl}^o - z_j^o)$$

Through transformation the following formula is obtained

$$u_j = u_j^* + L_j^u \ \sin (c_j t + \varphi^o)$$

where $\varphi^o = \text{arc} \ \sin \dfrac{u_j^o - u_j^*}{L_j^u}$

$$L_j^u = \frac{1}{c_j} \sqrt{c_j^2 (u_j^o - u_j^*)^2 + (x_j^o - \sum_l Y_{jl}^o - z_j^o)^2}$$

It can easily be seen that the mathematical forms of the behavioural rules in the transformed version of the model are similar to differential equations describing harmonic oscillation where is no damping. In view of the above form of the solution we can make statements on the stock level of economic units with the behavioural equations given in the model, which will be similar to those of characteristics of harmonic oscillation.

The important caracteristics of this autonomous control are:[1/]

i/ The value of production stock is a periodic function of time for any positive value of the control parameters. The centre of oscillation is the pre-fixed norm u^*.

ii/ The amplitude of the periodical oscillation is constant. Its magnitude depends on the actual value of the control parameters and on the given initial value of the variables.

iii/ The period of oscillation is constant, too.

The solution of the model gives rise to two issues:

1/ In what follows we shall examine only the production stock variables, since the other variables can easily be explained in a similar manner. For detailed analysis see the papers referred to.

1. With the given behavioural rules can the functioning of the system be ensured in accordance with a definition to be given later.

2. What properties will the solution of the model have if the behavioural rules are changed.

The article of Kornai - Martos was followed by a comprehensive work to study autonomous control. These works were connected primarily with issue 2. /Virág, 1971./. The fact that the behavioural equations of the transformed model are identical with those of harmonic oscillation provides the possibility for defining behavioural equations ensuring the dampening of oscillation. One solution is that a dampening factor is built in the equation which corresponds to the frictional force in the case of harmonic oscillation. Behavioural equation obtained in this manner can be given good economic interpretations. The solutions of the new system produce results similar to damped oscillations. /Dancs - Hunyadi - Sivák, 1973. Sivák, 1974/.

These investigations have aimed primarily at the stability properties of the solution and less attention has been devoted to the workability of the model.

3. The workability of the system

The concept of workability is interpreted in respect of the economic contents of the model.

D e f i n i t i o n : system I /or II/ is regarded workable if the following conditions hold for its solutions:

(3.1.) $x > 0$,

(3.2.) $u > 0$,

(3.3.) $V > 0$,

(3.4.) $w > 0$.

1. T h e o r e m :

In a system satisfying conditions 1. - 6. the model I/and thus also the model II/ has a solution which is workable in the sense of the above definition i.e. the values of u^*, V^* and w^* as well as C, have such a system in which 3.1 - 3.4 conditions are satisfied.

P r o o f : To satisfy condition (3.2) the following relationship should be ensured

$$(3.5.) \qquad u^* > L^u$$

Writing it for one co-ordinate

$$u_j^* > L_j^u$$

i.e. $$u_j^* > \frac{1}{c_j}\sqrt{c_j^2(u_j^o - u_j^*)^2 + (x^o - \sum_l Y_{jl}^o - z_j^o)^2}$$

Utilizing that $\dot{u}(0) = x^o - \sum Y_{jl}^o - z_j^o$,

after transformation the following formula is obtained:

$$c_j u_j^* > \sqrt{c_j^2(u_j^o - u_j^*)^2 + \dot{u}_j(0)^2}$$

Similarly, to satisfy (3.3.) or (3.4.) it is necessary that

$$c_j V_{jl}^* > \sqrt{c_j^2 (V_{jl}^o - V_{jl}^*)^2 + \dot{V}_{jl}(0)^2}$$

or $$c_j w_j^* > \sqrt{c_j^2(w_j^o - w_j^*)^2 + \dot{w}_j(0)^2}$$

Let us take that

$$(3.6.) \qquad \begin{aligned} u_j^* &= u_j^o \\ V_{jl}^* &= V_{j\ell}^o \\ w_j^* &= w_j^o, \end{aligned}$$

and the values of the c_j parameters according to the following formula

$$(3.7.) \qquad c_j > \max\left\{\frac{\dot{u}_j(0)}{u_j^o}\ ;\ \max_l \frac{\dot{V}_{jl}(0)}{V_{jl}^o}\ ;\ \frac{\dot{w}_j(0)}{w_j^o}\right\}$$

With such values the condition $u_j^* > L_j^u$ /and with this also $V_{jl}^* > L_j^V$, $w_j^* > L_j^W$/ is satisfied which ensures that conditions (3.2.) - (3.4.) are also met.

With a similar line of argument we can guarantee that condition (3.1.) is also met.∎

Let us come back to our condition $u_j^* > L_j^u$. After rearrangement the following formula is obtained:

$$\frac{1}{2} c_j^2 (u_j^o - u_j^*)^2 + \frac{1}{2} \dot{u}(0)^2 < \frac{1}{2} c_j^2 u_j^{*2} \qquad (3.8.)$$

If we make use of the energy concept of harmonic oscillation apart from the analogy found in the solution another one can be discovered.

We know, that the sum of the kinetic (E_{kin}) and potential energy (E_{pot}) constitutes the energy (E) of the oscillating body.

Utilizing the fact that the equation of movement[1/] of our system is as follows:

$$\ddot{u}_j = c_j^2 u_j^* - c_j^2 u_j$$

the "energy of production stocks" will be

$$E^u = E^u_{kin} + E^u_{pot} = \frac{1}{2} \dot{u}^2 + \frac{1}{2} c^2 (u - u^*)^2 \qquad (3.9.)$$

Making use of this latter formula the analogy is self evident. The formula (3.8.) obtained from the condition $u_j^* > L_j^u$ after rearrangement is nothing else than

$$E^u(0) < E^{u^*}_{pot} \qquad (3.1o.)$$

where $E^u(0)$ is the energy at the starting-point and $E^{u^*}_{pot}$ the potential energy associated with the stock norm. Making use of this analogy the following consequences are encountered.

Consequences:

The necessary and sufficient condition of system I /and II/ being workable according to conditions (3.1.)-(3.4.) is that the following

1/ The equation is given here for u only. In a similar manner it can be given for the other variables, too.

relationships are met

$$(3.2.) \qquad E^{u}(0) < E^{u^{*}}_{pot}$$

$$(3.3.) \qquad E^{V}(0) < E^{V^{*}}_{pot}$$

$$(3.4.) \qquad E^{w}(0) < E^{w^{*}}_{pot}$$

In a special case e.g. when $u_j^o = u_j^*$ the condition (3.2.) takes the following form $E^u_{kin}(0) < E^u_{pot}(0)$.

4. A possible generalization of the model

After having examined the workability of the system let us focus our attention to the second issue. Supposing some modification in the behavioural rules a generalization of the model can be discussed.

In the above investigations the desired or pre-fixed stock level was considered constant. However, it seems reasonable to assume that it also changes over time. The desired stock level of the consumer or producer units may be different in the different economic situations. The stock level held constant in the model so far will be treated differently.

Two possible cases will be examined. The first one is a rather general case where the function describing the desired stock level is not specified. The other case is a special one.

1. Let us take first the case where the actual stock level has an influence on the desired stock level. We will try to illustrate it with an example.

Let us take a consumer who has a certain amount of stock. His opinion of the prospectives varies depending on whether he has a small or large stock. Let us assume that the consumer in question has a stock of food sufficient for a week. In view of this he is optimistic concerning the situation at the market and he feels a stock for five days would be sufficient. On the other hand if his stock of food is at the zero level he is more anxious and less optimistic. Perhaps at first he tries to ensure a stock for one or two days but given the possibility of similar emergency situations, he may want to purchase stock for eight-ten days. Naturally it is difficult to put this relationship in a formula, however, we may assume that it does not distrort very much the actual stock level.

It is uncertain even in this case, however, how this effect appears over time. This may be defined so that if f is a function expressing the desired stock levels how far the resultant stock $(u_1(t), u_2(t))$, may be from one another?[1/]

Let us consider the following a s s u m p t i o n for the function f:

$$(*) \quad \| f[u_1(t)] - f[u_2(t)] \| \leqq \gamma \| u_1(t) - u_2(t) \|$$

where $\gamma > 0$ is a scalar.

In accordance with the above conditions the assumption expresses that small stock level differences /right hand side/ are accompanied with small differences /left hand side/ in the desired stock level.

Let us define the behavioural equation formulated in the above sense:

$$\ddot{u}(t) = C^2 \left[f(u(t)) - u(t) \right]$$

The task cannot be solved in an explicit form. In the following we try to give an upper estimate for the possible divergence.

The solutions of the model can implicitly be expressed in the following form:

$$(4.1.) \qquad u_1(t) = e^{Qt} u_1(0) + e^{Qt} \int_0^t e^{-Q\tau} f(u_1(\tau)) \, d\tau$$

$$(4.2.) \qquad u_2(t) = e^{Qt} u_2(0) + e^{Qt} \int_0^t e^{-Q\tau} f(u_2(\tau)) \, d\tau$$

1/ Further on we are going to analyze only one variable of the model. However, due to the special structure of the model the analysis does not loose generality.

where

$$e^{Qt} = \begin{pmatrix} \cos Ct & C^{-1} \sin Ct \\ -C \sin Ct & \cos Ct \end{pmatrix}, \quad Q = \begin{pmatrix} 0 & E \\ -C^2 & 0 \end{pmatrix}$$

Differences of the solutions can be measured with the norm of deviation. The behaviour of the deviation over time can be estimated with the help of the norm as a scalar.

Let us make use of the following lemmas:

1. L e m m a : Let φ, ψ, χ be real-valued continuous /or piecewiese continuous/ functions on a real t interval $I: a \leq t \leq b$. Let $\chi(t) > 0$ on I, and suppose for $t \in I$ that $\varphi(t) \leqq \psi(t) + \int_a^t \chi(s)\varphi(s)\,ds$ then $\varphi(t)$ can be estimated in the form:

$$\varphi(t) \leqq \psi(t) + \int_a^t \chi(s)\psi(s) \exp\left[\int_s^t \chi(u)\,du\right] ds$$

/Coddington-Levinson, 1955/

2. L e m m a : Let $\|\cdot\|$ denote the matrix norm induced by the euclidean norm /known as spectral norm/ and, if $A \in C_{nxn}$, let λ_A be the spectral radius of A^*A, then $\|A\| = \lambda_A^{1/2}$. /Lancaster, 1969/.

3. L e m m a : A constant upper bound can be found for the operator norm of the e^{Qt}. /Dancs - Ligeti,1973/.

2. Theorem: If f satisfies the (*) assumption and (4.1.), (4.2.) hold for $u_1(t)$ and $u_2(t)$, the estimation for the solution growths exponentially, if $t \to \infty$.

P r o o f :

Let us take the difference between (4.1.) and (4.2.)

$$u_1(t) - u_2(t) = e^{Qt}\left[u_1(0) - u_2(0)\right] + e^{Qt}\int_0^t e^{-Q\tau}\left[f(u_1(\tau)) - f(u_2(\tau))\right] d\tau$$

Let us take the norm of the expression and use the (*)assumption

$$(**)\ \|u_1(t)-u_2(t)\| \leqq \|e^{Qt}\|\ \|u_1(0)-u_2(0)\| + \|e^{Qt}\| \int_0^t \|e^{-Q\tau}\|\ |\gamma|\ \|u_1(\tau) -$$

$$- u_2(\tau)\|\, d\tau$$

Let us use the following notations:

$$\varphi(t) = \|u_1(t) - u_2(t)\|$$

$$\psi(t) = \|e^{Qt}\|\ \|u_1(0) - u_2(0)\|$$

$$\chi(t) = \|e^{Qt}\|\ e^{-Q}\ |\gamma|$$

In accordancne with the 3. lemma the majorant for e^{Qt} is a constant

$$\psi(t) = K_1\ \|u_1(0) - u_2(0)\|$$

$$\chi(t) = K_2\ |\gamma|$$

where K_1, K_2 are properly chosen constants.

Using the above notations we may apply the lemma 1. for (**):

$$\varphi(t) \leqq K_1 \|u_1(0) - u_2(0)\| + K_1\ \|u_1(0) - u_2(0)\| \cdot K_2|\gamma| \int_0^t e^{\int_\tau^t K_2|\gamma|\,du}\, d\tau$$

After integration we can obtain the following expression:

$$\varphi(t) \leqq K_1\ \|u_1(0) - u_2(0)\|\ e^{K_2 \gamma t}\ \blacksquare$$

2. Let us examine such a case where we assume that the function f is known. Let us assume that there is an excess supply of a certain commodity at the market. The producer and consumer unit see their supply ensured, therefore they aim at a lower stock level. However, sooner or later these reserves are depleted and in some cases shortages appear. As a consequence the behaviour of the consumer and of the producer units changes, they try to achieve higher stock levels. Let us assume that this behaviour can be described with following function:

$$f(t) = u^* + \bar{u}\ \cos At$$

where: $\bar{u}$ and A are the parameters of changing behaviour, A is diagonal.

The function of behaviour can be formulated in the following form:

$$\ddot{u} = C^2(u^* - \bar{u} \cos At - u(t))$$

Let us see how this system behaves in this case. It is known that the solution of the original system can be given in the following form:

$$u_j = u_j^* + K_j \sin (c_j t + \varphi_j^o)$$

For the complete solution we have to know the correction factor, the periodic part which is determined by the following integral

$$\int_0^t e^{Q(t-\tau)} \begin{pmatrix} 0 \\ \bar{u} \cos A\tau \end{pmatrix} d\tau$$

After the integration is performed we are left with

$$\int_0^t e^{Q(t-\tau)} \begin{pmatrix} 0 \\ \bar{u} \cos A\tau \end{pmatrix} d\tau = (\cos At - \cos Ct)(C^2 - A^2)^{-1} \bar{u} =$$

$$= \frac{t^2}{2} \bar{u} \frac{\sin \frac{A+C}{2}t \sin \frac{A-C}{2}t}{\frac{A+C}{2}t \cdot \frac{A-C}{2}t}$$

We can examine by components those cases where the C and A parameters are close to each other.

Since

$$\lim_{a_j \to c_j} (\cos a_j t - \cos c_j t)(c_j^2 - a_j^2)^{-1} \bar{u}_j = -\frac{\bar{u}_j}{2c_j} t \sin c_j t$$

is a function with increasing periodicity over t. The complete solution of the system oscillates with increasing amplitude.

Analyzing the interpretation of the C and A parameters it can be pointed out that if the two behavioural parameters are close to each other similarly to the physics, r e s o n a n c e as such occurs also in the economy. The value of the A parameter if inadequately chosen

/measures taken at wrong time or unexpected reaction of the consumers and producers/ may bring about resonance also in the economy.

References

CODDINGTON, A. - LEVINSON, N.: Theory of Ordinary Differential Equations, Mc Graw-Hill Book Co. 1955.

DANCS I. - LIGETI I.: Gazdasági rendszer stabilitásának vizsgálata. /Stability analysis of a dynamic economic system,/ Institute of Economic Planning, Hungary, Working Paper,1973.

DANCS,I. - HUNYADI, L. - SIVÁK,J.: Készletjelzésen alapuló szabályozás egy Leontief tipusu gazdaságban /Control based on stock signals in a Leontief-type economy/, Szigma, Vol.VI. No.3. /1973/. pp. 185-2o7.

LANCASTER, P.: Theory of matrices, Academic Press, New-York-London,1969.

KORNAI,J. - MARTOS,B.: Autonomous functioning of an economic system. Econometrica, Vol. 41. No.3. /1973/ pp. 5o9-529.

KORNAI,J.: Anti-equilibrium. North-Holland Publishing Co.Amsterdam,1971.

SIVÁK,J.: Control Based on Stock Signals, Paper presented on the Winter Symposium of Econometric Society, Budapest, January 1974.

VIRÁG, I.: Gazdasági rendszerek vegetativ müködése sztochasztikus külső fogyasztással /Autonomous functioning of an economic system with external stochastic consumption/ Szigma, Vol.VI. No.4. /1971/ pp. 261-268.

MODELLING AND OPTIMIZATION TECHNIQUES IN ACCORDANCE WITH THE INFORMATION REQUIREMENTS FOR SOCIO-ECONOMIC DEVELOPMENT

W.H. de Man

ITC-Unesco Centre for Integrated Surveys
Enschede, The Netherlands

ABSTRACT

The main objective of this paper is to attempt to indicate in what way concepts such as modelling, simulation, optimization, etc. can be applied as a tool in the design of policies for socio-economic development.

A model as a basis for the design of policies should be in accordance with the existing administrative, statistical, political and sociological infrastructures.
The objectives of the development should be reflected by the model.

Both the frequent unavailability of data of good quality, as well as the fact that policy and decision makers should have some insight in the structure of the model, ask for the application of simple methods.

As an illustration of the considerations as laid down in this paper, two case studies are presented.

INTEGRATED SURVEYS

In general, the stagnation of development in a particular area is caused by an intricate complex of problems. The identification and analysis of these problems need to be carried out in a coordinated and integrated way. The importance of integration in the study of natural resources for development purposes was emphasised during the Unesco Conference on "Principles and Methods of Integrating Aerial Survey Studies of Natural Resources for Potential Development" in Toulouse, France in 1964. In this conference it was recommended that survey team leaders and other experts should be trained in the concepts, methods, techniques and practical operation of integrated surveys of natural resources, together with economic and sociological aspects of the intended development.

In order to provide such training facilities, and to ensure the further development of efficient, comprehensive survey procedures, Unesco and the International Institute for Aerial Survey and Earth Sciences (ITC) in The Netherlands, decided to establish the ITC-Unesco Centre for Integrated Surveys. This Centre commenced its activities in 1965.

Although many different definitions of the term "integrated surveys" do exist, within the scope of this paper "integrated surveys" include:

(1) all activities related to the formulation of the survey objectives, survey tasks, and survey activities, and

(2) the subsequent collection, analysis, and interpretation of all kinds of relevant information needed for the (re)formulation of concrete action programmes (or their alternatives) for development purposes.

The objective of integrated surveys is to ensure that the interrelated (often mono-disciplinary) survey activities are in accordance with the common survey goals.

A detailed examination of the concept of integrated surveys, as well as its relation to concepts like modelling, simulation, etc. is presented elsewhere (for example, see 1/, 2/, 3/).

FOR WHOM IS THE MODELLING AND OPTIMIZATION EXERCISE SET UP?

Within the context of this paper, applications of modelling and optimization are viewed in their relation to socio-economic development. Modelling and optimization techniques may be applied to the domain of socio-economic development as powerful tools in demonstrating the consequences of specific policy measures. One should keep in mind that these policy measures have to be proposed by policy and decision makers, and that they are, after all, responsible for the decision. Using the words of HALTER and MILLER 4/: "Our conclusion (...) was that computer simulation is a powerful tool to be used in the decision-making process, but that it is not a replacement for the decision maker".

Policy and decision makers are responsible for the implementation of certain policies for development. The environment in which they act is characterized by a set of political and administrative conditions, typical for developing countries. Although it is rather difficult to give one single definition of "a developing country", one may observe that most developing countries are characterized by mass poverty, malnutrition, diseases, illiteracy, bad housing, great unemployment, rural-urban migration, a mainly agricultural based economy, unbalanced income distribution, poor management in both the public and private sectors.

Within this scope, the objectives for development may be formulated, as Zambia's President Kaunda does 5/: "National development is meaningless if it does not develop each one of our four million people in the country". He summarizes the Zambian objectives as follows:

(a) Every individual should receive sufficient food both in quantity (no starvation) and in quality (no malnutrition).

(b) Every individual should have a decent two or three-room brick house.

(c) Every individual should have adequate clothing and footwear.

The President of the World Bank, McNAMARA, speaking about rural development, expressed his view as follows 6/: "Essential elements of any comprehensive programme are:
- acceleration in the rate of land and tenancy reform
- better access to credit
- assured availability of water
- expanded extension facilities backed by intensified agricultural research
- greater access to public services
- and most critical of all, new forms of rural institutions and organizations that will give as much attention to promoting the inherent potential and productivity of the poor as is generally given to protecting the power of the privileged".

He also said: "We intend to continue to invest in large projects but we will emphasize on-farm development incorporating a maximum of self-financing so that the benefits of irrigation can reach small farmers more quickly".

These quotations may serve as an illustration of the type of development objectives that are relevant to developing countries.

It is obvious that the performance (and the control) of the various development activities have to be made explicit in accordance with the foregoing-mentioned development objectives. HALTER and MILLER made use of the following performance measures in their study of the Venezuelan cattle industry 7/: discounted net cash flows on farm level, foreign exchange balances, farm income, net beef imports, and domestically produced nutrient outputs. ROSSMILLER, et al. used as performance measures for the Korean Agricultural Sector Analysis 8/: agriculture gross product, value added, per-capita incomes, per-capita calories and proteins, profit per hectare (by crop), profit per man/year (by crop), seasonal labour demand profits (by crop and total), exports and imports, agricultural production (by commodity and region), etc.

Moreover, it is extremely important to have some idea about the capital investment requirements (and its availability).

Furthermore, the performance measures should be in accordance, to some extent, with the statistical concepts as used by the policy and decision makers. Otherwise these measures become isolated variables.

In every society, regional or national, there exist specific administrative, political, and social infrastructures. Although these structures may be weak, it is very important that they are considered carefully when studying development possibilities.

APPLICATION OF MODELLING AND SIMULATION TO SOCIO-ECONOMIC DEVELOPMENT

From the foregoing, it is clear that modelling and simulation methods can be applied fruitfully to socio-economic development only if this application is made in close cooperation with the responsible policy and decision makers, and if it fits within the existing infrastructures. In addition, many methods of modelling, simulation, optimization, etc. make use of sophisticated procedures which can hardly be applied in situations where sufficient and reliable quantitative data are missing. It should be noted that in developing countries in particular, sufficient and reliable statistical data are often lacking. For example, time series, if available, are incomplete; different statistical concepts are used when describing the same phenomena.

The lack of data, however, should not lead to a "data hunger" for masses of unrelated data. SHAH suggests: before any data collection programme is started, it is very important to consider questions such as what the data are required for, and how they will be processed and used. What is the necessary format and to what accuracy are the data to be collected. 9/

Note that the application of systems analysis facilitates in first defining the important elements to be investigated and subsequently in evaluating the accuracy to which the data have to be collected. In addition to the problem of unavailability of data, experience shows that it is necessary to have local professional talent with the capability of applying modelling and simulation methods. Too often these studies are conducted by foreign experts and take place completely isolated from local professionals in the fields of modelling, simulation and optimization.
Such studies easily stop if the experts leave. If an expert recommends the application of (sophisticated) methods and procedures, the training of local professionals, in order to enable them to use these procedures by themselves, should be kept in mind. Quoting MAJOR, when he speaks about the MIT-Argentina Project 10/: "The group of Argentine professionals is now fully capable of further developing and utilizing the system of models constructed for the case study, and of developing other sets of models for water resources planning programmes in Argentina. The effort of this aspect of the programme was to present the Argentine Government with a "living report". To facilitate the work of these men after their return to Argentina, all of the models developed for the case study were designed so that they can be run on computation equipment currently available in Buenos Aires."

DIFFERENT TYPES OF MODELS

Models can be classified in various ways. A specific classification depends on the purpose this classification has to serve. Some examples of classification are:

- according to the model "language"
  - verbal model
  - analogue model
  - mathematical model
  - scale model
  - graphical (visual) model
- according to the change of the object (system) with respect to time
  - static model
  - dynamic model.

CLARK suggests the classification of many models presented in the hydrological literature as follows 11/:

- four main classes
  1) stochastic-conceptual
  2) stochastic-empirical
  3) deterministic-conceptual
  4) deterministic-empirical
- any of these main classes may be sub-classified in several ways
  a) linear or non-linear in the systems-theory sense
  b) linear or non-linear in the statistical regression sense
  c) lumped or probability-distributed or geometrically distributed.

The distinction stochastic/deterministic is according to CHOW 12/: "When the probability of hydrologic data is ignored, the mathematical model is known as a deterministic model. When the hydrologic uncertainty is considered, the model is called a stochastic model." The distinction conceptual/empirical is according to whether the model is or is not suggested by consideration of the physical process acting upon the input variable(s) to produce the output variable(s). (The term "black-box" corresponds to "empirical").

THORBECKE 13/ presented a classification of agricultural sector-models. He recognizes five distinctive classes.

(1) Non-formal, general equilibrium-consistency models. This type of approach relies on a general equilibrium-consistency framework rather than on formal quantitative models. This approach is used, among others, by FAO for the Country Perspective Studies.

(2) Linear programming models. Examples are the "Colombia Agricultural Sector Analysis" by a USAID team and the "Agricultural Sector Analysis in Thailand" by Iowa State University.

(3) Micro dynamic recursive programming models. The term "micro" refers to the fact that this type of model is built from "the bottom up": the maximization procedure is at farm level. The dynamic elements are introduced through recursive programming. An example is the Punjab Region Analysis.

(4) Multilevel planning models. The main characteristic of these models is the formal linkage of the agricultural sector model upwards with an economy-wide model and downwards with agricultural district sub-models. An example is the Mexican CHAC model.

(5) Systems-science, simulation models. These models are basically simulation-type models. The results of changes in exogenous variables, policy instruments and technology can be simulated within the model. In that way a number of "development plans" can be generated. An example is the Korean Agricultural Sector Analysis by Michigan State University (ROSSMILLER et al.).

The main advantage of classifying examples of available models like THORBECKE does, is obviously the possibility to catalogue these examples in a systematic way. This enables development study teams to find easily examples applied on similar situations that they are themselves confronted with. In this respect, HEADY made a plea in the Bucharest Planning Seminar 1971 to develop a handbook on overall and sub-system models. 14/

In the same way, SHAH and the author put forward a recommendation to report case studies and examples of cases where the methodology and concepts of systems analysis, modelling and model validation, simulation, etc., were developed and adopted for situations where sufficient and reliable data are not available. 15/

The author wishes to add one type of model to this list. A variation of the non-formal, general equilibrium-consistency model is formed by the "model" of "back-of-the-envelope calculations". In fact, one could often feel satisfaction already if one is able to find just some orders of magnitude of the phenomena under investigation.

TO WHAT EXTENT CAN THE APPLICATION OF MODELLING AND OPTIMIZATION SERVE AS AN AID TO POLICY AND DECISION MAKERS,

In the previous sections the environment in which modelling and optimization techniques may be applied to socio-economic development has been described. Here, the application of modelling and optimization techniques as an aid to policy and decision makers is considered. Broadly speaking, there are two important aspects: a) the purpose it has to serve (viz. being an aid to specific users) and b) the availability of quantitative data of good quality. In particular with respect to developing countries, both aspects ask for the application of simple methods. It should be clear to the users of the results of this application how these results are obtained. They should have confidence in the results. This is the only way to understand what these results really mean. Insight into the structure of a model is very often directly useful for solving the problem.

Besides this, the model has to reflect the relevant policy instruments and political constraints. In this respect AHLUWALIA distinguishes six different "areas of intervention" open to governments in the implementation of development plans. 16/

1) Factor markets determine prices, utilization levels, and income of labour and capital.

2) Ownership and control of assets determine the distribution of personal income. Human capital in the form of skills is influenced by education.

3) Taxation of personal income and wealth operates on personal income as a fiscal corrective on market-determined income.

4) Provision of public consumption goods, or direct income transfers by the state, complement post-tax income distribution patterns and, jointly with taxation of personal income and wealth, determine the net fiscal impact on the distribution of personal income.

5) Commodity markets are closely linked to the equilibrium in the factor markets. The commodity composition of final demand obviously affects the pattern of demand for factors and therefore factor incomes. Conversely, the income distribution directly determines commodity demand through consumption patterns.

6) Less subject to government influence is the state of technology. This determines the level of total output and the degree of substitutability between factors.

The choice of intervention depends to a large extent on the choice of strategy. The choice of strategy, in turn, depends on the chosen aims of development. Obviously, the applied model should reflect goals, strategies and policy instruments, as are relevant to the specific case.

Often it is difficult, or even impossible, to make the goals (or targets), strategies and instrumental variables explicit in quantified terms. One should remember that in the process of socio-economic development, many non-rational phenomena (such as human and social behaviour) take place and change in relation to an accelerating world. If this is the case, it is rather dangerous to build one mathematical model describing the entire system, or to apply sophisticated optimization methods. One could far better try to split up the entire complex system into smaller (and simpler) sub-systems. And, instead of applying mathematically oriented optimization techniques in such cases, one could study the physical consequences of the system under pre-set assumptions and conditions. By changing these assumptions and conditions, different alternative consequences can be obtained and compared by the policy and decision makers.

In this respect it is relevant to mention a study undertaken by DE FIGUEIREDO and GABUS of the Batelle Institute, Geneva. 17/ They represent future developments as the result of two types of factors: trends and events. Trends are used in the normal sense, events include all phenomena (economic, social, political, technological, etc.) which do not fit a general trend, and whose occurence may be outside but have an effect on the system. These two components constitute an "integrated" model (as they call it). This integrated model uses two types of complementary information: (a) statistical information as used in a traditional econometric model in order to explain relations between trends, and (b) intuitive information based on experts' evaluation of the probability of important events for a given economic development.

By using this integrated model, simulations can be carried out which take into account the interrelation between events and trends.

TWO CASE STUDIES

In this section the foregoing considerations are illustrated by two case studies.

In April, 1974 a team of the ITC-Unesco Centre for Integrated Surveys undertook field investigations in one of the Gouvernorats of Northern Tunisia. In April, 1975 another team of the Centre undertook field investigations in one of the Gouvernorats of the Sahel region of Tunisia. In both cases the team consisted of staffmembers of the Centre, as well as participants of the Standard Course.

The 1974 Survey 18/

The region under investigation is one of the most important agricultural areas of the country. Tourism has developed rapidly over the past five years and continues to expand. The demand for water is anticipated to exceed the locally available water resources representing eventually a major constraint upon development.

The purpose of this reconnaissance survey was to collect basic quanitative and quantitative data for the formulation of development alternatives with emphasis on the optimization of water utilization in the context of a regional development plan.

The survey included:

1) Evaluation of the present agricultural practices and scope for future development of rainfed and irrigated agriculture, livestock, forestry, and fisheries, in view of physical, technical and socio-economic constraints.
2) Evaluation of the present situation and scope for further development of tourism in view of physical, technical and socio-economic constraints and its impact on urbanization.
3) Evaluation of present and future surface and ground water resources, and the possibility of maintaining the present level of development and the scope of further development, eventually in conjunction with other sources of water supply.

From the beginning, it was clear that no sophisticated mathematical procedure could be applied in order to define the optimal water use within the gouvernorat. At least at that phase of the survey, no objective function could be expressed in mathematical terms and essential data were missing. However, several policy measures open to the decision makers for implementation could be fairly accurately described in a quantitative way. For instance, the area of certain types of soils under cultivation of specific crops. The consequences of such policies were described in terms of employment opportunities.

According to the classification set up by THORBECKE, the type of model that was applied could be called a "non-formal, general equilibrium-consistency model" (modified to the "back-of-the-envelope" method).

Through a comparison with the projected development of the labour supply and taking into account the labour requirements in tourism and services, indications could be obtained about the relevance of certain alternative policies of agricultural development. As the limit of the time horizon, the year 1986 was agreed upon. For the analysis and interpretation of the collected data, the gouvernorat was subdivided into four regions.

With respect to agriculture, three different types of resources were relevant in that phase of the survey: land, water, and human resources.

a) Land resources. The soils of the area were subdivided into a number (6) of classes according to their agricultural capabilities. The total acreage per soil capability class was measured.

b) Water resources. The amount of available surface and ground water was obtained with a high and a low estimate. The domestic water use for 1986 was anticipated. Subsequently the available water resources for agriculture could be estimated.

c) Human resources. For the year 1986 the total labour force was estimated. For the same year the employment in tourism was estimated with a high and a low estimate. Subsequently estimations for the residual to be employed in agriculture, services, transport and communications, industry and mines could be obtained.

Besides the information on the available resources, some characteristics of cultivated crops were known. For example, the required labour and irrigation water inputs per hectare, per year, and to what soil capability class the crop is restricted.

Based on the above-mentioned data, the consequences of some policy measures were calculated. In this specific case, some extreme policy goals were selected: maximum employment in agriculture, maximum citrus cultivation, minimum water use with maximum employment in rainfed agriculture, and minimum water use with maximum vineyards. For each of these policy goals the employment consequences were calculated.

The 1975 Survey 19/

The area of the 1975 survey is one of the most developed regions of Tunisia. Agriculture, tourism, industry, and services are the main economic activities.

The purpose of the survey was to identify, based on the investigation of land, water and human resources, various development alternatives and to determine their consequences, with emphasis on the employment situation to be expected by 1986.

The survey included:

1) Evaluation of available data of land and water resources in the survey area, which are relevant to development.

2) Analysis of the present state of agriculture and scope for agricultural development based on the present and possible future land and water resources.

3) Analysis of the actual situation of some second and third order "(sub)urban centres", and the identification of possibilities for promoting these centres in relation to agricultural and regional development potential.

4) Analysis of the present and projected social and economic situation in the principal sectors of economic activity with emphasis on the employment situation.

5) Analysis of alternative use of resources, in particular land and water, within the principal sectors of economic activity and the impact of employment.

As relevant to the scope of this paper, the format of the collected data was almost the same as in the case of the 1974 survey. The model that was applied in this case was, according to the classification set up by THORBECKE, a combination of the "non-formal, general equilibrium-consistency model" (modified to the "back-of-the-envelope" method) and the "linear programming model". The latter approach was selected because it was to be expected that the relevant policy goals were of the maximization type.

The linear programming problem may be represented in the following manner.

The objective function

maximize $$Z = C_1X_1 + C_2X_2 + \dots + C_nX_n$$

is subject to a set of constraints.

$$A_{i1}X_1 + A_{i2}X_2 + \dots + A_{in}X_n \leq B_i \qquad (i = 1, 2, \dots k)$$

$$A_{p1}X_1 + A_{p2}X_2 + \dots A_{pn}X_n = B_p \qquad (p = k + 1, K + 2, \dots, m)$$

$$X_j \geq o \qquad (j = 1, 2, \dots, n)$$

In this particular case, two different policy objectives were considered: maximum employment and maximum total gross value added. Therefore, Z can represent either the total employment or the total gross value added.

X_j $(j = 1, 2, \dots, n)$ are the activities. Both the (8) industrial activities as the touristic activity are defined in terms of creating gross value added in addition to the present situation. The agricultural activities are defined in terms of the amount of hectares under a specific number (8) of crops.

C_j $(j = 1, 2, \ldots, n)$ are the value coefficients. In fact, there is a specific set of value coefficients in case of employment maximization and another one in case of gross value added maximization.

B_i $(i = 1, 2, \ldots, k)$ are the constraints referring to the water, recycled water, and land resources.

B_p $(p = k + 1, k + 2, \ldots, m)$ are constraints in the sense that the present levels of certain activities have to be maintained.

A_{ij} $(i = 1, 2, \ldots, m; j = 1, 2, \ldots, n)$ are coefficients relating to the activities and the constraints.

Some Comments on the 1974 Survey and the 1975 Survey

In both cases, before any attempt could be made at optimization, the reliability of the collected data was checked by a non-formal, general equilibrium-consistency approach. The data base as obtained in this way forms a tool in showing policy and decision makers easily some consequences of policy measures proposed by them.

In the 1975 survey an attempt was made to consider also the spatial consequences of proposed policy measures. It is felt at the ITC-Unesco Centre that much more research has to be devoted to this aspect.

Furthermore, it is felt with respect to both surveys, that information about the capital investment requirements and the possibilities to meet these requirements was almost lacking. (Likely this is mainly due to the short time the team was really on the spot).

CONCLUSION

The application of modelling and optimization techniques can serve as an aid to policy and decision makers, both in understanding better the existing situation as well as in selecting policies for development.

In the process of modelling and optimization, the policy and decision makers should play an active role. They are, after all, responsible for the ultimate policies for development. Technical specialists should avoid smuggling in their own subjective values under the slogan of scientific knowledge.

The model should reflect the existing relevant policy instruments and political conditions in which the policy and decision makers act. The model and optimization procedures should also be in agreement with the quality (reliability) of the available statistical data.

These considerations often may lead to the application of simple methods. Simple methods does not have a great scientific appeal. However, these simple methods may contribute to the solution of the urgent problems much more than the bulk of cases do where highly sophisticated methods and procedures are applied.

oOo

REFERENCES

1/ BAKKER A.J. — Trends and Developments in Integrated Surveys, Proceedings of the 5th International Seminar, March, 1971 Publication of the ITC-Unesco Centre for Integrated Surveys.

2/ SCHULZE F.E. — Integrated Surveys and Development Planning. ITC Journal 1973, No.2 (Special Issue)

3/ de MAN W.H. — Integrated Surveys of Land and Water Resources for Development Purposes, Proceedings of the First IFIP Working Conference on Computer Simulation of Water Resources, Ghent, 1974. North Holland Publishing Company, 1975.

4/ HALTER A.N. & MILLER S.F. — Simulation in a Practical Policy-Making Setting: The Venezuelan Cattle Industry, Systems Approaches to Developing Countries, IFAC-IFORS Conference, Algiers, 1973.

5/ de GAAY FORTMAN B. — Rural Development in an Age of Survival, Occasional Paper No.21, Institute of Social Studies, The Hague, 1972.

6/ McNAMARA R. — President of the World Bank's Address to the Board of Governors 1973 Meeting, Nairobi.

7/ HALTER A.N. & MILLER S.F. — ibid

8/ ROSSMILLER G.E. et al. — Korean Agricultural Sector Analysis and Recommended Development Strategies, 1971-1985. Seoul and East Lansing, 1972.

9/ SHAH M.M. — Systems Engineering Approach to Agricultural and Rural Development Systems, Proceedings of the First IFIP Working Conference on Computer Simulation of Water Resources Systems, Ghent 1974. North Holland Publishing Company, 1975.

10/ MAJOR D.C. — Investment Criteria and Mathematical Modelling Techniques for Water Resources Planning in Argentina: The MIT-Argentina Project, Systems Approaches to Developing Countries, IFAC-IFORS Conference, Algiers, 1973.

11/ CLARKE R.T. — Mathematical Models in Hydrology. Irrigation and Drainage Paper No.19, F.A.O. Rome, 1973.

12/ CHOW V.T. ed. — Handbook of Applied Hydrology. McGraw-Hill Book Company, 1964.

13/ THORBECKE E. — Sector Analysis and Models for Agriculture in Developing Countries. Food Research Institute Studies in Agricultural Economic, Trade and Development, Vol. XII No.1, 1973.

14/ — Planning Methodology Seminar, Bucharest, 1971. Irrigation and Drainage Paper No.11, F.A.O. Rome, 1972.

15/ SHAH M.M. & de Man W.H. — Proceedings of the First IFIP Working Conference on Computer Simulation of Water Resources Systems, Ghent, 1974. North Holland Publishing Company, 1975.

16/ AHLUWALIA M.S. et al. — Redistribution with Growth, A Joint Study by the World Bank Development Research Centre and the Institute of Development Studies at the University of Sussex. Oxford University Press, 1974.

17/ de FIGUEIREDO J.B. & GABUS A. — Why and How to Introduce the Event Dimension into the Simulation of Development Policies Systems Approaches to Developing Countries, IFAC-IFORS Conference, Algiers, 1973.

18/, 19/ — The Fieldwork Reports are unpublished internal documents of the ITC-Unesco Centre for Integrated Surveys.

Population Planning; a Distributed Time Optimal Control Problem

G.J. Olsder and R.C.W. Strijbos
Department of Applied Mathematics
Twente University of Technology
P.O. Box 217, Enschede
The Netherlands

Abstract

The time evolution of the age profile of a group of people, for instance the population of a certain country, can be described by a first-order partial differential equation. A time optimal control problem arises when the population must be brought from a given age profile to another desired one as quickly as possible. The birth rate, i.e. the number of births per unit of time, is the control variable and it serves as a boundary condition for the partial differential equation. To prevent the age distribution to become undesirable from an economical point of view during the transient to the final situation we require the working population to exceed a given fraction of the total population at each instant of time. This introduces a state constraint to the problem.

For the cases considered the following facts turn out. a) If age and time are discretized properly, a linear programming problem results, the solution of which equals an optimal solution of the continuous version of the problem. b) The time optimal control is not necessarily unique. A complete characterization of the class of all optimal controls can be given. c) Under certain conditions the class of all optimal controls contains a unique non-increasing control.
Two examples are solved analytically.

1. Introduction.

The evolution of a certain group of people, say for instance the population of a country, can be described by a partial differential equation in which the independent variables are time and age. If the initial age profile is given as well as the birth rate and the mortality function, then the evolution is completely determined. The mortality function depends on time and age and is assumed to be known. Immigration and emigration are not considered in the model, though this could easily be built in.

Given a certain initial age profile the population must be "steered" as quickly as possible to another, prescribed, final age profile by means of a suitable chosen birth rate. In this way a time optimal control problem has been formulated. The problem is stated in terms of an overpopulation which should be reduced. The other way around can be dealt with equally well.

The optimal birth rate may unbalance the age distribution during the time interval concerned, which could give rise to economic and social problems. Therefore it is assumed that the working population, which must support the non-working population, must exceed a given fraction of the total population at each instant of time. This becomes a state constraint in the mathematical formulation. It will turn out that the addition of this state constraint makes the control problem nontrivial. Another constraint which is considered is that the birth rate, obviously nonnegative, must be a nonincreasing function of time in order to avoid possible peaks.

This paper is not concerned with the social and political problems involved in establishing the best mechanism for a program of population management. Instead of this, it focusses upon the mathematical solution of the time optimal control problem.

The mathematical problem has not quite been solved in its generality; the mortality function and the definition of the working population should satisfy certain restrictions.

Related problems have been treated by for instance Langhaar [1] and Falkenburg [2]. Instead of time optimality Falkenburg considers a quadratic criterion and no state constraints are included. In [3] a similar control problem is considered using the Leslie model, with demografic data of the Netherlands.

2. The model describing the population dynamics.

The quantity p will stand for population density and it depends on the independent variables time t and age r. The number of people of ages in the age interval (r, r+dr] at a certain time t is given by p(t,r)dr. Suppose t increases with dt and hence the age of an individual increases with dr = dt as well. Now

$$p(t+dt,\ r+dt)dr = p(t,r)dr - p(t,r)\mu(t,r)dr\ dt, \tag{1}$$

where $\mu(t,r)$ is the mortality function, i.e. $\mu(t,r)dt$ is the fraction of people of the age class (r,r+dr] who die in the time interval [t,t+dt). If $dr = dt \to 0$, eq. (1) yields

$$\frac{\partial p(t,r)}{\partial t} = - \frac{\partial p(t,r)}{\partial r} - \mu(t,r)p(t,r) \tag{2}$$

which is a linear partial differential equation of the hyperbolic type. It is assumed that μ and the boundary conditions are sufficiently smooth in order for $\partial p/\partial r$ and $\partial p/\partial t$ to exist almost everywhere. The following boundary and initial conditions will be used:

$$p(0,r) = p_0(r) \quad , \quad 0 < r \leq 1, \tag{3}$$

$$p(t,0) = u(t) \quad , \quad 0 \leq t \leq T, \tag{4}$$

where $p_0(r)$ is the given initial age distribution; $u(t)$ is the birth rate and T is the final time. It has been assumed that the age r has been scaled in such a way that nobody reaches an age of $r > 1$. The time t will be measured with respect to the same scale.

From now on it will be assumed that $\mu(t,r)$ is independent of t and by abuse of notation we will now write $\mu(r)$, which is assumed to be known. The solution of eqs. (2)-(4) is

$$p(t,r) = p_0(r-t)\exp(-\int_{r-t}^{r} \mu(s)ds) \quad , \quad 0 \leq t < r, \tag{5}$$

$$p(t,r) = u(t-r)\exp(-\int_{0}^{r} \mu(s)ds) \quad , \quad t \geq r. \tag{6}$$

Because nobody reaches $r = 1^+$, the mortality function should satisfy

$$\exp(-\int_{0}^{1^+} \mu(s)ds) = 0$$

However, this is not the case for the functions $\mu(r)$ considered in this paper. For these imperfect $\mu(r)$-functions it will be assumed that those people who reach an age of $r > 1$, simply leave the model and are not considered any longer.

The age distribution is called stationary at $t = t_s$ if

$$p(t_s,r) = c.\ \exp(-\int_{0}^{r} \mu(s)ds), \quad 0 \leq r \leq 1 \tag{7}$$

where c is a positive constant. A stationary age distribution corresponds to a constant birth rate $u(t) = c$ for $t_s - 1 \leq t < t_s$.

In the remainder of the text the following abbreviations will be used

$$e(r) = \exp(-\int_0^r \mu(s)ds) ,$$

$$ei(a;b) = \int_a^b e(r)dr .$$

3. Statement of the problem.

We will consider the following problem. Bring the population from a given initial age profile to another desired one as quickly as possible by properly choosing the birth rate. More precisely, given eqs. (2) and (3), the boundary condition (4) should be chosen in such a way that at time $t = T$ the age distribution $p(T,r)$ equals a prescribed function $p_T(r)$ for all $r \in (0,1]$. Moreover the final time T must have its minimal value. It is easily shown that $p(T,r)$, $0 \leqslant r \leqslant 1$ is completely determined by $u(t)$ with $t \in [T-1,T]$ because the people who were born between $t = 0$ and $t = T-1$ have all died at time T and hence do not show up in $p(T,r)$. It is tacitly assumed here that $T \geqslant 1$.

From now on it will be assumed that both $p_0(r)$ and $p_T(r)$ are stationary. Apart from a multiplicative constant p_0 and p_T are equal; we assume that $p_0(r) > p_T(r)$, $0 \leqslant r \leqslant 1$.

The final time T must be minimized and it is clear from above that the minimal T, to be denoted by T^*, equals 1; simply choose $u(t) = u_T$ on $0 \leqslant t \leqslant 1$, where the constant u_T corresponds to the stationary age distribution $p_T(r)$.

The optimal control problem defined above is trivial. However, the solution may unbalance the age distribution and therefore the following state constraint will be added:

$$\int_a^b p(t,r)dr \geqslant \alpha \int_0^1 p(t,r)dr, \qquad 0 \leqslant t \leqslant T,$$

which can be rewritten as

$$h(t) \triangleq \int_0^1 \gamma(r)p(t,r)dr \geqslant 0, \qquad 0 \leqslant t \leqslant T. \tag{8}$$

This ineq. can be thought of as an economic constraint; the working population, defined as all people aged between a and b, should be at least a given percentage of the total population.

Quantities a and b are constants with $0 \leq a < b \leq 1$; $\gamma(r)$ is a stepfunction; $\gamma(r) = -\alpha$ for $0 \leq r < a$ and $b \leq r < 1$ and $\gamma(r) = 1-\alpha$ for $a \leq r < b$. The parameter α is a constant within the bounds

$$0 < \alpha < \bar{\alpha} \triangleq \frac{ei(a;b)}{ei(0;1)}, \tag{9}$$

where the second inequality has been obtained from the fact that ineq. (8) should be valid for a stationary age distribution.
We will also assume that

$$u(t) \geq 0, \qquad 0 < t \leq T$$

If we use eq. (6), the problem can be completely restated in terms of the birth rate u(t);

minimize T subject to

$$u(t) = u_0 \geq 0, \ -1 \leq t < 0,$$
$$u(t) = u_T \geq 0, \ T-1 \leq t \leq T,$$
$$u(t) \geq 0, \ 0 \leq t < T-1,$$
$$h(t) = \int_0^1 \gamma(r)u(t-r)e(r)dr \geq 0, \ 0 \leq t \leq T.$$

Here u_0 and u_T are the constant birth rates, corresponding to $p_0(r)$ and $p_T(r)$ respectively. Without loss of generality we will take $u_0 = 1$. In a later stage sometimes the condition that the optimal birth rate must be nonincreasing will be added.

The problem will be approached in a slightly different manner. The roles played by the quantities T and u_T are interchanged, i.e. in obtaining a solution we assume that T is fixed and that u_T must be minimized. This trick is justified by the fact that the mapping $T \to u_T$ is nonincreasing and continuous which can be proved for the problems treated. Our problem now reads

minimize u_T subject to

$$u(t) = 1 \quad , -1 \leq t < 0, \tag{10}$$
$$u(t) = u_T \quad , T-1 \leq t \leq T, \tag{11}$$
$$u(t) \geq 0 \quad , 0 \leq t < T-1, \tag{12}$$
$$h(t) = \int_0^1 \gamma(r)u(t-r)e(r)dr \geq 0 \quad , 0 \leq t \leq T. \tag{13}$$

4. Elucidation of the constructive solution scheme.

Because the function to be minimized and the constraints (10)-(13) are all linear in u_T and $u(t)$, the problem just stated can considered to be a Linear Programming problem in an abstract space. So a saddlepoint theorem can be applied which gives necessary and sufficient conditions for the optimal solution u_T^*, $u^*(t)$. A start in this direction has already been made [4].

In this paper however we want to follow a more direct approach, although the class of problems to which it can be applied is not as wide as the class for which the attack in [4] is valid.

We want to make clear certain features of the proposed method by treating two examples. The first example, though not very realistic, serves well to illustrat the method.

Example I.

In this example we take $\mu(r) = 0$ for $0 \leq r < 1$, $a = 0$, $b = \frac{1}{2}$, $\alpha = \frac{1}{3}$, $T = 2$. The problem now is to minimize u_T subject to

$$u(t) = 1 \quad , \qquad -1 \leq t < 0, \tag{14}$$

$$u(t) = u_T \quad , \qquad 1 \leq t < 2, \tag{15}$$

$$u(t) \geq 0 \quad , \qquad 0 \leq t < 1, \tag{16}$$

$$h(t) = \int_0^{\frac{1}{2}} u(t-r)dr - \frac{1}{3} \int_0^1 u(t-r)dr \geq 0, \; 0 \leq t \leq 2 \tag{17}$$

Consider ineq. (17) only for $t = \frac{1}{2}$, 1 and $\frac{2}{3}$ respectively;

$$\int_0^{\frac{1}{2}} u(t)dt \geq \frac{1}{4} , \tag{18}$$

$$\int_{\frac{1}{2}}^1 u(t)dt \geq \frac{1}{2} \int_0^{\frac{1}{2}} u(t)dt, \tag{19}$$

$$\frac{1}{2} u_T \geq \frac{1}{2} \int_{\frac{1}{2}}^1 u(t)dt, \tag{20}$$

from which it follows that $u_T^* \geq \frac{1}{8}$. However, $u_T^* = \frac{1}{8}$, because the piecewise constant control deduced from ineqs. (18)-(20) by imposing the equality-sign

$$u(t) = \frac{1}{2} \quad , \quad 0 \leqslant t < \frac{1}{2}$$

$$u(t) = \frac{1}{4} \quad , \quad \frac{1}{2} \leqslant t < 1$$

$$u(t) = u_T = \frac{1}{8} \quad , \quad 1 \leqslant t \leqslant 2$$

satisfies all the conditions (14)-(17) and hence is optimal (see figure 1).

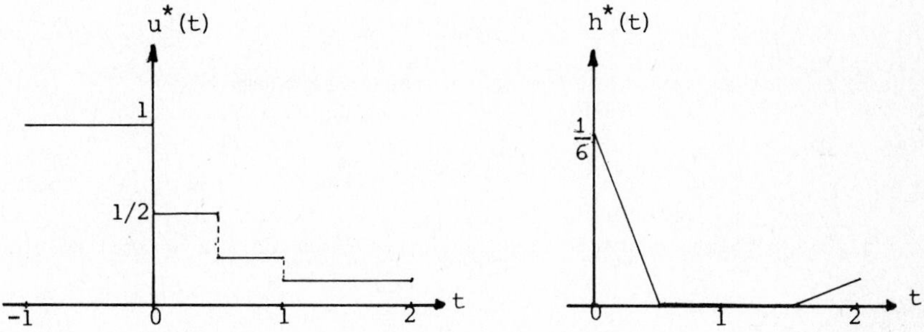

Figure 1. An optimal solution for the first example.

However, the optimal solution is not unique. Another possible solution is for instance

$$u^*(t) = \frac{5}{12} \quad , \quad 0 \leqslant t < \frac{1}{4} ,$$

$$u^*(t) = \frac{7}{12} \quad , \quad \frac{1}{4} \leqslant t < \frac{1}{2} ,$$

$$u^*(t) = \frac{1}{6} \quad , \quad \frac{1}{2} \leqslant t < \frac{3}{4} ,$$

$$u^*(t) = \frac{1}{3} \quad , \quad \frac{3}{4} \leqslant t < 1 ,$$

$$u^*(t) = u_T^* = \frac{1}{8} , \quad 1 \leqslant t \leqslant 2.$$

This optimal solution is sketched in figure 2.

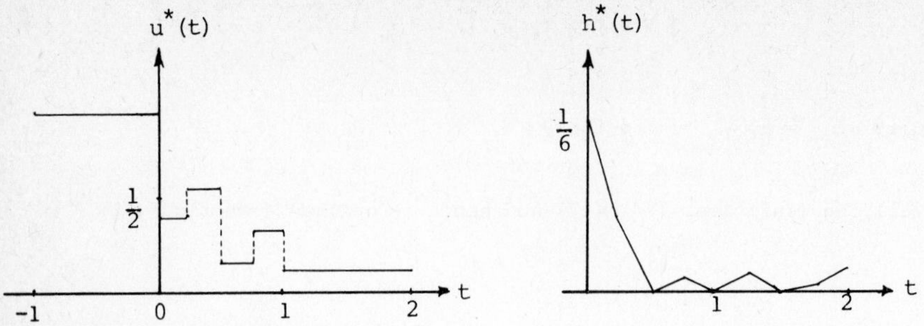

Figure 2. Another optimal solution for the first example.

In order to give a complete characterization of the class of all optimal solutions we define

$$f(t) = \int_0^t u(t)dt, \qquad t \geq 0$$

and

$$x_i(\tau) = f(\tau+(i-1)\tfrac{1}{2}), \qquad i = 1,2, \quad 0 \leq \tau \leq \tfrac{1}{2}.$$

It follows from (18)-(20) with equality-signs that $x_2(\frac{1}{2}) = f(1) = \frac{3}{8}$. On the intervals $\frac{1}{2}(i-1) \leq \tau \leq \frac{1}{2}i$, $i = 1,2,3,4$ ineq. (17) becomes:

$$\left.\begin{aligned} x_1(\tau) &\geq \tau - \tfrac{1}{4} \\ 2x_2(\tau) - 3x_1(\tau) &\geq \tfrac{1}{2} - \tau \\ -3x_2(\tau) + x_1(\tau) &\geq -\tfrac{1}{4}\tau - \tfrac{3}{4} \\ x_2(\tau) &\geq \tfrac{1}{8}\tau + \tfrac{1}{4} \end{aligned}\right\} \quad 0 \leq \tau \leq \tfrac{1}{2}, \tag{21}$$

where $u_T^* = \frac{1}{8}$ and $x_2(\frac{1}{2}) = \frac{3}{8}$ have been substituted.

In the three dimensional space, spanned by x_1-, x_2- and τ-axes, the points (x_1, x_2, τ) satisfying ineqs. (21) form a bounded set; this set is a tetrahedron and has been drawn in figure 3. For $\tau = 0$ only one point (x_1, x_2) satisfies ineqs. (21), viz. $x_1 = 0$, $x_2 = \frac{1}{4}$. For $\tau = \frac{1}{2}$ again only one point satisfies ineqs. (21), viz. $x_1 = \frac{1}{4}$, $x_2 = \frac{3}{8}$. For intermediate τ, however, infinitely many points (x_1,x_2) satisfy ineq. (21). For each τ, $0 \leq \tau \leq \frac{1}{2}$, we choose a point (x_1,x_2) subject to the ineqs. (21) in such a way that $x_i(\tau_1) \leq x_i(\tau)$ for all $\tau_1 \leq \tau$ and $i = 1,2$ in order for ineq. (16) to be satisfied; then the points constitute an optimal solution. Because the optimal $x_i(\tau)$ may have jumps, even optimal birth rates are possible which possess delta-functions.

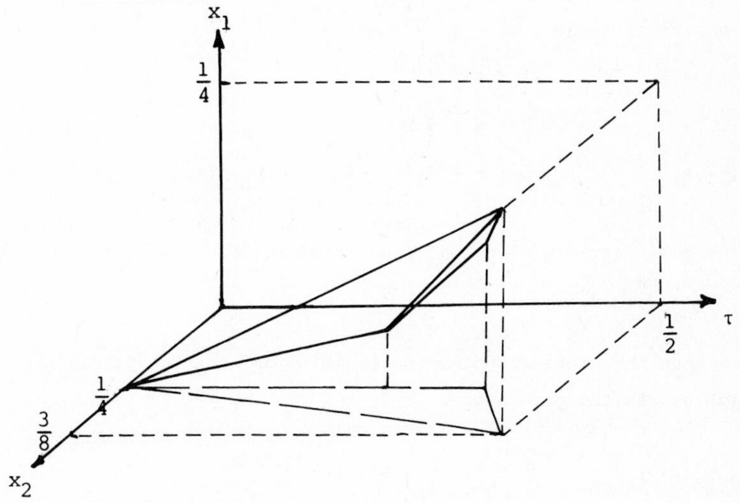

Figure 3. Set of all optimal solutions.

It is easily seen that, if only non-increasing $u(t)$ functions are allowed, the solution is unique and equals the one of fig.1.In fact, if $u(t)$ is nonincreasing, then $x_i(\tau)$ is concave (a connecting bar lies below or on the curve) and the only possibility then is the straight line connecting ($\tau=0$, $x_1=0$, $x_2=\frac{1}{4}$) and ($\tau=\frac{1}{2}$, $x_1=\frac{1}{4}$, $x_2=\frac{3}{8}$); see also figure 3.

We conclude this example by summarizing the facts proved.

(i) An optimal solution (piecewise constant) can be found by considering the ineq. $h(t) \geq 0$ only at a finite number of <u>characteristic</u> points ($t = \frac{1}{2}, 1, \frac{3}{2}$).

(ii) The class of all optimal solutions can be completely characterized with the help of the $x_i(\tau)$-functions.

(iii) This class contains a unique non-increasing control.

The above analysis can be extended to more realistic situations. For example the mortality function may be taken constant and the final time T arbitrary. Instead of going through this problem in quite its generality, only a rough sketch of the solution method and the results for a specific example will be given. For a more detailed discussion and other generalizations one is referred to [4].

Example II.

In this example we take $\mu(r) = \bar{\mu}$ = constant for $0 \leq r < 1$, $a = \frac{1}{3}$ and $b = \frac{2}{3}$. The parameter α is a constant satisfying the ineq. (9). The final time T is taken arbitrarily. In this case the problem reads

minimize u_T subject to

$$u(t) = 1 \quad , \; -1 \leq t < 0 , \tag{22}$$

$$u(t) = u_T \quad , \; T-1 \leq t < T, \tag{23}$$

$$u(t) \geq 0 \quad , \; 0 \leq t < T-1 \tag{24}$$

$$h(t) = \int_{\frac{1}{3}}^{\frac{2}{3}} u(t-r)e(r)dr - \alpha \int_0^1 u(t-r)e(r)dr \geq 0 \quad , \; 0 \leq t \leq T. \tag{25}$$

It turns out that the critical points on the time axis, which play a crucial role in the analysis, are the points given by

$$t_k = k.\nu \quad , \; k = 1,\dots, N+1 ,$$

and $\tilde{t}_k = (k-1).\nu + \sigma, \; k = 1,\dots, N+1,$

with $\nu = \frac{1}{3}$, $N = [T/\nu]$ and $\sigma = T-N.\nu$, where $[T/\nu]$ is the largest natural number less then or equal to T/ν.

Now define

$$f(t) = \int_0^t u(t-r)\exp[-\bar{\mu}r]dr \quad , \; 0 \leq t \leq T , \tag{26}$$

$$x_i(\tau) = f[t_{i-1} + \tau(\tilde{t}_i - t_{i-1})], \; i = 1,\dots, N-2; \; 0 \leq \tau \leq 1, \tag{27}$$

$$\tilde{x}_i(\tau) = f[\tilde{t}_i + \tau(t_i - \tilde{t}_i) \qquad i = 1,\dots, N-3; \; 0 \leq \tau \leq 1, \tag{28}$$

$$\bar{x} = x_{N-2}(1) \quad , \; t_0 = 0 \tag{29}$$

The ineq. (25) can be transformed into restrictions on the functions $x_i(\tau)$ and $\tilde{x}_i(\tau)$. In a compact way the restrictions are given by the following matrix inequality

$$A(\tau)\; x\;(\tau) \geq b(\tau) \qquad , \quad 0 \leq \tau \leq 1 \tag{30}$$

with

$$x(\tau) = (x_1(\tau),\tilde{x}_1(\tau),x_2(\tau),\ldots\ldots,\tilde{x}_{N-3}(\tau),\; x_{N-2}(\tau),\; \bar{x},\; u_T)' \tag{31}$$

Matrix $A(\tau)$ has size (2N+1) x (2N-3) and its elements, as well as the components of $b(\tau)$, are given in the appendix.
An optimal solution can be obtained in the following way

1) Minimize u_T subject to the economic constraint (30) at the characteristic points only, i.e. subject to the constraint

$$A(0)x(0) \geq b(0). \tag{32}$$

Note that $x_1(0) = 0$. This is a finite-dimensional linear programming problem which can be solved by standard techniques, Call the solution of this LP-problem

$$x^*(0) = (x_1^*(0),\; \tilde{x}_1^{\,*}(0),\ldots\ldots,\; x_{N-2}^{\;*}(0),\; \bar{x}^*,\; u_T^*)' \tag{33}$$

2) Now choose $u(t)$, $0 \leq t < T-1$, to be piecewise constant, i.e.,

$$u(t) = u_i \qquad , \quad t_{i-1} \leq t < \tilde{t}_i \qquad , \quad i = 1,2,\ldots,N-2$$
$$u(t) = \tilde{u}_i \qquad , \quad \tilde{t}_i \leq t < t_i \qquad , \quad i = 1,2,\ldots,N-3$$

The quantities u_i and $\tilde{u}_i$ are uniquely determined by eq. (33) and the formulas (27)-(28). For $\mu = 0$ the calculations have been carried out analytically and the result is

$$u_T = \frac{\nu(1-\xi^N)(1+\xi)\xi^{N-2} + \sigma(1+\xi^{N-1})(\xi^2-1)\xi^{N-2}}{\nu(1-\xi^N)(1+\xi^{2N-3}) + \sigma(1+\xi^{N-1})(\xi^2-1)\xi^{N-2}} \tag{34}$$

$$u_i = \frac{(\nu-\sigma)\xi^{N-2}(1-\xi^2)(1+\xi^{N-1}) + \nu(\xi^i+\xi^{2N-1-i})(1-\xi^{N-2})}{(\nu-\sigma)(1-\xi^N)(1+\xi^{2N-3}) + \sigma(1+\xi^{2N-1})(1-\xi^{N-2})} \quad , \tag{35}$$

$$i = 1,2,\ldots,N-2$$

$$\tilde{u}_i = \frac{\nu(1-\xi^N)(\xi^i+\xi^{2N-3-i}) + \sigma(1+\xi^{N-1})(\xi^2-1)\xi^{N-2}}{\nu(1-\xi^N)(1+\xi^{2N-3}) + \sigma(1+\xi^{N-1})(\xi^2-1)\xi^{N-2}}, \tag{36}$$

$$i = 1,2,\ldots,N-3$$

where ξ is defined as the largest root of

$$-\alpha\xi^2 + (1-\alpha)\xi - \alpha = 0$$

3) It can be easily shown that

$$u_1 > \tilde{u}_1 > u_2 > \ldots\ldots > \tilde{u}_{N-3} > u_{N-2} > u_T > 0$$

So the constraint (24) is satisfied. Moreover it can be proved that the solution (34)-(36) satisfies the economic constraint (30) for all $\tau \in [0,1]$, and hence the solution (34)-(36) is an optimal solution.

Some remarks will be made on the uniqueness for the piecewise constant solution $u^*(t)$ found. Because $\bar{x}$ and u_T are not time dependent and are known from (34)-(36) they will be substituted in (30) with as result:

$$\hat{A}\,\hat{x}(\tau) \geq \hat{b}(\tau) \quad , \quad 0 \leq \tau \leq 1, \tag{37}$$

where $\hat{x}(\tau) = (x_1(\tau), \tilde{x}_1(\tau), \ldots, x_{N-2}(\tau))'$ and the size of the constant matrix $\hat{A}$ is (2N+1) x (2N-5); $\hat{b}(s)$ is reconstructed from b, $\bar{x}$ and u_T.

In the 2(N-2)-dimensional space spanned by the components of $\hat{x}$ and the parameter τ an admissible region for $\hat{x}$ and τ exists with $0 \leq \tau \leq 1$; one can imagine a figure similar to figure 3. Such a region of admissible $\hat{x},\tau$ points, i.e. those $\hat{x}$ and τ which satisfy (37), will now be bounded by curved hypersurfaces because in general $\mu \neq 0$. So the admissible region will be banana-shaped. For each $\tau \in [0,1]$ all the admissible $\hat{x}$ of course constitute a convex set.

As was shown in the first example, the optimal control is unique if only non-increasing solutions are allowed. Is this also true in this example? The answer is affirmative. One has to investigate a matrix D, which can be constructed from the matrix A, on inverse-monotonicity [4].

We conclude this example by sketching the function $u_T(\tau)$ for different values of $\bar{\mu}$ and α. For $\bar{\mu} \neq 0$ the function values has been obtain numerically.

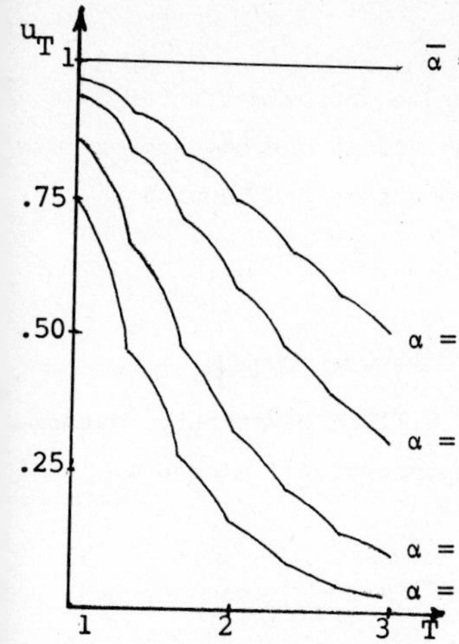

Figure 4, The values of $u_T(T)$ for $\bar{\mu} = 0$ and several values of α,

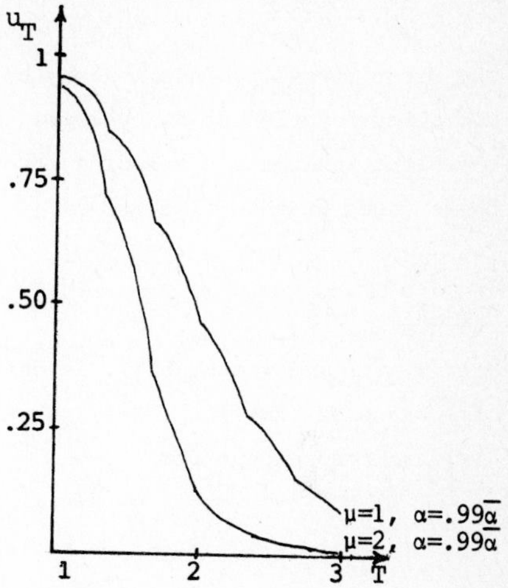

Figure 5. The values of $u_T(T)$ for $\bar{\mu} = 1$ and 2 respectively and $\alpha = .99\bar{\alpha}$.

Note that for $\alpha = \bar{\alpha}$ the working population can just support the non-working population. There is no freedom left to reduce u_T.

5. Conclusion.

In this paper some mathematical features of a population planning problem have been investigated. An open loop control has been found which decreases (or increases) the number of people to a desired level and distribution as quickly as possible subject to the condition that the working population must be at least a given percentage of the total population at each instant of time. Remarkably, the optimal solution to this dynamic problem can be obtained by linear programming provided the working population and mortality function satisfy suitable prerequisities.

A constraint, which has not been considered in this research, is a minimum level of fertility (or maternity functions), i.e. u(t) should satisfy

$$u(t) \geq \int_0^1 \delta(t,r)p(t,r)dr, \quad 0 \leq t \leq T, \text{ for some function } \delta(t,r).$$

Only constant mortality functions have been considered. Some mortality functions somewhat closer to reality may be $\mu(r) = \frac{\pi}{2} \operatorname{tg} \frac{\pi r}{2}$, with corresponding stationary population $p(r) = c. \cos \frac{\pi r}{2}$, or $\mu = \frac{1}{1-r}$ with corresponding $p(r) = c(1-r)$.

The first mortality-function may be considered as a crude approximation of a mortality-function of a developed country, whereas the second one may approximate the situation for a developing country. No analytic solutions are known for these cases at this time.

6. Appendix.

Matrix $A(\tau)$ and vector $b(\tau)$, as defined in ineq. (30) will be given here. Matrix $A(\tau)$ has size $(2N+1) \times (2N-3)$ and $b(\tau)$ has $(2N+1)$ components. All elements a_{ij} of $A(\tau)$ are zero except for

$$a_{ii} = -\alpha,\ a_{i+2,i} = e(\nu),\ a_{i+4,i} = -e(\nu)^2,\ a_{i+6,i} = \alpha e(\nu)^3;$$

$$i = 1,2,\ldots.,2N-5;$$

$$a_{i,2N-4} = -\alpha.e(\sigma(\tau-1) + \nu(i-N+3));\ a_{i,2N-3} = -\alpha.ei(0;\sigma(\tau-1) + \nu(i-N+3))$$

$$i = 2N-3;2N+1;$$

$$a_{i,2N-4} = (1-\alpha).e(\sigma(\tau-1) + \nu(i-N+3));\ a_{i,2N-3} = (1-\alpha).ei(0;\sigma(\tau-1) + \nu(i-N+3));\quad i = 2N-1;$$

$$a_{i,2N-4} = -\alpha.e(\tau(\nu-\sigma) + \nu(i-N+2));\ a_{i,2N-3} = -\alpha.ei(0;\tau(\nu-\sigma) + \nu(i-N+3));$$

$$i = 2N-4;\ 2N;$$

$$a_{i,2N-4} = (1-\alpha).e(\tau(\nu-\sigma) + \nu(i-N+2));\ a_{i,2N-3} = (1-\alpha).ei(0;\tau(\nu-\sigma) + \nu(i-N+2));\quad i = 2N-2;$$

The components b_i of the vector b are zero except for

$$b_1 = \alpha.ei(\tau\sigma;\nu) - (1-\alpha).\ ei(\nu;2\nu) + \alpha.ei(2\nu;1)\ ;$$

$$b_2 = \alpha.ei(\tau(\nu-\sigma) + \sigma;\nu) - (1-\alpha).ei(\nu;\ 2\nu) + \alpha\ ei(2\nu;1)\ ;$$

$$b_3 = -(1-\alpha).ei(\tau\sigma+\nu;2\nu) + \alpha.ei(2\nu;1) ;$$

$$b_4 = -(1-\alpha).ei(\tau(\nu-\sigma) + \sigma + \nu;2\nu) + \alpha.ei(2\nu;1) ;$$

$$b_5 = \alpha.ei(\tau\sigma + 2\nu;1) ;$$

$$b_6 = \alpha.ei(\tau(\nu-\sigma) + \sigma + 2\nu;1).$$

7. References.

[1] Langhaar, H.L.; General Population Theory in the Age-Time Continuum, J. of the Franklin Inst., vol. 293, no. 3, March 1973, pp. 199 - 214.

[2] Falkenburg, D.R.; Optimal Control in Age Dependent Populations, Proceedings 1973 J.A.C.C., Columbus, Ohio, pp. 112 - 117.

[3] Kwakernaak, H.; Population policy as an optimal control problem, Memorandum nr. 94, Twente University of Technology, The Netherlands, 1975 (in Dutch).

[4] Olsder, G.J. and Strijbos, R.C.W.,; Population Planning; a distributed time optimal control problem, Memorandum nr. 64, Twente University of Technology, The Netherlands, 1975.

ON THE OPTIMALITY OF A SWITCH-OVER POLICY FOR CONTROLLING THE QUEUE SIZE IN AN M/G/1 QUEUE WITH VARIABLE SERVICE RATE *)

Henk Tijms
Mathematisch Centrum
Amsterdam

ABSTRACT

This paper considers an M/G/1 queue in which a finite number of service types are available for controlling the queue size. There is a linear holding cost, a service cost rate, and a fixed reward for each customer served. The purpose of this paper is to show that under the assumption of stochastically ordered service times there is an average cost optimal stationary policy having the property that the service type used is a non-decreasing function of the queue size.

1. INTRODUCTION

Consider a single-server station where customers arrive in accordance with a Poisson process with rate λ. For each new service to be started the server must choose one of a finite number of different service types $k = 1,\ldots,M$. For service type k the service time is a positive random variable S_k with probability distribution function $F_k(t)$. It is assumed that S_k is stochastically smaller than S_j for all k and j with $k > j$, that is, $F_k(t) \geq F_j(t)$ for $t \geq 0$ when $k > j$, so type k is "faster than type j for $k > j$. Further we assume that $\lambda ES_M < 1$ and $ES_k^2 < \infty$ for all k. The following costs are considered. There is a holding cost of $h > 0$ per customer per unit time, a service cost rate $r_k \geq 0$ when the server is busy and uses service type k, a service cost at rate $r_0 \geq 0$ when the server is idle, and a fixed reward of $R_k \geq 0$ for each customer served by using service type k.

Define the state of the system as the number of customers present. The system is only observed at the epochs where a new service must be started and the epochs where the server becomes idle. When the system is observed in state $i \geq 1$, then one of the actions $k = 1,\ldots,M$ must be chosen where the choice of action k means that service type k is used for the new service to be started. For notational purposes, we say that action 0 is chosen when state 0 is observed. Let $C(i,k)$ be the expected cost incurred until the next review when in state i action k is chosen. Then, $C(i,k) = hiES_k + h\lambda ES_k^2/2 + r_k ES_k - R_k$ for all $i \geq 1$ and $1 \leq k \leq M$, and $C(0,0) = r_0/\lambda$.

Since we will consider the average cost criterion, it is no restriction to assume that immediate costs $C(i,k)$ are incurred when action k is taken in state i. A policy π is any rule for choosing actions, where a policy f is said to be stationary

---

*) This paper appeared as Mathematical Centre Report BN 25/75.

if it chooses a single action $f(i)$ whenever the system is in state i. A stationary policy f is called a switch-over policy when $f(i)$ is non-decreasing in $i \geq 1$.

Let $V(\pi,i,t)$ be the total expected cost incurred in $[0,t)$ when policy π is used and the initial state is i, and, for any i and π, let

$$\bar{V}(\pi,i) = \limsup_{t\to\infty} t^{-1} V(\pi,i,t) \text{ and } V_\alpha(\pi,i) = \int_0^\infty e^{-\alpha t}\, dV(\pi,i,t)$$

for $\alpha > 0$, so, for initial state i and policy π, $\bar{V}(\pi,i)$ is the long-run average cost and $V_\alpha(\pi,i)$ is the expected total discounted cost when the discount factor is α. A policy π^* is called average cost optimal when $\bar{V}(\pi^*,i) \leq \bar{V}(\pi,i)$ for all i and π, and a policy π^* is called α-optimal when $V_\alpha(\pi^*,i) \leq V_\alpha(\pi,i)$ for all i and π. Let $V_\alpha(i) =$ $= \inf_\pi V_\alpha(\pi,i)$, $i \geq 0$.

The existence of an average cost optimal switch-over policy was shown in CRABILL [3], LIPPMAN [8,9] and SOBEL [14] for the case where the service times are exponential and the service rate can also be chosen at arrival epochs, cf. also BEJA & TELLER [1]. SCHASSBERGER [13] considered the case of stochastically ordered service times and, assuming a finite waiting room and no holding cost, he proved that there is an average cost optimal switch-over policy. His proof, however, fails for the model of this paper. The purpose of this paper is to demonstrate that using recent work of LIPPMAN [8,10] the average cost optimality of a switch-over policy can be readily shown. It seems reasonable to conjecture that the results of this paper also hold under the weaker assumption of decreasing mean service times. However, this case will probably require a quite different argumentation. A more complex policy will be optimal when there are fixed costs for switching from one service rate to another. This problem has been studied in CRABILL [4] under the assumption of exponential service times. In the above references the control variable is the queue size. For the case where the control variable is the total amount of work remaining to be processed in the system related work was done in DOSHI [5], MITCHELL [11], THATCHER [15] and TIJMS [16].

2. PROOF

We first give some preliminaries. The notation $X \subset Y$ means that the random variable X is stochastically smaller than the random variable Y. We have (see [17])

LEMMA 1. *Let* $X \subset Y$. *Then, for any non-decreasing function* f, $Ef(X) \leq Ef(Y)$ *provided the expectations exist.*

Let A_k be distributed as the number of arrivals during a service time S_k. Since $P\{A_k > n\} = \int_0^\infty P\{A_k > n \mid S_k = t\}\, dF_k(t)$, lemma 1 implies

LEMMA 2. $A_k \subset A_j$ *for all* k *and* j *with* $k > j$.

Denote by $Z_1(t)$ the total holding and service costs incurred in $[0,t)$ and denote by $Z_2(t)$ the total rewards received for servicing customers during $[0,t)$. Then $Z(t) = Z_1(t) - Z_2(t)$ is the total cost incurred in $[0,t)$. Let T be the epoch of the first return of the system to state 0. Denote by $E_{i,\pi}$ the expectation when policy π is used and the initial state is i.

LEMMA 3. *Let* f *be a stationary policy such that* $f(i) = M$ *for all* i *sufficiently large. Then both* $E_{i,f}(T)$ *and* $E_{i,f}(Z_2(T))$ *are bounded by a linear function of* i *and* $E_{i,f}(Z_1(T))$ *is bounded by a quadratic function of* i.

PROOF. Consider the basic M/G/1 queue in which the traffic intensity is less than 1 and the service time has a finite second moment. Suppose that at epoch 0 a service starts when $s \geq 1$ customers are present. From queueing theory it is well known that both the expectation of the first epoch at which the system becomes empty and the expected number of customers served up to that epoch are linear functions of s. Further the expected total time spent in the system by the customers up to the first epoch at which the system becomes empty is a quadratic function of s. Since for our model $\lambda ES_M < 1$ and $ES_M^2 < \infty$, the lemma now follows easily.

LEMMA 4. *Consider the basic* M/G/1 *queue with* $\lambda ES < 1$ *and* $ES^2 < \infty$ *where* λ *is the arrival rate and* S *is the service time of a customer. Denote by* N_n *the number of customers present when the* nth *service starts. Then* EN_n^2/n *converges to* 0 *as* $n\to\infty$.

PROOF. Denote by L_n the number of customers present just after the nth service completion epoch. Further, let ν_{k+1} be the number of customers arriving during the service time of the kth customer, let $\delta(0) = 0$, and let $\delta(x) = 1$ for $x > 0$. Since $0 \leq N_n \leq L_{n-1} + 1$ for $n \geq 2$, it suffices to prove that EL_n^2/n converges to 0 as $n\to\infty$. Now this follows easily by working out the obvious identity

$$\frac{1}{n}\sum_{k=1}^{n} EL_{k+1}^2 = \frac{1}{n}\sum_{k=1}^{n} E(L_k - \delta(L_k) + \nu_{k+1})^2 \qquad \text{for } n \geq 1$$

and using the fact that $\lim_{n\to\infty} EL_n = \lambda ES + \lambda^2 ES^2/2(1-\lambda ES)$ and $\lim_{n\to\infty} E\delta(L_n) = \lambda ES$ (e.g. COHEN [2]).

I am indebted to Professor J.W. COHEN for suggesting the proof of this Lemma.

To prove that there is an average cost optimal switch-over policy, we first consider the discounted model. For the semi-Markov decision model with unbounded costs HARRISON [6,7] and LIPPMAN [8,10] have given conditions under which for each $\alpha > 0$ an α-optimal stationary policy exists and the optimality equation applies. It is straightforward to verify that for this problem both the conditions in [6] and those in [10] hold. This implies that for any $\alpha > 0$ and $i \geq 1$,

$$(1) \qquad V_\alpha(i) = \min_{1\leq k\leq M} \{C(i,k) + \int_0^\infty e^{-\alpha t} \sum_{j=0}^{\infty} V_\alpha(i-1+j)\, e^{-\lambda t} \frac{(\lambda t)^j}{j!}\, dF_k(t)\},$$

where $V_\alpha(0) = r_0/\lambda + \int_0^\infty e^{-\alpha t} V_\alpha(1)\lambda e^{-\lambda t}dt$. Also, for any $\alpha > 0$, let f_α be a stationary policy such that $f_\alpha(i)$ minimizes the right side of (1) for all i, then f_α is α-optimal. Using lemmas 1 and 2 and making a minor modification of the first part of the proof of Theorem 6 in [8], we get that there is an $\alpha^* > 0$ and a bound $B < \infty$ such that $f_\alpha(i) = M$ for all $0 < \alpha < \alpha^*$ and $i > B$. This implies

LEMMA 5. *There is a stationary policy* f^* *with* $f^*(i) = M$ *for all* $i > B$ *and a sequence* $\{\alpha_k\}$ *with* $\alpha_k \to 0$ *as* $k \to \infty$ *such that* $f_{\alpha_k} = f^*$ *for all* k.

The next theorem can be readily obtained from a close examination of the analysis of the average cost criterion in [8,10]. However, since this analysis is rather complicated by its generality and needs some modifications, it might be helpful to outline a simple proof that suffices for the present problem.

THEOREM 1. *The policy* f^* *is average cost optimal, and* $\bar{V}(f^*,i) = g$ *for all* i *for some constant* g. *There is a function* h *with* $h(0) = 0$ *and*

$$(2)\qquad |h(i)| \le \alpha i^2 + \beta i + \gamma \qquad \textit{for } i \ge 0,$$

for some constants α, β *and* γ, *such that* $h(0) = r_0/\lambda - g/\lambda + h(1)$ *and*

$$(3)\qquad h(i) = \min_{1\le k\le M} \{C(i,k) - gES_k + \sum_{j=0}^{\infty} h(i-1+j)p_j^{(k)}\} \qquad \textit{for } i \ge 1,$$

where $p_j^{(k)} = P\{A_k = j\} = \int_0^\infty e^{-\lambda t}\{(\lambda t)^j/j!\}dF_k(t)$. *Moreover,* $f^*(i)$ *minimizes the right side of* (3) *for all* i.

PROOF. Let $g = E_{0,f^*}(Z(T))/E_{0,f^*}(T)$. Then, by Lemma 3 and Theorem 3.16 in ROSS [12], we have that $t^{-1}V(f^*,i,t)$ has the finite limit g as $t \to \infty$ for all i. Now, from Lemma 5 and a standard Abelian theorem (see pp.181-182 in [18]) it follows that, for all i and π,

$$\bar{V}(\pi,i) = \limsup_{t\to\infty} t^{-1}V(\pi,i,t) \ge \limsup_{a\to 0} \alpha V_\alpha(\pi,i) \ge$$
$$\ge \limsup_{k\to\infty} \alpha_k V_{\alpha_k}(i) = \lim_{k\to\infty} \alpha_k V_{\alpha_k}(f^*,i) = \lim_{t\to\infty} t^{-1}V(f^*,i,t).$$

This proves the first part of the theorem. As a byproduct we find

$$(4)\qquad \lim_{k\to\infty} \alpha_k V_{\alpha_k}(i) = g \qquad \text{for all } i \ge 0.$$

Following the proof of Theorem 4 in [8] (cf. also p.148 in [12]) and using (4), we find that, for some constant δ,

$$(5)\qquad -E_{i,f^*}(Z_2(T)) + \delta E_{i,f^*}(T) \le V_{\alpha_k}(i) - V_{\alpha_k}(0) \le E_{i,f^*}(Z_1(T)) \text{ for all } k,i.$$

So, for each i, $\{V_{\alpha_k}(i) - V_{\alpha_k}(0)\}$ is a bounded sequence. Now by Cauchy's diagonalization method, there is a subsequence $\{\alpha'_k\}$ of $\{\alpha_k\}$ and a function h such that

$$(6) \qquad h(i) = \lim_{k\to\infty}\{V_{\alpha'_k}(i) - V_{\alpha'_k}(0)\} \qquad \text{for all } i \geq 0.$$

By (5), (6) and Lemma 3 we have that h satisfies (2). Next we observe that, by (2) and $ES_k^2 < \infty$,

$$(7) \qquad \sum_{j=0}^{\infty} |h(i-1+j)|\, p_j^{(k)} < \infty \qquad \text{for all } i \geq 1 \text{ and } 1 \leq k \leq M.$$

Finally, subtracting $V_\alpha(0)$ from both sides of (1) with $\alpha = \alpha'_k$, letting $k \to \infty$, and using (4), (6), (7) and the construction of f*, we find the other assertions of the theorem (we note that (7) is needed for applying the bounded convergence theorem).

A repetition of the second part of the proof of Theorem 6 in [8] shows

<u>LEMMA 6</u>. $h(i+1) - h(i) \geq h(i) - h(i-1)$ *for all* $i \geq 1$, *i.e. the function* h *is convex.*

Denote by h(i,k) the expression between brackets in (3). Then

<u>LEMMA 7</u>. *For all* k_1, k_2 *with* $k_1 > k_2$, $h(i,k_1) - h(i,k_2)$ *is non-increasing in* $i \geq 1$.

<u>PROOF</u>. Fix k_1, k_2 with $k_1 > k_2$ and fix $i \geq 1$. Using (7), we have

$$h(i+1,k_1) - h(i+1,k_2) - \{h(i,k_1) - h(i,k_2)\} = hES_{k_1} - hES_{k_2} +$$
$$+ \sum_{j=0}^{\infty} \{h(i+j) - h(i-1+j)\}p_j^{(k_1)} - \sum_{j=0}^{\infty} \{h(i+j) - h(i-1+j)\}p_j^{(k_2)}.$$

By lemma 6, $h(i+j) - h(i-1+j)$ is non-decreasing in $j \geq 0$. Now, the lemma follows from the Lemmas 1 and 2 and the fact that $ES_{k_1} < ES_{k_2}$.

We are now in a position to state our main result.

<u>THEOREM 2</u>. *For any* $i \geq 1$, *let* $f_0(i)$ *be the largest value of* k *for which the right side of* (3) *is minimal. Then,* f_0 *is an average cost optimal switch-over policy which uses service type* M *for all* i *sufficiently large.*

<u>PROOF</u>. It easily follows from Lemma 7 that $f_0(i+1) \geq f_0(i)$ for all $i \geq 1$, and, by Lemma 5 and Theorem 1, $f_0(i) = M$ for all i sufficiently large. Since g is the minimal average cost, the switch-over policy f_0 is optimal when $\bar{V}(f_0,i) = g$ for all i. To prove this, we first observe that Lemma 3 and the proof of Theorem 7.5 in [12] imply that, for all i,

$$(8) \qquad \bar{V}(f_0,i) = \bar{V}(f_0,0) = \lim_{n\to\infty} E_{0,f_0}\left(\sum_{j=1}^{n} Z_j\right)/E_{0,f_0}\left(\sum_{j=1}^{n} \tau_j\right),$$

where Z_k denotes the cost incurred at the (k-1)th review and τ_k denotes the time between the (k-1)th and the kth review. Let X_k be the state at the kth review. Since $f_0(i) = M$ for all i sufficiently large and $\lambda ES_M < 1$, it follows from Lemma 4 and (2) that

$$\lim_{k\to\infty} k^{-1} E_{0,f_0}(h(X_k)) = 0.$$

Now the proof of Theorem 7.6 in [12] implies that the right side of (8) equals g (cf. p.727 in [8]). This completes the proof.

REFERENCES

[1] BEJA, A. & TELLER, A., "Relevant Policies for Markovian Queueing Systems with Many Types of Service", *Management Sci.*, Vol. 21 (1975), 1049-1051.

[2] COHEN, J.W., *The Single Server Queue*, North-Holland, Amsterdam, 1969.

[3] CRABILL, T.B., "Optimal Control of a Service Facility with Variable Exponential Service Time and Constant Arrival Rate", *Management Sci.*, Vol. 18 (1972), 560-566.

[4] ——————, "Optimal Hysteric Control of a Stochastic Service System with Variable Service Times and Fixed Switch-Over Costs", University of North Carolina (1973).

[5] DOSHI, B.T., "Continuous-Time Control of Markov Processes on an Arbitrary State Space", Technical Summary Report No. 1468, Mathematical Research Center, University of Wisconsin, Madison, Wisconsin (1974).

[6] HARRISON, J.M., "Countable State Discounted Markovian Decision Processes with Unbounded Rewards", Technical Report No. 17, Department of Operations Research, Stanford University, Stanford, California (1970).

[7] ——————, "Discrete Dynamic Programming", Ann. Math. Statist., Vol. 43 (1972), 636-644.

[8] LIPPMAN, S.A., "Semi-Markov Decision Processes with Unbounded Rewards", *Management Sci.*, Vol. 19 (1973), 717-731.

[9] ——————, "Applying a New Device in the Optimization of Exponential Queueing Systems" (to appear in *Operations Res.*).

[10] ——————, "On Dynamic Programming with Unbounded Rewards", *Management Sci.* Vol. 21 (1975), 1225-1233.

[11] MITCHELL, B., "Optimal Service-Rate Selection in an M/G/1 Queue", *Siam J. Appl. Math.*, Vol. 24 (1973), 19-35.

[12] ROSS, S.M., *Applied Probability Models with Optimization Applications*, Holden-Day, Inc., San Francisco, 1970.

[13] SCHASSBERGER, R., "A Note on Optimal Service Selection in a Single Server Queue", *Management Sci.*, Vol. 21 (1975), 1326-1331.

[14] SOBEL, M.J., "Optimal Operation on Queues", in: *Mathematical Methods in Queueing Theory*, Lecture Notes in Economics and Mathematical Systems, No. 98, Springer-Verlag, Berlin, 1973.

[15] THATCHER, R.M., "Optimal Single-Channel Service Policies for Stochastic Arrivals", Report ORC 68-16, Operations Research Center, University of California, Berkeley (1968).

[16] TIJMS, H.C., "On a Switch-Over Policy for Controlling the Workload in a Queueing System with Two Constant Service Rates and Fixed Switch-Over Costs", Report BW 45/75, Mathematisch Centrum, Amsterdam (to appear in *Zeitschrift für Operations Res.*).

[17] VEINOTT, A.F., Jr., "Optimal Policy in a Dynamic, Single Product, Non-Stationary Inventory Model with Several Demand Classes", *Operations Res.*, Vol. 13 (1965), 761-778.

[18] WIDDER, D.V., *The Laplace Transform*, Princeton University Press, 1946.

OPTIMIZATION OF RESOURCE ALLOCATION IN R+D PROJECTS

Ryszard Waśniowski
Technical University of Wrocław
Wrocław, Poland

While formulating R+D programmes we came across the problem of optimal resource allocation among separate disciplines concerned with realization of a defined number of subjects and tasks. Optimal decisions on financing the research projects is a much complex problem and requires the application of mathematical programming algorithms. To use the algorithms of optimal resource allocation such input values as realization costs of a given subject, probability of its effective realization, and its priority within the whole research programme should be definied. The estimation accuracy of the input data depends on the assumed optimization time horizon. For this reason resource allocation methods should be classified according to the models used, i.e. either static or dynamic ones.

1. Formulation of the problem

We assume the programme of research aiming to achieve the realization of global goal to be defined. The programme is constituted by subjects subdivided into particular tasks. By an optimal resource allocation we mean the distribution of limited budget among the separate subjects that ensures the maximum quality index of global problem.

2. Static models of resource allocation into R+D projects

Static models are used to establish the programmes of R+D projects for time periods not longer than 3÷6 years. This constraint results from the fact that at a longer optimization timehorizon the input data to a given model lose their validity becoming stale. Let us assume that the research programme consiwts of a set of N projects. For the above set we have defined the vector of weights $a = (a_1, a_2, \ldots, a_N)$, where a_i denotes the weight of the i-th project from the set N. The realization cost of a separate project is given by the vector $k = (k_1, k_2, \ldots k_N)$, k_i being the cost of the i-th project. Both weight and cost of separate projects are estimated by the experts.

Let us introduce zero-one variable, then

$$x_i = \begin{cases} 1, \text{ if the i-th project was accepted to realization} \\ 0, \text{ otherwice} \end{cases}$$

Optimization problem is reduced to determining the set $x=(x_1,x_2,\dots,x_N)$ with respect of the maximum of quality criterion

$$J = \max_{\{x_i\}} \sum_{x=1}^{N} a_i x_i$$

at budget constraint $\sum_{i=1}^{N} k_i x_i \leqslant B$,

where B-budget assigned to the realization of the programme.

To solve this problem the Balas, Dragan, and Mylen [1] procedures have been used. The solution of linear zero-one programming problem allows to obtain collection selected from the set N projects differing in validity and realization cost.

In mathematical models of optimal resource allocation a specific character of the programme of research project should be often taken into consideration. Consequently, such models can be applied solely to a defined class of problems e.g. a static model for the optimization of allocation of resources designed for the realization of the collection of projects conditioning the achievement of defined military goals has been presented by Dean and Hauser [2]. By simulating the model on computer and by repeatedly solving the problem at different levels of global budget the global quality index can be determined as a function of budget J(B). This allows to establish the upper limit of the budget. Above this limit any financing of the research projects becames inexpedient.

3. Resource allocation based on aggregation of the project networks

At first let us introduce some basic definitions. The activity is a proces described by the following equation:

$$v_i(t) = \frac{dx_i(t)}{dt} = f_i\left[h_{ij}(t),t\right]$$

where: $x_i(t)$ is the state of the i-th activity at the moment $t; x_i(t_o)=0$ $x_i(t_k) = w_i$, t_o and t_k are the initial and the final moments of an activity, respectivelly, w_i is the volume of the i-th activity, $v_i(t)$ is the rate of the i-th activity at the moment t, $h_{ij}(t)$ are the resources group parameters of the i-th activity, $h_i(t) = \{h_{ij}(t)\}$ is the m-vector of the i-th activity resource group. If the modulus of the vector $h_i(t)$ depends only on the value t, then the latter can be represented as $h_i(t) = \rho_i(t)\alpha_i$, where $\rho_i(t)$ is the power of the i-th activity resource group at the moment t, $\alpha_i = \{\alpha_{ij}\}$ is the m-vector of resource group parameters for the i-th activity, and resource group parameter α_{ij} is the value of the j-th resource when $\rho_i(t) = 1$. Project is a set partially ordered consisting of final number of activities. It can be represented by a network. The project is said to be realized if its state x(t) changes its value from the initial value x(0) = 0 up to the final value x(T) = W being the volume of the project, and T the final moment of the project. We will assume further that the project is finished if all its activities are finished. Multiproject is a set of independet projects, which must be realized by common resources. There are two types of resource constraints.

$$\sum_{p=1}^{l} \sum_{i=1}^{n_p} \alpha_{ij}\, \rho_i(t) \leqslant N_j(t) \quad , \quad j=1,2,\ldots, m, \tag{1}$$

$$\sum_{p=1}^{l} \sum_{i=1}^{n_p} \alpha_{ij}\, q_i \leqslant S_j \quad , \quad j=1,2,\ldots, m. \tag{2}$$

where $q_i = \int_0^T \rho_i(t)dt$ is the power consumption of the i-th activity $(i=1,2,\ldots, n_p)$, S_j is the permissible consumption of the j-th resource in the multiproject, N_j is the given value of the j-th resource in the multiproject at the moment t, i is the number of the project activity $(i = 1,2, \ldots, n_p)$, p is the number of the project $(p = 1,2, \ldots, l)$. The project aggregation is a network of projects represented by one activity.

Let us assume that the multiproject consisting of l projects, each having the volume $w_1, w_2, \ldots, w_l$, must be realized under definite constraints of resources. The problem is to allocate the resources to project activities so that the criterion (1) or (2) be minimized. As criterion several functions may be used e.g. min max T_p and $\sum_{p=1}^{l} \beta_p(T_p)$, where T_p is the final moment of the p-th project and $\beta_p(T_p)$ is a non-decreasing function of the T_p. The aggregation of the project networks permits to obtain the solution of the problem as a sequence of the following actions: I Aggregate the project networks, i.e. given the values of w_i, α_i and functions $v_i(t) = f_i [\rho_i(t),t]$ for each activity, define the values of w_p, α_p and functions $v_p(t) = f_p[\rho_p(t),t]$.

II When aggregation is completed solve the resource allocation problem with l independet activities. This step gives the values of $N_{pj}(t)$ and S_{pj} for each project.

III Using the values found in previous step solve the allocation problem for each project separately.
Thus the problem of resource allocation with $n = \sum_{p=1}^{l} n_p$ activities is transformed to l resource allocation problems with n_p activities.
As an example of such an approach consider the solution of the resource allocation problem in the multiproject, when the resources are of financial means and the criterion min max T_p. It is assumed that each activity in the network is subject to a continuous upward-concave time-cost relationship. Each $S_p(T_p)$ being a non decreasing function of T_p, all the projects have the some final moment, i.e.
$T_1 = T_2 = \ldots = T_l = T$, if the final moment of the multiproject is minimized. Hence, the value of T may be found from the equation $S_1(T) = S_2(T) = \ldots S_l(T) = S$.

4. Dynamic models of optimal resource allocation into R+D projects

The problem of optimal financial allocation of resources among separate realization periods of one project can be also solved by a dynamic programming method [3].
Let us assume that the project (programme) is to be realized in the course of N periods, e.g. during N years.
Let us introduce the following denotations:
x_i-budget assigned for the i-th (from the end) period of time,
y_i-budget used till the i-th period of time, i.e. in the course of N-i time intervals,
Q_i-expected value of the income at the accomplishment of the project in the i-th (from the end) period of time, i.e. the difference between the expected market and current prices,
$P(x_i,y_i)$ - probability of realization of projects in the i-th (from the end) period of time as a function of x_i,y_i,
C_i - market price of the project, provided that the latter was realized in the i-th (from the end) period of time.

The problem of optimalization consists here in an optimal budget allocation to the separate periods of project realization, i.e. in determining an optimal vector $X_1^*, X_2^*, \ldots, X_r^*$ with respect to the expected value of the income consummed. Given initial budget X_N the optimal sequence $X_{N-1}^*, X_{N-2}^*, \ldots, X_1^*$ will be obtained according to the Bellman recurrent algorithm:

$$Q_i(y_i) = \max_{0 \leq X_i} \left\{ C_i P_i(x_i, y_i) - X_i + \gamma_i \left[1 - P_i(x_i, y_i)\right] f_{i-1}(y_{i-1}) \right\} \qquad (3)$$

where $y_{i-1} = y_i + x_i$ and $\gamma_i \in [0,1]$ is coefficient of punishment for the delay in realization of project, fixed by the experts. Coefficient γ_i can either be constant or increase with time.
The component $\left[C_i P_i(x_i, y_i) - X_i\right]$ in (3) denotes the expected value of income, if the given project is in the i-th (from the end) period of time, whereas $\gamma_i \left[1 - P_i(x_i, y_i)\right] f_{i-1}(y_{i-1})$ is the expected value of the income in case when the project is finished in time interval following the i-th one from the end. Parameters C_i and relations $P_i(x_i, y_i)$ are estimated by the experts.

5. Conclusions

The optimization methods of financing the research projects presented in the paper have been adopted by the Technical University of Wrocław. ALGOL programmes implementing the procedures described have been developed. A listing and implementation on the use of the programmes are available from the author. It should be emphasized that the application of static models is not related with any computational difficulties, while the methods of complex of operations and dynamic programming required complex numerical calculations. The performed investigations allow to state that more efficient algorithms of a dynamic resource allocation into R+D should be found.

6. References:

[1] KUCHARCZYK J., SYSŁO M., Algorytmy optymalizacji w jązyku ALGOL 60, (Algorithms of optimization in ALGOL 60), PWN Warszawa (in Polish).

[2] DEAN B.V., HAUSER L.E., Advanced Material Systems Planning. IEEE Trans.on Eng.Man. Vol.EM-14, NO 1, March 1967.

[3] BELLMAN R.E., DREYFUS S.E., Applied Dynamic Programming. Princeton University Press, Princeton, New Jersey, 1963.

Optimal Ocean Navigation

C. de Wit
University of Technology
Subdep. of Mathematics
Delft - Netherlands.

Abstract.

A merchant or navy ship is to cross a wide ocean in minimum time. With the available data regarding input disturbances and system's - i.e. ship's - performance, this paper is mainly dedicated to the practical implementation of the solution of this non-linear problem. An account of the incompleteness of the various data, while the ship' master and his officers are primarily responsible for damage to ship and cargo, the description of the solution method is given in a most plausible form, so that it is well understandable to the practical navigator.
This was one of the reasons for using the concept of timefronts. The rather frequent occurrence of conjugate points on tracks, that can be constructed on the basis of the usual necessary conditions as well as the fair possibility that such a curve without conjugate points is only time-optimal in a local sense were other arguments to make a search for the global solution of this problem by means of timefronts.

1. Optimization criterion.

The problem of navigating a ship across a wide ocean has been an adventurous challenge throughout the centuries. In the old days the main feature of this problem was the question of feasibility without substantial damage to ship, crew and cargo. In the past 25 years however, the emphasis has been shifted to the search for an "optimal" solution in some sense.

By far the most important criterion of optimization has until now been the time itself, i.e. the trip's duration. Other criteria could be to minimize the fuel consumption or the occurrence of bad weather and high waves. Mainly on account of the lack of reliable data, these criteria have until now not been taken into study for practical application.

2. The least time problem.

2.1. Preliminary data.

The search for a ship's least time track across an ocean needs a fair knowledge of the following things.

(1) In the first place we have the disturbing inputs, like the significant wave heig the mean directions of wave propagation, the wind speeds and directions all over th area for a timelast of at least the mean trip's duration.

(2) Secondly we need to know the system's performance, i.e. the ship's maximum speed under these weather conditions into various directions, possibly taking account of restrictions, caused by safety considerations.

Considering the weather data, the availability is restricted to a future time period of at most 72 hours. This implies that f.i. for a trip with a minimal duratio of 6 days, the initial estimate of a least time track can only be time optimal for the first 2-to-3-days' part. Practical experience has shown, that there is little or no sense in making any assumptions for the later part.

As for the ship's performance data, figure 1 shows an example of the ship's attainable speed into various directions, when a wind of 35 knots (1 knot = 1852 m/h) has been prevailing long enough and with sufficient fetch to develop a stationary field of wind waves. This polar speed graph is called the "original velocity indicatrix".

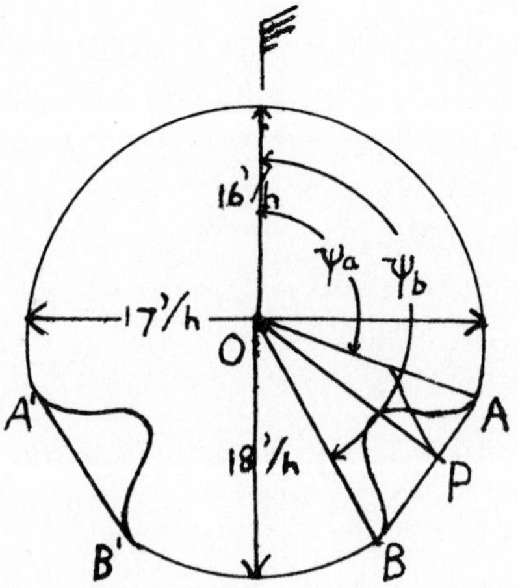

Figure 1.

Original velocity indicatrix for a ship with a nominal speed of 20 knots in waves, generated by a wind speed of 35 knots.

The forward part of this speed graph, with ship's courses differing at most 50^0 from the wind direction, can be determined by means of computations, based on a theory of energy dissipation. The rest of the graph has to be acquired by means of practical or at least full scale measurements, because for these cases there is no satisfactory model available.

The concave dents in the "wind-free-parts" are a result of the fact, that the apparent frequency of the waves - coming in between the beam and the stern - is rather low. With an unfavourable static stability, the ship is liable to get a considerable list during several minutes without the presence of a sufficiently restoring torque. This phenomenon can only be prevented by a considerable speed reduction in that sector. With these reduced speeds however, these courses cannot be selected for a time-optimal track.

We now replace - see fig. 1 - the original velocity indicatrix by its convex envelope.

In fig. 1 the concave arcs AB and A'B' are then replaced by straight line segments, that are tangents to the original indicatrix.

When a ship should wish to proceed as fast as possible into the direction OP, she would have to tack on the courses ψ_a and ψ_b.

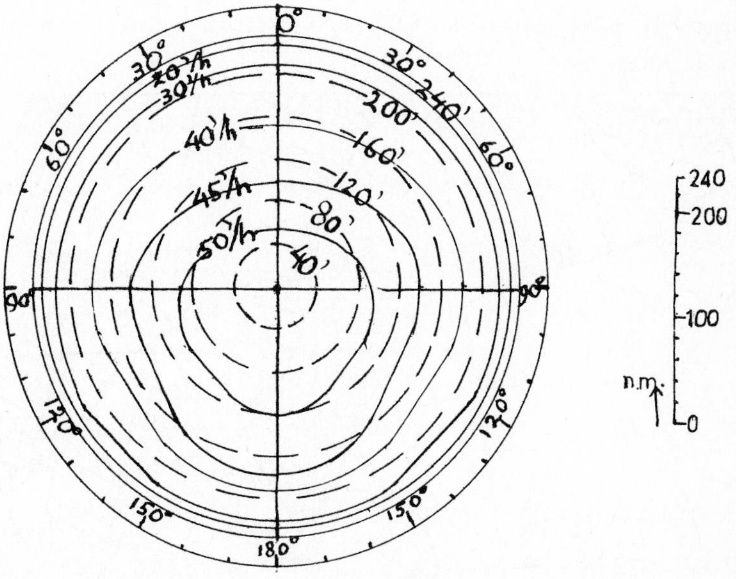

Figure 2.

Effective 12^h-position indicatrices for a vessel with a nominal speed of 20 knots in waves, generated by wind velocities of 0, 20, 30(5)50 knots.

Figure 2 shows a ship's performance in 12 hours for various courses-relative to the wind direction - and for various wind velocities. The 12^h-interval has been chosen because most weather stations broadcast weather prognoses for times with mutual intervals of 24 hours.

2.2. Construction of subsequent timefronts.

The construction of (the initial estimate of) a least time track can be carried out by using the concept of timefronts. A timefront ∂H_t can be defined as the bound of the attainable region H_t at time t, when starting in $\underline{x}_o$ at time t_o.

The main problem now is the construction of a timefront ∂H_{k+1}, for a time $t_{k+1} = t_o + (k+1)\ 24^h$, when the previous timefront ∂H_k is given.
For this construction, one needs the weather maps M_k and M_{k+1} made up for times t_k a t_{k+1}.
Figures 3 and 4 give a view of this construction.
Weather map M_k shows the situation at time t_k. From timefront ∂H_k as a start we firs construct timefront $\partial H_{k+\frac{1}{2}}$ for a time $t_k + 12^h$. To find the timefront, we need the weather situation at time $t_k + 6^h$ as an average during the time interval $[t_k, t_{k+\frac{1}{2}})$. Therefor we compare M_k with M_{k+1} and give M_k a 6^h-forward shift.

From ∂H_k we now draw a sufficiently dense collection of line segments perpendicular to ∂H_k and pointing to the outside of H_k. On these segments the wind direction and speeds can now be fairly estimated, i.e. derived from the directions and mutual distances of the isobars.

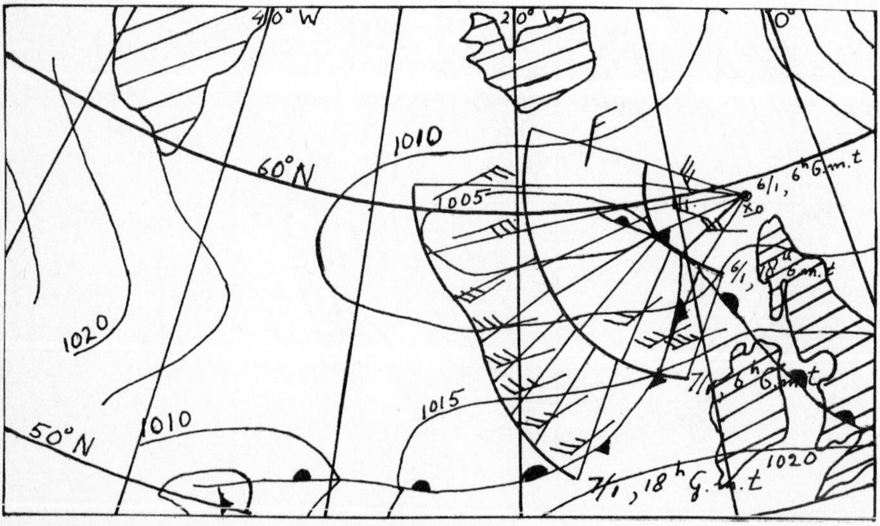

Figure 3.

Starting at $59^o_{}$N, 5^oW on jan. 6th, 6^h G.m.t., the timefronts for jan. 6th, 18^h G.m.t and for jan. 7th, 6^h G.m.t. have been constructed. With the estimated weather situation for jan. 7th, 12^h G.m.t. the timefront for jan. 7th, 18^h G.m.t. is constructed.
Wind speed code : : 25 knots, : 30 knots.

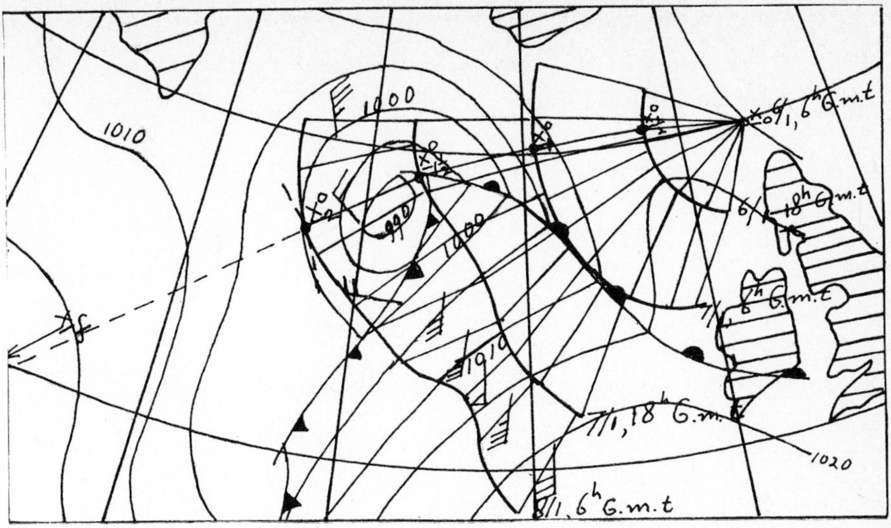

Figure 4.

From the timefront of jan. 7th, 18^h G.m.t. and with the use of the weather map for jan. 8th, 0^h G.m.t. the timefront is constructed for jan. 8th, 6^h G.m.t.

With the aid of the 12^h-performance diagram (fig.2) the ship's ultimate position, sailing along one of these lines during 12 hours, can now be found. These points can be connected by a smooth curve, which is the relevant part of $\partial H_{k+\frac{1}{2}}$.

From this intermediate timefront, one can now obtain ∂H_{k+1} in the same manner, only now the time interval is $[t_k + 12^h, t_k + 24^h)$ with $t_k + 18^h$ as the midpoint. This means that we now have to use M_{k+1} with a 6^h-shift backward.

2.3. Estimation of the initial course.

With $\underline{x}_0$ at time t_0 as a starting point and with the weather maps M_0^0, M_1^0 and M_2^0 at our disposal, we can now construct the timefronts $\partial H_{\frac{1}{2}}^0$, ∂H_1^0, $\partial H_{1\frac{1}{2}}^0$, ∂H_2^0. Now when the destination $\underline{x}_f$ is situated outside of H_2^0, we can determine the point $\underline{x}_2^0$ of the last timefront ∂H_2^0, that is closest to $\underline{x}_f$ in a purely geodesic sense. From $\underline{x}_2^0$ we can then work backwards. i.e. we can determine $\underline{x}_{k-\frac{1}{2}}^0$ from $\underline{x}_k^0$ by drawing a line from $\underline{x}_k^0$ perpendicular to $\partial H_{k-\frac{1}{2}}^0$ for $k = 2, 1\frac{1}{2}, 1$. The initial course is then given by the vector $\underline{x}_{\frac{1}{2}}^0 - \underline{x}_0$ and the ship takes the track from $\underline{x}_0$ via $\underline{x}_{\frac{1}{2}}^0$ to $\underline{x}_1^0$ as a schedule for the first 24 hours.

At time t_1 the ship receives new weather information in the form of weather maps M_1^1, M_2^1 and M_3^1. Also, a position fix may give an updating $\underline{x}_1^1$ of the planned position $\underline{x}_1^0$. With these new data the entire procedure is repeated, until the destination $\underline{x}_f$ lies

in between ∂H_k^{k-2} and $\partial H_{k-\frac{1}{2}}^{k-2}$ for some k.
In that case we can determine $\underline{x}_{k-\frac{1}{2}}^{k-2}$ by drawing a perpendicular line from $\underline{x}_f$ onto ∂H_{k-}^{k-}
then find $\underline{x}_{k-1}^{k-2}$ aso in the same manner.

3. Practical implementation.

The entire procedure can be carried out either by the ship's navigator, in which case one can speak of "weather navigation" or by a shore weather institute. In this last case the weather station sends a routeing advice to the ship, explains it briefly and adapts it whenever necessary. This is called "weather routeing".

Both systems have their advantages. In the case of autonomous navigation the ship's officers are better able to adapt their constructions whenever the ship's performance turns out to deviate from the expectations. On the other hand, a weather bureau is able to obtain a better view on the expected weather and sea situations, as it can dispose of more meteorological information.

4. Automation.

The author of this paper designed a computer algorithm for calculations of a least time track. (Ref. 1,2). The co-state differential equations were bypassed by using the property, that the costate vector $\underline{p}$ is positively proportional to the time-front's gradient. Moreover, the time-optimal course $\psi_o(t)$, following at a certain tin t from the given state $\underline{x}(t)$ and a certain co-state $\underline{p}(t)$ by $\rho\underline{p}(t)$, where ρ is an arbitrary positive scalar.

In areas of strong winds, high waves and consequently low ship's performances, the timefronts may overwash each other, like indicated in figure 5.

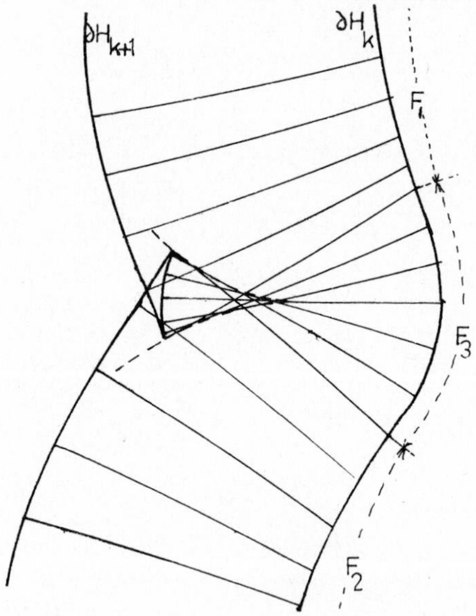

Figure 5.

A concave dent in ∂H_k frequently results in a splitting up of all the least time trajectories into two families of (still least time) trajectories F_1 and F_2 and a collec tion of trajectories, that are not even local time extremals past a certain conjugate point.

The difficulty then arises that the timefront's gradient may not exist. This difficulty was overruled by Bijlsma (Ref. 4), who determined the coefficients of the co-state differential equations of numerical differentiation.

References.

1. de Wit, C. - Mathematical Treatment of Optimal Ocean Ship Routeing; Rotterdam, 1968. (Ph.D. Thesis).
2. de Wit, C. - Optimal Meteorological Ship Routeing; Report 142 S, Neth. Ship Resear Centre T.N.O., Delft, 1970.
3. de Wit, C. - Progress and Development of Ocean Weather Routeing; Report 201 S, Net Ship Res. Centre T.N.O., Delft, 1974.
4. Bijlsma, S.J. - On minimal time ship routing; Staatsdrukkerij The Hague, 1975.

DESIGN AND APPLICATION OF AN INTERACTIVE SIMULATION LANGUAGE

M. Alfonseca
IBM Scientific Center
P. Castellana,4.Madrid-1 (SPAIN)

The name SIAL/74 stands for two different concepts:

1. A digital continuous simulation language.
2. The system interactively implementing such language.

We shall subsequently explain both parts with some detail.

1. THE LANGUAGE

SIAL/74 is a block oriented analog-logical simulation language. We shall describe it with the help of a convenient example.

1.1. Description of the example.

The following system of differential equations is to be solved:

$$y'' = \frac{K^2}{y^3} - \frac{1}{2y^2}$$

$$\theta' = -\frac{K}{y^2}$$

The system defines the movement of a moving object which leaves the point of polar coordinates $(y(0),\theta(0))$ with an initial radial velocity $y'(0)$ and which is attracted by an inmobile body situated at the origin of the coordinates.

The constant K is proportional to the initial tangent velocity of the moving object. Note that when $K = 0$ (the initial tangent velocity is null), the system above is reduced to the following one:

$$y'' = -\frac{1}{2y^2}$$

$$\theta = \theta(0)$$

which defines the movement of a body falling directly towards another body.

The given system can be solved using standard analog computer procedures, by means of the following steps:

1. The differential equations are solved for the highest derivative term in every variable.(In our example, the equations are already given in that form).

2. The highest derivatives are supposed to be known, and integrated as many times as needed.

3. The second members of the equations obtained in 1. are constructed, and the loops are closed.

Although analog computer blocks use to introduce sign changes, these will not be considered in our language, as this will make programming easier. On the other hand, the symbols we shall use for our elementary blocks will be the commonly accepted ones in analog computer literature.

Applying steps 2. and 3. to the given system of differential equations, the following block diagram is obtained:(see figure 1)

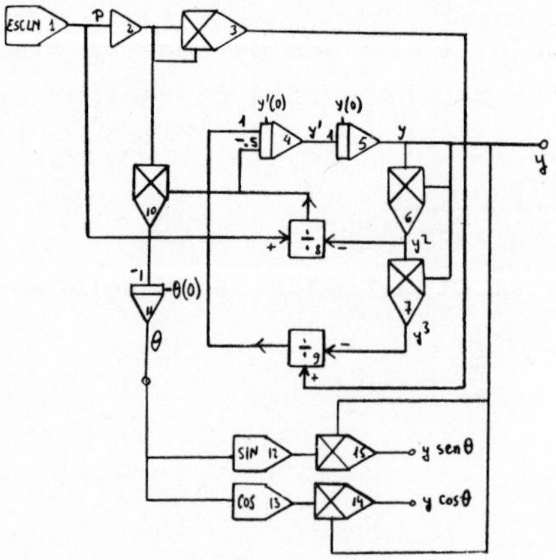

FIGURE 1. Block diagram for the gravity problem

1.2. SIAL/74 solution

The SIAL/74 program consists of the following parts:

1. A title which will head the print out of the results of the execution of the program.

2. The description of the block diagram, which consists of so many block descriptions as there are blocks in the diagram. A block des-

cription consists of a "code",defining the type of the block, and of two lists of numbers, one or both of which may not exist: a list of in tegers, giving the numbers of those blocks whose outputs are inputs for the block under consideration, and a list of parameters for the block. In the case of existence of only one list for a given type of block, the list will be given at the right of the block code. If both lists exist, the parameter list will appear to its left.

Each block will be assigned a number, its position within the block diagram description. Blocks may be numbered arbitrarily, that is to say, they may be defined in any order.

In our example, the description of the block diagram will consist of the following lines, in which the numbering appearing in figure 1 has been kept:

```
[1]   ESCLN ¯1
[2]   =0 SUM 1
[3]   MULT 2 2
[4]   ¯1.471 ¯.5 1 INTEGR 8 9
[5]   .316 1 INTEGR 4
[6]   MULT 5 5
[7]   MULT 5 6
[8]   DIV 1 6
[9]   DIV 3 7
[10]  MULT 2 8
[11]  1.5708 ¯1 INTEGR 10
[12]  SIN 11
[13]  COS 11
[14]  MULT 13  5
[15]  MULT 12  5
```

Block number 1 is defined as a step function with the step occurring at time = -1 (that is to say, before initial time for the simulation run; in this way, its output is assured to be the constant 1). In the definition of block number 2, another property of SIAL/74 is apparent: the definition of adjustable parameters. As soon as a value is encountered which is preceded by an equals sign, the parameter to which this value corresponds will be considered to be an adjustable parameter, with initial value the number after the equals sign. This feature is useful for the solving of automatic adjustment of parameters problems. Blocks number 2 defines thus an adder whose output is equal to the product of the adjustable parameter (initial value 0) times the output of block number 1.

Block number 3 multiplies by itself the output of block number 2.

(Squares it). Block number 4 defines an integrator. Its input is defined as the difference of the output of block number 9 and half the output of block number 8 (¯.5×Z[8]+1×Z[9]) and an initial output of¯1.471 is given. The remaining block descriptions are self explaining.

56 different block types ("codes") may be used in the construction of SIAL/74 models. The number of blocks in a model is only limited by the work space size of the actual system where SIAL/74 is implemented.

3.After the description of the block diagram, a set of global data must be given. In our example, the following ones where defined:

```
Δ←1E¯3
II←.02
TM←.3
INTEG←RECT
I←5 11 4
PLOT←15 14
```

where Δ is the elemental time interval for the simulation run, II is the results print-out interval, TM is the final (end run) time, the value of I is a list with the numbers of the blocks whose outputs are to form part of the results of the execution, INTEG defines the integration method desired, and PLOT contains a list of block numbers. At the end of the execution a plot will be drawn of the outputs of all the blocks in the list but the last one, against the output of that one. If the plot is desired against time, the last number in the list must be 0.

2. THE SYSTEM

SIAL/74 has been implemented as an APLSV work space, containing a compiler which accepts SIAL/74 programs and translates them into equivalent APL programs, capable of execution on the same interpreter executing the compiler.

Two modes of compilation are possible: interactive and self-controlled. In the interactive mode, the source program sentences must be given individually and successively. This mode is specially useful at the time a program is entered for the first time. If an error is detected during the compilation, it is pointed out, and the same instruction corrected must be input again. In this way, at the end of the process, we have the corrected source program and the complete corresponding object program will be available.

Once a program has been entered for the first time, in case we wish to correct it, it will be better to change directly the source program and to compile it once it has been corrected, instead of having to rewrite it. The compilation will be done in this case in the self-controlled mode; any error encountered now will be signaled, but it will not be possible to correct it during compilation.

We shall make this concept clearer with an example.

```
          COMPILAR
      INTERACTIVE COMPILATION?
      YES
      SIAL→APL COMPILATION
      TITLE:BESSEL EQUATION
      [1]    RAMPA .0001
      [2]    0 ¯1 ¯1 INTEGR 3 4
      [3]    1 1 INTEGR 2
      [4]    DIV 2 1
      [5]    ¯1 SUM 2
      [6]    //
      //
      [1]    TM←10
      [2]    II←.5
      [3]    Δ←.05
      [4]    I←3 5
      [5]    PLOT←3 5 0
      [6]    INTGR←RECT
      [7]
```

At this point, compilation is completed and we have the source program in the variable *FUENTE*.

```
             LISTAR FUENTE
      [0]    ESSEL EQUATION
      [1]    RAMPA .0001
      [2]    0 ¯1 ¯1 INTEGR 3 4
      [3]    1 1 INTEGR 2
      [4]    DIV 2 1
      [5]    ¯1 SUM 2
      [6]    //
      [7]    TM←10
      [8]    II←.5
      [9]    Δ←.05
      [10]   I←3 5
      [11]   PLOT←3 5 0
      [12]   INTGR←RECT
```

To make changes in the input program, we may use the function CAMBIAR in the following way:

```
        FUENTE←CAMBIAR FUENTE
INSTRUCTION NUMBER:0
ESSEL EQUATION
/
?
BE
INSTRUCTION NUMBER:1
RAMPA .0001
         /
?
0000001
INSTRUCTION NUMBER:7
TM←10
   //
?
5
INSTRUCTION NUMBER:¯1
      LISTAR FUENTE
[0]   BESSEL EQUATION
[1]   RAMPA .0000000001
[2]   0 ¯1 ¯1 INTEGR 3 4
[3]   1 1 INTEGR 2
[4]   DIV 2 1
[5]   ¯1 SUM 2
[6]   //
[7]   TM←5
[8]   II←.5
[9]   Δ←.05
[10]  I←3 5
[11]  PLOT←3 5 0
[12]  INTGR←RECT
      COMPILAR
INTERACTIVE COMPILATION?
NO
PROGRAM NAME?
⎕:
      FUENTE
[0]   BESSEL EQUATION
[1]   RAMPA .0000000001
[2]   0 ¯1 ¯1 INTEGR 3 4
[3]   1 1 INTEGR 2
[4]   DIV 2 1
[5]   ¯1 SUM 2
[6]   //
[7]   TM←5
[8]   II←.5
[9]   Δ←.05
[10]  I←3 5
[11]  PLOT←3 5 0
[12]  INTGR←RECT
SIAL→APL COMPILATION
```

At this point the source program has been corrected and recompiled. The pair of object programs are contained in the variables PO and POI.

3. SAMPLE SESSION

In this sample session, we shall solve the gravitational problem explained before, corresponding to Figure 1.

```
      COMPILAR
DESEA COMPILACION INTERACTIVA?
NO
QUE PROGRAMA DESEA COMPILAR?
⎕:
      GRAVITACION
[0]   GRAVITACION
[1]   ESCLN ¯1
[2]   =0 SUM 1
[3]   MULT 2 2
[4]   ¯1.471 ¯.5 1 INTEGR 8 9
[5]   .316 1 INTEGR 4
[6]   MULT 5 5
[7]   MULT 5 6   *ESTE ES EL CUBO DE Y
[8]   DIV 1 6
[9]   DIV 3 7
[10]  MULT 2 8
[11]  1.5708 ¯1 INTEGR 10
[12]  SIN 11
[13]  COS 11
[14]  MULT 13 5
[15]  MULT 12 5
[16]  //
[17]  Δ←1E¯3
[18]  II←.02
[19]  TM←.3
[20]  INTEG←RECT
[21]  I←5 11 4
[22]  PLOT←15 14
COMPILACION SIAL→APL
      EJEC POI
      TM←.13
      'GRAV'DEF PO
GRAV
      GRAV
GRAVITACION
TIEMPO           5           11           4
   .0000  3.160E¯01  1.571E00  ¯1.471E00
   .0200  2.856E¯01  1.571E00  ¯1.581E00
   .0400  2.527E¯01  1.571E00  ¯1.719E00
   .0600  2.167E¯01  1.571E00  ¯1.899E00
   .0800  1.764E¯01  1.571E00  ¯2.157E00
   .1000  1.297E¯01  1.571E00  ¯2.583E00
   .1200  7.026E¯02  1.571E00  ¯3.610E00
```

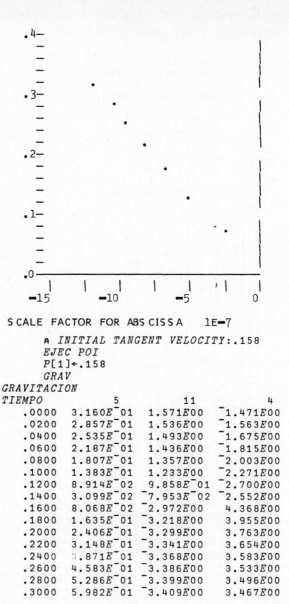

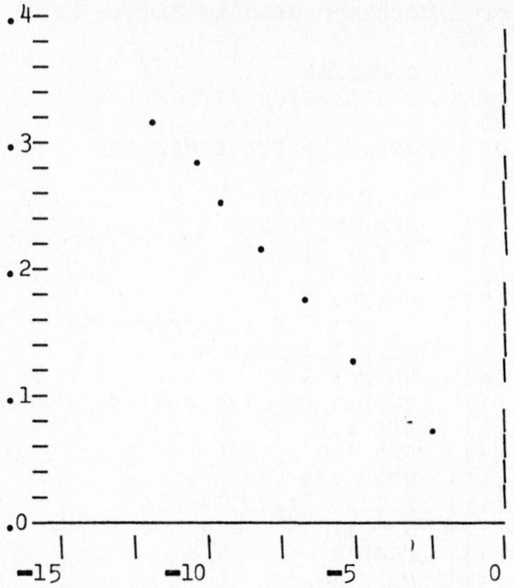

SCALE FACTOR FOR ABSCISSA 1E¯7

```
     ⍝ INITIAL TANGENT VELOCITY:.158
     EJEC POI
     P[1]←.158
     GRAV
GRAVITACION
```

TIEMPO	5	11	4
.0000	3.160E¯01	1.571E00	¯1.471E00
.0200	2.857E¯01	1.536E00	¯1.563E00
.0400	2.535E¯01	1.493E00	¯1.675E00
.0600	2.187E¯01	1.436E00	¯1.815E00
.0800	1.807E¯01	1.357E00	¯2.003E00
.1000	1.383E¯01	1.233E00	¯2.271E00
.1200	8.914E¯02	9.858E¯01	¯2.700E00
.1400	3.099E¯02	¯7.953E¯02	¯2.552E00
.1600	8.068E¯02	¯2.972E00	4.368E00
.1800	1.635E¯01	¯3.218E00	3.955E00
.2000	2.406E¯01	¯3.299E00	3.763E00
.2200	3.148E¯01	¯3.341E00	3.654E00
.2400	3.871E¯01	¯3.368E00	3.583E00
.2600	4.583E¯01	¯3.386E00	3.533E00
.2800	5.286E¯01	¯3.399E00	3.496E00
.3000	5.982E¯01	¯3.409E00	3.467E00

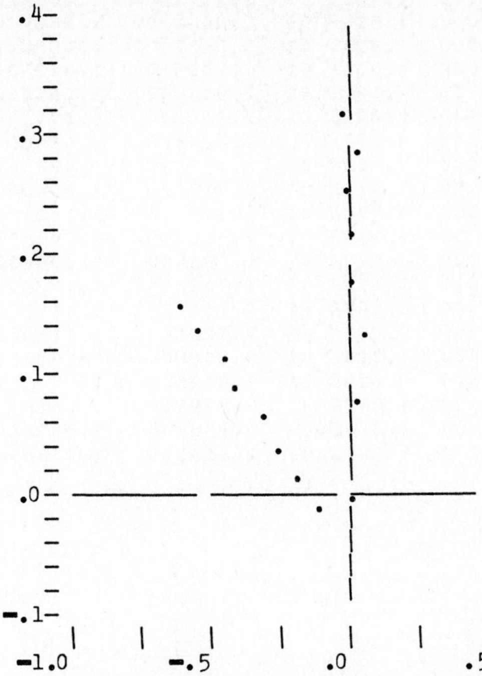


```
⍝ (A HYPERBOLIC MOVEMENT AROUND THE ORIGIN
⍝  CAN BE SEEN)
```

```
⍝ IN THE NEXT CASE, THE INITIAL TANGENT
⍝ VELOCITY WILL BE EQUAL TO .316

EJEC POI
P[1]←.316
TM←1
II←.05
```

GRAV
GRAVITACION

TIEMPO	5	11	4
.0000	3.160*E*¯01	1.571*E*00	¯1.471*E*00
.0500	2.402*E*¯01	1.364*E*00	¯1.560*E*00
.1000	1.616*E*¯01	9.604*E*¯01	¯1.541*E*00
.1500	1.013*E*¯01	¯6.345*E*¯02	¯4.820*E*¯01
.2000	1.331*E*¯01	¯1.440*E*00	1.443*E*00
.2500	2.132*E*¯01	¯2.007*E*00	1.651*E*00
.3000	2.942*E*¯01	¯2.260*E*00	1.575*E*00
.3500	3.707*E*¯01	¯2.406*E*00	1.485*E*00
.4000	4.430*E*¯01	¯2.502*E*00	1.408*E*00
.4500	5.118*E*¯01	¯2.572*E*00	1.344*E*00
.5000	5.776*E*¯01	¯2.625*E*00	1.291*E*00
.5500	6.410*E*¯01	¯2.668*E*00	1.245*E*00
.6000	7.023*E*¯01	¯2.703*E*00	1.206*E*00
.6500	7.618*E*¯01	¯2.733*E*00	1.172*E*00
.7000	8.197*E*¯01	¯2.758*E*00	1.142*E*00
.7500	8.761*E*¯01	¯2.780*E*00	1.116*E*00
.8000	9.313*E*¯01	¯2.800*E*00	1.092*E*00
.8500	9.854*E*¯01	¯2.817*E*00	1.070*E*00
.9000	1.038*E*00	¯2.832*E*00	1.051*E*00
.9500	1.090*E*00	¯2.846*E*00	1.033*E*00
1.0000	1.142*E*00	¯2.859*E*00	1.016*E*00

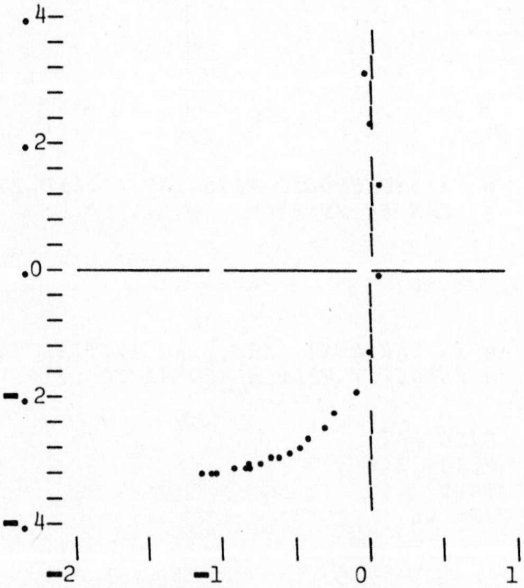

⍝ *A HYPERBOLIC MOVEMENT WITH LARGER*
⍝ *EXCENTRICITY CAN BE SEEN*

```
⍝ IN OUR LAST EXAMPLE, THE MOVING POINT
⍝ HAS A POSITIVE RADIAL VELOCITY OF .5,
⍝ AND AN INITIAL TANGENT VELOCITY OF .25

EJEC POI
P[1]←.25
CI[1]←.5
II←.1
TM←2
GRAV
```

GRAVITACION

TIEMPO	5	11	4
.0000	3.160E¯01	1.571E00	5.000E¯01
.1000	3.519E¯01	1.349E00	2.216E¯01
.2000	3.614E¯01	1.154E00	¯3.157E¯02
.3000	3.457E¯01	9.569E¯01	¯2.879E¯01
.4000	3.030E¯01	7.220E¯01	¯5.772E¯01
.5000	2.279E¯01	3.694E¯01	¯9.480E¯01
.6000	1.116E¯01	¯5.689E¯01	¯1.292E00
.7000	1.349E¯01	¯3.636E00	1.390E00
.8000	2.534E¯01	¯4.345E00	9.652E¯01
.9000	3.326E¯01	¯4.637E00	6.331E¯01
1.0000	3.829E¯01	¯4.831E00	3.803E¯01
1.1000	4.100E¯01	¯4.989E00	1.637E¯01
1.2000	4.163E¯01	¯5.135E00	¯3.927E¯02
1.3000	4.023E¯01	¯5.283E00	¯2.452E¯01
1.4000	3.668E¯01	¯5.450E00	¯4.718E¯01
1.5000	3.066E¯01	¯5.669E00	¯7.470E¯01
1.6000	2.143E¯01	¯6.039E00	¯1.125E00
1.7000	8.520E¯02	¯7.383E00	¯1.069E00
1.8000	1.697E¯01	¯1.018E01	1.406E00
1.9000	2.883E¯01	¯1.068E01	9.854E¯01
2.0000	3.719E¯01	¯1.091E01	7.009E¯01

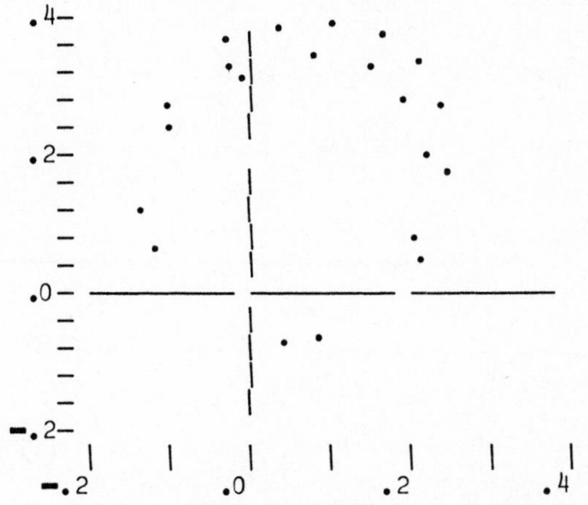


```
⍝ IN THIS CASE, THE MOVING POINT IS CAPTURED
⍝ AND DESCRIBES AN ELLYPSE.
```

4. CONCLUSSIONS

An interactive simulation language has been developed. Trough applications such as the gravity problem described above, and several biological simulations such as a conditional reflex model and the system for the regulation of body-water volume, its flexibility has been demonstrated.

REFERENCES

M.Alfonseca "SIAL/74: Lenguaje de simulación digital contínua", PCI-06.74, Nov.1974, UAM-IBM Scientific Center Publications.

A Functional Package for Monitoring Branching Methods in Combinatorial Optimization

J.P. A. Barthès

Department of Applied Mathematics and
Computer Science
University of Technology of Compiègne
60200 COMPIEGNE, France

This note announces the development of a set of computer functions for studying a wide class of combinatorial optimization problems by solving them interactively. A first implementation has been done at UTC and presently runs on a DEC PDP 11 minicomputer.

Combinatorial optimization methods such as Branch and Bound, Branch Search, etc., are used extensively because of their efficiency. Furthermore they yield good results in complex cases when sub-optimal techniques are used coupled with heuristics. It has been shown that it is possible to specify a given problem as well as the strategy to be implemented, by using a small number of parameters. Consequently, this paper presents a package of functions for implementing various branching strategies and for monitoring the search during the optimization process. The package contains a general branching mechanism which can be specialized by specifying parameters. It also provides a number of possibilities for outputting significant intermediate data or statistics.

The package may be considered a fundamental tool for the study of the interaction between the data structure and the type of strategy and in particular for the choice of heuristics for a given class of problems. This step is necessary if one wants to write efficient code for solving some classes of combinatorial optimization problems.

1. General Branching Algorithm

This paragraph is a short summary of previous work [1]. Combinatorial problems considered here consist of

(i) a set Σ of objects called solutions

(ii) a finite set $P = \{P_i\}$ of p properties, such that each property P_k partitions Σ into a finite number q_k ($q_k > 1$) of equivalence classes noted Σ/P_k.

(iii) a set of feasibility conditions $C = \{C_j\}$

(iv) a procedure which allows to extract from $\Sigma/P_1 \ldots P_p$ an optimal feasible solution if there is one.

A well known representation of the search process is the search tree whose nodes represent successive examined solution classes.

Algorithm Basically the algorithm examines a solution class obtained by using some property P_i. It tries to locate an optimal solution in the class, or to determine whether or not there is any feasible solution. Possibly it computes additional information such as upper bound, lower bound, evaluation function,... After a termination test the algorithm then goes into the process of selecting another solution class by choosing one of the previously examined classes and a new property. This property is used to obtain subclasses and one of them is selected to be examined at the next iteration.

In many places choices are made that depend on the user, who by doing so defines the strategy. They are indicated below by the qualifier *rule*, meaning a user defined procedure. For instance the *partitioning rule* corresponds to the choice of next property to be used, while the *priority rule* corresponds to the choice of the next solution class to be examined among the generated subclasses. It is worth noticing that such rules may be dynamically produced in the context of Branching Algorithms, i.e. they

may be context dependent.
The indicator and branching function mentioned in step 1.4 of the following algorithm play a crucial rule. They are used to evaluate the desirability from exploring further a given solution class and play a fundamental part in step 3.1. Actually they dictate the strategy.
The algorithm is stated in the case of a maximization problem.

Step 0

The original problem is examined first. The whole set of solutions Σ is assigned to the root of the search tree. At each iteration a solution class is examined as follows starting with Σ.

Step 1 Node Analysis

1.1. Check feasibility. If it is determined that the solution class does not contain any feasible solution, close the node and go to step 2.

1.2. Compute an upper bound for the solution class.

1.3. Update the state of the node. If closed (for example if terminal) then go to step 2 ; otherwise go to 1.4.

1.4. Compute a node indicator by evaluating the branching function. Go to step 2.

Step 2 Termination Test

Determine whether or not the search has terminated by examining the pending nodes of the search tree and by using the termination rule. If yes, then stop ; otherwise go to step 3.

Step 3 Node Generation

3.1. Use the pending node indicators to determine the branching node. Go to 3.2.

3.2. Use the partitioning and priority rules to determine the new node. Go to 3.3.

3.3. Update the state of the branching node and set the state of the new node to 0.

This is the end of an iteration, go to step 1 for the next iteration.

It is worth noticing that once the branching function has been defined all strategic decisions are taken in step 3 of the algorithm, while all information related to the problem data is acquired at step 1. This situation allows to write easily adequate code for implementing this type of general branching algorithm.

2. Implementation - SICOBA

General Approach SICOBA (SImulation of Combinatorial Optimization Branching Algorithms) is a set of about 30 functions written as FORTRAN subroutines which allow the user to solve any problem that can be set up as defined in (i) through (iv) of paragraph 1. Any strategy that can be implemented by a branching function can then specified and information about how the problem is being solved is obtained through SICOBA.

The user is left free to organize its data as he likes and must therefore provide routines for interfacing with the external world (input/output routines) as well as with SICOBA. The complexity and sophistication of those routines depend solely on the particular problem to be studied and on the user's programming skills. Generally it can be fairly simple. To illustrate this approach it suffices to give the names of the required routines which are called at various moments by SICOBA.

. Input/Output routines

RDDAT reads data in

PRTPB prints data for checking it

MODDAT modifies data (optional)

MOVSOL moves a feasible solution into a user's defined solution area

WRTSOL prints part of the solution area (user controlled)

. Search Parameters

INIPRM transmits search parameters to SICOBA as arguments.

. Data Information (needed in Node Analysis Step)

FSULB computes upper, lower bound, optimality over solution subclass

BRFCN implements a branching function

. Structural Information (needed both in Node Analysis and Node Generation Steps)

NXPIMI implements partitioning and priority rules

MAXPI returns the maximum member of generated subsets for a given property

. Dynamic management of property area (optional)

PINCNT increment and decrement a property reference counter

PDCCNT in user's area.

Any number of additional routines may be included by the user within the limit of the machine capacity.

Once the problem has been formulated the rest is taken care of by SICOBA.

Working Modes and Available Commands. SICOBA works in two possible modes Batch or Interactive, although it was really intended to be used interactively. In batch mode SICOBA simply solves the particular problem and prints additional information such as:

. Total number of explored nodes

. Total elapsed time

. Maximum number of nodes at any given time (core requirement)

. Number of explored nodes before reaching the optimal solution

. Maximum depth of search (interesting for complex dynamic property definition cases)

. Display of tree width versus time (are requirement)

. Display of tree depth versus time.

In interactive mode SICOBA works on a question/command answer basis and its possibilities can be best illustrated by giving a list of commands.

- . Exit
- . show list of commands
- . show data
- . perform single step (i.e. only node analysis for example)
- . perform n iterations
- . show current node content (examined subclass, upper-bound, lower bound, feasible solution, etc.)
- . give number of pending nodes (Instantaneous core requirement)
- . show best solution so far
- . show elapsed time
- . give number of free cells left
- . change data (user routine MODDAT)
- . start again
- . change search parameters (user routine INIPRM)
- . change tree width sampling frequency
- . change tree depth sampling frequency
- . display tree width versus time so far
- . display tree depth versus time so far
- . switch node trace flag
- . go into advanced command mode.

There is a set of about 25 advanced commands which allow the user to change pieces of information at very low level, that is to experiment on the structure. It is possible to change data but also structures (pointers) and proceed from there with standard commands. This is a dangerous but useful possibility.

In Conclusion It was found that SICOBA could be used mainly for the three following purposes

- . for testing various strategies on various combinatorial optimization problems
- . for helping to find better heuristics
- . for solving directly complex problems without using mathematical models.

Reference

. Barthès Jean Paul A., "Branching Methods in Combinatorial Optimization", PhD Thesis, Stanford (1973).

SCORPION : SYSTEME DE MODELISATION ET D'OPTIMISATION

D. DELPUECH
A. GIRES
B. PERE-LAPERNE
M. SOUBIES

Département Informatique
Institut de Recherche Economique et de Planification
Université des Sciences Sociales de Grenoble
B.P. 47 Centre de tri
38040 Grenoble-Cédex FRANCE.

RESUME

Le système SCORPION est un outil informatique qui permet de résoudre des problèmes d'optimisation et de simulation sur des modèles dynamiques représentables sous la forme de graphes orientés.

Un utilisateur définit son problème au moyen d'un programme écrit en langage SCORPION L'activation (session) comprend trois phases :

La phase de modélisation qui permet :

- de construire le graphe orienté schématisant le modèle,
- d'introduire les données associées au modèle ; ces données sont attachées aux noeuds et arcs du graphe, elles dépendent ou non du temps (modèle dynamique ou statique).
- de générer un ensemble d'équations qui traduisent les relations du modèle (ensemble de contraintes, fonction objectif).
- d'afficher le graphe et les données associées, partiellement ou entièrement.

La phase d'optimisation permet d'effectuer l'optimisation au moyen d'un algorithme mathématique qui donne des valeurs aux inconnues - stratégiques et de flux - telles que la fonction objectif soit optimale sur l'espace défini par les contraintes.

La phase d'analyse permet à l'utilisateur d'exploiter les résultats de l'optimisation dans l'ordre et au niveau d'agrégations qui lui conviennent.

Le système SCORPION présente trois aspects essentiels :

- La possibilité d'enchainer plusieurs sessions : les résultats, l'ensemble des données, la structure du graphe étant conservée d'une session à l'autre.
- La possibilité de l'utiliser soit en "batch" soit en conversationnel.
- La possibilité d'étendre le langage de référence.

MOTS-CLES : Modélisation, simulation, graphe, optimisation, expressions formelles, extensions syntaxiques et sémantiques, base de données.

Contrat IRIA-SESORI n° 72/48

I - LES CONCEPTS DE MODELISATION, D'OPTIMISATION ET D'ANALYSE .

La phase de modélisation a pour but de permettre à l'utilisateur de décrire le modèle de son application. Ceci implique en général :

- définir un domaine - structure et données - sur lequel il veut travailler (domaine économique, d'entreprise, des réseaux, etc...).
- définir une politique de fonctionnement et de développement ou de façon générale une politique qu'il veut appliquer à ce domaine.

Ces deux définitions caractérisent le scénario propre à l'application. Une succession de scénarios consistera en :

- une modification du domaine : ceci se traduisant par un changement de la structure du graphe ou des données,
- une définition de politiques différentes.

Dans le cas où le domaine étudié est représentable sous forme de graphe - c'est-à-dire qu'il se définit comme un ensemble d'opérations (les noeuds du graphe) et de relations entre ces opérations:les transferts (les arcs du graphe)- l'utilisateur dans un premier temps aura à décrire ce graphe, ses différents composants.

Dans un deuxième temps :

- il associera aux opérations et transferts des données : les attributs, qui les caractérisent, et leur affectera une valeur. Les attributs peuvent être définis de façon externe au graphe, c'est-à-dire indépendamment des opérations ou des transferts ;
- il exprimera par les "macro-attributs" les relations qui existent entre :
  . les inconnues implicites du modèle (les flux) ou les inconnues stratégiques (toute autre inconnue du modèle), et,
  . les données, les attibuts qu'il a défini.

Dans un troisième temps :

A l'aide des macros-attributs, des attributs et des inconnues il traduira la politique qu'il a retenu pour le modèle et l'exprimera par des contraintes et ûne fonction objectif à optimiser.

I.1. DEFINITION DU GRAPHE.

I.1.1. Les opérations.

Notion d'opération et mode de fonctionnement.

Une "opération" est une entité mettant en jeu un équipement qu'elle utilise selon un ou plusieurs modes de fonctionnement.

Un "mode de fonctionnement" est la manière dont l'équipement associé à une opération donnée est utilisé afin de produire un ou plusieurs "biens" (ou services) en sortie à partir d'un ou plusieurs "biens" admis en entrée.

A un instant donné l'équipement est utilisé selon un seul mode de fonctionnement. Dans le cas où l'opération possède plusieurs modes de fonctionnements ceux-ci seront mis en jeu alternativement durant une période donnée.

Opération monomode.

C'est une opération qui ne possède qu'un seul mode de fonctionnement, celui-ci admettant :

en entrée : zéro, un ou plusieurs biens.
en sortie : zéro, un ou plusieurs biens.

Nous la représenterons (cas général) :

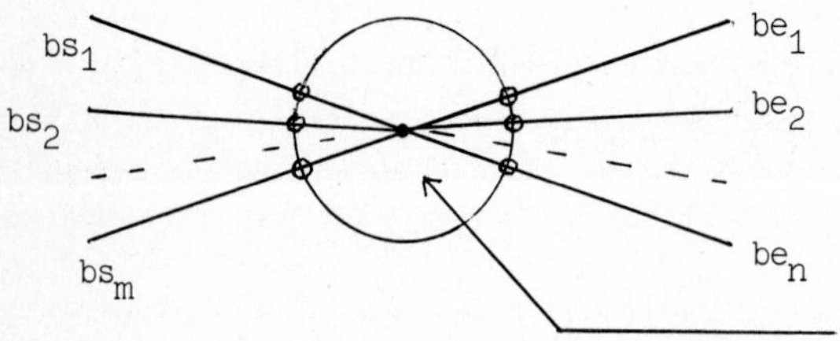

opération : un mode de fonctionnement.

Les relations entre les biens en entrée et ceux en sortie de l'opération sont décrites par l'équation :

$$be_1 + be_2 + \dots + be_n \longrightarrow bs_1 + bs_2 + \dots + bs_m$$

et les relations entre les flux (quantité de biens qui circulent dans les transferts) sont décrites par le système suivant :

$$\text{Flux }(bs_1) = a_{11}\text{ flux }(be_1) + a_{12}\text{ flux }(be_2) + \ldots + a_{1n}\text{ flux }(be_n)$$

...

...

$$\text{flux }(bs_m) = a_{m1}\text{ flux }(be_1) + a_{m2}\text{ flux }(be_2) + \ldots + a_{mn}\text{ flux }(be_n)$$

<u>Opération multimode</u>.

C'est une opération susceptible d'agir selon plusieurs modes de fonctionnement, chaque mode de fonctionnement étant homogène à une opération monomode.

Nous la représentons (cas général):

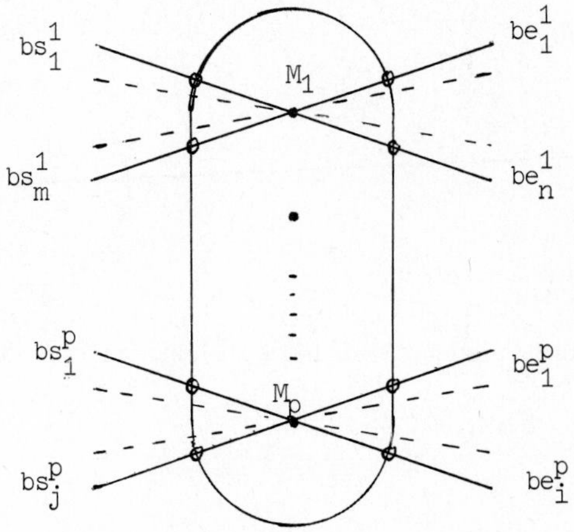

opération :
plusieurs modes de
fonctionnement.

Les relations entre les biens sont décrites par un ensemble d'équations (une par mode de fonctionnement) et les relations entre les flux sont décrites par un ensemble de systèmes d'équations.

I.1.2. Les transferts.

- Notion de transfert.

Un transfert exprime l'existence d'une relation entre les biens "sortant" d'une opération et les biens "entrant" dans une autre. Il traduit la possibilité d'utiliser les biens en sortie de la première par la deuxième opération

- Transfert élémentaire.

Un transfert élémentaire traduit la possibilité d'utiliser un bien d'un mode de fonctionnement d'une opération par un mode de fonctionnement d'une autre opération.

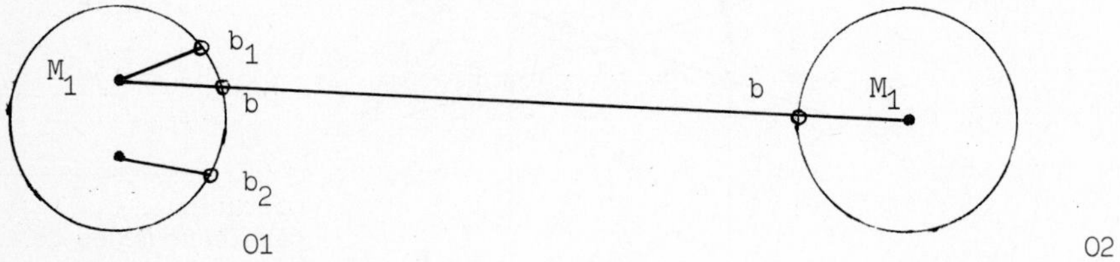

Ceci s'exprime en caractérisant l'origine et l'extrémité du transfert.

b. M1. 01 ⟶ M1. 02

- Transfert multiple.

Un transfert multiple traduira la possibilité d'utiliser tous les biens issu d'un mode de fonctionnement d'une opération par un autre mode de fonctionnement d'une autre opération. Ceci s'exprime en caractérisant l'origine et l'extrémité du transfert. L'origine et l'extrémité sont :

. un mode de fonctionnement d'une opération,
. ou une opération.

Dans ce cas tous les transferts réalisables sont créés.

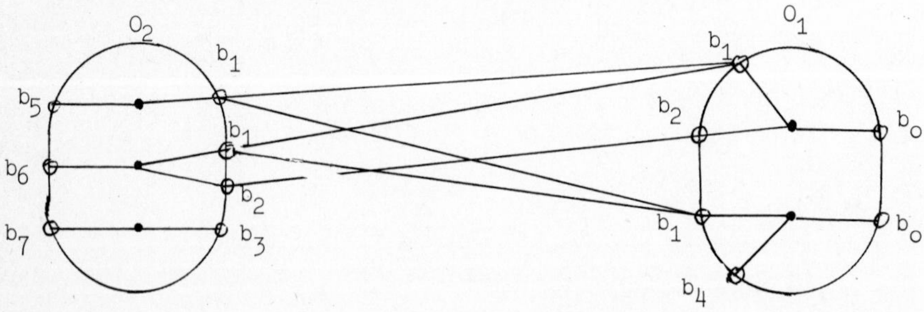

Dans le cas du schéma précédent où les opérations sont décrites par :

pour 01 - M1 : $b_o \longrightarrow b_1 + b_2$

M2 : $b_o \longrightarrow b_1 + b_4$

pour 02 - M1 : $b_1 \longrightarrow b_5$

M2 $b_1+b_2 \longrightarrow b_6$

M3 : $b_3 \longrightarrow b_7$

le transfert multiple 01 → 02 sera équivalent à cinq transferts élémentaires.

.1.3. Les secteurs.

- Notion de secteur.

Un secteur est un ensemble d'opérations et/ou de transferts élémentaires du graphe complet. Il est caractérisé par un nom. Cet ensemble est en général défini par référence à des caractéristiques communes que possèdent différents éléments. L'utilisateur peut composer un secteur, d'opérations et de transferts élémentaires quelconques.

- Trois types de secteur sont définis implicitement.

. Le secteur TRANSF : ensemble des transferts élémentaires du graphe.

. Le secteur ØPER : ensemble des opérations du graphe.

. L'opération est définie comme un secteur composé d'un seul élément: elle-même.

I.2. DEFINITION DES DONNEES.

I.2.1. La période.

La définition de modèles dynamiques pour lesquels les données dépendent du temps exige que l'utilisateur spécifie la période sur laquelle il veut décrire son modèle. La période sera précisée par les deux dates limites de validité du modèle.

I.2.2. Les attributs.

Un attribut est une caractéristique élémentaire, dépendante ou non du temps, qui peut être associée :

- au mode de fonctionnement d'une opération du graphe,
- a un transfert élémentaire du graphe,
- de façon externe au graphe.

Dans les deux premiers cas ils seront dits localisés, dans le dernier cas non localisés.

L'utilisation de ces attributs apparaît lors de leur déclaration et de leur affectation.

- Déclaration.

C'est à ce moment que l'utilisateur définit l'ensemble des attributs qu'il utilisera pour le modèle qu'il décrit. Il spécifie s'il s'agit d'attributs qui sont attachés aux éléments du graphe (attribut localisé) ou non (attribut non localisé).

Il précise si ceux-ci peuvent prendre différentes valeurs dans le temps ou non.

- Affectation.

L'affectation d'un attribut localisé est sa réalisation pour un élément du graphe(mode de fonctionnement d'une opération ou transfert élémentaire) et la définition d'une valeur pour celui-ci.

L'affectation d'un attribut non localisé sera la définition d'une valeur po celui-ci.

La valeur d'un attribut peut être définie par une expression faisant référence à des attributs déjà définis.

La définition peut être formelle : A = B * C, si la valeur de B ou C est modifiée après cette définition la valeur de A sera aussi modifiée,

ou numérique : A = ? B * C prend la valeur B* C lors de la définition, des modifications ultérieures de B et C n'affecteront pas A.

I.2.3. Les inconnues.

Le système permet de prendre en compte deux catégories d'inconnues :

- Les "inconnues implicites" liées à la structure du modèle (graphe).
- Les "inconnues stratégiques" qui comme les attributs peuvent être localisés en des éléments du graphe ou non. Elles représentent toutes les autres inconnues du système.

- "Inconnues implicites" :

Les inconnues implicites sont les inconnues associées au flux qui circulent dans le graphe.

- Inconnues ARC : ce sont les inconnues flux mesurant la qualité de bien qui circule dans un tansfert élémentaire.
- Inconnues CHEMIN : ce sont les inconnues flux mesurant la quantité qui circule d'un mode de fonctionnement d'une opération initiale à un mode de fonctionnement d'une opération finale.

(Un mode de fonctionnement d'une opération initiale est un mode de fonctionnement qui n'a pas de bien en entrée.

Un mode de fonctionnement d'une opération finale est un mode de fonctionnement qui n'a pas de bien en sortie sauf dans le cas où le graphe possède des cycles où ce sera un mode de fonctionnement d'une opération quelconque).

L'utilisateur dispose de ces deux types d'inconnues implicites.

Dans le premier cas une inconnue est associée à chaque transfert élémentaire du graphe, dans le deuxième cas à chaque chemin du graphe et ceci pour les les années "repère".

La notion "repère" permet d'indiquer les années de la période pour lesquelles une inconnue est définie, (sauf indication explicite d'un sous-ensemble d'années à considérer comme années repère. Le système considère par défaut toutes les années de la période comme des repères).

Le choix du type d'inconnues dépend de la nature du problème à résoudre. Les inconnues chemin fournissent des éléments d'analyse plus complets mais sont plus nombreuses.

A partir de ces notions élémentaires d'inconnues sont définies les "inconnue agrégées" qui sont également des notions du système.

(Voir l'annexe pour l'ensemble des inconnues agrégées qui peuvent être utilisées).

"Inconnues stratégiques" :

Ces inconnues peuvent être localisées ou non, datées ou pas.

Leur utilisation impose leur déclaration et leur réalisation.

- Déclaration :

  La déclaration consiste à indiquer le type de l'inconnue stratégique : localisée ou non et si celle-ci dépend du temps ou non.

- Réalisation :

  La réalisation d'une inconnue stratégique localisée consiste en la spécification des éléments auxquels on souhaite associer cette inconnue.

  Si l'inconnue stratégique a été déclarée comme dépendant du temps sa réalisation ne sera effective que pour les années repère.

  Dans ce cas il y aura pour l'élément considéré autant d'inconnues que d'années repère.

I.2.4. Les macros-attributs.

Un macro-attribut est une notion définie comme une expression quelconque des ATTRIBUTS et/ou des INCONNUES avec la mention d'au moins une inconnue dans l'expression.

Par exemple on définira :

- le coût-de-fonctionnement comme le produit d'un coût-unitaire-de-fonctionnement (attribut) par le flux entrant dans une opération (inconnue implicite) ;

- le coût-d'-investissement comme le produit d'un coût-unitaire-d'-investissement (attribut) par l'accroissement de capacité de l'opération (inconnue stratégique) ;

- le macro-attribut-Z comme égal a : attribut-a/inc-strat-x + attribut-b * LOG (FS-d'opération).

Un macro-attribut peut être localisé ou non et peut dépendre du temps ou non.

Pour l'utiliser il faudra le déclarer puis l'affecter.

Déclaration :

La déclaration consiste à préciser le type de l'attribut.

Affectation : L'affectation consiste :

- dans le cas où le macro-attribut est localisé à spécifier les éléments du graphe (mode de fonctionnement d'opération, transfert élémentaire) où il existe et à donner sa définition par une expression des attributs et des inconnues ;

- dans le cas où il n'est pas localisé à donner sa définition.

I.3. DEFINITION D'UNE POLITIQUE - GENERATION D'EQUATIONS

La structure du domaine, les données ayant été définies l'utilisateur peut désormais traduire :

- les contraintes techniques du domaine global,
- la politique qu'il désire appliquer à celui-ci.

Cette politique s'exprime par un ensemble de contraintes et une fonction objecti à optimiser.

I.3.1. Les contraintes.

Une contrainte est une relation entre deux expressions composées d'attributs, d'inconnues, de macro-attributs, de nombres (avec la mention d'au moins une inconnue ou macro-attribut).

I.3.2. La fonction objectif.

La fonction objectif sera définie comme une expression des attributs, des inconnues, des macro-attributs et de nombres à optimiser.

I.3.3. Génération d'équation.

A partir de la forme externe des contraintes et de la fonction objectif qu'aura défini l'utilisateur, le système gènèrera un ensemble d'équations,

ou les attributs prendront les valeurs affectées lors de leur définition,

ou les inconnues agrégées seront remplacées par les inconnues élémentaires,

ou les macros-attributs auront été remplacés par leur expression.

C'est cet ensemble d'équations, qui peut s'exprimer sous la forme d'un programme d'optimisation,

min (ou max) $g\ (x_{ie},\ x_s)$

sur le domaine définit par

$$f_j\ (x_{ie}, x_s)\ R\ h_j\ (x_{ie},\ x_s) \text{ pour } j = 1 \text{ à } n$$

(ou x_{ie} représente les inconnues implicites élémentaires.

x_s représente les inconnues stratégiques .

R est un opérateur de raltion : $<$, $=$, $>$, $<=$, $>=$.

n est le nombre de contraintes définies par l'utilisateur), qui sera résolu par un algorithme d'optimisation.

I.4. ALGORITHMES - OPTIMISATION .

Le modèle ayant été décrit - par la définition de sa structure des données, d'une politique - l'ensemble des données, des contraintes, de la fonction objectif est transformé en un système d'équations dépendant des inconnues élémentaires qui se présente sous la forme :

$$\begin{cases} \text{Min } g\ (x_{ie}, x_s) \\ f_j\ (x_{ie}, x_s)\ R\ h_j\ (x_{ie}, x_s) \text{ pour } j = 1 \text{ à } n. \end{cases}$$

Ce problème sera traité par un algorithme d'optimisation.

Dans l'état actuel du système SCORPION, en raison de la meilleure connaissance des algorithmes d'optimisation linéaires qui permettent de traiter un très grand nombre d'inconnues et de contraintes, le problème doit se traduire en terme linéaire c'est-à-dire que les fonctions f_j, h_j et g doivent être linéaires en x_{ie} et x_s.

Dans ces conditions, une solution sera obtenue par un algorithme de simplexe qui fournira comme résultat essentiel, les différentes valeurs des inconnues et les valeurs duales des contraintes.

Toutefois, tous les concepts développés permettent de générer des équations non linéaires des inconnues, une parfaite connaissance et une généralisation des algorithmes non linéaires permettraient alors de résoudre tout problème d'optimisation.

L'aspect génération d'équations/essentiel dans le système SCØRPIØN peut également convenir à la résolution de modèle de simulation se définissant à l'aide de fonctions des inconnues, seuls les algorithmes sont à adapter.

I.5. ANALYSE DES RESULTATS.

Bien souvent, l'analyse des résultats est considérablement ralentie par le volume énorme des valeurs numériques à compiler. La possibilité d'utiliser le système de façon conversationnelle pour rechercher les informations est précieuse lors de cette phase.

Cette partie est la plus ouverte et l'extensibilité du système prend ici tout son sens dans la mesure où il est impossible de prévoir à l'avance tous les besoins. L'utilisateur par le moyen de macro-commandes peut créer de nouveaux outils d'analyse qui lui sont propres.

Néanmoins, certains outils d'analyse sont prévus.

L'algorithme d'optimisation fournit toutes les valeurs des inconnues élémentair l'utilisateur peut obtenir :

- l'ensemble des inconnues agrégées.
- l'évaluation de tous les macros-attributs.
- L'évaluation de toute expression des inconnues, des attributs, des macros-attributs, des valeurs duales, des nombres.

D'autres possibilités telles que l'analyse statistique des résultats ou la sortie de ceux-ci sous forme de tableaux sont envisagées, mais ne sont pas actuellement réalisées.

II - LE LANGAGE LANSCO.

II.1. Présentation du langage.

L'interface entre l'utilisateur et le système SCORPION est assuré par le langage LANSCO qui permet à l'utilisateur :

- l'initialisation et la sauvegarde de ces données en début et en fin de session.
- la modification du langage LANSCO lui-même.
- L'interprétation de commandes par rapport à l'état courant du langage.

Un aspect important réside dans les possibilités de modifications inhérentes au langage. Ces possibilités sont au nombre de deux.

- définition (ou suppression) de macrosyntaxe.
- définition (ou suppression) de macrocommande.

La première fait intervenir des notions de la théorie des langages ; elle sera très rarement mise en oeuvre par un utilisateur mais est plutôt destinée aux personnes chargées d'adapter le système SCØRPIØN à un environnement donné.

La deuxième possibilité offre, au contraire, l'avantage classique de pouvoir définir des ellipses du langage de base.

L'utilisateur peut être amené à définir sa propre syntaxe par équivalences à la syntaxe de base, celle-ci restant inchangée.

Ces deux mécanismes d'extension du langage implique la notion de dialecte. A un instant donné d'une session le dialecte est constitué du langage de base ainsi que des macrosyntaxes et des macrocommandes définies par l'utilisateur ; seules les commandes écrites dans le dialecte courant peuvent être reconnues et interprétées à un moment donné.

D'un point de vue interne au système, la technique retenue pour traiter les extensions du langage de base est celle de la génération d'un code sous forme d'automate à pile d'états-finis. La totalité du langage de base a été définie sous forme de macrosyntaxes. Le langage de base est donc codifié dans la syntaxe propre au générateur d'automate.

II.2. Les expressions.

Les expressions, au sens classique d'expressions arithmétiques jouent un rôle fondamental dans le système SCORPION.

En effet, à part la structure d'un graphe, l'ensemble des données, organisées en base de données, est constitué d'un ensemble de notions (attributs, inconnue macro-attributs...) et des valeurs numériques ou des expressions formelles de ces notions.

Dans la phase d'optimisation, l'écriture de la fonction objectif et des contrai tes consiste à traiter des expressions pour générer des équations ; de même dan la phase d'analyse, il s'agit d'évaluer des expressions pour obtenir des résultats numériques.

D'un point de vue syntaxique, une expression est une combinaison algébrique tout à fait classique d'opérandes (les notions et/ou des nombres) et d'opérateurs.

Une notion peut être définie directement par une valeur numérique ou par une expression numérique :

ex. a = 5
a = 2 * 10 ⟵ expressions de type numérique

ou bien par référence à d'autres notions :

ex. c = ? (a + b) / 2 ⟵ expression de type numérique
d = 2 * (b + f) ⟵ expression de type formel

Le traitement d'une expression diffère suivant son type numérique ou formel ; en effet, celle de type numérique est reconnue puis évaluée, seul le résultat étant conservé tandis que celle de type formel est reconnue, puis conservée sous une forme particulière pour être évaluée dans une phase ultérieure.

La reconnaissance d'une expression consiste :

- à l'exprimer sous forme postfixée,
- à générer le pseudo-correspondant.

Dans le cas d'une expression formelle, c'est le pseudo-code qui est conservé et rattaché à la notion qu'il définit.

II.3. Les S et T itérations.

Les S-itérations sont des itérations sur l'espace liées au graphe et les T-itérations sont des itérations liées au temps dans les modèles dynamiques. Les itérations apparaissent comme des préfixes - éventuellement vides - de certaines instructions du langage.

Une S-itération a pour signification la répétition pour un certain nombre d'opérations et/ou de transferts (liste de lieux) regroupés ou non en secteurs d'une même instruction de définition ou d'évaluation.

Ex. pours op_1, op_2,...op_n : a = b/c ;

↖ préfixe d'une S-itération : instruction de définition.

? pours op_1, op_2,...op_n : a ;

↖ préfixe d'une S-itération : instruction d'évaluation.

↖ évaluation.

de même, une T-itération a pour signification la répétition suivant une série de dates d'une instruction de définition ou d'évaluation.

ex : pour t = d_1, d_2,...d_m : f = (1 + a) ** (t - d_1) ;

↖ préfixe d'une T-itération : instruction de définition.

Une S-itération et une T-itération peuvent être imbriquées :

ex. pours op_1, op_2...op_n :

pour t = d_1 à d_m : f (t) = (1 + a) ** (t-d_1) ;

Une autre forme de S-itération et de T-itération apparaît lors de l'utilisation des <u>macro-opérateurs</u> (somme, produit...) qui permettent d'évaluer une expression qui porte sur une liste de lieux et/ou sur une série de dates.

ex. SOM (op_1, op_2,...op_n : SOM (t = d_1 a d_m : 1/f (t))) ;

↖ macro-opérateur, S-somme ↖ macro-opérateur, T-somme

III - ARCHITECTURE GENERALE DU SYSTEME.

Le système SCORPION peut être activé suivant deux modes.

Le premier est le mode interprétatif ; c'est celui que connaît l'utilisateur lorsqu'il travaille sur un modèle et ses données à l'aide du dialecte prédéfini

Les modules suivants sont alors activés : (voir schéma du système).

- le moniteur et le module d'entrée/sortie avec l'utilisateur,
- l'interpréteur d'automate,
- les modules-algorithme d'optimisation, fonction de gestion de la base de données, fonction de gestion des expressions formelles -qui interagissent avec la base de données grâce à la fonction d'entrée/sortie.

Le modèle, les notions entrées et celles calculées se trouvant dans la base de données.

Le deuxième mode de fonctionnement est celui de définition ou de modification du dialecte courant.

Dans ce cas, les modules suivants sont activés : (voir schéma du système)

- le moniteur et le module d'entrées/sorties avec l'utilisateur,
- le générateur d'automate qui est chargé de définir un nouvel automate à pile,
- l'interpréteur d'automate.

Architecture générale du système : schéma

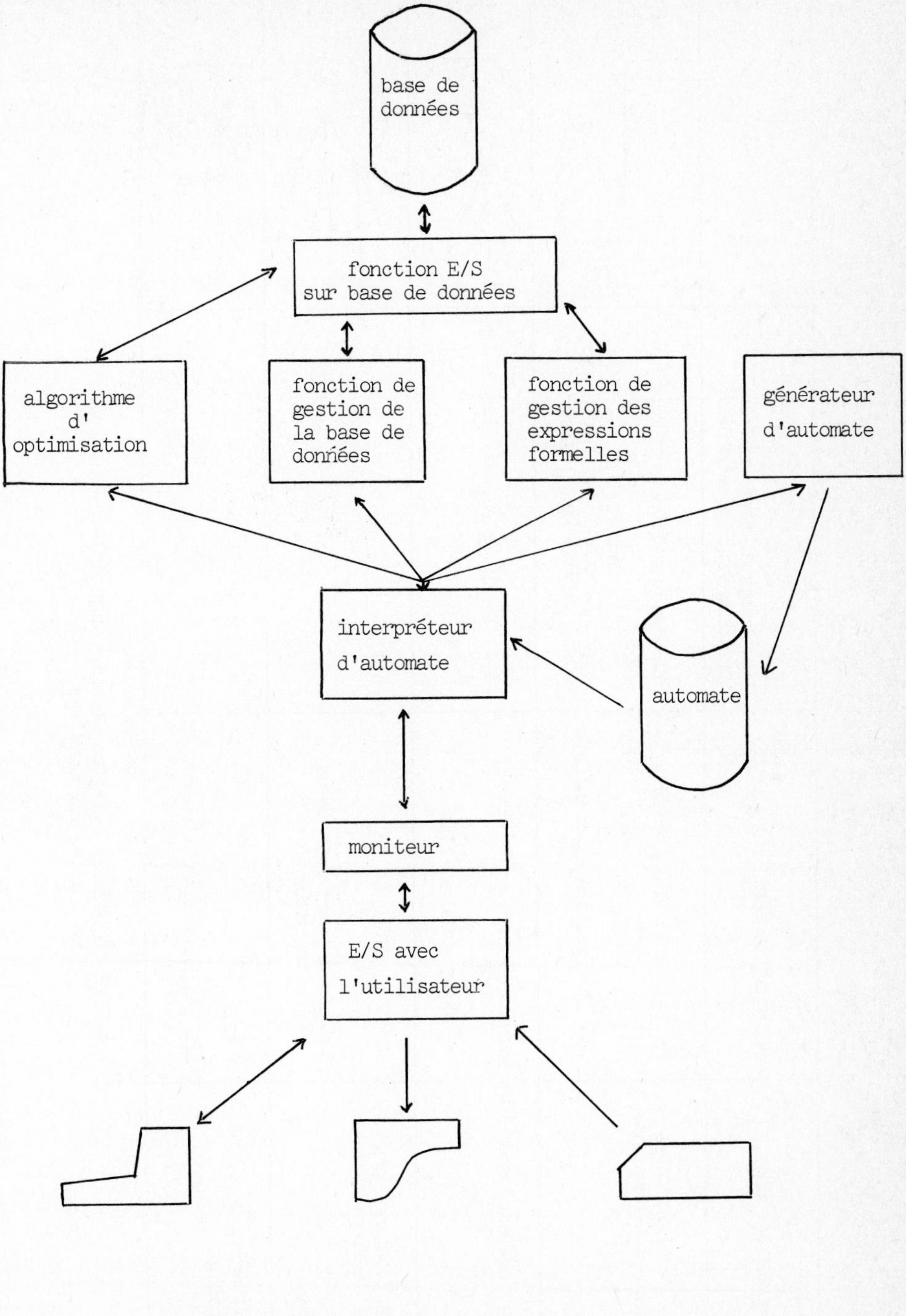

Inconnue agrégée	Désignation dans le système	Expression en fonction de inconnues élémentaires ou inconnues agrégées définies	
Flux "entrant" dans un transfert élémentaire	FE <u>de</u> b_1.M1.01 → M2.02 ↗ désignation du transfert	Si l'on considère des inconnues Arcs - l'inconnue Arc, sinon la somme des inconnues chemin traversant l'Arc.	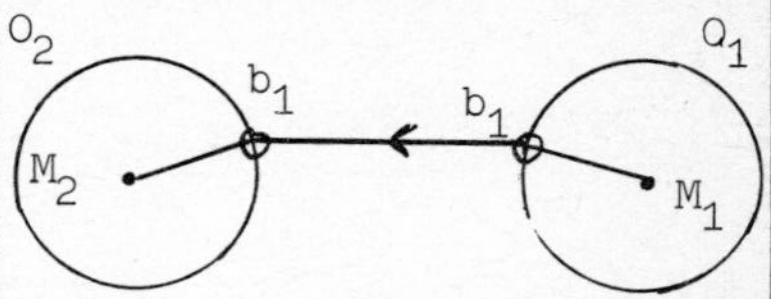
Flux "sortant" d'un bien	FS <u>de</u> b_1.M1.01 ↗ désignation du bien	$= \sum_j \sum_i$ FE <u>de</u> b_1.M1.01 → Mi.Oj	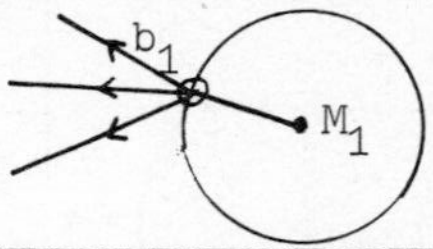
Flux "sortant" d'un mode de fonctionnement	FS <u>de</u> M1.01 ↗ désignation du mode de fonctionnement	$= \sum_i$ FS <u>de</u> b_i.M1.01	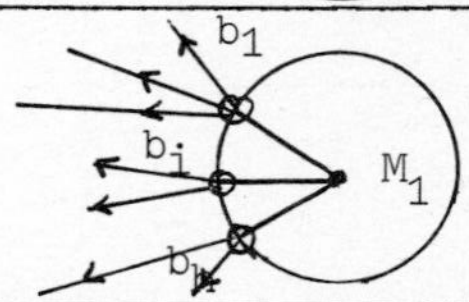
Flux "sortant" d'une opération	FS <u>de</u> 01 ↗ désignation de l'opération	$= \sum_i$ FS <u>de</u> $M_i.O_1$	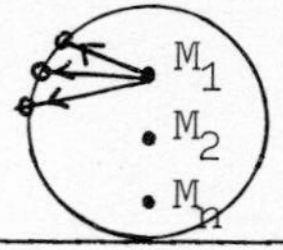

I - <u>ANNEXE</u> Inconnues agrégées définies à partir des inconnues implicites élémentaires.

Inconnue agrégée	Désignation dans le système	Expression en fonction des inconnues élémentaires ou inconnues agrégées définies	
Flux "sortant" d'un transfer élémentaire	FS <u>de</u> $b_1.M_1.O_1 \rightarrow M_2.O_2$	$= RDT * FE$ <u>de</u> $B_1.M_1.O_1 \rightarrow M_2.O_2$ (RDT : Rendement du transfert)	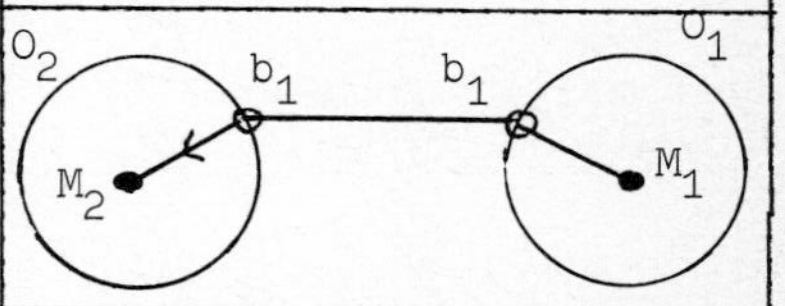
Flux "entrant" dans un bien	FE <u>de</u> $M_2.O_2$	$= \sum_j \sum_i FS$ <u>de</u> $b_1.M_1.O_j \rightarrow M_2.O_2$	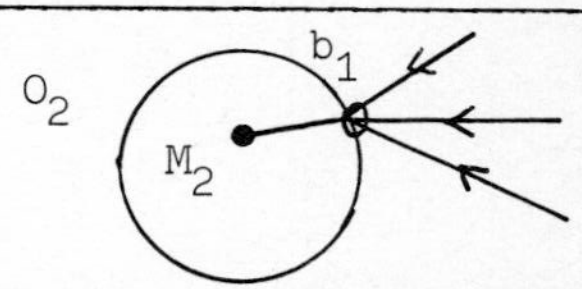
Flux "entrant" dans un mode de fonctionnement	FE <u>de</u> $M_2.O_2$	$= \sum_i FE$ <u>de</u> $b_i.M_2.O_2$	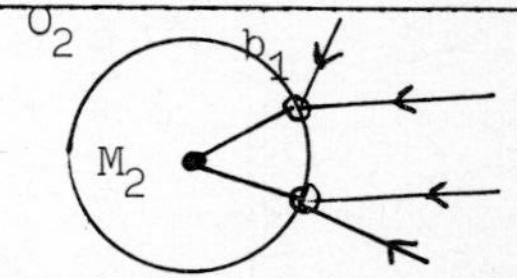
Flux "entrant" dans une opération	FE <u>de</u> O_2	$= \sum_i FE$ <u>de</u> $M_i.O_2$	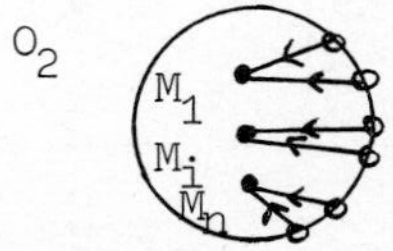

II - ANNEXE - Inconnues agrégées définies à partir des inconnues implicites élémentaires.

AN INTERACTIVE SYSTEM FOR MODELING

I. Galligani - L. Moltedo
Istituto per le Applicazioni del Calcolo "M. Picone", CNR
Rome, Italy

ABSTRACT

Recently some authors have proposed to introduce a pattern recognition approach in the modeling process, especially for the study of populations of species, within a compartimental representation, in aquatic ecosystems and for the water pollution control.

In order to implement this approach on a computer, it is necessary to develop "interactive systems" which are composed by a special language for modeling, a collection of data management procedures and a collection of numerical procedures. These systems give the possibility of integrating the data base handling techniques with mathematical methods for constructing models in an interactive manner in order to take into account the analyst's appreciation and understanding of the determining features of the prototype system during the different stages of the modeling process.

In this paper, we describe the main characteristics of such an interactive system with graphical facilities designed for a minicomputer which includes different algorithms for integrating ordinary differential equations. These algorithms have been chosen after an analysis which was not only oriented to the selection of the most significant methods but also to the study of their feasibility within a procedure which gives local and global error estimations. Some "standardization" problems in the implementation of this system have been taken into account.

INTRODUCTION

Various models have been proposed for the study of populations of species in ecosystems, within a compartimental representation, for the management of underground water reservoirs and for the improvement of the water quality. Most of them are lumped parameter models in which we have to identify the state-variables and the parameters. Direct and indirect methods have been developed for solving these identification problems. The indirect methods are essentially trial and error procedures which seek to improve an existing estimate of the variables and parameters in an iterative manner until the model response is sufficiently close to that of the real prototype system. This improvement generally is accomplished with the aid of empirical criteria or by formal mathematical procedures (gradient algorithms, random searches, etc.). However the indirect methods are effective only for a limited class of identification problems. They often breack down, especially when the "starting" model is not a sufficiently close representation of the prototype system and the excitation-response data available from the observations of the reality are of low quality. Besides they do not adequately utilize the large amount of potentially-valuable and useful information contained in the excitation-response data available from experiments or observations of the prototype system. Thus some authors have proposed to introduce a pattern recognition or learning approach in the modeling process (see, for example [1] , pg.32 and [2]).

In order to implement this approach on a computer, it is necessary to develop "Interactive Systems"(+) which are composed by:

- a special language for modeling;
- a collection of numerical procedures for solving classes of problems;
- a collection of data management procedures which provide a comprehensive set of data base management capabilities, including the ability to define new data bases, modify the definition of existing data bases,

(+) - We note that the word "system" is used in two different senses (both allowed due to common usage): physical system which we observe and computer software system.

retrieve and update values in these data bases and to extract from the data base those items that are used by the numerical procedures.

Indeed the advantages accrued by working on an interactive system with graphical capability are the very fast turnaround, the immediate graphical display, the simplicity of the control of the calculations and the possibility of various attacks on the problem and of various choices of the mathematical method. Especially for this "possibility", the analyst's appreciation and understanding of the prototype system's determining features may be taken into account during the different stages of the modeling process.

The construction of an interactive system with an effective high level language for modeling and with a well structured package for integrating data base handling techniques with mathematical methods is a very difficult task, especially when it is required to implement such a system on a minicomputer.

In this paper we describe the main characteristics of a "special" interactive system with graphical facilities designed to work on a minicomputer for solving ordinary differential initial value problems.

In this system we have restricted at the maximum the "descriptive" aspects of the modeling process, by designing the interaction to require only very simple actions by the user, which are anticipated by the system.(+) The interaction by anticipation on a "special" system has been taken into consideration in order to attempt to solve to some extent the dilemma between the system's "effectiveness" versus the "simplicity of use". Notwithstanding this restriction,with this system it is possible to develop in reasonable computing time many "significant lumped parameter models for different application areas, as dynamics of populations, environment, chemical kinetics, etc.

The system has been made self-helping and self-explanatory by giving the possibility to inquire optionally many tutorial displays.

The implementation of this system on a minicomputer allows the user to test simply and economically the above models in-house.

(+) - The interaction by anticipation allows the user to select a desired action rather than specify that action.

The system includes a rather great number of modern numerical procedures for solving initial value problems associated with ordinary differential equations. These algorithms take into consideration many different factors, as stiffness, cost of function evaluations, perturbation to linearity, estimation of the time-constants, etc., and are implemented within a procedure with automatic step-size and order determination.

The interactive system has been designed and written with portability in mind. For this the system has been written in Fortran by using the graphics package MINING [3]. With the MINING package a high degree of machine independence and an easement of programming have been achieved. (For example, the layout of each picture is done automatically; there are many automatic features, as "zooming", movement of items behind the "viewing window", etc.).

The machine-dependent subroutines on which MINING is based are constructed with some form of standardization.

Besides all the numerical procedures reflect a same structure in order to make these programs relatively easy to maintain or to modify.

Recently some systems similar to that described in this paper (see, for example [4] and [5]) have been developed, but in none of these all the above features are taken into account at the same time.

2. THE INTERACTIVE SYSTEM

2.1 Structure of the System

The interactive system performs a certain number of logical distinct activities which can be depicted by the following flowchart. At each block of the flowchart, i.e. module of the system, corresponds a logical distinct activity.

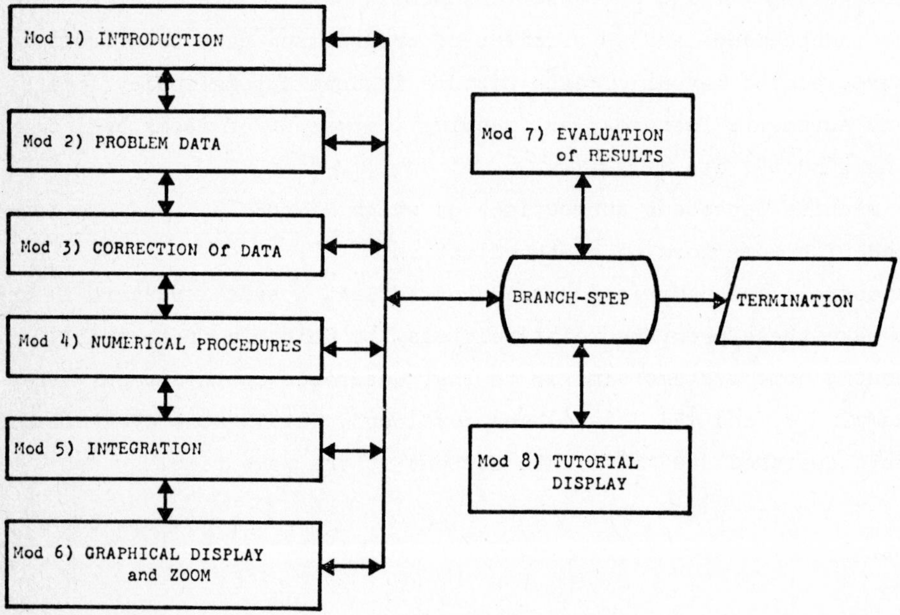

The connection among the different modules is performed through the three commands CONTINUE, BACK and BRANCH-OUT, which transfer the program control to the next, previous and Branch-Step modules, respectively. The Branch-Step module playes a significant role in the management of the modules.

The numerical procedures included in the system solve the initial value problem, written in normal form:

$$\underline{y}'(t) = \underline{f}(t, \underline{y}(t)) \qquad t \in (t_0, t_f] \quad \text{with} \quad \underline{y}(t_0) = \underline{y}_0 \tag{A1}$$

In module 1, INTRODUCTION, some introductory remarks are given.These remarks briefly summarize the flow of the program, give the built in limits on the number of equations, parameters, initial values, etc., and facilitate the user to verify the correct storage of the user's subroutines DE, JAC and FUNCT, which describe the function $\underline{f}(t,\underline{y}(t))$, the Jacobian matrix $\underline{f}_{\underline{y}}(t, \underline{y}(t))$ and the objective function, respectively. A typical objective function is $\|\underline{y}(t) - \underline{\tilde{y}}(t)\|^2$, where $\underline{\tilde{y}}(t)$ is an "estimate of the solution" $\underline{y}(t)$. In a same job, it is possible to declare many quite different functions.

In module 2, PROBLEM DATA, the values of the variables appearing in $\underline{f}(t,\underline{y}(t))$ which are susceptible of variations during a parametrical study and the initial conditions of the problem (A1) are assigned.

The module 3, CORRECTION of DATA, allows corrections of some problem data, as modification of the values, deletion and addition of some data. This module is useful for parametrical studies of the problem.

In module 4, NUMERICAL PROCEDURES, the choice of the method is performed either automatically or by the user and the parameters of the method, as step-size, order, error bound, time-constants, etc., are assigned.

In module 5, INTEGRATION, the integration process is carried out. If there is an interruption in the integration process, some diagnostic messages are displayed; otherwise the user must assign the mesh-points, belonging to $[t_0, t_f]$, in which the solution $\underline{y}(t)$ has to be represented.

In module 6, GRAPHICAL DISPLAY and ZOOM, the graphic displays of the solution $\underline{y}(t)$ and, optionally, of the "estimate of the solution" $\underline{\tilde{y}}(t)$ are performed.

In module 7, EVALUATION of RESULTS, the objective function is evaluated in correspondence of the current values of the problem data. In this module, it is possible to assign the values of an "estimate of the solution" $\underline{\tilde{y}}(t)$ and to plot the values of the objective function in correspondence of different values of a same problem data.

The module 8, TUTORIAL DISPLAYS, contains many tutorial informations which may help the user to interact more profitably with the system.

With the module BRANCH-STEP it is possible to perform a set of different activities to allow initiation of a new problem or a new attack on the problem at hand. This module is reached in two ways: either in the natural order of steps after Module 6 or by means the command BRANCH-OU which is available in all modules 1-8.

The module TERMINATION stops the process of solving different initia value problems, i.e. the job.

2.2 Numerical Procedures

The interactive system includes a rather great number of numerical procedures for solving initial value problems associated with ordinary differential equations.

These algorithms are based on well known methods which have been selected after a comparative experimental analysis characterized by the following main criteria:

- stability properties;
- cost of function evaluations;
- local truncation error expressions and possibility of obtaining good and not expensive global error estimates;
- reasonable criteria for choosing a proper step-size and order.

The results of this analysis have suggested to take into consideration the following algorithms.

1) An explicit Runge-Kutta method with a global error estimation based on the Stetter theorem [6] . For perturbed linear problems, including stiff ones, the Lawson formula [7] has been included. This method has been chosen in alternative to the explicit Runge-Kutta method with minimum truncation error bounds [8] and the explicit Runge-Kutta described in [9] §§ 2.8 - 2.10. We have also considered a variant of the formulas in § 2.10 suggested by Lawson for the error estimation and control.

2) A semi-implicit Runge Kutta method based on the A-stable Radau-type formula. An a-posteriori error estimate technique by Dahlquist [10] has been incorporated.

3) A multistep Adams-Bashforth-Moulton predictor-corrector method.

4) A method based on backward differentiation formulas developed by Gea

5) The polynomial and rational extrapolation method by Bulirsch and Stoer.

6) The exponential fitted A-stable formulas by Liniger and Willoughby.

The implementation of the methods 3) and 4) is a modified version of the well known programs developed by Gear [11]. The implementation of the methods 5) and 6) is a modified version of the programs included in [4]. The methods 2), 4) and 6), which are convenient for stiff problems, have been compared with the Jain's method [12] . While Jain's method is an A-stable of higher accuracy, it is costly to use. The method 5) is convenient for non stiff problems when function evaluations are not very expensive [13] .

2.3 Implementation of the System

The interactive system has been designed for the minicomputer PDP11/40 with a Tektronix 4010 display with portability in mind. For this, it has been written in Fortran with the graphics package MINING [3] (+); so the programming of the system was very easy, reaching a highly portable software. The machine dependent subroutines on which MINING is based are written in Fortran by using a Basic Graphics Package, which has been defined with some form of standardization by a CNR working group. The subset of subroutines of this package constructed for a display device with only Keyboard input (in the lowest common denominator approach [14]) is composed by:

- the "initialization and termination subroutines" INIT to establish communication between the user's program and the graphic display (*) and FINIT to terminate the use of the display device;
- the "image generation subroutines" WIND to define the screen window, TPLOT to plot a dark or bright vector, CHOUT to display a character, EXTCHR to extract characters from a character string and ANSTR to display a character string;
- the "attention-related subroutines" CHIN to introduce by Keyboard a character and TINSTR to introduce by Keyboard a character string.

The subroutine CHOUT is used also to define the operating mode (alphanumeric mode, graphic input mode, graphic plot mode, etc.) by addressing the proper control character.

(+) - Some few modifications to the original MINING package are carried out for its implementation on the minicomputer.

(*) - In this subroutine some "device-dependent" and "machine-dependent" informations must be made available.

The subroutines CHOUT, EXTCHR and CHIN are written in machine language. The subroutines TPLOT and WIND may be used in two versions: real and virtual tracking modes . Real tracking is intended to be performed on a "real screen" (i.e. the display screen) with the absolute coordinate system; virtual tracking is referred to a "virtual screen" (limited by the floating point precision of the computer) with an implicit cartesian coordinate system. This basic package may be extended with subroutines which take into account some special display features, as the cross hair in the Tektronix 4010 display.

The numerical procedures of the system have been structured in a standard form, which reflect the pattern of the well known program DIFSUB by Gear [15] . They perform one integration step and can be subdivided into four main sections. The first concerns the initialization operations, the second the calculations for one step, the third the estimate of the accuracy of the result and the fourth the determination of the step-size and order for the successive step.

The formal parameter part (or "calling sequence") of the numerical procedures is standardized in the form suggested by Hull in [16] .

3. SOME APPLICATIONS

a) An important problem in hydrology is to identify the parameters α_1, α_2 and α_3 of the following non linear model describing the fluid flow in a river basin $(\varphi \equiv \varphi(t),\ f \equiv f(t))$:

$$\frac{d^2\varphi}{dt^2} + \alpha_2 \varphi^{\alpha_1} \frac{d\varphi}{dt} + \alpha_3 \varphi = f \qquad t \in (t_o, t_f]$$

$$\varphi(t_o) = \beta_1 \qquad \frac{d\varphi(t_o)}{dt} = \beta_2$$

An estimate $\tilde{\varphi}(t)$ of the solution $\varphi(t)$ is known.

If we put $y_1 = \varphi$ $\quad y_2 = \frac{d\varphi}{dt}$ $\quad y_3 = \alpha_1$ $\quad y_4 = \alpha_2$ $\quad y_5 = \alpha_3$, this problem may be formulated: to find a vector $\underline{y} \equiv \underline{y}(t) = (y_1\ y_2\ y_3\ y_4\ y_5)$ which extremizes the function $F(\alpha_1\,\alpha_2\,\alpha_3) = \int_{t_o}^{t_f} |y_1(t) - \tilde{\varphi}(t)|^2 dt$ along a trajectory of the equation set:

$$\begin{cases} \dfrac{dy_1}{dt} = y_2 \\[2ex] \dfrac{dy_2}{dt} = -y_1^{y_3} y_2 y_4 - y_1 y_5 + f \\[2ex] \dfrac{dy_3}{dt} = \dfrac{dy_4}{dt} = \dfrac{dy_5}{dt} = 0 \end{cases} \tag{A2}$$

$$\begin{cases} y_1(t_o) = \beta_1 \\ y_2(t_o) = \beta_2 \\ y_3(t_o) = \alpha_1 \\ y_4(t_o) = \alpha_2 \\ y_5(t_o) = \alpha_3 \end{cases} \tag{A3}$$

This problem may be solved with the interactive system described in §2. by using the following iterative process.

Given an initial guess for the parameters α_1^o, α_2^o and α_3^o, we solve the problem (A2) - (A3) and we calculate the objective function $F(\alpha_1^o\ \alpha_2^o\ \alpha_3^o) = \int_{t_o}^{t_f} |y_1(t) - \tilde{\varphi}(t)|^2 dt$. Now the parameters α_2^o and α_3^o are held fixed and we calculate for different values of α_1 belonging of the interval $[\alpha_1^o - \delta\alpha_1^o \quad \alpha_1^o + \delta\alpha_1^o]$, $\delta\alpha_1^o$ is given, the objective function $F(\alpha_1\ \alpha_2^o\ \alpha_3^o)$. Let us plot $F(\alpha_1\ \alpha_2^o\ \alpha_3^o)$ as a function of α_1 alone. A minimum point on this curve, say at $\alpha_1 = \alpha_1^1$ will correspond to a value of α_1 at which $\partial F/\partial\alpha_1 = 0$; thus the value α_1^1 minimizes F with respect to α_1 . Now the parameters α_1^1 and α_3^0 are held fixed and we calculate for different values of α_2 belonging to the interval $[\alpha_2^0 - \delta\alpha_2^0 \quad \alpha_2^0 + \delta\alpha_2^0]$, $\delta\alpha_2^0$ is given, the objective function $F(\alpha_1^1\ \alpha_2\ \alpha_3^0)$. Let us plot $F(\alpha_1^1\ \alpha_2\ \alpha_3^0)$ as a function of α_2 alone. A minimum point of this curve, say at $\alpha_2 = \alpha_2^1$, minimizes F with respect to α_2 . Now the parameters α_1^1 and α_2^1 are held fixed and we calculate for different values of α_3 belonging to the interval $[\alpha_3^0 - \delta\alpha_3^0 \quad \alpha_3^0 + \delta\alpha_3^0]$, $\delta\alpha_3^0$ is given, the objective function $F(\alpha_1^1\ \alpha_2^1\ \alpha_3)$. Let us plot $F(\alpha_1^1\ \alpha_2^1\ \alpha_3)$ as a function of α_3 alone. From this graph we can choose $\alpha_3 = \alpha_3^1$ such that minimizes F with respect to α_3 . All these actions form the first step and at the point $(\alpha_1^1\ \alpha_2^1\ \alpha_3^1)$ the objective function $F(\alpha_1\alpha_2\alpha_3)$ has been reduced but probably not yet minimized. With the new guess α_1^1, α_2^1 and α_3^1 for the parameters, we repeat the above step to obtain the point $(\alpha_1^2\ \alpha_2^2\ \alpha_3^2)$ and so on until the relative changes in the parameters are small enough to claim convergence. Some useful convergence propertie of this Gauss Sidel interactive minimizer are given by Elkin [17] . Some times the convergence of this process is slow: however it gives always a global view of the behaviour of the objective function with respect to the parameters.

b) The difficulty in ecosystem modeling is that the systems are so compl depending on so many parameters, that to treat them as a whole is a very awkward problem. The techniques of the multicompartimental analysis are very useful because they allow to construct a prototype model as a seque ce of ecological models of increasing complexity. Generally, each of these models is described by a set of ordinary differential equations. By observing the difference between the compartimental evolution in the model and that in the system as determined by experiments, it is possible to identify the more significative parameters of the model. These models are utilized for "reducing" the experimental observations into a few parameters in order to simulate the behaviour of the system even in conditions not already experimented.

The interactive system described has been used to formulate some mathematical models for mass transfer in aquatic ecosystems as those developed in [18] . The transfer of a specific radionuclide in microecosystems in which biotic and abiotic complexity may be varied, has been analyzed. In this case a sequence of models may be formulated increasing the complexity of the system by increasing the number of system elements, the number of connections between them and the complexity of transfer functions (continuous linear, non linear, discrete).

c) An other use of the above interactive system was related to elaborate different variations of the Lotka-Volterra model which describes the dynamical behaviour of predator-prey populations in a closed ecosystem. Many improvements on this model have been suggested for the purpose of increasing its realism to reproduce population trends by fitting in the best way the measured values of the population-sizes available in a fixed period. The rationale for the construction of such a model is to propose initially between the predator species and the prey species the interaction mechanism of Lotka-Volterra. If this model reproduces well the available experimental observations, it may be considered a satisfactory description of the population trends; otherwise some deficiences of this model must be corrected. A deficiency is the non existence of a saturation level of the prey species in the absence of the predator species: a population in a limited space cannot exceed some saturation level. An other deficiency is the non existence of a saturation effect due to the limited appetite of the predator species. An other deficiency is the non existence of a time-lag between a prey kill and a predator birth and a seasonal variation of the populations. An other deficiency is the non existence of an age-specificity. This age-specificity is particularly important because of the different vulnerability of the various age groups of prey (very young, adults, etc.) to predation.(+)

Each elaboration to the initial Lotka-Volterra model requires to identify the parameters which characterize the new model: this problem is solved by the interactive system with the Gauss Sidel minimizing process described in a).

(+) - When we correct this deficiency in the original model, we have to change not only the structure of the differential equations (as for the other corrections) but also the number of these.

REFERENCES

[1] Sage A.P., Melsa J.L. : System Identification. Academic Press, New York (1971).

[2] Karplus W.J. : System Identification and Simulation. A pattern Recognition Approach. Comp. Sc. Dept. Report, Univ. of California (1971), Los Angeles.

[3] Smith L.B. : An example of a pragmatic approach to portable interactive graphics. Comput. & Graphics 1 (1975), 49-53.

[4] Dalle Rive L., Merli C. : FALCON-A conversational polyalgorithm for ordinary differential equation problems. Information Processing 74, North-Holland Publ. Comp., Amsterdam (1974).

[5] Edsberg L. : Integration Package for Chemical Kinetics. Stiff Differential Systems (ed. R.A. Willoughby). Plenum Press, New York (1974).

[6] Stetter H.J. : Local estimation of the global discretization erro SIAM J. Numer. Anal. 8 (1971), 512-523.

[7] Lawson J.D. : Generalized Runge-Kutta processes for stable system with large Lipschitz constants. SIAM J. Numer. Anal. 4 (1967), 372-380.

[8] Ralston A. : Runge-Kutta methods with minimum error bounds. Math. Comput. 16 (1962), 431-437.

[9] Lapidus L., Seinfeld J.H. : Numerical Solution of Ordinary Differential Equations, Academic Press, New York (1971)

[10] Dahlquist G. : Stability and error bounds in the numerical integr tion of ordinary differential equations. The Royal Inst. of Techn logy n.130, Stockholm (1959).

[11] Gear C.W. : Numerical Initial Value Problems in Ordinary Differential Equations. Prentice Hall, N.J. (1971).

[12] Jain R.K. : Some A-stable methods for stiff ordinary differentia equations. Math. Comput. 26 (1972), 71-78.

[13] Hull T.E. et al. : Comparing numerical methods for ordinary differential equations. SIAM J. Numer. Anal. 9 (1972), 603-637.

[14] Caruthers L.C., Bergeron R.D.: Device independent graphics, SEAS 1974 Session Report.

[15] Gear C.W. : The automatic integration of ordinary differential equations. Comm. ACM 14 (1971), 176-179

[16] Hull T.E. : Numerical solutions of initial value problems for ordinary differential equations. Numerical Solution of Boundary Value Problems for Ordinary Differential Equations (ed.A.K. Aziz), Academic Press, New York (1975).

[17] Ortega J.M., Rheinboldt W.C. : Iterative Solution of Nonlinear Equations in Several Variables. Academic Press, New York (1970).

[18] Argentesi F., Di Cola G., Verheyden N. : Parameter estimation of mass transfer in compartimented aquatic ecosystems. Identification and System Parameter Estimation Part 1 (ed. P. Eykhoff), North-Holland Publ. Comp., Amsterdam (1973).

A NETWORK COMBINING PACKET SWITCHING AND TIME DIVISION CIRCUIT SWITCHING IN A COMMON SYSTEM

Joe de Smet, Consultant, & Ray W. Sanders, Computer Transmission Corporation

Digital data transmission systems have quite rationally followed the patterns established by the older voice and telegraph transmission systems. Thus we find the more complex data transmission systems in use today are generally based on dial-up telephone networks or on polling systems over multipoint channels as used in earlier tele graph and teletypewriter networks.

The need to consider new approaches became apparent in studying the digital communica tion requirements of the State of California. Like governments in the world today, t use of computers has grown dramatically over the past few years. The need for remote access to and from these computers has grown exponentially. Each agency has been sol ing its own data communication problems based on voice grade dial or on digital polli schemes or a combination of both. As could be expected, growth of individual overlapping networks resulted in an inefficient maze when viewed as an overall system.

In 1973, the California State Universities and Colleges (CSUC) published a system description based on CSUC's present and forecasted data transmission requirements. This proposed system combined the attributes of voice type dial networks with digital on line call routing of the polling systems. Connections would be established by digital signals on line, but once a connection was established there would be no depe ence on the protocol of the transmitted data by the switching media. Additional features stipulated included error correction, 300 millisecond turnaround time, and the integration of asynchronous time share traffic with synchronous batch traffic for lin transmission efficiency.

Using this CSUC proposal as a base and reviewing the existing data systems in use by other agencies, The Pacific Telephone Company, one of the Bell System operating companies, in cooperation with the State Department of General Services developed the following features as a basis for a potential statewide interdepartmental data networ The network was designed to be capable of growing to meet the data transmission needs of all agencies.

Let's take a look at the interfaces required for a fully integrated system. From a user terminal point of view, such a system must provide basic supervisory and control functions. That is, it must be able to turn the user terminal on and off. It must recognize demand for service from the terminal. It must establish connections to oth terminals or computer ports either on a demand or on a prescription basis.

Also for maintenance of service it must provide a means of self checking and for remote testing.

Additional terminal features of an integrated system should include: autobaud, echoplex, abbreviated dialing, service queue with automatic cut through for busy connections, as well as service messages for failed lines or down computers.

Any new system should, of course, be capable of supporting all varieties of terminals now in use; but it should also provide flexibility for supporting new and unknown terminals without extensive reprogramming.

At the start, a new system must fully support teletypewriters (TTY) and cathode ray tubes (CRT) in both time share and inquiry response services. It must also simultaneously support remote job entry (RJE) devices in remote batch service. As the former are generally asynchronous while the latter are generally synchronous, both modes must be supported.

Interfaces to computer ports will require essentially all of the above user terminal features plus the ability to band groups of ports so they may be addressed with a single acronym. In addition, a multiplex scheme should be available so that several remote terminals can be simultaneously delivered to one computer port for software demultiplexing.

From an overall system point of view, if maximum line efficiency is to be obtained, traffic from various terminals must be consolidated on one line and routed to distant terminals or computers. A network of switching nodes, each capable of concentrating and routing traffic, is an obvious requirement. Such switching nodes must provide the terminal interfaces mentioned above. They must also concentrate, multiplex and switch data on demand or by pre-assignment. Switching nodes must be interconnected by data links or lines. Nodes must switch data traffic either directly or via other nodes for efficient traffic handling and minimum line costs. Interface to such data links should include error detection and correction, synchronous and asynchronous terminals served over the same data link, and automatic alternate routing for traffic overload or line failure.

In order to make a viable system, we must specify certain limits for call connection and data delivery. These include partitioning, priority, set-up time, and response time.

An integrated system must provide a means of preventing illicit connections as well as for establishing desirable connections. This ability to restrict access is called partitioning. Both flexibility in assignment and security in operation are fundamental requirements for partitioning. The security must be of a nature that even if the mod operandi becomes known, security will still be maintained.

Priority is required between various groups or agencies. For example, law enforcemen may need a completely unblocking system while college student time share service migh afford ten second, or more likely five minute, delay in call set-up. Priority should also be available within individual groups. For example, administrative messages mig take precedence over routine traffic between the same subset of stations. Dynamic priority of data link bandwidth must also be available. Time share and inquiry respo service demand immediate attention while batch traffic can be delayed.

Set-up time was not found to be critical; however, the traffic offered indicated tha ten connections per second must be established by the system. Response time was defined as the interval after the last bit of a character from a terminal is received a a switch node until the start of the first bit of that character back toward the same terminal with the distant switch looped back at a terminal interface. This round tri delay was requested by CSUC as not more than 300 milliseconds.

Even while the new system was being defined, additional customer requirements became evident. This indicated a need for extreme modularity and flexibility for growth in new and unsuspected directions. It also became apparent that a communication system which had to follow and react to the variety of line protocols now in use by the computer industry was doomed to everlasting reprogramming. Following a review of these factors and the variety of requirements discussed above, a systems philosophy was evolved:

All interfaces would meet the EIA RS 232C/CCITT V.24 standard.

Only ASCII and EBCDIC codes would be specified as requirements.

No speed or code conversion would be provided.

The new system would be transparent. That is, once a connection has been established, the data transmitted would be delivered to the receiving station exactly as transmitted by the sending station. Any and all line protocols would be up to the two connected stations.

All connections through the system would be completely full duplex. Whether or not stations sent simultaneously in both directions would be entirely up to the connected stations.

The new system must be completely modular. It must be capable of being changed without disruption of existing data services. Not only must it be modular so that stations could be added or deleted, but so that data link and data switches could be added, deleted or rearranged while other stations and switches are enjoying service without interference.

Last, but by no means least, the system must be maintainable. This means, maintainable at remote locations where maintenance men skilled in complex data systems are not readily available. A network control center capable of down line assignment changes, network self test features with centralized reporting, and complete down line test capability were deemed as mandatory. The network itself must be self checking and self healing to the extent feasible, and above all must report any deviations to the network control center.

Following development of the above features and philosophy, a search was initiated for existing hardware and software which could be adapted to provide a statewide integrated data system. While not dwelling on the selection process, it might be well to note that relatively standard steps were followed in issuing a request for price quotation (RPQ), evaluating the proposals received, and on the second attempt finding a system which could economically meet these specifications. This is the Computer Transmission Corporation TRAN® M3200 system.

The M3200 Network Switching and Management System PACUIT$_{tm}$ switching has been developed to provide the advantages of both circuit-switching and packet-switching, while eliminating many of their disadvantages. The fundamental design objective is that of minimizing delays in the network. To this end, the M3200 system incorporates many important new concepts, in conjunction with the best established techniques from TRAN's extensive experience in implementing networks. Highlights of the system are summarized below.

a. The PACUIT switching concept for reducing node buffering requirements by providing cyclic redundancy checking only at source and destination nodes.

b. Synchronous master-clock operation on all internode trunks.

c. Concurrent transmission of PACUITized data and simple time division circuit-switched data (non-PACUITized), on the same trunk.

d. Dynamic bandwidth allocation for optimum utilization of internode trunks, based on statistical multiplexing.

e. Optional fixed bandwidth for dedicated channels.

f. "Dynamic multiplexing option" available on tail-circuits (i.e., local distribution from a node), for efficient line utilization.

g. Full duplex transmission implemented by independent (simplex) transmission of data messages/responses in each direction.

TRAN® is a registered trademark of Computer Transmission Corporation

PACUIT$_{tm}$ is a trademark of Computer Transmission Corporation

h. Highly efficient PACUIT acknowledgement technique, for minimizing delays when trans mission retries are necessary.

i. Alternate routing capability when individual trunks are overloaded, or giving high error rates, or are out of service.

j. Continuous performance monitoring of traffic and error rates.

k. Port selection and contention for synchronous and/or asynchronous traffic, to eith individual ports or "hunt groups".

l. Logical network partitioning into user "access groups" for security.

m. "Abbreviated dial-in" within access group, for fast resource selection from a terminal.

n. "Camp-on" queuing of new users (if necessary) to avoid user retries during peak traffic periods.

o. Network statistics and diagnostics available on system console at each node.

p. Preassigned network management bandwidth for efficient system control.

q. Network Management System available (intended for large networks) for complete centralized control, including statistics, diagnostics, and network reconfiguratio

r. Basic network is transparent to user protocol and code to avoid overloading switch Protocol and/or code conversion can be added to switch modules or performed in sep rate utility modules, connected to one or more nodes as necessary.

s. Switching function and PACUIT assembly/disassembly are assisted by specially desig microprocessors, for optimum node efficiency.

t. General purpose bus architecture of switch allows highly flexible configuration capability, giving significant economic advantages and easy expandability.

PACUIT - THE HYBRID APPROACH

A major advantage of packet-switching is that of powerful error checking and recovery However, the classical means of forming and transmitting packets is a significant sou of transmission delay and excessive network overhead for low speed terminal traffic. Circuit-switching systems do not provide error checking, and therefore do not suffer from such delays and network inefficiencies. To provide the best of both systems, TR has introduced the hybrid PACUIT technique:

PACket + circUIT = PACUIT

A PACUIT is a highly efficient packet structure containing data traveling between the same source and destination nodes. The PACUIT structure is a variable length entity which effectively compacts data in an optimum manner. Because all data in a PACUIT have common source and destination nodes, there is no need to perform error checking or to store packets at each intermediate node along the path. Instead, only the sour and destination switches perform packet control functions, while all intermediate nodes operate in a purely time division circuit-switched mode for through traffic. That is, acknowledgement is performed only on a network end-to-end basis. The effect of this is to minimize end-to-end delays, while reducing the buffer storage requirements at each intermediate node. The latter follows from queuing theory in that the less time PACUIT's spend in each node, the less that queues will build up. The logical link established between any source/destination node pair is referred to as a "virtual connection".

Buffer storage requirements at end nodes are also reduced, as a result of another difference between the PACUIT and packet approaches. This is that PACUIT's are transmitted at regular intervals on each virtual connection emanating from the source node, whereas packets (in most earlier systems) are not transmitted until they contain a certain minimum amount of data. To understand why this is important, it must be remembered that data enters or leaves end nodes (to/from resources) at various rates.

In pure packet systems, the time that each buffer remains allocated depends on this rate. Since buffer sizes are predefined (e.g., equal to the minimum packet size), slow terminals may tie up considerable amounts of buffer storage for relatively long periods.

In the M3200 system, however, only small buffers need be allocated, since they will be emptied at regular intervals (each time a PACUIT is formed and transmitted). If no data is entered from a particular terminal between transmission of one PACUIT and the next, almost no space will be wasted for it in the new PACUIT. In other words, the PACUIT compaction technique ensures a minimal overhead for inactive terminals. It is also worth noting here that when a terminal completely disconnects from the network, it is completely de-allocated from the PACUIT channel.

Since PACUIT's may contain multiple-channel data, a well chosen transmission rate will result in a high probability that some channels will have data to send, even if others have not. Referring to Figure 1, the mean data content of a PACUIT must clearly be sufficiently high to ensure that the percentage overhead (due to structural information) is low. On the other hand, it must not be too high; otherwise the advantage of low buffer requirements will be lost.

The PACUIT transmission rate is, in fact, dynamically controlled by the M3200 switch software, using a monitoring and feedback technique. The same technique is used to control dynamic bandwidth allocation, and is explained in more detail below.

As was previously indicated, the use of packetizing is not always necessary. For transmission protocols which include their own powerful error detection codes, the use of packets is not as easily justified as it is for nonchecking protocols. In practice, it

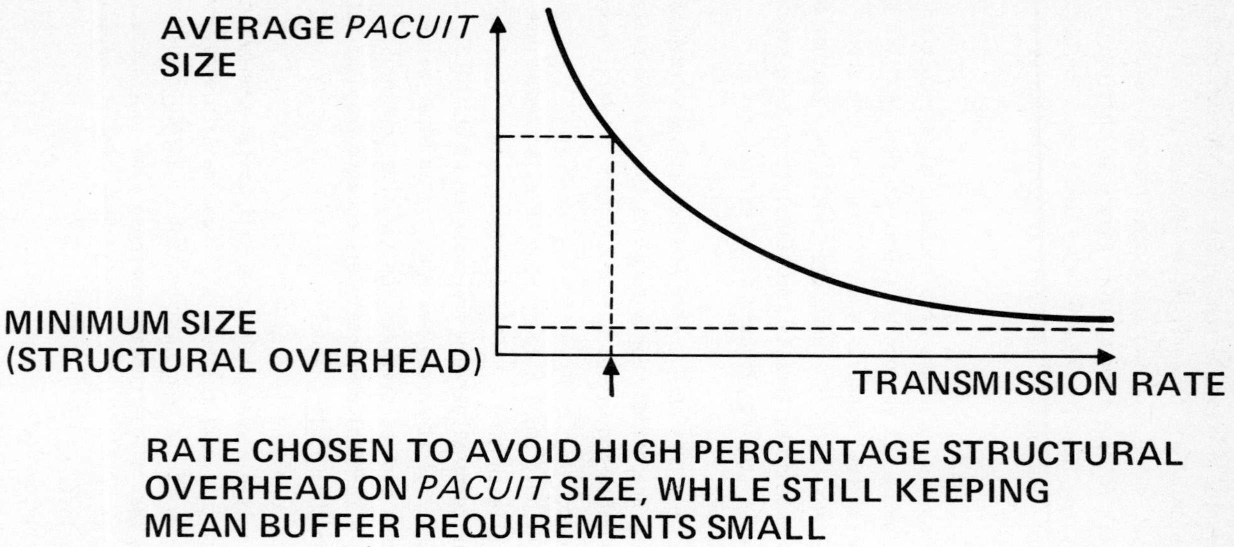

Figure 1 - Control of *PACUIT* Transmission Rate

is generally useful to packetize asynchronous data, since asynchronous terminals tend to offer weak or no error checking. Synchronous terminals, however, often include powerful detection codes such as cyclic redundancy checking.

The M3200 is the first system to offer the ability for mixing both packetized (PACUIT) data and individual time division circuit-switched channels, concurrently on the same internode trunks (see Figure 2).

STRUCTURE OF NODAL EQUIPMENT

The Nodal Equipment consists of two major units - a Digital Switch and a stored Program Controller.

The Digital Switch provides all data I/O to both terminals and lines while the Controller controls all assignments in the Digital Switch.

For example, a terminal requesting service would be automatically connected through the Switch to the Controller. The Controller would determine routing and notify the Digital Switch which output to connect to the terminal. All data originated by that terminal will continue to be relayed in both directions by the Digital Switch without further reference to the Controller, regardless of the data content. Disconnect is handled in a similar manner.

The Controller obtains all routing information from programmable tables. It also provides continuous test in background and logs traffic information.

DYNAMIC BANDWIDTH ALLOCATION

The technique used for intermixing PACUIT and pure circuit-switched data on trunk lines is that of time division multiplexing on a character-by-character basis. In earlier systems, the TDM technique results in less efficient trunk bandwidth utilization. This is due to the fact that time slot allocations are fixed within the repetitive channel selection sequence used for inserting data on the line. Thus, while no data is being entered from a terminal, its time slots will be unused, and are generally filled by "idle" characters.

TRAN has developed a new technique for the M3200 system which permits the dynamic reassignment of time slots to different data sources. This technique is knows as "dynamic bandwidth allocation". The decision to perform reassignment is based on a data traffic monitoring method referred to as "statistical multiplexing". This is implemented in the M3200 system by software in the switch minicomputer. The statistical multiplexing routines within a source node monitor the outgoing traffic at frequent intervals, on a channel-by-channel basis. In this case, each active PACUIT connection is treated as a single channel. The technique is, in effect, a "feedback" system - the higher a

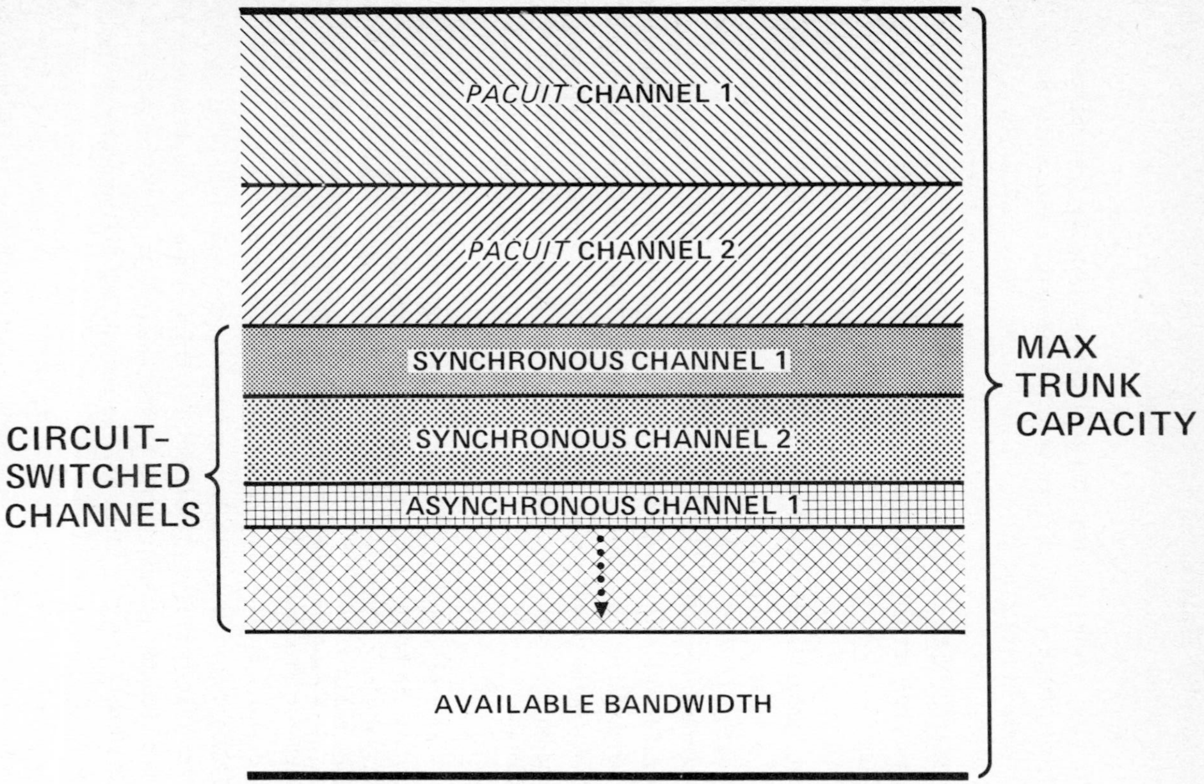

Figure 2 - Use of Trunk Bandwidth

channel composite traffic rate, the greater the bandwidth allocated to it; and vice-versa.

The M3200 system offers two types of synchronous circuits, one with flow control, and one without flow control (fixed bandwidth). For flow controlled synchronous channels, message transmission results in bursts of data from a buffer. In this case though, the buffer is that of the originating terminal, and not of its network entry node. The rate at which a synchronous terminal buffer is emptied is dependent on the available transmission capacity. A Remote Terminal Interface Unit (RTIU) controls the terminal clock to make use of this capacity. An RTIU may be used between each synchronous terminal and its point of entry to the network if circuit-switched service is required. The unit also serves a second function, that of resource addressing. If fixed bandwidth, dedicated (i.e., non-switched) service is required, then no RTIU is necessary.

DYNAMIC MULTIPLEXING

When several terminals are grouped together at some distance from their nearest node of an M3200 network, they may enter the network via a multiplexed tail-circuit (see Figure 3). In order to make optimum use of the tail-circuit trunk bandwidth, a technique is used that resembles dynamic bandwidth allocation in that it allows continual reassignment of time slot positions in the multiplexed channel selection sequence. The technique is called "dynamic multiplexing". A current specification of time slot/channel assignments is reloaded dynamically from the M3200 switch.

The effect of dynamic multiplexing is that the tail-circuit trunk bandwidth may be considerably less than the sum of the bandwidths of all terminals attached to the multiplexers. This can result in considerable cost savings, where line and modem costs are bandwidth-dependent.

FULL DUPLEX OPERATION

Trunk lines between M3200 nodes are both physically and logically full duplex. That is, they are capable of carrying data or response information in both directions concurrently. Moreover, data and responses need not be alternating. In the case of a synchronous circuit-switched channel, this will depend on the originating terminal type. For example, most Binary Synchronous Communication (BSC) terminals do not, in fact, work in a true full duplex manner. At best they perform in a "conversational" manner, with alternating messages in each direction (i.e., an output message may be sent instead of a positive acknowledgement to the preceding input message).

PACUIT operation, however, is logically full duplex. Consecutive PACUIT's may be transmitted in either direction, without waiting for the response to each one in turn. A proprietary TRAN technique permits a single five-bit response to fully identify the sequence of acknowledgements (positive and/or negative) up to four consecutive received

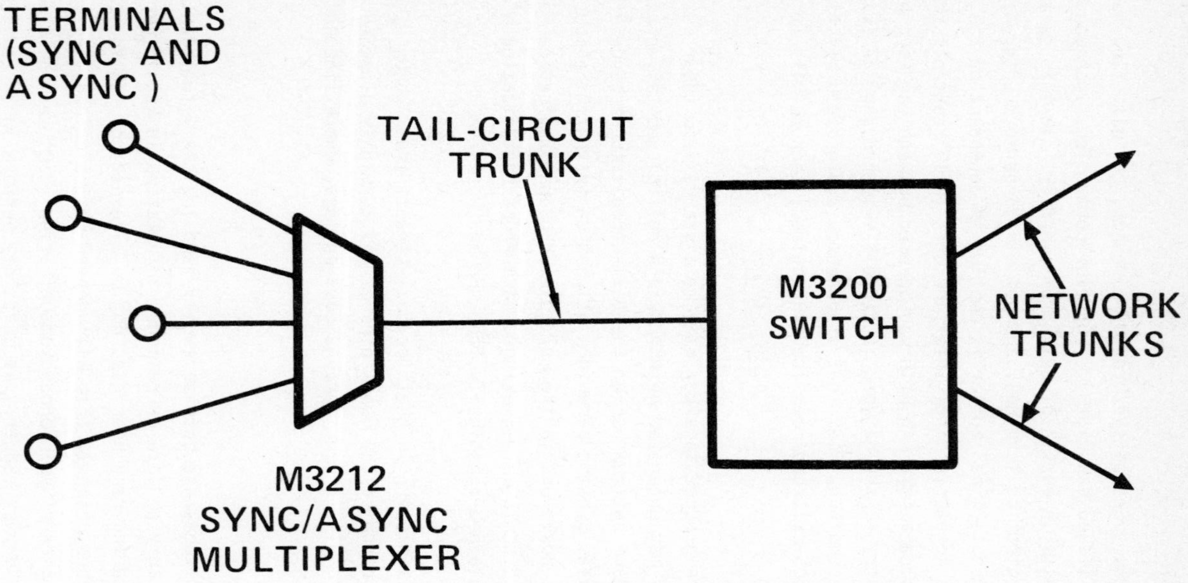

Figure 3 - Multiplexed Tail-Circuit for Network Access

PACUIT's. Such a response is usually carried within a PACUIT being transmitted on the same connection, in the opposite direction to the received PACUIT's. This is illustrated in Figure 4. Labels A1, B1, etc., represent PACUIT numbers, while RAn, RBn, etc., represent the single or accumulated responses. Note in this example that response RA2-4 identified good receipt of PACUIT's A2 and A3, but an error in A4. The latter is therefore retransmitted.

Such is the independence of the two directions of a PACUIT virtual connection, that they may not even follow the same physical trunk paths. In other words, the full duplex capability is implemented by independent simplex transmission of data in each direction. Thus, in Figure 5, PACUIT's traveling from node A to node D pass along the path ABD, while PACUIT's traveling from D to A use the path DCA. Simplex operation is particularly advantageous for the new class of split-speed terminals which operate up to 300 bps on the transmit side, and up to 9600 bps on the receive side.

ALTERNATE ROUTING

The term "virtual connection" is used to describe the logical link between any node pair for an active user channel. Thus, at the time network operation is started from cold, no virtual connections exist. Normally, the first ones to be established will be those for preassigned dedicated channels. Subsequently, as each new circuit-switched or PACUIT channel is initiated, it will either be added to an existing physical connection, or (if necessary) a new physical connection will be established to "contain" it.

Along the path of an established physical connection, the source and destination nodes are logically defined to the switch software as being PACUIT assembly/disassembly nodes. Any intermediate nodes are set up for time division circuit-switching only. (Note that an intermediate node of one physical connection may also be the source node of another.)

A source node is responsible for control of the connection. In the first place, the physical connection is set up by the source node minicomputer, based on optimum path tables contained in the software. The choice of the physical route depends not only on geographical considerations, but also on the current status of the relevant inter-node trunks. If any trunk in the potential route is either too heavily loaded, or out of service, an alternative route will be selected.

The connection approach used guarantees that no circuit-switched channels will be "dropped", in the event of trunk failures during operation. Any such failure (including detection by any node along the path of an unacceptable error rate) will be signaled to the source node, which will then set up an alternative route, and switch traffic onto it.

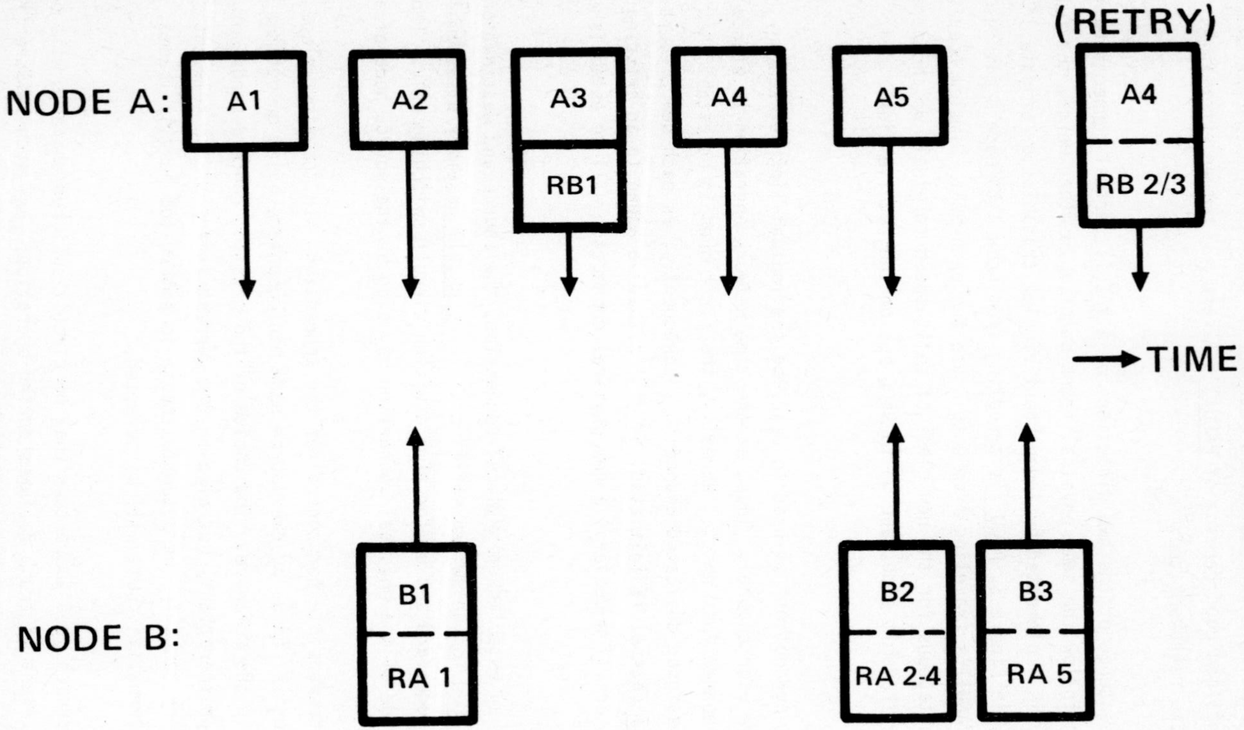

Figure 4 - Full Duplex *PACUIT* Transmission with Accumulated Responses

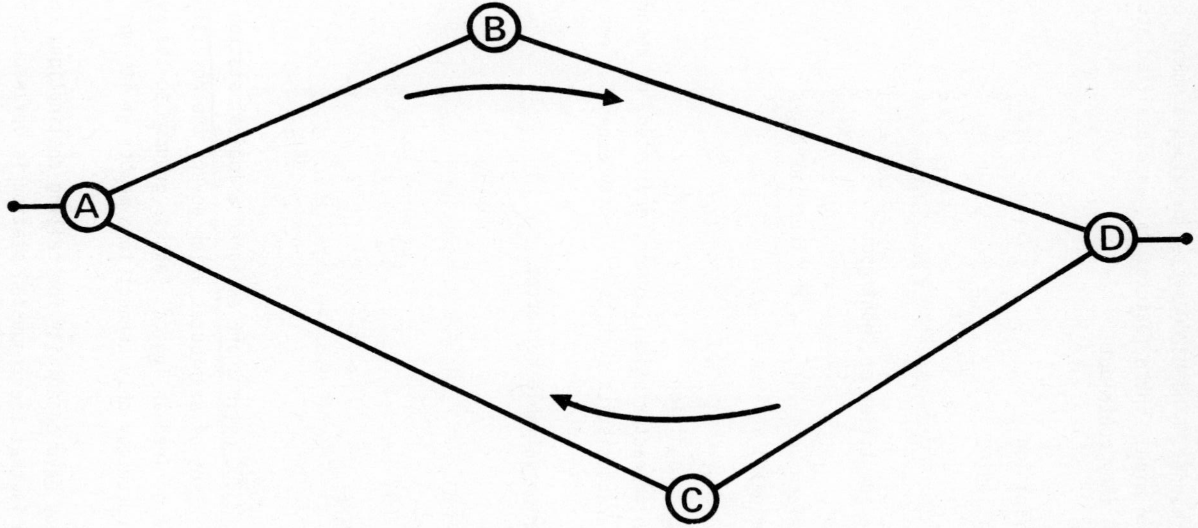

Figure 5 - Logical Full Duplex Connection Using Simplex Paths

NETWORK ACCESS AND PARTITIONING

It is worth recalling, at this point, that the fundamental objective of a switched ne work is to allow one resource to select and access another resource (e.g., terminal t computer), in a simple secure manner. The M3200 system provides a number of features designed with this objective in mind. These features may be classified according to the general functions to which they contribute.

a. Access Security
   1. "Access group" specification
   2. Logical network partitioning

b. Resource Identification
   1. Abbreviated dial-in
   2. Selection by specific identifier or "hunt group"
   3. Symbolic identifiers
   4. Remote Terminal Interface Unit (RTIU) with "touchpad" keys (for synchronous terminals)

c. Connection Assistance
   1. "Autobaud" line-speed recognition
   2. Preassigned bandwidth characteristics (common, dedicated, or reserved)
   3. Other preassigned characteristics such as "priority access", "emergency access", etc.
   4. "Camp-on" queuing for unavailable resources
   5. Resource messages

d. Additional Services
   1. Broadcast messages
   2. Message "echo"
   3. Local loop parity checking

a. Access Security

All resources connected to an M3200 network are assigned a logical station number by which they may be called, and a set of attributes which govern the resulting connect Sets of station numbers may be defined as logical "access groups" to the switch soft ware. In most cases, any resource may only connect to a member of its own access gr

However, selected resources may have capability for calling destinations in other sp cific groups. The limitation is that the requested station is defined as being able to receive the external call.

The access group facility effectively provides a means of partitioning the physical network into a set of smaller logical networks. Each of these logical networks may be entirely independent, or may have limited access to others. Partitioning is an important facility for networks that are shared by several independent organizations - for example, public data network services offered by the telephone companies.

b. Resource Identification

In a partitioned network, the number of resources in an access group is usually a small proportion of the total system resources. Thus, the number of characters or digits required to specify intragroup addresses may be somewhat less than the number required for intergroup addressing. This is analogous to the public telephone network in which seven digits are usually required for dialing a local call; whereas ten are required for long distance calls. The analogy is, however, incomplete inasmuch as the "abbreviated dial-in" facility of an M3200 network is not dependent on distance.

A further analogy exists between M3200 resource identification and telephone dialing. This is the "hunt group" concept. Often, in the major centers of large companies, a number of telephone trunks will be assigned to the central switchboard. An external caller dialing the company number will not necessarily be serviced on one particular line; if the first trunk is busy, then an automatic "hunt" for an unoccupied line will commence. Only if all lines are occupied will the caller receive a "busy" signal.

Analogously, multiple ports in an M3200 network which are in the same access group, and which offer access to similar resources, may be specified as members of a common hunt group. Typically, a hunt group will comprise several ports connected to the same computer, and offering access to the same application program(s). Again, however, the analogy with the telephone service is incomplete, since members of an M3200 hunt group may be widely distributed. For example, in Figure 6 identical time sharing services (TSO) are offered by two IBM computers at different nodes of a network. Nonetheless, the total of fifty ports shown may be specified as members of a common hunt group. A terminal user at node A who simply requests a TSO service (see below), may be connected by the system to either of the computers - he does not know or care which one.

The manner in which a terminal user requests a connection depends on his terminal type. Typically, asynchronous terminals are equipped with keyboards through which resource identifiers may be entered. An identifier can be either the station or hunt group number of the resource; or it may be a symbolic equivalent (i.e., alphabetic instead of numeric). Referring again to Figure 6, the name TSO would be a useful symbolic identifier. The switch minicomputer software contains tables of all such identifiers and their equivalent group of station numbers. The identifiers are defined as required, for any given network.

Synchronous terminals tend to have more diverse configuration characteristics than asynchronous terminals. For example, an RJE batch terminal does not require a key-

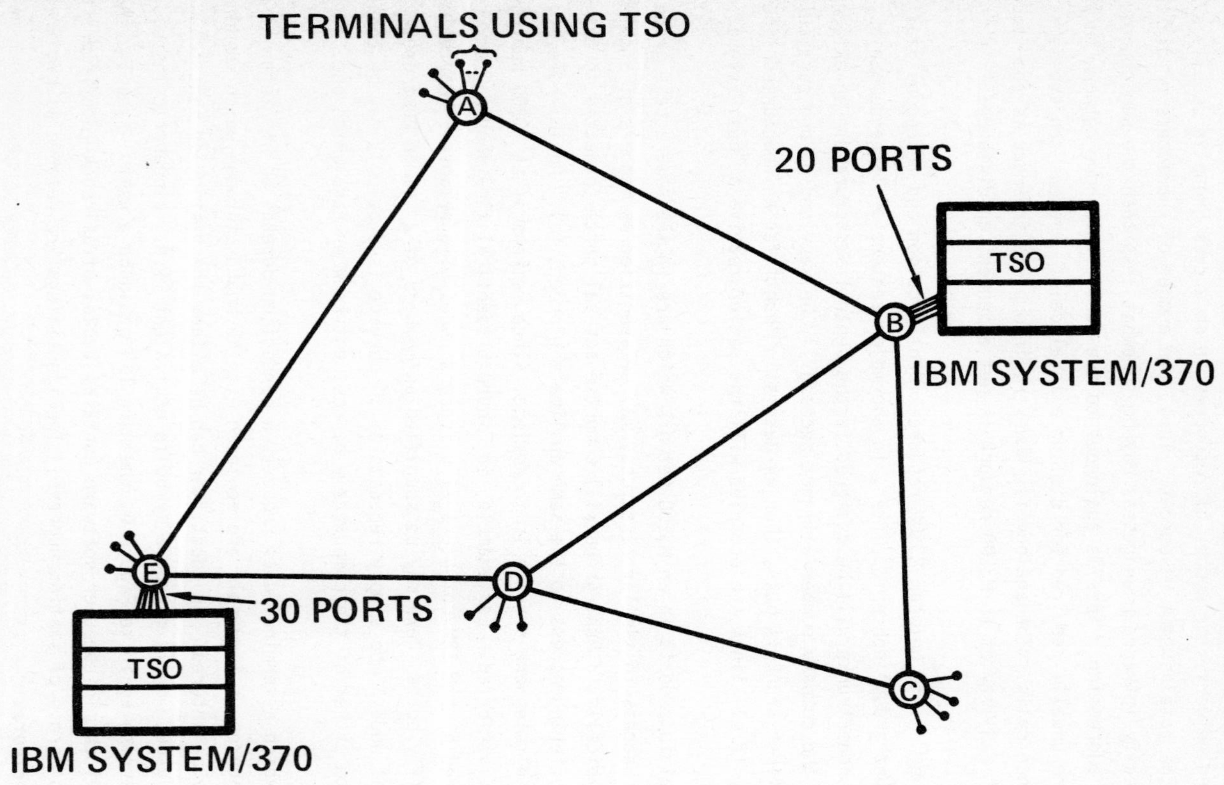

Figure 6 - Distributed "Hunt Group"

board. For this reason, resource addressing from synchronous terminals makes use of the Remote Terminal Interface Unit referred to before. The RTIU has a "touchpad" keyboard through which resource identifiers may be entered.

SOFTWARE ARCHITECTURE

The M3200 system runs under a highly efficient real time operating system developed especially for it. This is the Data Switch Operating System (DSOS). The software system, like its hardware counterpart, is modular in structure. Through a system generation process, the functional and I/O facilities required by each switch in the network are defined. This allows the building of a tailored version of DSOS for each switch which will be economic in terms of memory requirements, and will have a minimum performance overhead.

The diverse functions to be performed by DSOS are each handled by one or more "tasks". These tasks are grouped into multiple priority "levels", which are almost completely independent of one another. Each task runs under control of a Task Control Block (TCB). The TCB's contain all necessary status information for their related tasks to be run. Because levels are independent, each has its own Task Dispatcher and queue of ready-tasks (i.e., pointers to status information for tasks awaiting scheduling). Figure 7 illustrates the way in which level and task dispatching operates.

a. Suppose that a hardware interrupt occurs while a task in Level "n" is active. The switch minicomputer uses an automatic vector system for branching to the appropriate entry point in the Interrupt Processor. At the same time, it automatically stores interrupt status information in a queue in reserved memory.

b. The Interrupt Processor immediately calls a "Save" subroutine to locate the Level Control Table (LCT) of the interrupted Level "n" and saves all its volatile information therein (e.g., registers, program counters, etc.).

c. Interrupts are of two basic types:
   1. Nonsignificant, which do not require any special servicing (e.g., arrival of a data character from a terminal).
   2. Significant, which do require special service (e.g., completion of a message or PACUIT transmission).

   In the former case, the Interrupt Processor simply calls "Restore" (to perform the reverse of the "Save" function) and makes an immediate return to the interrupted task in Level "n". However, for significant interrupts, control is passed to the "Dispatch" routine.

d. "Dispatch" simply performs the minimum necessary housekeeping functions and passes control to Level 1, the Software System Scheduler. The latter is in effect a second-level interrupt handler. It scans all the accumulated interrupt status

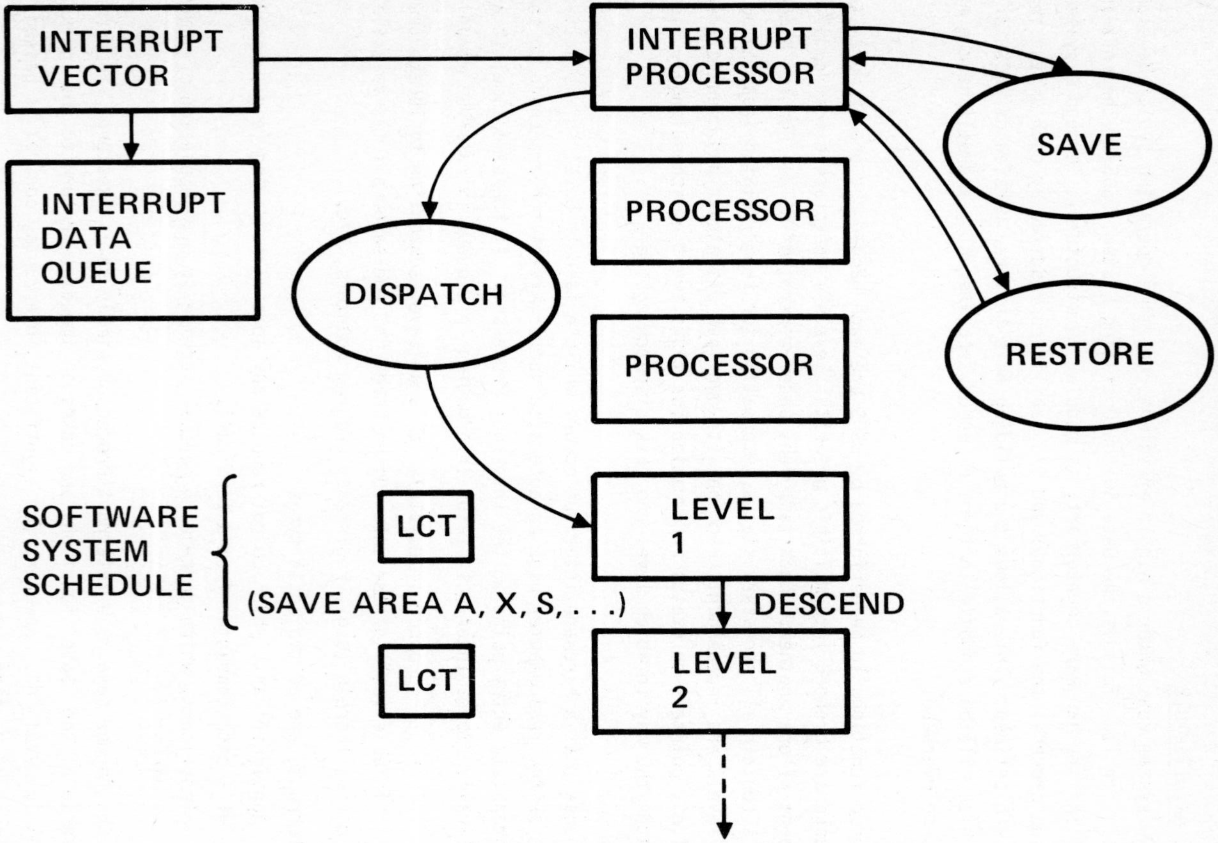

Figure 7 - Level and Task Dispatching in DSOS

information in reserved memory, and moves it to the appropriate level for later scheduling. This is the function of building the queue of ready-tasks within each level, referred to earlier. Note that the hardware stores status information even when interrupts are lost; hence the need for Level 1 to perform a scan for multiple status elements.

e. After completing its work, Level 1 executes the "Descend" routine. This passes control to the next lower level (2), after restoring volatile information from that level's LCT.

f. If Level 1 was active when the interrupt occurred (i.e., n = 2), its interrupted task will directly receive control and resume execution. If not, the Task Dispatcher for Level 2 will receive control and will scan its own ready-task queue. If an entry is present, the Task Dispatcher will locate the appropriate TCB (or build one, if necessary) and run the task. As long as no further significant interrupt occurs, all ready-tasks at Level 2 will be run in turn. This done, the Task Dispatcher will execute a "Descend" to the next level (3), and so on.

g. When all tasks at higher levels have been run, the lowest level is entered to perform general network monitoring and diagnostic functions. These tasks always have work to do, and will retain control until a significant interrupt occurs.

The DSOS dispatching mechanism thus ensures that high priority tasks receive immediate service, and that all tasks of any one priority receive service before all lower priority tasks. The current system priority levels are as follows:

a. Software System Scheduler: Distributes status information for level scheduling.

b. Communication Line Level: One TCB for each PACUIT channel.

c. Error Recovery Level: TCB's are generated as required to service error conditions.

d. Connect/Disconnect Level: A TCB is generated each time a terminal or port requests a connection or disconnection.

e. Network Management Level: Includes all tasks communicating with the central Network Management System (NMS). If no Network Control Center exists, this level is absent.

f. Operations Level: Tasks include operator communications and all operator-initiated functions.

g. Background Level: Includes initialization, monitoring, and diagnostic tasks.

Many of the actual program functions to be performed by the DSOS software are common to several tasks in a single level, or even to tasks in different levels. To avoid duplication of coding, such functions are programmed as separate "processors" from the main task coding. The twelve processors are illustrated in Figure 8, which also shows the overall software structure. The nesting structure shown signifies that a high level processor may call one at a lower level, but not vice-versa. Not all call are shown, since some processors are used by almost all tasks (e.g., the General Tabl Processor).

The coding of DSOS is fully reenterable, even though the dispatching mechanism only requires serial reusability. This is because the system is essentially table-driven. The major groups of tables are shown at the right of Figure 8. The software interfac to the M3200 hardware architecture is via the two powerful microprocessors shown at the top of Figure 8.

The microprocessors are the PACUIT Processing Unit (PPU) and the Switch Processing Unit (SPU). The PPU functions are structuring and destructuring PACUIT's, at regular intervals for each PACUIT channel. Transmission and reception of both PACUIT and cir cuit-switched data is handled by the SPU. The latter obtains routing information fro Channel Address Tables (CAT's) built and maintained by the software.

As mentioned earlier, many DSOS functions are optional, to allow tailoring of the system to a particular user's requirements. These functions are available in the for of more than thirty optional packages. Adding an optional package to the basic syste in effect, means adding tasks to one or more of the priority levels. Many of the options are related to network diagnostics and management, and are discussed in the nex paragraph.

NETWORK TESTING AND DIAGNOSTICS

Being an "intelligent" system, the M3200 network has many built-in self diagnostic an monitoring capabilities. This "real time" surveillance is automatically initiated by the DSOS software. Active diagnostics, such as loopback tests of available ports, ar performed on a time-available basis (in the background level), while monitoring and response to system generated alarms are performed at a high priority level.

Each switch monitors its own internal operation, and the operations of any multiplexe and trunks that it serves. The real time diagnostics are designed to locate most fau conditions before the user is aware of them. The test repertoire includes:

a. Switch diagnostics, with powerful and diverse self tests of the PPU, SPU, mini-computer, and RTD Bus.

b. Trunk monitoring of PACUIT channel error rates to ensure that a user-specified threshold is not exceeded. Also, monitoring for loss of frame synchronization.

c. Port diagnostics, with self testing of channel I/O modules and driver/receiver logic. Also, external monitoring such as parity checking on tail-circuits

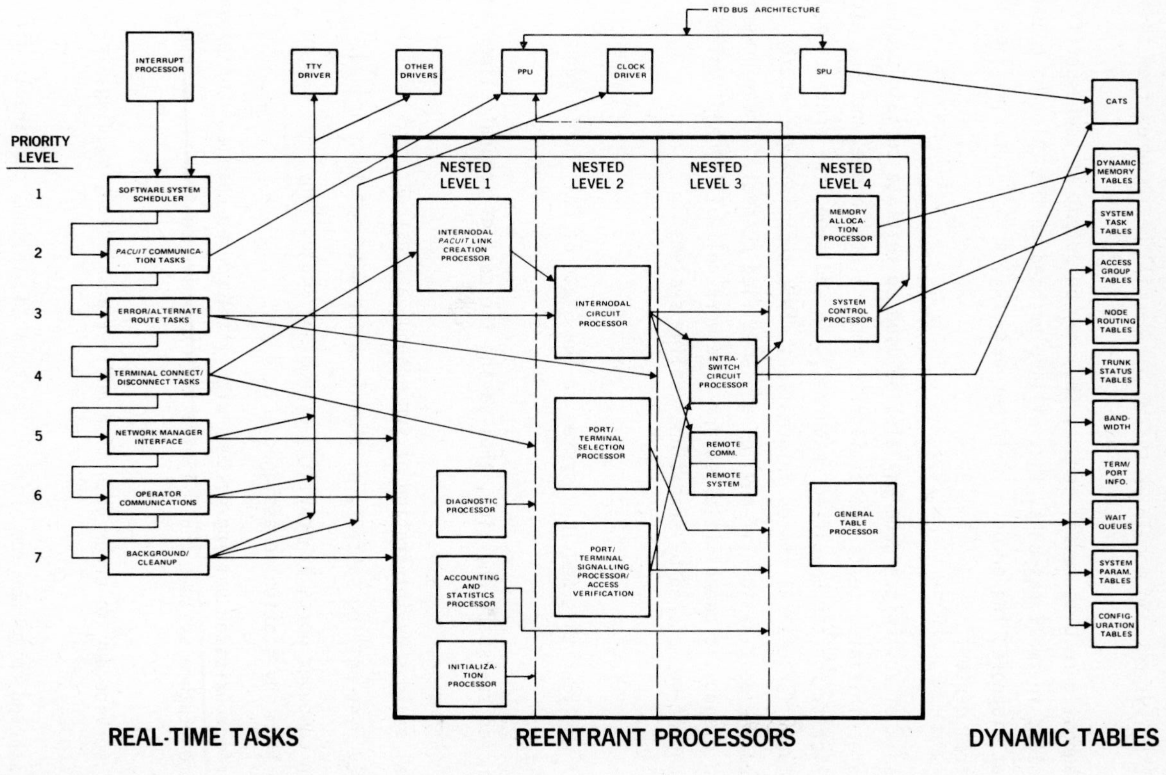

Figure 8 - DSOS Software Structure and its Interfaces with the M3200 Hardware

(optional), repetitive testing of computer ports that fail to respond to "ringing" by the switch, and remote loopback tests.

d. Configuration checks, to detect insertion of modules in wrong chassis positions or a working system. No module or system damage will be incurred from this erro

When these diagnostic results reveal errors, they may be output at user-specified loc tions. Typically, in small networks, they will be printed on the teletype console of the switch that diagnosed the error. In larger networks, error alarms will be sent t a Network Control Center.

The local console of any switch node may also be used to initiate certain tests. Man of these operator-initiated tests are similar to those listed above, but are executed with higher priority for the specified resources. In addition, the operator may inte rogate the network for channel status information; this test is a connection trace that identifies the destination (if any) of any specified channel. These powerful monitoring and diagnostic capabilities ensure a network reliability and system availability that cannot be matched by traditional online systems.

CONCLUSION

The results of applying this new TRAN system to the State of California requirements may be summarized:

Many agencies can share one line, thus saving the cost of separate lines and data sets.

Additional savings by integration of synchronous and asynchronous traffic.

Efficiency over polling systems, no time lost for data set turn around.

Saving in computer ports by providing economy of scale; any port can be accessed from any station so assigned.

Can interface existing polling systems with little or no change. Can provide control for future systems thus eliminating expensive controllers at each station.

Improved service due to error detection and retransmission, queuing, improved access.

Getting started costs for the initial few hundred stations comparable with the cost of existing systems. Incremental costs decrease as the systems grows.

This system has now been tested. The initial service starts March 1, 1976, for the California State Universities and Colleges. Four switches and nineteen multiplexers will serve one hundred fifty stations remotely to two computers for time share and remote batch service. Within two months thereafter, a second agency with additional computers and sixty stations will be added to the net. Figure 9 is a sketch of the initial layout. Figure 10 shows the expected three-year growth.

Here then is a digital system which improves service and is competitive in cost for a small layout. It has the desirable feature of decreased per station costs as the network grows combined with the flexibility to meet virtually any data transmission requirement.

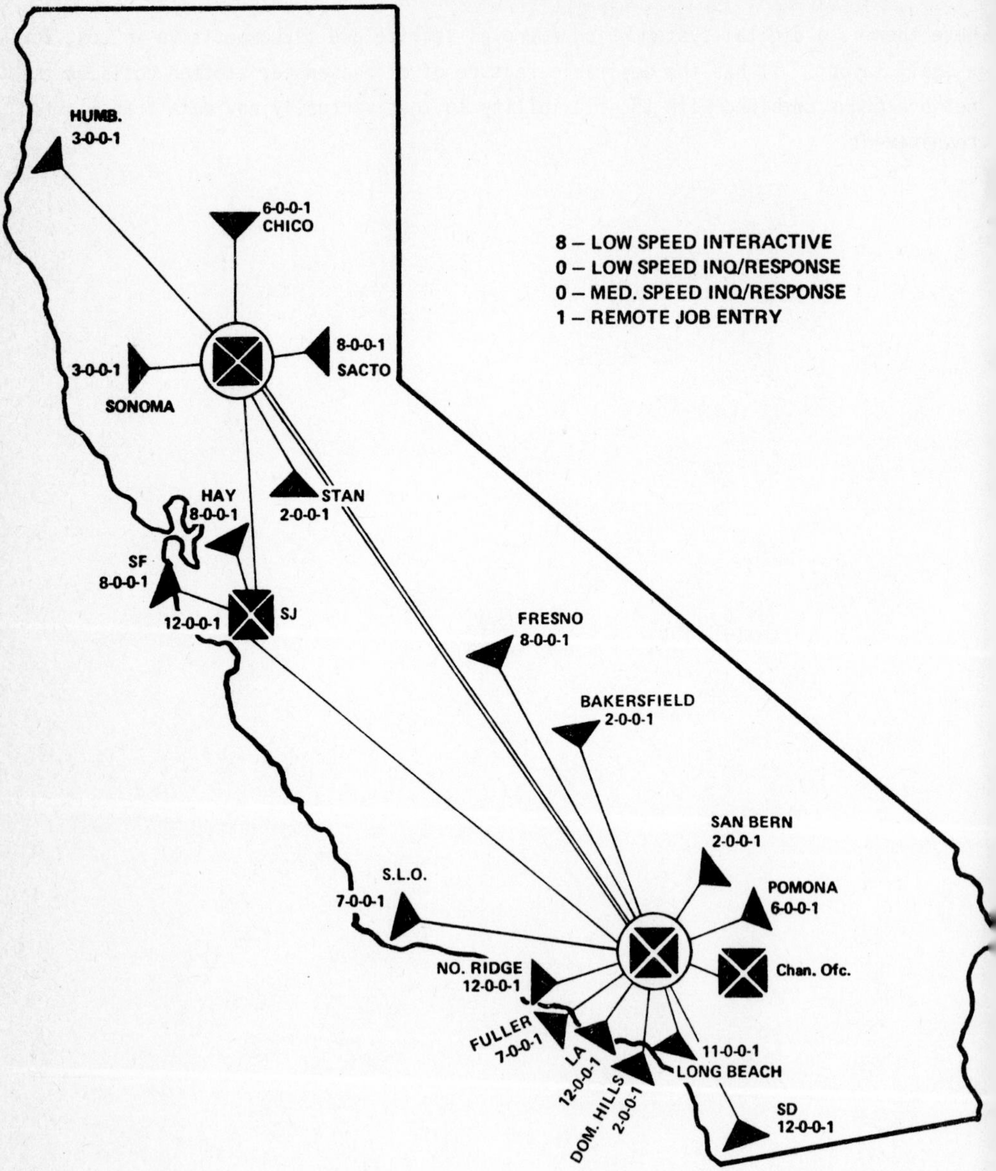
HUMB.
3-0-0-1
6-0-0-1
CHICO
8 – LOW SPEED INTERACTIVE
0 – LOW SPEED INQ/RESPONSE
0 – MED. SPEED INQ/RESPONSE
1 – REMOTE JOB ENTRY
3-0-0-1
SONOMA
8-0-0-1
SACTO
STAN
2-0-0-1
HAY
8-0-0-1
SF
8-0-0-1
12-0-0-1
SJ
FRESNO
8-0-0-1
BAKERSFIELD
2-0-0-1
SAN BERN
2-0-0-1
POMONA
6-0-0-1
S.L.O.
7-0-0-1
NO. RIDGE
12-0-0-1
Chan. Ofc.
FULLER
7-0-0-1
LA
12-0-0-1
DOM. HILLS
2-0-0-1
11-0-0-1
LONG BEACH
SD
12-0-0-1

Figure 9

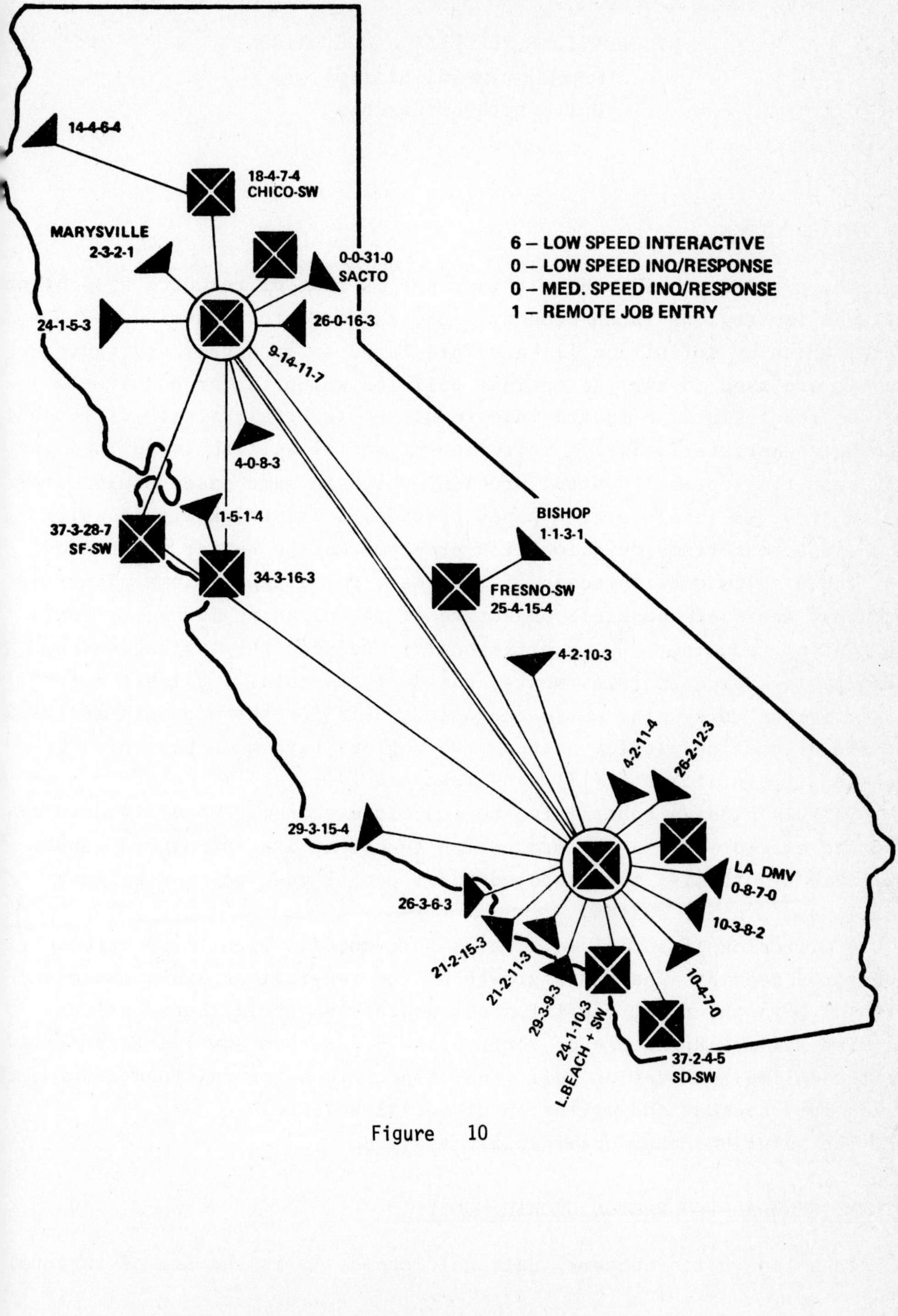
14-4-6-4
18-4-7-4
CHICO-SW
MARYSVILLE
2-3-2-1
0-0-31-0
SACTO
24-1-5-3
26-0-16-3
9-14-11-7
6 – LOW SPEED INTERACTIVE
0 – LOW SPEED INQ/RESPONSE
0 – MED. SPEED INQ/RESPONSE
1 – REMOTE JOB ENTRY
4-0-8-3
1-5-1-4
37-3-28-7
SF-SW
34-3-16-3
BISHOP
1-1-3-1
FRESNO-SW
25-4-15-4
4-2-10-3
4-2-11-4
26-2-12-3
29-3-15-4
LA DMV
0-8-7-0
26-3-6-3
10-3-8-2
21-2-15-3
21-2-11-3
29-3-9-3
24-1-10-3
L.BEACH + SW
10-4-7-0
37-2-4-5
SD-SW

Figure 10

OPTIMUM ALLOCATION OF INVESTMENTS IN A TWO - REGION ECONOMY

B.NICOLETTI, F.PEZZELLA and G.RAICONI
Dipartimento di Sistemi
Università di Cosenza
Cosenza, Italy

1. INTRODUCTION

The problem considered in this paper is that of resource allocation between two regions in an economy. Neo-Classic Macro Economic Growth models, which by definition |1| are formulated at an highly aggregated level, are used to analyse optimal policies which, under a suitable set of constraints, allocate investments to two regions with different economic characteristics. A criterion of social welfare is defined and the resulting optimal control problem, which in same cases admits singular arcs, is resolved This paper provides a framework within which such important resource allocation problems may be better understood.

The problem considered is of interest, for example, in a planified economy, where one possible objective of the planning authority could be that of reducing economic differentials between the two regions by a suitable choice of investments, based on the total available capital.

Previous work, using macro economic models for the economic analysis of the allocation problem between two regions, have been presented by Rahman |2|, Intriligator |3|, and Takayama |4|.

In this paper, a general two-region macro economic model is developed and assumptions on the production functions are introduced. Under suitable hypothesis, the proposed model can be modeled by a bilinear continuous dynamic system.

A criterion of social welfare is introduced, which takes into account the need of a balanced growth of the two regions and a maximizazion of both the final capital stock and of the social consumptions.

The Maximum Principle of Pontryagin |5| is then applied to determine the optimal allocation policy on respect to a general functional which takes into account the criterion of social welfare.

The solutions thus obtained are analyzed.

2. THE GENERAL TWO REGION GROWTH MODEL

In a two region economy, national income, Y, is the sum of regional incomes, $Y_i (i = 1,2)$:

$$Y = Y_1 + Y_2 \tag{1}$$

Each of the regional incomes is assumed |2,3,4| to be determined as a product of the regional capital stock, k_i, and the constant regional output-capital ratio, α_i:

$$Y_i = \alpha_i k_i \tag{2}$$

National investment, I, the sum of regional increases in capital stocks, $\dot{k}_i$, equals national savings, S, the sum of the products of incomes and constant regional savings ratio, s_i:

$$I \equiv \dot{k}_1 + \dot{k}_2 = S \equiv s_1 Y_1 + s_2 Y_2 \tag{3}$$

Using the production function (2):

$$\dot{k}_1 + \dot{k}_2 = g_1 k_1 + g_2 k_2 \tag{4}$$

where $g_i = s_i \alpha_i$ is the constant regional growth rate.

Two allocation parameters $u_i (i = 1,2)$ are defined as the proportions of investment allocated to region i, leaving $(1 - u_1 - u_2)$ as the proportion allocated to a third sector which refer to social consumptions.

Assuming that there is neither investments external to the system, or delay between investment and capital stock, or shift of capital from one region to another, when placed in either region, the equations of the system become:

$$\begin{aligned} \dot{k}_1 &= u_1 (g_1 k_1 + g_2 k_2) - \mu_1 k_1 \\ \dot{k}_2 &= u_2 (g_1 k_1 + g_2 k_2) - \mu_2 k_2 \\ \dot{k}_3 &= (1 - u_1 - u_2)(g_1 k_1 + g_2 k_2) - \nu k_3 \end{aligned} \tag{5}$$

with:

$$\begin{aligned} &0 \leq u_i \leq 1 \qquad i = 1,2 \\ &0 \leq u_1 + u_2 \leq 1 \end{aligned} \tag{6}$$

In the following, for simplicity, it is assumed that ν is negligible. The case of $\nu \neq 0$ is not substantially different.

The problem facing the economic planner is then to choose an optimal time path for the allocation parameters, $u_1(t)$ and $u_2(t)$, which achieves some objectives of the economy subject to the above constraints and certain initial conditions on capital stocks and social consumptions:

$$k_i(o) = k_{io} \tag{7}$$

The system to be studied is represented in a schematic way in fig.1.

A constant rate of growth n is assumed for the whole populations in both regions, $N_i (i = 1,2)$:

$$\dot{N}_1 = n\, N_i \qquad i = 1,2 \tag{8}$$

$N_{io} (i = 1,2)$ are the populations at time $t = 0$

3. THE CHOICE OF A CRITERION OF SOCIAL WELFARE

For economic planners the choice of a criterion of social welfare which can guide the establishment of economic policies is a complex problem.

It is possible to evaluate in different ways the performance of an economic system. Some Authors want to maximize a functional of the global consumption flow per capita or of the global income or of a linear combination of the two, over the planning horizon considered. As a matter offact, global indices may cause large unbalances between the two regions. In order to consider this fact, in this paper a general functional is considered which takes into account the following three factors, all along the fixed planning horizon T:

1) a "balanced growth", taken into account by minimizing, all along the fixed planning horizon T, the quadratic deviation between the incomes of the two regions, weighted according to their population:

$$\int_o^T \left(\frac{N_1 \alpha_1 k_1}{N_1 + N_2} - \frac{N_2 \alpha_2 k_2}{N_1 + N_2}\right)^2 dt \tag{9}$$

Taking into account (8) and with $\gamma = \frac{N_1(t)}{N_2(t)} \frac{\alpha_1}{\alpha_2} = \frac{N_{10}}{N_{20}} \frac{\alpha_1}{\alpha_2} > o$, (9) can be written:

$$\left(\frac{N_{10}\alpha_1}{N_{10}+N_{20}}\right)^2 \int_0^T \left(k_1 - \frac{k_2}{\gamma}\right)^2 dt \tag{10}$$

2) a global income at time T, to be maximized:

$$\alpha_1 k_1(T) + \alpha_2 k_2(T) \tag{11}$$

3) the social consumption, to be maximized at the final time T

$$k_3(T) \tag{12}$$

eventually discounted along the planning horizon:

$$\frac{1}{N_o} \int_0^T (1 - u_1 - u_2)(g_1 k_1 + g_2 k_2)\, e^{-(\nu+\rho)t}\, dt \tag{13}$$

where ρ is a suitable discounting factor.

For simplicity, only the first case is considered. The second case does not lead to solutions substantially different once a current value Hamiltonian |6| is considered.

The hole functional considered is:

$$\max_{\substack{u_i \\ i=1,2}} \{I = -\omega \int_0^T \left(k_1 - \frac{k_2}{\gamma}\right)^2 dt + (1-\beta)|\alpha_1 k_1(T) + \alpha_2 k_2(T)| + \beta k_3(T) \tag{14}$$

where ω and β are suitable weights, which satisfy:

$$0 \le \omega \le \infty \qquad 0 \le \beta \le 1 \tag{15}$$

4. THE OPTIMAL CONTROL PROBLEM

Once some values for ω and β are chosen, the maximization of I (14) subject to the dynamic state equations (5) along with the constrants on the controls (6) defines an optimal control problem. Since the controls u_1 and u_2 appear linearly in the state equations and the performance index, the problem could admit singular extremal arcs. Con sider the Hamiltonian:

$$H = - \omega\left(k_1 - \frac{k_2}{\gamma}\right)^2 + |(\lambda_1 - \lambda_3)u_1 + (\lambda_2 - \lambda_3)u_2| \; |g_1k_1 + g_2k_2| + \\ + \lambda_3(g_1k_1 + g_2k_2) - \mu_1\lambda_1k_1 - \mu_2\lambda_2k_2 \tag{16}$$

The three adjoint variables are defined by:

$$\lambda_1 = - \frac{\partial H}{\partial k_1} = - g_1|(\lambda_1 + \beta)\,u_1 + (\lambda_2 + \beta)\,u_2| + \lambda_1\mu_1 + g_1\beta + 2\omega\left(k_1 - \frac{k_2}{\gamma}\right)$$

$$\lambda_2 = - \frac{\partial H}{\partial k_2} = - g_2|(\lambda_1 + \beta)\,u_1 + (\lambda_2 + \beta)\,u_2| + \lambda_2\mu_2 + g_2\beta - \frac{2}{\gamma}\,\omega\left(k_1 - \frac{k_2}{\gamma}\right) \tag{17}$$

$$\lambda_3 = - \frac{\partial H}{\partial k_3} = 0$$

with transversality conditions:

$$\lambda_1(T) = (\beta - 1)\alpha_1$$

$$\lambda_2(T) = (\beta - 1)\alpha_2 \tag{18}$$

$$\lambda_3(T) = - \beta$$

From the last equ. of (17), one gets:

$$\lambda_3(t) = \text{const} = - \beta \tag{19}$$

the maximization of H with respect to (u_1, u_2) gives rise to the following possibilities:

$$\begin{aligned} &A: \quad \lambda_1 < - \beta, \quad \lambda_1 < \lambda_2 \quad \Rightarrow \quad u_1^* = 1,\; u_2^* = 0 \\ &B: \quad \lambda_2 < - \beta, \quad \lambda_2 < \lambda_1 \quad \Rightarrow \quad u_1^* = 0,\; u_2^* = 1 \\ &C: \quad \lambda_1 > - \beta, \quad \lambda_2 > - \beta \quad \Rightarrow \quad u_1^* = 0,\; u_2^* = 0 \end{aligned} \tag{20}$$

$$D: \quad \lambda_1 = \lambda_2 < - \beta \quad \Rightarrow \quad u_1^* + u_2^* = 1 \tag{21}$$

E: $\lambda_2 = -\beta,\ \lambda_1 > -\beta \quad \Rightarrow \quad u_1^* = 0,\ u_2^* \varepsilon\ |0,1|$ (22)

F: $\lambda_1 = -\beta,\ \lambda_2 > -\beta \quad \Rightarrow \quad u_2^* = 0,\ u_1^* \varepsilon\ |0,1|$ (23)

G: $\lambda_1 = \lambda_2 = -\beta \quad \Rightarrow \quad u_1^* \varepsilon\ |0,1|\ i = 1,2$ (24)

In cases D,E,F,G, singular arcs are defined. To study the optimal strategies from these conditions, one can perform a phase plane analysis of $\underline{\lambda}$. The preceding cases correspond to different regions in this plane. Following the optimal trajectories of $\underline{\lambda}$, when one goes from one region to another, there is a switching in the optimal solution.

5. THE OPTIMAL SOLUTION WHEN W = 0

5.1 Optimal Control

The analysis of the behaviour of $\underline{\lambda}$, in the cases considered in the preceding paragraph is done under the following hypothesis:

1. $\omega = 0$
2. region two has a larger growth rate ($g_2 > g_1$)
3. growth rates are larger than the corresponding depreciations, in both regions ($g_i > \mu_i$, i = 1,2).

$\underline{A}$: $\lambda < -\beta \quad \lambda_1 < \lambda_2$

$$\dot{\lambda}_1 = -g_1\lambda_1 + \mu_1\lambda_1 \qquad\qquad (25)$$
$$\dot{\lambda}_2 = -g_2\lambda_1 + \mu_2\lambda_2$$

The eigenvalues are:

$$\xi_1 = -(g_1 - \mu_1) < 0 \qquad\qquad (26)$$
$$\xi_2 = \mu_2 \qquad > 0$$

which correspond to a saddle point with asymptotes:

$$\lambda_1 = 0 \qquad\qquad (27)$$
$$\lambda_2 = \lambda_1 \frac{g_2}{g_1 - \mu_1 + \mu_2}$$

$\underline{B}$: $\lambda_2 < -\beta, \quad \lambda_2 < \lambda_1$

$$\dot{\lambda}_1 = -g_1\lambda_2 + \mu_1\lambda_1 \qquad (28)$$

$$\dot{\lambda}_2 = -(g_2 - \mu_2)\lambda_2$$

The eigenvalues are:

$$\xi_1 = \mu_1 > 0$$

$$\xi_2 = -(g_2 - \mu_2) < 0 \qquad (29)$$

which correspond to a saddle point with asymptotes:

$$\lambda_1 = 0 \qquad (30)$$

$$\lambda_2 = \lambda_1 \frac{g_2 - \mu_1 + \mu_2}{g_1}$$

$\underline{C}$: $\lambda_1 > -\beta, \quad \lambda_2 > -\beta$

$$\dot{\lambda}_1 = \mu_1\lambda_1 + g_1\beta \qquad (31)$$

$$\dot{\lambda}_2 = \mu_2\lambda_2 + g_2\beta$$

with an equilibrium point:

$$\lambda_1 = -\frac{g_1\beta}{\mu_1} \quad \text{and} \quad \lambda_2 = -\frac{g_2\beta}{\mu_2} \qquad (32)$$

after a translation of the origin to point (32), equ. (31) become:

$$\dot{\bar{\lambda}}_1 = \mu_1\bar{\lambda}_1$$

$$\dot{\bar{\lambda}}_2 = \mu_2\bar{\lambda}_2 \qquad (33)$$

with eigenvalues:

$$\xi_1 = \mu_1 > 0$$

$$\xi_2 = \mu_2 > 0 \qquad (34)$$

oth positive, so that one has an instable node.

Since the rates of capital depreciation could be very similar in oth sectors, il could be $\mu_1 = \mu_2 = \mu$, which correspond to an unstable tar. In fig. (2), this case is shown when $g_2 > g_1$.

The remaining cases correspond to possible singular solutions:

$$\underline{D}: \lambda_1 = \lambda_2 < -\beta$$

$$\dot{\lambda}_1 = -g_1\lambda_1 + \mu_1\lambda_1 \qquad (35)$$

$$\dot{\lambda}_2 = -g_2\lambda_2 + \mu_2\lambda_2$$

hich is admissible only if:

$$-g_1 + \mu_1 = -g_2 + \mu_2 \quad \Rightarrow \quad g_1 - \mu_1 = g_2 - \mu_2 \qquad (36)$$

$$\underline{E}: \lambda_2 = -\beta, \quad \lambda_1 > -\beta$$

$$\dot{\lambda}_1 = \mu_1\lambda_1 + g_1\beta \qquad (37)$$

$$\dot{\lambda}_2 = \mu_2\lambda_2 + g_2\beta = 0 = -\beta\mu_2 + g_2\beta$$

missible only if $g_2 = \mu_2$, a rather unrealistic case.

$$\underline{F}: \lambda_1 = -\beta, \quad \lambda_2 > -\beta$$

imilar to the previous case and admissible only if $g_1 = \mu_1$, which is unealistic.

$$\underline{G}: \lambda_1 = \lambda_2 = -\beta$$

missible only if $g_1 = \mu_1$ and $g_2 = \mu_2$, which once again is unrealistic.

As a conclusion, when $\omega = 0$, singular solutions are not present, general.

2. State Phase Plane Analysis.

To analyse the optimal solution on the state phase plane, it is cessary to study the behaviour of the equations (5) in the various cases considered in the preceding paragraph.

Attention is restricted only to the admissible cases A, B, and C. Only the first two equations are considered, since k_3 does not influence them.

A:

$$\dot{k}_1 = (g_1 - \mu_1)k_1 + g_2k_2$$
$$\dot{k}_2 = -\mu_2k_2 \tag{38}$$

The eigenvalues are:

$$\xi_1 = g_1 - \mu_1 > 0$$
$$\xi_2 = -\mu_2 < 0 \tag{39}$$

which correspond to a saddle point with asymptotes:

$$k_2 = 0$$
$$k_2 = -\frac{g_1 - \mu_1 + \mu_2}{g_2} k_1 \tag{40}$$

B:

$$\dot{k}_1 = -\mu_1k_1$$
$$k_2 = g_1k_1 + (g_2 - \mu_2)k_2 \tag{41}$$

The eigenvalues are:

$$\xi_1 = -\mu_1 < 0$$
$$\xi_2 = (g_2 - \mu_2) > 0 \tag{42}$$

which correspond to a saddle point with asymptotes:

$$k_1 = 0$$
$$k_2 = -\frac{g_1}{g_2 - \mu_2 + \mu_1} k_1 \tag{43}$$

C:

$$k_1 = -\mu_1k_1$$
$$k_2 = -\mu_2k_2 \tag{44}$$

The eigenvalues are:

$$\xi_1 = -\mu_1$$
$$\xi_2 = -\mu_2 \tag{45}$$

If $\mu_1 = \mu_2$, one has a stable star centered in the origin.

It is now possible to perform an analysis of the results. The case of a region 2 with a larger rate of growth ($g_2 > g_1$) is considered. The behaviour of the optimal solution can be studied by following the trajectories of λ in their phase plane. Taking into account the econo̲mical interpretation of $\lambda(t)$ as shadow prices, one should consider only negative values for both λ_1 and λ_2. As a matter of fact, the final values of $\lambda(t)$ (18):

$$\lambda_1(T) = -(1-\beta)\alpha_1 < 0$$

$$\lambda_2(T) = -(1-\beta)\alpha_2 < 0$$

are negative. A study of the optimal trajectories also show rather clearly that it is possible to arrive to them only from negative values of $\lambda(t)$. The actual trajectory depends on $\lambda(t)$ and on the lenght of the planning horizon T.

In fig.2, the phase plane of $\underline{\lambda}$ is divided in regions named according to the cases considered in paragraph 4. In principle, three cases are possible:

1. $\lambda(t)$ is situated in A, that is the output-capital ratio is larger in region 1 and $-(1-\beta)\alpha_1 < -\beta$.

Two subcases are possible according to the lenght of the planning period T:

a. $u_1 = 1 \quad \forall \quad t \in |0,T|$

b. $u_2 = 1 \quad \forall \quad t \in |0,t^*), \; u_1 = 1 \quad \forall \quad t \in (t^*,T|$

t^*, obtained by solving the adjoint equs., is given by:

$$t^* = T - \frac{1}{g_1} \ln \left[\frac{\frac{\alpha_2}{\alpha_1} - \frac{g_2}{g_1}}{1 - \frac{g_2}{g_1}} \right] \tag{46}$$

Of course, b. is possible only if $t^* > 0$.

Possible trajectories for the two cases considered are shown in fig.3, for the state variables k_1 and k_2. The optimal policy consists in investing in the region with a larger output-capital ratio. If planning horizon is long enough it could be convenient to invest before in region 2 and then in region 1.

2. $\lambda(T)$ is situated in B, that is the output-capital ratio is larger in region 2 ($\frac{\alpha_2}{\alpha_1} > 1$), and $-(1-\beta)\alpha_2 < -\beta$. In such a case, the optimal trajectory is always $u_2 = 1 \;\forall\; t \in |0,T|$.

The optimal policy consists in investing always in the region with a regional growth rate larger ($g_2 > g_1$) and a regional output-capital ratio also larger ($\alpha_2 > \alpha_1$).

A possible optimal trajectory is shown in fig.4

2. $\lambda(T)$ is situated in B, that is: $\frac{\alpha_2}{\alpha_1} > 1$, $-(1-\beta)\alpha_2 < -\beta$. In such a case the optimal trajectory is always $u_2 = 1$ for $t \in |0,1|$.

3. $\lambda(T)$ is situated in C, that is: $\alpha_2 < \frac{\beta}{1-\beta}$; $\alpha_1 < \frac{\beta}{1-\beta}$.

This consists in giving a larger weight in the optimization of the social consumptions on respect to the increase in the level of capital in both regions, If the planning horizon T is long enough, the following cases are possible:

a. $\lambda(T) \in C - c^*$ that is $\alpha_2 < \frac{\beta}{1-\beta}$ and $\alpha_1 < \frac{g_1+\mu}{g_2+\mu}\alpha_2 + \frac{g_1-g_2}{g_2+\mu}\;\frac{\beta}{1-\beta}$

$$u_2(t) = 1 \quad \forall \quad t \in |0,t^*)$$

$$u_3(t) = 1 \quad \forall \quad t \in (t^*,T|$$

where:

$$t^* = T - \frac{1}{\mu}\ln\left(\frac{\frac{g_2}{\mu} + (1-\frac{1}{\beta})\alpha_2}{\frac{g_2}{\mu} - 1}\right) \tag{47}$$

and $t^* < T$ for $\alpha_2 < \frac{\beta}{1-\beta}$

$u_2 = 1$ is possible only if $t^* > 0$

b. $\lambda(T) \in C^*$, that is $\alpha_1 < \frac{\beta}{1-\beta}$ and $\alpha_2 < \frac{g_2+\mu}{g_1+\mu}\alpha_1 - \frac{g_2-g_1}{g_1+\mu}\;\frac{\beta}{1-\beta}$

$$u_3(t) = 1 \quad \forall \quad t \in |0, t^*)$$

$$u_1(t) = 1 \quad \forall \quad t \in (t^*, t^{**})$$

$$u_3(t) = 1 \quad \forall \quad t \in (t^{**}, T|$$

where:

$$t^{**} = T - \frac{1}{\mu} \ln\left(\frac{\frac{g_1}{\mu} + (1 - \frac{1}{\beta})\alpha_1}{\frac{g_1}{\mu} - 1}\right) \tag{48}$$

$$t^* = t^{**} - \frac{1}{g_1}\ln\left(\frac{\frac{\alpha_2}{\alpha_1} - \frac{g_2}{g_1}}{1 - \frac{g_2}{g_1}}\right) = T - \frac{1}{\mu}\ln\left(\frac{\frac{g_1}{\mu} + (1 - \frac{1}{\beta})\alpha_1}{\frac{g_1}{\mu} - 1}\right) - \frac{1}{g_1}\ln\left(\frac{\frac{\alpha_2}{\alpha_1} - \frac{g_2}{g_1}}{1 - \frac{g_2}{g_1}}\right) \tag{49}$$

Clearly, if $t^{**} < 0$ only the policy $u_3(t) = 1$ and if $t^* < 0$ $u_1(t) = 1 \quad \forall \quad t \in |0, t^{**})$ and $u_3(t) = 1 \quad \forall \quad (t^{**}, T|$.

Possible trajectories for the two cases considered are shown in fig.5. In both of them, one begins always investing in the two regions to increase the global income and then in social consumptions $(u_3 = 1)$.

If, in the problem considered, one sets $\beta = 0$, one is considering the maximization of the global income at T. Now, only the cases I and II are possible. The problem reduces to that examined in |2,3,4|. All the results derived there are now particular cases.

CONCLUSIONS

In this paper an economy has been modeled with a two-sector. Macro Economic model where one sector, disaggregated in two regions, produces goods which are destined to be either invested or consumed, while the other sector, considered globally for the entire nation, produces goods which can only be used as social consumptions. The policy variable is the allocation of investments between sectors and regions.

A criterion of social welfare has been defined and the resulting optimal control problem is risolved.

REFERENCES

|1| Deistler,M., and Oberhofer,W. *"Macroeconomic Systems"*,Proceedings 1972 IFAC 5th World Congress, Paris, June 1972, Survey Paper.

|2| Rahman,M.D. *"Regional Allocation of Investments"*, Quartely Journal of Economics, Vol.77, Feb. 1963

|3| Intriligator, M.S. *"Regional Allocation of Investments"*, Quarterly Journal of Economics, Vol.78, Nov. 1964

|4| Takayama, A. *"Regional Allocation of Investments: A Further Analysis"*, Quarterly Journal of Economics, Vol.81, May 1967

|5| Pontryagin,L., and Gamkrelidze *"The Mathematical Theory of Optimal Processes"*, J.Wiley and sons, (Interscience Publishers), New York, 1962

|6| Haurie,A., Polis,M.P., and Yansouni,P.*"On Optimal Convergence to a Steady-State-Zero-Growth Economy with Pollution and Consumption Control"*, Proceedings 1973 IFAC/IFORS International Conference on Dynamic Modelling and Control of National Economies, Warwick, Great Britain, July 1973

FIGURE CAPTIONS

Fig.1 The economical system considered.

Fig.2 $\underline{\lambda}$ phase plane analysis for $\omega = 0$.

Fig.3 Phase plane analysis of the state variables (k_1, k_2) when $\frac{\alpha_2}{\alpha_1} < 1$ and $-(1-\beta)\alpha_1 < -\beta$.

Fig.4 Phase plane analysis of the state variables (k_1, k_2) when $\frac{\alpha_2}{\alpha_1} > 1$ and $-(1-\beta)\alpha_2 < -\beta$.

Fig.5 Phase plane analysis of the state variables (k_1, k_2) when $\alpha_i < \frac{\beta}{1-\beta}$ $(i = 1,2)$.

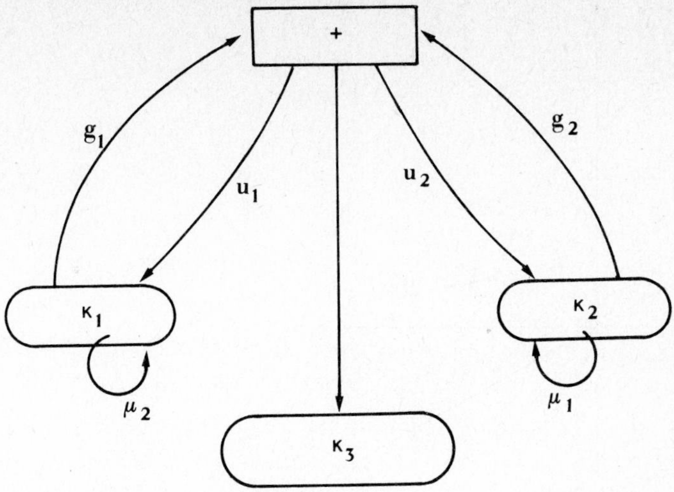
+
g_1
u_1
u_2
g_2
κ_1
κ_2
μ_2
μ_1
κ_3

FIG.1

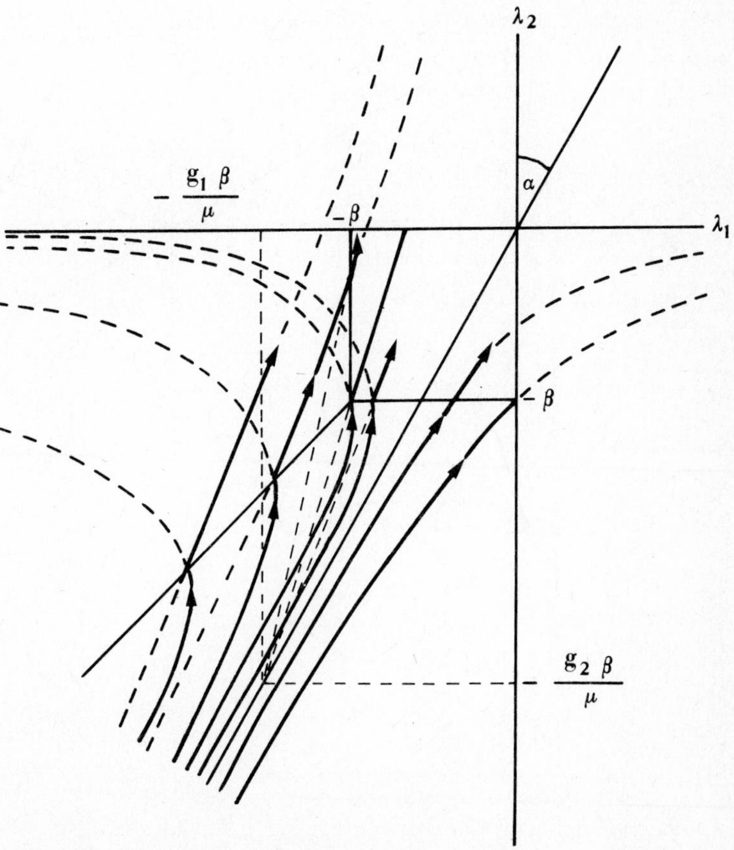
λ_2
$-\frac{g_1\ \beta}{\mu}$
α
$-\beta$
λ_1
$-\beta$
$\frac{g_2\ \beta}{\mu}$

FIG.2

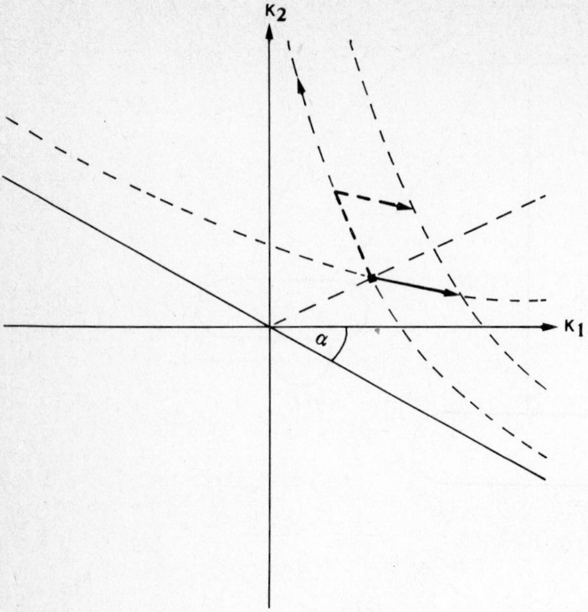

FIG.3

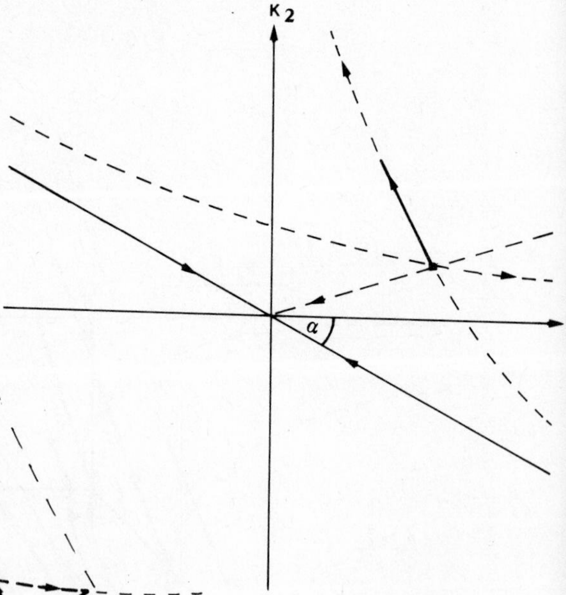

FIG.4

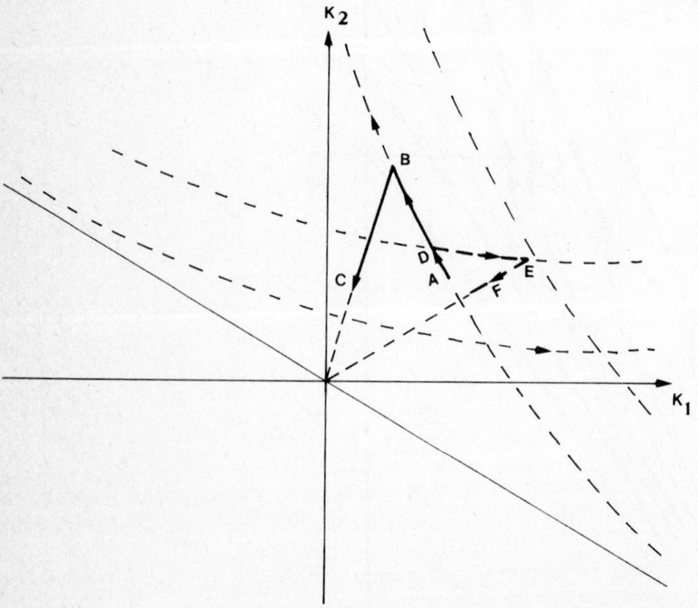

FIG.5

LIST OF AUTHORS

	Part	Page
AGBALAJOBI, F.B.	1	368
ALANDER, O.	1	506
ALFONSECA, M.	1	757
AL-JANABI, T.H.	2	510
ARMAND, J.L.	2	9
ARNAUD, Ch.	1	131
AUBIN, J.P. *	2	
BARON, G.	1	229
BARTHES, J.P.A.	1	769
BARTOLI, J.A.	1	537
BARTON, C.F.	1	59
BECK, M.B.	1	246
BLANVILLAIN, P.	2	636
BLUM, J.	1	71
BONNEMAY, A.*	1	
BRDYS, M.	2	656
BRUNI, C.	2	471
BUI, T.D. *	1	
CARASSO, C.	2	268
CASTI, J.	1	388
CHRYSOCHOIDES, N.	2	250
CIRINA, M.	2	283
COBELLI, C.	1	88
COLORNI, A.	1	557
COOPER, R.L.	1	368
CROUCH, P.E.	2	566
CURTAIN, R.F.	2	685
DELFOUR, M.C.	2	700
DELPUECH, D.	1	774
DENEL, J.	2	293
DERCKSEN, J.W.	1	470
DERVIEUX, A.	2	63
DRUD, A.	2	312
DUBOIS, D.M.	1	407

---

*paper not received

	Part	Page
EL-FATTAH, Y.M.	1	570
ESCUDERO, L.F.	1	264
FALLSIDE, F.	1	283
FAURE, R.	1	608
FAVIER, G.	2	636
FLIESS, M.	2	496
FRAEIJS DE VEUBEKE, B.	1	1
FRIEDMAN, M.	1	589
FRONZA, G.	1	292, 557
FURET *	1	
GALLIGANI, I.	1	794
GATTO, M.	1	103
GAUTIER, M.	1	110
GENESIO, R.	2	720
GERMANI, A.	2	471
GHIGGI, C.	1	116
GIORGI (de), C.	1	637
GIRES, A.	1	774
GIULIANELLI, S.	2	86
GONZALEZ, R.	2	587
GOTTESMANN, Cl.	1	131
GOULD, F.J.	1	455
GRAY, J.O.	2	510
GROSSMAN, Z.	1	145
GUIDA, G.	2	98
GUMOVSKI, I.	1	145
GUTMAN, S.	2	729
HARTUNG, J.	2	1
HATKO, A.	2	522
HAURIE, A.	1	646
HEE (van), K.M.	2	22
HELLMAN, O.	2	756
HEURGON, E.	1	622
HIRRIART-URRUTY, J.B.	2	763
HORST, R.	2	330
HSU, C.S.	1	59
HUNG, N.M.	1	646

	Part	Page
ICHIMURA, M.	1	363
JACOBSEN, S.E.	2	337
JELASKA, M.	1	657
JOHNSON, O.G.	1	676
JONG (de), J.L.	1	470
KALLIAUER, A.	1	496
KARLIN, A.	1	292
KFIR, M. *	1	
KIRKHAM, P.	1	131
KIUKAANIEMI, E.	1	506
KLUGE, R. *	2	
KOCH, G.	2	471
KOUKIS, M. *	1	
KOVACS, A.	2	353
KURCYUSZ, S.	2	362
LACOSTE, G.	1	131
LASIECKA, I.	2	522
LASRY, J.M.	2	790
LEDENT, J.	1	31
LEITMANN, G.	2	729
LEMAIRE, J.	2	130
LEPSCHY, A.	1	88
LEUENBERGER, D.G. *	2	
LEVAN, N.	2	538
LEVIEN, R. *	2	
LEVIEUX, F.	2	151
LIGETI, I.	1	691
LINKENS, D.A.	1	155
LITT, F.X.	1	315
LORENT, B.	1	331
LUCERTINI	2	86
MAFFIOLI, F.	2	389
MALENGE, J.P.	2	229
MALINOWSKI, K.B.	2	397
MAN (de), W.H.	1	705
MANDRIOLI, D.	2	98

	Part	Page
MANGIN, X.	1	676
MARCHUK, G.I.	1	13
MARTELLI, A. *	1	
MAURER, H.	2	555
MAURIN, S.	2	169
MIELLOU, J.C.	2	192
MIFFLIN, R. *	2	
MIGLIARESE, P.	1	637
MILLER, B.L.	2	799
MINOUX, M.	1	419
MOHLER, R.R.	1	59
MONSION, M.	1	110
MONTANARI, U. *	1	
MORANDI-CECCHI, M.	1	350
MOREL, P.	2	37
MORIOU, M.	2	130
MOSCA, E. *	2	
MOLTEDO, L.	1	794
MUKAI, H.	2	426
MURAT, F.	2	54
NICOLAS, P.	1	170
NICOLETTI, B.	1	834
OLSDER, G.J.	1	721
PACI, A.	2	98
PALERMO, P.C.	1	637
PALMERIO, B.	2	63
PATRONE, F.	2	560
PERE-LAPERNE, B.	1	774
PERKINS, J.D.	2	820
PERRY, P.F.	1	283
PETROVIC, R.	1	518
PEZZELLA, F.	2	834
PIERRA, G.	2	200
POLAK, E.	2	426
POLAK, E. *	1	
POME, R.	2	720
POUGET, J.	2	130